American Arts at
The Art Institute of Chicago

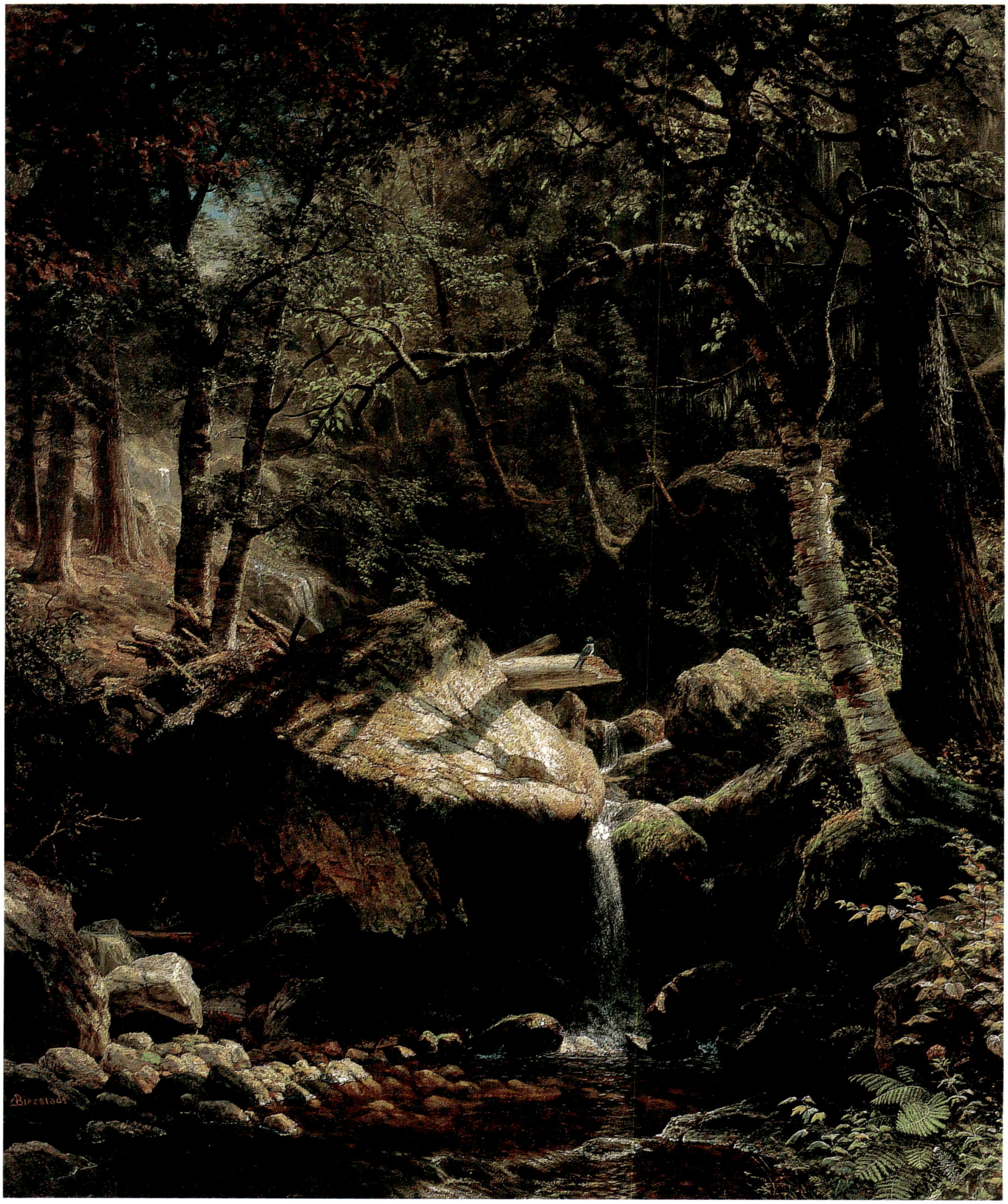

American Arts at The Art Institute of Chicago

From Colonial Times to World War I

Judith A. Barter, Kimberly Rhodes, and Seth A. Thayer,
with contributions by Andrew Walker

THE ART INSTITUTE OF CHICAGO

Distributed by Hudson Hills Press, New York

Produced by the Publications Department of The Art Institute of Chicago,
Susan F. Rossen, Executive Director
Edited by Michael Sittenfeld, Associate Editor; Catherine A. Steinmann, Assistant Editor; and
Robert V. Sharp, Associate Director of Publications
Production by Sarah E. Guernsey, Assistant Production Manager
Designed and typeset by Dean Bornstein, Peacham, Vermont
Color and duotone separations by Professional Graphics, Inc., Rockford, Illinois
Printed by Meridian Printing, East Greenwich, Rhode Island
Bound by Acme Bookbinding, Charlestown, Massachusetts

Unless otherwise indicated in the captions, all illustrations were produced by
Robert Hashimoto, Gregory Williams, Christopher Gallagher, and Robert Lifson in the
Department of Imaging, Alan B. Newman, Executive Director.

First Edition
Printed in the U.S.A.

Published by The Art Institute of Chicago, 111 South Michigan Avenue,
Chicago, Illinois 60603-6110
Distributed by Hudson Hills Press, Inc., 122 East 25th Street, 5th Floor,
New York, N.Y. 10010-2936
Editor and Publisher: Paul Anbinder
Distributed in the United States, its territories and possessions, and Canada
through National Book Network. Distributed in the United Kingdom,
Eire, and Europe through Art Books International Ltd.

Library of Congress Catalog Card Number: 98-74338

ISBN 0-86559-172-5

Frontispiece: Albert Bierstadt, *Mountain Brook*, 1863, oil on canvas
(cat. no. 87; see p. 190)

Illustration on page 6: John Quincy Adams Ward, *The Freedman*, modeled 1863,
bronze (cat. no. 88; see p. 193)

CONTENTS

8
Foreword
James N. Wood

9
Preface
Judith A. Barter

12
American Art in the "Great Grey City":
The Evolution of a Collection at The Art Institute of Chicago
Judith A. Barter

The American Arts Collection
Entries by Judith A. Barter, Kimberly Rhodes, and Seth A. Thayer, with contributions by Andrew Walker

47
From Colony to Nation

107
The Young Republic

165
The Civil War Era and the Gilded Age

261
The Modern Era

345
Glossary of Decorative Arts Terms

352
Index

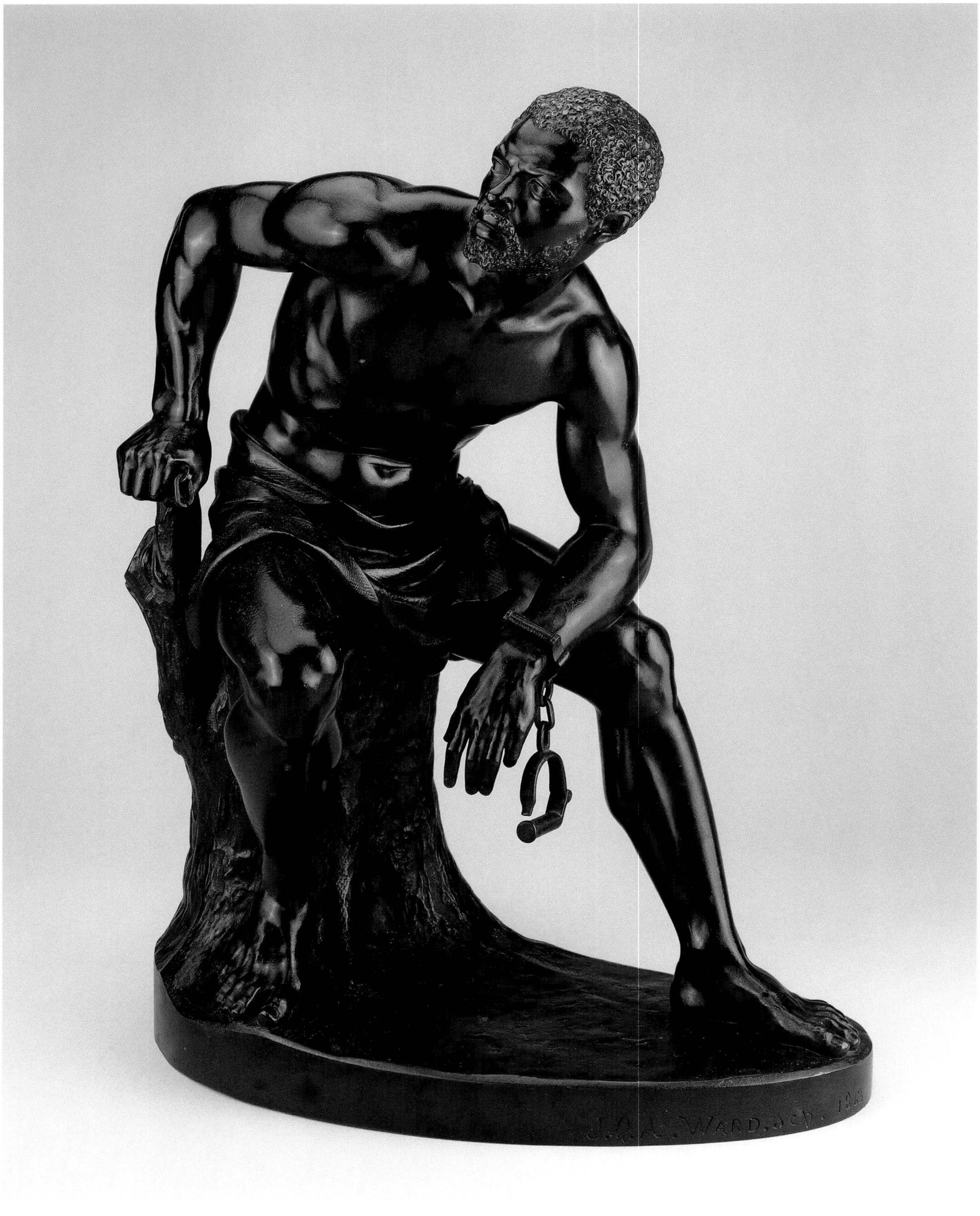
J.Q.A. WARD. Scp.

SPONSORS

The Henry Luce Foundation, Inc.

Chauncey and Marion Deering McCormick Foundation

Christie's

An anonymous donor

This volume is dedicated to the memory of
J. Peter McCormick

FOREWORD

CHICAGO IS CONSIDERED BY MANY to be the epitome of nineteenth-century American urbanism. After the Great Fire of 1871, the rough-and-tumble midwestern capital reinvented itself—and it has continued to reshape itself ever since. Constantly tearing down and rebuilding, Chicago displayed unbridled energy and served as a magnet for immigrants seeking opportunities. One hundred and five years ago, in the midst of a remarkable fair called the World's Columbian Exposition, the Art Institute opened its new home on Michigan Avenue. The museum has remained at the heart of the city and at the center of Chicago's cultural life ever since. It is therefore fitting that we now publish a volume dedicated to American arts and culture, reflecting the growth of the city's interest in the arts and the generosity of its patrons. Like Chicago itself, the Art Institute's collection of American arts is heavily weighted toward the second half of the nineteenth century and reflects the diverse artistic experiences of that period. This volume joins a series of volumes that focus on other departmental collections, but, unlike those catalogues, this book brings together many media—paintings, sculptures, and the decorative arts—to show the range of American cultural and aesthetic production.

We are grateful to Judith A. Barter, Field-McCormick Curator of American Arts, who envisioned and initiated this project. Her enthusiasm and energy brought the many pieces of this project together in short order. Over a three-year period, she and her staff—Kimberly Rhodes, Seth A. Thayer, and Andrew Walker—applied their scholarly skills to an insufficiently studied collection, shed new light on important objects, and prepared for publication many recent acquisitions. The realization of the volume was made possible by generous grants from the Henry Luce Foundation, Inc., the Chauncey and Marion Deering McCormick Foundation, Christie's, and an anonymous donor. Support from the Getty Conservation Trust in 1996 provided for the conservation of more than twenty major pieces of furniture and the reupholstery of a dozen eighteenth-century chairs. Working with Robert Mussey Associates, the curatorial staff selected period fabrics and restored original hardware. While these objects were off view, the staff of the American Arts Department completely reinstalled the permanent collection, making it more accessible and educational for our audience. It is my hope that the conclusion of the reinstallation and the publication of this volume will encourage scholars, students, and museum visitors to appreciate the range and importance of American arts at The Art Institute of Chicago, and will ensure that the collection continues to grow in the museum's second century.

James N. Wood
Director and President

PREFACE

THIS CATALOGUE PRESENTS a selection of notable objects from the almost three thousand works in the collections of the Department of American Arts at The Art Institute of Chicago. In recent years other catalogues have featured the museum's holdings of Italian, French, and British paintings, Italian drawings, and twentieth-century American paintings and sculpture. American architectural drawings, architectural fragments, and textiles have also been presented over the years in exhibition catalogues and various issues of the Art Institute's journal, *Museum Studies*, but this volume is the first book devoted specifically to the museum's important American paintings, sculpture, and decorative arts from roughly 1650—the era of early Puritan settlements in New England—to World War I, the onset of the modern era.

The diverse holdings of the Department of American Arts are reflected in the wide range of objects and media included in this catalogue. This volume is also unusual because it mixes in equal proportion the fine and decorative arts. In addition, many of the American paintings executed just before World War I that are housed in the Department of Twentieth-Century Painting and Sculpture have been included in acknowledgment of their importance to the history of American art.

Although the Department of American Arts was not formed until 1975, the Art Institute has collected American art of all types since it moved into its distinguished Michigan Avenue building in 1893. The introductory essay to this catalogue describes the formation of the American collection, traces its growth, and discusses some of the important patrons and support groups who have so generously and enthusiastically given objects and funds for the acquisition of works in this area. The catalogue entries themselves attempt to describe the aesthetic importance of the objects and to place them within a cultural and historical context. It is my hope that this discussion of paintings, sculpture, and decorative arts will make the American arts collection accessible to a broad audience and provide a basis for further scholarship, study, and interpretation. Ideally, the selection presented in this book will whet the appetites of its readers to visit the galleries often and see many more fine examples of American art on view at the Art Institute.

The realization of this book was a team effort in every sense. The goal of producing a catalogue of the most important American objects at the Art Institute was made possible by the generous support from the Henry Luce Foundation, Inc., and the guidance of Ellen Holtzman; the Chauncey and Marion Deering McCormick Foundation, directed by Charles E. Schroeder, Brooks McCormick, Charlotte McCormick, Mrs. Abby O'Neil, and Ms. Hilary Hunt; Christie's, with the help of Andrew Schoelkopf; and an anonymous donor. James N. Wood, Director and President of the Art Institute, and Deputy Director Teri J. Edelstein were supportive throughout the undertaking. Invaluable grant-writing support was provided by Karin Victoria, Meredith Miller Hayes, Gregory Perry, and Ellen Nedzel, and former staff members Mary Jane Keitel and Gregory Cameron. We also thank the Getty Conservation Trust for providing conservation funds for the restoration of many objects, enabling us to ensure their preservation and bring them to their proper period appearance. Furniture conservation services were performed by Robert Mussey, Christine Tompson, John Driggers, Melissa Carr, Tatiana Wilcke, Georgette Iannuzi, and Gerald Nadeau of Robert Mussey Associates, Boston. Under the direction of Frank Zuccari, the Conservation Department staff at the Art Institute—Faye Wrubel, Barbara Hall, Emily Dunn, Suzanne Schnepp, Steven Starling, and Kurt Vuillemot—worked tirelessly to make every object look its best. We also thank the conservators in the Department of Prints and Drawings, David Chandler and Harriet K. Stratis, and preparator Caesar Citraro. Christopher Fitzgerald of the American Arts staff prepared and moved objects for examination and photography, with the help of Reynold Bailey and the art-handling staff. Arrangements for the transporting of objects were handled by the Department of Museum Registration, Mary Solt, Executive Director, and her staff: Sally-Ann Felgenhauer, Frances Baas, and Vicki Wodarcyk. The photography of the collection was expertly executed by Alan Newman, Executive Director of Imaging, and his staff: Christopher Gallagher, Robert Hashimoto, Gregory Williams, Iris Wong, Robert Lifson, and former members Julie Zeftel and Anne Morse.

This book could not have come to fruition without the extraordinary research and interlibrary loan support provided by the staff of the Ryerson and Burnham Libraries, Jack Perry Brown, Executive Director. In particular, we thank Susan

Perry and Matt Crawford, former members Maureen Lasko, Natalia Lonchyna, and Alexis Petroff, and all the members of the reference and circulation staff. The staff of the library's archives division provided myriad sources for research as well. Thanks go to Archivists Bart Ryckbosch and Mary Woolever and assistant Deborah Webb. Curatorial colleagues at the Art Institute provided their expertise as well as encouragement. In the Department of Textiles, Christa C. Mayer Thurman, the Christa C. Mayer Thurman Curator of Textiles; Cynthia Cannon; and conservator Lorna Filippini were most helpful. Stephen Little, Pritzker Curator of Asian Art; Ian Wardropper, Eloise W. Martin Curator of European Decorative Arts and Sculpture; and Ghenete Zelleke, Curator of European Decorative Arts, all patiently answered questions. Marilyn Conrad, Kirsten Darnton, Bill Gross, and Mark Booth of the Department of European Decorative Arts and Sculpture, and former staff member Nora Buriks also provided support. In the Department of American Arts, additional help was provided by Kevin Sharp and Linda Pryka and former interns Carla Dunham, Elizabeth Kessler, Jennifer Miliken Downs, Merrill Falkenberg, and Gregory Foster-Rice.

The editing of the manuscript for this book and the production of the finished catalogue were expertly rendered by the Department of Publications, Susan F. Rossen, Executive Director. I wish to acknowledge the expertise of Michael Sittenfeld, Catherine Steinmann, Robert V. Sharp, and freelance editor Faith Hart, who shaped the text and brought refinement to our discussion of every object. I also owe thanks to a team of individuals who meticulously checked facts and tracked down obscure references: Susanne Breckenridge, Morgen Cheshire, Suzanne Gould, Katherine Irvin, and Laurie White. The elegant design of this book is the work of Dean Bornstein, and its splendid production is a reflection of the exacting standards of Sarah Guernsey, and the printing of Daniel Frank of Meridian Printing. Britt Salvesen of the Publications Department crafted the index, and Cris Ligenza provided assistance in numerous ways throughout the production of this book.

To our many colleagues at other institutions we owe an enormous debt of gratitude. Special thanks go to Morrison Heckscher, Peter Kenny, H. Barbara Weinberg, Thayer Tolles, and Stephanie Herdrich at the Metropolitan Museum of Art; Deborah Dependahl Waters, Museum of the City of New York; Jack Lindsay, Philadelphia Museum of Art; Donald Fennimore, Wendy Cooper, Janice Carlson, and Bert Denker, Henry Francis DuPont Winterthur Museum; Kevin Stayton, Barry Harwood, Linda Ferber, Barbara Gallati, and Teresa Carbone, Brooklyn Museum of Art; Patricia Kane and David Barquist, Yale University Art Gallery; Theodore E. Stebbins, Jr., Erica E. Hirshler, Ellenor Alcorn, Jeannine Falino, and Gerald W. R. Ward, Museum of Fine Arts, Boston; Professors Kathleen Swaim and James Freeman, University of Massachusetts, Amherst; Anna T. D'Ambrosio, Munson-Williams-Proctor Institute; Manon Theroux, Library Company of Philadelphia; Christopher Wilk, Victoria and Albert Museum; Philip Zea, Historic Deerfield; Christopher Gilbert, Temple-Newsam House; Ronald Hurst and Jonathan Prown, Colonial Williamsburg; Emily Neff and Katherine Howe, Museum of Fine Arts, Houston, and David Warren and Michael Brown, Bayou Bend Collection, Museum of Fine Arts, Houston; Lorna Condon and Richard Nylander, Society for the Preservation of New England Antiquities; Rodney Roland, Strawbery Banke Museum; Anna-Marie Sandecki, Louis Bann, and Ruth Cacvale, Tiffany and Company Archives; Marge Exton, Lenox, Inc., Archives; Thomas Sudbank, Diplomatic Reception Rooms, United States Government Department of State; Jackie Kenyon, Kendall College of Art and Design; Pamela Lucas, Grand Rapids Public Library; Leslie Greene Bowman, Los Angeles County Museum of Art; Elizabeth Broun and Richard Murray, National Museum of American Art, Smithsonian Institution; Nancy Anderson, National Gallery of Art; James Cook, University of Illinois; Marc Simpson, the Getty Information Institute; Susan Strickler, Currier Gallery of Art; David Brigham, Worcester Art Museum; David Park Curry, Virginia Museum of Fine Arts; Michael Shapiro and H. Nichols B. Clark, High Museum of Art; Sylvia Yount, Pennsylvania Academy of the Fine Arts; V. Scott Dimond, Bowdoin College Museum of Art; Elizabeth Kornhauser, Wadsworth Atheneum; Nancy Sojka, Detroit Institute of Arts; David Stetford, Norton Museum of Art; Elizabeth Oustinoff and Richard Ormond, John Singer Sargent Catalogue Raisonné Project, New York; Michael Boonstra, independent scholar, Titusville, Florida; James Cooke, independent scholar, Baltimore; and Dr. Roger W. Robinson, Willard House and Clock Museum.

Collectors, dealers, and colleagues in auction houses have also shared their knowledge generously. In particular I want to thank Janis Connor and Joel Rosenkranz, Peter Hill, Margaret Caldwell and Carl Florentino, Peter Sawyer, Charles Buckley, and Margo Johnson; Frank Levy, Deanne Levison, Robert Lionettei, Martin Grubman, Anne Haley, Stuart Feld, and William Kingsland; Arlene Palmer Schwind; Diana and Garry Stradling; and Peter Brant and Jean Bickley. Thanks also go to

Dean Failey, Jeanne Sloane, John Hayes, Ralph Carpenter, Jr., and Martha Willoughby of Christie's.

For their patient and enthusiastic support of this project I would like to thank the members of the Committee on American Arts and Chairman Marshall Field, and the members of the Antiquarian Society of The Art Institute of Chicago.

My deepest gratitude goes to my department personnel and fellow authors. Former staff members Kimberly Rhodes, now Assistant Professor of Art, Hollins University, and Seth A. Thayer, currently an independent consultant, researched the objects selected for publication and wrote the major portion of the catalogue entries. Assistant Curator of American Painting and Sculpture Andrew Walker meticulously edited entries and added others as new acquisitions entered the collection. All three labored to make information accessible to layman and scholar alike. Without them, the goal of our volume—to present American art of all types within an historical and cultural context—could not have been realized.

Finally, I wish to express, on behalf of all the authors, our gratitude to our families, who patiently sacrificed weekends, holidays, and other pleasures to support the research and writing of this volume.

Judith A. Barter
Field-McCormick Curator of American Arts

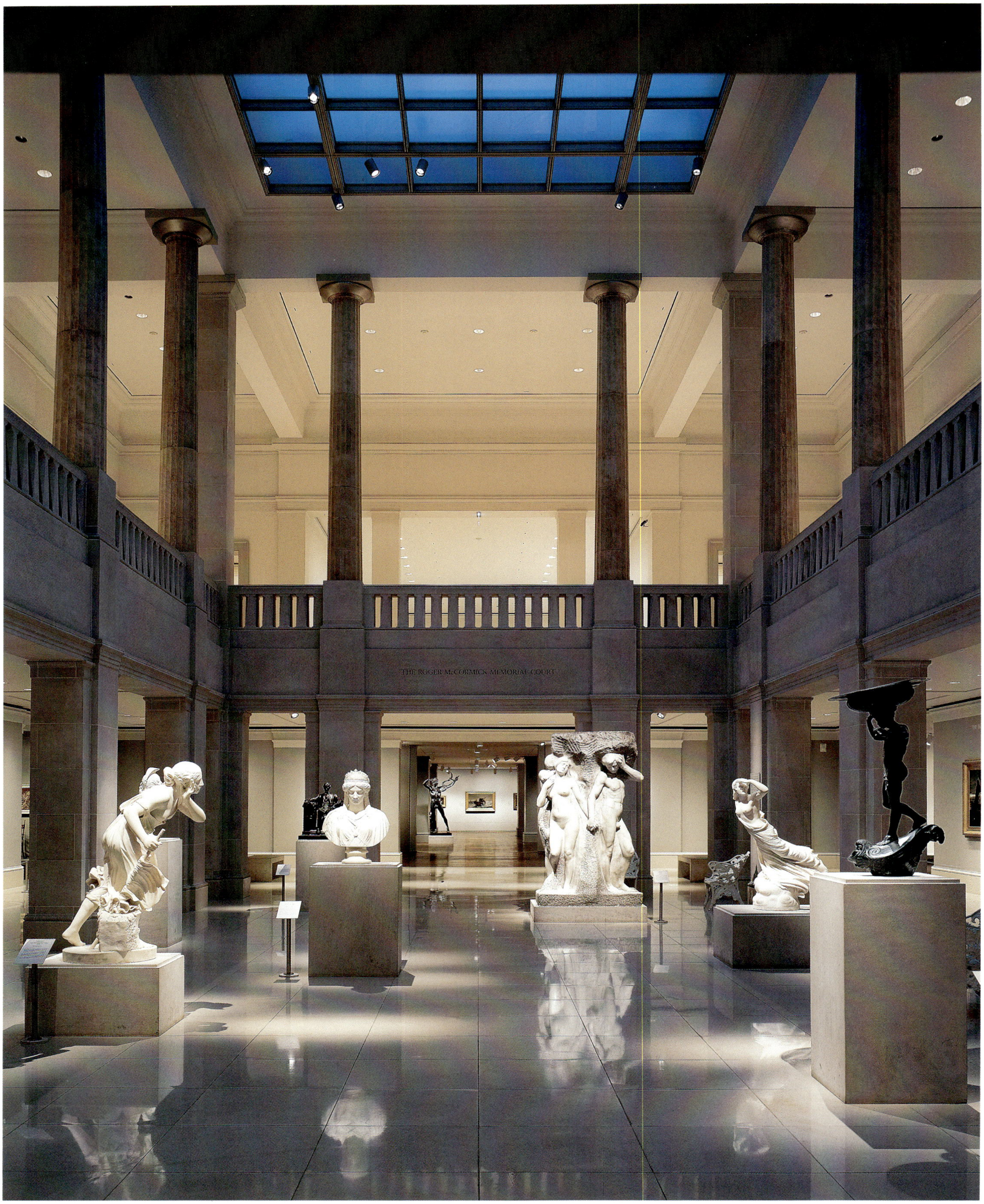
THE ROGER McCORMICK MEMORIAL COURT

AMERICAN ART IN THE "GREAT GREY CITY": THE EVOLUTION OF A COLLECTION AT THE ART INSTITUTE OF CHICAGO

JUDITH A. BARTER

Field-McCormick Curator of American Arts

CHICAGO IS THE QUINTESSENTIAL AMERICAN metropolis. It was wholly the invention of nineteenth-century commerce and industry, and its influence has been widespread. In his realist novel *The Pit* (1903), an unsparing description of the fierce world of commodity trading, Frank Norris described Chicago as the "Great Grey City," one that "imposed its dominion upon a reach of country larger than many a kingdom of the Old World." All regions of the vast country met in Chicago, on the lakefront and in the railway terminals. It served as the commercial and cultural link between eastern business and western industry, between southern mining, midwestern farming, and the city's own steel and machines. As Norris wrote, "Here, midmost in the land, beat the Heart of the Nation, whence inevitably must come its immeasurable power, its infinite, infinite, inexhaustible vitality . . . the true power and spirit of America . . . in its courage indomitable; subduing the wilderness in a single generation, defying calamity, and through the flame and debris of a commonwealth in ashes, rising suddenly renewed, formidable, and Titanic."[1]

Like a phoenix ascending from its ashes, Chicago reinvented itself after the Great Fire of 1871 as the modern, cosmopolitan American city. Business boomed, and there was no lack of money. Forward-looking citizens worried about the dearth of cultural institutions, which made them feel culturally inferior to their counterparts in the already centuries-old cities of Boston, New York, and Philadelphia. By the late 1870s, Chicago's leaders keenly felt the lack of a history. Very deliberately, they set out to ennoble commerce with the trappings of monuments and traditions: a symphony, a library, a university, and a museum.

The history of the museum they built—The Art Institute of Chicago—and its collection of American arts is inextricably tied to the rise of Chicago after the Great Fire, to the insecurities of a midwestern city without the grand traditions of New York or Boston, and to the program of education devised by wealthy Chicagoans for the city's working class. The growth of this collection was often marked by the conservatism of the museum's trustees and donors, although, as the reader will see, there were daring acquisitions and controversial exhibitions throughout the century.

The Chicago Society of Decorative Art and the Founding of the Art Institute

The ground for establishing a great art museum was prepared by the Chicago Society of Decorative Art, which was formed in 1877 at a meeting in the house of Dr. Ralph Isham, a tireless community leader who possessed the finest private library in Chicago at the end of the century.[2] Isham founded the society with the aid of Candace Wheeler, a follower of the principles of William Morris and the English Arts and Crafts movement, and a national authority on decoration and needlework design.[3] Like similar groups in eastern cities, the Chicago Society of Decorative Art was organized to "create in this community a desire for artistic decoration, and for a knowledge of the best methods of ornamentation; to provide training in artistic industries, and enable decorative artists to render their labor remunerative."[4] The membership fee was five dollars and anyone could join. Organizing directors Mrs. J. J. Glessner, Mrs. S. M. Nickerson, Mrs. Potter Palmer, and Mrs. J. Young Scammon, and members Mrs. Cyrus McCormick and Mrs. Martin Ryerson, were all to be instrumental supporters of the Art Institute.

FIG. 1. The J. Peter McCormick Sculpture Court, Field-McCormick Galleries of American Arts, in the Daniel F. and Ada L. Rice Building at The Art Institute of Chicago, 1997. Photograph © 1997 by Judith Bromley.

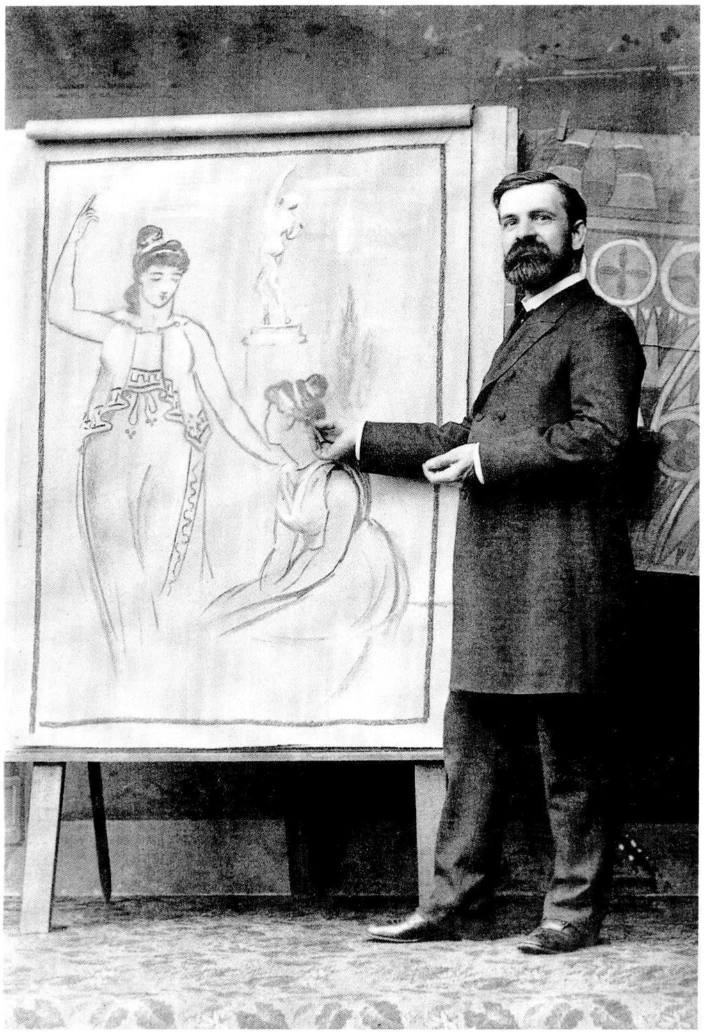

FIG. 2. William M. R. French (1843–1914), first director of the Art Institute, from 1885 to 1914.

In echoing aesthetic values prevalent in England and the eastern United States, the Chicago Society of Decorative Art was responding to the lack of a strong aesthetic sensibility in its native city. Since Chicago's essential purpose was to attract trade, the society attempted to create a link between commerce and culture, and thereby to temper their incompatibility. The society's substantial female membership reflected the nineteenth-century belief that men should confine themselves to the sphere of commerce while women should become involved in cultural pursuits. The captains of industry made money in the public world, and their wives beautified the domestic environment and provided cultural values for the next generation through clubs and civic organizations. Those cultural values were an important form of social control in Chicago. By 1880 nearly ninety percent of Chicago's population were first- or second-generation immigrants—the largest proportion of any American city.[5] Amidst such diversity, Chicago's elite promoted its societal views by determining the educational opportunities for the recently arrived populace.[6]

The Chicago Society of Decorative Art not only raised standards of taste but also created a market in Chicago for women's work. It exhibited painting, sculpture, needlework, wood carvings, tapestries, and decorative objects in all media made by women. It offered free classes, as well as exhibitions, and trained teachers to carry good decorative design sense and artistic inspiration back to their charges.[7] The Chicago Society of Decorative Art first rented rooms at 170 South State Street, and within a few years shared the premises of the newly formed Chicago Academy of Fine Arts, housed in a Romanesque Revival building designed by Burnham and Root at the southwest corner of Michigan Avenue and Van Buren Street. The civic leaders who in 1879 founded the Chicago Academy of Fine Arts, like those responsible for the Chicago Society of Decorative Art, envisioned an institution containing a permanent collection and devoted to teaching art and design. The academy would make it possible for young midwesterners to study art without having to go to Munich, Paris, or London. To do this, the new academy needed a collection of both Old Master and contemporary painting and sculpture. In December 1882 the academy was renamed The Art Institute of Chicago; its first director was William M. R. French (fig. 2), brother of sculptor Daniel Chester French.

In the meantime, the mission of the Chicago Society of Decorative Art had proved overwhelming for its members, forcing them to shift course in the late 1880s. In 1894 the society became a purchasing affiliate of the Art Institute, and eventually changed its name to the Antiquarian Society of The Art Institute of Chicago. As the oldest museum support affiliate in the country, it continues to provide funds for the purchase of decorative arts and sculpture. Many of the objects featured in this volume entered the museum's collection through the generosity and enthusiasm of the Antiquarian Society.

William M. R. French and the New Collection

The young museum director embodied Chicago's peculiar blend of civic progressivism and artistic conservatism. French was essentially interested in historical subjects, and was slow to champion contemporary art that was not figurative. Like many serious American collectors and artists of the late nineteenth century, he very deliberately looked to Paris for inspiration. In fact, as one historian observed, Chicagoans had a

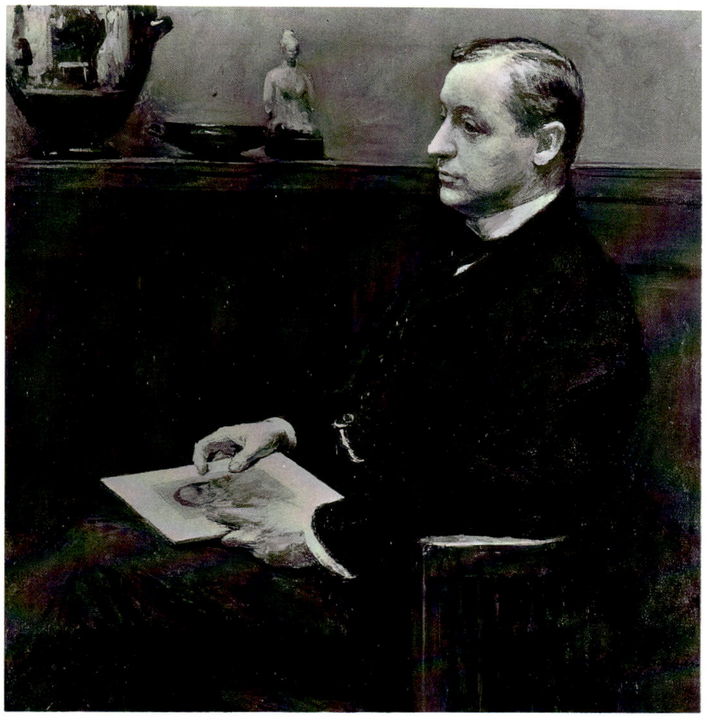

FIG. 3. Gari Melchers (1860–1932). *Charles L. Hutchinson*, c. 1902. Oil on canvas; 101.6 x 99.4 cm (40 x 39⅛ in.). Gift of Charles L. Hutchinson (1902.105). Unless otherwise noted, all artworks illustrated here are in the collection of The Art Institute of Chicago.

knack for bypassing New York and heading directly for France.[8] Henry James wrote in 1887, "When to-day we look for 'American art' we find it mainly in Paris. When we find it out of Paris, we at least find a great deal of Paris in it."[9] The number of expatriate American painters working in France had grown steadily since the Civil War, with significant colonies established in Concarneau, Giverny, and Pont-Aven. Indeed, at the 1889 Paris Exposition Universelle, so many American artists were represented that they received the highest number of awards—after the French, of course.

In March and April of that year, William French visited Paris with Art Institute President Charles L. Hutchinson (fig. 3).[10] Their trip had several purposes. First and foremost, French was looking at the Paris Exposition for acquisitions of contemporary art. Second, French and Hutchinson were sizing up the Paris exhibition because prominent Chicago civic leaders were planning for the 1893 World's Columbian Exposition.[11] The upcoming fair was viewed as a critical opportunity to put Chicago on the cultural and artistic map, and to present it as the most progressive and sophisticated of American cities.

French's travel notes show that he viewed the contemporary American painting section at the Paris Exposition and admired many of the pictures. At this point, French, heavily influenced by the art of the French realist painter Jules Breton, preferred genre scenes of peasants depicted along the rugged coasts of France or Holland, or in crude interiors. Perhaps such references to a simpler, preindustrialized past moved French and his captains-of-industry companions.[12] That he taught anatomy at the Art Institute, in addition to his directorial duties, also explains his predilection for figural compositions.

Several of the figure paintings that the director saw at the Paris Exposition—by William Merritt Chase, William Turner Dannat, George Hitchcock (a former Chicagoan), and Elihu Vedder—eventually entered the Art Institute's collection. Hitchcock's *Annunciation Lilies* (c. 1887; fig. 4) was singled out by critics for its excellent evocation of an outdoor setting and contemporary interpretation of a religious theme. The year after the Paris Exposition, Hitchcock sold it to Chicago's cultural doyenne, Mrs. Potter Palmer, who lent it to the 1890 Inter-State Industrial Exposition in Chicago. It came to the museum through Potter Palmer, Jr., in 1930. Vedder's *Fates Gathering in the Stars* (cat. no. 137), which was more to French's taste because of its classically inspired figures, was purchased for the Art Institute in 1919.[13]

While in Paris, French also thought a great deal about how to create museum installations. In the back of his travel notebook, he retained two Jeffrey and Company wallpaper samples used for the "Grande Bretagne" Fine Arts section of the Paris Exposition. The flocked, burgundy paper and olive-drab floral motif of the second sample provide an idea of the dark back-

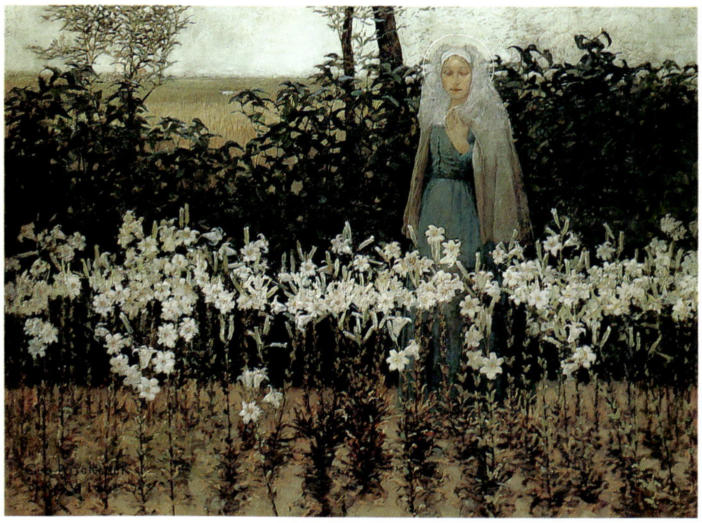

FIG. 4. George Hitchcock (1850–1913). *Annunciation Lilies*, c. 1887. Oil on canvas; 158.7 x 204.5 cm (62½ x 80½ in.). Potter Palmer Collection (1930.1289).

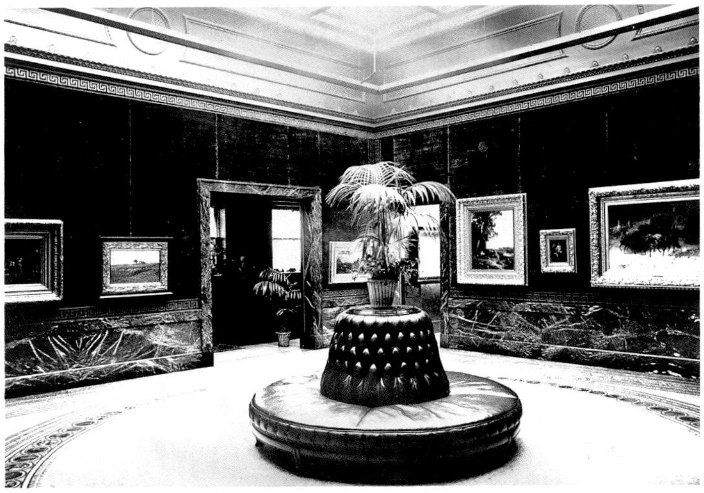

FIG. 5. The Elizabeth Hammond Stickney Room on the second floor of the Art Institute, 1901.

grounds upon which large Victorian pictures were later hung at the Art Institute. French made copious notes about wall colors he saw during his Paris sojourn. He described the walls at the Luxembourg sculpture gallery as a dull Pompeian red, the floor as a gray mosaic, and the dado as composed of several shades of gray. He also noted that the wooden pedestals were painted to look like variegated marble.

At the Musée du Louvre, French was especially taken with the Etruscan gallery. In his notebook, he made a pencil sketch of the flat, octagonal cases in the center of the room, with slightly inclined glass covers and, in the center, a vase resting atop a column. By the time he left Paris for London to see James McNeill Whistler's retrospective exhibition, he had very specific ideas for the Art Institute's galleries. He ordered pedestals from Bellman and Picadilly "in good colors . . . reds, Genoa greens, verde antique, and the beautiful shape called Thern."[14] He also acquired plaster copies of Greek vases, and anatomy and ornament books for teaching. French's taste and his admiration for the displays of Parisian museums and expositions no doubt influenced the work of Louis Millet, head of the design department at the School of the Art Institute. A decade later, he produced a design for the museum's Stickney memorial gallery (fig. 5) that featured a dark burgundy-brown wall color; a variegated black-and-gray marbleized dado; a gold, Greek-key-patterned stencil below the cornice; and a gray mosaic floor.[15]

French's interest in contemporary American art prompted the Art Institute to organize the first of its annual exhibitions of American oil paintings in May 1888. This began a tradition of annual, and later biennial, shows of contemporary American art.[16] These exhibitions brought to Chicago examples by American painters working at home and abroad, and established the city as a new center for contemporary American art. At first the American painting and sculpture exhibitions favored more traditional trends. Appearing occasionally among the highly finished genre scenes by such artists as Charles Courtney Curran, Henry Moeller, or Harry Siddons Mowbray were high-keyed Impressionist works by Chase or John Twachtman.

In his diary, French had noted only the more traditional figurative works at the Paris Exposition; and even though he visited the galleries of Paul Durand-Ruel, the dealer who championed Impressionism, he did not mention the movement. Yet one year later, French invited the Society of American Artists to exhibit at the Art Institute. Considered quite radical, the artists of this group had left the conservative National Academy fourteen years earlier.[17] The Chicago newspapers were either shocked or elated by the look of the Society of American Artists exhibition. The *Journal* moaned about meaningless, modern, "colorist" works, while the *Tribune* hailed the Impressionist pictures, saying, "At last our artists are learning that this young nation need not be ashamed to acknowledge her youth . . . [their works have] spontaneity, freshness . . . superb exuberance of feeling . . . [and convey a] rapture of life."[18] The American exhibitions sparked local debate over the nature of contemporary American art, a debate that would be continued and amplified by the World's Columbian Exposition in 1893.

The World's Columbian Exposition and the New Art Institute

By the time the United States had chosen Chicago as the site of the World's Fair, it was clear that the Art Institute had outgrown its home at Michigan Avenue and Van Buren Street. Not only did the selection of Chicago as the location of the fair focus international attention on the city, but it pushed the Art Institute's trustees to build a new museum on the east side of Michigan Avenue.

During the early 1890s, Chicago was quickly becoming the home of the tall office building, and the center of the movement to abandon historical architectural forms.[19] Yet even as new architecture came to the fore in the city, the museum looked to Europe and particularly to France for an historical, aesthetic direction. A photograph of Chicago's lakefront taken around 1895 shows the Art Institute building situated in the

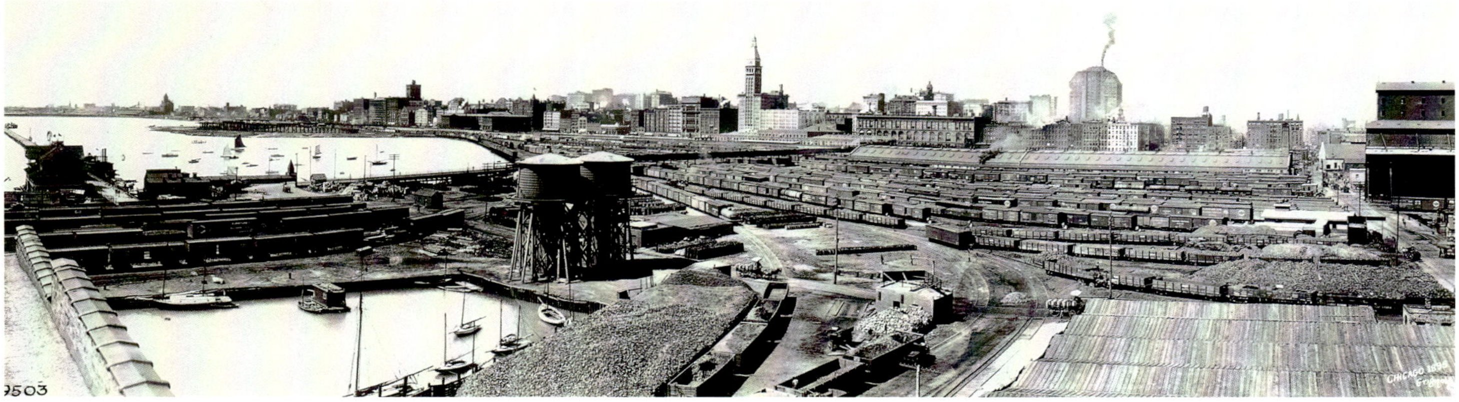

FIG. 6. View of Chicago lakefront, c. 1895, showing Illinois Central Railroad yards surrounding the Art Institute.

railroad yards (fig. 6). The Renaissance-inspired classicism of the museum is at odds with the tall buildings, water towers, train sheds, and smokestacks of the working city.

The Beaux-Arts or neo-Renaissance style of the Art Institute building, like that of most of the structures built for the World's Fair, constituted a rejection of the iron structures of the 1889 Paris Exposition such as the Palais des Machines or the Eiffel Tower. Rather, the designers of the World's Fair considered the look of ancient temples and courts and the ideals of the Renaissance as fitting models for American culture.[20] Most of the buildings for the World's Columbian Exposition, as well as the Art Institute itself (designed by Shepley, Rutan and Coolidge in 1891), were constructed in an architectural style that included temples, arches, and columns.

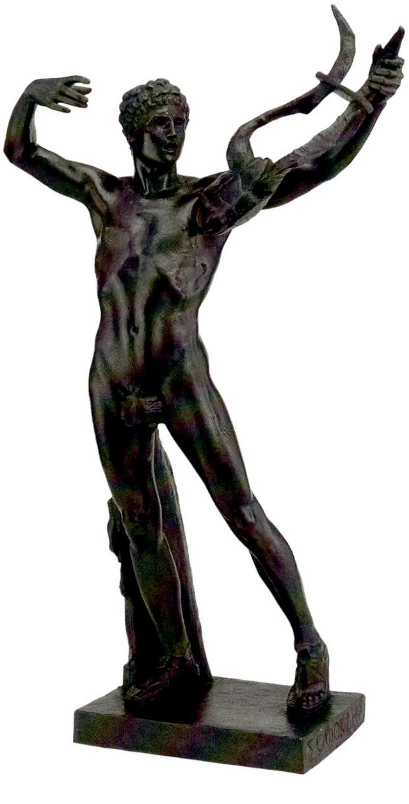

FIG. 7. John Donoghue (1853–1903). *Young Sophocles Leading the Chorus of Victory after the Battle of Salamis*, modeled 1885, cast 1911. Bronze; 238.8 x 134.6 cm (94 x 53 in.). Gift of Robert Allerton (1911.583).

Visitors to the World's Fair saw one of the largest selections of contemporary American art ever assembled. By contrasting late nineteenth-century American culture with the historical commemoration of Columbus's voyage, the organizers of the World's Fair hailed American painting and sculpture as the best the new world had to offer, worthy of a place alongside that of Europe.[21] The art shown at the World's Fair—including that in the American displays—was overwhelmingly conservative. Those who responded to the neoclassical vision of the fair included Chicago sculptor John Donoghue. His plaster cast *Young Sophocles Leading the Chorus of Victory after the Battle of Salamis* (1885), which was displayed at the fair and then at the Art Institute, recalled the idealized male nude of the ancient world. Chicago collector Robert Allerton had the piece cast in bronze in 1911, and that is the version now in the Art Institute's collection (fig. 7). Other neoclassically inspired American sculptures came to the museum shortly after the fair: Horatio Greenough's *Abdiel* (1838/43; cat. no. 68) entered the collection in 1894, and Randolph Rogers's *Nydia, the Blind Flower Girl of Pompeii* (1858; cat. no. 79) arrived at the museum in 1896.

The classical idealism of these works was complemented by acquisitions reflecting the influence of French naturalism promoted by sculptor Lorado Taft, a professor at the School of the Art Institute (see below). In 1899 the museum received a group of small bronzes of animals by the self-taught Chicago artist Edward Kemeys. His work was compared to that of France's

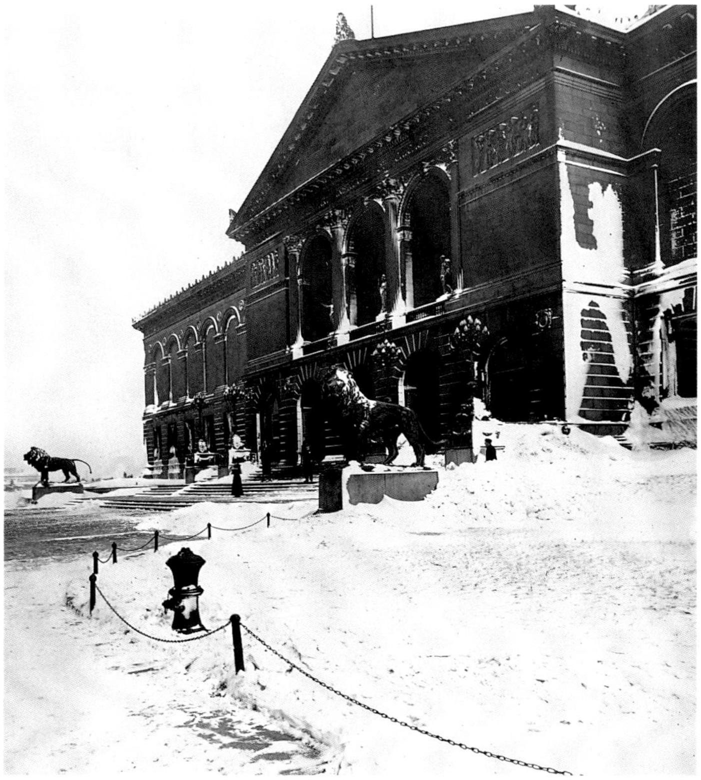

FIG. 8. Front view of the Art Institute, c. 1894, with the bronze lions sculpted by Edward Kemeys (1843–1907).

most famous *animalier*, Antoine-Louis Barye, whose sculptures William French had seen in Paris earlier. But Kemeys' popularity at the end of the century was also due to his scientific attention to detail and to presenting animals in an appropriate physical setting. His work at the World's Fair was admired by Hutchinson and by trustee Bryan Lathrop. The board suggested that Kemeys' heroic-sized, paired lions be cast at the American Art Bronze Foundry in Chicago. Lathrop's sister, Mrs. Henry Field, gave the bronze lions to the museum, whose exterior on Michigan Avenue they have guarded ever since (fig. 8).[22]

Popular American paintings at the World's Fair included Walter Shirlaw's *Toning the Bell* (1874; cat. no. 96), lent by J. H. Willing of Chicago. The picture reflects the somber hues and tactile brushwork of artists who studied in Munich. Chase's oil portrait *Alice* (c. 1892; fig. 9) is distinguished by a similarly dark, dramatic palette. The *Chicago Tribune* exclaimed that Chase's painting represented the "whole kingdom of Childhood" and possessed the "rare tenderness of a poem by Longfellow."[23] After the fair, *Alice* was purchased for the Art Institute by Chicago banker Ernest Hamill.

Also shown at the World's Fair was John Singer Sargent's

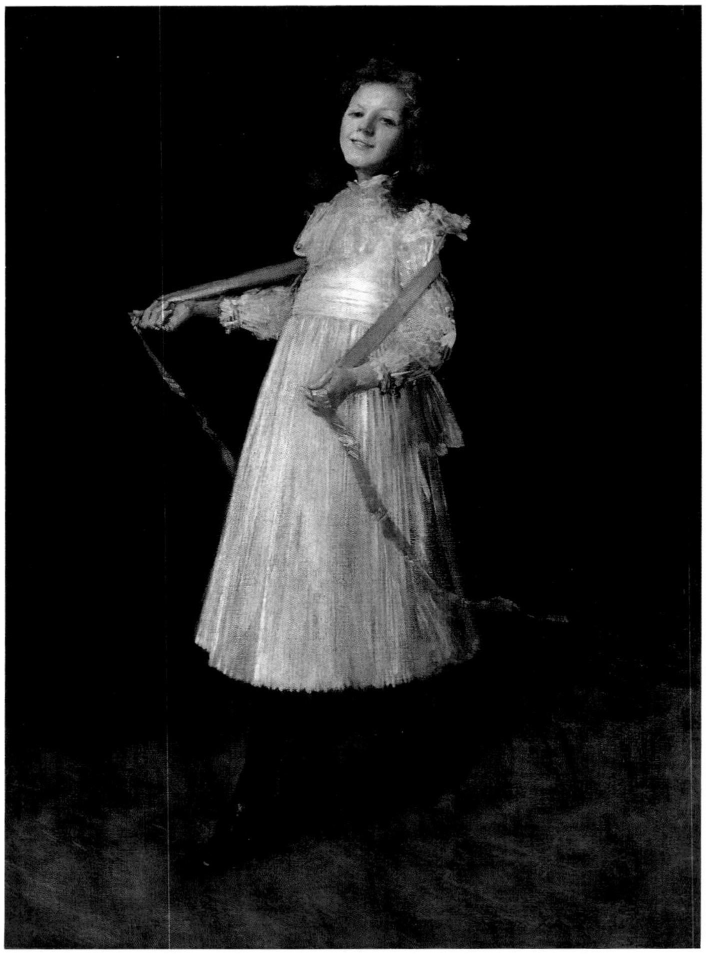

FIG. 9. William Merritt Chase (1849–1916). *Alice*, c. 1892. Oil on canvas; 171.8 x 125.5 cm (67 5/8 x 49 3/8 in.). Gift of Ernest A. Hamill (1893.107).

Study from Life (1891; fig. 10), a depiction of a young, nude Egyptian woman that is the polar opposite of *Alice*. Sargent painted it at a moment when he was gathering material for his Boston Public Library murals and exploring the exotic cultures of the Middle East. *Study from Life* reveals the Victorian acceptance of overt sexuality within a distant and therefore contained cultural framework. A rare departure from Sargent's bravura society portraits, the picture exudes a naturalism and intimacy that stem from the model's seeming unawareness of her audience.

Early Chicago Collecting

One of Sargent's closest friends, and the eventual owner of *Study from Life*, was Chicagoan Charles Deering (fig. 11), who collected and later donated many important works to the Art Institute. In 1876, while serving in the Navy, Deering met

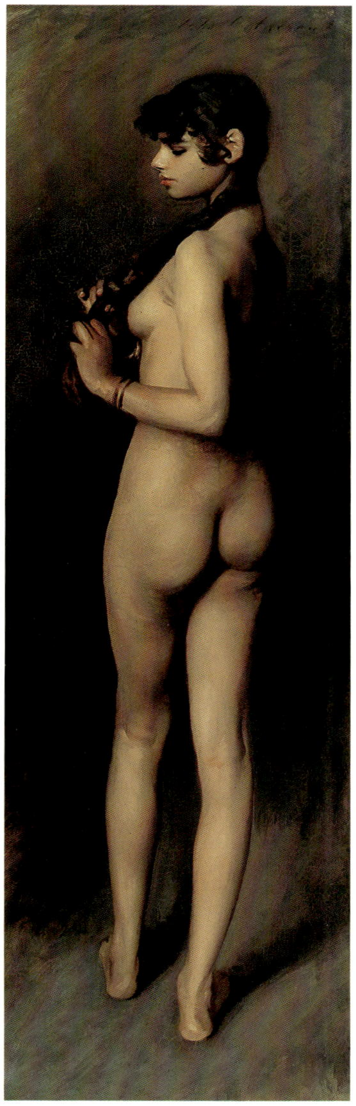

FIG. 10. John Singer Sargent (1856–1925). *Study from Life*, 1891. Oil on canvas; 185.4 x 58.4 cm (73 x 23 in.). Anonymous loan (82.1972).

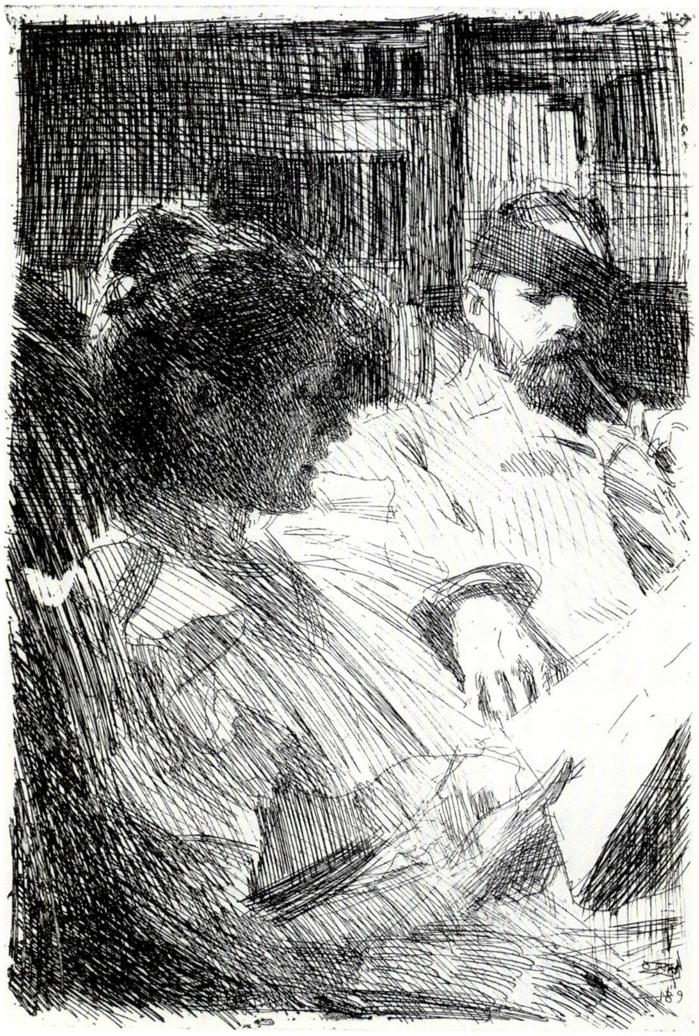

FIG. 11. Anders Zorn (Swedish, 1860–1920). *Reading: Mr. and Mrs. Charles Deering*, 1893. Etching; 24 x 16 cm (9 7/16 x 6 5/16 in.) (plate); 26.7 x 21.2 cm (10 1/2 x 8 3/8 in.) (sheet). Wallace L. DeWolf and Charles Deering Collections (1927.1851).

Sargent in Newport, Rhode Island.[24] Sargent introduced Deering to artists J. Carroll Beckwith and Augustus Saint-Gaudens. Deering's fondness for Sargent may explain why he made a concerted effort to own one of Saint-Gaudens's bas-reliefs of the painter's sister, Violet Sargent (c. 1908; cat. no. 131).[25] Deering and his brother James also formed close friendships with Walter McEwen and Gari Melchers, American artists working abroad. Melchers and the Deerings motored through Europe together; and Melchers was a frequent guest at Vizcaya, the Mediterranean-style villa James built near Miami. The Art Institute would eventually benefit from the friendship between James Deering and Melchers when the collector bequeathed to the museum a number of representative works by this artist spanning the period between 1885 and 1915.

During the 1893 World's Columbian Exposition, Charles Deering met the painter and printmaker Anders Zorn, who was the Swedish commissioner of fine arts. Soon thereafter, Deering rented Zorn's Paris studio with the intention of establishing himself as a painter, but eventually gave up art to join his father's business, Deering Harvester Company (which later became International Harvester Company). Henceforth, Deering's contribution to the visual arts was that of a discriminating collector and benefactor. He collected the work of his friend Sargent and amassed a complete collection of Zorn's graphic works. Included among the more than four thousand prints he bequeathed to the Art Institute were important examples by Americans central to the etching revival of the 1870s and 1880s: Otto Bacher, Joseph Pennell, Charles Adams Platt, and Whistler.

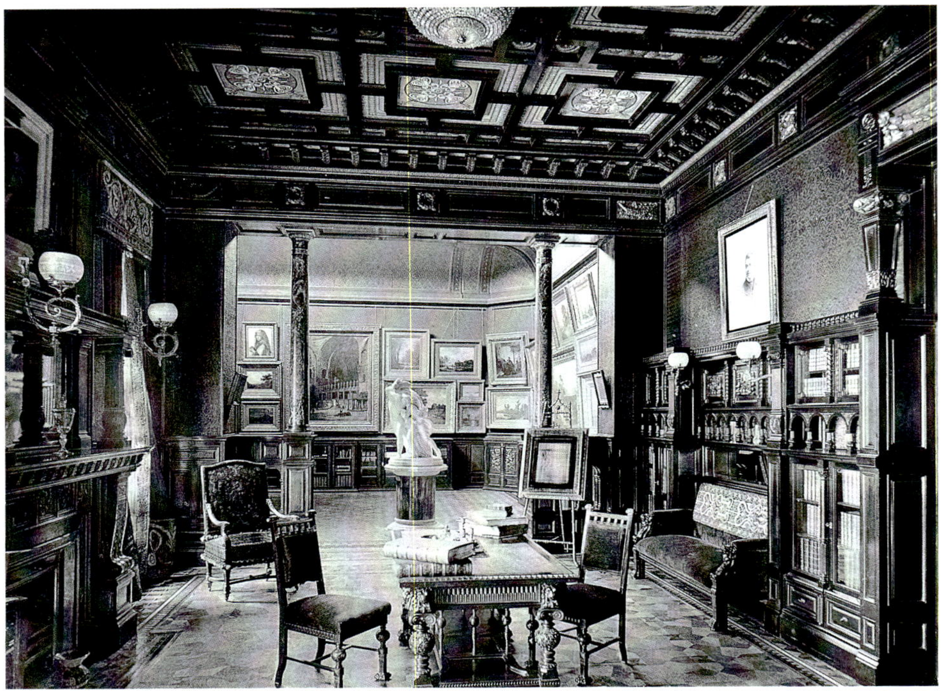

FIG. 12. Samuel M. Nickerson's library and gallery. On the back wall is David Neal's 1869 painting *Interior of St. Mark's, Venice* (fig. 13). Photograph from *Artistic Houses* (New York, 1884), vol. 2, pt. 1, pl. 25.

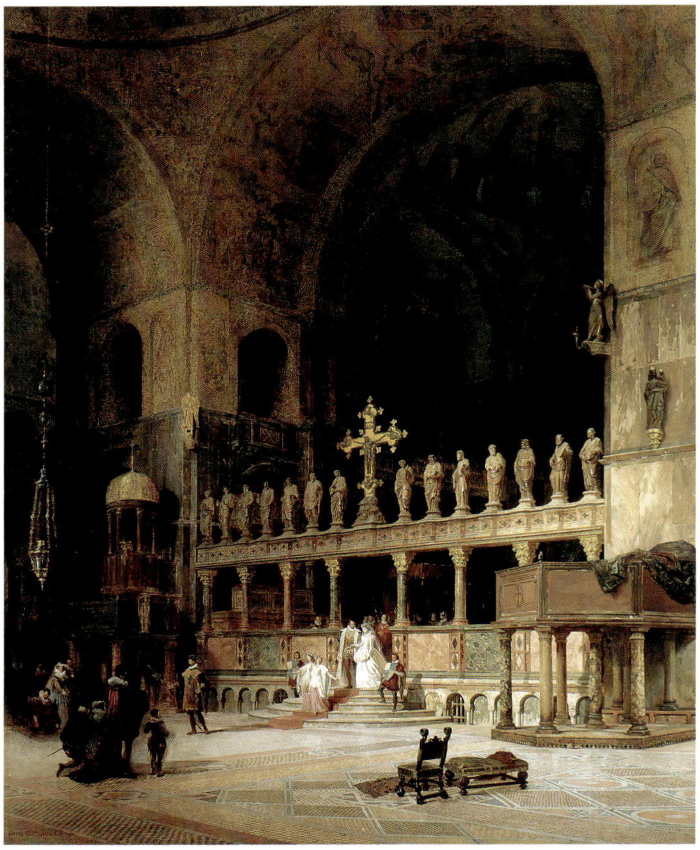

FIG. 13. David Neal (1838–1915). *Interior of St. Mark's, Venice*, 1869. Oil on canvas; 184.2 x 148.7 cm (72½ x 58½ in.). Mr. and Mrs. Samuel M. Nickerson Collection (1887.232).

While the Deering brothers acquired figurative works produced at the end of the nineteenth century, Samuel Mayo Nickerson, a distiller and banker who had arrived in Chicago in 1857, formed an art collection that included European portraits, genre paintings, and American landscapes. By the early 1880s, Nickerson's collection was the largest in the Midwest. His sumptuous home was included in *Artistic Houses* (1884), a large-format book that documented the houses of wealthy Americans; on the back wall of Nickerson's library, as seen in one of the book's illustrations (fig. 12), hung David Neal's *Interior of St. Mark's, Venice* (1869; fig. 13).[26] Neal's monumental painting was consistent with the Italianate theme of the library, which was finished in ebony and had walls covered in gold and olive silk. When Nickerson left Chicago for New York in 1900, he donated his entire collection to the Art Institute. Among the American selections were landscapes by Thomas Cole, Samuel Coleman, George Inness, William Trost Richards, and Elihu Vedder (1875; cat. no. 114). These provided the basis of the museum's American painting collection, as well as a counterpoint to the figurative works collected for the museum by William French. Nonetheless, when compared to the modern French landscapes that the Palmers were buying and giving to the museum at this time, the Nickerson Collection is striking for its conservative character.

Sara Hallowell, Bertha Honoré Palmer, and Impressionism

Among the most adventurous collectors of the period was Bertha Honoré Palmer (fig. 14), wife of the Chicago real estate magnate Potter Palmer. A pillar of the Art Institute and one of Chicago's most powerful and important art patrons, she was an organizer of the women's art exhibits at the 1893 World's Fair. Her legendary collection of French Impressionist paintings began with her friendship with Sara Tyson Hallowell (fig. 15), an art critic and consultant who lived in both Chicago and Paris.

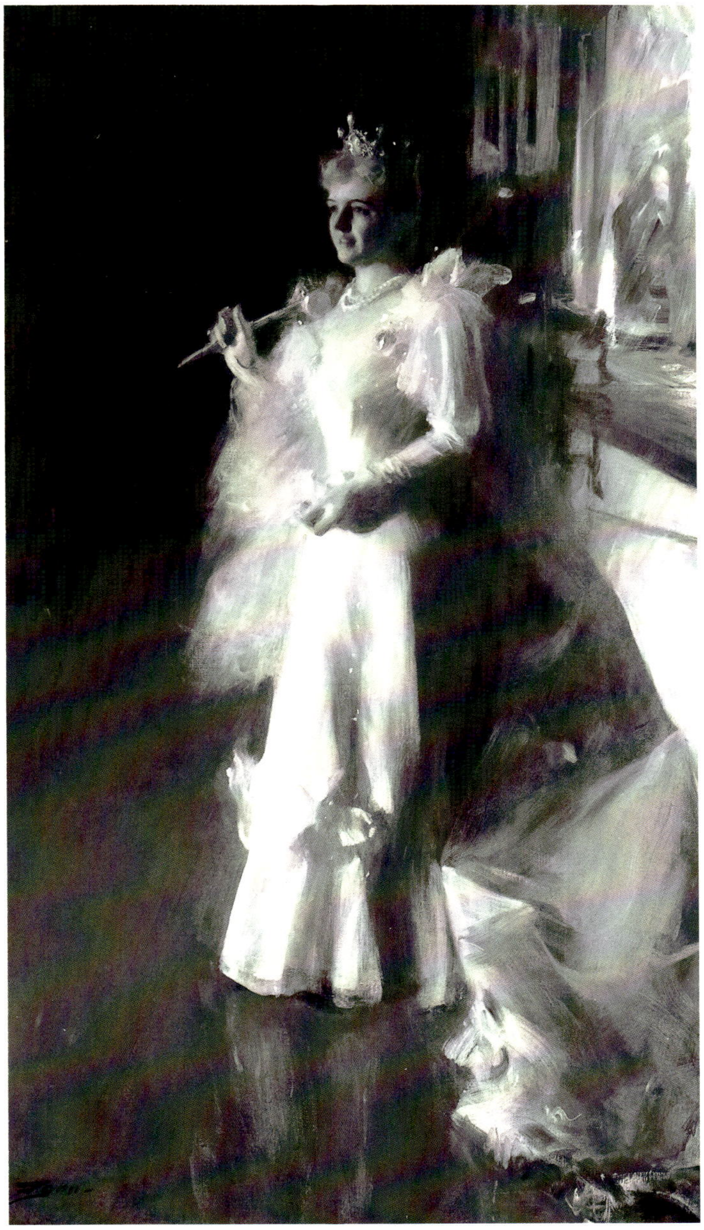

FIG. 14. Anders Zorn. *Mrs. Potter Palmer*, 1893. Oil on canvas; 258 x 141.2 cm (101⅝ x 55⅝ in.). Potter Palmer Collection (1922.450).

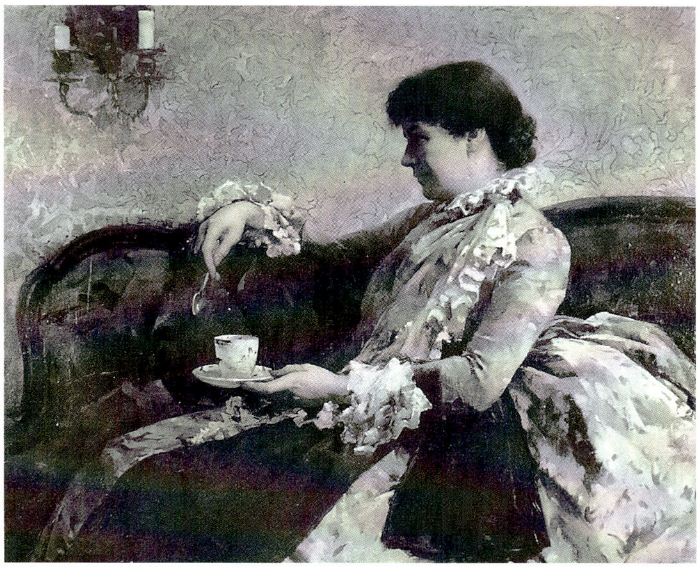

FIG. 15. Mary Fairchild MacMonnies (1858–1946). *Portrait of Mlle. S. H. (Sara Tyson Hallowell)*, 1886. Oil on canvas; 97.2 x 111.8 cm (38¼ x 44 in.). Cambridge University, Robinson College, Gift of Marion Hardy.

Hallowell moved to Chicago from Philadelphia in 1873 and became secretary of the art department of the Inter-State Industrial Expositions in Chicago during the 1870s. A New York critic said of the 1885 exposition, which Hallowell managed, that it had bested New York, Boston, and Philadelphia by featuring the most important pictures of the Paris Salon. "Bravo Chicago," he wrote, "and particularly bravo, Miss Sara Hallowell!"[27] By 1888 French had engaged Hallowell to select art for the annual American exhibitions at the Art Institute. In this capacity, she visited the studios of Americans abroad, made selections, and arranged for these works to be shipped directly to the Art Institute (she eventually settled in France in the 1890s).[28]

Around 1889 Hallowell began to serve as an adviser to Mr. and Mrs. Potter Palmer, and in that year the Palmers made their first purchase of a pastel by Edgar Degas.[29] Hallowell also introduced the Palmers to a friend of hers from Philadelphia who had lived almost exclusively in France, the artist Mary Cassatt. In 1892 the couple purchased a set of Cassatt's 1890–91 color prints and her pastel *Young Mother* (now in the Art Institute's collection).[30] Until that time, the Palmers' collecting interests had been more traditional, encompassing French Barbizon pictures as well as American works. They had commissioned portrait busts by Hiram Powers (1871; figs. 16–17) and had purchased landscapes by Eastman Johnson (1876; cat. no. 106) and Hitchcock (1887; cat. no. 129).[31] But after Mrs. Palmer met Sara Hallowell, she committed herself to French Impressionism.[32]

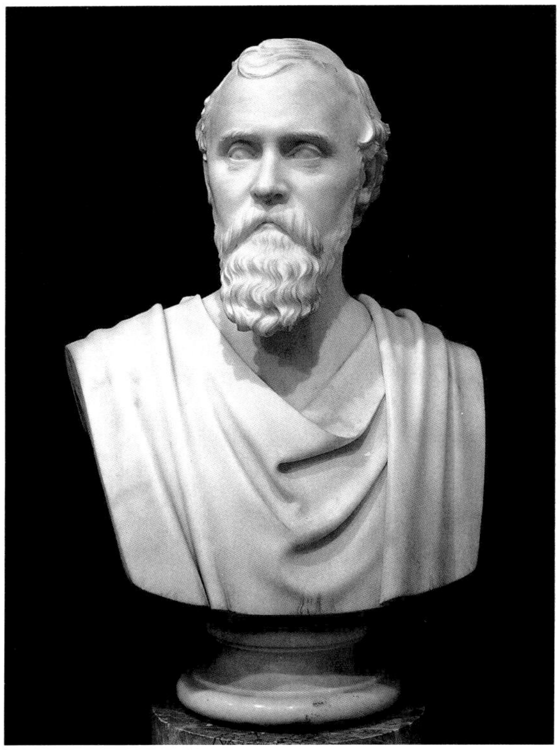

FIG. 16. Hiram Powers (1805–1873). *Potter Palmer*, 1871. Marble; 72.4 x 44.3 x 29.5 cm (28½ x 17⁵⁄₁₆ x 11⅝ in.). Gift of Gordon and Janis Palmer (1900.494.1).

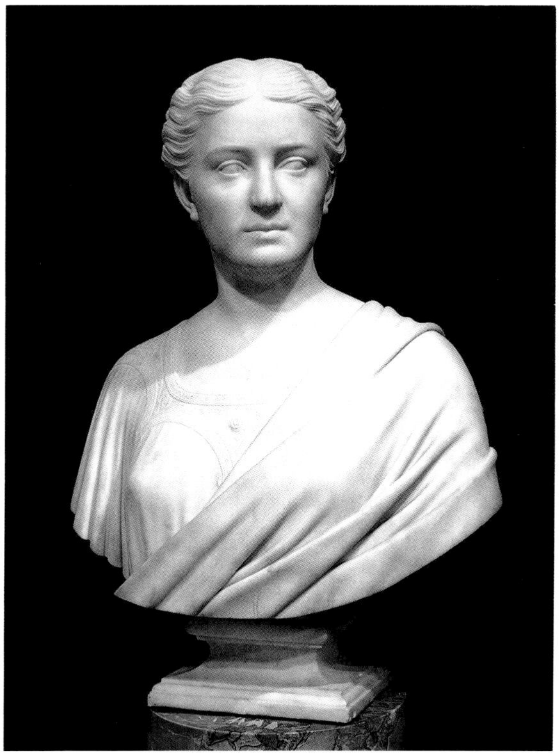

FIG. 17. Hiram Powers. *Mrs. Potter Palmer*, 1871. Marble; 69.5 x 49.5 x 29.5 cm (27⅜ x 19½ x 11⅝ in.). Gift of Gordon and Janis Palmer (1900.494.2).

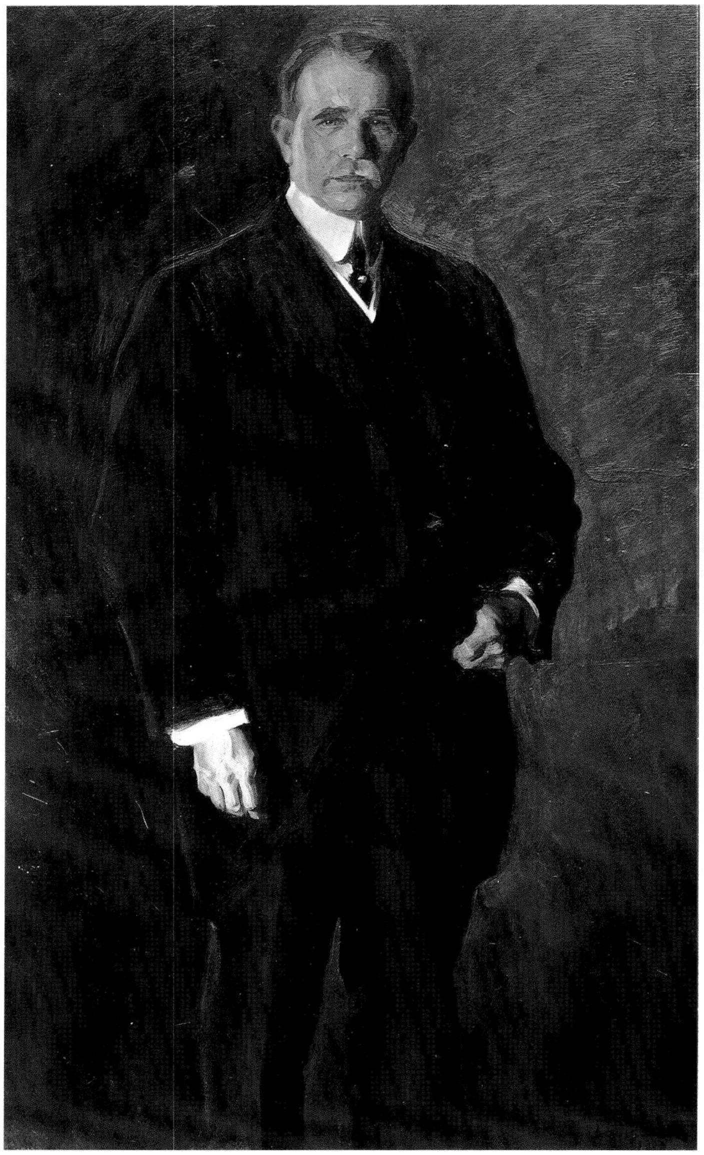

FIG. 18. Louis Betts (1873–1961). *Martin A. Ryerson*, 1913. Oil on canvas; 168.3 x 96.5 cm (66¼ x 38 in.). Mr. and Mrs. Martin A. Ryerson Collection (1933.1183).

Hallowell had persuaded the Paris dealer Paul Durand-Ruel to exhibit paintings by Degas, Claude Monet, and Camille Pissarro at the Illinois Inter-State Industrial Exposition of 1890.[33] This elicited such excitement that she became a leading contender for the position of director of the Department of Fine Arts for the 1893 World's Fair. Mrs. Palmer lobbied on her behalf, but Hallowell's candidacy fell victim to gender discrimination. Nonetheless, Hallowell served as assistant to the director of the Department of Fine Arts, Halsey Ives, and was influential in the selection of American artworks at the fair, particularly those displayed in the Woman's Building.[34]

While the American art at the fair was hardly avant-garde, Mrs. Palmer tried to make sure the women's art displayed was more exciting. She approached two American women artists living in France, Cassatt and Mary Fairchild MacMonnies, to create murals for the Woman's Building.[35] Large murals by women were unusual at the time. Cassatt, the only American woman to show with the original Impressionist group, was selected to depict "modern woman." No doubt Mrs. Palmer liked Cassatt's modernism, as well as her independence. The admiration was mutual. "I suppose," said Cassatt, "it is Mrs. Palmer's French blood which gives her organizing powers and her determination that women should be *someone* and not *something*."[36] Cassatt's mural was a triptych that addressed the lives of contemporary women. She depicted women picking fruit from the tree of knowledge and playing music. Although classical in feeling, and greatly influenced by the murals of the French artist Pierre Puvis de Chavannes and the frescoes of the Italian Renaissance painter Sandro Botticelli, the figures appeared in contemporary dress; and the color scheme, which included pinks, greens, purples, and golds, seemed shockingly modern to fairgoers. This work and MacMonnies' accompanying mural celebrating "primitive woman," which was more traditional in style, were important because they brought attention to contemporary work by women. It is a mystery and a tragedy that both murals, which have been lost, did not enter the Art Institute or another local institution after the World's Fair closed.[37]

The French-American connections at the turn of the century led to interesting friendships and collecting opportunities. Cassatt's association with Hallowell, Bertha Palmer, and the American Impressionist circle at Giverny resulted in her acquaintance with Art Institute President Charles Hutchinson, who purchased some of her drypoints for himself in 1911. She also knew trustee Martin A. Ryerson (fig. 18), who amassed an extraordinary collection of works of art from the fifteenth to the twentieth century, including paintings, sculptures, tex-

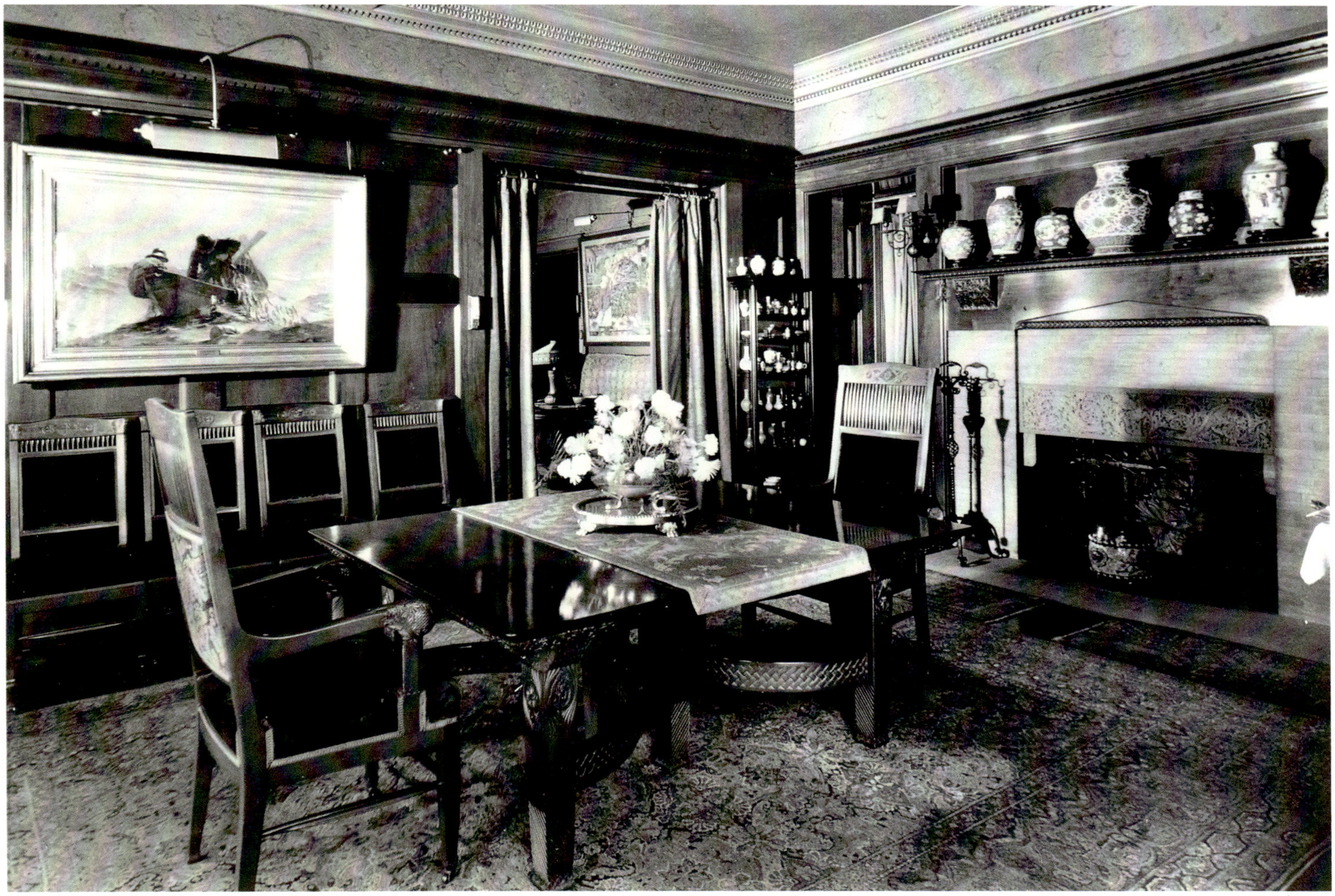

FIG. 19. Residence of Martin A. Ryerson, c. 1930. On the wall to the left is Winslow Homer's 1885 painting *The Herring Net* (cat. no. 110).

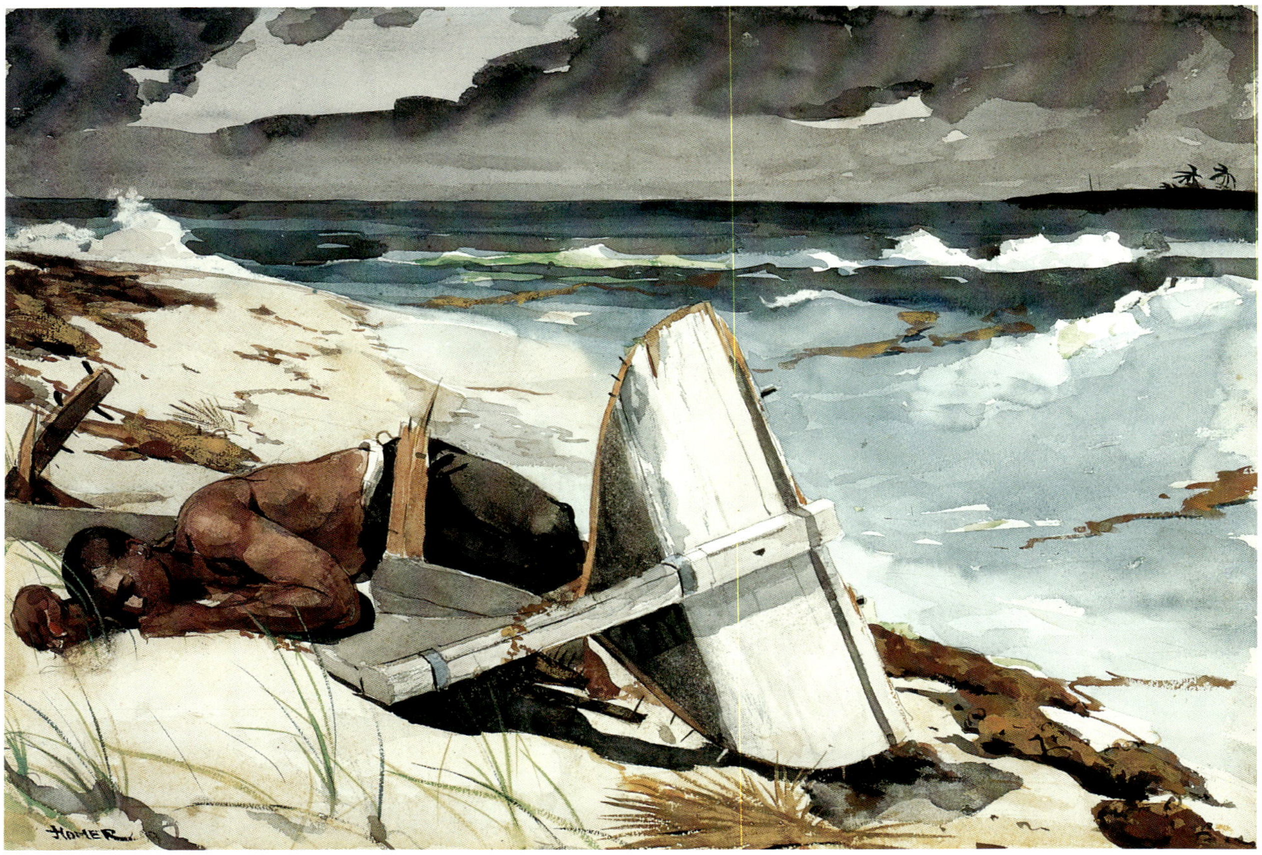

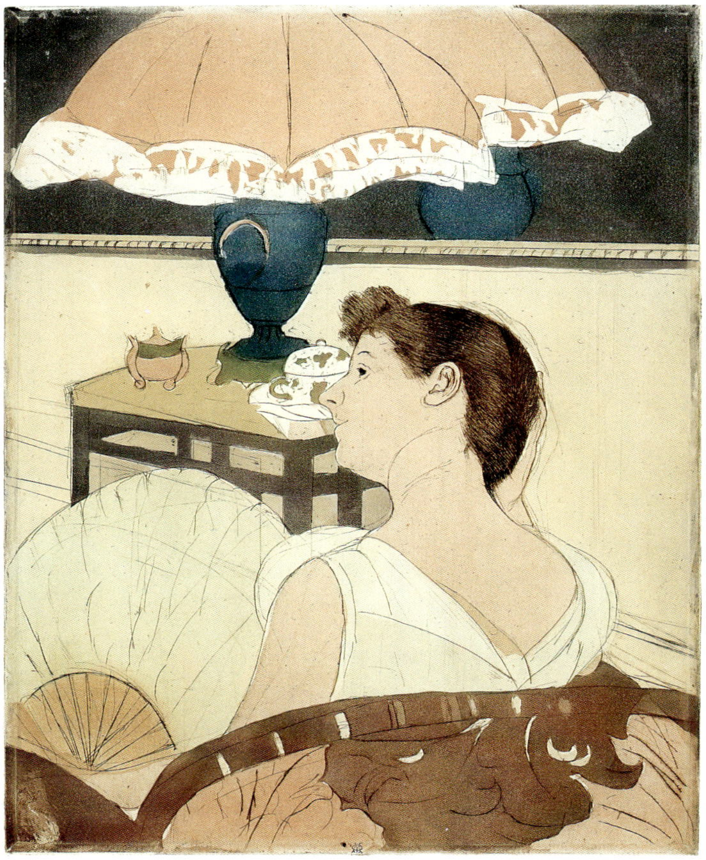

FIG. 20. Winslow Homer (1836–1910). *After the Tornado, Texas,* 1899. Watercolor; 37.8 x 54.4 cm (14⅞ x 21⅜ in.). Mr. and Mrs. Martin A. Ryerson Collection (1933.1235).

tiles, prints and drawings, Asian art, and European decorative arts. In the area of American art, Ryerson acquired numerous paintings by Arthur B. Davies; and he was drawn to the monumental heroicism of Winslow Homer's *Herring Net* (1885; cat. no. 110), which was shown at the World's Fair, purchased by Ryerson in 1915 (see fig. 19), and later given to the Art Institute. He was also interested in the Impressionist qualities of Homer's light-filled watercolors, such as *After the Tornado, Texas* (1899; fig. 20), and of Twachtman's landscapes, such as *The White Bridge* (after 1895; cat. no. 134); and he was fascinated with Sargent's bravura brushwork in *Venetian Glass Workers* (1880/82; cat. no. 98) and the modernism in Cassatt's Japanese-inspired color prints of 1890–91 (see fig. 21). While Cassatt's work was collected by the museum's trustees, and her

FIG. 21. Mary Cassatt (1844–1926). *The Lamp,* 1890–91. Drypoint and aquatint on cream laid paper; 32.3 x 25.2 cm (12 11/16 x 10 in.). Mr. and Mrs. Martin A. Ryerson Collection (1932.1290).

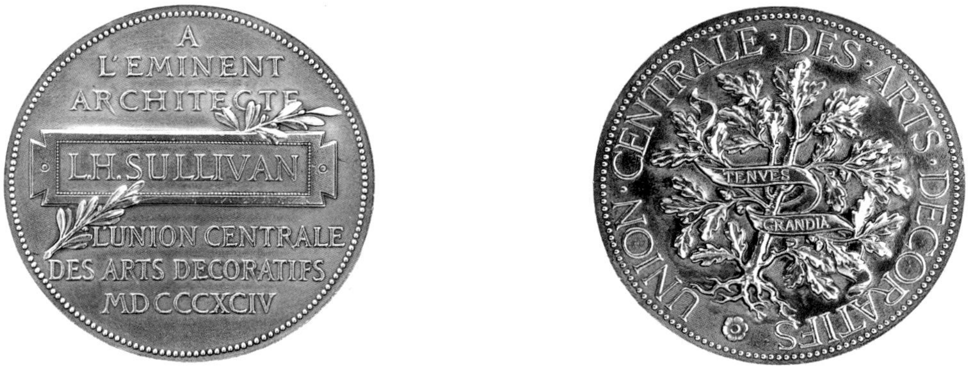

FIG. 22. Medal awarded to Louis Sullivan by the French government in 1894. The Art Institute of Chicago, Ryerson and Burnham Libraries, Sullivaniana Collection.

counsel was sought on acquisitions,[38] it was not until 1910 that the Art Institute purchased one of her most famous pictures, *The Child's Bath* (1893; cat. no. 128).

Ryerson's American paintings collection reflected the tension between nativist realism (of a work like Homer's *Herring Net*) and the Francophile, flattened, decorative qualities of Twachtman's landscapes and Cassatt's Japanese-influenced color prints. In fact, *japonisme* (that is, the intense interest in Japanese culture) took hold early in Chicago. Louis Gonse's groundbreaking book *L'Art japonaise*, published in Paris in 1883, was translated and published in Chicago by 1891. And Deakin's Art Rooms in Chicago showed Japanese prints in 1896.[39] Through Chicago's interest in *japonisme*, the Paris–Chicago connection was strengthened.

Chicago and Internationalism, 1895–1910: The Arts and Crafts Movement

The many Chicago–Paris connections promoted by the Art Institute and its patrons during the 1880s and 1890s were strengthened by architects and designers working in Chicago in the same period. Daniel Burnham's "Chicago Plan," which he first proposed to the city's park commissioners in 1897 and published in 1909, was indebted to Baron Georges Eugène Haussmann's 1854–70 design for Paris with its wide boulevards.[40] Burnham envisioned transforming Chicago into a Paris by Lake Michigan. Images of the French capital appear throughout his plan. And yet internationalism began to cut both ways, as Chicago became known in Europe as an important design center. In 1894 architect Louis Sullivan was awarded a medal by the French government (fig. 22); in the same year, he donated some of his organic architectural plaster molds for ornaments to the Union Centrale des Arts Décoratifs in Paris, where they were displayed in a "Sullivan Room" and formed a link between the abstracted naturalism of early Chicago Prairie School decoration and French Art Nouveau.[41]

Sullivan's aesthetics provided a transcendental component to modern, pragmatic buildings. For architects, his firm became a training ground and the philosophical foundation for Prairie School design. Sullivan influenced three men who were to become leaders of the Prairie School: George Grant Elmslie, George Washington Maher, and Frank Lloyd Wright. While their designs varied widely, these individuals shared the viewpoint that a structure's function should determine its form, and that exterior and interior spaces should be fully harmonious. Consequently, Prairie School architects designed furniture, fabrics, lighting fixtures, and other features for their buildings.

The Prairie School architects and interior designers at first drew their inspiration from the English Arts and Crafts movement and the philosophy of William Morris and Company. British design was readily available to the Prairie School in the Chicago publication *House Beautiful*, the New York magazine *International Studio*, and London's *Art Journal*. In 1891–92 the Englishman Walter Crane lectured in Chicago, and his work was exhibited at the Art Institute. C. F. A. Voysey, another British designer, displayed his work at the 1893 World's Fair.

In 1898 the Art Institute, which because of the strength of its female supporters had always been more sympathetic to modern decorative arts and design than to avant-garde painting and sculpture, exhibited examples from British designer C. R. Ashbee's communal Guild of Handicraft, as well as the work of Morris's Kelmscott Press. Two years later, when Ashbee lectured at the Art Institute, he met Wright, and a friendship developed over the next decade. The reform ideology of the English Arts and Crafts movement found a sympathetic audience in the Midwest, an area of the country that had been hospitable to earlier utopian thinkers such as the Fourierists, Mennonites, Owenites, and Christian Socialists. The combination of the Midwest's utopian tradition and its progressive attitude toward educating and training immigrants and the poor produced institutions such as Hull House, founded in Chicago by Jane Addams and Ellen Gates Starr in 1889. The Chicago Arts and Crafts Society had its beginning at Hull House in 1897 (Boston and Chicago founded America's first arts and crafts societies in the same year).[42] The membership of the organization cut across social strata. Members included prominent professional and business people, faculty from the University of Chicago (founded in 1891) and the Art Institute, and architects and artists.[43] In 1900 the Art Institute hosted the earliest museum exhibition of Arts and Crafts metalwork in the United States.[44] Among those who showed work at the society's annual exhibitions at the Art Institute were interior designers George Mann Niedecken and Louis J. Millet, painter Ralph Clarkson, and silversmiths Robert Jarvie (see cat. nos. 158–60) and Clara Barck (later Clara Barck Welles).

Louis Julian Millet, nephew of the French painter Jean François Millet, had a studio in Chicago as early as 1883 and became head of the Department of Design at the Art Institute in 1892. The stylized natural motifs of his work reflect Prairie School aesthetics. Most importantly, he was a teacher to an entire generation of Chicago artisans. Among his students was Clara Barck Welles, who opened the Kalo Shop in 1901 (*kalo* is Greek for beautiful). She modeled her enterprise, which became very successful, on Ashbee's Guild of Handicraft, and combined the Arts and Crafts philosophy of handmade beauty with social progressiveness (see cat. no. 161).[45]

While the membership of the Chicago Arts and Crafts Society included some art and architecture professionals, its mission was to provide opportunities for the common citizen.[46] Gifted amateurs exhibited alongside the professionally trained members. Eventually, philosophical differences between two groups—industrial-oriented modernist architects and craftsmen who emphasized handwork—led to the waning of the society. By 1905 the society was no longer exhibiting at the Art Institute.[47]

The Cliff Dwellers

Another organization, the Cliff Dwellers Club, proved to be more influential than the Chicago Arts and Crafts Society in the cross-pollination of contemporary American art and architecture in Chicago. The club was founded by Hamlin Garland, a Wisconsin-bred novelist who moved to Chicago in 1892.[48] Several of Garland's books were published in Chicago by Stone and Kimball, which was also the publisher of *Chap-Book* (1894–98), a magazine that featured the French-inspired Art Nouveau decorations of the graphic designer and illustrator Will Bradley.

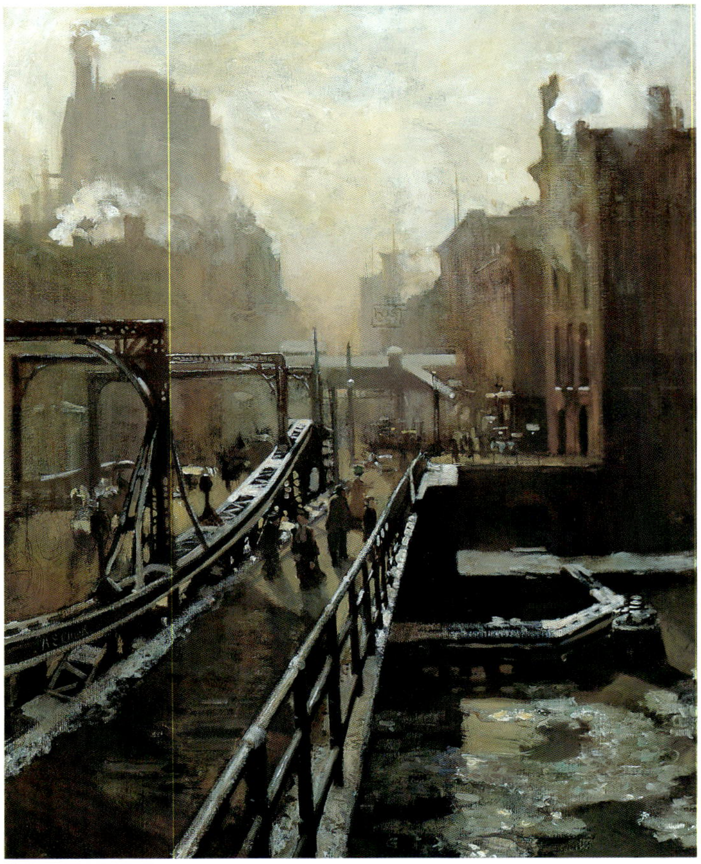

FIG. 23. Alson Skinner Clark (1876–1949). *Coffee House*, c. 1905. Oil on canvas; 97 x 76.5 cm (38 3/16 x 30 1/8 in.). Gift of Mr. and Mrs. Alson E. Clark (1915.256).

Garland met his future brother-in-law and lifelong friend, sculptor Lorado Taft, when he was invited by the Cliff Dwellers to lecture on "Impressionism in Art." Taft was an important teacher who wrote the first history of American sculpture. In addition to having a position on the faculty of the School of the Art Institute, he ran a bohemian summer colony called the Eagle's Nest in Oregon, Illinois, where artists lived and worked in communal fashion in the woods along the Fox River. Young sculptors who frequented Taft's Chicago studio as a center of intellectual exchange included Edward Kemeys, Herman Atkins MacNeil, and Bessie Potter (before her marriage to painter Robert Vonnoh; see cat. nos. 144–45). Taft was a friend of Daniel Chester French and a proponent of naturalism combined with heroic and universal themes. His plaster group of 1901, *The Solitude of the Soul* (cat. no. 143), was exhibited at the

Pan-American Exposition in Buffalo in 1901, won the gold medal at the St. Louis Universal Exposition in 1904, and was on loan to the Art Institute until 1911, when the Friends of American Art bought the cast and commissioned Taft to sculpt it in marble.

Besides Taft and Garland, other founding members of the Cliff Dwellers Club included painters Charles Francis Browne and Ralph Clarkson, Art Institute President Charles Hutchinson, architect Irving Pond, publisher Herbert S. Stone, and four University of Chicago professors. They wanted to "bring together men of artistic and literary tastes who are now widely scattered among the various social and business organizations of Chicago and unite them with artists, writers, architects and musicians of the city in a club whose purposes are distinctly and primarily aesthetic."[49]

The club was located on top of Orchestra Hall, high above Michigan Avenue and in close proximity to the dozens of studios stacked in the hub of Chicago's artistic life.[50] In 1910 Hutchinson, Cliff Dweller president at that time, commissioned silversmith Robert Jarvie to fashion a large punch bowl. Jarvie's design emulates a coiled Indian basket, in tribute to the club's name, which associated the modern studios of downtown Chicago with cliff-dwelling Indians, whose industrious artisanry and modernist-looking designs for textiles and ceramics were well known. Local pride in the history of the midwestern United States, its ancient cultures and indigenous decorative themes, and its forward-looking viewpoint came together in the Cliff Dwellers, the Arts and Crafts Society, and the Prairie School architects and designers.[51]

Building an American Painting Collection at the Beginning of the Century

This blending and reinterpretation of European art movements and other cultural influences made Chicago a center for the exploration of modernist art early in the century.[52] The Annual Exhibition of American Painting and Sculpture assumed a symbolist and realist rather than Impressionist flavor. Arthur B. Davies and Robert Henri displayed their work in the annual exhibitions as early as 1894; John Sloan was represented in 1900, George Luks in 1904, and George Bellows in 1908. Pictures such as Chicagoan Alson Skinner Clark's *Coffee House* (c. 1905; fig. 23) made poetic such mundane subjects as the fog and smoke rising over the Clark Street Bridge.[53] At the turn of the century, the Art Institute initiated a prize system and began to purchase works directly from the exhibitions.[54]

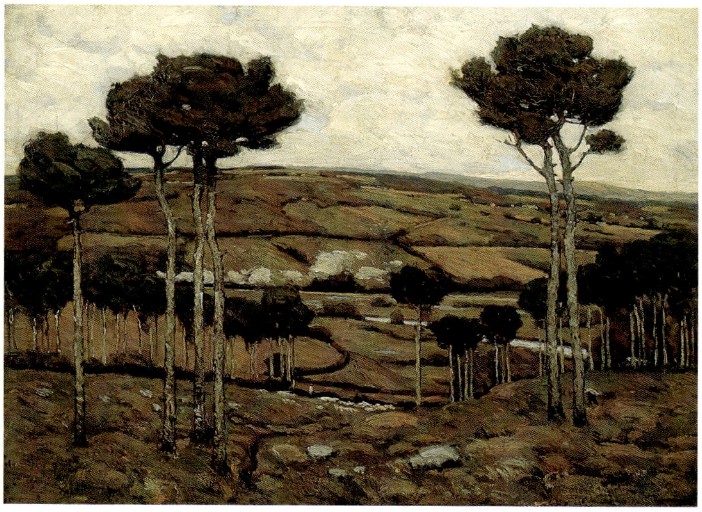

FIG. 24. William A. Harper (1851–1910). *Normandy Pines*, c. 1900. Oil on canvas; 76.2 x 101.6 cm (30 x 40 in.). Lent by the Oregon Public Library, Eagle's Nest Art Colony Collection (19.1993).

In 1906 the museum purchased Henry O. Tanner's symbolist *Two Disciples at the Tomb* (cat. no. 176), painted the same year. It was the first picture by this important African-American artist to be acquired by an American museum, and its purchase gave early support to his career. During the 1890s, Tanner had moved to France, where he found acceptance of his work in more racially tolerant circles. He also helped other African-American artists such as Chicago-based painter William A. Harper (see fig. 24). Harper, one of Taft's protégés at the Eagle's Nest art colony, studied in France from 1903 to 1905 and from 1907 to 1908. In 1910, after Harper's untimely death, the Art Institute mounted a memorial exhibition of his lyrical, symbolist landscape paintings—the first one-person exhibition of the work of an African-American artist in a major American museum.

The following year, a lover of landscape paintings, museum trustee Edward Butler, presented the Art Institute with his large collection of pictures by George Inness (see fig. 25 and cat. nos. 74–75 and 147). Butler had purchased a group of eighteen paintings by Inness through dealer Henry Reinhardt.[55] Butler, like Inness, was a follower of Emanuel Swedenborg, a philosopher who argued that the natural and spiritual worlds were connected by profound similarities. Thus, for Inness, art had to express mystical as well as physical truths. The delicate balance between objective (seen) and subjective (felt), between geometry (fact) and poetry (sentiment), is present in all his work. Inness's late works are plotted in imagined gridlike patterns, not unlike music.

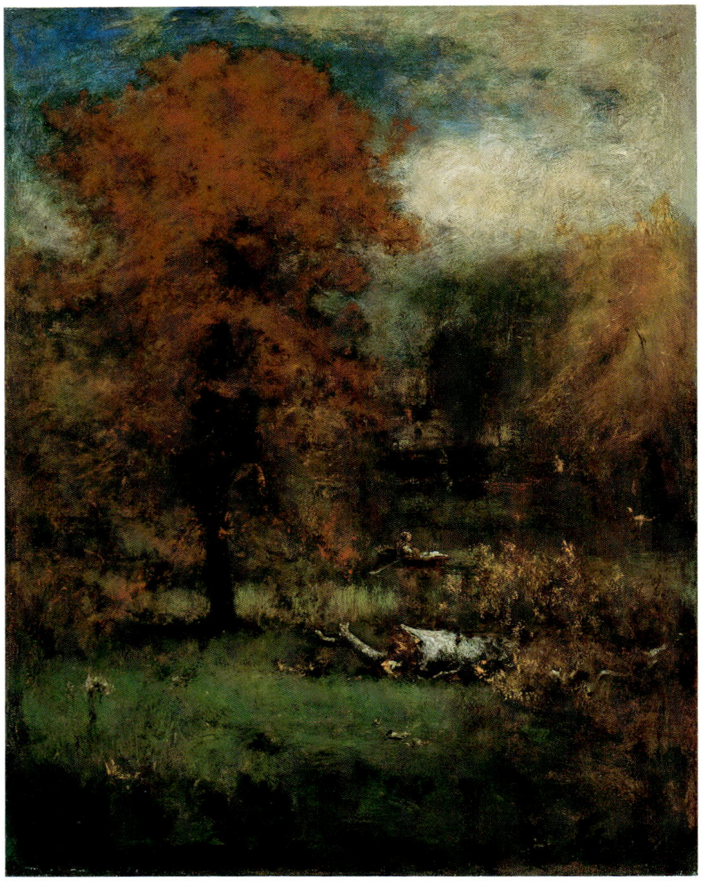

FIG. 25. George Inness (1825–1894). *The Mill Pond*, 1889. Oil on canvas; 95.9 x 74.3 cm (37¾ x 29¾ in.). Edward B. Butler Collection (1911.30).

The Art Institute's pictures by Inness date from different periods in the artist's career, beginning with *The Old Mill* (1849; cat. no. 74) and concluding with the dreamlike pictures of the 1890s, such as *The Home of the Heron* (1893; cat. no. 147). The late paintings of Inness, like those of Winslow Homer, are remarkably abstract. They bridge the gap between naturalism and spiritualism in nineteenth-century painting, and prefigure the symbolism and abstraction of twentieth-century works of art.

By 1910 enthusiasm for contemporary American art in Chicago was so great that a group of approximately one hundred seventy-five public-spirited collectors raised over thirty thousand dollars and began the Friends of American Art. Over the four decades the group existed, it purchased almost one hundred fifty works to add to the fifty-five already in the collection. Major objects acquired by the group for the museum during the 1910–11 inaugural year ranged from symbolist to Impressionist to realist, including Thomas Wilmer Dewing's *Lady in Green and Gray* (1911; cat. no. 166), Frank Weston Benson's *Rainy Day* (1906; fig. 26), and Robert Henri's *Young Woman in Black* (1902; see cat. nos. 177–78).

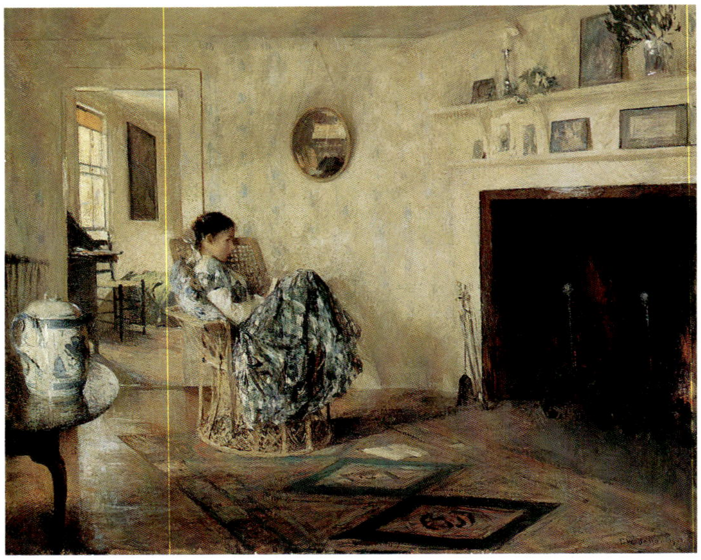

FIG. 26. Frank Weston Benson (1862–1951). *Rainy Day*, 1906. Oil on canvas; 63.6 x 76.3 cm (25 x 30 in.). Friends of American Art Collection (1910.314).

The Friends of American Art attempted to strike a balance between buying contemporary American art and purchasing older pictures to fill gaps in the Art Institute's collection. In the main, they concentrated on contemporary artists. Purchases included Twachtman's *Icebound* (c. 1889; cat. no. 133), William Glackens's *At Mouquin's* (1905; cat. no. 169), Sargent's *Fountain, Villa Torlonia, Frascati, Italy* (1907; cat. no. 171), and Bellows's *Love of Winter* (1914; cat. no. 186).

Contemporary American painting at the museum was considerably strengthened by gifts from Mr. and Mrs. Paul Schulze. Paul Schulze opened a bread bakery during the 1893 World's Fair, and it quickly became one of the largest in the country. He collected primarily American realist works during the early years of the century and knew personally most of the artists represented in his collection. The Schulzes' son Walter died on the day the armistice that ended World War I was signed, and the family donated fifteen paintings in his memory, among which were Robert Henri's uncompromising portrait pair, *Himself* and *Herself* (1913; cat. nos. 177–78).

The Armory Show of 1913 and Arthur Jerome Eddy

The Friends of American Art purchases and the Schulze gift strengthened the collections of Impressionist and realist painting, but the 1913 International Exhibition of Modern Art, now commonly called the Armory Show (because it was first shown in the New York Armory), introduced European modernism

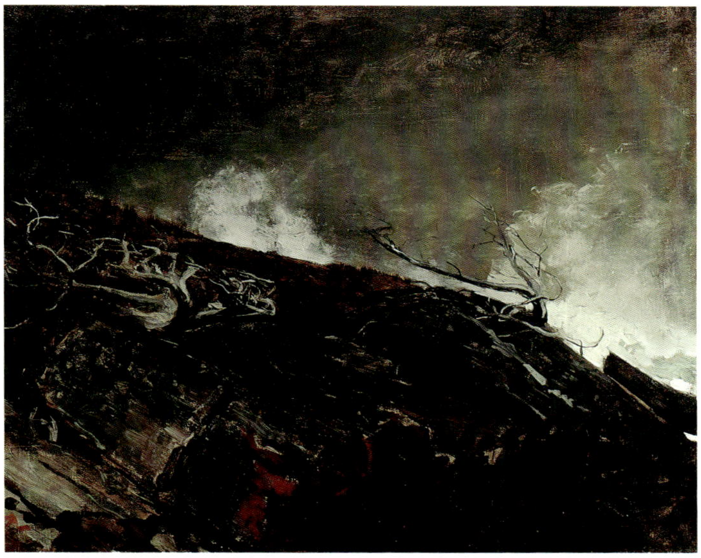

FIG. 27. Winslow Homer. *Coast of Maine*, 1893. Oil on canvas; 61 x 76.2 cm (24 x 30 in.). Arthur Jerome Eddy Memorial Collection (1931.505).

to Chicago. The Art Institute became the first art museum to host the exhibition, and almost two hundred thousand visitors came to see the controversial paintings in the show, among which was Marcel Duchamp's *Nude Descending a Staircase, No. 2* (1912; now in the Philadelphia Museum of Art).[56]

Poetry magazine's Harriet Monroe and Chicago collector Arthur Jerome Eddy were among those who tirelessly defended exhibited works by Paul Cézanne, Wassily Kandinsky, Henri Matisse, and others. But the majority of visitors, including faculty and students of the School of the Art Institute, were shocked by the new art. The students even burned effigies of Matisse paintings. The widespread hostility prompted Eddy to retire from business in order to write *Cubists and Post-Impressionism* (1914), the first English-language book that attempted to explain the modern movement.

Eddy first formed his opinions about modern art at the 1893 World's Fair. Completely devoted to modernism, he considered the American painter James McNeill Whistler to be the link between Impressionism (of which Eddy was critical) and Post-Impressionism. Whistler's art, according to Eddy, possessed the faithfulness of vision of the Impressionists, yet also incorporated an abstract sense of line and color, the "music" that went beyond nature.[57] The American works in the collection that he bequeathed to the Art Institute include outstanding Whistler prints,[58] and Whistler's *Arrangement in Flesh Color and Brown: Portrait of Arthur Jerome Eddy* (1894; cat. no. 154). The Eddy bequest also includes the most abstract painting by Winslow Homer in the Art Institute's collection, the brooding, powerful *Coast of Maine* (1893; fig. 27).

In 1922, the same year that the Arthur Jerome Eddy Memorial Exhibition was mounted at the Art Institute, two important, early Whistler paintings entered the collection through the sons of Mr. and Mrs. Potter Palmer: *Gray and Silver: Old Battersea Reach* (1863; cat. no. 99) and *Trouville (Gray and Green, the Silver Sea)* (1865; cat. no. 100), which Mrs. Palmer had purchased in 1892 and 1901, respectively.

By the 1920s, then, the American painting collection included Impressionist, symbolist, and realist pictures assembled by prominent collectors such as Butler, Eddy, Palmer, Ryerson, and the Schulzes, and strong supporters within the Friends of American Art circle. The Art Institute's Frank G. Logan Prize resulted in purchases for the American art collection from the museum's Annual Exhibition of American Painting and Sculpture. George Bellows's *My Mother* (1921), for example, won the prize in 1923 before entering the collection. Despite such purchases, in general the Art Institute continued to take an essentially conservative approach to collecting at this point. Still lacking a long history, Chicagoans revered the eighteenth-century roots of the eastern seaboard, and their museum reflected this bent in its activities.

Forming a Collection of American Decorative Arts, 1920–1950

Among the forces against which modernism had to struggle in Chicago in the first four decades of the century was the strong appeal of historicism. Years before, in the mid-nineteenth century, the interest in colonial America was mostly the province of a few antiquarians. In popular works such as Henry Wadsworth Longfellow's poems "Paul Revere's Ride" (1863) and "The Old Clock on the Stairs" (1845), and in novels such as Nathaniel Hawthorne's *The House of the Seven Gables* (1851), the history of the colonies was closely associated with the kinds of objects that antiquarians coveted. As the nation celebrated its centennial in 1876, interest in the colonial past grew, as reflected in the works of Edward Lamson Henry, who specialized in history paintings such as *Attack on the Chew House* (1878; fig. 28). Within a few years of the centennial, other artists were turning to similar subjects, including realist painter Thomas Eakins, who sculpted plaster casts depicting a colonial tea table and spinning wheel (1882–83; cat. nos. 107–08), and Frederick MacMonnies, who portrayed the hero Nathan Hale (1890; cat. no. 138).

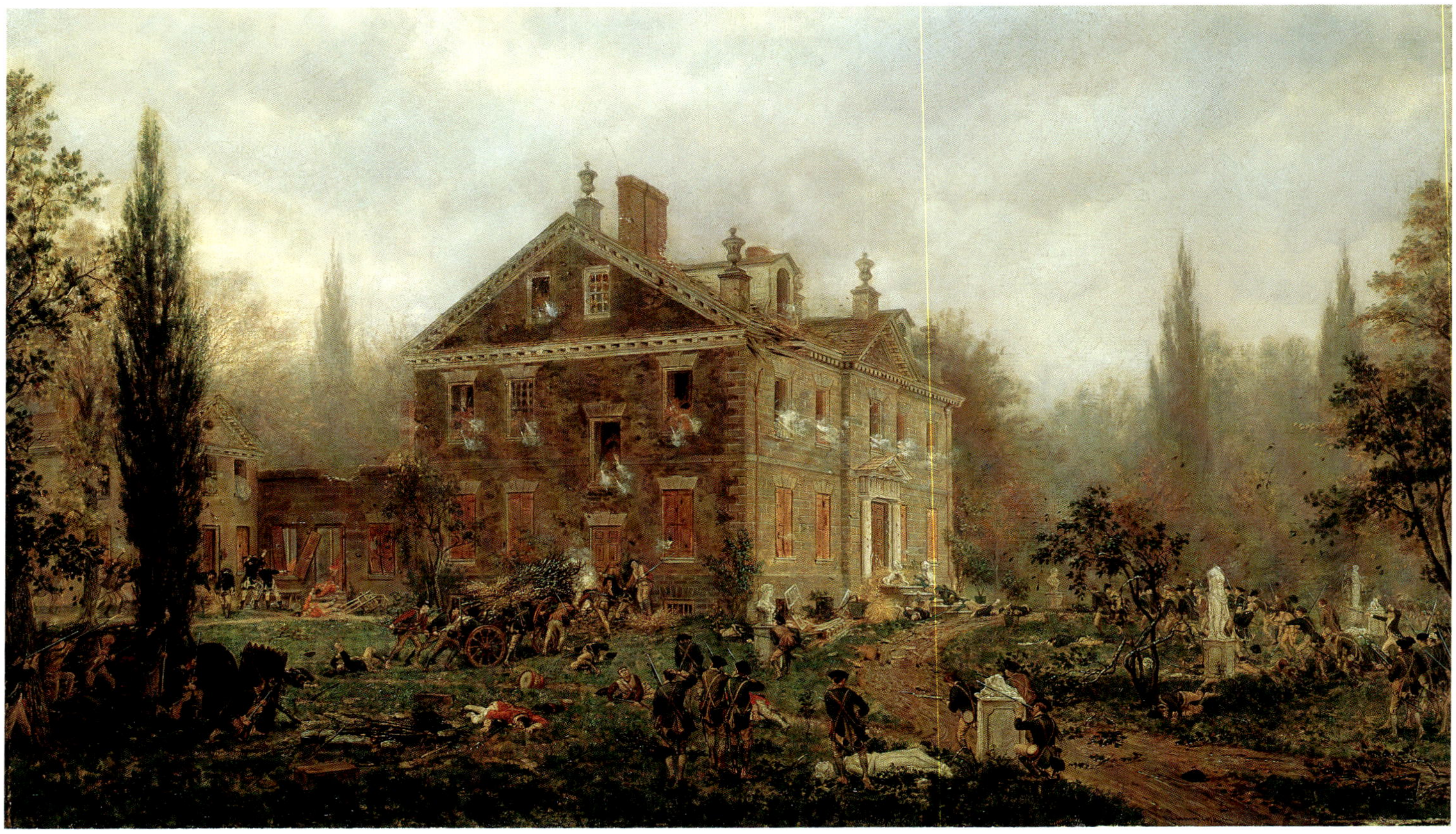

FIG. 28. Edward Lamson Henry (1841–1919). *Attack on the Chew House*, 1878. Oil on canvas; 63.5 x 107 cm (25 x 42⅛ in.). George F. Harding Collection (1982.77).

In the early years of the twentieth century, interest in the colonial era was partly a reaction to increasing immigration and, eventually, the Great Depression. Such nostalgia prompted the prominent businessmen John D. Rockefeller and Henry Ford to preserve a romantic view of American eighteenth-century life in new enterprises such as Colonial Williamsburg in Virginia (1926) and Greenfield Village in Dearborn, Michigan (1929). Among the Art Institute's patrons, renewed enthusiasm for American culture resulted in the museum's acquisition of private holdings of American decorative arts.

This development coincided with a shift to a new professionalism within the museum world. The role of curators in forming taste and guiding museums' acquisitions and exhibitions increased in importance. Robert Harshe assumed the directorship of the Art Institute in 1922. Believing the director and curators to be solely responsible for acquisitions, exhibitions, and installations, he appointed curators knowledgeable in various fields, encouraged the separation of the tasks of professional staff from the fiduciary responsibilities of the trustees, and strengthened his own office. Harshe also expanded the collecting activities of the museum and emphasized the importance of exhibitions.

The first Curator of Decorative Arts was the metalworker and jewelry designer Bessie Bennett, who occupied this position from 1914 until her death in 1939. A student of Louis Millet, she worked as a designer for the Chicago jewelry firm Juergens and Anderson and exhibited in the Arts and Crafts exhibitions at the Art Institute. At the beginning of her tenure, she formed a collection of contemporary pottery with funds raised by the Atlan Ceramic Club, a group of amateur potters.

The fact that the Art Institute assembled a strong decorative arts collection by the early twentieth century is due to the vigor of the Arts and Crafts movement in Chicago and the influence of Bennett. In addition to acquiring textiles, ivories, enamels, ceramics, furniture, glass, silver, period rooms, and wallpaper, she installed exhibitions of modern decorative arts from Sweden (1927), Empire furniture (1928), and folk art from Central and Eastern Europe (1939). A Chicago architect associated with the Arts and Crafts movement was Arthur Heun, a devotee of American blown, molded, and pressed glass; he donated his collection of glass to the Art Institute in 1933 (see cat. no.

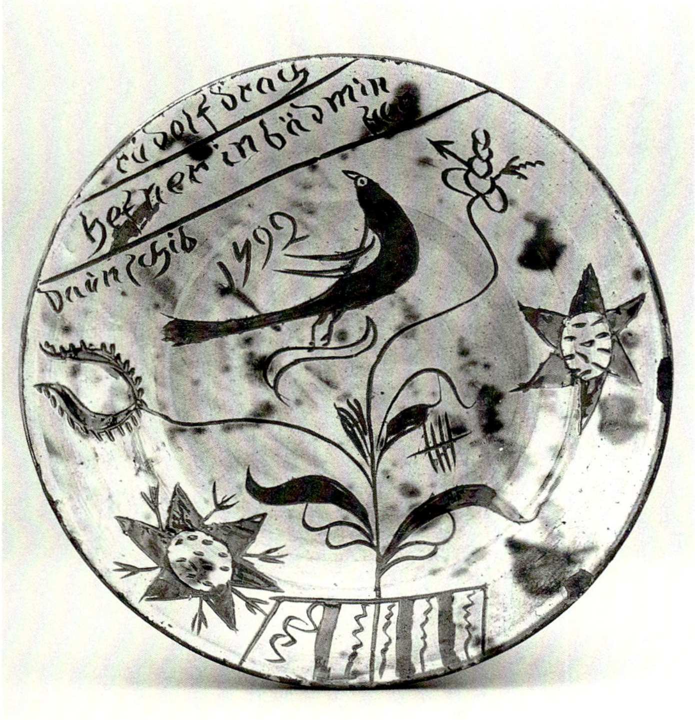

FIG. 29. Rudolph Drach (b. 1759). *Dish*, 1792. Earthenware; diam. 28.7 cm (11 5/16 in.). The Art Institute of Chicago by exchange (1907.122).

90). His gift was supplemented in 1935 by Mrs. Justus Johnson's collection of pressed pattern glass.[59]

The Art Institute's early patrons of American decorative arts included Emma B. Hodge, who donated early New England redware, Bennington ware, and a magnificent group of American nineteenth-century quilts to the Department of Textiles in 1907.[60] Hodge's ceramic collecting coincided with Edwin Atlee Barber's pioneering studies on the subject of early American ceramics.[61] An important scholar of the time, Barber sold early ceramics to the Field Museum of Natural History in 1894, which were given to the Art Institute in 1907 (see fig. 29). Another key patron of the museum in the 1910s and 1920s was Reverend Frank W. Gunsaulus, minister of Chicago's Central Church and a social reformer, who gave his extraordinary collection of sixty-two nineteenth-century American woven coverlets (see fig. 30).[62]

One of the most interesting collectors associated with Chicago in the 1920s, 1930s, and 1940s was Emily Crane Chadbourne. She was the daughter of Richard T. Crane, who built the Crane plumbing empire and was a founder of the Chicago Civic Opera.[63] After her marriage ended in divorce in 1905, Chadbourne left Chicago for Europe, and divided her time between apartments in London and Paris until 1924. During those years, she frequented the social circles of the American expatriate writers Natalie Clifford Barney and Gertrude Stein.

Chadbourne's Paris sojourn coincided with the artistic and musical flowering of the Montparnasse area. Tsugouharu Foujita's uncharacteristically restrained portrait of Chadbourne (1922; fig. 31) shows her in a pose that echoes both Jacques Louis David's *Portrait of Madame Récamier* (1800; Musée du Louvre, Paris) and Édouard Manet's *Olympia* (1863; Musée d'Orsay, Paris). Chadbourne's collecting activities at this point ranged from eighteenth-century European decorative arts to contemporary paintings. Between 1922 and 1926, she gave to the Art Institute watercolors from Gauguin's Tahitian period, which she had collected as early as 1908 and had exhibited at the 1913 Armory Show; drawings by Matisse; paintings by Davies; and French and English ceramics and antiques.

Chadbourne and her longtime companion, Ellen LaMotte, returned to the United States around 1924. They divided their time between Washington, D.C., and a farm in the Hudson River Valley, near Kingston, New York. Thereafter, the two women devoted themselves to collecting American art. The

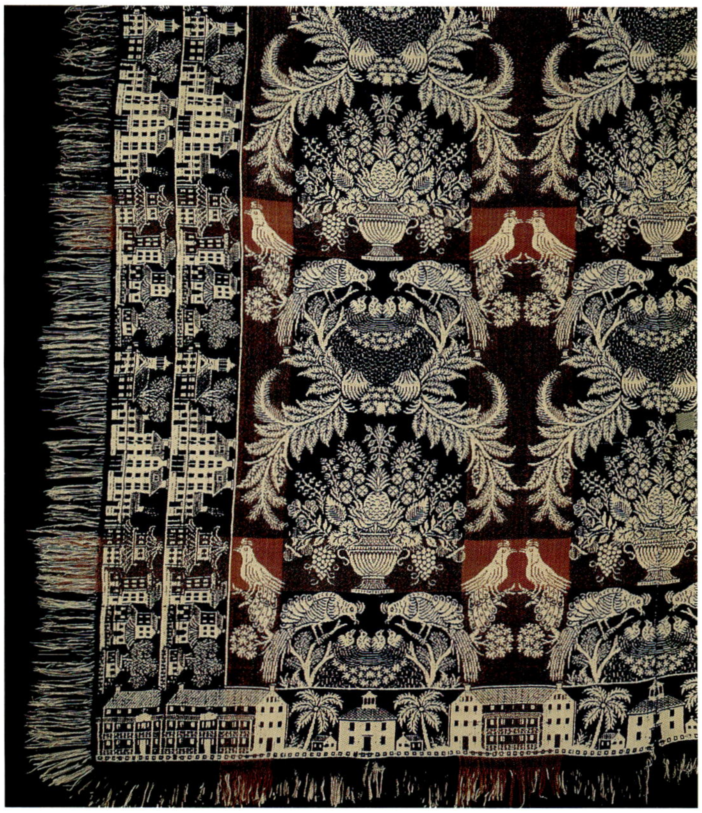

FIG. 30. Ohio. *Coverlet* (detail), 1840/45. Cotton and wool, plain weave double cloth; warp and weft fringe; woven on a loom with a Jacquard attachment; 233.4 x 203 cm (92½ x 80¼ in.). Gift of Frank W. Gunsaulus (1913.496).

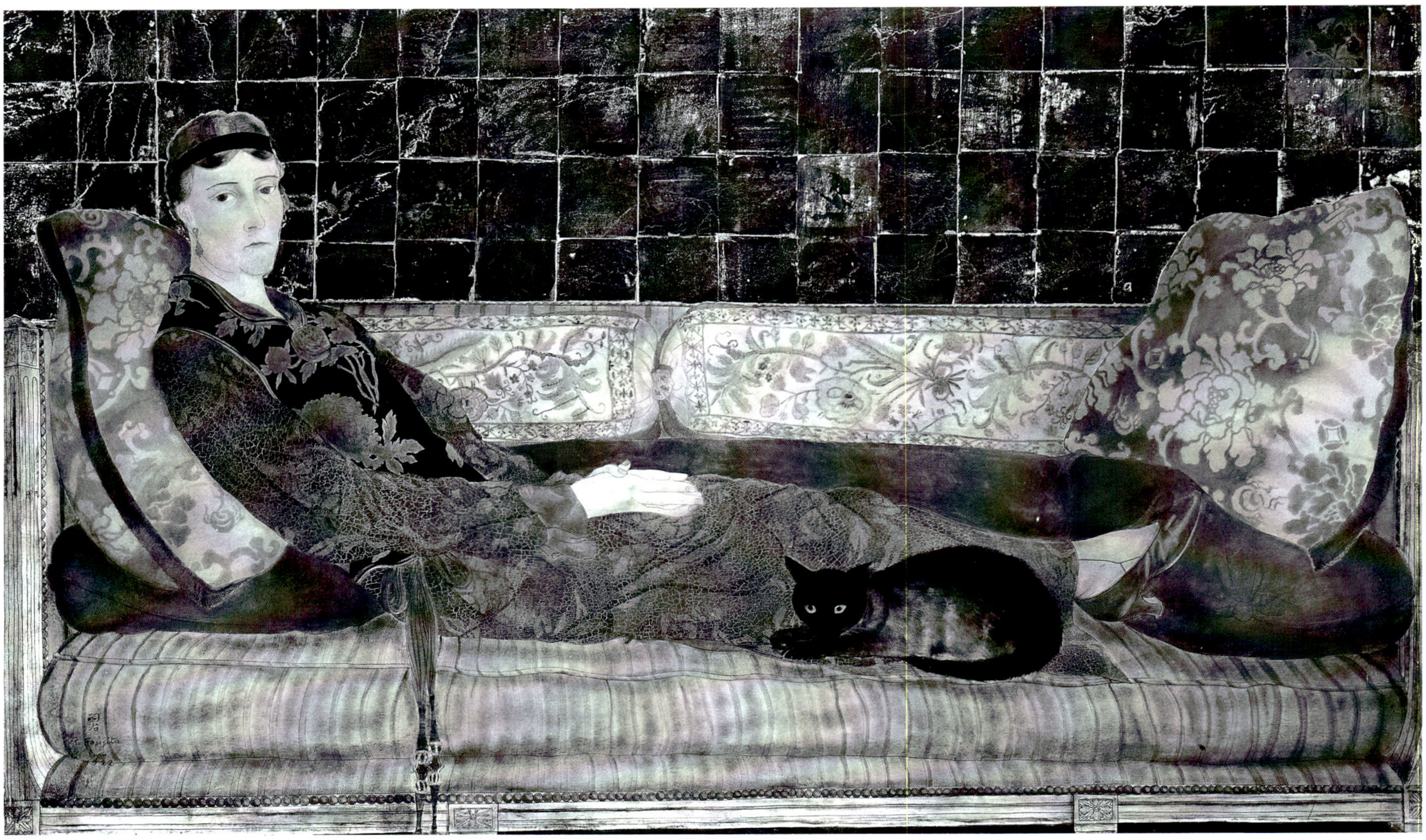

FIG. 31. Tsugouharu Foujita (Japanese, 1886–1968). *Portrait of E. C. Chadbourne*, 1922. Tempera on canvas; 89.2 x 146.1 cm (35⅛ x 57½ in.). Gift of Emily Crane Chadbourne (1952.997).

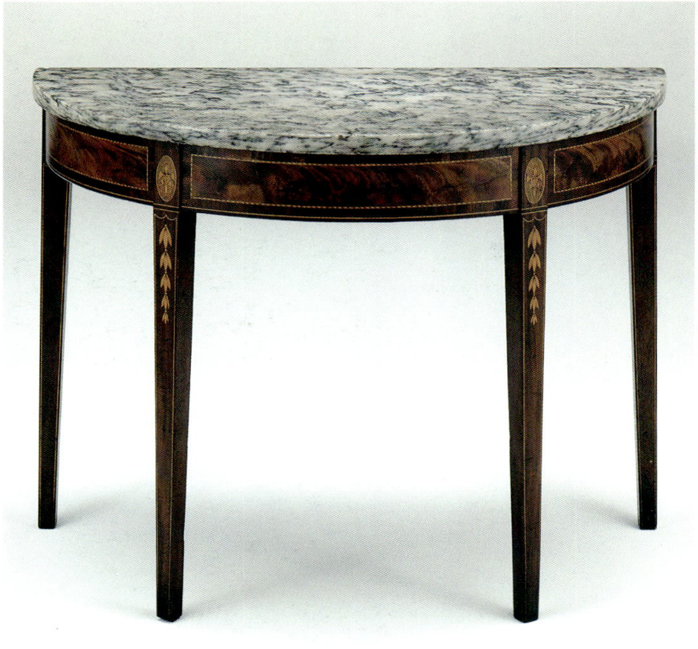

FIG. 32. Baltimore. *Pier Table*, 1790/1810. Mahogany, yellow poplar, white oak, yellow pine, marble; 73.7 x 99.4 x 51.8 cm (29 x 39⅛ x 20⅜ in.). Gift of Miss Ellen LaMotte (1952.950).

Art Institute eventually received furniture from Maryland and Pennsylvania inherited by LaMotte, including a fine eighteenth-century marble-topped pier table from Baltimore (1790/1810; fig. 32). Between 1928 and 1956, Chadbourne honored her Chicago ties by donating to the Art Institute examples of Massachusetts and New York furniture, Ohio blown glass, silver, nineteenth-century folk paintings and watercolors, Chinese export porcelain, and Whistler's *Study for Arrangement in Gray and Black, No. 2: Thomas Carlyle* (1872–73).

Among the most important collections of American decorative arts that came to the Art Institute in these years was that of Elizabeth Vaughan, the sister of Art Institute trustee Russell Tyson. She left her residence, Hamilton House in South Berwick, Maine (fig. 33), to the Society for the Preservation of New England Antiquities, but she bequeathed her outstanding collection of folk art, which she had assembled for her garden cottage, to the Art Institute in 1950 (see fig. 34). It comprised fine animal carvings, redware bowls, weather vanes, and early and exceptional Windsor chairs from Philadelphia (cat. no. 38) and New England.

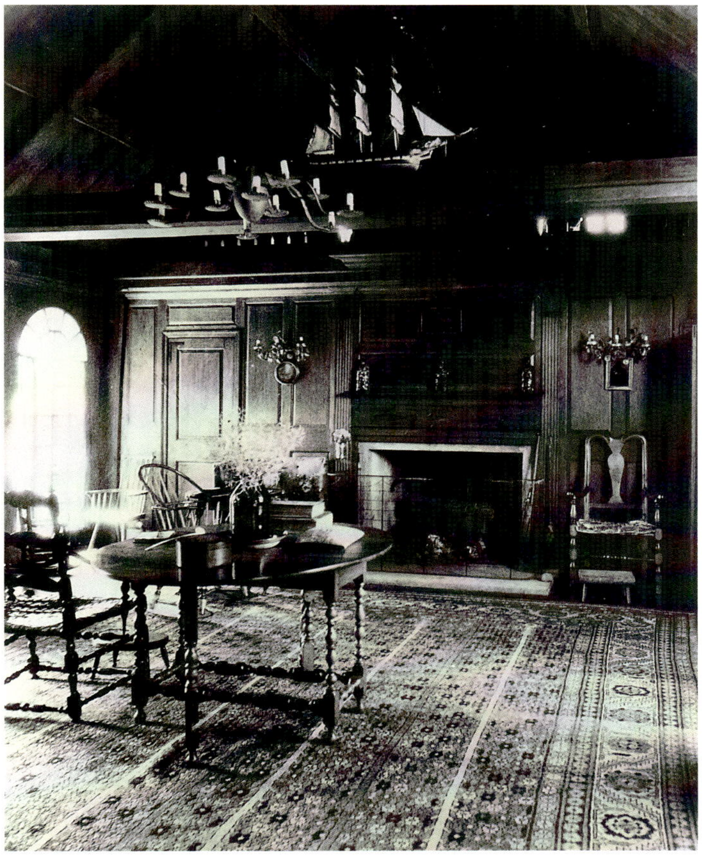

After Bessie Bennett's death in 1939, Meyric Rogers, Director of the St. Louis City Art Museum, assumed the curatorship of the Department of Decorative Arts. Trained at Harvard University's School of Architecture, Rogers also served as curator of a second, newly founded department, Industrial Arts, one of the earliest of its type in American museums.[64] Rogers organized exhibitions of contemporary ceramics from the Rookwood Pottery (1940), the sculpture of Swedish-born Carl Milles (1941), and architectural drawings of the American Institute of Architects (1942), the latter curated with Chicago architect and art collector Samuel Marx.[65]

Despite the curatorial interest in modernist design, Chicago's decorative arts collectors continued to favor earlier periods. In a city where little predated the 1871 fire, the passion for collecting seventeenth-and eighteenth-century American decorative arts was understandable. Rogers, whose grasp of the history of design was broad, augmented the historical collections. He had already worked with the collector Francis P.

FIG. 33. Interior of garden cottage, Hamilton House, South Berwick, Maine, built around 1907. Photograph by Paul J. Weber, taken before 1929, courtesy of the Society for the Preservation of New England Antiquities.

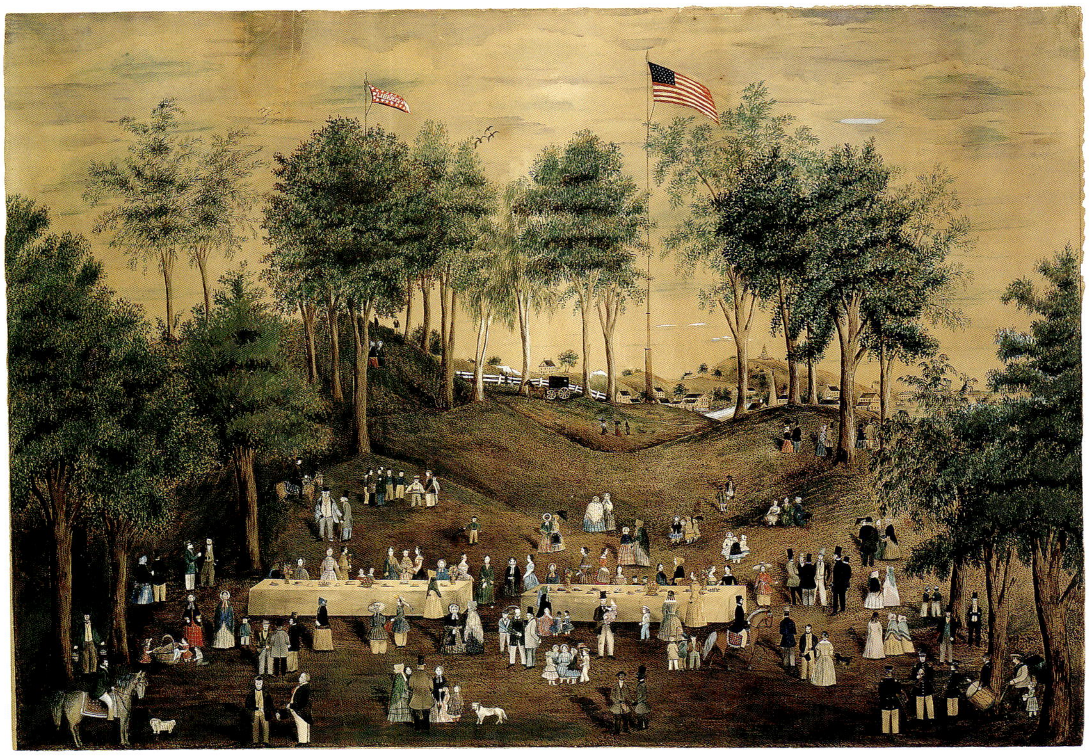

FIG. 34. Susan Merritt (1826–1879). *Fourth of July Picnic at Weymouth Landing*, 1845. Watercolor and collage on paper; 74.9 x 100 cm (29½ x 39⅜ in.). Gift of Elizabeth R. Vaughan (1950.1846).

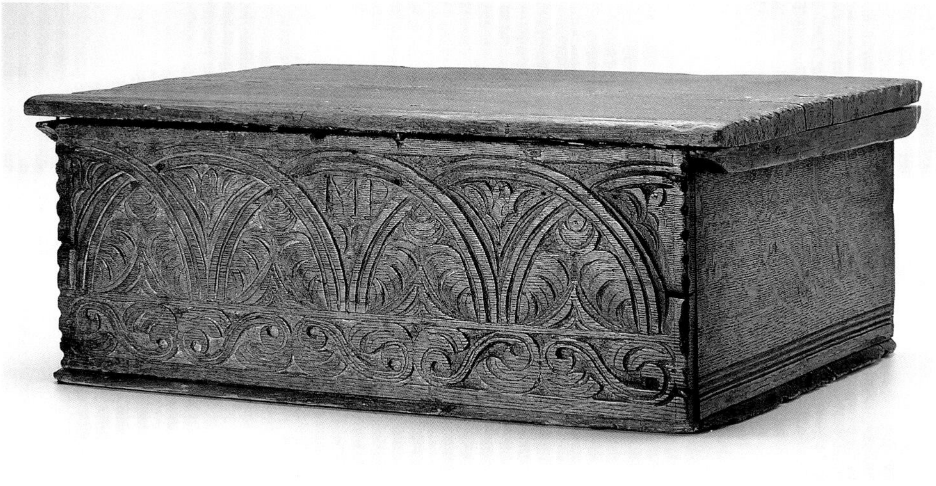

FIG. 35. Massachusetts. *Box*, 1650/1700. Oak with white pine; 24.8 x 63.5 x 45.7 cm (9¾ x 25 x 18 in.). Wirt D. Walker Fund (1946.564).

Garvan to form the Garvan Collection of American seventeenth- and eighteenth-century furniture and silver at Yale University.[66] When Rogers came to Chicago, the Art Institute's holdings of American furniture and silver were sparse and his mission was to build in these areas as he had with Garvan. As a result, in 1946 the museum acquired several seventeenth-century, or "Pilgrim," pieces from Mr. and Mrs. B. A. Behrends, private collectors in Connecticut.[67] Two of the most important objects are a rare, carved Massachusetts box (1650/1700; fig. 35) and a Hartford-area maple great chair.

From its inception to 1910, the Antiquarian Society had purchased mostly European and Middle Eastern textiles and other non-American decorative arts, probably owing to the leadership of Mr. and Mrs. Martin A. Ryerson. In 1911 the society collaborated with the Colonial Dames in mounting an exhibition that traced the history of looking glasses. Chicago was only slightly behind the national interest in forming exhibitions and collections of American decorative arts in the first three decades of the century.[68] In this context, the Art Institute's May 1926 loan exhibition of American furniture is of particular interest because it predates by three years the important Girl Scout Loan Exhibition of American furniture and decorative arts held in New York at the galleries of the American Art Association. Unfortunately, no catalogue of the 1926 exhibition was published even though objects were lent by major Chicago collectors—Robert Allerton and Emma Hodge—and by museums such as the Metropolitan Museum of Art in New York.

While the Antiquarian Society had broadened its exhibition interests in the 1920s and 1930s, its acquisitions for the museum had remained predominantly European. In 1942, under

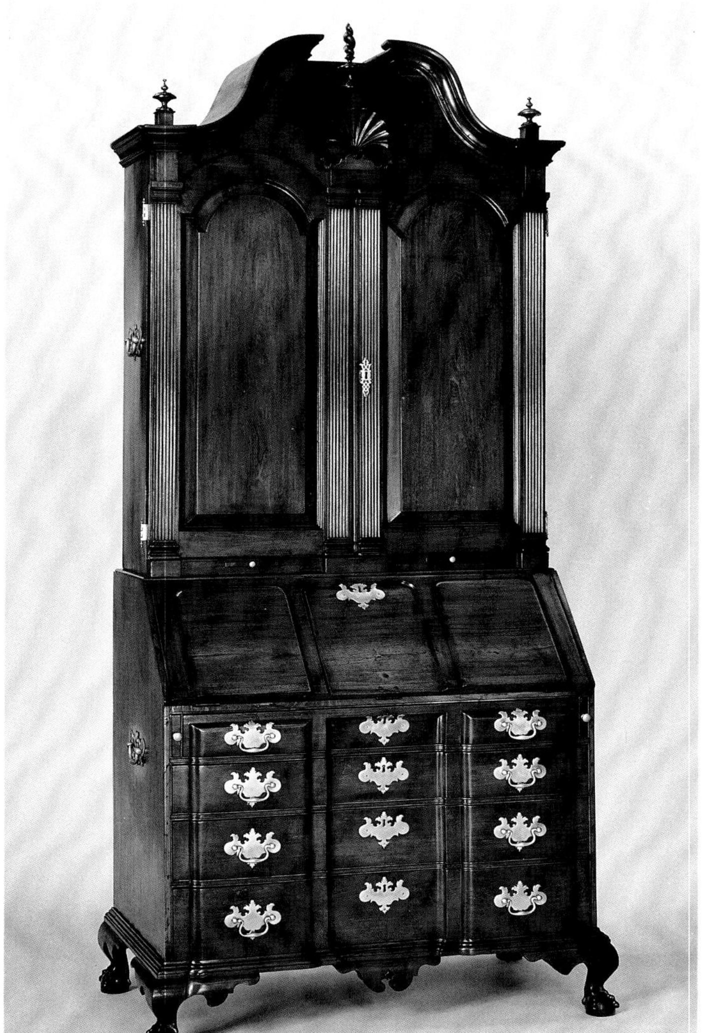

FIG. 36. Salem, Massachusetts. *Desk-and-Bookcase*, 1760/70. Mahogany with white pine; 257.7 x 115.6 x 64.7 cm (101½ x 45 x 25½ in.). Gift of the Antiquarian Society (1945.82).

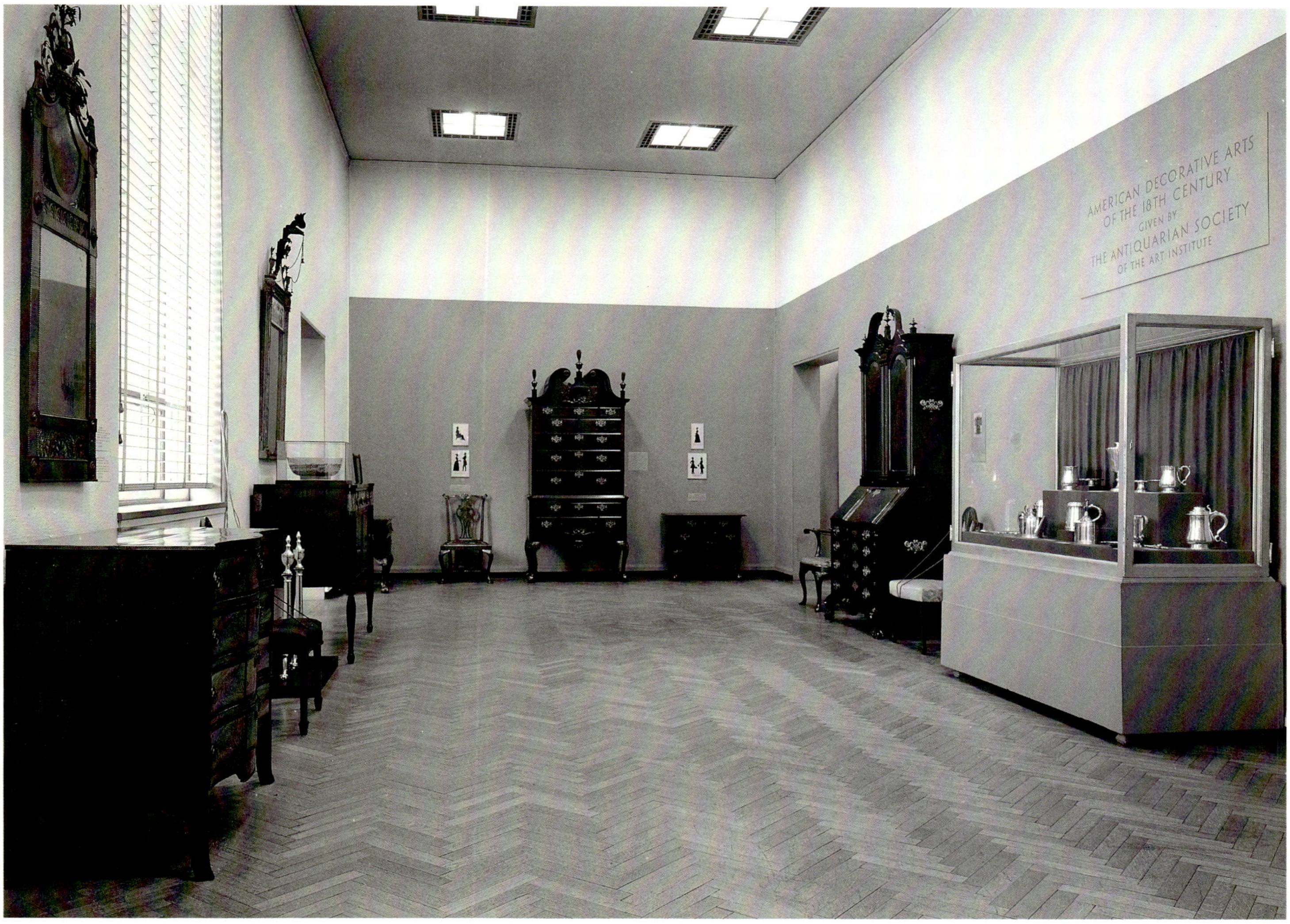

FIG. 37. Gallery of eighteenth-century American decorative arts given to the Art Institute by the Antiquarian Society, photographed in 1951. Among the pieces displayed in this gallery: on the far left, the serpentine-front chest of drawers from Portsmouth, N.H. (cat. no. 45); at the back wall, the matching Philadelphia high chest of drawers and dressing table; and on the right, the Salem block-front desk-and-bookcase (see fig. 36).

Rogers's direction, the Antiquarians embarked on a policy of building the American decorative arts collections. Three of the earliest purchases were a Salem block-front desk-and-bookcase (1760/70; fig. 36), and a matching Philadelphia high chest of drawers and dressing table (see fig. 37). By 1949 the society had purchased enough major pieces that the museum could inaugurate a new gallery devoted solely to American decorative arts (fig. 37).

Rogers assumed responsibility for a collection that lagged behind the great collections of silver that had been acquired by the Museum of Fine Arts in Boston, the Metropolitan Museum of Art, and Yale University from 1910 onward. Rogers encouraged the Antiquarians to rectify this situation somewhat during the 1940s and 1950s. In this period, the Mr. and Mrs. Edwin A. Seipp Fund provided for the acquisition of early silver, including a rare New York silver tankard by Cornelius Kierstede (1698/1722; cat. no. 7), a Jacob Hurd sauce boat (1740/58), a Jeremiah Dummer caudle cup, and a John Coney tankard. The Antiquarians also purchased an Edward Winslow salver (1710/40; cat. no. 8). The Antiquarians, along with Dr. and Mrs. C. Phillip Miller, provided funds for the purchase of a monumental, two-handled engraved cup Cornelius van der Burch made for the Van Cortlandt family (1674/99; cat. no. 1). In 1959 these important purchases were augmented by the acquisition of Ephraim Brasher's monumental, pear-shaped, three-tapped Rococo urn (1765/75; cat. no. 33).

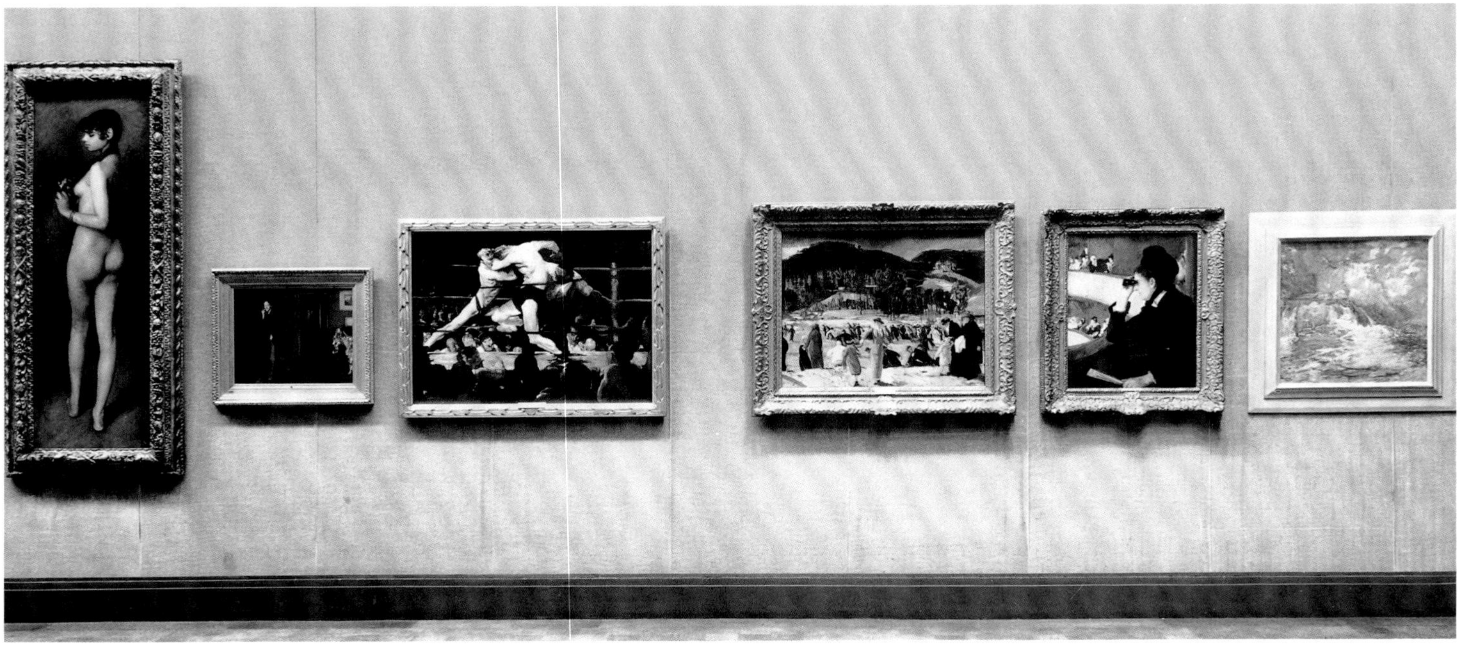

FIG. 38. Gallery in the Century of Progress "Exhibition of Paintings and Sculpture" at the Art Institute, 1933. Left to right: John Singer Sargent, *Study from Life* (1891; see fig. 10 above); Sargent, *Mr. and Mrs. Robert Louis Stevenson* (1885; Estate of Mrs. John Hay Whitney); George Bellows, *Stag at Sharkey's* (1909; Cleveland Museum of Art); Bellows, *Love of Winter* (1914; cat. no. 186); Mary Cassatt, *At the Français, a Sketch* (1877–78; Museum of Fine Arts, Boston); and John Twachtman, *The Waterfall* (c. 1895; private collection).

American Exhibitions at the Art Institute, 1930–1950

The growing prominence of American painting and decorative arts was also due to a number of major exhibitions at the Art Institute. The first was the Century of Progress Exhibition of 1933, which included the works of more than five hundred artists of many nationalities (see fig. 38). Its purpose was to show the development of Western painting in an unbroken sequence, and the "progress" of American collecting. All the works except for "Whistler's Mother" were from American collections. American and European works were hung together in the galleries.[69] The exhibition was so popular that a second exhibition, with a particularly strong American section, took place the following year. Most of the American paintings in the Art Institute's collection were on view in the 1934 exhibition, holding their own against works borrowed from collections all over the country. The roster of artists represented was particularly weighted toward a more traditional taste, with numerous works by such Chicago favorites as Cassatt, Eakins, Homer, Ryder, Sargent, Twachtman, and Whistler. But numerous works were included by such twentieth-century American artists as Bellows, John Steuart Curry, Davies, Glackens, Edward Hopper, Rockwell Kent, Yasuo Kuniyoshi, Georgia O'Keeffe, Charles Sheeler, Tanner, Max Weber, and Grant Wood.

It is important to note that, during the 1940s, little was known about American art: as a field of scholarship, it was barely fifty years old. Thus, the achievements in the area of American arts of Frederick A. Sweet, who joined the museum's staff as Assistant Curator of Painting and Sculpture in 1939, are especially noteworthy. To celebrate the fiftieth anniversary of the annual American painting and sculpture exhibitions, he assembled "Half a Century of American Art." The exhibition featured a selection of paintings and sculptures that had been displayed at the museum between 1888 and 1938, and served as an impressive history of the annual American art exhibitions. During the 1940s Sweet continued to focus on American art. His pathbreaking "Hudson River School and the Early American Landscape Tradition" (1945) featured one hundred sixty-four paintings by fifty artists. It was the first major exhibition to focus on early nineteenth-century American landscape painting and its connections to, and differences from, its European counterpart. Sweet's presentation included a discussion of the relationship between American painting and works of literature by the American authors William Cullen Bryant, James Fenimore Cooper, and Washington Irving.

Rogers and Sweet pioneered the combination of various media in exhibitions whose focus extended beyond the fine arts. In 1949 they organized "From Colony to Nation: Exhibi-

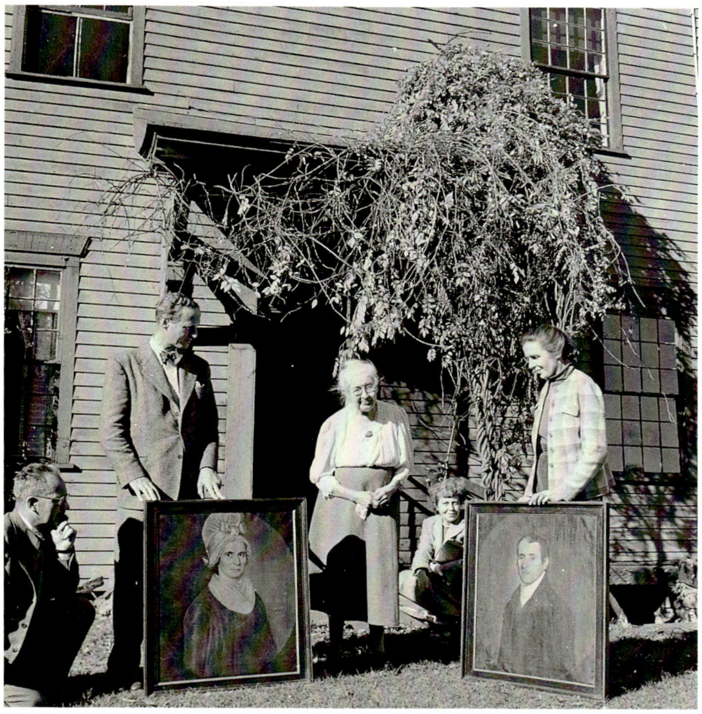

FIG. 39. Curators Hans Huth and Frederick A. Sweet visited Mrs. George A. Fuller (center) and her daughter Elizabeth (far right) in Deerfield, Massachusetts, to view paintings in their collection for possible inclusion in the 1949 exhibition "From Colony to Nation." The painting on the right, William Jennys' *Dr. William Stoddard Williams* (1801), was eventually selected for the show. (The seated woman is unidentified.)

tion of American Painting, Silver, and Architecture from 1650 to the War of 1812," one of the earliest aesthetic and historical surveys of developing American culture (see fig. 39). Sweet and Rogers's survey of silver, painting, and architecture attempted to show the distinctive forms and indigenous styles produced by the new nation that were unique and not purely reflective of European models.[70]

A New Collecting Emphasis

Among the acquisitions made during the late 1940s are paintings that are crucial parts of the collection today: John Singleton Copley's portraits of Mr. and Mrs. Daniel Hubbard (1764; cat. nos. 26–27); Homer's *Croquet Scene* (1866; cat. no. 104); and two major works by Eakins—a watercolor, *The Zither Player* (1876), and an oil, *Mary Adeline Williams* (1899; cat. no. 152). These purchases underscored the importance of the realistic tradition in eighteenth- and nineteenth-century American painting.[71] Sweet emphasized the ties between American and European painting in the late nineteenth century in his well-received exhibitions "Sargent, Whistler, and Mary Cassatt" (1954) and "James McNeill Whistler" (1968). American art in Chicago had come of age.

With the appointment in 1969 of David Hanks as Assistant Curator of Western Art (responsible for the decorative arts), the focus of collecting shifted to works created in Chicago, especially by early Prairie School designers and artisans. By 1970 many of the great turn-of-the-century Prairie School houses had been altered or demolished and their contents auctioned. Only a handful of architects, curators, and historians cared about the preservation of such buildings and their contents.[72] One of the homes destroyed, for example, was Sullivan and Elmslie's 1912 Babson House in Riverside, Illinois; its fireplace andirons, tall clock (cat. nos. 164–65), and carpet designed by Elmslie, however, survived and were later purchased at auction for the Art Institute by Mrs. Theodore Tieken. Generous Chicagoans donated Prairie School objects that had been in their families. Among the works that came to the museum in the early 1970s were Robert Jarvie's great punch bowl (1911; cat. no. 160) and pitcher, works by Clara Barck Welles's Kalo Shop (see cat. no. 161), and furniture by Elmslie and Wright (cat. nos. 157 and 163). Hanks augmented those gifts with major purchases of Wright furniture (see cat. no. 156).

A New American Arts Department

In 1975 a restructuring of museum departments included the formation of a new Department of American Arts, which combined the collections of American painting and sculpture through 1900 and American decorative arts to the present. The joining of works in so many media into a single department was unusual at the Art Institute, where departments were traditionally defined by medium. Milo Naeve served as the first curator of the newly formed department. His interest in eighteenth-century furniture and silver built upon and complemented Meyric Rogers's earlier formation of an eighteenth-century collection. Among the objects that entered the collection during Naeve's tenure are a fine bombé chest of drawers by John Cogswell of Boston (1780/95; cat. no. 24); a Boston Rococo mahogany side chair (1770/85; cat. no. 30); an important high chest from Newport, Rhode Island (1755/75; cat. no 22); and the John Wood, Jr., tall-case clock (1765/75; cat. no. 31). All of these major purchases were made possible by the Helen Bowen Blair Fund.

Throughout the 1980s, the Antiquarian Society continued to be one of the most important support organizations for

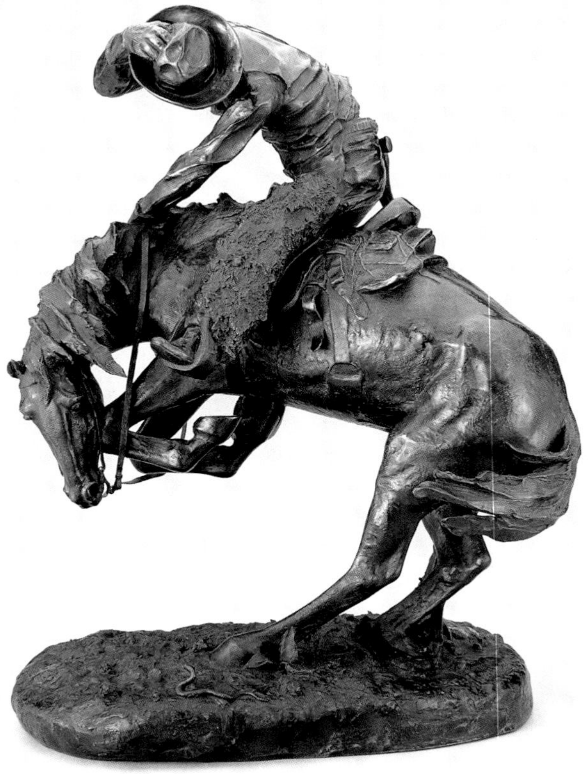

FIG. 40. Frederic Remington (1861–1909). *The Rattlesnake*, modeled 1905, cast 1905/09. Bronze; 61 x 42.6 x 27 cm (24 x 16¾ x 10⅝ in.). George F. Harding Collection (1982.818).

the growth of the decorative arts collections. Naeve encouraged the Antiquarians to expand their interests to include nineteenth-century objects. Two magnificent high-style pieces from New York—a rosewood Herter Brothers cabinet (1878/80; cat. no. 119) and a bird's-eye maple chest of drawers (1878/84; cat. no. 116)—are among the gifts made by the society. The maple chest, as well as an extraordinary Tiffany presentation punch bowl and pair of candelabra (1873; cat. no. 103), were given by the Antiquarians through the Mr. and Mrs. William Y. Hutchinson Fund.

In 1982 the collection of George F. Harding came to the Art Institute. A prominent figure in Chicago real estate early in the twentieth century, Harding collected arms and armor and war-related works of all types and eras. He had founded his own museum, which was located on the South Side of Chicago. Before the collection entered the Art Institute, it had resided for a number of years in an office building on Michigan Avenue. This enormous collection contained works by Frederic Remington, including the bronzes entitled *The Broncho Buster* (modeled 1895; cast 1895/98) and *The Rattlesnake* (modeled 1905; fig. 40); and paintings such as the grisaille series the artist executed for *Cosmopolitan Magazine* in 1905–06 (which accompanied his own story "The Way of an Indian"). Harding's interest in these romanticized Western images reflects Chicago's pivotal position, at the turn of the century, between the eastern and western parts of the United States. Chicago was situated at the opening of what was, in the nineteenth century, the western frontier. It is no accident that the historian Frederick Jackson Turner chose to deliver his famous 1893 address on the influence of frontier life on American character at the World's Columbian Exposition in Chicago. As the country's population moved further west and Chicago grew, it assumed a key role in bicoastal commerce and trade.

Another important development in the Art Institute's presentation of American arts was the construction from 1985 to 1988 of the Daniel F. and Ada L. Rice Building. This addition, which was steered to completion by Art Institute Director James N. Wood, includes an enlarged, thirty-thousand-square-foot area devoted exclusively to American painting, sculpture, and the decorative arts. The museum also established new acquisition funds to ensure the continued growth of interest in American art and culture. Eloise Martin and her family supported major purchases of Massachusetts and Maryland case pieces (cat. nos. 16 and 48). The interest of Mary Oldberg and Morris and Jane Weeden in furniture, silver, glass, and ceramics contributed to the growth of the collections in these areas (see cat. no. 168). Fern and Manfred Steinfeld and the family of Gertrude and Perry Herst provided funds to acquire modernist (post-1914) decorative arts that will be featured in a future publication. American Arts Department committee members as a group have been instrumental in the purchase of works in new collection areas, such as the decorative arts of the Southwest.

Since my appointment in 1992 as Field-McCormick Curator of American Arts, the entire collection has been reinstalled (see figs. 41–42). The creation of a large Beaux-Arts-style gallery for post-1860 paintings balanced the neoclassical symmetry of the sculpture court in the Rice Building. The Department of American Arts has continued to purchase important nineteenth- and twentieth-century objects. Our primary focus has been to develop the strengths of the collections while filling gaps in the areas of twentieth-century design, ceramics, glass, early nineteenth-century furniture, and American painting and sculpture before 1860. The Antiquarian Society provided funds for the purchase of a labeled Alexander Roux

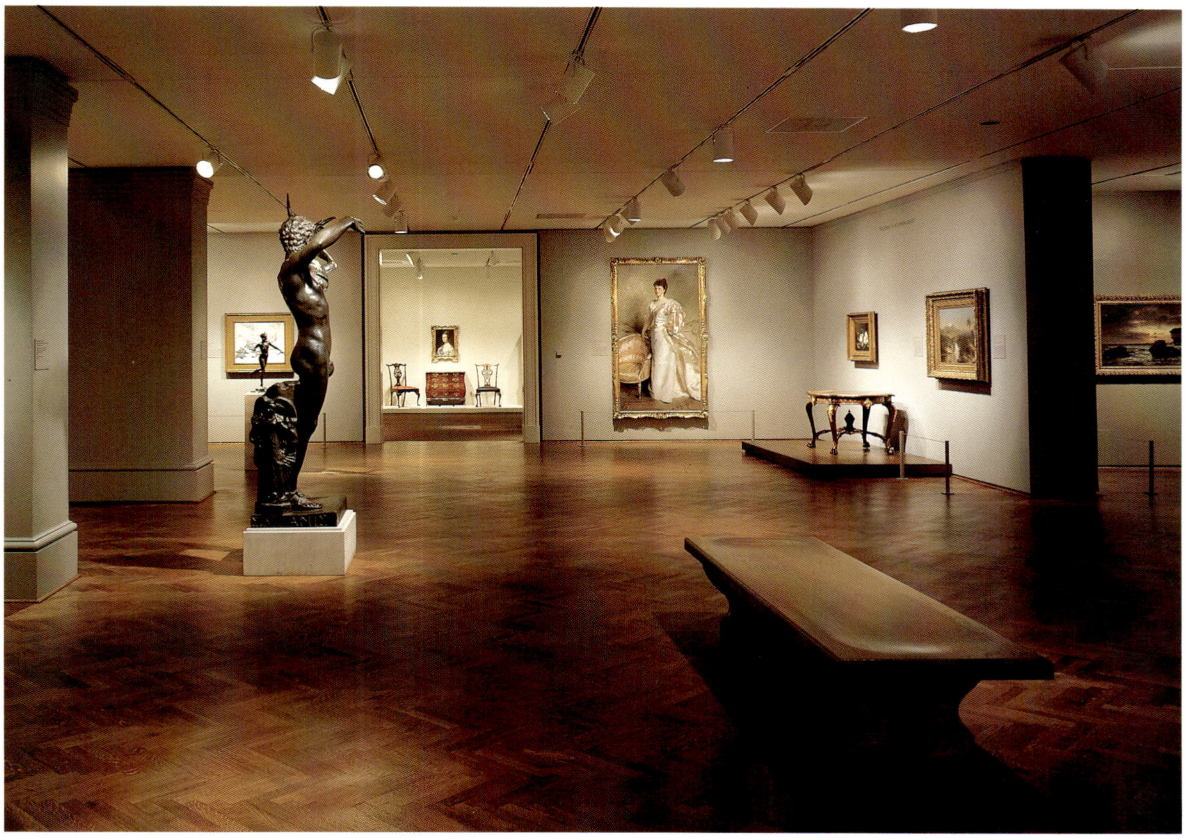

FIGS. 41–42. Field-McCormick Galleries of American Arts in the Rice Building at the Art Institute, 1997. Photographs © 1997 by Judith Bromley.

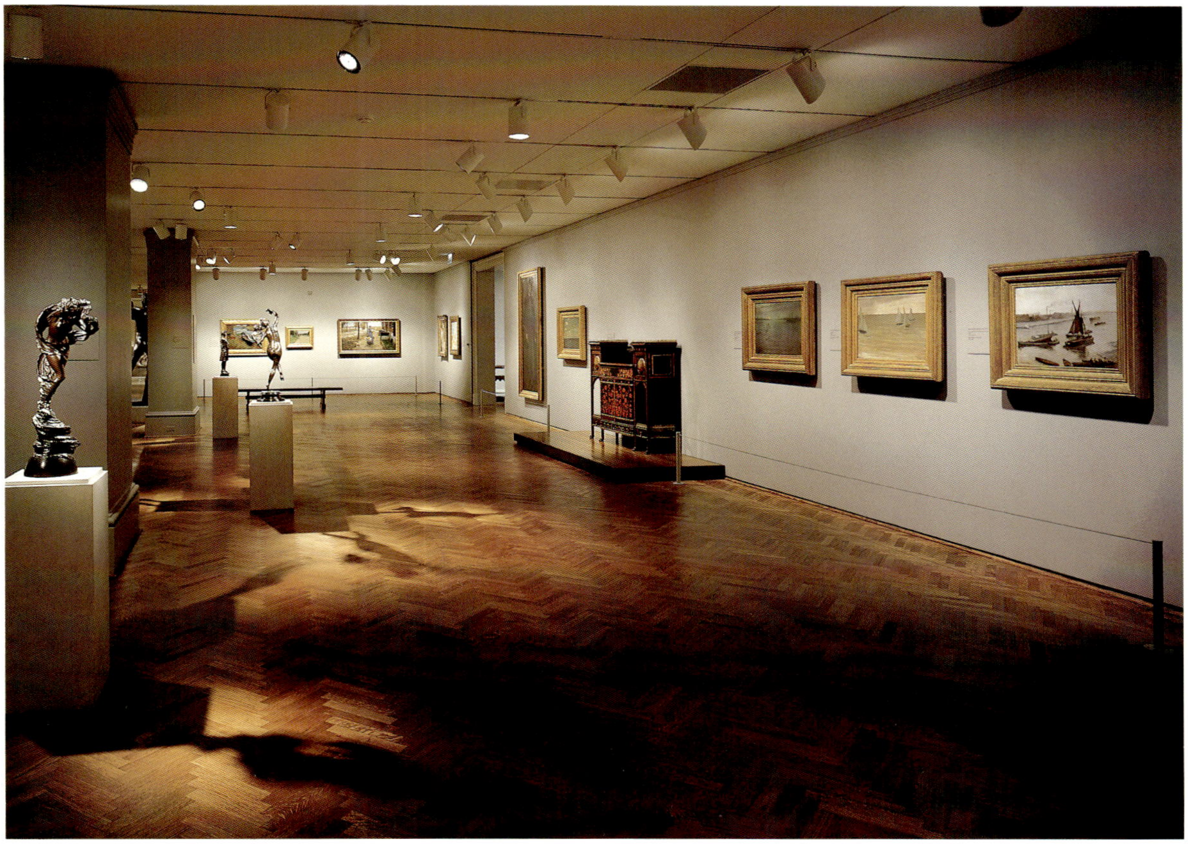

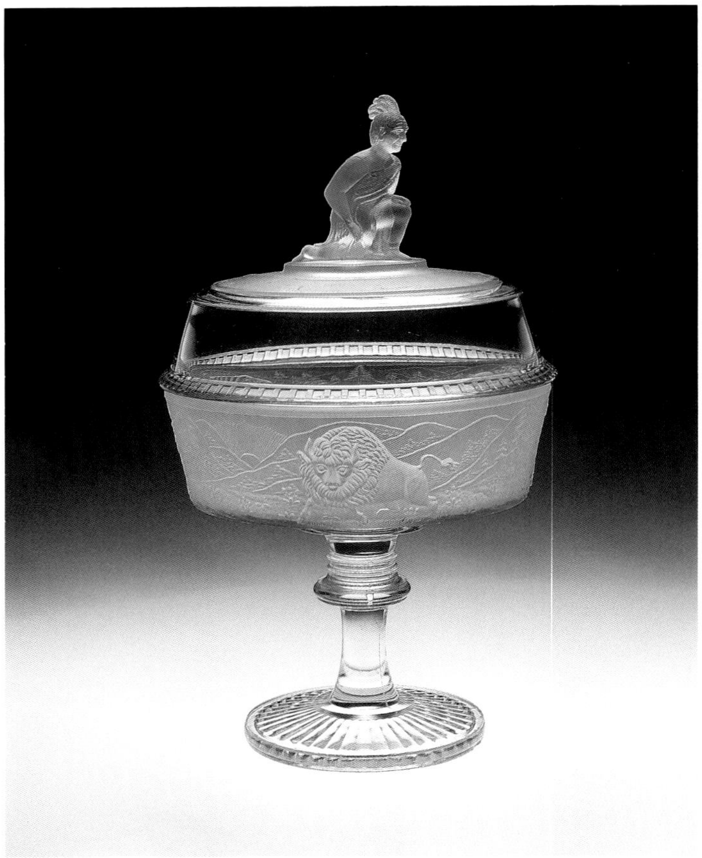

FIG. 43. Gillinder and Sons (Philadelphia; active 1864–1885). *Covered Compote in the Pioneer Pattern*, 1876. Glass; 40 x 23.2 cm (15¾ x 9⅛ in.). Gift of Harold Allen (1997.508).

rosewood sideboard (1850/57; cat. no. 85); a diminutive Emmons and Archibald Boston pier table (1813/25; cat. no. 60); a pair of Tiffany wine coolers (1873; cat. no. 103) that completed the presentation suite already in the collection; and Harriet Hosmer's *Zenobia, Queen of Palmyra* (c. 1857; cat. no. 78).

In the area of glass, purchases have ranged from a monumental Boston and Sandwich Glass Company double-plated lamp (c. 1865; cat. no. 91) to contemporary glassmaker Tom Patti's *Red Lumina with Concentric Disc* (1991). Chicago photographer Harold Allen, a former professor at the School of the Art Institute, donated his comprehensive collection of American pressed glass in 1997 (see fig. 43).

Funds provided by Wesley Dixon and Mrs. Herbert Vance have steadfastly supported the growth of the American paintings collection. Major acquisitions such as Rembrandt Peale's *Samuel Fisher Bradford* (1803/08; cat. no. 51), John F. Francis's *Wine, Cheese, and Fruit* (1857; cat. no. 84), and Albert Bierstadt's *Mountain Brook* (1863; cat. no. 87) filled large gaps in the collection's representation of the pre–Civil War era. Supported in part by the Grainger Fund, the department has also purchased examples of vernacular design and folk art that built upon the gifts left by Emily Crane Chadbourne, Emma Hodge, and Elizabeth Vaughan.

For generations important purchase funds have been provided by two families, the Fields and the McCormicks, both mainstays of Chicago's cultural life. The two families joined to endow the curatorial chair in American Art in 1984. From 1987 to 1993, Marshall Field served as Chairman of the Board of Trustees and enthusiastically supported major acquisitions in the department, including Raphaelle Peale's *Still Life—Strawberries, Nuts, &c.* (1822; cat. no. 56), William Rush's terracotta portrait of Andrew Jackson (1819; cat. no. 63), and a block-front bureau table from Newport, Rhode Island, attributed to John Townsend (1780/90; cat. no. 23). The support of Jamee J. and Marshall Field also made possible the acquisition of two of the most important pieces of furniture to enter the collection in the last few years: a New York inlaid center table with signed marquetry top by French-born master Joseph Cremer (c. 1862; cat. no. 89); and a labeled Charles-Honoré Lannuier card table (c. 1815; cat. no. 52).

Members of the McCormick family, which has produced generations of collectors and philanthropists from the nineteenth century on, established important acquisition funds for decorative arts and sculpture. The opening in 1988 of a new sculpture court in the Art Institute's Rice Building provided an opportunity to build the sculpture collection. Brooks McCormick gave works from his own collection, such as the aforementioned Saint-Gaudens bas-relief portrait of Violet Sargent, and enabled the museum to acquire sculpture through the Brooks and Hope McCormick Foundation. His brother, Roger McCormick, gave endowed and foundation funds to support acquisitions such as Henry Kirke Brown's rare bronze *The Filatrice* (1850; cat. no. 76) and John Quincy Adams Ward's sculpture *The Freedman* (1863; cat. no. 88). Funds given in memory of Roger's son, J. Peter McCormick, have provided for recent purchases of sculpture such as Joseph Mozier's full-length *Pocahontas* (1868; cat. no. 92) and Edward Sheffield Bartholomew's neoclassical *Hagar and Ishmael* (1856; cat. no. 77). Many of the gifts of the McCormick family are on view in the recently reinstalled J. Peter McCormick Sculpture Court and the Field-McCormick Galleries of American Arts at the Art Institute (fig. 1).

The gleaming white nineteenth-century marbles of the McCormick Sculpture Court sit squarely in the heart of Frank Norris's great gray city. All roads still lead to Chicago, even though today they often cross only at O'Hare International Airport. Chicago has epitomized the nineteenth and twentieth centuries' industrial and commercial might, the cross-fertilization of cultures, and the yearning for modern intellectual and aesthetic expression. The Art Institute is a monument born from those crosscurrents and from the determination and vision of civic leaders after the Great Fire. And as they did then, Chicagoans still strive to marry commerce and culture. The words of Thomas Curtis Clark's poem "Chicago," written in 1920, ring true to this day: "Our destined task is not to reckon gold, / To build wide marts where goods are bought and sold. / Let Beauty bloom! Let Art here have her way / Amid these towers and battlements of gray."

Notes

1. Frank Norris, *The Pit: A Story of Chicago* (New York, 1903), pp. 62–63.

2. Isham became a prominent surgeon during the Civil War and was one of the organizers of the United States Sanitary Commission. His interest in art may have been sparked by the art shows at the many fund-raising Sanitary Fairs held in Chicago and other major cities during the 1860s and 1870s.

3. In 1879 Wheeler joined Louis Comfort Tiffany and Samuel Colman in forming the Associated Artists, an interior-design firm modeled after William Morris and Company, London. Wheeler had admired the craft work of the South Kensington School of London shown at the 1876 Philadelphia Centennial Exposition. At South Kensington, women were taught needlework and other crafts to encourage them to produce beautiful objects and to be self-sufficient.

4. *Constitution and By-Laws of the Chicago Society of Decorative Art with Officers and Members* (Chicago, 1881), p. 3.

5. Witold Rybczynski, *City Life: Urban Expectations in a New World* (New York, 1995), p. 121.

6. A number of Chicagoans no doubt read Clarence Cook's *House Beautiful* (1878), a collection of essays published in 1875–77 in *Scribner's Monthly Magazine*. Like Wheeler, Cook had assimilated English notions about achievements and craftsmanship prior to the Industrial Age, but he used these ideas, as Elizabeth Stillinger wrote, to invest the artifacts of colonial America with romantic associations. See Stillinger, *The Antiquers: The Lives and Careers, the Deals, the Finds, the Collections of the Men and Women Who Were Responsible for the Changing Taste in American Antiques, 1850–1930* (New York, 1980), p. 57.

7. Florence Lowden Miller, "Historical Notes," in *The Antiquarian Society of The Art Institute of Chicago: The First One Hundred Years* (Chicago, 1977), p. 10.

8. Aline B. Saarinen, *The Proud Possessors: The Lives, Times, and Tastes of Some Adventurous American Art Collectors* (New York, 1958), p. 6.

9. Henry James, "John S. Sargent," *Harper's Magazine* (Oct. 1887), reprinted in John L. Sweeney, ed., *The Painter's Eye: Notes and Essays on the Pictorial Arts by Henry James* (Cambridge, Mass., 1956), p. 216. Director French's early acquisitions were paintings by contemporary American artists working abroad, such as William Dannat, George Hitchcock, and Charles Sprague Pearce. See "The Art Institute of Chicago: Modern Paintings II," *Art Amateur* (Dec. 1894), p. 19.

10. Charles L. Hutchinson served as president of the Art Institute from 1882 until his death in 1924.

11. French also visited the thirteen Art Institute students who were studying in Paris. Among them were Alice De Wolf Kellogg and Lawton Parker. See William Merchant Richardson French, "Notes [on a] journey to Europe with Mr. & Mrs. C. L. Hutchinson starting from New York Sat'y Mch. 9, 1889–" (unpub. travel diary, The Art Institute of Chicago Archives [hereafter referred to as AIC Archives]), for the list of Art Institute students whom French saw.

12. For further information on this theme, see D. Dodge Thompson, "'Loitering Through the Paris Exhibition': Highlights of the American Paintings at the Universal Exposition of 1889," in Annette Blaugrund, ed., *Paris 1889: American Artists at the Universal Exposition*, exh. cat. (Philadelphia, Pennsylvania Academy of the Fine Arts, 1989), pp. 58–59.

13. Chase's *City Park* (c. 1887; cat. no. 121), which shares the bright, high-keyed, plein-air palette of Hitchcock's work, did not find its way to the Art Institute until 1968. Dannat's *Study for "An Aragonese Smuggler"* (1881) entered the collection in 1887 because of the artist's friendship with French; the full-length portrait is now in the collection of the Metropolitan Museum of Art, New York. For more information on Hitchcock's work at the Paris Exposition, see Annette Blaugrund, "George Hitchcock (1850–1913)," in Blaugrund (note 12), p. 169.

14. See entries for Mar. 19 to May 17, 1889, in French (note 11), pp. 6–7, 67.

15. Photographs of the installation show that Millet also incorporated the pedestals ordered by French in London.

16. Similar exhibitions were organized in other midwestern cities because of "a general feeling amongst the artists of the Western States that they were at a disadvantage as compared to those of the more closely connected communities in the East" (St. Louis Art Museum, *Catalogue of the First Annual Exhibition of the Society of Western Artists* [1897], p. 4).

17. Daniel Catton Rich, "Half a Century of American Exhibitions" (1939), in Peter Hastings Falk, ed., *The Annual Exhibition Record of The Art Institute of Chicago, 1888–1950* (Madison, Conn., 1990), p. 9.

18. Ibid.

19. Henri Loyrette, "Chicago: A French View," in John Zukowsky, ed., *Chicago Architecture, 1872–1922: Birth of a Metropolis*, exh. cat. (The Art Institute of Chicago, 1987), p. 127.

20. Daniel Burnham directed the historicizing conception of the fair, and he called in mostly out-of-towners to assist in the planning and setting of the grounds and buildings. These included architects Richard Morris Hunt, Charles McKim, and Frederick Law Olmsted, and sculptors Daniel Chester French and Augustus Saint-Gaudens. Only sculptor Lorado Taft and architects Henry Ives Cobb and Louis Sullivan were local.

21. Elizabeth Broun and Alan Fern, "Introduction," in Carolyn Kinder Carr and George Gurney, eds., *Revisiting the White City: American Art at the 1893 World's Fair*, exh. cat. (Washington, D.C., National Museum of American Art and National Portrait Gallery, Smithsonian Institution, 1993), pp. 13–14.

22. See Jane Clarke, "The Art Institute's Guardian Lions," *The Art Institute of Chicago Museum Studies* 14, 1 (spring 1988), pp. 47–55. Mrs. Field was the sister-in-law of Marshall Field, founder of the Field Museum of Natural History, and the widow of Henry Field, whose important collection of Barbizon School and British paintings came to the Art Institute in 1894. See letter from Bryan Lathrop to Charles Hutchinson, Sept. 24, 1892, AIC Archives. Included in the gift were John Constable's *The Lock*, which was exhibited at the World's Columbian Exposition; Jules Breton's *Song of the Lark*; Eugène Delacroix's *Wounded Lioness, Tiger Resting*; and over thirty other examples by Camille Corot, Jules Dupré, Jean François Millet, Henri Rousseau, Constant Troyon, and others. Some of the works were lent to the 1889 Exposition in Paris; in his travel diary, William French duly noted the way they were displayed; see French (note 11), pp. 78, 98.

23. *Chicago Tribune*, Aug. 20, 1893, p. 24. Another critic commented: "Naturally Mr. Chase's Alice attracts us . . . she is so wholesome. Like a beautiful cultivated flower, she is the product of the guiding and pruning of a wise parent—a beautiful cultivated child of nature. She moves with . . . ease and grace . . . perfectly unconscious of self, which is the height of perfected art"; see L. M. Bryant, *American Pictures and Their Painters* (New York, 1917), pp. 114–15.

24. As a mark of their mutual interest in Japanese culture, Deering sent Sargent fans and costumes obtained during his trip to Japan in 1878; see letter from John Singer Sargent to Charles Deering, May 2, 1878, Deering–Sargent Correspondence, Ryerson and Burnham Archives, The Art Institute of Chicago.

25. Deering's correspondence with Saint-Gaudens's wife, Augusta, reveals that the cast of the bas-relief of Sargent's sister was made posthumously for Deering. See Augustus Saint-Gaudens papers, roll 5 (Archives of American Art, Washington, D.C.), Jan. 24 and 29 and Feb. 11, 1908.

26. See *Artistic Houses: Being a Series of Interior Views of a Number of the Most Beautiful and Celebrated Houses in the United States, with a Description of the Art Treasures Contained Therein* (1883; reprint, New York, 1971), pp. 106–07, fig. 104.

27. Quoted in Jeanne Madeline Weimann, *The Fair Women* (Chicago, 1981), p. 182. See also "Sara Hallowell: Unique in the Art World," *New York Times*, Dec. 31, 1915, pt. 3, p. 6.

28. The correspondence between Hallowell and French regarding the arrangements for the annual American exhibitions is in the AIC Archives.

29. For further information on Hallowell's relationship with the Palmers, see John Kysela, "Sara Hallowell Brings 'Modern Art' to the Midwest," *Art Quarterly* 27, 2 (1964), pp. 150–67; and Margo M. Hobbs, "Bertha Palmer's Philanthropy in the Arts" (M.A. thesis, The School of The Art Institute of Chicago, 1992), pp. 64–65.

30. Archives Durand-Ruel, Paris, sales records for Mr. and Mrs. Potter Palmer.

31. See The Art Institute of Chicago, *Catalogue of the Loan Collection of Paintings Exhibited by The Art Institute of Chicago at the Opening of the New Art Museum* (Nov. 19, 1887), p. 18, which mentions Hitchcock's painting.

32. Mrs. Palmer met Claude Monet in 1891 and purchased seven of his pictures that same year. By the summer of 1893, the Palmers owned thirty-three paintings by Monet; yet mysteriously, although the Palmers lent other pictures to the World's Fair, they lent none by this great Impressionist. Their collecting seems to have been driven by their interest in contemporaneity and in investment potential. Their most intense collecting period coincides with the building of their Lake Shore Drive mansion. Palmer, astute businessman that he was, confided to American Impressionist painter Theodore Robinson in 1893 that he wanted to invest in pictures that "he wouldn't lose money on." See Charles F. Stuckey, *Claude Monet, 1840–1926*, exh. cat. (The Art Institute of Chicago, 1995), p. 221; Richard R. Brettell, "Monet's Haystacks Reconsidered," *The Art Institute of Chicago Museum Studies* 11, 1 (fall 1984), pp. 4–21; and Frances Weitzenhoffer, *The Havemeyers: Impressionism Comes to America* (New York, 1986), p. 88.

33. Hallowell purchased Saint-Gaudens's bas-relief portrait of Jules Bastien-Lepage (cat. no. 130) directly from the artist in 1888. She lent the sculpture to the Art Institute in 1891 and gave it to the museum in 1908.

34. See Carolyn Kinder Carr, "Prejudice and Pride: Presenting American Art at the 1893 World's Columbian Exposition," in Carr and Gurney (note 21), pp. 65–71.

35. MacMonnies was married to sculptor Frederick MacMonnies (see cat. nos. 138–39), who created the massive fountain for the basin of the 1893 World's Columbian Exposition. She summered, and eventually lived year round, in Giverny.

36. Frederick A. Sweet, *Miss Mary Cassatt: Impressionist from Pennsylvania* (Norman, Okla., 1966), p. 136.

37. MacMonnies' *Primitive Woman* showed the influence of her teacher, Pierre Puvis de Chavannes. Described as almost Pre-Raphaelite, with a lighter palette and a continuous landscape background, MacMonnies' more traditional mural was preferred by critics to that of Cassatt. When the World's Fair was dismantled, Mrs. Palmer paid to have the murals stored in Chicago. They seem to have disappeared around 1911. For the history of the murals after the close of the World's Fair on October 31, 1893, see Sally Webster and Carolyn Kinder Carr, "Mary Cassatt and Mary Fairchild MacMonnies: The Search for Their 1893 Murals," *American Art* 8, 1 (winter 1994), pp. 53–69.

38. Both Cassatt and Ryerson were drawn to the recently rediscovered mannerist artist El Greco. Celebrated by such contemporary critics as Roger Fry and Clive Bell, El Greco was given the role of forerunner to modernist art. The artist's singular vision and spiritual expression, along with the abstract elements of his pictures, were compared to those of Paul Cézanne. Cassatt had seen El Greco's *Assumption of the Virgin* (1577) while traveling in Spain with her New York patrons and friends Mr. and

Mrs. H. O. Havemeyer. After this altarpiece was purchased by Durand-Ruel in 1904, she carried on a persuasive correspondence with Ryerson and Hutchinson regarding its availability, and urged the Art Institute to purchase it. See letter from Mary Cassatt to Charles Hutchinson, Jan. 9, 1905, AIC Archives; and Weitzenhoffer (note 32), pp. 156–57.

39. See *Catalogue of Japanese Engravings: An Important Collection of Old Prints in Color, Hokusai Sketches, Albums, Kakemonos, Rare Books and Modern Water Colors Belonging to Mr. H. Deakin, of Yokohama* (Chicago, 1896).

40. See Joan E. Draper, "Paris by the Lake: Sources of Burnham's Plan of Chicago," in Zukowsky (note 19), pp. 114–15.

41. See Lauren S. Weingarden, "Louis H. Sullivan's Ornament and the Poetics of Architecture," in Zukowsky (note 19), pp. 229–49; and Robert Twombly, *Louis Sullivan: His Life and Work* (New York, 1986), pp. 267–68.

42. See Eileen Boris, *Art and Labor: Ruskin, Morris, and the Craftsman Ideal in America* (Philadelphia, 1986), p. 33.

43. The Chicago Arts and Crafts Society provided an audience for the Art Institute's new journal, *Brush and Pencil* (1897–1905). Among those intellectuals interested in the Arts and Crafts movement was Oscar Lovell Triggs, an English professor at the University of Chicago and admirer of William Morris and Walt Whitman. Triggs wrote one of the earliest histories of the movement. Also active in the society were architects Frank Lloyd Wright and Allen and Irving Pond. See T. J. Jackson Lears, *No Place of Grace: Antimodernism and the Transformation of American Culture, 1880–1920* (New York, 1981), p. 67.

44. W. Scott Braznell, "Metalsmithing and Jewelrymaking, 1900–1920," in Janet Kardon, ed., *The Ideal Home, 1900–1920: The History of Twentieth-Century American Craft* (New York, 1993), p. 59.

45. Barck's mission, like that of Addams and Starr at Hull House, was to provide employment for women and immigrants. Tremendous immigration after 1870 had led to a backlash of nativism in the workplace. Immigrants were often viewed as anarchists or socialists after the violence and strikes of the 1880s. Many of Barck's designers were women, and her skilled workers were typically first-generation Scandinavians.

46. See "Training in New Lines: Profitable Field of Labor Open to People of Good Taste," *Chicago Inter-Ocean*, Mar. 27, 1898, in the chronological scrapbooks housed in the Ryerson and Burnham Libraries, The Art Institute of Chicago, vol. 9 (Aug. 22, 1897–June 5, 1898), pp. 148–49.

47. This rift was apparent when Wright addressed the society at Hull House on Mar. 1, 1901, calling his lecture "The Art and Craft of the Machine." He believed not only that the machine was useful for production and efficiency, but that it promoted the clean-cut, geometric, modernist aesthetic he espoused. Wright's lecture was reviewed in the *Chicago Tribune* on Mar. 4, 1901 (its date has been erroneously published as Mar. 6 in various sources). For the text of the lecture, see Bruce Brooks Pfeiffer, ed., *Frank Lloyd Wright: Collected Writings* (New York, 1992), vol. 1, pp. 58–69.

48. During the last decade of the century, young writers attracted to the radical literary climate of Chicago included George Ade, Theodore Dreiser, Peter Finley Dunne, Eugene Field, Henry B. Fuller, and Harriet Monroe.

49. Quoted in Henry Regnery, *The Cliff Dwellers: The History of a Chicago Cultural Institution* (Chicago, 1990), pp. 8–9. Because the Cliff Dwellers Club did not accept women members until the 1980s, there was little overlap with the Arts and Crafts Society, whose members were predominantly female.

50. The exterior of the penthouse on the eighth floor of Orchestra Hall was planned by Daniel Burnham, and the interior was designed by Howard Van Doren Shaw, with some hardware provided by Louis Sullivan; see Regnery (note 49), p. 13. In 1996 the Cliff Dwellers Club moved from Orchestra Hall to the penthouse of the Borg-Warner Building next door.

51. It should also be noted that *japonisme* was, like the Arts and Crafts movement, a powerful influence on modern design in the city. One of the most popular and spectacular exhibits at the 1893 World's Fair was the Japanese Pavilion, which was called the Ho-o-den. It made a great impact in particular on Wright and Elmslie, whose subsequent attitudes about interior space reflected the open, flowing plan of Japanese architecture. This was illustrated in Wright's installation at the Art Institute for an exhibition of his own collection of Hiroshige prints in 1906. He designed another installation for the large loan exhibition of Japanese Ukiyo-e prints held at the museum in 1908, which featured works from the collection of the discerning Chicagoan Clarence Buckingham. See David A. Hanks, *The Decorative Designs of Frank Lloyd Wright* (New York, 1979), p. 20; Frank Lloyd Wright, "Introduction," in The Art Institute of Chicago, *Hiroshige: An Exhibition of Colour Prints from the Collection of Frank Lloyd Wright*, exh. cat. (Mar. 29, 1906), unpag.; and The Art Institute of Chicago, *Catalogue of a Loan Exhibition of Japanese Colour Prints*, exh. cat., intro. by Frederick William Gookin (Mar. 5–25, 1908), p. 20.

The influence of Japanese aesthetics was also apparent in Wright's installations in the Dial Bookshop and the Thurber Gallery, both in the Fine Arts Building in downtown Chicago. Winfield Scott Thurber had opened an art gallery in the city as early as 1880. The gallery showed contemporary American and European paintings and prints, and had gained a reputation for quality. In 1909 Thurber opened a new gallery in the Fine Arts Building and chose Wright to design the space. See "Art Gallery Designed by Frank Lloyd Wright, Architect," *International Studio* 39 (Feb. 1910), pp. 95–96; and Evelyn Marie Stuart, "Development of Art in the West—Thurber Galleries," *Fine Arts Journal* 21, 6 (Dec. 1909), pp. 285–90.

52. The first two decades of the century were a watershed period in the literary milieu of Chicago as well. Margaret Anderson arrived from Columbus, Indiana, and by 1914 she was publishing the avant-garde literary magazine *The Little Review*, which included stories and poems by Sherwood Anderson, James Joyce, Vachel Lindsay, and Ezra Pound, among others. Harriet Monroe began *Poetry* magazine in 1912 with the aid of subscribers such as Bertha Palmer and Daniel H. Burnham. *Poetry* published Carl Sandburg's "Chicago" in 1914 and T. S. Eliot's "Love Song of J. Alfred Prufrock" in 1915.

53. Rich (note 17), p. 11.

54. In 1904 a prize was awarded to Mary Cassatt, who still held fast to her "independent" stance critical of juries and awards. Declining to accept it, she asked that the money be applied to benefit a Chicago art student in Paris. See the letters of Durand-Ruel and Mary Cassatt to William M. R. French, Nov. 23 and Dec. 4, 1904, Correspondence of William M. R. French, AIC Archives.

55. He may have seen two of these paintings by Inness—*The Mill Pond* (1889) and *Threatening* (1891)—at the 1893 World's Fair.

56. See Andrew Martinez, "A Mixed Reception for Modernism: The 1913 Armory Show at The Art Institute of Chicago," *The Art Institute of Chicago Museum Studies* 19, 1 (spring 1993), pp. 30–57.

57. Arthur Jerome Eddy, *Recollections and Impressions of James A. McNeill Whistler* (Philadelphia, 1904), pp. 178–82.

58. These joined the 134 Whistler etchings and lithographs bequeathed by Bryan Lathrop in 1917 to make the Art Institute's Whistler holdings among the best in the world.

59. Mildred Davison, "Some Nineteenth-Century American Glass," *Bulletin of The Art Institute of Chicago* 30, 4 (Apr.–May 1936), pp. 52–54.

60. See Mildred Davison, *American Quilts from The Art Institute of Chicago*, exh. cat. (The Art Institute of Chicago, 1966), unpag.

61. See Edwin Atlee Barber, *Pottery and Porcelain of the United States: An Historical Review of American Ceramic Art from the Earliest Times to the Present Day* (New York, 1893); and idem, *Tulip Ware of the Pennsylvania-German Potters: An Historical Sketch of the Art of Slip-Decoration in the United States* (Philadelphia, 1903).

62. See Mildred Davison and Christa C. Mayer Thurman, *Coverlets: A Handbook on the Collection of Woven Coverlets in The Art Institute of Chicago*, exh. cat. (Chicago, 1973), p. 9.

63. Emily's sister, Frances Crane Lillie, became interested in social progressivism and funded charitable organizations for orphans and widows, as well as the Crane Day Care Center at Hull House. See "Notes Dictated by Margaret Crane-Lillie Gildea, Sept. 1978, about Emily Crane Chadbourne and other members of the Crane Family" (unpub. MS, Ryerson and Burnham Libraries, The Art Institute of Chicago).

64. The new department was conceived after the exhibition of George Fred Keck's tubular-steel furniture in the "House of Tomorrow" at the 1933 Century of Progress Exhibition.

65. Architectural drawings, fragments, and models in the Art Institute's collection were eventually placed in the care of the museum's Department of Architecture after its establishment in 1981. Marx, an Art Institute trustee and a collector of School of Paris paintings, left to the museum furniture by Donald Deskey and his own furniture designed for client Leigh Block. The impact of modernist industrial design in Chicago was felt mainly at the Association of Arts and Industries, which, in 1937, hired László Moholy-Nagy, the Bauhaus teacher and painter-photographer, to direct a venture that was called the "New Bauhaus." Eventually the New Bauhaus reorganized and renamed itself the School of Design, and in 1950 it became part of the Illinois Institute of Technology.

66. Garvan was one of a number of wealthy individuals who turned their private collections into institutional ones at the beginning of the century. Garvan's patronage in connection with Yale began in the late 1920s.

67. The Behrends' Massachusetts home was featured in *Antiques* 40, 5 (Nov. 1941), pp. 288–90.

68. In 1904 the Museum of Art at the Rhode Island School of Design received the Pendleton Collection. In 1909 the Metropolitan Museum's Hudson-Fulton exhibition displayed American decorative arts, and the museum began to collect American furniture for its projected American Wing, instigated by the acquisition in 1909 of the Eugene Bolles collection of over six hundred pieces of furniture. In 1922 the family of Robert W. de Forest gave funds for the construction of the American Wing, which opened to the public in 1924.

69. See Ethelred Abbot, "The Century of Progress Exhibition of Art for 1934," *Bulletin of The Art Institute of Chicago* 28, 4 (Apr.–May 1934), p. 38; and The Art Institute of Chicago, *Catalogue of a Century of Progress Exhibition of Paintings and Sculpture: Lent from American Collections*, exh. cat. (1933).

70. See Hans Huth, "Pictures and Critics," pp. 7–9; and Daniel Catton Rich, "Introduction," p. 3, in The Art Institute of Chicago, *From Colony to Nation: An Exhibition of American Painting, Silver, and Architecture from 1650 to the War of 1812*, exh. cat. (1949).

71. They were featured in an article by the distinguished architectural historian Henry-Russell Hitchcock on the Art Institute's American paintings collection, which notes the connections between American artists such as Cassatt, Hassam, Homer, Sargent, and Whistler and their French counterparts. Hitchcock suggested that American and European pictures be hung together at the Art Institute. See Hitchcock, "American Painting at the Art Institute," *The Art Institute of Chicago Quarterly* 45, 3 (Sept. 15, 1951), p. 43.

72. Architectural photographer Richard Nickel documented the demolition of Louis Sullivan's great Stock Exchange Building in 1971. The building's trading room was salvaged and reconstructed in the Art Institute in 1976–77, and the entrance arch of the building was installed in the museum's East Garden in 1977. See John Vinci, *The Trading Room: Louis Sullivan and the Chicago Stock Exchange* (Chicago, 1989). Other locally prominent preservationists have included John Eifler, Timothy Samuelson, and John Vinci.

THE AMERICAN ARTS COLLECTION

Entries by Judith A. Barter, Kimberly Rhodes, and Seth A. Thayer, with contributions by Andrew Walker

FROM COLONY TO NATION

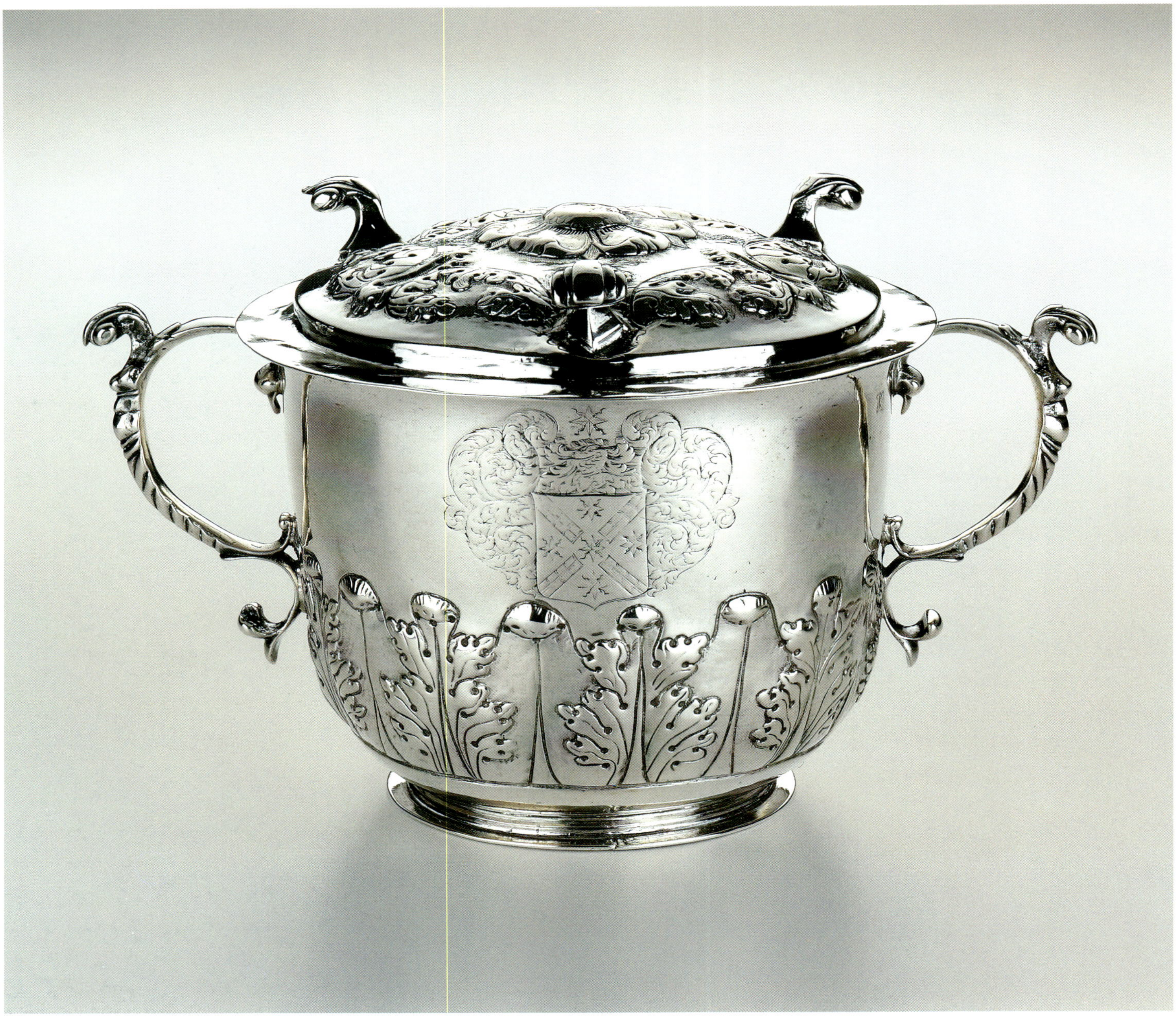

CAT. NO. 2

1. CORNELIUS VAN DER BURCH (1652–1699)

Caudle Cup, 1674/99

New York

Silver; 14 x 23.5 cm (5½ x 9¼ in.)

Marked on bottom three times: *CVB* (cojoined inside a heart); engraved on the body with the Van Cortlandt family arms

Gift of the Antiquarian Society and Dr. and Mrs. C. Phillip Miller, 1955.651

2. CORNELIUS KIERSTEDE (1675–1757)

Two-Handled Covered Cup, 1698/1720

New York

Silver; 14 x 22.9 cm (5½ x 9 in.)

Marked on side of each handle and three times on lid: *CK* (in a rectangle); engraved on body of cup: the Van Cortlandt family arms; engraved on bottom of cup: >*M C L*< and *Petrus Stuyvesant / married / M. C. Livingston / 1730*; engraved on underside lip of cover: *MCL*[1]

Restricted gift of Mrs. James W. Alsdorf, Pauline Seipp Armstrong, Marshall Field, Charles C. Haffner III, Mrs. Burton W. Hales, Mrs. Harold T. Martin, Mrs. C. Phillip Miller, Mr. and Mrs. Milo M. Naeve, Mrs. Eric Oldberg, Mrs. Frank L. Sulzberger, and the Ethel T. Scarborough Fund, 1984.1132

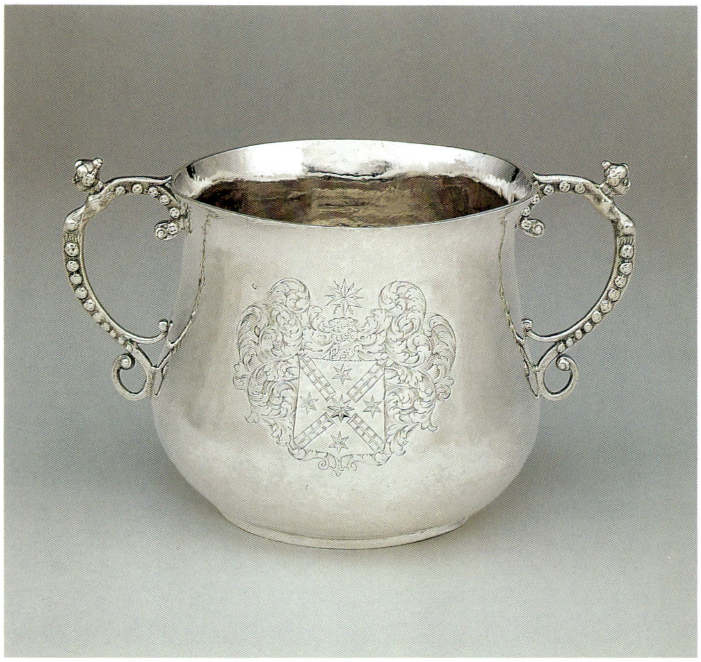

CAT. NO. 1

Throughout the colonial period, family members and friends gathered to celebrate a wedding; the birth of a child; the lying in, or resting, of a new mother; or a child's baptism.[2] To mark the occasion, celebrants often presented gifts. In prosperous households, silver pieces such as these two cups were given as tokens of good luck, and for the purpose of toasting one's health, happiness, or fertility.[3] The guests shared various hearty drinks known as caudle, syllabub, and posset—which consisted variously of hot wines, sugar, spices, eggs, cream, beer, bread, and oatmeal—from these cups. Such communal ceremonies strengthened the bonds of the assembled group and kept European traditions alive.[4]

One of the most common Dutch customs celebrated in the colonies was *kindermaal.* This festivity took place within ten days of the birth of a child and involved a mostly female group gathered at the bedside of the mother to toast her and her baby. The guests passed among themselves a caudle cup or bowl filled with a mixture of brandy and raisins, either drinking straight from the cup or using a spoon. The newborn child sometimes received gifts of silver or gold.[5]

Caudle cups were popular in Boston and the surrounding areas; surprisingly few survive from outside New England. Most of the region's caudle cups are small, perhaps indicating personal use. They may have been used to feed a hearty, warm mixture of oats, wine, and eggs to an invalid or a young child, or to nourish an adult on cold days. Such a small-scale cup, crafted by Jeremiah Dummer, is in the museum's collection.[6] The monumental size of the caudle cup made by Cornelius van der Burch (cat. no. 1), however, indicates that it was most likely reserved for special occasions. Its large handles would have allowed it to be passed easily among a group of people.

Oral tradition indicates that this cup was made for the baptism of Philip Van Cortlandt in 1683. Although this cannot be substantiated, several factors suggest that it may be true. First, the date of the baptism fits comfortably within van der Burch's working dates. Second, Stephanus Van Cortlandt (1643–1700), Philip's father, possessed his own large caudle cup—one made by New York silversmith Gerrit Onckelbag. The two cups are almost identical, suggesting that van der Burch may have used the Onckelbag cup as a model.[7] Though Philip Van Cortlandt inherited his family's house, their land, and the title Lord of the Manor, the Onckelbag caudle cup descended from Stephanus to another son—an indication perhaps that Philip possessed a cup of his own.

The two-handled covered cup by Cornelius Kierstede (cat. no. 2) is one of a small group of similarly decorated pieces from New York that were adapted from English cups dating from the 1680s. The form appears nowhere else in the colonies. Like the caudle cup, this piece, too, was made for the Van Cortlandt family. The cup and the cover are both engraved with the initials *MCL*, for Margaret C. Livingston, who in 1764 married Petrus Stuyvesant, scion of the Stuyvesant family. The cup descended in the family until acquired by the Art Institute.[8] Together, these two cups document the family's fascination with celebration rituals practiced in the Netherlands and England.

NOTES

1. The initials *MCL* engraved on the bottom of the cup and on the underside of the lid are those of Margaret C. Livingston. However, the nineteenth-century engraving on the bottom of the cup giving the date of her marriage to Petrus Stuyvesant as 1730 is inaccurate; see Roderic H. Blackburn and Ruth Piwonka, *Remembrance of Patria: Dutch Arts and Culture in Colonial America, 1609–1776*, exh. cat. (Albany, N.Y., Albany Institute of History and Art, 1988), p. 286.

2. Louise Conway Belden, *The Festive Tradition: Table Decoration and Desserts in America, 1650–1900* (New York, 1983), p. 138.

3. Other forms of silver, such as porringers, tankards, and small whistles, were also popular celebratory gifts. See entry on the Cornelius Kierstede tankard (cat. no. 7) for more information on symbols.

4. Gerald W. R. Ward, "The Dutch and English Traditions in American Silver: Cornelius Kierstede," in Francis J. Puig and Michael Conforti, eds., *The American Craftsman and the European Tradition, 1620–1820*, exh. cat. (Minneapolis Institute of Arts, 1989), p. 146, cat. no. 57.

5. Blackburn and Piwonka (note 1), pp. 189, 278.

6. It was a gift of the Antiquarian Society through the Mr. and Mrs. Edwin A. Seipp Fund (1952.167).

7. The cup by Gerrit Onckelbag, now in the collection of the Yale University Art Gallery, New Haven, Conn., measures only ¼-inch taller and ⅛-inch wider; see Kathryn C. Buhler and Graham Hood, *American Silver: Garvan and Other Collections in the Yale University Art Gallery* (New Haven, Conn., 1970), vol. 2, pp. 24–27, no. 572.

8. Information regarding the descent of the cup after Margaret Livingston married Petrus Stuyvesant was provided by Stuyvesant Butler; see his letter to Milo Naeve, Dec. 17, 1985, Files of the Department of American Arts, The Art Institute of Chicago.

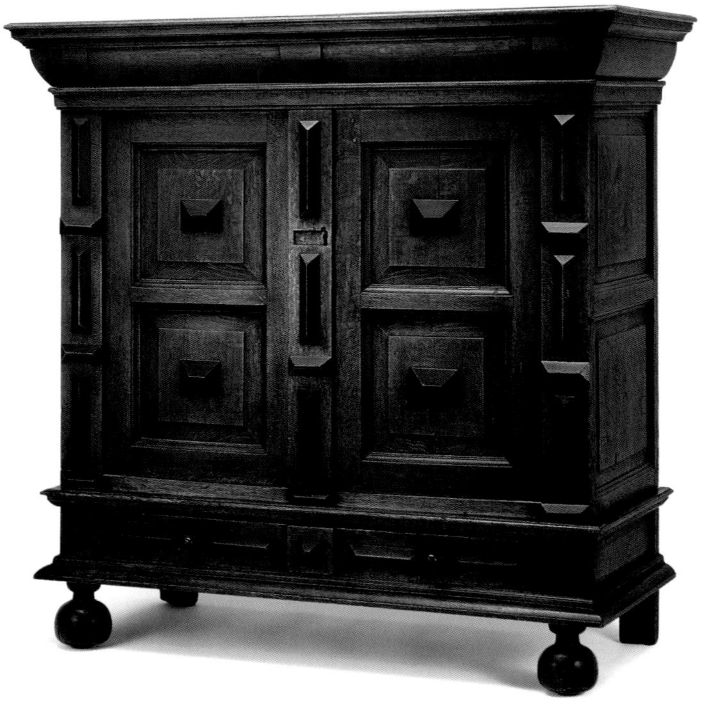

CAT. NO. 3

3. KAST, 1650/1700

New York area

Oak and walnut; 170.8 x 168.3 cm (67¼ x 66¼ in.)

Sanford Fund, 1949.489

The New Netherland colony was founded in 1623 by the employees of the Dutch West India Company, a commercial venture established in 1621 to oversee Dutch interests in the Western Hemisphere. Settlers in New Netherland brought to the New World their religious beliefs, in the guise of the Dutch Reformed Church, and their cultural attitudes toward business and everyday life.[1]

Even after the English wrested control of the colony in 1664, Dutch settlers remained tied to the Netherlands. Well into the nineteenth century, isolated pockets of Dutch influence continued to exist, in communities in western and central Long Island, northern New Jersey, and the Hudson River Valley. Ministers of the Dutch Reformed Church advocated the use of Dutch language in everyday speech and promoted a close identification with Dutch cultural traditions.[2] These attitudes certainly contributed to an enduring preference for certain fine and decorative art forms, such as the kast in the Art Institute's collection.

This kast is an American interpretation of a popular sixteenth- and seventeenth-century piece of Dutch furniture.

Kasten were made in the predominantly Dutch-settled areas of New York, New Jersey, and Connecticut from the mid-seventeenth century to the first quarter of the nineteenth century. Probably the largest piece of furniture in the Dutch-American home, the kast was an impressive symbol of prosperity.[3] Period inventories indicate that these large cupboards were used primarily to store linens and clothing. Usually imported, fine linens were among the most expensive items in the home.[4] Each shelf in a kast was lined with two long pieces of linen—running lengthwise and crosswise—folded over other linens to keep them clean.[5]

The Art Institute's kast is one of the earliest extant American examples, and it is closely related to Dutch prototypes. Its design may have been inspired by a Dutch pattern book, such as *Officina Arcularia* by Crispin de Passe the Younger (see fig. 1).[6] Like de Passe's design, the Art Institute's kast is architecturally inspired. The emphasis on proportion and symmetry, seen in the four identical square panels and in the simple, applied geometric ornament, echoes the classical orders. Furthermore, the bold Baroque form of this piece recalls a classical temple facade, and the addition of an entablature further emphasizes its architectural connotations.

The interior of the kast retains two of the three original shelves and the original drawer. The exterior drawer is also original and, like the interior one, is side-hung and nailed together. The backboards are of clapboard construction, nailed to the top and bottom rails of the kast. The feet are also original. The applied ornament on the front of the cupboard is walnut; it made a striking contrast to the lighter oak of the cupboard before, early in this century, it was stripped of its finish and the surface made a uniform brown.[7]

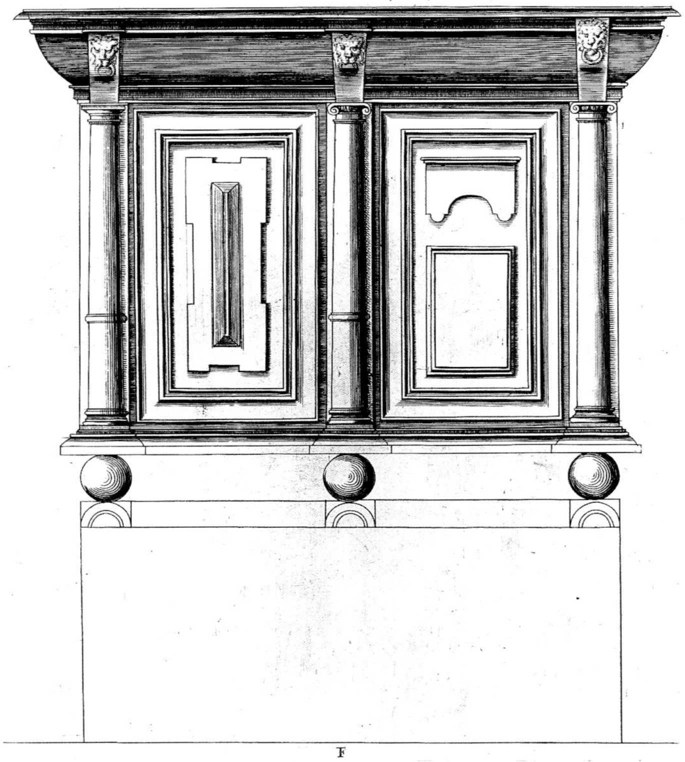

FIG. 1. Crispin de Passe the Younger (Netherlandish, c. 1565–1637). Plate from *Officina Arcularia in qua sunt . . . boutique menuserie* (Amsterdam, 1642). Metropolitan Museum of Art, New York, Harris Brisbane Dick Fund (23.34.1).

NOTES

1. Roderic H. Blackburn and Ruth Piwonka, *Remembrance of Patria: Dutch Art and Culture in Colonial America, 1609–1776*, exh. cat. (Albany, N.Y., Albany Institute of History and Art, 1988), pp. 35, 43.

2. Peter M. Kenny, Frances Gruber Safford, and Gilbert T. Vincent, *American Kasten: The Dutch-Style Cupboards of New York and New Jersey, 1650–1800*, exh. cat. (New York, Metropolitan Museum of Art, 1991), p. 1.

3. Ibid., pp. 1, 15.

4. An inventory of a Dutch woman's possessions, dated 1818, lists "fifteen tablecloths, forty-one sheets, twenty-eight pillowcases, forty-four towels, eleven rolls of linen, and an unspecified amount of weaving material"; see Dean F. Failey, *Long Island Is My Nation: The Decorative Arts and Craftsmen, 1640–1830*, exh. cat. (Setauket, N.Y., Society for the Preservation of Long Island Antiquities, 1976), p. 109.

5. Joyce Geary Volk, "The Dutch Kast and the American Kast: A Structural/Historical Analysis," in Roderic H. Blackburn and Nancy A. Kelley, eds., *New World Dutch Studies: Dutch Arts and Culture in Colonial America, 1609–1776* (Albany, N.Y., 1987), p. 108.

6. Kenny, Safford, and Vincent (note 2), p. 43.

7. Ibid.

4. CHEST, 1700/1710

Hatfield or Deerfield, Massachusetts
Oak with white pine; 82.5 x 122.5 x 48.2 cm (33½ x 48¼ x 19 in.)
Robert R. McCormick Charitable Trust Fund, 1979.1459

This chest is one of a large group of related boxes, tables, and chests made along the Connecticut River Valley, from Hartford, Connecticut, to Deerfield, Massachusetts.[1] They are sometimes called Hadley chests because the American antiquarian Henry Wood Erving discovered a similar chest in Hadley, Massachusetts, in 1883. Within this group, the use of similar carved motifs and construction techniques reflects the familial ties of the craftsmen who made the chests.[2] Further, at least three joiners in Hampshire County, Massachusetts, had

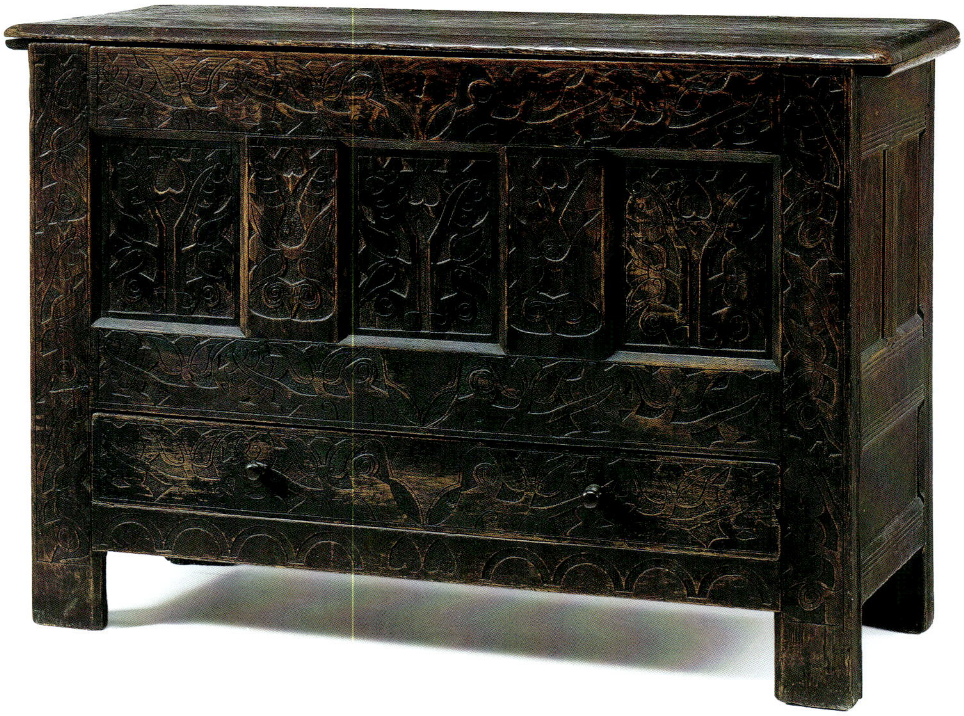

CAT. NO. 4

relatives in northern England, where furniture was made featuring similar carved motifs.[3]

The simple pinned frame and panel construction of this chest is called joined-work because it was fabricated by a craftsman known as a joiner. The joiner used his skill much in the way a housewright would frame a house. Using mortise and tenon joints to secure rails and stiles of a piece of furniture together, the joiner created a frame to which carved panels, lids, seats, or chair backs could be attached. A tenon is a small, projecting portion at the end of a length of wood that fits into a cavity, or mortise, in the end of an opposing piece of wood. The tenon is then fastened into the mortise with wooden pegs, creating a sturdy joint.

Scholars have suggested that pieces such as the Art Institute's served as dower chests for storing valuable linens, plates, and other possessions that a young woman brought to her marriage. At least eight related chests have the full maiden name of a woman carved or painted on the surface; the ownership of several other chests with carved initials and secure provenance histories can also be traced to unmarried young women.[4] The symmetrical, meandering vine-and-flower decoration of the Art Institute's chest has its roots in the designs found in Netherlandish Renaissance prints, which influenced English joiners who emigrated to the colonies. The tulip motif, repeated often on the surface of the chest, appears frequently in the decoration of English textiles, ceramics, and furniture of the sixteenth and seventeenth centuries.[5] The motif originated in ancient Persia, where the flower symbolized perfect love. Turkish pottery, enlivened with tulip designs, was present in England in the early seventeenth century.[6] On the chest, the tulip motif is used to create pictorial vignettes that reinforce the theme of love. The three inset panels and corresponding dividing boards incorporate the tulip motif into a tree pattern. Each tree has two branches separated by an inverse heart, suggesting both love and fertility. Vestiges of the original green and red paint on the surface indicate that originally the chest was brightly decorated, perhaps in the celebratory spirit of a wedding.

NOTES

1. Philip Zea, "The Fruits of Oligarchy: Patronage and the Hadley Chest Tradition in Western Massachusetts," in *New England Furniture: Essays in Memory of Benno M. Forman* (Boston, 1987), p. 1.

2. This was true of approximately forty of the over three hundred craftsmen recorded in Hampshire County, Mass., between 1636 and 1730; see Philip Zea and Suzanne L. Flint, *Hadley Chests* (Deerfield, Mass., 1992), p. 11.

3. Zea (note 1), p. 10.

4. Zea and Flint (note 2), p. 18.

5. Patricia E. Kane, "The Seventeenth-Century Furniture of the Connecticut Valley: The Hadley Chest Reappraised," in Ian M. G. Quimby, ed., *Arts*

of the Anglo-American Community in the Seventeenth Century (Charlottesville, Va., 1975), p. 84. Kane's study discusses typical construction techniques on these chests. She also grouped known Hadley chests together by visual similarities. The Art Institute's chest appears as no. 101 in the appendix.

6. On the tulip's symbolism, see J. C. Cooper, *An Illustrated Encyclopaedia of Traditional Symbols* (London, 1978), p. 182. See Wendy A. Cooper in Boston, Museum of Fine Arts, *New England Begins: The Seventeenth Century*, vol. 3 (1982), p. 394, cat. no. 397; and Michael Archer, "The Dating of Delftware Chargers," in English Ceramic Circle, *Transactions* 11, 2 (1982), p. 118.

5. ARMCHAIR, 1670/1700

New York area

Maple and ash; 101.6 x 57.2 x 48.3 cm (40 x 22½ x 19 in.)

Sewell L. Avery Fund, 1946.507

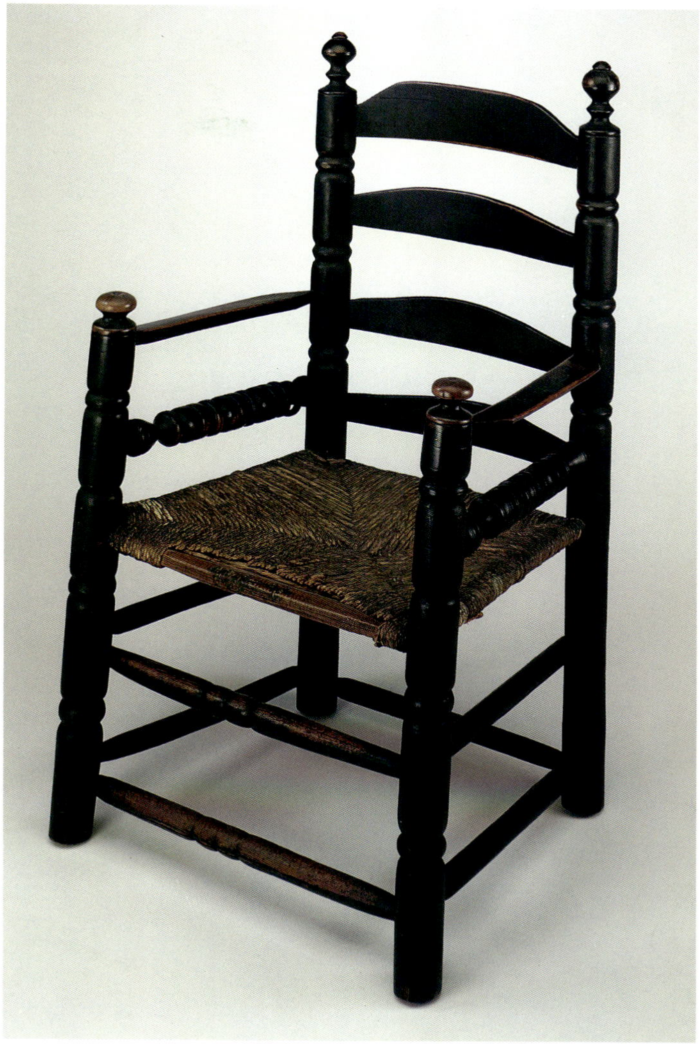

CAT. NO. 5

Although the New York area was settled by the Dutch in 1623, by the time the English took control of the region in 1664, there were eighteen different languages being spoken on the streets of New Amsterdam (present-day Manhattan), as settlers from France, Germany, Scandinavia, and elsewhere flocked to the colony to create new lives for themselves.[1]

This turned, slat-back chair is part of a small group of similar examples produced in the New York area. It is related to one now in the collection of the Museum of the City of New York which was, according to oral tradition, once owned by Abraham Riker, who was born in 1655 in New Amsterdam and died at his farm on Long Island sometime in the eighteenth century. The museum purchased the chair from a descendant of Riker. Another similar chair, now at the Brooklyn Museum of Art, was purchased on Long Island in the 1930s.[2] Turned, slat-back chairs have been produced in northern Europe for centuries. These chairs appear in early manuscript drawings and stone carvings. A carved English panel dating from 1590 documents the interior of a wood-turner's shop, complete with a lathe.[3]

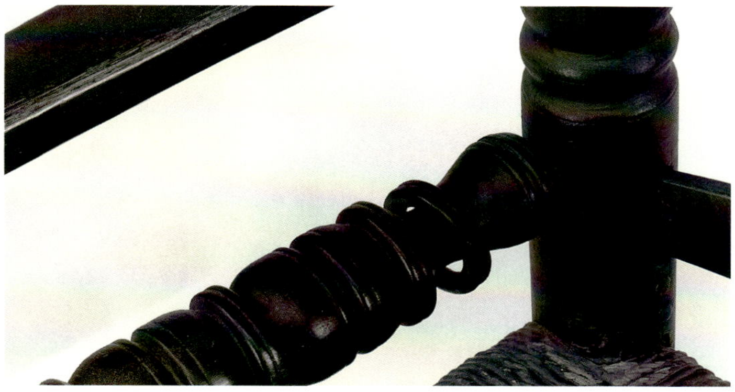

CAT. NO. 5, DETAIL

This New York chair exhibits stylistic traits long established in craft traditions. For example, its finials resemble the high, pointed knobs, thick stiles or legs with shallow, turned decoration also seen in a Norwegian twelfth-century chair (fig. 2). A remarkable surviving feature on the New York chair is the free-floating ring on the rear of the right arm-turning (see detail). This ring, turned on a lathe with the rest of the arm, attests to the turner's skill. Over twenty such rings appear on the back of the Norwegian chair, showing the vitality of the turner's traditional craft.[4]

The turner who crafted the New York chair would have been primarily involved in making stools and table legs—in addition to chairs—as well as staircase balusters and spokes for wheels. A turner's main tools were a lathe and a set of tools known as gouges. A block of wood would be set into the lathe, which would then be set spinning either by an apprentice turning a hand crank, or by the master craftsman operating a foot pump. Gouges of varying widths were used to form the design on the wood being turned.[5]

Although the Art Institute's chair was originally painted red, its current blue-green color has been on the chair for several generations and is now an integral part of its history. The rush seat may have been rewoven when the chair was painted its present color. All the finials, slats, and turned members are original to the chair, although the legs once had small, bulbous turnings for feet that were cut or broken off sometime in the early twentieth century.

NOTES

1. Roderic H. Blackburn and Ruth Piwonka, *Remembrance of Patria: Dutch Arts and Culture in Colonial America, 1609–1776*, exh. cat. (Albany, N.Y., Albany Institute of History and Art, 1988), p. 36.

2. Benno Forman, *American Seating Furniture, 1630–1730* (New York, 1988), p. 128; and Dean F. Farley, *Long Island Is My Nation: The Decorative Arts and Craftsmen, 1640–1830*, exh. cat. (Setauket, N.Y., Society for the Preservation of Long Island Antiquities, 1976), p. 23. Other chairs are at the Henry Francis du Pont Winterthur Museum, Winterthur, Del., and the Museum of Fine Arts, Boston.

3. Forman (note 2), pp. 45, 67.

4. Richard Ryder, "Four-Legged Turned Chairs," *Connoisseur* 191 (Jan. 1976), p. 47.

5. Forman (note 2), p. 44.

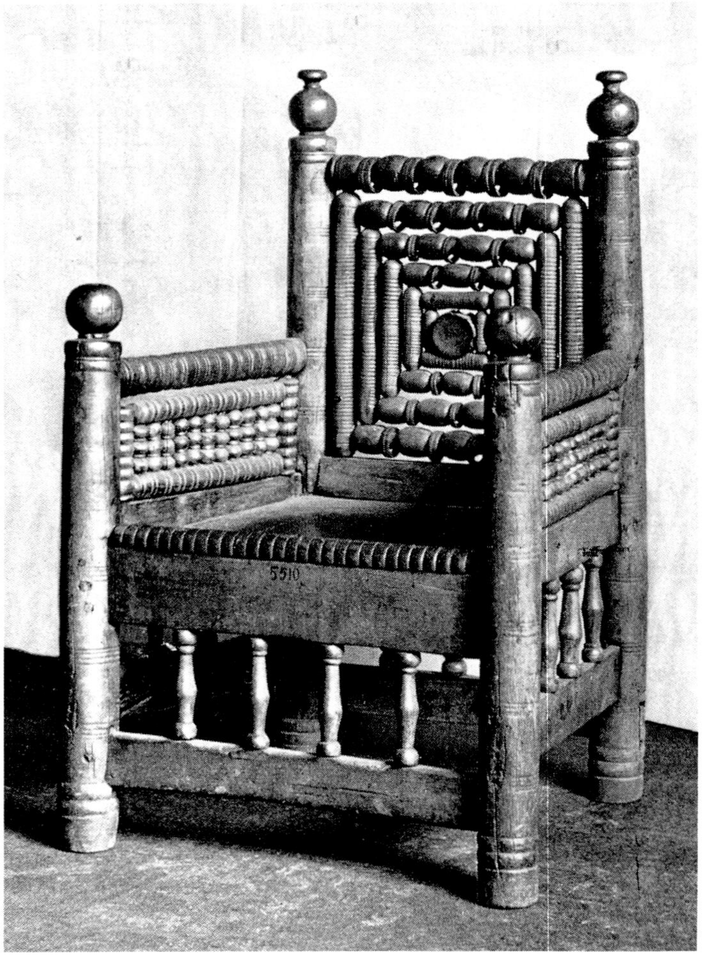

FIG. 2. Norwegian. *Chair from Baldishol Church*, c. twelfth century. Photograph from Richard D. Ryder, "Four-Legged Turned Chairs," *Connoisseur Magazine* 191 (Jan. 1976), p. 46.

6. JEREMIAH DUMMER (1645–1718)

Tankard, 1696/1705

Boston

Silver; h. 15.5 cm (6 in.)

Marked on lid and left side of handle: *ID* (in a heart with a star below initials); engraved on top of handle: *I* ^{B} *E*

Gift of the Antiquarian Society through the Mr. and Mrs. William Y. Hutchinson Fund, 1985.780

7. CORNELIUS KIERSTEDE (1675–1757)

Tankard, 1698/1722

New York

Silver; 16.5 x 19.4 (at base) cm (6½ x 7⅝ in.)

Marked once on either side of handle: *CK* (in a square); engraved with an unknown crest and coat of arms

Gift of the Antiquarian Society through the Mr. and Mrs. Edwin A. Seipp Fund, 1946.220

Tankards were one of the most popular silver objects during the colonial era. They were commonly presented as wedding gifts, and on festive occasions were filled and passed from person to person so that all could join in the celebration.[1] During this time they enjoyed such popularity that they went through many stylistic changes, departing from the plainer, traditional English form introduced to the colonies in the seventeenth century.

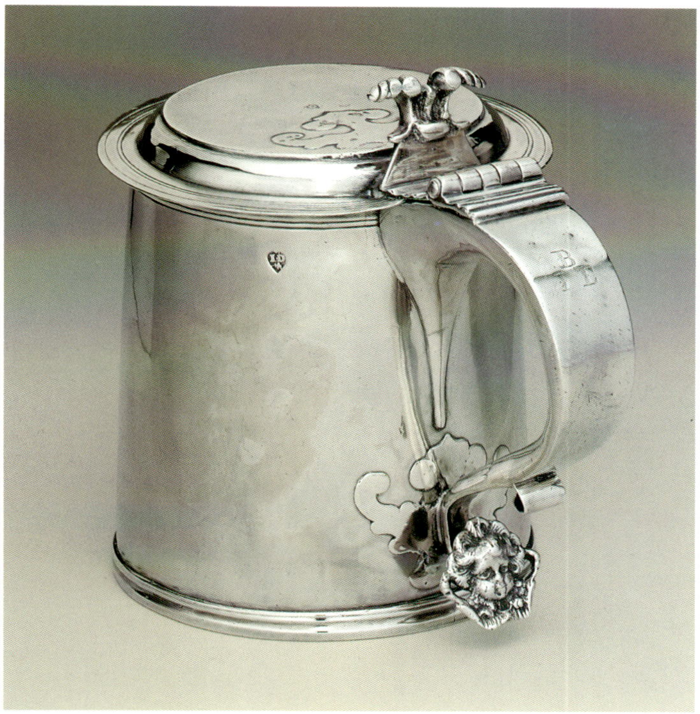

CAT. NO. 6

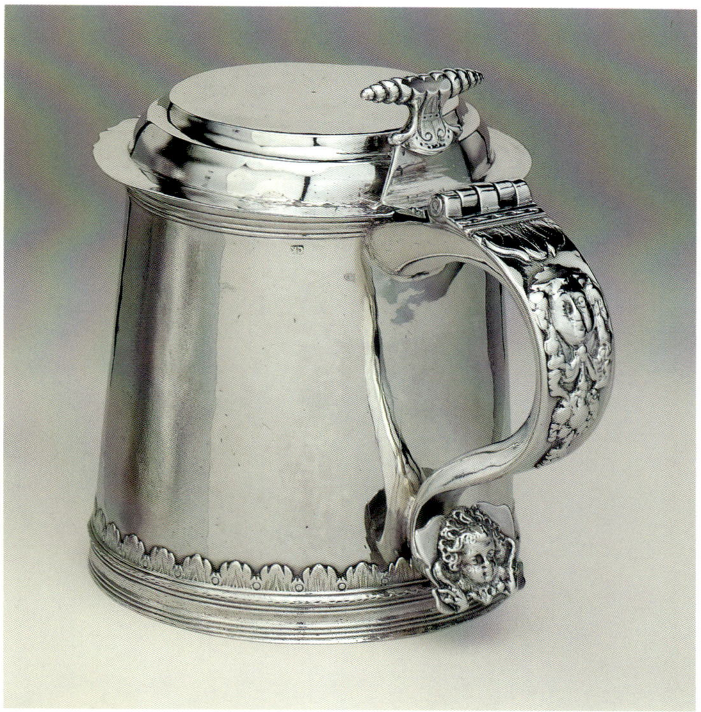

CAT. NO. 7

In urban areas such as Boston, Newport, New York, and Philadelphia, both silversmith and patron adapted and refined the English model to fit local style. Two tankards in the Art Institute's collection represent the earliest American types, and both are good examples of regional differences and design preferences. Jeremiah Dummer's tankard (cat. no. 6), for example, adheres closely to its English antecedent, revealing Boston's Puritanical roots, while Cornelius Kierstede's (cat. no. 7) combines the standard English form with distinctly Dutch-inspired decoration, consistent with its New York origin.[2]

Jeremiah Dummer was America's first native-born silversmith. He was born near Boston and apprenticed to John Hull, who not only taught Dummer the art of silversmithing but also tutored him to be a successful merchant and entrepreneur.[3] The Art Institute's tankard, like its English counterparts, has a slightly tapering, conical body with an applied, molded base; a flat, stepped lid with a serrated lip; and a double-spiral thumbpiece. The handle, which is a broad, curving band, ends with a cherub's head. The whole is devoid of engraved decoration, save for the unknown patron's initials on the top of the handle. The only flourishes of decoration on the tankard are the two cut-card foliate designs that adorn the lid and the lower handle juncture. This decorative touch also graces several other Dummer tankards.[4]

Born in New York, Cornelius Kierstede completed his apprenticeship there in 1698. His known body of work reflects an English silversmithing tradition influenced by the Dutch style. His tankard resembles Dummer's in form, although the applied decoration features devices associated with the New York area. Both the meander wire and the applied leaf band at the tankard's base appear on Dutch silver of the seventeenth and early eighteenth centuries.[5] In addition, the corkscrew thumbpiece, elaborate engraved decoration, and applied handle ornament are all common on New York tankards. The frequent use of corkscrew thumbpiece and leaf-band molding may indicate that one silversmith shop produced and sold these elements to colleagues around the city.[6] Likewise, the elaborate, engraved mantling of the crest appears on many New York tankards. The coat of arms on the Kierstede tankard remains unidentified, but the engraving closely matches that on a tankard Jan Van Nieu Kirke made for the Lansing family, and another tankard Kierstede executed for an unknown family.[7] This too may indicate that, like thumbpiece and leaf band, the engraving on many of these tankards originated in one shop.

The two tankards' ornamentation and engraving indicate that they were most likely presented as wedding gifts. Traditionally, initials on a tankard handle, were those of bride and groom, the uppermost *B* on the Dummer tankard being for

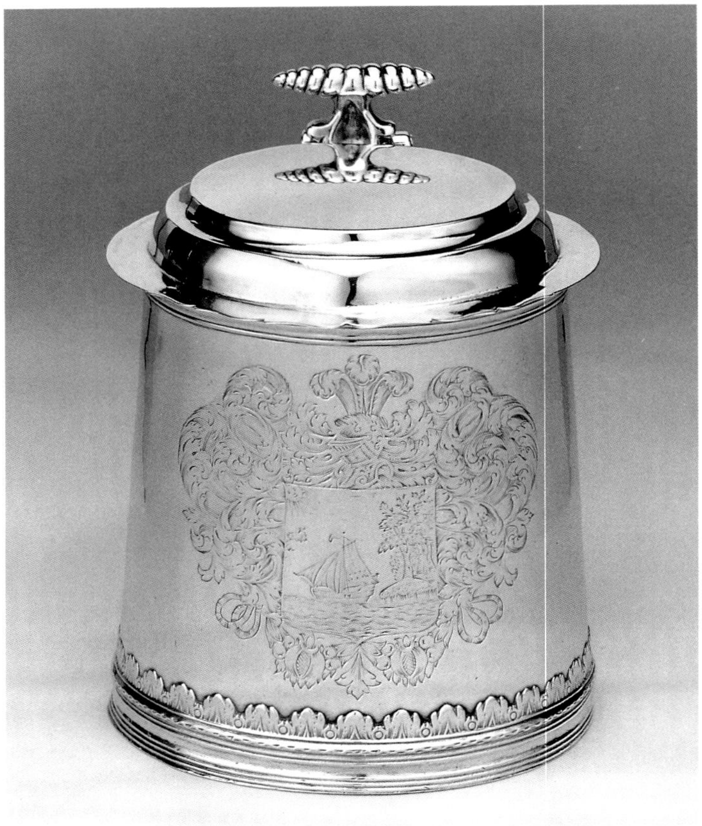

CAT. NO. 7, FRONT

the family name and the *I* and *E* below being the first-name initials of the groom and bride.[8] The cherub's head on both tankards symbolizes love and hope.[9] In addition, the Kierstede tankard features an applied head of a female angel with swags of flowers and fruit on the handle, and pomegranates with two pairs of overlapping loops of ribbons in the engraved manteling on the body of the tankard (see illustration). Together, these motifs signify fidelity, love, fertility, and union.[10]

NOTES

1. One type, called a "peg tankard," features small silver pegs descending the interior of the tankard. These markers indicated how much one could drink before passing the tankard on to the next celebrant. See Richard B. K. McLanathan, ed., *Colonial Silversmiths: Masters and Apprentices*, exh. cat. (Boston, Museum of Fine Arts, 1956), cat. no. 193.

2. In 1630 nine hundred Puritan settlers sailed from England to America to escape religious persecution. They established Boston under the leadership of John Winthrop. New York was settled by the Dutch West India Company in 1623 and was under Dutch rule until 1664, when the colony was taken over by the British. By 1700 the population of New York was almost equally represented by the two nationalities; see C. Louise Avery, *Early American Silver* (1930; reprint, New York, 1968), p. 118.

3. Both Hull and Dummer were successful merchants. At the height of his career, Dummer purportedly owned shares in eleven trading ships; see Hermann F. Clarke, "Jeremiah Dummer, Silversmith, 1645–1718," in Jane Bentley Kolter, ed., *Early American Silver and Its Makers* (New York, 1979), p. 64.

4. Cut-card work involves cutting a pattern from a "card" of thinly rolled silver and applying it to the silver form with liquid silver, or solder.

5. For a Dutch or Flemish beaker (c. 1700) with an applied leaf band at its base, see Avery (note 2), p. 144.

6. Barbara McLean Ward and Gerald W. R. Ward, eds., *Silver in American Life: Selections from the Mabel Brady Garvan and Other Collections at Yale University*, exh. cat. (New Haven, Conn., Yale University Art Gallery, 1979), p. 127.

7. The Lansing tankard is now at the Albany Institute of History and Art; see Roderic H. Blackburn and Ruth Piwonka, *Remembrance of Patria: Dutch Arts and Culture in Colonial America, 1609–1776*, exh. cat. (Albany, N.Y., Albany Institute of History and Art, 1988), p. 288. The second Kierstede tankard is now in the Milwaukee Art Museum; see Gerald W. R. Ward, ed., *American Furniture with Related Decorative Arts, 1660–1830: The Milwaukee Art Museum and the Layton Art Collection* (New York, 1991), pp. 95–98, cat. no. 38.

8. From the seventeenth through the early nineteenth century, a first or last name beginning with a *J* was represented by the letter *I*, so the groom's first name more probably began with a *J*.

9. David D. Hall, "The Gravestone Image as a Puritanical Culture Code," in Boston University, *Puritan Gravestone Art* (Boston, 1977), p. 25; and Blackburn and Piwonka (note 7), p. 288.

10. Ward and Ward (note 6), p. 127; and Gerald W. R. Ward, "The Dutch and English Traditions in American Silver: Cornelius Kierstede," in Francis J. Puig and Michael Conforti, eds., *The American Craftsman and the European Tradition, 1620–1820*, exh. cat. (Minneapolis Institute of Arts, 1989), p. 150. Pomegranates were a symbol of Juno, who was the goddess of marriage and childbirth, as well as the protector of women. See also Peter M. Kenny, Frances Gruber Safford, and Gilbert T. Vincent, *American Kasten: The Dutch-Style Cupboards of New York and New Jersey, 1650–1800*, exh. cat. (New York, Metropolitan Museum of Art, 1991), p. 30.

8. EDWARD WINSLOW (1669–1753)

Salver, 1710/40

Boston

Silver; 5.4 x 17.8 x 8.2 (at base) cm (2⅛ x 7 x 3¼ in.)

Marked on the top side of the tray, lower edge: *EW* (over a fleur-de-lis in a shaped shield); engraved at the center of the tray: a unicorn head

Gift of the Antiquarian Society, 1948.107

Small salvers usually served as stands for tea- or coffeepots. But the clover shape and diminutive size of this salver suggest that it may have been fashioned to hold four small, stemmed glasses for liquor or wine (see fig. 3). One glass would have been

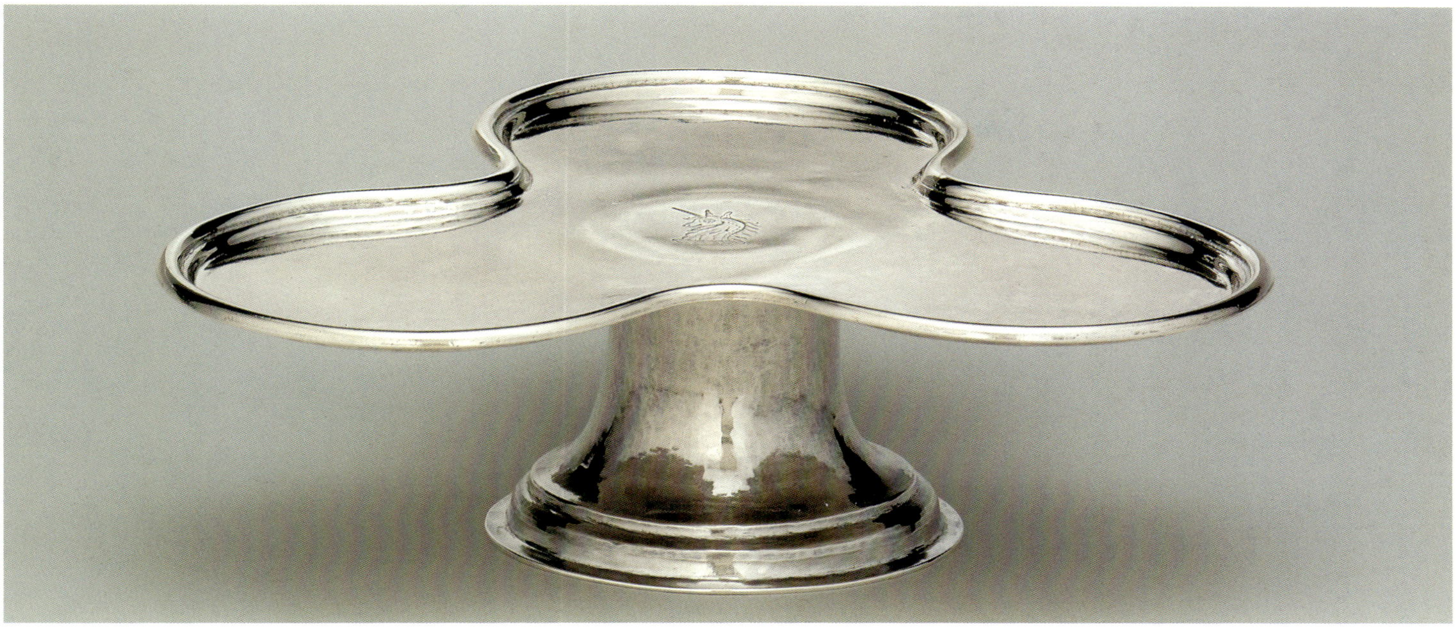

CAT. NO. 8

placed on each of the three lobes, with a fourth in the middle. A silver salver crafted to hold cordial glasses bespoke the status and importance of the owner. Only the wealthy could afford imported liquors; they stocked their cellars with Madeiras, ports, and sherries. The 1683 inventory of Thomas Kelland's house in Boston, for example, records "one hogshead, five butts, and thirteen pipes of malaga, sherry, canary, port, madeira, and fayal."[1]

There was a paucity of successful glass factories in America until late in the eighteenth century; glassware was imported from Europe. Boston clergyman Cotton Mather owned a set of Venetian glasses; excavations near Albany, New York, and in Maryland yielded fancy stemmed glassware from Italy and the Netherlands dating to the end of the seventeenth century.[2]

This salver exhibits the solidity and boldness of early Baroque design, combined with the flowing, curvilinear outlines of late Baroque aesthetics. Winslow focused on form rather than on decoration. The undulating outlines of the edges and the dramatically rising trumpet-shaped pedestal achieve a subtle balance of parts. The engraved unicorn head in the center of the tray is a common feature of eighteenth-century crests and provides no clues to the identity of the salver's original owner.

The silversmith Edward Winslow was descended from one of the founding families of Boston. His paternal grandparents, members of the Old South Church, lived next to Governor John Winthrop; his mother was the granddaughter of the spiritual leader Anne Hutchinson.[3] In 1702, after Winslow completed his apprenticeship to Jeremiah Dummer, he became a freeman; he is now regarded as one of the most accomplished early colonial silversmiths.[4]

Like many craftsmen of his time, Winslow pursued other interests to supplement his income. In 1728 he became the sheriff of Suffolk County; in 1743 he was chief justice of the Massachusetts Inferior Court of Common Pleas. His political career left little time for silversmithing, and his shop produced little of importance after 1740. He died in 1753, leaving a shop inventory of only four pounds' worth of tools.[5]

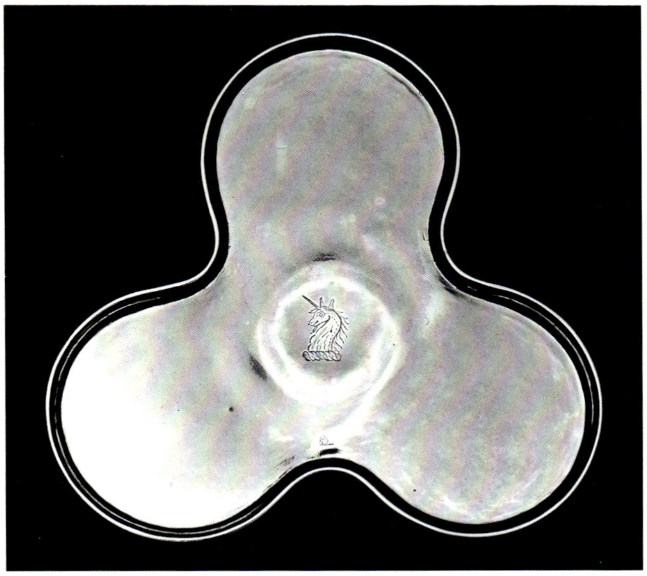

CAT. NO. 8, TOP

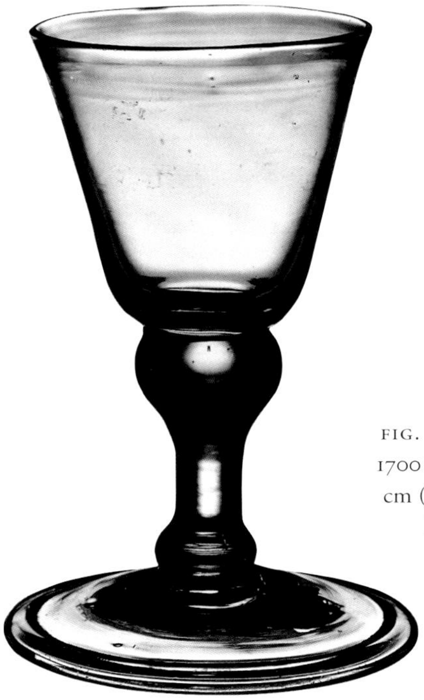

FIG. 3. English. *Drinking Glass*, 1700/1720. Lead glass; 10.5 x 6.8 cm (4⅛ x 2$^{11}/_{16}$ in.). Winterthur Museum, Winterthur, Del. (76. 0311).

NOTES

1. Madeira, canary, and fayal were named for the Portugese islands from which they came; malaga, for the southeastern Spanish port of the same name. A hogshead was a cask that held between 60 and 150 gallons; butts contained approximately 126 gallons each; and pipes held the equivalent of two hogsheads. See Louise Conway Belden, *The Festive Tradition: Table Decoration and Desserts in America, 1650–1900* (New York, 1983), pp. 233, 312, 314, 316.

2. Ibid., p. 233; and Arlene Palmer, *Glass in Early America: Selections from the Henry Francis du Pont Winterthur Museum* (New York, 1993), p. 6.

3. Helen Comstock, "Silver by Edward Winslow of Boston, 1669–1753," *Connoisseur* 108 (Dec. 1941), p. 206. Anne Hutchinson preached a religious doctrine that de-emphasized the clergy and focused on inner spirituality. She was tried for sedition and contempt in Boston and was subsequently banished. She and her followers founded Portsmouth, Rhode Island, as a religious haven in 1638.

4. Henry N. Flynt and Martha Gandy Fales, *The Heritage Foundation Collection of Silver with Biographical Sketches of New England Silversmiths, 1625–1825* (Old Deerfield, Mass., 1968), p. 361.

5. Barbara McLean Ward and Gerald W. R. Ward, eds., *Silver in American Life: Selections from the Mabel Brady Garvan and Other Collections at Yale University*, exh. cat. (New Haven, Conn., Yale University Art Gallery, 1979), p. 143; and Barbara McLean Ward, "Boston Goldsmiths, 1690–1730," in Ian M. G. Quimby, ed., *The Craftsman in Early America* (New York, 1984), pp. 132, 136.

9. JOHN SMIBERT (1688–1751)

Richard Bill, 1733

Oil on canvas; 127.6 x 102.2 cm (50¼ x 48¼ in.)
Friends of American Art Collection, 1944.28

Originally trained as a house painter and plasterer in Edinburgh, Scotland, John Smibert developed his formal portrait style in Sir Godfrey Kneller's academy on Great Queen Street in London and through study abroad in Italy.[1] He spent the years before his move to the colonies in London, maintaining a studio from 1725 to 1728 in Covent Garden, where Peter Pelham, the stepfather of John Singleton Copley (see cat. nos. 26–27), was his neighbor. Smibert left England in 1728; he arrived in Newport in the company of the Irish philosopher and clergyman George Berkeley. Dean Berkeley and his party had planned to travel on from Newport to Bermuda in order to establish a college for educating the children of colonists. Smibert was to serve as the college's professor of fine arts. The trip to Bermuda never took place, and Berkeley returned to Ireland in 1731. Smibert, however, chose to settle in nearby Boston, where English colonists, primarily merchants, demanded high-style portraits of themselves and their families. With few highly trained artists at hand, Smibert thrived as a portraitist and dealer of prints and art supplies.

Richard Bill, painted during Smibert's early Boston years, is an arresting example of the artist's style, which merged Baroque conceits with forthright likenesses of prosperous patrons. Smibert recorded Bill's commission in his account book, noting that the sitter requested a half-length portrait in March 1733 and paid fifty pounds for it.[2] A prosperous merchant and member of the Ancient and Honorable Artillery Company, Bill represented the Province of Massachusetts as a commissioner at the signing of a peace treaty with the Abenaki Indians in 1714.[3] In Smibert's portrait, Bill is a fashionably attired and forceful presence. A letter lying on the table next to the sitter's right hand identifies him as "Richard Bill, Esq." of Boston. Other objects further symbolize his subject's vocation. A sailing ship on the right, probably copied from an engraving, alludes to shipping and trade, while the desk and writing implements behind denote Bill's working environment.[4] Bill's confident bearing and the cumulative effect of the attributes combine to present the sitter as an important and powerful man. Four years after Smibert painted his portrait, Bill was elected a member of the Colonial Council of the Province of Massachusetts. Bill's good fortune did not last, however, and he died insolvent in 1757.

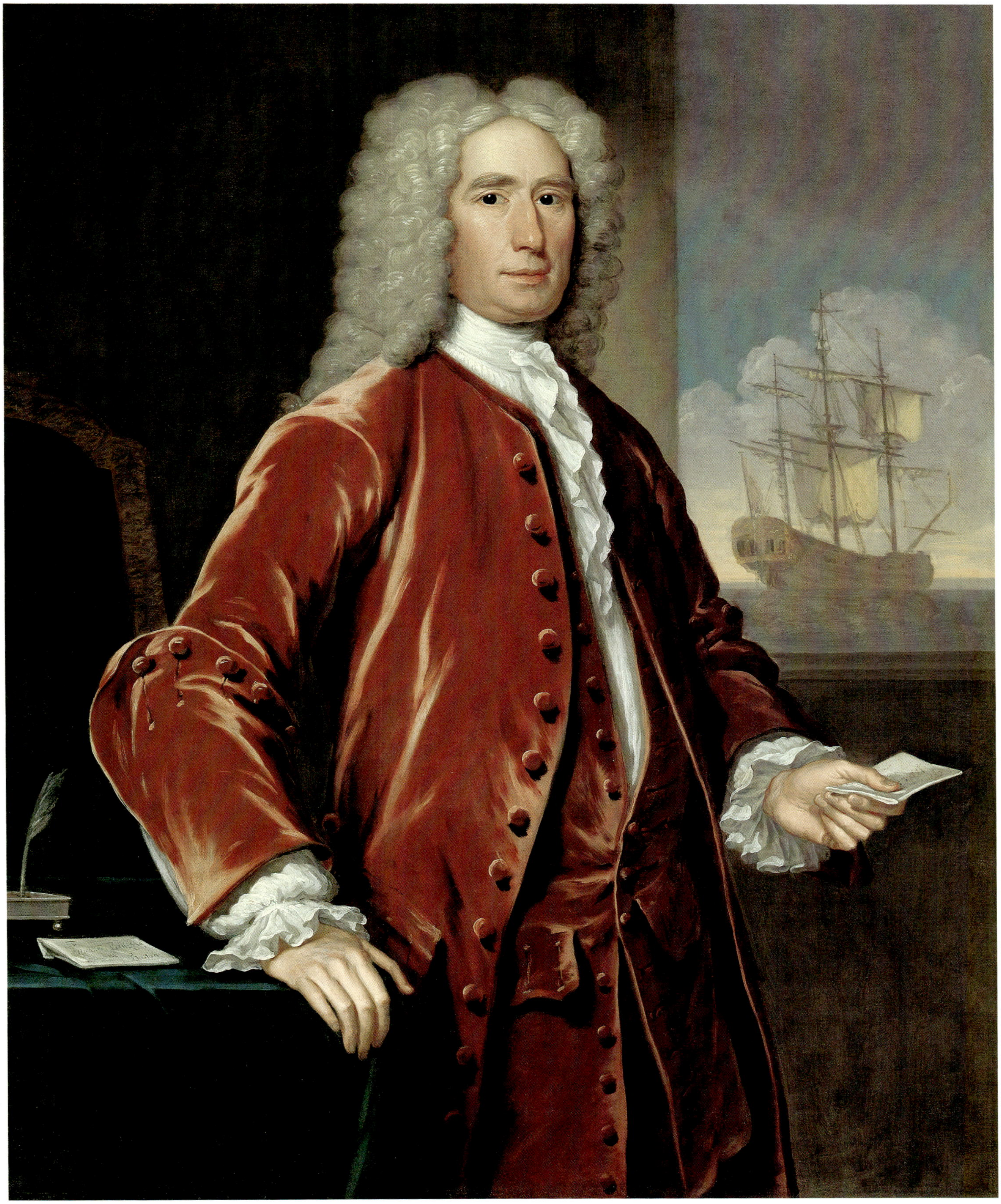

CAT. NO. 9

Although Smibert used a standard pose and props to identify Bill as a merchant, *Richard Bill* is more striking and satisfying than others the artist produced during the same period.[5] Richard Saunders attributed the painting's strength to Smibert's grasp of "principles of proportion, compositional balance, and dynamism," qualities evident in the vitality of the paint handling, smooth transitions between foreground and background, and solid placement of the sitter slightly at an angle to the picture plane.[6] Bill's countenance is also notable for its realism and complexity. Smibert recorded his sitter's thick eyebrows, long knobbed nose, and slight double chin with precision and a feel for character. Bill's mouth, however, is his most intriguing feature. At first glance, the merchant appears to be sternly gazing at the viewer, but the corners of his mouth seem slowly to turn upward into a bemused smile. This effect renders Richard Bill one of Smibert's most affable and lifelike sitters.

NOTES

1. For complete biographical information on Smibert, see Richard H. Saunders, *John Smibert: Colonial America's First Portrait Painter* (New Haven, Conn., and London, 1995).

2. John Smibert, *The Notebook of John Smibert* (Boston, 1969), p. 91, no. 73: "Mr. Bill H.P. 1/2 50-0-0."

3. Ledyard Bill, ed., *History of the Bill Family* (New York, 1867), p. 110.

4. Smibert's use of ship engravings as models for his paintings is documented in a letter, dated March 24, 1744, in which the artist requested from Arthur Pond, his London dealer, "a set of Ships published by Lempriere and sold by H. Toms in Union court Holburn. . . . These ships I want sometime for to be in a distant view in Portraits of Merchts etc who chuse such, so if there be any done since send them but they must be in the modern construction"; cited in Richard H. Saunders, "The Portrait in America, 1700–1750," in Richard H. Saunders and Ellen G. Miles, *American Colonial Portraits, 1700–1776*, exh. cat. (Washington, D.C., National Portrait Gallery, 1987), p. 24.

5. Other portraits of merchants produced by Smibert that feature similar compositions include *Jacob Wendell* (1731; Milwaukee Art Museum) and *Joseph Turner* (1740; property of Cliveden, a co-stewardship property of the National Trust for Historic Preservation).

6. Saunders (note 1), p. 87.

10. DESK-AND-BOOKCASE, 1700/1735

Boston

Walnut and white pine; 228.6 x 104.1 x 61.3 cm (90 x 41 x 24⅛ in.)

Gift of the Antiquarian Society through the Mr. and Mrs. William Y. Hutchinson Fund, 1985.517

From the early colonial period until the second half of the eighteenth century, Boston was the largest and busiest of the colonial cities, controlling the majority of the imported goods that flowed to the colonies from Europe. Although both New York and Philadelphia traded directly with London and Portugal, both cities still relied on Boston's merchants for many imported goods.[1] The War of Spanish Succession (1702–13) created an economic boom for Boston's merchants and craftsmen. In 1705 England began to import more dry-good and naval supplies from the colonies, owing to trade restrictions with France and Spain. Boston's merchants increased their trade with British ports outside England and built more ships to meet the demand. Boston's craftsmen were called upon to outfit these vessels with furniture and execute the carved and turned details.[2]

Merchants also called upon craftsmen to make furniture for their residences, which usually consisted of several rooms on the first floor with bedrooms above. Often the owner of the house conducted his principal business affairs in a room on the first floor, furnished with practical pieces such as this desk-and-bookcase. Locks on the drawers, doors, and fall front suggest that the desk-and-bookcase held important papers and valuable possessions. Contemporary inventories of desks belonging to Bostonians reveal that larger drawers held valuable, bulky objects such as linens, while the small drawers contained everything from money and jewelry to shoe buckles and snuff boxes.[3] A period inscription inside a small, interior drawer of this piece confirms its function: "I took 3 £ coin in one / 6 s in another / F___ took 2 s in another / 3.8 total." The inscription suggests that the drawer served as the family's bank or cash drawer. Usually upper bookcases used for business purposes contained long, vertical slots to accommodate large ledgers. For personal use, shelves were often horizontal to hold diaries, smaller books, and personal items.[4]

This desk-and-bookcase was executed in the Baroque style, often referred to as the William and Mary style, in honor of the reigning English monarchs. Furniture makers working in this mode rejected the applied or carved ornament that joiners pre-

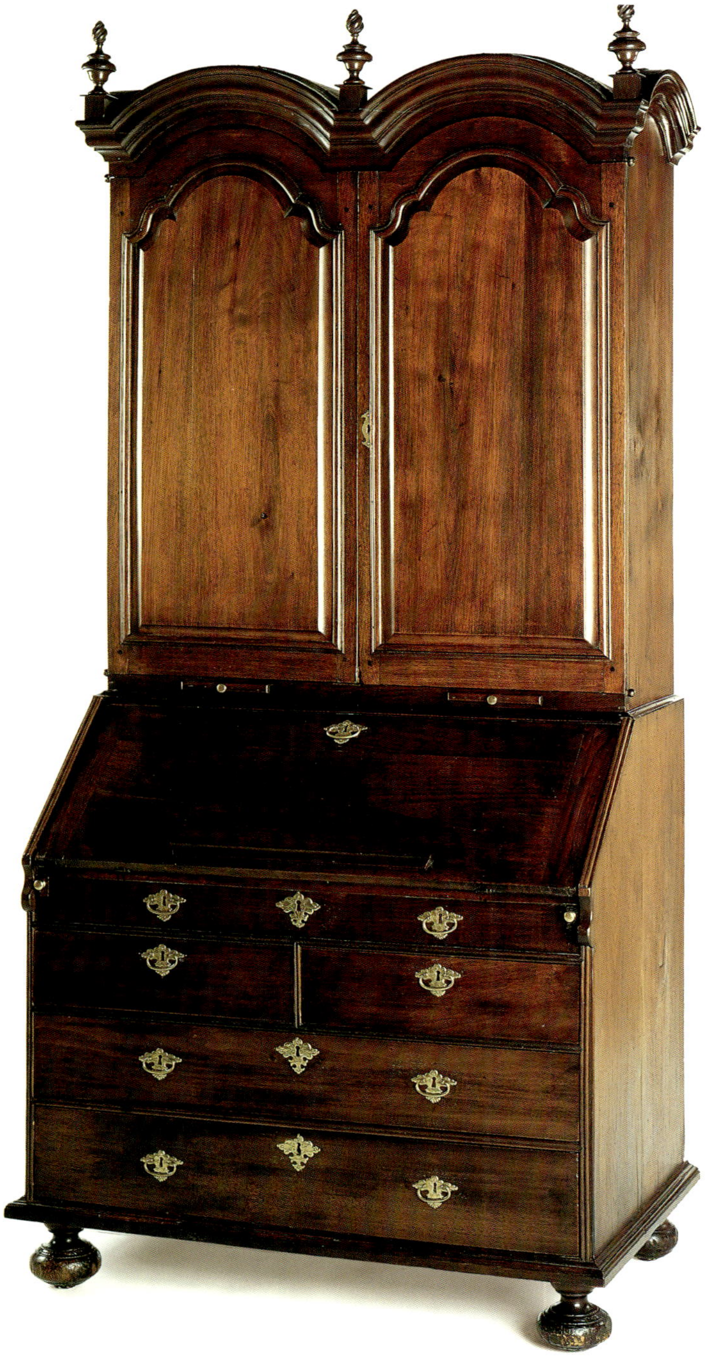

CAT. NO. 10

ferred. They favored rich woods, such as walnut and mahogany, and contrasting veneers for surface decoration. The period saw the birth of the cabinetmaker, whose techniques in crafting furniture differed from those of the joiner, who dominated the furniture-making trade of the seventeenth century. A cabinetmaker used board construction and dovetail joints to secure the case. To make a dovetail joint, he cut several small, flaring tenons shaped like a dove's tail at the end of one board and a corresponding number of open mortises at the end of another board. When put together, the joint acted like a permanent zipper, locking the two boards together.

The desk-and-bookcase is an elegant example of this new type of craftsmanship. The soft brown color and broad expanse of unembellished walnut boards give the piece a sumptuous character. Flourishes such as the slight curve of the molding on the bookcase doors and the double-domed pediment with flame finials complement the blocky severity of the lower case. The bun feet, derived from Dutch furniture of the previous century, accentuate the desk's vertical attenuation.

The American double-domed desk-and-bookcase form was inspired by similar English examples. An English japanned desk of the same form was owned by the Bowdoin family of Boston in the early part of the century, and may have inspired the patron of the Art Institute's desk.[5] English-trained cabinetmakers who possessed the skills to make such a piece were immigrating to the colonies to find work. A double-domed English desk signed and dated by William Price was made in London in 1713. Price immigrated to Boston a year later, and at least one scholar has speculated that Price made this desk.[6]

NOTES

1. Carl Bridenbaugh, *Cities in the Wilderness: The First Century of Urban Life in America, 1625–1742* (New York, 1960), pp. 178–79.

2. Brock Jobe, "The Boston Furniture Industry, 1720–1740," in Walter M. Whitehill, ed., *Boston Furniture of the Eighteenth Century* (Charlottesville, Va., 1974), p. 4.

3. For a complete list of the contents of the desks of Anthony Stoddard and George Rogers, see Brock Jobe and Myrna Kaye, *New England Furniture: The Colonial Era* (Boston, 1984), pp. 226–29, cat. no. 45.

4. Shelves inside bookcases such as this were often reconfigured to suit other purposes. The shelving in the Art Institute's bookcase is in its original position, as evidenced by the cabinetmaker's scribe lines and the fact that the shelves were dadoed in from the back of the case and are in their original dados.

5. Philip M. Johnston, "The William and Mary Style in America," in Reinier Baarsen et al., *Courts and Colonies: The William and Mary Style in Holland, England, and America*, exh. cat. (New York, Cooper-Hewitt Museum, 1988), p. 74.

6. Baarsen et al. (note 5), p. 158, cat. no. 108. The present whereabouts of the desk signed by William Price are unknown. For an English desk that closely resembles the Art Institute's, see R. W. Symonds, *Old English Walnut and Lacquer Furniture* (New York, 1923), p. 165. Benno Forman believed the desk to be the work of William Price; see correspondence between David Stockwell and Milo Naeve, Mar. 6, 1985, Files of the Department of American Arts, The Art Institute of Chicago.

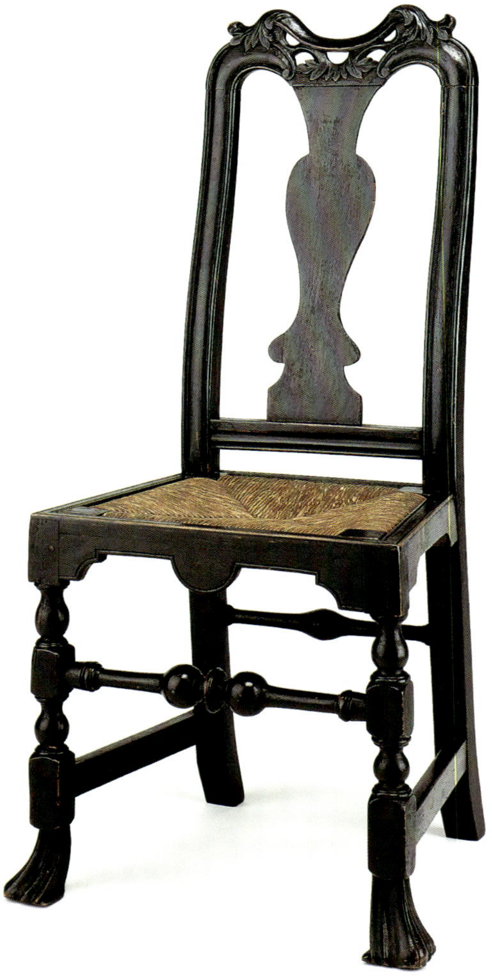

CAT. NO. 11

11. ATTRIBUTED TO JOHN GAINES III (1702–1743)

Side chair, 1730/40

Portsmouth, New Hampshire

Maple; 108 x 45.7 x 44.5 cm (42½ x 18 x 17½ in.)

Promised gift of Jamee J. and Marshall Field, 14.1994

As the gateway to upper New England, the coastal town of Portsmouth, New Hampshire, was a thriving commercial center. The upper valley of the Piscataqua River was a rich resource for both hard and soft timber. By 1720 over seventy water-powered lumber mills lined the Piscataqua, and the region exported nearly a million board feet of lumber annually.[1] Merchants made their fortunes with locally built ships that carried timber, provisions, and dry goods from the valley and exchanged them for fish and other goods in Newfoundland and for silks, sugar, and spices in the Caribbean.[2] Because of Portsmouth's wealth, large houses lined the waterfront, and there was great demand for fashionable furniture.

John Gaines III was trained as a turner in his father's chair-making shop in Ipswich, Massachusetts, where he worked until 1724, when he traveled to Portsmouth to ply his trade and seek his fortune. Within a few years, Gaines had married, built a house, and established himself in a large chair-making enterprise. He took advantage of Portsmouth's trading status by producing chairs for export, as well as for local patrons.[3]

Gaines learned to turn banister-back chairs in the blocky, early Baroque manner from his father, John Gaines II.[4] The younger Gaines brought this aesthetic tradition with him to Portsmouth but soon incorporated the graceful, curvilinear forms of the late Baroque style. This chair represents a transition between the two approaches. The legs and stretchers are of a type employed in Massachusetts banister-backed chairs of the early Baroque era, a popular form that was produced throughout the eighteenth century. However, the vase-shaped splat, the curve of the carved crest rail, and the shaped seat rail show the emergence of the undulating classicism of the late Baroque style. The crest rail itself differs slightly from other John Gaines III chairs, where each end of the yoke rail is connected to the shoulder of the chair by a bold scroll.[5] Here a carved-leaf motif breaks up the lines of the chair back and lends a lightness that is echoed in the elevated, carved feet.

The work of John Gaines III remained transitional. He died at the age of forty-one, before he could fully develop his interpretation of the new fashion.

NOTES

1. James L. Garvin, "That Little World Portsmouth," in Brock Jobe, ed., *Portsmouth Furniture: Masterworks from the New Hampshire Seacoast* (Hanover, N.H., 1993), p. 15.

2. Peter Ralph Barry, "The New Hampshire Merchant Interest, 1609–1725" (Ph.D. diss., University of Wisconsin, 1971), p. 355.

3. Surviving records indicate that within a six-year period, Gaines sold over 250 chairs for export to a local merchant, John Moffit, and another five dozen to William Pepperill. See Brock Jobe, "Furniture Making in Eighteenth-Century Portsmouth," in Jobe (note 1), p. 43.

4. For examples of the work of John Gaines II, see Robert E. P. Hendrick, "John Gaines, II, and Thomas Gaines, I, 'Turners' of Ipswich, Massachusetts" (M.A. thesis, University of Delaware, 1964). For examples of Boston chairs of this period, see Benno Forman, *American Seating Furniture, 1630–1730* (New York, 1988), pp. 335–38, cat. no. 76.

5. The chair is attributed to Gaines on the basis of four similar chairs, with different crest rails, that he made for the parlor of his own house and that are still owned by his descendants. See Jobe (note 1), p. 295, cat. no. 77. There are over thirty chairs that survive with related crest rails; see Jobe (note 1), p. 297 n. 4.

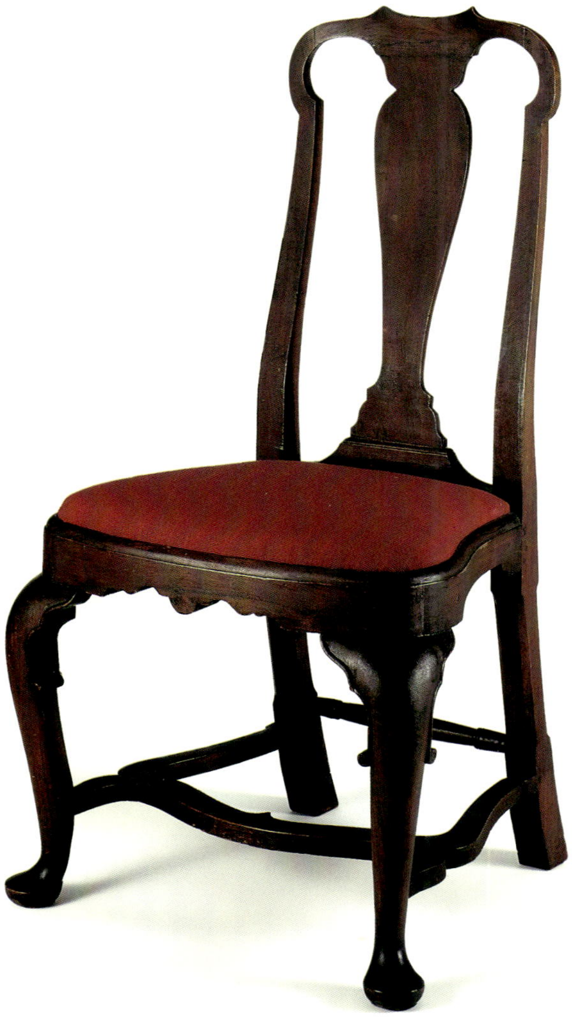

CAT. NO. 12

12. SIDE CHAIR, 1730/60

Newport, Rhode Island
Walnut with pine or maple slip seat;
106.4 x 52.7 x 40.6 cm (41⅞ x 20¾ x 16 in.)
Robert Allerton Fund, 1979.54

Newport, Rhode Island, was an insular community in the eighteenth century. Outsiders who attempted to establish businesses within the town often found their pursuits difficult, for the populace, which was predominantly Quaker, preferred to conduct business with relatives or with others of their own religion. In 1776, for example, the Newport clergyman Ezra Stiles wrote to a friend who had inquired about opening a medical practice in the town that most entrepreneurial newcomers were rebuffed unless they connected themselves in some way with a local family: "[Dr.] Hunter came about 1752 and did no thing to Effect in the first 10 years till he married Col. Malebon's Daughter, [a] Shur Anchor is a Petticoat."[1] The last words allude to the power of kinship ties in eighteenth-century Newport, where marriages were frequently made as commercial alliances.

In the Rhode Island cabinetmaking business, the families that took the greatest advantage of their kinship ties were the Goddards and the Townsends. Solomon Townsend had moved from Long Island, New York, to Newport in 1707, and there married the widow of Col. James Almy. His two sons, Job and Christopher, became the first of the Townsend line of cabinetmakers. Job married Rebecca Casey, and Christopher married Patience Easton, both of whom were daughters of prominent Newport merchant families. When Job's daughter Hannah married John Goddard in 1746, a well-known craftsman and one of Job's former apprentices, the two families were cemented together.[2] By 1800 there were twenty prominent furniture craftsmen linked by marriage or direct descent to Job Townsend and John Goddard. The kinship ties that connected these craftsmen enabled lesser known or younger cabinetmakers to gain access to designs, new ideas, materials, templates, and tools with which to carry out their trade. Given these advantages, there was no reason for apprentices of succeeding generations to look outside the family for a master and conversely little reason for the masters to look outside of the family for apprentices.[3] Information passed down within the family explains why there are such striking similarities in much of the furniture attributed to Newport and to the Goddard–Townsend clan.

The Art Institute's chair is part of a sizable group of Rhode Island chairs with a yolk crest rail; rolled shoulders; carved C-scrolls and beading on the knees of the front legs; chamfered rear legs; shaped, flat stretchers; and pad feet. The one feature that varies within this group is the shape of the front seat rail. Many chairs in this group have been attributed to the workshop of Job Townsend, in light of a similar set and other furniture that descended in the Eddy family of Newport.[4] The Art Institute's piece was once thought to be part of a set that also included chairs now in the Colonial Williamsburg and the Bayou Bend collections.[5] But the Art Institute's example has a more elaborately shaped front seat rail and is constructed differently from these other chairs.[6] A comparison of the construction of several chairs from this related group is revealing: the number and placement of the support pegs used to hold the legs' mortise-and-tenon joints together, as well as the shape and placement of the corner glue blocks under the slip seat on the Art Institute chair, the Bayou Bend chair, and a related chair with a plain front seat rail at the Henry Francis du Pont Winterthur Museum, are completely different.[7] These variations in the methods of construction indicate that the three related chairs were most likely made in different shops. Had the chairs been made in the same shop, these features would have been consistent.

NOTES

1. Quoted in Margaretta M. Lovell, "'Such Furniture as Will be Most Profitable': The Business of Cabinetmaking in Eighteenth-Century Newport," *Winterthur Portfolio* 26, 1 (spring 1991), p. 52.

2. Ibid., pp. 53–55.

3. Ibid., p. 42.

4. A note in a 1932 auction catalogue entry for the Eddy chairs states that descendants of the Eddy family still retained a labeled Job Townsend piece that was part of the set. See New York, American Art Association, Anderson Galleries, *Colonial and Early Federal Furniture, Silver and Porcelains of Distinguished Provenance* (Jan. 9, 1932), lot 80, pp. 110–11.

5. Colonial Williamsburg is in Williamsburg, Va., and the Bayou Bend Collection is owned by the Museum of Fine Arts, Houston. See Barry A. Greenlaw, *New England Furniture at Williamsburg* (Charlottesville, Va., 1974), pp. 60–61, cat. no. 52; and David B. Warren, *Bayou Bend: American Furniture, Paintings, and Silver from the Bayou Bend Collection* (Boston, 1975), p. 24, cat. no. 39. Both catalogues state that the chair now at the Art Institute is a matching example. Another chair with the same crest rail as the Bayou Bend and Williamsburg examples was owned by Leigh Keno American Antiques; see *Antiques* 47, 5 (May 1995), p. 642.

6. The emergence of the Keno chair (see note 5) has revealed that the Williamsburg and Bayou Bend chairs are also not from the same set, indicating the existence of two separate sets of chairs with the same front seat rail. The Keno and Williamsburg chairs are both numbered "III" on the front seat rail. While the Bayou Bend and the Keno chairs are approximately the same height, the Williamsburg chair is a full two inches higher, which includes an inch added to both its rear legs sometime in its history (see note 5).

7. On the Art Institute's chair, the side seat rails are pegged twice to the front legs in a vertical line and three times to the rear posts in a triangular pattern. The front legs are each pegged only once to the front rail, and the rear seat rail is pegged once to the rear posts, with the peg located high up on the rear posts. The triangular front-corner glue blocks under the slip seat appear to be original. The rear-corner blocks are replacements. The Bayou Bend chair has only one peg in each of the front legs, and one peg each where the side and rear seat rails attach to the rear posts. There is no indication that the seat interior ever had corner blocks. The Winterthur chair has two pegs in each front leg attaching the side and front seat rails to the legs, and only one peg in the side of each rear post, and no peg on the rear seat rail. Like the Bayou Bend example, this chair seems never originally to have had corner blocks. For information on the Bayou Bend chair, see correspondence between Michael K. Brown, Curator, Bayou Bend, and Seth A. Thayer, Mar. 13, 1995, Files of the Department of American Arts, The Art Institute of Chicago. For information on the Winterthur chair, see correspondence between Donald Fennimore, Curator, Henry Francis du Pont Winterthur Museum, and Seth A. Thayer, Mar. 27, 1995, Files of the Department of American Arts, The Art Institute of Chicago.

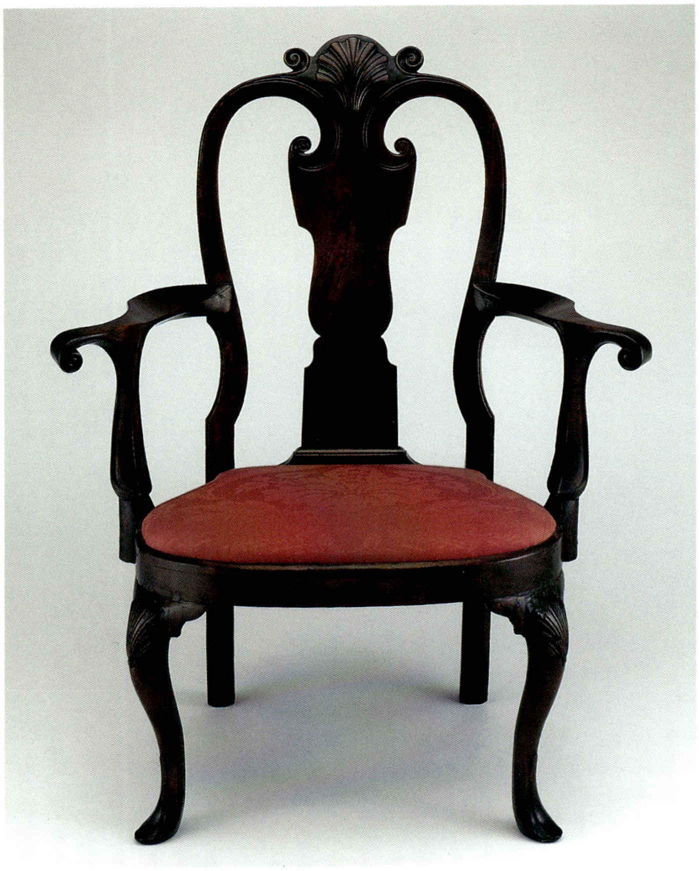

CAT. NO. 13

13. ARMCHAIR, 1730/40

Philadelphia

Walnut; 107.9 x 60.4 x 47.6 cm (42½ x 23¾ x 18¾ in.)

Gift of the Antiquarian Society through the Jessie Spalding Landon Fund, 1944.207

Beginning in the late 1720s, Philadelphia experienced an era of extraordinary expansion. Though established less than fifty years before, the city could boast of the creation of several important institutions: the cornerstone of Christ Church, for example, was laid in 1727; the Philadelphia Hospital was founded in the early 1730s; the Library Company was instituted in 1731 (with the assistance of Benjamin Franklin); and construction of the State House (now Independence Hall) was begun in 1732.[1] In 1731 naturalist John Bartram created the first botanical garden in America at his country house below Gray's Ferry Bridge on the west bank of the Schuylkill River. Prosperous merchants began to build grand townhouses in the city and manor houses in the country.[2] The city's population grew rapidly, with most of the inhabitants coming from the British

Isles and Germany. By 1740 Philadelphia was second only to Boston in population, and within twenty years it had surpassed the city to the north to become the colonies' busiest port and one of the four largest cities in the British Empire. Artisans flocked to Philadelphia to answer the demand for new buildings and furnishings.

The influx of immigrants and the rise in commercial activity transformed this predominantly Quaker town into a religiously and philosophically diverse commercial center.[3] The Art Institute's late Baroque-style Philadelphia chair is an excellent illustration of the shift in ideology that was taking place, for it successfully blends the Quaker taste for elegant simplicity and functionality with decorative flourishes that were prevalent in English work of the period. Several key decorative features of the chair offer hints that it was most likely made by an English or Irish cabinetmaker who had recently immigrated to Philadelphia. The front slipper feet, for example, are similar to those found on Irish chairs.[4] The incised lines that curl from the ears of the back splat, beneath the shell-carved crest rail to the outer edge of the shoulders of the chair, are also unusual features, and are more common on English and Irish furniture than on Philadelphia pieces.[5]

Though the craftsman who made the chair may have used skills he learned in England or Ireland to create some of the details, the simplicity of the gracefully curving lines, the lack of excessive ornamental embellishment, and the functional nature of the chair reflect the Quaker background of the settlers of Philadelphia.[6] Some of the decorative elements that embellish the Art Institute's chair are found on other early Philadelphia "fiddleback-splat" chairs, so named for the curve on the bottom of the back splat that is reminiscent of a violin.[7] Chairs in this group all have slipper feet with stockings; lamb's-tongue-shaped supports on the arm chairs; boldly curving balloon seats; octagonal rear legs and stump feet; and round-shouldered crest rails that lead into stiles conforming to the general curve of the splat. The interior seat frame of the museum's chair is laid out in a typical Philadelphia manner and its components tenoned together; the front legs, too, are tenoned through the seat rails. The major differences within this group of chairs are stylistic, and include the shape of the splat; the decorative carving, if any, on the crest rail; and the carving on the knees. These differences most likely reflect the price a patron was willing to pay for his chair.[8]

NOTES

1. William MacPherson Hornor, Jr., *Blue Book, Philadelphia Furniture: William Penn to George Washington* (1935; reprint, Washington, D.C., 1977), pp. 33–34.

2. Harold Donaldson Eberlein and Cortlandt Van Dyke Hubbard, *Portrait of a Colonial City: Philadelphia, 1670–1838* (Philadelphia, 1939), pp. 206–07, 226–30.

3. Edwin B. Bronner, "Village into Town, 1701–1746," in Russell F. Weigley, ed., *Philadelphia: A Three-Hundred-Year History* (New York, 1982), p. 43.

4. David Stockwell, "Irish Influence in Pennsylvania Queen Anne Furniture," *Antiques* 79, 3 (Mar. 1961), p. 269. The molded edge support around the front legs on the interior of the seat rail is also a particularly English and Irish construction detail.

5. For an example of an English chair with a similar treatment, see Percy Macquoid and Ralph Edwards, *The Dictionary of English Furniture: From the Middle Ages to the Late Georgian Period* (London, 1924), vol. 1, p. 225, fig. 64.

6. The interior frame of the chair was originally fitted as a closestool, perhaps indicating that it was commissioned for an infirm member of the family for whom it was made.

7. See Morrison H. Heckscher, *American Furniture in the Metropolitan Museum of Art, Vol. 2: Late Colonial Period: The Queen Anne and Chippendale Styles* (New York, 1985), pp. 79–84, cat. nos. 36–39, for similar examples of such chairs. Other examples are in the collection of the Museum of Fine Arts, Boston (see John T. Kirk, *American Chairs: Queen Anne and Chippendale* [New York, 1972], p. 70, cat. no. 49); the Bybee Collection at the Dallas Museum of Art (see Charles Venable, *American Furniture in the Bybee Collection* [Austin, Tex., 1989], pp. 44–45, cat. no. 19); and several private collections.

8. For information on Philadelphia price books for cabriole chairs, see Hornor (note 1), pp. 190–230.

14. DESK-AND-BOOKCASE, 1740/50

Boston

Mahogany with oak and white pine;
238.7 x 104.8 x 61 cm (94 x 41¼ x 24 in.)

Written in pencil across top board of lower case, in an eighteenth-century hand: *Jos. L*

Major Acquisitions Centennial Fund, 1986.414

This desk-and-bookcase is related to a small number of pieces of Massachusetts case furniture that have been linked by similarities in their construction, carving, and types of woods.[1] Several stylistic traits of the Art Institute's desk indicate that it is one of the earliest pieces in the group.[2] The blocked configuration of the interior of the desk, for example, though similar to early Boston (see cat. no. 10) and English work, is earlier than the stepped (or "amphitheater") interiors of all the other

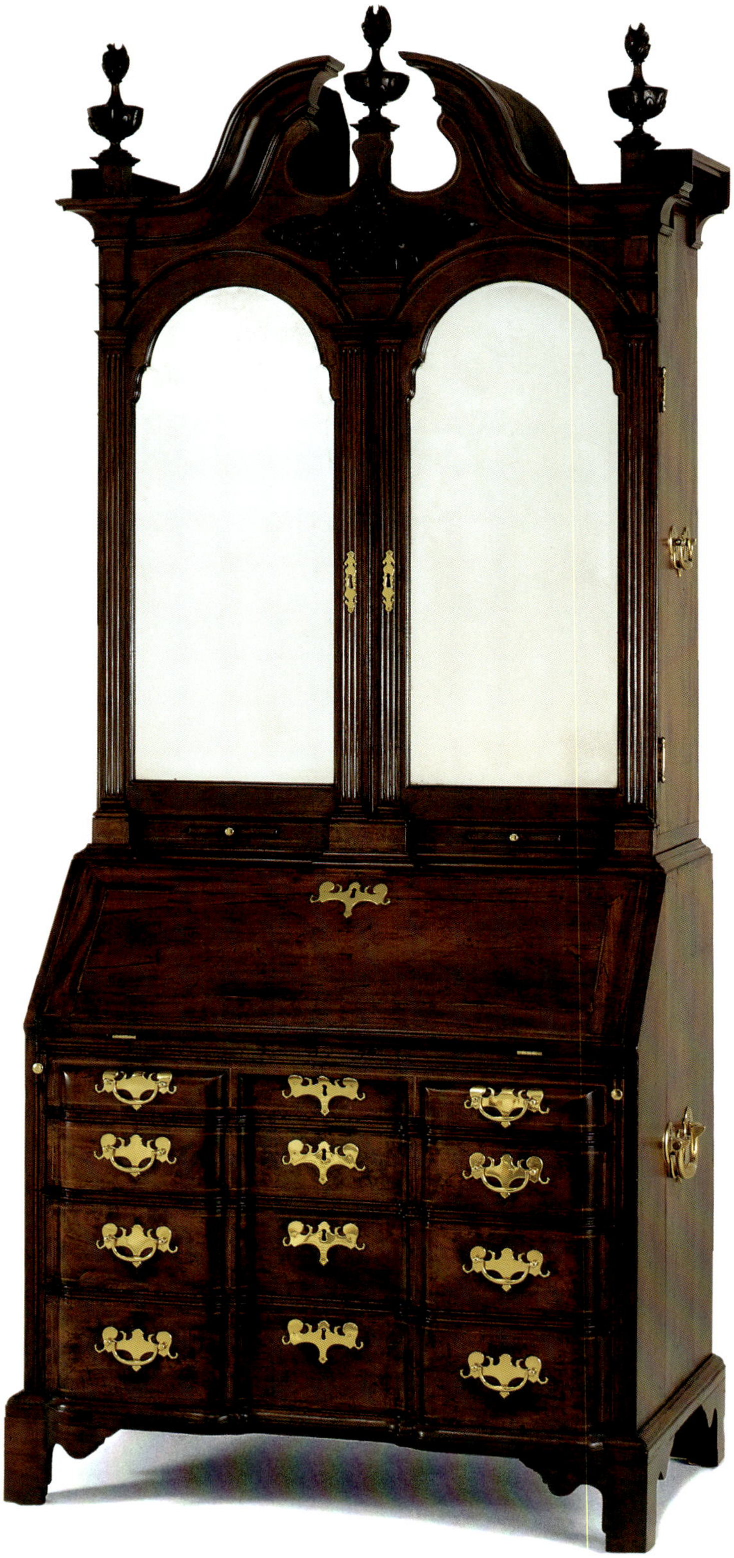

CAT. NO. 14

related desks. The naturalistic carving of fruits and flora on the tympanum of the bookcase section recalls seventeenth-century English prototypes, while the related examples all exhibit a lighter shell-and-vine carving typical of the mid-eighteenth century.[3]

Several features of the construction of the Art Institute's desk-and-bookcase suggest that its cabinetmaker was English-trained. The vertical backboards on both the upper and lower units; the blocky, projecting side moldings on the cornice; and the three-quarter dustboards between the drawers are characteristic of English work.[4] The maker may have arrived in Boston only shortly before producing this piece, and therefore used design and construction methods learned in England rather than those current in Boston.

This desk-and-bookcase has had numerous restorations over its long life. The earliest known records date from the late 1940s, when it was owned by the Pennsylvania antiques dealer Joseph Kindig. At that time, the desk had empire ball feet; all but three of the interior valences on the desk cubby holes were missing, as were the central finial and plinth on the bookcase and the tip of the uppermost leaf in the tympanum carving; the doors had clear glass panes; the original hardware was removed; and the gilded shells on the scooped-out sections under the tympanum were worn away (see fig. 4). Subsequently the piece received new bracket feet, a new central plinth and finial, mirrored doors with wooden back panels, and refreshed gilding on the interior of the bookcase.[5]

Shortly before this piece entered the Art Institute's collection in 1986, the brass hardware was again replaced, with the exception of the locks, hinges, and escutcheon plates on the bookcase doors. The replacement brasses were much smaller than the original hardware, and shadows delineating the original backplate patterns showed through the lighter finish on the wood's surface. Tracings of these hardware shadows revealed that the desk-and-bookcase originally had a very distinctive pattern of brass backplates. Unique to Boston furniture, this brass pattern, or a slight variant of it, appears on a small number of case pieces dating from the early 1740s to late 1750s. The brasses are hand-cut from unusually thick sheets of metal, and no two are identical.[6] In 1996 Israel Sack, Inc., from which the Art Institute had purchased the desk-and-bookcase, turned up a box containing most of the original hardware, save for the side-carrying handles.[7] Each backplate was carefully matched with its shadow, and the handles are once again in their proper positions on the desk.

NOTES

1. See Frank M. Levy and Philip D. Zimmerman, "An Important Blockfront Desk by Richard Walker of Boston," *Antiques* 147, 3 (Mar. 1995), pp. 436–41; Alan Miller, "Roman Gusto in New England: An Eighteenth-Century Boston Furniture Designer and His Shop," in Luke Beckerdite, ed., *American Furniture* (Hanover, N.H., 1993), pp. 161–200; and Brock Jobe, "A Boston Desk-and-Bookcase at the Milwaukee Art Museum," *Antiques* 140, 3 (Sept. 1991), pp. 412–19.

2. Miller (note 1), p. 167. There are at least ten related desks-and-bookcases within the group; for a list of these examples, see the entry on the piece in the Milwaukee Art Museum by Brock W. Jobe in Gerald W. R. Ward, ed., *American Furniture with Related Decorative Arts, 1660–1830* (New York, 1991), pp. 122–26, cat. no. 45.

3. Miller (note 1), p. 169; and Jobe (note 2), pp. 125–26.

4. Jobe (note 2), p. 125; and Georgette Rudes, "Condition Report," May 31, 1996, Files of the Department of American Arts, The Art Institute of Chicago.

5. In 1996 microscopy revealed that the desk retained a resin finish embedded in the wood cells, probably shellac with an overcoating of tinted wax. Testing also showed the intrusion of solvents, an indication that the piece had been refinished at least once. With this information on hand, the desk-and-bookcase was cleaned of surface dirt and wax; small mars to the surface of the wood were blended to match surrounding areas; cracks were filled; and the piece was given a coat of tinted wax. See Robert Mussey, Jr., "Ultraviolet Microscopy Finish Exam Report," Dec. 1, 1993, p. 1, Files of the Department of American Arts, The Art Institute of Chicago; and Georgette Iannuzzi, "Treatment Report," June 1996, Files of the Department of American Arts, The Art Institute of Chicago.

6. Robert Mussey supplied information on the brasses, which are the subject of ongoing research by him. For Boston case pieces with related hardware, see Gilbert T. Vincent, "The Bombé Furniture of Boston," in Walter Muir Whitehall, ed., *Boston Furniture of the Eighteenth Century* (Boston, 1974), pp. 137–96.

7. Deanne Levison of the firm of Israel Sack, Inc., New York, kindly located and provided the original hardware to The Art Institute of Chicago.

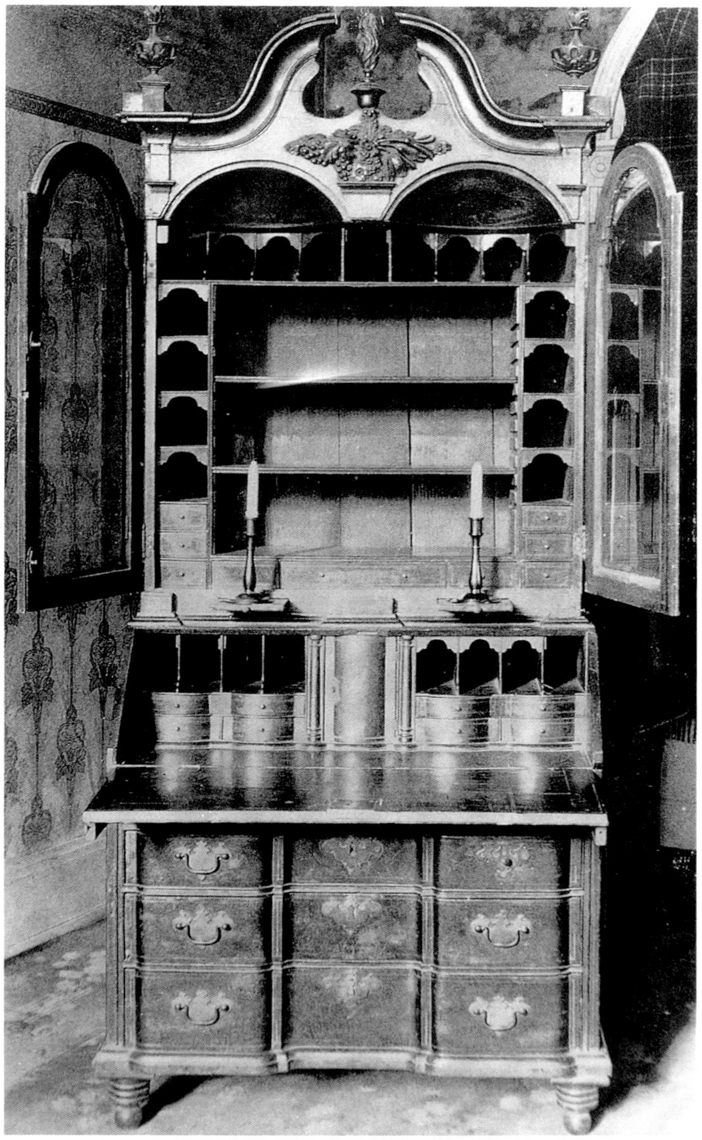

FIG. 4. Cat. no. 14, before its restoration, late 1940s. Photograph from Alan Miller, "Roman Gusto in New England: An Eighteenth-Century Boston Furniture Designer and His Shop," in Luke Beckerdite, ed., *American Furniture* (Hanover, N.H., 1993), p. 168.

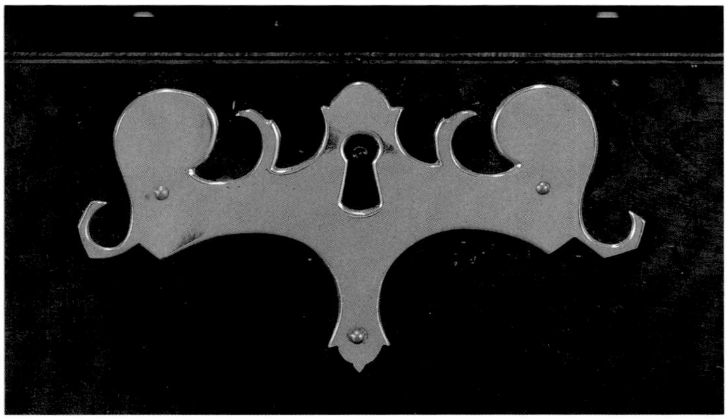

CAT. NO. 14, DETAIL

15. HIGH CHEST OF DRAWERS, 1745/65

North shore of Massachusetts, possibly Salem
Mahogany with white pine and cedar;
153.7 x 67.3 x 36.5 cm (60½ x 26½ x 14⅜ in.)
Inscribed in pencil on the proper right drawer side of the proper right drawer on the base: *Sally Kings draw she keeps her shifts in* and *Salem*
Gift of the Antiquarian Society through the Mrs. Edgar J. Uihlein Fund, 1987.11

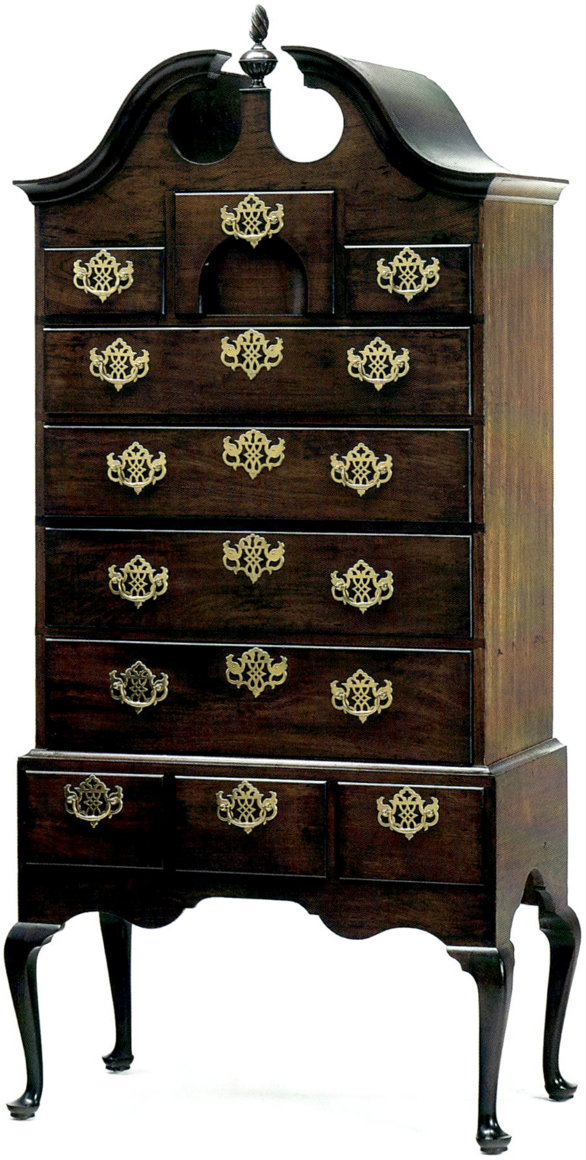
CAT. NO. 15

Small-scale case furniture is very rare.[1] Too large to have served as a cabinetmaker's model, and lacking locks on the drawers, this piece was not made for the safe-keeping of valuables or spices; it was made for use by a child. A reduced version of comparable furniture used by adults, it is as finely and solidly crafted as any full-size high chest of drawers.

The chest bears an inscription in one of the small lower drawers that identifies this compartment as one in which Sally King of Salem kept her "shifts." The pencil markings are those of a child; the hand is shaky and unsure, and there were several preliminary attempts at producing a florid *S* before the writer inscribed her name. There also appears a progression of letters that may be part of a penmanship lesson or some sort of rhyme.[2] Records indicate that indeed a Sally King lived in Salem in the late eighteenth century.[3] Born on March 27, 1783, to James and Judith Norris King, she was probably the second owner of the chest after either her father or her mother, both of whom would have been children when the earlier Baroque style of this chest was in vogue. James King was a prominent merchant in Salem who spent a substantial amount of money on rebuilding and outfitting the frigate *Essex*. His son, Sally's brother John, graduated from Harvard, practiced law in Salem, and became a senator in the Massachusetts legislature.[4]

When acquired, the chest was thought to be an example of Newport, Rhode Island, craftsmanship.[5] The piece shares many construction details with Newport cabinetwork, including the exposed dovetails of the drawer dividers and the placement of the drawers. However, a number of examples of Boston and Salem furniture exhibit the characteristics of Newport workmanship. In Salem, especially, local knowledge and ideas blended with Newport design principles and construction techniques to produce a style that is totally distinct from Boston cabinetwork.[6] But while many of its construction features reflect those of Newport work, the high chest exhibits other traits that are typical of pieces from Massachusetts. The graceful sweep of the cabriole legs, the crisp lines on the knees, and the round pad feet on discs are similar to those on the Art Institute's Salem dressing table (cat. no. 16). In addition, the three large drawers in the base and the large pediment drawer flanked by two smaller drawers are also characteristic of Salem work—though not of Newport.[7] The design and construction of the pediment of the child's high chest also relate closely to the museum's full-size high chest from Salem (fig. 5).[8]

In 1996 tracings of the original hardware patterns were taken from shadows on the surface of the drawer fronts. The

NOTES

1. For a smaller chest from Pennsylvania that is labeled as a cabinetmaker's model and that lacks locks on the drawers, see the Philadelphia Museum of Art, *Philadelphia: Three Centuries of American Art*, exh. cat. (1976), p. 25, cat. no. 21.

2. When the Conservation Department at the Art Institute examined the side of the drawer with an infrared camera, the letter progression "Busy uny ayun asy" was revealed.

3. The name Sally King does not appear in the vital records of Salem prior to 1780; see letter from MaryAnn T. Campbell, Librarian and Archivist at the Peabody-Essex Museum, Salem, Mass., to Seth A. Thayer, Mar. 10, 1997, Files of the Department of American Arts, The Art Institute of Chicago.

4. Ibid.

5. The finial, typical of a Newport design, was replaced when the piece entered the collection of the Art Institute.

6. For examples of Boston work with Newport characteristics, see Margaretta Markle Lovell, "Boston Blockfront Furniture," in Walter Muir Whitehall, ed., *Boston Furniture of the Eighteenth Century* (Boston, 1974), pp. 116–20.

7. The child's chest has full dust boards underneath the top three drawers, a construction feature common to Salem cabinetry of the period.

8. The pitch is higher than that of most Newport high chests. The top boards on the pediment do not go all the way to the top of the pediment, but rather stop three-quarters of the way up; and a small two-piece block of wood completes the span from the boards to the top of the pediment.

9. Shadow tracings, like those done for cat. no. 14, were executed by Robert Mussey Associates in 1996, and indicate that the hardware shadows on the wood match the pierced pattern of the backplates. Robert Lionetti located the original brasses in his warehouse.

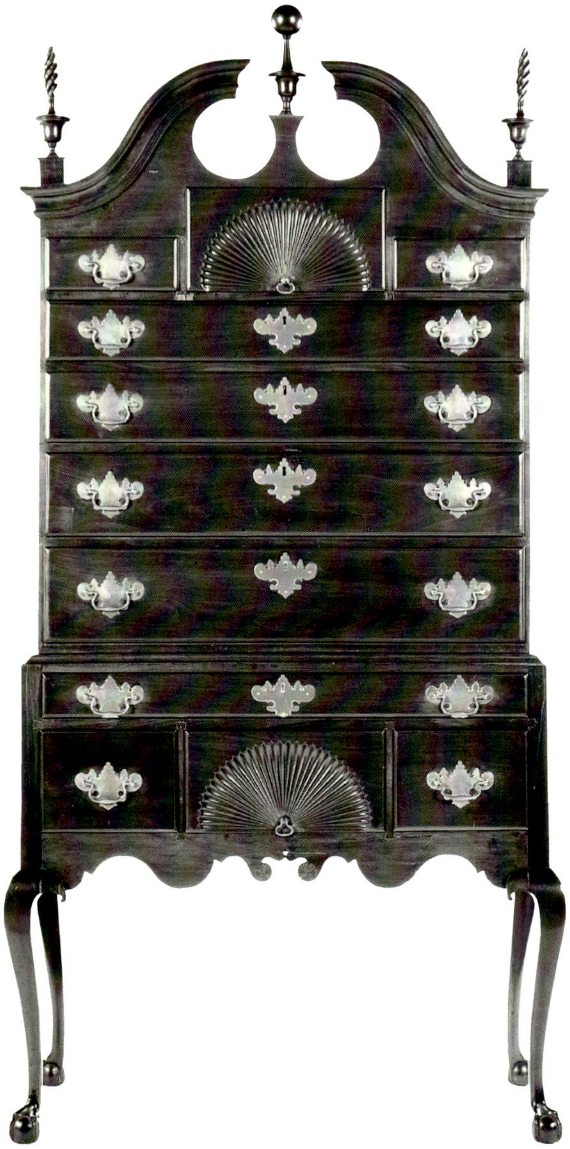

FIG. 5. American (Salem, Massachusetts). *High Chest of Drawers*, 1760–65. Mahogany with white pine; 217.2 x 102.8 cm (85½ x 40½ in.). The Art Institute of Chicago, Gift of William McCormick Blair (1984.714).

tracings revealed an elaborate, pierced pattern. The original backplates, posts, and bails were recovered from the dealer who sold the piece to the Art Institute and were placed back on the chest. The original escutcheons, or lock plates, were not found, and those now on the chest are modern replacements.[9] The hardware pattern used on the chest appears as stock no. 681 in an English hardware catalogue dating from approximately 1775 (fig. 6). Although the catalogue was printed in the 1770s, the hardware most likely dates from an earlier period, for pierced brasses appear on English furniture from the 1730s and 1740s and were available to cabinetmakers in this country as well.

FIG. 6. Engraved plate from an English manufacturer's catalogue, c. 1775. Metropolitan Museum of Art, New York, Harris Brisbane Dick Fund (35.41.1).

16. DRESSING TABLE, 1750/70

Salem, Massachusetts

Mahogany and white pine;

78.2 x 88.9 x 57.2 cm (30¾ x 35 x 22½ in.)

Signed in chalk across the underside of the top board: *Stephen* [?]

Gift of the Antiquarian Society through the Mrs. William O. Hunt, Jessie Spalding Landon, Mrs. Harold T. Martin, Adelaide Ryerson, and Mrs. H. Alex Vance funds, 1977.517

Dressing tables were most often made en suite with high chests of drawers. Both were normally used in the bed chamber, the high chest to store valuable linens and textiles and the dressing table to hold articles for grooming.[1] The dressing-table drawers held objects such as combs, brushes, powders, ribbons, pieces of lace, and patch boxes.[2] A looking glass was often hung above the table, or a small dressing glass set upon it. Below the mirror, these dressing glasses usually had drawers for extra storage (see fig. 7). The dressing table and mirror would have been separated by a textile known as a *toilette*, which was used to protect the surface of the table from the implements of grooming. Usually made from muslin, silk, baize, linen, or velvet, *toilettes* were popular in England, and period inventories from Boston indicate that they were present in American homes as well.[3]

This dressing table was made in Salem, Massachusetts, and has several Salem characteristics in the design, including the diamond cut out in the center of the front and side aprons, and the scrolled, voluted knee brackets.[4] The table also takes some inspiration from Newport craftsmanship of the period. The shell carving in the lower drawer is reminiscent of work from Newport, as are the exposed dovetails of the drawer dividers. Salem and Newport were closely connected through the meetings of the New England Society of Friends that took place three times a year in Salem, Newport, and Sandwich, Massachusetts.[5] Both Salem and Newport were important trading ports in the eighteenth century, and local design customs and ideals were certainly assimilated by visitors to either port.

The usually blocky design of many Boston-area dressing tables of the Queen Anne period is tempered in this example by the sophisticated, lively, exuberant outline of the skirt and side aprons and the elegant, elongated cabriole legs.[6] The table

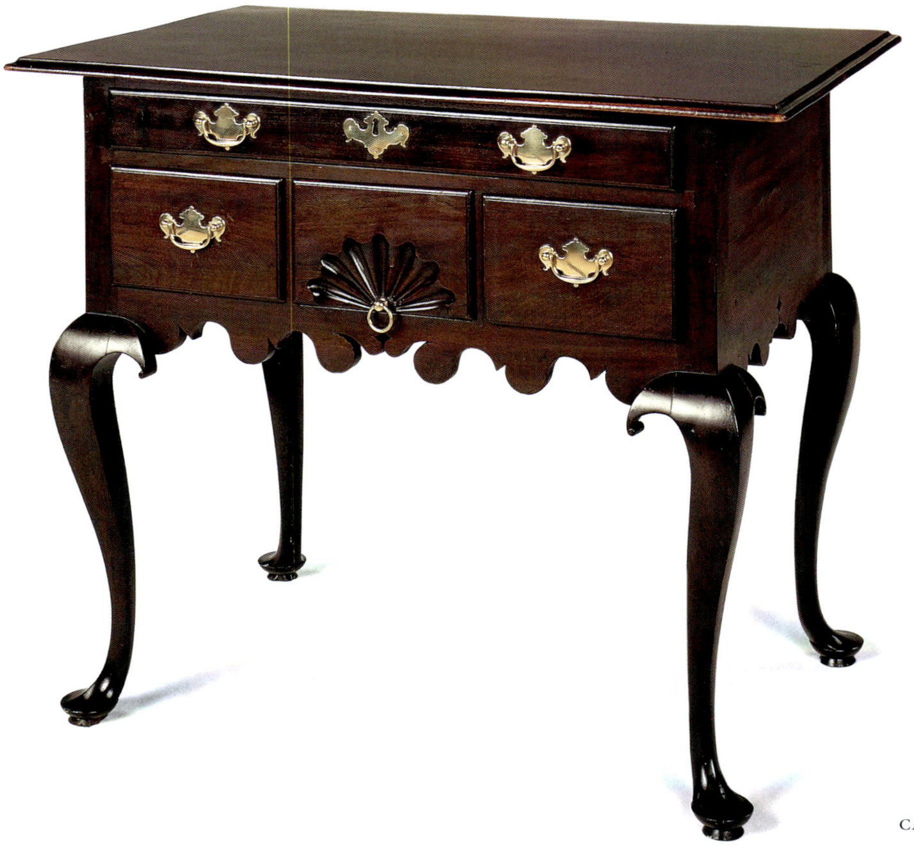

CAT. NO. 16

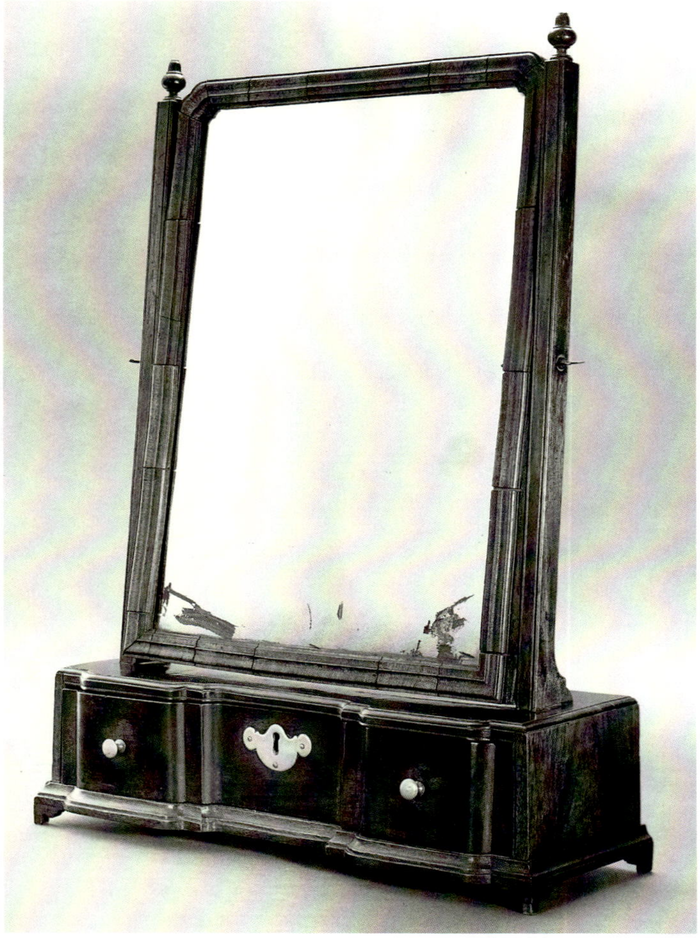

FIG. 7. American (Boston area). *Dressing Glass*, 1740/60. American black walnut with white oak and white pine; 65.7 x 47.8 cm (25⅞ x 18¾ in.). The Art Institute of Chicago, Gift of the Antiquarian Society (1944.423).

epitomizes the graceful, double-curved lines advocated by the artist William Hogarth in his *Analysis of Beauty*, published in London in 1753. In elaborating his notion of the "line of beauty," Hogarth observed, "That the waving line, or line of beauty, varying still more, being composed of two curves contrasted, becomes still more ornamental and pleasing."[7]

NOTES

1. Morrison H. Heckscher, *American Furniture in the Metropolitan Museum of Art, Vol. 2: Late Colonial Period: The Queen Anne and Chippendale Styles* (New York, 1985), p. 231.

2. Patch boxes were usually made of silver and held small pieces of cut velvet, satin, or silk that could be applied to areas of the face to hide small-pox scars or to satisfy one's vanity; see Barbara McLean Ward and Gerald W. R. Ward, eds., *Silver in American Life: Selections from the Mabel Brady Garvan and Other Collections at Yale University*, exh. cat. (New Haven, Conn., Yale University Art Gallery, 1979), p. 133. The Art Institute's collections contain two American silver patch boxes, one by John Dixwell of Boston (1985.245) and an unmarked example, possibly from Newport, R.I. (1983.790).

3. Benno M. Forman, "Furniture for Dressing in Early America, 1650–1730," *Winterthur Portfolio* 22, 2–3 (summer/autumn 1987), p. 158. A Pennsylvania dressing table dating from about 1740 in the Art Institute's collection (1991.264) has small, contemporary tack holes on the underside of the top where a textile was once attached.

4. Albert Sack, *The New Fine Points of Furniture: Early American* (New York, 1993), p. 209.

5. Margaretta Markle Lovell, "Boston Blockfront Furniture," in Walter Muir Whitehill, ed., *Boston Furniture of the Eighteenth Century* (Boston, 1974), p. 120.

6. For examples of other Boston area dressing tables of the period, see Dean A. Fales, Jr., "Boston Japanned Furniture," in Whitehill (note 5), pp. 60, 62; and Lovell (note 5), pp. 96–98.

7. William Hogarth, *The Analysis of Beauty* (London, 1753), p. 38.

17. JOSEPH BLACKBURN (ACTIVE 1752–C. 1778)

Abigail Chesebrough (Mrs. Alexander Grant), 1754

Oil on canvas; 127.6 x 101.5 cm (50 x 40 in.)

Signed on bottom of window at right: *I Blackburn Pinxt 1754*

Bequest of Miss Amelia Peabody, 1984.725

18. COSMO ALEXANDER (1724–1772)

Alexander Grant, 1770

Oil on canvas; 127.7 x 101.6 cm (50¼ x 40 in.)

Signed, lower right on base of column: *Alex^{r} p* [?] *A D 1770*

Ada Turnbull Hertle Fund, 1977.2

Joseph Blackburn's portrait of twenty-year-old Abigail Chesebrough of Newport, Rhode Island, is a scintillating example of the refined, Rococo manner Blackburn brought to the colonies from England. It is unclear whether the artist was English by birth, but the conventions of his portraiture—stock poses, an emphasis on lustrous drapery, and theatrical backgrounds—point to a familiarity with English portrait painting and perhaps training or apprenticeship in that country.[1] Blackburn painted his first colonial portraits in Bermuda and from there proceeded to Newport, Rhode Island, where wealthy merchants enjoyed a thriving trade with the Caribbean island colony.[2]

Blackburn's English connections and sophisticated painting style contributed to his popularity in the colonies between the

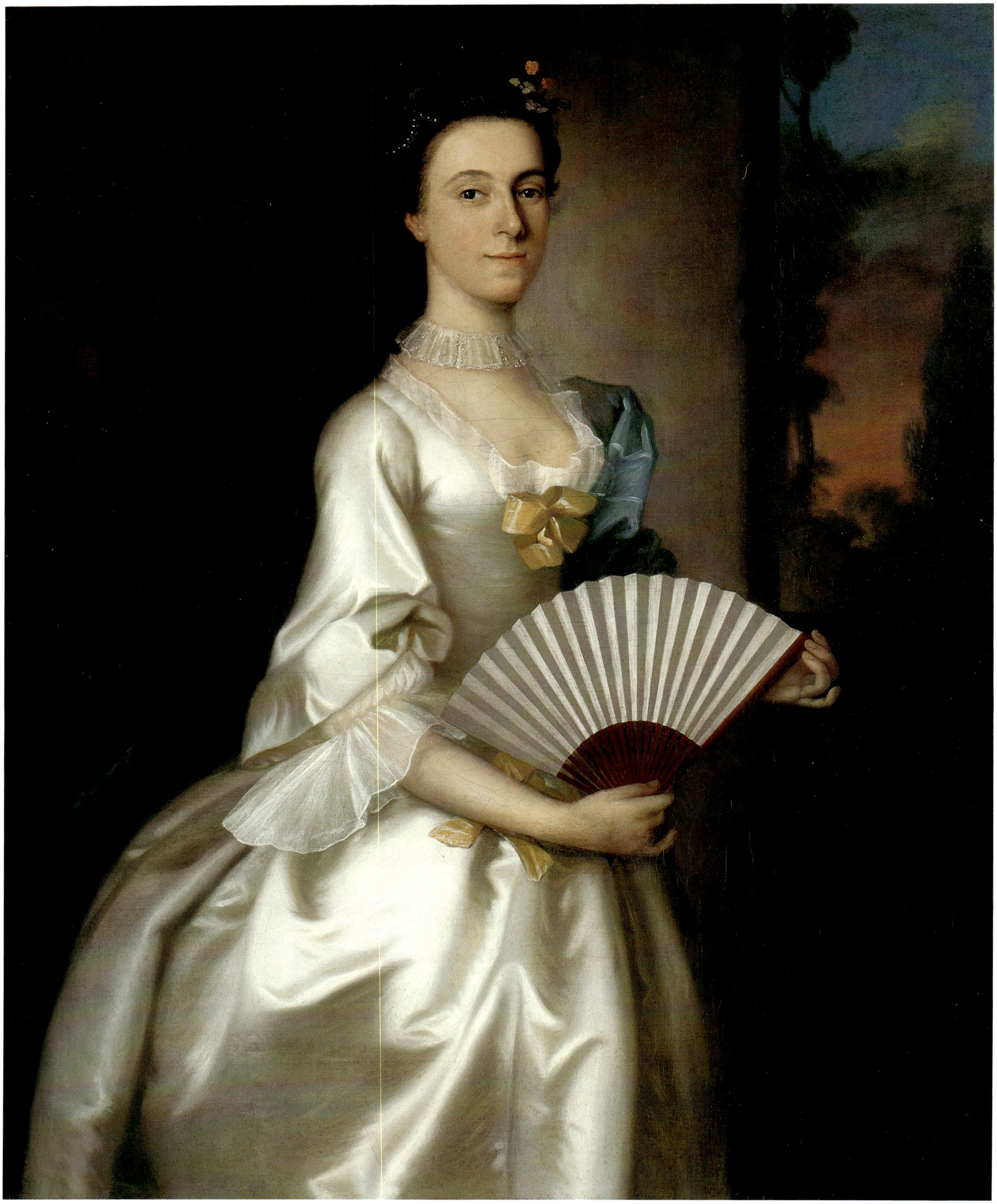

CAT. NO. 17

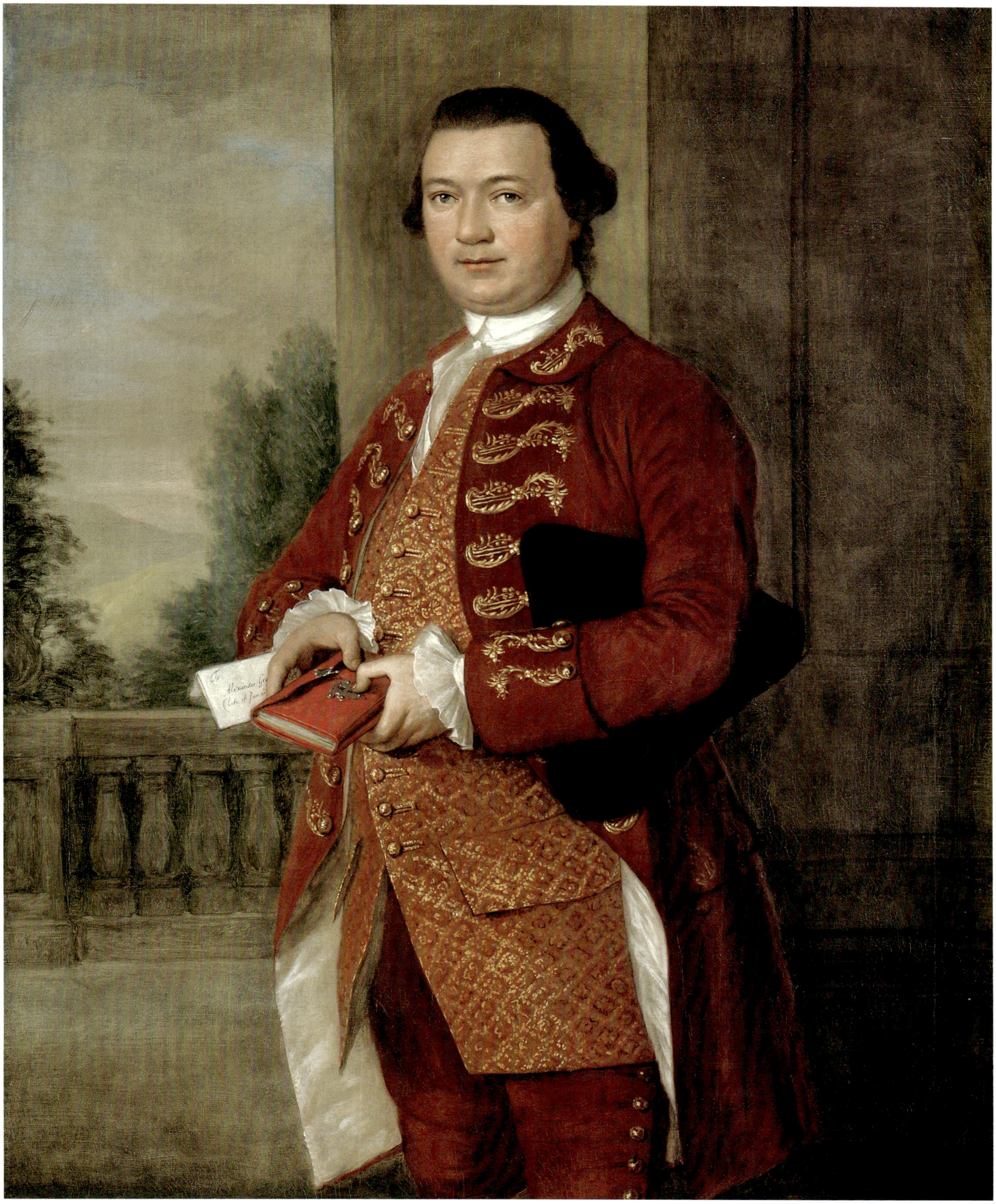

CAT. NO. 18

death of John Smibert in 1751 and John Singleton Copley's rise to fame ten years later in Boston (see cat. nos. 26–27). Abigail Chesebrough was the daughter of "King David" Chesebrough, so-named for his mercantile wealth and economic dominance in Newport. Although he commissioned Smibert to paint his portrait in 1732 (Stonington Historical Society, Connecticut), Chesebrough selected Blackburn to paint the likenesses of other members of his family. At least two orders for portraits were placed with the ambitious young Blackburn in 1754: the Art Institute's of his daughter and one of his second wife, Abigail's stepmother, Margaret Chesebrough (née Sylvester), now in the Metropolitan Museum of Art, New York (fig. 8).[3]

Blackburn's portrait of Abigail Chesebrough accentuates her youthful femininity. Whereas Margaret Chesebrough is identified as a married woman by ivy twining around a tree in the background, Abigail personifies virginal beauty.[4] The open fan draws attention to her social status and unifies her costume by echoing the ribbing of her lace collar and the soft folds of her cuffs. The fan form is also closely associated with the Rococo style and was used to ornament furniture from the same period.[5] Abigail's pose cannot be traced to an exact model, but it is reminiscent of those used by fashionable English portrait painters such as Thomas Hudson and Joseph Highmore.

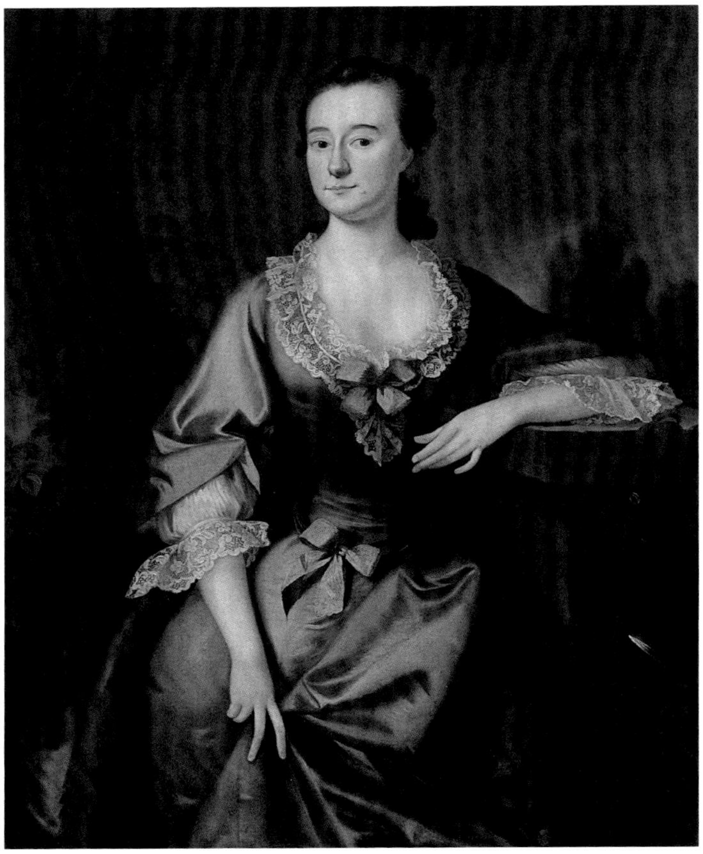

FIG. 8. Joseph Blackburn (c. 1730–after 1774). *Mrs. David Chesebrough*, 1754. Oil on canvas; 126.7 x 101.9 cm (49⅞ x 40⅛ in.). Metropolitan Museum of Art, New York, Gift of Sylvester Dering (16.68.3).

Abigail Chesebrough married Alexander Grant, a Scottish merchant, in October 1760. Alexander's portrait is perhaps a later pendant to Blackburn's picture; the two are the same size and their background features and frame styles coalesce.[6] Like Chesebrough, Grant stands on a balcony overlooking a fanciful landscape, engages the viewer directly, is elegantly dressed, and is accompanied by props that define his high station in Newport society. If Blackburn's painting accentuates Chesebrough's vibrant youth, then Cosmo Alexander's portrait of Grant stresses his mature self-confidence. Grant grasps a letter tightly in his hands; it reads: "To Alexander Gra[nt] / Late of Jamai[ca]." He also holds an unclasped wallet. These signify both his personal and professional identities. His lavish red-and-gold brocade suit and comfortable heft reinforce his image as a prosperous man.

Cosmo Alexander was a Scottish artist who is perhaps best known as Gilbert Stuart's first instructor in Newport (see cat. no. 57).[7] He plied his trade in Newport between 1769 and 1771, after which he and Stuart embarked for the southern colonies and, eventually, Scotland. The elder artist died suddenly in Edinburgh, leaving his protégé to fend for himself.

Biographical information about Alexander Grant is scant, although his wife's movements were recorded by Ezra Stiles, pastor of the Second Congregationalist Church in Newport and later president of Yale University. Between 1770 and 1786, Stiles noted Mrs. Grant's expeditions to London, where she and her husband were apparently forced to reside during the Revolutionary War. On May 6, 1775, Stiles wrote that he "saw a Letter of 4th March from Mrs Grant in London: she says many Mouths there breath Fire and Flame, and that nothing will satisfy but the Destruction of Boston or its surrend[er] into their Hands."[8] Stiles recorded the death of Abigail's father in his diary, and apparently served as leasing agent for her father's property after his death.[9]

It is unclear whether these portraits remained in David Chesebrough's Newport home during the war (he was forced to flee to Stonington, Connecticut, to escape British occupation of Newport), were brought to Stonington, or traveled to London with the Grants. They remained in the Chesebrough family until 1916, when a descendant bequeathed them to the Stonington Historical Society because of the family's historical significance in the town.

NOTES

1. For more biographical information about Blackburn, see Wayne Craven, *Colonial American Portraiture: The Economic, Religious, Social, Cultural, Philosophical, Scientific, and Aesthetic Foundations* (Cambridge, 1986), pp. 296–304.

2. See William B. Stevens, Jr., "Joseph Blackburn and His Newport Sitters, 1754–1756," *Newport History* 40 (summer 1967), pp. 95–107, for more about connections between Newport and Bermuda and Blackburn's career in Newport.

3. Blackburn also painted a portrait of Margaret Chesebrough's sister Mary Sylvester, probably in 1754 (Metropolitan Museum of Art, New York).

4. John Caldwell and Oswaldo Rodriguez Roque with Dale T. Johnson, *American Paintings in the Metropolitan Museum of Art, Vol. I: A Catalogue of Works by Artists Born by 1815* (New York, 1994), p. 31.

5. For more about the Rococo style in colonial America, see Morrison H. Heckscher and Leslie Greene Bowman, *American Rococo, 1750–1775: Elegance in Ornament*, exh. cat. (New York, Metropolitan Museum of Art, 1992).

6. The frames, probably English, are of the same gilded, Rococo style, but their carving does not match.

7. See Pam McLellan Geddy, "Cosmo Alexander's Travels and Patrons in America," *Antiques* 112, 5 (Nov. 1977), pp. 972–77, for more about Alexander's career.

8. Franklin Bowditch Dexter, ed., *The Literary Diary of Ezra Stiles, D.D., LL.D.* (New York, 1901), vol. 1, pp. 547, 659.

9. Ibid., vol. 3, p. 163.

19. BENJAMIN BURT (1729–1805)

Communion Dish, 1781

Boston

Silver; 3.8 x 33.2 (diam.) cm ($1\frac{1}{2}$ x $13\frac{1}{16}$ in.)

Marked near center on underside of bowl: *B·BURT* (in rectangle); engraved around rim of dish: a cherub's head and the words *The Legacy of the Honble Isaac Royall Esq. to the Church of Christ in Medford 1781.*

Gift of the Antiquarian Society, 1989.65

20. SAMUEL EDWARDS (1705–1762)

Baptismal Basin, 1755

Boston, Massachusetts

Silver; 7.5 x 30.1 (diam.) cm ($2\frac{15}{16}$ x $12\frac{1}{16}$ in.)

Marked near the center on interior of bowl: *S · E* (under a crown and above a device in shaped shield); engraved around rim of basin: *The Bequest of Mr. John Willis to the Church of Christ in Medford 1755.*

J. Peter McCormick Fund, 1988.445

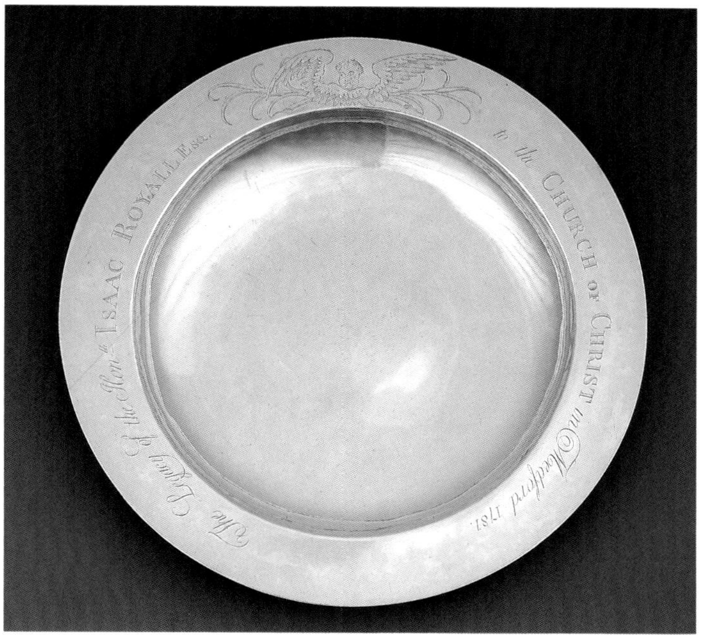

CAT. NO. 19

These two pieces of plate—as silver was called in the seventeenth and eighteenth centuries—from the Church of Christ in Medford, Massachusetts, were commissioned by the church with funds bequeathed by parishioners. Between 1719 and 1863, the Medford Church of Christ, founded in 1712, was given, or commissioned, at least twenty-two such pieces of silver for communion and baptismal services.[1] Many other colonial churches that were not as wealthy as this one, however, had to use wooden or pewter communion vessels, which were considered to be acceptable for services until more desirable silver forms could be procured.[2]

In the seventeenth and early eighteenth centuries, Congregational churches in America practiced a form of communion that allowed only certain members of the church to participate—namely, those who had had conversion experiences.[3] Although almost everyone in the community was required to attend services, full membership in the church was granted only to those who "have not only attained the knowledge of the principles of Religion, and are free from gros and open scandals, but also do together with the profession of their faith and Repentance, walk in the blameles obedience to the Word."[4] For the act of communion, individual vessels were laid out on an altar or a small table, and communicants partook of the bread and wine, in imitation of the Last Supper.[5]

The beginning of the eighteenth century, however, saw a broadening of the communion ritual to include the entire congregation. So that large numbers of people could participate in

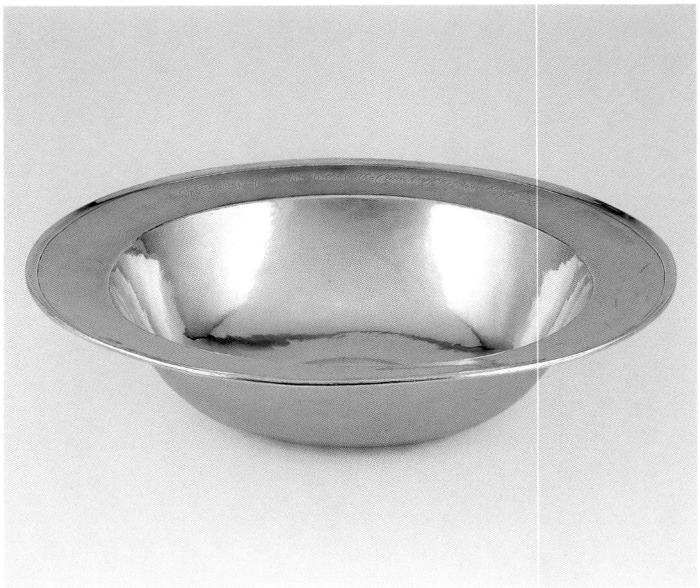

CAT. NO. 20

the ceremony, new vessel forms such as the communion dish were required. Two-handled standing cups were also used to facilitate passing the wine among communicants.[6]

Isaac Royall, the donor of the communion dish in the Art Institute's collection, was a prominent loyalist; forced to flee the colonies at the beginning of the Revolutionary War, he never returned. At his death in 1781, he bequeathed a large, two-handled English silver cup to the Church of Christ in Medford, together with a sum of money that the church used to commission the communion dish from Benjamin Burt.[7] The bold and elegant style of the inscription across the rim of this otherwise plain vessel appears on several communion dishes from other churches.[8] The winged head of a cherub, an ornament adopted by Congregational churches in the mid-eighteenth century and used as well in church interiors and on gravestones, represents resurrection. The palm branches beneath the cherub's wings symbolize divine blessing, resurrection, and victory over sin and death.[9]

The rite of baptism was always a significant event for a family, because a child was named, it was believed, in the presence of God and was welcomed into a Christian community. According to the records of colonial New England towns, children were usually baptized within six months of their birth.[10] Like the sacrament of communion, baptism was restricted to the children of full members of the Congregational church until the mid-eighteenth century, when those of nonmembers were allowed to be baptized.[11]

The silver baptismal basin in the Art Institute was commissioned from Samuel Edwards with funds bequeathed by John Willis, whose brother Thomas was a deacon in the Medford Church of Christ. John Willis had settled in Medford and married into the Tufts family. His 1755 bequest stipulated that one hundred pounds be donated to the church one year after his death; a portion of that bequest was used for this elegant basin.[12]

NOTES

1. The church purchased its first silver communion objects, a pair of two-handled cups, from silversmith John Dixwell in 1719; see E. Alfred Jones, *The Old Silver of American Churches* (Letchworth, 1913), pp. 271–73; and the collection of research materials from the First Church of Christ in Medford, in the Files of the Department of American Arts, The Art Institute of Chicago.

2. Barbara McLean Ward, "In a Feasting Posture: Communion Vessels and Community Values in Seventeenth- and Eighteenth-Century New England," *Winterthur Portfolio* 23, 1 (spring 1988), p. 3.

3. Ibid., p. 2.

4. From the Cambridge Platform of 1648, as quoted in Harry S. Stout, *The New England Soul: Preaching and Religious Culture in Colonial New England* (New York, 1986), p. 18.

5. Barbara McLean Ward and Gerald W. R. Ward, eds., *Silver in American Life: Selections from the Mabel Brady Garvan and Other Collections at Yale University*, exh. cat. (New Haven, Conn., Yale University Art Gallery, 1979), p. 91.

6. A two-handled cup by Benjamin Pierpont, one of ten similar cups made for the First Congregational Church in Hatfield, Mass., is in the Art Institute's collection (1948.105).

7. Charles Brooks, *History of the Town of Medford* (Boston, 1855), pp. 173–76, 265–66. Brooks misdates the communion dish as being given in 1789, instead of 1781.

8. For other examples from Boston, see Kathryn C. Buhler, *American Silver, 1655–1825, in the Museum of Fine Arts, Boston* (Greenwich, Conn., 1972), vol. 1, p. 316, cat. no. 272, and p. 364, cat. no. 321.

9. For more information on the iconography of the cherub's head, see Dell Upton, *Holy Things and Profane: Anglican Parish Churches in Colonial Virginia* (Cambridge, Mass., 1986), pp. 119–20; and James Deetz and Edwin S. Dethlefsen, "Death's Head, Cherub, Urn and Willow," in Thomas J. Schlereth, ed., *Material Culture Studies in America* (Nashville, Tenn., 1982), pp. 195–205. For the meaning of palm branches, see J. C. Cooper, *An Illustrated Encyclopaedia of Traditional Symbols* (London, 1978), p. 125.

10. John Demos, "Infancy and Childhood in the Plymouth Colony," in Michael Gordon, ed., *The American Family in Social-Historical Perspective* (New York, 1978), p. 157.

11. Ward (note 2), p. 4.

12. Jones (note 1), p. 276.

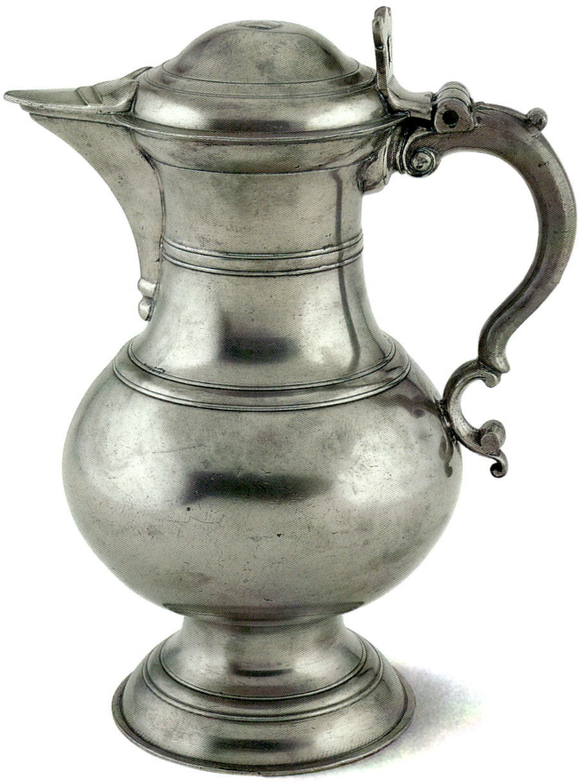

CAT. NO. 21

21. ATTRIBUTED TO WILLIAM WILL (1742–1798)

Flagon, 1765/80

Philadelphia
Pewter; 28.5 x 20.3 cm (11¼ x 8¼ in.)
Gift of Mrs. William O. Goodman, 1938.847

William Will was the fourth son of the German-born pewterer John Will (c. 1707–1774), who immigrated to the colonies in 1752. Born in Nieuwied, Germany, William was most likely apprenticed to his father in New York. By 1763 William had moved to Philadelphia with his brother Philip, also a pewterer. William became one of the most prolific and talented pewterers of the eighteenth century; his work is characterized by its ambitious design, fine workmanship, and originality.[1] He had a reputation for using his pewter molds to create beautiful and unusual forms like the flagon in the Art Institute's collection.

Until the beginning of the nineteenth century, pewter forms were cast from molds. Because these molds were expensive, a pewterer was forced to be as versatile as possible with what he had. In pewtering families like the Wills, molds were often passed from one generation to the next until they were worn out. In addition, pewterers used a single mold interchangeably for different purposes.[2] Hollow ware such as this flagon typically comprise several molded pieces joined together with solder and polished so that the solder marks are invisible. For example, the mold for the flagon's lid, minus the dome portion, was also used to make the base.

Some scholars have attributed the Art Institute's flagon to William's father, John, on the basis of two pewter flagons that are thought to have been made by him (see fig. 9).[3] The style of these pieces, however, appears to be earlier than that of the Art Institute's flagon. Differences in craftsmanship indicate that another pewterer made the Art Institute's piece. The rounded bellies of John Will's flagons—flared at the center and flattened at both top and bottom—look as though they were fashioned from two opposing porringer bowls or small basins. The belly of the Art Institute's flagon, on the other hand, is more globular in shape and was most likely adapted from a round teapot form. The two flagons attributed to John Will, with their angular lines and ungainly proportions, seem less successful in design than the Art Institute's flagon. Both John Will flagons exhibit thick bands, called midbands, that encircle

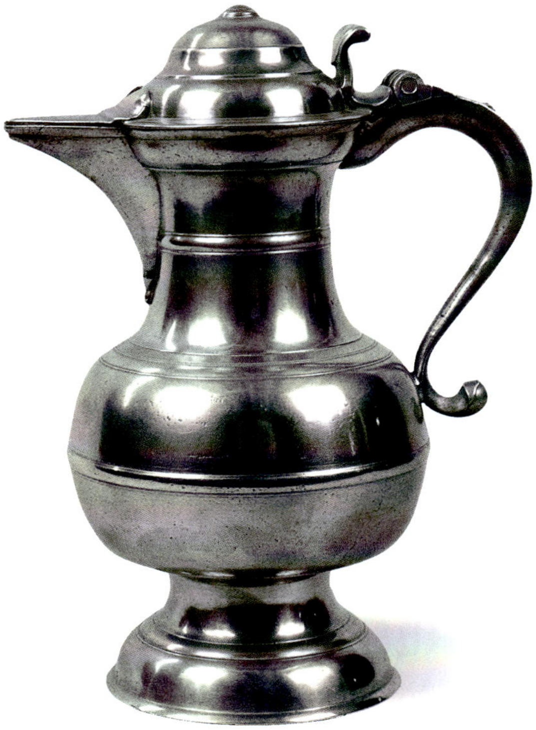

FIG. 9. John Will (c. 1707–1774). *Flagon*, 1752/74. Pewter; 30.5 x 13.3 (diam. at base) cm (12 x 5¼ in.). Collection of Dr. and Mrs. Melvyn D. Wolf.

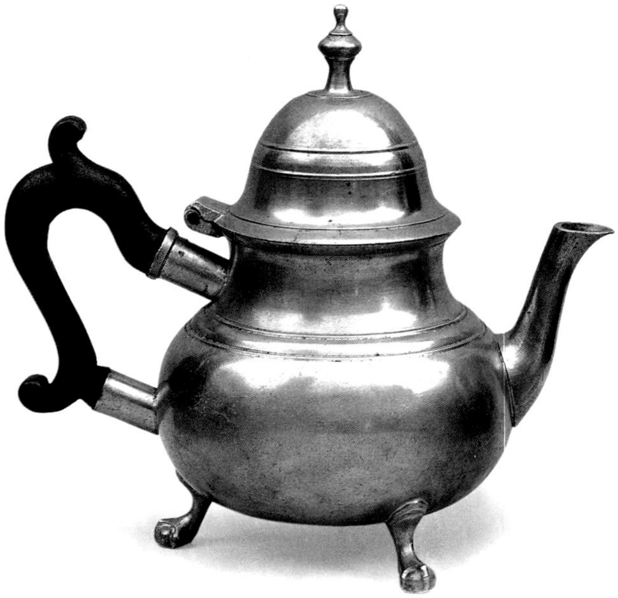

FIG. 10. William Will (1742–1798). *Teapot: with mark of maker; wood handle*, 1764/98. Pewter; h. 21.6 cm (8½ in.). Metropolitan Museum of Art, New York, Gift of Mrs. J. Insley Blair (49.2).

the middle of their bodies, and S-curve handles, features found on Baroque silver of the early eighteenth century. Moreover, sections that make up the flagons do not flow together as well as they do in the Art Institute's piece, indicating that their maker was less skilled than the pewterer who produced the museum's flagon.

Although unmarked, the Art Institute's flagon relates closely to pieces documented to William Will. A communion service that he made for the Salem Lutheran Church in Aaronsburg, Pennsylvania, includes a pitcher whose form is similar to the Art Institute's flagon.[4] So, too, the pitcher has a globular belly, flaring neck, and broken scroll handle with a small C-scroll at the lower handle juncture. C-scrolls were favored motifs during the Rococo period, and this type of handle was typically seen on silver tankards and mugs from the mid to late eighteenth century. The round bellies of the Art Institute's flagon and the Aaronsburg pitcher may have been made from the same mold or molds as a footed, pear-shaped teapot with a globular belly made by William Will (fig. 10). At least five such teapots bearing Will's identifying mark are known to survive.[5]

Though flagons were used in the home during the seventeenth and early eighteenth centuries, by 1750 most flagons were commissioned by or given to churches for use in the communion service.[6] Will made several flagons, a few of which survive with documentation of their early church history. Unfortunately the early history of the Art Institute's flagon is not known.[7]

NOTES

1. Suzanne Hamilton, "The Pewter of William Will: A Checklist," *Winterthur Portfolio* 7 (1972), pp. 129–30.

2. Charles V. Swain, "Interchangeable Parts in Early American Pewter," *Antiques* 83, 2 (Feb. 1963), p. 212.

3. The second flagon is illustrated in Charles V. Swain, "Three Flagons Attributed to John Will," *Antiques* 179, 5 (May 1972), p. 853.

4. Paul M. Auman, "New Finds in Old Pewter by William Will: The Aaronsburg Communion Service," *Antiques Magazine* 57, 4 (Apr. 1950), p. 274.

5. Hamilton (note 1), pp. 157–58, nos. 170–74.

6. Charles F. Montgomery, *A History of American Pewter* (New York, 1973), p. 60.

7. The Art Institute's flagon was used by the Congregational church in Farmington, Ohio, after which it was purchased by the donor. See Files of the Department of American Arts, The Art Institute of Chicago.

22. ATTRIBUTED TO JOHN GODDARD (1723–1785)

High Chest, 1755/75

Newport, Rhode Island

Mahogany with chestnut and white pine;
219.4 x 101.6 x 54.6 cm (86⅜ x 40 x 21½ in.)

Helen Bowen Blair Fund, 1989.158

Newport grew rapidly from a small seacoast village with a population of 1,500 in the early years of the eighteenth century to a thriving seaport town of 9,000 inhabitants by 1770.[1] By 1740 Newport had established itself on the coastal trade routes between England and the West Indies. The merchants of Newport established a triangular barter system whereby they imported commodities such as sugar, molasses, and cotton from Barbados, and exported beef, pork, butter, cheese, and horses from the colonies; they then used the surplus these trades produced to purchase goods from England to sell to inland towns in the colonies.[2] In the decades before the American Revolution, Newport merchants were among the wealthiest and most influential figures in the colonies. The furniture produced there attests to this fact, for mid-eighteenth-century Newport furniture is of the highest quality, style, and design.

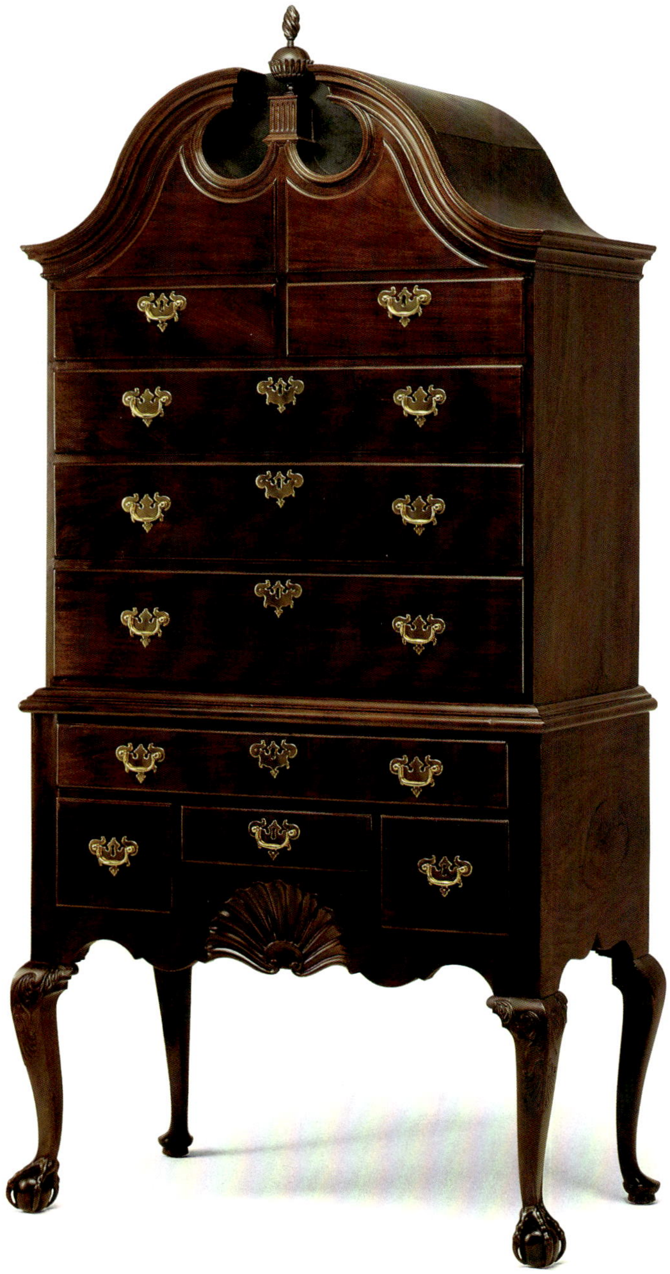

CAT. NO. 22

Well after the high chest fell out of favor in England, it was still popular in America. Craftsmen developed and redefined the form, which was introduced to America by the 1690s, until it reached its apogee in the mid-eighteenth century. But while the chest's basic elements were the same, each furniture-producing center developed its own decorative vocabulary for the form.

This high chest is an excellent example of Newport's stylistic interpretation of the high-chest form and a testament to the genius of the Goddard–Townsend school (see cat. nos. 12 and 23). It succeeds in resolving many problems inherent in the design of the bonnet-top. The applied, raised panels at the top of the facade harmoniously integrate the bonnet into the design of the rest of the chest. These panels are a feature on Rhode Island furniture that rarely appears elsewhere.[3] Compared with the two other high chests in the collection, from Massachusetts and Philadelphia (see p. 35, fig. 37), the Newport high chest is better proportioned, achieving an equal balance between the body of the chest and the thickness and length of the legs. The bulk of the Newport piece rests on its superb ball-and-claw feet. These feature elongated balls, rigid tendons and knuckles on the claws, and undercut talons, which are associated with Rhode Island furniture making.[4] The ornament is subdued, accentuating the form of the chest rather than fighting it; the simple yet exquisitely carved shell and the cyma and ogee-shaped curve of the apron serve to soften the lines of the lower portion of the chest and draw attention to the main body. The deliberate absence of side finials on the bonnet-top and strong curve of the bonnet help direct attention back to the chest. Because Newport was a predominantly Quaker community, the emphasis on the strong, sparsely ornamented Baroque facade would have appealed to clients. This is true of most pieces of furniture produced in Newport.

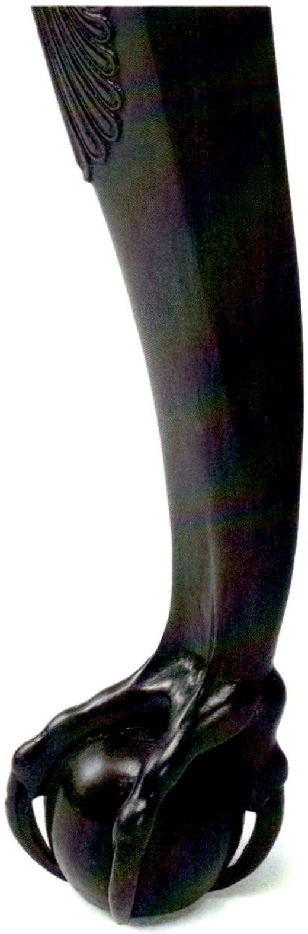

CAT. NO. 22, DETAIL

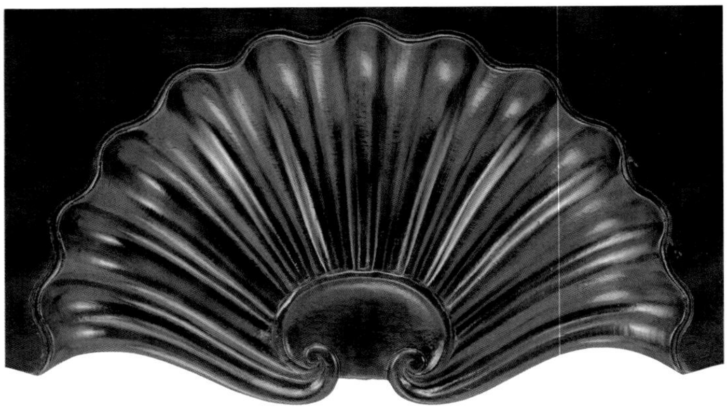

CAT. NO. 22, DETAIL

John Goddard moved to Newport from Massachusetts prior to 1737. Before becoming apprenticed to Job Townsend (1699–1765), he served as a captain on a trading sloop between Philadelphia and Newport.[5] In 1746 he married Job Townsend's daughter Hannah, with whom he had some fifteen children, three of whom became cabinetmakers. It was the apprenticeship and marital links between Job Townsend and John Goddard that tied the two cabinetmaking families together for over a century. The Townsend–Goddard group is the most identifiable of the over one hundred cabinetmakers working in Newport in the mid-1700s; this is true primarily because the group signed or labeled select pieces of their work and those marks have survived. Aided by the marked examples, scholars have been able to attribute many unmarked pieces of furniture to one or another craftsman in the group through similarities of construction techniques or type and quality of decorative motif. Although this chest cannot conclusively be attributed to John Goddard, it shares many attributes with furniture documented to him, such as the carving of the central shell, the knees, and the ball-and-claw feet.

NOTES

1. Michael Moses, *Master Craftsmen of Newport: The Townsends and Goddards* (Tenafly, N.J., 1984), p. 3.

2. Margaretta M. Lovell, "'Such Furniture As Will Be Most Profitable': The Business of Cabinetmaking in Eighteenth-Century Newport," *Winterthur Portfolio* 26, 1 (spring 1991), pp. 28–29.

3. Other cabinetmaking areas where such panels are known to have been used are in central Connecticut and Long Island, both regions where Goddards and/or Townsends are known to have lived.

4. Ralph E. Carpenter, Jr., *The Arts and Crafts of Newport, Rhode Island, 1640–1820*, exh. cat. (Newport, R.I., Preservation Society of Newport County, 1954), p. 22.

5. Ibid., p. 13.

23. ATTRIBUTED TO JOHN TOWNSEND (1732–1809)

Bureau Table, 1780/90

Newport, Rhode Island

Mahogany with maple, chestnut, and white pine; 86.6 x 93.4 x 58 cm (34⅛ x 36¾ x 20 in.)

Gift of Jamee J. and Marshall Field, 1984.1387

This form of case furniture was one of the most popular with Newport patrons: over fifty bureau tables are known to exist.[1] The appeal of the bureau table may be attributed to its compactness and virtuosity. Having both large and small drawers, a wide top surface, and a central storage cupboard, the bureau table's features would have appealed to the practical nature of the Quaker citizens of Newport. Bureau tables were kept in the bed chamber and most likely functioned as dressing tables. The long top drawer and smaller side drawers held combs, brushes, powders, and other accoutrements. The central door opens up to a compartment that may have held a wig stand.[2] Several other bureaus have fall-front top drawers that pull out to reveal small, blocked drawers and writing surfaces that serve as desks.[3]

This is one of six Newport bureau tables that can be attributed to John Townsend on the basis of construction and design features in similar, labeled pieces by the maker.[4] In this example, the top board of the bureau is attached to a subtop with nails and screws rather than dovetails, a feature found on pieces from the 1790s.[5] On the top drawer of the museum's piece, the three carved shells have central C-scrolls featuring petals and crosshatched baskets, all indicative of Townsend's later work.[6]

The attribution to John Townsend is strengthened by distinctive calligraphic symbols on several of the interior drawer bottoms and on the drawer dividers that are also seen on labeled or signed pieces by Townsend.[7] The symbols on the Art Institute's bureau are written in both chalk and graphite as they are on a high chest dated 1759 documented to John Townsend.[8] Because of normal wear, most of the symbols are barely legible, but they appear to be letters of the alphabet with many of the same scrolling flourishes that characterize Townsend's writing.[9]

The Art Institute's bureau is an elegant piece that epitomizes the late Baroque style that flourished for years in Newport. The top is integrated into the case by the cove-and-bead molding, with smaller cavetto molding underneath, a feature

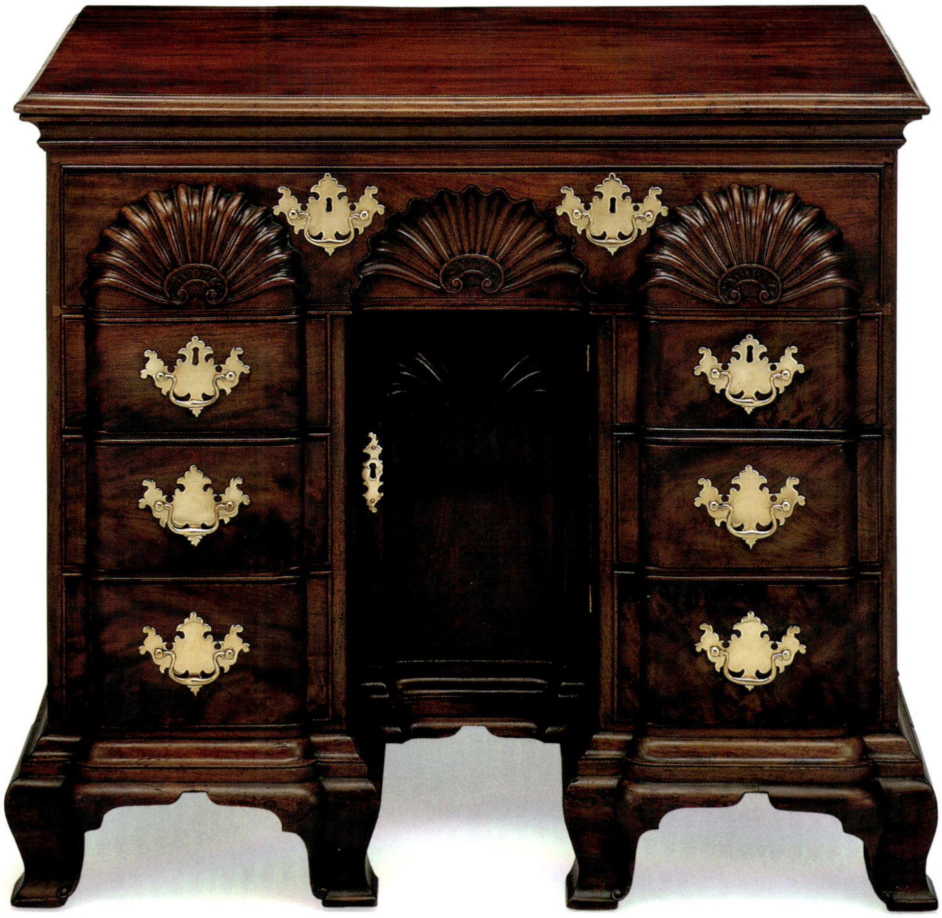

CAT. NO. 23

particular to Townsend's work. The carved shells were boldly executed by an experienced hand; the lobes are sharply defined, yet appear to flow freely outward (see detail). The blocking of the upper drawer continues through the side drawers and into the graceful double scroll of the bracket feet providing an unbroken visual plane that succeeds in harmonizing the design elements of the entire bureau.

According to oral tradition, Samuel Fowler was the original owner of this bureau.[10] Fowler, a successful merchant, conducted business with several members of the Townsend family, including John. An entry from Fowler's diary illustrates his success as a merchant: "Attended to business of Samuel Fowler and Sons. Had warf built out and large store there on, also contracted with Sam'l Tobey of Berkley to build a ship called 'Hope'—200 tons. Importation of goods from this year and last amt'd to $57,500."[11] Contained in Samuel Fowler's petty ledger (dated 1783 to 1788), around the date of the bureau table, is a list of clients, goods sold, and payment methods. From Fowler, John Townsend bought hinges worth three shillings, four pence, on May 1, 1786. In 1786 and 1787 his purchases included nails and sundries.[12] The fact that Townsend purchased cabinetmaking supplies from Fowler bolsters the argument that Fowler owned this bureau table. Surviving records indicate that patronage loyalty resulting from familial, religious, or trading ties was the norm in eighteenth-century Newport.[13]

NOTES

1. Michael Moses, *Master Craftsmen of Newport* (Tenafly, N.J., 1984), p. 7.

2. Morrison Heckscher, *American Furniture in the Metropolitan Museum of Art, Vol. 2: Late Colonial Period: The Queen Anne and Chippendale Styles* (New York, 1985), p. 209.

3. Moses (note 1), p. 7.

4. The other bureaus are in the following collections: the Metropolitan Museum of Art, New York; the Henry Francis du Pont Winterthur Museum, Winterthur, Del.; Yale University Art Gallery, New Haven, Conn.; the Bayou Bend Collection, Museum of Fine Arts, Houston; and a private collection.

5. Morrison Heckscher, "John Townsend's Block-and-Shell Furniture," *Antiques* 121, 5 (May 1982), p. 1151.

6. The Metropolitan Museum of Art's bureau is the earliest piece in the group. For the identifying construction features of Townsend's bureaus, all

CAT. NO. 23, DETAIL

of which are present on the Art Institute's chest except for the double-dovetail top boards, see Heckscher (note 5).

7. Moses (note 1), p. 88.

8. Ibid.; Gerald W. R. Ward, *American Case Furniture in the Mabel Brady Garvin and Other Collections at Yale University* (New Haven, Conn., 1988), p. 266, cat. no. 140.

9. For examples of Townsend's writing, see Moses (note 1), pp. 102–04.

10. John Walton Antiques, Inc., advertisement, *Antiques* 110, 1 (July 1976), p. 4.

11. The entry for 1785 is from typescript pages entitled, "1774–1829 Extracts from Pa Fowler's diary—Records of a Past Time," in the Newport Historical Society.

12. Petty ledger of Samuel Fowler, dated 1783–88, p. 121, Newport Historical Society. Fowler also sold eighteen shillings' worth of sundries to Edmund Townsend in 1785 (ibid, p. 119).

13. For an explanation of patronage loyalty, see Margaretta M. Lovell, "'Such Furniture as Will Be Most Profitable': The Business of Cabinetmaking in Eighteenth-Century Newport," *Winterthur Portfolio* 26, 1 (spring 1991), p. 56.

24. ATTRIBUTED TO JOHN COGSWELL (1738–1819)

Chest of Drawers, 1780/95

Boston

Mahogany and white pine;

79.7 x 91.8 x 50.8 cm (31⅜ x 36⅛ x 20 in.)

Helen Bowen Blair Fund, 1979.499

American furniture in the colonial period was most often derived from existing European forms. These designs spread throughout the colonies, and each furniture-producing center then developed that form in its own particular style. Certain forms only fully developed in one center, and did not become fashionable elsewhere. This is true of New York serpentine-front card tables, Newport block-and-shell-front furniture, and Boston bombé furniture.[1] The influence of French taste and style in Boston during the American Revolution, as well as the insularity of the cabinetmaking community, may explain how the bombé form came to Boston and why it was distinctive to that city.

During the American Revolution, Boston Harbor was protected by the French navy. Bostonians welcomed French officers their homes during their stays in the colonial city. Established merchants began trading goods with France and Belgium, importing fabrics, furniture, and other goods from those countries. The city's tastemakers expected local artisans to familiarize themselves with French tastes and styles, and to be conversant with the newest French furniture and other artistic forms.[2]

As an artisan center, Boston was one of the most insular communities in the colonies. Once an artisan was attached as an apprentice or by marriage to a Boston family, there was little reason for him or succeeding generations of his family to leave the city in search of work. Thus, the knowledge of styles and of craftsmanship was kept within the immediate community.[3] Favorite forms developed in the Boston area, such as the bombé chest, often remained local, and were not adapted by other colonial cabinetmaking centers.

Of the over sixty-five surviving examples of bombé furniture made in colonial Boston, thirteen are chests with serpentine fronts. Six of these are similar in design and construction to the chest at the Art Institute. Although no two chests are identical, these six have identically shaped fronts, sides, tops, and bases.[4] Recently all of these chests have been attributed to John Cogswell based on a signed chest-on-chest now in the Museum of Fine Arts, Boston.[5] Besides sharing several similar construction techniques with the group of chests, the swell of the case sides is almost identical in profile. Cogswell most likely used a template to cut and shape the boards for his sides. Unlike the work of other Boston bombé furniture designers, Cogwell's case sides begin their swell higher up on the boards to reduce the heavy appearance of the case bottom.[6]

The Art Institute's chest is an exceptional example of this rare serpentine-front, bombé form.[7] Like all the related chests, the sides of the case were carved from solid, four-inch-thick mahogany boards. The white pine drawer sides and the mahogany drawer fronts are both curved to conform to the shape of the case. These features reveal Cogswell's masterful craftsmanship, for he not only had to curve the dovetails in the interior of the drawers, but also had to match perfectly the individual curves of the case and drawer sides.

The bold, clean lines of the chest and the absence of decoration illustrate Cogswell's brilliance. The robust, red, swirl-grained mahogany on the drawer fronts and the oversized original brasses, in conjunction with the serpentine surface and swelled case sides, create a strong visual interplay of material, color, and shape. The carved central drop connects the rolling swell of the case sides and brings the viewer's eye back to the center while the sturdy ball-and-claw feet anchor the chest to the ground.[8]

NOTES

1. Bombé is a modern appellation for these forms; it was taken from the French verb *bomber*, meaning to bulge or swell. See Harold Sack, "The Bombé Furniture of Boston and Salem, Massachusetts," *Antiques* 135, 5 (May 1989), p. 1187 n. 2.

2. Robert Mussey and Anne Rogers Haley, "John Cogswell and Boston Bombé Furniture: Thirty-Five Years of Revolution in Politics and Design," in Luke Beckerdite, ed., *American Furniture* (Hanover, N.H., 1994), p. 81.

3. For example, successive generations of the Coit, Perkins, and Frothingham families all entered the cabinetmaking trade in Boston, with the Frothingham family producing over fifteen cabinetmakers over four generations, all of whom established themselves in Boston or nearby Charlestown. See Brock Jobe, "The Boston Furniture Industry, 1720–1740," in Walter M. Whitehill, ed., *Boston Furniture of the Eighteenth Century* (Boston, 1974), pp. 9–11.

4. Robert D. Mussey, in Clement Conger and Alexandra Rollins, eds., *Treasures of State* (New York, 1991), pp. 189–90, cat. no. 99. Other related chests are in the following collections: the Dietrich Americana Foundation Collection, Philadelphia (on loan to the Metropolitan Museum of Art, New York); the U.S. Department of State, Diplomatic Reception Rooms, Washington, D.C. (acc. no. 69.103); and the Collection of Julian Wood Glass, Jr. Two were on the market in 1995: see New York, Christie's, *The Collection of Mr. and Mrs. Eddie Nicholson* (Jan. 1995), lot 1063; and Portsmouth, N.H., Northeast Auctions, *Collection of Marjorie Doyle Rockwell* (Nov. 5, 1995), lot 501.

5. The chest is signed on the top board of the lower case, "Made By John / Cogswell in midle street / Boston 1782."

6. Mussey and Haley (note 2), p. 87. For examples of Boston bombé furniture by other makers, see Conger and Rollins (note 4), cat. nos. 13, 73, 82.

7. The bombé shape has been used for centuries on various chest forms. The earliest known use is found in classical sarcophagi. The shape reemerged in Renaissance marriage chests, and was subsequently reinterpreted in early

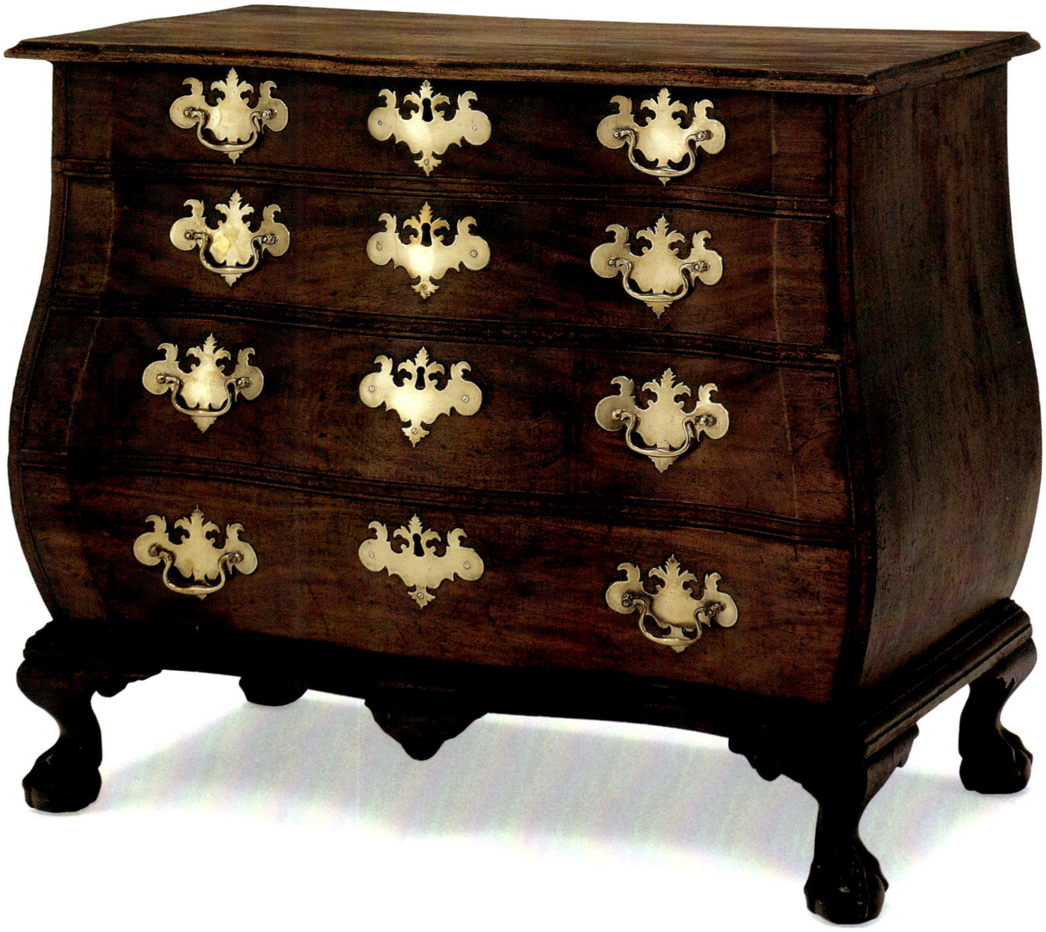

CAT. NO. 24

eighteenth-century French chests-of-drawers, or *commodes en tombeau* ("chests in the style of a sarcophagus"). See Gilbert T. Vincent, "The Bombé Furniture of Boston," in Walter M. Whitehill, ed., *Boston Furniture of the Eighteenth Century* (Boston, Mass., 1974), p. 143.

8. The dovetails on all the chests are identically angled and cut into the case sides within an eighth of an inch of the outer surface. A majority of the chests have large triangular glue blocks at each corner of the underside of the chest, and "chalk inscriptions on the undersides of the bottom boards" that read "Bottom," or utilize a chevron mark (^) or an X; see Mussey and Haley (note 2), p. 87. The chest at the Art Institute has "Bottom" scrawled across the boards.

25. SIDE CHAIR, 1750/55

Philadelphia
Mahogany with tulip poplar;
97 x 56.5 x 40 cm (39¼ x 22¼ x 15¾ in.)
Incised, on inside rear seat rail: *V*
Robert R. McCormick Charitable Trust Fund, 1979.1029

This chair is part of a larger suite of at least eight chairs that descended in the John Wister family. Four of these are still in the Wister house, Grumblethorpe, in Germantown, Pennsylvania.[1] Wister was a German immigrant who followed his brother, Caspar, to the colonies in 1727. When he arrived in Philadelphia, he established himself on Market Street, where he began selling blackberries and importing wine.[2] His business prospered, and in 1744 he built Grumblethorpe, a summer refuge from the heat of Philadelphia. The house is made of stone with oak paneling and pine floors throughout. It was large and elegant for its time, having four main rooms on the first floor, with a bedroom above each on the second, five bedrooms in the attic, and two over the kitchen for the servants.[3]

The Art Institute's chair may have been made soon after John Wister's house was completed and as such is an early example of Rococo taste in Philadelphia. The pierced splat and concave, ruffled shell on the seat rail were popular treatments on compass-shaped seat chairs in the Baroque style; a splat of the same design as that on the Art Institute's chair appears on one of the finest Baroque chairs produced in Philadelphia.[4] The trapezoidal seat, interior seat construction, rectangular back with fluted stiles, and shell-and-vine carving on the crest rail on the Art Institute's chair, however, were mainstays of chair design in the Rococo period. It appears that the unknown craftsman who made this suite was comfortable with the late Baroque style, but wanted to craft the chairs in the newest style—the Rococo—with which he was less familiar. Perhaps he did not have an opportunity to study Thomas Chippendale's *Gentleman and Cabinet-Maker's Director*, one of the most important sources of inspiration for Philadelphia cabinetmakers, who used designs from the pattern book to create high-style furniture and carvings in the Rococo taste (see cat. no. 31). Chippendale's pattern book was published in London in 1754, but was probably not publicly available in Philadelphia until after its third printing, in 1762, after which the Library Company of Philadelphia acquired a copy for its collection.[5] At this point, Philadelphia chairs began to assume a more "gothic" appearance, as dictated by Chippendale's patterns.[6]

Certainly, Rococo designs appeared in Philadelphia in the early 1750s, before Chippendale's book was first published in London. One of the earliest documented pieces exhibiting naturalistic carving is a high chest signed by Henry Clifton and dated 1753.[7] It is similar in design and ornament to a Philadelphia high chest and matching dressing table in the Art Institute's collection. Chairs with "Carved Claw and Knee open back" were ordered from John Elliott in 1754 by Philadelphian Edward Shippen.[8] Whether these were imported from England or made in Philadelphia is not known, but we can be certain that chairs in the Rococo manner were available in Philadelphia very early in the history of this style. It is conceivable then that John Wister may have ordered the set of chairs as early as 1750/55 for use in his new house.

NOTES

1. Jack Lindsey, Curator of American Decorative Arts, Philadelphia Museum of Art, supplied this reference. Another chair is in a private collection, on loan to the Philadelphia Museum of Art, and two are in private hands; see New York, Christie's, *Fine American Furniture, Silver, Folk Art and Decorative Arts* (Jan. 24, 1987), lot 289, p. 133.

2. Harold D. Eberlein and Horace M. Lippincott, *The Colonial Homes of Philadelphia and Its Neighborhood* (Philadelphia, 1912), pp. 217–18.

3. Harry M. and Margaret B. Tinkcom and Grant M. Simon, *Historic Germantown: From the Founding to the Early Part of the Nineteenth Century* (Philadelphia, 1955), pp. 56–57.

4. See William MacPherson Horner, Jr., *Blue Book of Philadelphia Furniture* (1935; reprint, Washington, D.C., 1977), pl. 41.

5. Morrison H. Heckscher and Leslie Greene Bowman, *American Rococo, 1750–1775: Elegance in Ornament*, exh. cat. (New York, Metropolitan Museum of Art, 1992), p. 183.

6. For examples, see Horner (note 4), pls. 271–78.

7. The Clifton high chest is in the collection of the Colonial Williamsburg Foundation, Williamsburg, Va. (1975-154).

8. Heckscher and Bowman (note 5), p. 182.

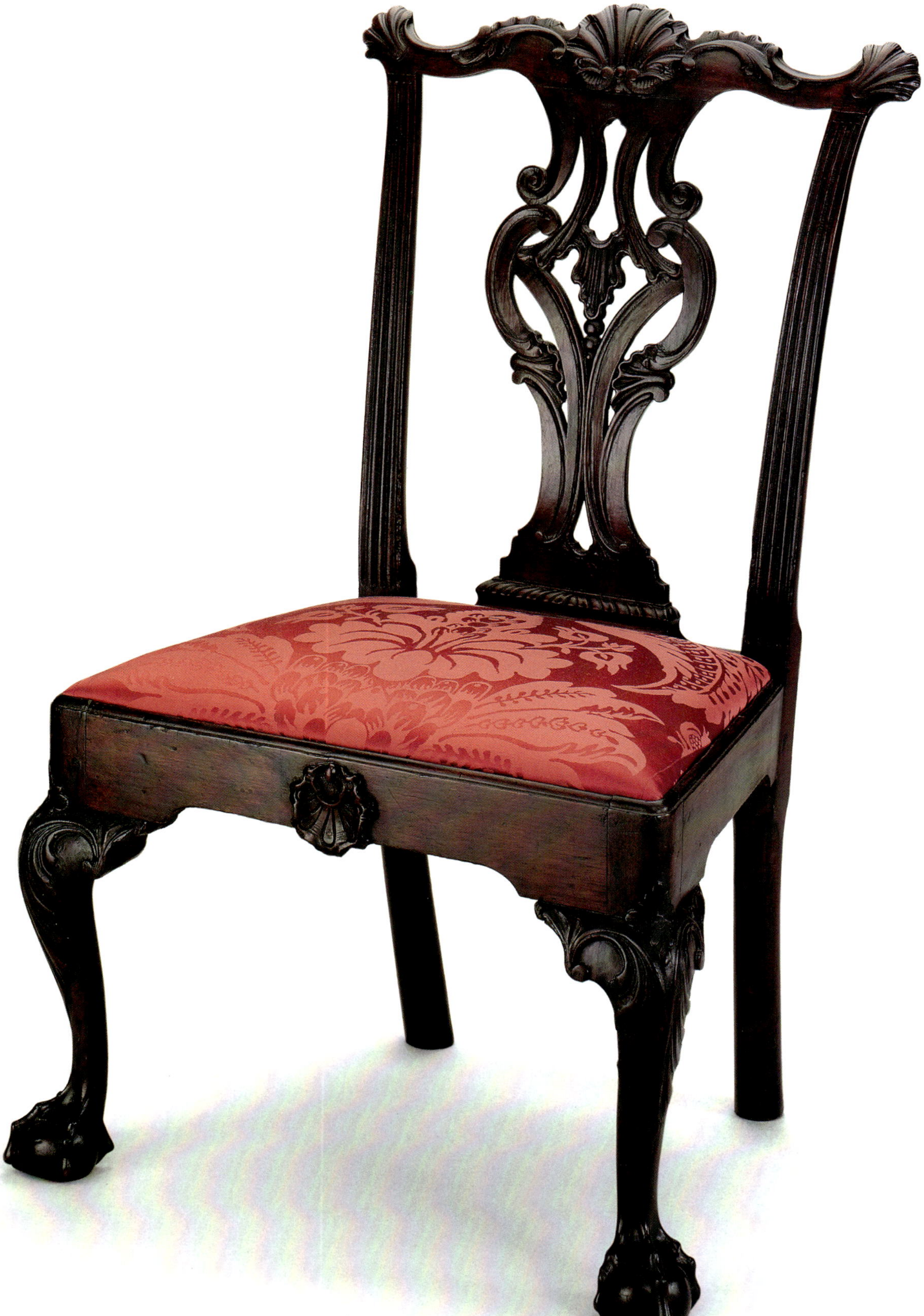

CAT. NO. 25

26. JOHN SINGLETON COPLEY (1738–1815)

Daniel Hubbard, 1764

Oil on canvas; 127.2 x 100.8 cm (50⅛ x 39¹¹⁄₁₆ in.)
Signed on base of column: *John S. Copley pinx. 1764*
The Art Institute of Chicago Purchase Fund, 1947.27

27. *Mrs. Daniel Hubbard (Mary Greene)*, c. 1764

Oil on canvas; 127.6 x 100.9 cm (50¼ x 39¾ in.)
The Art Institute of Chicago Purchase Fund, 1947.28

Between 1753 and 1774, when he left the colonies for England because of his Loyalist sympathies, John Singleton Copley painted 350 portraits, primarily of Bostonians. Copley received his only formal art training from his stepfather, Peter Pelham, an English graphic artist who specialized in mezzotint engraving. Pelham encouraged the aspiring artist to learn to draw by copying English prints and to produce his own mezzotints. By 1764, when *Daniel Hubbard* and presumably *Mrs. Daniel Hubbard (Mary Greene)* were painted, Copley had established a popular portrait style, influenced by imported mezzotints of fashionable English portraits, which attracted to him the patronage of Boston's merchant aristocracy. Art historian Paul Staiti noted that, during his Boston years, "Copley's unmatched success as a producer in a culture of consumption was built on his ability to sell dream material that told consumers in visual terms what it was possible for them to believe about themselves."[1] Hubbard, a merchant who earned between 100 and 500 pounds per year, and his wife were part of this world.[2] Accordingly, Copley presented them as sumptuously dressed, confidently posed, and surrounded by objects that allude to their social status.

Mr. Daniel Hubbard is depicted in his professional capacity. Seated in an anonymous, imaginary interior embellished with neoclassical furnishings, he gazes directly at the viewer.[3] Copley's attention to the idiosyncrasies of his facial features, especially his mouth, renders his likeness distinct. Resting under the sitter's left arm is a thick, leather-bound book, perhaps a ledger.[4] Hubbard's right arm is cocked on his hip, an assertive gesture of a confident man that also reveals the lustrous, white silk waistcoat he wears under his conservative, brown wool suit. Expensive silks, velvets, and brocades, imported from England during the colonial period, are displayed conspicuously in Copley's paintings to indicate the wealth and anglophiliac sentiments of his sitters.[5]

For the same reasons, he adapted poses and costumes from English mezzotints. In addition to ennobling his sitters and emphasizing their ties to British culture, such borrowing increased the artist's proficiency and productivity. *Mrs. Daniel Hubbard (Mary Greene)* is indebted to John Faber's mezzotint of Thomas Hudson's *Mary Finch, Viscountess Andover* from 1746 (fig. 11), as is Copley's portrait of *Mrs. John Amory (Katherine Greene)* (fig. 12). Mary Greene Hubbard and Katherine Greene Amory were first cousins; Mrs. Hubbard, whose likeness was probably painted after Mrs. Amory's, may have admired her cousin's portrait and chosen one in the same style.[6]

Although Copley used the same source for these two portraits, he individualized each woman's appearance. He seems to have copied both women's dresses directly from the print, but painted Mrs. Hubbard's olive green and Mrs. Amory's ocher yellow.[7] The facial shape and hairstyle of the two women are strikingly similar and echo those of the mezzotint, but the features are highly particularized. Mrs. Hubbard's presence is invigorated by its placement close to the picture plane, in contrast to Mrs. Amory, who is seen further back in the composition. The artist departed from the mezzotint in embellishing Mrs. Amory's dress with a double lace cuff and Mrs. Hubbard's with a lace ruff, further underscoring their affluence and social position.

Of the two portraits based on Faber's mezzotint, *Mrs. Daniel Hubbard (Mary Greene)* is the more faithful to its source. In the mezzotint, the drawing ability of the subject is indicated by the pen she holds to a blank sheet of paper, as well as by the cupid carved on the table below, who holds a landscape drawing. Mrs. Hubbard leans on papers adorned with a delicate needlework pattern that echoes her lace sleeves and implies her feminine accomplishments. Embroidery and drawing were viewed as suitable avocations for upper-class urban women, and were included in their education as decorative rather than practical skills.[8]

The Hubbard portraits appear to retain their original frames, although they have new backings and have been regilded.[9] These molded white pine frames are distinguished by elaborate all-over carving and gilding and were probably manufactured in Boston. The frames were costly, and they complement the mixture of neoclassical and Baroque elements as well as the opulent details in these portraits.

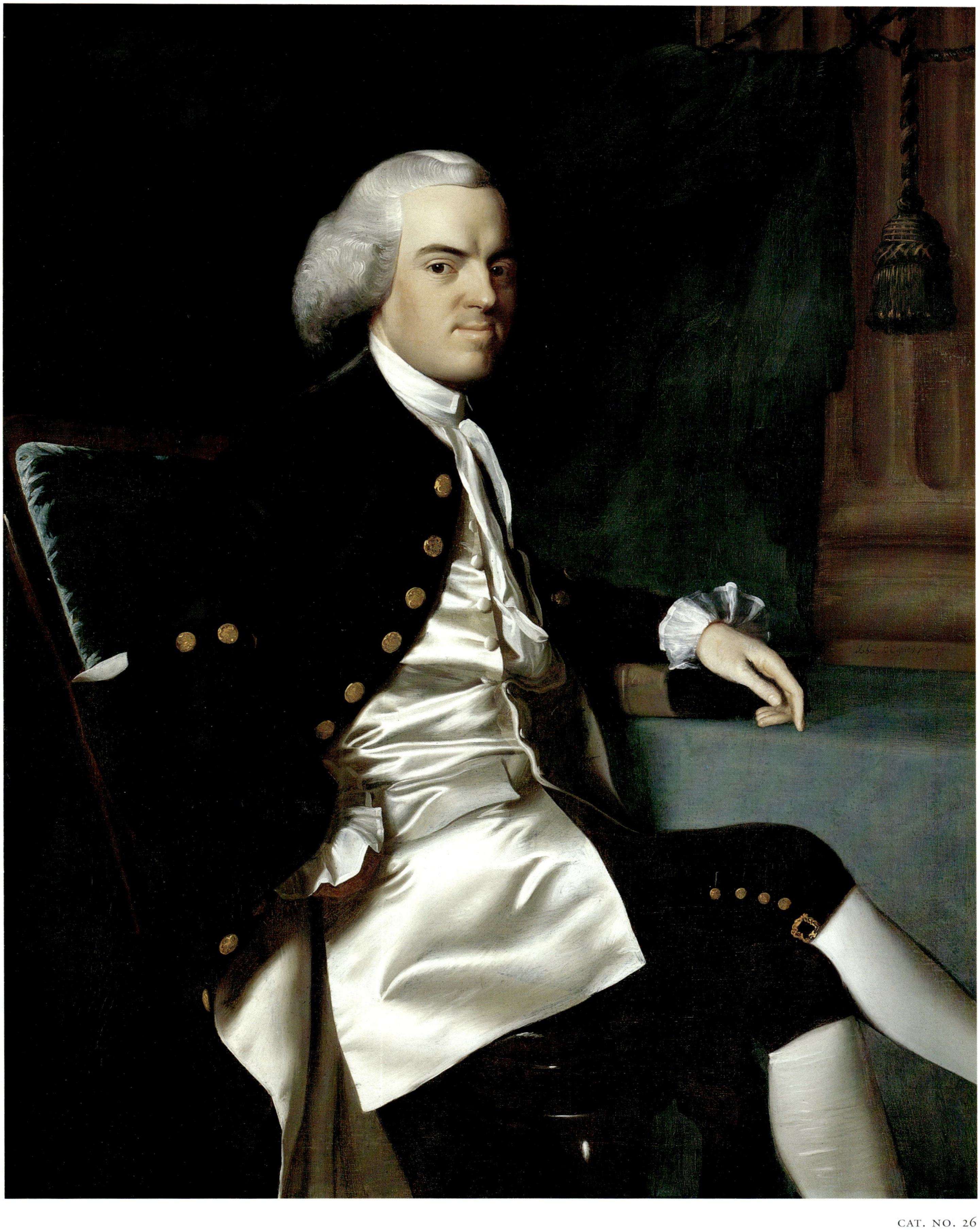

CAT. NO. 26

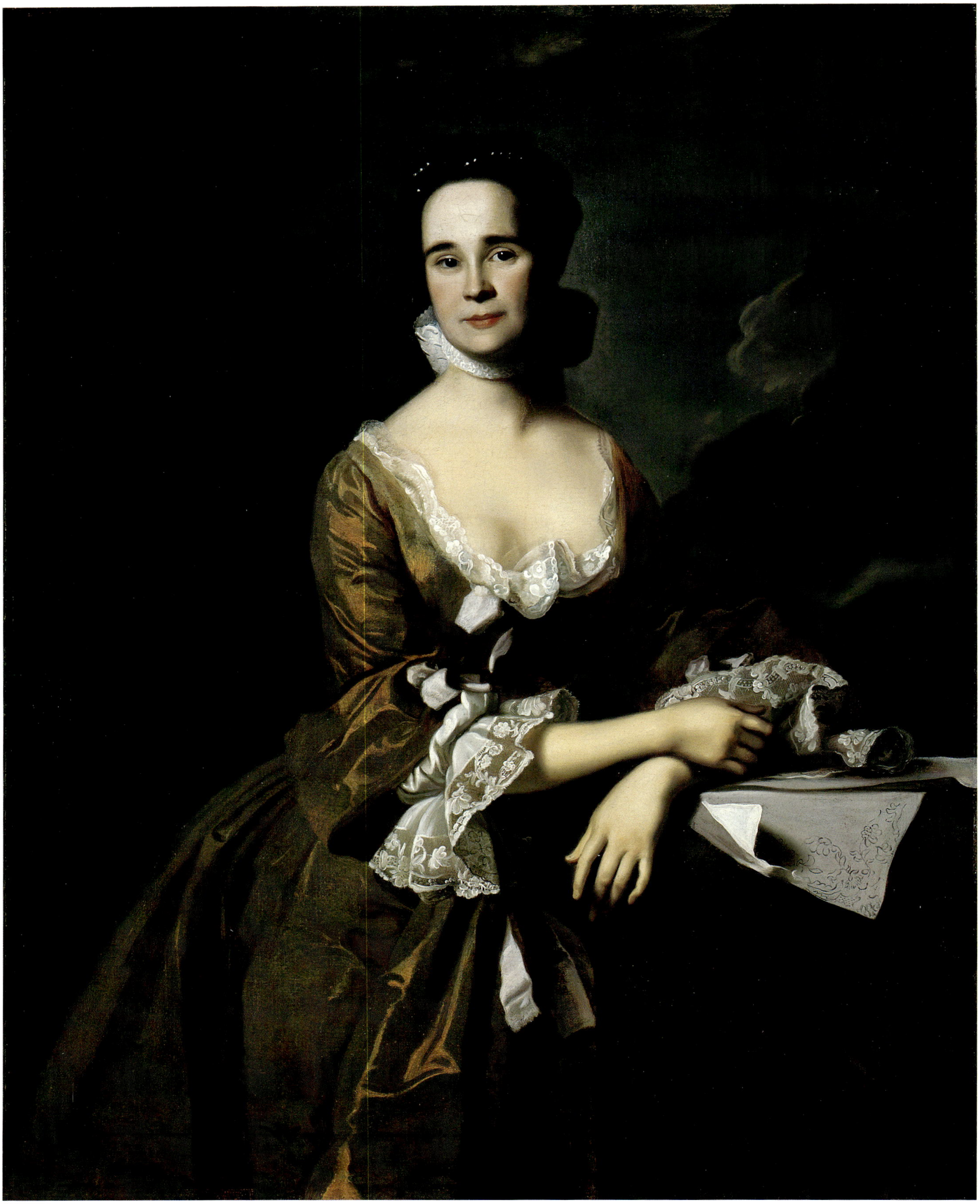

CAT. NO. 27

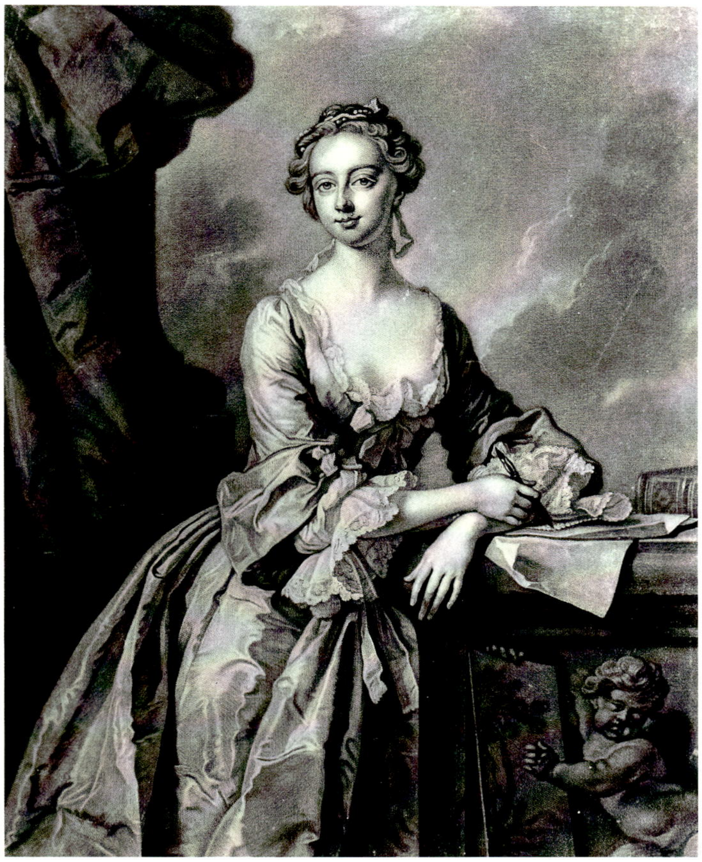

FIG. 11. John Faber (English, 1684–1756), after Thomas Hudson (English, 1701–1779). *Mary Finch, Viscountess Andover*, 1746. Mezzotint; 31.1 x 25.1 cm (12¼ x 9⅞ in.). The Trustees of the British Museum, London.

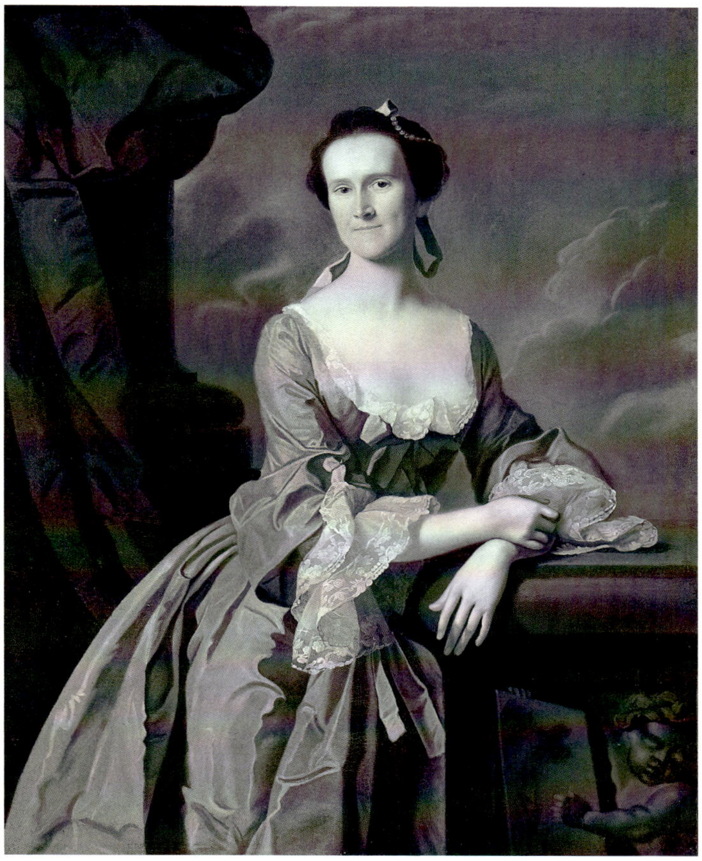

FIG. 12. John Singleton Copley (1738–1815). *Mrs. John Amory (Katherine Greene)*, c. 1763. Oil on canvas; 125.7 x 101.6 cm (49½ x 40 in.). Museum of Fine Arts, Boston (37.36).

NOTES

1. Paul Staiti, "Accounting for Copley," in Carrie Rebora et al., *John Singleton Copley in America*, exh. cat. (New York, Metropolitan Museum of Art, 1995), p. 35.

2. Jules Prown, *John Singleton Copley* (Cambridge, Mass., 1966), vol. 1, pp. 164, 127. According to Prown, Copley painted fourteen members of the Greene family, to which the Hubbards belonged. Daniel Hubbard's annual income was a large sum for a merchant, when compared to that of a professional craftsman, who might earn forty pounds in a year.

3. For Theodore Stebbins, these portraits of the Hubbards differ from those of other couples Copley painted, because "the woman takes the customary masculine standing position and holds papers; Mrs. Hubbard strikes us as ready to take charge, and her husband sits and waits"; see Theodore E. Stebbins, Jr., "An American Despite Himself," in Rebora et al. (note 1), p. 87.

4. Another portrait of a merchant by Copley featuring this prop is *Nicholas Boylston* (1767; Harvard University Portrait Collection, Cambridge, Mass.).

5. Rebora et al. (note 1), pp. 68–70, 84.

6. Mary and Katherine Greene were both married in 1757. Prown noted ([note 2], p. 127) that the income of John Amory, Katherine's husband, was "very high" compared to that of Daniel Hubbard, which was "medium." The Hubbards may have chosen the same pose for Mary to express family affinity and to emulate their wealthier relations. Both date and style indicate that Mrs. Hubbard's portrait was painted later than her cousin's.

7. There is some debate over whether the dresses in these paintings were copied directly from the print, were props in Copley's studio, or were custom-made for the women to wear during their sittings. For more on these questions, see Trevor J. Fairbrother, "John Singleton Copley's Use of British Mezzotints for His American Portraits: A Reappraisal Prompted by New Discoveries," *Arts Magazine* 55, 7 (Mar. 1981), pp. 122–30; and Frederick A. Sweet, "Mezzotint Sources of American Colonial Portraits," *Art Quarterly* 14 (summer 1951), pp. 148–57.

8. See Mary Beth Norton, *Liberty's Daughters: The Revolutionary Experience of American Women, 1750–1800* (Boston, 1980), pp. 20–26, for more about the role of needlework in the lives of urban women.

9. Morrison H. Heckscher, "Copley's Picture Frames," in Rebora et al. (note 1), p. 158 n. 11.

28. CARD TABLE, 1755/90

New York

Mahogany with tulip poplar, white oak, and white pine; 69.9 x 88.3 (open) x 87.6 cm (27½ x 34¾ x 34½ in.)

Restricted gifts of Mr. and Mrs. Robert Brown and Mrs. Potter Palmer IV; Estate of Annie Dunlop in memory of Annie Wisner; Robert Allerton and Bessie Bennett endowments, 1973.564

Card playing in America was a popular pursuit among all classes during the eighteenth century. While card games were enjoyed in many fashionable homes, they were also played in taverns and assembly halls. The activity became so widespread that legislation was passed to halt the increasing amount of time devoted to it. In 1788 lawmakers in New York made tavern-keepers subject to fines and imprisonment if they allowed card playing in their establishments. Nonetheless, the gentry continued to play nightly games of whist and loo in the privacy of their parlors. A young socialite from Philadelphia, Rebecca Franks, visited New York in 1781 and wrote home to her sister that "few New York ladies know how to entertain company in their houses unless they introduce the card table."[1] Frequent advertisements appeared in papers throughout the colonies announcing new shipments of playing cards and gaming pieces. In 1810 the *Columbia Centinel*, a Boston newspaper, advertised "50 sets of Loo counters, playing cards of the first quality, by the groc dozen, or single pack."[2]

Over one hundred New York serpentine-front card tables survive. As with the Boston bombé chest (see cat. no. 24), production of these tables was confined to a particular area and was not known outside that region.[3] To date, the table has no known European prototype.[4] The gadrooned moldings around the bottom of the serpentine skirt were a common decorative motif on Dutch silver of the seventeenth and early eighteenth centuries and may reflect the influence of immigrant Dutch craftsmen. The heavy, blocked feet, with thick webbing around the talons and a straight rear talon, resemble one of several types of New York claw-and-ball feet.[5]

When opened, the table top has four inset square corners for candlesticks. Four recessed oval wells held playing pieces that were used to keep score in various games. The pieces were usually round, oval, or in the shape of fish, and made of mother-of-pearl or ivory. Many of these tables have or had a small drawer located behind the swing leg that would have held the gaming pieces and the playing cards when not in use. The drawer on the Art Institute's example is still intact. A baize or felt playing surface was a normal feature on most of these

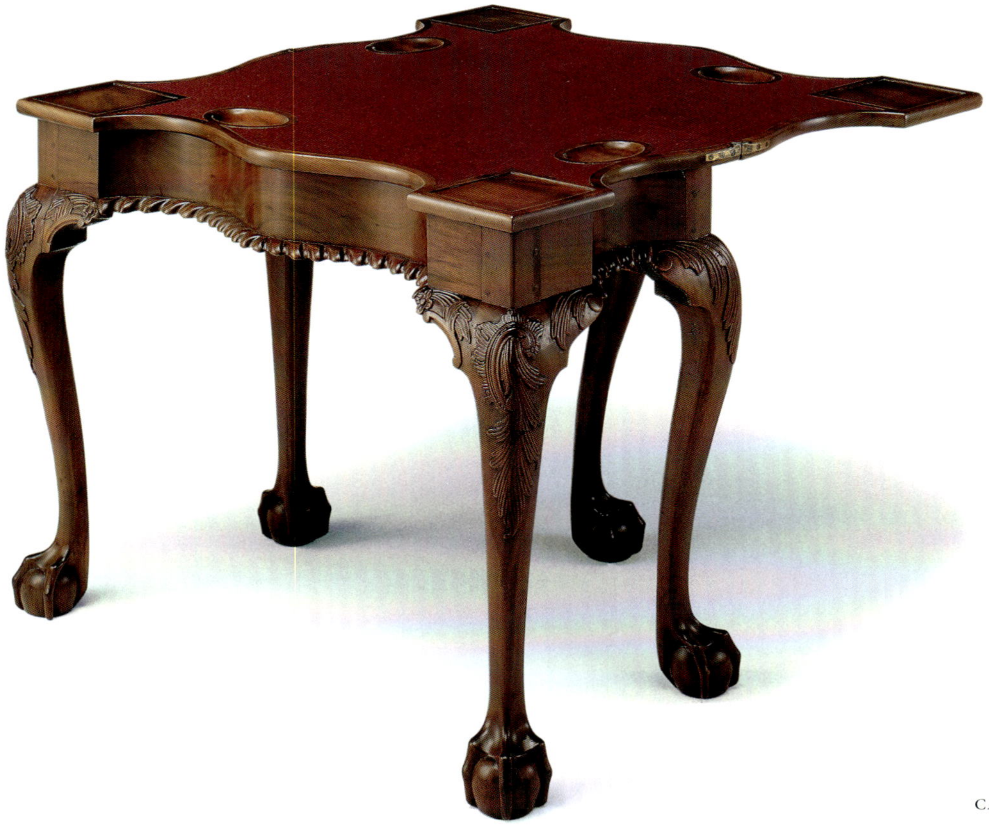

CAT. NO. 28

tables; however, few survive, and the crimson felt on the Art Institute's example is a replacement.

Among the surviving New York serpentine-front, five-legged card tables, there are several methods of construction, suggesting that more than one shop produced these tables. The Art Institute's example is part of a group with identical construction techniques, and similar decorative and functional features. Scholars have labeled this group the "Van Rensselaer" type, after the example at the Metropolitan Museum of Art, New York, which belonged to the family of that name. The design for these tables is the boldest among the several distinct groups.[6] The serpentine shape of the skirt is deeper, and the gadrooned moldings are the most pronounced, having between nine and twelve lobes on either side of the central element on the front of the table. The only feature that varies within the Van Rensselaer group is the decorative treatment of the knee carving, indicating that the tables were most likely made in the same shop but carved by different craftsmen.[7]

The decorative elements of the table unify its design. On the front apron of the table, the projecting blocks at either end bracket the serpentine curve and give the table its sturdy appearance. The applied, gadrooned moldings unite the graceful cabriole legs with the more massive gaming top. Without the gadrooning, the proportions of the table would appear awkward and clumsy. The rhythm created by the gadrooning extends through the shallow carving on the knee and knee returns, continues down the boldly curving legs and ends at the elongated, fingerlike claws that firmly grip the balls of the feet.

NOTES

1. Gerald W. R. Ward, "'Avarice and Conviviality': Card Playing in Federal America," in Benjamin A. Hewitt et al., *The Work of Many Hands: Card Tables in Federal America*, exh. cat. (New Haven, Conn., Yale University Art Gallery, 1982), p. 17.

2. Catherine Perry Hargrave, *A History of Playing Cards and a Bibliography of Cards and Gaming* (Boston, 1930), p. 309.

3. Two serpentine-front card tables were displayed at Temple-Newsam House in Leeds, England. One was part of the Stannus collection, owned by the Society for the Protection of Ancient Buildings (SPAB) in London. Unfortunately, the table was stolen in 1986; see letter from Philip Venning, Secretary of SPAB, to Seth A. Thayer, Jan. 23, 1995, Files of the Department of American Arts, The Art Institute of Chicago. The Stannus table was identified as English in John Kirk, *American Furniture and the British Tradition to 1830* (New York, 1982), p. 18; and Morrison Heckscher, "The New York Serpentine Card Table," *Antiques* 103, 5 (May 1973), p. 982. Its place of origin, however, cannot be verified. According to Christopher Gilbert, Curator of Furniture at Temple-Newsam House, another serpentine-front card table is still on display there. Catalogued as an English reproduction, but thought by scholars to be a period New York card table, the table's integrity has been compromised by extensive restoration. Christopher Gilbert and Frank Levy assisted with this reference.

4. An earlier, rectilinear, square-cornered card table form does exist in England and New England; see David Barquist, *American Tables and Looking Glasses in the Mabel Brady Garvin and Other Collections at Yale University* (New Haven, Conn., 1992), p. 169; for an example, see, pp. 165–66, cat. no. 72.

5. John T. Kirk, *American Chairs: Queen Anne and Chippendale* (New York, 1972), p. 45.

6. Known tables in the Van Rensselaer group include one in a private collection and one each in the following public collections: the Metropolitan Museum of Art, New York (47.35), the Henry Francis du Pont Winterthur Museum, Winterthur, Del. (59.2843), the Chipstone Foundation, Milwaukee, Wis. (1958.3), and the New Jersey Historical Society, Newark, N.J. For more information on the varying shop traditions, see Frank M. Levy, "The Most Opulent Form: A Structural Analysis of New York Five-Legged Card Tables" (M.A. thesis, University of Delaware, 1991).

7. Levy (note 6), pp. 45, 51. The Art Institute table has gadrooning with eleven lobes and carved C-scrolls and acanthus leaves on the knees.

29. SIDE CHAIR, 1742/70

New York area

Mahogany, white oak, white pine, and beech; 108.6 x 58.4 x 54.6 cm (41¾ x 23 x 21½ in.)

Inscribed, on right interior seat rail: *IIII*

Richard T. Crane, Jr., Memorial Fund, 1971.25

This New York side chair is one of eight known to survive with the "RML" cipher-pierced back splat.[1] Scholars differ in their opinions of the date of the chairs and to whom the cipher refers. The chairs may have been made to commemorate the marriage of Judge Robert and Margaret Beekman Livingston in 1742 or that of their son Robert Livingston, Jr., to Mary Stevens in 1770.[2]

The first Robert Livingston to reside in America was granted a royal land patent by the governor of New York in 1686 to control forested lands along the Hudson River. These lands eventually grew to encompass 160,000 acres, known as Livingston Manor, and extended between the Hudson River and the Massachusetts border. A portion of this property eventually passed to Judge Robert Livingston and, in turn, to his son Chancellor Robert Livingston, Jr., grandson and great-grandson, respectively, of the original Robert.[3] Both father and son were prominent, powerful men in their eras, and such a stylish set of chairs could have been made for either one.

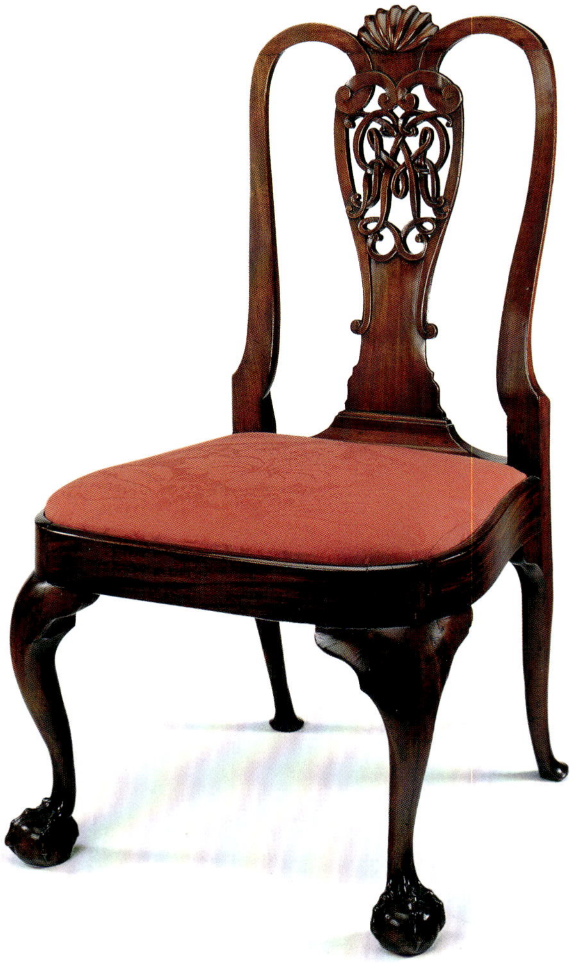

CAT. NO. 29

The chair is an amalgam of regional styles. From the seat up, it exhibits New England design traits, particularly with the rounded shoulders of the stiles and the carved shell at the crest rail. From the seat down, the chair follows New York design characteristics, having delicate rear legs ending in pad feet, reverse-curve knee brackets, and large, round, ball-and-claw feet.[4]

The chair exhibits a mixture of crude carving techniques and well-executed cabinetry elements. A close examination of the cipher-pierced splat reveals the carving to be a credible attempt at a sophisticated design by a naive craftsman. The cipher was most likely carved by an apprentice or rural cabinetmaker using a saw and chisel.[5] The scrolls that surround the cipher are simple and heavy, and reveal the lack of technical skill on the part of the carver. The same may be said of the seven-lobed shell that surmounts the crest rail: it lacks the vibrancy of carved shells from Philadelphia and the grace of those from Newport or Boston.

In contrast to the unskilled carvings are the strong and elegant curves of the stiles, legs, and seat of the chair. The well-proportioned round shoulders of the crest rail drop perfectly into the sweeping lines of the conforming stiles, which transform themselves into the round, inwardly curving rear legs and pad feet. The broad, undecorated horseshoe-shaped seat flows into the uncarved knees of the front cabriole legs, perhaps the most successful part of this chair. The legs of the cipher chair have a movement rarely encountered on other New York chairs of the period, whose legs tend to be blocky and heavy. The broad expanse of uncarved mahogany at the top of the knee flows effortlessly into the delicate ankles, which turn inward toward the center of the chair, only to be brought forward again by the large, round ball-and-claw feet. Powerful talons with inch-long claws grip the ball feet. This contrast to the ungainly carving on the back of the chair may indicate that more than one hand was responsible for the carved elements on the chairs.

NOTES

1. Five chairs are in public institutions, and three are in private collections. Aside from The Art Institute of Chicago, the museums that have the chairs in their collections are Yale University Art Gallery, New Haven, Conn., Mabel Brady Garvin Collection (marked "I" on the seat rail; see John Kirk, *American Chairs: Queen Anne and Chippendale* [New York, 1972], no. 127);

CAT. NO. 29, DETAIL

Henry Francis du Pont Winterthur Museum, Winterthur, Del. (marked "I+" on the seat rail; see Charles F. Hummel, "Queen Anne and Chippendale Furniture in the Henry Francis du Pont Winterthur Museum, Part 2," *Antiques* 48, 12 [Dec. 1970], p. 904); Museum of Fine Arts, Houston, Bayou Bend Collection (marked "III" on the seat rail; see David Warren, *Bayou Bend* [Houston, 1975], p. 25); Cleveland Museum of Art (marked "VI" on the seat rail; see Henry Hawley, "A Livingston Chair," *Bulletin of the Cleveland Museum of Art* 76, 9 [spring 1989], p. 327); and Metropolitan Museum of Art, New York (marked "o" on the seat rail), where it is on loan.

2. Cleveland, Yale, Winterthur, and Bayou Bend all date their chairs between 1742 and 1760, and contend that their chairs were made for Judge Robert Livingston and his wife. Cleveland bases its dating on the needlework seat cover, which bears the initials of another child of Judge Robert and Margaret Livingston; see Hawley (note 1), p. 329. Yale's and Winterthur's chairs are so dated because their overall design follows the style of mid-century furniture and silver; see Patricia Kane, *Three Hundred Years of American Seating Furniture* (Boston, 1976), p. 81, cat. no. 61, and Hummel (note 1), p. 904. Bayou Bend bases its dating on the theory that the chair design would have been out of fashion by 1770; see Warren (note 1), p. 25.

3. Ruth Piwonka, *A Portrait of Livingston Manor, 1686–1750* (New York, 1986), pp. 21–51.

4. For more information on regional characteristics of chairs, see Kirk (note 1).

5. Hummel (note 1), p. 906.

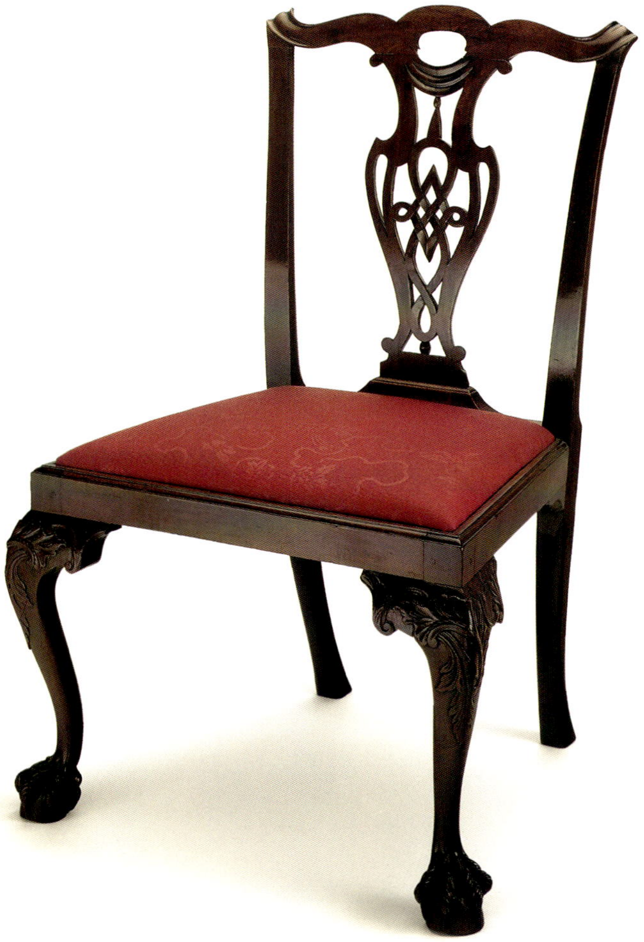

CAT. NO. 30

30. SIDE CHAIR, 1770/85

Boston

Mahogany with oak and maple;

93.3 x 54.6 x 44.8 cm (36¾ x 21½ x 17⅝ in.)

Incised on rear seat rail: *V*; original maple slip seat incised on rear rail: *VIII*

Helen Bowen Blair Fund, 1991.266

The design of this chair is based both on an English prototype that was exported to Boston in the mid-eighteenth century and on a plate in the third edition of Thomas Chippendale's pattern book, *The Gentleman and Cabinet-Maker's Director*, published in 1762. Sometime around 1750, William Phillips of Boston imported a set of chairs from England for his own use (see fig. 13). The chairs have the same asymmetrical leaf carving on the knees and similar hairy-paw feet as the chair in the Art Institute's collection. The museum's chair also incorporates the general design of the English chairs' crest rails and certain portions of the back splat.

Portions of this Boston chair were also derived from plate 11 in Chippendale's *Director* (fig. 14). The plate's three chair designs all exhibit elements in common with the Art Institute's chair. The museum's chair blends these illustrated elements: undecorated stiles; a crest rail with scrolled ears; a pierced back splat; flared rear feet; and a thin, trapezoidal seat.

This chair is part of a small group of Boston hairy-paw-footed furniture that includes three other chairs from the same set, a drop-leaf table, and a set of chairs that belonged to the Marquand family of Boston and Newburyport.[1] The chair is also related to pieces with similar features, but with ball-and-claw feet. The two types of furniture were most likely made by one shop, for chairs in both groups share the same template for the crest rail. The corner blocks on many chairs and two settees from both groups are all triangular, with slightly chamfered edges; the blocks are attached with either two or four large-headed nails. The front legs of all the furniture in both groups measure 14⅝ inches and have the same asymmetrical C-scroll carving on the knees.[2]

The Art Institute's chair illustrates the transition from the Rococo style beginning just before the American Revolution to the neoclassical style, which predominated in the colonies after the Revolution. The elaborate carving, so pervasive during the height of the Rococo era, is relegated on this chair to the knees and feet, where the crisp, bold carving provides a striking contrast to the flat plane of the chair back. One would expect the stiles on this chair to be stop-fluted, as they are on related high-style Rococo examples from Boston.[3] Instead, the stiles provide a simple framework for the elegant, classical, urn-shaped back splat, which has been cut and pierced but, with the exception of the swag at the top of the splat, not carved. The swag-and-tassel motif at the top of the urn, usually much more pronounced and highly carved, has been reduced here to an outline.[4]

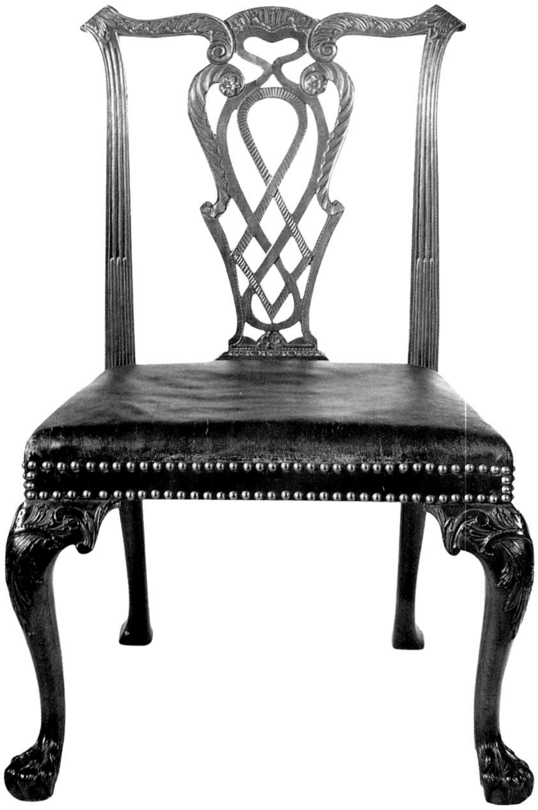

FIG. 13. "T. Hooper." *Side Chair*, c. 1750. Mahogany with beech; 94.6 x 48.9 cm (37¼ x 19¼ in.). Museum of Fine Arts, Boston, Gift of Mrs. Joshua Crane, Sr., in memory of her husband (30.726).

NOTES

1. One chair is in the collection of the Henry Francis du Pont Winterthur Museum (see Joseph Downs, *American Furniture: Queen Anne and Chippendale Periods* [New York, 1952], p. 151); one is in the collection of Barry Freedman (see *Antiques* 147, 1 [Jan. 1995], p. 62); and one is in a private collection. The drop-leaf table is illustrated in Rodriquez Roque, *American Furniture at Chipstone* (Madison, Wis., 1984), p. 291, cat. no. 135. The Marquand chairs are illustrated in New York, Israel Sack, Inc., *Opportunities in American Antiques* 4, 25 (June 1, 1974), p. 1080.

2. Mary Ellen Hayward Yehia, "Ornamental Carving on Boston Furniture of the Chippendale Style," in Walter M. Whitehill, ed., *Boston Furniture of the Eighteenth Century* (Boston, 1974), p. 206. For illustrations of the related furniture, see Yehia, pp. 197–214; Luke Beckerdite, "Carving Practices in Eighteenth-Century Boston," in *Old-Time New England: New England Furniture* (Boston, 1987), pp. 128–36; and Morrison H. Heckscher and Leslie

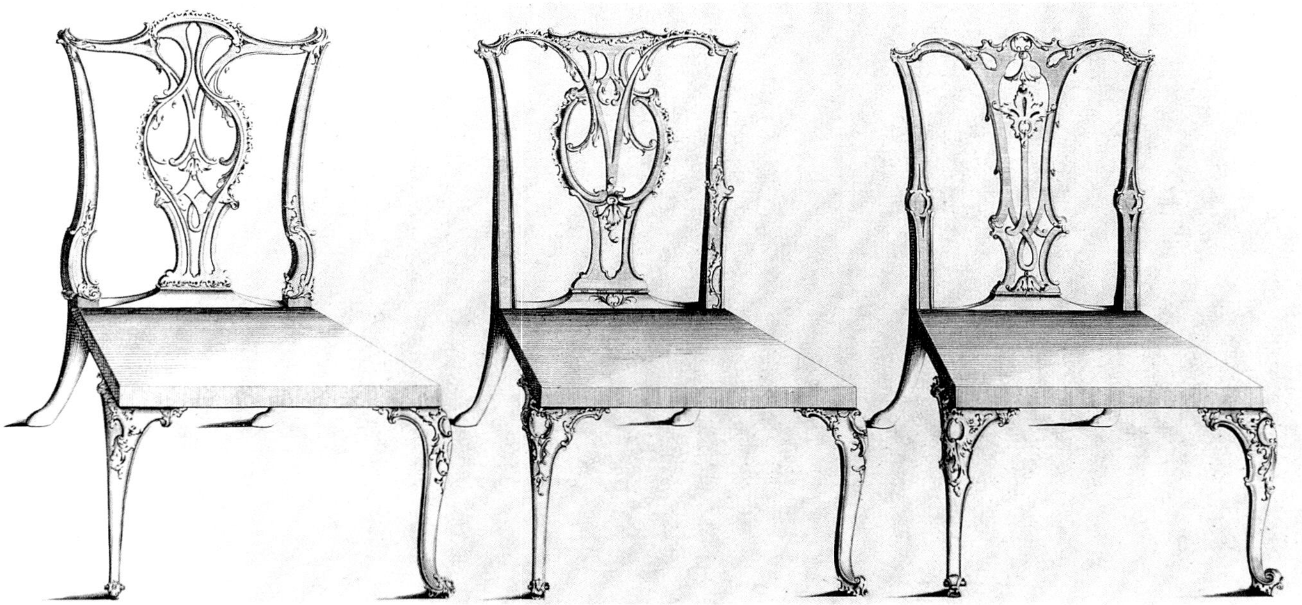

FIG. 14. Thomas Chippendale, *The Gentleman and Cabinet-Maker's Director* (London, 1762), pl. 11. Collection of Ryerson and Burnham Libraries, The Art Institute of Chicago.

Greene Bowman, *American Rococo, 1750–1775: Elegance in Ornament*, exh. cat. (New York, Metropolitan Museum of Art, 1992), pp. 147–51.

3. Israel Sack (note 1), p. 1080; and Brock Jobe and Myrna Kaye, *New England Furniture: The Colonial Era* (Boston, 1984), p. 393, pl. 114a.

4. Jobe and Kaye (note 3), p. 392.

31. MOVEMENT BY JOHN WOOD, JR. (1736–1793)

Tall-Case Clock, 1765/75

Philadelphia

Mahogany and tulip wood, brass, iron, and glass;
254 x 47.6 x 22.9 cm (100 x 18¾ x 9 in.)

Helen Bowen Blair Fund, 1990.175

By 1765 tensions between the colonies and England had escalated to a breaking point. A series of taxes on imported goods were instituted by King George III to defray the cost of maintaining a British army in the colonies during and after the French and Indian War (1754–63). Such so-called taxation without representation led colonists to take their first steps toward rebellion. Early in 1769, over three hundred Philadelphia merchants, along with merchants in other colonies, signed nonimportation agreements that placed embargoes on British-made goods shipped to the colonies.[1] The agreements were a boon to local industry. While merchants bemoaned the loss in income, local craftsmen scrambled to produce colonial-made goods that would replace British-made ones.[2]

Foreseeing tremendous opportunities in the colonies, English and European-trained craftsmen emigrated in droves to Philadelphia, Boston, New York, and other cities and towns. Many of these craftsmen were unable to establish themselves in their own businesses and instead became attached to local shops. Knowing the importance that wealthy colonists put on having items in the latest fashions from Europe, many craftsmen placed advertisements in local papers that announced their own arrivals from London, or those of new workmen. Before the signing of the nonimportation agreements, John Wood, Jr., had advertised a variety of clocks and watches, as well as parts for them, that were both imported and of his own making. After 1769, however, his advertisements emphasized Philadelphia-made goods and the expansion of his business to include London-trained craftsmen.[3]

John Wood's clock works and case in the museum's collection are excellent examples of the high style embraced by

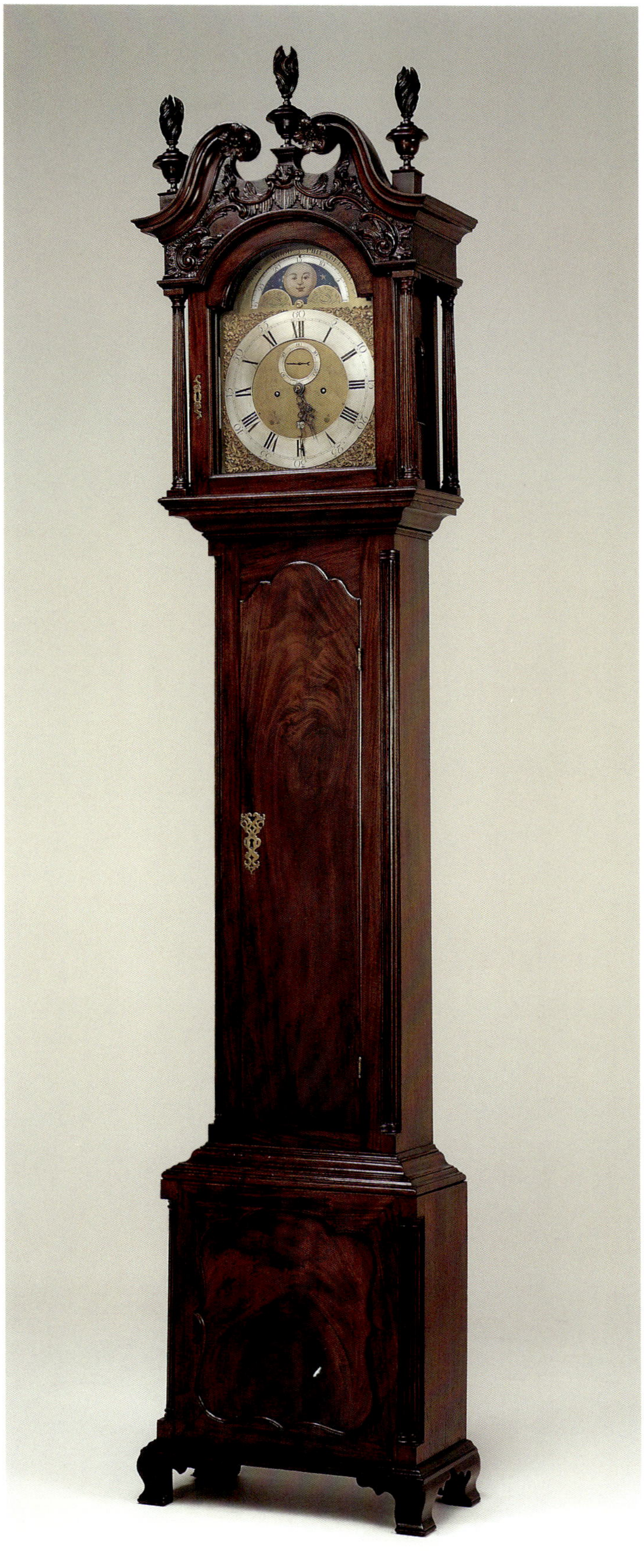

CAT. NO. 31

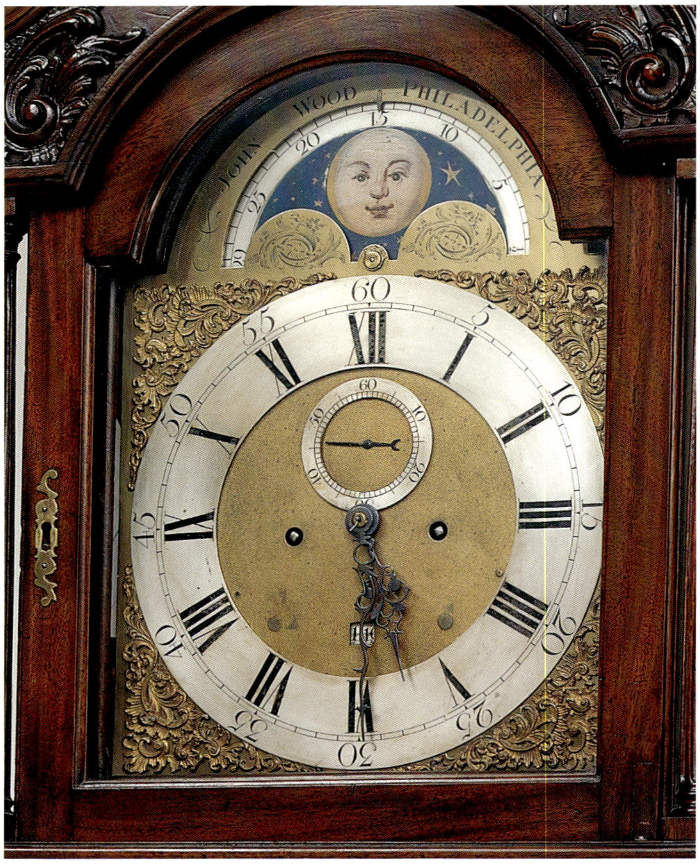

CAT. NO. 31, DETAIL

Philadelphians in the final decades of the eighteenth century. The urn-and-flame finials are masterfully carved, though only the proper right flame and the two side urns are original. The delicate nature of the turnings required that the finials be constructed out of three separate pieces; the flame, the urn, and the base of the urn are all attached by dowels. Visually, the three distinct portions of the clock are linked through careful planning of the design. The arch of the bonnet door is echoed in both the waist door and in the inset panel in the base. Freestanding columns are visually extended down the clock by the carved, attached quarter-columns at both waist and base. The beautifully constructed inset panel at the base was much more complicated to execute than the applied panels usually seen on Philadelphia clocks of the period.[4]

There are no known records that identify the craftsman who made this clock case for Wood. From the style of the case, we know that maker and carver were both well versed in Rococo design and may have learned the style through pattern books they either owned or could find in local libraries. Between 1764 and 1769, for example, the Library Company of Philadelphia had acquired for its collection the third edition of Thomas Chippendale's pattern book, *The Gentleman and Cabinet-Maker's Director*, a major source book for Philadelphia Rococo design. Founded in 1731, the Library Company was the first subscription library in America, and in 1769 it counted among its members nine prominent cabinetmakers and many other craftsmen, including John Wood, Jr.[5] In addition to *The Gentleman and Cabinet-Maker's Director*, there were numerous other design books available in Philadelphia from which craftsmen could find inspiration.[6] If the carver of the clock case had consulted Chippendale's book, he may have taken his designs for the carving on the tympanum of the clock from plates 194–95, "Designs of Borders for Paper Hangings &c." (see fig. 15).[7] The borders in the Chippendale book employ such Rococo ornamental motifs as leaves, C- and

FIG. 15. Thomas Chippendale, *The Gentleman and Cabinet-Maker's Director* (London, 1762), pl. 194. Collection of Ryerson and Burnham Libraries, The Art Institute of Chicago.

S-scrolls, foliage, and shells. The lively, tightly controlled carving of the foliage and C-scrolls on the tympanum of the clock reflects the same spirit found in Chippendale designs. Most likely, the carver took his inspiration from several of these designs. Designs inspired by pattern books rarely followed the source line for line.

The brass face of the clock is standard for the period. Approximately twelve inches across, it has a large applied brass ring to mark the hours and minutes and a smaller ring to mark the seconds. Both rings are silvered for legibility.[8] A most remarkable feature of the face is the brilliant blue and gold dial proclaiming the phases of the moon. The captivatingly simple rendering of the face painted on the surface of the full moon functions as a transitional plane between the face of the clock and the tympanum carving. The paint appears to be original and is in excellent condition.

Such an exquisite clock was surely made for an important Philadelphia client to display in a public room. A mahogany clock case with "Scroll pediment head," "Column corners," and "Fret Dentils Shield Roses and Blazes" cost anywhere between 10 and 12 pounds.[9] This price does not include the works or the glass for the bonnet, which may have increased the cost by 6 to 8 pounds, resulting in a final price of 16 to 20 pounds, a mighty sum considering craftsmen and laborers of the period made 35 to 60 pounds a year in wages.[10]

NOTES

1. Harry M. Tinkcom, "The Revolutionary City, 1765–1783," in Russell F. Weigley, ed., *Philadelphia: A Three-Hundred-Year History* (New York, 1982), p. 115.

2. For a more complete description of the events surrounding the signing of the nonimportation agreements, see chapter 1 in Morrison H. Heckscher and Leslie Greene Bowman, *American Rococo, 1750–1775: Elegance in Ornament*, exh. cat. (New York, Metropolitan Museum of Art, 1992), pp. 1–15.

3. See Wood's advertisement in the *Pennsylvania Journal* (Oct. 24, 1771), in Alfred Coxe Prime, *The Arts and Crafts in Philadelphia, Maryland, and South Carolina, 1721–1785: Gleanings from Newspapers* (Topsfield, Mass., 1929), p. 270.

4. For a variety of examples, see James W. Gibbs, *Pennsylvania Clocks and Watches: Antique Timepieces and Their Makers* (University Park, Pa., 1984).

5. Wood had previously been a member of the Union Library Company of Philadelphia, which merged with the Library Company in 1769; see letter from Manon Théroux, Reference Librarian and Rare Book Cataloguer, Library Company of Philadelphia, May 3, 1995, Files of the Department of American Arts, The Art Institute of Chicago.

6. Morrison H. Heckscher, "English Furniture Pattern Books in Eighteenth-Century America," in Luke Beckerdite, ed., *American Furniture* (Milwaukee, Wis., 1994), pp. 184–97.

7. Thomas Chippendale, *The Gentleman and Cabinet-Maker's Director: Being a Large Collection of the Most Elegant and Useful Designs of Household Furniture in the Most Fashionable Taste*, 3rd ed. (1762; reprint, New York, 1938), pls. 194–95.

8. For a description of the standard Philadelphia clock face, see Heckscher and Bowman (note 2), p. 66.

9. William Macpherson Horner, Jr., *Blue Book of Philadelphia Furniture: William Penn to George Washington* (1935; reprint, Washington, D.C., 1977), p. 129.

10. Gary B. Nash, "Artisans and Politics in Eighteenth-Century Philadelphia," in Ian Quimby, ed., *The Craftsman in Early America* (New York, 1984), p. 65.

32. BANCROFT WOODCOCK (1732–1817)

Sugar Dish with Cover and Cream Pot, 1765/75

Wilmington, Delaware

Silver; sugar dish: 18.6 x 6.7 (diam. at base) cm (7 5/16 x 2 5/8 in.); cream pot: 10.8 x 5.7 (diam. at base) cm (4 1/4 x 2 1/4 in.)

Sugar dish marked on bottom: *B:WOODCOCK* (in a conforming rectangle); inscribed: *S·W to E·R*; cream pot marked on bottom: *B·WOODCOCK* (in a conforming rectangle)

Gift of the Antiquarian Society, 1978.137a–b, 1978.138

Bancroft Woodcock was born in 1732 in Wilmington, Delaware, into a devout Quaker family that had emigrated from Ireland. He opened a silver shop in Wilmington in 1754, and over the following decades his business prospered. Like many craftsmen in colonial America, Woodcock had other sources of income besides his main trade. From 1772 to 1794, he was paid yearly by the Borough of Wilmington to take care of the town fire engines. He also owned and leased no fewer than six lots of property in Wilmington.[1] By the end of his career as a silversmith, he was being issued warrants by the state of Pennsylvania to conduct land surveys on over 3,000 acres of land in the southwestern portion of the state where he may have been involved in land speculation.[2]

The Art Institute's covered sugar dish and cream pot probably date from before the Revolution, when the prevailing taste in the area surrounding Philadelphia was for the elaborate Rococo style fashionable in Europe. The two pieces are superlative examples of the "double-bellied" form favored throughout the colonies during the Rococo period and preva-

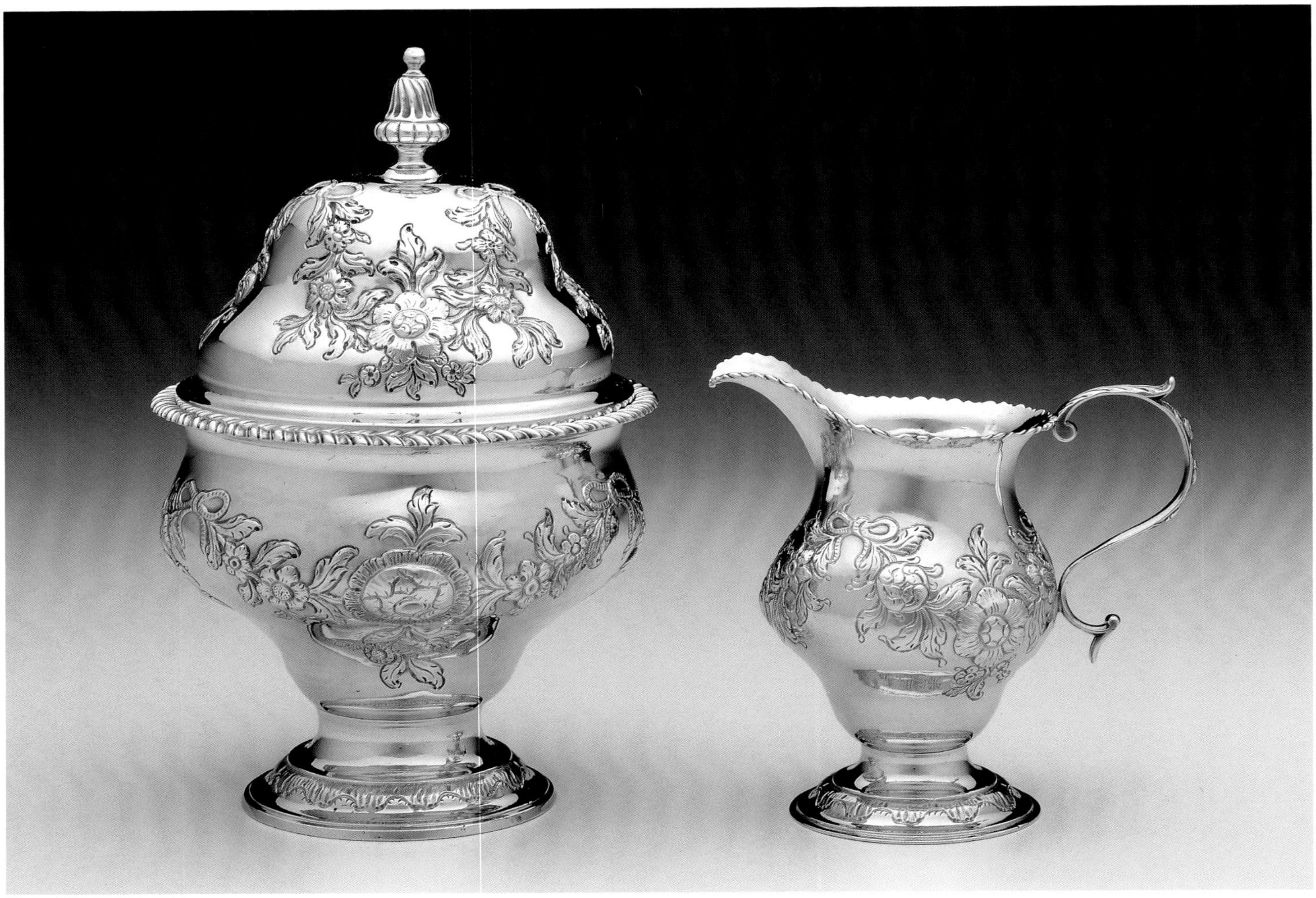

CAT. NO. 32

lent in Woodcock's oeuvre until about 1785, when he began designing in the newly popular neoclassical style.[3] The chased surface decoration was worked with a small hammer and chisels, which involved both raising and inscribing the flat surface to attain a bolder and more sculptural decorative effect than could be achieved through engraving; no silver was removed and no cutting device employed in the process.[4] The naturalistic design of the flower garland is typical of the Rococo decoration found on American objects of this period. The foliate design is carefully controlled and spare in its naturalism, never veering from the intended pattern.

It is not uncommon to find matching silver sugar dishes and cream pots surviving from eighteenth-century America, because they were often ordered to complement an English or Asian porcelain teapot and matching cups.[5] Because of the costliness of silver, it was usual to order one's silver piecemeal, and therefore to have a tea or coffee service comprising pieces from different periods. While the Art Institute's sugar dish and cream pot are identical to each other in style and decoration, there are indications that the pieces may have been made at different times. Engraved initials of the original owners appear only on the underside of the sugar dish and Woodcock's touch mark, on the bottom of each piece, varies. In the chronology of Woodcock's marks, the double-pellet mark (on the sugar dish) predates the single-pellet mark (on the cream pot).[6] Otherwise, the pattern of the sugar dish differs only in the number and size of the flowers on the garlands; two blossoms appear on either side of the large flower, instead of one, as on the cream pot.

Because these two examples are the only known pieces by Woodcock with such elaborately chased decoration, it is unlikely that he would have executed the garland motif himself. Either he or his client may have had the decoration added by another craftsman after both objects were completed. Several pieces of Philadelphia silver by other makers exhibit similar garland chasing.[7]

NOTES

1. David Warren, "Bancroft Woodcock: Silversmith, Friend, and Landholder," *Bancroft Woodcock: Silversmith*, exh. cat. (Wilmington, Del., Historical Society of Delaware, 1976), unpag.

2. Stuart L. Warter, "The Wandering Woodcocks of Pennsylvania: Bancroft, Isaac, and John (Part I)," *Silver* 24, 5 (Sept./Oct. 1991), p. 9.

3. A neoclassical, helmet-shaped cream pot by Woodcock dating between 1791 and 1800 is also in the Art Institute's collection (1941.94).

4. Morrison H. Heckscher and Leslie Greene Bowman, *American Rococo, 1750–1775: Elegance in Ornament*, exh. cat. (New York, Metropolitan Museum of Art, 1992), p. 73.

5. Barbara McLean Ward and Gerald W. R. Ward, eds., *Silver in American Life: Selections from the Mabel Brady Garvan and Other Collections at Yale University*, exh. cat. (New Haven, Conn., Yale University Art Gallery, 1979), pp. 104–06.

6. David Warren, Director of the Bayou Bend Collection at the Museum Fine Arts, Houston, supplied this reference to the marks. See also Louise C. Belden, *Marks of American Silversmiths in the Ineson-Bissell Collection* (Charlottesville, Va., 1980), p. 454.

7. A cream pot by Abraham DuBois is in the collection of the Philadelphia Museum of Art; two sauce boats by Joseph Richardson, Sr., are illustrated in Philip H. Hammerslough, *American Silver Collected by Philip H. Hammerslough*, vol. 4 (Hartford, Conn., 1973), p. 6.

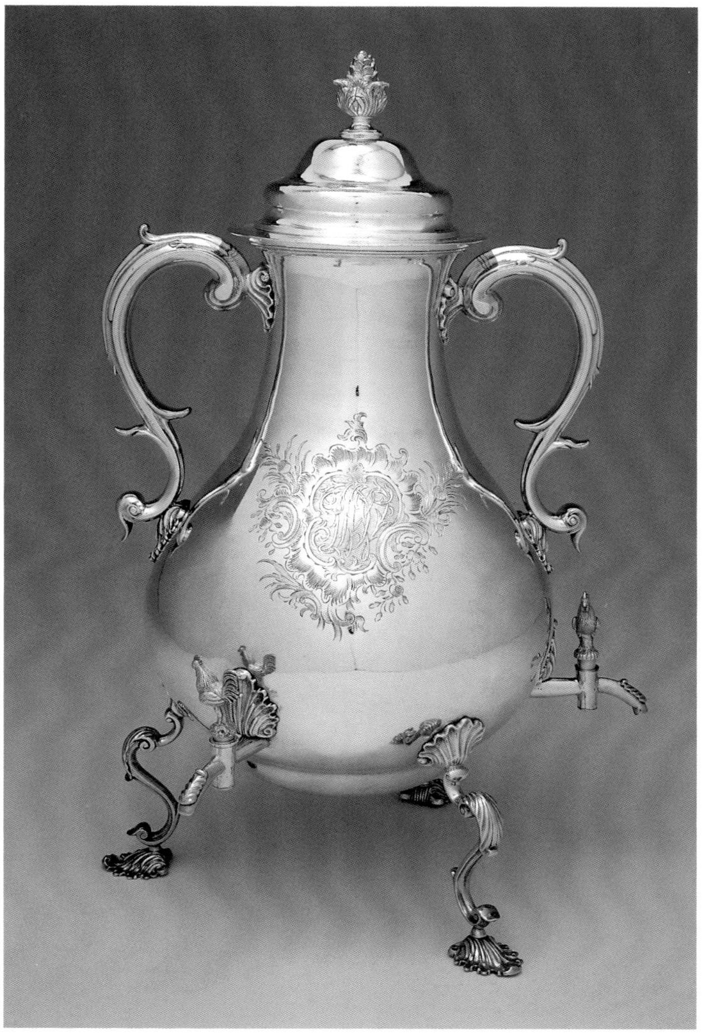

CAT. NO. 33

33. EPHRAIM BRASHER (1744–1810)

Urn with Cover, 1765/75

New York

Silver; 43.8 x 28.1 x 21.4 (diam.) cm (17¼ x 11 1/16 x 8 7/16 in.)

Stamped on bottom twice: *BRASHER*; and once: *N–YORK* (all three in rectangles)

Gift of the Antiquarian Society, 1959.58

Often described as a coffee or tea urn, this object may actually have been used as a wine or punch pot.[1] Two features of the urn support this theory: the absence of a heating apparatus to keep tea or coffee warm; and the presence of a deep convex bottom, which creates a well for sediment from alcoholic beverages. Silver wine fountains appeared in small numbers in England during the Baroque period. These usually took the form of an urn or covered cup, complete with handles and spigot.[2] Punch equipage was on the more elaborate afternoon tea tables in eighteenth-century America. Writing in 1781 about his experiences traveling in America, Baron Cromot du Bourg reported that "about five o'clock they [Americans] take more tea, some wine, madeira [and] punch."[3] Punch was a popular concoction, made from fruit juices, spices, sugar, and spirits, usually rum. In America, it was considered a true sign of hospitality to serve the beverage to one's guests. Bostonian Harrison Gray Otis was known to keep a porcelain bowl filled with punch on his front stair landing every afternoon so that his guests would not be thirsty.[4]

This American urn is the only one known to survive from the colonial period. It was most likely a special commission for an as yet unidentified owner who was familiar with English wine fountains (see fig. 16). The pear-shaped form on three legs was popular in the Netherlands and in England in the early eighteenth century, and was introduced to those two countries by Huguenot goldsmiths who were trained in France but did not remain there, fleeing after 1685 to escape religious persecution.[5] The Huguenots were familiar with the styles that

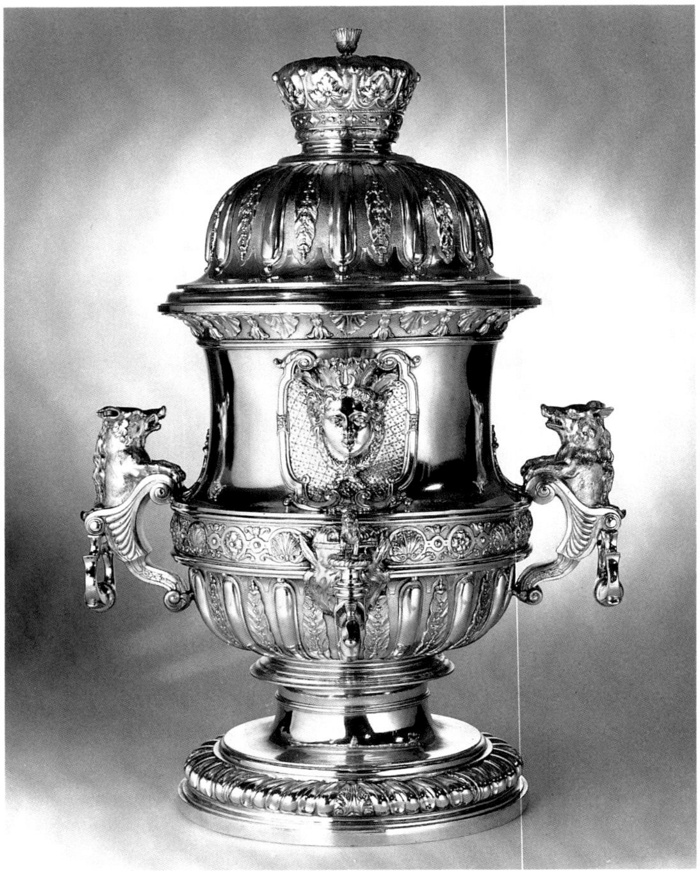

FIG. 16. Peter Archambo (English, active 1720–1749). *Wine Fountain*, 1728. Silver; 70 x 50 cm (27½ x 19⅝ in.). The Worshipful Company of Goldsmiths, London.

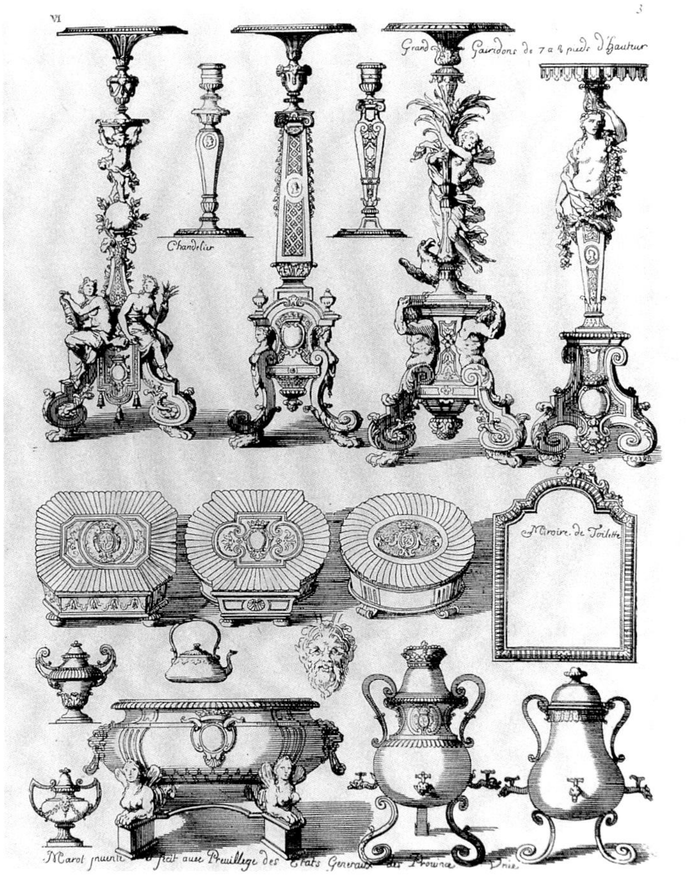

FIG. 17. Daniel Marot (Netherlandish, 1661–1752). *Designs for Silver*, c. 1712. Etching; 28 x 20.3 cm (11 x 8 in.). Collection Le Soufache, École National Supérieure des Beaux-Arts, Paris.

dominated the courts of the French kings and were highly trained in techniques such as casting and applying ornament to the surface of their forms, making their work extremely desirable to Dutch and English patrons.

Using the earlier urn form, Brasher added the element of Rococo asymmetry to his later interpretation. The irregular placement of legs and spigot gives the urn a slightly unbalanced appearance. The cast shells on the feet, spigots, and handles; the acanthus leaves on the ends of the spouts and on the knees of the broken-scroll legs; and the vibrant cartouche engraving—are all commonly identified with the Rococo. Brasher probably took the design from a pattern book such as Daniel Marot's *Nouveaux Livre d'ornements, pour l'utilitée des sculpteurs, et orfèvres,* published in 1712 (see fig. 17). Here, along with designs for candlesticks, mirrors, and small dressing boxes, are two designs for urns. Like other American silversmiths and cabinetmakers, Brasher may have combined elements from several pattern-book plates to create a colonial interpretation of this European form.

NOTES

1. This possibility was suggested in a letter from Peter Guille, then Director of the Sterling and Francine Clark Art Institute in Williamstown, Mass., Aug. 4, 1964, to Vivian J. Scheidemantel, then Associate Curator of Decorative Arts at the Art Institute, Files of the Department of American Arts, The Art Institute of Chicago.

2. Reinier Baarsen et al., *Courts and Colonies: The William and Mary Style in Holland, England, and America,* exh. cat. (New York, Cooper-Hewitt Museum, 1988), p. 119, cat. no. 45.

3. Rodris Roth, "Tea Drinking in Eighteenth-Century America: Its Etiquette and Equipage," *United States National Museum Bulletin* 225 (1961), p. 66.

4. Louise Conway Belden, *The Festive Tradition: Table Decoration and Desserts in America, 1650–1900* (New York, 1983), pp. 237–39.

5. In 1685 Louis XIV revoked the Edict of Nantes, which had protected French Protestants from religious persecution. Holland, ruled by the Protestant William of Orange, later William III of England, became a haven for the persecuted Huguenots. In 1688 William and his queen, Mary, ascended the throne of England, creating another refuge for the Huguenots. See Baarsen et al. (note 2), p. 118, cat. no. 44.

34. JOSEPH RICHARDSON (1711–1784)

Coffeepot, c. 1770

Philadelphia

Silver and wood; 29.5 x 11.6 (diam. at base) cm (11 5/8 x 4 9/16 in.)

Marked twice on underside of base: *IR* (in rectangle); inscribed: *S / I M / 1770*; nineteenth-century engraving on side of coffee pot: *A.S. / to / J.M.M.*

Gift of the Antiquarian Society through the Lena Turnbull Gilbert and Jessie Spalding Landon funds, 1984.50

In June 1767 the British Parliament passed a series of taxes, known as the Townshend Acts, to be imposed upon the American colonies. These taxes were levied as import duties on such staples as paint, glass, and tea. In response, colonists effectively slowed or stopped the import of British goods and turned to locally manufactured products or goods imported from other countries. Tea, which was popular among Americans, was summarily sacrificed in the name of patriotism. A humorous poem entitled "A Lady's Adieu to Her Tea Table" appeared in colonial newspapers shortly before the outbreak of war:

> No more shall my teapot so generous be
> In filling the cups with this pernicious tea,
> For I'll fill it with water and drink out the same
> Before I'll lose LIBERTY that dearest name.[1]

Coffee rapidly replaced tea as the social beverage of choice. A young Virginia gentleman wrote in 1773 in his journal, "After dinner and an agreeable walk. . . . Drank coffee at four, they are now too patriotic to drink tea."[2] Account books for both Boston silversmith Paul Revere and Joseph Richardson reveal that their orders for coffeepots increased tremendously before the Revolution.[3]

Joseph Richardson was the son and apprentice of Philadelphia silversmith Francis Richardson, who died when Joseph was eighteen. In his 1729 will, Richardson's father directed that Joseph carry on the family trade and support his stepmother until he attained the legal age of twenty-one.[4] The elder Richardson bequeathed all his silversmithing tools to Joseph, bypassing his older son Francis Richardson, Jr., who had just finished his apprenticeship with his father. Joseph carried on the silversmithing business until his retirement in 1777, when he was able to pass the business his father had begun seventy-five years earlier to his sons, Joseph, Jr., and Nathaniel, making it the oldest goldsmithing business in Philadelphia at the time.[5]

This coffeepot was most likely fashioned for the wedding of Joseph and Mary (Burling) Smith, who were married in Philadelphia in 1770. The attenuated neck of the body; somewhat flat, double-domed lid; applied, cast shell and acanthus leaf ornaments; and swirled, bell-shaped finial are firmly Rococo in style.

The subtle and graceful curves of the coffeepot are echoed in the smooth flow of the lines of the double-domed lid. The strong, vertical thrust of the spout is mirrored by the inverted shape of the broken-scroll handle, while the mouth of the spout is lightly balanced by the thumb scroll at the top of the handle. The applied ornament complements the pot rather than overwhelms it. The bell finial repeats the form of the pot and continues its verticality. The piece is perfectly placed on a low, trumpet base, which Richardson conceived more as an extension of the pot than as a straightforward stand.

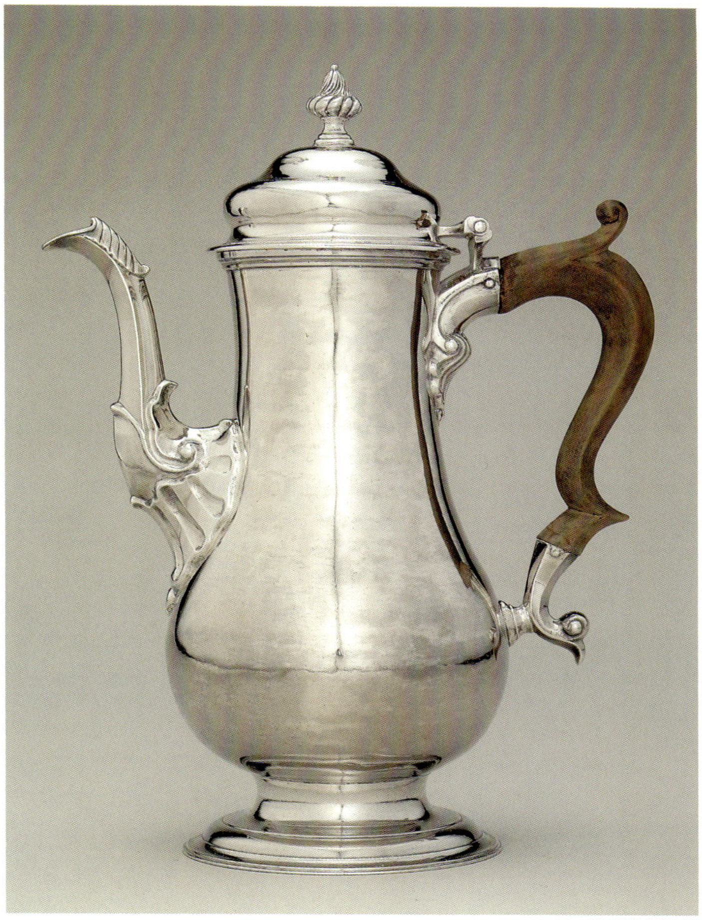

CAT. NO. 34

NOTES

1. The poem appears in its entirety in Rodris Roth, "Tea Drinking in Eighteenth-Century America: Its Etiquette and Equipage," *United States National Museum Bulletin* 225 (1961), p. 68.

2. As quoted in ibid., p. 67.

3 Morrison H. Heckscher and Leslie Greene Bowman, *American Rococo, 1750–1775: Elegance in Ornament*, exh. cat. (New York, Metropolitan Museum of Art, 1992), pp. 95–96; and Martha Gandy Fales, *Joseph Richardson and Family: Philadelphia Silversmiths* (Middletown, Conn., 1974), p. 78.

4. Fales (note 3), p. 32.

5. Ibid., p. 153. See cat. no. 42 in the present volume for an example of the work of Joseph Richardson, Jr., and Nathaniel Richardson.

35. ATTRIBUTED TO THE CHAPIN SCHOOL OF CABINETMAKERS

Pair of Side Chairs, 1771/90

East Windsor, Connecticut

Mahogany with white and yellow pine;
96.7 x 53.3 x 42.5 cm (38 1/8 x 21 x 16 3/4 in.)

Incised in Roman numerals, on the inside rear seat rails: *IIII* (of 1970.33) and *V* (of 1970.32); inscribed in pencil, once on each interior seat rail: *4* (of 1970.33); once on the front and side interior seat rails: *V* (of 1970.32); and on interior rear seat rail: *5* (of 1970.32)

Gift of the Antiquarian Society, 1970.32–33

These chairs are part of large group of furniture pieces that has been attributed to the Chapin school of cabinetmakers of East Windsor and Hartford, Connecticut. In most cases, the furniture cannot be definitively linked to one maker because the craftsmen in the Chapin school, like the Frothinghams in Boston and the Goddards and Townsends in Newport, were linked by marriage and apprenticeship ties. Younger members were trained by fathers, uncles, and cousins. The stylistic and construction features of objects that normally might be attributed to a single maker were, instead, shared among the members of the Chapin family, thus making it impossible to link a piece with a particular craftsman unless that piece was signed.[1]

The most famous members of the Chapin school of cabinetmakers, Eliphalet and Aaron Chapin, were second cousins who lived and worked closely together from 1774 to 1783.[2] Eliphalet was employed as a journeyman in Philadelphia from 1766 to 1770. When he returned to Connecticut in 1771, he bought land and a house in East Windsor and began his cabinetmaking business. Aaron was several years younger and entered Eliphalet's shop as a journeyman at age twenty-one.[3]

In 1783 Aaron moved to Hartford, where he advertised his "Chair Making business, in as great variety perhaps as is done in any one shop in the State, in both Mahogany and Cherry Tree."[4] Most of the surviving furniture from the Chapin group is made from cherry wood, with a secondary wood of pine, but a handful of pieces, such as the Art Institute's chairs, are made from mahogany.

As is true of other pieces of Connecticut furniture (see, for example, cat. no. 36), the style of the museum's Chapin chairs was inspired by the craftsmanship in Boston, Newport, New York, and Philadelphia. The through-tenon construction of the side seat rails into the back posts, the shape and construction of the glue blocks (see detail), and the shapes of the rear legs, feet, and back-splat are similar to features of Philadelphia furniture of the period (see cat. no. 25). The interior glue blocks are quarter-round, made of two pieces in front and one piece in the rear, like those of Philadelphia chairs, but each block is glued and nailed with two large rosehead nails, a feature specific to the Chapin school. The use of Philadelphia construction techniques on these chairs may stem from Eliphalet's time as an apprentice in that city.[5] The heavy treatment of the carved shell recalls chairs from New York (see cat. no. 29), while the central groove in the ears of the crest rail is seen in both New York and Newport chairs. The carving on the splat and middle portion of the crest rail resembles that of several chairs from Massachusetts.[6]

The Art Institute's chairs also exhibit characteristics that are peculiar to the Chapin school of cabinetmaking. An X-ray of one of the chairs (see detail) shows that the chair back was constructed by fitting round tenons on the stiles into round mortises in the crest rail, enabling the chairmaker to interchange chair parts and facilitate the chair-making process.[7] This technique is rare in joined cabinet work of the eighteenth century.[8] The shape of the ball-and-claw feet is also particular to this group; the round ball is cut off at the bottom and grasped by four geometrically carved, thick talons, each with three distinct knuckles.[9]

NOTES

1. For a discussion of all the familial links, see Joseph Lionetti and Robert Trent, "New Information about Chapin Chairs," *Antiques* 129, 5 (May 1986), pp. 1084–88.

2. Emily M. Davis, "Eliphalet Chapin," *Antiques* 35, 4 (Apr. 1939), p. 172.

3. Lionetti and Trent (note 1), p. 1087.

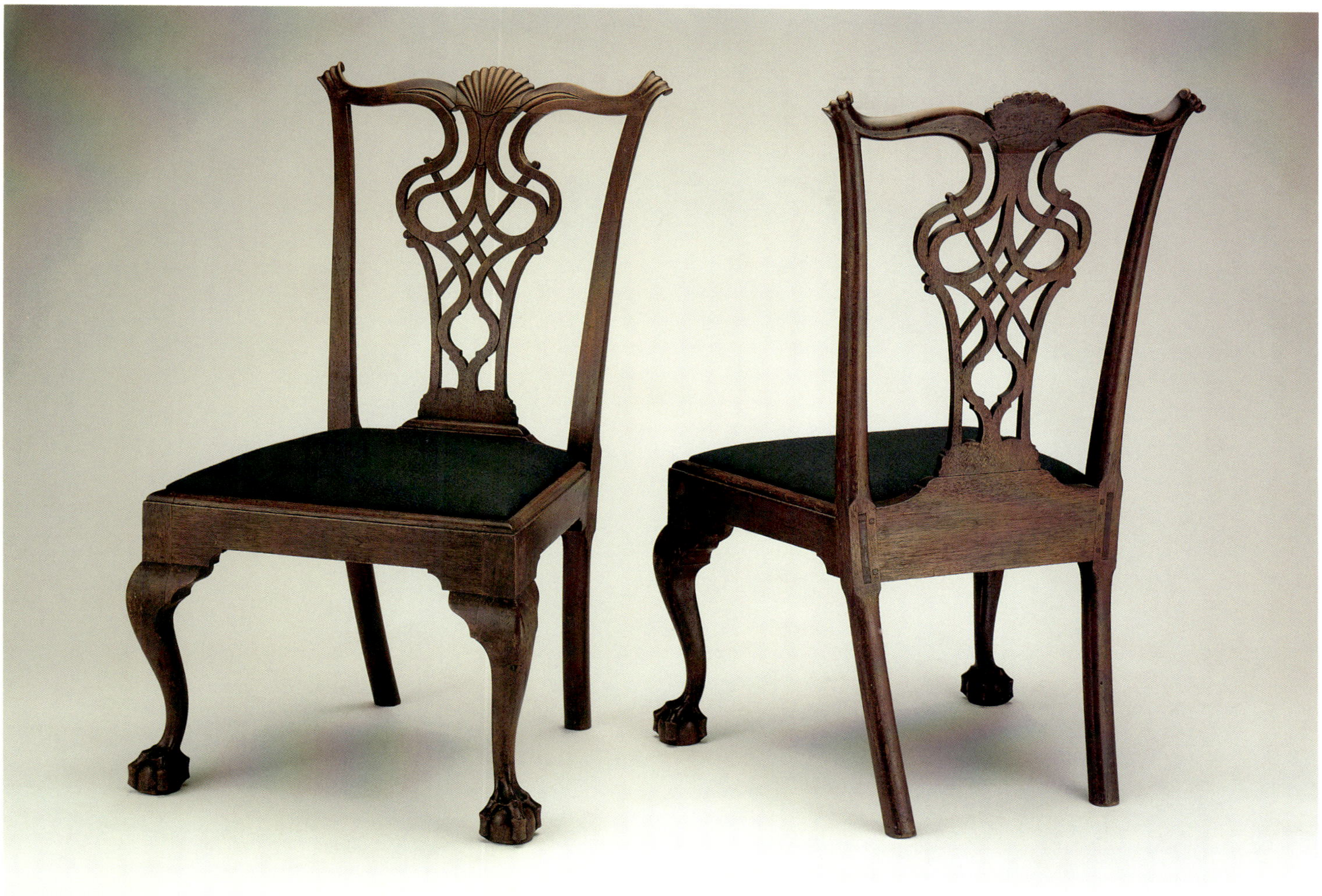

CAT. NO. 35

4. As quoted in Morrison H. Heckscher, *American Furniture in the Metropolitan Museum of Art* (New York, 1985), p. 46, cat. no. 10.

5. For a discussion of the construction of a Philadelphia chair, see entry on cat. no. 25.

6. John Kirk, *American Chairs: Queen Anne and Chippendale* (New York, 1972), pp. 55, 187.

7. Philip Zea in Hartford, Conn., Wadsworth Atheneum, *The Great River: Art and Society of the Connecticut River Valley, 1635–1820*, exh. cat. (1985), p. 229, cat. no. 109.

8. X-rays of other Connecticut chairs of the time, and of chairs from Boston, Newport, New York, and Philadelphia, do not reveal this construction feature. Most chairmakers used rectangular mortise and tenon joints. See Lionetti and Trent (note 1), p. 1093.

9. Like related chairs in the Chapin group, the rear glue blocks are carved to conform to the flat arch of the side rails. The rear seat rail is made of two pieces and is double-pegged to the stiles. These construction features and type of ball-and-claw feet are found on other chairs in the group; see Patricia E. Kane, *Three Hundred Years of American Seating Furniture: Chairs and Beds from the Mabel Brady Garvan and Other Collections at Yale University* (Boston, 1976), pp. 138, 141, cat. nos. 117–18; and Heckscher (note 4), pp. 46–47, cat. no. 10. Chairs with similar back splats are in the collections at

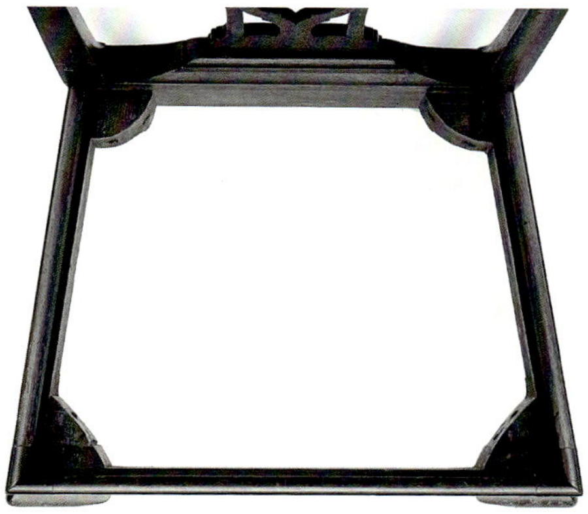

CAT. NO. 35, DETAIL

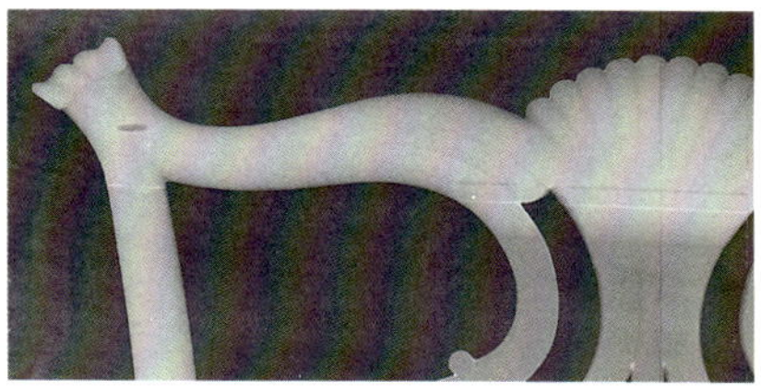

X-RAY OF CAT. NO. 35

Western Reserve Historical Society in Cleveland, Ohio; Wadsworth Atheneum in Hartford, Conn.; and Historic Deerfield in Deerfield, Mass.; see records of the Decorative Arts Photographic Collection, Henry Francis du Pont Winterthur Museum, Winterthur, Del. A possible mate to the Art Institute's chairs is illustrated, with two other chairs that have the same back splat, in a 1939 issue of *Antiques*; see Davis (note 2), pp. 172–73.

36. DESK, 1770/90

Norwich, Connecticut

Mahogany, white pine, and zebrawood;

109.8 x 112.5 x 56 cm (43¼ x 44¼ x 22 in.)

Gift of the Antiquarian Society through the Jessie Spalding Landon Fund, 1948.122

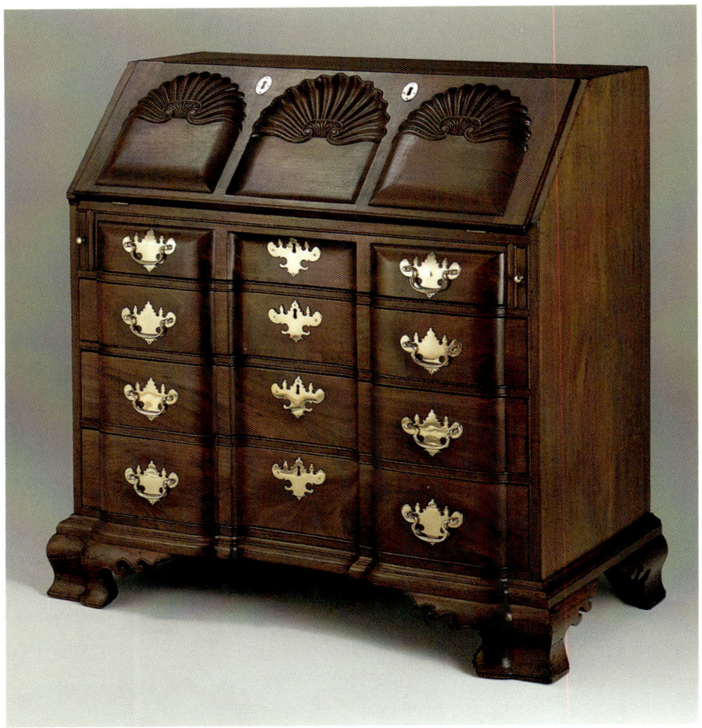

CAT. NO. 36

This desk is one of a number of furniture pieces made in and around Norwich, Connecticut, that were influenced by both Rhode Island and Massachusetts design and craftsmanship. The carved shells, curved bracket feet, blocked front drawers, and case construction of the desk were modeled on contemporary Newport furniture such as the Art Institute's bureau table (cat. no. 23). The squared, blocked front; base moldings; use of exotic woods; "amphitheater" style of the desk interior; fan carving on the interior drawer behind the central door; and certain construction features were inspired by Massachusetts craftsmanship, specifically that of Boston and Salem.[1]

The Massachusetts and Newport influences on this desk might be explained by the location of Norwich. The town was an important river port situated along overland trading routes between Boston and New York, and between Newport and New York.[2] Other outside influences would have come through Norwich's port. Norwich was one of the largest towns in Connecticut in 1782, with a population of 7,325, second only to New Haven, with nearly 8,000.[3] Located on the Thames River, Norwich served as the gateway for trade to the middle and upper portions of eastern Connecticut. Most of the merchandise distributed throughout the region passed through the merchants of Norwich, whose stores of supplies included rum, beeswax, furs, linens, dry goods, silver, pewter, and products from Europe.[4]

The Norwich desk exhibits construction and design traits that are rooted in Connecticut as well, including the desk's oversized proportions; applied, carved, and blocked shell panels on the lid; and scrolled volutes with beaded edges on the feet.[5] Such volutes appear on a number of pieces of Norwich furniture, including an elaborate tall-case clock with works by Thomas Harland now in the Detroit Institute of Arts.[6]

The first known owner of this desk, General Ebenezer Huntington, was a direct descendant of one of the founders of Norwich, and was himself a Revolutionary War hero. He was a major general of the Connecticut militia and was made a brigadier general of the United States Army in 1799 by President John Adams. In 1810, and again in 1817, he was elected a member of Congress. Huntington had four unmarried daughters, known as the "Ladies Huntington," who lived in his house in Norwich until the last one died in 1885.[7] The desk was most likely in the house until that time, when it was sold by the Huntington heirs to George Smith Palmer (1855–1934), an important early collector of American furniture.

NOTES

1. The facing strips applied to the exposed dovetails on the drawer dividers on the case front are a particular Boston feature.

2. Bruce C. Daniels, *The Connecticut Town: Growth and Development, 1635–1790* (Middletown, Conn., 1979), p. 149.

3. Houghton Bulkeley, "Norwich Cabinetmakers," in *Contributions to Connecticut Cabinet Making* (Hartford, Conn., 1967), p. 34.

4. Daniels (note 2), p. 147.

5. Because of its size, there was speculation that this desk once had a bookcase top. However, no physical evidence on the desk top, such as nail holes or prominent scuff marks, suggests such a possibility. Other desks from Nor-

wich, at the Metropolitan Museum of Art and Yale University, are similarly oversized. See Robert F. Trent, "The Colchester School of Cabinetmaking, 1750–1800," in Francis J. Puig and Michael Conforti, eds., *The American Craftsman and the European Tradition, 1620–1820*, exh. cat. (Minneapolis Institute of Arts, 1989), p. 119, cat. no. 43; and Gerald W. R. Ward, *American Case Furniture in the Mabel Brady Garvan and Other Collections at Yale University* (New Haven, Conn., 1988), p. 308, cat. no. 160.

6. Ada B. Chase and Houghton Bulkeley, "Thomas Harland's Clock—Whose Case?" *Antiques* 87, 6 (June 1965), p. 700.

7. Huntington may be the original owner of the desk; however, he purchased his house from his half-brother, General Jedidiah Huntington, in 1789. Jedidiah may have also sold the desk to Ebenezer. Genealogical information comes from Mary E. Perkins, *Old Houses of the Antient Town of Norwich, 1660–1800* (Norwich, Conn., 1895), pp. 221–28.

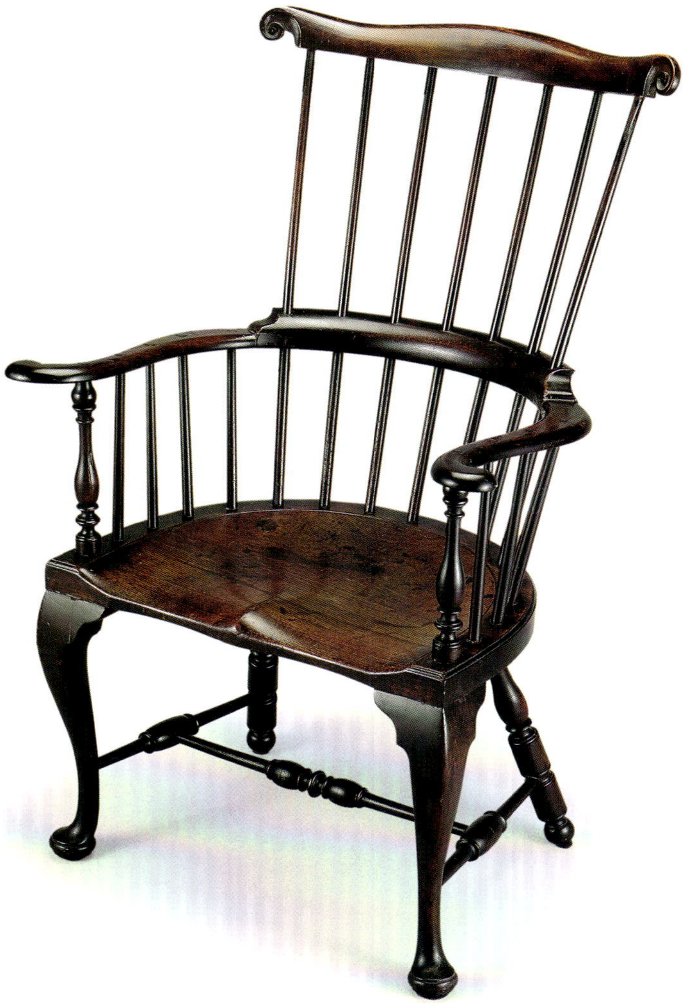

CAT. NO. 37

37. HIGH-BACK WINDSOR CHAIR, 1760/68

Philadelphia

Walnut; 109.2 x 65.7 x 43.2 cm (43 x 23⅞ x 17 in.)

Gift of Mrs. Christopher Brown, Marshall Field, Mrs. Harold T. Martin, Mrs. H. Alex Vance, and the Mary Waller Langhorne Fund, 1979.22

38. FAN-BACK WINDSOR CHAIR, 1760/70

Philadelphia

Tulip seat, maple legs, hickory spindles, and oak arms; 102.4 x 49.1 x 44.5 cm (40⅜ x 19⅜ x 17½ in.)

Bequest of Elizabeth R. Vaughan, 1950.1713

In 1733 Jacques Rigaud made a drawing of the gardens at Stowe in Buckinghamshire, England.[1] The drawing documents one of the earliest uses of Windsor chairs. As depicted, the chairs were placed on wheeled platforms with tillers so the sitter could be pushed around the gardens while steering. The sturdy, lightweight chairs developed into more comfortable alternatives to benches and stools; they were used in gardens, hallways, galleries, and, later in the century, in taverns and other public establishments.[2]

Windsor chairs were probably first introduced to America when Englishman Patrick Gordon arrived in Philadelphia to take up residence as the lieutenant governor of Pennsylvania in the early 1730s. When he died in 1736, his estate inventory listed five Windsors.[3] As the most fashionable of the American colonial cities, Philadelphia looked to London for the latest styles. By the early 1740s, its craftsmen copied and modified the English designs and began what was to become a brisk business in the manufacture of Windsor chairs. The popularity of the chairs was such that by 1790 the revenue from exports to the West Indies and the southern American colonies exceeded that of all other furniture construction combined. By the early 1800s, Windsors were made throughout the country.[4]

Two chairs in the Art Institute are among the most stylish windsors produced in Philadelphia in the mid- to late eighteenth century. Based on English models, the Art Institute's high-back Windsor (cat. no. 37) is a rare American example that has cabriole legs and is made entirely from walnut.[5] Generally, American chair producers seemed to favor the simpler, sharply angled, raked legs such as those on the museum's fan-back Windsor (cat. no. 38).

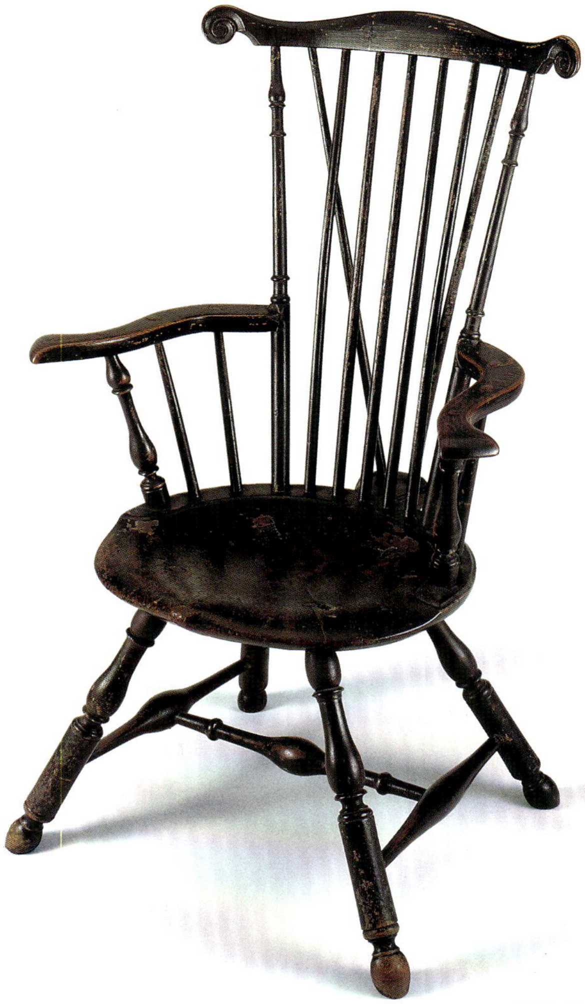

CAT. NO. 38

This latter chair retains its original green paint under later layers of red and brown. The carved volutes on the crest rail, the S-curves of the arms, and the dynamic splay of the legs acknowledge the high-style Rococo furniture that was so popular in Philadelphia at the time. Unlike the high-back Windsor, which derives its back support from the rail running through the middle of the spindles, this chair's support results from the two spindles that form a triangle behind the back spindles and that run from the crest rail to the rear of the seat. The chair is almost identical to one in the collection of the Henry Francis du Pont Winterthur Museum.[6]

NOTES

1. Simon Jervis, "The First Century of the English Windsor Chair: 1720–1820," *Antiques* 65, 2 (Feb. 1979), p. 361.

2. For more on the early use of Windsor chairs, see Nancy Goyne Evans, *American Windsor Chairs* (New York, 1996), pp. 38–50.

3. Ibid., p. 65.

4. Ibid., p. 13.

5. Alfred Coxe Prime, *The Arts and Crafts in Philadelphia, Maryland, and South Carolina, 1721–1785: Gleanings from Newspapers* (Topsfield, Mass., 1929), pp. 18–89.

6. Evans (note 2), p. 93.

THE YOUNG REPUBLIC

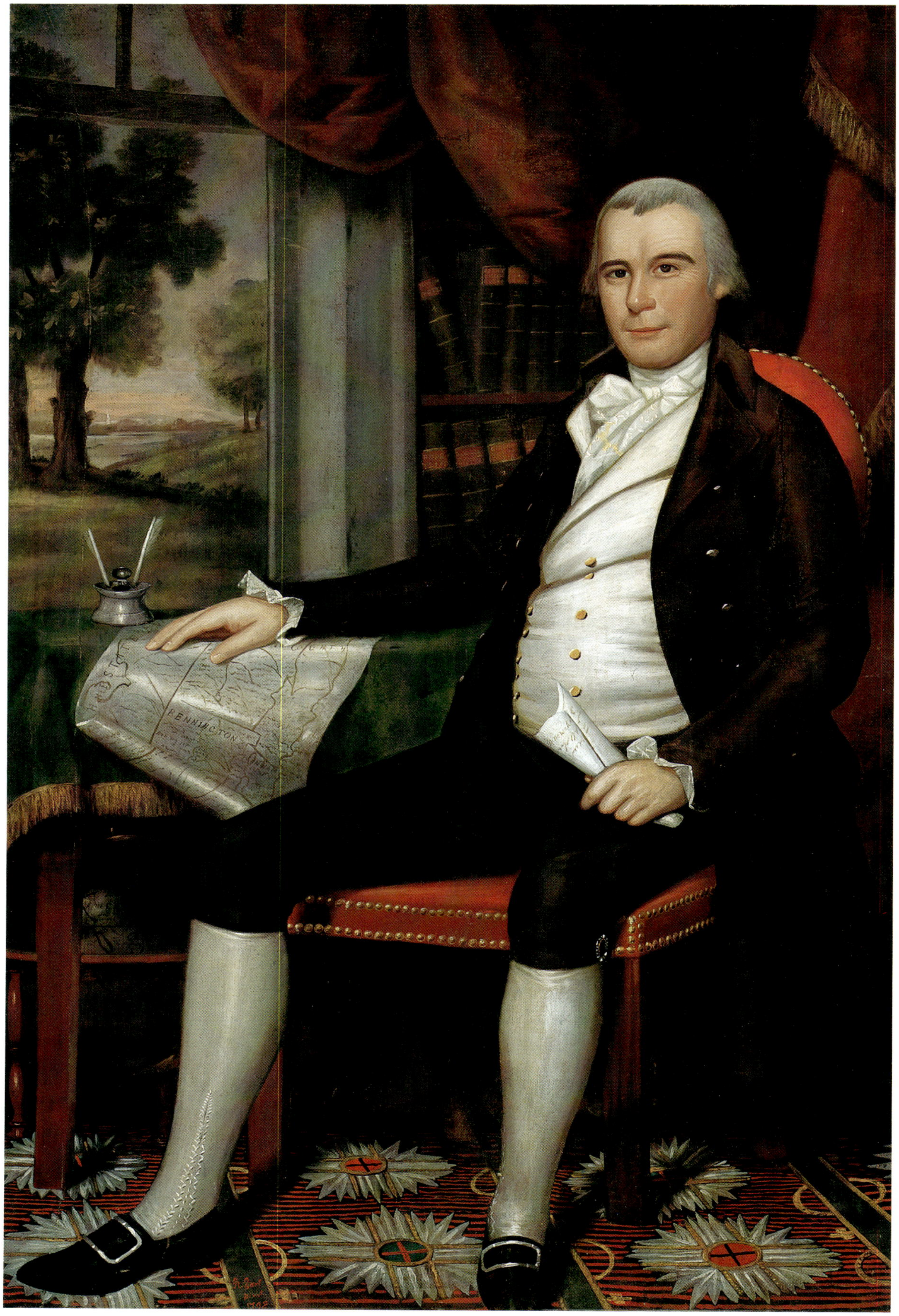

CAT. NO. 39

39. RALPH EARL (1751–1801)

Noah Smith, 1798

Oil on canvas; 163.2 x 107.3 cm (64¼ x 42¼ in.)

Signed, lower left: *R. Earl / Pinxt / 1798*

Goodman Fund, 1956.126

During a period when highly skilled portrait painters normally worked in urban centers, Ralph Earl cultivated a clientele consisting primarily of wealthy rural landowners. Patrons in Connecticut, New York, and Vermont responded favorably to his knowledge of fashionable English portrait styles and his sensitivity to their simple, refined tastes. Their steady commissions sustained Earl's career. Toward the end of his life, Earl painted a portrait of Noah Smith of Bennington, Vermont, which vividly captures the spirit of both its subject and the post-Revolutionary era in which the artist prospered.

After leaving Worcester County, Connecticut, to avoid enlistment in his father's militia company, Earl spent much of his early career in New Haven painting prominent citizens associated with Yale College. A Loyalist, Earl refused to take up arms for the colonies and later claimed to have been a spy for the British government. Forced to leave New Haven for not paying taxes, Earl escaped to London in the spring of 1778 with Captain John Money, quartermaster general of the British Army. He remained in England until 1785, studying with Benjamin West and practicing as a portraitist in Norwich, Windsor, and London.[1]

Like his contemporary John Singleton Copley, whom he admired and emulated, Earl found that contact with English artists had a formidable impact on the development of his portrait style.[2] The works he produced in England and New York City, where he settled upon returning from England in 1785, exhibit the influence of Thomas Gainsborough, Allan Ramsay, and Sir Joshua Reynolds.[3] However, when he retreated to the Connecticut countryside in 1788, after being incarcerated in debtor's prison in New York, Earl was forced to temper his academic style to satisfy his new patrons. The elaborate wigs, bonnets, and rich fabrics favored by his urban subjects were replaced by discreet accoutrements and pointed allusions to property ownership.

Noah Smith epitomizes Earl's depiction of New England's rural gentry. A native of Suffield, Connecticut, and a 1778 graduate of Yale College, Smith was acquainted with many of Earl's Connecticut patrons and was related by marriage to the New Milford Boardmans painted by Earl in 1789. He joined the Vermont bar in 1779, and took up residence in Bennington in 1781. His distinguished career included terms as clerk of Bennington County Courts (1781–84), and as Vermont supreme court justice (1789–90). He also presided as the first grand master of the Grand Lodge of Vermont Freemasons (1794–97).[4]

Smith's election to chief justice of the Vermont Supreme Court in 1798 probably precipitated his patronage of Earl, who had relocated with his wife and children to nearby Troy, New York. The accumulation of details in Earl's portrait of Smith emphasizes the judge's worldly knowledge, material wealth, and status. Seated against a backdrop of drapery, learned books (such as Samuel Johnson's *Lives of the Poets* and Alexander Pope's translation of Homer's *Iliad*), and a window overlooking an expanse of pastoral scenery, Smith exudes amiable self-confidence. His right hand anchors a map of Vermont with "Bennington" clearly legible, while he clasps an unidentifiable piece of paper in his left. A map of the world displaying the New World is tucked away under the table, suggesting Smith's prominent position in the affairs of the new nation.

Earl's accomplished portrait *Mrs. Noah Smith and Her Children* (fig. 18) was executed as a pendant to *Noah Smith*.[5] The family portrait is the same height and shares similar background features with its pendant: a richly patterned rug and compatible furniture. Although group portraits such as this were rare in eighteenth-century America, even more unusual was Smith's choice to have his portrait painted separately from that of his family.[6] The two canvases were perhaps meant to hang across the room from each other instead of side by side.[7]

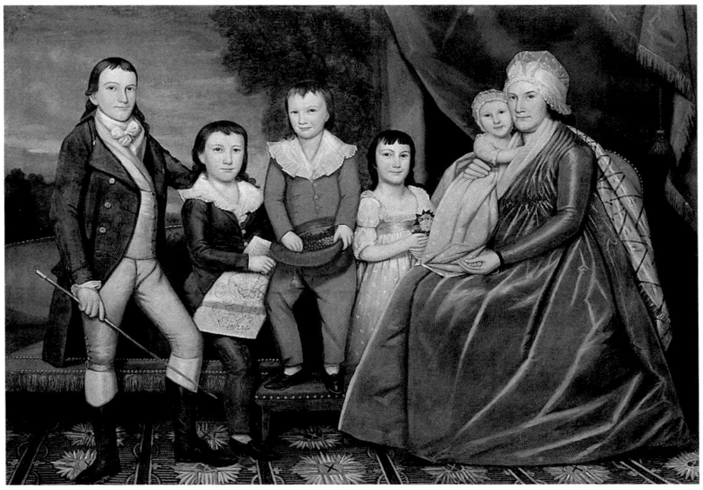

FIG. 18. Ralph Earl (1751–1801). *Mrs. Noah Smith and Her Children*, 1798. Oil on canvas; 162.6 x 217.8 cm (64 x 85¾ in.). Metropolitan Museum of Art, New York, Gift of Edgar William and Bernice Chrysler Garbisch (64.309.1).

Henry and Daniel Smith, on the left side, resemble their father: Henry's erect posture, adult clothing, and grasp of a riding crop suggest his father's assertiveness, and Daniel holds a foldout map of the world on his lap.

Earl depicted Noah Smith as optimistic, affluent, and powerful. Unfortunately, this state of affairs did not last. Around 1801 Smith moved from Bennington to Milton, Vermont, where he was a large landowner. After a number of financial setbacks, he was put into debtor's prison in Milton, and died shortly after his release in 1811.

NOTES

1. The primary source for Ralph Earl's biography and body of work is Elizabeth Mankin Kornhauser, *Ralph Earl: The Face of the Young Republic*, exh. cat. (Hartford, Conn., Wadsworth Atheneum, 1991).

2. Ibid., pp. 16–30.

3. Works that exhibit these characteristics include *Reclining Hunter* (c. 1783/84; Collection of Drs. Caroline and Peter Koblenzer, Philadelphia); *Dr. Joseph Trumbull* (1784; Historic Deerfield, Mass.); and *Mrs. John Johnston (Martha Spear)* (1785; Anderson House, Washington, D.C.).

4. Biographical details for Noah Smith have been culled from Franklin Bowditch Dexter, *Biographical Sketches of the Graduates of Yale College* (New York, 1885), pp. 52–54; and John Spargo, *The Rise and Progress of Freemasonry in Vermont* (Burlington, Vt., 1944), pp. 31–32.

5. Nineteenth-century copies of these two works, probably painted by Ezra Ames of Albany, N.Y., in the 1840s, are in the collection of The Art Institute of Chicago (*Mrs. Noah Smith and Her Family*) and the Bennington Museum, Vt. (*Noah Smith*).

6. For an excellent analysis of the social significance of early American family portraits, see Margaretta M. Lovell, "Reading Eighteenth-Century American Family Portraits: Social Images and Self-Images," *Winterthur Portfolio* 22, 4 (winter 1987), pp. 243–64.

7. John Caldwell and Oswaldo Rodriguez Roque with Dale T. Johnson, *American Paintings in the Metropolitan Museum of Art, Vol. 1: A Catalogue of Works by Artists Born by 1815* (New York, 1994), pp. 146–48.

40. CARVING ATTRIBUTED TO SAMUEL McINTIRE (1757–1811)

Pair of Side Chairs, 1795/1811

Salem, Massachusetts

Mahogany with ash and birch;

97.2 x 54 x 47 cm (38¼ x 21¼ x 18½ in.)

Gift of the Antiquarian Society through the Edith Almy Adams Fund, 1938.1321–22

The design of these chairs derives from George Hepplewhite's 1788 edition of *The Cabinet-Maker and Upholsterer's Guide* (see fig. 19). Though Samuel McIntire's probate inventory did not list a copy of Hepplewhite's pattern book, that of his colleague Jacob Sanderson did. Sanderson and his brother Elijah moved to Salem in the late eighteenth century and set up a cabinetmakers' cooperative that was patronized by many of the best craftsmen in town, including McIntire. The cabinetmakers grouped their furniture together and sent them out as venture cargo in Salem's ships, sharing in the profits when the ships returned. McIntire and the Sandersons worked closely together on several projects, so it may be that McIntire used Sanderson's books for inspiration.[1]

In creating these chairs, McIntire and the cabinetmaker refined—and improved—the design in Hepplewhite's drawing. The addition of the spade-front feet and the pendant-husk carving on the front legs serves to balance the ornate carving of the vases-of-wheat-and-swag motif on the chair back. The slight thickening of the back splat and the wider spacing of the rear stiles give the chair a more robust appearance. The pointed tips of the shield backs and the beaded edges of the chair backs and stiles add to the strength of the conception.

This pair of chairs is part of a set of eight[2] that may have originally been made for Elias Hasket Derby, a wealthy Salem merchant to whom a related set of chairs by McIntire has been firmly documented. A bill for services rendered from Samuel McIntire, dated February 17, 1798, lists carving work executed for Derby: "To carving eight chairs @ 10/6 each ——— £4:4:0."[3] The date of the bill corresponds to the completion of Derby's new house (see below). The number of chairs matches the number purchased by the West family from the Derby household in the early nineteenth century,[4] as well as the number of chairs known today with the same motifs. Though it cannot be said with certainty that the Art Institute's chairs are two of the eight listed in the McIntire bill, this is a distinct possibility.

The last house owned by Elias Hasket Derby and his wife was designed and built between 1795 and 1798 by Samuel McIntire. The Derbys died in 1799, a few months after they took possession of the residence.[5] Their seven children purchased objects from their father's estate in July 1800.[6] Elizabeth Derby, daughter of Elias, married Nathaniel West, and together they built Oak Hill, a house also designed by Samuel McIntire. The Wests most likely purchased the set of eight chairs for their new house. The chairs descended in the West family until sold by the estate of Abby C. West to the Art Institute in 1938.

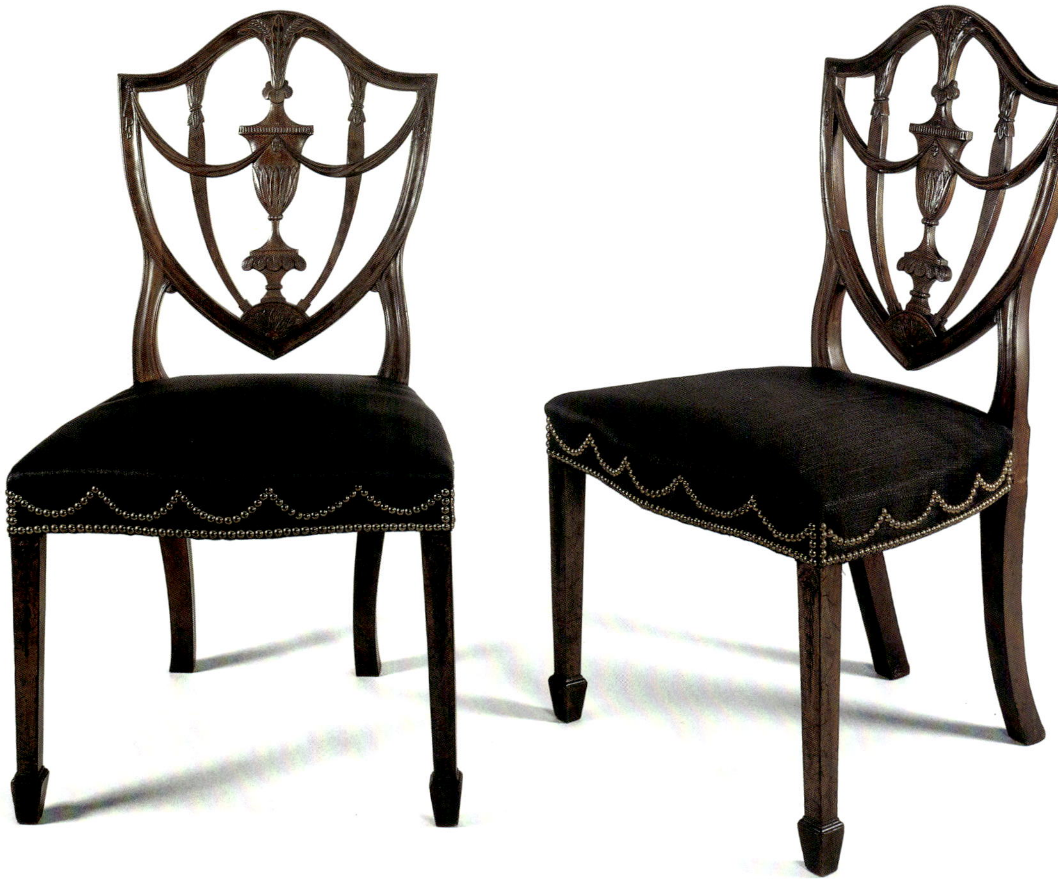

CAT. NO. 40

NOTES

1. Dean A. Fales, "The Furniture of McIntire," in Benjamin W. Labaree, ed., *Samuel McIntire: A Bicentennial Symposium, 1757–1957* (Salem, 1957), pp. 56–58, 60.

2. Two are in the Museum of Fine Arts, Boston; two are in the Metropolitan Museum of Art, New York; one is in the Henry Ford Museum, Dearborn, Mich.; and another is in the Peabody Essex Museum, Salem, Mass.

3. Mabel M. Swan, *Samuel McIntire, Carver, and the Sandersons, Early Salem Cabinet Makers* (Salem, Mass., 1934), p. 16.

4. A letter from the executor of Mrs. Abby West's estate, from whom these chairs were acquired, states, "The chairs were part of a set of eight which were purchased by Mrs. West's family ancestors at the auction sale of the Derby household which was held very early in the nineteenth century." See letter from Charles C. Buckham to Edward Hipkiss, Jan. 7, 1945, quoted in Wendy A. Cooper, "The Furniture and Furnishings of the Farm at Danvers," *Bulletin of Museum of Fine Arts, Boston* 81 (1983), p. 35.

5. Fiske Kimball, "Samuel McIntire," in Labaree (note 1), p. 15.

6. Cooper (note 4), p. 24.

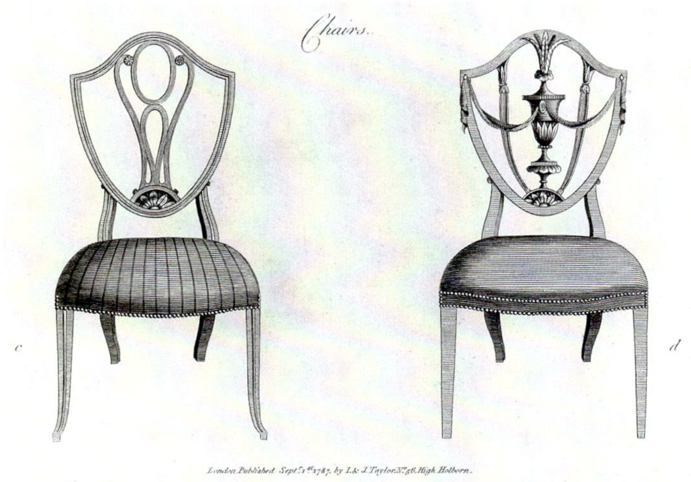

FIG. 19. A. Hepplewhite and Company, *The Cabinet-Maker and Upholsterer's Guide* (London, 1788), pl. 2. Collection of Ryerson and Burnham Libraries, The Art Institute of Chicago.

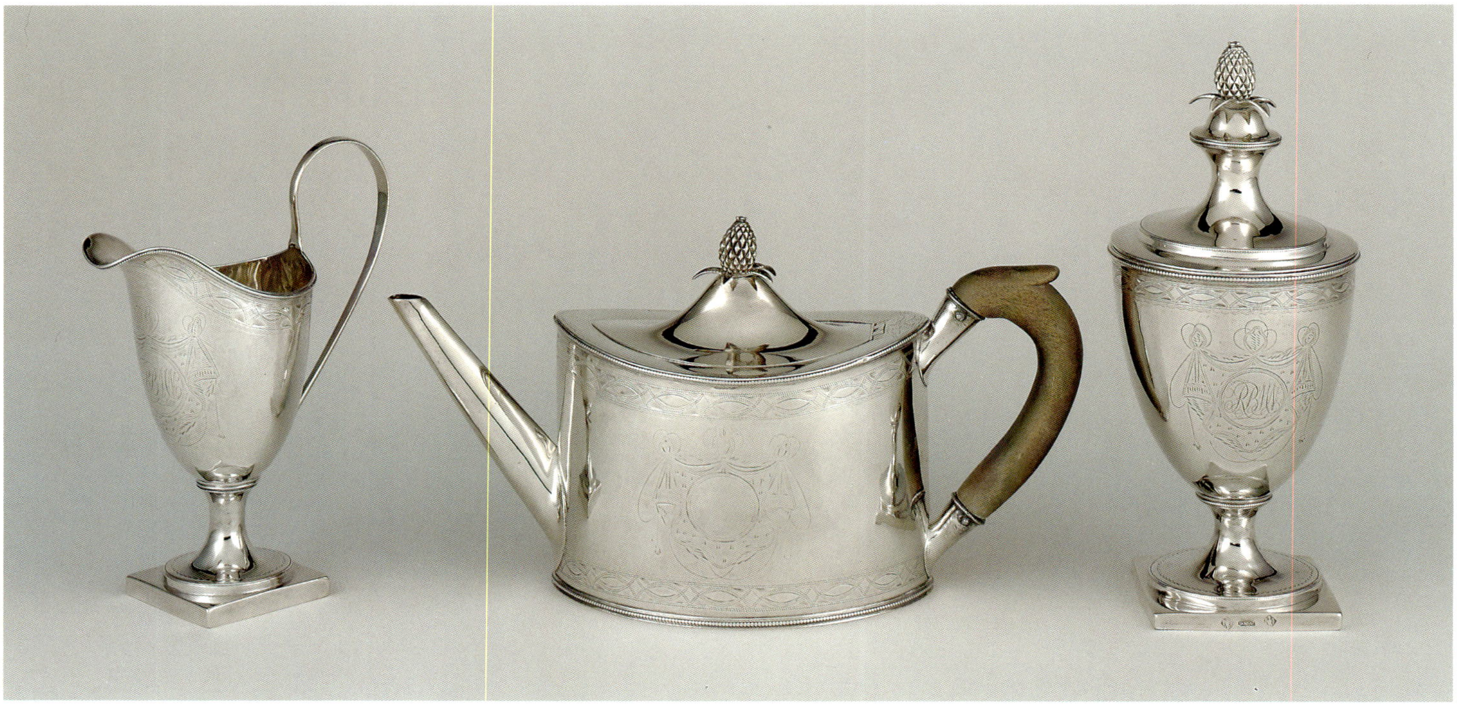

CAT. NO. 41

41. DANIEL VAN VOORHIS (1751–1824)

Tea Set, 1788/1805

New York

Silver; teapot: 15.9 x 28.6 x 10.8 cm (6¼ x 11¼ x 4¼ in.); sugar basin: 24.1 x 10.2 (diam.) cm (9½ x 4 in.); cream pot: 19 x 6 x 6 (at base) cm (7½ x 2⅜ x 2⅜ in.)

Teapot marked on underside: *D. V. VOORHIS* (in rectangle), with two eagles within diamonds appearing above and below name; sugar basin and cream pot marked on underside: *D. V. V.* (in rectangle), with two eagles within diamonds on either side of initials

Gift of the Antiquarian Society through Mrs. Cyrus H. Adams and Mrs. James C. Hutchins, Jr., 1950.1584 (teapot) and 1950.1648a–c (sugar basin and cream pot)

For a silversmith working in America in the first decades of the nineteenth century, native and foreign competition was strong. In some instances, as in the case of Daniel Van Voorhis, silversmiths tried many different ways to keep their businesses profitable. Van Voorhis's career was complicated. Born on Long Island, he was most likely apprenticed to a silversmith from New York City. He plied his trade in Philadelphia, New Jersey, New York, and Vermont. He had numerous partners, and moved his shop several times in each city where he worked. Besides fabricating silver pieces himself, he augmented his income by importing English silver and jewelry.[1] From 1775 to 1780, Van Voorhis worked closely with Philadelphia silversmith Thomas Shields, filling orders for Shields's clients.[2]

Advertisements placed in local newspapers during his career indicate the frustration Van Voorhis experienced by trying to keep pace with his competition. In 1782 he advertised his own shop in the *Pennsylvania Packet*: "Daniel Van Voorhis, Goldsmith, Informs the Public, that he has removed from his late dwelling house on Market Street to the west side of Front Street. . . . He flatters himself, from his close attention, to give general satisfaction to all who may please to favor him with their custom." By the end of that year, he was forced to relocate to Princeton, New Jersey, where he advertised in the *New Jersey Gazette* that "he has now opened shop in Princeton . . . where he intends carrying on his business in all its branches and shall always be happy to receive the commands of those who choose to employ him. . . . Their work will be executed with dispatch, in the neatest manner, the newest fashions, and on the most reasonable terms, he being enabled to execute his work at lower prices than it can be done in Philadelphia." At the end of the advertisement Van Voorhis listed thirty silver forms he could make in his shop.[3] By 1784 Van Voorhis had moved to New York City and taken on two partners, Simeon

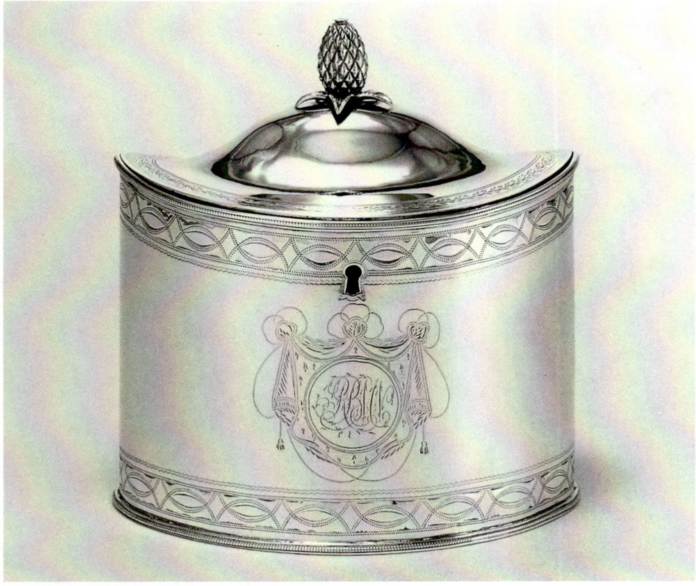

FIG. 20. William Black and Erastus O. Tomkins (active 1839–1851). *Tea Caddy*, 1839/51. Silver; h. 15.7 cm (6⅜ in.). The Art Institute of Chicago, Gift of the Antiquarian Society through Mrs. James C. Hutchins, Jr. (1950.1585).

Bailey and William Coley. The three men advertised themselves as "Real Manufacturers in Gold, Silver, Jewellery &c.... They have procured the best workmen from Europe, and flatter themselves that the Goods they manufacture will be sold on much lower Terms than those imported, and will be found equal in point of Workmanship."[4] The next year Van Voorhis is listed in partnership with Coley only. They advertised in the *New York Daily Advertiser* that "it is a particular point with them to sell for the smallest profit which their constant attention to their business, and the number of workmen they employ, enable them to do."[5] Coley and Van Voorhis moved to Rupert, Vermont, in 1787, and began minting copper coins. Van Voorhis became the cashier for the firm during the year it was in business.[6] In 1788 he was back in New York, where he spent the rest of his career, the last decade of which was in partnership with his son. It is from this period that the Art Institute's tea set dates.

The style of the tea set was a popular one in New York, New Jersey, and Philadelphia at the turn of the nineteenth century. The shapes and decoration of the set were inspired by classical Roman designs unearthed at Herculaneum and Pompeii during the 1730s. The decorative vocabulary of these finds was reinterpreted by antiquarians such as English architect Robert Adam, who published a book of designs, *The Works in Architecture of Robert and James Adam* (London, 1773–79). Adam's renditions of Roman ornament were copied and disseminated in the popular furniture designs of Thomas Sheraton (*The Cabinet-Maker and Upholsterer's Drawing-Book, in Three Parts* [London, 1793]) and George Hepplewhite (*The Cabinet-Maker and Upholsterer's Guide* [London, 1788]). This early neoclassical style has been called "Federal" in the United States because it corresponded with the growth of the young nation. Americans identified with shapes and symbols such as the urn, swag, and oval, which they believed were associated with the Roman republic.

The cannister forms of the tea set were made with thin sheets of rolled silver manipulated into the appropriate shape and soldered, a much faster process than raising the form from an ingot of silver.[7] Compared to other three-piece tea sets of similar design, those comprising the Van Voorhis set are well balanced, both in proportion to each other and in the style and amount of engraving on each piece.

The bright-cut engraving is typical of the period. The Van Voorhis pieces employ a large drapery swag as a background to the central circular medallion containing engraved initials of the original owner. The border band design appears to mimic the swag effect of the central medallion. A companion tea caddy by William Black and Erastus O. Tomkins was made to match the three-piece set between 1839 and 1851, when Black and Tomkins were in active partnership (fig. 20). Though the engraving on the caddy looks the same as those on the rest of the set, close examination reveals that it is by a different hand.

NOTES

1. For a list of working dates and partnerships, see Ian M. G. Quimby with Dianne Johnson, *American Silver at Winterthur* (Charlottesville, Va., 1995), p. 313.

2. Ibid.

3. Alfred Coxe Prime, *The Arts and Crafts in Philadelphia, Maryland, and South Carolina, 1721–1785: Gleanings from Newspapers* (Topsfield, Mass., 1929), p. 94.

4. Rita S. Gottesman, *The Arts and Crafts in New York, 1777–1799* (New York, 1954), p. 75.

5. Ibid., p. 77.

6. Jane B. Burrage, "Early Silversmiths in Vermont," *Antiques* 67, 2 (Feb. 1955), p. 154.

7. Henry J. Kauffman, *The Colonial Silversmith: His Techniques and His Products* (Camden, N.J., 1969), p. 127.

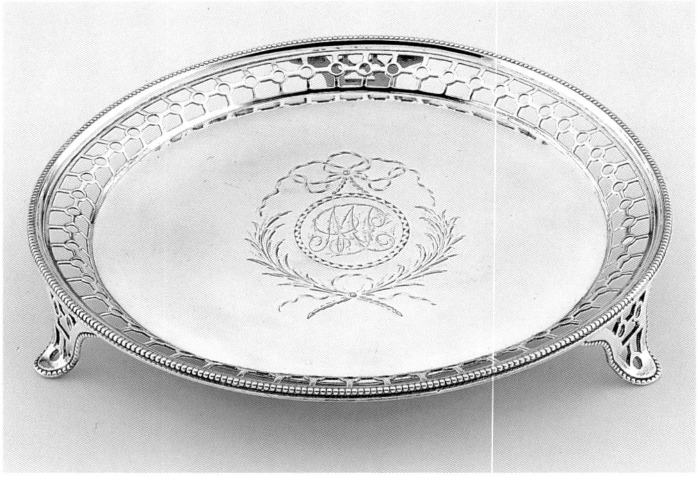

CAT. NO. 42

42. JOSEPH RICHARDSON, JR. (1752–1831) AND NATHANIEL RICHARDSON (1754–1827)

Salver, 1784/90

Philadelphia

Silver; 3.2 x 19.3 (diam.) cm (1¼ x 7⅝ in.)

Stamped, underneath, three times: *I•NR* (in rectangle); bright-cut engraving on surface: *MP* (in script within a circle of ribbon)

Alyce and Edwin DeCosta, and Walter E. Heller Foundation funds, 1983.17

The neoclassical style of this salver appeared in American silver in 1774 when Richard Humphries, a silversmith from Philadelphia, used an antique urn form ornamented with circles, ovals, squares, and other geometric shapes to fashion a tea urn.[1] The style flourished at the end of the Revolutionary era, when Americans began to identify with the republican ideals of ancient Rome. The civilizations and cultures of classical antiquity had become increasingly familiar because of archaeological discoveries at Herculaneum and Pompeii in the 1730s and the popularity of the ancient city of Paestum with European and American travelers at the end of the eighteenth century.[2]

Technological innovations made it relatively easy for silversmiths to adapt the neoclassical style to silver designs. Rolled sheet silver could be cut and shaped in innumerable ways. The geometric pierced-work band on the edge of this salver was cut from a strip of silver, shaped into a curve and soldered onto the edge of the circular tray. The beaded decoration and the pierced French feet were likewise cut from thin strips and soldered onto the pierced portion.[3] Because pierced work such as this is characteristic of silver made in Philadelphia, Baltimore, Wilmington, and Annapolis, it has been suggested that one firm or several supplied pierced bands to silversmiths in the mid-Atlantic region.[4] Indeed, the American Bullion and Refining Office of Philadelphia advertised for several types of machines in the *Pennsylvania Packet* on October 23, 1789: "Wanted, the following tools and utensils: . . . a peircing press."[5] A press utilizes a shaped die to cut into a thin sheet of silver to produce a very regular pattern.[6]

The bright-cut engraving in the center of the salver is different from simple engraving because the lines are not just incised into the silver, but are made using a small, beveled gouge with two cutting points to chip-carve the decoration into the surface, creating faceted lines that catch and reflect light.[7] The engraving, a circle of ribbons with two crossed wheat sheaves enclosing another circle, is typical of the period. The initials MP in the center of the salver are for Mary Pemberton, in whose family this salver descended until it was acquired by the Art Institute.

Joseph, Jr., and Nathaniel Richardson were brothers, and the last members of a family of silversmiths working in Philadelphia since 1701—the longest continuous running goldsmith shop in that city. Their grandfather, Francis, worked in the Baroque style, while their father Joseph Richardson, Sr., created silver masterpieces in the Rococo style (see cat. no. 34).[8] Like many craftsmen, the brothers did not support themselves solely with their craft; they imported and sold English silver, clocks, and measuring scales. The pair also invested in dry goods imported from the West Indies, such as sugar, cotton, wool, and animal hides.[9] Nathaniel left the silversmithing business in 1790, and Joseph, Jr., continued until 1801; President George Washington appointed him assayer of the United States Mint in 1795.[10]

NOTES

1. The urn is in the collection of the Philadelphia Museum of Art; see Graham Hood, *American Silver: A History of Style, 1650–1900* (New York, 1971), pp. 160, 162.

2. For more information about the influence of these cities on the arts and culture of North America, see Wendy A. Cooper, *Classical Taste in America, 1800–1840*, exh. cat. (Baltimore Museum of Art, 1993).

3. Martha Gandy Fales, *Joseph Richardson and Family, Philadelphia Silversmiths* (Middletown, Conn., 1974), p. 167.

4. Charles F. Montgomery and Patricia E. Kane, eds., *American Art: 1750–1800: Towards Independence*, exh. cat. (New Haven, Conn., Yale University Art Gallery, 1976), p. 56; and Stephen K. Victor, "'From the Shop to

the Manufactory': Silver and Industry, 1800–1970," in Barbara McLean Ward and Gerald W. R. Ward, eds., *Silver in American Life: Selections from the Mabel Brady Garvan and Other Collections at Yale University*, exh. cat. (New Haven, Conn., Yale University Art Gallery, 1979), p. 25.

5. Alfred Coxe Prime, ed., *The Arts and Crafts in Philadelphia, Maryland, and South Carolina, 1786–1800: Gleanings from Newspapers* (Topsfield, Mass., 1932), p. 143.

6. Victor (note 4), p. 25.

7. Henry J. Kauffman, *The Colonial Silversmith: His Techniques and His Products* (Camden, N.J., 1969), p. 135.

8. Francis Richardson set up shop off Market Street in Philadelphia in 1701; see Fales (note 3), p. 153.

9. Ibid., p. 155.

10. Beatrice B. Garvan, in Philadelphia Museum of Art, *Philadelphia: Three Centuries of American Art*, exh. cat. (1976), p. 158.

43. JOHN RITTO PENNIMAN (c. 1782–1841)

Meetinghouse Hill, Roxbury, Massachusetts, 1799

Oil on canvas; 73.6 x 94 cm (29 x 37 in.)

Centennial Year Acquisition and the Centennial Fund for Major Acquisitions, 1979.1461

John Ritto Penniman's view of Roxbury, Massachusetts, his first recorded easel painting featuring a landscape, provides a rare glimpse of life in a prosperous New England town at the turn of the eighteenth century. A suburb of Boston settled in 1630, Roxbury was home to many distinguished colonists and artisans. Trained as a decorative painter, Penniman did his ear-

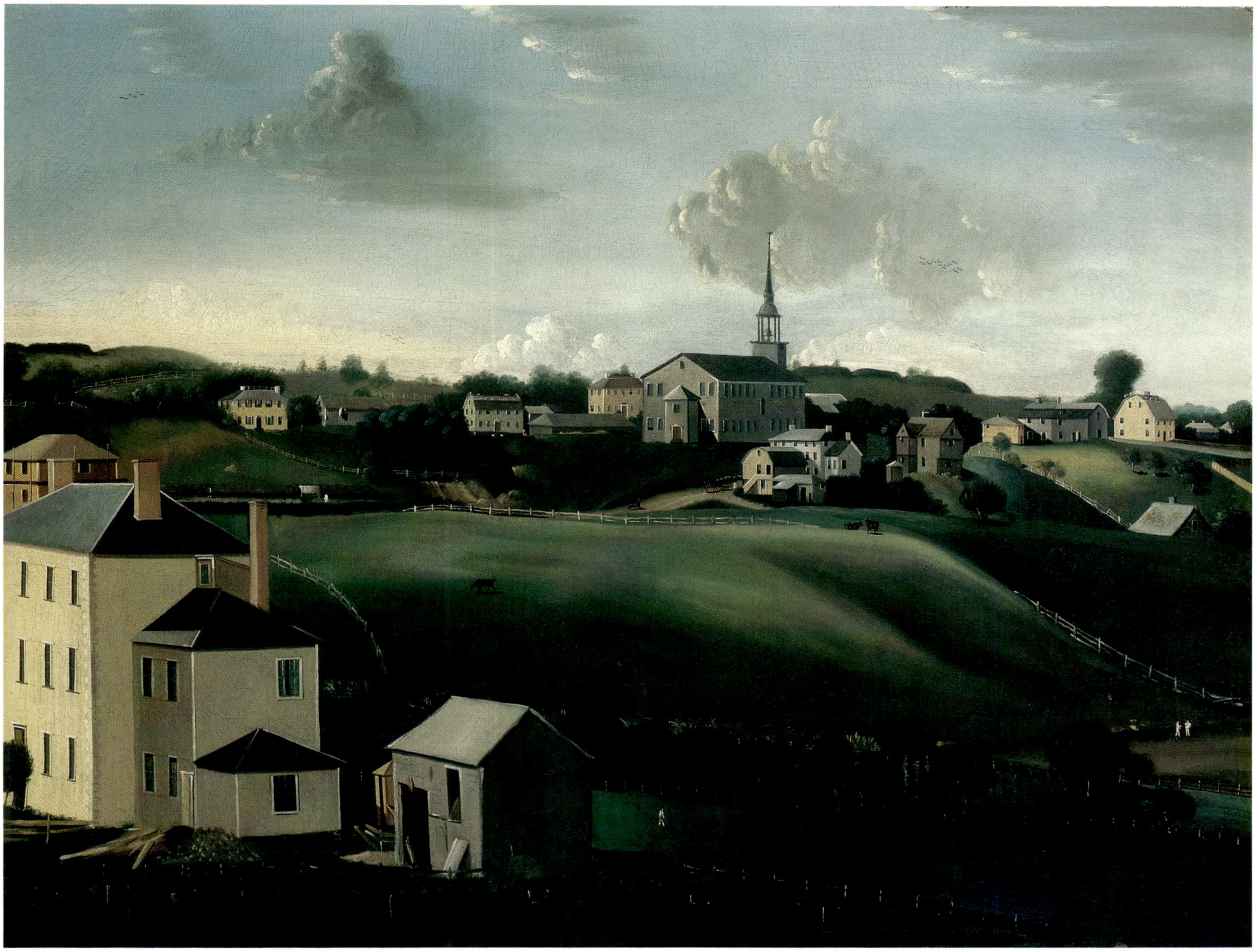

CAT. NO. 43

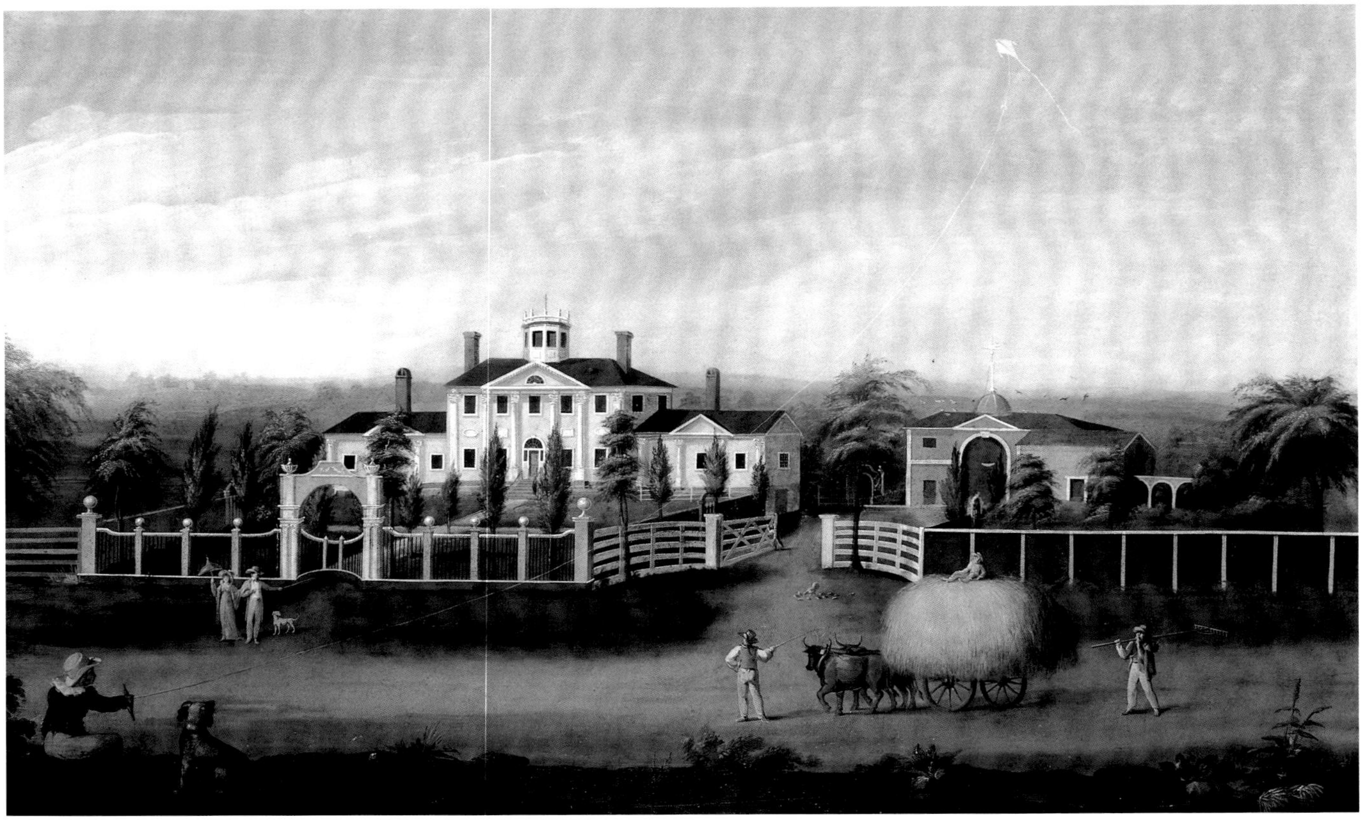

FIG. 21. Unidentified artist. *New England Country Seat*, 1800/1810. Oil on panel; 58.6 x 91.8 cm (23 x 36⅛ in.). The Art Institute of Chicago, Gift of Robert Allerton (1946.391).

liest work painting clock dials for Roxbury-based clockmaker Aaron Willard, who commissioned *Meetinghouse Hill* from the young artist.[1] Willard's shop was situated on Washington Street, the center of the thriving artisan community. Penniman is reported to have painted his view from the residence of Deacon Moses Davis on Washington Street, thus providing Willard with a panorama of the town as he experienced it daily.[2]

Penniman's gently pastoral painting is formally indebted to both topographical and picturesque styles of landscape painting.[3] By recording details of architecture, roads, and the physical features of the land, Penniman visually re-created the town, while the rolling hills and keenly ordered composition created an engaging picture. The clarity with which Penniman delineated each element was a hallmark of decorative artists who painted documentary views of towns and estates. *New England Country Seat* (fig. 21), painted by an unidentified artist after 1800, shares the same hard lines of the structures, bright palette, and slightly skewed perspective evident in Penniman's Roxbury view.

The artist's topographical accuracy makes it possible to identify many of the buildings in *Meetinghouse Hill*. The meet-

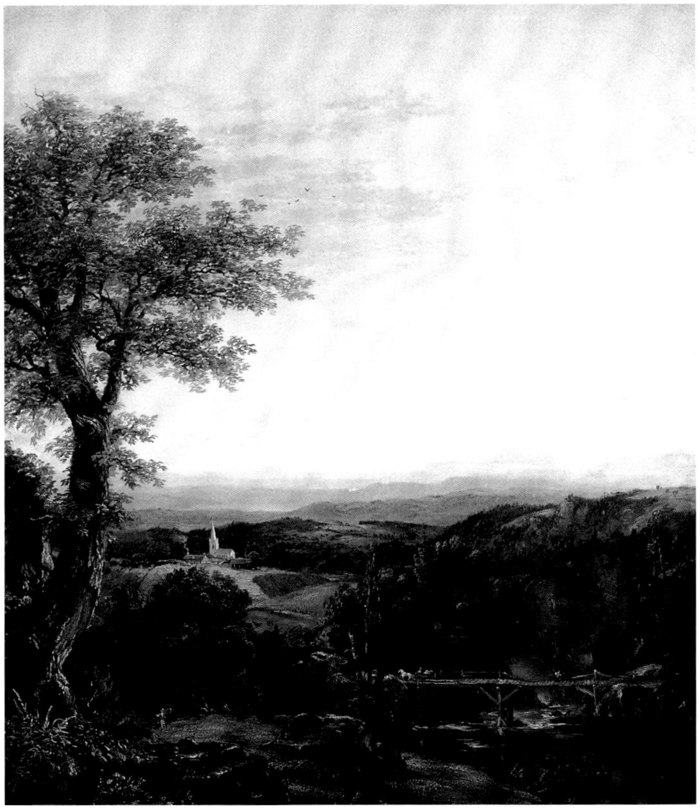

FIG. 22. Thomas Cole (1801–1848). *New England Scenery*, 1839. Oil on canvas; 57.1 x 46.7 cm (22½ x 18⅜ in.). The Art Institute of Chicago, Mr. and Mrs. Samuel M. Nickerson Collection (1900.558).

inghouse at the center of the composition is the fourth to have been built on the hill; it was destroyed in 1803 and replaced the following year with the fifth and final church erected on the spot. The Spooner-Lambert-Taber house, still standing in Roxbury, is located to the immediate left of the meetinghouse; the gambrel-roofed parsonage, built in 1751, is off to the right.[4] A nineteenth-century historian also identified the Mears house on the left and a grocery store on Eliot Square.[5] Earthworks erected for the defense of Boston during the Revolutionary War can be discerned immediately to the right of the meetinghouse and on the painting's far left edge.

In addition to Penniman's exacting transcription of Roxbury's built environment, he also recorded the daily activity in and around the town. A covered wagon travels on the road at the center of the composition; livestock graze in the enclosed common; a man pushes a wheelbarrow directly in the center of the canvas; and a hunter stands in the center foreground. A pile of lumber in the left foreground suggests industry and building. The land is cultivated and tamed, and it harmoniously merges with the Federal-style architecture to present a vision of an ordered society.

The presence of the meetinghouse at the center of the composition reinforces this theme by unifying the town around the symbolic authority of the church. Silhouetted by clouds, its spire marks the highest point on the horizon and perhaps suggests the spiritual aspirations of the community. While traveling up Meetinghouse Hill in his old age, John Eliot—a noted colonial clergyman who preached at the First Church of Roxbury—is rumored to have said: "This is very like the way to heaven, 'tis up hill; the Lord, by his grace, fetch us up."[6] The theme of North America as a sacred place and of its citizens as the chosen people of God was further explored in the landscapes of the Hudson River School painters. Thomas Cole's 1839 *New England Scenery* (fig. 22) depicts a pastoral village scene viewed from afar. But the meetinghouse—which Penniman displayed so prominently—is located in the distant middleground of Cole's work and greatly reduced in size. While the church retains its symbolic power as an intimation of the promise of America, Cole included mountains and wilderness to suggest that nature can also be a place of worship and an emanation of spiritual values.

NOTES

1. Penniman's earliest signed work is a clock dial dated 1793; see Carol Damon Andrews, "John Ritto Penniman, 1782–1841: An Ingenious New England Artist," *Antiques* 120, 7 (July 1981), p. 148.

2. Francis S. Drake, *The Town of Roxbury: Its Memorable Persons and Places* (Roxbury, Mass., 1878), p. 287. An engraving of *Meetinghouse Hill, Roxbury, Massachusetts* serves as frontispiece for this book. An apparently apocryphal story regarding Willard's commission of this painting relates that the clockmaker ordered it before he and his family moved to another town, so that his wife would not be homesick; see letter from Dr. Roger W. Robinson to Kimberly Rhodes, Nov. 21, 1995, Files of the American Arts Department, The Art Institute of Chicago.

3. For more about early landscape painting in America, see Edward J. Nygren and Bruce Robertson, *Views and Visions: American Landscape Before 1830*, exh. cat. (Washington, D.C., Corcoran Gallery of Art, 1986).

4. The meetinghouse depicted in this painting was built in 1746, and a bell cast at Paul Revere's foundry was installed in the steeple in 1798; see Eleanor H. Gustafson, "Museum Accessions," *Antiques* 120, 7 (July 1981), p. 90.

5. Drake (note 2), p. 287.

6. Ibid., p. 265.

44. ATTRIBUTED TO LANGLEY BOARDMAN (1774–1833)

Serpentine-Front Chest of Drawers, 1800/1810

Portsmouth, New Hampshire

Mahogany, mahogany and oak veneers, eastern white pine, and stamped brass pulls; 90.2 x 110.5 x 59.7 cm (35½ x 43½ x 23½ in.)

Restricted gift of Mrs. Eric Oldberg and Timm R. Reynolds; gift of Edmund J. Doering II in honor of Mrs. Eric Oldberg; R. T. Crane, Jr., Memorial Fund, 1994.536

45. SERPENTINE-FRONT CHEST OF DRAWERS, 1800/1815

Portsmouth, New Hampshire

Mahogany, birch and mahogany veneers, eastern white pine, and stamped brass pulls; 95.9 x 103.5 x 58.4 cm (37¾ x 40¾ x 23 in.)

Inscribed in ink, on backboard: *J. Wentworth*

Gift of the Antiquarian Society, 1948.108

The area surrounding Portsmouth, New Hampshire, was known as the Piscataqua River Valley. The region was settled in 1620 and quickly became known for its rich timber resources. Portsmouth shipbuilders excelled in their boat-building skills, producing sturdy, quick ships of all sorts. In peacetime, Portsmouth's shipbuilding industry was situated at a hub of trade between Newfoundland and points north, and the southern colonies and Caribbean islands. In wartime, pri-

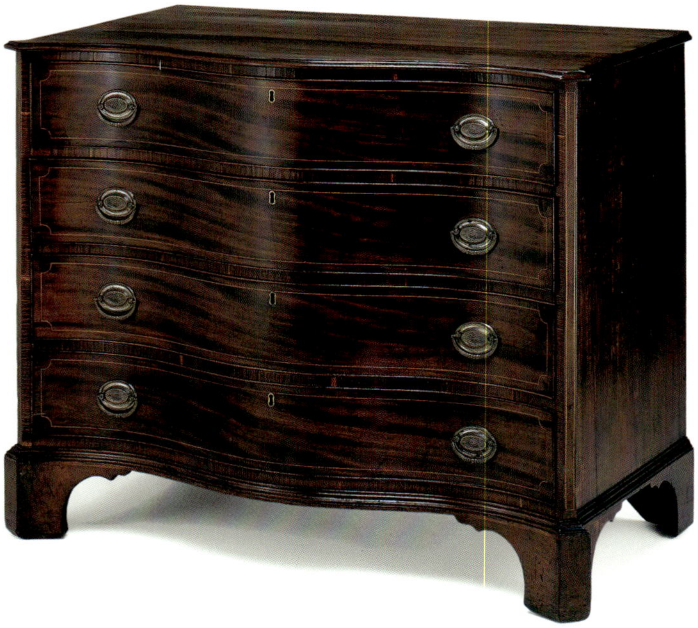

CAT. NO. 44

vateers, or private war ships, were officially sanctioned by the local government, and they preyed on foreign commercial ships. After they were confiscated, those ships and their cargos were sold at auction. Many of Portsmouth's prominent citizens invested in privateering expeditions and built large homes on the waterfront with their profits.[1]

Langley Boardman, newly arrived from Ipswich, Massachusetts, announced the opening of his Portsmouth cabinetmaking business in the local paper, the *Oracle of the Day,* on July 14, 1798.[2] Just twenty-four years old, Boardman was conversant with the English neoclassical style, which favored motifs drawn from Roman antiquity, light-colored inlay in geometric patterns, and contrasting colors in paints and veneers. Within a year of his arrival, Boardman had an impressive array of furniture for sale, including sideboards, desk-and-bookcases, bureaus, card tables, and chairs.[3]

The canted-cornered, serpentine-front chest of drawers appears to have been a popular form with Boardman's clients, for over a dozen, including the Art Institute's, are still known to exist. All have four drawers of equal height, figured mahogany veneers, canted front corners, and C-shaped bracket feet with a slight cusp along the inner edge.[4] Surviving chests of this pattern descended in the well-to-do Wendell, Langdon, Rundlet, and Parrott families of Portsmouth, and today remain in historic houses there.[5]

The Art Institute's Boardman chest (cat. no. 44) retains much of its original finish, to which a later coat of shellac has been applied. The brasses, with chased decorations of grape clusters, are original. The horizontal, wavy-grained, mahogany veneer and the vertical oak veneer are employed to their utmost effect on this chest. The alternating shades of red-brown and chocolate-brown color in the mahogany veneer and the vertical striations of the oak veneer catch and diffuse reflections to create the illusion of depth within the wood and the sensation of movement across the surface. These effects are complemented by the gracefully flowing serpentine front.

Providing a sharp visual contrast to the Boardman chest is another Portsmouth chest in the museum's collection (cat. no. 45). Its compartmentalized, veneered surface and striking contrast of flame-birch veneer with mahogany banding were popular among local cabinetmakers and their clients. The French feet and the central drop pendant show the influence of English designer George Hepplewhite.[6] This regional neoclassical style was popular with the Piscataqua River Valley clientele, as seen in numerous examples that survive today. This chest is part of a large group of pieces featuring such boldly contrasting veneers. Though most chests in this group closely follow Hepplewhite's bow-front chest design, the Art Institute's example has a gently sweeping serpentine curve that accentuates its geometric surface.

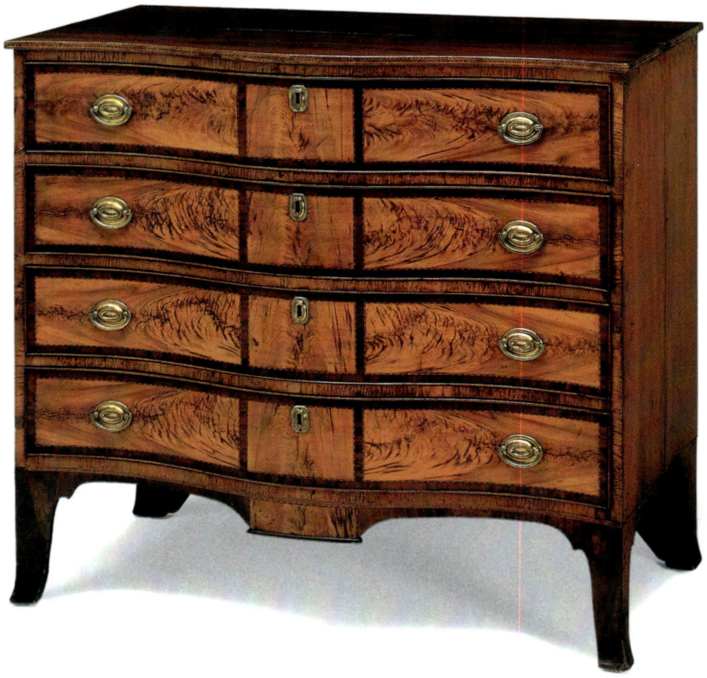

CAT. NO. 45

Though the maker of this second chest is unknown, the inscription "J. Wentworth" on the upper backboard may be the name of an early owner. There were several Wentworths who had ties to Portsmouth, including Governor John Wentworth, who was the last royal governor, in 1775.[7]

NOTES

1. For example, after 1812 Langley Boardman became a partner in several privateering expeditions. He and other prominent citizens owned shares in the privateering ship *Fox*. See Richard E. Winslow III, *"Wealth and Honour": Portsmouth During the Golden Age of Privateering, 1775–1815* (Portsmouth, N.H., 1988), pp. 152–53.

2. Brock Jobe, in Jobe, ed., *Portsmouth Furniture: Masterworks from the New Hampshire Seacoast*, exh. cat. (Boston, Society for the Preservation of New England Antiquities, 1993), pp. 106–07.

3. Johanna McBrien, "Portsmouth Furniture Making, 1798–1837," in Jobe (note 2), p. 59.

4. See Clement Conger, *Treasures of State: Fine and Decorative Arts in the Diplomatic Reception Rooms of the U.S. Department of State* (New York, 1991), pp. 203–04, cat. no. 115.

5. According to Conger (note 4), "The Wendell chest is now owned by the Strawbery Banke; the Langdon and Rundlet chests are in the collections of the Society for the Preservation of New England Antiquities; the Parrott chest is at the Moffatt-Ladd House, a property operated by the National Society of the Colonial Dames in America" (p. 204). Related chests are also in the Yale University Art Gallery (1962.32.22); the Diplomatic Reception Rooms, U.S. Department of State (see Conger [note 4], cat. no. 115); and a private collection, through Bernard and S. Dean Levy, Inc. (inv. no. 33478). Three were sold at auction by Sotheby's in New York: sale no. 3539, June 1973, lot 453; sale no. 4316, Nov.–Dec. 1979, lot 1188; and sale no. H-2, May 1980, lot 1134 (see Jobe [note 2], p. 108). Another related chest, branded several times with the name "C. Hardy," is in the Museum of Fine Arts, Boston.

6. See George Hepplewhite, *The Cabinet-Maker and Upholsterer's Guide* (1794; reprint, New York, 1969), pl. 76. Its central drop is most likely a holdover from the late Baroque and Rococo periods in American furniture design, when elements such as finials, fans, and carved scallop shells appeared below the apron on many case pieces. See Anne Rogers Haley and Brock Jobe, in Jobe (note 2), p. 114.

7. See Jobe (note 2) for more information on the Wentworth family.

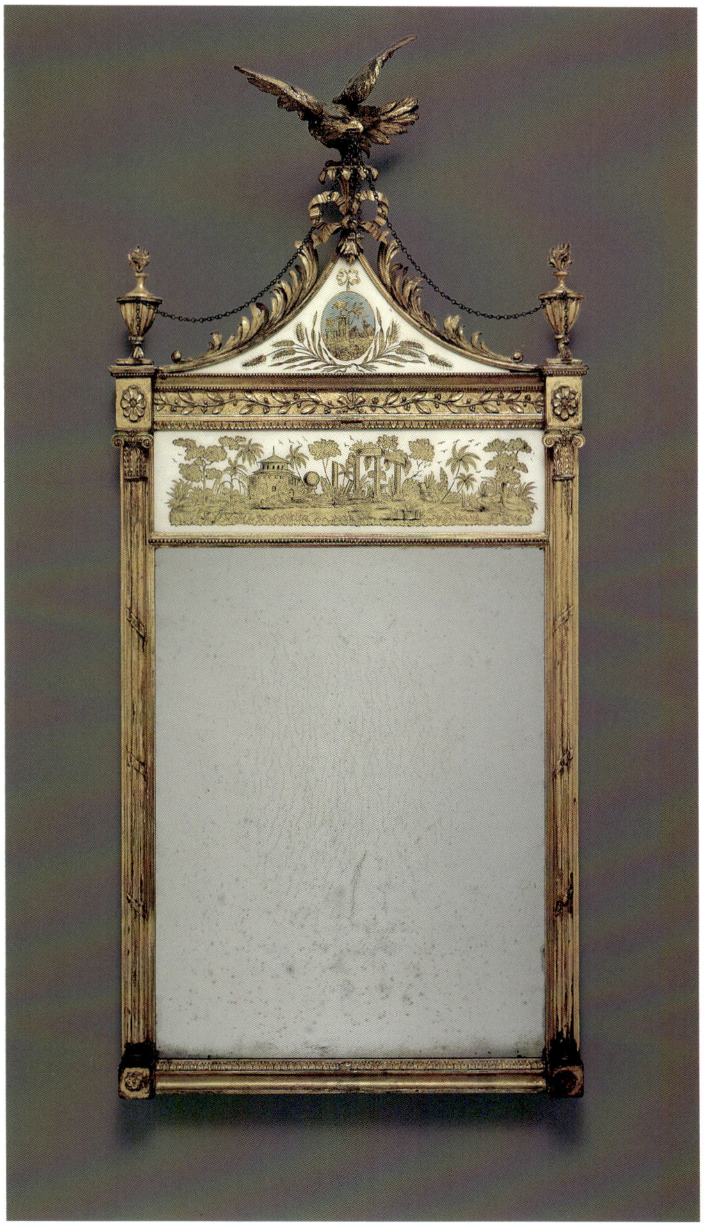

CAT. NO. 46

46. LOOKING GLASS, 1790/1810

New York
White pine with silvered, gilt and painted glass;
170.2 x 71.2 x 5.7 cm (67 x 28¼ x 2¼ in.)
Gift of the Antiquarian Society, 1925.100

Prior to the American Revolution, most looking glasses were imported from England and other countries. American glass makers were unable to produce a glass smooth or clear enough to be silvered.[1] By 1790, however, technological advances made possible the domestic manufacture of looking glasses. An article published in a New York newspaper in 1790 documented the progress that one American glass manufacturer had made: "It is with pleasure we learn that the glass manufactory in Maryland is thriving fast. The glass lately manufactured there is equal in quality to that imported from Europe. . . . We learn that Looking Glasses will be manufactured at these works in the spring."[2] And, as another newspaper article shows, large glasses were being made in New York City by 1794.[3]

It is sometimes difficult to determine whether a looking

glass is of American or European manufacture. The use of eastern white pine (*Pinus strobus*) in the frame of the Art Institute's glass argues for an American origin, since it was a wood favored for carved surfaces in America.[4]

This looking glass was called a pillar glass because it was designed as a vertical interior element to harmonize with architectural elements such as door frames or chimney breasts.[5] Some of its details are drawn from neoclassical architecture, including its engaged columns with Ionic capitals and its square plinths below flaming urns. The eagle was favored by American carvers as a symbol of freedom and the young republic. There are also painted motifs inspired by the work of the eighteenth-century architect Robert Adam, such as the oval suspended from a bow knot, surrounded by wheat stalks. The rectangular, reverse-painted glass panel, called an *eglomisé* panel, is similar to a frieze on an architectural entablature.[6] The panel's scene evokes classical antiquity, but the crumbling ruins surrounded by exotic vegetation relate the image to Romanticism.

In addition to its original gilded surfaces and silvered glass, this work retains its original finials, carved branches, and chains. The *eglomisé* panels have both been largely repainted, which is not unusual for panels of this age.

NOTES

1. David L. Barquist, *American Tables and Looking Glasses in the Mabel Brady Garvan and Other Collections at Yale University* (New Haven, Conn., and London, 1992), pp. 294–95.

2. *Gazette of the United States*, Apr. 7, 1790, as quoted in Rita Susswein Gottesman, ed., *The Arts and Crafts in New York, 1777–1799: Advertisements and News Items from New York City Newspapers* (New York, 1954), pp. 98–99.

3. *The Diary; or Evening Register*, July 17, 1794, as cited in Gottesman (note 2), p. 119.

4. The brace for the eagle finial is made from red pine, a wood found in both America and England, but may have been added at a later date. Wood samples were taken from five areas on the looking-glass frame: two areas on the frame, one from the finial, one from the eagle, and one from the brace supporting the eagle. The samples were analyzed by the Center for Wood Anatomy Research, U.S. Forest Products Laboratory, Madison, Wis., in April 1976.

5. Helen Comstock, *The Looking Glass in America, 1700–1825* (New York, 1968), p. 19.

6. Barquist (note 1), p. 323.

47. CYLINDER DESK AND BOOKCASE, 1800/1810

Northeastern Massachusetts, probably Boston

Mahogany with white pine and mahogany, birch, and maple veneers; 196.8 x 91.2 x 55.9 cm (78½ x 35⅞ x 22 in.)

Inscriptions: lower case, on underside of proper left short drawer bottom in script: *R*; on underside of proper right short drawer bottom in script—both in pencil: *L*; on interior of drawer bottom on long drawer in chalk: *FOR BOOKS*

Gift of the Antiquarian Society through the Jessie Spalding Landon Fund, 1957.453

During the eighteenth century, literacy rates remained low in the colonies—only a third of women and about half of the men could sign their names. However, the influence of the Enlightenment, with its emphasis on universal education, had begun to improve the situation in New England by the end of the century. In the colonial era, most pedagogical efforts were made on behalf of boys. But by the first decades of the nineteenth century, a number of girls' schools with serious educational aims were founded in the Northeast. By 1840 literacy was almost universal among New England men and women.[1]

This new emphasis on female education and accomplishment was chronicled in portraiture between 1790 and 1830. The flowers and embroidery that accompanied eighteenth-century female sitters were replaced by books and letters (see fig. 23). New furniture forms were produced to provide for these activities. In 1803 the English designer Thomas Sheraton provided a drawing for a lady's bureau bookcase in his *Cabinet Dictionary*, in which he wrote, "This design is intended for the use of a lady and should be executed in black rosewood, and brass ornaments, to give it a proper appearance." Sheraton also provided a design for a cylinder writing table, "which is for a lady to write at."[2] George Hepplewhite's *Cabinet-Maker and Upholsterer's Guide* included a design for a tambour writing table and bookcase (fig. 24). The tambour desk is small in scale and so may also have been intended for use by a woman.

In its reliance on contrasting veneers for ornamentation, this desk and bookcase is typical of pieces in the early neoclassical taste. The carved and reeded legs, mullions separating the glass panes, and dentil molding under the cornice are subtle complements to the contrasting mahogany, birch, and maple veneers.[3] The cabinetmaker took full advantage of his skills by employing both light and dark veneers, as well as veneers of different figures and grains. A horizontally grained crotch

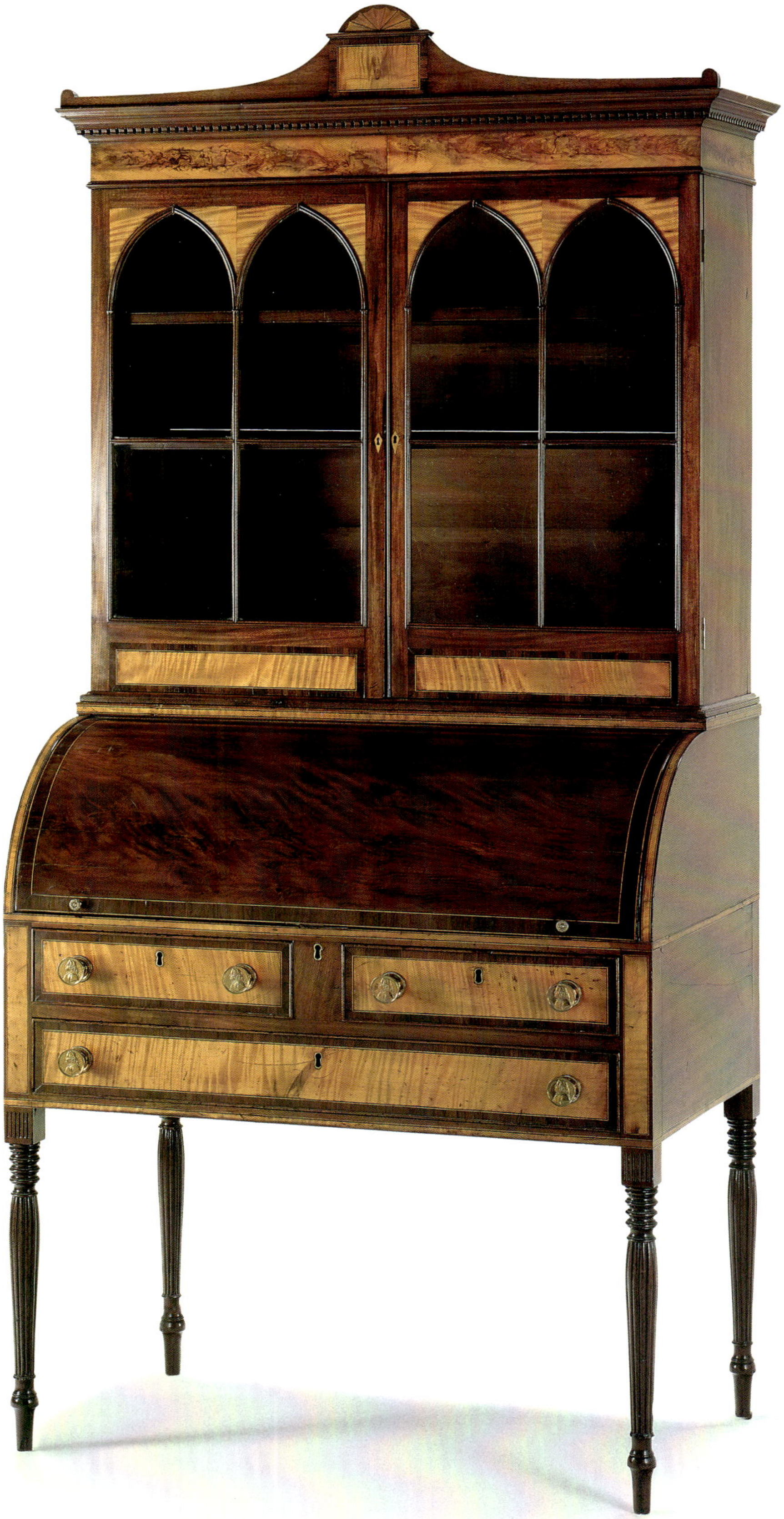

CAT. NO. 47

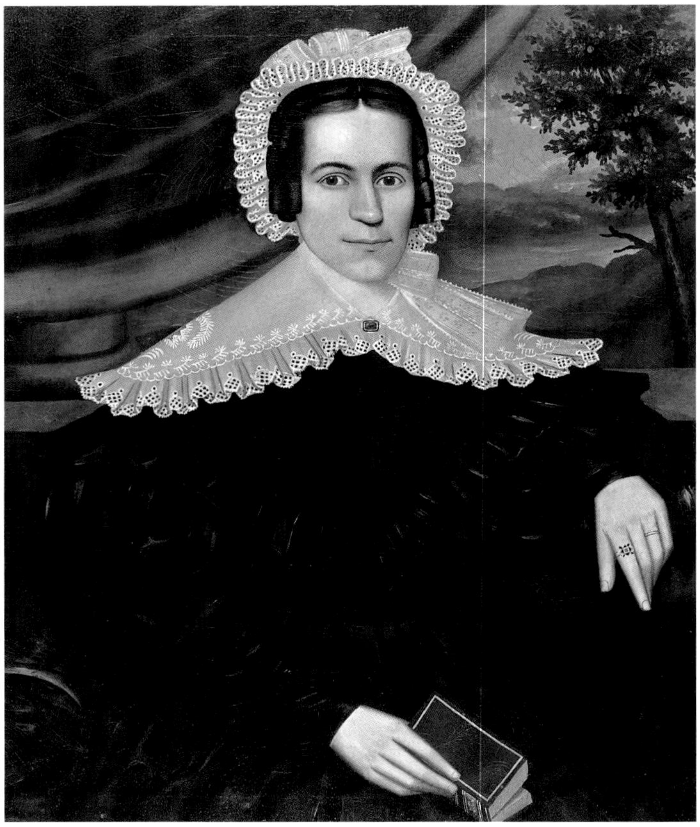

FIG. 23. Erastus Salisbury Field (1805–1900). *Woman with Green Book*, 1836/40. Oil on canvas; 89 x 74.4 cm (35 x 29¼ in.). The Art Institute of Chicago, Gift of Edgar William and Bernice Chrysler Garbisch (1980.746).

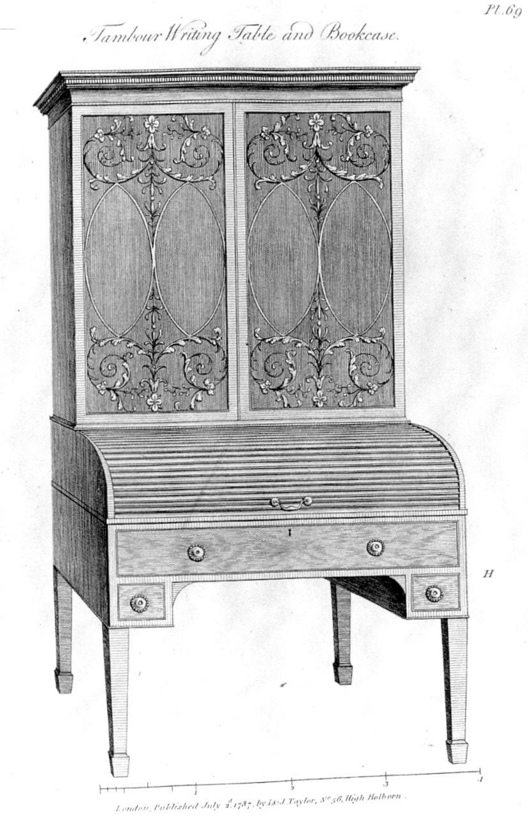

FIG. 24. A. Hepplewhite and Company, *The Cabinet-Maker and Upholsterer's Guide* (London, 1788), pl. 69. Collection of Ryerson and Burnham Libraries, The Art Institute of Chicago.

mahogany veneer,[4] framed by a stringing of light wood and a larger border of vertically grained mahogany veneer, appears on the cylinder front. In contrast is the vertically grained maple veneer accentuating the cylinder top. Maple veneer is also used on the drawer fronts.

The craftsman who made this piece paid particular attention to minor details of construction and design. The lower rail of the cylinder fall has matching maple and ebonized inlay, which creates a visual harmony with the overall design when the desk is open. The orderly configuration of the drawers and cubby holes on the desk interior extend the compartmentalization of the desk's exterior. Each of the interior and exterior drawers has mahogany front, side, and back boards with a pine bottom board. The two uppermost interior drawers are cut at an angle to accommodate the cylinder top. The English stamped, brass knobs are ornamented with a likeness of Benjamin Franklin. Franklin organized the first subscription library in America in 1731 by founding the Library Company of Philadelphia. He lived in England sporadically from 1757 to 1775; after he became famous, his image was widely circulated in print, on miniatures, and on ceramics. The depiction of Franklin may have been modeled after a miniature painted by Isaac Gossett in London in 1766, which was then copied and mass-produced in ceramic by Josiah Wedgwood.[5]

NOTES

1. Nancy F. Cott, *The Bonds of Womanhood: "Woman's Sphere" in New England, 1780–1835* (New Haven, Conn., and London, 1977), pp. 101–03, 115–17.

2. Thomas Sheraton, *The Cabinet Dictionary* (1803; reprint, New York, 1970), pp. 111–13, 188.

3. Wood veneers are thin slices of plank wood. Expensive and highly figured woods such as mahogany and maple were sliced into veneers and glued to less expensive woods such as pine to make the expensive materials go further. See Herbert L. Edlin, *What Wood Is That? A Manual of Wood Identification* (London, 1969), p. 14.

4. A crotch veneer is taken from the area of the tree where the trunk separates into two limbs.

5. Donald L. Fennimore, "Brass Hardware on American Furniture, Part II: Stamped Hardware, 1750–1850," *Antiques* 140, 1 (July 1991), p. 86; and Fennimore, *Metalwork in Early America: Copper and Its Alloys from the Winterthur Collection* (Winterthur, Del., 1996), p. 330.

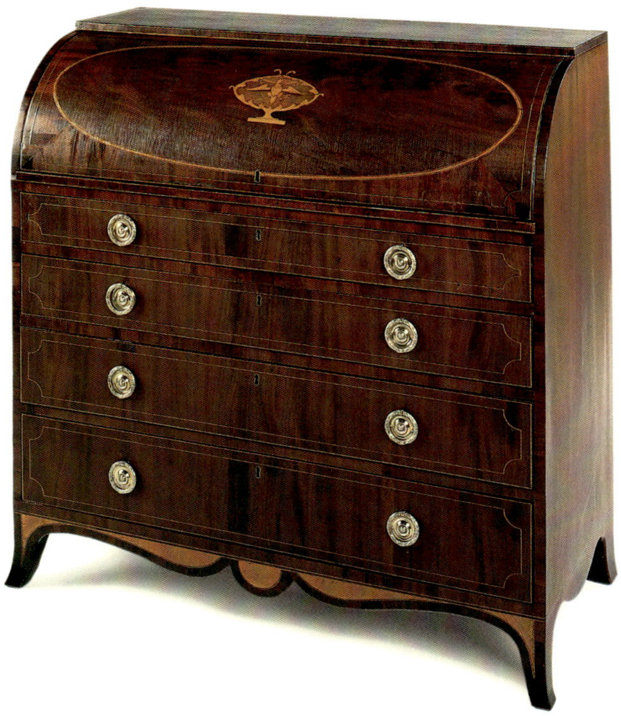

CAT. NO. 48

48. CYLINDER DESK, 1800/1810

Baltimore

Mahogany with mahogany and satinwood veneers and tulip wood; 112.3 x 107.2 x 52.3 cm (44¼ x 42¼ x 20⅝ in.)

Signed on the proper right interior small proper left drawer, on right drawer side in script: *Jas Haillon*

Gift of the Antiquarian Society through Joyce Martin Brown, Mrs. Harold T. Martin, Mrs. Edgar J. Uilhein, and Melinda Martin Vance, 1981.291

Federal Baltimore was a city with a variety of specialized craft industries: cabinetmakers, chairmakers, carvers, gilders, and inlay makers.[1] The inlay trade was an important part of the Federal furniture-making industry in Baltimore. Three principal suppliers provided the city's cabinetmakers with stringing, shells, eagles, and other decorative patterns. Among these, Thomas Barrett was particularly successful; when he died in 1800 his estate inventory contained over 1,300 "shells for inlaying in furniture" and over 600 yards of banding. Much of the inlay work from Barrett's estate was purchased by local cabinetmakers for use in their own furniture.[2]

Baltimore pictorial inlay work is very distinctive. The most common images used in the Federal period were multiple three-part husks, or bellflowers, shells, eagles, and floral-leaf motifs.[3] The craftsman of the museum's desk employed vertically grained mahogany veneers on the drawer fronts, thin bands of satinwood inlay around the edges of the drawers and cylinder top, and large sections of satinwood inlay with a border of mahogany on the skirt to provide a stimulating but simple visual complement to the large oval inlay on the cylinder top, the focal point of the desk.

The oval decoration on the cylinder top has a ground of horizontally grained mahogany veneer. In the center of the oval is a smaller foliate oval on a trumpet foot containing an eagle with spread wings holding a shield, a banner, an olive branch, and an arrow—symbols of the new republic. The eagle motif and a conch shell also appear on the interior prospect door. By 1800 the eagle was a popular device used in American and Baltimore furniture. In fact, in 1798 the First Troop of the Baltimore Light Dragoons honored America's new symbol with a toast and six rousing cheers at a banquet. A toast to President Adams only garnered three cheers.[4]

The Art Institute's cylinder desk is one of only a handful of related examples. It is closest to a desk in the collection of the Baltimore Museum of Art, and was most likely made by the same hand. The inlay on its cylinder front depicts a similar eagle, but with its head facing the opposite direction.[5] The desk may have been inspired by several plates from George Hepplewhite's *Cabinet-Maker and Upholsterer's Guide.* Plate 76c depicts a four-drawer chest with a similar apron design and the

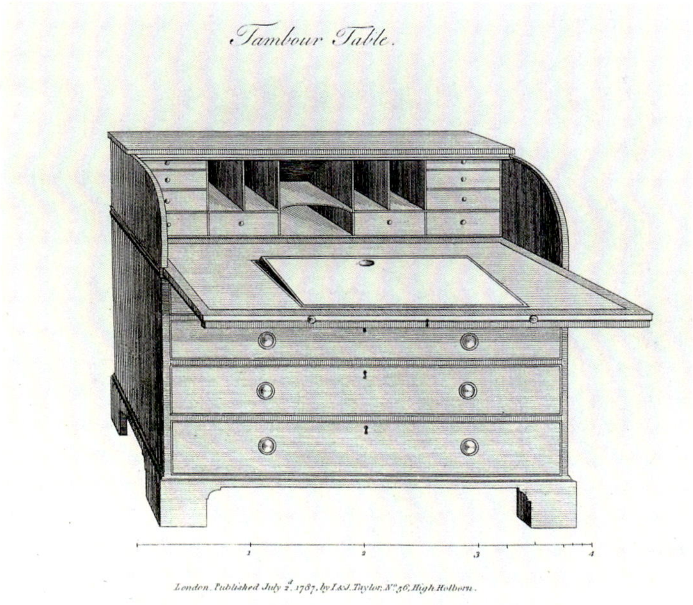

FIG. 25. A. Hepplewhite and Company, *The Cabinet-Maker and Upholsterer's Guide* (London, 1788), pl. 68. Collection of Ryerson and Burnham Libraries, The Art Institute of Chicago.

curved French feet that were popular in Baltimore. Plate 68 shows a design for a tambour desk that, like the Art Institute's cylinder desk, has a slide-out writing surface, flat top, curved front, and four-drawer front (fig. 25). Tambour doors were not a popular design element in Baltimore; the cabinetmaker who followed Hepplewhite's design substituted the cylinder for the tambour top in the finished product.[6]

NOTES

1. Gregory R. Weidman, *Furniture in Maryland, 1740–1940* (Baltimore, 1984), pp. 72–73.

2. Ibid., p. 73; and Charles F. Montgomery, *American Furniture: The Federal Period* (New York, 1966), p. 40.

3. Montgomery (note 2), p. 40.

4. Mabel Munson Swan, "Wings Over Baltimore," *Antiques* 42, 1 (July 1942), p. 17.

5. The related desk appears on the cover of William Voss Elder III and Jayne E. Stokes, *American Furniture, 1680–1880, in the Collection of the Baltimore Museum of Art* (Baltimore, 1987); however, the image was mistakenly reversed. Other related pieces are a desk and bookcase in the Maryland Historical Society (see Weidman [note 1], p. 136); a miniature cylinder desk in the Winterthur Museum (see Montgomery [note 2], p. 239); a cylinder desk formerly owned by Joe Kindig, Jr. (see advertisement in *Antiques* 46, 4 [Oct. 1944], inside front cover); and a cylinder desk in a private collection.

6. The cylinder top is constructed with curved, veneered boards of mahogany that are strengthened on the underside by glued linen fabric. The same construction appears on the desk in the Baltimore Museum of Art. See Elder and Stokes (note 5), pp. 103–04.

49. CHARLES WILLSON PEALE (1741–1827)

Mrs. John Nicholson (Hannah Duncan) and John Nicholson, Jr., 1790

Oil on canvas; 91.5 x 69.3 cm (36 x 27 5/16 in.)

Gift of Mr. and Mrs. Carter H. Harrison, 1952.1001

50. JAMES PEALE (1749–1831)

Mary (Polly) Lawton Bringhurst, 1790

Watercolor on ivory; 6.3 x 5.2 cm. (2 1/2 x 2 1/16 in.)

Signed, lower right: *I P 1790*

Verso: *Mourning Scene*

Mary Louise Stevenson Fund, 1958.410

51. REMBRANDT PEALE (1778–1860)

Samuel Fisher Bradford, 1803/08

Oil on canvas; 68.5 x 55.9 cm (27 x 22 in.)

Restricted gift of Mr. and Mrs. Herbert Alexander Vance Fund, 1986.21

Among John Nicholson's papers, now in the Pennsylvania State Archives in Harrisburg, is a card listing the sizes and corresponding prices for Charles Willson Peale's portraits of ladies and gentlemen. Nicholson chose a fairly modest three-quarters size for the portraits of himself and his family, described by Peale's card as "two Feet six Inches, by two Feet one Inch" and as costing ten guineas.[1] When Peale painted the Nicholsons, John was comptroller general of Pennsylvania, a post he held from 1782 to 1794, and a wealthy landowner, with 3,700,000 acres to his name. By 1800, however, Nicholson's fortunes had sharply declined, and he was incarcerated in debtor's prison.[2]

Peale fared better than Nicholson, although his beginnings were quite modest. Apprenticed early in life to a saddler in Annapolis, Maryland, he did not begin painting until he was in his early twenties.[3] Sensing his talent, a group of patrons sent the amateur artist to London, where Benjamin West aided the young Peale's artistic training. In 1776 he and his family settled in Philadelphia, the city that came most closely to be associated with the artist and his talented offspring. Peale's vast enthusiasms and achievements encompass both the arts and the sciences, including the founding of the first American natural history museum, in July 1786.[4] Father of a large brood of children named for renowned artists and scientists, male and female alike, Peale united family and work, training many of his progeny to be artists and to perform horticultural studies both in his museum and at his farm, Belfield.

Peale wrote "An Essay to Promote Domestic Happiness" in 1812, and historian Lillian B. Miller suggested that he "enjoyed finding examples of . . . domestic happiness in the family pictures he was asked to paint."[5] *Mrs. John Nicholson (Hannah Duncan) and John Nicholson, Jr.* personifies the artist's ideas about domestic happiness, which he expressed in his essay, as well as those popularized by the eighteenth-century French philosopher Jean Jacques Rousseau. Among the many strategies for domestic bliss, Rousseau promoted lenient child-rearing practices and a strong connection to nature for mother and child.[6] Mrs. Nicholson and her son embody this Rousseauean bond to nature by the generic outdoor scene behind them and other less obvious details. Rather than being covered by a wig,

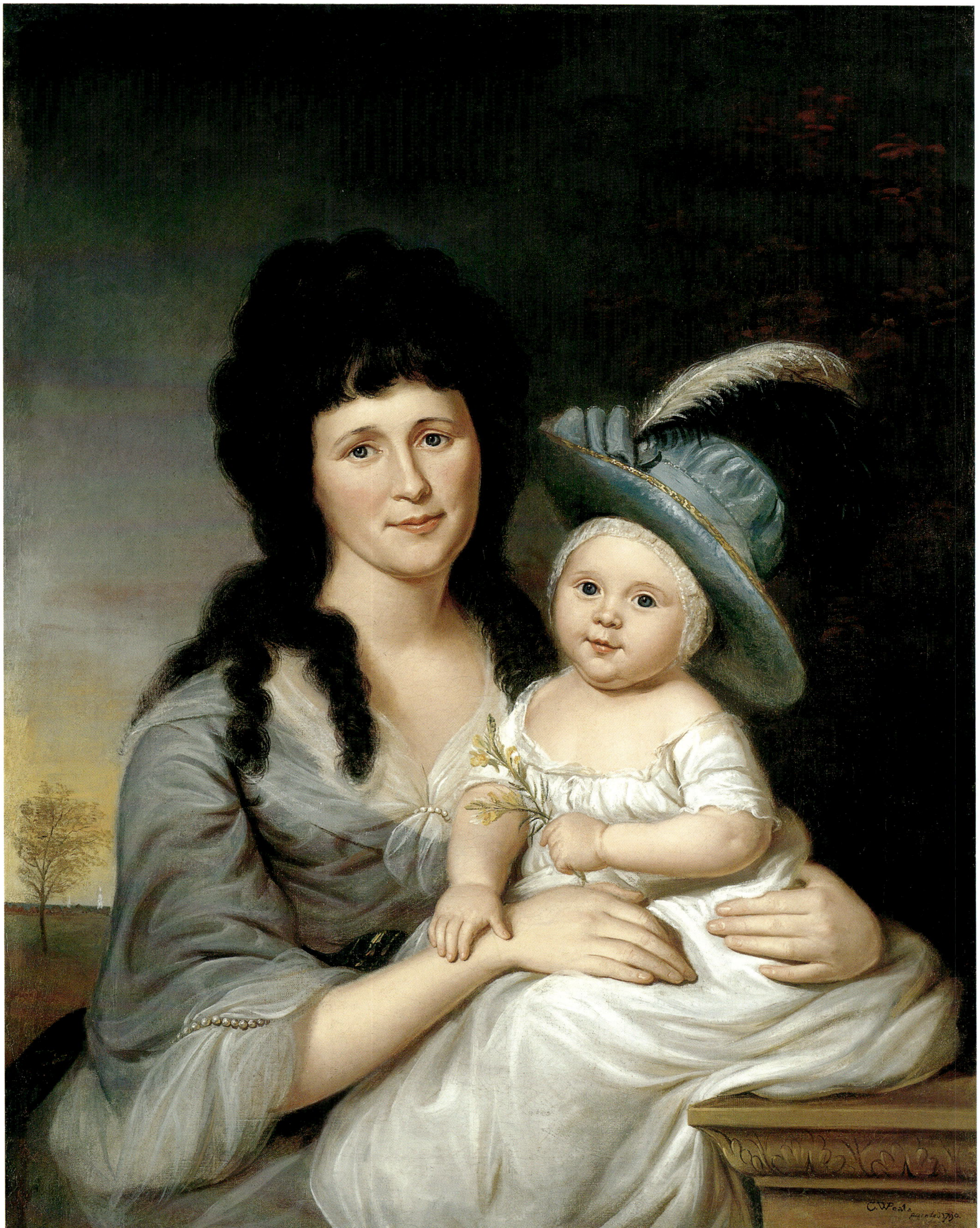

CAT. NO. 49

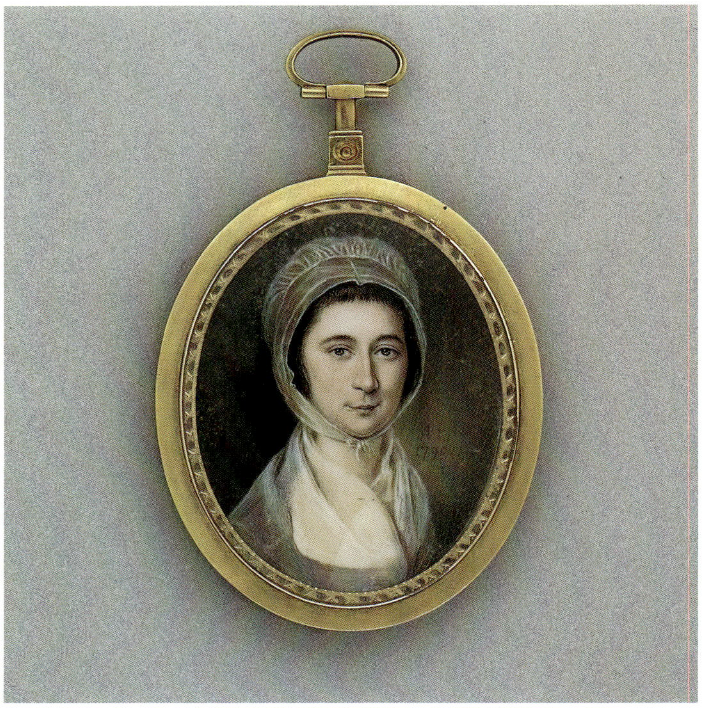

CAT. NO. 50, RECTO

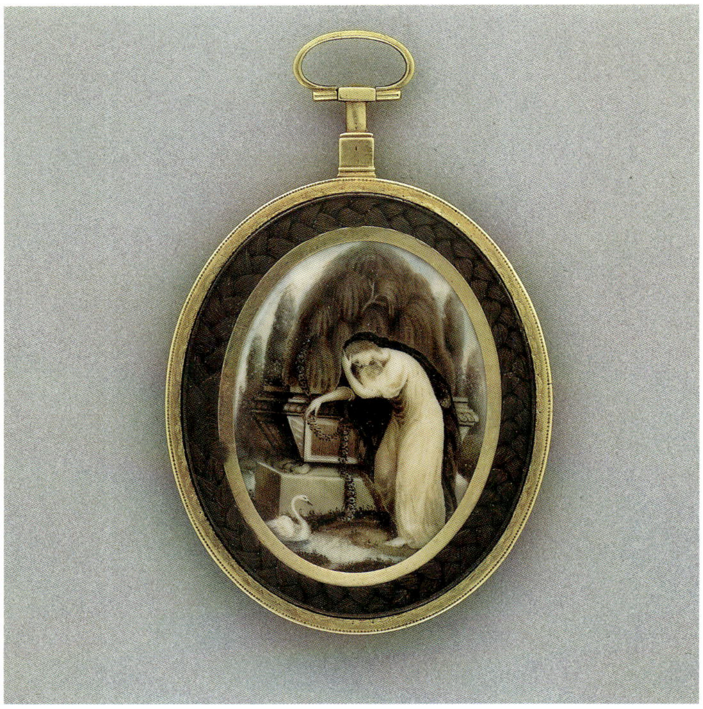

CAT. NO. 50, VERSO

her hair falls freely to her shoulders; her dress is elegantly soft and loose; and the baby wears a feather in his cap and holds a sprig of flowers in his chubby, dimpled fist. The two touch each other tenderly and smile sweetly, without a trace of stiffness. In contrast Mr. Nicholson (fig. 26) poses formally indoors; he holds a quill pen and rests his arm on an open book, suggesting his role as provider for his family. Whereas his wife and son directly engage the viewer, Mr. Nicholson looks off to the side.

Charles Willson Peale taught his younger brother James the art of miniature painting. In 1786 the two reportedly decided to divide the market for portraits in Philadelphia between them, James specializing in miniatures and Charles in larger works on canvas. The same year that Charles painted the Nicholson family likenesses, James Peale produced a miniature of Mary (Polly) Lawton Bringhurst, using the traditional method of painting in watercolor on ivory.[7] The ivory's smooth opacity provides a luminous ground for the subtle layers of transparent colors applied in a stippled fashion.

A Quaker originally from Newport, Rhode Island, Mary Lawton married John Bringhurst, a Philadelphia merchant, in 1789 and died four years later.[8] Mrs. Bringhurst wears a simple bonnet and shawl, which attest to her Quaker heritage and married status. Portrait miniatures were produced as portable keepsakes usually for family members and spouses; they functioned as intimate, cherished reminders of loved ones before

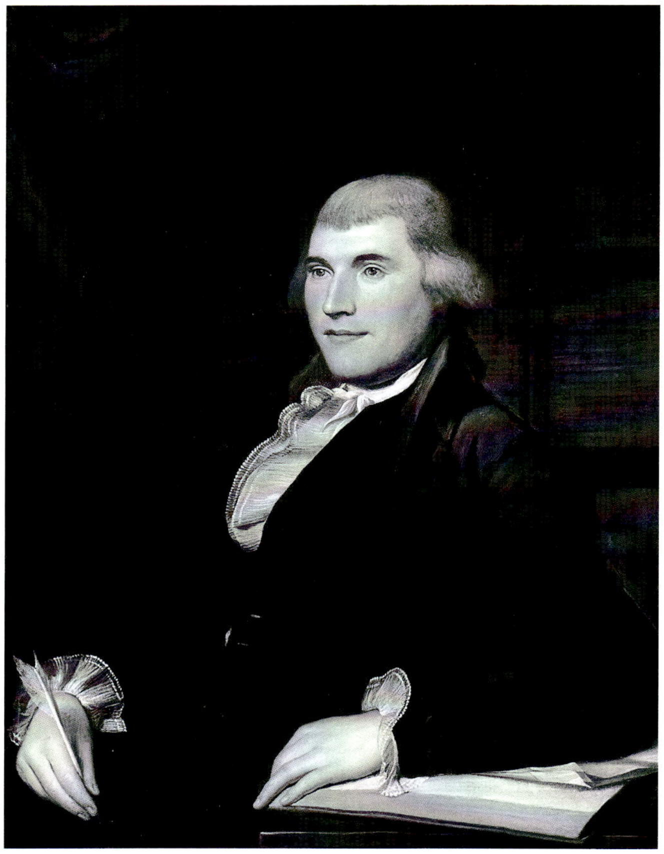

FIG. 26. Charles Willson Peale (1741–1827). *John Nicholson,* 1790. Oil on canvas; 91.5 x 70 cm (36 x 27½ in.). The Art Institute of Chicago, Gift of Mr. and Mrs. Carter H. Harrison (1952.1000).

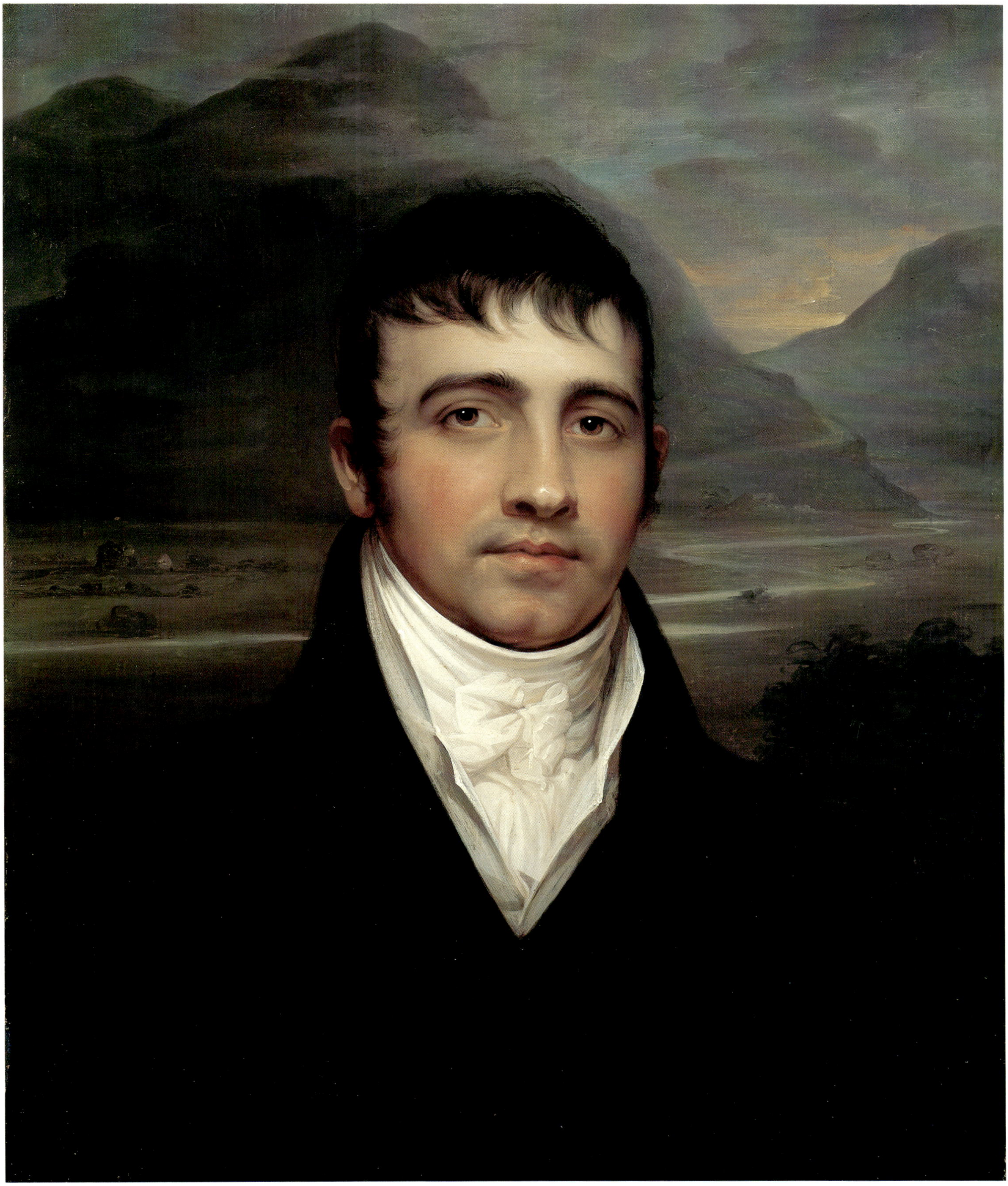

CAT. NO. 51

photographs usurped their popularity in the mid-nineteenth century. Mrs. Bringhurst's early death explains the traditional mourning scene, painted on the reverse, of a woman with loose hair weeping over a tomb.

When Charles Willson Peale announced his retirement from portrait painting in *Claypoole's American Daily Advertiser* on April 24, 1794, he recommended his sons Rembrandt and Raphaelle to the public for future portrait commissions.[9] Raphaelle became better known for his elegant still-life compositions (see cat. no. 56) than his portraits, but his brother dutifully followed his father's lead and established himself as a portraitist early in his career, gaining renown for the extraordinary number of likenesses he made of George Washington. Later, however, Rembrandt turned to history painting to satisfy his longing to make a more significant contribution to American art.

Rembrandt painted *Samuel Fisher Bradford* sometime after his 1803 return from London, where he studied, like his father, with Benjamin West, and before his 1808 trip to Paris. Bradford was a descendant of William Bradford, who traveled to the colonies with William Penn and established the *New York Gazette* in 1725.[10] In this family of printers, Samuel Fisher Bradford's most important contributions include the editing and publication of Abraham Rees's *Cyclopaedia* and artist-ornithologist Alexander Wilson's illustrated, multi-volume *Ornithology*. The Bradfords and Peales had long-standing personal and professional relationships: the Bradfords often published materials for the Peale Museum, and the families collaborated on various other printing projects as well.

Bradford is depicted bust-length in front of evocative scenery that augments the romantic tone established by the sitter's loose white tie, casually arranged hair, and sensitive, finely modeled features. Carol Hevner suggested a connection between the landscape and Bradford's relationship with Alexander Wilson, whom Bradford hired in 1806 to tutor his sons. Wilson believed that, according to Hevner, "the beauties and particulars of American nature could be a just expression of a proud nationalism."[11] The portrait anticipates the predominant role that landscape would come to play in the shaping of American art during Peale's lifetime.

These three portraits demonstrate not only the versatility and preeminence of the Peale family, but also the dominance of portraiture in American art production during the early republic. Calculating, but always creative, the Peales stimulated and saturated an art market that kept them prospering economically and artistically.

NOTES

1. This card is reproduced in Edgar P. Richardson, Brooke Hindle, and Lillian B. Miller, *Charles Willson Peale and His World*, exh. cat. (Washington, D.C., National Portrait Gallery, 1982), p. 73.

2. David A. Hanks, "American Paintings at The Art Institute of Chicago, Part I: The Eighteenth Century," *Antiques* 104, 3 (Sept. 1973), p. 414.

3. For more biographical information on Peale, see Richardson, Hindle, and Miller (note 1).

4. For a study of Peale's Museum, see David Brigham, *Public Culture and the Early Republic: Peale's Museum and Its Audience* (Washington, D.C., 1995).

5. Richardson, Hindle, and Miller (note 1), p. 202.

6. See Carol Duncan, "Happy Mothers and Other New Ideas in French Art," *Art Bulletin* 55, 4 (Dec. 1973), pp. 570–83, for more about Rousseau's impact on images of women in the eighteenth century.

7. This portrait miniature was long thought to depict James Peale's first wife, Rachel Brewer Peale, who died in 1790. For a complete account of the reattribution of this piece by Lance Humphries, see Eleanor H. Gustafson, ed., "Collectors' Notes," *Antiques* 148, 2 (Aug. 1995), p. 142. Mr. Humphries generously shared his research with us.

8. For more about John Bringhurst and his mercantile activity, see Harwood A. Johnson and Diana Edwards, "Ornamental Wedgwood Wares in Philadelphia in 1793," *Antiques* 145, 1 (Jan. 1994), pp. 166–73.

9. Lillian B. Miller, ed., *The Selected Papers of Charles Willson Peale and His Family*, vol. 2, pt. 1 (New Haven, Conn., and London, 1988), p. 91.

10. In addition to his own portrait, Bradford commissioned one of his wife, Abigail Inskeep Bradford (now in a private collection). For more about the Bradford family and printing, see Rosalind Remer, *Printers and Men of Capital: Philadelphia Book Publishers in the New Republic* (Philadelphia, 1996).

11. Carol Eaton Hevner, "Samuel Fisher Bradford," in Robert Devlin Schwarz, *A Gallery Collects Peales*, exh. cat. (Philadelphia, F. S. Schwarz and Son, 1987), p. 24.

52. CHARLES-HONORÉ LANNUIER (1779–1819)

Card Table, c. 1815

New York

Mahogany with rosewood veneer, giltwood, brass and ebony inlay, ormolu; 74.9 x 91.1 x 45.1 cm (29½ x 35⅞ x 17¾ in.)

Inscribed on the engraved label on the underside of the table top: *Hre. Lannuier Cabinet Maker from Paris Kips [H]is Whare house of new fashion fourniture Broad Street, No. 60, New-York. / Hre. Lannuier Ebèniste, de Paris Tient Fabrique & Magasin de Meubles les plus à la Mode, New-York.* (see detail)

Promised gift of Jamee J. and Marshall Field, 1994.712

Charles-Honoré Lannuier was a French émigré who trained in Paris as an *ébèniste*, or cabinetmaker, under his brother

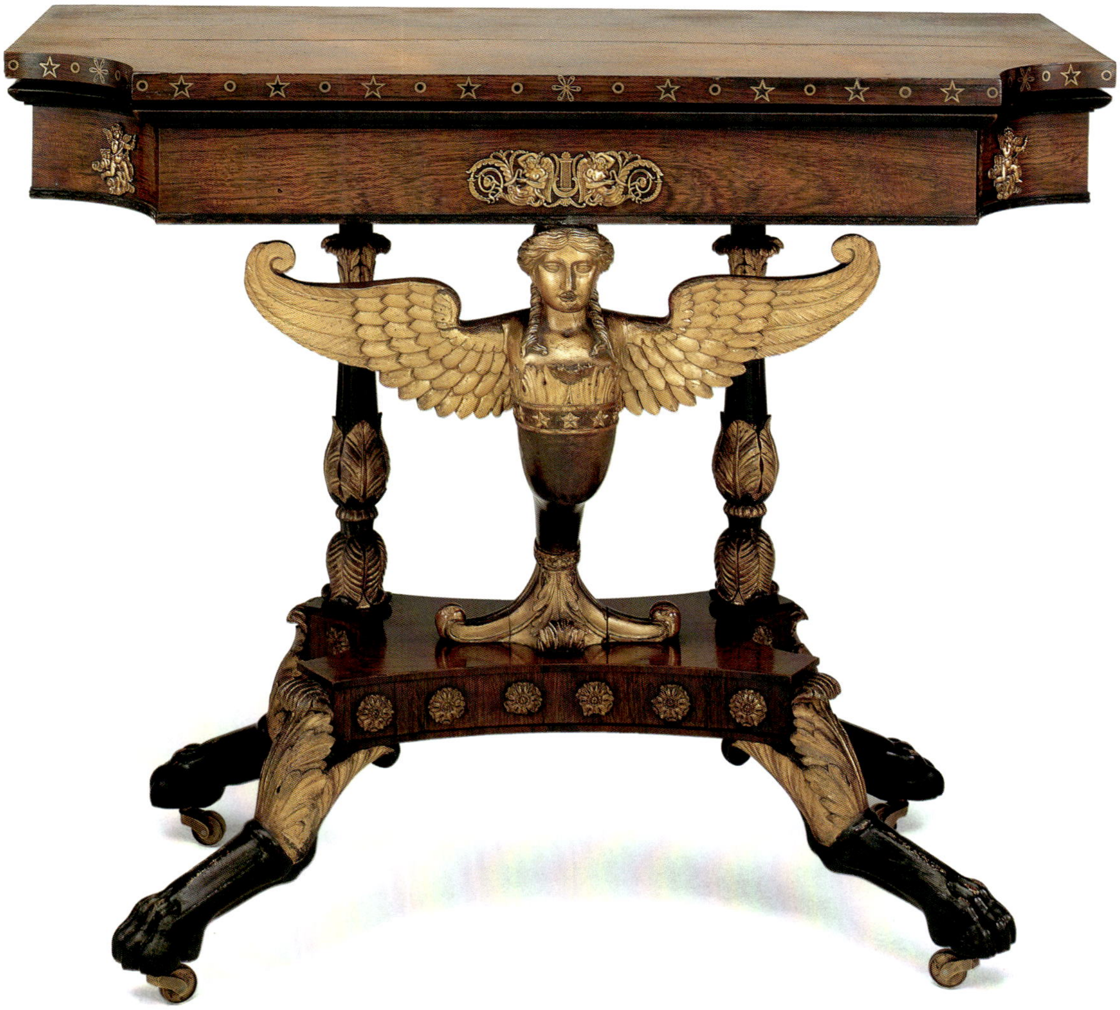

CAT. NO. 52

Nicholas. He arrived in New York in 1803, bringing with him an array of new ideas and styles from France. This labeled card table is part of a group of furniture pieces, including at least eighteen similar tables, that epitomize the American taste for French fashion at the turn of the nineteenth century. Lannuier derived the decorative elements he employed from designs in pattern books, such as *Recueil de décorations intérieures*, which Napoleon's chief designers, Charles Percier and Pierre F. L. Fontaine, first published in 1801 and then reissued in 1812, about the same time that Lannuier began to produce this group of related tables. Another publication he must have known is Pierre de la Mésangère's book of furniture-design, *Collection des meubles et objets de goût*, released serially between 1796 and 1830.

These new pattern books reflected the impact of the Napoleonic campaigns between 1798 and 1801, and a new archaeological approach to the culture of ancient Greece, Egypt, and Turkey. Replacing the lighter, fanciful neoclassical designs of Robert Adam, Thomas Sheraton, and George Hepplewhite, the early Empire style favored sculptural solidity, sweeping curves, and richness of materials and veneers. This later stage of neoclassicism also interpreted antiquity more literally, basing design ideas on actual objects or architectural elements such as Egyptian pylons, Greek saber-legged chairs, and Roman curule stools.

When Lannuier arrived in America, he advertised that he made furniture in "the newest and latest French fashions; and that he has brought for that purpose . . . new patterns."[1] Lannuier may have seen and been inspired by plate 62 in the 1812 edition of Percier and Fontaine's book (fig. 27).[2] The plate includes classical elements that Lannuier incorporated into his card tables: at the top, the winged caryatid supporting an

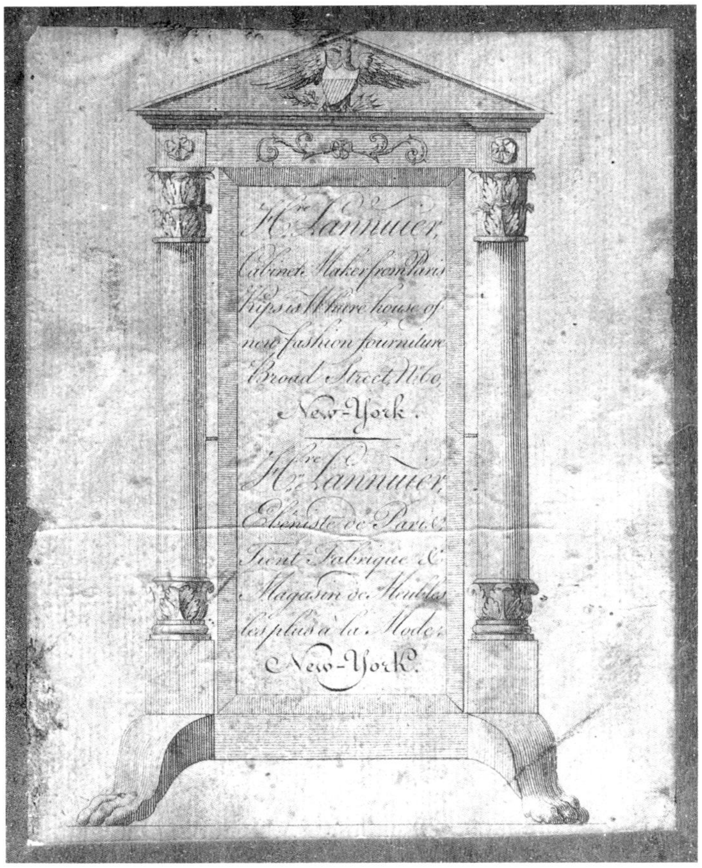

CAT. NO. 52, DETAIL

entablature is similar to the central figure on the card table; at the lower right, the female sphinx may also have inspired Lannuier's winged figure; the hair of the sphinx, which falls down around its shoulders and is gathered up and tied in a loose knot at the top of its head, is similar to that of the Lannuier figure. Lannuier adapted bed designs from plate 21 of Mésangère's volume (fig. 28) for his designs of French bedsteads commissioned by Mrs. Isaac Bell of New York and Stephen Van Rensselaer IV of Albany.[3] Lannuier may also have adapted and simplified several of the decorative elements from this plate for his card tables, including the four outstretched animal paw feet, with acanthus leaves sprouting from the ankle of each foot, the columnar supports at the rear of the table, and the stars around the caryatid figures.

The Art Institute's table is in pristine condition. There has been no major regilding or repainting of any of the table's surfaces. Microscopy conducted on the finish of the legs of the table revealed that the original surface remains intact.[4] Lannuier painted the legs a greenish-black color known as *vert antique* which was meant to resemble patinated bronze.[5] Lannuier used both oil and water gilding to accentuate some of the carved surfaces of the table. Oil gilding produces a matte, or dull, finish because the gold leaf is applied to a red- or yellow-tinted oil-based varnish that has been previously affixed to the surface being gilded. Once applied, the gold cannot be burnished because of the nature of the oil varnish. Water gilding is a more complex process. The wood surface is built up with layers of gesso—a mixture of chalk and glue—and bole—a mixture of clay and glue. The bole surface can be burnished or rubbed to a high sheen with a stone. When ready, the bole surface is moistened with a mixture of water and glue to which the gold leaf can be applied. The leaf will take on the appearance of the burnished bole layer underneath to produce a very shiny surface. On this table, Lannuier oil-gilded the acanthus leaves on the feet and water-gilded the caryatid figure. He burnished the gilded areas on the short, flat feathers to increase the contrast and heighten the three-dimensionality of the wings.

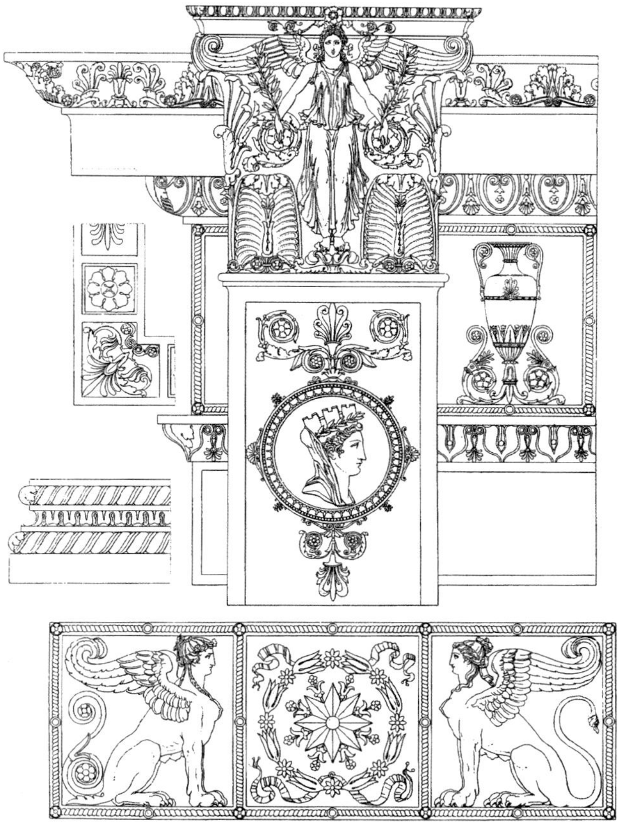

FIG. 27. Charles Percier and Pierre F. L. Fontaine, *Recueil de décorations intérieures* (Paris, 1812), pl. 62. Collection of Ryerson and Burnham Libraries, The Art Institute of Chicago.

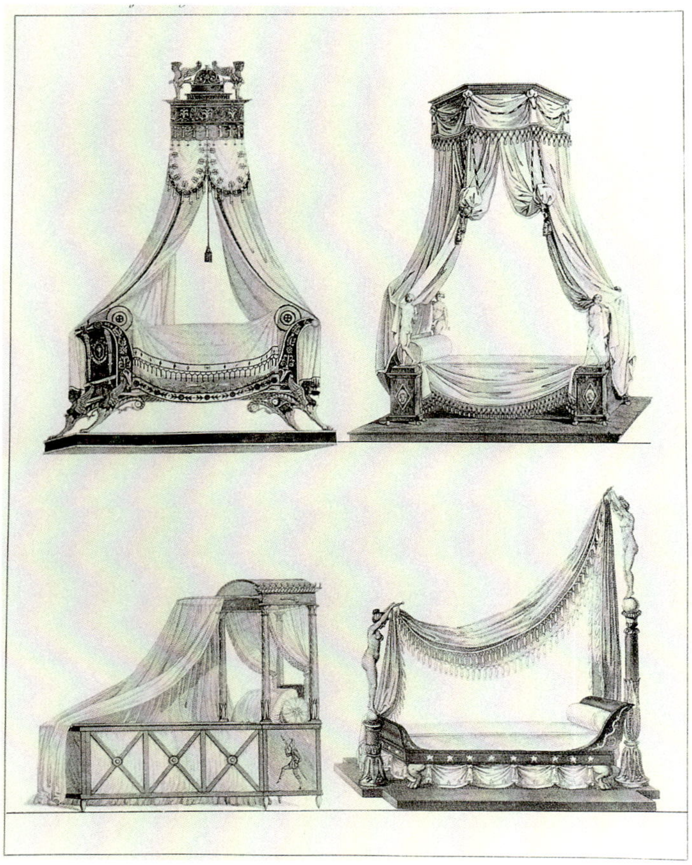

FIG. 28. Pierre de la Mésangère, *Collection des meubles et objets de goût*, ed. Paul Cornu (1796–1830; reprint, Paris, [1920s]), pl. 21. Collection of Ryerson and Burnham Libraries, The Art Institute of Chicago.

The inlaid band of stars and circles along the edge of the table top is an unusual embellishment.

NOTES

1. Charles F. Montgomery, *American Furniture: The Federal Period* (New York, 1966), p. 365.

2. The plate features the details in a room designed for the King of Spain; see Charles Percier and Pierre F. L. Fontaine, *Recueil de décorations intérieures* (Paris, 1812), p. 41.

3. The Bell bedstead is now in the collection of the Bartow-Pell Mansion Museum, Bronx, N.Y. The Van Rensselaer bedstead is now in the collection of the Albany Institute of History and Art, Albany, N.Y.; see Wendy A. Cooper, *Classical Taste in America, 1800–1840*, exh. cat. (Baltimore Museum of Art, 1993), pp. 129–31, cat. nos. 89–90.

4. Conservation research files of the Department of American Arts, The Art Institute of Chicago.

5. Peter M. Kenny, Frances F. Bretter, and Ulrich Leben, *Honoré Lannuier: Cabinetmaker from Paris*, exh. cat. (New York, Metropolitan Museum of Art, 1998), pp. 190–92.

53. ARMCHAIR, c. 1815

New York
Mahogany; 83.8 x 49.5 x 53.3 cm (33 x 19½ x 21 in.)
Gift of the Antiquarian Society in honor of Perry H. Wheeler, 1993.121

54. SETTEE, 1815/20

New York
Mahogany with caning;
90.2 x 183.3 x 58.4 cm (35½ x 72⅜ x 23 in.)
Robert Allerton Fund, 1978.301

Post-revolutionary New York grew more rapidly than any other city in the new republic. In 1789 the city was chosen as the nation's temporary capital, and George Washington was inaugurated as the first President in Federal Hall.[1] A major port for the mid-Atlantic states, New York's harbor supplied goods and services for most of New Jersey and Connecticut. As a result, the city's merchant elite grew and prospered, creating a desire for goods in the most fashionable European tastes. Craftsmen, mostly from France, England, and Scotland, settled in lower New York and began to produce furniture in the latest European style. The most notable among them were Michael Allison, Charles-Honoré Lannuier, and Duncan Phyfe. Motifs from the ancient world—Greek klismos, or sabre legs; Roman hairy paw feet; and classical symbols such as the lyre, harp, swags of flowers and leaves, and wheat sheaves tied with bow knots—epitomized the new neoclassical fashion. The standard design for New York chairs of this period combined curved front and rear legs with a scrolled back incorporating a lyre, harp, or cross in its design. The most expensive of these chairs had carved front legs and paw feet. In 1807 Duncan Phyfe crafted some of the first known New York chairs to be made in this fashion for William Bayard.[2] The design had great popular appeal, for many variations survive, not all of them produced by Phyfe's shop. Phyfe established his business on what is known today as Fulton Street, an area that had a large concentration of cabinet and chairmaking firms; he owned several properties in the vicinity that he rented to other cabinetmakers.[3] These cabinetmakers could see Phyfe's furniture displayed in his showrooms.

Both the armchair and the settee in the Art Institute's collection are excellent examples of the Grecian style introduced by Phyfe and copied by his competitors. With its beautifully scrolled arms, lyre-shaped back splat, turned crest and splat

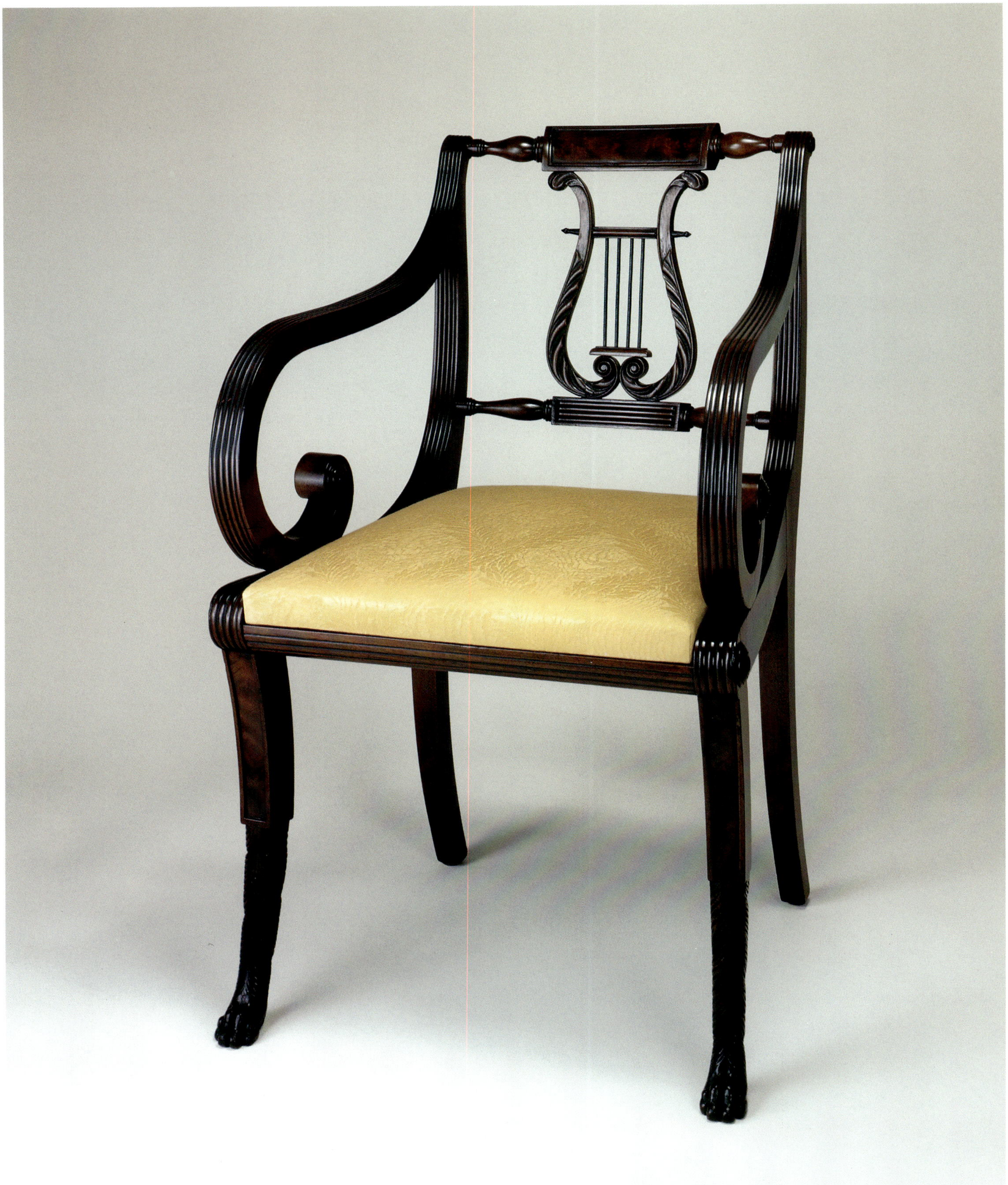

CAT. NO. 53

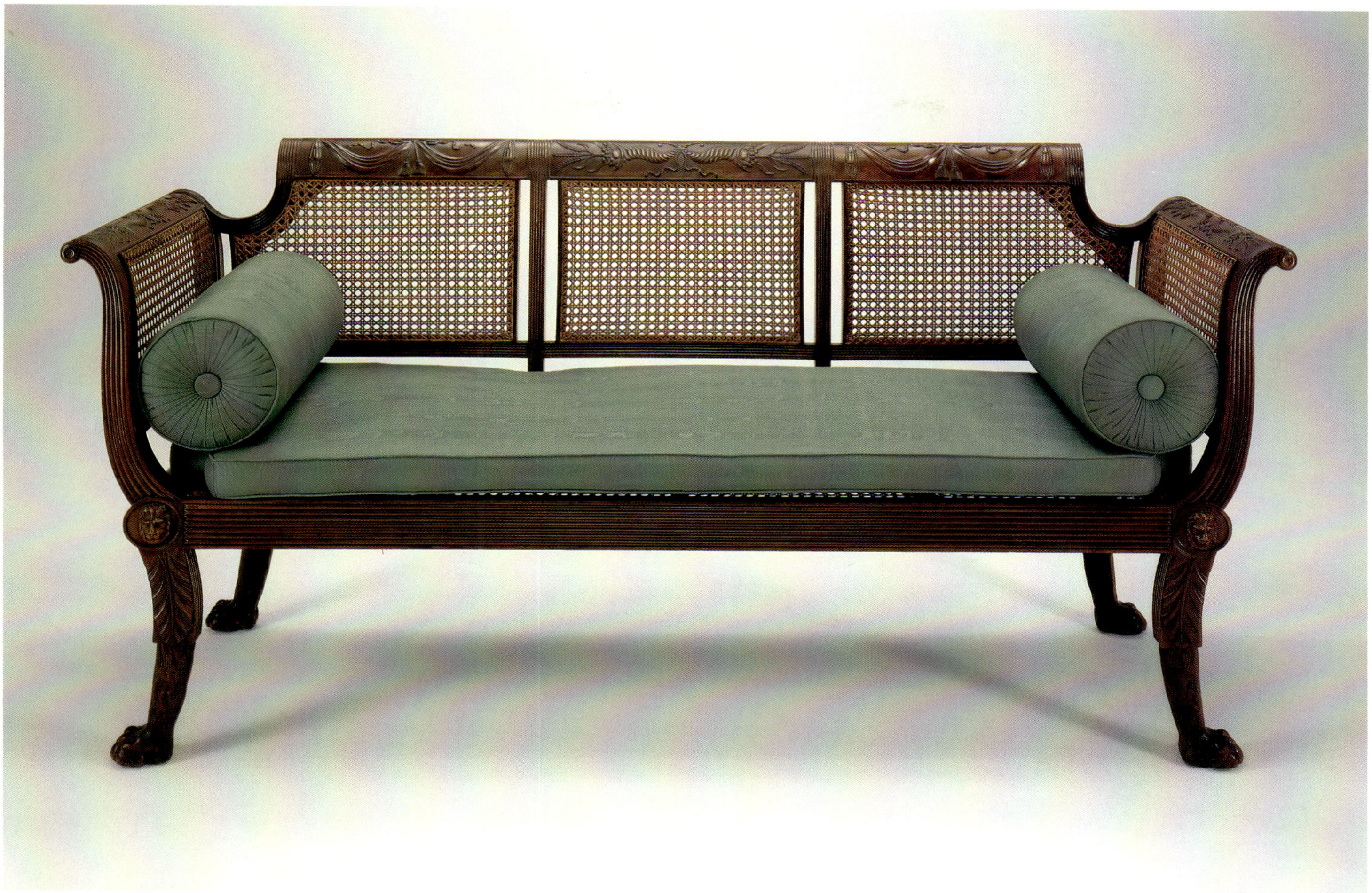

CAT. NO. 54

rails, and carved legs and paw feet, the armchair represents the pinnacle of this classically inspired design.

The settee was part of a larger suite of parlor furniture made for Henry McFarlan, who lived on Vesey Street, several doors from cabinetmaker Michael Allison, and around the corner from the shops of Phyfe and Lannuier.[4] The design of this settee may have been interpreted from one of the many pattern books coming from London at the beginning of the century. The motifs of lion masks, hairy carved legs, and animal paws appear throughout pattern books by Thomas Hope, George Smith, and Thomas Sheraton, all of whom interpreted antique forms for the use of others.[5] The curving sweep of the reeded arms and back, the carved ornament, and the overall lightness of the form make this an elegant and sophisticated piece. The settee is one of several related examples with caned seats and outwardly curving animal paw feet that have been attributed to Phyfe's shop.[6] The museum's settee, however, is somewhat different in construction and quality of carving from the other known examples, and therefore cannot be firmly attributed to Phyfe's shop.[7]

NOTES

1. Because New York was thought to be too far north to best represent the nation as the capital, the seat of government was moved south to Philadelphia in 1790, where it remained for ten years while Washington, D.C., was being constructed.

2. Charles F. Montgomery, *American Furniture: The Federal Period* (New York, 1966), p. 117; and Wendy A. Cooper, *Classical Taste in America: 1800–1840*, exh. cat. (Baltimore Museum of Art, 1993), p. 109.

3. For a list of cabinetmakers to whom Phyfe rented space, see Michael K. Brown, "Duncan Phyfe" (M.A. thesis, University of Delaware, 1978), pp. 6–7.

4. Four matching chairs survived with the settee until 1944, when they were sold at Sotheby Parke Bernet Galleries, New York (May 20, 1944: lots 761–62). Those chairs were sold again in 1998; see Sotheby's, New York, *Important Americana: American Furniture and Folk Art* (Jan. 18, 1998), lot 1558, unpag.

5. Paige Talbott, in Clement Conger and Alexandra Rollins, eds., *Treasures of State: Fine and Decorative Arts in the Diplomatic Reception Rooms of the U.S. Department of State* (New York, 1991), p. 230, cat. no. 138.

6. Other examples are one in the collection of the Diplomatic Reception Rooms of the U.S. Department of State (see Conger and Rollins [note 5], p. 230, cat. no. 138); one sold at auction at Christie's, New York (June 17, 1997), lot 429; and one formerly in the collection of Dr. C. Ray Franklin, which was sold at auction at Sotheby's, New York (Jan. 17 and 19, 1997), lot 951.

7. The museum's settee has a front seat rail ornamented with seven notch-ended reeds; the lion's head masks on the legs are fully contained in an oval and are carved from wood; the ornamental carving is flat and stylized; the underside of the seat rails is unchamfered; there are chamfered glue blocks in each corner of the underside of the seat; there are three seat braces set with half dovetails into the front and rear seat rails with no cabinetmaker's marks present. In the three related settees, the front seat rails are ornamented with five stump-ended reeds; the ornamental carvings are more robust and detailed; the underside of the side seat rails are chamfered; none of the related settees originally had glueblocks underneath the seat. The settees from Christie's and Sotheby's have lion's head masks on the legs made out of composition, or plaster. The Sotheby's settee has three braces with full dovetails underneath the seat; the settees from Christie's and the Department of State have four braces underneath with half dovetails, the Department of State's having cabinetmaker's marks on the braces that correspond to matching scribe lines on the seat rails. Thomas Sudbank of the Diplomatic Reception Rooms at the U.S. Department of State provided the information on the settee in that collection.

55. JEAN-SIMON CHAUDRON (1758–1846) AND ANTHONY RASCH (c. 1778–1859?) (ACTIVE 1809–1812)

Tea and Coffee Service, 1809/12

Philadelphia

Silver and ebonized wood; coffeepot: h. 29.2 cm (11½ in.); teapot: h. 26.7 cm (10½ in.); cream pot: h. 18.4 cm (7 1/4 in.); sugar basin: h. 23.5 cm (9¼ in.)

Each piece marked on underside of base in banners: *CHAUDRON'S & RASCH* and *STER•AMER•MAN•* [Sterling American Manufacture]

Robert Allerton Endowment, 1989.156.1–4

Jean-Simon Chaudron was born in Vignery, France, in 1758. He learned the art of watchmaking in Switzerland, where he may have also learned to fabricate jewelry and silver objects. In

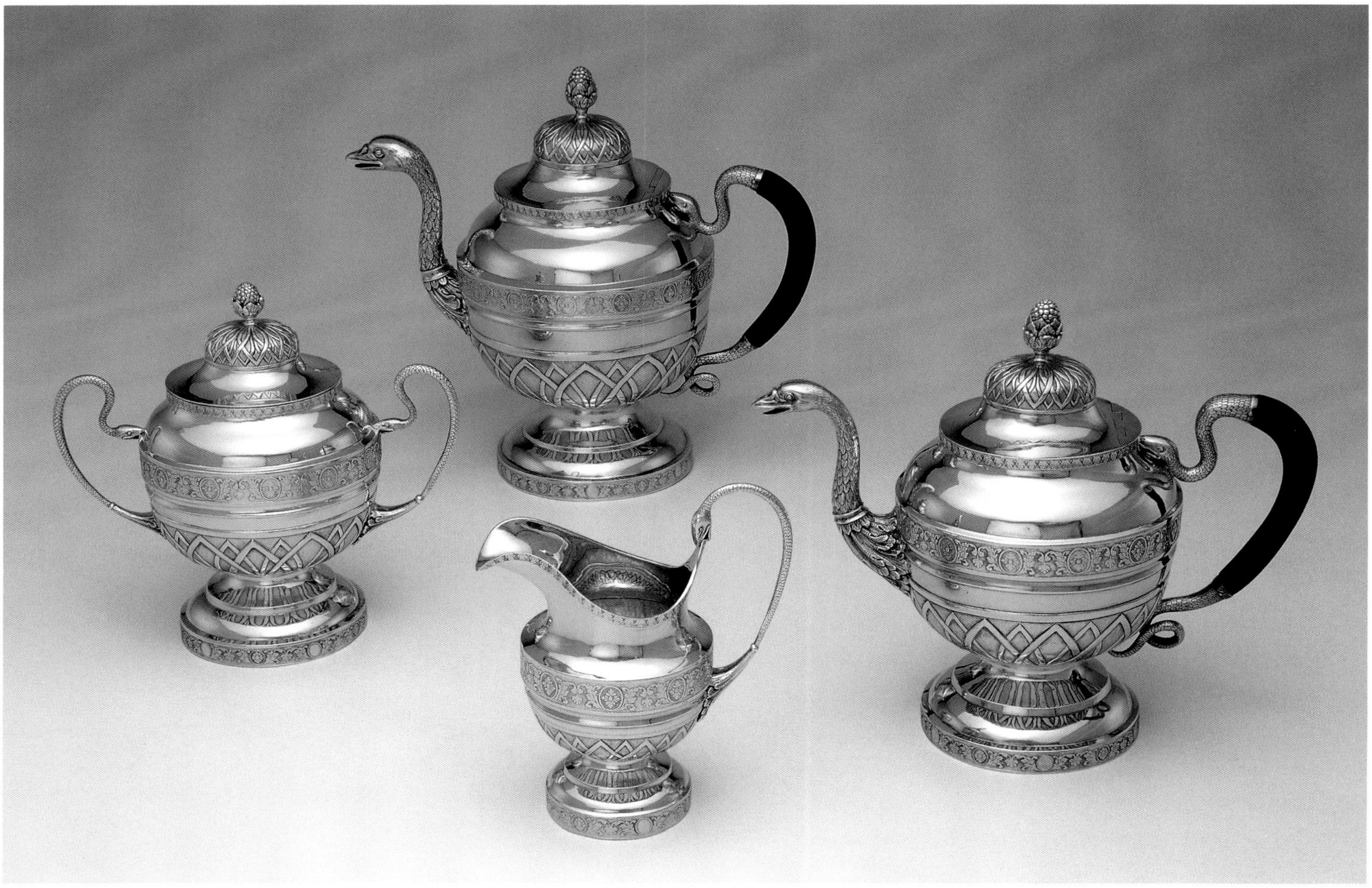

CAT. NO. 55

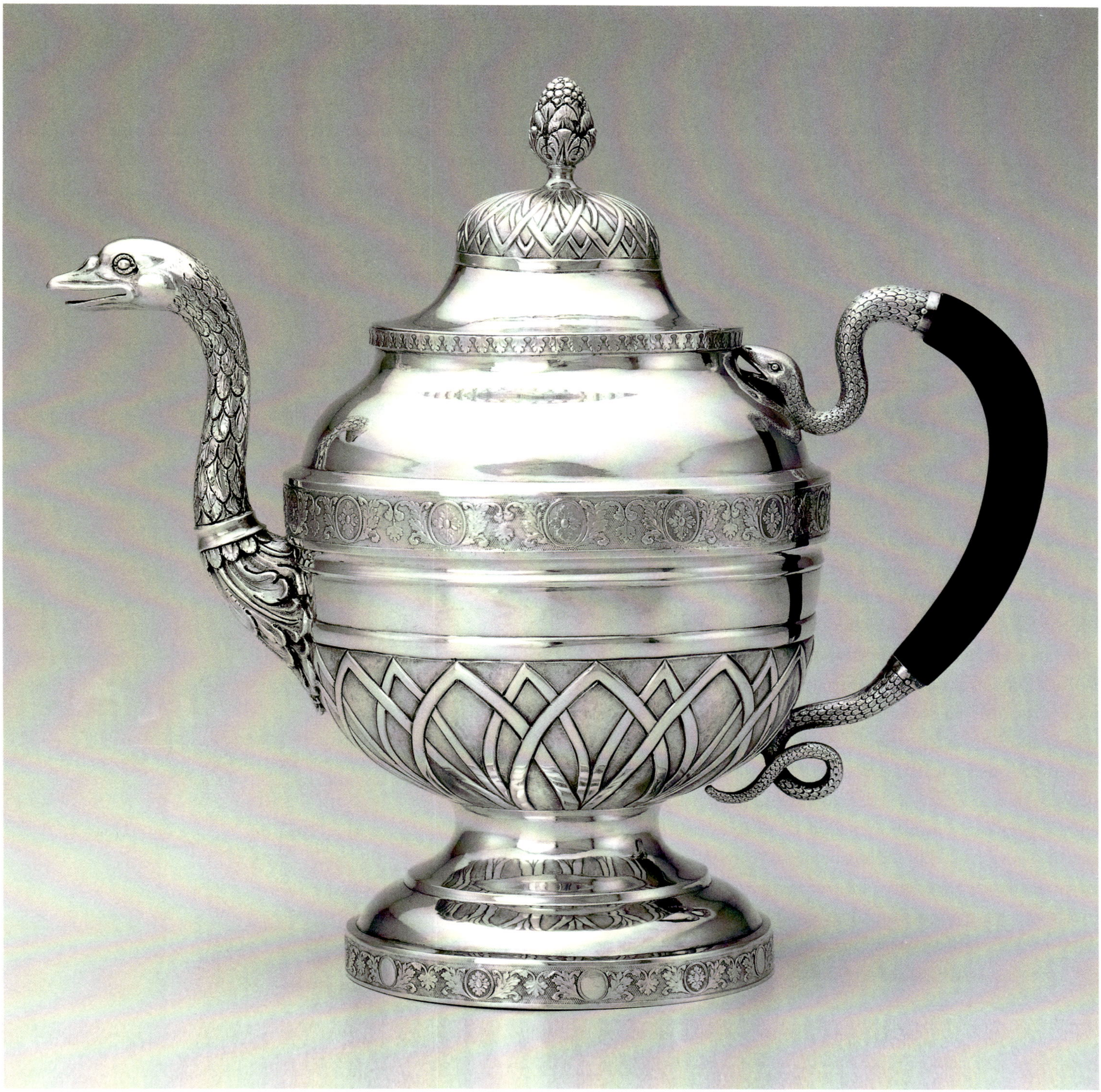

CAT. NO. 55 (COFFEEPOT)

1780 he left France and emigrated to Haiti, where he lived for thirteen years before moving with his new wife to Philadelphia to escape political strife in the French colony.[1] By 1799 Chaudron had established himself as a silversmith and advertised in the *Philadelphia Federal Gazette* as having for sale "A large Assortment of Elegant Watches, Gold Chains and Jewellery."[2] In 1809 he announced his partnership with Anthony Rasch, a Bavarian immigrant who had trained as a silversmith in Germany. The two men worked together until 1812, when they dissolved their partnership.[3]

Rasch may have been indentured to Chaudron after his arrival in Philadelphia.[4] At that time, a master living in America

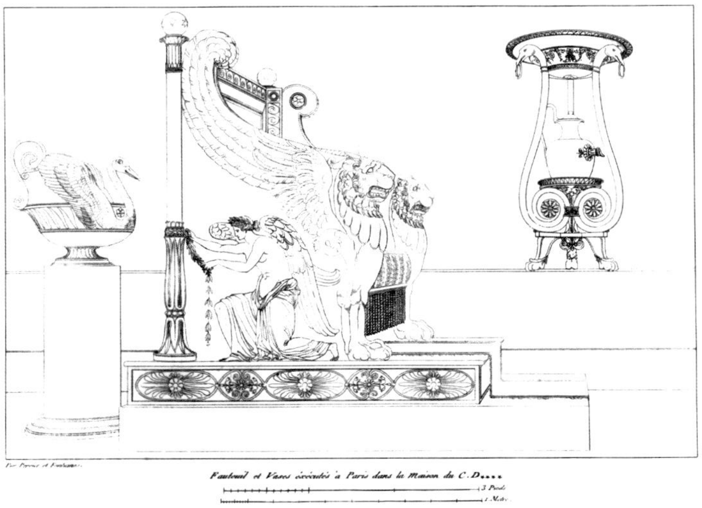

FIG. 29. Charles Percier and Pierre F. L. Fontaine, *Recueil de décorations intérieures* (Paris, 1812), pl. 6. Collection of Ryerson and Burnham Libraries, The Art Institute of Chicago.

in need of skilled labor at inexpensive prices would often pay for an immigrant's passage in exchange for a specified period of work. A contract between master and laborer typically stated the terms of servitude and what the laborer could expect to receive in return, usually food and clothing.[5] Rasch arrived in Philadelphia in 1804; Chaudron made him a partner five years later.[6] Together the two silversmiths made use of each other's talents to create intricately detailed silver objects.

Utilizing technical advances that developed during the first decades of the nineteenth century, Chaudron and Rasch were able to produce a number of objects using many of the same decorative motifs. The bands of ornament surrounding each piece of the tea and coffee service at the mid-band and at the base were cut from a thin sheet of silver using a roller wheel with a continuous pattern cut into it; this is known as die-rolling. The small die-rolled band featured on the lip of the creamer and the edge of the lids on all the pieces in the Art Institute's service appear again on another Chaudron and Rasch tea and coffee service of the same form.[7] Each piece of both sets, as well as a cream pot in the collection of the Museum of the City of Mobile, Alabama, includes a chased, pointed-arch motif around the lower body and lids.[8]

During their short partnership, Chaudron and Rasch created some of the most ambitious neoclassical silver in America. They took many of their decorative elements directly from French and English silver designs from the early years of the nineteenth century. The swan motif on the spouts of the tea and coffee pots appears in French Empire designs by Charles Percier and Pierre F. L. Fontaine, designers to the Empress Josephine, whose personal symbol was a black swan. The swan, symbolizing love, was associated with both Apollo and Venus.[9] Several of the plates published in their 1801 *Recueil de décorations intérieures* employed swans heads as the principal decorative motif. Design for a pedestal table with swan-head supports in the 1812 edition (fig. 29) shows a collar around the swans' necks similar to collars on the spouts of the silver service. In addition to the swan, the silversmiths also used the serpent in their compositions. Both motifs appear in Greek and Roman mythology.

NOTES

1. James R. Cormany, "Jean Simon Chaudron: Silversmith, Poet, and American Pioneer," *Silver* 25, 4 (July–Aug. 1992), pp. 8–9.

2. Whether these were pieces of his own fabrication is not known. See Alfred Coxe Prime, *The Arts and Crafts in Philadelphia, Maryland, and South Carolina, 1786–1800*, 2d ser. (Topsfield, Mass., 1932), p. 98.

3. Ian M. G. Quimby, *American Silver at Winterthur* (Charlottesville, Va., 1995), p. 339.

4. David Hanks, in Philadelphia Museum of Art, *Philadelphia: Three Centuries of American Art*, exh. cat. (1976), p. 227; and Quimby (note 3), p. 339.

5. For more information on indenture and apprenticeship, see Ian M. G. Quimby, *Apprenticeship in Colonial Philadelphia* (New York and London, 1985).

6. The possessive form of "Chaudron" on the silver marks of the Art Institute's tea and coffee service may indicate that Chaudron actually owned the business and Rasch was a trained artisan in the former's employ. Quimby (note 3), p. 342.

7. The service was once in the collection of the Hirschl and Adler Galleries, New York.

8. See photographs and letter from the Hirschl and Adler Galleries, New York, May 30, 1990, Files of the Department of American Arts, The Art Institute of Chicago. The principal die-rolled band of ornament that appears around the mid-band of the Hirschl and Adler service appears again in a service of a different form owned by the Henry Francis du Pont Winterthur Museum, Winterthur, Del.; see Quimby (note 3), p. 340.

9. Wendy A. Cooper, *Classical Taste in America, 1800–1840*, exh. cat. (Baltimore Museum of Art, 1993), pp. 144–45.

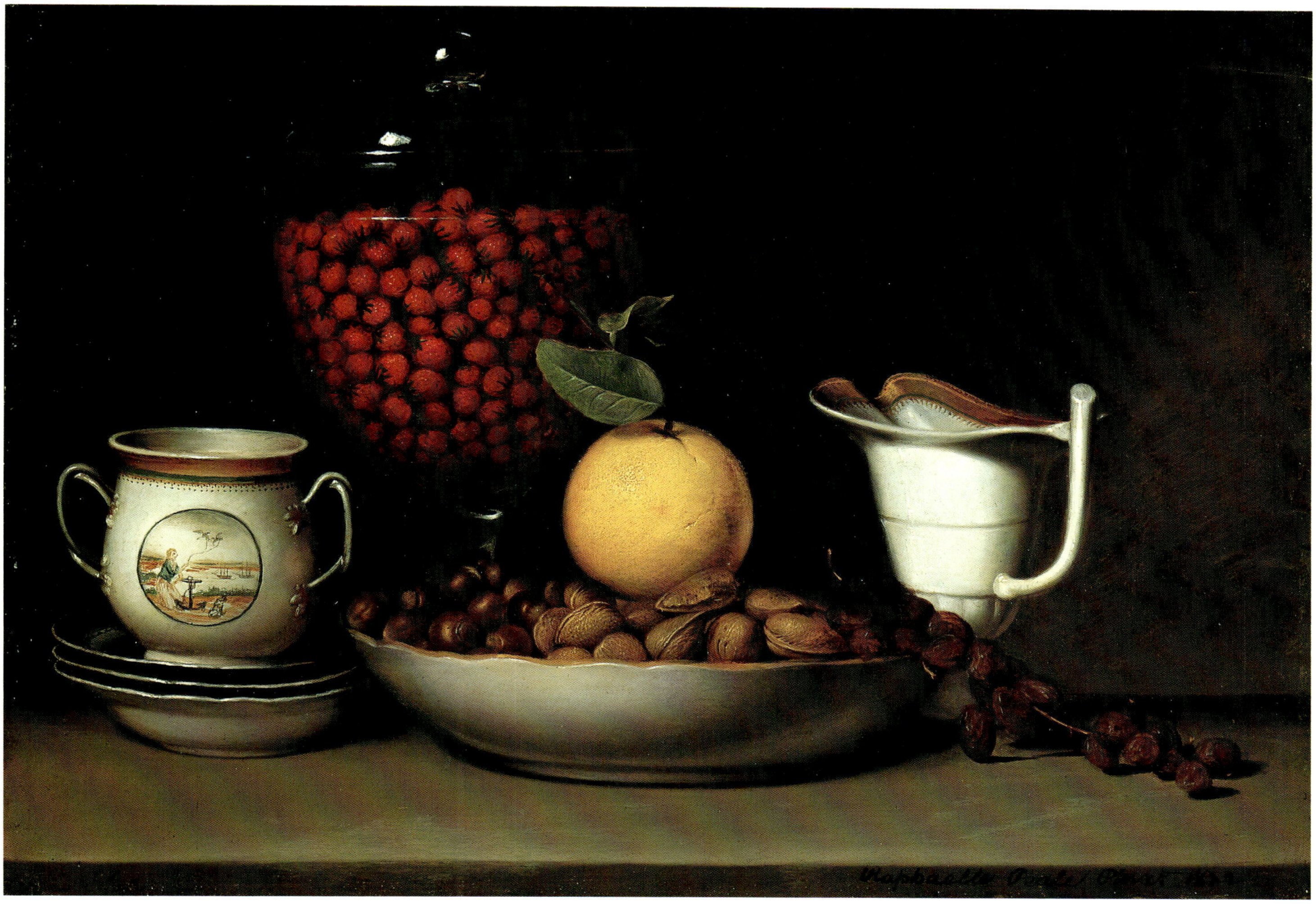

CAT. NO. 56

56. RAPHAELLE PEALE (1774–1825)

Still Life—Strawberries, Nuts, &c., 1822

Oil on wood panel; 41.1 x 57.8 cm (16⅜ x 22¾ in.)
Signed, lower right: *Raphaelle Peale / 1822*
Gift of Jamee J. and Marshall Field, 1991.100

When Charles Willson Peale (see cat. no. 49) retired from portrait painting in 1794, he referred potential patrons to his sons Raphaelle and Rembrandt; Rembrandt thrived in this trade (see cat. no. 51), but Raphaelle floundered. He tried his hand at miniature painting, made some money making cut-paper silhouettes, and finally turned to still life, producing highly distilled, illusionistic compositions.[1] From 1812 until the year before his death, Raphaelle exhibited still lifes regularly at the Pennsylvania Academy of the Fine Arts, hoping to sell them and earn a living. Although his persistence did not lead to fame and fortune during his lifetime, it did result in his recognition two decades later as the United States' first professional still-life painter.[2] Today, however, examples of Raphaelle's work are rare; of the one hundred and fifty still-life paintings he is thought to have completed, only fifty are known.[3]

As the eldest son of Charles Willson Peale, whose voracious intellectual appetites embraced natural science, art, and philosophy, Raphaelle was introduced early in life to his father's many interests and served as his apprentice in the arts of painting and taxidermy. The elder Peale often expressed his frustration at his son's misspent talent.[4] Raphaelle's manifold personal problems included an unhappy marriage, alcoholism, gout, mental illness (perhaps caused by poisoning during taxidermy), and perpetual debt.[5] Because of his woes and physical impairments, Raphaelle's still lifes have often been interpreted as therapeutic, attempts to impose order and beauty on an agitated life. When attempting to decode a still-life painting, however, we must consider each element equally as a piece of a puzzle: one object may carry more symbolic associations than another, but each is essential to the overall effect. This is also the case with Raphaelle's career, which must be viewed from many angles in order to be understood.

In *Still Life—Strawberries, Nuts, &c.,* Peale achieved a delicate balance between personal, natural, and national history that is embodied by both his choice of objects and his exquisitely elegant style. Like all of Raphaelle's mature still-life compositions, the Art Institute's painting is painstakingly balanced, with forms layered horizontally and vertically. Comprising the horizontal strata are the Chinese export porcelain creamer, dish, and sugar bowl. The raisins that have strayed from the bowl, the luscious orange, and the glinting glass compote filled with red strawberries are aligned vertically. The viewer's eye can move around the composition, taking it all in, but without haste.

The foods Raphaelle portrayed in this painting have led some to speculate on how they reflect the artist's life and the world in which he lived. In 1810 Charles Willson Peale bought an estate outside Philadelphia and named it Belfield. Here, he and his son Rubens turned their attentions to horticulture and established greenhouses where they experimented with the cultivation of many plants, including strawberries. Annie V. F. Storr convincingly demonstrated that the strawberries depicted in the Art Institute's painting are probably the hothouse rather than the wild variety, thus linking them to activities at Belfield.[6] Storr also attached meaning to the combination of food displayed: all are associated with different seasons and thus, if grown "naturally," would not be available at the same time. Their inclusion here is not just fanciful but rather suggests the Enlightenment era's fascination with the natural world and the power of humans to shape it.

Raphaelle's choice of still life as a subject can be seen as an attempt to influence taste and create a new clientele; his emphasis on consumable goods, whether food or export porcelain, made his painting particularly marketable. The decoration of the export porcelain also features a sign of the times: a sailor releasing doves and supporting an anchor, symbolizing the hope and promise of the new Republic.

NOTES

1. For more about the many facets of Raphaelle's career, see Nicolai Cikovsky, Jr., *Raphaelle Peale Still Lifes*, exh. cat. (Washington, D.C., National Gallery of Art, 1988).

2. Nicolai Cikovsky, Jr., "Democratic Illusions," in ibid., p. 45.

3. The Art Institute's painting has been known by many names over the years; the title it bears now is thought to be the one under which it was exhibited at the 1824 Pennsylvania Academy of the Fine Arts annual exhibition. See Annie V. F. Storr, "Raphaelle Peal's *Strawberries, Nuts, &c.*: A Riddle of Enlightened Science," *The Art Institute of Chicago Museum Studies* 21, 1 (1995), p. 29, for an excellent overview of the history of the painting's titles.

4. For a fascinating discussion of Charles Willson and Raphaelle Peale's relationship, see Lillian B. Miller, "Father and Son: The Relationship of Charles Willson Peale and Raphaelle Peale," *American Art Journal* 25, 1–2 (1993), pp. 4–61.

5. Phoebe Lloyd, "Philadelphia Story," *Art in America* 76 (Nov. 1988), pp. 155–70, 195–98, 200–202.

6. Storr (note 3), pp. 31–34.

57. GILBERT STUART (1755–1828)

Major-General Henry Dearborn, 1812

Oil on mahogany panel; 71.5 x 57.1 cm (28 3/16 x 22 1/2 in.)
Friends of American Art Collection, 1913.793

Gilbert Stuart's idealized portrait of Major-General Henry Dearborn (1751–1829) depicts an aging, yet still robust, military figure invigorated by the challenge of the War of 1812. A Revolutionary War hero who served as Secretary of War during Thomas Jefferson's two presidential terms (1801–09), Dearborn was appointed senior major-general of the army by President James Madison in January 1812. During Dearborn's tenure as Secretary of War, many forts were named for him, including Chicago's Fort Dearborn, erected in 1803. As commander of the northeastern frontier forces during the first year of the War of 1812, though, Dearborn initiated unsuccessful military strategies; he was relieved of his command on July 6, 1813.[1] Dearborn concluded his public service as minister to Portugal.

Like his sitter, Stuart was nearing the end of a long, successful career when this work was commissioned.[2] The artist received his earliest training with the Scottish portraitist Cosmo Alexander (see cat. no. 18) in Newport, Rhode Island, and later studied with Benjamin West in London. Stuart entered West's studio in 1777 with raw talent and little discipline, but by 1780 he was his teacher's principal assistant and most successful student. Upon inaugurating his own studio in 1782, Stuart began to receive portrait commissions from some of England's most distinguished gentlemen, such as William Grant of Congalton (1982; National Gallery of Art, Washington, D.C.). Stuart remained in the British Isles until 1793,

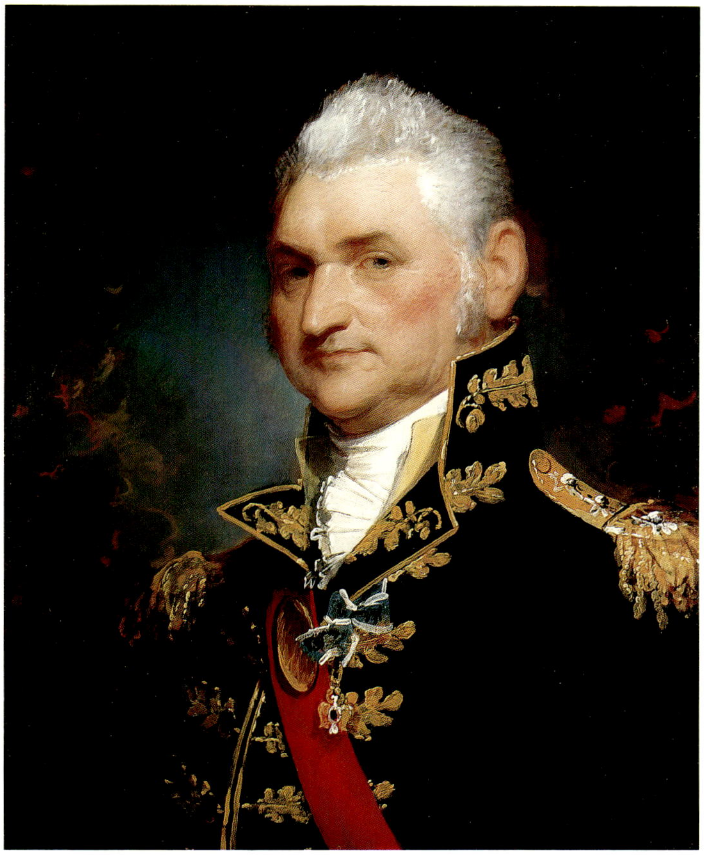

CAT. NO. 57

when the political upheaval caused by the French Revolution forced him to return to his native land.

Major-General Henry Dearborn is one of several portraits Stuart painted of American military and political figures after his return to the United States.[3] Stuart's skillful, vigorous portraits from the post-Revolutionary period are realistic images that express the force of the new country's fervent nationalism. The most iconic of these are his portraits of George Washington, which Stuart repeated and other artists copied to meet the demand for the first president's likeness. A number of the Revolutionary War heroes Stuart depicted, such as Dearborn, are shown wearing the medal of the Society of the Cincinnati. The society was named after the Roman citizen-soldier Cincinnatus, who left his plow to defend his country, returning to his life of farming when danger had passed. Washington served as the society's first president.

Many of Stuart's paintings from this period, including *Major-General Henry Dearborn*, are painted on mahogany panel rather than on canvas. In December 1807, Thomas Jefferson barred American ships from leaving harbor so they would not become involved in the Napoleonic wars, which initially prevented the fine English canvas generally used by Stuart from entering the country.[4] Escalating hostilities between the United States and England, which resulted in the War of 1812, kept English canvas and other goods out of the United States for many years. Stuart compromised by scoring his panels to simulate the look of canvas and to help the paint adhere to the surface.

By the time Dearborn's portrait was commissioned, Stuart had settled in Boston, where he remained for the rest of his life. Dearborn resided in nearby Roxbury. The general sat for his portrait three times, an hour for each sitting.[5] Stuart did not prepare preliminary sketches of his subjects, but painted their faces directly onto the canvas or panel as he entertained them with his social patter. Later, he filled in the background and body in the studio. This method accounts for the fresh realism of Dearborn's face and the tacked-on feeling of the body. By highlighting the clouds that surround the general with a bellicose red, however, Stuart heightened the drama of Dearborn's portrait.

Contemporary written accounts of Dearborn's appearance and an 1818 portrait bust of Dearborn by J. B. Binon (fig. 30)

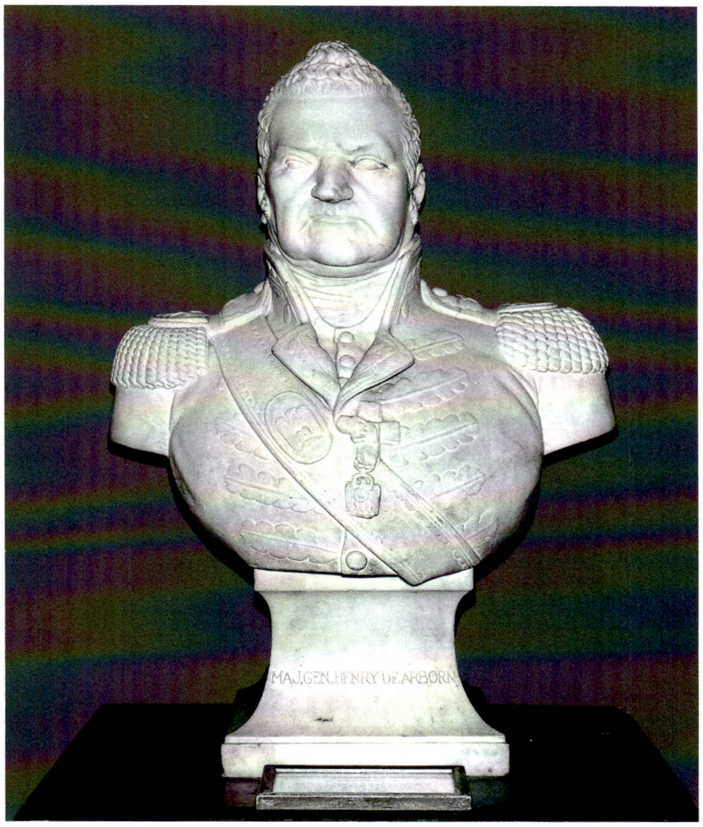

FIG. 30. J. B. Binon. *Portrait Bust of Major-General Henry Dearborn*, 1818. Marble; 58.4 x 57.2 x 28.6 cm (23 x 22½ x 11¼ in.). Chicago Historical Society, Gift of John H. and Octavia C. Carroll (1896.8a–b).

show that Stuart idealized his subject's appearance. In 1812 Dearborn was sixty-one years old and weighed two hundred fifty pounds.[6] Binon's bust documents the general's considerable girth and pugnacious countenance with an adroit realism that contrasts with Stuart's more refined image of Dearborn's figure. Stuart also chose a more flattering three-quarter profile pose that conceals the small eyes, broken nose, and drooping jowls, more apparent in Binon's straight-forward bust.

Stuart's portrait appealed to many, and seven replicas are documented: two by Stuart and five by other artists.[7] The Art Institute's portrait is the version that was painted from life; because of Dearborn's significance in local history, it was acquired by the Chicago Commercial Club late in the nineteenth century.

NOTES

1. For information about Dearborn's military career, see Richard Alton Erney, *The Public Life of Henry Dearborn* (New York, 1979).

2. For biographical information about Stuart, see Richard McLanathan, *Gilbert Stuart* (New York, 1986).

3. Other portraits of military heroes by Stuart include *General Matthew Clarkson* (c. 1794; Metropolitan Museum of Art, New York) and *Master Commandant James Lawrence, U.S.N.* (1812; United States Naval Academy, Annapolis, Md.).

4. Charles Merrill Mount, *Gilbert Stuart: A Biography* (New York, 1964), p. 283.

5. Francis S. Drake, *The Town of Roxbury: Its Memorable Persons and Places* (Roxbury, Mass., 1878), p. 337. Stuart also painted portraits of Dearborn's son Major-General Henry Alexander Scammell Dearborn and his wife around the same time. Both of these portraits are in the Bowdoin College Museum of Art in Brunswick, Maine.

6. Pierre Berton, *The Invasion of Canada* (Boston, 1980), pp. 152–53. Berton also remarked that "Dearborn's size, of course, is borne out by the fact that there were on the farms of America following the War of 1812, small wheeled vehicles known as 'dearborns'—copies of the little cart with which the soldiers used to trundle the General about because he was too fat and perhaps too sick to walk" (letter from Pierre Berton to Milo Naeve, Mar. 2, 1982, Files of the Department of American Arts, The Art Institute of Chicago).

7. See Lawrence Park, *Gilbert Stuart* (New York, 1926), vol. 1, pp. 268–70.

58. THOMAS SULLY (1783–1872)

Dr. Joseph Klapp, 1814

Oil on canvas; 91.4 x 71.1 cm (36 x 28 in.)
Gift of Annie Swan Coburn to the Mr. and Mrs. Lewis L. Coburn Memorial Collection, 1950.1363

59. *Mrs. Klapp (Anna Milnor)*, 1814

Oil on canvas; 92.1 x 71.5 cm (36 1/4 x 28 1/8 in.)
Gift of Annie Swan Coburn to the Mr. and Mrs. Lewis L. Coburn Memorial Collection, 1950.1362

Thomas Sully, one of America's most prolific artists, painted more than two thousand portraits over the course of his seventy-year career. English by birth, he emigrated to the United States with his family in 1792 and became a naturalized citizen in 1809.[1] The artist painted *Dr. Joseph Klapp* and *Mrs. Klapp (Anna Milnor)* during the early years of his career, soon after he returned from a trip to England (1809–10). Though primarily self-taught, Sully immersed himself, while in London, in the study of contemporary English painting and assiduously copied works by Benjamin West and Sir Joshua Reynolds, among other Royal Academy luminaries. The paintings he produced upon returning to his home in Philadelphia are freely handled and stylish, and portray their prosperous subjects as confident and accomplished.

Joseph Klapp was born and raised in Albany, New York, studied medicine at the University of Pennsylvania with the esteemed physician Benjamin Rush, and subsequently settled in Philadelphia.[2] In this portrait, Klapp rests his elbow on Rush's *Works*, indicating his own profession and paying homage to his mentor. The texts lining the background of the painting further attest to the sitter's intellectual interests. Klapp's costume and romantic countenance are typical of American fashionable portraiture of the early nineteenth century that frequently reflects British styles. Sully's debt to Gilbert Stuart (see cat. no. 57) and the English painter Thomas Lawrence is evident here, particularly in his free paint handling.

Sully's portrait of Anna Milnor Klapp attests to the artist's special skill in depicting women. Mrs. Klapp was from a prominent Philadelphia family; her father, William Milnor, is said to have been acquainted with George Washington.[3] As lovely as her husband is dashing, Mrs. Klapp wears a silvery gray Empire-style dress with a starched white stand-up collar that frames her face. She holds in her lap a cloth that obscures

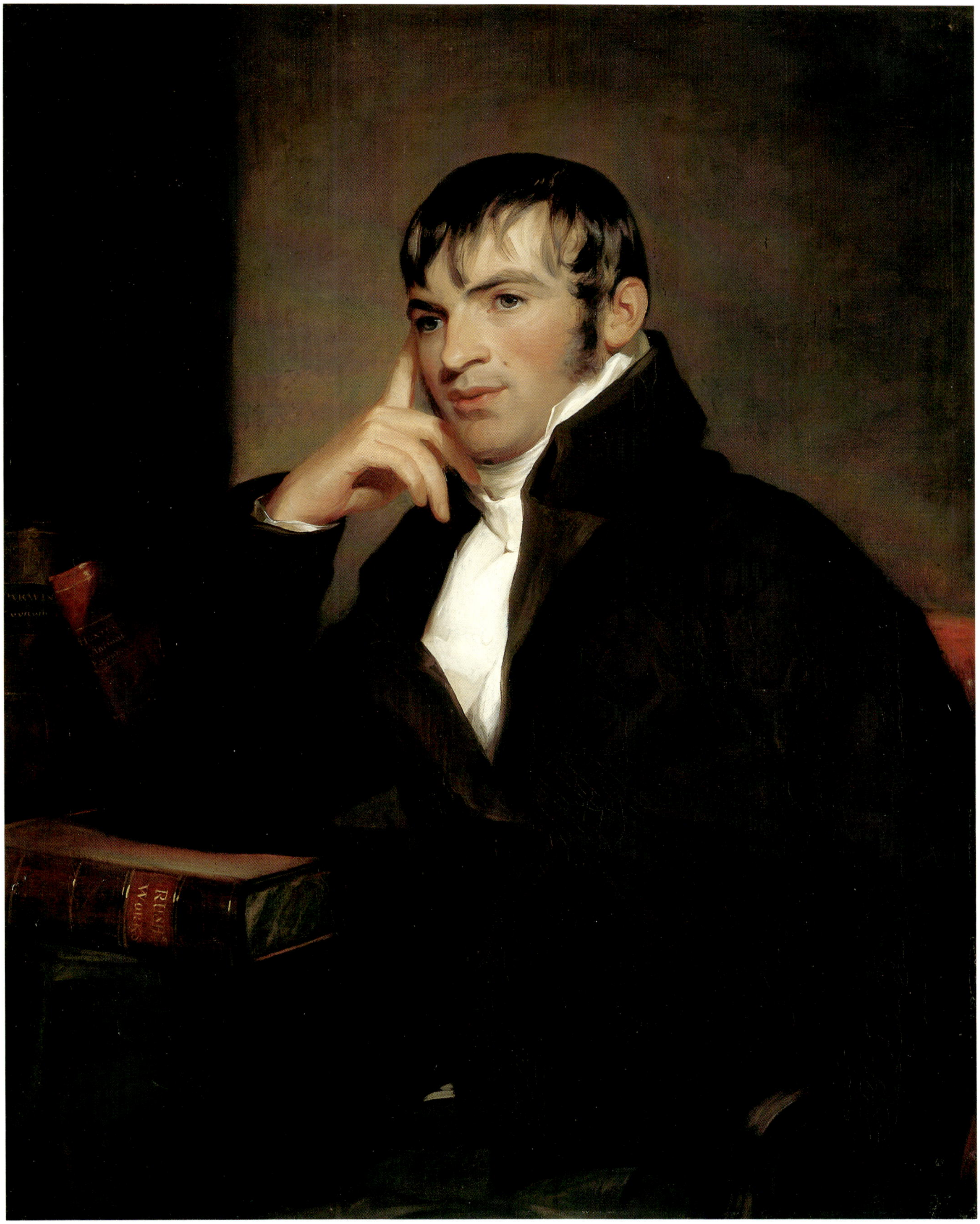

CAT. NO. 58

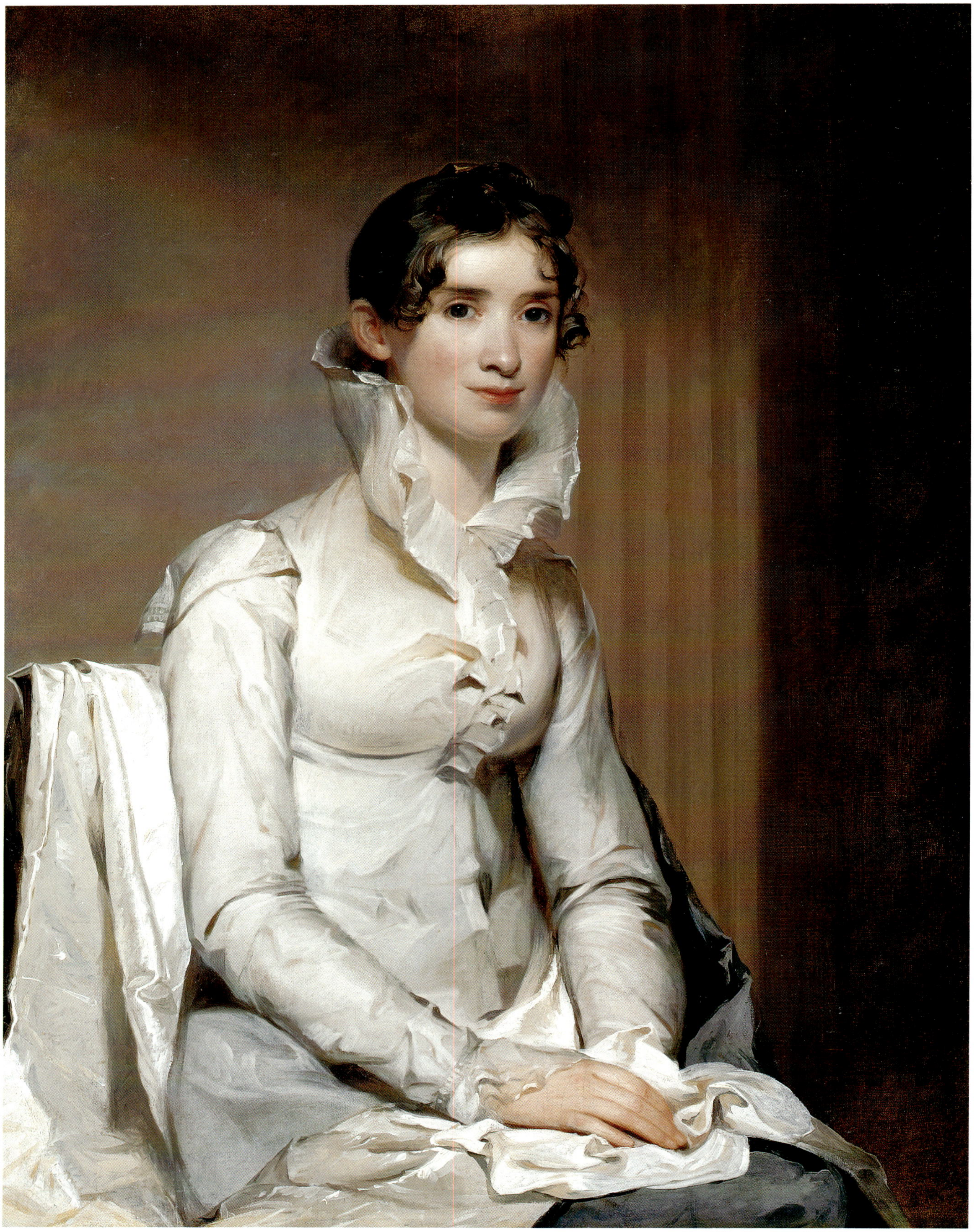

CAT. NO. 59

her left hand, and diverts our attention from the awkwardly rendered arm. On the right, a single column underscores the neoclassical elegance of the painting.

Throughout his long career, Sully kept a detailed account book and recorded all the commissions he received, how long each took to execute, and how much he was paid. According to this book, Sully began the portraits of Dr. and Mrs. Klapp on June 3, 1814, and completed them on July 6; they cost one hundred dollars each and were both "Kit Cat," or three-quarter, size.[4] Sully also kept a journal, and reported on September 23, 1814: "Dr. Klapp & his wife's portraits sent home."[5] This schedule adheres to the formula the artist set out in his *Hints to Young Painters*: "I find that two hours is long enough to detain the sitter. I seldom exceed that time; and six sittings of two hours each is the time I require."[6] The formula he established also prescribes the use of a harmoniously limited color scheme, which is most apparent in the portrait of Mrs. Klapp.

Sully's popularity, like John Singleton Copley's (see cat. nos. 26–27) and Gilbert Stuart's (see cat. no. 57), was due to his absorption of English portrait painting and his ability to portray his subjects in a fashionably flattering manner. The breathless, romantic quality of Sully's work and the staggering number of portraits he produced during his lifetime demonstrate that in the young Republic, it was possible for an artist to excel at painting and the business of art.

NOTES

1. On Thomas Sully's oeuvre, see Edward Biddle and Mantle Fielding, *The Life and Works of Thomas Sully, 1783–1872* (Philadelphia, 1921); and Charles Henry Hart, ed., *A Register of Portraits Painted by Thomas Sully* (Philadelphia, 1909). A manuscript copy of "Account of Pictures" can be found in the Thomas Sully Papers, roll N18, Archives of American Art, Washington, D.C.; and the Manuscript Division of the New York Public Library. For more biographical information on Sully, see Biddle and Fielding; and Monroe H. Fabian, *Mr. Sully, Portrait Painter: The Works of Thomas Sully, 1783–1872*, exh. cat. (Washington, D.C., National Portrait Gallery, 1983).

2. Sully also painted the portrait *Benjamin Rush, M.D.* (1813; Pennsylvania Hospital, Philadelphia). Klapp and Rush are portrayed in a similar pose, surrounded by books, although Rush's portrait is full-length.

3. Typescript of Clapp [*sic*] Family Genealogy, p. 15, Files of the Department of American Arts, The Art Institute of Chicago.

4. "Account of Pictures" (note 1).

5. Ibid.

6. Thomas Sully, *Hints to Young Painters* (1873; reprint, New York, 1965), pp. 10, 16.

60. THOMAS EMMONS AND GEORGE ARCHIBALD (ACTIVE 1813–1825)

Pier Table, 1813/25

Boston

Mahogany and mahogany veneer on chestnut and pine, black marble, ormolu and brass; 81.9 x 88.3 x 39.7 cm (32¼ x 34¾ x 15⅝ in.)

Stenciled on interior top board: *Emmons and Archibald / no. 39 Orange Street / Boston / Cabinet, Chair, & Upholstery / Manufactory*

Gift of the Antiquarian Society through bequests of Lena Turnbull Gilbert, Harriet Jones, Jessie Spalding Landon, and Adelaide H. Ryerson; 1994 Philadelphia trip fund, 1994.538

61. SECRÉTAIRE À ABATTANT, 1820/25

Boston

Mahogany, mahogany veneer, black marble, ormolu, and brass; 145.4 x 133 x 48.4 cm (57¼ x 52⅜ x 19 1/16 in.)

Gift of the Antiquarian Society through the Lena T. Gilbert Fund, 1983.30

62. JAMES STEWART (ACTIVE 1813–1819)

Pianoforte, 1818

Baltimore

Mahogany and mahogany veneer with poplar and oak, ebony, ivory, ormolu, and brass; 83.2 x 170.2 x 64.1 cm (32¾ x 67 x 25¼ in.)

Labeled: *J. Stewart / Baltimore / Hanover Street*

Gift of Mrs. Herbert McLaughlin, 1970.430

These three pieces of furniture epitomize the American interpretation of the full-blown, late French Empire, or Restoration, style. Architecturally inspired, each contains elements drawn from classical sources, such as colonnades, capitals, and entablatures. Indeed, their architectural counterpart in the United States is the Greek Revival style, which was based on severe, plain facades punctuated by Doric columns and pillars and embellished with Greek key designs. The three pieces of furniture discussed here—a table, a secretary, and a pianoforte—display a massive quality, a simplicity of form, and a linear severity inspired by the language of buildings. For decoration these objects rely on heavy, bright ormolu mounts and expanses of matched veneers intended to reflect light.

The Emmons and Archibald pier table is distinguished by its unusually diminutive scale.[1] Using the design vocabulary of Pierre de la Mésangère, this American firm managed to create a pier table of great strength and presence for a small space. Its petite size is enhanced by the reflective qualities of the black marble, mahogany veneers, and bright ormolu mounts. The mirrored back surface creates additional depth. In a room brightly lit by candles, the surfaces of the table must have had a dramatic effect.

The table is labeled with the firm's stencil on the top board, underneath the marble top. Thomas Emmons and George Archibald occupied a shop at 39 Orange Street (renamed Washington Street in 1824) in Boston from 1813 to 1825. In 1818 they announced in the *Columbian Centinel* that they "employed a first-rate upholster and are now available to furnish with upholstery work done in the best style. They have on hand couches, sofas, mahogany chairs and a variety of fashionable furniture."[2]

The Art Institute's large case piece, called a *secrétaire à abattant*, was once owned by David Sears of Boston, and was probably ordered to complement the decor of his new home on Beacon Street.[3] Sears first traveled to Europe between 1811 and 1814, and developed a taste for current Parisian fashions. Upon his return to Boston, Sears hired noted French émigré architect Alexander Parris to build his Beacon Street house.[4] A perspective rendering of the Sears's house, executed in 1822 (fig. 31),

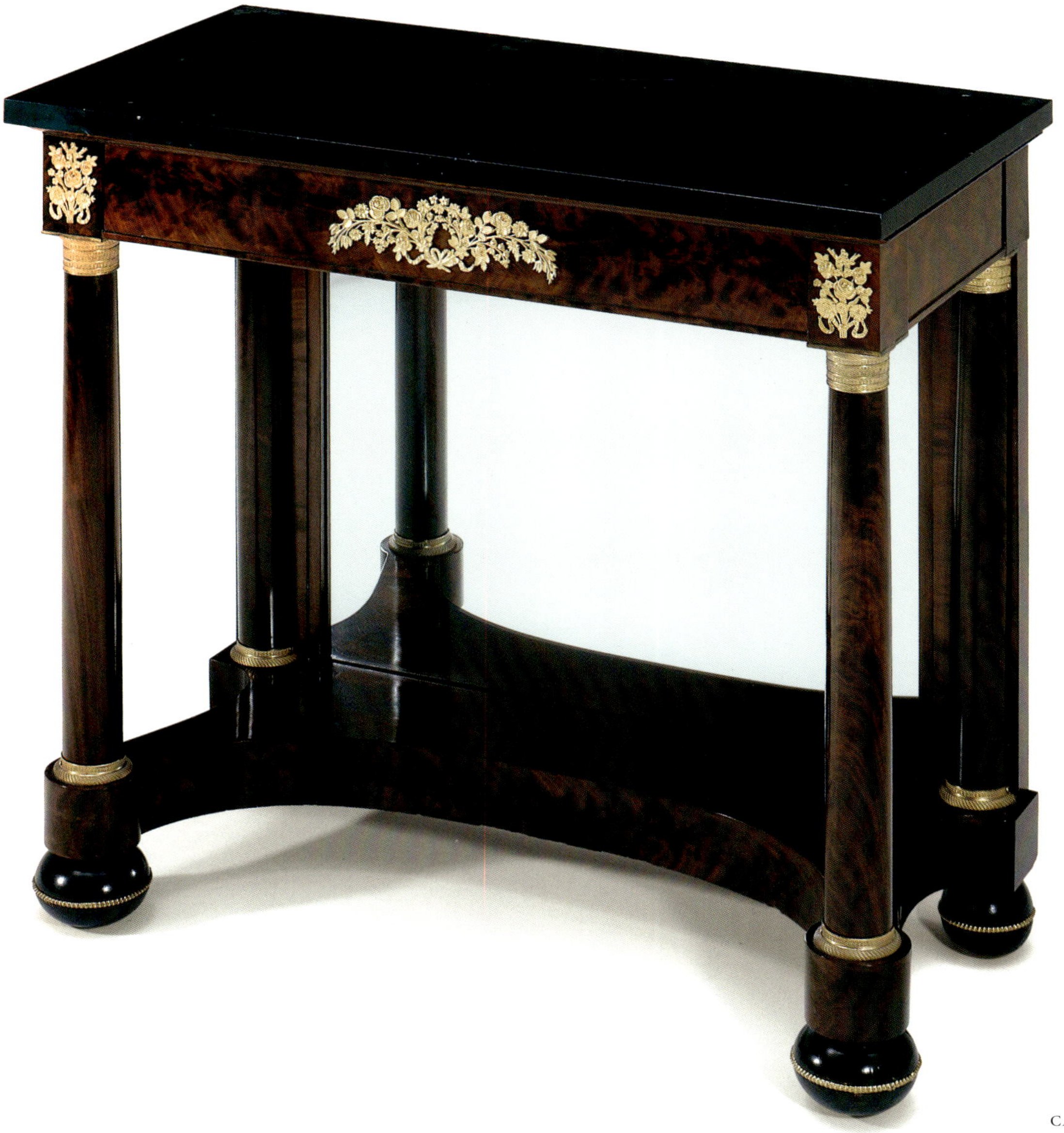

CAT. NO. 60

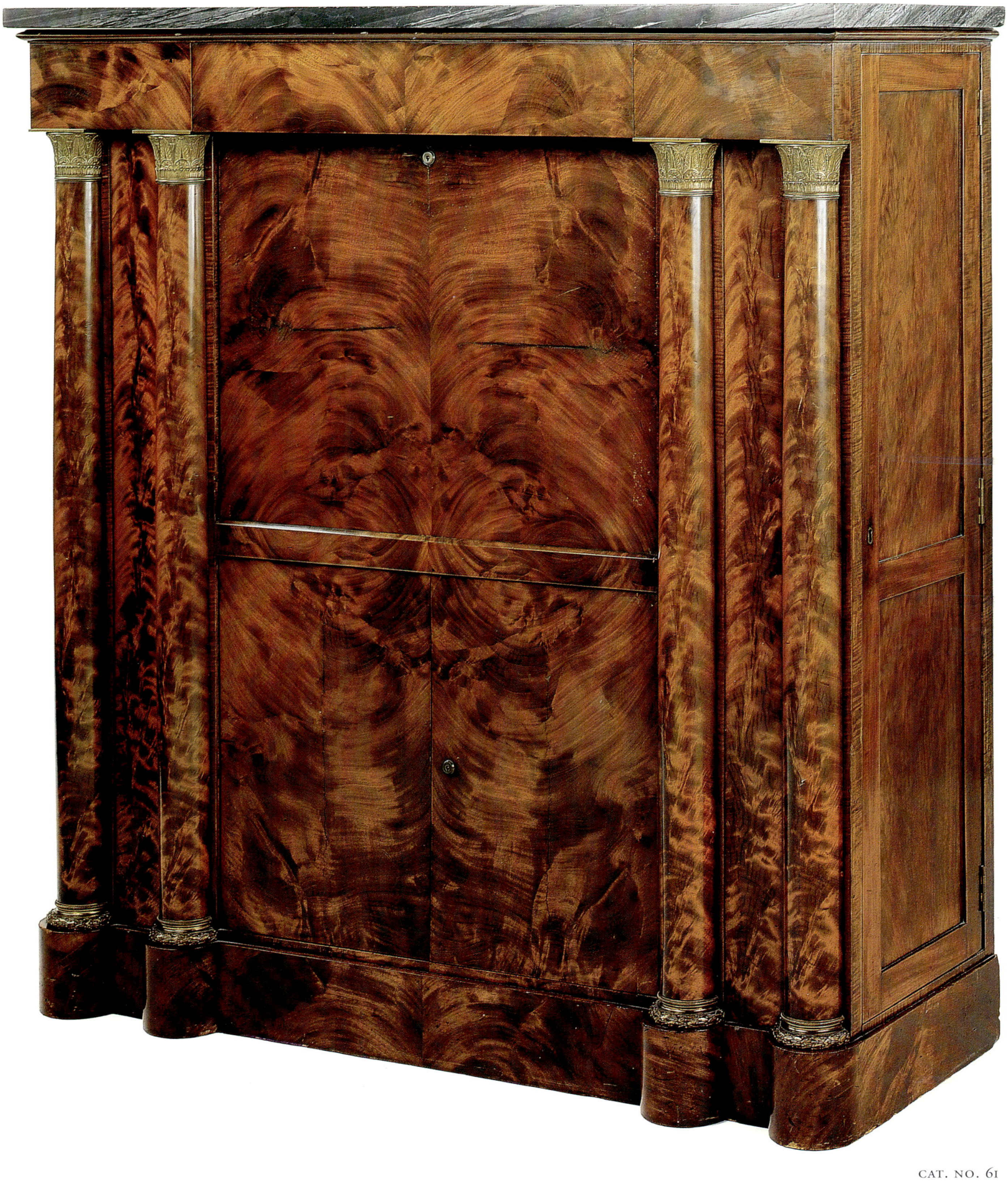

CAT. NO. 61

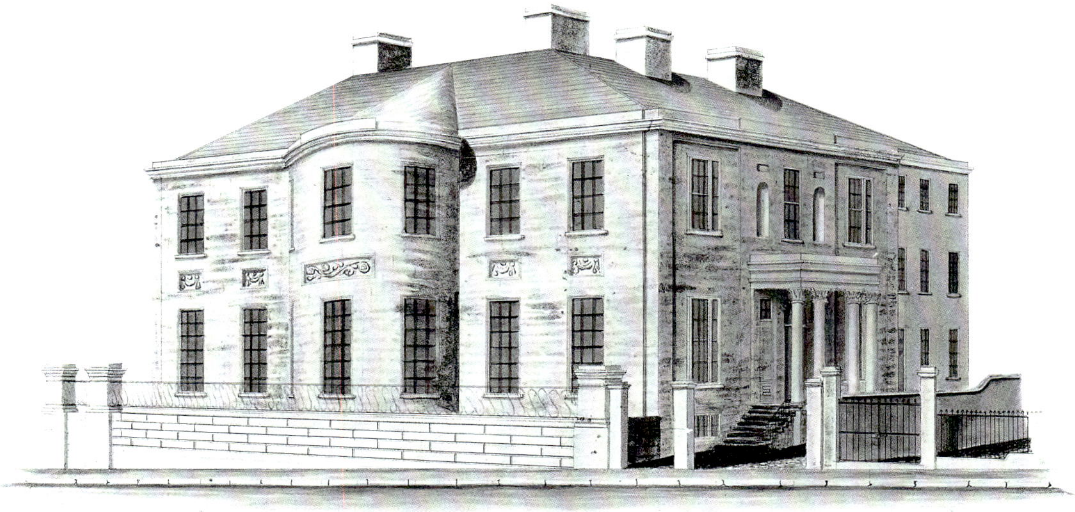

FIG. 31. Frederick P. Leverett. *Perspective Drawing of the David Sears House*, 1822. Photograph courtesy of Harvard University Archives, Cambridge, Mass.

shows a double-columned portico with Composite capitals similar to those of the *secrétaire*. Sears or the craftsman of the desk may have wanted to accentuate the symbolic quality of a front portico, which welcomed visitors to the home of a prosperous family, by echoing the design of the portico in the design of the *secrétaire*.[5]

Like David Sears of Boston, Baltimoreans were familiar with current French styles. The pianoforte by James Stewart is

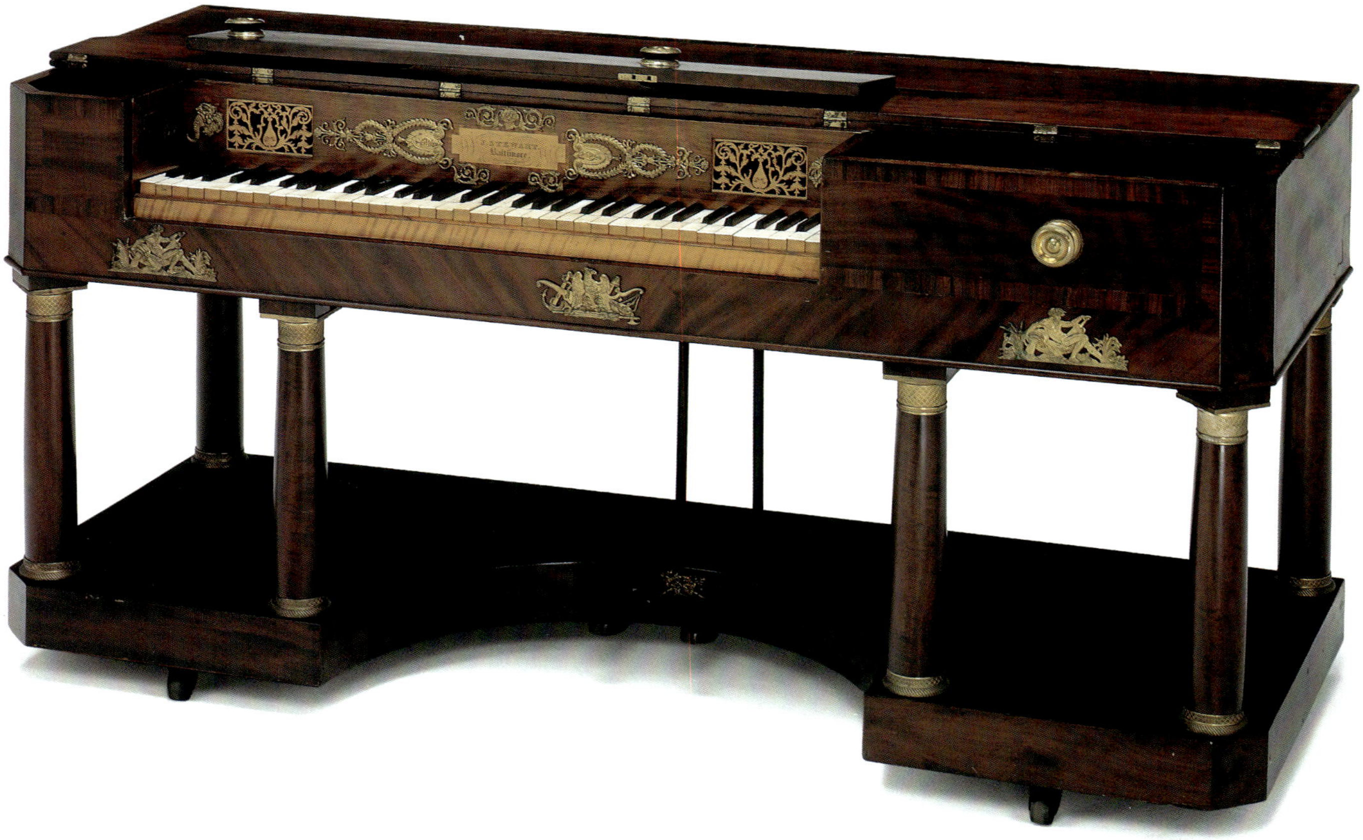

CAT. NO. 62

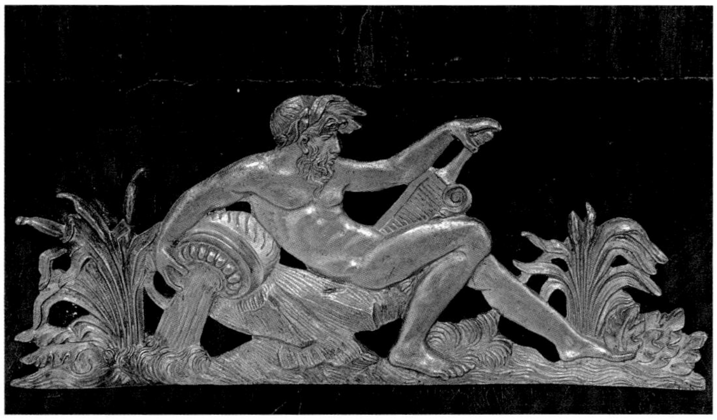

CAT. NO. 62, DETAIL

also architecturally inspired, using columns to support the works, which are enclosed within an entablaturelike casing. The placement of the English stamped-metal decorations alluding to musical themes suggests a classical frieze.[6] Stewart was trained in England, where he was surely conversant with the designs contained in Thomas Hope's *Household Furniture and Interior Decoration* (1807), which was expressly indebted to Percier and Fontaine's earlier archaeological plates. He emigrated to Baltimore in 1812 but moved to Boston after the financial panic of 1819, when his business failed. He subsequently returned to England for the remainder of his life.[7]

NOTES

1. Another Emmons and Archibald pier table of similar scale is at the Museum of Fine Arts, Boston (1977.839).

2. See Page Talbott, "Boston Empire Furniture," *Antiques* (May 1975), p. 879. Prior to 1913, Thomas Emmons was in partnership with James Cogswell at the same address. In 1825 Emmons went into business for himself, taking over the shop of Isaac Vose and Son at 705 Washington Street in Boston. He died in April 1825, one month after dissolving his partnership with George Archibald.

3. Correspondence with family descendants in the files of the Department of American Arts at The Art Institute of Chicago confirms that the desk remained in the house on Beacon Street until it was sold sometime in the 1960s or 1970s.

4. Wendy A. Cooper, *Classical Taste in America, 1800–1840*, exh. cat. (Baltimore Museum of Art, 1993), p. 40.

5. See ibid, p. 163.

6. See Jillian Ehninger, "Furniture Hardware from the Boston Workshop of Henry K. Hancock," *Antiques* 147, 5 (May 1995), p. 735.

7. Gregory R. Weidman et al., *Classical Maryland, 1815–1845: Fine and Decorative Arts from the Golden Age*, exh. cat. (Baltimore, Maryland Historical Society, 1993), p. 138.

63. WILLIAM RUSH (1756–1833)

General Andrew Jackson, 1819

Terracotta; h. 50.5 cm (19⅞ in.)

Restricted gift of Jamee J. and Marshall Field, the Brooks and Hope B. McCormick Foundation, and the Bessie Bennett, W. G. Field, Ada Turnbull Hertle, Laura T. Magnuson, and Major Acquisitions funds, 1985.251

William Rush's bust of Andrew Jackson, completed nine years before Jackson's successful bid for the presidency of the United States, captures the strong character and emotional intensity of the acclaimed general who had already led his troops to victory in two important battles against the Indians. It is recognized as one of only three terracotta busts surviving from Rush's mature period.[1] In 1817 Jackson and his army charged into Spanish Florida, defeated the Seminole Indians, and captured two Spanish forts. Despite his conquest, Jackson was criticized for allowing the execution of two British subjects, an action that threatened to involve the United States in conflicts between Great Britain and Spain. A month of congressional investigation threatened to blacken Jackson's military career. Only the staunch defense of Secretary of State John Quincy Adams saved him from censure. During the inquiries, the general's popularity with the American public soared as he was lauded for his courage and patriotism.

After his exoneration, Jackson traveled to Philadelphia; it was during this successful visit that William Rush began his portrait of the fifty-two-year-old military hero.[2] One of the country's first sculptors, Rush began his career as a carver of wooden figureheads for ships. By 1810 he had made the transition to the portrait bust, creating images of the nation's new leaders including Samuel Adams, Benjamin Franklin, and George Washington. Unlike many artists of the period, Rush did not study abroad; instead, he received his early training from Edward Cutbush, an English artist living in Philadelphia.[3]

In the spirit of neoclassicism, Rush perceived himself and the men around him as builders of a new world, and he chose as his portrait subjects great patriots of the young nation—botanists, prominent physicians, educators, ministers, statesmen, and military heroes.[4] The simplicity and dignity of Rush's portrait of Jackson are reminiscent of Roman busts, and may reflect the influence of the French sculptor Jean-Antoine Houdon. Scholars are divided, however, as to how strongly Rush was influenced by the larger neoclassical movement.[5] The unpretentiousness, strong expression, and naturalism of

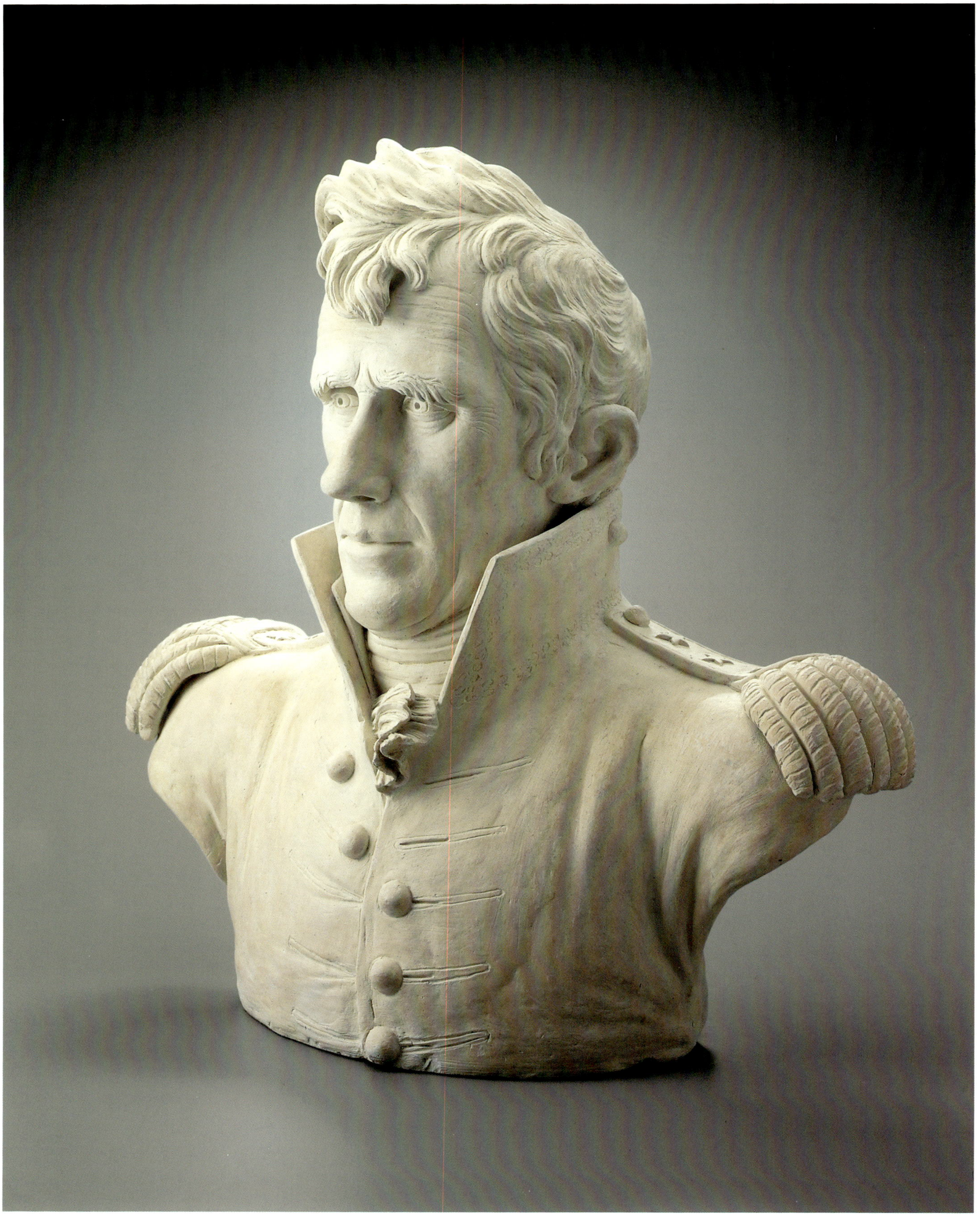

CAT. NO. 63

the sculptures are unique to the style Rush developed in his portraits.

Rush chose to work in terracotta—clay that is fired in a kiln—presumably because it was less expensive and easier to work with than marble. It also enabled the artist to achieve a greater degree of modeling and detail and to create molds from which plaster casts could be made. For his portrait of Jackson, Rush meticulously carved the lines around the subject's eyes and mouth, as well as the thick, stiff curls of his hair. The artist transferred a method he used to carve eyes in wood, "incising the circular line of the iris and removing a ball of clay from the center to form a deep shadow for the pupil."[6] Jackson peers out at the viewer, his seriousness and concentration reinforced by the furrowed brow. Terracotta, which lacks the smooth quality of marble or plaster, was an appropriate choice for an image of "Old Hickory," who was known for his rugged, country manner. His strong features, including a slightly crooked nose and double chin, indicate the skill with which Rush could infuse an individual physiognomy and unique character with a sense of heroism and patriotism.

Rush exhibited his original terracotta statue in the spring of 1819 and then accepted commissions for replicas, producing as many as the market would bear.[7] The bust was immediately lauded by critics not only as a portrait of a great man but as an outstanding accomplishment by one of North America's preeminent sculptors. A report in the *Daily Intelligencer* of December 14, 1819, comments that "the likeness is perfect, and the work another proof that the nation progresses not less in arts than in arms. This probably will rank as Rush's masterpiece."[8]

NOTES

1. This terracotta original was believed lost until the catalogue of a William Rush exhibition at the Pennsylvania Academy of the Fine Arts in 1982 included a photograph of a plaster cast and a description of the lost terracotta, and the Burlington County Historical Society in New Jersey recognized it as the terracotta that had been donated to their collection in 1940 and erroneously attributed to Jean-Antoine Houdon. See Milo M. Naeve, "William Rush's Terracotta and Plaster Busts of General Andrew Jackson," *American Art Journal* 21, 1 (1989), pp. 28–36, for a complete account of the history, discovery, and conservation of this piece.

2. See James G. Barber, *Andrew Jackson: A Portrait Study* (Seattle and London, 1991), for more on this piece and other portraits of the general executed by Philadelphia-based artists in 1819.

3. Rush played an important role in fostering the artistic community in Philadelphia, collaborating with Charles Willson Peale and his sons in 1795 to form one of the earliest American art academies, the Columbianum. Ten years later, Rush helped found the Pennsylvania Academy of the Fine Arts and served as its director until his death in 1833. See Linda Bantel, "William Rush, Esq.," in Bantel, ed., *William Rush, American Sculptor*, exh. cat. (Philadelphia, Pennsylvania Academy of the Fine Arts, 1982), p. 16.

4. Frank Goodyear, "'Tolerable Likeness: The Portrait Busts of William Rush," in Bantel (note 3), p. 48.

5. Wayne Craven described Rush's work as representative of the American vernacular, a style that emerged in the United States independently of design developments in Europe; see Craven, *Sculpture in America* (New York, 1968), p. 24. Frank Goodyear, however, wrote that Rush's sculpture can best be interpreted against the backdrop of neoclassicism, and that to label his work "American vernacular" not only diminishes its quality but overlooks its origins; see Goodyear (note 4), p. 47.

6. Virginia Norton Naude, "Toolmarks and Fingerprints: A Technical Discussion," in Bantel (note 3), p. 87.

7. Bantel (note 3), p. 26.

8. Cited in ibid., p. 157.

64. THOMAS COLE (1801–1848)

Distant View of Niagara Falls, 1830

Oil on panel; 47.9 x 60.6 cm (18⅞ x 23⅞ in.)
Signed, lower right: *Thomas Cole / 1830*
Friends of American Art Collection, 1946.396

For centuries Niagara Falls has served as an enduring North American icon. Still a place of pilgrimage for tourists, the grandeur of the falls inspired nineteenth-century artists and writers to celebrate the sublime power of nature and the American landscape. Thomas Cole recognized the beauty and significance of the falls, which he described in a letter to his patron Robert Gilmor before leaving on a journey to Europe: "I am very anxious to be on my voyage. Next Wednesday I intend setting off for the Falls of Niagara. I cannot think of going to Europe without having seen them. I wish to take a 'last lingering look' at our wild scenery."[1] Cole's letter relates to a poem William Cullen Bryant wrote the same year, "To Cole, the Painter Departing for Europe": "Thine eyes shall see the light of distant skies: / Yet, Cole! thy heart shall bear to Europe's strand / A living image of thy native land, / Such as on thy own glorious canvass lies."[2]

Cole has long been known as the patriarch of the Hudson River School of landscape painting, and his reputation as a painter of the untamed American wilderness was well established by 1829. Admirers such as Bryant, who advised Cole in the same poem to "keep that earlier, wilder image bright," feared that the artist's trip to Europe to study the Old Masters would corrupt his vision. Others, such as Gilmor, saw the po-

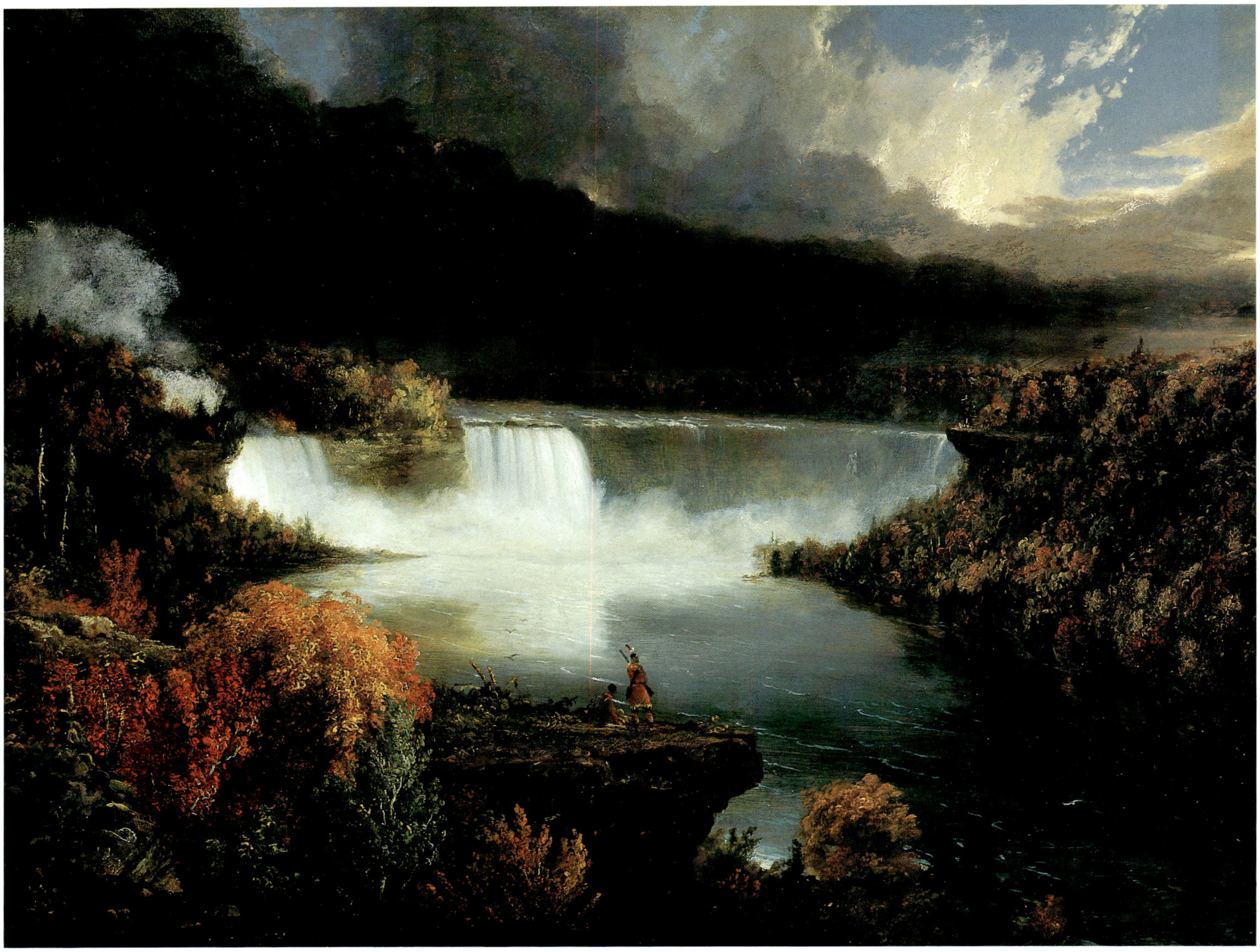

CAT. NO. 64

tential for sales in Europe of American views. He encouraged Cole: "Prepare yourself with original sketches of our scenery, particularly such as is known & remarkable, which you can make pictures of abroad to be disposed of to the collectors of American scenes & subjects."[3]

Cole arrived on the American side of Niagara Falls on May 8, 1829, and stayed for a week; cold and ice prevented him from crossing to the Canadian side on this trip. He commented in his notebook, "I anticipated much—but the grandeur of the falls far exceed anything I had been told of them—I am astonished that there have been no good pictures of them—I think the subject a sublime one."[4] Cole sketched numerous views of the falls from a variety of vantage points and, as was his practice, annotated them with color and compositional notes. A sheet in a notebook of the artist's now housed in the Detroit Institute of Arts (fig. 32) includes tree studies, rock formations, the edge of the falls seen from above, and a vista labeled "Niagara 2 miles off." The latter foreshadows the Art Institute's *Distant View of Niagara Falls.*[5]

Cole departed for England on June 1. In London, where he resided for three years, he painted at least two works based on on-site drawings of Niagara Falls. One, now lost, was a seven-foot-long canvas exhibited in the 1830 exhibition of the British Institution. The surviving work is the Art Institute's panel, which John Howard Hinton commissioned as one of a set of twelve views to be engraved for his book *The History and Topography of the United States* (London, 1830–32). A meticulous record-keeper, Cole kept a notebook that listed the delivery date for each view; he deposited "The Falls of Niagara" with Hinton in January 1831.[6] Attesting to the popularity of his

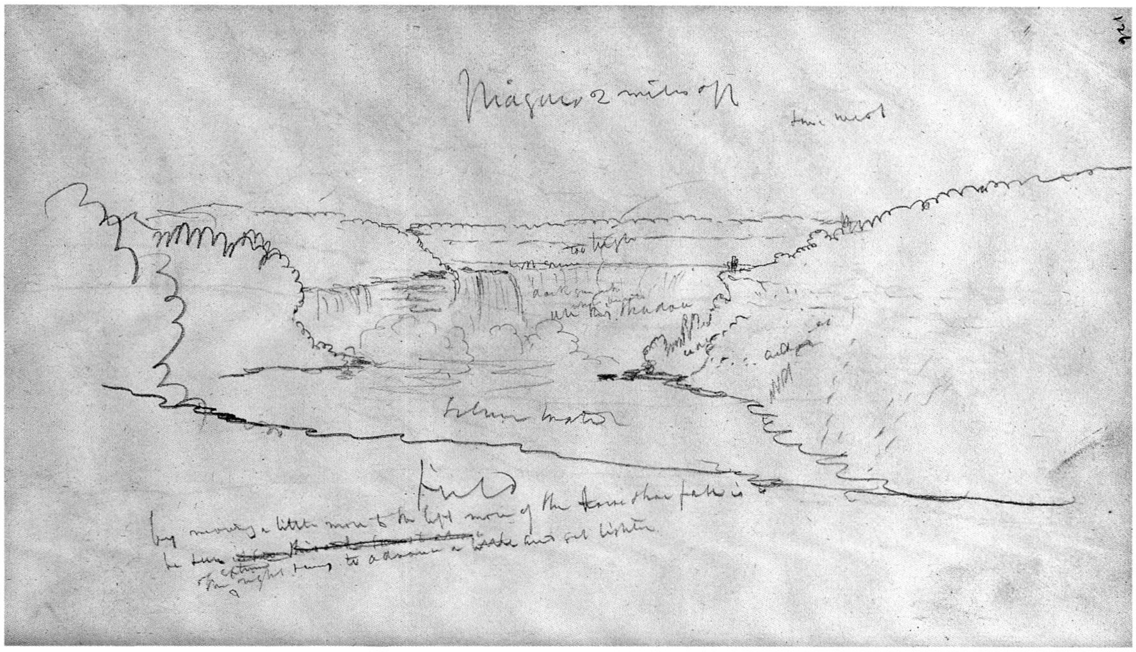

FIG. 32. Thomas Cole (1801–1848). *Niagara, Two Miles Off*, 1828. Graphite pencil on wove paper; 12.1 x 19.7 cm (4¾ x7¾ in.). Detroit Institute of Arts, Founders Society Purchase, William H. Murphy Fund (39.560.126).

American landscape views in England, Cole's illustrations for Hinton's book were also used to decorate Staffordshire china.[7]

The potency of Cole's image of Niagara lies in its depiction of unspoiled nature. *Distant View of Niagara Falls* bears little resemblance to the actual landscape surrounding the falls at the time of the artist's visit, which was marked by factories, scenic overlooks, and hotels to accommodate a growing number of tourists. Instead, Cole constructed a timeless vision of the national landmark that he later described in lines of poetry: "Ages untold thy voice broke forth unheard; / But by the shrinking wolf, or the tim'rous deer / Or wandering savage of the echoing wild."[8] The autumn foliage, thunderclouds, and Native Americans surveying the scene comprise a romanticized view of Niagara Falls, a wistful look back at the vanishing American wilderness. A poetic interpretation rather than an objective description, *Distant View of Niagara Falls* presents a symbolic image of America.

NOTES

1. Letter from Thomas Cole to Robert Gilmor, Jr., Apr. 26, 1829; in Howard S. Merritt, "Correspondence Between Thomas Cole and Robert Gilmor, Jr.," *Baltimore Museum of Art Annual* 2 (1967), p. 67. For excellent accounts of the significance of Niagara Falls in American culture, see Jeremy Elwell Adamson, *Niagara: Two Centuries of Changing Attitudes, 1697–1901*, exh. cat. (Washington, D.C., Corcoran Gallery of Art, 1985); and Elizabeth McKinsey, *Niagara Falls: Icon of the American Sublime* (Cambridge, 1985).

2. William Cullen Bryant, "To Cole, the Painter Departing for Europe," in Graham Clarke, ed., *The American Landscape: Literary Sources and Documents* (Mountfield, East Sussex, 1993), vol. 2, p. 166.

3. Letter from Robert Gilmor, Jr., to Thomas Cole, Dec. 5, 1827, in Merritt (note 1), p. 53.

4. Thomas Cole Papers, roll D39, frame 0228, Archives of American Art, Washington, D.C. Cole visited Niagara Falls a second time, in August 1847.

5. Nancy Sojka, Associate Curator of Graphic Arts, Detroit Institute of Arts, provided detailed descriptions of these drawings.

6. For Cole's comments on this project, see his letter to Thomas S. Cummings dated Oct. 19, 1830, in Thomas Cole Papers, roll D6, frame 0033, Archives of American Art, Washington, D.C. For his delivery of "The Falls of Niagara," see Thomas Cole, Sketchbook and Diary (1829), p. 40, in Lesley–Cole Papers, box 7, New-York Historical Society. The engraving of *Distant View of Niagara Falls* was published as the frontispiece to the second volume of the first English edition of Hinton's book with the legend "from an original picture in the possession of Joshua Bates, Esq." An American edition, published in 1834 by Samuel Walker in Boston, features an engraved version of Cole's image by T. S. Woodcock, who slightly altered the scene. Cole's view was published in all four editions of the book.

7. Henry H. Glassie, "Reevaluation of a Thomas Cole Painting," *The Art Institute of Chicago Museum Studies* 8 (1976), p. 98.

8. Thomas Cole, "Niagara" (1829), in Marshall B. Tymn, ed., *Thomas Cole's Poetry* (York, Penn., 1972), pp. 50–51.

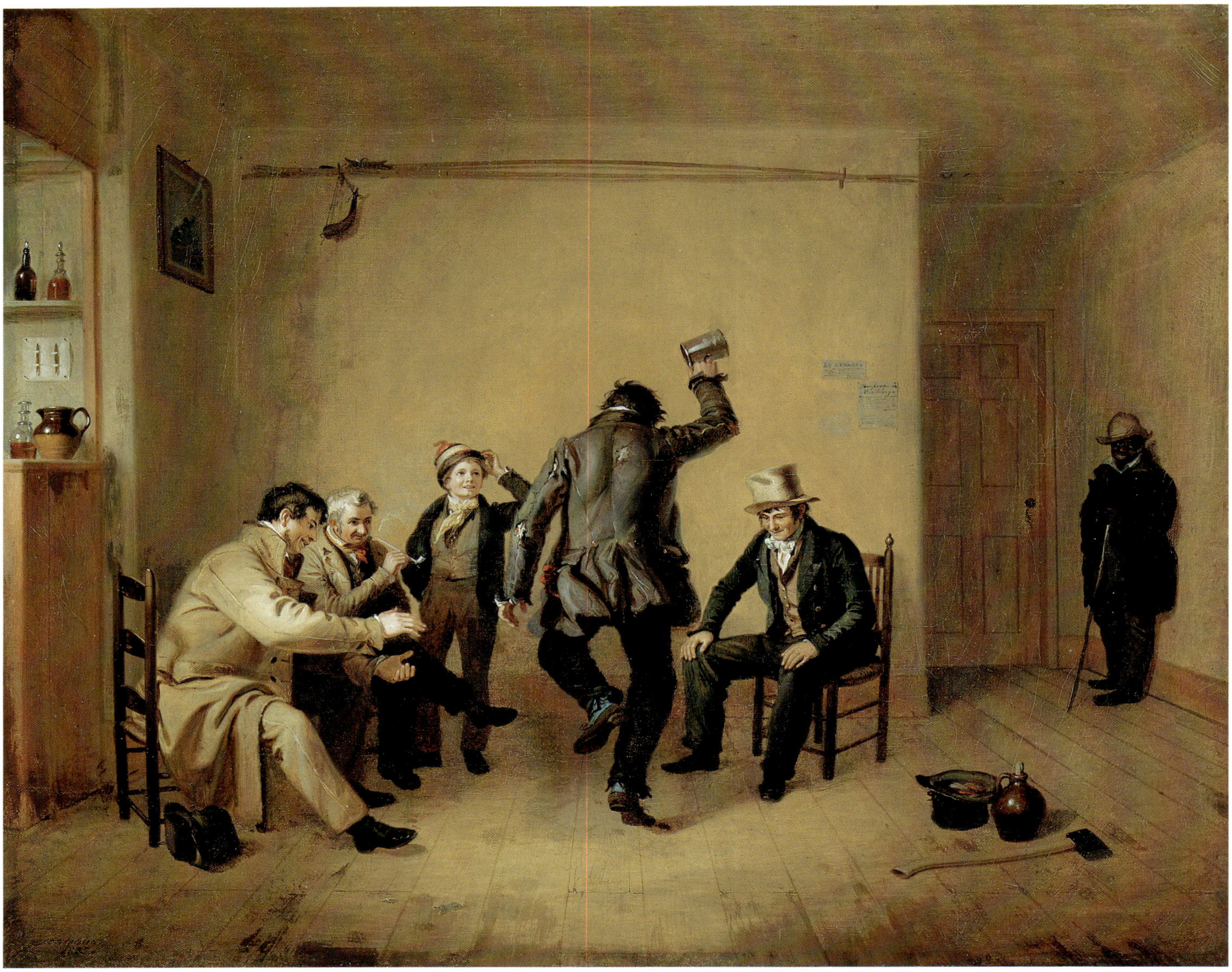

CAT. NO. 65

65. WILLIAM SIDNEY MOUNT (1807–1868)

Bar-room Scene, 1835

Oil on canvas; 57.4 x 69.7 cm (22⅝ x 27⁷⁄₁₆ in.)
Signed, lower left: *W. S. Mount / 1835*
The Goodman Fund, 1939.392

In his popular genre paintings, William Sidney Mount slyly commented on American social and political issues, such as temperance and the abolition of slavery.[1] *Bar-room Scene* is an early example of the artist's socially engaged work. Exhibited at the National Academy of Design in New York City in 1835, the painting received favorable reviews from both art critics and the larger public. The themes of the painting, set in a country tavern, and the rustic types depicted are familiar in Mount's oeuvre and embody the vernacular, yet complexly textured, character of his work.

Unlike most artists of his generation who rose to prominence in the New York art world, Mount, a native of Setauket, Long Island, did not train in Europe. Instead, he apprenticed to his brother Henry as a sign painter between 1824 and 1827 in New York City, took courses at the National Academy of Design during 1826 and 1827, and spent one week studying in Henry Inman's studio around 1828. That same year, he was elected an associate member of the National Academy of Design, where he exhibited for the first time. By 1835, when

Mount exhibited *Bar-room Scene*, he had developed critical, popular, and collecting audiences for his work who responded to his artistic skill and wry wit. As one biographer noted, "[Mount] was an enthusiastic American in his feelings, and a lover of fun and humor, and these qualities were almost invariably visible in his productions."[2]

According to Mount, he painted *Bar-room Scene* "in Setauket in 1835 at the house of Gen. Satterlee by the aid of two south windows and separated (in winter) by a curtain to divide the two lights. The artist by one window and the model by the other."[3] This arrangement accounts for the strong light that outlines and accentuates the revelers gathered in the tavern interior who encourage the drunken, and perhaps itinerant, figure in the center to dance. The illuminated, central portion of the canvas contrasts sharply with the shadowed, right side, where a smiling African-American man watches the activity.

Peripheral African-American spectators are as common in Mount's work as white farmers and musicians, but inhabit a much more ambiguous position.[4] Although the figure in *Bar-room Scene* is a free black man, he does not participate in the revelry as an equal and his facial features are broadly stereotyped. Drawing his language from racial epithets, one reviewer commented: "Nor must young Cuffee [the African-American] be forgotten, who has a smile expressive of more mind than belongs to his race, and seems to think that Uncle Plats could do quite as well as the white man." Both "Cuffee" and "Uncle Plats" are derogatory slang terms. This same reviewer referred to the dancer as "Vestris," a satiric allusion to the renowned French ballet dancer Gaetano Vestris (1729–1808).[5]

From 1938 to the 1980s, Mount's painting was called *The Breakdown*, a title that further underscores the picture's perceived racial themes. The breakdown is a dance of African-American origin that was identified with both black and white "backwoodsmen" in the nineteenth century.[6] The reveler is dancing a breakdown, which the marginalized African-American recognizes and appreciates. A white man performing an African-American dance also brings to mind minstrel shows, an idea reinforced by the caricaturish "blackface" features of the observer. However appropriate these interpretations may be, Mount's more benign title, *Bar-room Scene*, suggests that he was also interested in showing the public house as a site of Jacksonian populism in action—a space open to all types of men.

Mount also alluded to temperance issues, not only in the title but also in the notice for a temperance meeting posted on the back wall. Temperance was an important social issue during this period (see also entry on cat. no. 84) and one that Mount comically commented on in more than one painting. *Loss and Gain* (1847; Museums at Stony Brook, New York) depicts a tattered drunk who has dropped his liquor jug while stumbling over a fence. *Bar-room Scene* is not as judgmental, appealing instead to the viewer's sense of irony that a temperance meeting should be advertised in a bar-room. Nonetheless, the artist clearly distinguished between the dancer and those who encourage his revelry, suggesting that a difference exists between moderation and intemperance.[7] As one nineteenth-century critic described it, "a *gem*, this, of which any collector might be proud,"[8] *Bar-room Scene* offers a complex view of antebellum social politics in the guise of a humorous genre painting.

NOTES

1. Called the "American Wilkie" during his lifetime, Mount is regarded as the first American artist to devote his career to genre painting. For more on genre paintings and socially engaged themes, see Elizabeth Johns, *American Genre Painting: The Politics of Everyday Life* (New Haven, Conn., and London, 1991).

2. Charles Lanman, *Haphazard Personalities, Chiefly of Noted Americans* (Boston, 1885), p. 170.

3. William Sidney Mount's diary, Nov. 14, 1852 (Stony Brook, N.Y., Museums at Stony Brook), quoted in Alfred Frankenstein, *William Sidney Mount* (New York, 1975), p. 249.

4. For more about depictions of African-Americans in Mount's paintings, see Karen M. Adams, "The Black Image in the Paintings of William Sidney Mount," *American Art Journal* 7, 2 (Nov. 1975), pp. 42–59.

5. "Exhibition of the National Academy of Design: Fifth Notice," *New York Mirror* 12 (June 13, 1835), p. 395. "Cuffee" probably refers to Paul Cuffee (1759–1817), an African-American sea captain who was the first black in Massachusetts to petition for the right to vote. "Uncle Plats" most likely refers to an African-American, as "plats" is another term for braids.

6. The title of this painting has changed a number of times during the last one hundred years. It was shown as *Bar-room Scene* at the 1835 National Academy of Design exhibition, came to the Art Institute as *The Breakdown* in 1939, and was retitled *Walking the Line* in the 1980s. We restore the original title of the painting with this publication. For a discussion of the breakdown, see Constance Rourke, *American Humor: A Study of the National Character* (New York, 1931), p. 90.

7. Newspaper clippings and broadsides about temperance are included in Mount's papers at the Museums at Stony Brook. See David Cassedy and Gail Shrott, *William Sidney Mount: Annotated Bibliography and Listings of Archival Holdings of the Museums at Stony Brook* (Stony Brook, N.Y., 1983), pp. 22–24.

8. "The Five Arts," *Knickerbocker* 5, 6 (June 1835), p. 554.

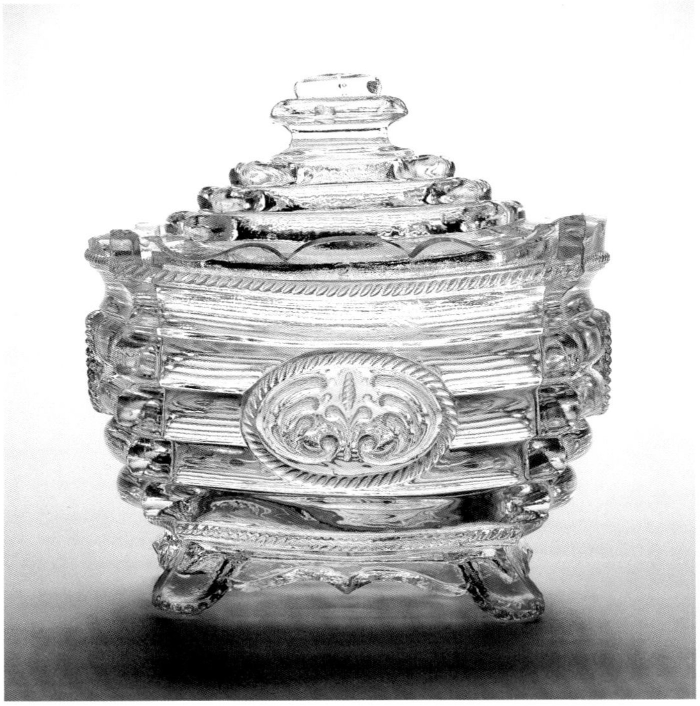

CAT. NO. 66

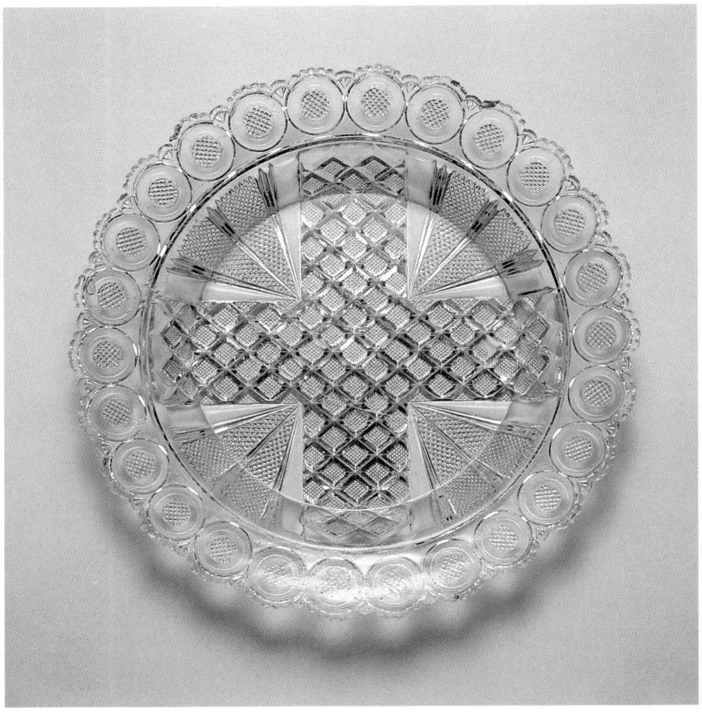

CAT. NO. 67

66. NEW ENGLAND GLASS COMPANY (1818–1888)

Covered Sugar Bowl, before 1830

East Cambridge, Massachusetts

Pressed glass; 13 x 12.4 x 9.8 cm (5⅛ x 4⅞ x 3⅞ in.)

Gift of the Antiquarian Society through Mr. and Mrs. Robert O. Delaney, 1995.40a–b

67. BOSTON AND SANDWICH GLASS COMPANY (1826–1888) OR NEW ENGLAND GLASS COMPANY (1818–1888)

Clear Strawberry Diamond Bowl with Cross, before 1830

Sandwich or East Cambridge, Massachusetts

Pressed glass; 4.5 x 30.5 (diam.) cm (1¾ x 12 in.)

Through prior acquisition of David Adler and Robert Allerton, Ada K. Rew in memory of her parents, Mr. and Mrs. Irwin Rew, The School of The Art Institute of Chicago, Elizabeth R. Vaughan, 1995.41

Early American glass firms were founded and operated by groups of immigrants from Germany, Italy, Poland, and the Netherlands who brought with them the technology and decorative vocabularies of their native countries.[1] Little information on these early glass manufactories has survived. Consequently, scholars have been able to pinpoint geographic regions for pieces based only on the similarity to documented objects.

The introduction of machine pressing at the beginning of the nineteenth century made molded and pressed glass an affordable alternative to labor-intensive, imported cut glass and crystal. The Art Institute's sugar bowl and strawberry-diamond bowl are typical of the earliest type of pressed glass produced in New England. The thickness of both pieces indicates that they were made before 1830, after which the device known as the cap ring was invented, which allowed makers to fashion thinner and more delicately worked glass.[2]

The sugar bowl is attributed to the New England Glass Company based on company invoices dated 1828 and 1829. At that time, this glass house was shipping creamers and sugar bowls by the dozen for $4.50 and $6.00, respectively.[3] The Art Institute's sugar bowl is pressed in a pattern of simple horizontal ribbing with a medallion relief on either side and a simulated ring handle at either end. The bowl is based on designs in contemporary use by Staffordshire potters in England, whose wares, depicting various American transfer-printed views, were popular in the United States.[4] The simple covered-box shape, with carrying handles at either end, refers to the form of an ancient sarcophagus and illustrates the American taste for neoclassical motifs in the first decades of the nineteenth century.[5]

The strawberry-diamond bowl is one of the largest early pieces of pressed glass known today. The patterned bowl came in a variety of sizes, the biggest being twelve inches in diameter. The museum's bowl is a rare, surviving example of this large size.[6] The diamond patterning of the cross refracts and diffuses the incoming light and gives the pattern a quality and depth that is rarely found in other American glass from this period.

NOTES

1. Arlene Palmer, *Glass in Early America: Selections from the Henry Francis du Pont Winterthur Museum* (New York, 1993), p. 9.

2. The cap ring governed the flow of molten glass out to the rim of the object and thus controlled the thickness of the rim of a plate, cup, or bowl during pressing. See James H. Rose, *The Story of American Pressed Glass of the Lacy Period, 1825–1850*, exh. cat. (Corning, N.Y., Corning Museum of Glass, 1954), p. 14.

3. Helen McKearin, "New England Glass Company Invoices, Part II," *Antiques* 52, 4 (Oct. 1947), p. 275.

4. Ibid., p. 276.

5. Wendy A. Cooper, *Classical Taste in America, 1800–1840*, exh. cat. (Baltimore Museum of Art, 1993), pp. 203–04.

6. The Corning Museum of Glass, Corning, N.Y., has another example.

68. HORATIO GREENOUGH (1805–1852)

Abdiel, 1838/43

Marble; h. 61 cm (24 in.)

Gift of Mrs. Elizabeth G. H. Bartol, 1894.562

In his 1851 essay "Aesthetics at Washington," Horatio Greenough wrote, "I believe that these States need art as a visible exponent of their civilization. They call for it as a salvation from merely material luxury and sensual enjoyment, they require it as the guide and ornament of inevitable structure and manufacture."[1] Greenough wrote extensively in order to educate Americans about art and culture and to encourage them to produce a national art that reflected democratic values. *Abdiel* is one of dozens of works in marble that the sculptor executed to illustrate his theories. He took his subject from Book 5 of John Milton's epic poem *Paradise Lost.* Abdiel, whose name means "servant of God," is an angel who refuses to accept Satan's claims of divinity and instead remains committed to God amidst the chaos of the rebel uprising in Heaven:

> Among the faithless, faithful only he,
> Among innumerable false, unmoved,
> Unshaken, unseduced, unterrified
> His loyalty he kept, his love, his zeal. . . .
> And with retorted scorn his back he turned
> On those proud towers to swift destruction doomed.[2]

Spending most of his adult life in Italy, Greenough was the first American to pursue marble sculpting as a profession. He arrived in Rome in 1825, after graduating from Harvard University, and studied with Bertel Thorvaldsen, the renowned Danish neoclassical sculptor. Returning to Boston in 1827, the young artist took advantage of his prosperous family's connections and obtained portrait-bust commissions from President John Quincy Adams and Boston's mayor Josiah Quincy. Throughout his career, Greenough's portrait busts provided the financial means to support his less lucrative experiments with imaginative subjects such as *Abdiel.*

In 1828 Greenough settled in Florence, where he became part of a close-knit community of American artists and writers, including Thomas Cole (see cat. no. 64), James Fenimore Cooper, and Samuel F. B. Morse. Greenough and his colleagues imagined that in Italy they would gain a more complete knowledge of Western civilization than they could expect to glimpse in the still young United States.[3] It was in this temperate, intellectual climate that Greenough conceived *Abdiel.*

The subject of the faithful seraph was first suggested to Greenough by the painter Washington Allston. A generation older than Greenough, Allston had traveled widely in Europe at the turn of the century and was a formidable intellectual presence in Cambridge, Massachusetts, during the sculptor's years at Harvard. He regaled students with his philosophical and aesthetic theories and encouraged them to travel abroad. Allston's avid pursuit of "moral beauty" in art and his interest in Miltonic themes may have led him to suggest Abdiel as a subject for his protégé.[4]

An erudite patron, Edward Elbridge Salisbury, commissioned Greenough to pursue a Miltonic theme, and in 1838

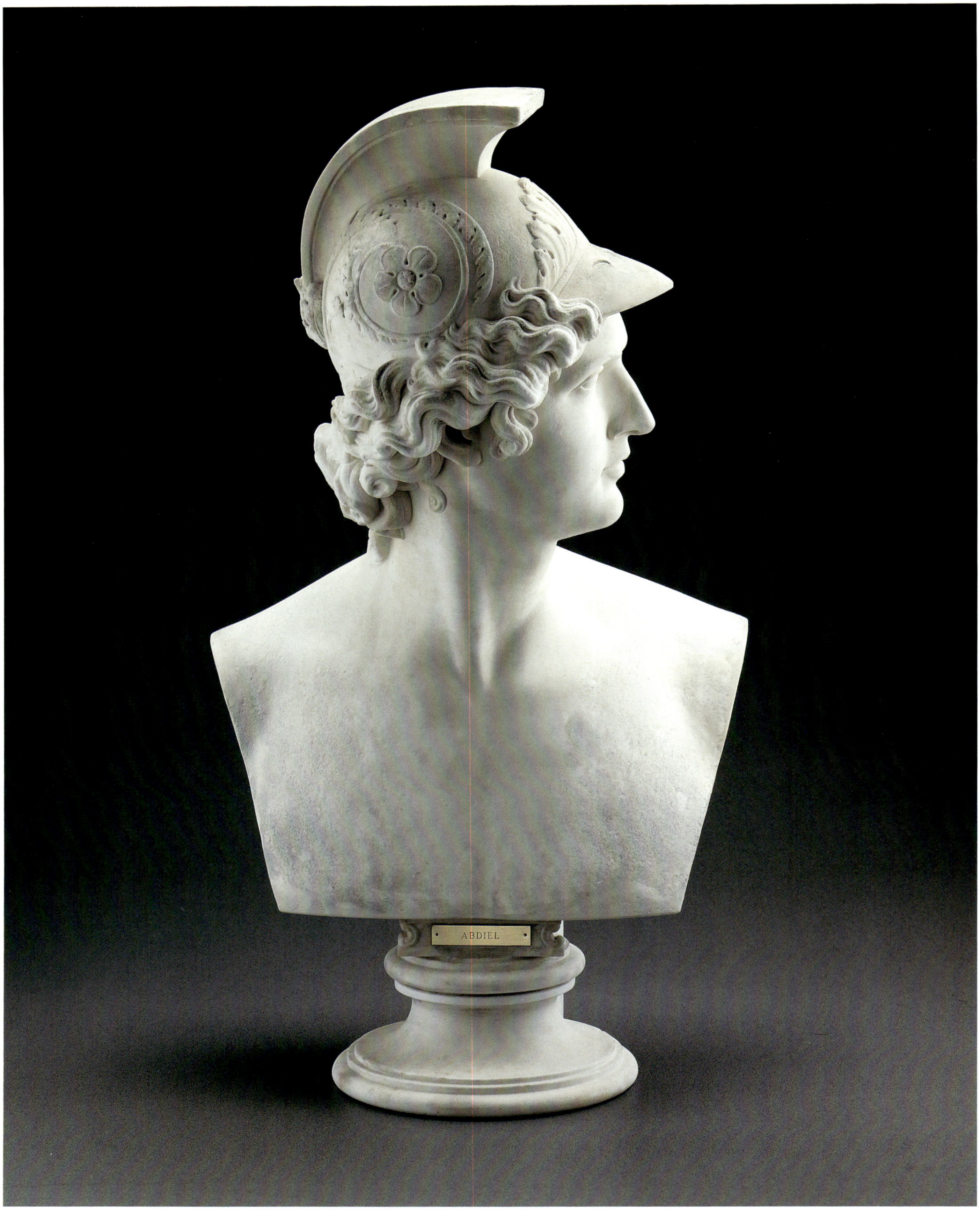

CAT. NO. 68

Greenough completed a full-length *Abdiel*, now in the Yale University Art Gallery. Owing to the expense of marble, Greenough was not able to execute a life-sized figure: the Yale statue stands only three-feet tall. However, the sister of a Boston friend, Mrs. Elizabeth G. H. Bartol (née Howard), commissioned Greenough to produce a statue of his choice for her collection; she received the oversized bust of *Abdiel* now in the Art Institute's collection.[5]

Greenough drew upon classical and Renaissance sculptural sources as well as Milton's biblically inspired text for his idealized bust.[6] Finely chiseled, beautifully proportioned, and attired in the garb of a Greek warrior, the colossal bust recalls in pose and execution both the antique *Apollo Belvedere* (Allston's favorite piece of classical sculpture) and Michelangelo's Renaissance bust of Giuliano de' Medici, a plaster cast of which the sculptor kept in his Florence studio. *Abdiel* skillfully conveys two opposing emotions: the subject's placid face reflects his calm resolve, while his severely turned head and straining neck muscles reveal the extreme emotions involved in his repudiation of Satan.

Greenough's learned visual quotations helped establish his reputation as an original and literary sculptor determined to elevate American taste in the visual arts. His life ended abruptly in 1852, when he contracted "brain fever" and died in a Cambridge hospital. On his death, Ralph Waldo Emerson wrote that Greenough was "one product of American soil, . . . one of the best proofs of the capability of this country."[7] An example of the aspirations of American artists in the early years of the Republic, Greenough's *Abdiel* represents staunch virtue, classical poise, and moral beauty as touchstones for art and culture in the New World.

NOTES

1. Horatio Greenough, *The Travels, Observations, and Experience of a Yankee Stonecutter* (Gainesville, Fla., 1958), p. 17.

2. John Milton, *Paradise Lost* (1667), bk. 5, ll. 897–900, 906–07, as quoted in Janet A. Headley, "Horatio Greenough's Heroic Subjects: *Abdiel* and *David*," *Yale University Art Gallery Bulletin* (1991), p. 35.

3. For more information on American sculptors in Italy, see Sylvia E. Crane, *White Silence: Greenough, Powers, and Crawford, American Sculptors in Nineteenth-Century Italy* (Coral Gables, Fla., 1972); and Theodore E. Stebbins, Jr., *The Lure of Italy: American Artists and the Italian Experience, 1760–1914*, exh. cat. (Boston, Museum of Fine Arts, 1992).

4. William H. Gerdts and Theodore E. Stebbins, Jr., *"A Man of Genius": The Art of Washington Allston, 1779–1843*, exh. cat. (Boston, Museum of Fine Arts, 1979), p. 103.

5. Mrs. Bartol actually had to be coached on the source. A letter from Greenough to his brother Henry, dated July 8, 1843, explains: "The head which Mrs. Bartol received is the Abdiel enlarged. If she will look at the close of the fifth book of the 'Paradise Lost' she will find the moment represented. He is threatening Satan as he turns to leave the rebel host." See Frances B. Greenough, ed., *Letters of Horatio Greenough* (New York, 1970), p. 152.

6. Abdiel, however, is not a biblical figure but an imaginative character created by Milton.

7. Quoted in Nathalia Wright, *Horatio Greenough: The First American Sculptor* (Philadelphia, 1963), p. 300.

69. MADE BY CORNELIUS AND COMPANY (1839–1851)

DESIGNED BY ISAAC F. BAKER

Girandoles, 1848/51

Philadelphia

Gilt bronze, marble, glass; max. h. 45.1 cm (17¾ in.)

Gift of the Antiquarian Society through Judith Carmack York, 1995.102a–c

Girandoles featuring historical and literary figures were widely produced in the nineteenth century.[1] Fashioned from gilded cast bronze and ornamented with glass prisms, girandoles were usually displayed before a mirror, atop a pier table, or as garniture on a fireplace mantel. The mirror behind allowed the lighted candles and prisms to reflect and magnify the gilded surfaces. A three- or five-branch central fixture flanked by two single fixtures was typical.

The Philadelphia firm Cornelius and Company was the largest nineteenth-century producer of girandoles in the United States. The firm's factory was five stories high, had a separate department for each type of fixture made, and employed several hundred workmen.[2] The firm patented their figural designs so they could not be replicated by rival organizations. The patent drawings of Isaac F. Baker, a partner in the Cornelius firm, for the Art Institute's set, complete with the identities of each figure, are on file with the United States Patent Office. Cornelius and Company patented the large candelabra on December 5, 1848, and the two accompanying candlesticks on April 10, 1849.[3]

These popular domestic objects glorified American mythology. The girandoles depict characters from James Fenimore Cooper's *Last of the Mohicans* (1826), a novel that takes place in the Hudson River Valley during the French and Indian War (1754–63). The main character, Natty Bumppo, is an accom-

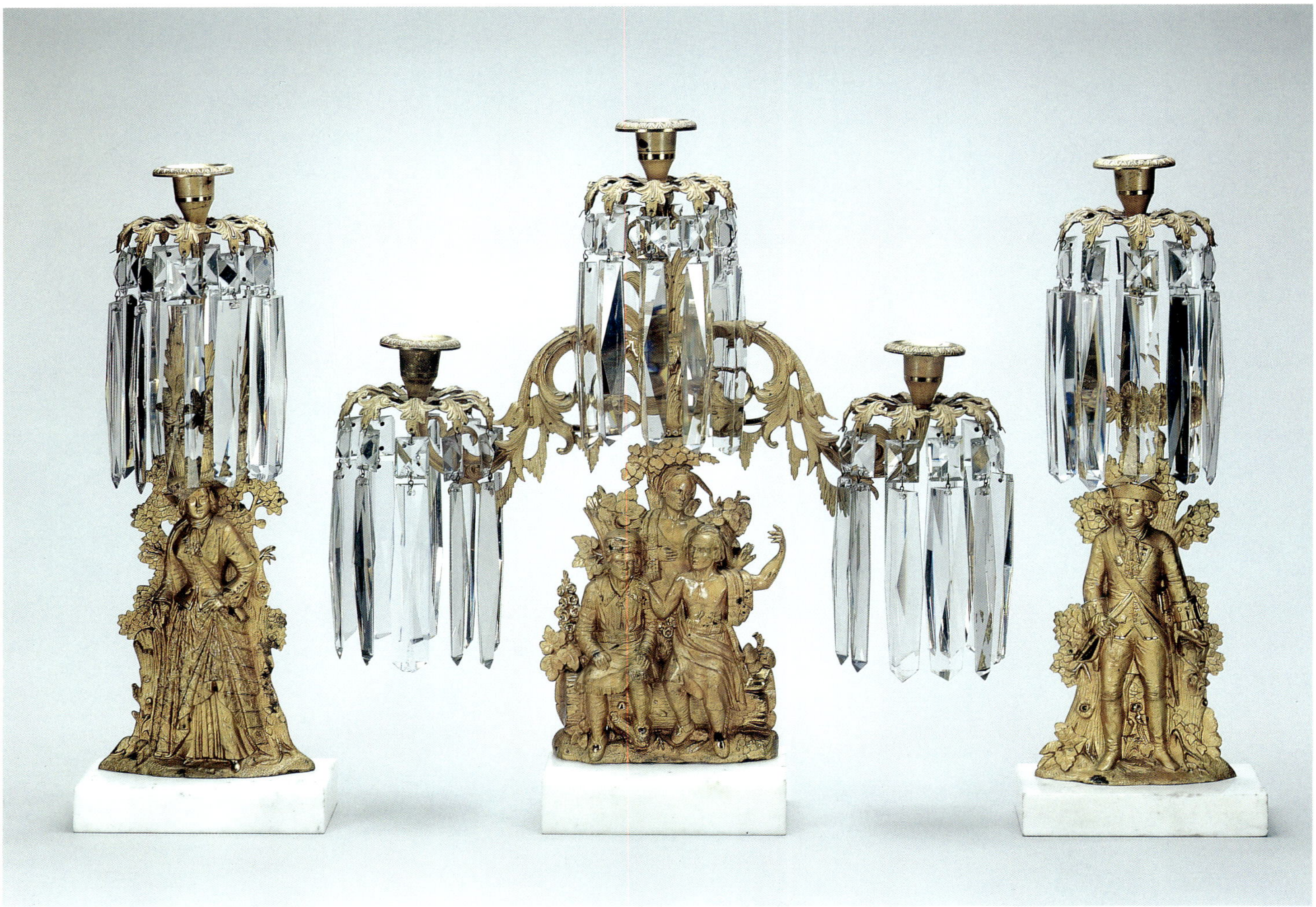

CAT. NO. 69

plished frontiersman who was raised by Chingachgook, the chief of a friendly Mohican tribe. As the story evolves, Cora Munro, the daughter of an English colonel, and her sister, Alice, are abducted by an unfriendly Indian tribe. Natty, Chingachgook, his son Uncas, and Major Duncan Heyward, an officer in the English army, set out to save the two women.

On the girandoles, Baker represented each character as Cooper described them in his novel. The single figures depict Cora Munro and Major Heyward. The central candelabra depicts Chingachgook, Natty Bumppo, and Uncas.[4] The figure of Chingachgook is, as Cooper described, "seated on the end of a mossy log. . . . His closely shaved head . . . was without ornament of any kind, with the exception of a solitary eagle's plume, that crossed his crown, and depended over the left shoulder. A tomahawk and scalping-knife . . . were in his girdle."[5] Baker also added his own interpretation of the chief of the Mohicans. Swathed in a togalike blanket, Chingachgook sits in a classical pose first used in the fifth century B.C. by the Greek sculptor Phidias in his monumental sculpture of Zeus. Baker's inspiration may have come from a more recent use of the pose: Horatio Greenough's larger-than-life statue of George Washington, executed between 1832 and 1841.[6] Chingachgook was modeled in a reverse position to that of the Washington sculpture, but the representation of the toga, his outstretched arm with the end of the toga thrown over his forearm, and the positioning of his feet are very similar to Greenough's sculpture.

The girandoles epitomize Cornelius and Company's mid-century production. Palmette-bordered bobèches and down-turned, water-leaf prism rings originated in Philadelphia, but were used by New York companies as well. The coffin-shaped glass prisms and original matte, gilt finish with burnished highlights reflect light, lending brilliance to these pieces.[7]

NOTES

1. The subjects of girandoles produced by Cornelius and Company include Pocahontas and John Smith, Ivanhoe, and George Washington.

2. Philadelphia Museum of Art, *Philadelphia: Three Centuries of American Art*, exh. cat. (1976), p. 334; and Donald L. Fennimore, *Metalwork in Early America: Copper and Its Alloys from the Winterthur Collection* (Winterthur, Del., 1996), p. 226.

3. Stamped on the back of each piece: 206 for the central fixture and 216 for the side fixtures. For the patent drawings, see Fennimore (note 2), p. 226.

4. Ibid., p. 227.

5. James Fenimore Cooper, *The Last of the Mohicans*, ed. William Charvat (Cambridge, Mass., 1958), p. 34.

6. Wayne Craven, *Sculpture in America*, rev. ed. (New York, 1984), pp. 105–08.

7. Garnitures could be purchased with either a matte or highlighted finish; highlighted examples were more expensive. A contemporary account of the factory documents the work of the burnishing department. See *Descriptions of the Establishment of Cornelius and Baker* (Philadelphia, 1860), as quoted in Pyne Press, *Lamps and Other Lighting Devices, 1850–1906* (Princeton, N.J., 1972), p. 9.

70. SIDEBOARD, 1825/35

Philadelphia or Baltimore

Mahogany with mahogany veneer, poplar, and eastern white pine; 124.5 x 186.4 x 59.7 cm (49 x 73⅜ x 23¾ in.)

Mrs. Alfred S. Burdick, Alfred T. Carton, Hibbard family heirs, Mrs. Paul B. Magnuson, and Decorative Arts Purchase Fund, 1974.8

The cabinetmaker who crafted this sideboard was inspired by the writings and designs of Englishman Rudolph Ackermann, whose *Repository of Arts, Literature, Fashions, Manufactures, &c.* appeared monthly from 1809 to 1828 and was widely distributed. In 1822 Ackermann published a design for a sideboard and cellaret (fig. 33), about which he wrote: "The engraving which accompanies this article represents a sideboard and cellarette [*sic*], suitable for the mansions of the great and opulent. The sideboard is of richly marked mahogany inlaid with bronze, which may, according to taste, or to suit the dining

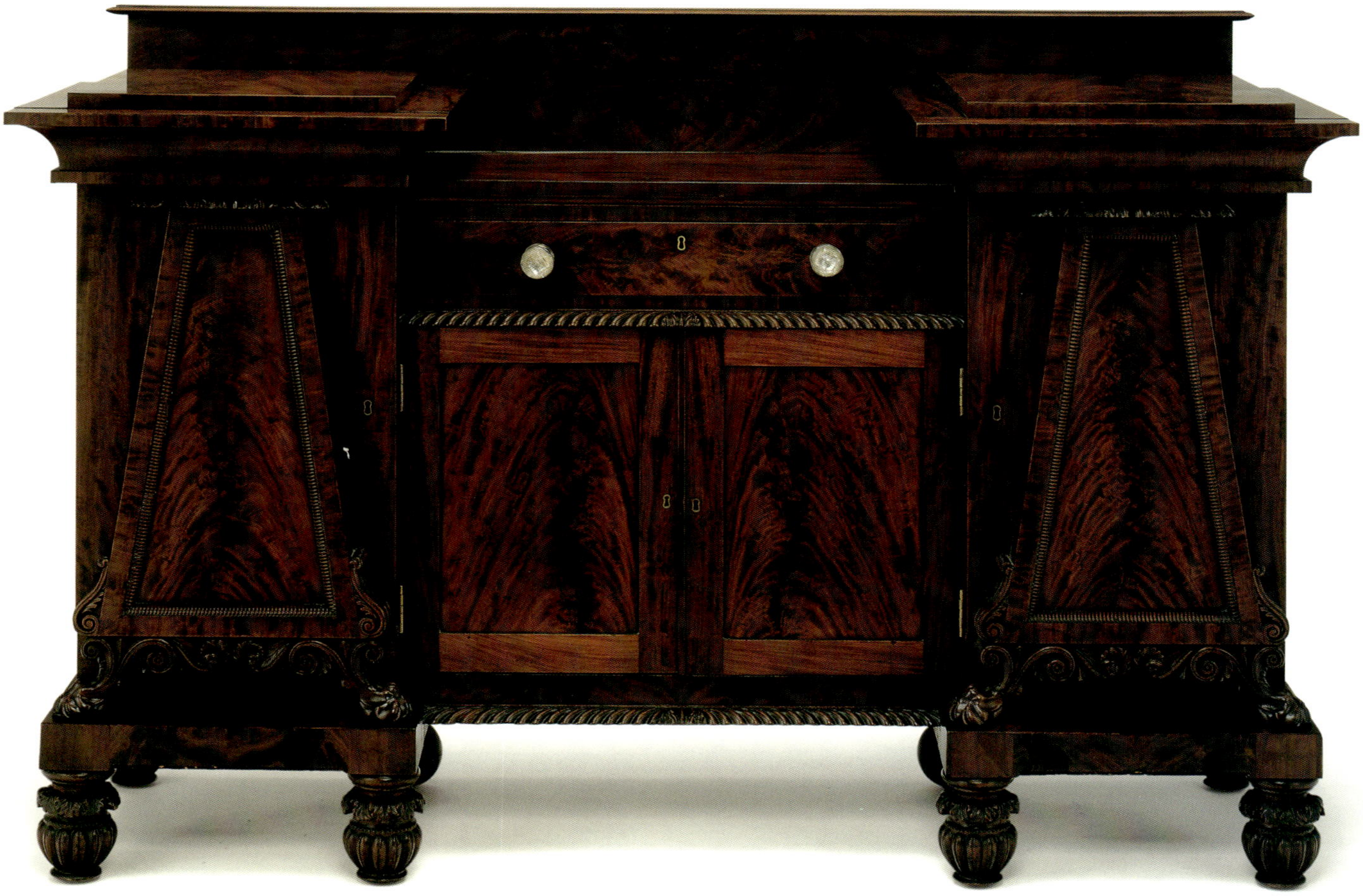

CAT. NO. 70

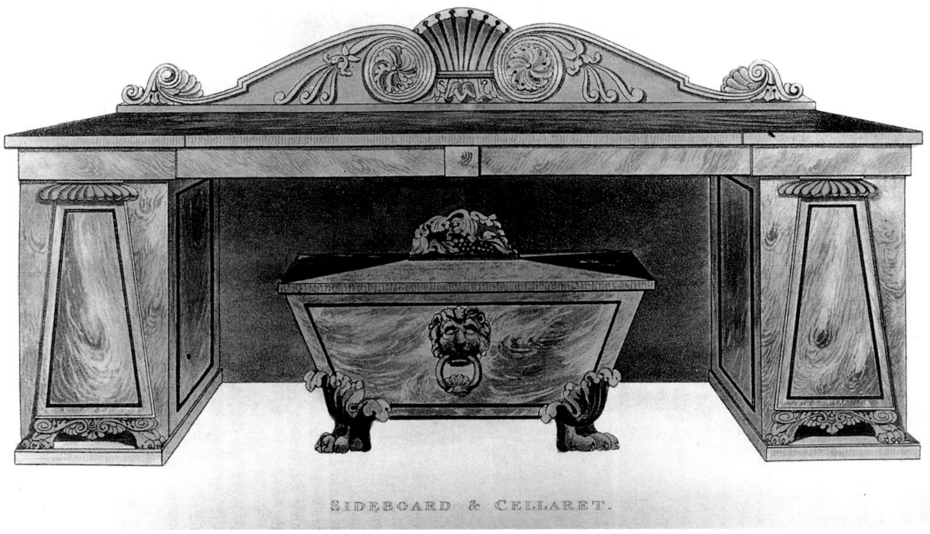

FIG. 33. Rudolph Ackermann, *The Repository of Arts, Literature, Fashions, Manufactures, &c.*, 2d ser., vol. 14, no. 82 (Oct. 1, 1822), p. 243.

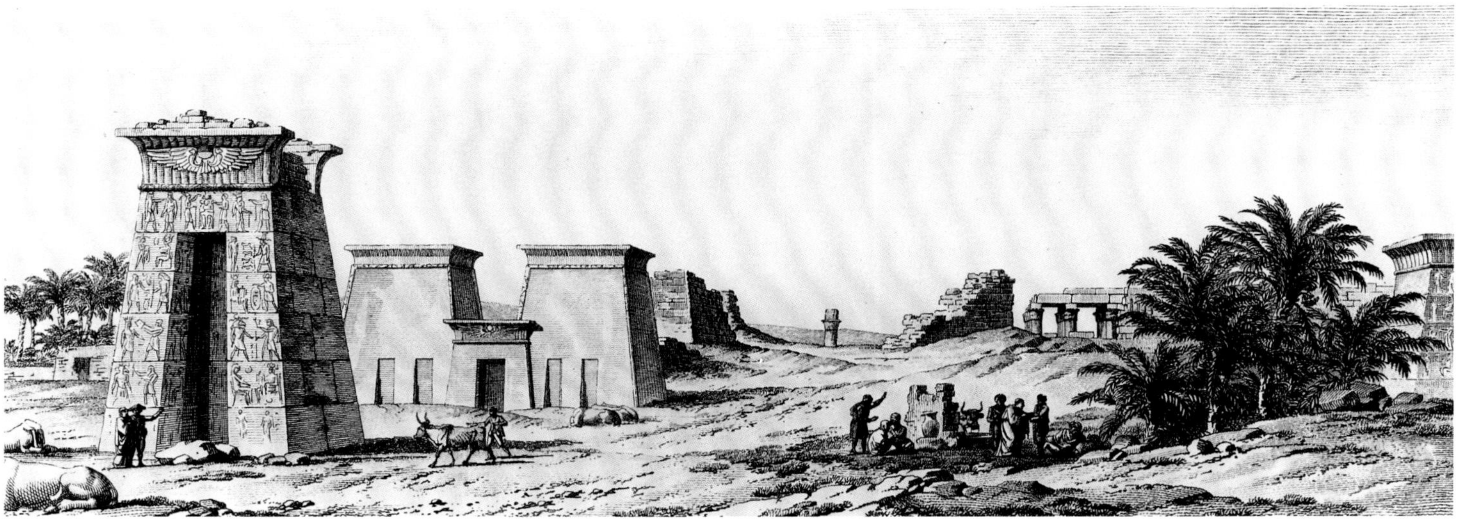

FIG. 34. Dominique Vivant Denon, *Voyage dans la Basse et la Haute Egypte, pendant les campagnes du général Bonaparte* (Paris, 1802), vol. 2, pl. 43, fig. 3. Photograph courtesy of Winterthur Library Printed Book and Periodical Collection, Winterthur, Del.

room furniture, be more or less so."[1] Like Ackerman's design, this sideboard uses highly figured mahogany, gadrooning, and Egyptian-inspired pylons supported by scrolled volutes and animal-paw feet.

Ackermann would have no doubt known of Egyptian designs from books such as Baron Dominique Vivant Denon's *Voyage dans la Basse et la Haute Egypte*, inspired by Napoleon's Egyptian campaign and published in 1802 (see fig. 34). Denon, who would become the first director of the Musée du Louvre, Paris, illustrated a pylon entrance at the temple of Thebes. The Philadelphia cabinetmaker responsible for the Art Institute's sideboard would have had an opportunity to see Denon's work at the Library Company of Philadelphia, which acquired *Voyage dans la Basse et la Haute Egypte* in 1828.[2]

The sideboard was originally owned by Dr. Arthur Rich (1779–1853) and his wife, Mary Wiltbank Rich (1802–1869). They were married in 1825 in Philadelphia and soon moved to Baltimore, where they lived until Dr. Rich's death. The sideboard may have been a wedding present to the couple, or may have been purchased to furnish their home in Baltimore.[3]

NOTES

1. Rudolph Ackermann, *The Repository of Arts, Literature, Fashions, Manufactures, &c.*, 2d ser., vol. 14, no. 82 (Oct. 1, 1822), p. 243.

2. The Library Company of Philadelphia was the nation's first public library, and counted among its members many of the city's craftspeople.

3. Letter from Hester Rich (great-granddaughter of the original owners) to Mary Bean, July 17, 1974, Files of the Department of American Arts, The Art Institute of Chicago.

71. AMMI PHILLIPS (1788–1865)

Cornelius Allerton, 1821/22

Oil on canvas; 84.1 x 69.5 cm (33 x 27½ in.)
Gift of Robert Allerton, 1946.394

72. *Mrs. Reuben Allerton (Lois Atherton)*, 1821/22

Oil on canvas; 84.1 x 69.5 cm (33 x 27½ in.)
Gift of Robert Allerton, 1946.395

Ammi Phillips was a self-taught, itinerant portrait painter who plied his trade in Connecticut, Massachusetts, and New York.[1] Traveling from county to county, Phillips produced likenesses of prominent rural citizens such as the Allertons: a mother and son from Dutchess County, New York. Phillips's style changed as he matured artistically; the Allerton portraits were painted during a period when he emphasized realism, perhaps under the influence of Albany artist Ezra Ames.[2]

Phillips executed his first Dutchess County portraits around 1820, and worked there regularly for more than thirty years, producing formulaic, yet individualized, portraits of the men and women of the region. A doctor in Pine Plains, New York, Cornelius Allerton served as Dutchess County Clerk in 1815–16, and was forty-two years old when Phillips depicted him.[3] His father, Reuben Allerton, had also been a physician in Dutchess County and had served in the Revolutionary War as a surgeon at the battle of Saratoga in 1777.[4] Phillips painted a portrait of Reuben's wife, Lois Atherton Allerton, when she was about sixty-four. Little else is known of her life.

Phillips portrayed both Cornelius and Lois Atherton Allerton three-quarter length, seated on painted chairs (probably the same chair), holding an identifying prop, and framed against a somber gray background. Compositional similarities aside, Phillips sharply contrasted the appearance of each sitter. The dour, wrinkled Mrs. Allerton wears a stiff bonnet denoting her age and widowhood. Cornelius appears as a middle-aged man with windswept hair and a jaunty jabot. Volume one of *Parr's Medical Dictionary* on his lap indicates his profession; the horse, in the left background, is probably included for the same reason.[5] In contrast, Mrs. Allerton holds the *Gospel Herald*, an evangelical newspaper edited by Henry Fitz and published in New York City between 1820 and 1827.[6] In its first issue, the *Gospel Herald* stated its mission "to vindicate 'the ways of God to man'—to pour the wine and oil of the joy of the salvation of our God into the wounded hearts of our brethren . . . who are groping in the darkness of error and unbelief."[7] Calvinism, excommunication, and bigotry are among the many topics the newspaper addressed over the years.

The *Gospel Herald* was only one of many mouthpieces of the early nineteenth-century evangelical movement that attracted primarily women.[8] Its inclusion here underscores Mrs. Allerton's religiousness and positions her as the moral backbone of her family, whereas her son's professional status suggests his role as the household's financial head. Phillips thus presented mother and son as opposites: a woman of religion and a man of science; an older, withered mother and her robustly attractive son; spiritual leader of the family and breadwinner. Many of the artist's paired portraits express similar dichotomies between male and female spheres, unified by similar dress, background colors, and furniture.

It is likely that Cornelius Allerton commissioned both his portrait and that of his mother. He evidently commissioned as well a now-unlocated portrait of his wife, Clarissa Husted Allerton.[9] Phillips's portraits of the Allertons epitomize this period of his career stylistically, but are also valuable social documents from the first quarter of the nineteenth century, not only illuminating male and female roles during this period but documenting the aspirations and appearance of the young nation's rural populace.

NOTES

1. For more about Phillips's biography and a chronological listing of his travels, see Stacy C. Hollander and Howard P. Fertig, *Revisiting Ammi Phillips: Fifty Years of American Portraiture*, exh. cat. (New York, Museum of American Folk Art, 1994).

2. See ibid., pp. 20–22, for more on Phillips's realistic style.

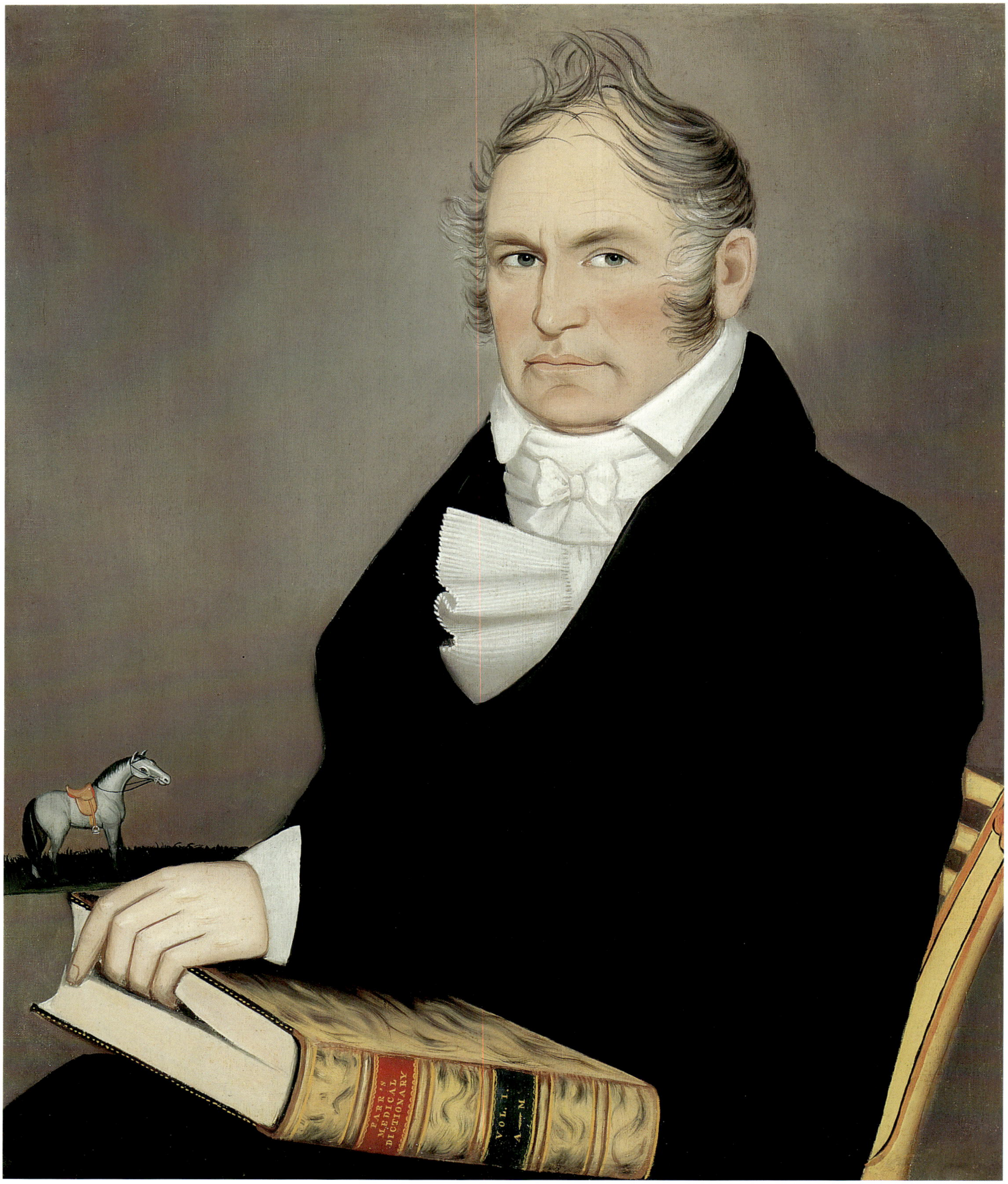

CAT. NO. 71

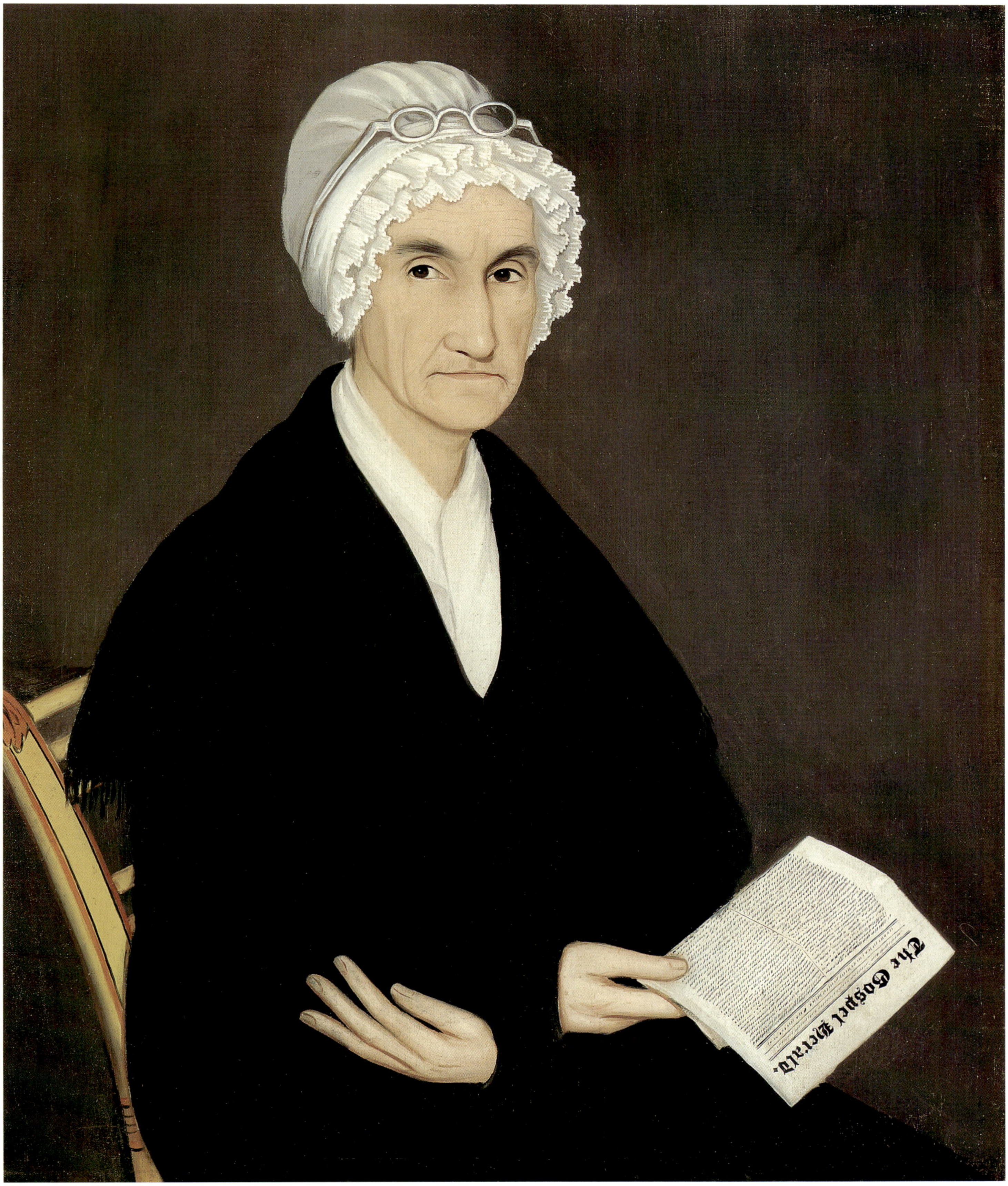

CAT. NO. 72

3. James H. Smith, *History of Dutchess County, New York* (Syracuse, N.Y., 1882), pp. 232, 244.

4. Ibid., pp. 345, 354. Reuben Allerton lived from 1753 to 1806.

5. The volume of *Parr's Medical Dictionary* held by Cornelius Allerton was published in Philadelphia in 1819. Allerton family lore suggests that Cornelius either painted the horse himself at a later date or commissioned the artist to add it; see letter from John Gregg Allerton to Milo Naeve, Apr. 6, 1981, Files of the Department of American Arts, The Art Institute of Chicago. In his portraits, the artist used primarily cats and dogs, typically posed with children. See Leigh Rehner Jones and Shirley A. Mearns, "Ammi Phillips's Portraits with Animals," *Hudson Valley Regional Review* 4, 2 (Sept. 1987), pp. 62–81.

6. These portraits have been dated according to the issue of the *Gospel Herald* held by Mrs. Allerton. Although no date is legible on the masthead, the typeface and masthead layout corresponds to volume 2 of the newspaper (Apr. 1821 to Apr. 1822).

7. *Gospel Herald* 1, 1 (Apr. 22, 1820), p. 1.

8. For more on evangelism and women, see Mary P. Ryan, *Cradle of the Middle Class: The Family in Oneida County, New York, 1790–1865* (Cambridge, Mass. 1981).

9. Hollander and Fertig (note 1), p. 61.

THE CIVIL WAR ERA
AND THE GILDED AGE

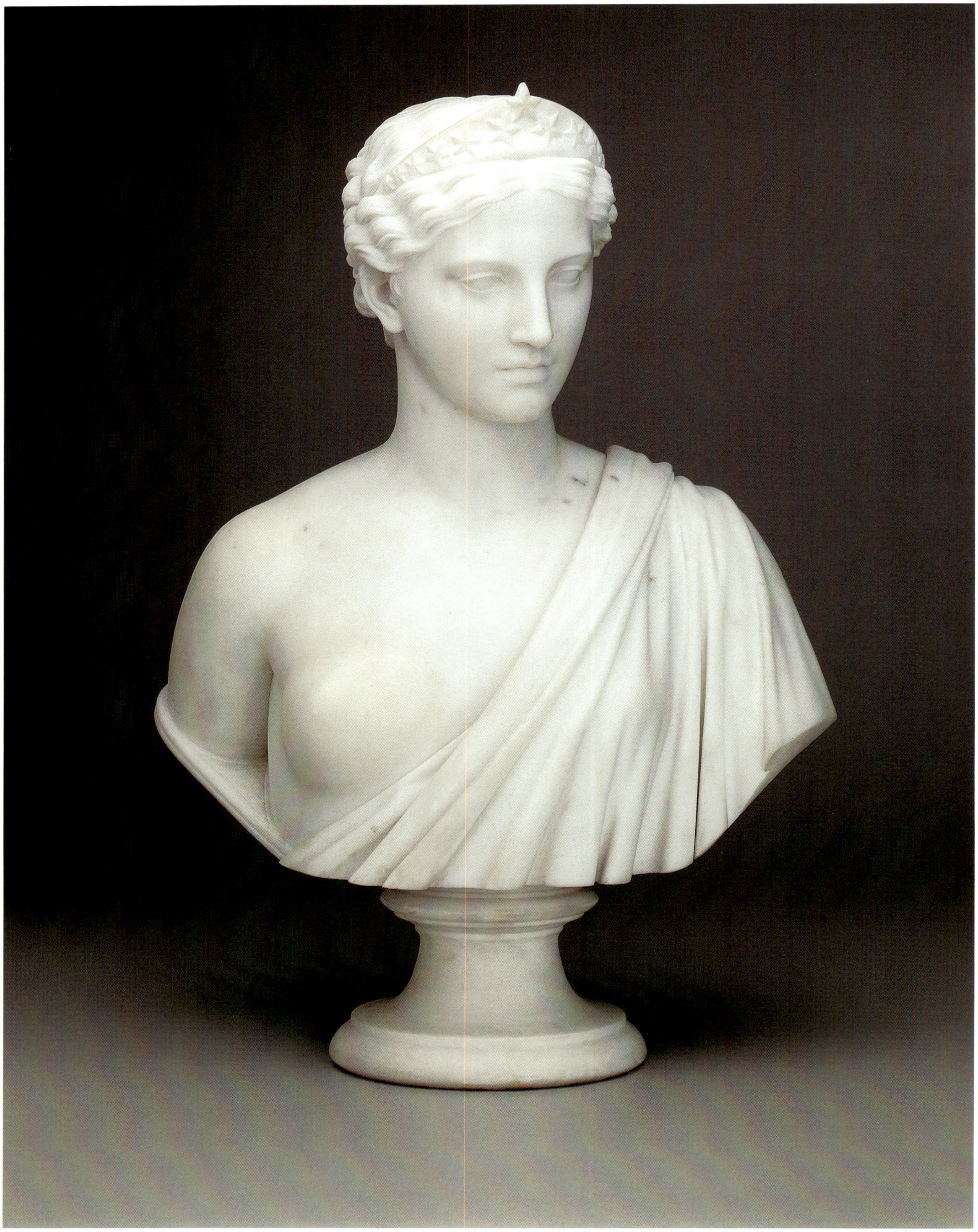

CAT. NO. 73

73. HIRAM POWERS (1805–1873)

America, 1850/54

Marble; h. 73.7 cm (29 in.)

The Art Institute of Chicago Purchase Fund, 1910.30

Hiram Powers's image of America is crowned with a diadem emblazoned with thirteen stars representing the Union's original states. Powers derived this bust from the full-length statue he made to memorialize the 1848 revolutions in Europe and celebrate the democratic values of the United States government. In 1848 Powers explained the theme of *America* to his Cincinnati patron Nicholas Longworth: "I am making a statue to suit the times, at least it ought to suit the times if Liberty is to triumph. . . . I wish her to say that where crowns are exalted I cannot abide, and if you would have me live with you, and you would enjoy the blessings which I can give, you must be united and you must trample in the dust, every semblance of despotism."[1] Powers changed the original title, *Liberty*, to *America* to identify more specifically the virtues of his home country. This made clear the sculptor's desire to honor the United States as a model for burgeoning democratic nations and, in so doing, to gain the one honor that had eluded Powers for years, a coveted government commission.

Living in Florence, Powers witnessed firsthand Italy's struggles for unification under the leadership of Giuseppe Garibaldi, and supported the insurrectionist activities of the broad international community concerned with the establishment of democratic nations in Europe. In the United States, support for the 1848 uprisings was overwhelmingly positive, for both political and economic reasons.[2] To the denizens of a country founded upon the principles of liberty and equality for all, the monarchical tyranny of the governments of France, Germany, and Italy was reprehensible. On a more pragmatic level, Americans expected favorable trade treaties to result from the initiation of republican leadership in these countries.

Powers's work was unusual in that it bridged a gap between the two cultures, American and Italian, toward which the sculptor felt patriotic allegiance. Begun in 1848, the full-sized marble version of *America* was not completed until 1858. A partially nude figure draped around the hips and with her left arm raised, *America* takes her pose from the classical *Venus de Milo*. Her symbolic attributes include a laurel wreath, a diadem, and the broken chains on which she stands. Powers did not add the chains until after Congress passed a resolution in 1855 to commission a work from him. He had previously left out this inflammatory detail to avoid provoking Southern patrons who might interpret the attribute as an anti-slavery statement. However, Powers was a vehement abolitionist, and he finally carved the chains as a response to the controversial Kansas–Nebraska Act of 1854, which allowed the two states to decide slavery issues by popular sovereignty.

At the time of the 1855 Congressional resolution, Powers was certain that *America* would be chosen by the government to adorn the Capitol. However, when President James Buchan-

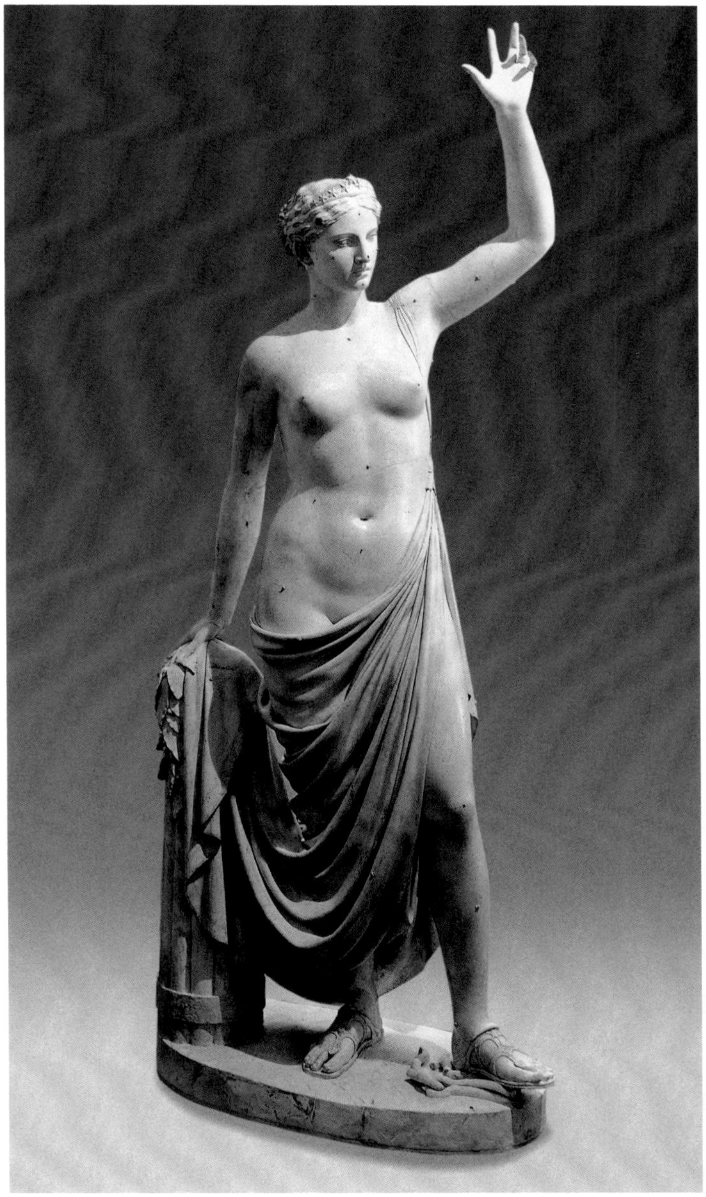

FIG. 35. Hiram Powers (1805–1873). *America*, 1848–50. Plaster; 226.5 x 89.3 x 42.8 cm (89½ x 35⅛ x 16⅞ in.). National Museum of American Art, Smithsonian Institution, Washington, D.C., Museum purchase in memory of Ralph Cross Johnson (1968.155.4).

an finally ordered work from the sculptor, in 1859, it was for two life-sized statues of Thomas Jefferson and Benjamin Franklin. *America* was not placed on public exhibition until 1861, when it was shown to acclaim at the first Italian National Exhibition in Florence. Critics overwhelmingly interpreted the statue as representing Italy's struggles for unity, achieved that same year.[3] Fire destroyed the full-sized marble *America* in 1865; the plaster cast (fig. 35) is now housed at the National Museum of American Art, Washington, D.C.

The Art Institute's *America* is one of twenty-eight busts produced by Hiram Powers between 1850 and 1873. Its patriotic subject and pronounced Greco-Roman elements, such as the himation, or cloth, draped over one breast and the slightly turned head, made it one of the sculptor's most popular pieces with mid-nineteenth-century American clients.[4] Stripped of most of the statue's iconographic detail, save for the crown of stars, the *America* bust is a simplified, more easily digestible symbol than its full-sized counterpart. The stars are also the only feature that distinguishes this work from other ideal busts fashioned by Powers such as *Faith* (c. 1872; Museum of Fine Arts, Boston), whose crown is decorated with an emblematic Greek cross.

Allegories of the United States as a dignified, classically beautiful woman date from the early years of the Union, when the country's leaders were searching for an apt symbolic depiction of democratic values. Hiram Powers's *America* bust embodies the nation that "Europe beholds afar off . . . , the light and hope of mankind."[5]

NOTES

1. Vivien Green Fryd, "Hiram Powers's *America*: 'Triumphant as Liberty and in Unity,'" *American Art Journal* 18, 2 (1986), p. 56.

2. See Merle Curti, "The Impact of the Revolutions of 1848 on American Thought," *Proceedings of the American Philosophical Society* 93, 3 (June 1949), pp. 209–15, for an informative synopsis of the American reaction to the European revolutions.

3. Albert Boime, *The Art of the Macchia and the Risorgimento* (Chicago, 1993), p. 172.

4. Cornelius C. Vermeule, "America's Neoclassic Sculptors: Fallen Angels Resurrected," *Antiques* 102 (Nov. 1972), pp. 873–75.

5. Fryd (note 1), p. 64.

74. GEORGE INNESS (1825–1894)

The Old Mill, 1849

Oil on canvas; 75.9 x 107 cm (29⅞ x 42⅛ in.)
Signed, lower right: *G. Inness 1849*
Goodman Fund, 1939.388

75. *Catskill Mountains*, 1870

Oil on canvas; 123.8 x 184.5 cm (48¾ x 72⅝ in.)
Signed, lower left: *G. Inness 1870*
Edward B. Butler Collection, 1912.1623

George Inness began his career as a landscape painter at a time when depictions of the untamed American wilderness were especially valued by artists, critics, and the general public. Yet throughout his professional life, Inness insisted equally on the importance of the cultivated landscape as a subject for artists. In 1879 he wrote that "the highest art is where has been most perfectly breathed the sentiment of humanity. Rivers, streams, the rippling brook, the hill-side, the sky, the clouds . . . can convey that sentiment. . . . The civilized landscape peculiarly can; and therefore I love it more and think it more worthy of reproduction than that which is savage and untamed."[1] Twenty years separate *The Old Mill* and *Catskill Mountains*, but both depict inhabited pastoral scenes, albeit in styles that reflect the artist's changing approach to landscape painting.

Before his debut as an artist in 1844, Inness worked with various teachers, including John Jesse Barker in Newark, New Jersey, and Régis François Gignoux in New York City.[2] Gignoux is believed to have exerted the most profound influence on the young artist, not so much stylistically as by introducing his pupil to the art of Old Masters such as Nicholas Poussin and Claude Lorrain. Using a dark, burnished palette, Inness painted his earliest compositions, including *The Old Mill*, following the formulas of Baroque landscape painting: large clumps of highly stylized trees, a diagonal element (in this case the stream) that directs the viewer into the middle-ground, and small figures for anecdotal detail. Although these early works were not well received by critics, who called them "artificial," the American Art-Union repeatedly purchased them for its annual distribution of paintings, supplying the young artist with a consistent source of income and publicity.[3]

The American Art-Union was established in New York in order to "seek out youthful genius and develope its energies. It has [an American] School to build up, in the midst of a popu-

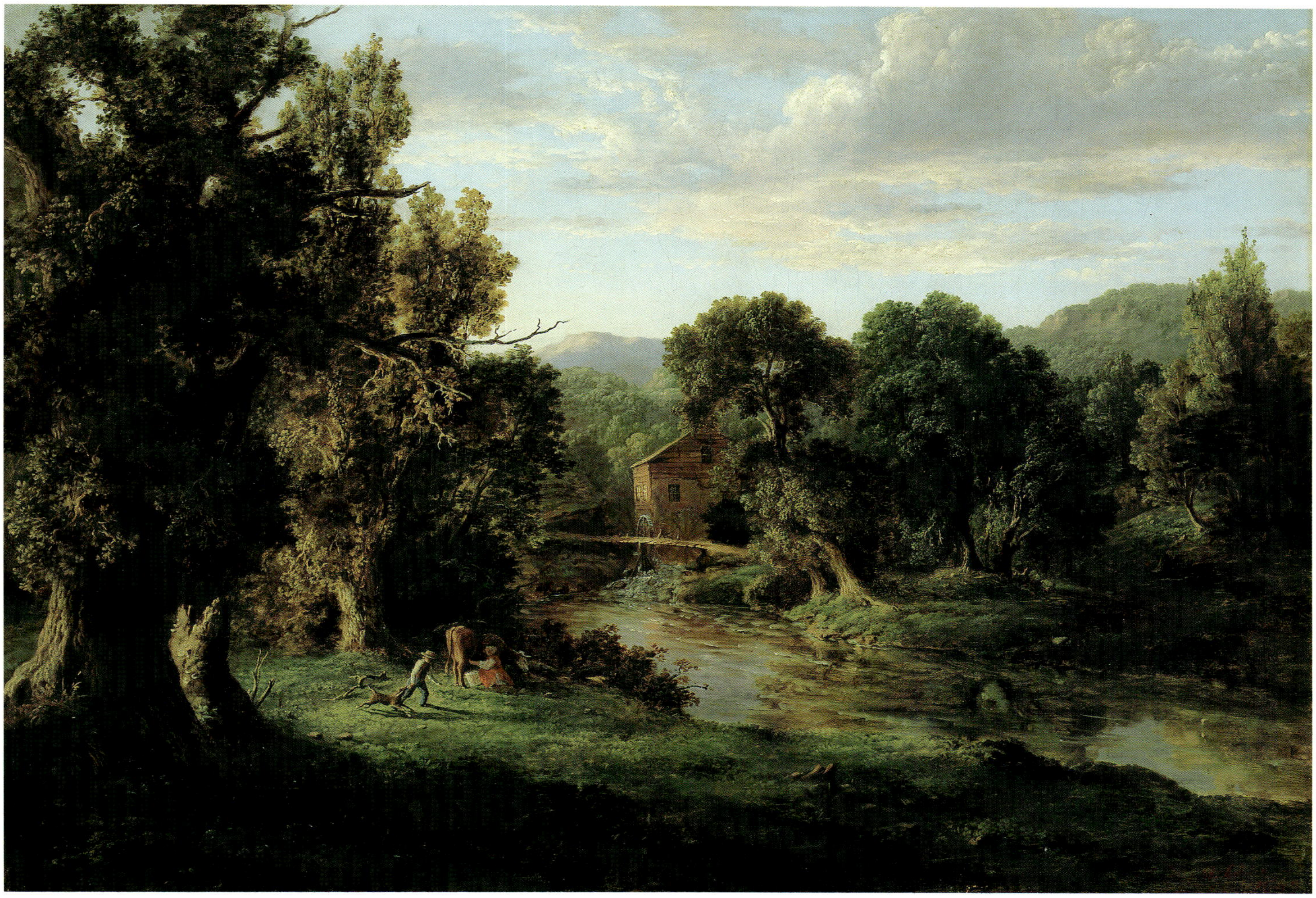

CAT. NO. 74

lation which is devoted to other and quite incongenial pursuits."[4] Inness was one of many artists who benefited from the Art-Union's policy of buying works directly from artists, exhibiting them in its free galleries, and then distributing the paintings by lottery to subscribers. Inness's first success with the Art-Union came in 1848, when it purchased *Crossing the Ford* (fig. 36), another of his early landscapes in the Art Institute's collection. In 1849, the year *The Old Mill* was acquired and distributed, Inness sold four other paintings to the Art-Union.[5]

In *The Old Mill*, Inness used patches of light to emphasize such details as a milkmaid, a boy, a running dog, and a decrepit mill, in contrast to the shadowy darkness of the trees. This play of light and dark not only illuminates the pleasures of rural life, but also suggests the potential for danger at the edge of the forest. That the mill is old establishes the location as settled and stable, although its state of disrepair may attest to its being an outmoded source of power and industry. It is a vision of rural life that celebrates its simplicity yet hints at its decline. Many American artists expressed a similar nostalgia during this period of rampant expansion and industrialization.

Inness executed *Catskill Mountains*, one of his largest canvases, in mid-career, just before his third extended trip to Europe.[6] Unlike other landscape artists who worked in the Catskills, Inness did not paint the sites made popular by the rising tide of tourists flocking to the region. The rolling hills and majestic mountains in the background resemble the topography of the area surrounding the village of Leeds.[7] As in *The Old Mill*, Inness represented a land tamed by human presence denoted by the church, the carefully tended fields, and the hayrick on the right. *Catskill Mountains*, however, contains underlying political and spiritual dimensions that the earlier painting lacks.

Immediately following the Civil War, Inness painted *Peace and Plenty* (1865; Metropolitan Museum of Art, New York), an even larger canvas than *Catskill Mountains*, in which he ex-

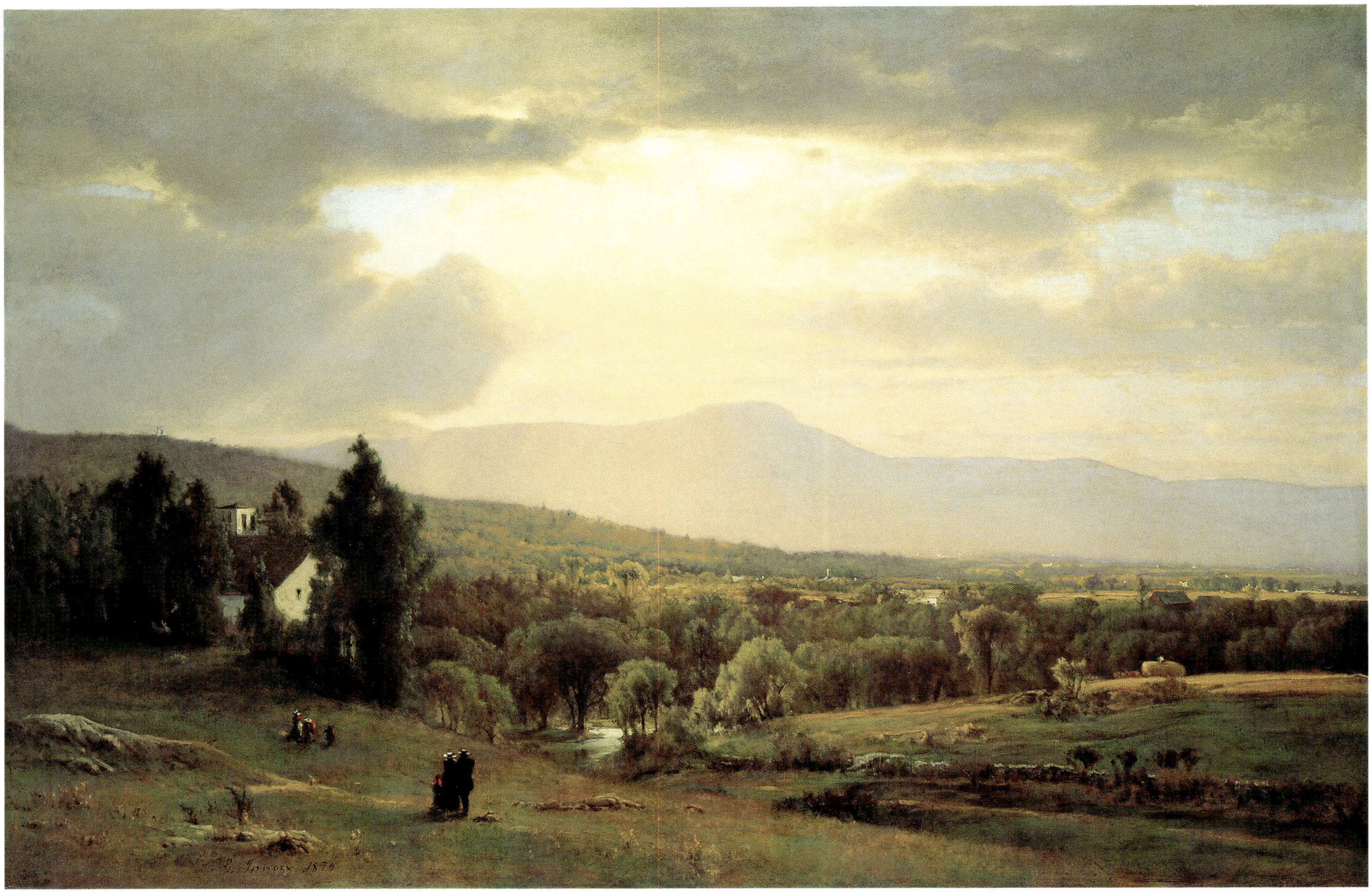

CAT. NO. 75

pressed his optimism in the aftermath of the conflict.[8] Like the Art Institute's landscape, the earlier work is a pastoral scene painted in a softly smudged manner reminiscent of French Barbizon School painting. In both works, the artist seems to have emphasized the therapeutic value of the cultivated landscape: it can heal and promise abundance.

In the mid-1860s—about the time he painted *Peace and Plenty*—Inness became involved with Swedenborgianism, a religious movement based on the writings of the eighteenth-century theologian Emmanuel Swedenborg. Swedenborg proposed that "each and all things in nature correspond to spiritual things," and suggested therefore that communion with the natural world can bring one closer to God.[9] Inness and his wife formally joined the Swedenborgian Church in 1867. That year the artist contributed an article to the *New Jerusalem Messenger* entitled "Colors and Their Correspondences," in which he described specific color combinations and their spiritual significance.[10] If we consider *Catskill Mountains* in the context of Inness's religious beliefs, it becomes clear that the wide ex-

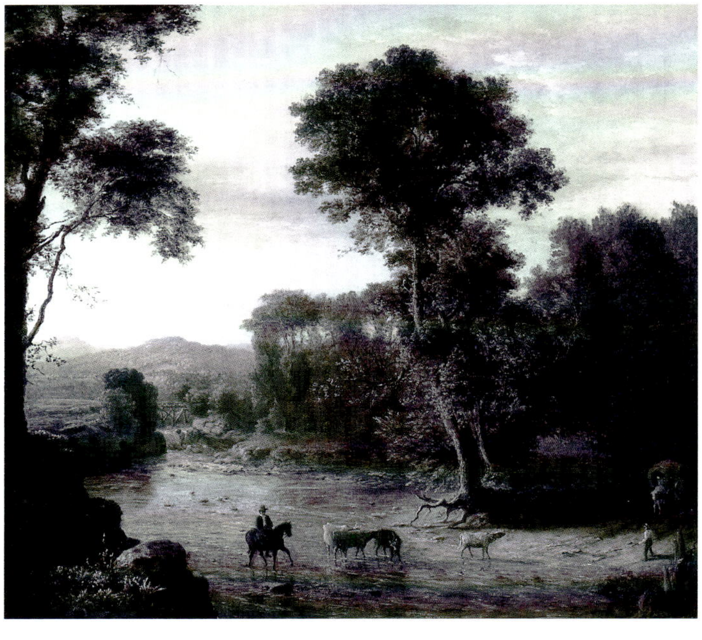

FIG. 36. George Inness (1825–1894). *Crossing the Ford*, 1848. Oil on canvas; 56.8 x 56.3 cm (22 7/16 x 22 1/4 in.). The Art Institute of Chicago, Gift of Mrs. Edith Kepke MacDonald (1977.487).

panse of blue sky that embraces the landscape is as symbolic of spirituality and worship as the picturesque church nestled in trees on the left. Inness's Swedenborgian investigation of landscape was lifelong; he painted some of his most transcendent works, including *Home of the Heron* (cat. no. 147), in his last years.

NOTES

1. "A Painter on Painting," *Harper's New Monthly Magazine* 56 (Feb. 1878), reprinted in Nicolai Cikovsky, Jr., and Michael Quick, *George Inness*, exh. cat. (Los Angeles County Museum of Art, 1985), p. 209.

2. For biographical information about Inness, see Nicolai Cikovsky, Jr., *George Inness* (New York, 1971).

3. See ibid., pp. 25–28, for more on the negative reception of Inness's early paintings.

4. *Bulletin of the American Art-Union* 2, 2 (May 1849), p. 12.

5. The other works bought by the American Art-Union in 1849 were *View in Berkshire Co., Massachusetts; Clearing Off After a September Storm*; *Moonlight*; *A Nook Near Our Village*; and *Early Recollections.*

6. Inness traveled to the Catskills at least twice between 1864 and 1869.

7. Kenneth Myers, *The Catskills: Painters, Writers, and Tourists in the Mountains, 1820–1895*, exh. cat. (Yonkers, N.Y., Hudson River Museum of Westchester, 1987), p. 151.

8. Inness very much wanted to fight with the Union Army during the Civil War but was rejected on grounds of health. He turned instead to his painting to express his nationalistic fervor.

9. Sally M. Promey, "The Ribband of Faith: George Inness, Color Theory, and the Swedenborgian Church," *American Art Journal* 26, 1–2 (1994), p. 49. This article provides a fine introduction to Inness's involvement with Swedenborgianism.

10. Ibid., pp. 46–47.

76. HENRY KIRKE BROWN (1814–1886)

The Filatrice (The Spinner), 1850

Bronze; 50.8 x 30.5 x 17.8 cm (20 x 12 x 7 in.)

Roger McCormick Endowment, 1989.59

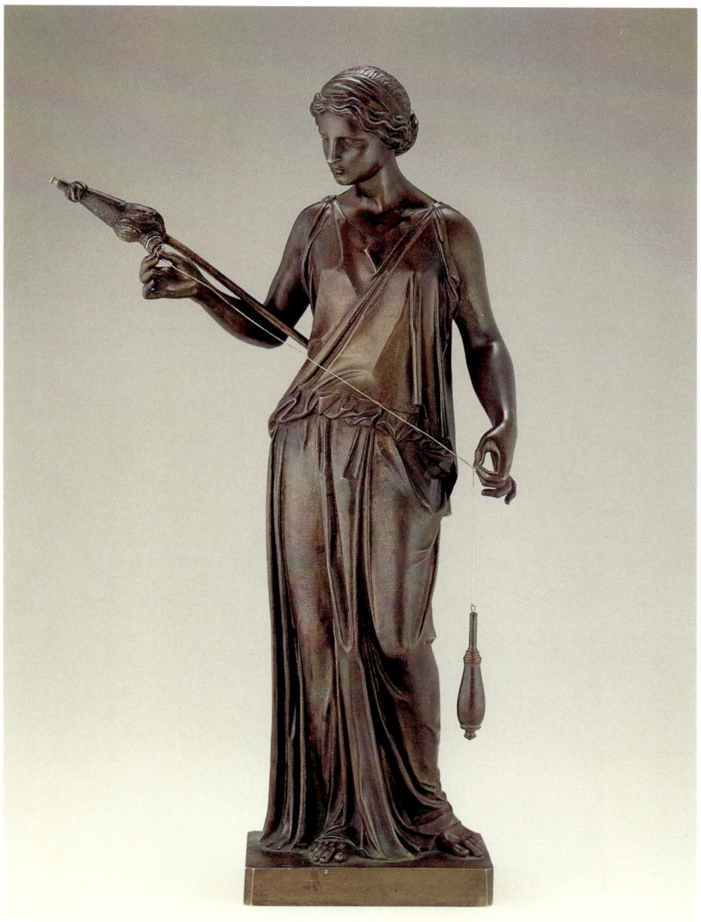

CAT. NO. 76

When Henry Kirke Brown returned to the United States in 1846 after a four year sojourn in Italy, he embarked upon a mission to produce sculpture in a neoclassical style that focused on American concerns and subject matter.[1] Brown fostered a relationship with the American Art-Union and opened a foundry for the manufacture of bronze sculpture in Brooklyn.[2] *The Filatrice* is a product of both of these enterprises: commissioned by the Art-Union in 1850 to be distributed by lottery to twenty of its members, it was cast in Brown's foundry. No records survive documenting how many of the twenty statues were actually produced, and only three are known today.[3]

Of the four commissions Brown received from the Art-Union between 1847 and 1850, *The Filatrice* was the most extensive. In July 1850, the *Bulletin of the American Art-Union* reported: "Mr. H. K. Brown, whose *Indian Hunter* was so much and so deservedly admired, has lately designed a female figure for this purpose, which has been adopted by a recent vote of the Committee. It represents a *Girl Spinning* in the graceful manner in which that occupation is carried on in Italy. . . . A famous work upon a similar subject, and called from it the *Filatrice*, adorns the Duke of Devonshire's collection at Chatsworth."[4] By referring to European models for the piece, the writer calls attention to the aspirations of Brown and other American artists during this period to elevate taste by adapting European models to American subjects. Using a strictly neoclassical design in *The Filatrice*, Brown transformed a homely subject (spinning) into an elegant one with mythic overtones of the Three Fates, one of whom spins the thread of life.

The neoclassical style of *The Filatrice* is also evident in Brown's more typically "American" subject matter.[5] *The Choosing of the Arrow*, the first of Brown's bronzes commissioned by the American Art-Union, depicts a Native American readying for the hunt. Both hunter and spinner stand in a contrapposto indebted to classical statuary and hold their distinguishing props (a bow and a distaff) diagonally to their bodies to create compositional tension. But where *The Filatrice* perpetuates a classical theme, *The Choosing of the Arrow* uses a conservative style to introduce innovative sculptural subject matter.

By eschewing marble for bronze, Brown helped introduce a new aesthetic in the United States that diverged from the traditional white marble so strongly associated with neoclassicism. *The Filatrice* was one of the first pieces Brown cast in bronze, and its distribution through the American Art-Union was strategically planned to promote the medium. The sculptor operated his Brooklyn foundry from 1848 with the assistance of two French founders named Lalouette and Bellenout.[6] However, the foundry also served as a workshop to train young American sculptors to work with bronze. John Quincy Adams Ward (cat. no. 88), one of Brown's first student apprentices, remained in the elder sculptor's studio until 1856 and in turn trained Daniel Chester French (see cat. nos. 142 and 174–75), establishing a tradition for the production of artistic bronzes in North America.

Brown went on to receive commissions for large bronzes, including one of De Witt Clinton, the New York State governor who initiated the construction of the Erie Canal; and an equestrian statue of George Washington. Both were cast by the Ames Foundry in Chicopee, Massachusetts. Brown seems to have abandoned his Brooklyn foundry after 1851, but the legacy of his innovative enterprise lives on in early works such as *The Filatrice*.

NOTES

1. Wayne Craven's articles remain the best sources for information about Brown; see Craven, "Henry Kirke Brown in Italy, 1842–1846," *American Art Journal* 1, 1 (spring 1969), pp. 65–77; and idem, "Henry Kirke Brown: His Search for an American Art in the 1840s," *American Art Journal* 4, 2 (Nov. 1972), pp. 44–58.

2. For more about the aims of the American Art-Union, see entry on George Inness's painting *The Old Mill* (cat. no. 74).

3. The two other known versions of *The Filatrice* are in private collections.

4. "Condition and Prospects of the American Art-Union," *Bulletin of the American Art-Union* 3 (July 1850), p. 51. The Chatsworth reference refers to Rudolf Schadow's marble *A Statue of a Spinning Girl* (1819), still in the collection of the Duke of Devonshire at Chatsworth. *The Filatrice* is also mentioned in "The Return to be Made to the Members of 1850," *Bulletin of the American Art-Union* 3 (Sept. 1850), p. 88; and reproduced in *Bulletin of the American Art-Union* 4 (July 1851), p. 57. Besides *The Filatrice*, Brown contributed to the Art-Union a marble bas-relief entitled *Christ Giving Sight to the Blind Man* in 1847, *Indian Hunter* in 1849, and *The Choosing of the Arrow* in 1850.

5. Brown traveled to Michigan to observe Menominee Indians before creating *The Choosing of the Arrow*, but produced a typically romanticized version of a Native American.

6. Michael Shapiro, *Bronze Casting and American Sculpture, 1850–1900* (Newark, Del., 1985), pp. 45–50.

77. EDWARD SHEFFIELD BARTHOLOMEW (1822–1858)

Hagar and Ishmael, 1856

Marble; 71.1 x 49.9 cm (28 x 19⅝ in.)

Inscribed, lower right: *BARTHOLOMEW ROME 1856*

J. Peter McCormick Fund and Roger McCormick Endowment, 1995.38

Edward Sheffield Bartholomew's career as a sculptor was cut short when he died in Naples, Italy, at the age of thirty-six. At the time of his death, he was beginning to be recognized by critics and patrons for his sensitive marble renderings of biblical and mythological scenes. *Hagar and Ishmael* was one such work. An 1856 article in the *Art Journal* focused attention on Bartholomew's bas-relief *Hagar and Ishmael*, characterizing it as "remarkably expressive, . . . the figures group well in the composition, all the lines [seem] to flow naturally yet picturesquely."[1]

Bartholomew traveled to Rome in 1850 and studied with Giorgio Ferrero, an Italian artist who specialized in bas-relief and who encouraged his talented student to travel to Greece and study the Parthenon friezes in order to hone his skills.[2] Between his arrival in Italy in 1850 and his death in 1858, Bartholomew maintained a studio in Rome and returned only twice to the United States. As part of the second wave of American sculptors who settled in Rome, Bartholomew enjoyed the patronage of many wealthy Americans traveling through Italy on the Grand Tour and the companionship of other ambitious American artists seeking inspiration and training there. These sculptors adhered to a neoclassical style that relied upon formal restraint and subtle effects to move and edify the viewer. An early visitor to his studio remarked that "Mr. Bartholomew has poetic sentiment, with taste, strength, and patience—he

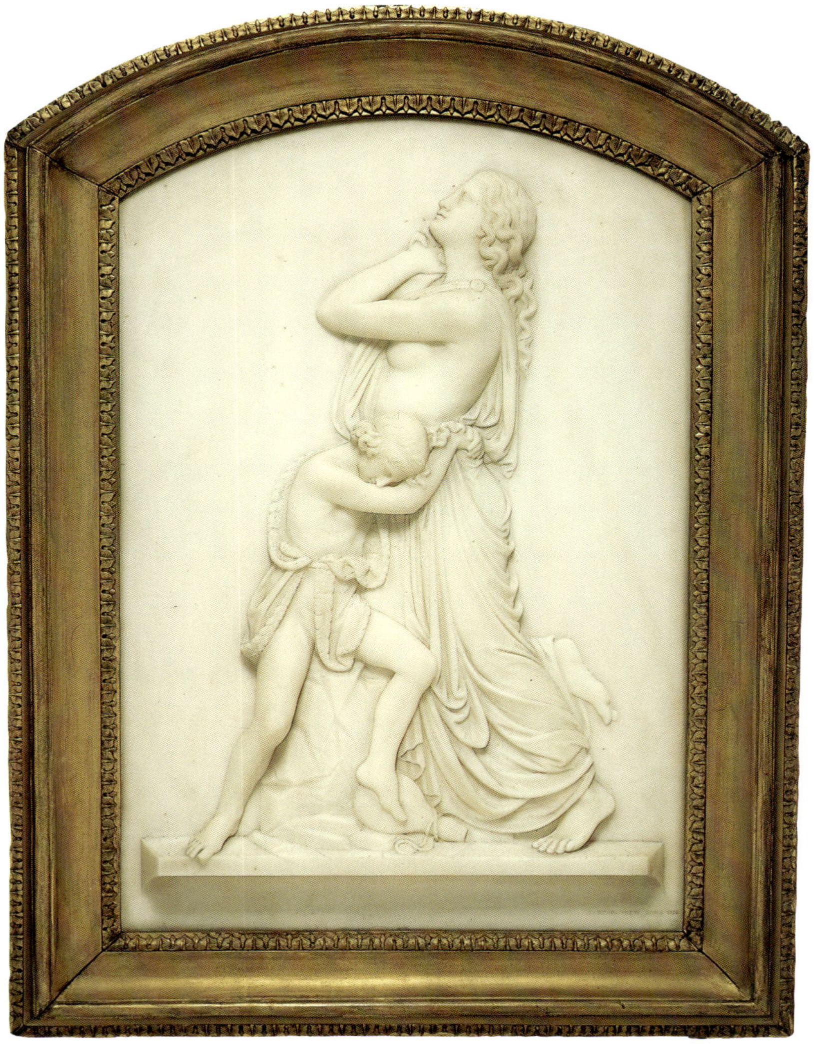

CAT. NO. 77

has a genuine reverence for his art, and a modest estimate of himself—beyond doubt an artist whom America will do well to encourage."[3] By 1856 Bartholomew could report the following to his friend the landscape painter Frederic Edwin Church: "I am full of orders and works of all kinds. I am making any number of portrait busts."[4]

During his brief career, Bartholomew created sculptures for many esteemed patrons; of these perhaps the most loyal were the city of Hartford and its museum, the Wadsworth Atheneum.[5] He was born in Colchester, Connecticut, in 1822, and moved to Hartford with his family when he was fifteen. In 1845 he became the first curator of the Wadsworth Atheneum, a post he held for three years. The city of Hartford honored Bartholomew with a testimonial dinner in 1857, along with Church, a Hartford native. When Bartholomew died suddenly in Naples (probably from tuberculosis), a subscription list was formed in Hartford to raise money to purchase the work left in the artist's studio and to pay his debts.[6] Among the pieces purchased from the studio was a plaster bas-relief of *Hagar and Ishmael* (1853; Wadsworth Atheneum, Hartford, Connecticut) that was the model for the Art Institute's marble version.[7] *Shepherd Boy* (fig. 37), a sculpture in the round, depicts a youth wearing a hide and possessing a body type that foreshadows that of Ishmael in *Hagar and Ishmael*.

Mid-nineteenth-century artists and patrons favored biblical, historical, and mythological narratives for their learned allusions and moral content.[8] Though not a particularly popular subject for sculptural compositions, the story of Hagar and Ishmael, recounted in Genesis, was morally attractive. Hagar was a handmaiden in the house of Abraham and Sarah who was chosen to bear Abraham's child because of Sarah's inability to conceive; Ishmael was the product of their union. Hagar and Ishmael lived with Abraham and Sarah for fourteen years, until Sarah became pregnant and gave birth to Isaac, Abra-

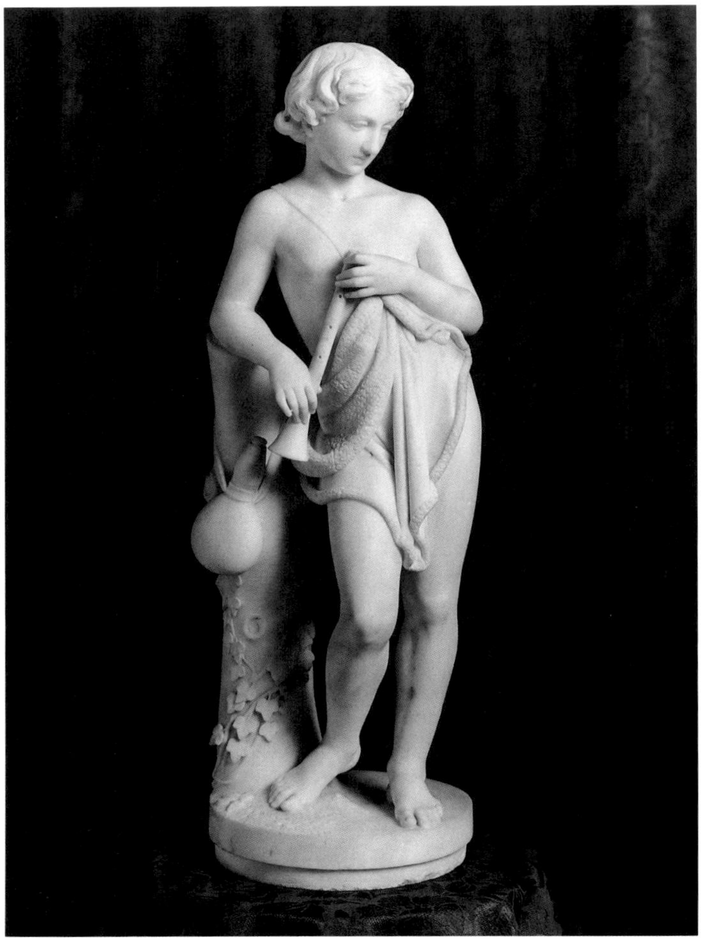

FIG. 37. Edward Sheffield Bartholomew (1822–1858). *Shepherd Boy*, 1854. Marble; 69.2 x 22.9 x 22.5 cm (27¼ x 9 x 8⅞ in.). Chrysler Museum, Norfolk, Va., Gift of James H. Ricau and Museum Purchase (86.460).

ham's legitimate heir. Fearing competition, Sarah had Hagar and Ishmael expelled to the desert, where they were rescued from certain death by God, who provided a well to quench their thirst. Bartholomew's bas-relief captures the moment of Hagar beseeching God to rescue her son. Her pose is one of earnest supplication, while Ishmael's clinging posture reveals his dependence on and attachment to his mother. The discarded jug at the bottom center of the composition alludes to their perilous thirst in the desert. Just a few years before the outbreak of the Civil War, the plight of Hagar and her son resonated with references to slavery and the oppression of African-Americans.[9]

NOTES

1. "Hagar and Ishmael," *Art Journal* 8 (Apr. 1, 1856), p. 116. This article was illustrated with an engraving by J. H. Baker of Bartholomew's *Hagar and Ishmael*. The measurements cited in this article ("three feet eight inches in height, by two feet two inches in width") correspond not to the Art Institute's marble bas-relief, but to the Wadsworth Atheneum's plaster version (46⅝ x 28½ in.).

2. For biographical information about Bartholomew, see Susan Underwood Crane, "Edward Sheffield Bartholomew," *Connecticut Quarterly* 2, 3 (July, Aug., Sept. 1896), pp. 202–14; and William G. Wendell, "Edward Sheffield Bartholomew, Sculptor," *Wadsworth Atheneum Bulletin*, 5th ser., 12 (winter 1962), pp. 1–18.

3. Grace Greenwood, *Haps and Mishaps of a Tour in Europe* (Boston, 1853), p. 223.

4. Letter from Edward Sheffield Bartholomew to Frederic Edwin Church, Mar. 11, 1856, in Archives, Wadsworth Atheneum, Hartford, Conn.

5. One of Bartholomew's most esteemed patrons was Enoch Pratt, a wealthy financier from Baltimore. For more on his patronage of Bartholomew, see Alexandra Lee Levin, "Enoch Pratt as Patron of Edward S. Bartholomew, Sculptor," *Maryland Historical Magazine* 51, 4 (Dec. 1956), pp. 267–72.

6. For details of this arrangement, see Wendell (note 2).

7. Although the dimensions of the plaster are slightly larger than those of the marble, pointing pin marks in the plaster suggest that it was carved in marble at least once. The details of the two pieces match as well.

8. Another nineteenth-century American sculptor who illustrated the story is Edmonia Lewis in *Hagar* (1875; National Museum of American Art, Washington, D.C.).

9. See Kirsten P. Buick, "The Ideal Works of Edmonia Lewis: Involving and Inverting Autobiography," *American Art* 9, 2 (summer 1995), pp. 10–11.

78. HARRIET HOSMER (1830–1908)

Zenobia, Queen of Palmyra, c. 1857

Marble; 86.4 x 57.2 x 31.8 cm (34 x 22½ x 12½ in.)
Inscribed on the back: *HARRIET HOSMER / FECIT ROMAE*
Gift of the Antiquarian Society, 1993.260

Harriet Hosmer was among the small group of nineteenth-century female sculptors in Rome later described by Henry James as "the white marmorean flock."[1] Hosmer, a leading figure at mid-century, is notable for both her skill as a sculptor and her unorthodox and pioneering spirit. Her work addressed the recurring theme of strong females whose power was thwarted by the injustices of society. A courageous individual who defied society's traditional expectations of her sex, she was attracted to historical women who broke the mold. One such subject was Zenobia, who ruled Palmyra (now Syria) from 268. During her reign, she conquered Egypt and much of Asia Minor, but was eventually defeated by the Roman Emperor Aurelian in 272. After her capture, Zenobia was marched through Rome in chains. Following neoclassical tradition,

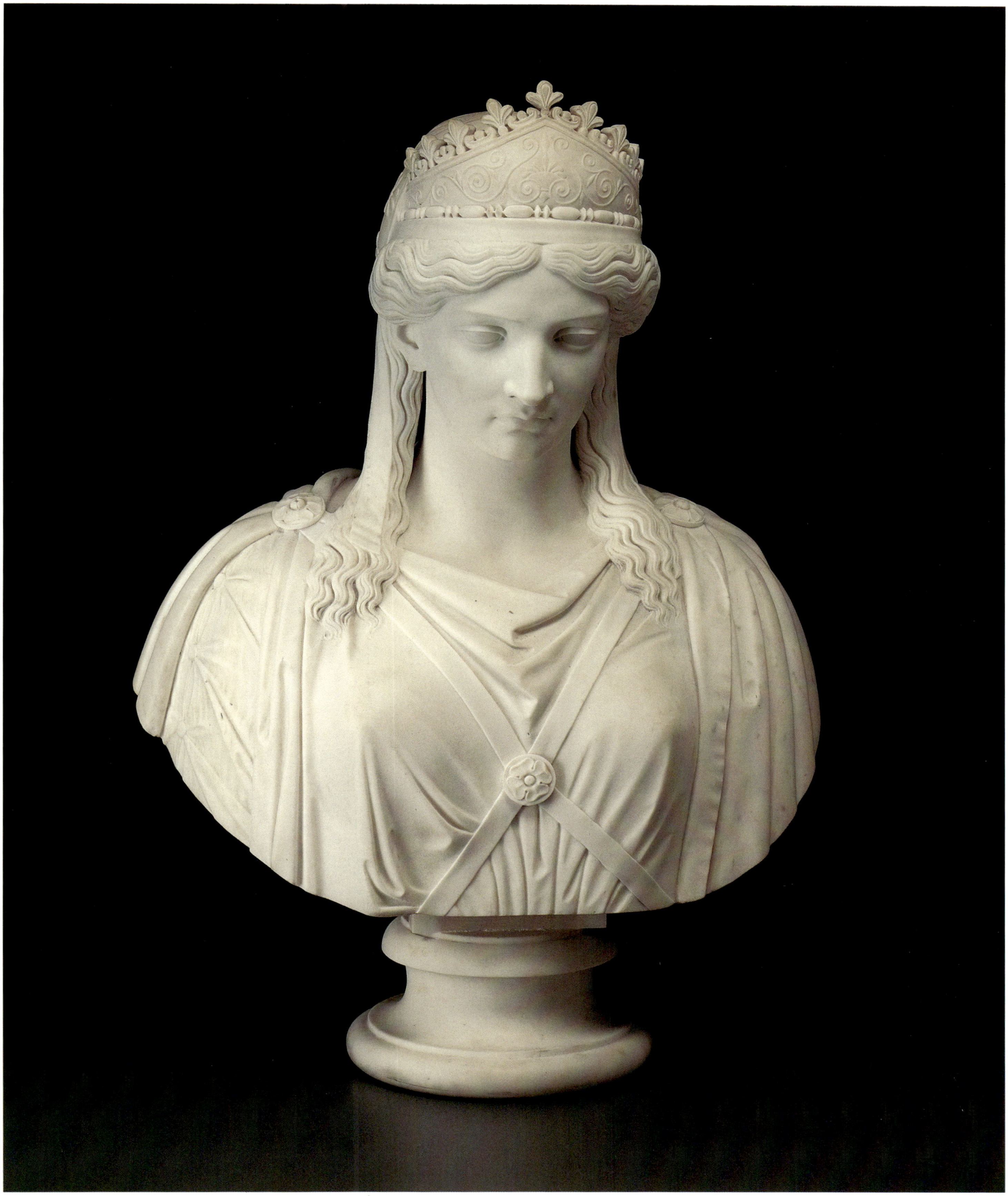

CAT. NO. 78

Hosmer's heroic bust of the ancient queen shows the subject's serene resolve.

Hosmer was born in Watertown, Massachusetts, and attended a progressive boarding school run by Elizabeth and Charles Sedgwick in Lenox, Massachusetts, which provided a more challenging education than generally offered to women in the nineteenth century. Her father, Hiram Hosmer, encouraged his daughter's interest in sculpture and allowed her to study drawing and modeling in Boston with the English-born sculptor Peter Stephenson. Like many artists, Hosmer wished to augment her training by studying anatomy. Strict local rules against women pursuing such study put an immediate stop to her efforts to enroll in anatomy classes at Boston Medical College. With the help of a school friend, however, she was able to study anatomy privately under Dr. J. N. McDowell at the Medical College in St. Louis, Missouri.

Hosmer returned to Watertown from St. Louis in 1852, established her own sculpture studio, and completed her first major composition in marble—an idealized portrait bust of *Hesper* (1852; Watertown Public Library, Massachusetts). She soon tired of the lack of artistic opportunities for women in North America and, like many of her male colleagues during this period, traveled to Rome to pursue her career and complete her training. She joined the classes of the English sculptor John Gibson, and her work soon rivaled her master's in restrained sentimentalism and exacting execution of detail. One American friend wrote that "it may gratify [Hosmer's] many American friends to hear that great interest is felt in her, and warm admiration expressed for her genius, not alone by Mr. Gibson, but by many of the first artists in Rome. She is a marvel to them for her industry, her modest confidence, her quiet enthusiasm."[2]

Hosmer completed several ambitious sculptures of female subjects before turning to *Zenobia* in 1857 when, on a trip home to Watertown, she began the extensive research necessary before beginning to model her heroic queen. She explored historical sources, asked the English art critic and writer Anna Jameson (who authored a book entitled *Memoirs of Celebrated Female Sovereigns* [London, 1831]) for advice, and probably read popular adaptations of Zenobia's story, such as Reverend William Ware's *Zenobia, Queen of Palmyra* (London, 1838).[3] Each of these sources presented a different facet of the queen: Ware portrayed Zenobia as beautiful and spirited, but also haughty and ambitious; while Edward Gibbon's *Decline and Fall of the Roman Empire* (1776–78) acknowledges her as "perhaps the only female whose superior genius broke through the servile indolence imposed on her sex by the climate and manners of Asia."[4] Hosmer's version of the queen portrayed a powerful woman in chains, but made her heroic in size, weighty in shape, and regal in manner.[5]

Hosmer worked on a larger-than-life, full-length version of *Zenobia* between 1857 and 1859. Nathaniel Hawthorne visited her studio in 1858 and wrote that "*Zenobia* stood in the centre of the room . . . a very noble and remarkable statue indeed, full of dignity and beauty . . . certainly I have seldom or never been more impressed by a piece of modern sculpture. . . . *Zenobia* is a high, heroic ode."[6] This version (later destroyed in a fire) marked the end of Hosmer's apprenticeship as a sculptor. By exhibiting it widely in Europe and the United States, she hoped to gain recognition as a major artist; her success was remarkable. *Zenobia* was exhibited prominently at the 1862 International Exhibition in London and toured the United States to great acclaim during 1864–65. Thousands of Americans viewed the sculpture during its tour, and numerous articles in newspapers and magazines celebrated the queen and the sculptor.[7]

The popularity of the full-sized version led to commissions for smaller replicas and heroic busts such as the Art Institute's. Hosmer wrote to her friend and patron Wayman Crow that she was selling full-length versions in reduced size for $1,200 and busts (with pedestal) for $1,000 through her Boston dealer, William Jenks.[8] The heroic bust displays delicate modeling of the toga and a sensitivity to the planes and surface of Zenobia's face. The artist carefully detailed the scrollwork on her crown, as well as the waves in her cascading hair. Although the chains of the full-length version are missing, the emotion of the piece is heightened by the emphasis on facial expression. Head tilted downward and lips slightly parted, the queen's reserved expression is one of melancholy and resignation rather than remorse.

NOTES

1. Henry James, *William Wetmore Story and His Friends* (London, 1903), vol. 1, p. 257. Departmental intern Merrill Falkenberg researched *Zenobia* and prepared a first draft of this entry.

2. Grace Greenwood, *Haps and Mishaps of a Tour in Europe* (Boston, 1853), p. 217.

3. More complete accounts of Hosmer's process in creating *Zenobia* can be found in Joy Kasson, *Marble Queens and Captives* (New Haven, Conn., and London, 1990), pp. 141–65; and Dolly Sherwood, *Harriet Hosmer, American Sculptor* (Columbia, Mo., 1991).

4. Quoted in Sherwood (note 3), p. 231. Gibbon's comment also provides insight into the racial stereotypes that pervaded discussions of Zenobia.

5. Kasson (note 3), p. 154.

6. Nathaniel Hawthorne, *The French and Italian Notebooks*, ed. Thomas Woodson (Columbus, Ohio, 1980), pp. 509–10.

7. For a complete account of *Zenobia*'s tour, see Sherwood (note 3), pp. 227–31.

8. A reduced-size version of the full-length sculpture is in the collection of the Wadsworth Atheneum, Hartford, Conn. Mrs. Potter Palmer owned a sixty-six-inch-high version of the full-length sculpture. See Chicago, Grant's Art Galleries, *Important Art Property*, sale cat. (June 3, 1942), p. 3; and letter from Harriet Hosmer to Wayman Crow, Nov. 30, 18[58?], Harriet Goodhue Hosmer Papers, roll 3, folder 98, Schlesinger Library and Research Center, Radcliffe College, Cambridge, Mass.

79. RANDOLPH ROGERS (1825–1892)

Nydia, the Blind Flower Girl of Pompeii, modeled 1855–56, carved 1858

Marble; h. 139.7 cm (55 in.)

Inscribed on base: *Rome 1858*

Bequest of Mrs. Uri Balcom, 1896.77

Randolph Rogers lived and worked in Rome from 1850 until his death in 1892. Raised in Ann Arbor, Michigan, the sculptor, like his fellow expatriate Hiram Powers, had little formal training before moving to Italy. Rogers arrived in Florence in 1848 and studied briefly with Lorenzo Bartolini. Bartolini's stylistic amalgam of neoclassical and naturalistic forms left its mark on Rogers, who was recognized for his ability both to evoke classical models and to impress an American public with dramatic, literary, and sentimentalized subjects.

One of the most popular sculptures of the second half of the nineteenth century, Rogers's *Nydia, the Blind Flower Girl of Pompeii* combines Victorian morality with archaeological interest in the buried cities of Pompeii and Herculaneum. *Nydia* is based on a character from Edward Bulwer-Lytton's historical novel *The Last Days of Pompeii*, a fictional account of the eruption of Vesuvius. First published in London in 1834, the book went through twenty-five editions and was translated into German and French by the turn of the century.[1] Aside from the novel's romantic and political intrigue, much of its enormous appeal can be attributed to the author's close attention to archaeological detail and his emphasis on the domestic aspects of life in the Roman Empire. Bulwer-Lytton visited Pompeii in 1833 during a trip to Naples, and his book combines first-hand knowledge of Pompeii with contemporary views on such issues as religion and the role of women in society.

One of his characters is a blind flower girl, Nydia. As Pompeii burns, Nydia's heightened sensitivity to sound helps her to save herself and her companions, Glaucus and Ione. As Mt. Vesuvius continues to erupt, Nydia becomes separated from Glaucus and Ione and bravely searches for them in the melee. It is this moment in the novel that Rogers depicted in his sculpture: "In vain she raised that plaintive cry so peculiar to the blind; it was lost amidst a thousand shrieks of more selfish terror. Again and again she returned to the spot where they had been divided—to find her companions gone, to seize every fugitive—to inquire of Glaucus—to be dashed aside in the impatience of distraction. . . . Poor girl!—her courage was beautiful to behold!—and Fate seemed to favour one so helpless."[2] Nydia at last locates Glaucus and Ione and accompanies them to the sea, where all three board a boat bound for Greece. When Nydia realizes that Glaucus loves Ione and not her, she throws herself overboard and drowns.

The pathos and drama of the scene are enhanced by Rogers's active composition and spare use of attributes. The fallen Corinthian column at Nydia's feet alludes to the danger that surrounds her, and the staff refers to her handicap. The way she strains forward—her gaze blank, her hand cupping her ear, and her drapery billowing about her—captures the desperateness and bravery of her search. Many classical sources have been proposed as models for Rogers's statue, including Hellenistic copies of the *Winged Psyche* in the Capitoline Museum and a fragment from the Niobe group in the Vatican.[3]

A visitor to Rogers's studio in 1869 commented, "I once went to his studio and saw seven *Nydias*, all in a row, all listening, all groping, and seven Italian marble-cutters at work cutting them out. It was a gruesome sight."[4] Rogers's biographer documented close to one hundred versions of *Nydia*, both full-sized and reduced in scale, in private and public collections. The sculptor amassed approximately $70,000 from the sale of replicas of *Nydia*.[5] The subject's popularity, like that of many literary heroines idealized in the nineteenth century—including Alfred Lord Tennyson's Elaine and William Shakespeare's Ophelia—was due to Nydia's pathos and tragic end. Most Victorian viewers interpreted the statue as an uplifting example of female courage and loyalty in the face of grave danger.

NOTES

1. See Alexandra R. Murphy, *Visions of Vesuvius*, exh. cat. (Boston, Museum of Fine Arts, 1978), p. 6.

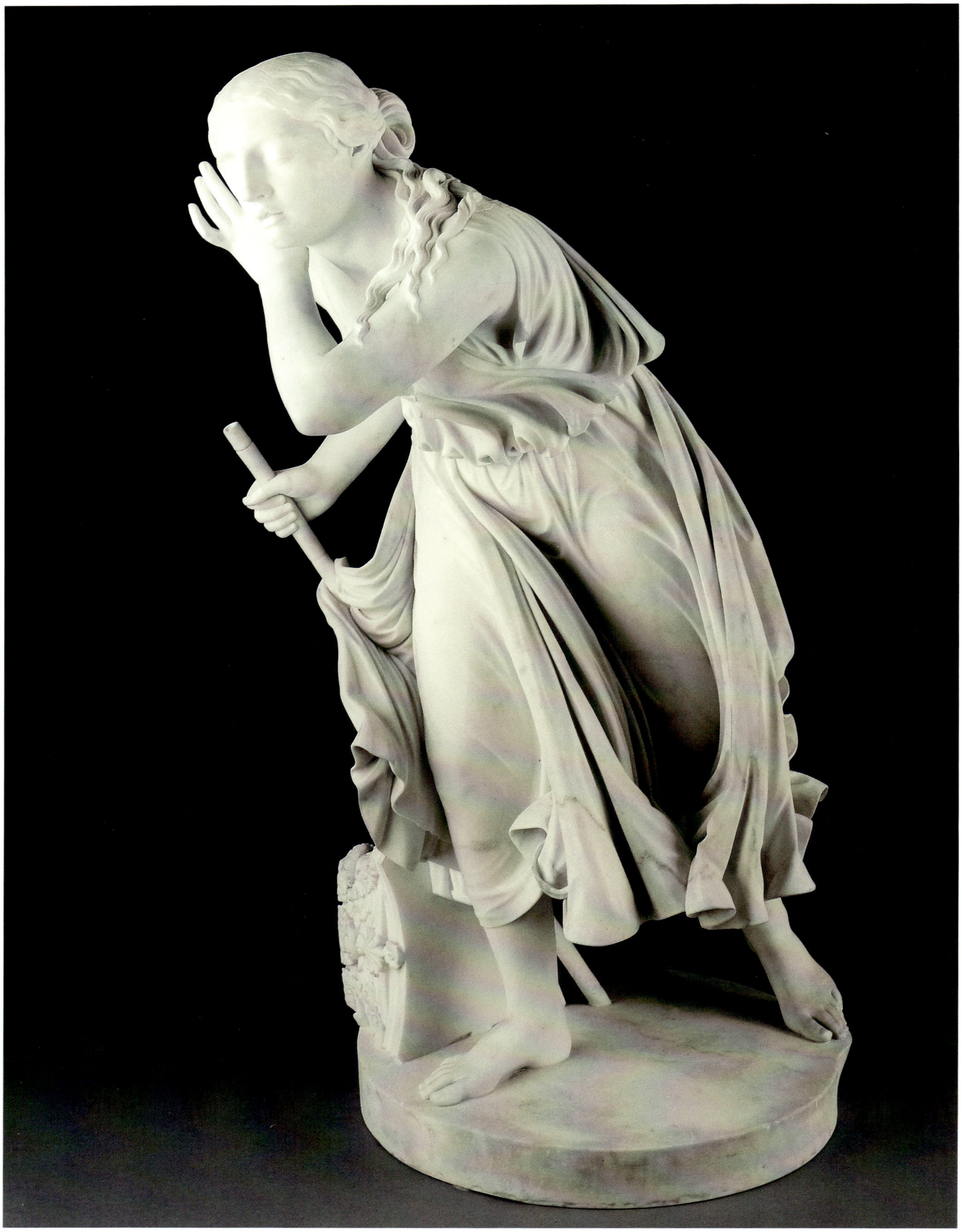

CAT. NO. 79

2. Edward Bulwer-Lytton, *The Last Days of Pompeii* (New York, 1946), p. 348.

3. Kathryn Greenthal, Paula M. Kozol, and Jan Seidler Ramirez, *American Figurative Sculpture in the Museum of Fine Arts, Boston* (Boston, 1986), p. 157.

4. Quoted in Joyce K. Schiller, "*Nydia*: A Forgotten Icon of the Nineteenth Century," *Bulletin of the Detroit Institute of Arts* 67, 4 (1993), pp. 42–43.

5. "Randolph Rogers, the Sculptor," *Harper's Weekly* 12 (Feb. 6, 1892), p. 465.

80. DESIGNED BY JOHN CANN AND DAVID DUNN (ACTIVE 1855–1860)

RETAILED BY JOHN COX AND COMPANY (ACTIVE 1817–1856)

Pitcher, 1855/56

Brooklyn, New York

Coin silver; h. 38.7 cm (15¼ in.)

Marked on bottom in Roman capitals: *J & I COX* / arm and hammer in oval / *COIN* (in losenge) / *C: &D* (in diamond) / *N. Y.* (in rectangle)

Bequest of Kate S. Buckingham, 1938.354

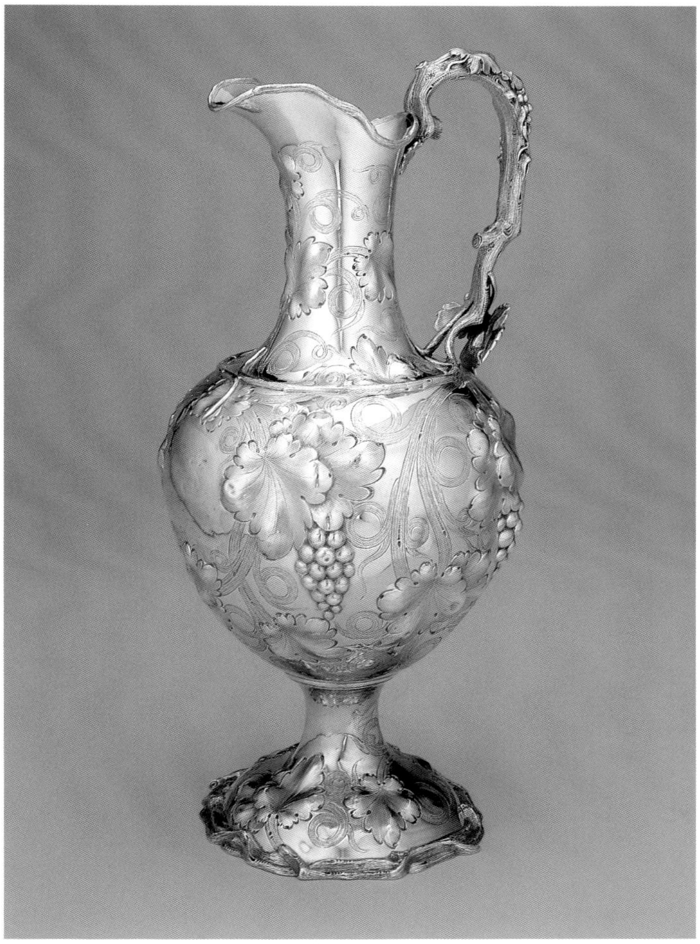

CAT. NO. 80

This pitcher, or ewer, was designed by the firm of Cann and Dunn, which manufactured hollow ware at their shop in Brooklyn. They were distinguished for the quality of their output and were well known for their presentation pieces.[1] Their advertisement in *Trow's New York City Directory* of 1855–56 proclaims the firm as "Manufacturers of silverware . . . vases, pitchers, tea services, cups, etc." John Cox and Company is listed in the same directory as being "Importers of gas fixtures, clocks, bronzes, plated wares &c., manufacturers of silverware" at their business address, 349 Broadway, New York.[2] Though Cox and Company was listed as a manufacturer of silverware, the presence of the Cann and Dunn mark on the pitcher indicates that Cox was merely a retailer for the piece.

The form of this pitcher is ancient, but the decoration of the piece is a revival of the French eighteenth-century ornamental style known as Rococo. In response to the severity of the earlier Empire style, the Rococo Revival advocated the florid, naturalistic style favored at the court of Louis XV.[3] The nineteenth-century American tastemaker Andrew Jackson Downing wrote: "The modern French [style] . . . stands much higher in general estimation in this country than any other. Its union of lightness, elegance, and grace renders it especially the favorite of the ladies. . . . [The style is] characterized by greater delicacy of foliate ornamentation, and greater intricacy of detail."[4] Favored by New York silversmiths, the repoussé pattern of clusters of grapes, twisting vines, and curling tendrils embodies characteristics of the Rococo Revival.

This pitcher may have been inspired by the solid gold tea service made for Edward K. Collins from gold discovered at the Mariposa mine in California (fig. 38); it was probably designed by John Chandler Moore and was retailed and displayed by Ball, Black, and Company at the Crystal Palace Exposition in London in 1851 and at the Crystal Palace Exposition in New York in 1853–54. Illustrated in several publications, the set was critically acclaimed for "the general excellence of the workmanship."[5]

NOTES

1. Charles L. Venable, *Silver in America, 1840–1940: A Century of Splendor*, exh. cat. (Dallas Museum of Art, 1994), p. 317.

2. *Trow's New York City Directory* (New York, 1856), p. 119.

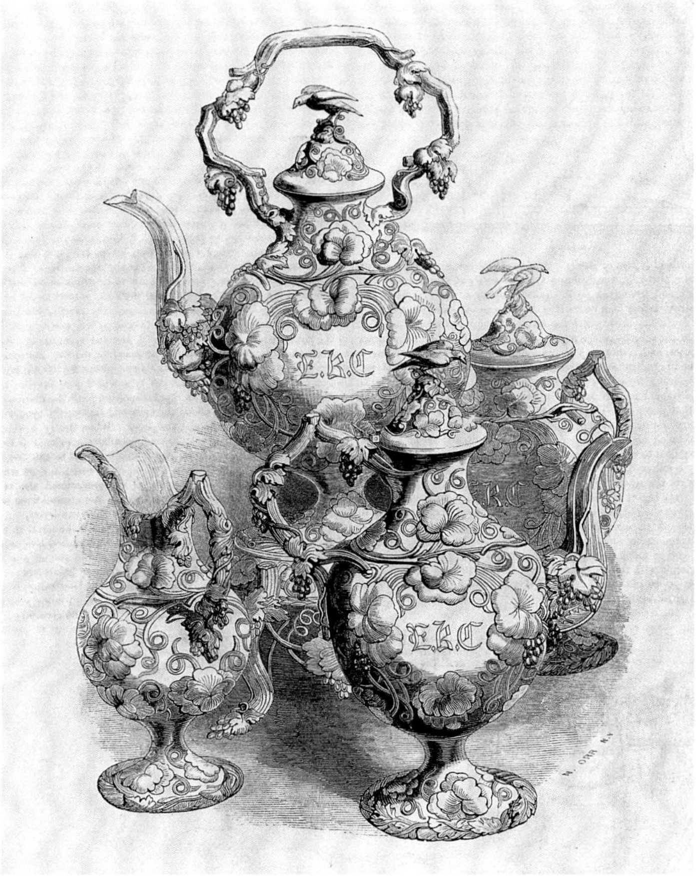

FIG. 38. Benjamin Silliman and C. R. Goodrich, *The World of Science, Art, and Industry Illustrated from Examples in the New-York Exhibition, 1853–54* (New York, 1854), p. 107. Collection of Ryerson and Burnham Libraries, The Art Institute of Chicago.

3. Metropolitan Museum of Art, *Nineteenth-Century America: Furniture and Other Decorative Arts*, exh. cat. (New York, 1970), p. xviii.

4. Andrew Jackson Downing, as quoted in Ed Polk Douglas, "Rococo Revival: John Henry Belter," *Nineteenth-Century Furniture: Innovation, Revival, and Reform* (New York, 1982), p. 26.

5. Venable (note 1), p. 40.

81. ARMCHAIR, 1840/60

New York

Oak; 152 x 63.5 x 56.5 cm (62 x 27½ x 24½ in.)

Restricted gift of Jeffrey Shedd, 1988.320

Gothic-inspired furniture first appeared in America in the mid-eighteenth century, after Englishman Thomas Chippendale published *The Gentleman and Cabinet-Maker's Director* in 1754. Chippendale's fanciful Gothic arches for chair backs had no basis in archaeological discoveries of the time, but instead evoked the spirit of the Middle Ages. The Gothic Revival style became popular again in the mid-nineteenth century; unlike the fanciful designs from Chippendale, however, this second awakening of interest in the late medieval era attempted more accurate borrowings of design and ornamentation from the Middle Ages.

English Gothic architecture became known to American craftsmen through pattern books and serial publications. The authors of these publications simplified the complex nature of the history and development of Gothic design in England so that it could be understood by a wide audience. One of the

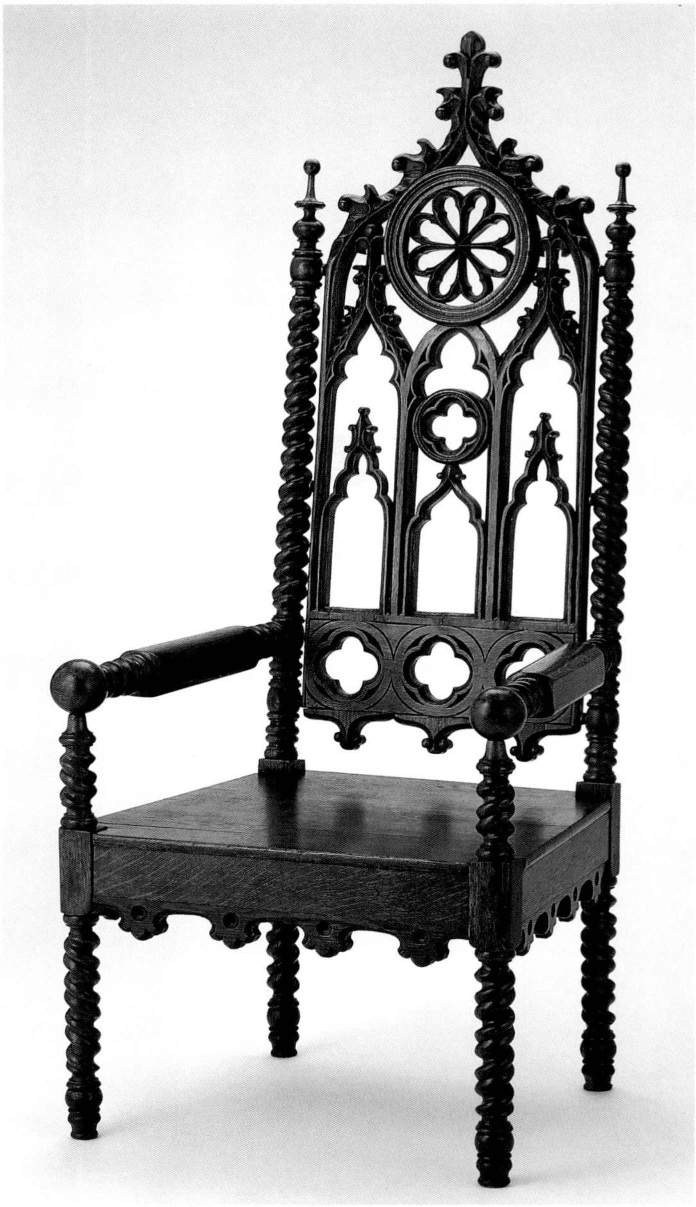

CAT. NO. 81

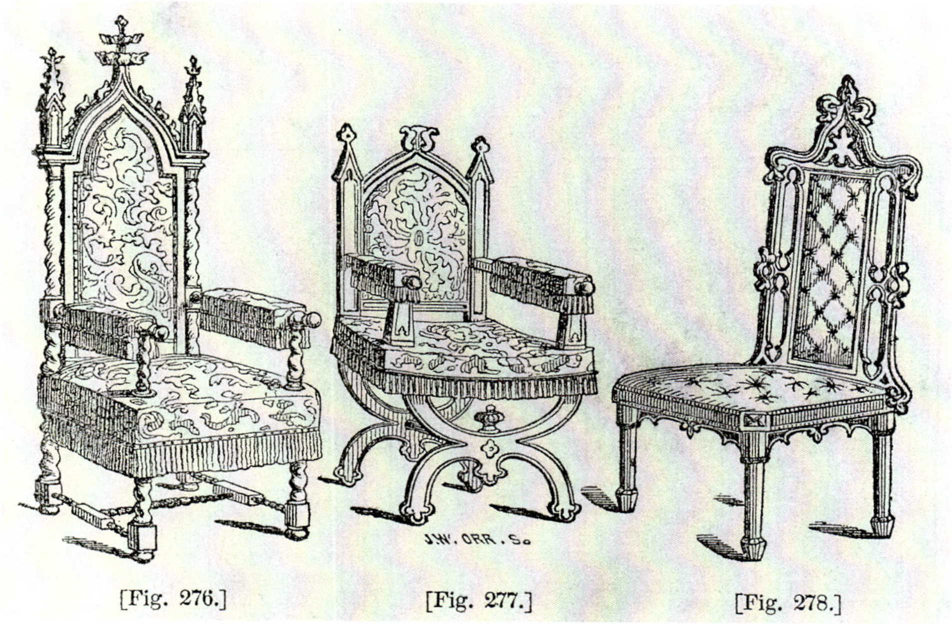

FIG. 39. Andrew Jackson Downing, *The Architecture of Country Houses* (New York, 1851), figs. 276–78. Collection of Ryerson and Burnham Libraries, The Art Institute of Chicago.

standard reference works on Gothic architecture in the nineteenth century was Thomas Rickman's *An Attempt to Discriminate the Styles of English Architecture from the Conquest to the Reformation.* First published in 1818, it went through seven printings by 1881. In 1833 John Claudius Loudon published *The Encyclopaedia of Cottage, Farm, and Villa Architecture and Furniture*, which was one of the most popular publications on design in the nineteenth century and was widely read in America.[1]

Two of the most important interpreters of the Gothic Revival style were the Englishmen Augustus Charles Pugin and his son Augustus Welby Northmore Pugin. A. C. Pugin first published his designs in Rudolph Ackermann's *Repository of Arts, Literature, Fashions, Manufacturers, &c.*, a widely read monthly serial devoted to design and fashion. In the 1830s A. W. N. Pugin published *Gothic Furniture*; a few years later, his *Gothic Furniture in the Style of the Fifteenth Century* appeared. Both authors published drawings for large-scale Gothic chairs based on architectural designs. A. W. N. Pugin suggested that furniture in the Gothic style befit a library: "In order to preserve unity of character, the wood is of light oak with gilt mouldings, relieved by rich crimson velvet cushions and tassels. This chair may be introduced with propriety into a church, prelate's mansion, or an extensive library."[2] Since libraries became associated with medieval knowledge,[3] the style became popular for American domestic libraries whose owners wished to appear learned.

American architects such as Andrew Jackson Downing and Alexander Jackson Davis, the most famous American proponents of the Gothic style, took the designs of Loudon, the Pugins, and others and reworked them for American purposes. Seventeen years after Loudon published his encyclopedia, Downing wrote *The Architecture of Country Houses.* His drawing for a library chair (fig. 39) incorporates several of the elements seen in English designs, and like the Art Institute's chair, recalls church architecture.

The arch of the chair back is shaped like a Gothic doorway or window, with a pinnacle featuring carved crockets up either side. Like a rose window, the central motif sits above a tripartite row of pinnacles which is repeated below. The center arch supports a quatrefoil, or four-lobed flower. The whole back is supported above a band of three quatrefoils with pendant cusps, or points.

NOTES

1. Megan Aldrich, *Gothic Revival* (London, 1994), pp. 107–10, 113.

2. A. W. N. Pugin, *Gothic Furniture; Consisting of Twenty-Seven Coloured Engravings* (London, [1830s]), p. 18.

3. Jane B. Davies, "Introduction," in Katherine Howe and David B. Warren, *The Gothic Revival Style in America, 1830–1870*, exh. cat. (Houston, Museum of Fine Arts, 1976), p. 8.

82. ÉTAGÈRE, 1850/70

New York
Rosewood, rosewood veneer, marble, and glass;
185 x 147.3 x 66 cm (73 x 58 x 26 in.)
Elizabeth R. Vaughan Fund, 1970.405

83. FIRESCREEN, 1850/60

New York
Rosewood with white pine and original cross-stitch embroidery panel; 170.1 x 108.6 cm (67 x 42¾ in.)
Mary Waller Langhorne Endowment, 1989.155

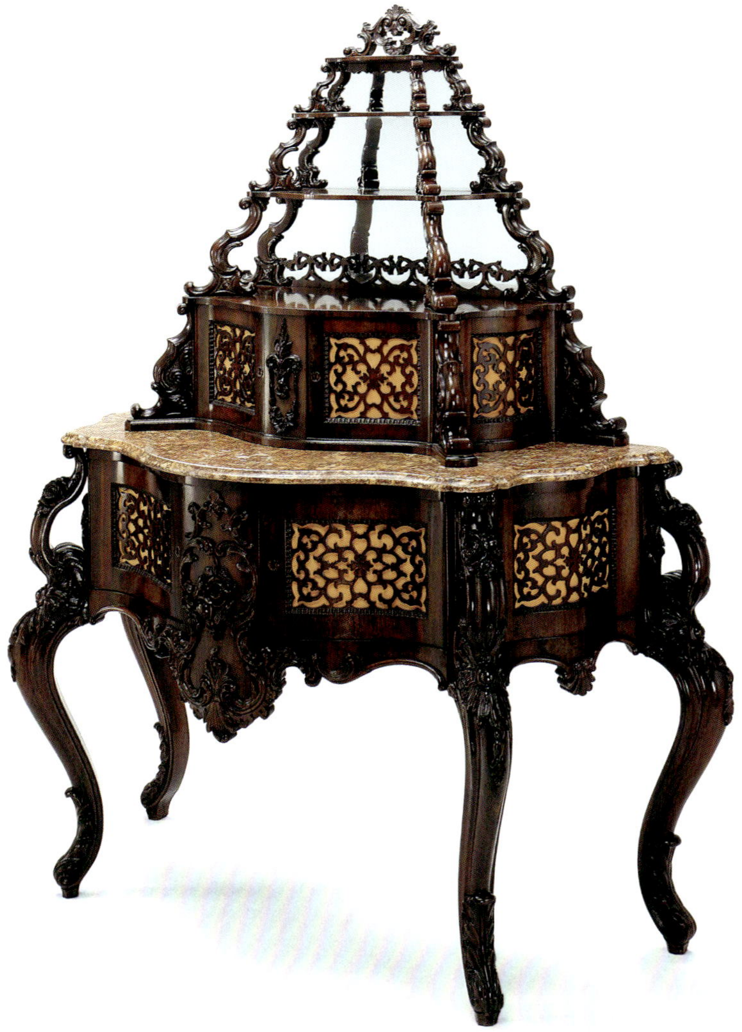

CAT. NO. 82

At the end of the eighteenth century, Americans developed a proclivity for formal parlors. Some families were wealthy enough to have two parlors; the "best parlor" was saved for special occasions and important guests, and the "second parlor" was used as the family sitting room. The best parlor contained most of the family's finest possessions. Andrew Jackson Downing described the ideal mid-nineteenth-century front parlor in his *Architecture of Country Houses*: "The *drawing-room* should always exhibit more beauty and elegance than any apartment in the house. . . . The furniture should be richer and more delicate in design, and the colours of the walls decidedly light, so that brilliancy of effect is not lost in the evening."[1] The most treasured furniture, as Downing described it, was usually made from rosewood or mahogany, was stiffly upholstered, and was rarely used by the family.[2] One "best parlor" from this period was described as "a store-room for household treasures. . . . Its furniture was the costliest and most modern, as well as the ugliest in the house. It was sort of a show-room."[3]

The Art Institute's étagère and firescreen were both likely made for use in best parlors. Étagères were well-suited for these rooms because, in a large space, they could be displayed to advantage. Downing described the étagère form as being "employed as a stand for little articles, curiosities, books, or whatever trifles of useful or ornamental character may accumulate, with no other special place devoted to them."[4] The focal point of this étagère is the balance between its carved decoration and its triangular shape and bold lines. The mirrors behind the shelves added a reflective background against which to display smaller objects.

Large firescreens served two functions: to hide the fireplace when it was not in use, and to shield portions of the room and guests from the heat of the fire. Casters enabled the large screen to be wheeled into different positions as required. The architectonic quality of these screens made them compatible with the architecture of their surroundings. Indeed, the design for the Art Institute's screen may have been adapted from an architectural plate in *The Cabinetmaker's Assistant*, published in 1853 in Glasgow and New York by Blackie and Son (fig. 40). This plate is a design for a mirror, which was to be placed above a mantel, that is similar in form to the screen, with carved vines winding up the side stiles and C-scrolls carved around the base.

Floral needlework was used in firescreens. The needlework in this firescreen was most likely made specifically for the piece. Its asymmetrical, foliate design was meant to mirror the carved details on the firescreen frame, such as the carved shells on the knees and the pierced vines on both sides of the frame.

Between 1847 and 1858, New York cabinetmaker John Henry Belter patented designs for Rococo Revival furniture that used

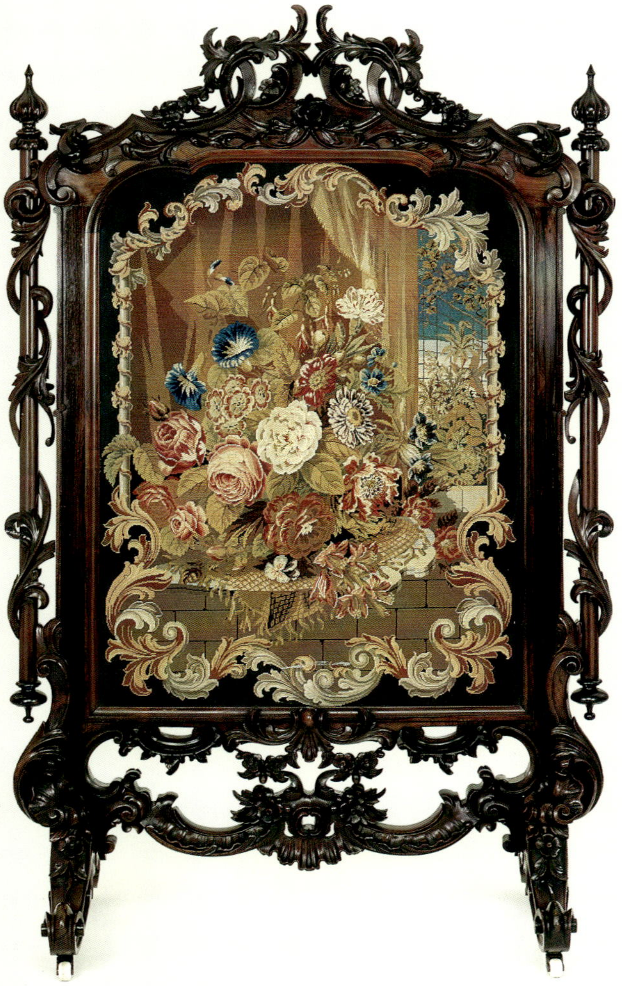

CAT. NO. 83

FIG. 40. Blackie and Son, *The Cabinetmaker's Assistant* (Glasgow and New York, 1853), pl. 51. Collection of Ryerson and Burnham Libraries, The Art Institute of Chicago.

lamination, a process in which thin layers of wood were glued together at right angles to create a strong, durable surface. The laminated boards could be steamed and pressed into a desired curvature and carved in minute detail.[5] Cabinetmakers who wanted to produce furniture in the "Belter style" frequently infringed upon Belter's patents. The craftsman who constructed the étagère took advantage of Belter's innovative lamination process, for although he carved the legs and the S-scrolls from solid wood, he used lamination to create the curvature of the apron and of the case sections. The étagère and the firescreen are both reminiscent of Belter's work and are attributed to New York craftsmen on the basis of their well-executed carving.

NOTES

1. Quoted in John C. Freeman, ed., *Furniture for the Victorian Home* (New York, 1968), p. 39.

2. Elizabeth D. Garrett, *At Home: The American Family, 1750–1870* (New York, 1990), p. 39.

3. As quoted in Jane C. Nylander, *Our Own Snug Fireside: Images of the New England Home, 1760–1860* (New York, 1993), p. 253.

4. Freeman (note 1), p. 53.

5. Marshall B. Davidson and Elizabeth Stillinger, *The American Wing at the Metropolitan Museum of Art* (New York, 1985), pp. 166–67; for information on Belter, see Ed Polk Douglas, "Rococo Revival: John Henry Belter," in *Nineteenth-Century Furniture: Innovation, Revival, and Reform* (New York, 1982), p. 26.

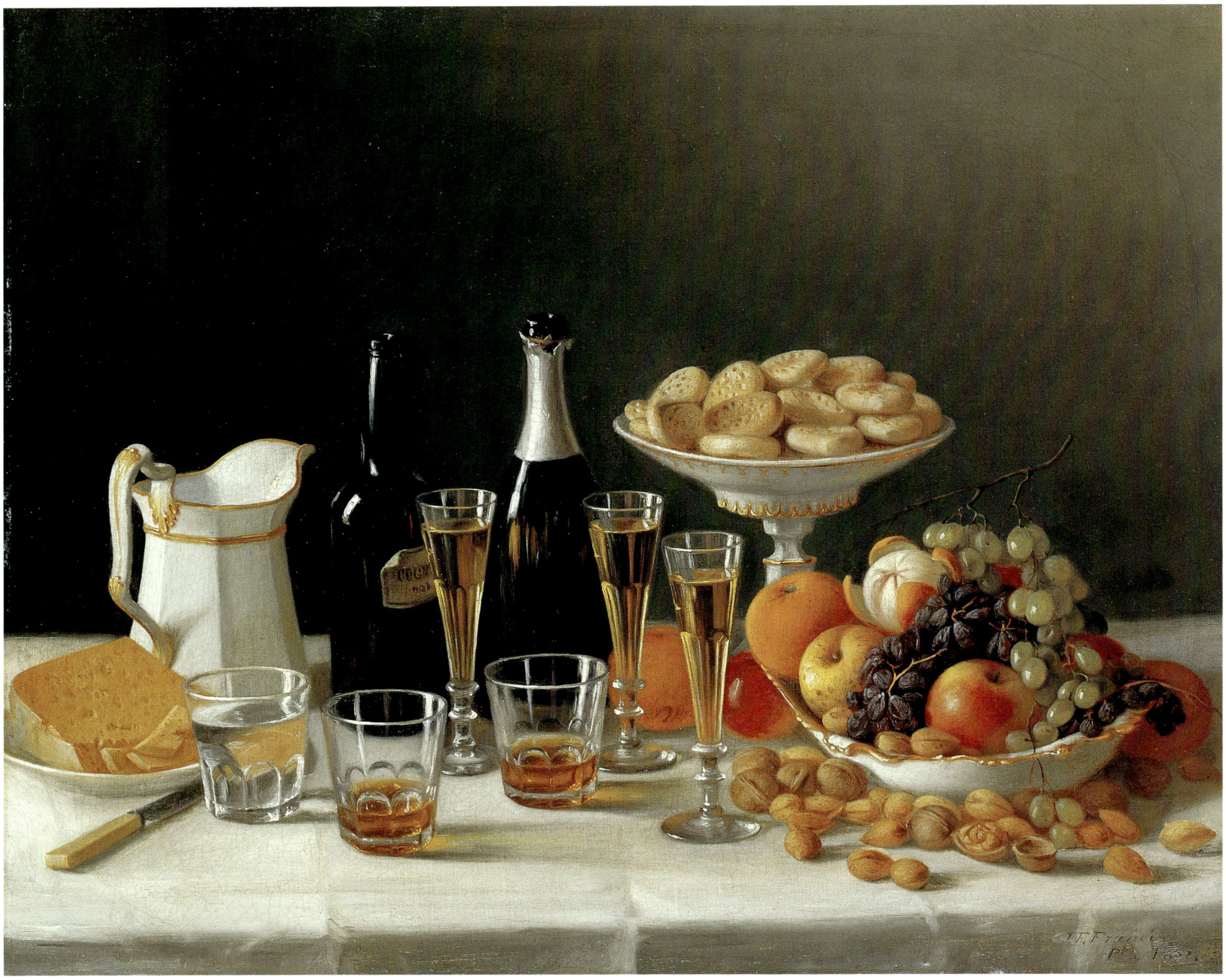

CAT. NO. 84

84. JOHN F. FRANCIS (1808–1886)

Wine, Cheese, and Fruit, 1857

Oil on canvas; 63.5 x 76.2 cm (25 x 30 in.)

Signed, lower right: *J. F. Francis / Pt. 1857*

Restricted gift of Charles C. Haffner III and Mrs. Herbert Alexander Vance; Wesley M. Dixon, Jr., Fund, 1994.239

A native of Philadelphia, the primarily self-taught painter John Francis worked as an itinerant portraitist until the late 1840s, when he settled in Jeffersonville, Pennsylvania, and turned his attention to still life.[1] Although he still traveled to ply his trade, Francis maintained his primary residence in Jeffersonville until the end of his life. *Wine, Cheese, and Fruit* is an elaborate and opulent type of still life, sometimes called a "luncheon" piece, produced when the artist was at the height of his skill and popularity. Painted in the standard size Francis chose for his still lifes, this picture is filled with objects—wine and liquor bottles, glassware, water pitcher, a ceramic compote and bowl, nuts, fruit, cheese, and "jawbreakers" (oyster crackers)—common to many of his works of this type.[2]

Francis's shift to still lifes was a smart entrepreneurial decision. The widening use of daguerreotypes encroached on the business of the itinerant portrait painter. On the other hand, still-life painting, with its decorative potential, was in demand. Increasing economic prosperity and a growing number of art exhibitions in cities such as New York and Philadelphia also helped create a market for still lifes.[3]

The most painterly and tactile of mid-century still-life painters, Francis preferred to emphasize the tone and texture of objects. Favoring pastel tones to heavier hues, Francis chose here to paint the cheese, fruit, liquor, and pottery in a harmony of yellows that creates a subtle and delicate glow. The artist also contrasted a wide variety of textures: succulent grapes and dried raisins; crumbling cheese and hard crackers; sleek stemware and peeling foil. Francis aligned the compositional elements on a table, in a narrow horizontal space that allows the viewer to enjoy each one, much as one can relish the components of a leisurely luncheon.

Like seventeenth-century Dutch still lifes, Francis's compositions speak both to material existence and moral issues. The table spread before the viewer in *Wine, Cheese, and Fruit* is dominated by bottles of wine and cognac and a number of glasses bearing spirits. Usually imported from France, wine and cognac were quite expensive.[4] Thus, here the liquor, commonly served at elaborate meals such as this, may symbolize tangible wealth. The painting, however, dates from a period when the temperance movement was particularly active and widespread.[5] In 1851 Maine passed laws barring the manufacture of liquor in that state; and in 1854 Pennsylvania only narrowly defeated a similar proposal. The growth of the temperance movement was accompanied throughout the 1850s by violence and coercion. Temperance societies, such as the all-male Washingtonians, tended to be composed largely of members of the artisan class. The middle class, on the other hand, generally interpreted temperance loosely, relying upon a collective morality and individual "self-control" to guide its drinking habits. By hanging a painting such as this one in his home, in which liquor is present in moderate amounts and water included as an alternative beverage, a middle-class man could assert both his economic class and "temperate" status.[6]

Francis was a religious man who stipulated in his will that his nephews Willie, Hubert, and Preston King use their five-hundred-dollar inheritance wisely and not "degrade their manhood by crime or the sin of intemperance."[7] *Wine, Cheese, and Fruit* is perhaps a recognition of his patrons' view of the temperance movement, as well as his own.

NOTES

1. For more biographical information about Francis, see David W. Dunn, *A Suitable Likeness: The Paintings of John F. Francis, 1832–1879*, exh. cat. (Lewisburg, Pa., Packwood House Museum, 1986); and Bruce Weber, "Who Was John F. Francis?" in Berry-Hill Galleries, Inc., *John F. Francis: Not Just Desserts*, exh. cat. (New York, 1990), pp. 2–5.

2. Other similar compositions by Francis include *Still Life with Wine Bottles and Basket of Fruit* (1857; Museum of Fine Arts, Boston), *Still Life with Glasses of Wine, Cognac, and Biscuits* (1851; Mellon Bank, Pittsburgh), and *Still Life—Grapes in a Bowl* (undated; Newark Museum, N.J.).

3. See Kenneth L. Ames, *Death in the Dining Room and Other Tales of Victorian Culture* (Philadelphia, 1992), for more about the role of still-life paintings in the decoration of Victorian homes.

4. Susan Williams, *Savory Suppers and Fashionable Feasts: Dining in Victorian America* (New York, 1985), p. 134.

5. For more about the temperance movement, see Jack S. Blocker, Jr., *American Temperance Movements: Cycles of Reform* (Boston, 1989).

6. Williams (note 4), p. 134, commented that "throughout the rest of the [nineteenth] century, hostesses were urged always to offer water as well as wine, and not to feel bound to serve wine if conscience advised against it."

7. Quoted in Alfred Frankenstein, *After the Hunt: William Harnett and Other American Still Life Painters, 1870–1900* (Berkeley and Los Angeles, 1953), p. 135.

85. ALEXANDER ROUX (c.1813–1886)

Sideboard, 1850/57

New York

Rosewood with walnut, tulip poplar, glass, and marble; 238 x 204.5 x 58.4 cm (93¾ x 80½ x 23 in.)

Marks or inscriptions: signed, on top board of lower case: *Emile*; inscribed, on underside of top board on lower case: *Mr. Tr—ing;* printed label on proper left interior drawer bottom reads: *A. ROUX / Cabinetmaker / 481 Broadway / New York*

Gift of the Antiquarian Society, 1995.245

American sideboards in the Renaissance Revival style were crafted to appeal to masculine sensibilities.[1] According to the Book of Genesis, man was supposed to claim dominance "over the fish of the sea, and over the fowl of the air, and over the cattle, and over all the earth."[2] Traditionally a man's role in his family was that of hunter and provider, and the iconographic carving on the Roux sideboard was designed to proclaim this to all who ate in its proximity. In the newly industrialized world of the early nineteenth century, the head of household no longer went out to hunt for food, but instead ventured into the wilds of the working world. His business acumen was measured in wealth. The domestic environment—that is, household management and child rearing—was turned over to

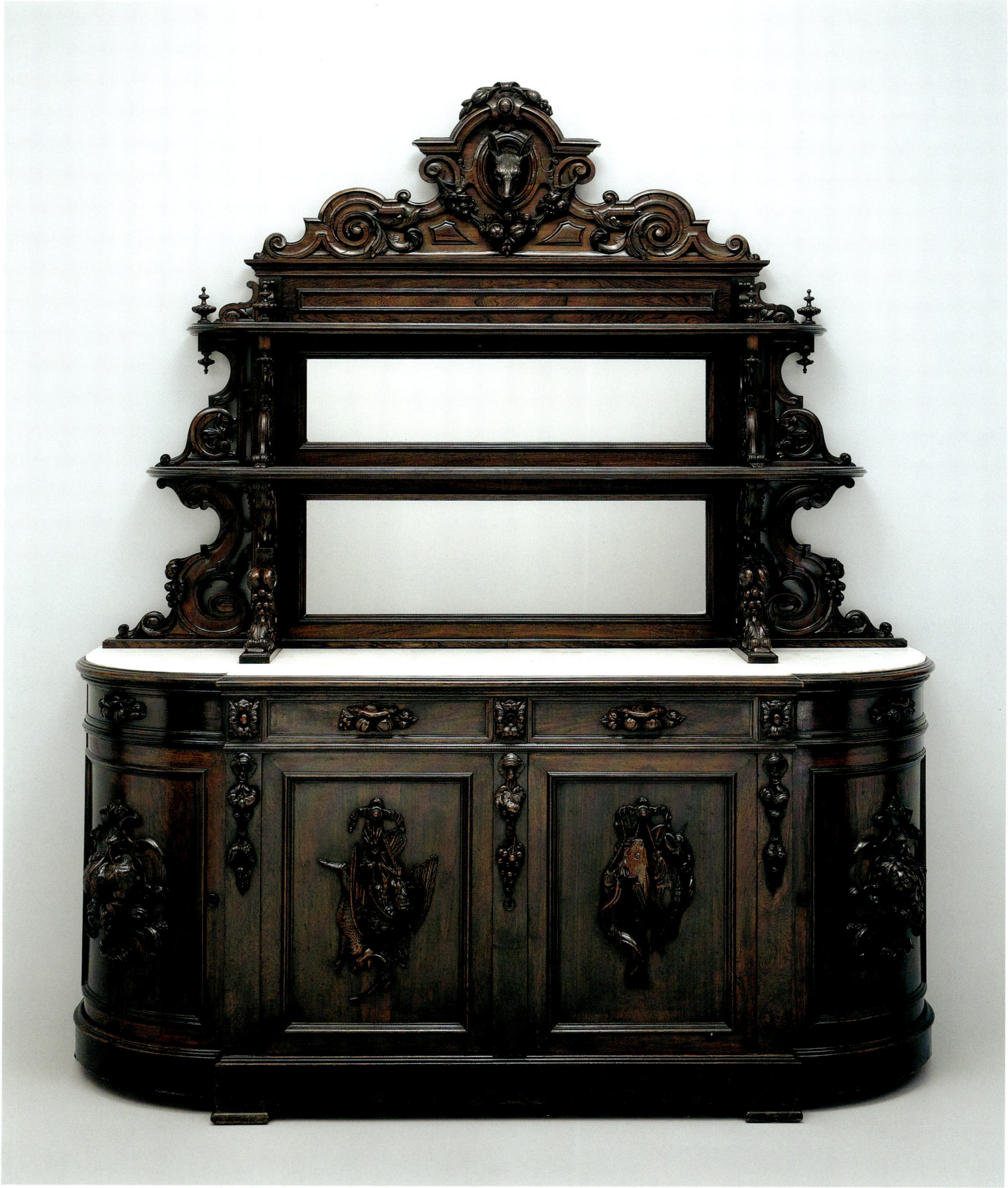

CAT. NO. 85

women, and the separation of private and public spheres was strictly maintained as the century progressed. Therefore the carving on the sideboard, its monumental size, and the rich rosewood and walnut surface were meant to announce the prominence and power of the owner.

This monumental sideboard has its roots in the 1844 Paris Exposition of Industry, where the designer Ringuet Leprince showcased a carved oak sideboard in the Renaissance style (fig. 41). The carved panels, scroll supports, and cornice of the Leprince sideboard are incorporated into the design of the Art Institute's sideboard. These highly carved sideboards became fixtures at every World's Fair from the 1851 Crystal Palace Exhibition in London through the Philadelphia Centennial Exhibition in 1876. Designers and furniture makers exhibited such lavishly decorated show pieces to demonstrate their abilities in the furniture-making industry. While most of the original exhibition pieces are now lost, many smaller sideboards, based on their designs, remain.[3]

The Art Institute's sideboard is closely related to one that Alexander Roux exhibited at the 1853 New York Crystal Palace Exhibition (fig. 42).[4] The carvings on the lower cases of the two Roux sideboards are very similar, depicting indigenous fish and wild game such as trout, lobster, eel, grouse, and rabbit. Both pieces also feature carved examples of fruits and nuts, perhaps symbolizing prosperity. As in the exhibition piece, the Art Institute's example has a two-tiered étagère with carved clusters of nuts surrounding the scroll supports but with the addition of mirrored back boards and a marble serving surface. Most likely the sideboard was the dominant piece of furniture in the dining room, which was hung with still lifes extolling the virtues of food and drink, much like the scene in a painting by John Francis of the same period in the Art Institute's collection (cat. no. 84).

Alexander Roux emigrated to the United States from Paris in 1837 and was listed in the New York directories that year as an upholsterer. He used his heritage to his advantage, touting himself in advertisements as a French cabinetmaker, a distinction that held much prestige among the wealthy patrons of New York's cabinetmaking industry. Roux was able to compete with all the large New York firms of the nineteenth century because of the quality and breadth of his products. By 1855 he was employing over one hundred workers, and by 1877 his firm was making over half a million dollars annually. Over the sixty-year period that Roux and his company were in business, the workrooms were forced to move to larger spaces several times. Each move can be documented by several different printed labels present on known Roux pieces. The printed label on this sideboard allows us to date it to the period between 1850 and 1857, before the firm changed its name from Alexander Roux to Roux and Company.[5]

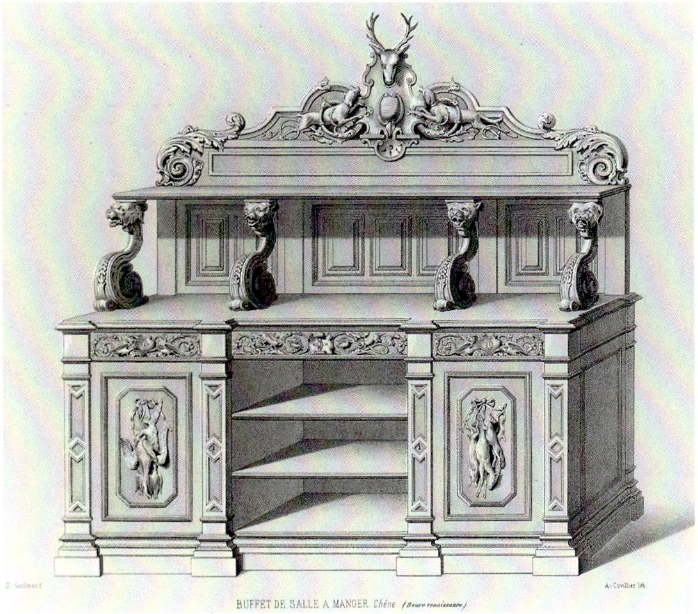

FIG. 41. Illustration of a sideboard by Ringuet Leprince, from *Le Garde-meuble album de l'exposition de l'industrie* (Paris, 1844), pl. 11. Photograph courtesy of Local History Department, Grand Rapids Public Library, Grand Rapids, Mich.

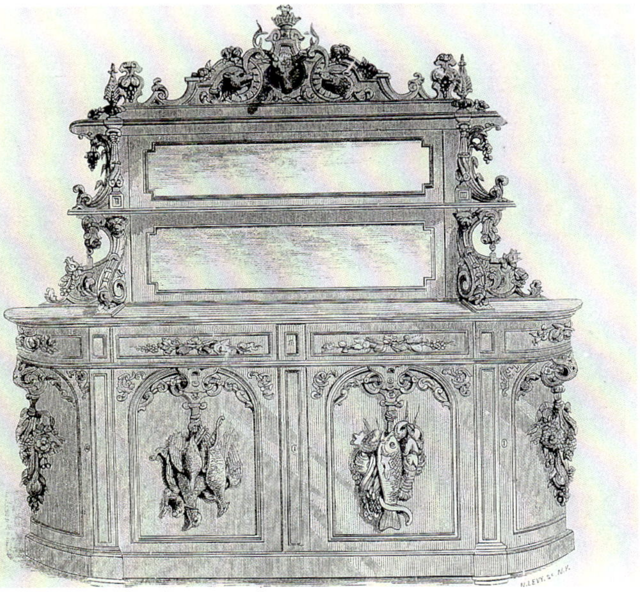

FIG. 42. Illustration of a sideboard by Alexander Roux, from Benjamin Silliman, Jr., and C. R. Goodrich, *The World of Science, Art, and Industry Illustrated from Examples in the New-York Exhibition, 1853–54* (New York, 1854), p. 162. Collection of Ryerson and Burnham Libraries, The Art Institute of Chicago.

NOTES

1. Kenneth L. Ames, *Death in the Dining Room and Other Tales of Victorian Comfort* (Philadelphia, 1992), p. 67. Highly carved, hunt sideboards similar in scale to the Roux sideboard are in the collections of the Museum of Fine Arts, Houston; Museum of Fine Arts, Boston; Yale University Art Gallery, New Haven, Conn.; Currier Gallery of Art, Manchester, N.H.; Cleveland Museum of Art; High Museum of Art, Atlanta; and Metropolitan Museum of Art, New York.

2. Genesis 1:26, as quoted in Ames (note 1), p. 71.

3. For an excellent discussion of the sideboards featured at expositions, see Ames (note 1), chap. 2.

4. An oak example recently acquired by the Metropolitan Museum of Art follows the line drawing so closely that it may be the one that Roux exhibited.

5. Dianne D. Hauserman, "Alexander Roux and his 'Plain and Artistic Furniture,'" *Antiques* 93, 2 (Feb. 1968), pp. 210, 213.

86. FREDERIC EDWIN CHURCH (1826–1900)

View of Cotopaxi, 1857

Oil on canvas; 62.2 x 92.7 cm (24½ x 36½ in.)

Signed, lower right: *F. E. Church '57*

Gift of Jennette Hamlin in memory of Mr. and Mrs. Louis Dana Webster, 1919.753

The German naturalist Alexander von Humboldt described the Ecuadorian volcano Cotopaxi as "the most beautiful and regular of the colossal summits in the high Andes . . . [but it] is also the most dreadful volcano in the kingdom of Quito, and its explosions the most frequent and disastrous."[1] In the mid-nineteenth century, the volcano exerted both an aesthetic and a metaphoric power over the landscape painter Frederic Edwin Church, who produced at least ten finished paintings of it.[2] Executed just before Church's second journey to Latin America, *View of Cotopaxi* is a symbolically layered landscape incorporating the scientific, religious, and political themes that preoccupied the artist throughout his career.

Church was familiar with Humboldt's influential 1848 scientific discourse *Cosmos*, which espoused a religious view of creation. Published a decade before Charles Darwin's evolutionary theories, Humboldt's book interprets the wonders of the natural world as evidence of God's role as Creator. Humboldt likened both the untamed wilderness of the United States and the dense rain forests of Latin America to the Garden of Eden; for him, they were sanctified landscapes intimately linked with ideas about creation and paradise.

Prompted by *Cosmos*, which encouraged artists to travel widely, Church embarked upon his first voyage to Latin America in April 1853 to record its botanical and geological marvels. He was accompanied by his patron Cyrus Field, a wealthy paper manufacturer who wished to investigate the region's economic potential. For six months, they followed the course of travel outlined by Humboldt; on September 10, they arrived at Señor Larrea's hacienda, on the west side of Cotopaxi, where Humboldt had stayed during his exploration of the area earlier in the century. On September 12, Church recorded his reaction when Cotopaxi's cone appeared from behind a shroud of clouds: "Waited patiently all day for the clouds to disappear from the summit of Cotopaxi and about sunset had the satisfaction of a partial view which was magnificent. Took a slight sketch."[3] Church departed the next day for Chimborazo with detailed sketches of the volcano, missing an eruption of Cotopaxi by a matter of days.

Realized almost four years after Church viewed the volcano, *View of Cotopaxi* is a synthetic landscape painted from sketches and memory, a process also used by the artist's teacher Thomas Cole in *Distant View of Niagara Falls* (cat. no. 64). Cole had written that "the most lovely and perfect parts of Nature may be brought together, and combined in a whole that shall surpass in beauty and effect any picture painted from a single view."[4] In following this compositional strategy, Church imbued his landscape scenes not only with natural beauty but also with metaphoric and historical resonance. The composition of *View of Cotopaxi* gradually leads the viewer from the foreground, teeming with tropical foliage, to snow-capped Cotopaxi rising above Ruminahui, the mountain skirting the west side of the volcano. The harmony of landscape elements conveys the majesty of the scene through conventional methods of composition that recall the pastoral works of the classical French landscapist Claude Lorrain. Church constructs the illusion of deep space through a rational progression of foreground, middleground, and background, all framed by a palm tree.

The creative and destructive force of volcanoes caused Humboldt to regard them as both links to terrestrial history and evidence of divine power.[5] Church applied Humboldt's geological theories to his artistic investigation of Cotopaxi, but exaggerated the volcano's slope in order to present it as a perfect cone. He also altered the terrain surrounding the volcano. Although the plants in the foreground of *View of Cotopaxi* are

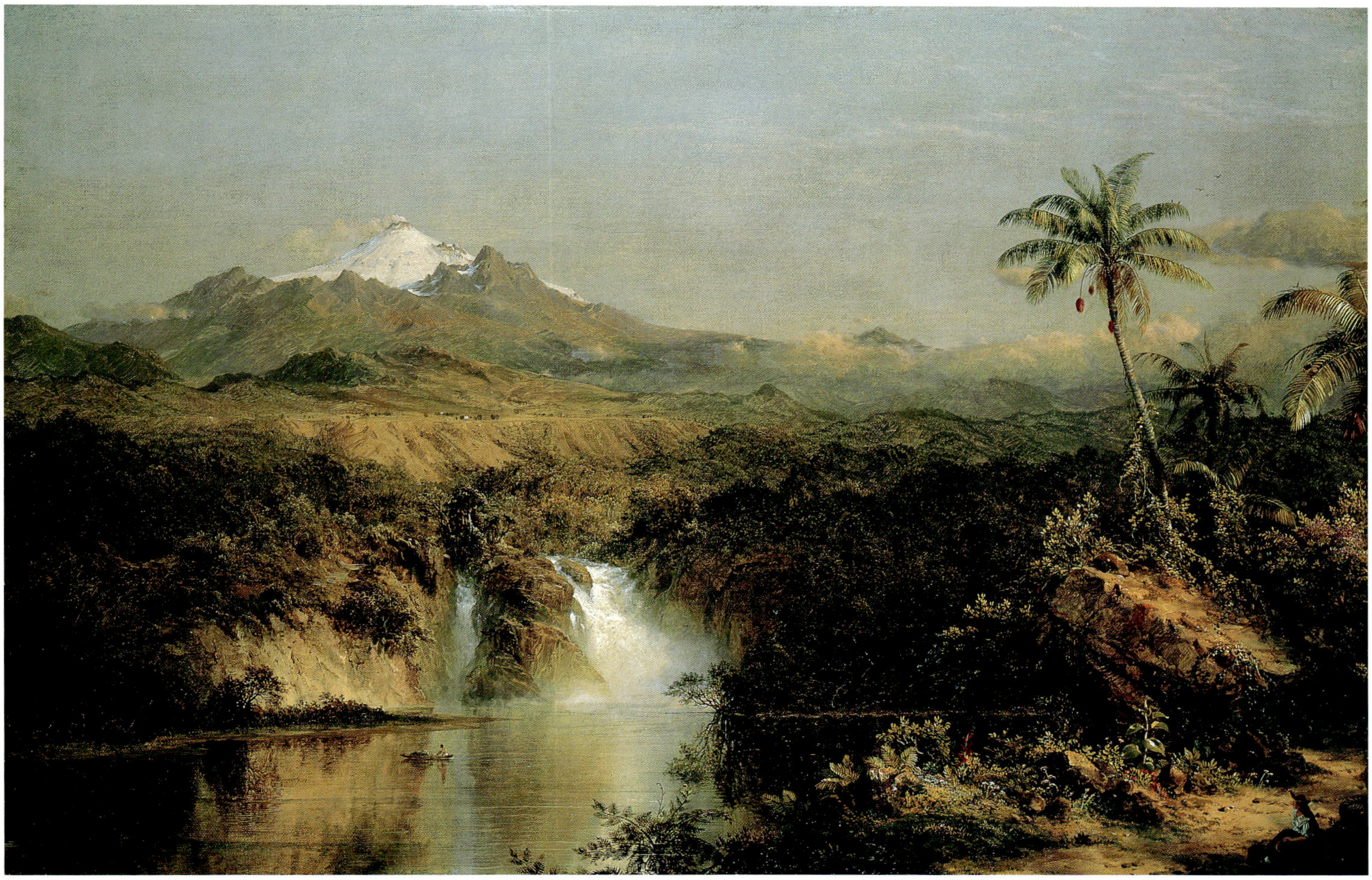

CAT. NO. 86

botanically accurate, they are geographically misplaced. Cotopaxi is located on a barren, treeless plain devoid of the lush vegetation Church painted. The palm tree on the right-hand side of the canvas has been identified as *Scheelea butyracea*, a species indigenous to the valleys of the Cuaca and Magdalena rivers in Colombia.[6] Church, who was knowledgeable about botany, may have included the palm tree as an emblem of Latin America, as well as a symbol of the Garden of Eden.[7] The artistic license he took with the volcano's shape and the anomalous palm tree increases the drama of *View of Cotopaxi* and emphasizes the religious nature of the scene.

While he was completing *View of Cotopaxi*, Church wrote to William Henry Osborn, "I am just completing a picture for Mr. Walter Wright which is better than anything that I ever did of the same size. You will see it shortly in Chicago."[8] Wright lent his picture in 1859 to the first art exhibition held in Chicago and established it as a benchmark for art collecting in the city.[9]

NOTES

1. Quoted in Katherine Manthorne, *Creation and Renewal: Views of Cotopaxi by Frederic Edwin Church*, exh. cat. (Washington, D.C., National Museum of American Art, 1985), p. 7.

2. This group of paintings includes *Cotopaxi* (1855; National Museum of American Art, Washington, D.C.); *Cotopaxi* (1855; Museum of Fine Arts, Houston); and *Cotopaxi* (1862; Detroit Institute of Arts).

3. Church is quoted in Katherine Emma Manthorne, *Tropical Renaissance: North American Artists Exploring Latin America, 1839–1879* (Washington, D.C., and London, 1989), p. 13.

4. Letter from Thomas Cole to Robert Gilmor, Dec. 25, 1826, Thomas Cole Papers, Archives of American Art, Washington, D.C.

5. Manthorne (note 1), pp. 31–33.

6. Letter from Timothy Plowman to Betty Blum, May 7, 1979, Files of the Department of American Arts, The Art Institute of Chicago.

7. On the symbolism of the palm tree, see Katherine Manthorne, "The Quest for a Tropical Paradise: Palm Tree as Fact and Symbol in Latin American Landscape Imagery, 1850–1875," *Art Journal* 44, 4 (winter 1984), pp. 374–82.

8. Letter from Frederic Edwin Church to William Henry Osborn, Feb. 23, 1857, Princeton University Libraries. He made a similar comment in a letter

to a friend named Austin, dated Mar. 5, 1857, which is now in the collection of the Olana State Historic Site, Hudson, N.Y.

9. See "The Art Exhibition," *Press and Tribune* (June 1, 1859), p. 2; and "Chicago's First Fine Arts Exhibition," *Chicago History* 2, 2 (spring 1951), pp. 321–27.

87. ALBERT BIERSTADT (1830–1902)

Mountain Brook, 1863

Oil on canvas; 111.8 x 91.4 cm (44 x 36 in.)

Signed, lower left: *A. Bierstadt*

Restricted gift of Mrs. Herbert A. Vance; fund of an anonymous donor; Wesley M. Dixon, Jr., Fund and Endowment; Henry Horner Straus and Frederick G. Wacker endowments; through prior acquisitions of various donors, including Samuel P. Avery Endowment, Mrs. George A. Carpenter, Frederick S. Colburn, Mr. and Mrs. Stanley Feinberg, Field Museum of Natural History, Mr. and Mrs. Frank Harding, International Minerals and Chemicals Corp., Mr. and Mrs. Ralph Loeff, Mrs. Frank C. Miller, Mahlan D. Moulds, Mrs. Clive Runnells, Mr. and Mrs. Stanley Stone, and the Charles H. and Mary F. S. Worcester Collection, 1997.365

In 1860, after having returned to New York City from his first trip to the Rocky Mountains, Albert Bierstadt set upon the difficult task of promoting a new genre of landscape that focused on the American West. By 1861 Bierstadt's Western scenes had gained acceptance among his peers, earning him the status of a full academician at New York's prestigious National Academy of Design. Although he had reached the pinnacle of his profession, Bierstadt did not rest on his laurels. In a masterful move, meant to give further dimension to his reputation, he painted views of more traditional New England subjects, particularly of the White Mountains. *Mountain Brook*, completed in 1863, ranks among the artist's most successful White Mountain compositions.[1]

Mountain Brook, an interior woodland scene, inverts the compositional formula evident in similar forest scenes painted by Asher B. Durand, a leader among landscape artists at the time. Bierstadt reversed Durand's paradigmatic pathway, which leads the eye out toward an expansive scene, by drawing the viewer down a mountain stream and into the heart of a forest interior. Pine, maple, and birch trees form a natural canopy pierced by a hazy, golden light, throwing the boulder and waterfall at the painting's center into sharp contrast. Bierstadt's palette is dominated by dark russet and muted shades of green and brown. In the midst of this subdued color scheme, a glimpse of blue sky, the white ribbon of the stream, and the sun's reflection off the boulder dramatically draw attention from the depths of the forest to the jewel-like foreground. As was typical of Bierstadt at the time, he worked out many of the painting's complicated compositional devices in an exquisite oil sketch (fig. 43).

The transition from a grandiose background to a more intimate foreground is punctuated in the Chicago canvas by a small blue-and-white tufted kingfisher perched on the edge of a fallen tree trunk, a detail absent in the artist's sketch. The bird not only provides a means to gauge scale, but also, along with the sensitively painted ferns in the lower right, inserts a note of delicacy in this wilderness scene. Throughout the 1860s, Bierstadt produced both interior forest scenes, such as *Franconia Notch* (1863; private collection, Woodstock, Vermont), and larger, more panoramic vistas, such as *The Emerald Pool* (1870; Currier Gallery of Art, Manchester, New Hampshire).[2]

Even while *Mountain Brook* remained on Bierstadt's easel in his New York studio, critical praise rang in the New York press. Barry Gray, writing for the *New York Leader* in January 1863, judged the painting to be the best Bierstadt had ever produced and predicted critical acceptance for the work when it finally went on public view. For Gray, Bierstadt was particularly successful in his deft contrast of "light and shade, warmth and coolness, strength and tenderness," which together resulted in the picture's heightened realism.[3] Small watercolor studies of ferns and other plant life that Bierstadt made during his 1860 White Mountain excursion document a careful process of study equaled at that time only by the American Pre-Raphaelites.[4] Gray's emphasis on the painting's combination of meticulous detail and strong contrast set the critical standard for the painting. Art critics reiterated his praise throughout the 1863 exhibition season.

Bierstadt publicly exhibited *Mountain Brook* in late January 1863 at the Century Club, New York. A critic for the *Boston Evening Transcript* confirmed Gray's prediction and declared the painting to be Bierstadt's "best work." After a passing compliment to Bierstadt on his conscientious study of nature, the critic turned to the painting's ability to conjure romantic literary associations: "This picture delineates just such a wild, retired spot as the 'melancholy Jacques' might have been disposed to haunt, and the trees, the brook and the stones the prototype of those in which the banished Duke in the forest of

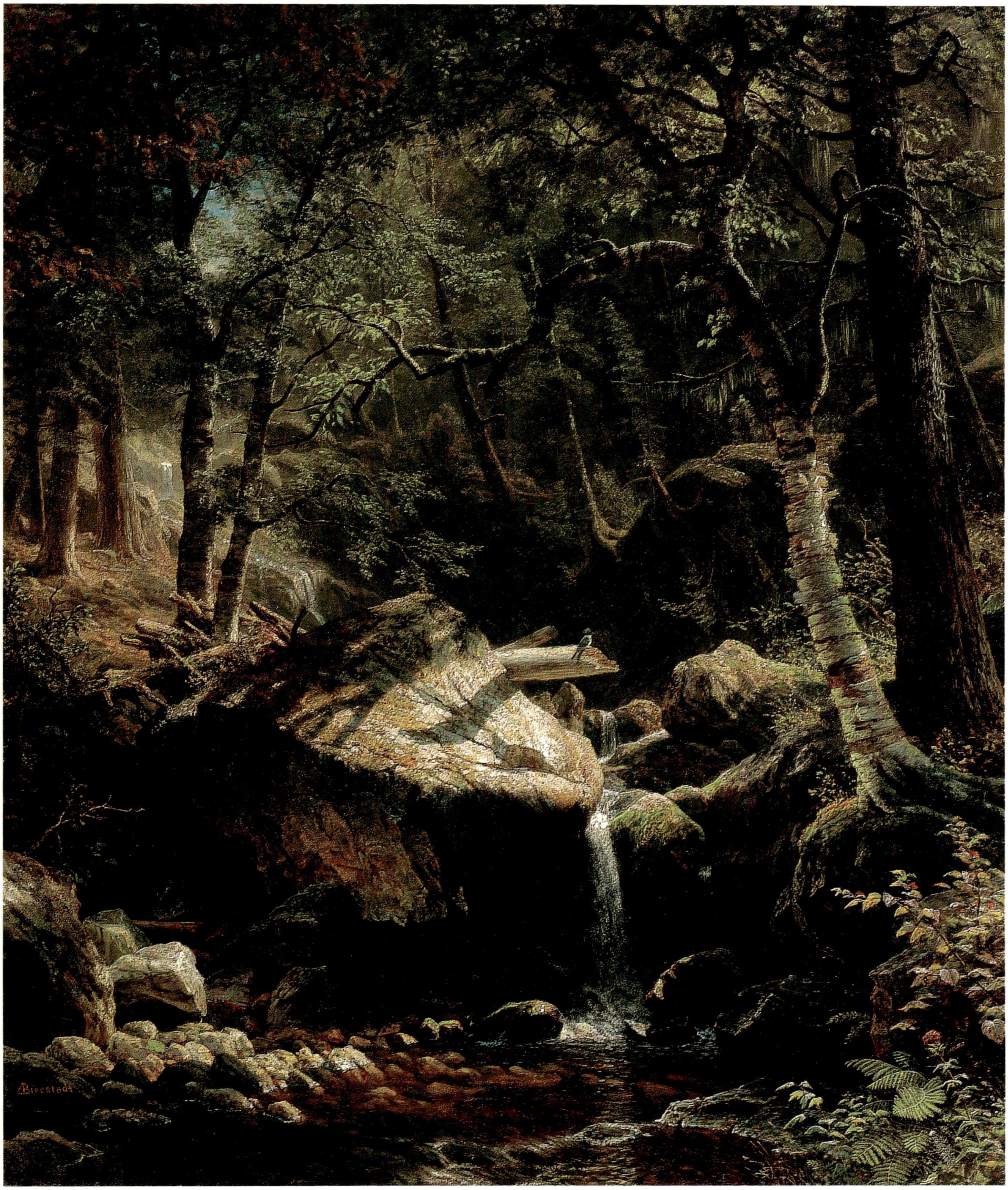

CAT. NO. 87

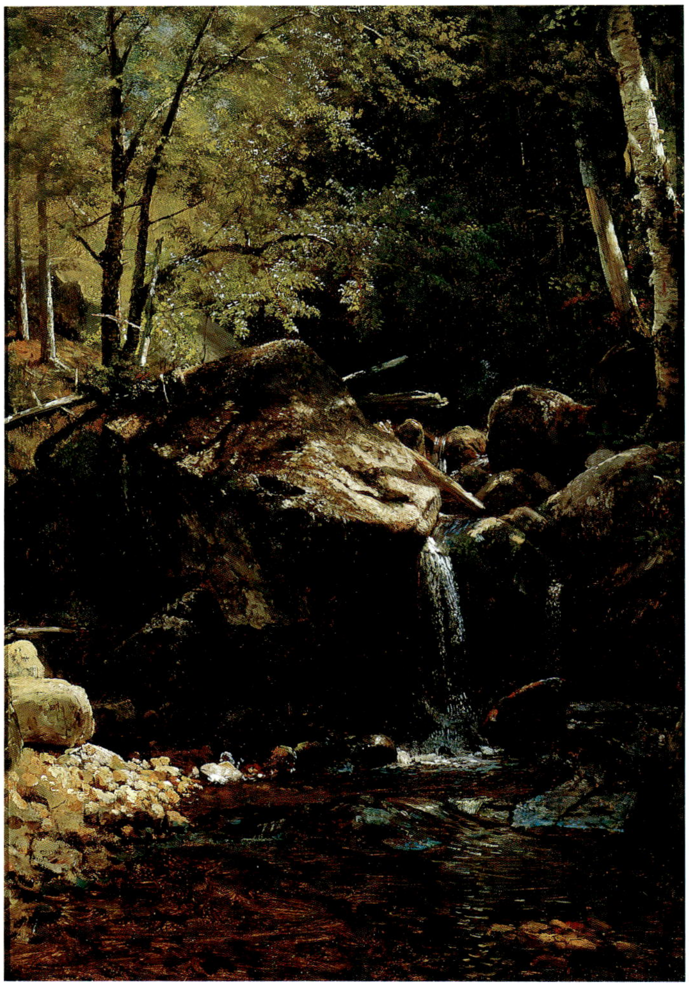

FIG. 43. Albert Bierstadt (1830–1902). *Mountain Brook,* 1862. Oil on paper on rag board; 48.3 x 35.6 cm (19 x 14 in.). Private collection, Seattle.

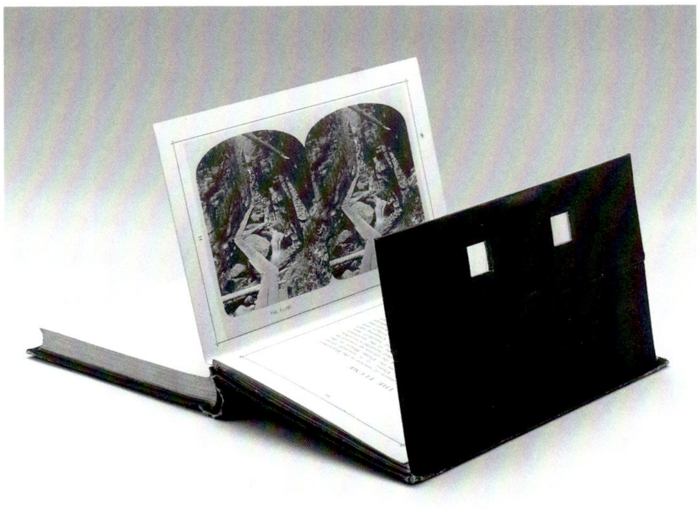

FIG. 44. Harroun and Bierstadt (active 1870s–1880s). *Gems of American Scenery, Consisting of Stereoscopic Views of the White Mountains,* 1878. The Art Institute of Chicago, Gift of Robert Jesmer (1980.224).

Arden found tongues, books, and sermons."[5] Apparently little effort was needed for this critic to envision characters from Shakespeare's *As You Like It* inhabiting Bierstadt's vision of the White Mountains.

Bierstadt's attraction to the White Mountains mirrored the region's growing status as one of America's premiere tourist attractions. By 1851 the White Mountains had begun to rival other American tourist sites, such as Niagara Falls and the Catskill Mountains. This once remote wilderness was accessible to New Yorkers and New Englanders, as well as European tourists.[6] Although Bierstadt made his first trip to the White Mountains in 1858, he probably developed the composition for *Mountain Brook* during an 1860 New Hampshire excursion he took with his younger brothers, Charles and Edward. From their base at the Crawford House, a fashionable hotel, the brothers conducted photographic experiments. In 1862 the three brothers published the volume *Stereoscopic Views Among the Hills of New Hampshire.* Both this 1862 and the later 1876 edition had a stereoscopic viewer built directly into the book's binding to ease leisured study (see fig. 44). The group of views served principally as a guide for tourists to the Franconia Notch region. In an announcement published in the *Crayon* for the first edition of the book, the elder Bierstadt's role in the venture is made clear: "The artistic taste of Mr. Albert Bierstadt, who selected the points of view, is apparent in them. No better photographs have been published in this country."[7] Comparison between the stereoscopic photographs and Bierstadt's *Mountain Brook* suggests that the painting is an imaginary composite that combines various features from a popular tourist site, The Flume, in the Franconia mountain region.

NOTES

1. Dr. Nancy K. Anderson, Associate Curator, Department of American Painting and Sculpture, National Gallery of Art, Washington, D.C., generously provided material from her extensive Bierstadt research files in assisting with this entry.

2. William C. Lipke and Philip N. Grime, "Albert Bierstadt in New Hampshire," *Bulletin of the Currier Gallery of Art* 2 (1973), pp. 20–37.

3. Barry Gray, "Bierstadt's *Mountain Brook,*" *New York Leader,* Jan. 17, 1863.

4. Bierstadt's work from this period is often compared to that of the American Pre-Raphaelites; see, for example, Linda Ferber and William Gerdts, *The New Path: Ruskin and the American Pre-Raphaelites,* exh. cat. (New York, Brooklyn Museum, 1985), pp. 232–35.

5. "The Century Exhibition," *Boston Evening Transcript,* Jan. 16, 1863.

6. For more on White Mountain tourism, see Donald Keyes, *The White*

Mountains: Place and Perception, exh. cat. (Durham, N.H., University Art Galleries, University of New Hampshire, 1980); and Dona Brown, *Inventing New England: Regional Tourism in the Nineteenth Century* (Washington, D.C., 1995), pp. 41–74.

7. "Domestic Gossip," *Crayon* 8 (Jan. 1861), p. 22.

88. JOHN QUINCY ADAMS WARD (1830–1910)

The Freedman, modeled in plaster 1863

Bronze; 49.9 x 40 x 23.9 cm (19⅝ x 15¾ x 9⅜ in.)

Signed, on base: *J. Q. A. Ward. Scp. 1863*

Roger McCormick Endowment, 1998.1

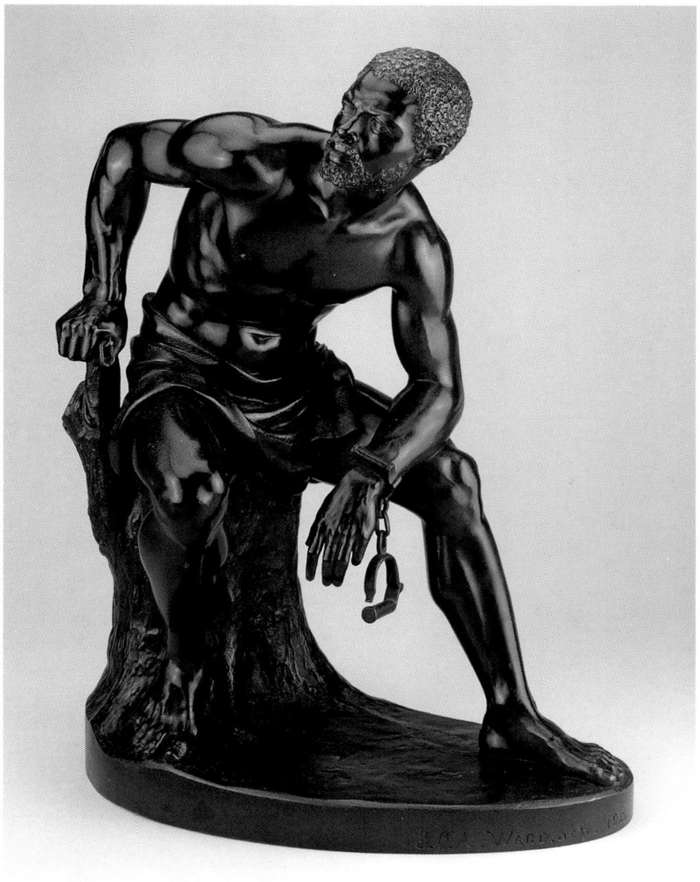

CAT. NO. 88

John Quincy Adams Ward began his professional career as a sculptor in 1849 at age nineteen, when he apprenticed in the Brooklyn studio of Henry Kirke Brown (see cat. no. 76). Like Brown, Ward was a leader of the second generation of American sculptors who pioneered efforts to cast both public and private sculpture in bronze while maintaining a commitment to the neoclassical tradition of Horatio Greenough (see cat. no. 66). As director of the National Academy of Design in 1874, first president of the National Sculpture Society, and trustee of the Metropolitan Museum of Art—all in New York—Ward exercised enormous influence in the art world over his long career.[1]

At no time was Ward's influence more keenly felt than during the period of national disillusionment produced by the Civil War. Increasingly the artist began to promote a new realism in sculpture to address pressing moral issues. In the fall of 1862, he began work on *The Freedman*. Modeled around the time of President Lincoln's Emancipation Proclamation (issued on September 22, 1862), this powerful work embodies Ward's desire to put into sculptured form the injustice of slavery and the plight of the African-American. In contrast to the popular neoclassical allegory found in Hiram Powers's marble *Greek Slave* (1844; Yale University Art Gallery, New Haven, Connecticut), Ward's bronze realistically depicts the twisting, muscular body of a seminude black man, seated on a tree stump. He has just broken free from the shackles that bound him to slavery; the remnants of the chains, potent reminders of his bondage, dangle from his wrist. Ward's statuette captures the slave's nobility through a combination of perfect classical proportion and physiognomic precision.

Modeled from life, *The Freedman* has generally been considered the first realist sculptural representation of an African-American. Although in general art critics did not note *The Freedman*'s exact classical prototype, Ward probably derived the twisting torso of the figure—the focal point of the composition—from the *Belvedere Torso* (Vatican Museums, Rome). What fascinated contemporary writers was the sculpture's physiognomic accuracy. As one critic stated, "The peculiar characteristics of the [black] race, as distinguished from the white man or the red Indian, are made prominent and form a chief subject of interest. [This work] symbolizes the African race of America, the birth of a new people within the ranks of Christian civilization."[2] Ward, who reportedly made studies from a number of African-American models during his travels through the South, brilliantly combined realism and classicism to fashion the "perfect" black body from the perspective of the ideal male nude.[3]

The original plaster cast of the sculpture was first exhibited in New York at the National Academy of Design's annual exhibition in 1863, not long after the official publication of the

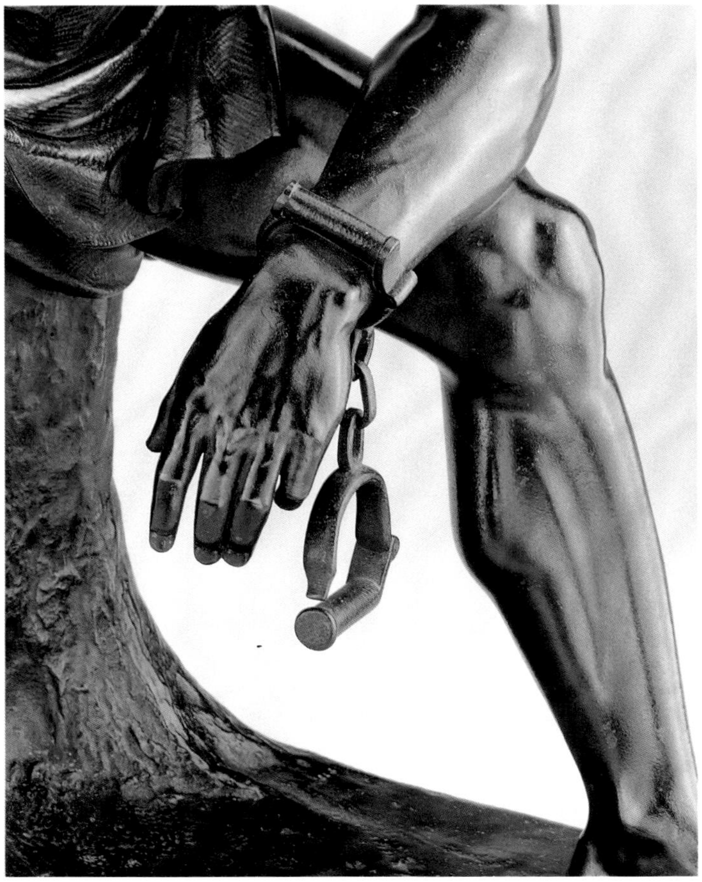

CAT. NO. 88, DETAIL

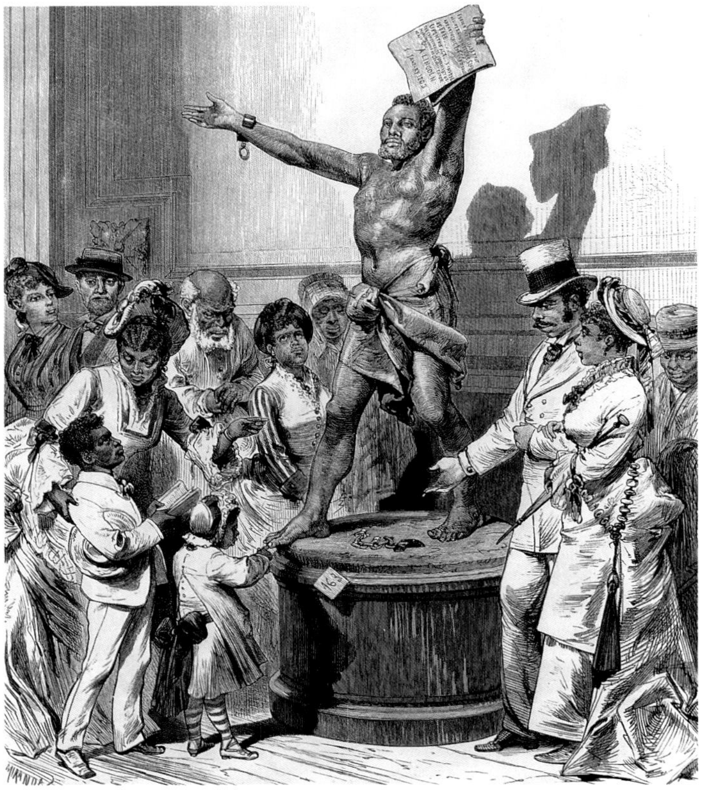

FIG. 45. "The Statue of 'The Freed Slave' in Memorial Hall," in *The Illustrated Historical Register of the Centennial Exhibition, Philadelphia, 1876* (Philadelphia, 1876), p. 133. Collection of Ryerson and Burnham Libraries, The Art Institute of Chicago.

Emancipation Proclamation.[4] An article praising *The Freedman* appeared in the *New York Times* review of the show; in recognition of its merits, Ward was elected an academician by his colleagues.[5] One year later, James Jackson Jarves, a prominent American art critic, wrote a glowing assessment of *The Freedman*: "A naked slave has burst his shackles, and with uplifted face thanks God for freedom. We have seen nothing in our sculpture more soul-lifting or more comprehensively eloquent. It tells in one word the whole sad story of slavery and the bright story of emancipation."[6]

The Freedman proved to be a popular piece in the North, and numerous bronze replicas from Ward's maquette were made over the years at three different foundries.[7] In 1867 historian Henry Tuckerman even suggested the sculpture be replicated cheaply and in small scale so that the widest possible audience could experience Ward's noble work of art.[8] No doubt *The Freedman* also inspired later sculptors interested in the subject. A display at the 1876 Centennial Exhibition in Philadelphia featured Italian sculptor Francesco Pezzicar's full-size bronze *The Freed Slave* (1873; Civico Museo Revoltella,

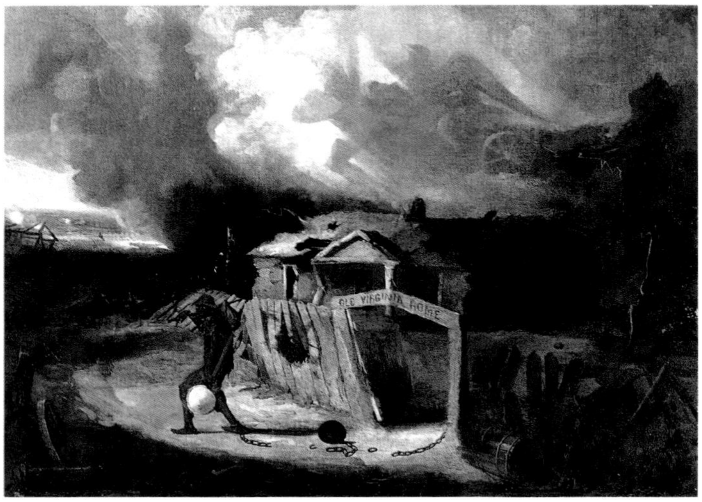

FIG. 46. David Gilmour Blythe (1815–1865). *Old Virginia Home*, 1864. Oil on canvas; 52.7 x 72.4 cm (20¾ x 28¾ in.). The Art Institute of Chicago, Ada Turnbull Hertle Fund (1979.55).

Galleria d'Arte Moderna, Trieste).[9] A souvenir register of the fair (fig. 45) illustrates the seminude male figure holding in triumph the Emancipation Proclamation while a crowd of finely dressed African-Americans displays a variety of reactions to the work.

In large part, *The Freedman's* popularity resulted from Ward's dignified presentation of his subject. Rarely shown as agents of their own liberation, freed slaves were commonly portrayed in the 1860s as being emancipated by either Abraham Lincoln or an allegory of liberty who smashes the chains of bondage.[10] The liberated African-American even became the focus of disturbing political allegory. David Gilmour Blythe's 1864 painting *Old Virginia Home* (fig. 46) depicts a caricatured black man leaving the war-torn plantation and dragging behind him the broken shackles of his ball and chain. Hunchbacked and wide-eyed, the freed slave trudges into an uncertain and dispirited future.[11] By contrast Ward's *The Freedman*, ready to stand and be counted, is a heroic representation and a poignant reminder of a tragic chapter in American history. The sculptor Lorado Taft's forceful words about the sculpture are as relevant today as they were when he wrote them in 1924: "But while we of the present please ourselves in analyzing the little figure, calmly dissecting its anatomy, it had quite a different appeal in the days of stress and struggle which gave it birth."[12]

NOTES

1. "John Quincy Adams Ward," *American Figurative Sculpture in the Museum of Fine Arts, Boston* (Boston, 1986), pp. 168–69.

2. Mr. Sturgis, cited in Lorado Taft, *The History of American Sculpture* (New York, 1924), p. 221.

3. Kurt Savage, *Standing Soldiers, Kneeling Slaves: Race, War, and Monument in Nineteenth-Century America* (Princeton, N.J., 1997), p. 57.

4. *Catalogue of the Thirty-Eighth Annual Exhibition of the National Academy of Design, 1863* (New York, 1863), p. 32, cat. no. 467, as "Freedman—Model for a Bronze Statuette." In 1863 Ward also displayed the maquette for *The Freedman* at the Pennsylvania Academy of the Fine Arts; see *Catalogue of the Fortieth Annual Exhibition of the Pennsylvania Academy of the Fine Arts, 1863* (Philadelphia, 1863), p. 25, cat. no. 394, as "Statuette—The Freedman (model for bronze)."

5. "The Academy Exhibition," *New York Times,* June 24, 1863, p. 2.

6. Furthermore, Jarves recommended that *The Freedman* be cast in "heroic size" and placed next to the statue by Horatio Greenough of George Washington in the Capitol, "to commemorate the crowning virtue of democratic institutions in the final liberty of the slave." For a full account of Jarves's comments, see James Jackson Jarves, *The Art Idea*, ed. B. Rowland, Jr. (Cambridge, Mass., 1960), p. 225.

7. These include the Ames Manufacturing Company of Chicopee, Mass.; Henry-Bonnard Company of New York City; and the Gorham Company Founders of Providence, R.I. As of 1985, when the art historian Lewis Sharp completed his catalogue raisonné of Ward's work, eight known copies had been located; see Lewis Sharp, *John Quincy Adams Ward, Dean of American Sculpture (with a Catalogue Raisonné)* (Newark, Del., 1985), pp. 153–56. Other versions of *The Freedman* are included in the public collections of the Boston Athenaeum; Metropolitan Museum of Art, New York; American Academy of Arts and Letters, New York; National Academy of Design, New York; Pennsylvania Academy of the Fine Arts, Philadelphia; Detroit Institute of Arts; and Cincinnati Art Museum.

8. Henry T. Tuckerman, *Book of the Artists: American Artist Life Comprising Biographical and Critical Sketches of American Artists, Preceded by an Historical Account of the Rise and Progress of Art in America* (1867; New York, 1967), pp. 581–82.

9. Hugh Honour, *The Image of the Black in Western Art*, vol. 4, pt. 1 (Cambridge, Mass., 1976), pp. 256–58.

10. Savage (note 3), p. 57.

11. For a full reading of Blythe's political allegory, see Bruce Chambers, *The World of David Gilmour Blythe*, exh. cat. (Washington, D.C., National Collection of the Fine Arts, Smithsonian Institution, 1981), pp. 94–95.

12. Taft (note 2), p. 221.

89. CENTER TABLE (MARQUETRY TOP BY JOSEPH CREMER, PARIS [ACTIVE 1836–1878]), C. 1862

New York

Rosewood with tulip poplar, white pine, maple, various other inlaid woods, mother-of-pearl, and ormolu mounts; 137.2 x 91.4 x 74.6 cm (54 x 36 x 29⅜ in.)

Top signed: *J. Cremer*; table frame impressed with the number *1007*

Restricted gift of Jamee J. and Marshall Field, Mrs. Eric Oldberg, and the Winnetka Associates of the Woman's Board of the Art Institute; Americana, Brooks and Hope B. McCormick, J. Peter McCormick, and Mrs. Frank L. Sulzberger funds; Mary Waller Langhorne Endowment; and through prior acquisitions of Ellen N. LaMotte, Elizabeth R. Vaughan, and the Wirt D. Walker Endowment, 1993.122

Joseph Cremer, the maker of the marquetry top of this center table, was one of the premier French *ébénistes* of the nineteenth century and was touted as "being amongst the best workers in the revived art of marquetrie" at the 1862 International Exhibition in London.[1] During his forty-plus years in business, Cremer successfully revived the French tradition of marquetry which had flourished during the reign of Louis XIV. This table top's oval marquetry panel is the first piece of American furniture incorporating a signed example of French marquetry: it bears Cremer's signature hidden in the floral decoration. Almost identical inlaid panels appear on at least three other cen-

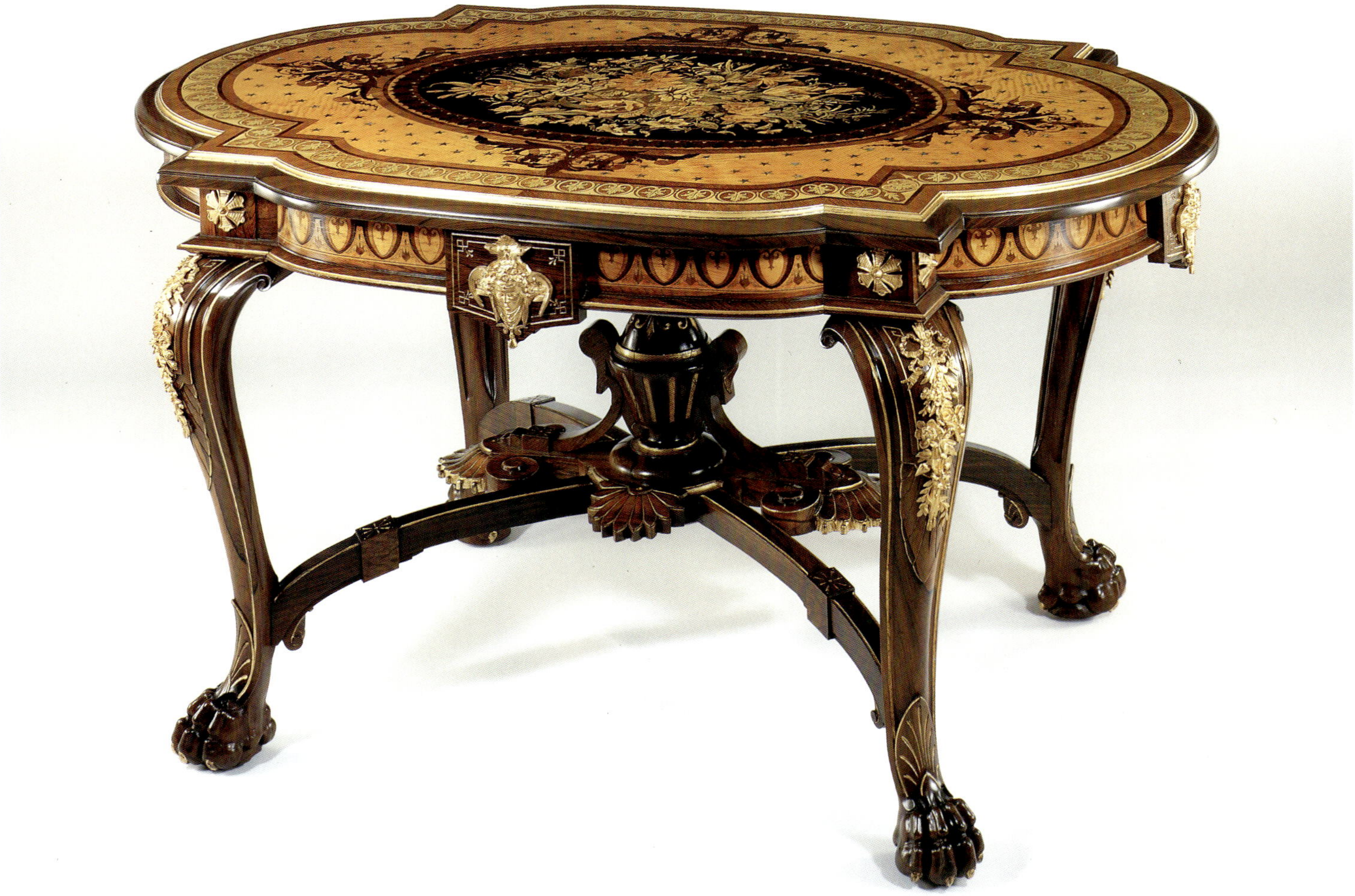

CAT. NO. 89

ter tables.[2] The Herter Brothers firm of New York also made several center tables with marquetry tops depicting birds and butterflies that are strikingly similar to one another. These have been attributed to Cremer on the basis of his documented work on French furniture.[3]

Scholars have attributed to Cremer inlaid panels on other pieces of American furniture, but there was no proof that he executed ready-made marquetry pieces for the American market until the appearance of the Art Institute's signed panel.[4] The proliferation of such panels indicates that Cremer's shop and possibly other French marquetry makers supplied the American market with their wares in far greater numbers than previously thought. The fact that there are so many almost-identical panels, varying only in the colors of the woods used and in a few small details, may indicate that Cremer and his contemporaries mass-produced their work for American furniture makers. The high cost of materials and the unavailability of skilled labor in their own land made it more cost-effective for them to import marquetry panels from France.[5]

It is likely that Cremer was responsible only for the central oval of the Art Institute's center table. Framing the signed, asymmetrical floral panel are several bands of maple and curly maple, with inlay patterns of mother-of-pearl stars and symmetrical maple C-scrolls overlaid with a foliate pattern in ebonized wood. The marquetry on the rest of the table top and on the apron is static and more geometric in design and was probably executed by a worker in the New York shop where the table was made.

The rich and varied motifs decorating the table are inspired by a number of styles. The table's overall heavy proportions, as well as the anthemion leaves, carved urn, paw feet, and inlay pattern around the apron, are derived from Renaissance proto-

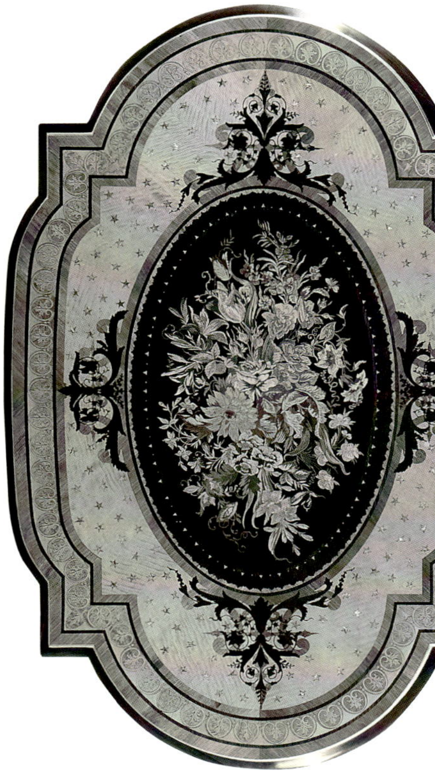

CAT. NO. 89, TOP

types. The ribbon and floral ormolu mounts on the knees, the female ormolu masks around the table top, and the intricate floral marquetry top are Rococo in nature. These embellishments provided an opulent feast for nineteenth-century eyes.

NOTES

1. J. B. Waring, *Masterpieces of Industrial Art and Sculpture at the International Exhibition, 1862*, vol. 1 (London, 1863), unpag.

2. One of these tables is in the Museum of the City of New York; see New York, Metropolitan Museum of Art, *Nineteenth-Century America: Furniture and Other Decorative Arts*, exh. cat. (1970), cat. no. 188. A second table is in the collection of Margot Johnson, Inc., New York, and a third is in the collection of the Cornell Fine Arts Center, Rollins College, Winter Park, Fla.; see Files of the Department of American Arts, The Art Institute of Chicago.

3. Katherine S. Howe et al., *Herter Brothers: Furniture and Interiors for a Gilded Age*, exh. cat. (Houston, Museum of Fine Arts, 1994), pp. 138, 142–43; and Henry Hawley, "American Furniture of the Mid-Nineteenth Century," *Bulletin of the Cleveland Museum of Art* 74, 5 (May 1987), pp. 195–96.

4. A cabinet with a retailer's label from the firm of Sypher and Co. of New York and attributed to Pottier and Stymus is now in the Museum of Fine Arts, Houston; it has a central figural marquetry panel identical to one on a French cabinet signed by Cremer and dated 1856. The cabinet was exhibited at the London Exhibition of 1862; it is now in the Toledo Museum of Art (1990.97). See London, Sotheby's, *Nineteenth- and Twentieth-Century Furniture and Decorations* (May 31, 1991), lot 122; and Howe et al. (note 3), pp. 114–15, 248 n. 10.

5. Howe et al. (note 3), p. 138.

90. COMPOTE, 1830/50

Massachusetts

Lead glass; 15.9 x 26.8 x 22.5 cm (6¼ x 10⁹⁄₁₆ x 8⅞ in.)

Gift of Arthur Heun, 1933.1323

By the first decades of the nineteenth century, elevated dishes, fashionably known as *compotes de fruits*, had become popular as centerpieces on dessert tables in North American dining rooms.[1] Typically these dishes held stewed fruits, a heated mixture of cooked fruit, sugar, water, and spices. They also seem to have been used to serve salads, nuts, and other foods.[2] The Art Institute's compote is made of machine-pressed lead glass.

Perhaps the most important technological advance in the history of glassmaking, machine pressing (see cat. nos. 66–67) made possible the mass production of forms, the interchangeability of parts, and the purchase of glassware by individual households at affordable prices. To operate a glass press, a worker would pull down a lever attached to a fulcrum and a guided plunger. This forced a quantity of molten glass into a mold with enough pressure to ensure that the glass filled all the crevices in the mold and replicated whatever pattern the plunger bore.[3] After the bowl on this compote was pressed, it was joined to the octagonal base by means of a thin, molten-glass wafer, which can be seen just under the base of the bowl.This type of compote was available in a number of colors, including yellow, amethyst, blue, and green, as well as colorless glass. This bowl type was also offered with several other types of bases.[4]

American pressed glass was popular in both the United States, where it was valued for its affordability and its similarity to more expensive cut glass, and Europe, where it was desirable as well for its elaborate patterning. German porcelain designs show the influence of American glass on porcelain modelers in the factories. In the 1830s, the Meissen factory purchased pressed glass to provide design inspirations for its ceramic modelers. In June 1835, Gotthelf Emil Frenkel, the manager of the Meissen porcelain factory's sales outlet in Leipzig, reported that some of the most popular items sold at the outlet were dessert services copied from American glass models. According to Frenkel's report, "a substantial quantity of pressed glass ware from North America with the most appealing designs on hollow wares and flat wares of a distinctive appearance . . . instantly sold." A Meissen shallow porcelain bowl (fig. 47) was modeled on an American "princess-feather" glass bowl or dish similar to the Art Institute's compote.[5]

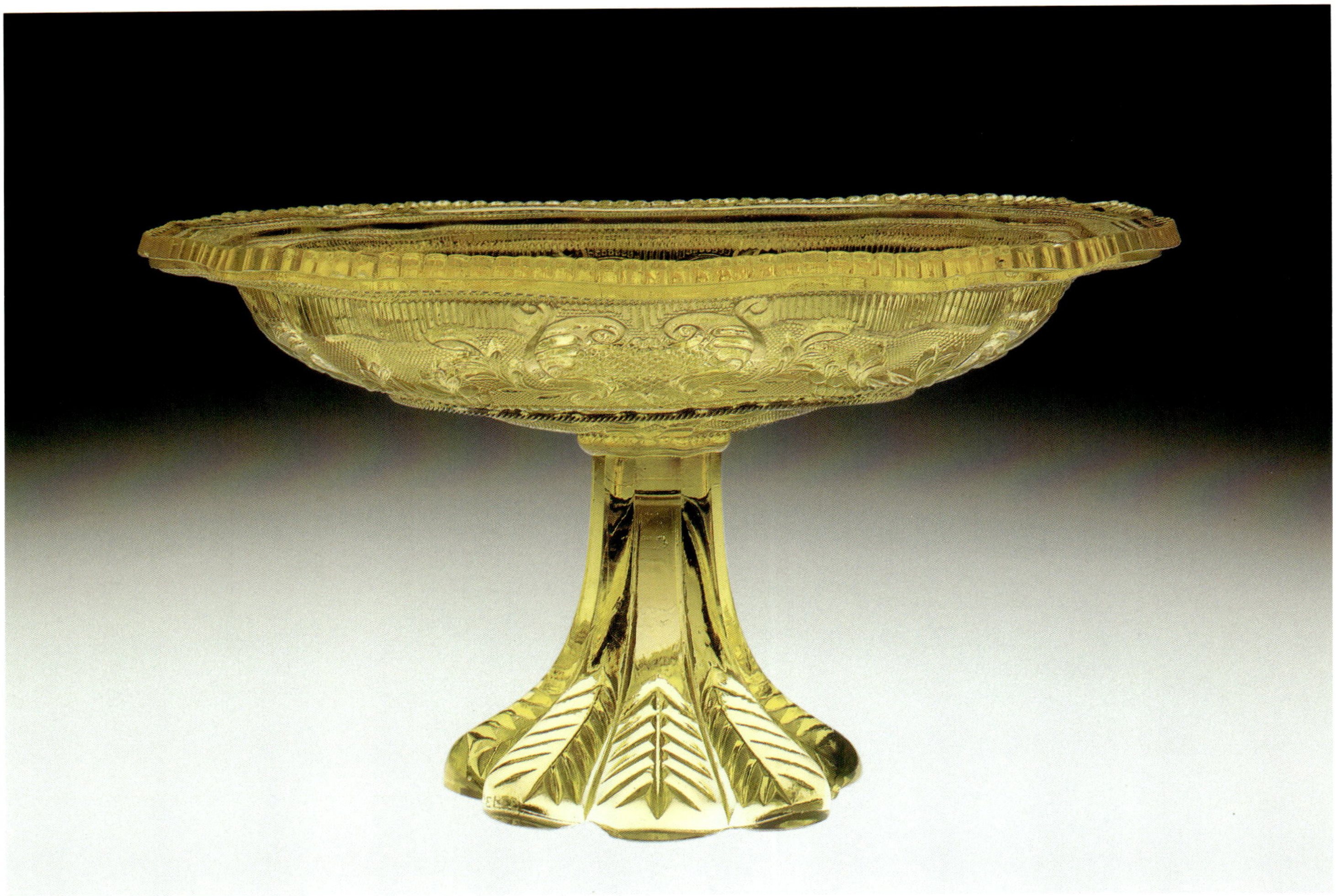

CAT. NO. 90

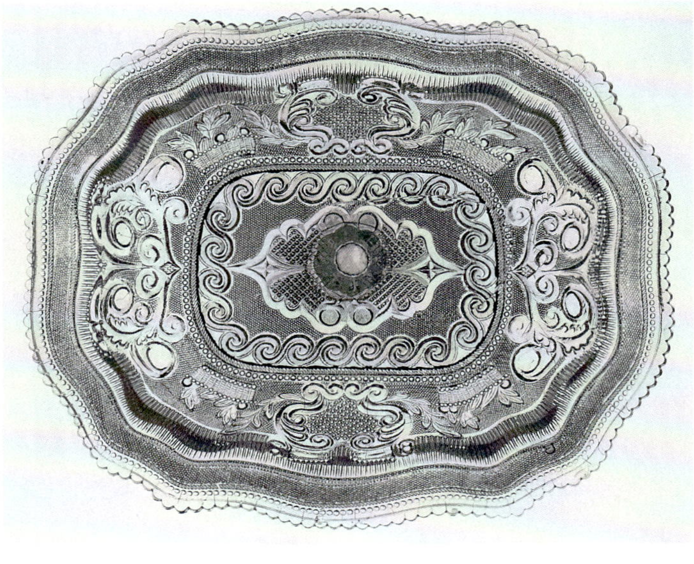

CAT. NO. 90, TOP

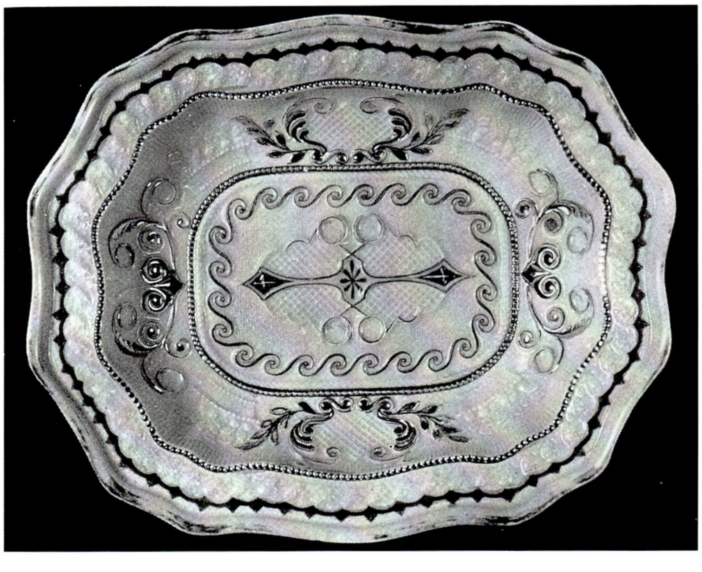

FIG. 47. Meissen porcelain dish, after 1830. Photograph from Ruth Webb Lee, *Sandwich Glass: The History of the Boston and Sandwich Glass Company*, 5th ed. (Northborough, Mass., 1947), p. 396, pl. 152.

This compote was pressed in the princess-feather pattern on a background of raised dots, called stipples. With an elaborate decorative scheme of scrolled volutes, waves, beads, incised lines, leaves, feathers, and hearts, the pattern covers almost the entire surface of the compote, reflecting light and hiding any imperfections or discoloration in the glass that may have resulted from the pressing process.[6] The lobes on the faceted base of the compote are in a fern pattern. The princess-feather pattern was not limited to these compotes, but was popular for vegetable dishes, plates, bowls, and other forms. It could be paired with other designs on individual glass forms to provide innumerable variants.[7]

NOTES

1. Louise Conway Belden, *The Festive Tradition: Table Decoration and Desserts in America, 1650–1900* (New York, 1983), pp. 59–60.

2. Arlene Palmer, *Glass in Early America* (New York, 1993), p. 237.

3. Kenneth M. Wilson, *American Glass, 1760–1930* (New York, 1994), vol. 1, pp. 265, 268.

4. George S. McKearin and Helen McKearin, *American Glass* (New York, 1941), p. 362, pls. 161–62.

5. Palmer (note 2), p. 243; and Joachim Kunze, "Meissen Porcelain Designed from Glass Patterns (1831 to 1855)," *Glass Club Bulletin* 153 (fall 1987), p. 5.

6. Amanda E. Lange, in Winterthur, Del., Henry Francis du Pont Winterthur Museum, *Eye for Excellence: Masterworks from Winterthur* (1994), p. 42.

7. For examples of other forms in the "princess-feather" pattern, see McKearin and McKearin (note 4), pls. 158–60.

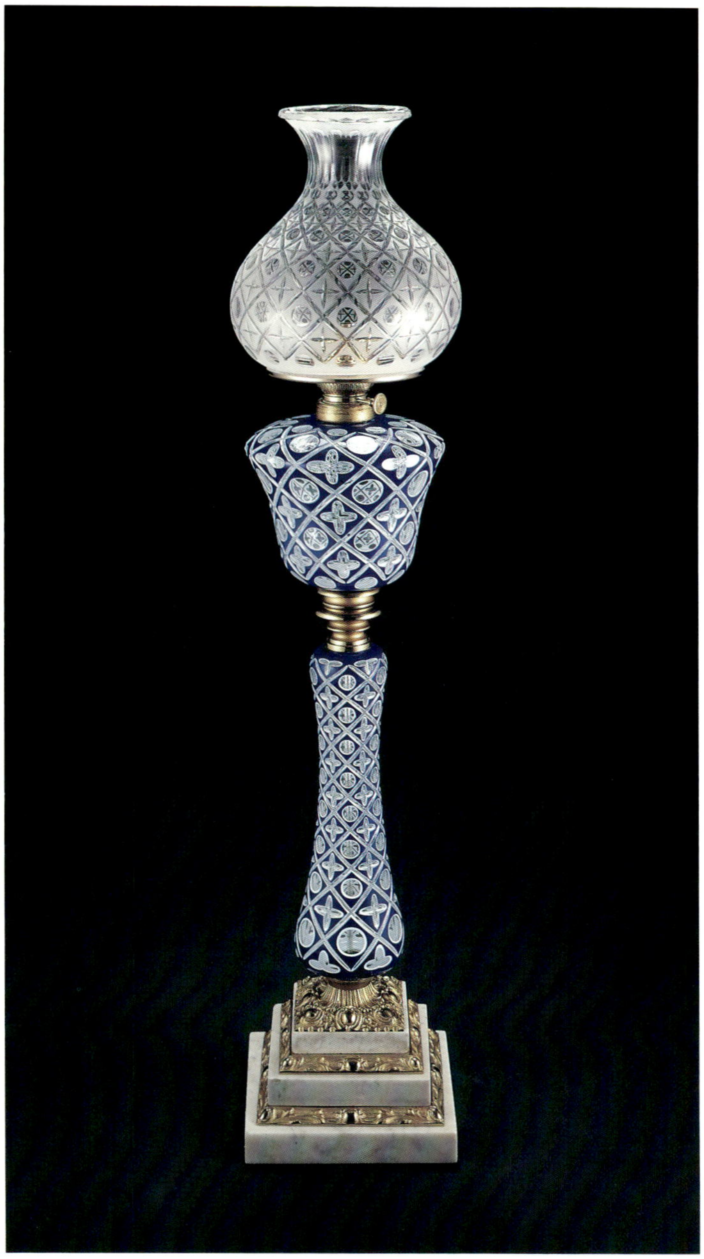

CAT. NO. 91

91. BOSTON AND SANDWICH GLASS COMPANY

Double-Plated Lamp, c. 1865

Sandwich, Massachusetts

Cobalt blue, opaque white, and colorless glass; gilt bronze; and marble; h. 97.8 cm (38½ in.) to top of shade

Through prior acquisition of Emily Crane Chadbourne, Arthur Heun, Mrs. Maurice B. Mandelbaum, Dr. and Mrs. Roy Nagle, and Mrs. Howard Peabody, 1994.5

After 1859, kerosene-burning glass lamps gradually replaced other oil-burning lamps and candles as sources of light and rapidly gained favor in most households. Kerosene produced less smoke and odor than animal-based oils and was also less expensive. Because of the time involved in cleaning the lamps, kerosene, like other oils, was used sparingly. Rooms were lit only when in use, and usually by a single source. The Boston and Sandwich Glass Company, which made this lamp, was one of the largest manufacturers of domestic glass in the United States during the mid-nineteenth century. Marketed for the urban home or large country house, this monumental piece was a crowning achievement for the company.

By the 1840s, the fashion in urban parlors called for placing a lamp on a circular table in the center of a room, thus taking greatest advantage of the light generated (see fig. 48). Small mats, called table rugs, were placed on the table tops to catch spills and leaks from the lamps.[1] When not receiving company, a family lit only one lamp or several candles. Because of the limited amount of illuminated space, family members would often gather together in one room to read, sew, play games, or tell stories.[2] During winter months, the light from the fireplace might add to the illumination of a room or even take the place of lamplight or candlelight.

Plated glass was perfected in Bohemia by the mid-1830s, and by the early 1840s examples had been exported to Boston, New York, and Philadelphia. The Boston and Sandwich Glass Company opened its first furnace expressly for the production of colored glass for plating in the early 1840s. Over the next several years, the company's experiments with glass formulas and plating techniques raised the quality of its products; by 1850 Boston and Sandwich plated glass was being produced in intricate designs and was superior to that of most other manufacturers.

Plated glass was produced by encasing a colorless, blown-glass shape in either one or two layers of colored, molten glass. The differently hued layers were fused together in the blowing process; while the blown glass was still soft, it was forced into a mold and then left to harden.[3] Patterns were cut through the top layers of colored glass to expose each color overlay and the colorless glass underneath. The 1865 Boston and Sandwich Glass Company catalogue described the pattern on the Art Institute's lamp as "Cut-Punty-and-Diamond-Flint."[4]

This lamp is one of fewer than a dozen examples that survive in this monumental size.[5] With its triple-stepped marble base and brass mounts, it weighs a staggering twenty-three pounds, not including fuel, burner, chimney, and globe.[6] The design of the lamp is especially harmonious: the solid marble base progresses inward, anticipating the gentle curve of the body of the lamp, which flares out again at the head, echoing the base. In adding the chimney and globe, the glass cutter accentuated the lamp's verticality. His mastery of the plating technique is evident in the decoration of this lamp. He expertly cut back the cobalt blue and opaque white-glass layers to reveal the layer underneath. The cut-punty-and-diamond-flint motif is uniform throughout the lamp, no small feat for a hand-cut design.

This piece comes from the distinguished collection of whale-oil and kerosene lamps assembled by W. Colston Leigh (1902–1992). It is one of the most spectacular pieces of nineteenth-century American glass.

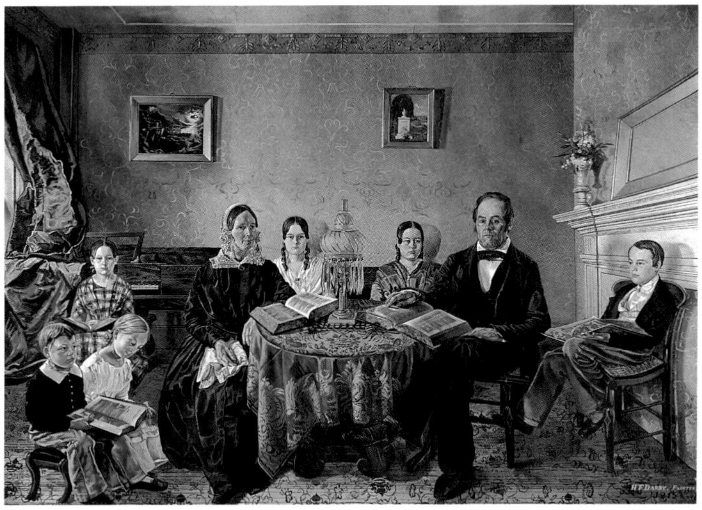

FIG. 48. Henry F. Darby (1829–1897). *The Reverend John Atwood and His Family*, 1845. Oil on canvas; 182.9 x 240.6 cm (72 x 96¼ in.). Museum of Fine Arts, Boston, Gift of Maxim Karolik for the M. and M. Karolik Collection of American Paintings, 1815–1865 (62.269).

NOTES

1. The rugs were made of small scraps of carpeting. See Jane C. Nylander, *Our Own Snug Fireside* (New York, 1993), p. 113.

2. Elizabeth D. Garrett, *At Home: The American Family, 1750–1870* (New York, 1990), pp. 150–51.

3. Raymond E. Barlow and Joan E. Kaiser, *The Glass Industry in Sandwich* (Windham, N.H., 1989), vol. 2, p. 195.

4. Punties are the cut circles, and diamond flints are the cut crosses. See Catherine M. V. Thuro, *Oil Lamps II: Glass Kerosene Lamps* (Paducah, Ky., 1983), p. 61.

5. Other examples are in the collections of the Sandwich Glass Museum, Sandwich, Mass.; Chrysler Museum, Norfolk, Va.; Detroit Institute of Arts; and Metropolitan Museum of Art, New York.

6. The glass areas serve as reservoirs for the kerosene. These held enough fuel for several days, after which the lamp was disassembled, cleaned thoroughly, refilled with fuel, and returned to its table. See Barlow and Kaiser (note 3), vol. 2, p. 208.

92. JOSEPH MOZIER (1812–1870)

Pocahontas, 1868 (after original, carved 1854)

Marble; h. 121.8 cm (48 in.) on original marble pedestal
Signed, dated, and inscribed (on base): *J. MOZIER. Sc:/ROME. 1868*
Titled (on base): *POCAHONTAS*
Roger McCormick and J. Peter McCormick funds, 1997.366

Born in Burlington, Vermont, to parents of French origin, and raised in central Ohio, Joseph Mozier began his career not as an artist but as a successful dry-goods merchant in New York City. Mozier's interest in art, however, finally led him to abandon his business and devote himself to sculpture. In 1845 the nascent artist sailed for Europe. Although not formally trained, Mozier opened a studio in Florence and by 1850 had settled in Rome, where he practiced his new profession until his death in 1870. Advised early on by Hiram Powers (see cat. no. 73) and free from financial concern throughout his twenty-five year career, Mozier produced a series of important full-length statues that reveal a reliance on literary themes and classical prototypes. Among the best known of these is his *Pocahontas.*[1]

The subject of the Indian maiden in general, and of Pocahontas in particular, interested Mozier from the outset of his career, as it had a number of other neoclassical sculptors during the mid-nineteenth century. Erastus Dow Palmer's *Indian Girl, or the Dawn of Christianity* (1853; Metropolitan Museum of Art, New York) was typical. A standing, partially nude female Indian gazes downward at a cross held in her hand; it represents the Native American woman as a noble princess open to Christian conversion.[2] Not surprisingly the story of Pocahontas reached new levels of celebrity at this time. According to popular retellings, the young Indian maiden not only saved the life of Captain John Smith, but also embraced the Christian faith, took the name Rebecca, and later married colonist John Rolfe. More than just a romantic tale, Pocahontas's life historically reaffirmed a concept central to the aim of western expansion in the nineteenth century: subjugating a native people was justified by the benefits of Christian progress that white civilization would bring.[3]

The Pocahontas subject proved a financial boon to Mozier's early career. After first completing an ideal bust of the subject in 1848, the sculptor began work on the full-length *Pocahontas* soon after moving to Rome. He completed the first marble by 1854, and its success was announced almost immediately by a correspondent for the *Art Journal.* The author recounted the Pocahontas story and praised the sculpture as being "full of

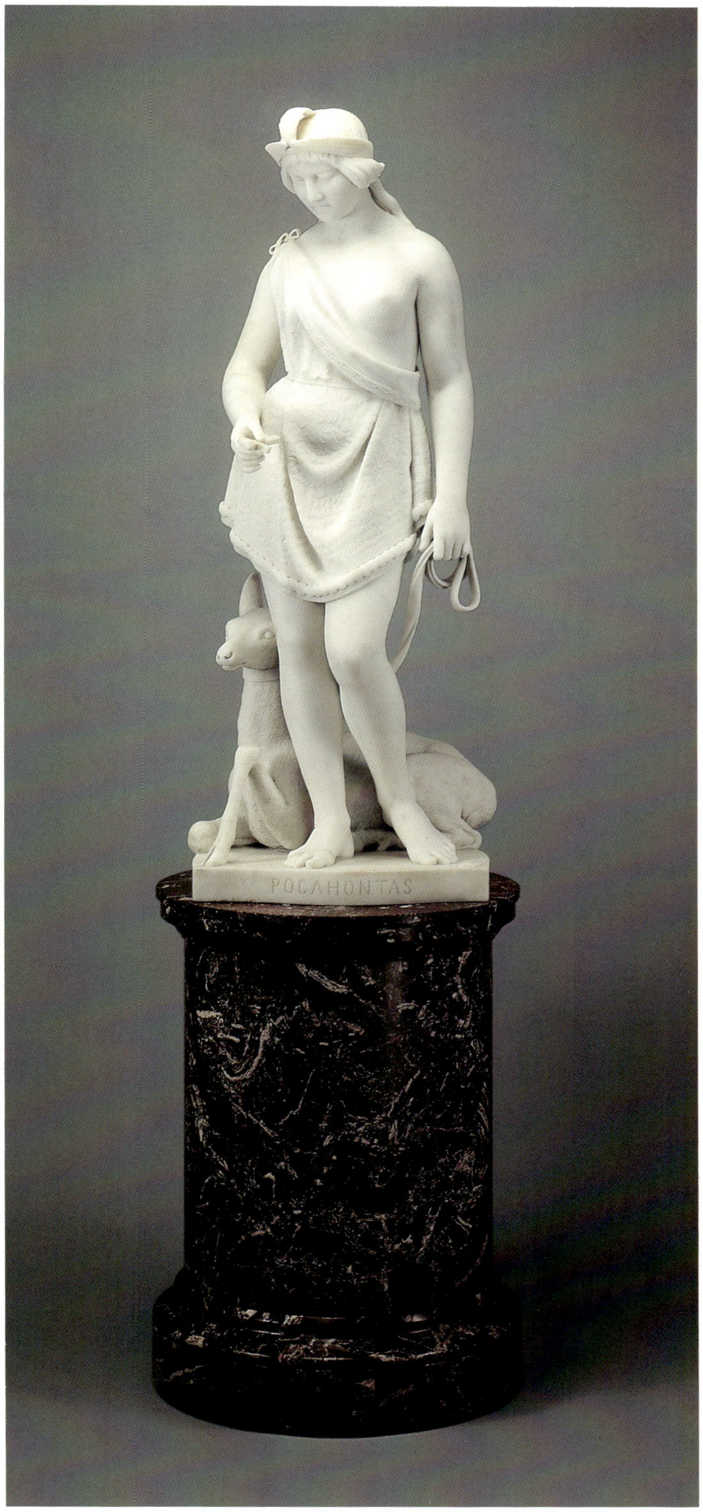

CAT. NO. 92

deep sentiment and unaffected purity, with a striking originality as to costume and treatment."[4] The subject proved popular with Mozier's clientele: when the writer Nathaniel Hawthorne visited the sculptor's studio in 1858, he observed "a figure of Pocahontas which has been repeated several times."[5] During his lifetime, Mozier's *Pocahontas* was consistently celebrated as one of his signature sculptures.[6]

Like Palmer's full-length Indian figure, Mozier's *Pocahontas* presents his subject at the moment of her spiritual conversion. The contrapposto pose, perhaps echoing Italian Renaissance prototypes, captures her hesitation as she pauses to contemplate a cross held in her right hand. Mozier took special care in rendering the accoutrements that helped signify Pocahontas's identity as a Native American. He executed the feathered headgear and deer-skin garment with precision to simulate tooled leather and tufted fur. Carved with equal accuracy, the fawn at Pocahontas's feet serves a narrative as well as a structural purpose. As the *Art Journal* correspondent observed, the animal reinforces a notion of Pocahontas's primitive innocence, "emblematic both of the chase and of her own untamed condition."[7] Audiences were fascinated with the statue's authentic details. In reviewing an 1859 exposition in Chicago that featured Mozier's statue, one newspaper critic noticed "how closely visitors were scrutinizing the face, to find out whether there was genuine, savage Indian expression to those fair features."[8]

Mozier's keen business aptitude helped him to market *Pocahontas* successfully to an eager clientele, and between 1859 and 1870, several versions of the statue were featured at important public exhibitions in the United States.[9] The noted Philadelphia collector Joseph Harrison possessed a copy, as did the financier LeGrand Lockwood, who prominently displayed his *Pocahontas* in the entrance hall of his Connecticut estate opposite a second Indian sculpture by Mozier, *The Wept of Wish-ton-Wish*.[10] The sculpture was even known in Chicago as early as 1859, where it was featured in the city's first fine-arts exposition and was lent by E. B. McCagg.[11] The existence of ample replicas of *Pocahontas* make tracing the Art Institute's version to its original owner next to impossible. Remarkably, this 1868 rendering still stands on its original marble base.

NOTES

1. For the most recent biographical overview of Mozier's life, see H. Nichols B. Clark's entry on the sculptor and his *Pocahontas* in *A Marble Quarry: The James H. Ricau Collection of Sculpture at the Chrysler Museum of Art* (New York, 1997), pp. 122–24, 128–31. Dr. Clark generously shared his work on Mozier's *Pocahontas* prior to the publication of the Ricau collection catalogue.

2. Another image of the female Indian common in popular novels, poems, and songs was that of a sexual temptress. For two important studies that examine how Native American women were represented in the nineteenth century, see Rayna Green, "The Pocahontas Perplex: The Image of Indian Women in American Culture," *Massachusetts Review* 16 (1975), pp. 699–714; and Mary V. Dearborn, *Pocahontas's Daughters: Gender and Ethnicity in American Culture* (New York, 1986).

3. For more on how Pocahontas's story has been manipulated since the nineteenth century, see William M. S. Rasmussen and Robert S. Tilton, *Pocahontas: Her Life and Legend*, exh. cat. (Richmond, Virginia Historical Society, 1994).

4. Florentia, "A Walk Through the Studios of Rome," *Art Journal* 66 (June 1854), p. 185.

5. Nathaniel Hawthorne, *Passages from the French and Italian Notebooks* (Boston, 1872), cited in Lorado Taft, *The History of American Sculpture* (New York, 1924), p. 110.

6. Albert Ten Eyck Gardner, *Yankee Stonecutters: The First American School of Sculpture, 1800–1850* (New York, 1945), p. 69. For references in Mozier's obituary to the importance of *Pocahontas*, see *Art Journal* 10 (Jan. 1871), p. 6. Other marble versions of *Pocahontas* are in the collections of the Museum of Fine Arts, Boston; J. V. Fletcher Library, Westford, Mass.; Joseph M. Napoli, Brooklyn; private collection, Louisiana; and Hirschl and Adler Galleries, New York.

7. Florentia (note 4), p. 185.

8. "The Art Exposition," *Chicago Press and Tribune* (June 21, 1859), p. 2.

9. William J. Clark, Jr., *Great American Sculptures* (Philadelphia, 1878), pp. 120–21. The important venues included the Chicago Exposition of Fine Arts (1859), the Philadelphia Sanitary Fair (1864), and the Brooklyn and Long Island Fair (1864).

10. On the recent theory that Mozier carved *Pocahontas* and *The Wept of Wish-ton-Wish* as pendants, see Eric W. Baumgartner, *A Marvellous Repose: American Neo-Classical Scupture, 1825–1876*, exh. cat. (New York, Hirschl and Adler Galleries, 1996), p. 28.

11. Clark (note 1), p. 130.

93. WILLIAM BRADFORD (1823–1892)

The Coast of Labrador, 1866

Oil on canvas; 72 x 113.3 cm (28⅜ x 44⅝ in.)

Signed, lower right: *Wm Bradford / 1866*

Ada Turnbull Hertle Fund, 1983.529

A native of Fairhaven, Massachusetts, a whaling town located near New Bedford, William Bradford devoted most of his career to painting arctic scenes such as *The Coast of Labrador*.[1]

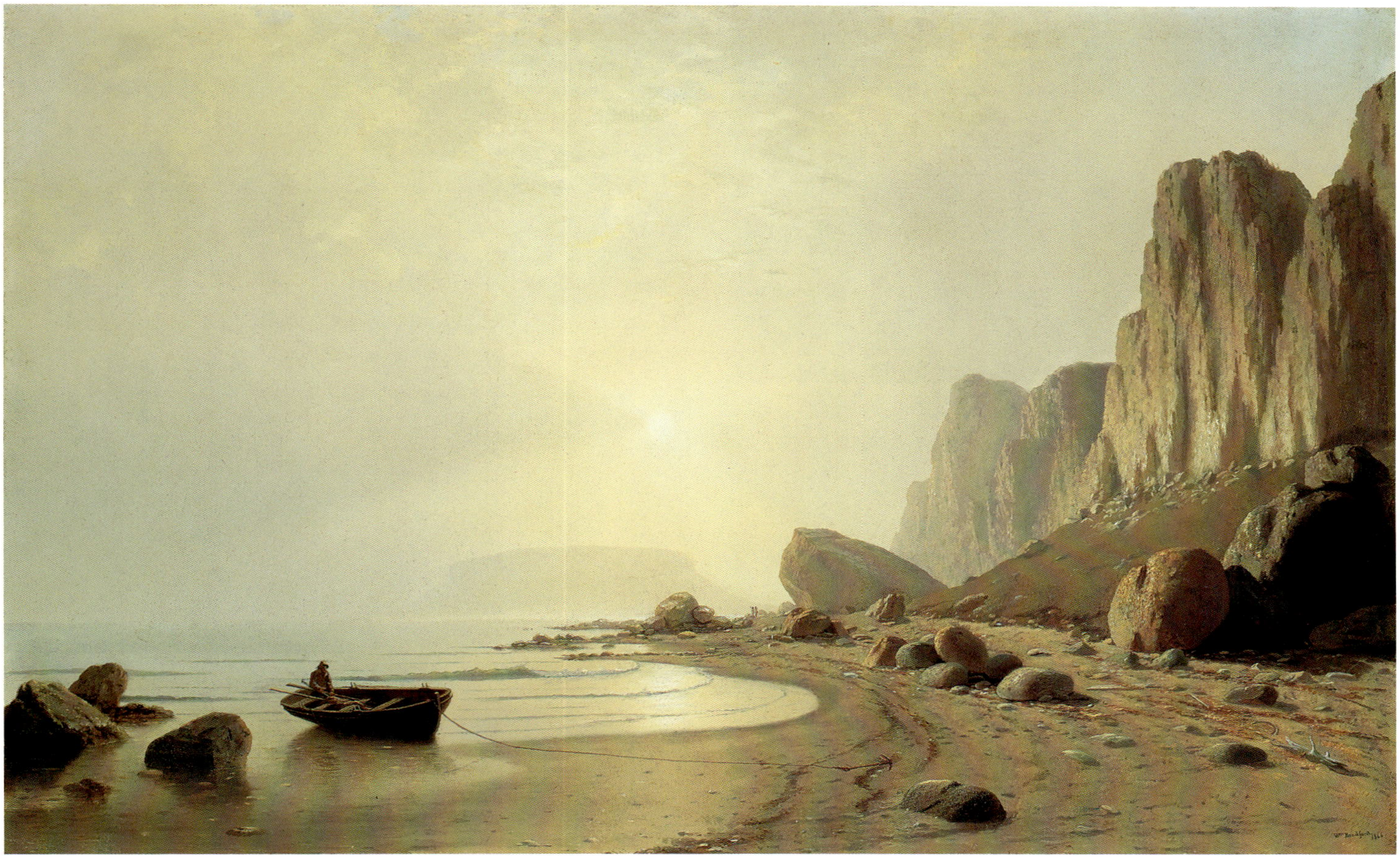

CAT. NO. 93

Rendered in minute detail and suffused with light, Bradford's arctic compositions share a common style with John Frederick Kensett's glowing views of the Rhode Island coast (see cat. no. 94). One of Bradford's earliest arctic scenes, the Art Institute's painting conveys the contemplative mood characteristic of the so-called luminist artists, such as Kensett, with whom the artist has long been compared.

In the mid-1850s, before his interest in the arctic region took hold, Bradford painted ship portraits (see fig. 49) heavily indebted to Dutch marine painting. Albert Van Beest, a Dutch painter with whom Bradford shared a studio, greatly influenced the young artist, and the two even collaborated on a number of commissions. While he painted ship portraits, Bradford also made his first journeys, between 1854 and 1857, to Labrador, in northeastern Canada. According to Bradford's daughter Mary, it was not, however, until the summer of 1861, when he returned to this region, that he plumbed it as a source of artistic inspiration and exploration.[2] After his 1861 trip, Bradford returned to the region eight times; his last and most ambitious excursion took place in 1869. Profits from the sale of his marine pictures enabled him to attract sponsors for the enormous expense of his excursions to the Arctic Circle.

Bradford was not the first American artist to travel to this region, and the popularity of his northern landscapes coincided with the success other prominent artists found painting arctic images.[3] Frederic Edwin Church (see cat. no. 86) went to Labrador and Newfoundland in 1859 accompanied by Reverend Louis Noble, who in 1861 published *After Icebergs with a Painter*, his account of the journey. Church's artistic study of the region culminated that same year with his monumental painting *The Icebergs* (Dallas Museum of Art). Both Noble's book and Church's painting capitalized on the sublime beauty of the Arctic, but also on its treacherous nature, which caused many nineteenth-century explorers to perish.

Although many of Bradford's early journeys were made to tap the artistic potential of Labrador, later in his career he lectured in the United States and England on the scientific significance of icebergs and arctic geology. The artist also published the book *The Arctic Regions* (London, 1873), in which his images illustrate detailed accounts of his voyages.[4] The

3. Judging from the artist's estate sale, the coastal scenes Kensett began painting in the mid-1850s comprise the bulk of his oeuvre; see *The Collection of Over Five Hundred Paintings and Studies by the Late John F. Kensett*, exh. cat. (New York, National Academy of Design, 1873). *Near Newport* was probably no. 178 in this sale.

4. For more on Kensett and Newport, see Mark W. Sullivan, "John F. Kensett at Newport: The Making of a Luminist Painter," *Antiques* 138, 5 (Nov. 1990), pp. 1030–41.

5. The main sources for information on luminism are Barbara Novak, "Luminism: An Alternative Tradition," in *American Painting of the Nineteenth Century: Realism, Idealism, and the American Experience* (New York, 1979), pp. 92–109; and John Wilmerding, ed., *American Light: The Luminist Movement, 1850–1875*, exh. cat. (Washington, D.C., National Gallery of Art, 1980).

4. Ralph Waldo Emerson, "Nature," in William H. Gilman, ed., *Selected Writings of Ralph Waldo Emerson* (New York, 1965), p. 189.

7. Mark White Sullivan, "John F. Kensett, American Landscape Painter" (Ph.D. diss., Bryn Mawr College, 1981), p. 132.

95. MARY CASSATT (1844–1926)

After the Bullfight, 1873

Oil on canvas; 82.5 x 64 cm (32 1/8 x 25 3/16 in.)

Signed, dated, inscribed: *M.S.C. / Seville / 1873*

Gift of Mrs. Sterling Morton, 1969.332

Mary Cassatt arrived in Spain, traveling alone, in early October 1872; she was twenty-eight years old. She had already completed an art curriculum at the Pennsylvania Academy of the Fine Arts, Philadelphia; studied in Paris with the fashionable and influential painter-educator Jean-Léon Gérôme; and traveled widely in Italy, settling in Parma, where she copied frescoes by Correggio. Eager to absorb more lessons from the Old Masters, Cassatt left Italy for Spain, specifically to see the works of Bartolomé Esteban Murillo and Diego Velázquez. At the Museo del Prado in Madrid, she copied Velázquez's *Don Baltasar Carlos*, and also *The Spinners*. The latter work, she wrote to a friend, was the most realistic picture she had seen, noting, "good heavens, why you can walk into the picture."[1]

After three weeks in Madrid, Cassatt moved on to Seville, where she arrived on October 26. She was armed with Théophile Gautier's popular 1845 travel guide to Spain, which describes at length the various figures and costumes associated with the bullfight. In the two paintings of bullfighters Cassatt executed in Seville, her treatment closely followed Gautier's description of their costume—a short jacket of orange, green, blue, or red velvet, embroidered with sequins and gold, adorned with silver filigree ornament, and left open in the front. Bullfighters wore a jabot, or shirt with a ruffle down the front, a loose, colorful, narrow tie, a silk belt, and leather pants. Typically tall and athletic, they carried a vivid, red silk cape hung over a horizontally held baton, used both to attract and to agitate the bull.[2]

Though infused with the realism of Velázquez, *After the Bullfight*, not unlike Gautier's small book, initially seems a skilled traveler's search for the exotic and the picturesque. The painting also, however, reveals an unexpectedly modern sensibility in its vigorous brushwork, and in the relaxed, seemingly unposed quality of the sitter. Cassatt was very likely familiar with the Spanish paintings of France's leading avant-garde painter, Édouard Manet, from her studies in Paris in 1866–67. Manet himself had visited Spain in 1865 and continued to draw upon Spanish themes long after his return to the French capital. His *Matador Saluting* (1866; Metropolitan Museum of Art, New York) was exhibited in 1867, along with at least fourteen other pictures exploring Spanish subjects in a major exhibition held at the Avenue d'Alma in Paris.[3] Like Gautier and Manet, and to some degree like her former teacher Gérôme, who also turned frequently to Spanish subjects for his popular Salon paintings, Cassatt saw both the aesthetic and commercial possibilities of this choice. She declared: "I see the immense capital that can be drawn from Spain, it has not been 'exploited' yet as it might be, and it is suggestive of pictures on all sides."[4]

The modernity of Cassatt's *After the Bullfight* is best understood in the context of two other paintings she executed in Seville. *The Flirtation: A Balcony in Seville* (1872; Philadelphia Museum of Art) was first exhibited with this title in 1873.[5] The narrative implied by the title emphasizes a potentially romantic relationship between the demure woman on the right who gazes over her shoulder and the man leaning forward out of the shadowy background. In a second painting, *Offering the Panal to the Bullfighter* (fig. 50), Cassatt represented another pair engaged in a flirtation. Here the woman offers water to a bullfighter in which to plunge his *panal*, or honeycomb, for sweet refreshment. The Art Institute's *After the Bullfight* may well have been conceived as a conceptual pendant to the second picture, since together they suggest a tale of imminent seduction and its somewhat amusing aftermath: in the Chicago picture, the woman has disappeared, the *torero* has now draped the red silk scarf loosely over a wooden support, and casually lights a cigarette. In her Spanish pictures, Cassatt revealed a sensuality and wit that have been largely overlooked.[6] Her

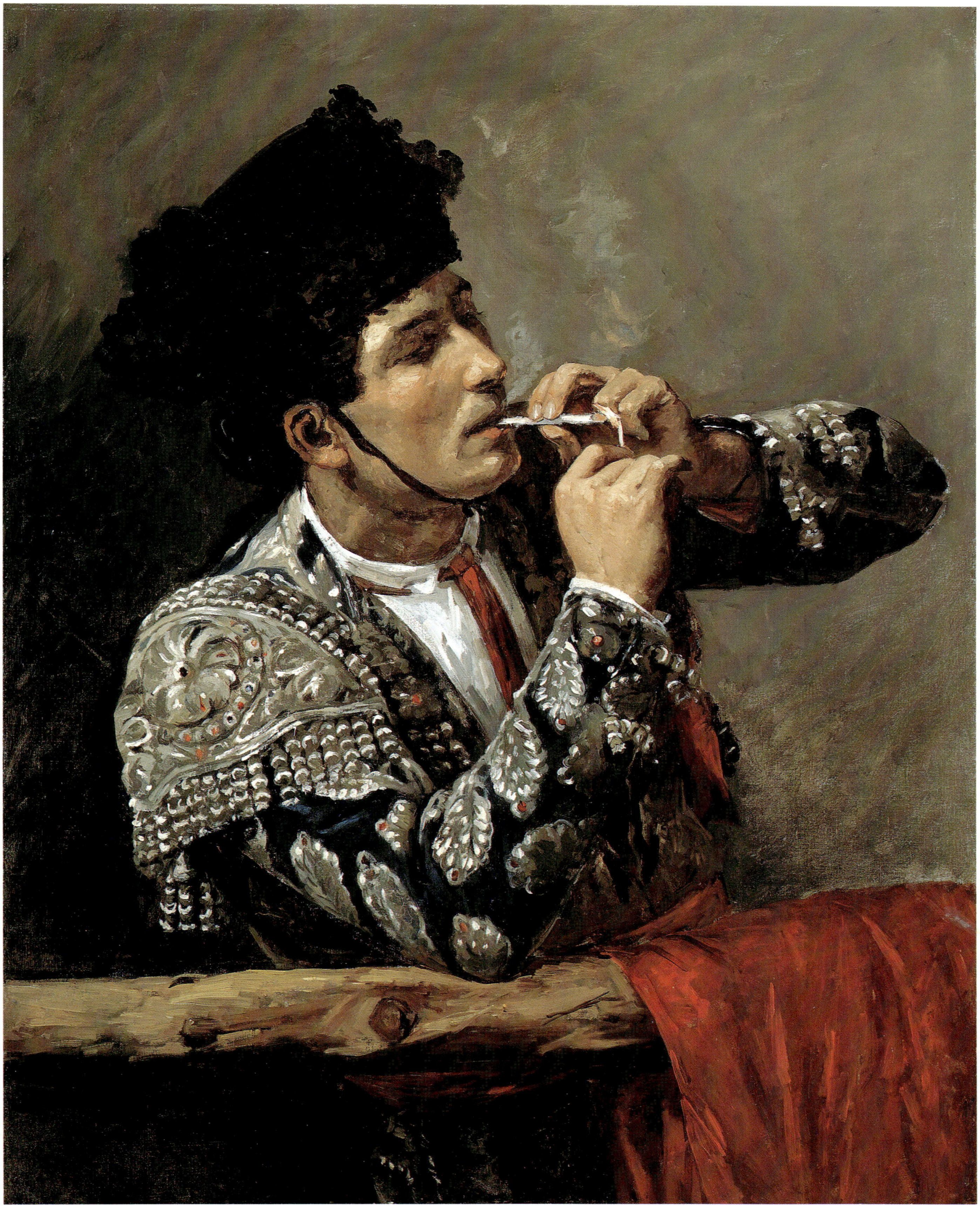

CAT. NO. 95

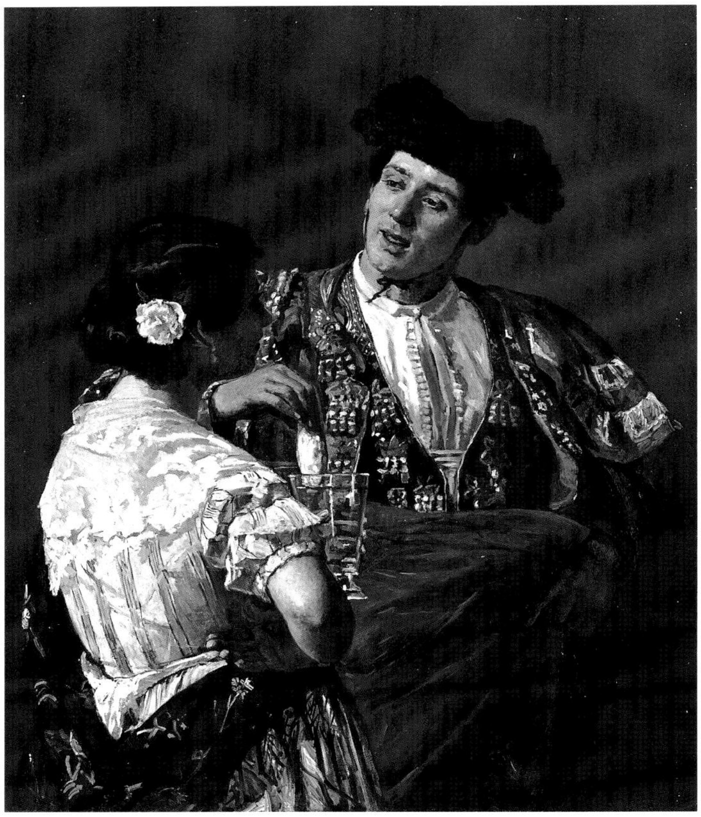

FIG. 50. Mary Cassatt (1844–1926). *Offering the Panal to the Bullfighter*, 1873. Oil on canvas; 100.6 x 85.1 cm (39⅝ x 33½ in.). Sterling and Francine Clark Art Institute, Williamstown, Mass. (1955.1).

subtle investigation of gender relations in Seville magnificently captures the romantic allure of a foreign culture. Having reconciled her admiration for the Old Masters with a more daring technical style, Cassatt approached the contemporaneity and ironic distance of Manet's finest canvases. She returned to Paris in March 1873, and within a few years met Edgar Degas and joined the French Impressionist circle.

NOTES

1. See letter from Mary Cassatt to Emily Sartain, Oct. 5, 1872, in Nancy Mowll Mathews, ed., *Cassatt and Her Circle: Selected Letters* (New York, 1984), p. 103.

2. Théophile Gautier, *Un voyage en Espagne* (Paris, 1908), pp. 73–77.

3. Joel Isaacson, *Manet and Spain: Prints and Drawings*, exh. cat. (Ann Arbor, Museum of Art at the University of Michigan, 1969), p. 9; and *Manet, 1832–1883*, exh. cat. (Paris, Réunion des Musées Nationaux, 1983), p. 240. The picture was purchased directly from the artist by the critic Théodore Duret in 1870, but eventually was acquired, at Cassatt's urging, by her close friends H. O. and Louisine Havemeyer in 1898. See Alice Cooney Frelinghuysen et al., *Splendid Legacy: The Havemeyer Collection*, exh. cat. (New York, Metropolitan Museum of Art, 1993), pp. 27, 30, 352–53.

4. Letter from Mary Cassatt to Emily Sartain, Oct. 27 [1872], in Mathews (note 1), p. 109.

5. See *Exhibition of Paintings, Engravings, Drawings, and Works of Household Art in the Cincinnati Industrial Exposition*, exh. cat. (1873), cat. no. 184, described in the catalogue as "The Flirtation: A Balcony in Seville. For Sale. A realistic yet picturesque group, whose dusky faces and brilliant Andalusian dress afford fine opportunity for rich contrasts of color. The firm and accurate drawing of the figures is specially noticable."

6. The exception is M. Elizabeth Boone, "Bullfights and Balconies: Flirtations and Majismo in Mary Cassatt's Spanish Paintings of 1872–73," *American Art* 9, 1 (spring 1995), pp. 54–71.

96. WALTER SHIRLAW (1838–1909)

Toning the Bell, 1874

Oil on canvas; 101.6 x 76.2 cm (40 x 30 in.)

Signed, lower left: *Walter Shirlaw / 1874*

Friends of American Art Collection, 1938.1280

Walter Shirlaw painted *Toning the Bell* during his student years in Munich, where in 1870 at age thirty-two he began his studies at the Royal Academy.[1] Perhaps Shirlaw's best-known work, the painting was exhibited to great acclaim at no fewer than three World's Fairs: the 1876 Centennial Exhibition in Philadelphia, the 1893 World's Columbian Exposition in Chicago, and the 1915 Panama–Pacific Exposition in San Francisco. On the occasion of Shirlaw's memorial exhibition in 1911, the painting was again singled out as the work that established his reputation. The artist spent his early years as a banknote engraver, first in New York City for the American Bank Note Company and then at the Western Note Engraving Company in Chicago.[2] During his apprenticeship at the American Bank Note Company, Shirlaw enrolled in evening classes at the National Academy of Design and debuted at its Annual Exhibition in 1861 with *Musical Appeal* (1861; private collection).[3]

From 1870 to 1877, Shirlaw followed a typical course of study in Munich: he studied life drawing, with George Raab; then painting, with Alexander Wagner; and finally composition, with Arthur Ramberg and Wilhelm Lindenschmidt. An early biographer commented on his choice of teachers: "Shirlaw liked Raab for his wonderful accuracy of characteristics; Wagner, for his movement, vim, and vitality; . . . Ramberg, for his refinement of composition."[4] More structured than the Parisian atelier system, the Munich Royal Academy imposed upon students a uniform course of instruction that emphasized the study of the Old Masters. The realistic figures, the

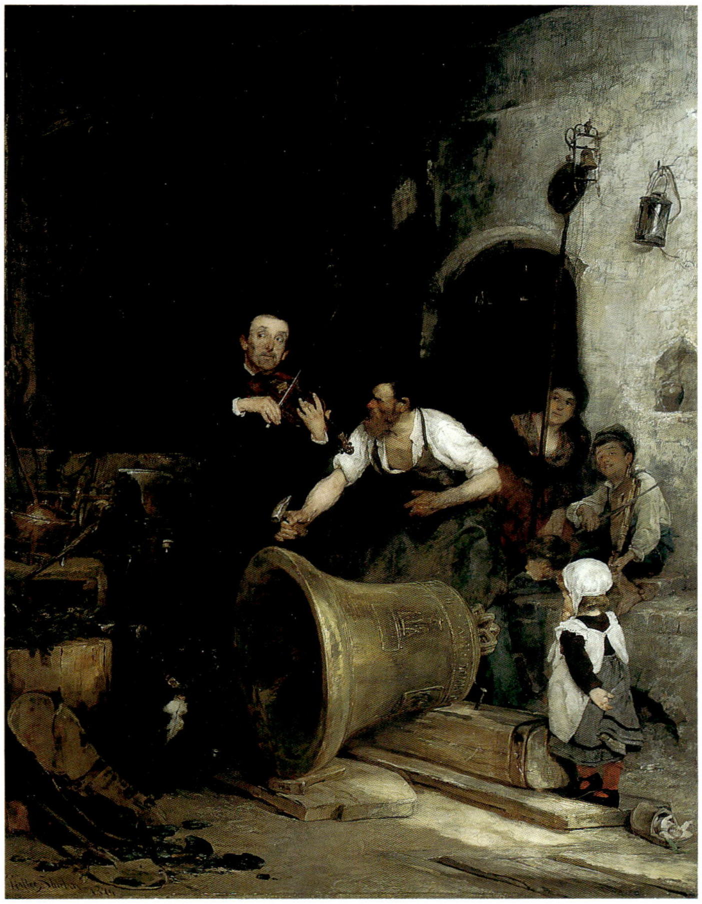

CAT. NO. 96

limited palette, and the strong contrasts of *Toning the Bell* all reflect the training students received in Munich.

Because of his considerable talent, Shirlaw received a great deal of support and attention at the Royal Academy. Around 1874, during his tenure with Ramberg, he won a scholarship that provided him with a studio and a stipend for models and material. In exchange for this generous package, the Academy required Shirlaw to exhibit work at the end of each term. *Toning the Bell* was the first canvas he completed to fulfill this obligation.[5] This work, like most of the artist's popular pictures from his Munich years—including *Sheep Shearing in the Bavarian Highlands* (1876; private collection) and *Good Morning* (c. 1876; Detroit Institute of Arts)—is a genre picture inspired by close observation of Bavarian peasant life.

Critics often praised Shirlaw for his exacting use of accessories and details to construct elaborate allegories. In a manner similar to that of seventeenth-century Dutch artists Jan Steen and Adriaen Brouwer, he used musical themes and scenes from everyday life to embody moral, religious, and social issues. In *Toning the Bell*, for example, the visual correspondence between bell founder and violinist alludes to the shared nobility of the craftsman and the fine artist. The laurel wreath that rests on the stone shelf to the left and the crow on a string directly above, both symbols that relate to the mythological god Apollo, help sustain this reading.[6]

The religious iconography of the painting adds to its meaning. The image visible on the side of the bell is the crucifixion of Christ, which is referred to as well by the nail protruding from the wooden beam on which the bell rests, with the words "Anno Domini" inscribed above. The figures gathered around the bell not only watch the bell founder and the violin-playing cleric, but form pairs of opposites: a young girl and her doll; this young girl and the woman in the door; and a dog and a crow.[7] The bell founder's extended arm intersects with the neck of the violin forming, in effect, a second cross; he has removed his hat and bends as if genuflecting to the cleric. These religious connotations liken the suffering of the artist (whether crafts-

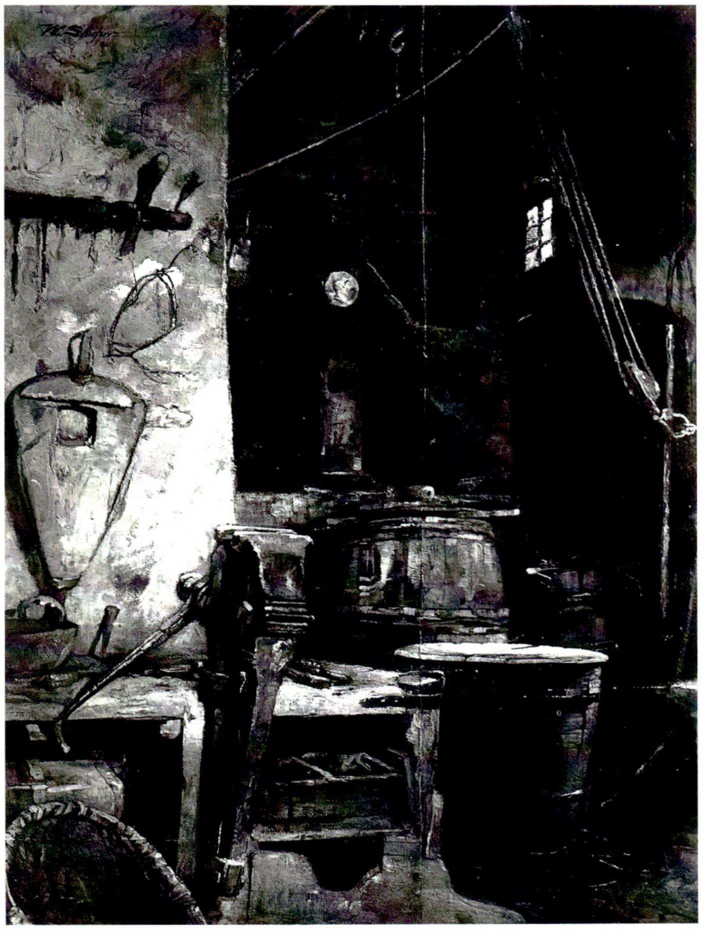

FIG. 51. Walter Shirlaw (1838–1909). *Bell Foundry, Germany*, c. 1874. Oil on paper board; 73.4 x 56.7cm (29¼ x 22⅜ in.). National Museum of American Art, Smithsonian Institution, Washington, D.C., Gift of Mrs. Walter Shirlaw (1913.11.2).

man, musician, or painter) to that of Christ and suggest that art ennobles all—human and animal alike.

Shirlaw produced many painted sketches for *Toning the Bell* that attest to his interest in the characterization and expressiveness of the violinist, and his careful planning of the composition. A page of drawings at the Cooper-Hewitt National Design Museum, New York, features detailed renderings of a violin, the fingering of a string on a violin, and a hand holding a mallet (probably a study for the bell founder). *Bell Foundry, Germany* (fig. 51), which explored the setting of *Toning the Bell*, exhibits a freedom of handling and vitality that the artist sought to restrain in the oil.[8]

NOTES

1. Other American artists who studied in Munich included William Merritt Chase, J. Frank Currier, Frank Duveneck, and Toby Rosenthal. Shirlaw was particularly close to Chase and Duveneck; they were sometimes referred to as the "Holy Triumvirate," "The Holy Trinity," and "The Father, Son, and Holy Ghost." For more on artists training in Munich, see Michael Quick, "Munich and American Realism," in *Munich and American Realism in the Nineteenth Century*, exh. cat. (Sacramento, Calif., E. B. Crocker Art Gallery, 1976), pp. 21–36.

2. Shirlaw worked at the American Bank Note Company as an apprentice between 1852 and 1858. He returned to the engraving firm in 1862 and stayed for eighteen months. In 1865 he accepted a position as superintendent at the Western Note Engraving Company, where he remained until 1868. While in Chicago, Shirlaw helped found the Chicago Academy of Design, precursor of The Art Institute of Chicago.

3. This painting anticipates *Toning the Bell* in its genre subject and its focus on a violinist, in this case a child. Other works by Shirlaw that portray musical themes include *Little Street Musicians* (1862; location unknown), *The Old Violinist* (date unknown; Davenport Museum of Art, Iowa), and *Kapellmeister* (date and location unknown).

4. T. H. Bartlett, "Walter Shirlaw," in Walter Montgomery, ed., *American Art and American Art Collections* (Boston, 1889), p. 57.

5. James Cooke, "Individualism and Tradition: Walter Shirlaw and the American Artist's Experience in Munich" (M.A. thesis, University of Illinois at Urbana-Champaign, 1988), pp. 19–20. Special thanks to Mr. Cooke for sharing his work and contributing his expertise to the writing of this entry.

6. Ibid., pp. 23–28.

7. The compositional practice of placing symmetrical pairs of opposites around the cross in a crucifixion scene can be traced to medieval iconography.

8. Other studies include a wash drawing of the violinist (Corcoran Gallery of Art, Washington, D.C.) and a small, polished oil sketch of the same subject (Mead Art Museum, Amherst College, Amherst, Mass.). A preliminary oil study for *Toning the Bell* was in the collection of William T. Evans in 1913 (see *Illustrated Catalogue of the Collection of American Paintings Formed by the Widely Known Amateur William T. Evans* [New York, 1913], no. 22); the location of this painting has been unknown since 1954.

97. JOHN SINGER SARGENT (1856–1925)

Rehearsal of the Pasdeloup Orchestra at the Cirque d'Hiver, 1876/78

Oil on canvas; 93 x 73 cm (36 5/8 x 28 3/4 in.)
Signed, lower left: *To G Henschel / John S. Sargent*
Anonymous Loan, 81.1972

Painted during Sargent's student years in Paris, *Rehearsal of the Pasdeloup Orchestra at the Cirque d'Hiver* epitomizes the energy of his early experiments with Impressionistic style. Vigorous brushwork, skewed perspective, and tonal control synthesize the artist's visual and aural perception of the scene; Sargent looked, listened, and recorded simultaneously. Fellow painter and friend William Coffin recalled the artist's frequent trips to the Cirque d'Hiver (Winter Circus) and his production of this painting:

> I remember how much we used to like to go to the Colonne concerts at the Châtelet, and to those given by Maître Pasdeloup at the Cirque d'Hiver, on Sunday afternoons. . . . Sargent, who dearly loved the music, was struck by the odd picturesqueness of the orchestra at Pasdeloup's, seen in the middle of the amphitheater, the musicians' figures foreshortened from the high point of view on the rising benches, the necks of the bass-viols sticking up above their heads, the white sheets of music illuminated by little lamps on the racks, and the violin-bows moving in unison. While he listened he looked, and one day he took a canvas and painted his impression. He made an effective picture of it, broad, and full of color.[1]

Coffin's description of the painting and its spontaneous brushwork suggest that it was painted on site. Paint is freely handled with little concern for the rendering of detail, thin washes collide with thick impasto, a phantom chandelier hangs from the ceiling, whole sections of musicians are suggested by broad strokes of black punctuated by spots of light, and the canvas displays many areas of nebulous paint. Curved maroon bands suggest the tiers of the amphitheater where audience members sit like notes on a musical score. The clowns in the foreground burst with color and allude to the dual purpose of the Cirque d'Hiver—a site where popular and "high" culture seamlessly converge.

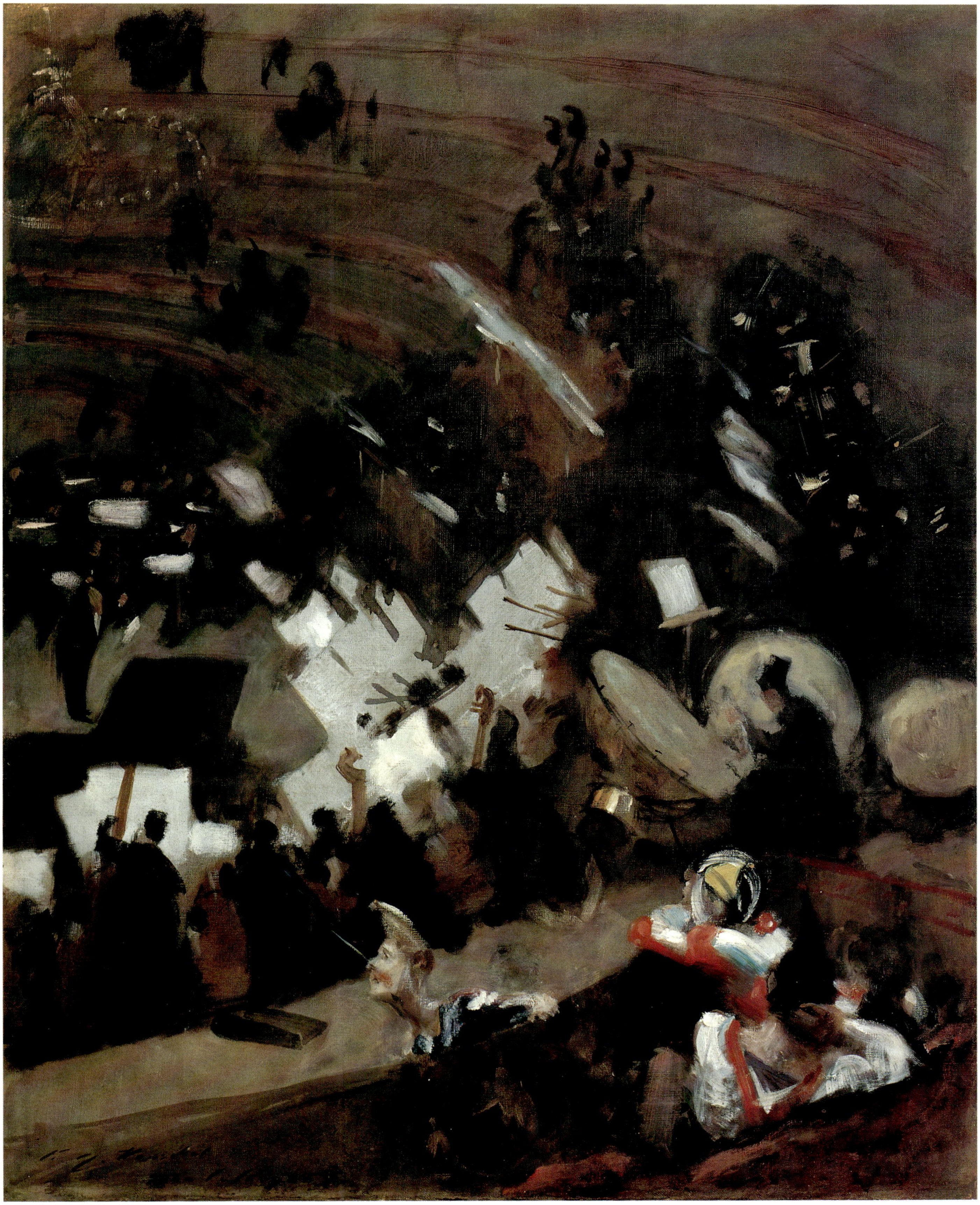

CAT. NO. 97

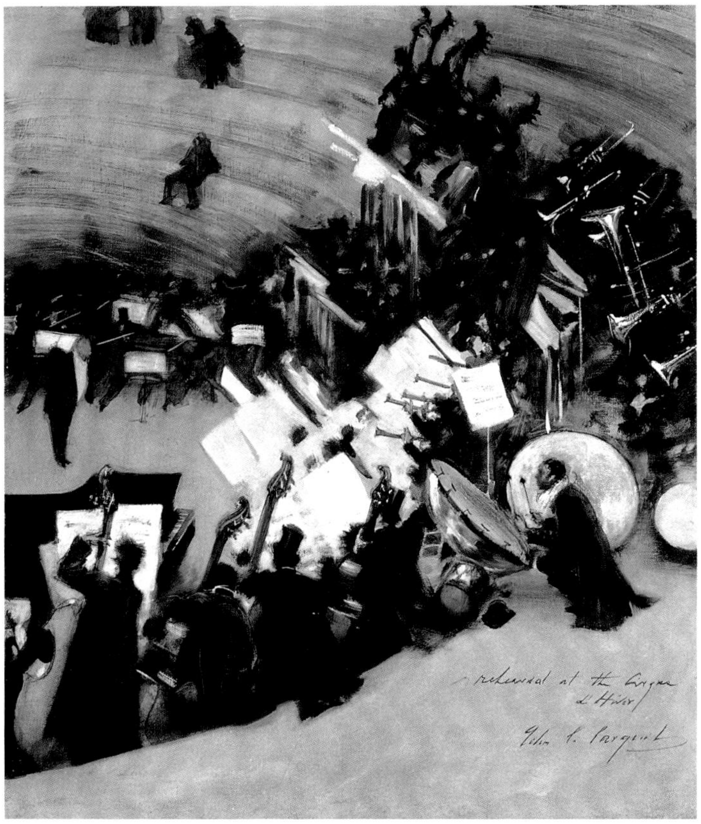

FIG. 52. John Singer Sargent (1856–1925). *Rehearsal of the Pasdeloup Orchestra at the Cirque d'Hiver,* 1876/78. Oil on canvas; 55.2 x 46.3 cm (21¾ x 13¼ in.). Museum of Fine Arts, Boston (22.598).

Jules Étienne Pasdeloup (1819–1887) conducted rehearsals of his orchestra, free to the public, at the Cirque d'Hiver on Sunday afternoons. Pasdeloup was best known for his Concerts Populaires, held at the Cirque Napoléon (the earlier incarnation of the Cirque d'Hiver) between 1861 and 1870, which aimed to introduce classical music to a broad public. During his lifetime, the conductor consistently showcased the work of composers such as Wagner and Schumann, who were little known in France.[2] Many years after it was painted, Sargent appropriately presented this work of a conductor and his orchestra to Sir George Henschel, a renowned English composer, conductor, and musician.[3]

The date of this work is unclear. Early Sargent biographers Evan Charteris and Charles Merrill Mount date the work 1876 and 1878 respectively, but cite no sources for their dates.[4] A provocative comparison with similar types of works exhibited in the 1876 Impressionist exhibition may provide clues to the date, however. That exhibition opened in April of that year at 11 Rue le Peletier in Paris—in time for Sargent to view the show before departing for the United States in mid-May. While there is no hard evidence that Sargent visited the exhibition, *Rehearsal of the Pasdeloup Orchestra* formally and thematically corresponds to two paintings Edgar Degas submitted to the Impressionist show: *The Dance Class* (1874; Metropolitan Museum of Art, New York) and *The Ballet from "Robert le Diable"* (1876; Victoria and Albert Museum, London).[5] Although Sargent painted many actors, actresses, musicians, and singers during his career, they were generally produced as portraits rather than public scenes of performance.[6]

When viewed alongside Sargent's composition, Degas's 1876 pictures provide a compelling formal comparison. Each uses an oblique vantage point that disorients the viewer by recreating the sensation of watching a performance from a balcony. Sargent employed this device very rarely in his work; it reflects the influence of Degas and, possibly, of Japanese prints.[7] Similarly, scenes of popular entertainment were unusual in Sargent's work (even though he regularly attended performances), but were favored subjects of the Impressionists—particularly Cassatt and Degas.[8] Sargent, who was not formally part of the Impressionist circle, nonetheless inhabited two distinct Parisian art worlds: the academic realm, represented by his portraiture and Salon entries; and the avant-garde, independent circle of the Impressionists.

The existence of a smaller, more detailed grisaille painting of the same subject at the Museum of Fine Arts, Boston (fig. 52) has further confused the dating of *Rehearsal of the Pasdeloup Orchestra.* The scholar Richard Ormond noted, "David McKibbin suggests that this [the Art Institute's picture] was probably the original, and that [the version in the Museum of

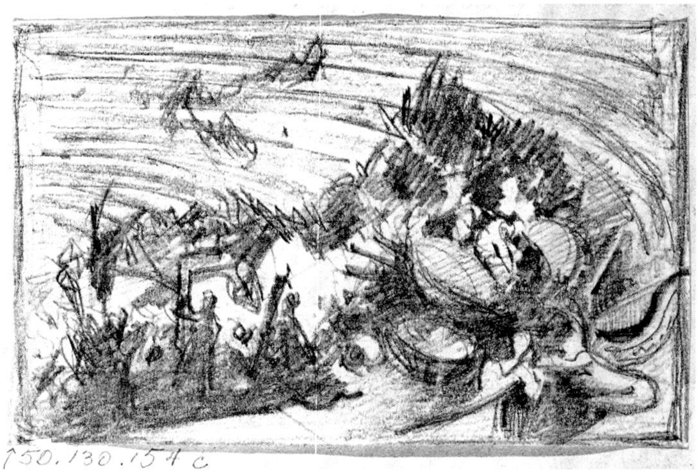

FIG. 53. John Singer Sargent. *Flower,* 1876. Pencil on paper; 8.6 x 13.7 cm (3⅜ x 5⅜ in.). Metropolitan Museum of Art, New York, Gift of Mrs. Francis Ormond, 1950 (50.130.154C).

Fine Arts, Boston] may have been specially painted for the black-and-white illustration in H. Bacon, *Parisian Art and Artists* (Boston, 1883)."[9] Like the Art Institute's version, the Boston painting has been dated both 1876 and 1878. A related sketch at the Metropolitan Museum of Art in New York (fig. 53) further supports an earlier date for the Art Institute's work. Although the painting has a more vertical format, the sketch shares a similar orchestral arrangement and includes the masked clowns sitting in the box seats in the lower left corner.[10]

NOTES

1. William A. Coffin, "Sargent and His Painting," *Century Magazine* 52, 2 (June 1896), p. 172.

2. For information on Jules Étienne Pasdeloup, see Elisabeth Bernard, "Jules Étienne Pasdeloup," in Stanley Sadie, ed., *The New Grove Dictionary of Music and Musicians* (London, 1980), vol. 14, pp. 259–60.

3. For more about George Henschel and his relationship with Sargent, see George Henschel, *Musings and Memories of a Musician* (London, 1918), pp. 331–36. Sargent and Henschel met in 1887, and Sargent painted Henschel's portrait in 1889 (now in the collection of Ira and Nancy Koger); it is not known when Sargent presented *Rehearsal of the Pasdeloup Orchestra* to Henschel.

4. Evan Charteris, *John Sargent* (New York, 1927), p. 43; and Charles Merrill Mount, *John Singer Sargent: A Biography* (New York, 1955), p. 442.

5. *The New Painting: Impressionism, 1874–1886*, exh. cat. (Fine Arts Museums of San Francisco and National Gallery of Art, Washington, D.C., 1986), pp. 144–86.

6. See entry on Sargent's *Mrs. George Swinton* (cat. no. 141) for more information on the artist's portraits of singers.

7. Sargent most likely viewed an array of Japanese prints while visiting the Centennial Exhibition in Philadelphia during his 1876 summer sojourn in the United States.

8. Patricia Hills notes that *Rehearsal of the Pasdeloup Orchestra at the Cirque d'Hiver* is one of the few subject pictures Sargent painted in Paris. Another she mentions is *In the Luxembourg Gardens* (1879; Philadelphia Museum of Art), which is also a Parisian scene. See Patricia Hills, "The Formation of a Style and Sensibility," in Hills, ed., *John Singer Sargent*, exh. cat. (New York, Whitney Museum of American Art, 1986), p. 31.

9. Richard Ormond, *John Singer Sargent: Paintings, Drawings, Watercolors* (New York, 1970), p. 236. The painting in the Museum of Fine Arts, Boston, was once owned by Henry Bacon; it was published in Bacon's 1883 Boston edition of *Parisian Art and Artists*.

10. Stephanie Herdrich, a research assistant in the Department of American Paintings and Sculpture at the Metropolitan Museum of Art, New York, first discovered the relationship between the sketch and the Art Institute's painting and generously brought it to our attention.

98. JOHN SINGER SARGENT (1856–1925)

Venetian Glass Workers, 1880/82

Oil on canvas; 56.5 x 84.5 cm (22¼ x 33¼ in.)
Signed, lower left: *John S. Sargent*
Mr. and Mrs. Martin A. Ryerson Collection, 1933.1217

Richly painted in gray and black tonalities illuminated by swathes of light, *Venetian Glass Workers* is one of John Singer Sargent's many genre scenes featuring workers painted at the beginning of the 1880s.[1] In this painting, Sargent shifts pictorial interest from the ostensible subjects—the workers—to the contrast between their dank surroundings and the scintillating products of their labor, subtly noting the separation of native production and tourist consumption of Venetian glassware. Sargent's emphasis on his artistic technique also subverts modes of the urban picturesque commonly practiced by artists working in the Italian city during the second half of the nineteenth century. Enigmatic and formally daring, the Venetian genre pictures are among the most satisfying in Sargent's oeuvre.

The laborers in *Venetian Glass Workers* are participating in a process that transforms long, thin glass tubes into beads. The woman in the right foreground is using a cutting tool, the *zocco*, to slice glass tubes into uniform lengths that will be placed in a metal drum with a mixture of lime, carbonate, sand, carbon, and water.[2] When the drum is heated and turned, the mixture acts as an abrasive that smooths the edges of the cut glass and forms rounded beads. Women employed as bead stringers, like those depicted by Sargent in *Venetian Bead Stringers* (1880–82; Albright-Knox Art Gallery, Buffalo, New York), prepared the multi-hued, sparkling bits of glass for sale.

Herman Melville rhapsodized about this process of making glass beads in an 1857 journal entry: "Drawing the rods like twine—making, cutting, rounding, polishing, coloring a secret."[3] Like Melville, Sargent captured the poetic expressiveness of glass. In *Venetian Glass Workers*, bundles of glass tubes are suggested by pale blue and white strokes of the brush; the marks left by the bristles delineate the separate tubes. The flash of the glass as it reflects the dim light admitted through the barred window in the upper left starkly contrasts with the deep black of the interior that shrouds the six workers. The entire composition is anchored spatially and thematically by the il-

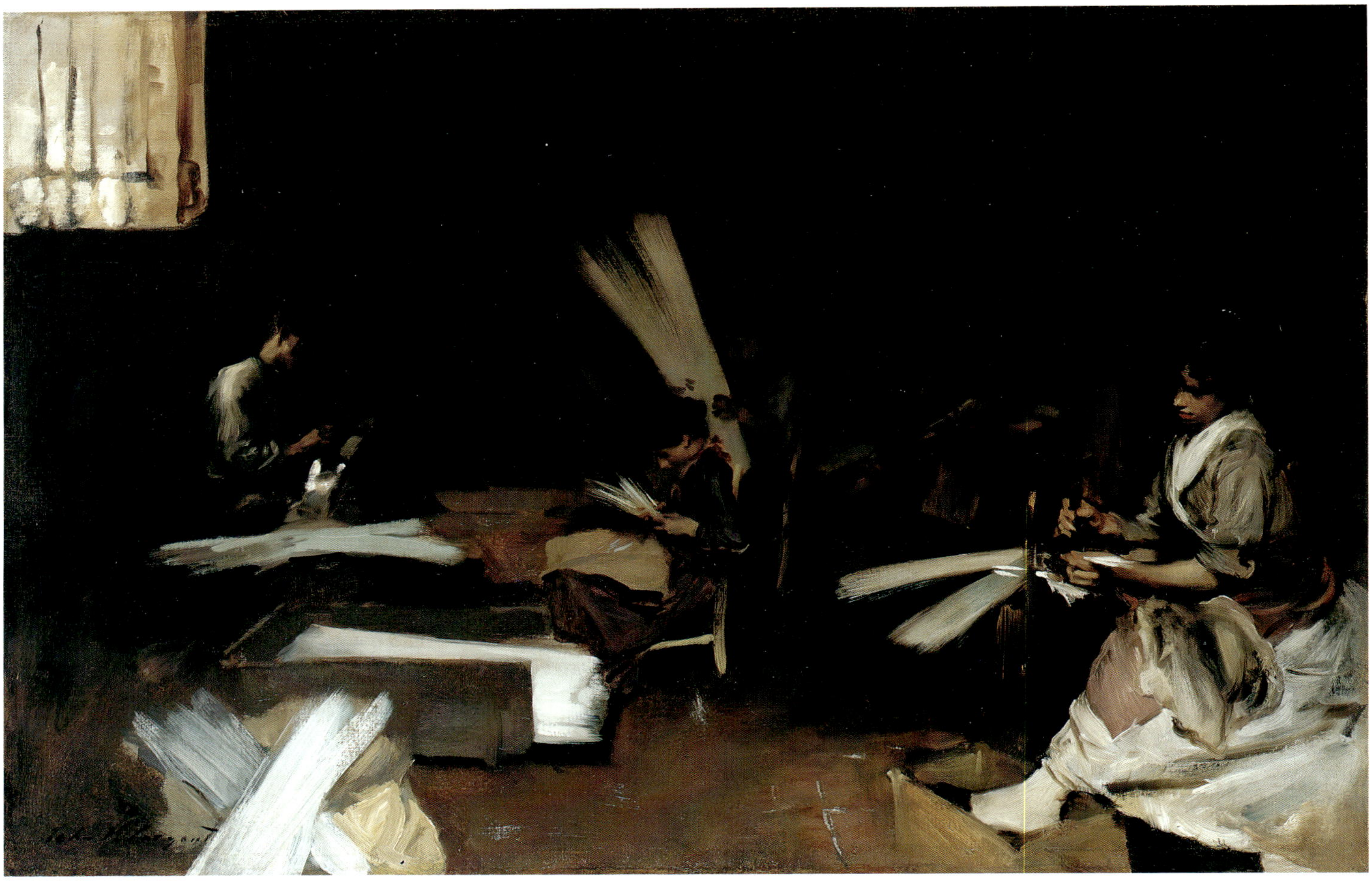

CAT. NO. 98

luminated female worker in the right foreground. The most visible figure, she is one point of a unifying triangle formed by one bundle of glass in the left foreground and another held aloft by the female worker in the center of the canvas.

As a whole, Sargent's Venetian scenes form a stylistically coherent group, but two in particular present labor in a manner similar to *Venetian Glass Workers*: *Venetian Bead Stringers* and *Venetian Water Carriers* (fig. 54).[4] The former represents the drudgery of stringing beads through the workers' slumped postures and the barren interior. Alternatively, *Venetian Water Carriers* depicts the strenuous task of hauling heavy buckets of water up from a deep well before carrying them to households without plumbing. The wide brushstrokes used to represent the glass bundles in *Venetian Glass Workers* reappear in the paving stones and derelict brick in *Venetian Water Carriers*. The women in all three paintings are not prettified by their labor; they strain their arms and backs in the awkward poses dictated by their tasks.

Sargent's Venetian scenes differ greatly in tone from Robert Frederick Blum's paintings of similar subjects. Like *Venetian Glass Workers*, Blum's *Venetian Lacemakers* (1887; Cincinnati Art Museum) depicts women working at an arduous task, but the saturated palette and garrulous atmosphere of the latter painting create the effect of workers enjoying their labor. Sargent's debt to Diego Velázquez, whose work he was introduced to in Émile Auguste Carolus-Duran's studio and through trips to Spain, may be partially responsible for his unusual approach. Sargent's use of a dark, tonal palette, avoidance of the picturesque, and manipulation of compositional features, such as using light for jarring psychological effect, have been cited as examples of Velázquez's influence on his work. Throughout the 1880s, Sargent combined these painterly techniques to great advantage, producing thrilling works like *El Jaleo* (1882; Isabella Stewart Gardner Museum, Boston) and *Venetian Glass Workers* that engage the viewer with their ambiguity and complexity.

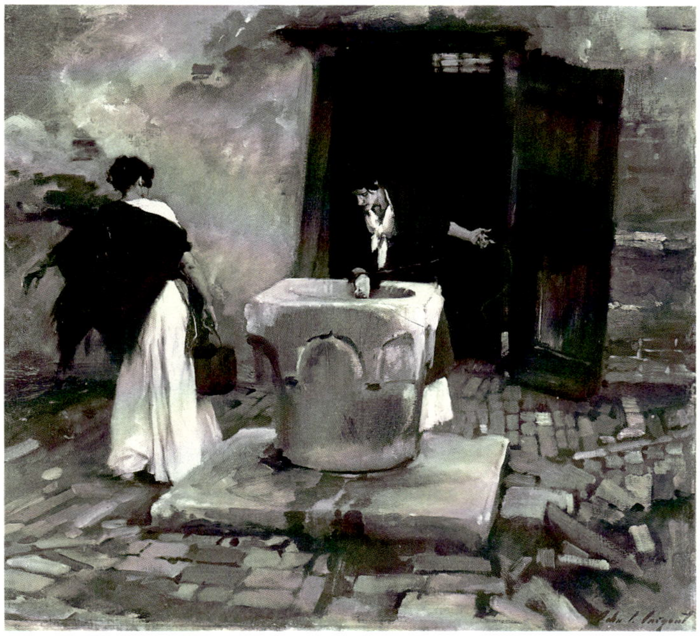

FIG. 54. John Singer Sargent (1856–1925). *Venetian Water Carriers*, c. 1882. Oil on canvas; 64.5 x 70.5 cm (25⅜ x 27¾ in.). Worcester Art Museum, Worcester, Mass. (1911.30).

NOTES

1. Other Venetian scenes include *Venetian Water Carriers* (c. 1882; Worcester Art Museum, Mass.); *Venetian Interiors* (c. 1882; Museum of Art, Carnegie Institute, Pittsburgh, Penn.); *Venetian Bead Stringers* (1880/82; Albright-Knox Art Gallery, Buffalo, N.Y.); and *The Bead Stringers of Venice* (n.d.; National Gallery of Ireland, Dublin). Sargent's Venetian scenes are notoriously difficult to date. He made two trips to Venice—in 1880 and then again in 1882. None of the works connected to either trip is dated. For an excellent overview of Sargent's career during these years, see Marc Simpson with Richard Ormond and H. Barbara Weinberg, *Uncanny Spectacle: The Public Career of the Young John Singer Sargent*, exh. cat. (Williams-town, Mass., Sterling and Francine Clark Art Institute, 1997).

2. Peter Francis, Jr., *The Story of Venetian Beads* (Lake Placid, N.Y., 1979), pp. 7–8.

3. Quoted in Margaretta Lovell, *Venice: The American View, 1860–1920*, exh. cat. (Fine Arts Museums of San Francisco, 1984), p. 103.

4. Another connection exists between *Venetian Glass Workers* and *Venetian Water Carriers*. According to a letter of Jan. 12, 1912, from John Singer Sargent to Charles Hovey Pepper, previous owner of *Venetian Glass Workers*, the Art Institute's painting was one of two he exchanged with the "late owner" (Friedrich Wilhelm Carl Bechstein) for "a piano of his make"; for this letter, see roll NMc 10 France 480, Archives of American Art, Smithsonian Institution, Washington, D.C. The other painting apparently was *Venetian Water Carriers*, as evidenced by a letter of Mar. 2, 1912, from William Macbeth to Phillip J. Gentner of the Worcester Art Museum; a copy of this letter is in the Files of the Department of American Arts, The Art Institute of Chicago, thanks to Susan Strickler and David Brigham of the Worcester Art Museum.

99. JAMES McNEILL WHISTLER (1834–1903)

Gray and Silver: Old Battersea Reach, 1863

Oil on canvas; 50.9 x 69 cm (20 x 27 in.)
Signed, lower left: *Whistler 63*
Potter Palmer Collection, 1922.449

100. *Trouville (Gray and Green, the Silver Sea)*, 1865

Oil on canvas; 51.5 x 76.9 cm (20¼ x 30⅜ in.)
Signed, lower right: *Whistler*
Potter Palmer Collection, 1922.448

101. *Nocturne: Blue and Gold—Southampton Water*, 1872

Oil on canvas; 50.5 x 76 cm (19⅞ x 29$^{15}/_{16}$ in.)
Signed, lower left: butterfly monogram
The Stickney Fund, 1900.52

James McNeill Whistler pursued marine themes throughout his long career as a painter and printmaker, and within them charted a course toward the modern, sophisticated, and often controversial aesthetic sensibilities that characterize his work. Painted only two years apart, *Gray and Silver: Old Battersea Reach* and *Trouville (Gray and Green, the Silver Sea)* show the artist's increasing interest in Japanese sources and abstract, tonalist sensibilities that culminated in the "Nocturnes" of the 1870s. The two earlier works also represent Whistler's dual loyalties to the depiction of British and French scenes, rivers and oceans, industrial and pleasure crafts. As an American who chose to live as an expatriate in Europe, Whistler is often considered in the company of John Singer Sargent and Mary Cassatt.[1] Born in Lowell, Massachusetts, in 1834, Whistler moved at the age of nine to St. Petersburg, Russia, where his father worked as a civil engineer.[2] The artist traveled to London during this period, and even lived there briefly before returning to the United States with his mother after his father's death in 1849. Whistler did not return to Europe until 1855, when he enrolled at the École Impériale et Spéciale de Dessin in Paris. The following year he entered Charles Gleyre's studio and became immersed in the Parisian art world, which at that time was dominated by realist painters such as Gustave Courbet.

Whistler traveled back and forth between Paris and London

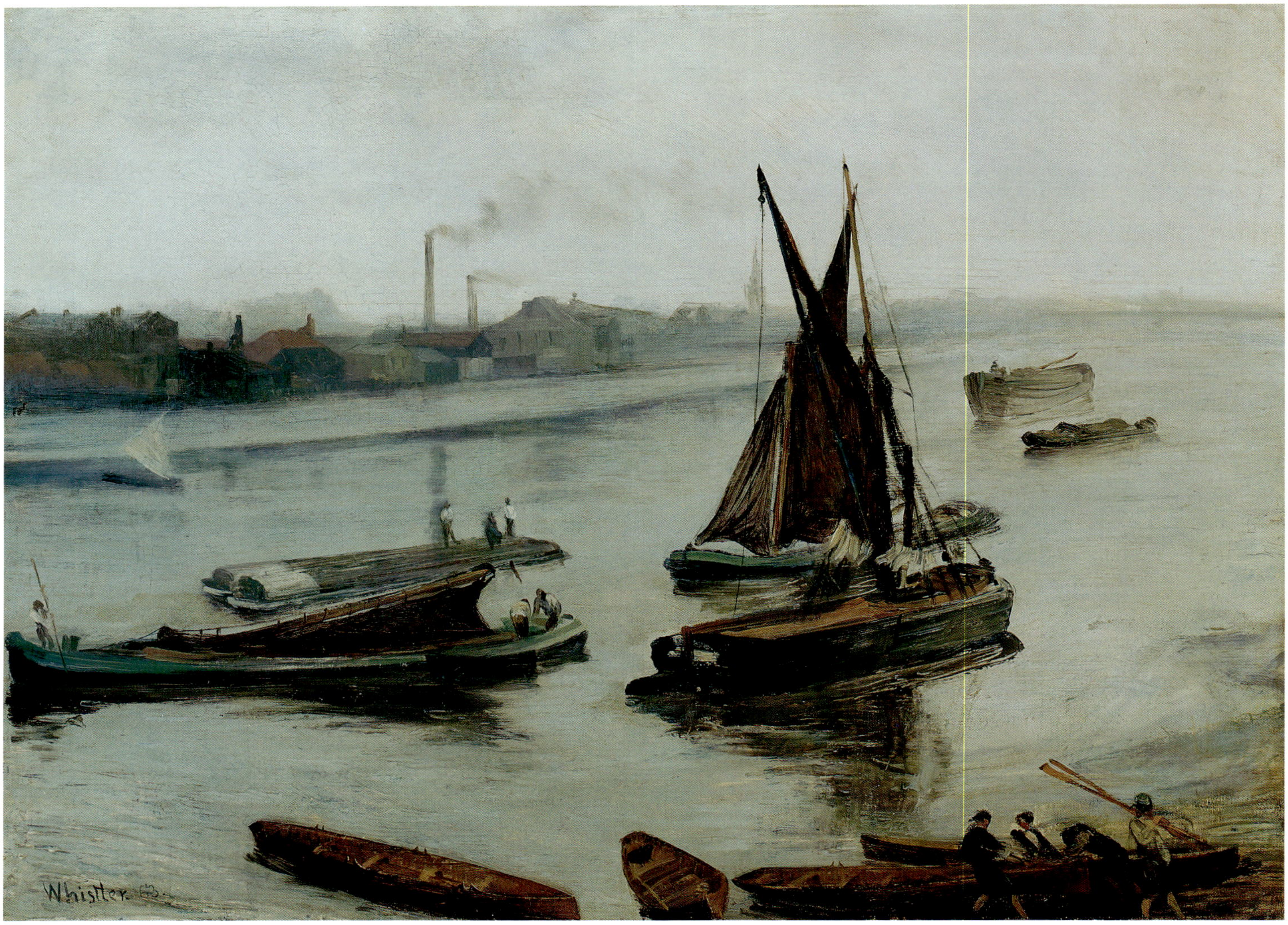

CAT. NO. 99

throughout his life, but this peripatetic existence was intense in the late 1850s and early 1860s. By December 1862, the artist had situated himself in the Chelsea area of London, perhaps at the suggestion of painter Dante Gabriel Rossetti and poet and critic Algernon Swinburne. In March 1863, he took up residence at 7 Lindsey Row, the vantage point from which he depicted Battersea and other Thames scenes.[3] These early Thames scenes show the river as a site of industry rather than of leisure.[4] His choice of a gray and brown palette emphasizes the fogs of pollution that hung over industrial London. Yet Whistler employed this miasma as a pictorial device that shrouds the scene and creates a soft, diffused atmosphere.

Although they appear smudged and blurred, some of the buildings depicted on the Battersea or south side of the river can be identified: the smoking chimneys belong to Morgan's Patent Plumbago Crucible Company's Works and the spire to St. Mary's Church.[5] Further down the river, toward the horizon, is the Battersea Railway Bridge, which opened in 1863. Art historian Robin Spencer described the barges traversing the center of the river as "coal-heavers, preparing to off-load their cargoes at Johnson's coal wharf downstream of Battersea Bridge" and speculated that "the boats in the foreground probably belonged to Greaves's boatyard, located on the Lindsey Row waterfront."[6] Thus Whistler painted a portrait of his new neighborhood and incorporated the scenes that passed by his window every working day, albeit filtering the realism through his interest in Japanese aesthetics.

Trouville (Gray and Green, the Silver Sea) is a seaside scene stripped to essentials: sky, water, and sailing yachts. Whistler traveled to the French resort town in the autumn of 1865 with his partner and model Joanna Hiffernan; there they met Gustave Courbet, who appears in another of Whistler's Trouville

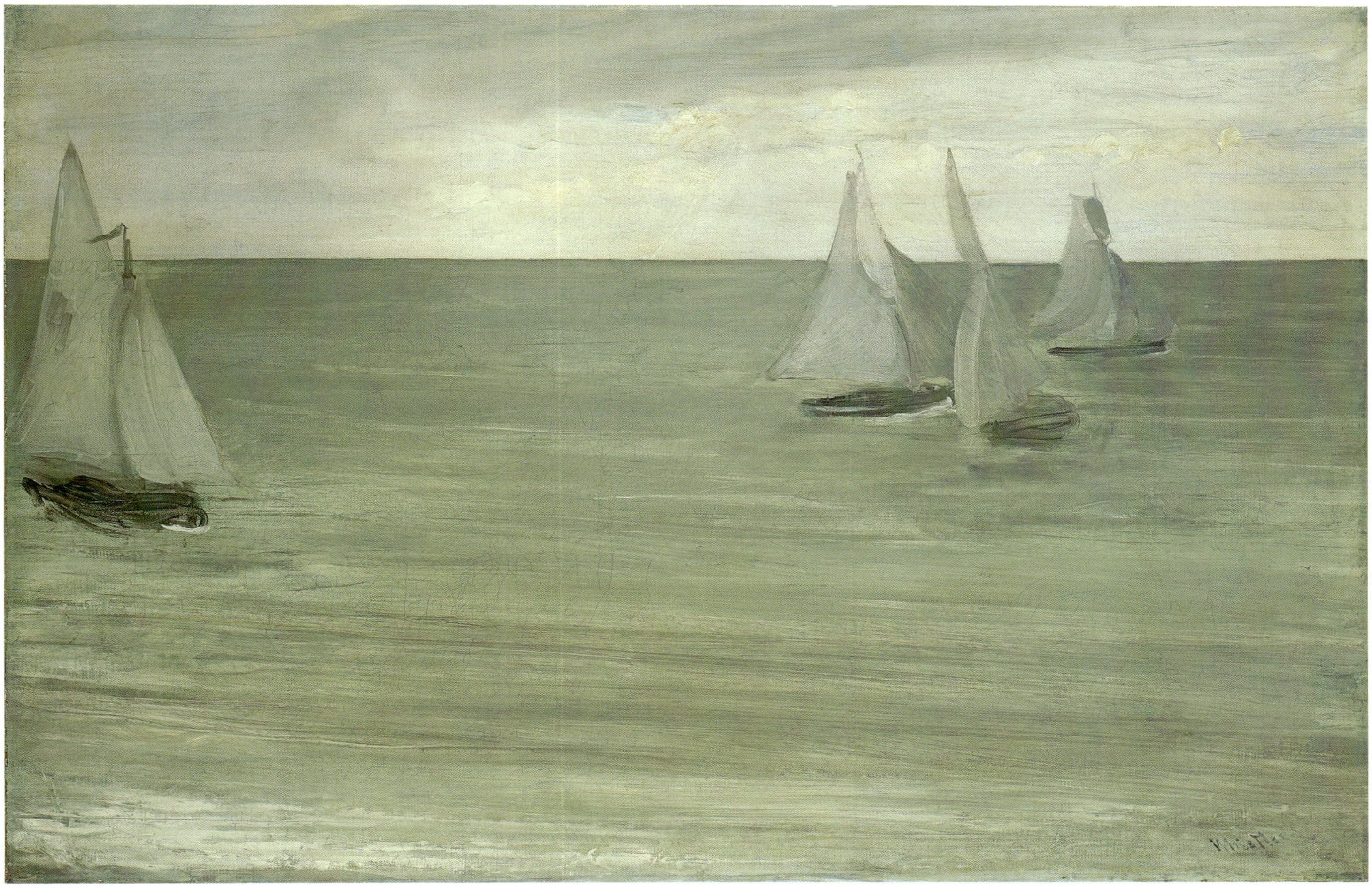

CAT. NO. 100

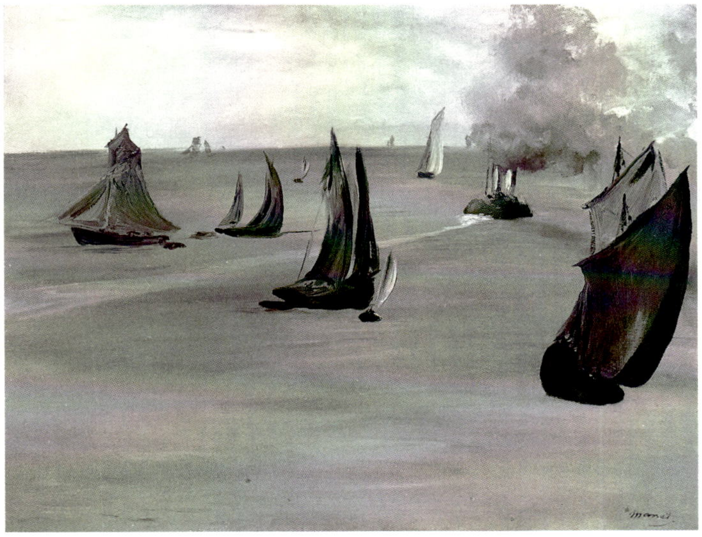

FIG. 55. Édouard Manet (French, 1832–1883). *Departure from Boulogne Harbor*, 1864/65. Oil on canvas; 73.6 x 92.6 cm (29 x 36½ in.). The Art Institute of Chicago, Mr. and Mrs. Potter Palmer Collection, 1922.425.

paintings.[7] Whistler painted at least five works in Trouville, each of which displays a very high horizon and tonalist palette.[8] The artist's sweeping, horizontal strokes reflect the movement of the sea and the yachts that race with the wind. Whistler's French contemporaries, most notably Édouard Manet, painted scenes similar to *Trouville.* Manet's *Departure from Boulogne Harbor* (fig. 55) bears a striking resemblance to Whistler's, although he utilized a more vivid palette and created a busier scene. Both artists were looking to Japanese prints for their compositional effects and painting out-of-doors to capture the spontaneity of their motifs. Interestingly, both of these paintings were owned by Chicagoan Bertha Honoré Palmer, a preeminent collector of Impressionist painting.

Whistler's fascination with the depiction of water culminated in his nocturnes: quiet, night-time scenes of daring simplicity and abstraction. *Nocturne: Blue and Gold — Southampton Water* shows an inlet of the English Channel about eighty miles southwest of London just as the moon is rising.

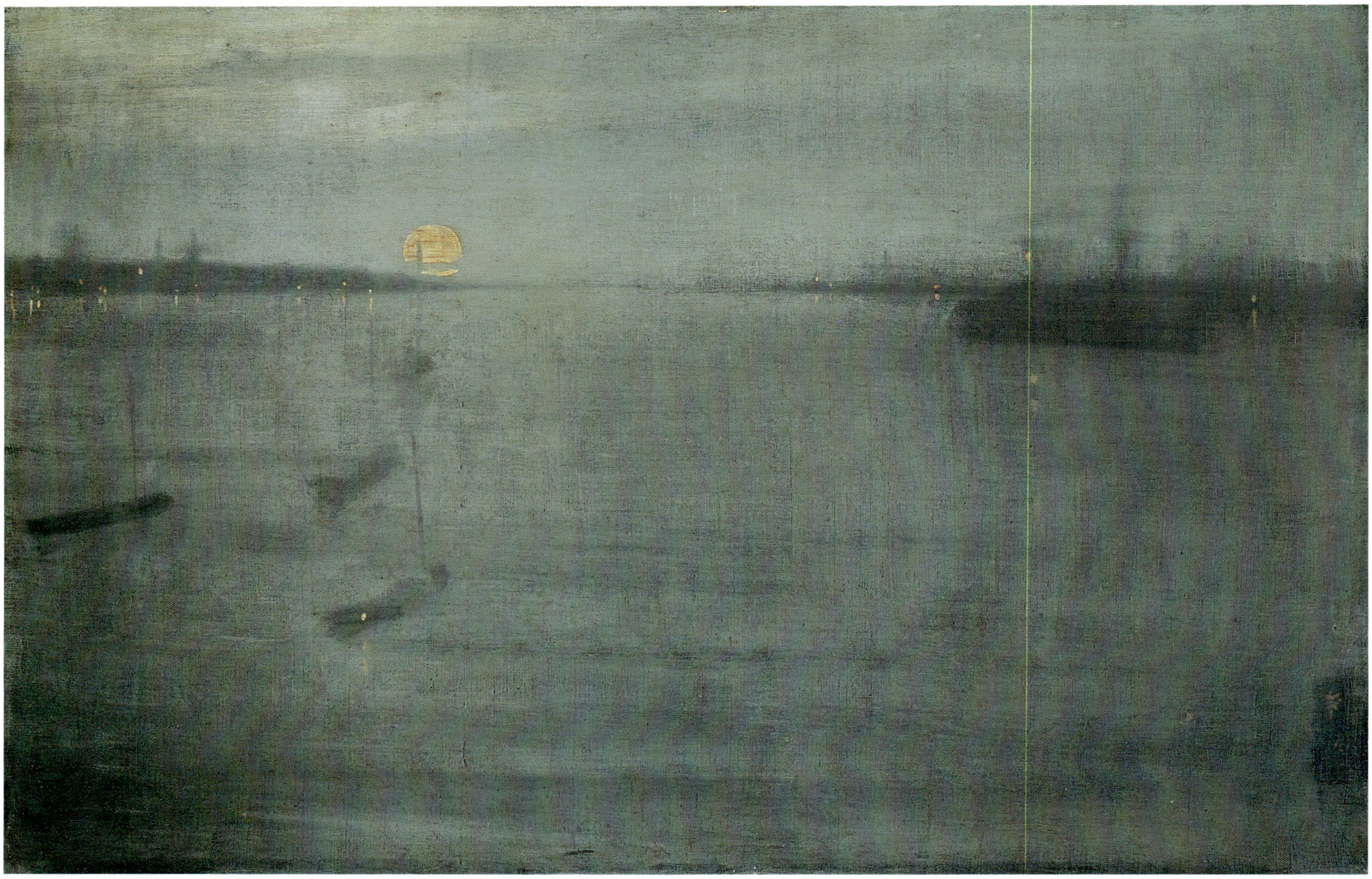

CAT. NO. 101

Although it is dusk, large ships and small boats hover in the port, taking on passengers and preparing to go to sea. Whistler's composition pays little attention to all of this activity; rather, the subtle variations in color and simplified forms create a serene and peaceful atmosphere. The nocturnes, titled in reference not only to their evening subjects but to musical compositions, created a stir when they were first shown in London.[9] Most notably, the critic John Ruskin attacked *Nocturne in Black and Gold: The Falling Rocket* (c. 1875; Detroit Institute of Arts) when it was exhibited at the Grosvenor Gallery. Whistler subsequently sued Ruskin for libel and won.[10]

The Art Institute's painting seems to have met with a more favorable response. Possibly one of the first nocturnes that Whistler exhibited publicly, at the Dudley Gallery in 1872, the canvas matches the description in the *Athenaeum* of one of the works at that venue: "multitudinous shipping on either side with the 'silent highway' in the centre and nearly deserted. The air might be said to be visible, so dense is the deep, warm twilight which obscures all things here. . . . The moon [is] near the dim horizon on our left. . . . The strength of this picture lies not in its verisimilitude, but in the super-subtle arrangement and exquisitely delicate nature of its colour."[11] A reviewer for the *Builder* took a more humorous approach to the nocturnes at the Dudley Gallery: "[Whistler's] 'Nocturn,' whether performed under the influence of 'Grey and Gold' (187) or 'Blue and Silver' (237), is noctidial enough to perplex a Thames waterman as to the time o' day, and that such a pretty blue or pale-grey fog could necessitate the lighting up of the moon and other lamps must perplex him more. . . . Moonshine; moonshine! what a great latitude there is for moonshine!"[12]

Whistler's nocturnes are emblematic of his modernity, showing subsequent generations one path toward nonobjective art. Color and light create a mood that becomes the subject of the work; the place depicted is nearly inconsequential. These three works demonstrate how Whistler gradually minimized the anecdotal details of his paintings to make more abstract paintings. Seen together, they present a coherent view of this artist's evolving vision.

NOTES

1. See, for example, Frederick A. Sweet, *Sargent, Whistler, and Mary Cassatt*, exh. cat. (The Art Institute of Chicago, 1954).

2. The biographical material available on Whistler is vast. Some recent, informative publications include Richard Dorment and Margaret F. MacDonald, *James McNeill Whistler*, exh. cat. (London, Tate Gallery, 1994); and Gordon Fleming, *James Abbott McNeill Whistler: A Life* (New York, 1991).

3. Other Thames scenes from this period include *The Last of Old Westminster* (1862; Museum of Fine Arts, Boston) and *Battersea Reach* (c. 1863; Corcoran Gallery of Art, Washington, D.C.).

4. For a provocative reading of Whistler's Thames scenes, see Kathleen Pyne, "Whistler and the Politics of the Urban Picturesque," *American Art* 8 (summer/fall 1994), pp. 60–77.

5. Robin Spencer, *Whistler* (London, 1990), p. 54.

6. Ibid.

7. Courbet appears in Whistler's *Harmony in Blue and Silver: Trouville* (1865; Isabella Stewart Gardner Museum, Boston).

8. Whistler's Trouville paintings include *Crepuscle in Opal: Trouville* (1865; Toledo Museum of Art, Ohio); *Harmony in Blue and Silver: Trouville* (1865; Isabella Stewart Gardner Museum, Boston); and *The Sea* (1865; Montclair Art Museum, N.J.).

9. Whistler's patron Frederick Leyland suggested the terminology to him.

10. For more about the Whistler/Ruskin trial, see Linda Merrill, *A Pot of Paint: Aesthetics on Trial in Whistler v. Ruskin* (Washington, D.C., 1992).

11. Quoted in Andrew McLaren Young, Margaret MacDonald, Robin Spencer, and Hamish Miles, *The Paintings of James McNeill Whistler* (New Haven, Conn., and London, 1980), p. 71.

12. "Winter Exhibition at the Dudley Gallery," *Builder* 30 (Nov. 23, 1872), p. 929.

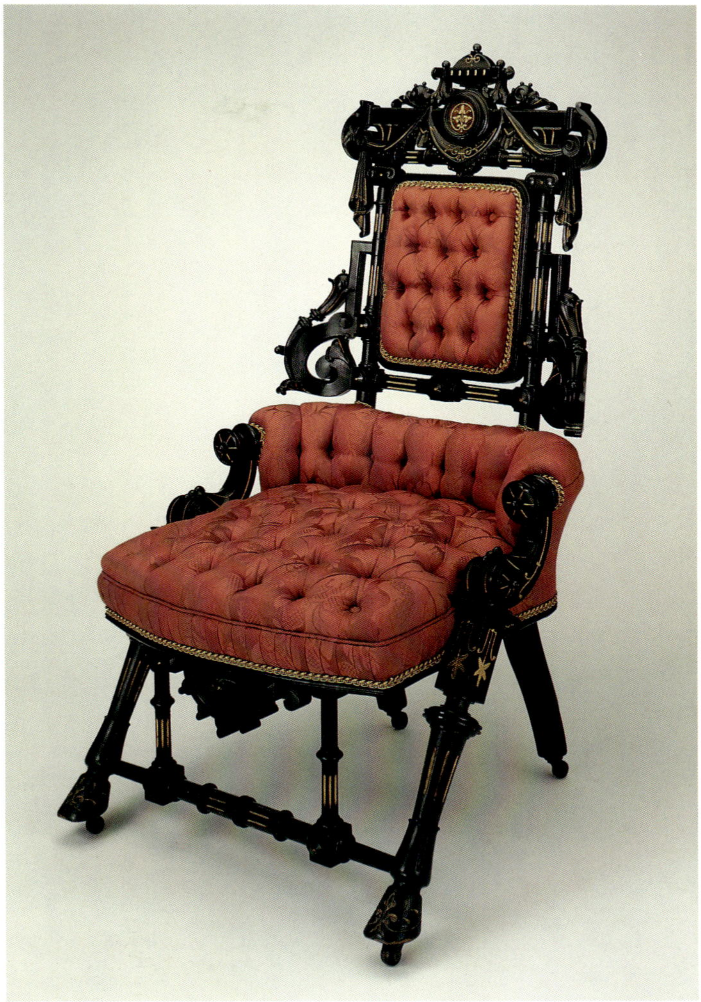

CAT. NO. 102

102. GEORGE JAKOB HUNZINGER (1835–1898)

Armchair, patented 1869

New York
Ebonized walnut with gilt decoration;
139.7 x 61 x 66 cm (55 x 24 x 26 in.)
Stamped on rear of left front leg: *HUNZINGER / N.Y. / PAT. MARCH 30 / 1869*
Perry and Gertrude Herst Endowment, 1996.439

George Hunzinger was born in Tuttlingen, Germany, where his family had been in the cabinetmaking business since the early seventeenth century. He apprenticed as a cabinetmaker in his hometown, but spent the early years of his career as a journeyman in Switzerland. In 1850, along with thousands of other German citizens, he emigrated to North America. He settled in Brooklyn, where in 1866 he opened his own furniture business; in two years, he built up a large and profitable business.[1]

Hunzinger began to apply successfully for patents for his innovative furniture designs by 1861. The patented device used on the Art Institute's chair, which Hunzinger developed in 1869, is a diagonal brace that stretches from the rear of the front feet to the midsection of the seat-back. In his patent application, Hunzinger explained why the brace was a necessary design modification: "The back legs of chairs are very liable to become loosened at the point of connection with the seat. . . . This looseness arises from pressure against the back of the chair, and from the tipping of the chair backward upon the hind legs."[2] This design innovation was a prominent feature in all of Hunzinger's chairs after 1869.

In a rare departure from his usual work, which was free of

historical references,[3] Hunzinger designed this chair in the then newly fashionable "neo-grec" style, which combined Egyptian, Greek, and Roman motifs. This style reflected the myriad combinations and stylistic revivals that abounded in the post–Civil War period. The ebonized and gilt-wood hoof feet incised with lotus blossoms and the pendant drop under the seat rail allude to Egyptian antiquity. The stylized Ionic columns, central medallion, and carved swag on the chair back are classically inspired.

An unusual feature of this Hunzinger design is the carved decoration on the crest rail. Most of his chairs relied instead on lathe-turned elements that resembled pieces of an engine or lengths of pipe fitted together.[4] The Art Institute's chair represents not only Hunzinger's best work but also his most expensive. His factory produced a wide range of chairs—from an eight-dollar maple rocker with a wire seat to a seventy-two-dollar ebonized and gilt walnut recliner with silk upholstery and fringe,[5] very close in design to that of the Art Institute's chair.

The chair is in excellent condition. The ebonizing over the walnut is original and has required only minimal conservation. The incised gilt lines are fourteen-carat gold and also in mint condition. Although the chair has been reupholstered, the underupholstery is original and intact. The silk-damask fabric was chosen using threads of the original fabric as a color guide. Most likely the chair was part of a larger suite of furniture including a settee and a larger gentleman's chair. Several of these suites survive in public collections.[6]

NOTES

1. Richard W. Flint, "George Hunzinger," in *Art and Antiques, Nineteenth-Century Furniture: Innovation, Revival, and Reform* (New York, 1982), pp. 124–26.

2. Ibid., p. 126.

3. Catherine Hoover Voorsanger in "Recent Acquisitions: A Selection," *Metropolitan Museum of Art Bulletin* 51, 2 (fall 1993), p. 59.

4. New York, Metropolitan Museum of Art, *Nineteenth-Century America: Furniture and Other Decorative Arts*, exh. cat. (1970), cat. no. 186 (entry by Marilyn Johnson).

5. Oscar P. Fitzgerald, *Four Centuries of American Furniture* (Radnor, Pa., 1995), p. 240.

6. The mate to the Art Institute's chair is in the collection of the Brooklyn Museum. Similar suites are in the Royal Ontario Museum in Toronto and the Margaret Woodbury Strong Museum in Rochester, N.Y.

103. TIFFANY AND COMPANY (FOUNDED 1837)

Candelabra signed by Eugene J. Soligny (C. 1833–1901)

The Geneva Tribunal Testimonial, 1873

New York

Silver; punch bowl: h. 41.9, diam. 67.3 cm (16½, 26½ in.); candelabra: 77.4 x 43.2 cm (30½ x 17 in.); wine coolers: h. 35 cm (13⅜ in.)

Inscriptions, marked under each base: *TIFFANY AND CO.* (in convex rectangle) / *2379* (punch bowl); *3180* (candelabra); *2963* (wine coolers) / *Quality 925.1000* (in rectangle) / gothic *M* (in oval) / *5200* / *UNION SQUARE* (in convex rectangle); each marked on underside of one foot: *No. 1*; signed on proper left side of base on each candelabra: *EJ* (conjoined) and *S*; punchbowl inscribed: *The United States of America / Viscount d'Itajubá / His Majesty, the Emperor of Brazil / Article 1 of the Treaty Between the United States and Her Britannic Majesty / Concluded at Washington May 8, 1871 as a Mark of Their Appreciation of the / Dignity, Learning, Ability and Impartiality with Which He Discharged His Arduous Duties at / Geneva*

Punch Bowl and Candelabra: Gift of the Antiquarian Society through the Mr. and Mrs. William Y. Hutchinson Fund, 1985.221a–c

Pair of Wine Coolers: Gift of the Antiquarian Society, 1996.15.1–2

In 1871 the United States government brought suit against Great Britain for breaching its vow of neutrality during the last years of the Civil War. The suit accused Great Britain of, among other things, building and selling five war vessels to the Confederate government, including the C.S.S. *Alabama*, one of the largest ships in the Confederate fleet. The lawsuit, dubbed the "Alabama Claims" by the press, sought reparations from Great Britain for aiding in the pursuit and destruction of Union ships, for insurance costs, and for prolonging the war. The last accusation called for Great Britain to pay for all the costs of war incurred by the Union government after the Battle of Gettysburg; the United States eventually dropped this claim for "indirect" costs.[1]

Under a treaty signed by Britain and the United States, a board of arbitrators was entrusted with judging the merits of the competing claims. To help settle the case, three neutral countries—Brazil, Italy, and Switzerland—each appointed one representative to the board: Viscount d'Itajubá for Brazil, Count Sclopis for Italy, and Jacques Staempfli for Switzerland.

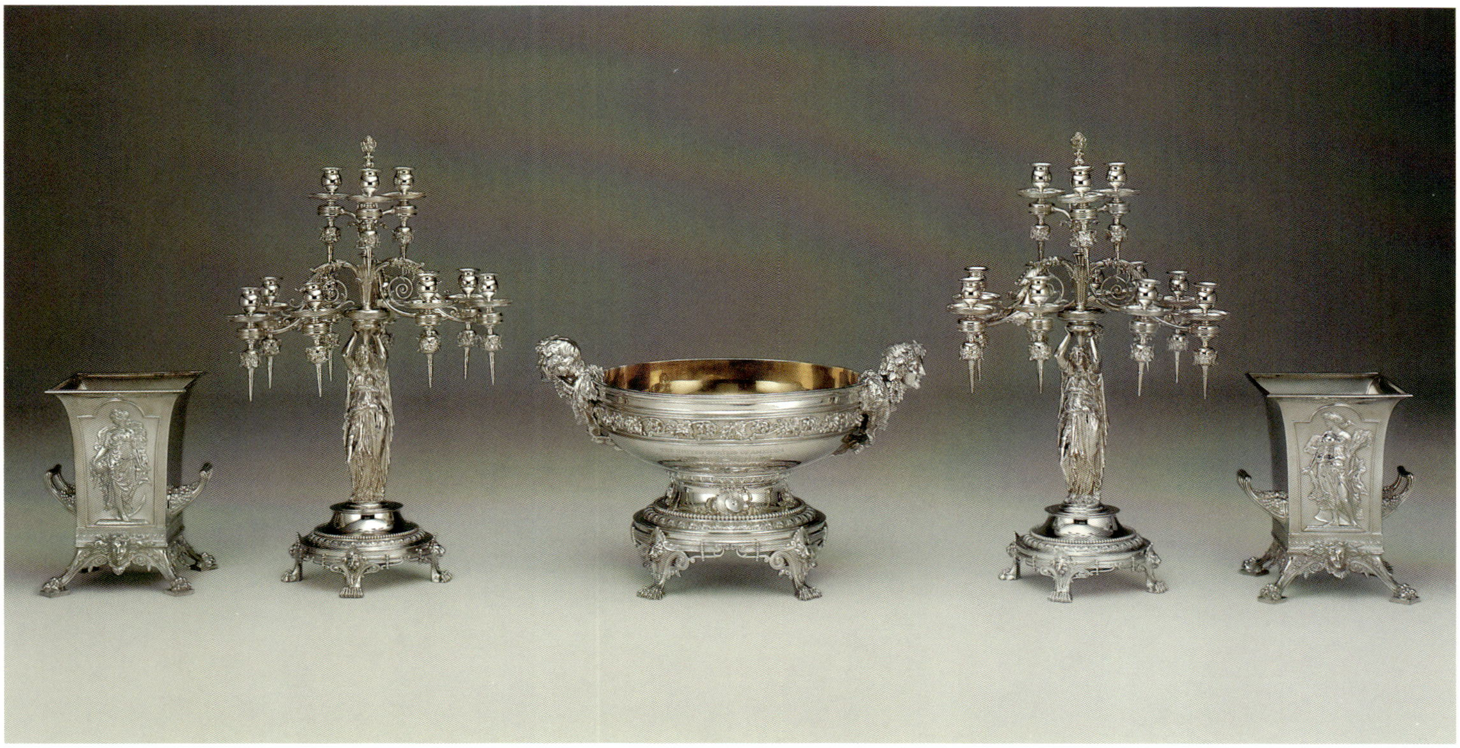

CAT. NO. 103

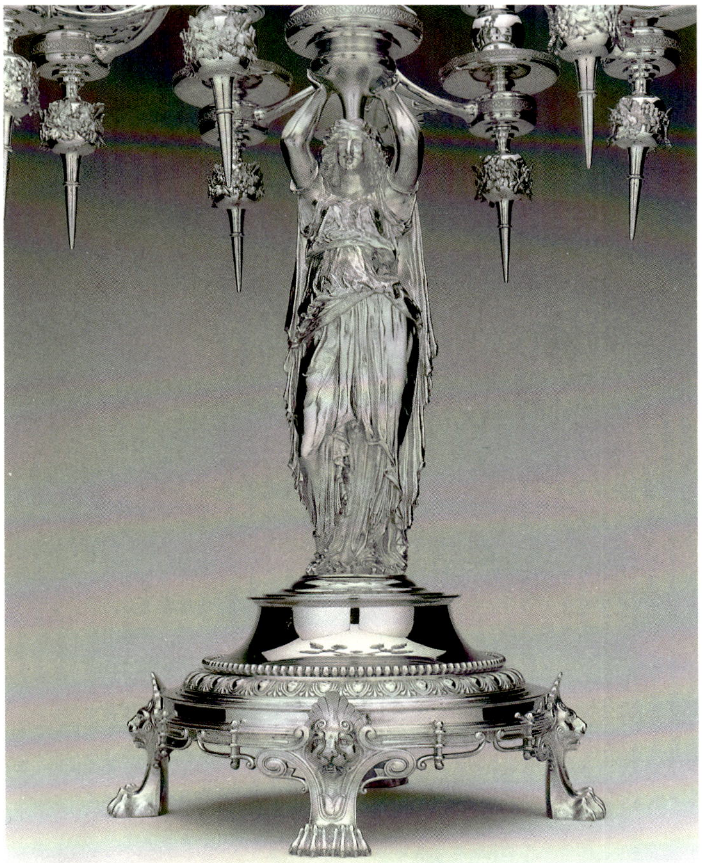

CAT. NO. 103, DETAIL (CANDELABRA)

The arbitrators met in Geneva during the winter of 1871–72. After all the evidence was presented, they found that Great Britain was legally at fault and ordered it to pay the United States war reparations amounting to fifteen million dollars.[2]

The Art Institute's suite of silver was one of three identical sets commissioned by the United States government and presented to the three neutral arbitrators of the "Alabama Claims" as a symbol of gratitude.[3] Before presenting the suites, Tiffany and Company exhibited them at the Vienna Exposition in 1873, where they were greeted approvingly by the press. One North American reviewer noted: "The testimonial to the Geneva arbitrators was a somewhat unusual proceeding, but one which the general voice of the nation heartily endorsed; and the feeling has been almost universal that the silver-ware manufactured for the purpose, by Tiffany, of New York, was worthy of our standing as a nation, and would reflect credit upon us wherever it went."[4]

The Art Institute's version of the Geneva Tribunal Testimonial was presented to the Brazilian viscount. It was the first one made by Tiffany and Company, as indicated on each piece of silver in the suite with a "No. 1" stamped on the underside of one foot. The Art Institute's version is the only one that was given to its recipient in a formal presentation ceremony.[5] United States Secretary of State Hamilton Fish instructed his

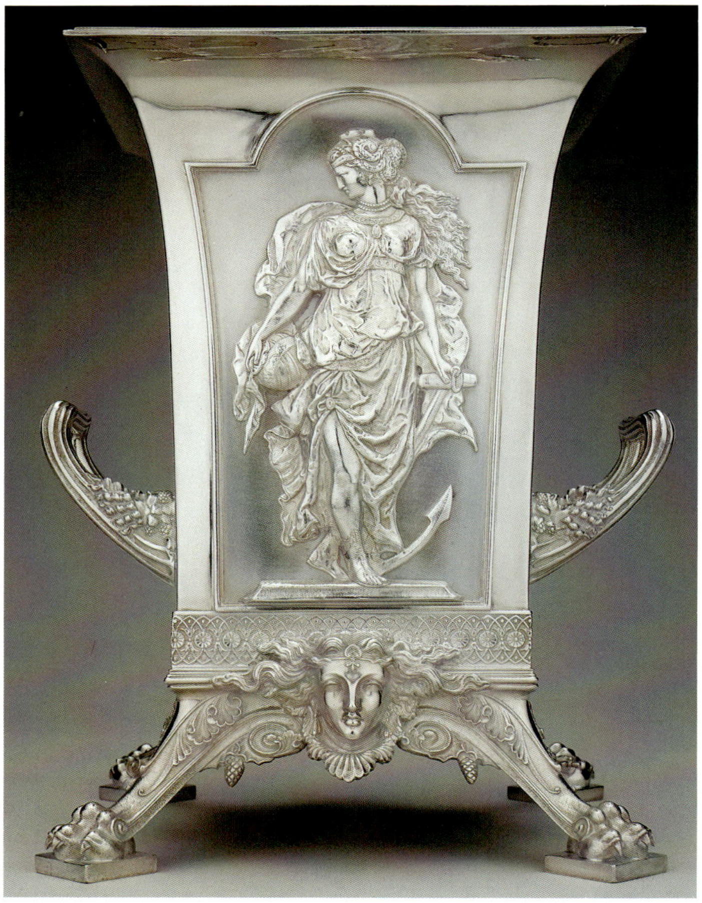

CAT. NO. 103 (WINE COOLER)

representative in Paris to present the suite to Viscount d'Itajubá: "On the receipt of the cases intended for the Viscount . . . , you will present them to him in the name of the United States as a mark of their appreciation of the dignity, ability, learning and impartiality with which he discharged his arduous duties at Geneva, and as an expression of the President's deep sense of the unselfishness with which he devoted his time and his great abilities to the solution of the difficult questions which had then arisen between Her Britannic Majesty and the United States, and which are now so happily laid at rest by the action of the Tribunal of Arbitration of which the Viscount d'Itajubá was so distinguished a member."[6]

The suite was executed in the "neo-grec" style, a popular revival of the classical taste from earlier in the century. Figures and symbols on the pieces of the suite represent ancient Greek themes. The handles of the punch bowl depict Dionysus, the god of wine, who can be identified by the grape vines encircling his head, the bemused expression on his face, and the lion skin tied around his neck. Gracing the handle junctures of the coolers are face masks of Silenus, a woodland god, mentor, and constant companion to Dionysus. The four legs of both coolers are each set on a lion's paw; scrolls and grape leaves adorn the knees. The grape-vine motif is continued in a wide band around the punch bowl, connecting the two heads of Diony-

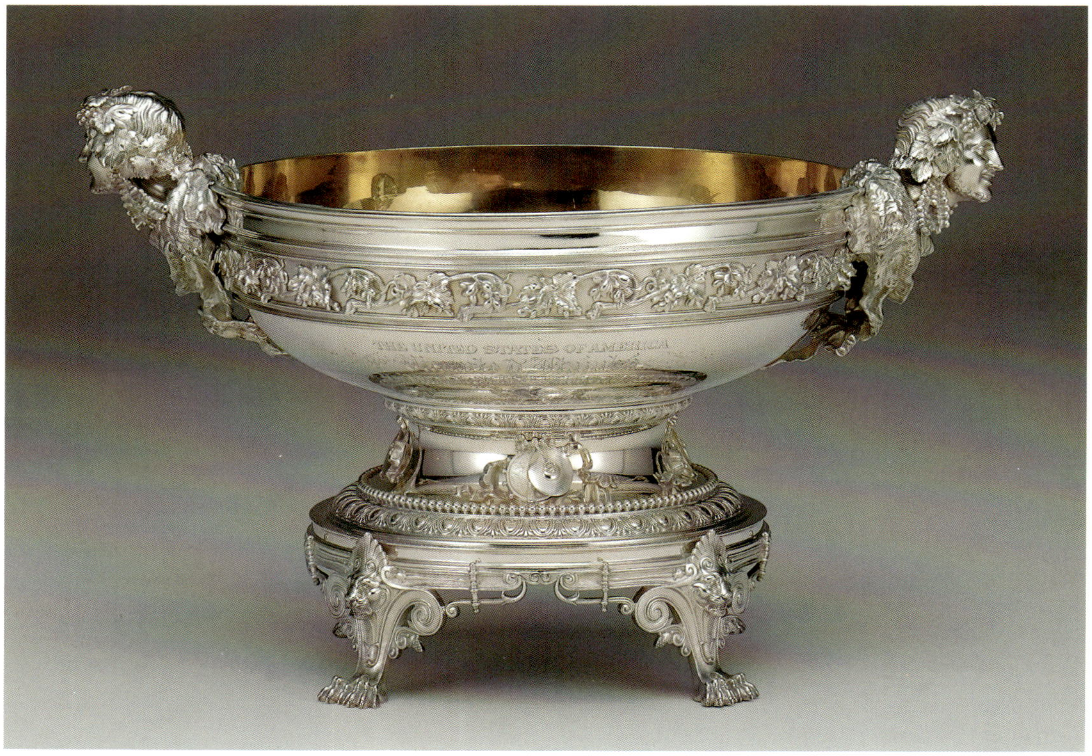

CAT. NO. 103 (PUNCH BOWL)

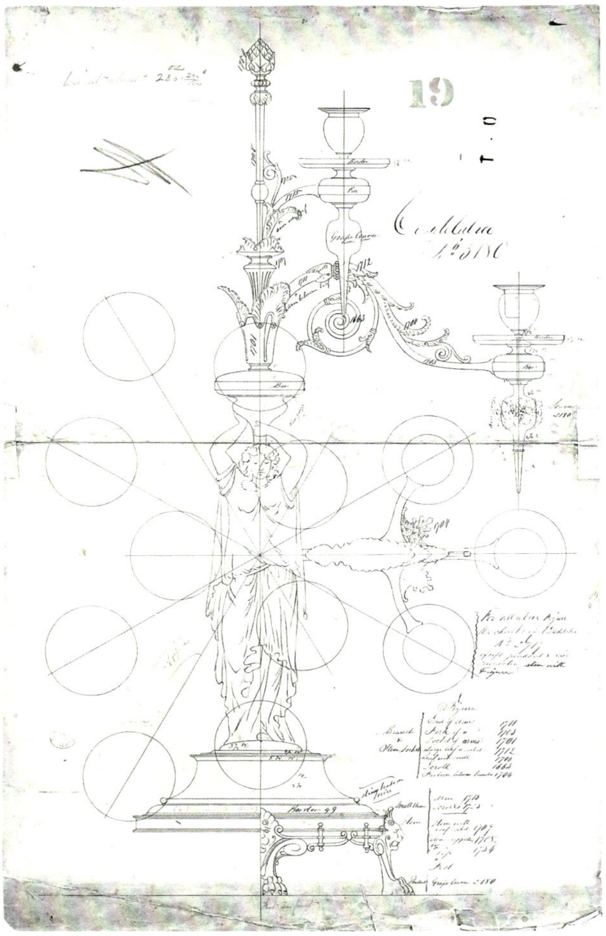

FIG. 56. Tiffany and Company. *Candelabra No. 3180*, 1873. Red sepia and black ink, and pencil on paper; 81.9 x 52.1 cm (33¼ x 20½ in.). The Art Institute of Chicago, Gift of Tiffany and Company (1986.200).

sus, and surrounds the pendant drops under each candle cup of the pair of candelabra. Encircling the base of the punch bowl are groups of ribbon-tied cymbals and tambourines representing the debauched festivals associated with the wine god and his followers. The figures holding the candle cups are representations of Ariadne, wife of Dionysus.[7] On the base, to the left of each figure, are the carefully inscribed initials of one of Tiffany and Company's most well known and talented chasers: Eugene J. Soligny. Though the initials are somewhat worn away, they match those found on the relief plaque of William Cullen Bryant on Tiffany and Company's Bryant vase, now at the Metropolitan Museum of Art, New York.[8] The pattern of the belt encircling the waist of Ariadne is repeated in the decorative bands surrounding the base of the candle cups and in the band around that of the wine coolers. Each wine cooler has two unsigned, chased plaques. On one, Demeter, the goddess of agriculture, is shown holding a sheaf of wheat and a plowshare. On the other, a personification of Commerce is represented in classical drapery holding a globe of the world with signs of the Zodiac in one hand; her other hand rests on an anchor.

Because of its remarkable craftsmanship and scale, and the importance of the occasion for which it was made, this suite of silver is one of the most important presentation suites produced by an American firm in the nineteenth century.

NOTES

1. Allan Nevins, *Hamilton Fish: The Inner History of the Grant Administration* (New York, 1957), vol. 2, pp. 519, 550; and William S. McFeely, *Grant: A Biography* (New York, 1981), pp. 332–36, 352–55.

2. McFeely (note 1), p. 355.

3. The suite made for the representative of Switzerland is now in the Musée d'Art et d'Histoire, Geneva. The whereabouts of the suite made for the Italian count are unknown.

4. As quoted in Christie's, New York, *Important American Furniture, Silver, Prints, Folk Art and Decorative Arts* (Jan. 27, 1996), lot 91, p. 52.

5. Letter from Hamilton Fish to E. B. Washburne, Mar. 14 ,1873, Hamilton Fish Letter Book, National Archives Trust Fund Board, Washington, D.C., Foreign Relations Branch.

6. Ibid.

7. The pattern for the candelabra is listed as "Pattern number 3180 Candelabra extra large figure—Ariadne" in Tiffany and Company Pattern Book (1873), p. 270, Tiffany and Company archives, Parsippany, N.J.

8. For an illustration of the initials on the Bryant vase, see Frances Gruber Safford and Ruth Wilford Caccavale, "E. J. Soligny, the Chaser of the Bryant Vase," *Antiques* 137, 3 (Mar. 1990), p. 691.

104. WINSLOW HOMER (1836–1910)

Croquet Scene, 1866

Oil on canvas; 40.3 x 66.2 cm (15⅞ x 26$\frac{1}{16}$ in.)
Signed, lower right: *WINSLOW HOMER / -66-*
Friends of American Art Collection, 1942.35

In 1865 Winslow Homer completed the first of five paintings he would devote to the subject of croquet. *Croquet Scene* is probably the fourth in the series and the most compositionally striking in its use of light and color to define space.[1] Homer's interest in depicting this game coincided with the rise in its popularity among the upper classes in the United States. His choice of subject matter, as well as his decision to paint the subject in series, reveals its modernity, as does the lack of ex-

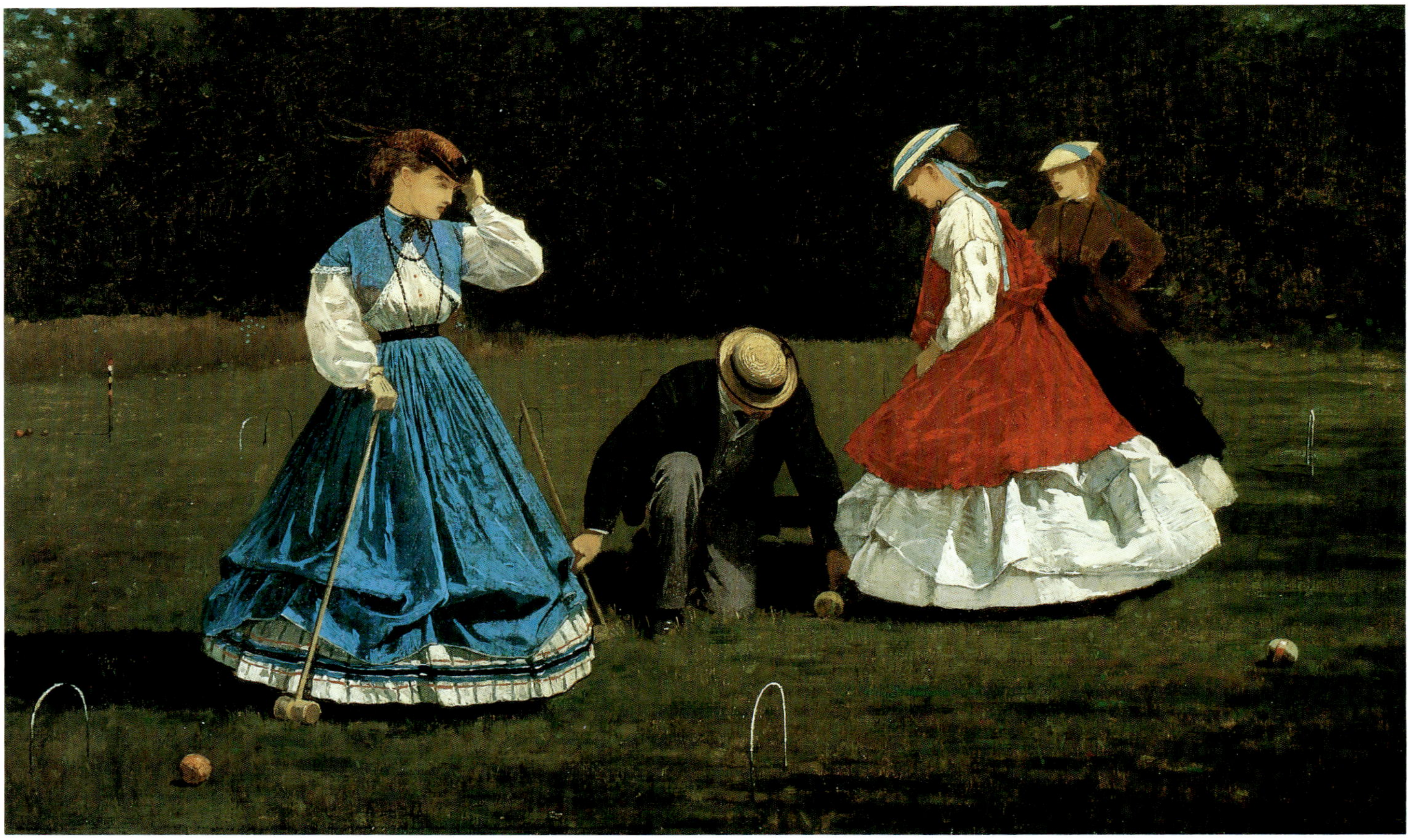

CAT. NO. 104

plicit narrative in the paintings. These works also have close ties to illustration, both to engravings in croquet rule books and to Homer's early graphic work.[2]

Homer received little formal training, but developed his artistic skills as an apprentice at John H. Bufford's lithography shop in Boston between 1854 and 1857.[3] He published his first illustration in *Harper's Weekly* in 1857, and was hired as the magazine's Civil War correspondent in 1861. The on-site drawings Homer made of battles and camp scenes were translated into engravings and subsequently published as illustrations; his earliest paintings also depict Civil War subjects, some of which closely relate to his illustrations.[4] The artist was elected a full academician of the National Academy of Design in 1865, and donated the first of his croquet pictures, *Croquet Player* (1865; National Academy of Design, New York), to the institution upon his appointment.[5]

Deriving from a fourteenth-century French peasant game called *paille maille*, the modern form of croquet was played in Ireland as early as the 1830s.[6] The Irish introduced it to the English around 1852, who in turn interested Americans in the game. In 1866 Milton Bradley, the American toy manufacturer, patented the first croquet set mass-produced in the United States. Homer's croquet paintings exhibit his familiarity both with the basic rules and with the more subtle social aspects of the game. Although the playing fields Homer depicted are not always believable, the strategic methods employed by the players in his paintings correspond to those described in popular rule books. Women predominate in these paintings, and their interaction with men is consistent with the etiquette of the game, which allowed females to compete with males, but required the former to conduct themselves with elegance and grace.

Croquet Scene is closely related to a larger, less finished composition at the Yale University Art Gallery (fig. 57). The two women in *A Game of Croquet* are almost identical to the two female figures in the foreground of the Art Institute canvas, although they stand alone before a low stone fence and a row of small trees. The Art Institute's smaller composition is more compressed, with a dense thicket of trees closing the space behind the figures. The woman in red raises her skirt at the front hem in order to set her foot upon the ball to begin the croquet stroke that is intended to knock the ball of her opponent—the

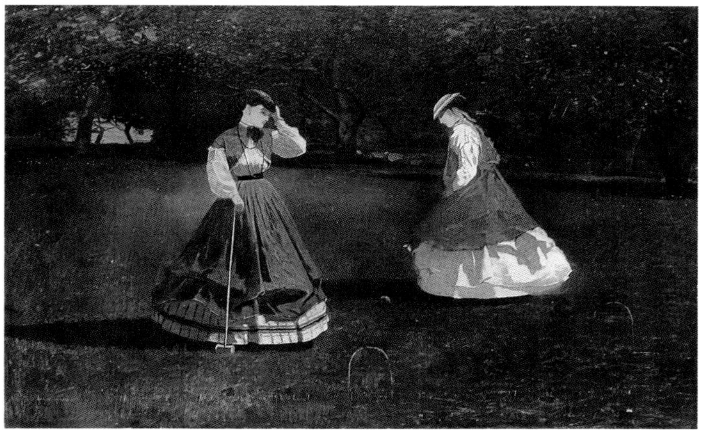

FIG. 57. Winslow Homer (1836–1910). *A Game of Croquet*, 1866. Oil on canvas; 48.3 x 76.2 cm (19 x 30 in.). Yale University Art Gallery, New Haven, Conn., Bequest of Stephen Carlton Clark, BA 1903 (1961.18.25).

woman in blue—off the field. In a chivalrous act, a man, whose face we cannot see, kneels down to adjust the ball so that the woman can maintain her dignified pose.[7] The long shadows extending to the left indicate that the game is being played in the afternoon, the preferred time of day for croquet matches. Homer's attention to these technical and social details reveals his sensitivity to the nuances of the game.

The artist also included visual rhymes in the painting: the two women at the right wear straw hats with blue ribbons that echo the stripes of the croquet balls, as does the man's straw boater and the bottom of the blue dress, which is ringed with blue, red, and black stripes. The diagonal from left to right formed by the figures provides the only sense of depth. The flattening effect of the trees in *Croquet Scene* does not appear in any of Homer's other croquet paintings, which feature landscapes peppered with more spaciously placed trees and glimpses into the distance. The dark, dense foliage of the Art Institute's painting also intensifies the colorful brilliance of the women's dresses. The red dress in particular stands out against the greens of the grass and trees.

The popularity of croquet was undermined in the 1870s by accusations that the opportunities the game provided the sexes to intermingle and women to display athletic prowess would encourage immoral behavior. The potential titillation afforded by viewing the foot and ankle of the woman in red as she prepares to execute her croquet stroke is alluded to by the subservient position and intense gaze of the kneeling male figure. Painted at the peak of the game's popularity, *Croquet Scene* both celebrates this pastime and hints at its controversial implications.

NOTES

1. David Park Curry, *Winslow Homer: The Croquet Game*, exh. cat. (New Haven, Conn., Yale University Art Gallery, 1984), unpag.

2. On Homer as an illustrator, see Philip C. Beam, *Winslow Homer's Magazine Engravings* (New York, 1979); and Lloyd Goodrich, *The Graphic Art of Winslow Homer* (New York, 1968).

3. On Homer's biography, see Nicolai Cikovsky, Jr., and Franklin Kelly, *Winslow Homer*, exh. cat. (Washington, D.C., National Gallery of Art, 1995).

4. For more about Homer and the Civil War, see Marc Simpson, *Winslow Homer: Paintings of the Civil War*, exh. cat. (Fine Arts Museums of San Francisco, 1988).

5. The inscription on the back of this painting reads: *Winslow Homer would like to have the privilege of painting . . . . a better picture.*

6. Historical information on croquet comes from Curry (note 1).

7. For illustrations from rule books including men in poses that closely correspond to those of the figures in Homer's painting, see Curry (note 1), figs. 9–11.

105. WINSLOW HOMER (1836–1910)

Mount Washington, 1869

Oil on canvas; 41.3 x 61.8 cm ($16\frac{1}{4}$ x $24\frac{5}{16}$ in.)
Signed, lower right: *Winslow Homer / -1869-*
Gift of Mrs. Richard E. Danielson and Mrs. Chauncey McCormick, 1951.313

Like *Croquet Scene* (cat. no. 104), Winslow Homer's *Mount Washington* explores themes of leisure in post–Civil War America that signal shifts in the roles of women. During the first half of the nineteenth century, the White Mountains of New Hampshire, of which Mount Washington is the highest peak, were celebrated by artists, travel writers, and naturalists for their sublime wilderness.[1] Thomas Cole (see cat. no. 64) traveled to the White Mountains for the first time in 1827 and was one of the first landscape painters to capture on canvas the quintessentially romantic features of the mountains. Many artists were attracted to the untamed scenery of the region, including John Frederick Kensett (see cat. no. 94) and Albert Bierstadt (see cat. no. 87). But by the time Winslow Homer arrived on assignment from *Harper's Weekly* in 1868, the landscape was dominated by tourists and the comforts they demanded: grand hotels, railroads, and well-groomed trails for walking and riding.

Homer traveled to the White Mountains in the summers of 1868 and 1869 specifically to document tourist activity; these

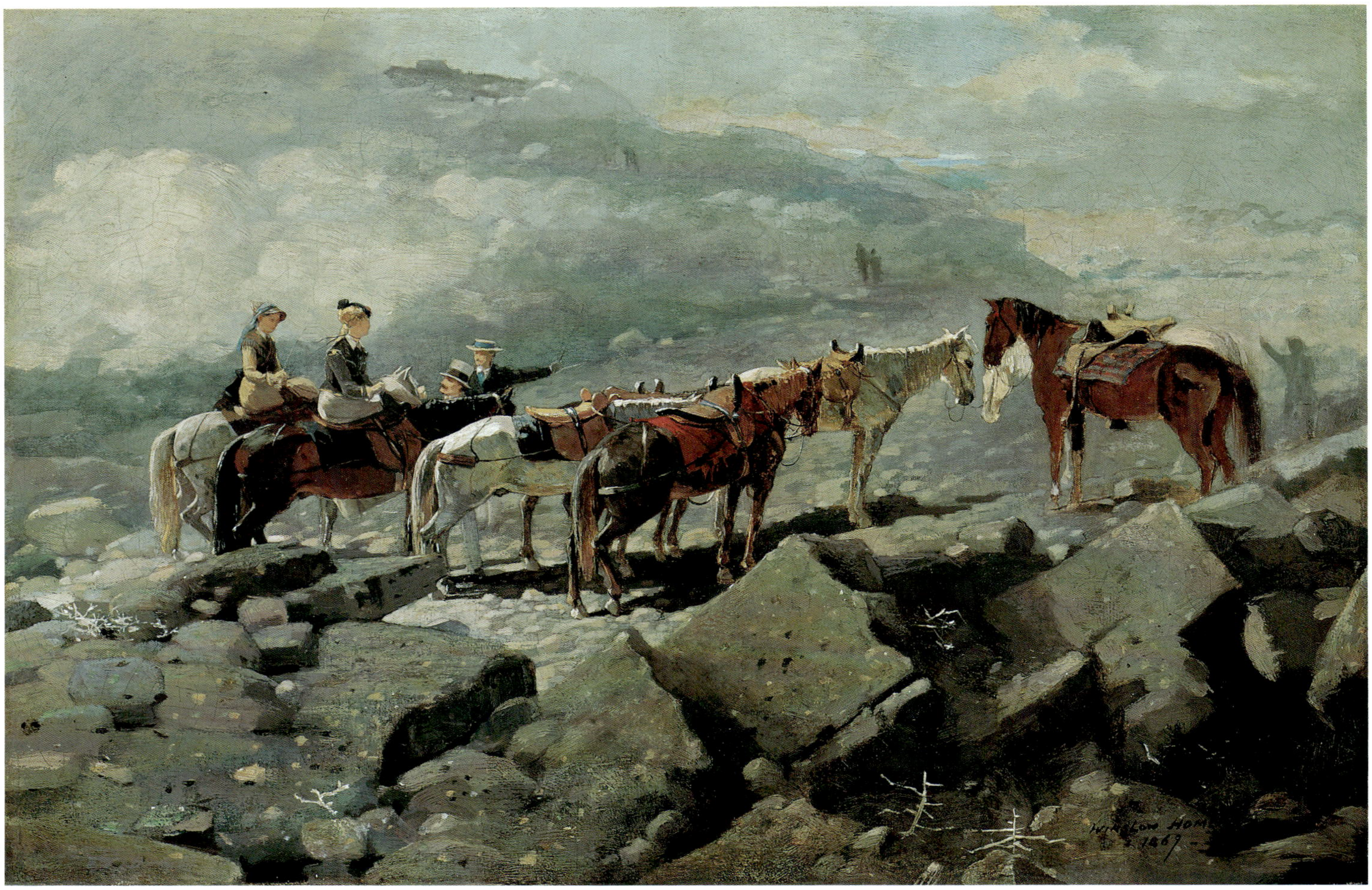

CAT. NO. 105

were the only trips he made to the region. The sketches, illustrations, and paintings that resulted from these journeys depict the interaction between people and the landscape, a relationship dominated not by nature, but by humankind. *Mount Washington* portrays a type of tourist activity known as scenic touring.[2] The women on horseback are accompanied by fashionably dressed male companions who point to designated spots with grand overlooks. The objective for both men and women was to undergo a memorable experience tinged with danger; the rocks surrounding the tourists and their horses produce a shadowy suggestion of peril. In a related painting, *Bridle Path, White Mountains* (1868; Sterling and Francine Clark Art Institute, Williamstown, Massachusetts), the artist used the same compositional device of forbidding rocks in the foreground to confine a lone female rider.[3] The sublimity of the Art Institute's painting is suggested by the cloud-shrouded summit of Mount Washington and the distant, sketchily rendered figures walking toward the Summit House, a hotel at the top of the mountain that opened in 1853. A drawing of the riderless horses and their tack, *Study for the Summit of Mount Washington* (1869; Cooper-Hewitt National Design Museum, Smithsonian Institution, New York), reveals Homer's reliance upon detailed drawings to compose his finished works.[4]

By 1869 hiking and riding were not the only two ways a traveler could ascend Mount Washington: the Cog Railway, which transported tourists to the summit, had been completed that same year. Homer's depiction of riders, then, documents a vanishing mode of travel and alludes to riding as a sport (for both men and women) rather than as a necessity. In *Mount Washington*, as in *Croquet Scene*, Homer explored both the social and aesthetic significance of his female subjects. Although they appear to be accompanied by men, women are the focal points of the composition. That they are independent and capable perhaps alludes to the emergence of women in the public sphere in the second half of the nineteenth century. Their clothing, while fashionable, is simpler and more practical than that of their counterparts in *Croquet Scene*, suggesting the freedom riding gave women, as well as the skill and sheer physical exertion involved.

The depiction of the eastern landscape as a stage for human activity, particularly that of tourism, rather than as a paradise charged with Christian and nationalistic associations, is characteristic of work produced after the Civil War. For Homer, who served during the conflict as an artist-journalist, the firsthand experience of a ravaged land and the dramas enacted upon it stood in contrast to the relatively benign character of his White Mountain scenes. The forceful presence of the rocks in the foreground anticipate Homer's powerful later seascapes, including *The Herring Net* (cat. no. 110).

NOTES

1. On the White Mountains and visual culture, see Robert L. McGrath and Barbara J. MacAdam, *"A Sweet Foretaste of Heaven": Artists in the White Mountains, 1830–1930*, exh. cat. (Hanover, N.H., Hood Museum of Art, Dartmouth University, 1988); and Donald Keyes, *The White Mountains: Place and Perceptions*, exh. cat. (Durham, N.H., University Art Galleries, University of New Hampshire, 1980).

2. For a cultural history of tourism in New England, see Dona Brown, *Inventing New England: Regional Tourism in the Nineteenth Century* (Washington, D.C., 1995), pp. 41–74.

3. For more on *Bridle Path, White Mountains*, see Margaret C. Conrads, *American Paintings and Sculpture at the Sterling and Francine Clark Art Institute* (New York, 1990), pp. 63–67. Homer borrowed the rider from *Bridle Path* for the figure on the far left in *White Mountains*.

4. Nicolai Cikovsky, Jr., and Franklin Kelly, *Winslow Homer*, exh. cat. (Washington, D.C., National Gallery of Art, 1995), p. 77. The drawing is dated 1869, which secures the date of the Art Institute's painting. An illustration published in the July 10, 1869, edition of *Harper's Weekly* is another image that relates closely to *Mount Washington*. The differences between it and the painting reveal Homer's diverse approaches, depending on the media, to the same subject.

106. EASTMAN JOHNSON (1824–1906)

Husking Bee, Island of Nantucket, 1876

Oil on canvas; 69.3 x 137 cm (27¼ x 54 3/16 in.)
Signed, lower left: *E. Johnson / 1876*
Potter Palmer Collection, 1922.444

A timeless evocation of agrarian peace and cooperation, *Husking Bee, Island of Nantucket* is one of Eastman Johnson's two genre paintings inspired by this rural scene.[1] Painted in 1876, during the nation's centennial year, this work addresses, in both form and content, issues of democratic idealism and nationalism during a time of enormous economic and social change.

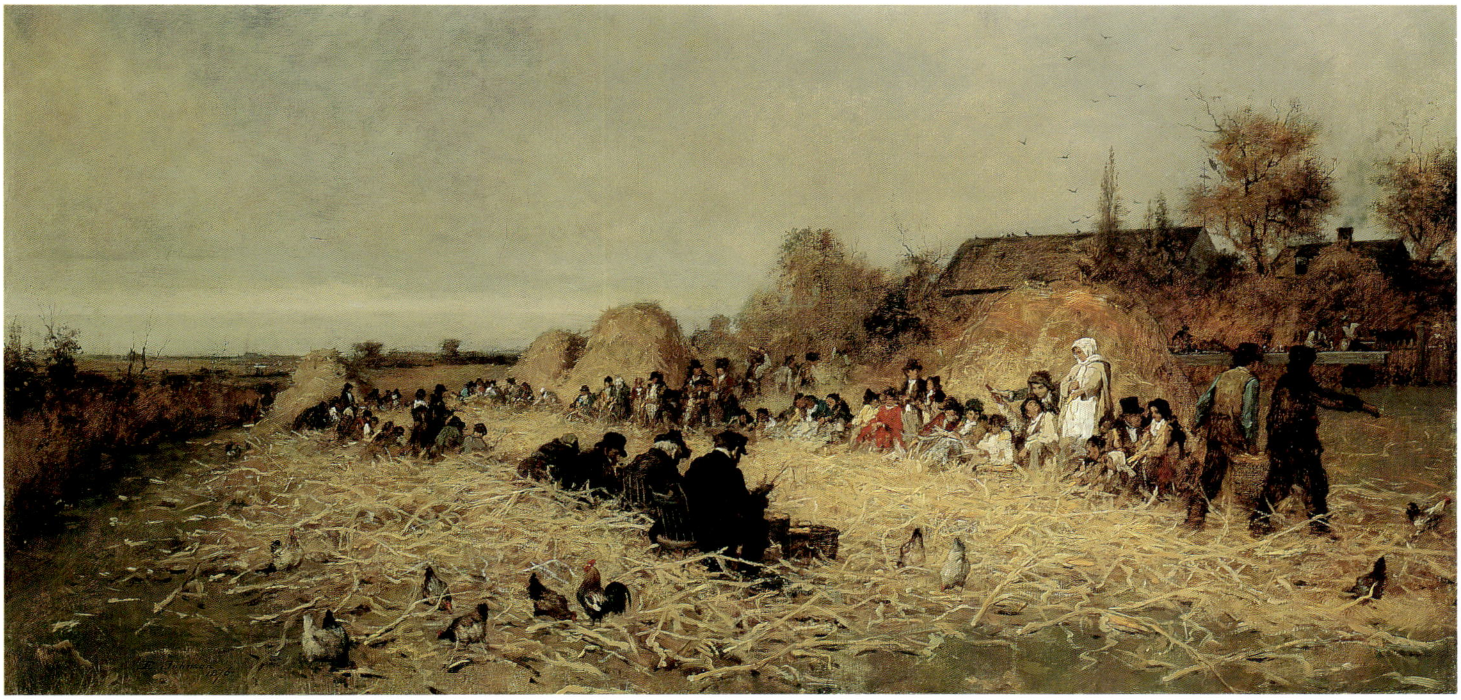

CAT. NO. 106

Johnson's artistic training in the 1850s in Düsseldorf, Holland, and Paris exposed him to a wide array of influences. In The Hague, he copied works by Rembrandt van Rijn and Anthony Van Dyck. One of the strongest influences, however, was the peasant paintings of Jean François Millet and Jules Breton. Johnson's genre paintings, imbued with the plein-air sensibility of the French Barbizon School, as well as a Romantic view of peasant life, were highly praised by critics for their apparent similarities to contemporary French art. Writing in 1882, S. G. W. Benjamin noted that "in tone and color and in the acute perception of rural human nature it [Johnson's work] loses nothing by comparison with the work of Jules Breton."[2] But other critics, such as William Walton, recognized an essential difference between American and French rural genre scenes, a difference that revealed Johnson's indigenous style and subject: "[Johnson's] conception of this rendering of 'the life of the poor,' of 'the tillers of the soil' (and ex-toilers of the sea), preaches no ugly gospel of discontent, as does so much of the contemporary French and Flemish art of this genre. . . . There is no 'cri de la terre' arising from his cranberry marshes or his hay-stuffed barns."[3] In other words, the abundance of the American landscape, the purity of the rural life Johnson depicted, struck such critics as a celebration of American life.

Situated off the Massachusetts coast, Nantucket Island was a prosperous whaling center until the mid-nineteenth century. With the rise in the use of steamships in the whaling industry, Nantucket's clipper ship captains were soon displaced from their jobs and the industry shifted to coastal cities such as Boston. Modest family farms could still be seen dotting Nantucket's landscape during this period; the island's Quaker heritage encouraged community participation in domestic activities such as cornhusking and quilting bees, all of which were reported in the local newspaper. Johnson is said to have witnessed a cornhusking bee during an autumn visit to Nantucket, where he bought a home in 1869 and regularly spent summers.[4]

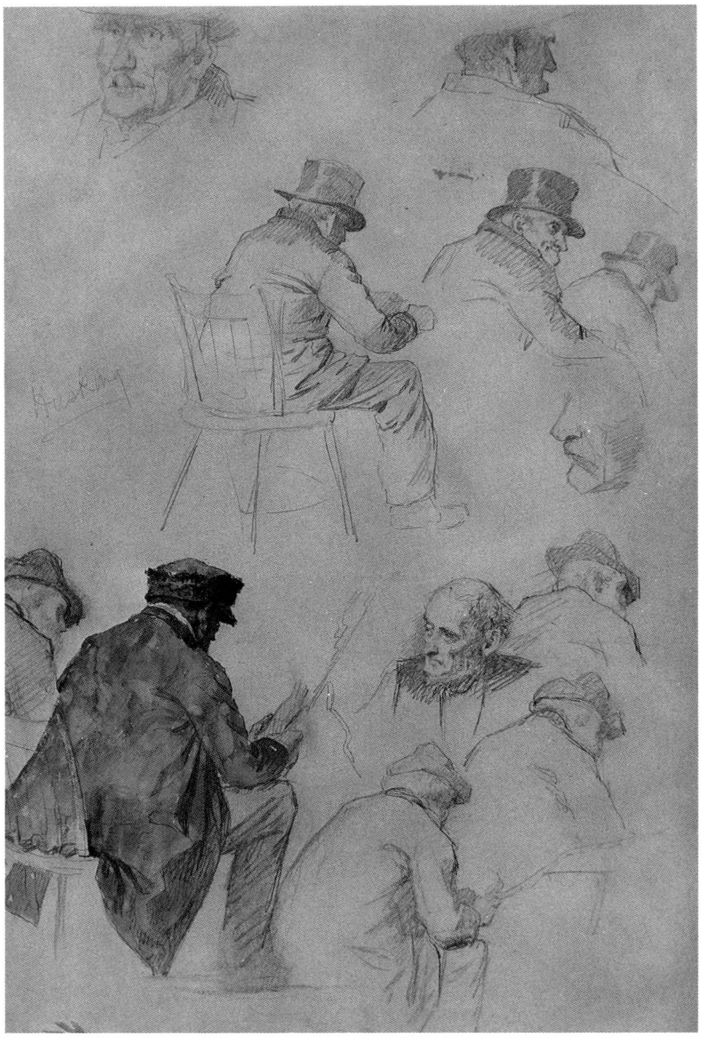

FIG. 58. Eastman Johnson (1824–1906). *Husking (Study for Corn Husking [Husking Bee])*, 1876. Pencil and watercolor; 47.9 x 28.6 cm (18⅞ x 11¼ in.). Free Library, Philadelphia, Rosenthal Collection.

A perfect balance is achieved in *Husking Bee* between foreground and background. Patches of clear red, blue, and green appear like sparks amid the shimmering gold of the cornhusks, whose texture is at once soft and brittle. Examples of harvest and Thanksgiving imagery permeate the canvas. In the right middle ground, a table is being prepared for a feast that will provide sustenance for those who have worked to harvest crops. Johnson included a woman discovering a red ear of corn, which, according to a folk tradition, allows her to kiss the person of her choice. This fusion of indigenous details and a sophisticated style based on European models proved a very successful formula for the artist.[6]

The artist used local models for the picture. Sketches related to this work in the Museum of Fine Arts, Boston, and the Free Library, Philadelphia (fig. 58), document his interest in native Nantucket islanders; one of those he drew has been identified as Captain Charles Myrick, the third figure on the left side of the finished painting.[7] Nonetheless, Johnson's painting contains an element of historical fiction in its suggestion of the love of the land and economic self-sufficiency that the colonial farmer or yeoman had helped to define as part of the American experience. Close examination of the figures in *Husking Bee* reveals little about the decade—or even century—in which they lived. Retired sea captains wear old-fashioned silk top hats; the woman in white who stands at the right wears an anachronistic, colonial kerchief and apron. The timelessness of the painting is further enhanced by the lack of evident mechanization on the farm. By the time this painting was executed, many American farms were modernized by machinery that replaced such tasks as cornhusking by hand.[8] As a result, small farmers were being forced to leave their land and move to cities in search of work. None of the social ramifications of urbanization or farm mechanization is apparent in *Husking Bee*. By 1876 tourism had replaced whaling and farming as Nantucket's economic base.[9] Thus by choosing to portray Nantucket and its denizens as a preindustrial, classless society involved in a cooperative task that involved the entire community, Johnson created a treatise on the American values of democracy, economic independence, and hard work—values that were widely celebrated in the nation's centennial year.

NOTES

1. The second is *The Cranberry Harvest, Island of Nantucket* (1880; Timken Art Gallery, San Diego).

2. S. G. W. Benjamin, "A Representative American," *Magazine of Art* 5 (1882), p. 489.

3. William Walton, "Eastman Johnson, Painter," *Scribner's Magazine* 40, 3 (Sept. 1906), pp. 270–71.

4. Letter from Mrs. Eastman Johnson to Mr. A. B. de St. M. d'Hervilly, Jan. 28, 1913, American Paintings Department, Metropolitan Museum of Art, New York. In this letter Mrs. Johnson wrote: "'The Corn Husking of Nantucket' was painted in late November. One day of dark skies and wind. [Johnson] came upon the scene when driving exactly like this—absolutely truthful the yellow corn and husks, the bright chickens running about the old sea captains with their silk hats of better days, figure in the center, too old to enjoy crouching by the hour on the ground."

6. *Husking Bee* was exhibited to wide acclaim at the Paris Exposition Universelle in 1878.

7. Patricia Hills identified Myrick in *The Genre Painting of Eastman Johnson: The Sources and Development of His Style and Themes* (New York, 1977), p. 147. An oil sketch for *Husking Bee* entitled *Corn Husking at Nantucket* is in the collection of the Metropolitan Museum of Art, New York.

8. See Sarah Burns, *Pastoral Inventions: Rural Life in Nineteenth-Century American Art and Culture* (Philadelphia, 1989); and Patricia Hills, *The Painters' America: Rural and Urban Life, 1810–1910*, exh. cat. (New York, Whitney Musem of American Art, 1974).

9. For information about Nantucket in the nineteenth century, see Marc Simpson, Sally Mills, and Patricia Hills, *Eastman Johnson, The Cranberry Harvest, Island of Nantucket: Twenty-Fifth Anniversary Exhibition*, exh. cat. (San Diego, Timken Art Gallery, 1990).

107. THOMAS EAKINS (1844–1916)

Spinning, modeled 1882–83, cast c. 1886

Painted plaster; 47 x 38.2 cm (18½ x 15 in.)
Marion and Samuel Klasstorner Fund Income, 1978.437

108. *Knitting*, modeled 1882–83, cast c. 1886

Painted plaster; 47 x 38.2 cm (18½ x 15 in.)
Marion and Samuel Klasstorner Fund Income, 1978.438

Although he is best known as a painter of genre scenes and portraits characterized by heightened physical and psychological realism, Thomas Eakins also experimented with sculpture. *Spinning* and *Knitting* were the first of seven works in relief he produced over the course of his career.[1] They were commissioned as fireplace ornaments in 1882 by Philadelphian James P. Scott. Modeled not long after the 1876 Centennial Exposition in Philadelphia, these relief sculptures capture the vogue for colonially inspired subjects that swept the nation following this event, which celebrated the one hundredth anniversary of the Declaration of Independence.[2] Eakins further produced a group of paintings in oil and watercolor featuring women spinning that relate to these reliefs and attest to his interest in this type of subject matter.[3]

A dedicated teacher who emphasized the study of the human figure, Eakins also explored the new medium of photography. He kept apprised of fellow Philadelphian Eadweard Muybridge's innovations in stop-motion photography, which he also employed. His approach to sculpture was equally innovative. The suggestion of depth and illusion that relief modeling entails makes it a particularly difficult sculptural technique. Fortunately the scientific precision Eakins brought to his study of painting and photography also helped him master this tricky medium. He eventually became so proficient in relief that he delivered a lecture entitled "The Laws of Sculptured Relief," in which he explained in great detail the correct perspectival rendering of a tip-top table such as the one depicted in *Knitting*.[4]

The Scott commission pleased Eakins; he is said to have commented, "the architect [Theophilus Parsons Chandler] . . . easily induced me, for the work was much to my taste."[5] He was attracted to the challenge of producing reliefs to be seen from multiple viewpoints. He explained to Scott, "The mere

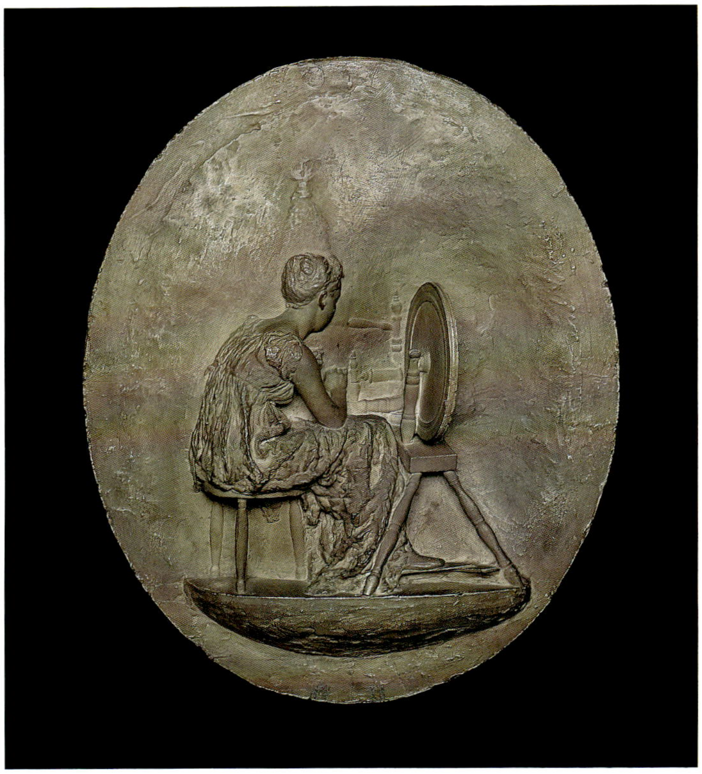

CAT. NO. 107

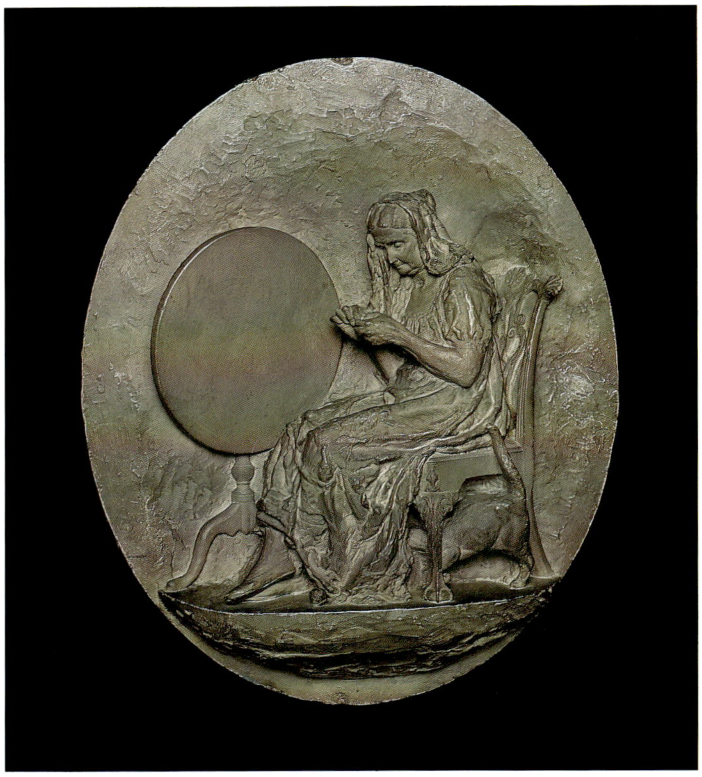

CAT. NO. 108

geometrical construction of the accessories in a perspective which is not projected on a single plane but in a variable third dimension, is a puzzle beyond the sculptors whom I know."[6] In the end, however, Scott rejected Eakins's final product; after extensive negotiations, the reliefs were returned to Eakins and he was paid $500. Ultimately another Philadelphia patron of Eakins, Edward Coates, purchased the bronze versions of *Spinning* and *Knitting* and presented them to the Pennsylvania Academy of the Fine Arts, where Eakins taught for many years.[7]

Eakins employed Mrs. King, who posed many times for him, as the model for *Knitting* and Ellen Wetherald Ahrens, a student at the Academy, for *Spinning*.[8] Although both works depict women engaged in handicraft, the figures differ in their age and class. The older woman knitting is surrounded by signs of affluence and comfort (including the cat playing underneath the chair), and the younger woman spinning sits on an austere stool with no other props beside her ever-turning wheel. In their modeling sessions, each woman performed the task depicted in the work, thus enabling the artist to attain the utmost verisimilitude. Eakins also chose his props with accuracy in mind; the chair in *Knitting* is an Affleck "Chippendale" chair, and the tip-top table originated in the colonial period.

Eakins's penchant for unflinching realism is evident in his rendering of the old woman's face and arm, the flesh of which is wrinkled and sagging. The rough handling of the surfaces—Eakins first worked in clay, after which the reliefs were cast in bronze and plaster—distinguishes these pieces from the smoothly polished, classically refined reliefs of Augustus Saint-Gaudens (see cat. nos. 130–32). Eakins took more chances with his reliefs than Saint-Gaudens by incorporating challenging props and attempting to define drapery three-dimensionally. These daring and vital pieces show Eakins both stretching himself in a new medium and treating themes that preoccupied him: aging, work, women, and colonial subjects.

NOTES

1. For more on Eakins and sculpture, see Moussa M. Domit, *The Sculpture of Thomas Eakins*, exh. cat. (Washington, D.C., National Museum of American Art, 1969).

2. See Christopher Monkhouse, "The Spinning Wheel as Artifact, Symbol, and Source of Design," in Kenneth L. Ames, ed., *Victorian Furniture: Essays from a Victorian Society Autumn Symposium* (New York, 1982), pp. 155–72, for more about the impact of the Centennial Exhibition.

3. These works include the watercolors *Spinning* (1881; Metropolitan Museum of Art, New York); *Seventy Years Ago* (1877; Art Museum, Princeton University, Princeton, N.J.); *Spinning* (1881; collection of Mrs. John Randolph Garrett, Sr.); and the oil *The Courtship* (1878; Fine Arts Museums of San Francisco).

4. Evan Turner, "Thomas Eakins: The Quest for Truth," *The Art Institute of Chicago Centennial Lectures, Museum Studies* 10 (1983), pp. 165–66.

5. Quoted in Phyllis D. Rosenzweig, *The Thomas Eakins Collection of the Hirshhorn Museum and Sculpture Garden* (Washington, D.C., 1977), p. 99.

6. Quoted in ibid.

7. Doreen Bolger, "'Kindly Relations': Edward Hornor Coates and Swimming," in Bolger and Sarah Cash, eds., *Thomas Eakins and the Swimming Picture*, exh. cat. (Fort Worth, Texas, Amon Carter Museum, 1996), p. 45.

8. Eakins used his sister Margaret as the model for his many drawings and paintings of spinning subjects; she died unexpectedly in 1881.

109. DECORATED BY URIAH DYER (1849–1927)

WORKS BY SILAS HOADLEY (1786–1870)

Tall-Case Clock, case c. 1820, decoration 1884

North Appleton, Maine

Painted pine, gilded copper alloy, iron; h. 195.6 cm (77 in.)

Signed on face: *S. HOADLEY, PLYMOUTH*; signed on case: *U. N. Dyer, House & Sign Painter. No. Appleton*

Bessie Bennett, Laura T. Magnuson, and Wendell Fentress Ott endowments, 1996.438

The style and construction of the case of this clock date its manufacture to the early part of the nineteenth century.[1] Its movements are the work of Silas Hoadley, a clockmaker who worked in Plymouth, Connecticut, between 1790 and 1840. Decades passed before the artist Uriah Dyer of North Appleton, Maine, painted the decoration on the case for the clock's owner, Dr. Phineas A. Crooker of Warren, Maine, in 1884.[2]

Dyer treated the surfaces of the case like a canvas, leaving no section undecorated, and in the process created an important social and historical document. He imbued his vignettes of the settling and history of the town of Warren with a Victorian taste for luxury. The areas painted in black are meant to suggest ebony. Other opulent touches include the elaborate silver-leafed surfaces, gold-painted cartouches framing each scene, and Japanese-inspired vignettes on both side panels of the clock. While Dyer was probably self-taught, the Japanese influence evident in his decoration of the clock suggests he was aware of contemporary fashion and may have turned to pat-

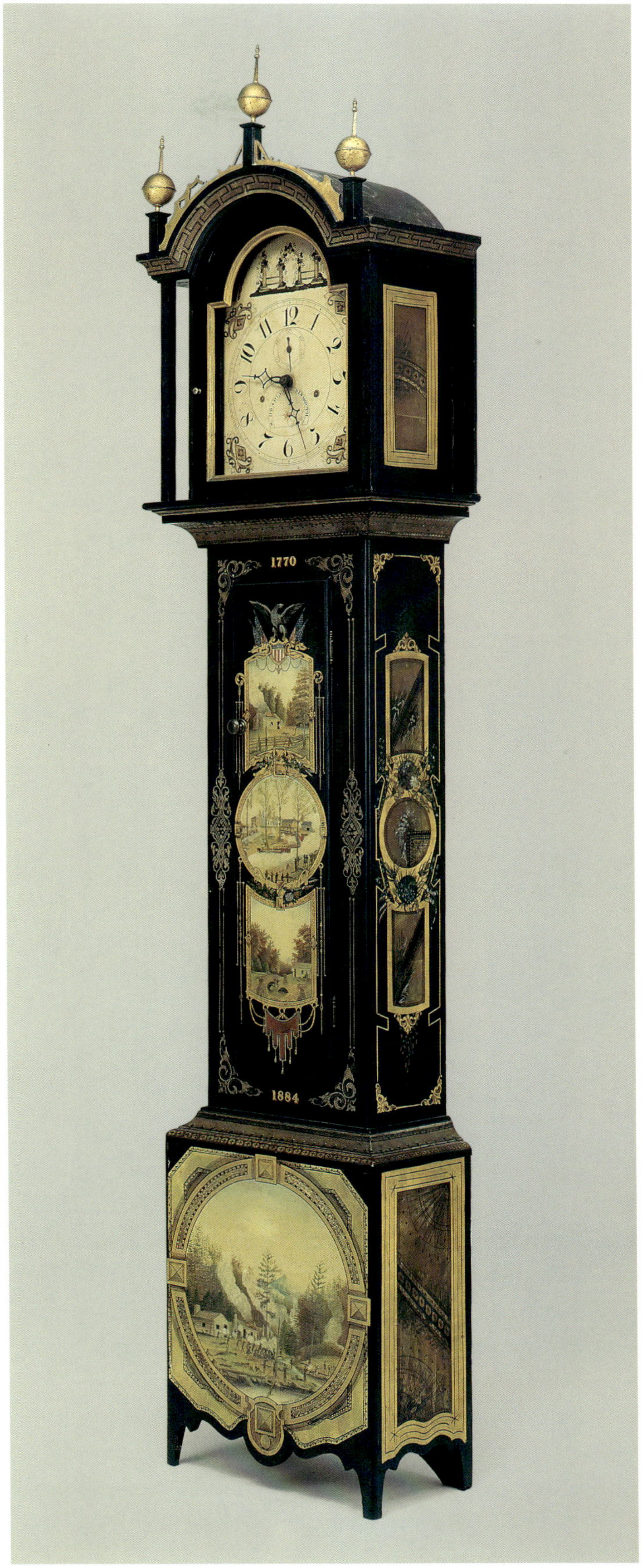

CAT. NO. 109

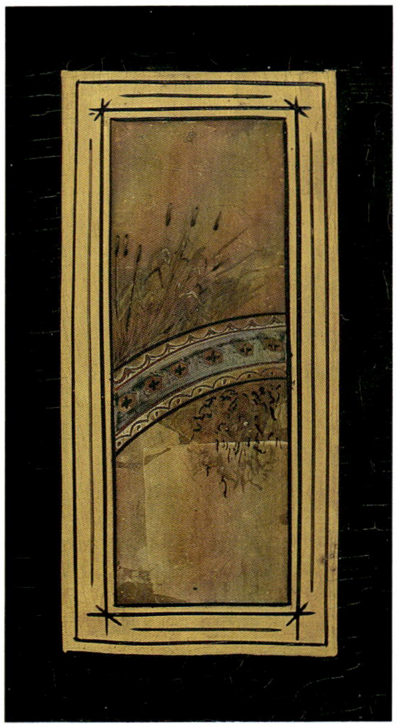

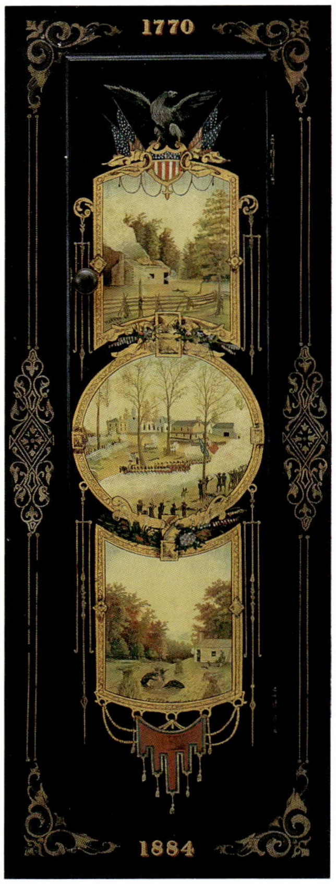

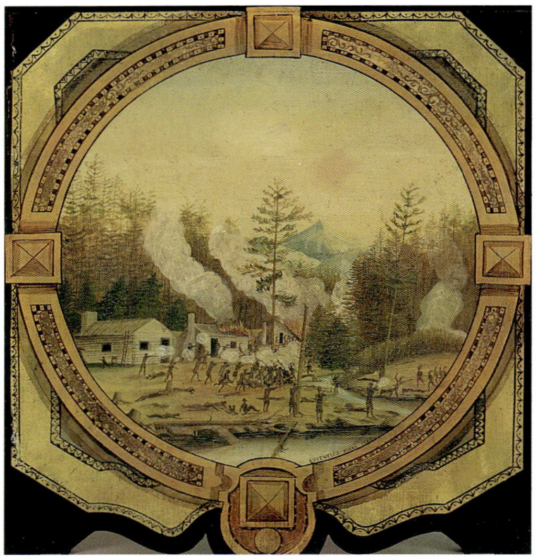

CAT. NO. 109, DETAILS (SIDE, DOOR, AND BASE)

tern books, book bindings, printed textiles, or period-painted ceramics for inspiration. He also may have intended to mimic panels from Japanese screens in his treatment of the sides of the clock.[3] In contrast, the scenes on the front of the clock depict the harsh, and often bloody, lives of the early residents of the area, first as settlers in the wilderness of Maine and then as rebellious colonists.

Three scenes painted on the clock depict images specific to Warren, Maine (see details). The upper and lower scenes on the door are both labeled "Warren, ME" and are dated 1645 and 1750, respectively. The upper vignette depicts a solitary log cabin engulfed in flames as two Native Americans and the white settlers battle for the land. In the lower image, Dyer painted a battle pitting man against nature in which several bears have ventured close to a cabin to forage in the harvest fields. A figure shoots at them from the cabin doorway as another figure, struck down by the bears, lies close by.

The image on the base of the clock, labeled "Lovewell's Fight 1725," illustrates another conflict between Native Americans and area settlers (see detail). Lovewell's Fight was actually a three-year-long war that began in 1722. According to an account of one battle, "a body of 200 Indians surprised and burnt the proprietor's sloop, killed one and took six men prisoners, burnt the saw-mill, some houses and frames, and made a vigorous attack upon the blockhouses, which with difficulty were saved by the bravery of the garrison."[4] Dyer's painting shows a similar, chaotic scene of burning buildings and fighting figures. Another resident of Maine, Henry Wadsworth Longfellow, described the war in one of his early poems, "Ode Written for the Commemoration at Fryeburg, Maine, of Lovewell's Fight."

Another scene, located in the center of the door, illustrates the Revolutionary battle at Lexington, Massachusetts. At the time of the Revolution, Maine was still part of the colony of Massachusetts.

A lifelong resident of Maine, Dyer was born on March 11, 1849, in Appleton, where he died on March 17, 1927. Recognition of his work during his own lifetime was limited to the state's mid-coastal region. His other artistic endeavors included sign painting, landscape painting, cabinetmaking, portraiture, and photography.[5]

NOTES

1. Elizabeth Kessler, a former intern in the Department of American Arts at the Art Institute, contributed to this entry.

2. Crooker's initials are painted on the inside of the waist door, above the trompe l'oeil trade card of Uriah Dyer.

3. For images of imported and domestic textile and ceramic designs that employ similar floral, border, and fan motifs, and for reproductions of four-panel screens, see William Hosley, *The Japan Idea: Art and Life in Victorian America*, exh. cat. (Hartford, Conn., Wadsworth Atheneum, 1990), pp. 79, 152–73.

4. Cyrus Eaton, *Annals of the Town of Warren* (Hallowell, Me., 1877), p. 38.

5. Mark Sisco, "Appleton, Maine, Folk Artist Uriah Dyer," *Maine Antique Digest* 20, 1 (Jan. 1992), pp. 2E–3E.

110. WINSLOW HOMER (1836–1910)

The Herring Net, 1885

Oil on canvas; 76.5 x 122.9 cm (30⅛ x 48⅜ in.)

Signed, lower right: *Homer 85*

Mr. and Mrs. Martin A. Ryerson Collection, 1937.1039

Almost two decades separate Winslow Homer's *The Herring Net* from *Croquet Scene* (cat. no. 104) and *Mount Washington* (cat. no. 105), and the changes that occurred in the artist's work over the course of these years are striking. Although his paintings were still based on observations of contemporary life, Homer's subject matter moved from land to sea, sport to work, and women to men. Formally, his palette became subdued and the scale of his figures and his canvases became monumental. Exactly why and how Homer's style shifted toward the heroic in the 1880s has been the subject of much discussion. The most persuasive arguments have linked the artist's style with his trips to the fishing towns of Gloucester, Massachusetts, in 1880 and Cullercoats, England, in 1881–82, and his permanent move to Prout's Neck on the rocky, desolate coast of Maine in 1883.[1]

Homer visited Prout's Neck for the first time in July 1875 and by August had published his final engraving, *The Family Record*, in *Harper's Weekly*.[2] By cutting his ties to illustration, Homer freed himself to pursue a variety of subjects unhampered by the necessity of pleasing his employers and working on assignment. By the summer of 1880, when he lived in solitude on Ten Pound Island in Gloucester Harbor, Homer had

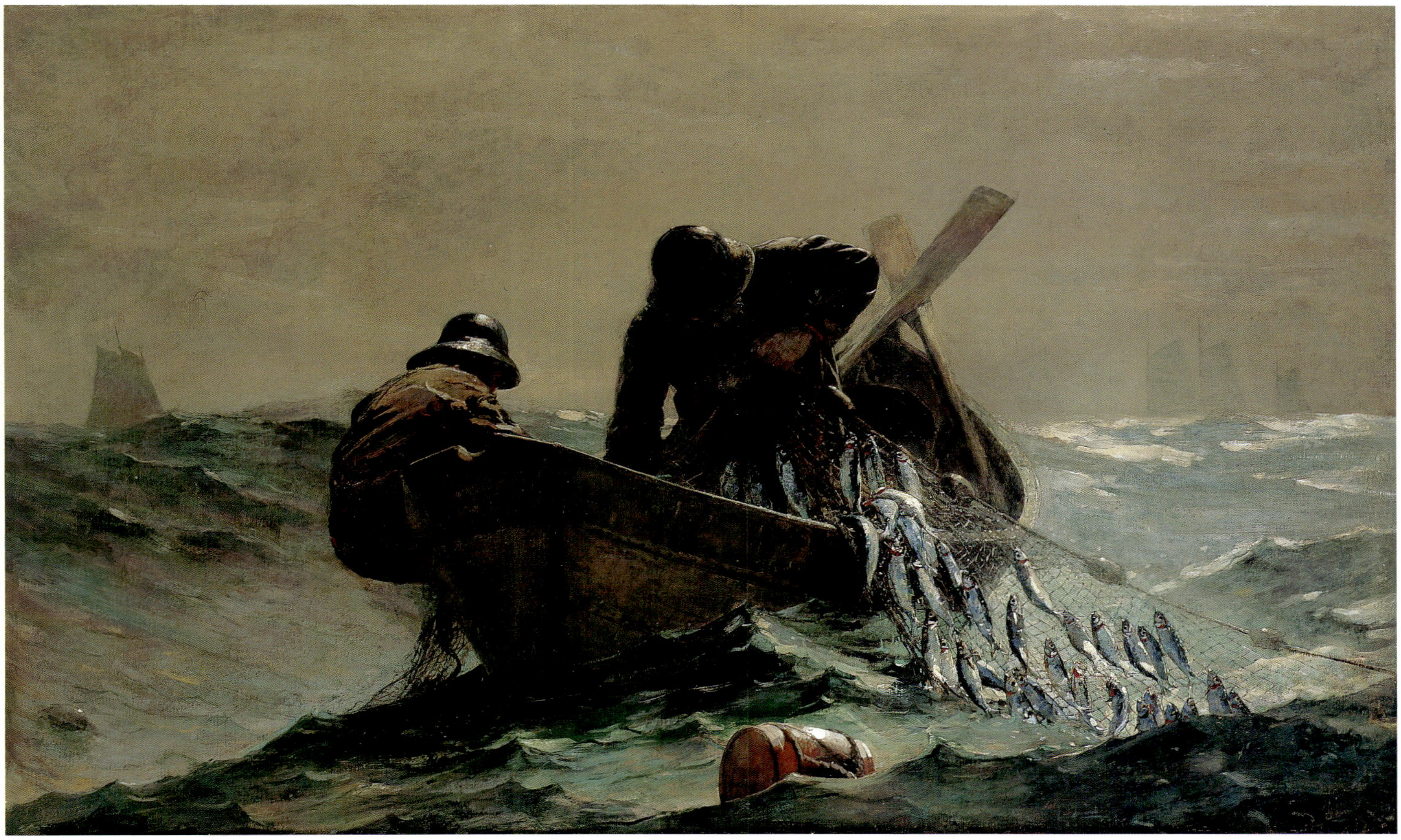

CAT. NO. 110

fully turned his attention to the sea, and to the men and women who depended upon it for their livelihood. In March 1881 he set sail for England to study further the fishing industry and settled in the small coastal village and artists colony of Cullercoats until the fall of 1882.[3]

Homer continued to explore these themes upon his return to the United States. In 1885 he produced three paintings in rapid succession, *The Herring Net*, *The Fog Warning* (1885; Museum of Fine Arts, Boston), and *Lost on the Grand Banks* (1885; private collection), that pit fishermen against the sea and invoke the timeless conflict between the forces of man and nature.[4] As one early twentieth-century critic suggested, "it was the struggle of men with the sea, of the waves with the land, . . . the poise of and buoyancy of boats among threatening billows . . . in general, a world of ceaseless strife and motion that engaged [his] imagination."[5] These paintings are all approximately the same size, and imply a narrative progression even though their protagonists differ.[6] They depict the three principal fish of the New England fishing industry: herring, halibut, and cod.[7] In the first, *The Herring Net*, two fishermen load a haul of herring onto their small dory. The second painting shows a lone fisherman in a dory weighed down by two large halibut, looking anxiously at the horizon darkening with fog and the schooner that awaits him. In the final picture fog has descended upon two cod fishermen who scan the sea for signs of life.

The Herring Net is by far the most optimistic of the three pictures and was praised for its "seriousness of aim" when it was shown for the first time at the 1885 National Academy of Design autumn exhibition.[8] Homer is believed to have painted this scene after observing local fishermen taking advantage of the presence of a large school of herring in the waters off Prout's Neck in the fall of 1884. He is reported to have hired a local boy, Roswell Googins, to row him out to the fishing fleet in order to make sketches of the fishermen at work.[9]

One of these sketches, also entitled *The Herring Net* (fig. 59), presents a vivid example of how Homer subtly altered his sedate drawings to compose dramatic paintings. The two fishermen are positioned similarly in both the drawing and the painting: one hauls the net teeming with silver herring into the dory while the other counterbalances the boat. Intent upon their task, both gaze down into the boat. In the painting, however, Homer has changed the location of the buoy and the nets, the size of the waves, and the distance of the dory from the schooners in order to enhance the precariousness of the fishermen's situation. What is portrayed as a routine commercial fishing outing in the sketch is elevated to the realm of the ideal on canvas. *The Herring Net* thus becomes an allegory with universal significance about the complex relationship between man and nature.

NOTES

1. On Homer in Prout's Neck, see Philip C. Beam, *Winslow Homer at Prout's Neck* (Boston, 1966).

2. Nicolai Cikovsky, Jr., and Franklin Kelly, *Winslow Homer*, exh. cat. (Washington, D.C., National Gallery of Art, 1995), p. 395.

3. For more on Homer in Cullercoats, see William H. Gerdts, "Winslow Homer in Cullercoats," *Yale University Art Gallery Bulletin* 36, 2 (spring 1977), pp. 18–35; and Tony Knipe et al., *Winslow Homer: All the Cullercoats Pictures*, exh. cat. (Sunderland, Tyne and Wear, Northern Centre for Contemporary Art, 1988).

4. On these three paintings, see Paul Raymond Provost, "Winslow Homer's *The Fog Warning*: The Fisherman as Heroic Character," *American Art Journal* 22, 1 (spring 1990), pp. 20–27.

5. Frank Jewett Mather, Jr., "The Art of Winslow Homer," *Nation* 92 (Mar. 2, 1911), p. 225.

6. For an informative discussion of the three works together, see Cikovsky and Kelly (note 2), pp. 226–30.

7. Ibid., p. 226.

8. "Fine Arts: The Autumn Academy," *Nation* 41 (Dec. 17, 1885), p. 516.

9. Beam (note 1), p. 66.

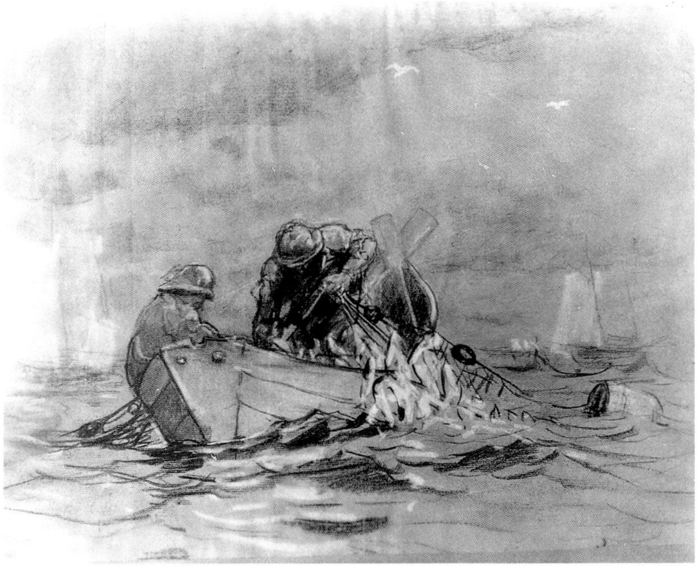

FIG. 59. Winslow Homer (1836–1910). *The Herring Net*, 1884. Black, brown, and white chalk on blue green laid paper; 42.2 x 52.4 cm (16⅝ x 20⅝ in.). Cooper-Hewitt National Design Museum, Smithsonian Institution/Art Resource, New York, Gift of Charles W. Gould (1916.15.2).

111. ATTRIBUTED TO POTTIER AND STYMUS (ACTIVE 1859–1888)

Armchair, 1870/75

New York

Ormolu mounts by Pierre E. Guerin (founded 1857)

Rosewood with ash, juniper, and burl maple veneer, ormolu mounts, original woven tapestry fabric; 98 x 64 x 58 cm (38½ x 25¼ x 22¾ in.)

Painted in black paint on crest rail, underneath upholstery: *3924. Ingersoll*

Suzanne Waller Worthy Fund, 1970.39

112. SOFA, 1860/70

New York

Ormolu mounts by Pierre E. Guerin

Rosewood, inlays of various woods, ormolu mounts, and porcelain plaques; 115.5 x 188 x 76.2 cm (45½ x 74 x 30 in.)

Gift of Robert R. McCormick Charitable Trust, 1985.7

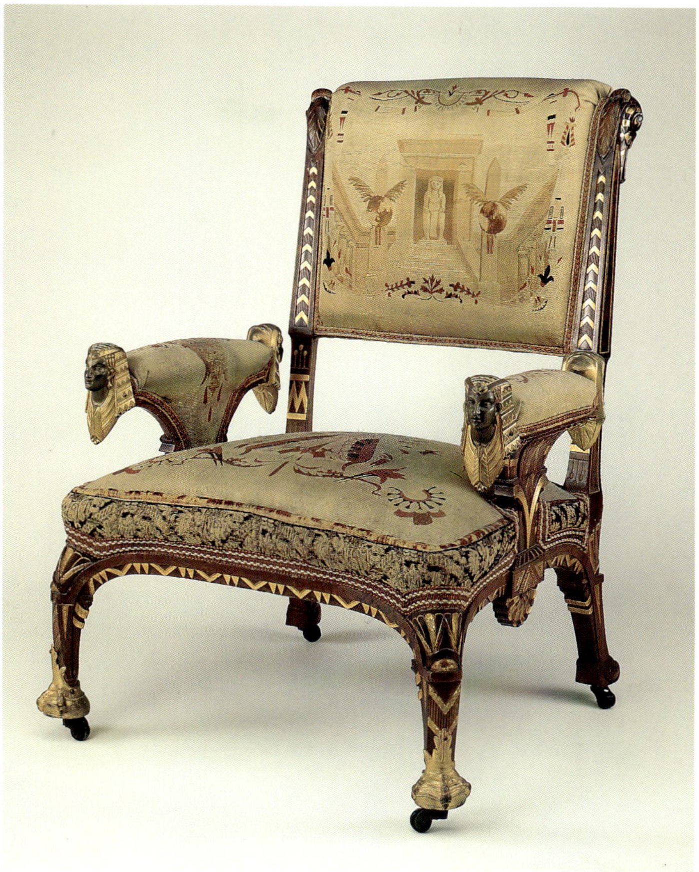

CAT. NO. III

The end of the Civil War opened an era of unprecedented economic growth throughout America. In the following decade, a manufacturing boom coupled with the continuing expansion of railroads and the exploration and exploitation of the vast natural resources of the Western frontier created a new social structure and a class of newly rich industrialists, bankers, speculators, and railroad magnates.[1]

To meet the demands of this new clientele, firms specializing in the complete decoration of interiors proliferated in the mid-nineteenth century. Among the largest and most famous of these firms, based in New York but accepting commissions throughout the country, was Herter Brothers (see cat. nos. 117–19).[2] For a brief period from 1851 to 1853, its founder, Gustave Herter, was in partnership with Auguste Pottier, though no examples of their work are known to survive. A few years later, Herter was joined by his brother Christian, and in 1859 Pottier formed a partnership with William Stymus. Together Pottier and Stymus became one of the Herter Brothers' most formidable competitors. By 1875 the Pottier and Stymus firm employed 750 people and had annual sales that surpassed a million dollars. Their factory and showrooms on Lexington Avenue took up a block-long, six-story building between 41st and 42nd Streets.[3] Some of their most important commissions included furnishings in the Renaissance Revival style for the President's Office and Cabinet Room at the White House during Ulysses S. Grant's term in 1869, furniture for Henry M. Flagler's house in New York and his house and hotels in Florida, and the redecoration in 1887 of Thomas Edison's home in New Jersey.[4]

Oddly Pottier and Stymus did not label their work, although attributions can be made on stylistic grounds. An unbridled contemporary account by rival cabinetmaker Ernest Hagen gives us an excellent idea of their production: "Their work was nearly all done in the 'Neo Grec' most awfull gaudy style with brass gilt Spinx head on the sofas and arm chairs, gilt engraved lines all over with porcailaine painted medalions on the backs, and brass gilt bead moldings nailed on. Other wise, their work was good; but the style horrible."[5]

The museum's Egyptian Revival armchair is characteristic of much of the surviving work from the Pottier and Stymus firm. The chair is closely related to another armchair, a side chair, and a rosewood, walnut, and marble center table, all three of which are attributed to the firm and now in the collection of the Metropolitan Museum of Art.[6] All four items

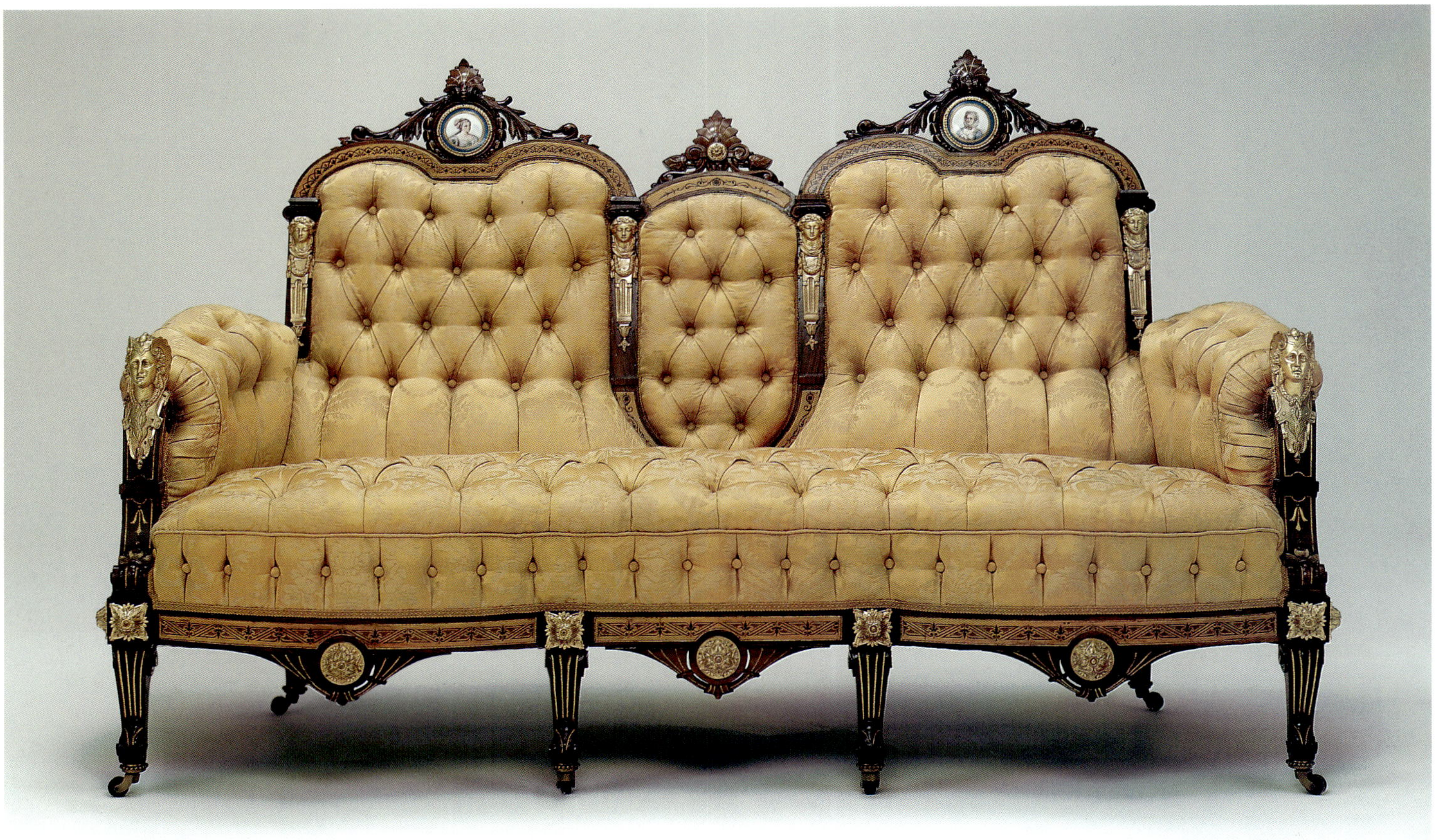

CAT. NO. 112

have very similar incised gilt decoration and ormolu Egyptian heads. The upholstery for the Art Institute's armchair is original and may have been produced by the firm. Before becoming a partner in the company, William Stymus worked as the foreman of the upholstery department at Rochefort and Skarren, a New York decorating firm from the 1850s. A contemporary description of the Pottier and Stymus factory indicated that there was a department devoted to chair upholstery, the execution of tapestries, and hangings and trimmings for chairs.[7]

The style of the sofa is best termed Renaissance Revival, a style that one critic from the nineteenth century thought "would seem to cover almost anything."[8] The form and overlying decoration of the sofa incorporates carved anthemion leaves and vines, inlay, gilt incised lines, and ormolu mounts that are characteristic of the Renaissance Revival style. However, the porcelain plaques on the crest rail recall the Louis XVI period. The carved ionic capitals and ormolu mounts with classical female heads and drapery swags on the sofa back take their inspiration from antiquity. The silk damask fabric with representations of baskets of flowers and foliate swags is a reproduction of the original fabric.[9] As many of New York's finest cabinetmaking firms worked in this high Renaissance Revival style, this sofa cannot be safely attributed to one firm.

After the 1876 Philadelphia Centennial, which introduced the Aesthetic Movement to the throngs of people who visited the fair, many firms such as Pottier and Stymus, Leon Marcotte, and Herter Brothers slowed their production of furniture, and by the mid-1880s, having dominated the furniture industry for decades, closed their doors.

NOTES

1. Eric Foner, *Reconstruction: America's Unfinished Revolution, 1863–1877* (New York, 1988), pp. 460–61.

2. See Katherine S. Howe et al., *Herter Brothers: Furniture and Interiors for a Gilded Age*, exh. cat. (Houston, Museum of Fine Arts, 1994).

3. Catherine Hoover Voorsanger, "From the Bowery to Broadway: The Herter Brothers and the New York Furniture Trade," in Howe et al. (note 2), p. 70.

4. These commissions are documented by surviving letters and bills of sale; see David A. Hanks, "Pottier & Stymus Mfg. Co.: Artistic Furniture and Decorations," *Art and Antiques* 7, 5 (Sept./Oct. 1982), pp. 85, 87–88.

5. Elizabeth A. Ingerman, "Personal Experiences of an Old New York Cabinetmaker," *Antiques Magazine* 84, 5 (Nov. 1963), pp. 579–80.

6. Marshall B. Davidson and Elizabeth Stillinger, *The American Wing at the Metropolitan Museum of Art* (New York, 1985), pp. 178–79, figs. 274, 277.

7. Hanks (note 4), pp. 84, 90.

8. Davidson and Stillinger (note 6), p. 176.

9. The original fabric for the sofa is preserved in the Department of American Arts at The Art Institute of Chicago.

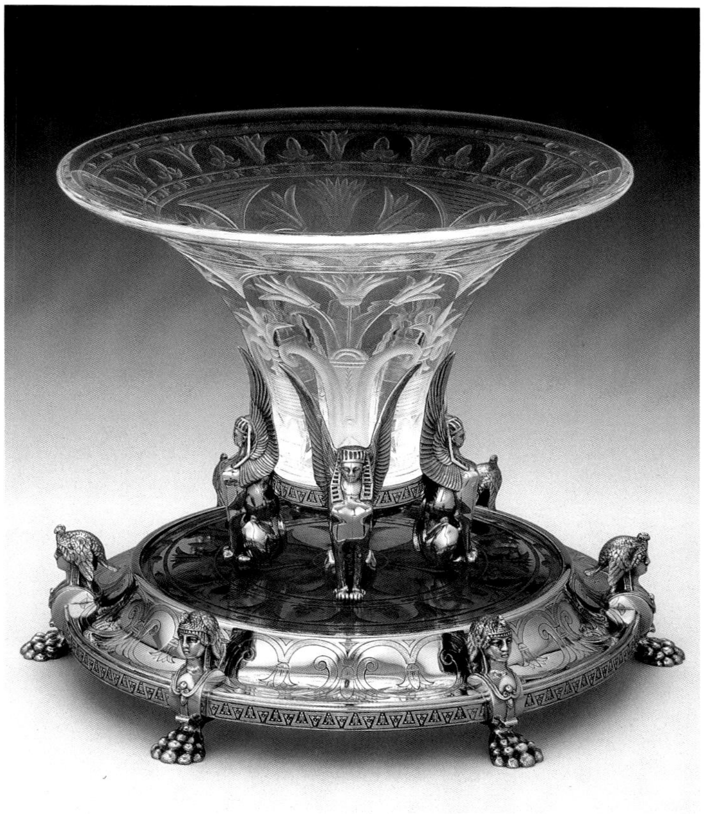

CAT. NO. 113

113. DOMINICK AND HAFF (ACTIVE 1872–1928)

RETAILED BY COWELL AND HUBBARD COMPANY, CLEVELAND, OHIO

Centerpiece, 1872/75

New York

Silver and etched glass; 28.3 x 30 (diam. of vase) cm (11⅛ x 1113/16 in.)

Marked on inner rim of base: *D. H.* (in square beside an empty diamond and circle); *STERLING / H 88 x 15 / THE COWELL & HUBBARD CO.*

Laura S. Matthews Fund, 1983.215

The earliest known example of the Egyptian Revival was executed in 1279 in central Italy, when stone carver Fra Pasquale carved one of four large sphinxes. From that time on, sphinxes and other Egyptian motifs were depicted in mural paintings and manuscripts and were used as decorative and structural supports on buildings, carved sarcophagi, cemetery gates, furniture, silver, and many other objects.[1]

Though Egyptian motifs continued to be used in architecture and the decorative arts throughout the late eighteenth and early nineteenth centuries (see cat. no. 70), the height of the Egyptian Revival in America took place in the second half of the nineteenth century. Americans had traveled to Egypt as part of their fascination with the Holy Land, but the opening of the Suez Canal in 1870 and the premiere in Cairo of Verdi's opera *Aida* in 1871, focused the attention on Egypt and its ancient civilization. *Aida* opened to great acclaim in New York in 1873.[2] The *New York Times*, for example, devoted several columns to a description of the scenery and performers in the production. The interest in Egypt also sparked a growth in tourism to the ancient land. Throughout the 1870s, Englishman Thomas Cook offered quick excursion trips to Cairo to see the pyramids and cruise along the Nile River.

Objects fashioned in the spirit of the Egyptian Revival were often not purely Egyptian in style. Many times Egyptian motifs were added to classical Greek- and Roman-inspired forms, or combined with ancient motifs from different cultures. Silversmiths Henry Blanchard Dominick and Leroy B. Haff created this centerpiece by using ancient Egyptian and Grecian motifs to guide the shape. The etched glass vase is in the shape of a lotus blossom, a flower associated in ancient Egyptian tradition with the sun and regenerative rites.[3] The form of the vase is repeated and reinforced by the etched lotus-flower patterning in the glass. The bowl is supported by four seated, female, winged sphinxes. Dominick and Haff's interpretation of the sphinx combines the original Greek female version with an Egyptian royal headdress. Sphinxes wearing the royal headdress, called a *nemes*, were originally manifestations of ancient Pharaohs, or rulers of Egypt, and traditionally were the guardians of temples and tombs.[4] Dominick and Haff represented the sphinxes as erect and alert, as if guarding the centerpiece or its contents. The sphinxes sit atop a roundel of glass etched with more lotus flowers. The whole is supported upon a base engraved with a band of scrolls and lotus flowers and six female heads wearing the vulture headdress that was reserved for female rulers and deities of Egypt.[5]

Dominick and Haff probably copied their motifs from published sources such as *La Description de l'Égypte*, a mammoth project incorporating all the information that scholars had gathered during Napoleon's march to Egypt in the early nineteenth century. This work was commissioned by the government of France and was issued in ten volumes between 1802 and 1829. Five of the ten volumes were devoted exclusively to antiquity and featured engraved representations of ancient bas-reliefs, temple facades, tomb paintings, and monumental sculptures, providing ample material for any revivalist.[6]

Successor to the famous silversmithing firm of William Gale and Son, Dominick and Haff were well respected among the trade in New York. Known primarily for their innovative flatware designs, they had a reputation for the quality of their special commissions and presentation hollow ware.[7]

NOTES

1. Kevin Stayton, "Revivalism and the Egyptian Movement," in Hudson River Museum, *The Sphinx and the Lotus: The Egyptian Movement in American Decorative Arts, 1865–1935*, exh. cat. (Yonkers, N.Y., 1990), p. 5.

2. Charles L. Venable, *Silver in America, 1840–1940: A Century of Splendor*, exh. cat. (Dallas, Dallas Museum of Art, 1994), p. 64; and Bernadette M. Sigler, "The Egyptian Movement in American Decorative Arts, 1865–1935," in Hudson River Museum (note 1), p. 14.

3. National Gallery of Canada, *Egyptomania: Egypt in Western Art, 1730–1930*, exh. cat. (Ottawa, 1994), p. 480, cat. no. 324.

4. Ibid., pp. 86–87.

5. Ibid., p. 562, cat. no. 380.

6. Wendy A. Cooper, *Classical Taste in America, 1800–1840*, exh. cat. (Baltimore, Baltimore Museum of Art, 1993), p. 66; Charles Coulston Gillispie and Michel Dewachter, eds., *Monuments of Egypt, the Napoleonic Edition: The Complete Archaeological Plates from La Description de l'Égypte* (Princeton, N.J., 1987).

7. Venable (note 2), p. 318.

114. ELIHU VEDDER (1836–1923)

Storm in Umbria, 1875

Oil on canvas; 33 x 114.3 cm (13 x 45 in.)
Signed, lower right: *Elihu Vedder Rome 1875*
Mr. and Mrs. Samuel M. Nickerson Collection, 1900.605

Elihu Vedder was one of countless American artists who, beginning in the nineteenth century, traveled to Italy to augment their educations and to steep themselves in the traditional setting of the Old World. From 1867 to 1875, Vedder and his family summered in Perugia, a city in Umbria, a region in central Italy located between Florence and their home in Rome. The artist produced a number of landscapes of the area, with its characteristic wide basins and river valleys, flanked by the Umbrian-Marchigian Appenines mountain range, as settings with dramatic atmospheric effects for pastoral activities such as goatherding.[1] Thus these works suggest both the specificity of place and the evocative qualities of the Italian landscape.

Although Vedder is best known for his enigmatic, literary pictures, such as those he painted to illustrate *The Rubáiyát of Omar Khayyám* (see cat. no. 137), the Umbrian landscape was a persistent subject throughout his career. Vedder first visited Umbria with the American landscape painter Thomas Hotchkiss in 1867. Their journey included a stop in Perugia to view works by Italian Renaissance masters; this experience deeply affected Vedder's perception of the Umbrian region. For Vedder, painters such as Perugino and Piero della Francesca captured the spiritual energy of the local landscape. When he returned to the region in the 1870s, Vedder continued to seek out their masterpieces as he traveled from town to town. Late in his life, Vedder's fascination with Italian landscapes continued, as his 1914 poem "In Umbria" reveals:

> Oft have I trod these silent Umbrian hills,
> Where neither grass nor tree is left to shade
> The awful desolation man has made,
> Silent, save where the Contadino's spade
> Breaks the hard soil, he singing cheers his toil,
> Or shouting, drives his meagre swine afield,
> To glean what food the starving land may yield.[2]

Storm in Umbria was painted in 1875, during Vedder's final summer stay in Perugia. The painting's emphatically horizontal format, strong contrasts of light and dark areas, and rich surface texture lend an air of immediacy to the view, even

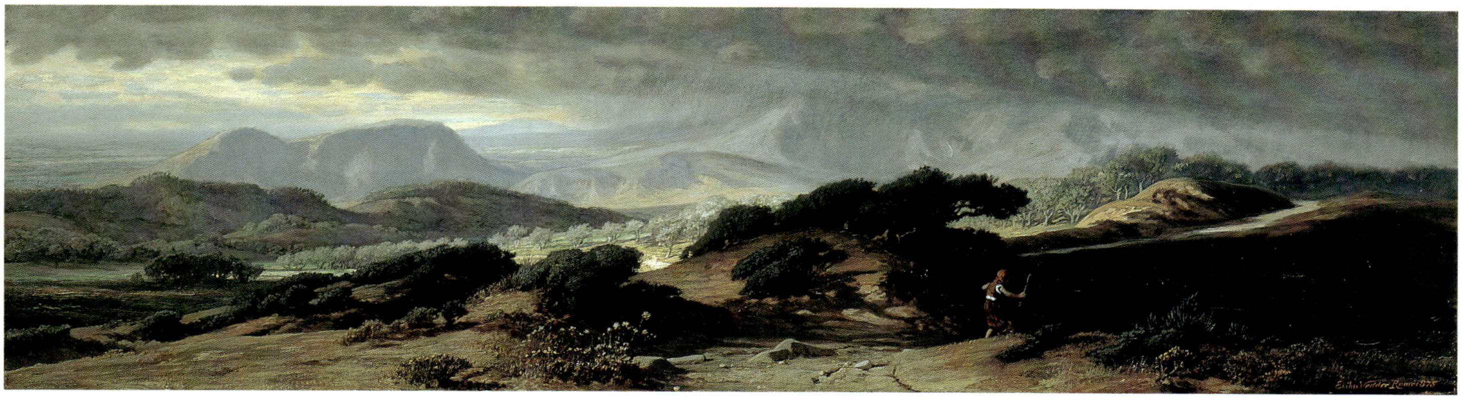

CAT. NO. 114

though Vedder developed the finished canvas from a series of sketches.[3] In this dramatic, even vengeful, landscape, the tiny goatherd in the right foreground seems about to be overpowered by the natural forces that surround her. Vedder employed landscapes similar to *Storm in Umbria* in his better-known literary pictures. For example, in *The Cumaean Sibyl* (fig. 60), the figure appears before a similar backdrop of mountains. By focusing on the figure, however, Vedder presented the sibyl as a potent force, equal to the threatening energy of nature.

Remarkably both *Storm in Umbria* and *The Cumaean Sibyl* were featured in a 1901 exhibition of Vedder's paintings held at The Art Institute of Chicago.[4] A writer for the *Chicago Record Herald* admired both paintings, but bestowed special praise on the Umbrian landscape, which he compared to the work of French artist Claude Lorrain: "It presents a fine sweep of valley . . . entirely filled with the play of light and shadow, and over all is a heavy, turbulent sky."[5] The painting had been donated to the Art Institute by Samuel M. Nickerson (1879–1914), a founder and trustee of the museum who gave it his entire collection in 1900. The artist's account books reveal that his Italian landscapes were particularly popular with American patrons. Nickerson even wrote to Vedder that "the picture I bought of yours in Rome is very much admired, and holds a first place in my small collection."[6]

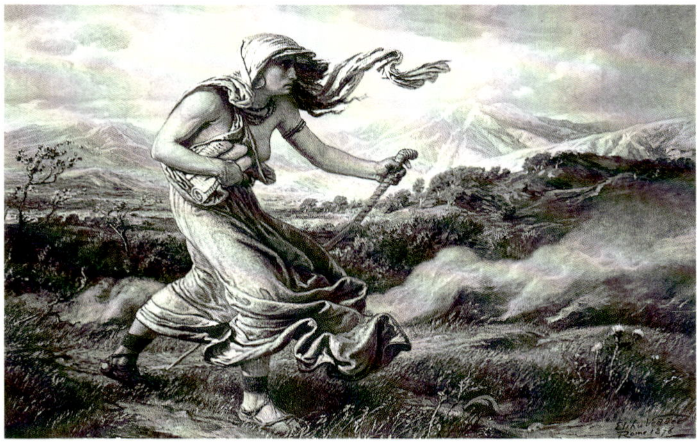

FIG. 60. Elihu Vedder (1836–1923). *The Cumaean Sibyl*, 1876. Oil on canvas; 96.5 x 149.9 cm (38 x 59 in.). Detroit Institute of Arts, Founders Society Purchase, Merrill Fund (57.235).

NOTES

1. Regina Soria recorded no fewer than thirty sketches, oils, and drawings executed by Vedder in Umbria between 1871 and 1875; see Soria, *Elihu Vedder: American Visionary Artist in Rome (1836–1923)* (Rutherford, N.J., 1970), pp. 90–101.

2. From Elihu Vedder, *Miscellaneous Moods* (1914); cited in *Visions of Italy*, exh. cat. (New York, Borghi and Company, 1988), p. 29.

3. A small oil sketch in the collection of the St. Augustine Historical Society in St. Augustine, Florida, entitled *Near Perugia* (dated "Aug. 15, '67") recalls the background mountain scenery in *Storm in Umbria*. A drawing titled *Landscape with Figures*, c. 1874 (Soria [note 1], p. 307, no. 242), replicates the subject of *Storm in Umbria* from a different point of view. The whereabouts of this work are unknown. A photograph of it, acquired from Regina Soria, is in the Files of the Department of American Arts, The Art Institute of Chicago.

4. The Art Institute of Chicago, *Exhibition of Works by Elihu Vedder*, exh. cat. (1901), cat. no. 24. *Storm in Umbria* was also included in the first exhibition of fine art held at the Art Institute in 1883; see The Art Institute of Chicago, *First Annual Exhibition of the Art Institute*, exh. cat. (1883), p. 11, cat. no. 63, as *Scene in Italy*.

5. *Chicago Record Herald*, Apr. 14, 1901, in Scrapbook, Ryerson and Burnham Libraries, The Art Institute of Chicago.

6. Elihu Vedder Papers, Archives of American Art, Smithsonian Institution, Washington, D.C., roll no. 518, fr. 542.

115. UNION PORCELAIN WORKS (c. 1863–1914)

DESIGNED BY KARL L. H. MÜLLER (1820–1887)

Poet's Pitcher, 1875/86

Greenpoint, Brooklyn

Parian porcelain; h. 21.8 cm (8⅞₁₆ in.)

Marked on underside of base with an eagle's head and the letter *S* with *Union Porcelain Works, Greenpoint, N.Y.* above *1 86* in a yellow circular decorator's mark

Gift of the Antiquarian Society through Mrs. Eric Oldberg, 1996.14

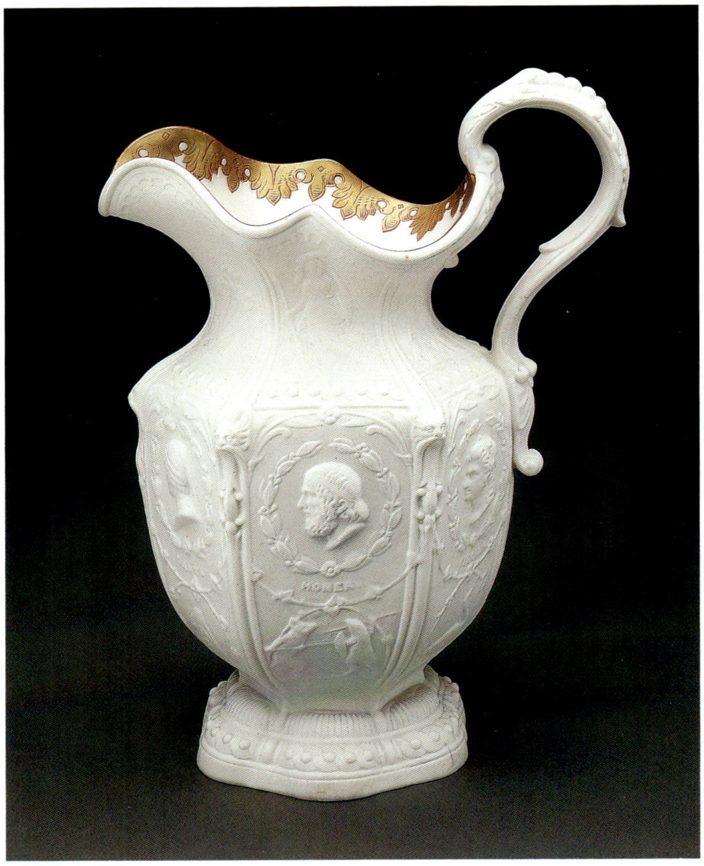

CAT. NO. 115

The Union Porcelain Company was purchased by Thomas C. Smith and reorganized into the Union Porcelain Works around 1863. Having taken over a company that was known for making porcelain door knobs, door plates, and other utilitarian wares, Smith experimented with different formulas to produce fine porcelain table wares that could compete with imported products from Meissen and Dresden. In 1865 he succeeded in making a white ware suitable for production, and in 1866, utilizing the skill of two porcelain painters, one English and one German, he placed his products on the market. By 1874 his successful enterprise employed 170 people and covered over an acre of land in Brooklyn.[1]

The first porcelain poet's pitcher was designed in 1875, most likely for the Centennial Exhibition in Philadelphia.[2] A poet's pitcher was later exhibited at the 1876 American Institute Fair in New York, where it received great praise from a critic from the *Crockery and Glass Journal*: "The poet's pitcher, in plain white porcelain, ornamented with wreaths and vines, and medallion heads is a chaste and beautiful affair."[3] Like most objects designed for display at international expositions, the poet's pitcher showcased the virtuosity of Union Porcelain Works products. The Art Institute's pitcher appears to be one of the more elaborate ones produced, having a gilded and painted foliate design around the rim of the opening. It is modeled out of parian porcelain, a hard-fired, unglazed biscuit porcelain that resembles marble.

The pitcher's name derives from the masterfully executed relief medallions that encircle the body. Each of the six faceted sides contains the profile of a poet within a laurel wreath and each is bordered on the top and the bottom by appropriate literary vignettes. The vignette above the head of John Milton, for example, depicts Eve and the Serpent conversing by the Tree of Knowledge, an obvious reference to *Paradise Lost*. The scene below is of a sheep recumbent against a triangle—probably an allusion to Milton's great pastoral poem "Lycidas."[4] Ossian, an apocryphal third-century Irish poet, is depicted between a harp and a shield and helmet.[5] The bust of Shakespeare appears below masks of comedy and tragedy and above the figure of Falstaff, the boisterous character who appears in both *Henry IV*, Parts I and II, and *The Merry Wives of Windsor*. The scene above the portrait of Dante depicts the condemnation of Paolo and Francesca taken from the *Inferno*. Below Dante is the figure of Beatrice who appears in both the *Inferno* and *La vita nuova*. Homer is shown below Achilles, most likely as a symbol of the *Iliad*, and above a dueling mouse and frog from a comic poem entitled "The Bactrians."[6] Above the head of Virgil are the figures of Romulus and Remus suckling a she-wolf, while below him is the image of a swan—both images drawn from the *Aeneid*.[7]

These references to ancient and Renaissance literary sources are indicative of the importance of literature to the educated middle class in America during the nineteenth century. Karl

Müller, who designed the pitcher, favored literary subjects for his works. Among his other surviving pieces are a bust of Shakespeare, a pedestal with the story of Electra now in the Metropolitan Museum of Art, New York, a vase with the figures of Comedy and Tragedy on the handle, a vase based on Longfellow's poem entitled "Keramos," and a portrait bust of actor Edwin Forrest as William Tell.[8] Karl Müller left his hometown of Koblenz, Germany, in the late 1840s after apprenticing in a goldsmith shop. He went to Paris to study at the Royal Academy and immigrated in 1850 to America, where he completed his studies at the National Academy of Design in New York. Müller began his career in New York crafting clock cases and small statuettes out of cast metal, which were then offered through art union magazines to subscribers around the country.[9] In 1874 the Union Porcelain Works hired Müller to design their ceramic products for display at the 1876 Philadelphia Centennial Exhibition. Prior to the Centennial, American ceramic manufacturers had been criticized by European firms for the lack of quality and inventiveness in their product lines. At the Centennial, however, the ceramics from the Union Porcelain Works and several other firms received widespread acclaim from international critics. One account described many of the works that Müller executed: "The cabinet trimmings are numerous and good. When visitors examine this display, they will see what can be done in art pottery on this side of the water."[10]

NOTES

1. Jennie J. Young, *The Ceramic Art: A Compendium of the History and Manufacture of Pottery and Porcelain* (New York, 1878), pp. 473–75.

2. An unpainted parian example with the incised initials and date "KLHM/1875" under the spout survives in a private collection. Alice Cooney Frelinghuysen, *American Porcelain, 1770–1920*, exh. cat. (New York, 1989), cat. no. 48, p. 154.

3. "The American Institute Fair," *Crockery and Glass Journal* 4 (Sept. 28, 1876), p. 14.

4. Letter from Kathleen M. Swaim, Professor of English, University of Massachusetts, Amherst, Mar. 19, 1997, Files of the Department of American Arts, The Art Institute of Chicago.

5. Ossian's poems were purportedly discovered and translated by the eighteenth-century Scottish poet James Macpherson. The poems tell the tales of Finn and his warrior band and were central to the development of the early Romantic movement in English literature. At the time of their publication, Samuel Johnson cast serious doubt upon the authenticity of Macpherson's claims, but it was not until late in the nineteenth century that it was revealed that Macpherson had written the poems himself.

6. Ian Wardropper, Eloise W. Martin Curator of European Decorative Arts and Sculpture and Ancient Art, The Art Institute of Chicago, provided this reference.

7. In the *Aeneid*, book 8, Venus presents Aeneas with his sacred armor. Vulcan has engraved an image of the she-wolf reclining in Mars's cavern with the twins Romulus and Remus nursing. The swan appears in the *Aeneid*, book 11. A reference is made to citizens acting like birds, especially rough-voiced swans croaking in Padua's fish-teaming ponds. Letter from James Freeman, Professor of English, University of Massachusetts, Amherst, Mar. 13, 1997, Files of the Department of American Arts, The Art Institute of Chicago.

8. Frelinghuysen (note 2), p. 154.

9. Ibid., p. 34.

10. As quoted in J. G. Stradling, "American Ceramics at the Philadelphia Centennial," *Antiques Magazine* (July 1976), p. 151.

116. CHEST OF DRAWERS, 1878/84

New York
Bird's-eye maple, tulip poplar, and cherry;
152.4 x 111.8 x 55.9 cm (60 x 44 x 22 in.)
Stamped on brass locks: *ROBINSON BOSTON*
Gift of the Antiquarian Society through the Mr. and Mrs.
William Y. Hutchinson Fund, 1986.186

This chest is part of a large suite of bedroom furniture made for the New York home of Henry G. Marquand.[1] A distinguishing feature of the Marquand residence was that each room of the house was decorated in a different revival style reflecting an interpretation of a historical period. The front hall, for example, was executed with a mixture of Renaissance and Gothic motifs, but there was also a Greek-inspired drawing room, a Saracenic, or Arabic, room, an Anglo-Japanese room, and an "English Renaissance"–style dining room.[2] In each case, the furniture harmonized with the architectural decoration.

The upstairs bedroom that housed the Art Institute's chest was described in a 1905 auction brochure as having "trim of bird's-eye maple and a tall carved chimneypiece of the same wood . . . [and a] door having a bird's-eye maple veneer on one side and a mahogany [veneer] on the other."[3] This room, believed to have been that of Marquand's daughter, Elizabeth, was apparently not given over to one fashion as the downstairs rooms were, for each piece of the maple bedroom suite was executed in a slightly different historical style.[4] On the bedstead were Renaissance Revival decorations of urns, paterae, and winged cupids. Four chairs were executed with Anglo-Japanese spindle backs and scrolled crest rails inspired by the designs of Englishman E. W. Godwin.[5]

The Art Institute's chest is inspired by many design sources, so intricately linked as to be almost undefinable. For example,

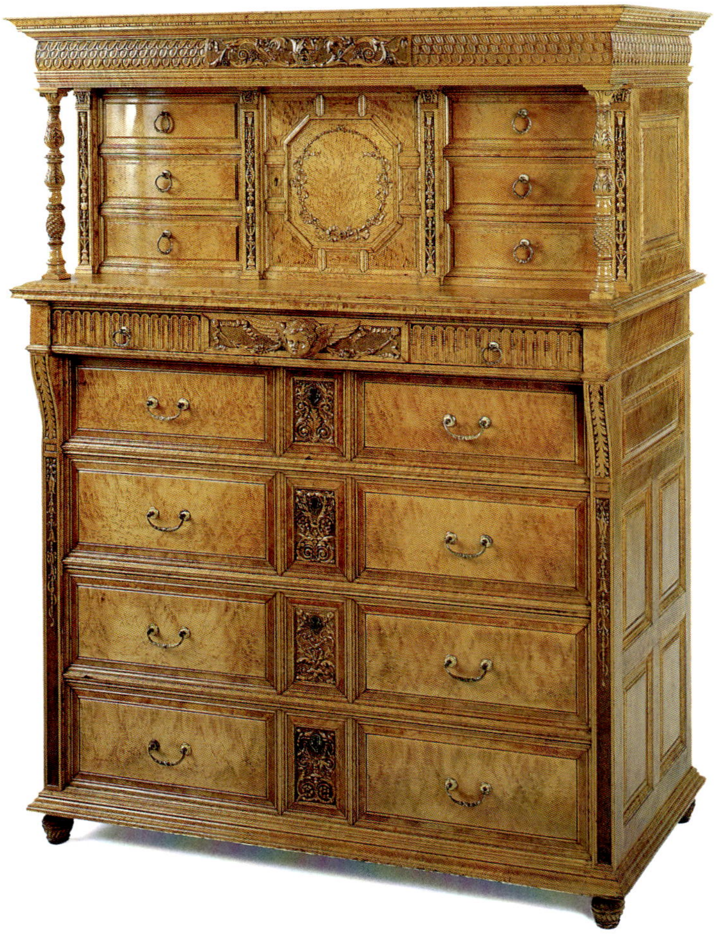

CAT. NO. 116

some of the carved motifs, swags, capitals, vines, and foliate forms are loosely drawn from the antique and interpreted in a "Renaissance" style. But featured images such as the cherub's head placed prominently in the center of the piece recall Baroque interpretations of these age-old symbols. The winged cherubs were found on seventeenth-century tombstones, and on church silver. The form of the chest, too, takes its inspiration from seventeenth-century Baroque court cupboards, particularly in the tripartite division of the upper section of the chest; the carved spindle supports of the upper case; the carved cornice; the raised moldings surrounding the drawer; and the paneled construction of the case sides. Not surprisingly, this chest of drawers was made at a time of great interest in American colonial history and combines this interest in historicism with the beautiful materials, skilled workmanship, and eclectic design vocabulary of the Aesthetic Movement.

Although the authorship of this elaborate suite of furniture is uncertain, several decorative motifs used on the Art Institute's chest of drawers are similar to those used on a gold-medal-winning cabinet exhibited by New York craftsman Leon Marcotte at the Paris Exposition of 1878 (see fig. 61).[6] The winged cherub's head; the narrow, carved, vertical panels depicting vases and sprouting vines; the carved panels of scrolling vines; and the drawer pulls on the bird's-eye maple chest are all present on the Marcotte cabinet. Indeed, decorative elements from all the pieces of the bird's-eye maple suite can be found on the Marcotte cabinet.[7] The publication of Marcotte's design in the *Art Journal* of 1878, however, opens up the possibility that other cabinetmakers used it as a design source.

NOTES

1. The house was built on 68th Street and Fifth Avenue between 1881 and 1884 by Richard Morris Hunt. It was demolished in 1912. See Susan R. Stein, "Some of the New York City Houses of Richard Morris Hunt," *Antiques* 129, 4 (Apr. 1986), p. 849.

2. The furniture for the Greek drawing, or music, room was ordered from London and decorated in the Greco-Roman style by Sir Lawrence Alma-Tadema. The furniture was made of ebony and inlaid with ivory, red cedar, mother of pearl, and shell. The suite was described as having "decoration in

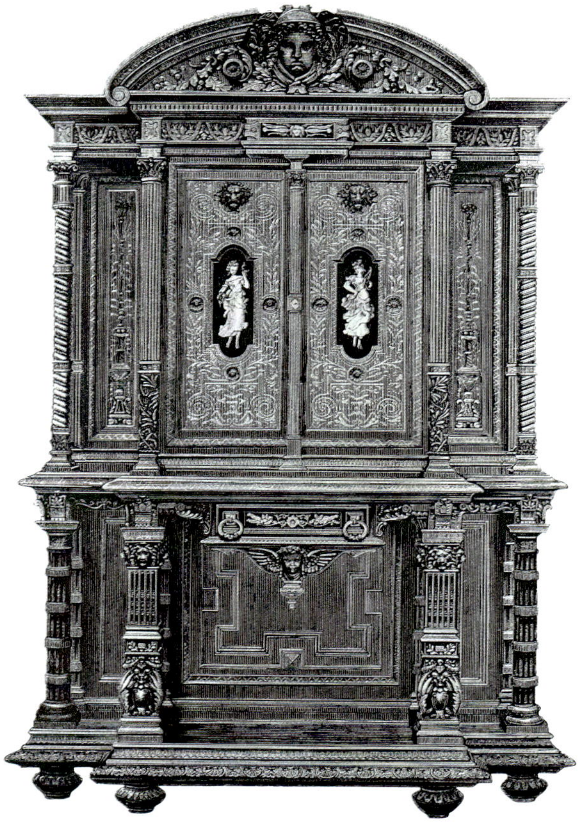

FIG. 61. Illustration of cabinet by Leon Marcotte exhibited at the 1878 Exposition Universelle in Paris. Photograph from *The Illustrated Catalogue of the Paris International Exhibition* (London, 1878), p. 144.

the best Pompeiian manner." See American Art Association, New York, *Catalogue of the Art and Literary Property Collected by the Late Henry G. Marquand* (Jan. 23–31, 1903), lots 1363–64. For illustrations of pieces from the suite, see Daniëlle O. Kisluk-Grosheide, "The Marquand Mansion," *Metropolitan Museum Journal* 29 (1994), pp. 159–61.

3. New York Real Estate Auction House, *The Marquand Residence* (New York, 1905), pp. 9–10.

4. A 1952 inventory of the contents of Cedarmere, the Long Island home of Elizabeth Marquand and her husband Harold Godwin, contains a notation by their daughter Elizabeth underneath the description of the suite stating "from Mommee's room in 68th Street." See Kisluk-Grosheide (note 2), p. 181 n. 88.

5. Doreen Bolger Burke et al., *In Pursuit of Beauty: Americans and the Aesthetic Movement,* exh. cat. (New York, Metropolitan Museum of Art, 1986), p. 160; and Kisluk-Grosheide (note 2), pp. 172–73.

6. *Art Journal* 17 (1878), p. 144.

7. For images of the other pieces in the suite, see Burke et al. (note 5), pp. 164–65.

117. HERTER BROTHERS (ACTIVE 1859–1906)

Sideboard, 1876/80

New York

Oak with white pine; 230 x 213.4 x 73.7 cm (91½ x 84 x 29 in.)

Robert R. McCormick Charitable Trust, 1982.1113

During the great European revolutions of 1848, Gustave Herter emigrated from his native Württemberg, Germany, to New York. A decade later he was firmly established in business, manufacturing heavily carved and ornate Renaissance Revival furniture. His half-brother Christian emigrated in 1860, and by 1865 had joined Gustave in the furniture-making business.

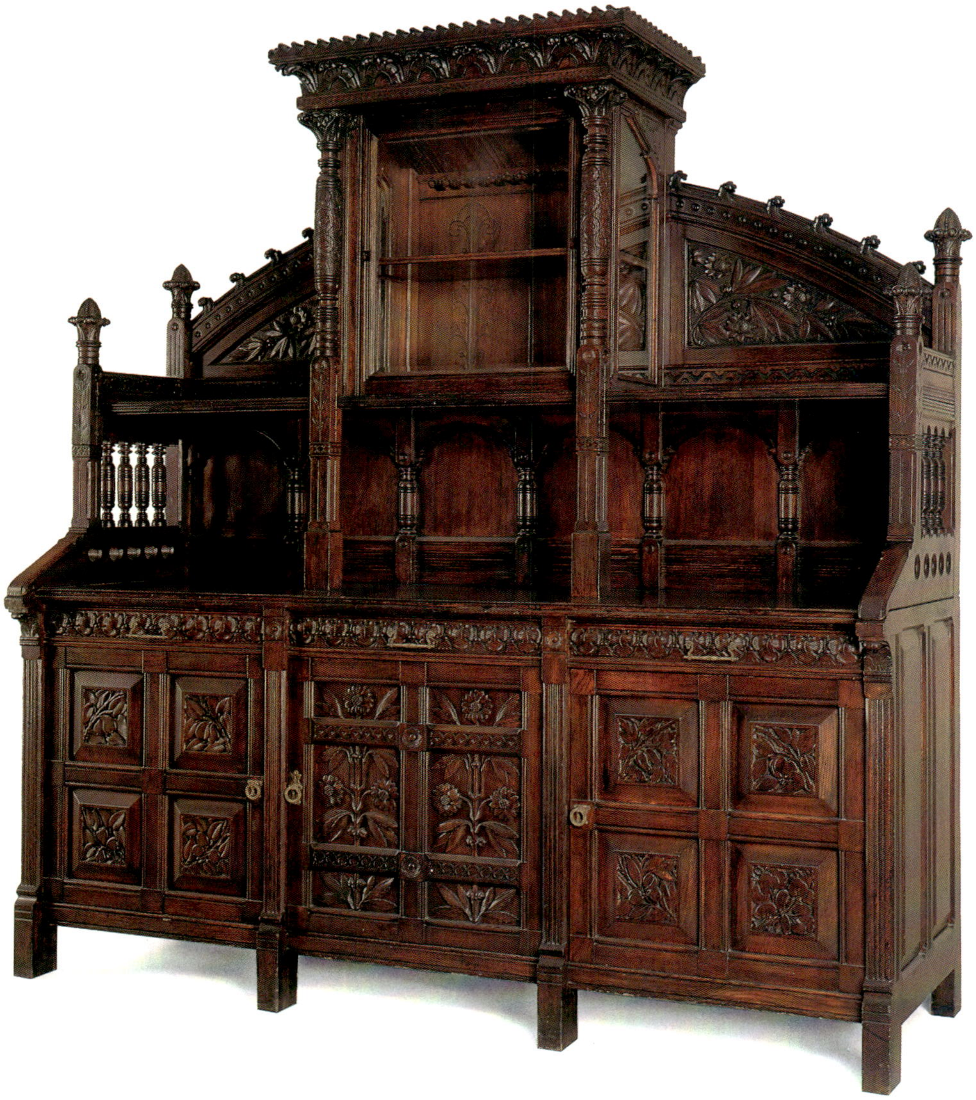

CAT. NO. 117

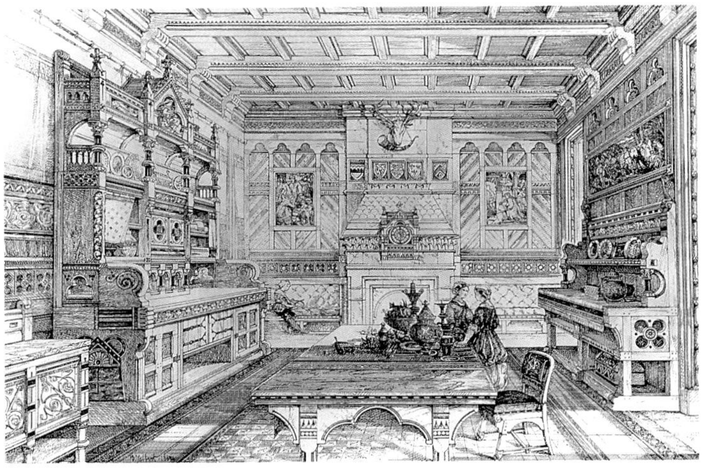

FIG. 62. Gothic Revival dining room designed by Bruce Talbert, illustrated in his book *Gothic Forms Applied to Furniture, Metal Work, and Decoration for Domestic Purposes* (Birmingham, 1867), pl. 11.

Christian returned to Paris to study painting during the years 1868–69, but upon his brother's retirement from the firm in 1870, Christian returned to New York to manage the company.

His European sojourn certainly made Christian Herter conversant with the aesthetic theories of the English reform movement and its reaction to the popular revival styles of the mid-nineteenth century. Reformers were concerned that the preponderance of heavy and superfluous ornament in such fashions obscured the original intent of the objects they adorned. Proponents of the reform movement wanted a return to simple, "honest" craftsmanship and functional as well as beautiful forms. They spread these ideals on both sides of the Atlantic through arts-and-crafts organizations, exhibitions, and publications. One of the most influential of these products was Charles L. Eastlake's *Hints on Household Taste*, published in London in 1868 and reprinted for the American market eight times between 1872 and 1886.[1] Eastlake argued that the fashionable revival designs of the previous decades were "absurd and mischievous," and he looked to every country except England for design inspiration.[2] Eastlake advised that the dining room sideboard should "consist of a wide and deep shelf fitted with one or two drawers, and resting at each end on a cellarette cupboard. If this piece of furniture were constructed in a plain and straightforward manner, and were additionally provided with a few narrow shelves for displaying the old china vases and rare porcelain . . . what a picturesque appearance it might present at the end of a room!"[3]

Another English designer, Bruce Talbert, issued a book of his own reform designs in 1867, *Gothic Forms Applied to Furniture, Metal Work, and Decoration for Domestic Purposes*, which was republished in Boston in 1873. For Talbert, the predominantly oak furniture of the Middle Ages represented a massive power and simple straightforward construction that could inspire cleaner contemporary design. Talbert illustrated such a modern English dining room complete with an immense, architectonic sideboard (see fig. 62). Like the Art Institute's sideboard, Talbert's designs incorporate crockets and finials, leafy column capitals, an arched colonnade, and paneled cupboard doors. Both sideboards incorporate ample storage, display, and serving space into their designs to make the pieces useful as well as beautiful.

The form and ornament of the Art Institute's sideboard is closely linked with the English and American cabinets that were shown at the 1876 Philadelphia Centennial Exhibition and illustrated in George Titus Ferris's *Gems of the Centennial Exhibition*.[4] These sideboards are impressive constructions, and their decorative vocabulary of carved sunflowers, lilies, spindles, and incised lines—all typical of the new fashion—

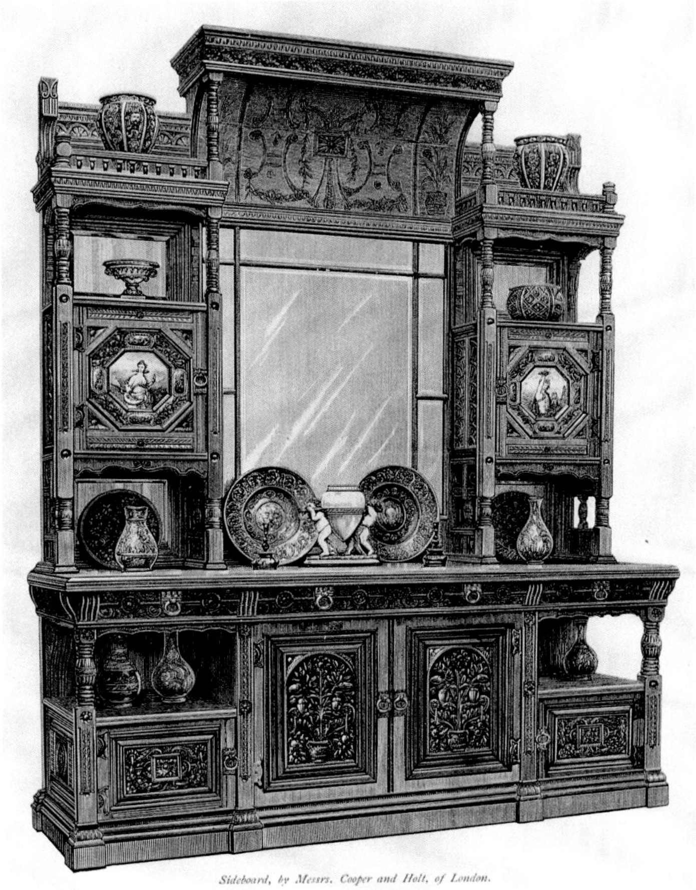

FIG. 63. Sideboard designed by Cooper and Holt, illustrated in George T. Ferris, *Gems of the Centennial Exhibition* (New York, 1877), p. 94.

reflects the emphasis placed upon natural forms by aestheticians such as John Ruskin. In particular, the Herter piece shares characteristics with the cabinet shown by London manufacturer Cooper and Holt (fig. 63). Both cabinets have similar vertical tripartite divisions; projecting central sections with carved cornice moldings; rows of carved and turned spindles on the case sides; carved, paneled doors on the lower sections below a single row of three drawers; and the repeated motif of a carved rosette on the vertical members of the lower case. Both sideboards also use virtually identical brass hardware on the cupboard doors.

Herter's decoration was not as spare as some critics would have liked. Clarence Cook, author of *House Beautiful,* lamented: "Mr. Herter has had some pieces made which were both well designed and thoroughly well made, as all his furniture is, however we may sometimes quarrel with his over-ornamentation."[5]

NOTES

1. Doreen Bolger Burke et al., *In Pursuit of Beauty: Americans and the Aesthetic Movement,* exh. cat. (New York, Metropolitan Museum of Art, 1987), p. 19.

2. Charles L. Eastlake, *Hints on Household Taste* (London, 1868; reprint, Boston, 1878), pp. 5, 75.

3. Ibid., p. 85.

4. For illustrations of these pieces, see Eastlake (note 2), pp. 97, 136.

5. Clarence Cook, *The House Beautiful: Essays on Beds and Tables, Stools and Candlesticks* (London, 1868; reprint, New York, 1878), pp. 223–24.

118. HERTER BROTHERS (ACTIVE 1859–1906)

Side Chair, 1869/70

New York

Rosewood with marquetry of various woods, and ivory;
90.5 x 45.7 x 41.9 cm (35⅝ x 18 x 16½ in.)

Written in script in pencil on the original muslin undercovering at the left rear of seat: *GH*

Wesley M. Dixon, Jr., Endowment, 1988.199

119. *Cabinet,* 1878/80

New York

Rosewood with ebonized cherry, maple, walnut, satinwood, marquetry of various woods, brass, gilding, and paint;
134.6 x 180.3 x 40.6 cm (53 x 71 x 16 in.)

Impressed twice on back boards: *HERTER BRO'S;* written in script in pencil on top boards: *N 238 Store*

Gift of the Antiquarian Society through the Capital Campaign, 1986.26

In addition to his years of working in the cabinetmaking business with his brother Gustave, Christian Herter studied painting in Paris in 1868 and 1869, and he was certainly familiar with the many great Parisian mural commissions executed during that period. Of particular interest was the work of the well-known muralist Pierre-Victor Galland (1822–1892), with whom Herter collaborated in 1868 on the decoration of the LeGrand Lockwood residence, Elm Park, in Norwalk, Connecticut.[1]

The Art Institute's sidechair is one of a suite of six reception chairs—lightweight, upholstered side chairs used in drawing rooms—that were used at Elm Park around 1869–70. After Lockwood's furnishings were auctioned in 1873, the house's new owner, Charles Drelincourt Mathews, used inventory lists to repurchase some of the original furnishings. He also commissioned more furniture from the Herter Brothers firm.[2] The musical motif on the crest rail of the museum's side chair is similar to those motifs used by Galland in the ceiling decoration of the drawing room at Elm Park. The classical motifs on the chair—the fluted columns and ionic capitals on the front legs, the repeated lotus blossoms on the legs and chair back, the swans' heads on the crest rail, the musical motif of the inlay, and the pattern of the original fabric—are all reminiscent of furnishings from the Louis XVI period in France.[3]

From the mid-1870s through the 1880s, many of Herter Brothers' designs were influenced by the Anglo-Japanese

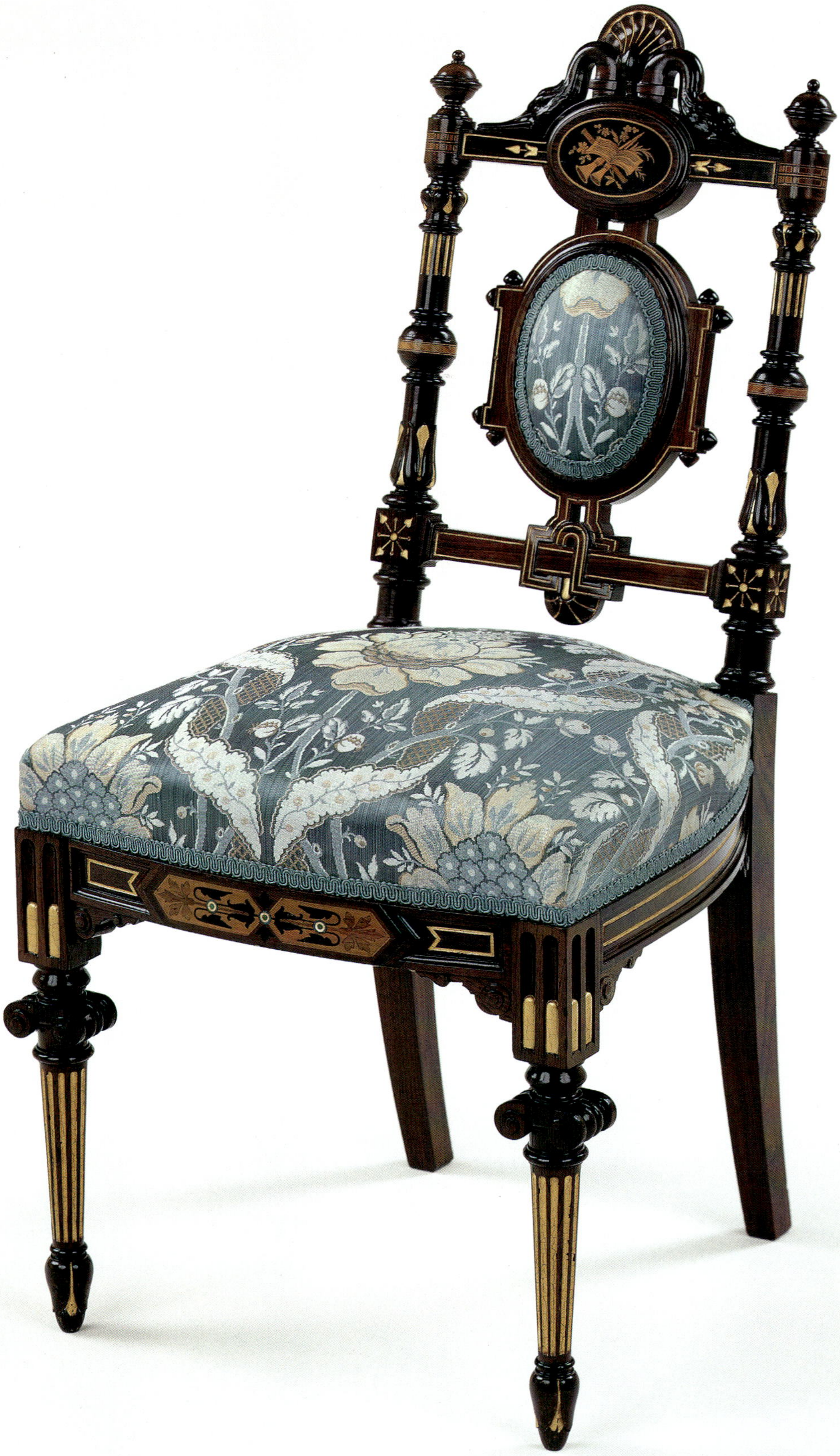

CAT. NO. 118

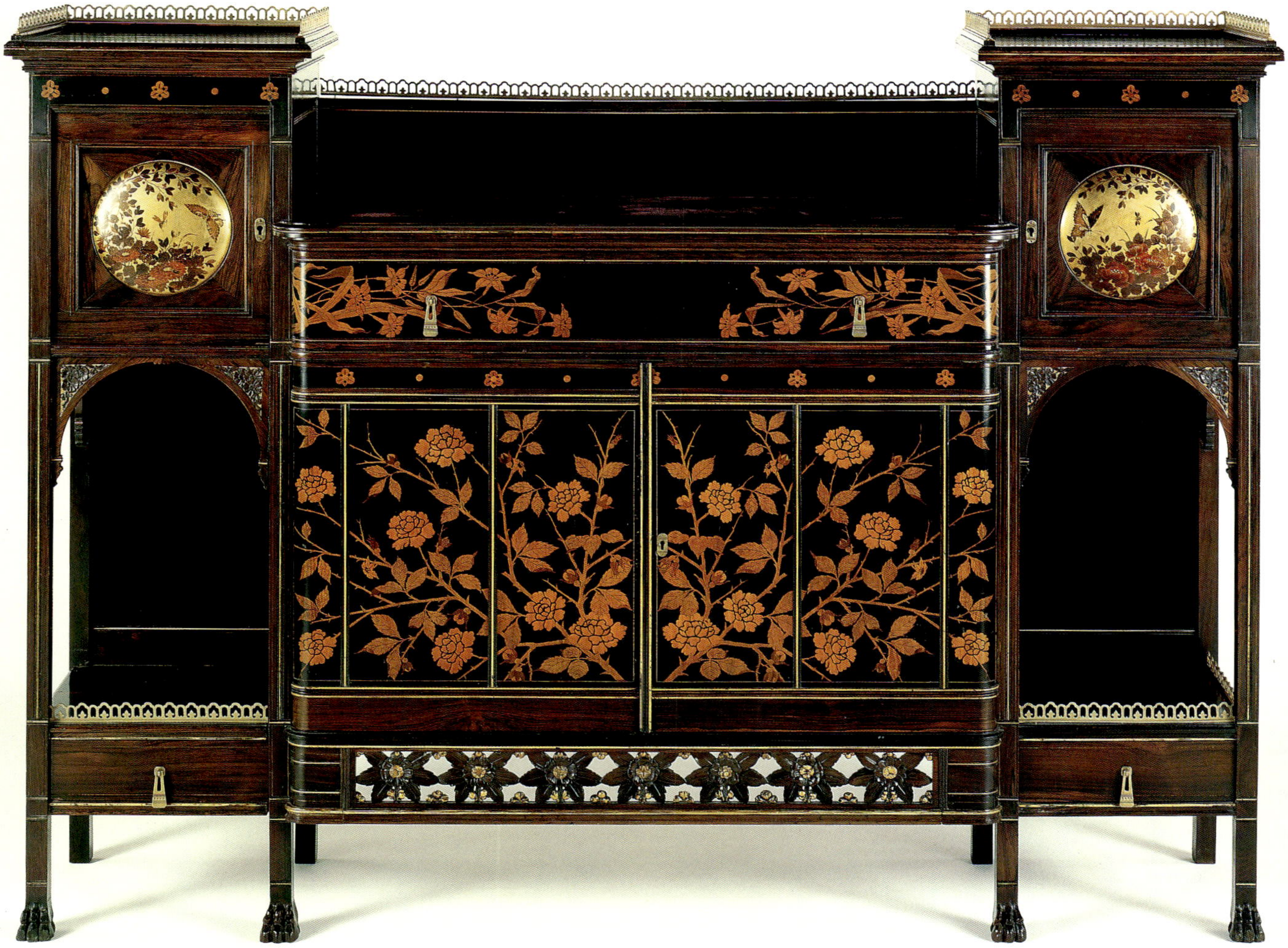

CAT. NO. 119

aestheticism prevalent in the paintings and decorative schemes of James McNeill Whistler (especially his Peacock Room of 1876–77) and the furniture of English designers such as E. W. Godwin, who was one of the first to produce Anglo-Japanese ebonized furniture. The Art Institute's cabinet dates from the late 1870s, and is a fine example of the Herter version of Anglo-Japanese style. The piece deceptively blends a symmetry and simplicity of design with extraordinary and rich materials: highly figured rosewood and ebonized cherry, inlaid brass, gilt and painted panels, and intricate marquetry.

The delicate, stylized marquetry door panels depicting roses are sectioned off by vertical brass strips, emulating a multi-paneled Japanese screen. The inlaid doors are complemented by the carved plum blossom spandrels over the arched openings and the seven pierced and carved flowers along the apron of the piece. The gilded and painted wooden roundels in each storage door are American imitations of Japanese lacquer work. Once thought to be the tops of Japanese mirror boxes, the painted detail is richer and more illusionistic than Japanese work of the period and has clear affinities to American china painting.[4]

Though its history is now lost, this cabinet, like the Elm Park sidechair, was most likely a special commission, the type of commission for which the Herter firm was best known: "Almost all the furniture made by [Herter Brothers] is made to order; they keep very little material in stock, and even their chairs and sofas, of which they keep more ready-made than of the other regulation-pieces, have to be covered to suit individual tastes."[5] After Christian Herter retired from the firm in 1882, however, Herter Brothers executed less and less special-commission work and concentrated on fabricating interior woodwork. For large-scale commissions, the firm then subcontracted to other furniture manufacturers the responsibility for furnishings. The firm put its remaining stock up for auction in 1905 and finally closed its doors the following year.[6]

NOTES

1. Katherine Howe et al., *Herter Brothers: Furniture and Interiors for a Gilded Age,* exh. cat. (Houston, Museum of Fine Arts, 1994), p. 31.

2. Ibid., pp. 144–45.

3. The original upholstery survived on the chair until 1985. Peter Hill, "Unique Masterpiece Chairs," Research files, Department of American Arts, The Art Institute of Chicago.

4. See the entry by Milo M. Naeve in Naeve and Lynn Springer Roberts, *A Decade of Decorative Arts: The Antiquarian Society of the Art Institute of Chicago,* exh. cat. (Chicago, 1986), p. 73. Stephen Little, Pritzker Curator of Asian Art at The Art Institute of Chicago, provided the revised analysis of these roundels. For examples of china painting, see Djennifer Michael, "Gender Struggles Shaped the Arts and Crafts Movement," *Arts and Crafts Quarterly Magazine* 3, 2 (spring 1990), pp. 22–25.

5. Clarence Cook, *The House Beautiful: Essays on Beds and Tables, Stools and Candlesticks* (London, 1868; reprint, New York, 1878), p. 322.

6. Howe et al. (note 1), p. 14.

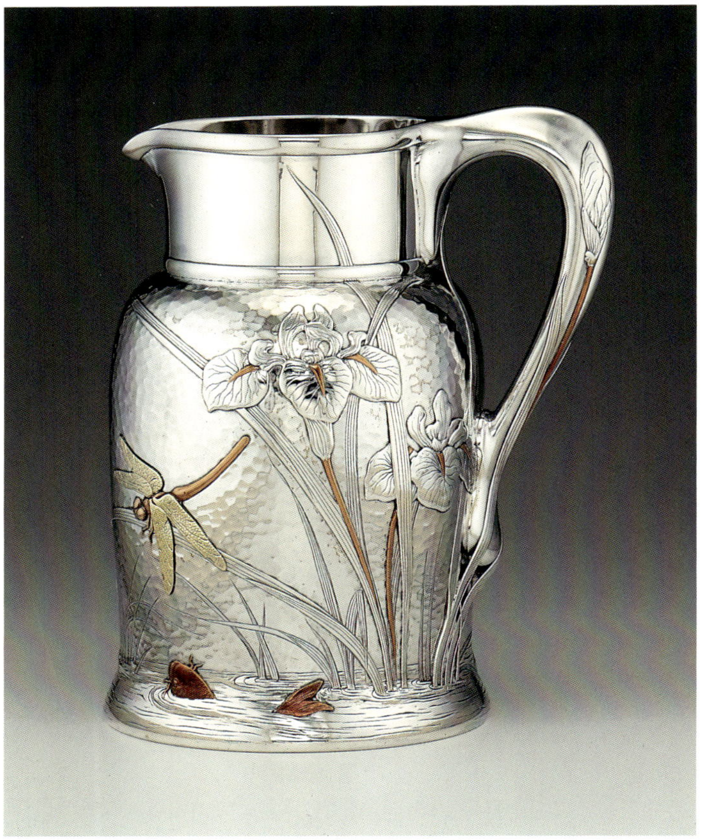

CAT. NO. 120

120. TIFFANY AND COMPANY (FOUNDED 1837)

Pitcher, 1878

New York

Silver, gold, and copper; 22.2 x 14 (diam. at base) cm (8¾ x 5½ in.)

Marked on bottom: *TIFFANY & CO. / 5051 MAKERS 9267 / STERLING SILVER / AND / OTHER METALS / 144*

Restricted gift of Mrs. Frank Sulzberger, 1984.240

In the last half of the nineteenth century, Orientalism enjoyed widespread popularity in Europe and the United States. After Admiral Perry opened Japan to foreign trade in 1854, Japanese objects permeated Western markets. At the 1876 Philadelphia Centennial Exhibition, a Japanese pavilion and dwelling illustrated examples of traditional Japanese life. Thousands of American artisans and art patrons filed through the exhibition, and the Japanese display was one of the most popular—and most publicized—attractions at the exposition.[1]

Tiffany and Company began producing silver in the Japanese taste as early as 1870 by engraving and chasing Japanese scenes and decorative elements on traditional European forms such as this pitcher. By the middle of the 1870s, the firm had begun experimenting with applied decoration on the body of silver wares. Flowers, fish, insects, and birds—fabricated from mixed metal alloys such as copper and gold—were soldered onto the forms, creating startling decorative contrasts to the hand-hammered surfaces of the objects.[2] The effect was the first such innovation for an American silver-making firm. At the 1878 Exposition Universelle in Paris, Tiffany and Company exhibited their Japanese-inspired, mixed-metal silver objects to an astonished European community. The English craftsman Christopher Dresser wrote to the company, commending their display: "No silversmith, that I know, has made the progress in art as applied to their industry that you have. . . . You occupy the proud position of being the first silversmith of the world."[3]

In 1876 and 1877 Dresser traveled extensively in Japan, purchasing metalwork and ceramics for Tiffany and Company for their retail operations, as well as collecting pieces that could provide design inspiration for their craftsmen.[4] For their efforts at the 1878 Paris Exposition, the firm was awarded the *Grand Prix* for silver, several medals were won by employees of the company, and Charles L. Tiffany, the company's founder, was made a Chevalier of the French Legion of Honor.[5] One of the inspirations for Tiffany and Company's success in translating Japanese decoration to Western forms was the Japanese art collection of Edward C. Moore, the head of Tiffany's design studio. His collection included textiles, ceramics, metalwork, papier-mâché, baskets, ivory figures, lacquer work, and woodblock prints.[6]

A pitcher similar to the Art Institute's was displayed in Paris at the 1878 Exposition Universelle.[7] The original design for the form is now also in the Art Institute's collection (see fig. 64). The design details the placement and type of the appliqués, called electrotypes, that were to be used on the pitcher. The appliqués were standardized decorative elements that could be used in many different silver designs, each one having its own inventory reference number. The applied decoration was almost certainly inspired by the woodblock prints of Katsushika Hokusai (1760–1849), one of the most popular Japanese printmakers of the period. Hokusai published numerous volumes of his work, three of which are in the Tiffany archives, no doubt having belonged originally to Edward Moore. The iris, one of Hokusai's favorite flower motifs and a Japanese symbol of success, is featured in many of his prints, including *Iris and Grasshopper* (fig. 65).[8] The flowers in the print have the same sharp lines and graceful arcs as the applied iris flowers on the pitcher. Hokusai's depiction of a dragonfly in another print (fig. 66) displays the same wing placement and prominent eyes as the image on the pitcher. The carp, another dominant motif in Hokusai's work that appears several times on the Tiffany pitcher, is a Japanese symbol of determination.[9]

The various organic designs picked for the pitcher and the naturalistic treatment of the handle are early manifestations of what would become the Art Nouveau style in the 1890s.

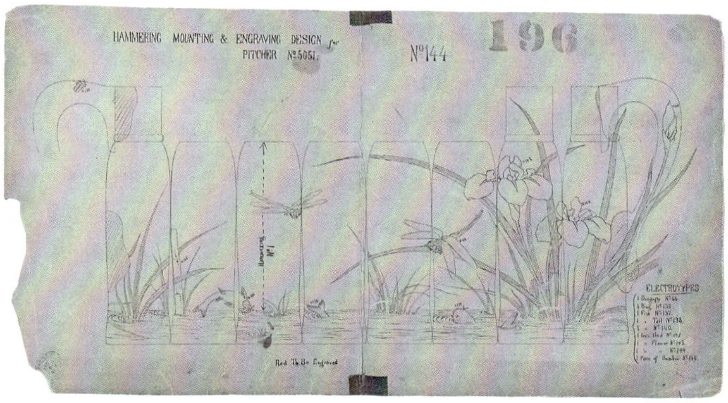

FIG. 64. Tiffany and Company (founded 1837). *Hammering, Mounting, and Engraving Design for Pitcher No. 5051*, 1878. Black and red ink, and colored pencils on paper; 33.3 x 59.7 cm (13⅛ x 23½ in.). The Art Institute of Chicago, Gift of Tiffany and Company (1986.199).

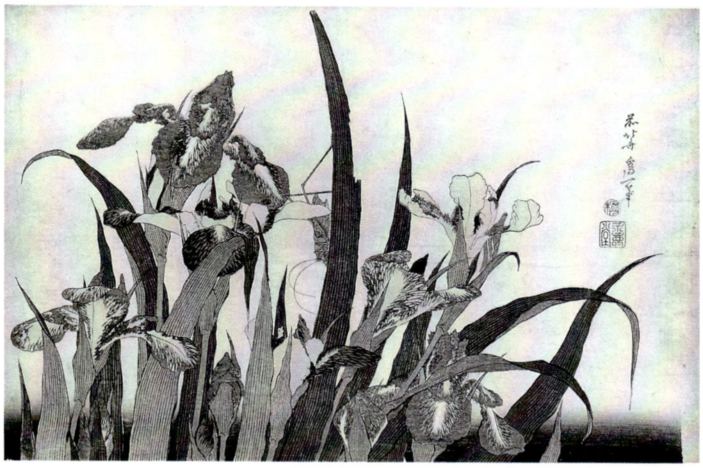

FIG. 65. Katsushika Hokusai (Japanese, 1760–1849). *Iris and Grasshopper*, n.d. Woodblock print; 26.8 x 39.4 cm (10⁹⁄₁₆ x 15½ in.). The Art Institute of Chicago, Gift of Mr. and Mrs. Gaylord Donnelley (1969.696).

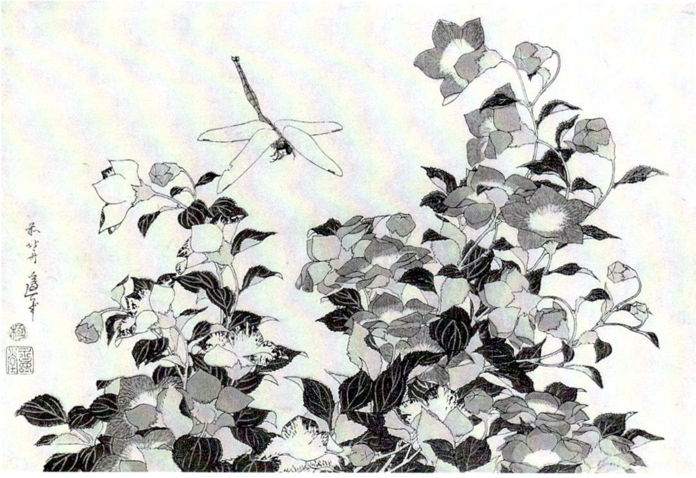

FIG. 66. Katsushika Hokusai. *Chinese Bell Flowers and a Dragonfly*, c. 1825. Woodblock print; 26 x 37.5 cm (10¼ x 14¾ in.). The Art Institute of Chicago, Clarence Buckingham Collection (1925.3377).

NOTES

1. Henry H. Hawley, "Tiffany's Silver in the Japanese Taste," *Bulletin of the Cleveland Museum of Art* (Oct. 1976), p. 240.

2. Charles H. Carpenter, Jr., and Mary Grace Carpenter, *Tiffany Silver* (New York, 1978), pp. 190–92; Charles H. Carpenter, Jr., and Janet Zapata, *The Silver of Tiffany & Co., 1850–1987*, exh. cat. (Boston, Museum of Fine Arts, 1987), p. 11.

3. As quoted in David A. Hanks and Jennifer Toher, "Metalwork: An Eclectic Aesthetic," in Doreen Bolger Burke et al., *In Pursuit of Beauty: Americans and the Aesthetic Movement*, exh. cat. (New York, Metropolitan Museum of Art, 1986), p. 260.

4. Ibid., pp. 255–56.

5. Hawley (note 1), p. 238.

6. Carpenter and Carpenter (note 2), pp. 182, 184.

7. Christie's, New York, *Important American Furniture, Silver, Folk Art and Decorative Arts* (June 19, 1996), lot 50. The Absence of a French control mark on the Art Institute's pitcher indicates that it was not the example that was in France for the exhibition. A pitcher of the same design and decoration, with the French control mark, was sold at Christie's, New York (see ibid.).

8. Matthi Forrer, *Hokusai: Prints and Drawings*, exh. cat. (London, Royal Academy of Arts, 1991), cat. no. 60.

9. Ibid., cat. no. 66.

121. WILLIAM MERRITT CHASE (1849–1916)

A City Park, c. 1887

Oil on canvas; 34.6 x 49.9 cm (13⅝ x 19⅝ in.)
Signed, lower right: *Wm M. Chase*
Bequest of Dr. John J. Ireland, 1968.88

William Merritt Chase's paintings of public parks in Brooklyn and Manhattan are intimate renditions of familiar locations that chart the artist's response both to America's rapid urban growth and to contemporary French painting. Although Chase studied at the Royal Academy in Munich from 1872 to 1877, his mature style, which evolved in the 1880s, was inspired by diverse international art movements.[1] An early example of Chase's park scenes, *A City Park* exhibits the dramatic spatial

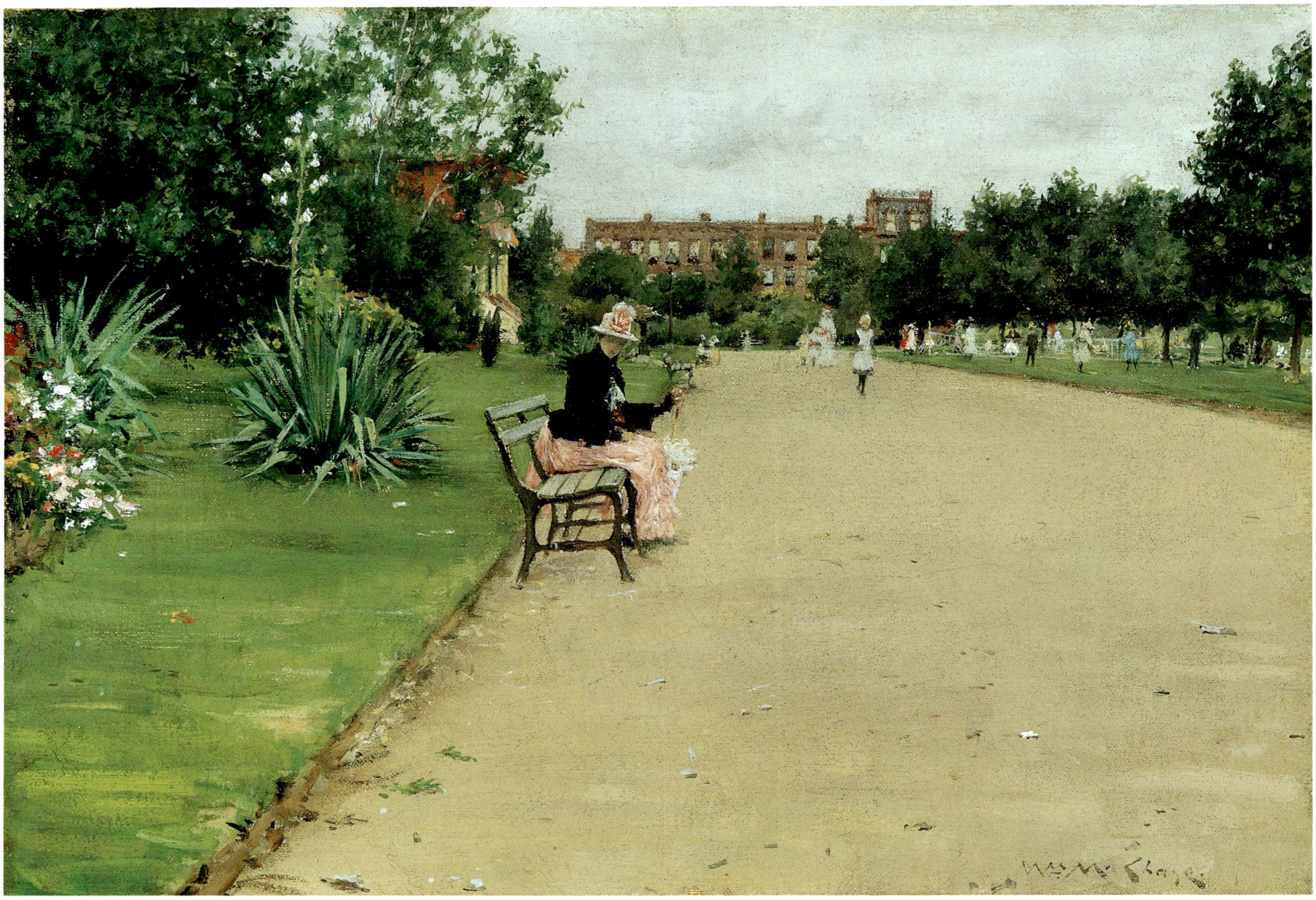

CAT. NO. 121

effects, high-keyed palette, and intimate scale of French Impressionist painting, as opposed to the dark palette and impasto brushwork promoted by the Munich School.[2]

The strong light, vivid color, and fluid handling of *A City Park* suggest a spontaneous method of composition rather than a studio production. Like the French Impressionists, Chase probably composed his composition *en plein-air*, as he indicated in comments on his own technique in the periodical *Art Amateur*: "When I start to paint out of doors I put myself in as light marching order as possible; that is, I have every thing made as portable and with as little weight as it can be. . . . I carry a comfortable stool that can be closed up in a small space, and I never use an umbrella. I want all the light I can get. When I have found the spot I like, I set up my easel, and paint the picture on the spot. I think that is the only way rightly to interpret nature."[3] The small scale of this work conforms to Chase's practice of painting outdoors unburdened by unnecessary or bulky materials. For twelve consecutive summers, from 1891 to 1903, Chase espoused the merits of plein-air landscape painting to students at Shinnecock Hills Summer School, which he had founded on Long Island.[4] Chase's method ultimately had widespread impact on succeeding generations of American painters.

New aspects of Chase's park scenes have recently been explored by Barbara Dayer Gallati, who traced the artist's use of familiar locations and family members in his paintings and concluded that "his art was most often the expression of external reality molded to portray his private world."[5] Gallati further noted that the subject of *A City Park* is most likely Tompkins Park, in Brooklyn, rather than Prospect Park, as previously assumed (see fig. 67). A David H. Chase—perhaps Chase's father, David Hester Chase—lived on a street bordering the park.[6] An 1888 *Art Amateur* review identifies several of Chase's paintings of "charming, sparkling bits of out-door life" as depicting locations in New York City. Perhaps directly referring to the Art Institute's canvas, the review adds: "The scene on a summer day in Tompkins Park, with the figures of a lady and child admirably introduced, is brilliantly executed and is full of atmosphere."[7]

Designed in 1870–71 by Frederick Law Olmsted and Calvert Vaux—the landscape architects who planned both Prospect and Central Parks—Tompkins Park in Brooklyn was intended to "form a cheerful, bright, and refreshing object to be observed from the adjoining streets and houses . . . [and accommodate] agreeable exercise, rest, and social intercourse in the open air."[8] *A City Park* adheres to Olmsted's dictum by showing a series of brownstones partially obscured by trees in the background. The brownstone-lined avenues visible in the painting delineate the boundaries of the park and define the space as a city square rather than Olmsted and Vaux's rambling parks with paths that twist and turn. The diagonally receding pathway that dramatically draws the viewer into *A City Park* further echoes the straight, gravel-paved arteries of Tompkins Park. A perspectival device favored by Chase, the strong diagonal creates the illusion of a wide spatial expanse more like a French boulevard than the path of a city park. Gustave Caillebotte and Giuseppe de Nittis, artists Chase admired, used this device to great effect in representing Paris after Baron Haussmann's 1854–70 renovation of the city. Chase's *A City Park* makes use of a combination of influences—from the artist's personal familiarity with the location to recent Impressionist innovations in painting method and subject matter—to depict a contemporary scene of a new urban landscape.[9]

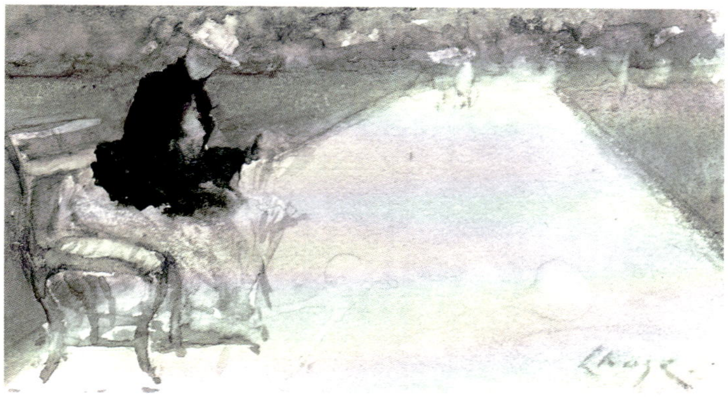

FIG. 67. William Merritt Chase (1849–1916). *Prospect Park*, c. 1886. Watercolor on paper laid down on paper; 8 x 12.2 cm (3 x 5¼ in.). Private collection, photograph courtesy of Spanierman Gallery, New York.

NOTES

1. For more about the Munich School, see cat. no. 95, and Michael Quick, *Munich and American Realism in the Nineteenth Century*, exh. cat. (Sacramento, Calif., E. B. Crocker Art Gallery, 1978).

2. Chase may have been influenced by French Impressionist paintings that the dealer Paul Durand-Ruel exhibited in New York City in 1886. This exhibition marks the first showing of French Impressionist work in the United States.

3. A. E. Ives, "Suburban Sketching Grounds," *Art Amateur* 25, 4 (Sept. 1891), p. 80.

4. For more on Chase at Shinnecock, see D. Scott Atkinson and Nicolai Cikovsky, Jr., *William Merritt Chase: Summers at Shinnecock, 1891–1902*, exh. cat. (Washington, D.C., National Gallery of Art, 1987).

5. Barbara Dayer Gallati, *William Merritt Chase* (New York, 1995), p. 10.

6. He is listed in the 1886–87 Brooklyn directories as living at 483 Marcy Avenue, one of the streets that border Tompkins Park. Other park scenes that have been identified by Gallati (note 5) as most likely of Tompkins Park are *Prospect Park, Brooklyn* (c. 1887; Parrish Art Museum, Littlejohn Collection, Southampton, N.Y.); *Prospect Park, Brooklyn* (Colby College, Waterville, Me.); and *Summer Scene in the Park* (location unknown). See Gallati (note 5), pp. 71–73.

7. Montezuma, "My Note Book," *Art Amateur* 18, 2 (Jan. 1888), p. 28.

8. David Schuyler and Jane Turner Censer, eds., *The Papers of Frederick Law Olmsted, Vol. 6: The Years of Olmsted, Vaux and Company, 1865–1874* (Baltimore and London, 1992), p. 395.

9. Chase produced a watercolor related to the Art Institute's painting; its inscription, "I'm glad my friend likes it so much," suggests that this work was created after the oil rather than as a preliminary study.

122. THEODORE ROBINSON (1852–1896)

The Valley of Arconville, c. 1887

Oil on canvas; 45.8 x 55.7 cm (18 x 21⅞ in.)

Signed, lower right: *TH. ROBINSON*

Friends of American Art Collection, 1941.11

In many of the paintings he produced in the 1880s and early 1890s, Theodore Robinson surveyed the poetic topography of France, especially Giverny and its environs. One of the first American artists to paint in Giverny, a town situated about two hours northwest of Paris, Robinson integrated the meth-

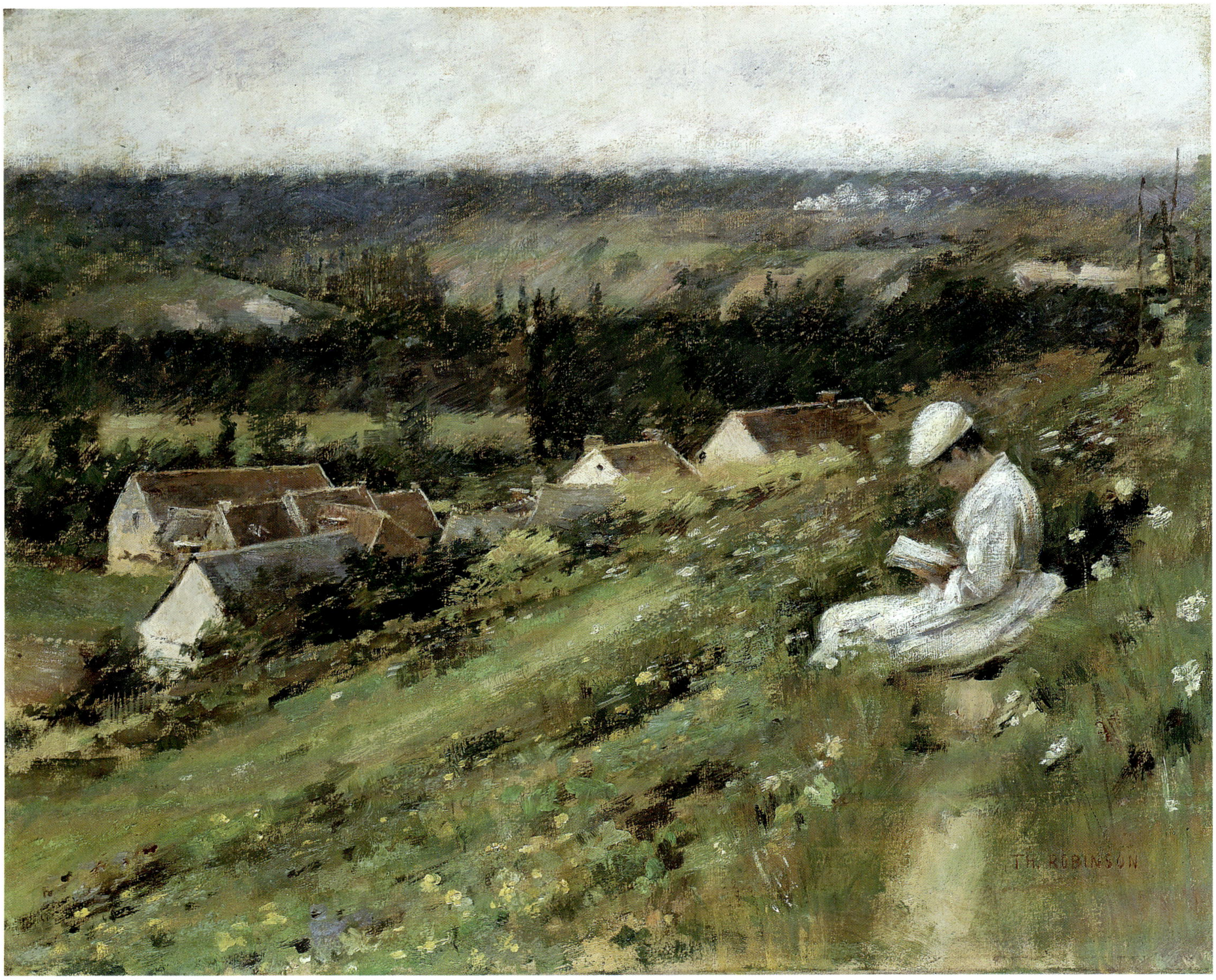

CAT. NO. 122

ods of the region's most famous resident, Claude Monet, into his work. Robinson helped to disseminate Impressionist painting techniques in the United States through his teaching and the exhibition of his paintings.[1] Although it was not painted in Giverny, *The Valley of Arconville* resembles many of Robinson's Giverny compositions. It demonstrates the artist's sensitivity to color, mood, and the more spontaneous gestures and high-keyed palette of French Impressionism.

Born in Irasburg, Vermont, Robinson was raised in Evansville, Wisconsin, and received his first artistic training at the Chicago Academy of Design.[2] He studied at New York's National Academy of Design in 1874 and 1875, and eventually traveled to Paris in 1876, where he trained in the atelier of Émile Auguste Carolus-Duran and at the École des Beaux-Arts with Jean-Léon Gérôme. He returned to the United States in 1879 and lived in New York City until 1884; between 1884 and 1892, he divided his time between France and the United States. Of all the American artists associated with Giverny, Robinson spent the most time in the town, living there for long stretches between 1887 and 1892. One of the few Americans who gained entrance into Monet's intimate circle, he was not only the French artist's student, but also a family friend. His art benefited greatly from this close relationship.[3]

The exact date Robinson met Monet is unknown, and accounts vary, but registry records from the Hôtel Baudy show that the American paid his first substantial visit to Giverny between September 18, 1887, and January 4, 1888.[4] During the spring and summer of 1887, Robinson worked in Barbizon, but he made a trip to Dieppe, where he sketched *On the Cliff* (fig. 68). This composition echoes the Art Institute's painting and probably depicts the same woman—Marie—who, like many models, has left little trace of her life.[5] His presence in Arconville, a small town southeast of Paris in the Champagne region of France, is documented only by the title of the Art Institute's painting; Robinson may have also visited Giverny that summer, before settling there in September.[6]

The panoramic, hillside vista of *The Valley of Arconville* recalls the format Robinson would use in many of his views of Giverny, all of which are devoid of figures. *On the Cliff* shows the artist experimenting with this format as early as June 1887. Although the palette of *On the Cliff* is more saturated than the Art Institute's pastel-hued canvas, the woman's pose is strikingly similar in both pictures—in one she is bent over sewing and in the other her head is bowed over a book—and in both pictures she sits on the sloping incline of a steep hill.

Robinson used the panoramic view to great effect in *The Valley of Arconville*. Seen from above, the landscape spreads out before us; the artist's layered, broken brushwork leads the eye down the slope, across the valley, and up into the background hills. Robinson captured both momentary effects—grasses and wildflowers blowing in the breeze, clouds moving across the sky—and solid structure, the geometry of the houses in the valley and the woman's serene figure.

When *The Valley of Arconville* was shown in the 1889 Society of American Artists exhibition, a critic for *Art Amateur* commented: "Mr. Theodore Robinson is one of those who have really gained a good deal by study of impressionistic methods. Of his seven contributions, there is none which does not show a solid advance beyond his work of previous years, and none that does not belong distinctly to the new school. The narrowing of his aim in this case, as in so many others, has been the saving of the artist."[7] Robinson's success with Impressionist methods and depictions of the French or American countryside continued until his premature death in 1896.

NOTES

1. For more about the artists' colony at Giverny, see William H. Gerdts, *Monet's Giverny: An Impressionist Colony* (New York, 1993).

2. For additional biographical information about Robinson, see John I. H. Baur, *Theodore Robinson, 1852–1896*, exh. cat. (Brooklyn Museum, 1946); and Sona Johnston, *Theodore Robinson, 1852–1896*, exh. cat. (Baltimore Museum of Art, 1973).

3. The diary Robinson kept between 1892 and 1896 (Frick Library, New York) documents his friendship with Monet.

4. Carol Lowrey, "Hôtel Baudy Guest Register," in Gerdts (note 1), p. 222.

5. Robinson's relationship with Marie is discussed by Baur (note 2), pp. 24–25, and Gerdts (note 1), p. 110. Robinson identified Marie as the woman in this painting in his diary on June 9, 1893: "Mrs. Bradley . . . told me of the

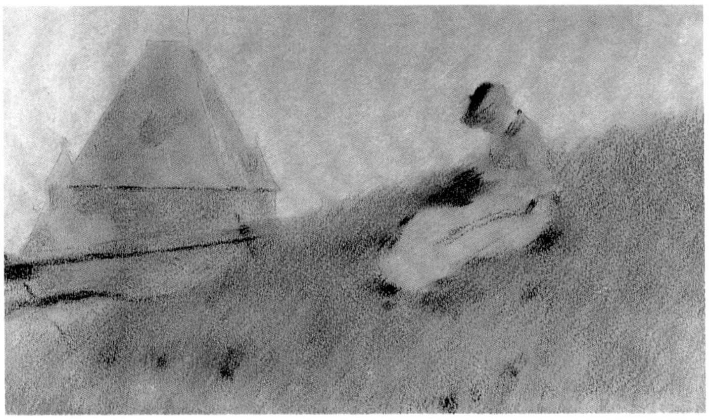

FIG. 68. Theodore Robinson (1852–1896). *On the Cliff*, 1887. Pastel; 20.3 x 33 cm (8 x 13 in.). Brooklyn Museum of Art, Gift of Michelle Murphy (54.38).

inspiration she got from a picture of mine (Carey's with Marie on the hillside)"; quoted in Baur (note 2), p. 78.

6. That *The Valley of Arconville* was painted in 1887 is supported by the presence of a thirty-year-old American, "Mr. Carrey," at the Hôtel Baudy, Giverny, Jan. 10–15, 1888. Arthur A. Carey (1857–1923) of Waltham, Mass., the first owner of the Art Institute's painting, studied in Europe between 1885 and about 1887 and probably acquired the painting from Robinson during this brief visit to Giverny. He is listed as the lender of *The Valley of Arconville* to an 1889 exhibition; see *Eleventh Exhibition of the Society of American Artists at the Fifth Avenue Art Galleries*, exh. cat. (New York, 1889), cat. no. 119.

7. "The Society of American Artists," *Art Amateur* 21, 2 (July 1889), p. 28.

123. MARTIN JOHNSON HEADE (1819–1904)

Magnolias on Light Blue Velvet Cloth, 1885/95

Oil on canvas; 38.6 x 61.8 cm (15¼ x 24⅜ in.)

Signed, lower right: *M. J. Heade*

Restricted gift of Gloria and Richard Manney; Harold L. Stuart Fund, 1983.791

Martin Johnson Heade's still life of magnolias lying on a blue velvet cloth was painted in St. Augustine, Florida, where the artist spent the last twenty years of his life. Over the course of his career, Heade painted portraits, landscapes, and still lifes that reflect his peripatetic lifestyle and wide variety of interests.[1] For example, his landscapes depict scenes ranging from the salt marshes of Newburyport, Massachusetts, to the volcanoes of Nicaragua to the Florida Everglades. When he settled in Florida in 1884, Heade found the climate suitable to both his temperament and his art production; in St. Augustine the artist received his first substantial patronage from the wealthy industrialist Henry Flagler.

The still lifes Heade painted after moving to Florida in 1884 were usually composed along a horizontal plane and depicted indigenous flowers: orange blossoms, cherokee roses, and magnolias. Of these tropical subjects, the magnolias are the most magnificent, opulent, and confidently painted.

Heade produced at least five variations on the magnolia-and-blue-velvet motif.[2] Although relatively modest-sized canvases, the scale of the flowers seen at close range gives these paintings a monumental presence. The Art Institute's example, which contains the most blooms of any of the similar compositions, shows four magnolias in different stages of blossom. The composition is lush and full of movement; the flowers seem slowly to open while the leaves project outward and ripple in all directions. The shiny leaves, rough bark, and smooth petals lying on blue velvet present a medley of strikingly tactile textures that, when combined with the flower bud and fully opened bloom, create an illusionistic effect similar to the modern process of stop-motion photography.

Although Heade did not produce many pencil sketches for his flower paintings, there do exist a number of oil studies of magnolias in the collection of the St. Augustine Historical Society.[3] Two of these correspond to the Art Institute's painting. *Study of a Single Magnolia Bud* (fig. 69), a delicately detailed rendering of the painting's central blossom, seems almost to have been directly transposed from the oil sketch to the finished canvas. Similarly the fully opened flower and its half opened mate appear in *Study of Three Blossoms of Magnolia* (1884/90). Absent from the sketches are the bed of leaves on which, in the finished pictures, the magnolias lie. Apparently Heade used the sketched flowers repeatedly for the larger paintings, altering only their number, arrangement, and density.[4] The magnolia leaves, however, were probably painted from life because they would not have withered as quickly as the blossoms.

The Art Institute's *Magnolias* can be interpreted in a variety of symbolic ways. Art historian Theodore Stebbins has attributed a sexual significance to Heade's flower paintings, likening them to reclining female nudes; he supports this reading by emphasizing that women and flowers were symbolically linked in the nineteenth century.[5] *Magnolias* could also represent the artist's reaction to the tropical exoticism of his adopted Florida home. Similar to the paintings of orchids and hummingbirds Heade made after having traveled through South America in the 1860s, the magnolia still lifes were related not only to the heightened scientific interest in unusual biological specimens, but also to Heade's own dedication to natural history.[6]

An obituary of Heade published in *Forest and Stream*, a weekly publication for which the artist wrote many articles under the pseudonym "Didymus," noted that "he turned with . . . success to studies of still-life, putting on canvas the Florida magnolia and the Cherokee rose with a vraisemblance so perfect as sometimes to be astonishing in the illusion."[7] This is the only mention of Heade's magnolia paintings in the press of his time, suggesting that these works were done for private collectors rather than exhibited publicly.[8] The magnolia paintings served several purposes: to decorate the homes of wealthy southerners, to reflect the lush Floridian flora, and to symbolize Heade's own late-life flourishing in St. Augustine.

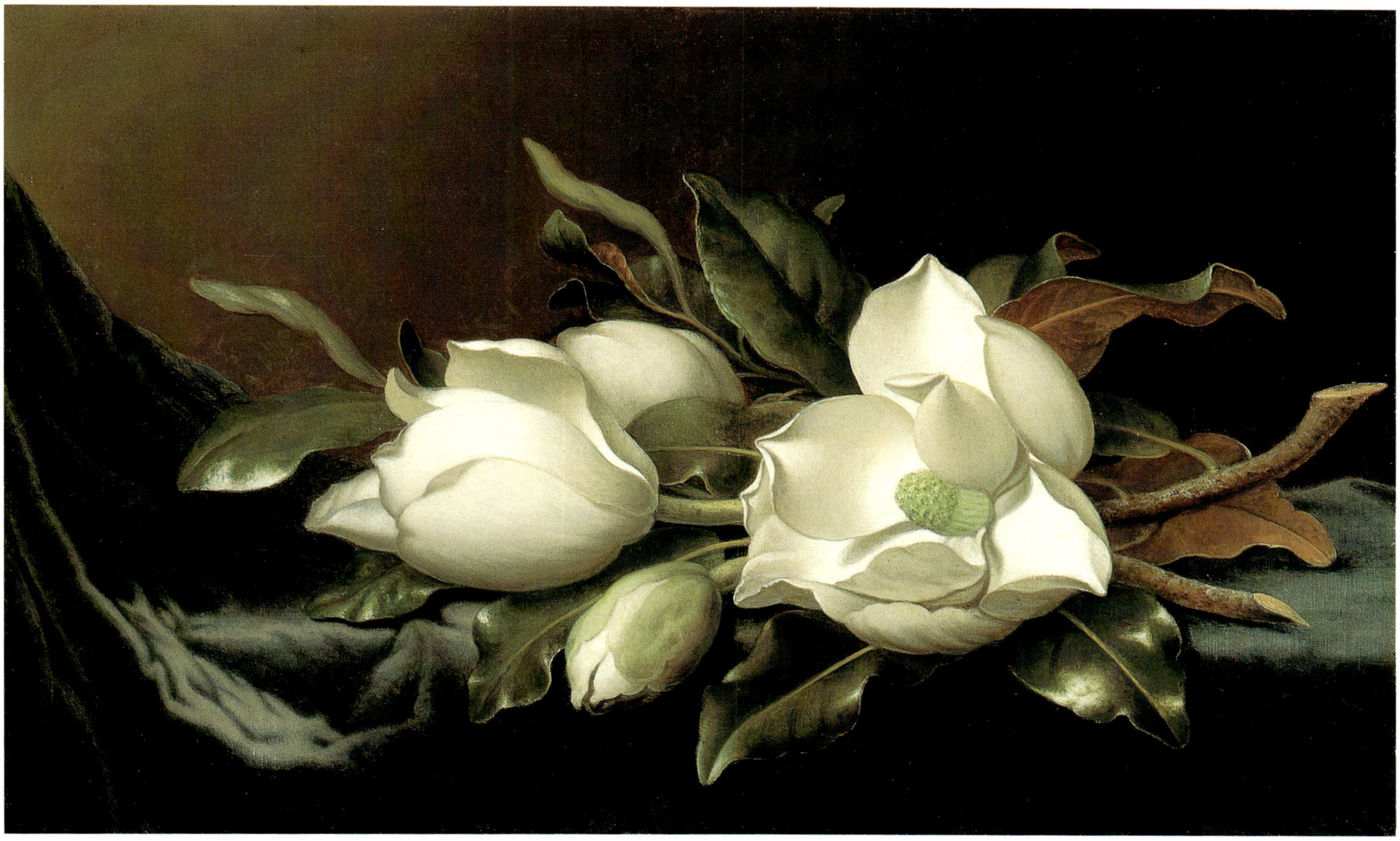

CAT. NO. 123

NOTES

1. The most complete source for information on Heade's life and work is Theodore E. Stebbins, Jr., *The Life and Works of Martin Johnson Heade* (New Haven, Conn., and London, 1975). Dr. Stebbins is currently at work on a revised edition of the Heade catalogue raisonné.

2. Ibid., p. 276.

3. For more information on Heade's magnolia studies, see Timothy A. Eaton, *Martin Johnson Heade: The Floral and Hummingbird Studies from the St. Augustine Historical Society*, exh. cat. (Boca Raton, Fla., Boca Raton Museum of Art, 1992).

4. The flowers in *Magnolias on Light Blue Velvet Cloth* resemble those in *Giant Magnolias on a Blue Velvet Cloth* (1885/95; private collection) and *Giant Magnolias* (1885/95; R. W. Norton Art Gallery, Shreveport, La.).

5. Stebbins (note 1), p. 176. Heade did not marry until 1883, and Stebbins asserts that the artist's conjugal bliss may also have added to the sensual appeal of the magnolia pictures.

6. Heade made three trips to South America—in 1863, 1866, and 1870. For more about the hummingbird and orchid pictures in the context of images of South America, see Katherine Emma Manthorne, *Tropical Renaissance: North American Artists Exploring Latin America, 1839–1879* (Washington, D.C., 1989), pp. 118–21. Regarding Heade's connections to the Charles Darwin's theory of evolution, see Ella M. Foshay, *Reflections of Nature: Flowers in American Art*, exh. cat. (New York, Whitney Museum of American Art, 1984), pp. 51–57.

7. "Martin J. Heade," *Forest and Stream* 63, 12 (Sept. 17, 1904), p. 1.

8. Heade's patron Henry Flagler, for example, was an industrialist who made his fortune first in railroads and then in hotel development in Florida.

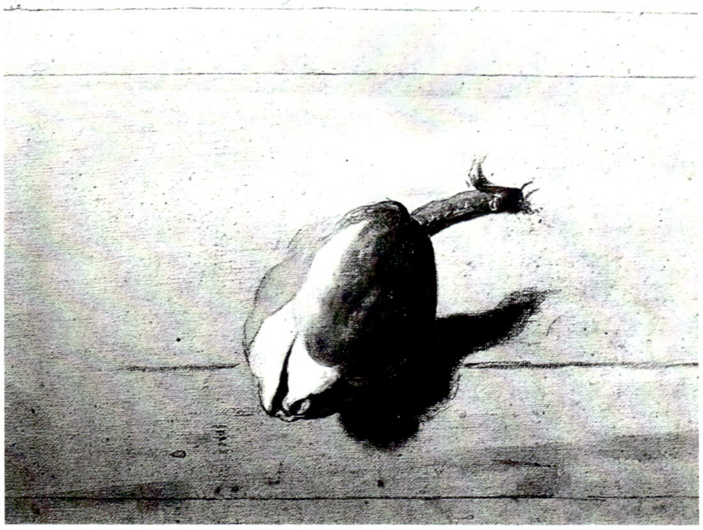

FIG. 69. Martin Johnson Heade (1819–1904). *Study of a Single Magnolia Bud*, 1884/90. Oil on unstretched canvas; 22.9 x 35.2 cm (9 x 13⅞ in.). St. Augustine Historical Society, St. Augustine, Fla.

124. WILLIAM M. HARNETT (1848–1892)

For Sunday's Dinner, 1888

Oil on canvas; 94.3 x 53.6 cm (37⅛ x 21⅛ in.)

Signed, lower left: *Harnett / 1888*

Wilson L. Mead Fund, 1958.296

125. *Just Dessert*, 1891

Oil on canvas; 56.6 x 68 cm (22¼ x 26¾ in.)

Signed, lower right: *Harnett / 1891*

Friends of American Art Collection, 1942.50

Still-life painter William Harnett excelled at trompe l'oeil, or "tricking the eye," and used the device in both his vertical and tabletop compositions.[1] His most renowned painting, *The Old Violin*, which was popularly reproduced as a chromolithograph (fig. 70), created the illusion of a violin hanging in front of a wooden door so effectively that viewers reportedly attempted to remove the instrument from the wall.[2] As popular as this magical technique was with the public, however, critics had mixed reactions to Harnett's reliance upon illusionism, just as earlier writers had disdained Raphaelle Peale's use of the same artifice (see cat. no. 56).[3] Both *For Sunday's Dinner* and *Just Dessert*, painted during the final years of Harnett's truncated career, exemplify the artist's skill at trompe l'oeil and the themes he repeatedly pursued in his work.

Like many American artists, Harnett's artistic training was varied and involved study in Europe.[4] He was born in Ireland in 1848, but emigrated with his family to Philadelphia before he was a year old. Between 1865 and 1875 he worked in Philadelphia and New York as an engraver to support himself and attended classes at the Pennsylvania Academy of the Fine Arts, the Cooper Union for the Advancement of Science and Art, and the National Academy of Design. In 1875 Harnett began successfully to exhibit and sell works, and by 1880 had saved enough money from the sale of his paintings to finance a trip to Europe. He settled in Munich for six years, making occasional visits to London and Paris. Harnett returned to the United States in 1886, and resided in New York City until his death six years later.

For Sunday's Dinner belongs to a body of work within Harnett's oeuvre that he developed during his years in Europe: depictions of objects (often dead animals) suspended illusionistically in front of a painted wooden door.[5] These paintings constitute Harnett's most virtuosic attempts at trompe l'oeil, and the Art Institute's painting was among the most highly praised. When it was shown at the National Academy of Design's autumn exhibition in 1888, one writer commented: "W. M. Harnett has never painted a better piece of still life than his plucked fowl."[6] *For Sunday's Dinner* was the artist's second attempt to depict a denuded rooster; the first, *Plucked Clean* (1882; Corcoran Gallery of Art, Washington, D.C.), is a more stark, but less graphic and complex, view of the subject.

Harnett's rooster hangs from a string with his throat cut and most of his feathers plucked—a few downy spots remain that contrast with his puckered, pimpled flesh. The metal door hinges on the right side of the canvas frame the rooster and echo his form, while the fixture that has slipped from its place covering the keyhole reveals the bare, scarred wood beneath just as the removal of the rooster's feathers has uncovered his unappealing skin. Harnett is perhaps commenting on illusionism and deceptive surfaces in this work: beneath every brilliantly executed painting is an unadorned canvas and an imperfect human hand. The painting's title and the rough, blemished surface of the door suggest a country dinner rather than a sophisticated urban affair—an unpolished, homely meal that nostalgically hints at a simpler past.[7]

One of only three works Harnett painted in the year before his death, *Just Dessert* also offers the viewer a display of foodstuffs, but presents them sumptuously arranged on a marble tabletop. The traditional tabletop composition is one that Harnett often employed, especially in his earlier works. In *Just Dessert*, the exotic clashes with the quotidian as maraschino liqueur, half a coconut, and Smyrna figs rest alongside a copper pitcher, pewter tankard, and ginger jar. Small crumbs of cork lie on the grapes, and fig seeds are smashed on the side of the wooden box, indicating that the dessert has been eaten and spotlighting Harnett's trompe l'oeil accuracy. The ginger jar and pewter tankard appear in many of the artist's tabletop compositions, but the copper pitcher is unique to *Just Dessert* and perhaps belonged to the first owner of the painting, Philadelphia hotel proprietor Peter Samuel Dooner.[8]

One of Harnett's obituaries reported that "a recent production from his brush is a fruit scene, which hangs in the corridor of Dooner's Hotel, and for which Mr. Dooner was offered and refused $1500," attesting to the value of the artist's work at the time of his death and the early ownership of the painting.[9] Dooner's ownership of *Just Dessert* is also significant to the interpretation of the painting. Harnett and Dooner were members of the Hibernian Society, a charitable

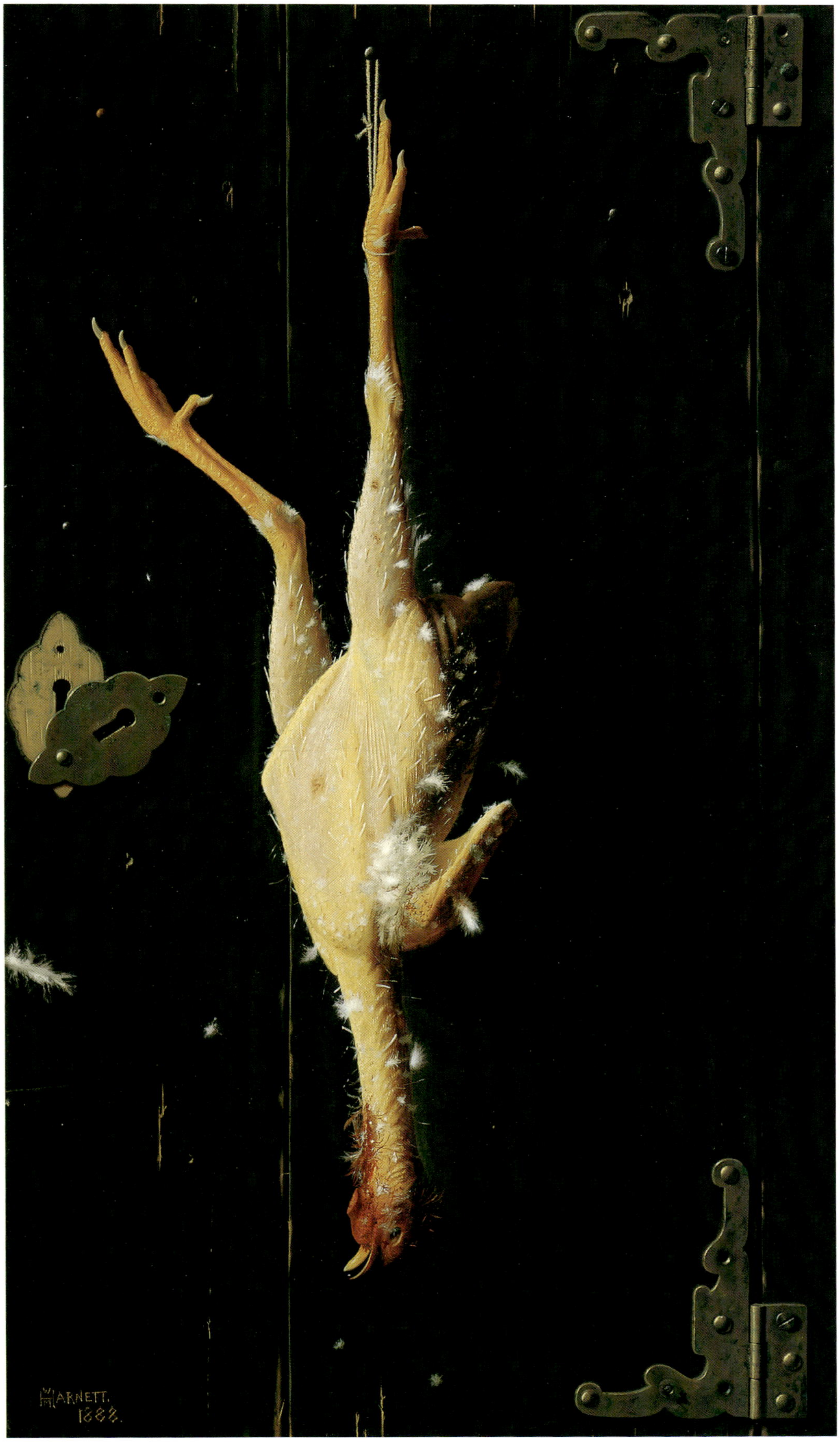

CAT. NO. 124

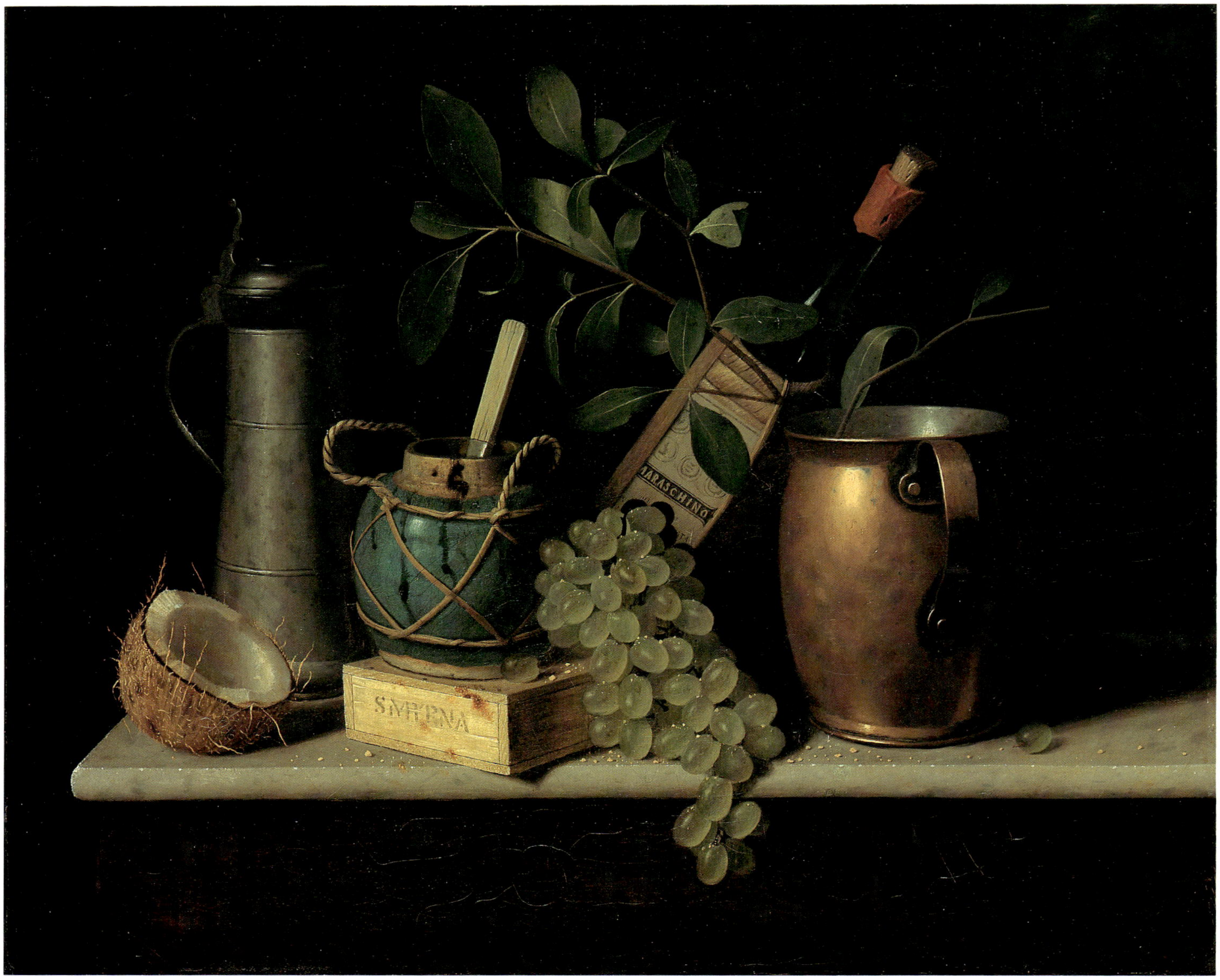

CAT. NO. 125

organization in Philadelphia that raised funds for Irish immigrants and often held their meetings at Dooner's Hotel.[10] The reference to a reward for hard work in Harnett's title may be a play on both artist's and patron's rise from their modest immigrant backgrounds to positions of status within their community. The branch of bay laurel that encircles the liquor bottle supports this interpretation; it was traditionally a symbol of outstanding achievement.

Whether he presented his still-life compositions suspended vertically or artfully arranged on a tabletop, William Harnett imbued his paintings with stunning illusionism, nostalgia, and playful yet probing observations. *For Sunday's Dinner* and *Just Dessert* epitomize these traits and justify the artist's reputation as one of America's most significant still-life painters.

NOTES

1. For an overview of the trompe l'oeil tradition in American painting, see William Frankenstein, *The Reality of Appearance: The Trompe l'Oeil Tradition in American Painting*, exh. cat. (New York, Whitney Museum of American Art, 1970).

2. Paul J. Staiti, "Illusionism, Trompe l'Oeil, and the Perils of Viewership," in Doreen Bolger, Marc Simpson, and John Wilmerding, eds., *William M. Harnett*, exh. cat. (New York, Metropolitan Museum of Art, 1992), p. 31.

3. For a general overview of Harnett's artistic reputation, see William H. Gerdts, "The Artist's Public Face: Lifetime Exhibitions and Critical Receptions," in Bolger, Simpson, and Wilmerding (note 2), pp. 87–99.

4. For more biographical information about Harnett, see Bolger, Simpson, and Wilmerding (note 2); and Alfred Frankenstein, *After the Hunt: William Harnett and Other American Still Life Painters, 1870–1900* (Berkeley and Los Angeles, 1953).

5. These vertical still-life compositions can also be seen as an extension of Harnett's letter-rack paintings of the late 1870s. The best known of Harnett's vertically composed still lifes are *The Old Violin* (1886, James H. Maroney, Jr.) and the four versions he did of *After the Hunt* (1883, Kennedy Galleries, Inc., New York; 1883, Columbus Museum of Art, Ohio; 1884, Butler Institute of American Art, Youngstown, Ohio; and 1885, Fine Arts Museums of San Francisco).

6. "In the Domain of Art: A Last Glance Around the Autumn Academy Display," *New York Herald*, Dec. 9, 1888, p. 19; quoted in Gerdts (note 3), p. 95.

7. David Lubin, "Permanent Objects in a Changing World: Harnett's Still Lifes as a Hold on the Past," in Bolger, Simpson, and Wilmerding (note 2), pp. 49–59. Lubin explored the issue of nostalgia in Harnett's paintings more fully in his book *Picturing a Nation: Art and Social Change in Nineteenth-Century America* (New Haven, Conn., and London, 1994), pp. 273–319.

8. Doreen Bolger, "The Patrons of the Artist: Emblems of Commerce and Culture," in Bolger, Simpson, and Wilmerding (note 2), p. 82.

9. "Art Loses a Master," *Philadelphia North American*, Nov. 1, 1892, p. 1. Another obituary noted, "A fruit scene, which hangs in the corridor of Dooner's Hotel, and for which Mr. Dooner was offered and refused $1,500, is one of his latest efforts. It is, without exception, one of the finest paintings of its kind in existence." See "William M. Harnett Dead," *Philadelphia Evening Bulletin*, Oct. 31, 1892, p. 6.

10. John H. Campbell and Daniel J. Dougherty, *History of the Society of the Friendly Sons of St. Patrick* (Philadelphia, 1952), p. 32. See also Thayer Tolles Mickel, "Permanent Perishables: The Artist's Fruit Paintings," in Bolger, Simpson, and Wilmerding (note 2), p. 219. Thayer Tolles Mickel greatly assisted in the tracking down of references for this entry.

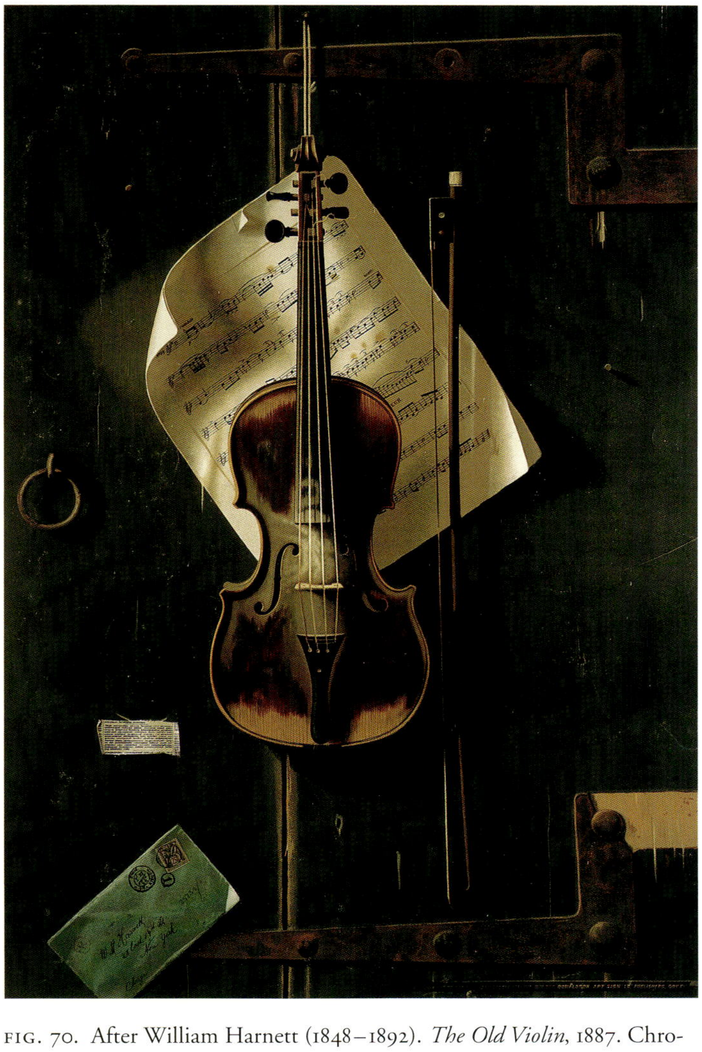

FIG. 70. After William Harnett (1848–1892). *The Old Violin*, 1887. Chromolithograph on paper; 88 x 58.5 cm (34⅝ x 23 in.). The Art Institute of Chicago, Mr. and Mrs. T. Stanton Armour Fund (1994.724).

126. ABBOTT HANDERSON THAYER (1849–1921)

Winged Figure, 1889

Oil on canvas; 130.8 x 95.9 cm (51½ x 37¾ in.)

Signed, lower right: *Abbott H. Thayer / 1889*

Simeon B. Williams Fund, 1947.32

Abbott Handerson Thayer's paintings of angels, virgins, and brides convey a conventional view of womanhood that fuses late nineteenth-century aesthetics with Italian Renaissance artistic models. *Winged Figure* was the second of over one dozen paintings of an angelic female figure that Thayer produced during his career.[1] He was originally an *animalier*, but after four years (1875–79) of study in Paris at the atelier of Jean-Léon Gérôme, he turned to figure painting—first portraits and then idealized subjects.

Later in his life, the artist expounded upon his inspiration for *Winged Figure* in a letter to a museum director: "Doubtless my lifelong passion for birds has helped to incline me to work wings into my pictures; but primarily I have put on wings probably more to symbolize an exalted atmosphere (above the realm of genre painting) where one need not explain the action of his figures."[2] The model for this canvas has been identified as Thayer's neighbor in Dublin, New Hampshire, Clara Adelaide May (1872–1946).[3] The artist often depicted recognizable models in his idealized works—including his children, servants, and family friends—thus uniting portraiture and allegory.

The sensitivity of Thayer's approach is tempered by the sensuous, painterly surfaces of his canvases and the vague eroticism of his subjects. In the Art Institute's painting, a monumental winged figure atop a cloud presides over the composition, her substantial wings spread out behind her, cradling her tilted head. While most of Thayer's winged figures face the

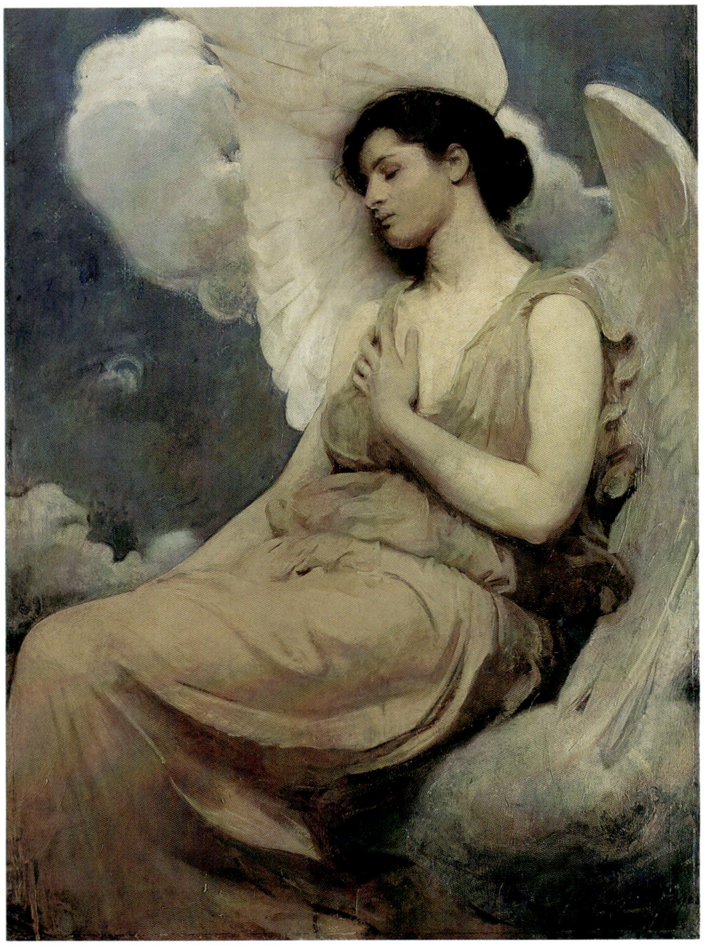

CAT. NO. 126

viewer directly, here the model looks down and is either sleeping or lost in reverie. The hand at her breast modestly reveals the flesh beneath her draped chiton, and she seems to yield to sacred or profane ecstasy.

Although to a late twentieth-century viewer Thayer's images of women exude carnality, nineteenth-century audiences and critics responded to these paintings with reverence. As American art critic Charles Caffin commented, "Thayer has done for the spiritual ideal of American womanhood what C. D. Gibson has done for the physical and mundane—created a type. . . . [She] is unconscious of her modesty, self-contained, but tender and unselfish. She is typical of the pure, frank outlook upon life, prepared to accept its responsibilities and renunciations, to lighten its grossness, and uphold a high ideal."[4] The artist himself professed only the most pure intentions for his subjects: "For *men*," he wrote, "the dawn, the day, girls, mothers and children, and brave kind men, all these things in their most familiar form are more ravishing every day come over again, through all time by virtue of the ever-deepening layers of heavenly connotations which they accumulate."[5] The late nineteenth-century penchant for depicting women as angels and other symbols of virtue is indicative of a desire to idealize women's traditional roles during a period when women were not only trading home and hearth for the workplace but also becoming politically active.[6]

Many of Thayer's New Hampshire neighbors were artists portraying similar themes in a related style. Perhaps formally closest to Thayer was the sculptor Augustus Saint-Gaudens, who also modeled monumental female angels such as *Amor Caritas*, a small bronze version of which is in the collection of The Art Institute of Chicago (cat. no. 131).

Thayer's angels depict women as vehicles for transcendence, guardians of morality, gentle nurturers, and objects of worship, yet their sheer weight and physicality and the richness of their depiction demand a more worldly reading. Although dismissed after his death by modernist critics for being hopelessly literal and literary, Thayer himself insisted upon the abstract values and painterly manner of his work.[7] These contradictions position Thayer's idealized, angelic women between traditional and modern artistic sensibilities.

NOTES

1. Other paintings of winged, female figures by Thayer include *Angel* (c. 1887; National Museum of American Art, Washington, D.C.); *Seated Angel* (1899; Wadsworth Atheneum, Hartford, Conn.); *Stevenson Memorial* (1903; National Museum of American Art, Washington, D.C.); *Angel* (1893; Milwaukee Art Museum); *Angel* (c. 1906; Museum of Fine Arts, Boston); and *A Winged Figure* (1911; Freer Gallery of Art, Washington, D.C.). The Art Institute of Chicago's *Winged Figure* most closely resembles *Winged Figure* (1912; unlocated, formerly in the John Braun Collection). Richard Murray, Senior Curator, National Museum of American Art, graciously shared his research on Thayer's angel subjects.

2. Letter from Abbott Handerson Thayer (written in Emma Thayer's hand) to the director of the Hillyer Gallery, Smith College, Northampton, Mass., c. 1916, Smith College Archives.

3. See Thomas B. Brumbaugh, "An Artist and His Model: Abbott H. Thayer and Clara May," *American Art Journal* 10, 1 (May 1978), pp. 24–32. In Ross Anderson, *Abbott Handerson Thayer*, exh. cat. (Syracuse, N.Y., Everson Museum, 1982), p. 61, the author stated that he was not wholly convinced that Clara May was the model for this picture.

4. Quoted in Rilla E. Jackman, *American Arts* (Chicago, 1947), p. 129.

5. Quoted in Anderson (note 3), p. 43.

6. For more on this topic, see Bailey Van Hook, *Angels of Art: Women and Art in American Society, 1876–1914* (University Park, Pa., 1996).

7. Anderson (note 3), p. 11.

THE MODERN ERA

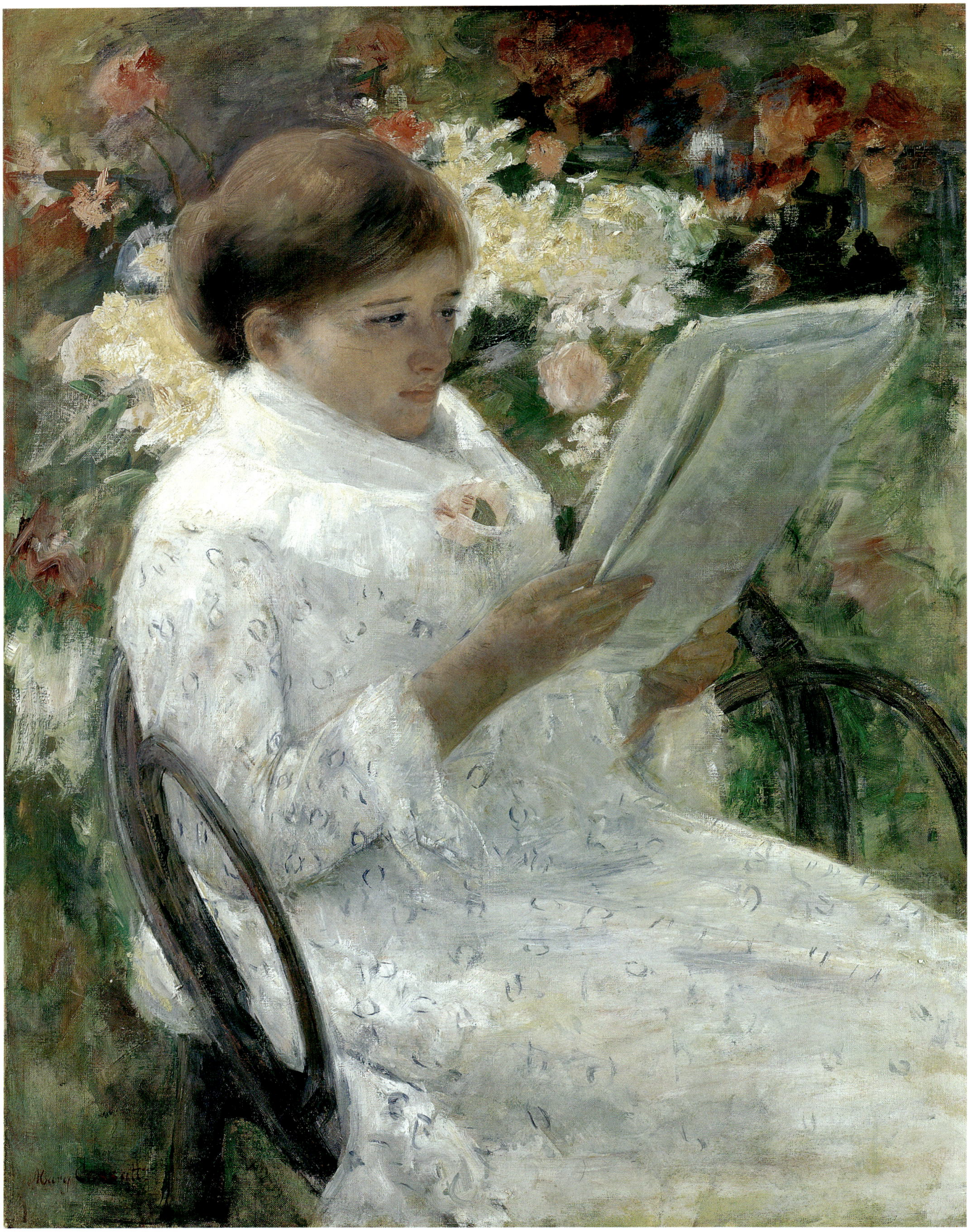

CAT. NO. 127

127. MARY CASSATT (1844–1926)

On a Balcony, 1878/79

Oil on canvas: 89.9 x 65.2 cm (35½ x 25⅝ in.)
Signed, lower left: *Mary Cassatt*
Gift of Mrs. Albert J. Beveridge in memory of her aunt, Delia Spencer Field, 1938.18

128. *The Child's Bath*, 1893

Oil on canvas; 100.3 x 66.1 cm (39½ x 26 in.)
Signed, lower left: *Mary Cassatt*
The Robert A. Waller Fund, 1910.2

After studying in Italy and Spain in the early 1870s, Mary Cassatt settled in Paris, then the capital of modern art, in 1873. In about 1877 she met Edgar Degas and soon thereafter joined the circle of Impressionist painters. She was one of just four women, and the only American, to become part of the French independent movement. She exhibited with the group in 1879, 1880, 1881, and 1886. *On a Balcony* was included in the 1880 exhibition.

During her early Impressionist years, Cassatt addressed subjects that showed the activities of middle-class women—at the theater, in domestic interiors and small gardens, taking tea, sewing, or reading. Some of these themes may have been suggested by the plethora of fashion magazines that appeared in Paris starting in the 1860s. In fact, Cassatt's own work was featured in an article written by Claude Monet's patron Ernest Hoschedé in *L'Art de la mode* in 1881.[1] Like the women in fashion plates, Cassatt's women reflect the activities of the modern world. Here, a female figure dressed in casual "deshabille" (a morning dress worn while at home) enjoys a private moment. This modern woman reads not one of the romantic novels associated with eighteenth-century portraits of women reading such as those by Jean-Baptiste Greuze or Jean-Honoré Fragonard, but rather a newspaper or contemporary periodical. Cassatt enjoyed painting such informality, and the morning dress provided an opportunity to lighten further the Impressionist palette. The barely visible green railing and the flowers surrounding her head are extensions of the privacy of the home, and they link Cassatt's female portraits with the intimacy and accoutrements of domestic spaces. Cassatt's female subjects are not simply decorative, however; they show an active intelligence and are absorbed in activity.

Japanese art was all the rage in Paris during and after the 1878 Paris Exposition Universelle, and many artists, including Edgar Degas, Félix Bracquemond, Édouard Manet, Claude Monet, James Tissot, and Alfred Stevens, collected Japanese prints.[2] The critic Armand Silvestre wrote of this picture that he liked "the woman reading on the balcony, where peonie shrubs frame her blonde head—a true model of Japanese art in its absence of distant space and the happy mixture of color in an entirely pleasant range."[3] He saw the influence of Japanese aesthetics in the flattened picture space, high-keyed palette, and broad, abstract geometrical forms, such as the circular arms of the chair and the pattern of the dress. In this early work, Cassatt experimented with the *japonisme* that would come to full flower a little more than a decade later in her masterpiece, *The Child's Bath* of 1893.

In April 1890 Cassatt visited the large exhibition of Japanese prints on view at the École des Beaux-Arts.[4] After returning to the exhibition several times (once with Degas, once with Berthe Morisot),[5] Cassatt approached her own painting with a new sensibility that combined the symbolism of the woman-and-child theme with a flattened, highly decorative, and graphically oriented aesthetic. *The Child's Bath* was a continuation of an experiment with Japanese aesthetics she had begun in a series of ten color prints that documented activities in a woman's day.[6] Many of the same props and compositional devices Cassatt used in her color prints were repeated, albeit on a grander scale and with greater chromatic variety, in *The Child's Bath*. Like her series of prints "à la Japonaise," this painting emphasizes decorative pattern and a plunging perspective that fills the flattened picture plane. The oriental carpet, the woman's striped dress, the geometry of the pitcher and bowl, and the Rococo Revival chest and wallpaper in the background meld together in a tapestry of pinks, whites, and greens. The abstract pattern negates the illusionistic depth of the picture space, pushing color and line to the surface of the canvas.

Throughout the 1890s and after the turn of the century, Cassatt's work became increasingly monumental and symbolic. Her work reflects the late nineteenth-century fascination with maternity and the new social emphasis on child care prevalent in the literature of the period. Cassatt concentrated on the theme of the nude child, arising from a nap or after a bath, always accompanied by a clothed female adult. The nude-child theme allowed the artist to explore the nature of innocence, and physical tenderness and sensuality outside a sexual context. The figures do not look at each other but rather at their reflections in the water. Intimacy is suggested through the tactile sensations of the water shared by mother and child and

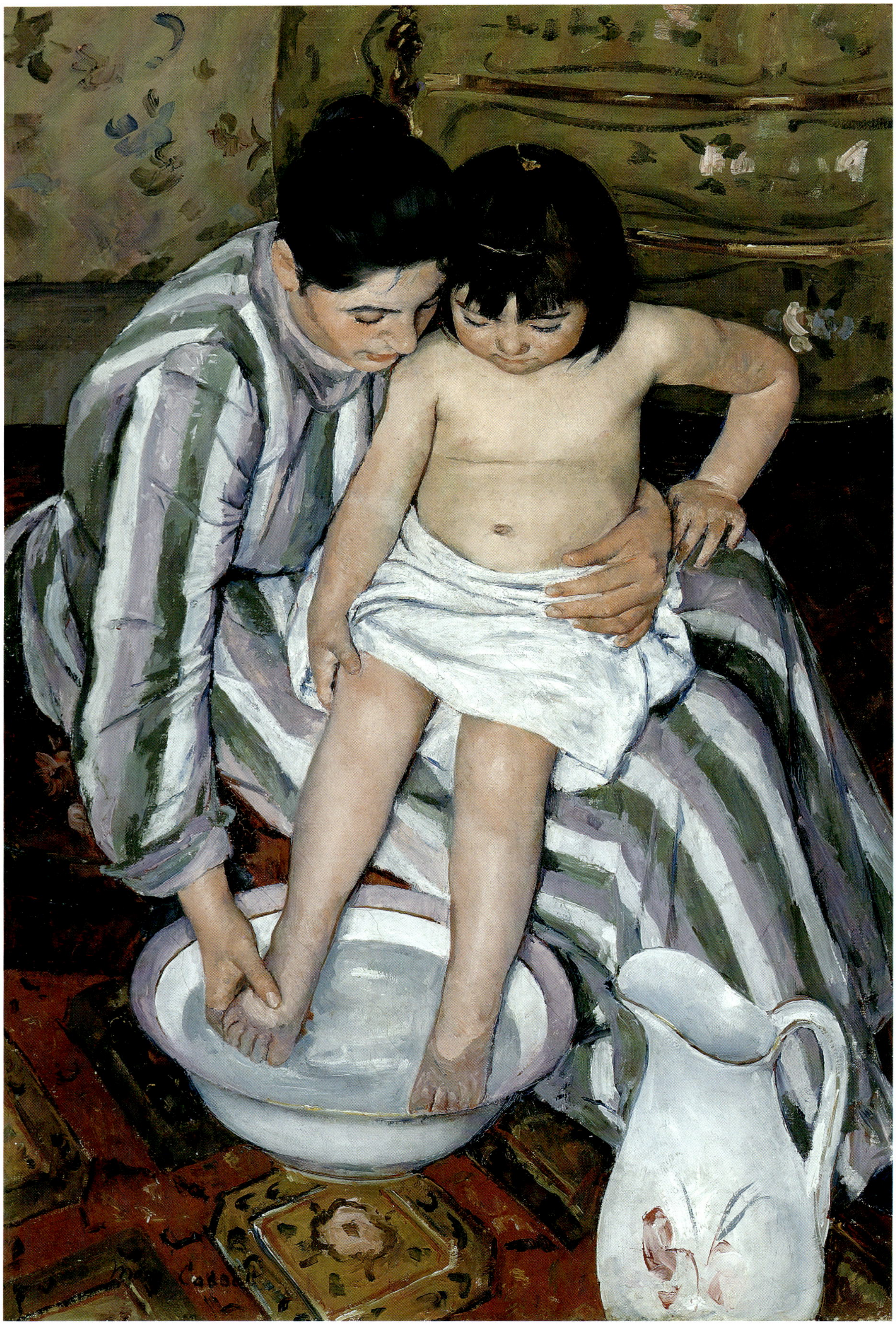

CAT. NO. 128

the touching of their hands and feet. Strong modeling, firm drawing, and the child's compact and oddly proportioned body impart an unequivocal, unidealized physicality to the scene, which produces a feeling of great tenderness. Focusing on the tactile qualities of Cassatt's maternal themes, the critic Félix Fénéon wrote: "And always, these large, beautiful, masculine hands that Cassatt likes to give her women, have decorative functions, especially when set against the bodies of naked infants, they disturb the lines, then blend with them to create unexpected arabesques."[7] Cassatt's studies of women and children together depicted the woman's sphere, but also alluded to the sexual life of women—not through sexuality itself, but through the nineteenth century's socially sanctioned emphasis on maternity.

Like many of the other original members of the Impressionist circle, Cassatt spent much of her time living in the countryside during the 1890s. She bought a chateau fifty miles northwest of Paris, and there, for the rest of her career, concentrated on images of children, or mothers and children, in both the pastel and oil media. Her female imagery was a socially conservative reflection of her own interest in early feminism and the women's suffrage movement. She lived to see women vote in the United States, but not in France, where universal suffrage was not adopted until after World War II. Historians today consider Cassatt, along with Whistler and Sargent, to be among the most important nineteenth-century American expatriate artists.

NOTES

1. Ernest Hoschedé, "Les Femmes Artistes," *L'Art de la mode* (Apr. 2, 1881), pp. 54–59.

2. Ernest Chesneau, "Exposition Universelle: Le Japon à Paris," *Gazette des Beaux-Arts* 18 (1878), p. 387.

3. Armand Silvestre, "Le Monde des arts," *La Vie moderne* (April 24, 1880), p. 262: "J'aime aussi beaucoup la femme lisant sur un balcon, dont les arbustes encadrent de pivoines sa tête blonde,—un véritable échantillon d'art japonais par l'absence des plans et le ragoût heureux de couleurs dans une gamme tout à fait riante."

4. See *Exposition de la gravure japonaise*, exh. cat. (Paris: École Nationale des Beaux-Arts, 1890). The exhibition was organized as a survey of seventeenth- and eighteenth-century Japanese woodblock prints and included 725 prints and 428 books.

5. For Cassatt's plans to view the exhibition with Edgar Degas, see letter from Degas to Paul Albert Bartholomé, undated, but inscribed by the recipient, "29 April 1890," in Marcel Guerin, ed., *Lettres de Degas* (Paris, 1945), pp. 151–52, letter no. 120. For a letter in which she strongly urges Berthe Morisot to come to the exhibition, see letter from Cassatt to Morisot, undated, but probably late April or early May 1890, in Nancy Mowll Mathews, ed., *Cassatt and Her Circle: Selected Letters* (New York, 1984), pp. 214–15. In her letter to Morisot, Cassatt becomes almost poetic about the Japanese prints and the exhibition: "I dream of it and don't think of anything else but color on copper. Fantin [Henri Fantin-Latour] was there the 1st day I went and was in ecstasy. I saw Tissot [James Tissot] there who also is occupied with the problem of making color prints."

6. Cassatt first exhibited her series of ten color prints in April 1891 at Galerie Durand-Ruel in Paris. The first print in the series, *The Child's Bath* (*Bain d'Enfant*), carried the subtitle or description: "An attempt to imitate the Japanese print" ("Essai d'imitation de l'estampe japonaise").

7. Félix Fénéon, "Cassatt, Pissarro," *Le Chat noir* (Apr. 11, 1891), p. 1728.

129. GEORGE HITCHCOCK (1850–1913)

Flower Girl in Holland, 1887

Oil on canvas; 79.1 x 147.3 cm (31⅛ x 58 in.)

Signed, lower left: *Geo. Hitchcock op. XXXV 1-8-8-7*

Potter Palmer Collection, 1888.169

The search for picturesque subjects took numerous American artists to rural regions of England, France, and the Netherlands during the last quarter of the nineteenth century. Originally trained as a lawyer, George Hitchcock settled in Egmond, a group of three towns in the West Friesland region of the northwest coast of Holland, in 1884 after spending brief periods studying art in London, Paris, and The Hague.[1] In the nearly twenty years he spent in Egmond, Hitchcock specialized in scenes featuring sacred and secular women juxtaposed with voluptuously blooming flowers, and he earned a reputation as a daring colorist. Hitchcock painted *Flower Girl in Holland*, one of the earliest examples of this theme in his work, when he was gaining international acclaim.[2]

With fellow American artist Gari Melchers (1860–1932), Hitchcock founded an art colony in Egmond that flourished between 1895 and 1905. Students from both Europe and the United States flocked there in the summer months, much as they did to Giverny and Pont-Aven in France. They relished the landscape of rural Holland, which offered an evocative mixture of sea, sand dunes, farms, and tulip fields. Hitchcock introduced Holland to American audiences in a series of articles he wrote between 1887 and 1891 for *Scribner's Magazine* entitled "The Picturesque Quality of Holland." Using terms familiar to late nineteenth-century tourists, Hitchcock described the country as a place to escape from modern, industrialized, urban life.[3]

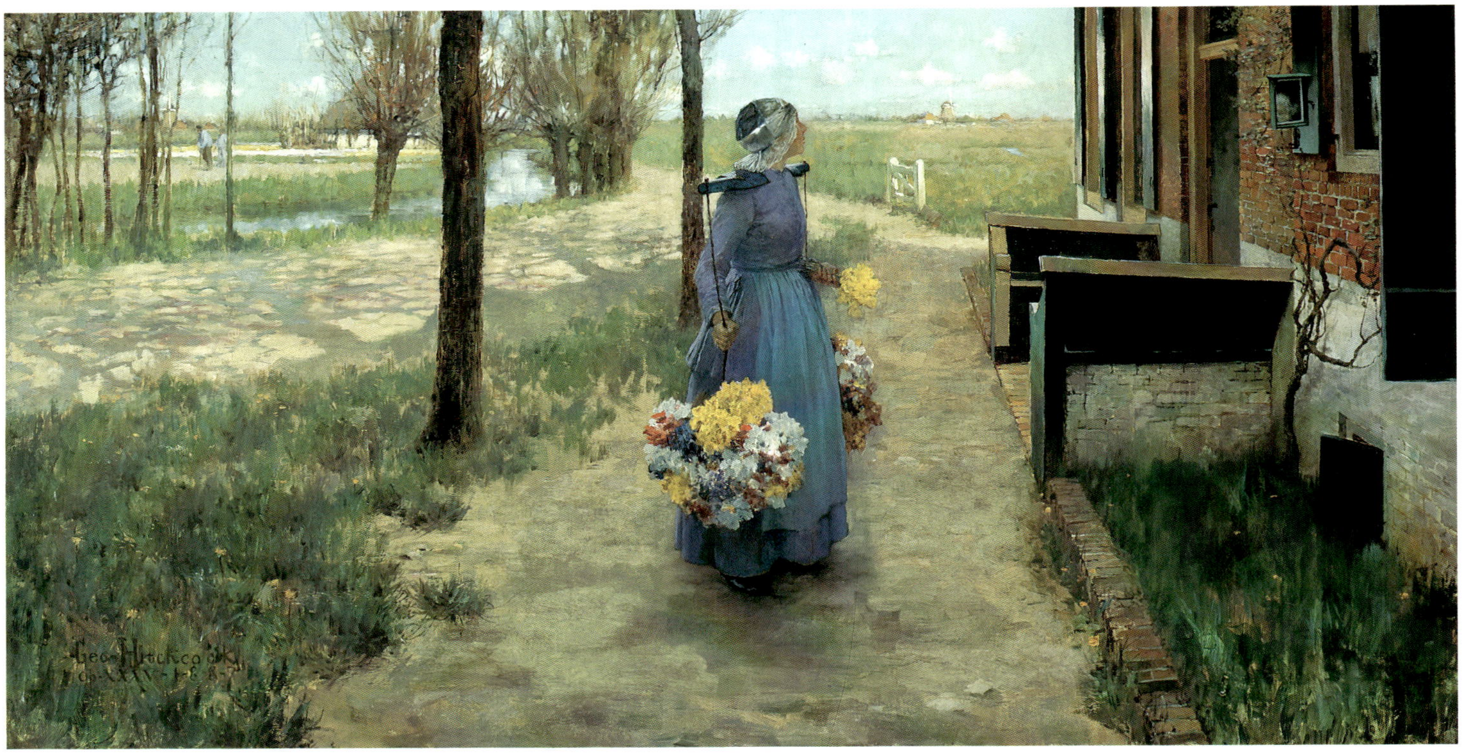

CAT. NO. 129

Egmond's economy was based in agriculture and fishing and its residents were generally poor, but artists reveled in their adherence to native costume and tradition. The glorification of the peasant by Hitchcock and his contemporaries also constituted a rejection of avant-garde trends in French art and an endorsement of realism.

Within this picturesque genre, artists were often drawn to the depiction of young female flower vendors. For example, Childe Hassam's *At the Florist* (fig. 71) bears a striking resemblance to Hitchcock's picture, although Hassam's scene situates a rural woman (or a woman dressed in rural costume) in an urban milieu and comments on, according to a recent analysis, "the commodification of nature in the city and . . . the transformation of nature from a necessity into a luxury."[4] In Hitchcock's painting, however, the flower seller's purpose is essentially decorative: she provides the opportunity to render a pleasing arrangement of colors and forms. Hitchcock's description of a similar subject in *Scribner's Magazine* reveals the formal qualities he admired in these figures: "A fresh-complexioned girl, with large balls of many-colored flowers, composed of separate bunches of tulips or hyacinths hanging at the ends of a milk-bucket yoke, is often seen in the spring turning an honest penny in a beautiful way by selling the useless blossoms

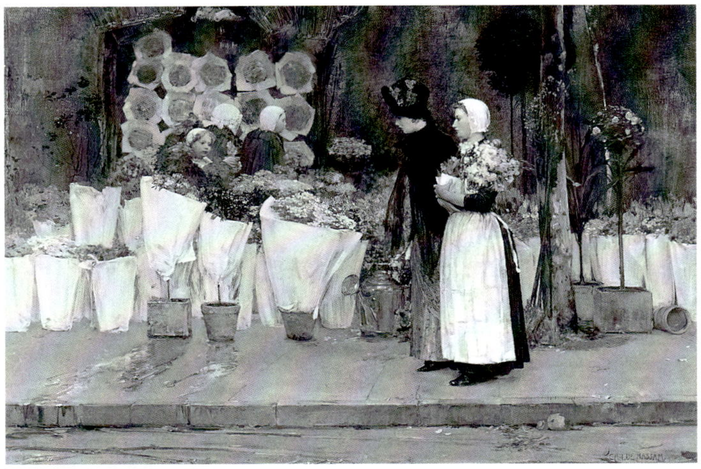

FIG. 71. Childe Hassam (1859–1935). *At the Florist*, 1889. Oil on canvas; 92.7 x 136.5 cm (36½ x 53¾ in.). Chrysler Museum, Norfolk, Va., Gift of Walter P. Chrysler, Jr. (71.500).

when the bulb has reached its maturity. . . . Whatever the female figures are doing, the lace head-dress adds always a charm and invites study."[5]

The costume of the vendor in Hitchcock's painting, especially the distinctive bonnet, is of a type indigenous to West Friesland. Regarding the delicate lilac dress, Hitchcock wrote:

"the favorite color for the women's working dresses is a variety of pale lilacs, faded again into numberless shades and tints, which are very harmonious among the pale, delicate greens of the sea-dunes or the glistening white sands of the almost endless sea-coast."[6] The care Hitchcock lavished on such details extended to his observation of local architecture. Still recognizable and standing in 1989, the house featured in Hitchcock's painting was actually part of a row of buildings that included the former Town Hall and village school.[7] Hitchcock's manipulation of the scene—which allows a clear view of the background landscape, complete with a windmill—is indicative of his concern for establishing an aura of authenticity through the presentation of select, familiar details rather than through an accretion of literal fact.

NOTES

1. Hitchcock arrived in London in 1877 and studied drawing privately with a Mr. Heatherley. In Paris he studied at the Académie Julian with Gustave Boulanger and Jules Joseph Lefebvre. In 1880 he settled in The Hague, where he studied briefly with Hendrik Willem Mesdag.

2. *Flower Girl in Holland*'s inscription, "Geo. Hitchcock op. XXXV 1-8-8-7," indicates that the painting is perhaps part of a series. Two other works inscribed similarly with an "op." number have been located: *The Annunciation* (1887; The Art Institute of Chicago), also known as *Annunciation Lilies*, inscribed "op. xxxvi"; and *The Tulip Garden* (1887; Jordan Volpe Gallery, New York), inscribed "op. 33."

3. For a complete account of this phenomenon in relation to Holland, see Annette Stott, "Dutch Utopia: Paintings by Antimodern American Artists of the Nineteenth Century," *Smithsonian Studies in American Art* 3 (spring 1989), pp. 47–61.

4. Barbara Weinberg, Doreen Bolger, and David Park Curry, *American Impressionism and Realism: The Painting of Modern Life, 1885–1915*, exh. cat. (New York, Metropolitan Museum of Art, 1994), p. 14.

5. George Hitchcock, "The Picturesque Quality of Holland: Figures and Costumes," *Scribner's Magazine* 10, 5 (Nov. 1891), p. 627.

6. Ibid., p. 625.

7. Letter from Ronald Van Vleuten to Lawrence A. Paul, Jan. 24, 1989, Files of the Department of American Arts, The Art Institute of Chicago.

130. AUGUSTUS SAINT-GAUDENS (1848–1907)

Jules Bastien-Lepage, modeled 1880, cast in copper and bronze 1881

Copper with bronze patina; 37.2 x 27 cm (14⅝ x 10⅝ in.)

Foundry: Magee Furnace Co., Chelsea, Mass.

Inscribed across top: *[I]VLES BASTIEN LEPAGE AETATIS XXXI PARIS MDCCCLXXX AVGVSTVS / SAINT-GAVDENS FECIT*

Gift of Sara Hallowell, 1908.83

131. *Violet Sargent*, modeled 1890, cast in bronze c. 1908

Bronze; 127.7 x 77.5 cm (50¼ x 30½ in.)

Inscribed on bench: *A ST G / MDCCCLXXXX / FECIT*

Gift of Brooks McCormick, 1976.685

132. *Amor Caritas*, modeled 1897, cast in bronze after 1899

Bronze; 131.4 x 80.7 cm (51¾ x 31¾ in.)

Inscribed, lower left: *AVGVSTVS. / SAINT-GAVDENS / MDCCCXCVII*

Roger McCormick Fund, 1982.211

These three pieces comprise a selective overview of Augustus Saint-Gaudens's development as a sculptor of bas-relief.[1] Although he created sculptures in the round as well, Saint-Gaudens excelled at bas-relief and was renowned as a portraitist who was expert with this technique. *Jules Bastien-Lepage* and *Violet Sargent* are impressive examples of the artist's ability to capture a likeness naturalistically and to suggest a mood sensitively in bronze. *Amor Caritas*, on the other hand, is an allegorical subject derived from a large-scale sculpture that demonstrates Saint-Gaudens's breadth of technique and subject matter. All of these pieces embody the sculptor's adherence to American Renaissance artistic ideals through his choice of media, subject matter, and classical form.[2]

Like many American nineteenth-century sculptors, Saint-Gaudens received his artistic training abroad. Before formally studying sculpture, however, he was apprenticed to the cameo cutter Louis Avet in New York City, which accounts in part for his skill with bas-relief. By the time he traveled to Europe in 1867, Paris had, owing to the advances in bronze casting being developed there, usurped Rome as the preeminent training ground for young sculptors. With Olin Levi Warner and Howard Roberts, Saint-Gaudens was among the first Americans to study sculpture in Paris; Saint-Gaudens entered François Jouffroy's atelier at the École des Beaux-Arts in 1868 and Warner followed suit in 1869. Saint-Gaudens remained with Jouffroy until 1870 and subsequently spent two years in Italy before returning to the United States. Italy offered Saint-Gaudens numerous opportunities to study Renaissance portrait reliefs and medals, to which his work has often been compared.

Saint-Gaudens's sojourn in Europe was the first of many he made during the course of his career. He occasionally exhibited at the Paris Salon, most notably in 1880 when his work (including a cast of *Jules Bastien-Lepage*) won an honorable mention. Saint-Gaudens met his fellow artist Bastien-Lepage during their student years in Paris and rekindled their relationship when Saint-Gaudens returned in 1878. Saint-Gaudens recalled that "Lepage was short, bullet-headed, athletic and . . . dandified in dress. . . . He asked if I would make a medallion of him in exchange for a portrait of myself."[3] Shown in profile holding a palette and paint brushes, the French artist is impeccably dressed and his hair and features are sharply defined and individualized. This relief was enormously successful with patrons, and more than twenty versions exist.[4]

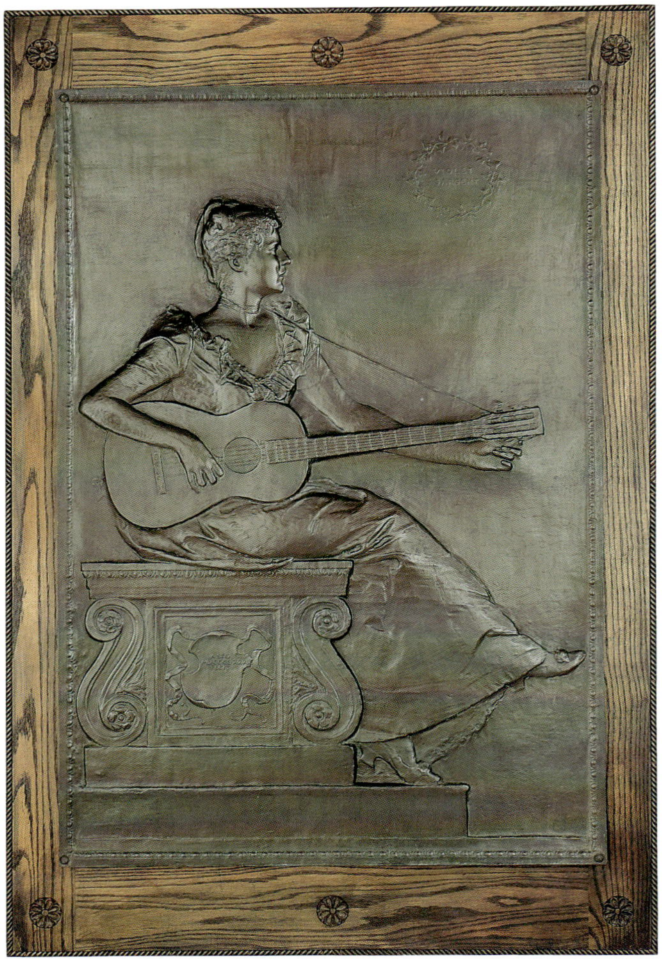

CAT. NO. 131

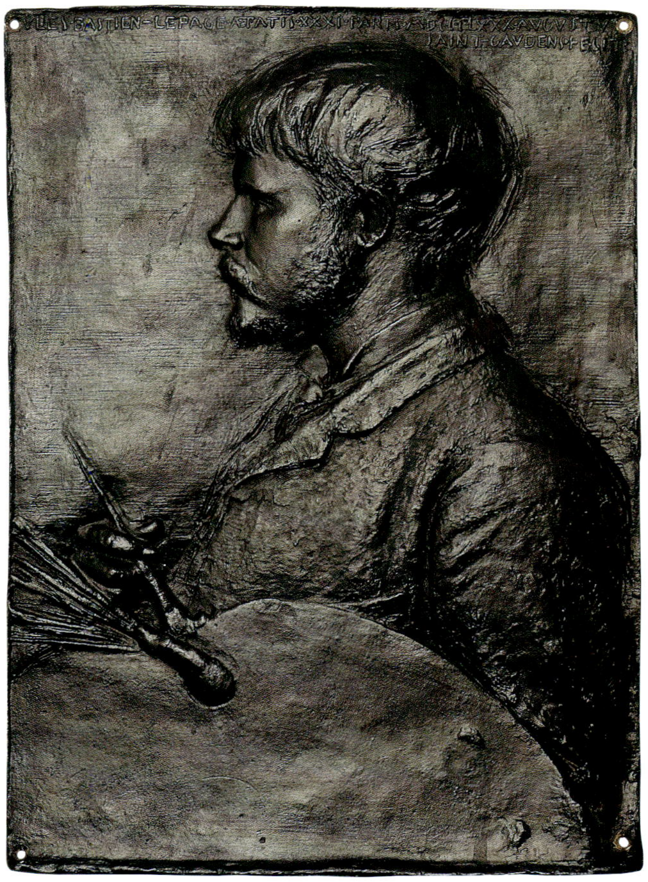

CAT. NO. 130

The Art Institute's version was purchased by Sara Hallowell from the artist in 1881; a letter from Saint-Gaudens to Hallowell dated November 14, 1881, reads: "Your letter of Nov 3 was duly received and I beg you will excuse any delay—I herein enclose receipt for the two hundred dollars for the Bastien."[5] Hallowell and Saint-Gaudens enjoyed a lasting friendship and worked together at the 1893 World's Columbian Exposition in Chicago, where Hallowell was Assistant Chief of Fine Arts and Saint-Gaudens was an adviser on sculpture and the designer of the Presentation Medal and figure of Columbus.[6] They shared a mutual admiration for the paintings of Bastien-Lepage, perhaps best expressed through the production and purchase of the portrait relief.[7]

Saint-Gaudens's mastery of materials and his international

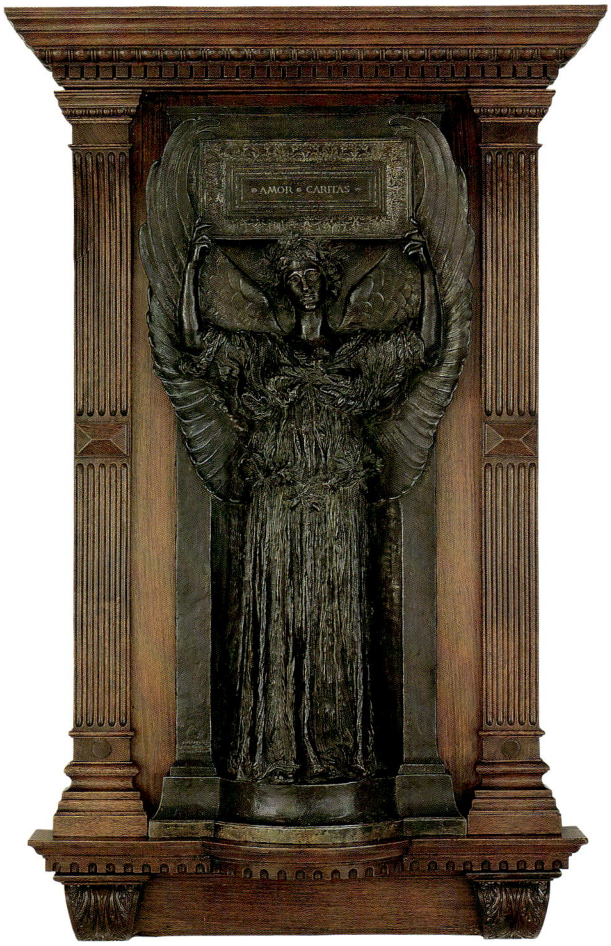

CAT. NO. 132

connections within the late nineteenth-century art world are also displayed in *Violet Sargent.* The relief depicts John Singer Sargent's younger sister at age twenty and was modeled at the sculptor's home in Cornish, New Hampshire, during a trip the Sargents made to the United States during the first half of 1890. In exchange for the relief of his sister, Sargent painted a portrait of Saint-Gaudens's son Homer, which is in the collection of the Carnegie Museum of Art in Pittsburgh.[8] Two versions of the bas-relief were made for the Sargent family, one in bronze (1890; National Museum of American Art, Washington, D.C.) and one in marble (1890; Saint-Gaudens National Historic Site, Cornish, New Hampshire). The Art Institute's version was cast after Saint-Gaudens's death for Sargent's friend and Art Institute trustee Charles Deering.[9]

Two sketches for *Violet Sargent* in the Cooper-Hewitt National Design Museum in New York show that Saint-Gaudens experimented with different poses before settling on the final version. In the bronze relief, Sargent appears charmingly beautiful and carefree sitting on a bench, apparently tuning her guitar, in a casual pose that emphasizes her youth. The shallow relief of the piece augments its delicacy and grace and demonstrates Saint-Gaudens working at the height of his powers.

Amor Caritas differs in both style and subject matter from the other pieces discussed in this essay. A heavily modeled and allegorical piece, the Art Institute's version is a reduction of a larger-than-life-size bronze sculpture that won the grand prize at the 1900 Exposition Universelle in Paris and was subsequently purchased by the French government for the Luxembourg Museum. Derived from designs for the Morgan tomb (Hartford, Connecticut) and the Ann Maria Smith tomb (Newport, Rhode Island), *Amor Caritas* probably depicts Davida Clark, the sculptor's mistress. Dressed in loose, classically inspired drapery with garlands of passion flowers around her waist and head, the figure holds a plaque inscribed with the words "Amor Caritas" above her head. Translated as "Love Charity," the loosely symbolic title personifies the idealized character of the winged women who inhabit numerous late nineteenth-century American paintings and sculptures.[10]

Saint-Gaudens and, after his death, his widow marketed these reductions and others at Doll and Richards in Boston and at Tiffany and Company in New York, where by 1917 they sold for five hundred dollars apiece.[11] This piece retains its original mahogany tabernacle frame, perhaps designed by the architect Stanford White, which emphasizes its classical features and its serene and stately presence.[12]

NOTES

1. For more information about Saint-Gaudens and bas-relief, see John Dryfhout and Beverly Cox, *Augustus Saint-Gaudens: The Portrait Reliefs*, exh. cat. (Washington, D.C., National Portrait Gallery, 1969).

2. See the entry on Daniel Chester French's *Truth* (cat. no. 142) for more information on the American Renaissance.

3. Augustus Saint-Gaudens, *The Reminiscences of Augustus Saint-Gaudens*, vol. 1 (New York, 1913), p. 215. Saint-Gaudens also recalled that Lepage's portrait of him was destroyed in a fire that burned Saint-Gaudens's studio in 1904.

4. John H. Dryfhout, *The Work of Augustus Saint-Gaudens* (Hanover, N.H., 1982), p. 108.

5. Letter from Augustus Saint-Gaudens to Sara Hallowell, Nov. 14, 1881, Augustus Saint-Gaudens Papers, reel 8, Library of Congress, Washington, D.C.

6. See Judith A. Barter's introductory essay (pp. 21–25) for more information about Hallowell and art collecting in Chicago.

7. At least two copies of the Bastien-Lepage relief are electrotypes; Electrotyping is a reproductive technique that is less costly than sand-casting because it involves adhering a bronze-type patina to other metals' surfaces. Michael Shapiro has noted that the Art Institute's version exhibits the characteristics of an electrotype, and its purchase date by Hallowell coincides

with the sculptor's experimentation with the technique; see Michael Edward Shapiro, *Bronze Casting and American Sculpture 1850–1900* (Newark, Del., 1985), p. 99. Also, an article mentioning Saint-Gaudens's use of electrotyping was published around the time of Hallowell's purchase of the Art Institute's relief; see "Art Casting," *Lawrence Daily American*, Nov. 3, 1881, p. 3.

8. Donald Miller, "Inspired Friendship: Sargent and Saint-Gaudens," *Carnegie Magazine* 53, 4 (Apr. 1979), pp. 4–11.

9. A series of letters between Augusta Saint-Gaudens, the sculptor's widow, and Charles Deering in the Augustus Saint-Gaudens papers establishes the circumstances under which the piece was cast. See, for example, letter from Charles Deering to Mrs. Augustus Saint-Gaudens, Jan. 24, 1908; letter from Mrs. Augustus Saint-Gaudens to Charles Deering, Jan. 27, 1908; and letter from Charles Deering to Mrs. Augustus Saint-Gaudens, Feb. 11, 1908; Augustus Saint-Gaudens Papers, reel 5, Dartmouth College Library, Hanover, N.H.

10. For more on nineteenth-century depictions of winged women, see the entry on Abbott Handerson Thayer's *Winged Figure* (cat. no. 126).

11. Letter from Augusta Saint-Gaudens to Messrs. Tiffany and Company, Sept. 17, 1915, Tiffany Archives, New York, N.Y.

12. Suzanne Smeaton stated without documentation that the frame on *Amor Caritas* was designed by Stanford White; see "American Picture Frames of the Arts and Crafts Period, 1870–1920," *Antiques* 136, 5 (Nov. 1989), p. 1127. This claim is strengthened by the similarity of the Art Institute's frame to a documented White gilded tabernacle frame on Thomas Wilmer Dewing's painting *Lady in Grey* (1911–12; Rhode Island School of Design, Providence, R.I.).

133. JOHN HENRY TWACHTMAN (1853–1902)

Icebound, c. 1889

Oil on canvas; 64.2 x 76.6 cm (25¼ x 30⅛ in.)
Signed, lower right: *J. H. Twachtman*
Friends of American Art Collection, 1917.200

134. *The White Bridge*, after 1895

Oil on canvas; 75 x 75 cm (29½ x 29½ in.)
Signed, lower left: *J. H. Twachtman*
Mr. and Mrs. Martin A. Ryerson Collection, 1937.1042

During the last decade of his life, John Twachtman painted numerous views of the landscape surrounding his home on Round Hill Road in Greenwich, Connecticut.[1] He bought seventeen acres of property around 1890 and painted outside year round to capture the effects of the changing seasons on his carefully cultivated land. *Icebound* and *The White Bridge* depict two different spots on the artist's property in winter and spring and demonstrate his changing formal response to each scene and time of year. Twachtman characterized the blanketed solitude of winter and the blossoming elegance of spring with varying compositional and paint handling effects that reveal his sensitivity to the natural world, Impressionistic tendencies, and commitment to representing his local landscape.

Like William Merritt Chase (see cat. no. 121), Twachtman received his initial artistic training in Munich in the mid-1870s. After his return to the United States in 1878, Twachtman's style evolved from one that made extensive use of the dark, heavy impastos characteristic of the Munich School to one favoring a lighter palette and thinner paint application and more in tune with modern French trends. To continue his instruction, Twachtman journeyed to Paris in 1883 and enrolled at the Académie Julian. Very few paintings survive from the years immediately following Twachtman's Parisian training, but those that do exhibit a tonalist, Whistlerian sensibility applied to depictions of the natural world. Additionally, they express not only the artist's involvement with Japanese aesthetics but also the popular idea that art could have a therapeutic effect on the lives of urban dwellers.[2]

Icebound is one of Twachtman's many Connecticut winter scenes that embody the idea of the season as conducive to contemplation and regeneration rather than as a dead, barren time.[3] In fact, views of winter comprise the largest portion of Twachtman's oeuvre, and most depict a frozen body of water. *Icebound* shows either Horseneck Brook or Hemlock Pool, two water holes that are part of a stream on the estate that he painted many times. In an often-quoted letter to fellow artist and close friend J. Alden Weir, Twachtman revealed his preference for the serenity of winter, writing: "We must have snow and lots of it. Never is nature more lovely than when it is snowing. Everything is so quiet and . . . All nature is hushed to silence."[4]

The dense, gradually built-up layers of paint in *Icebound* mimic the accumulation of snow on the frozen ground, while the sinuous curves that define the snow and ice against the water suggest movement in an otherwise tranquil environment. The deep blue of the water and the orange leaves that linger on the trees are the most vivid notes of color in this otherwise monochromatic canvas. Almost square in format, the painting's harmonious composition allows the viewer to contemplate the scene from several points of view—one can consider the water either receding into the background or spilling out of the canvas along the bottom left corner. *Icebound* may have been exhibited at the Art Institute in 1889; one critic's com-

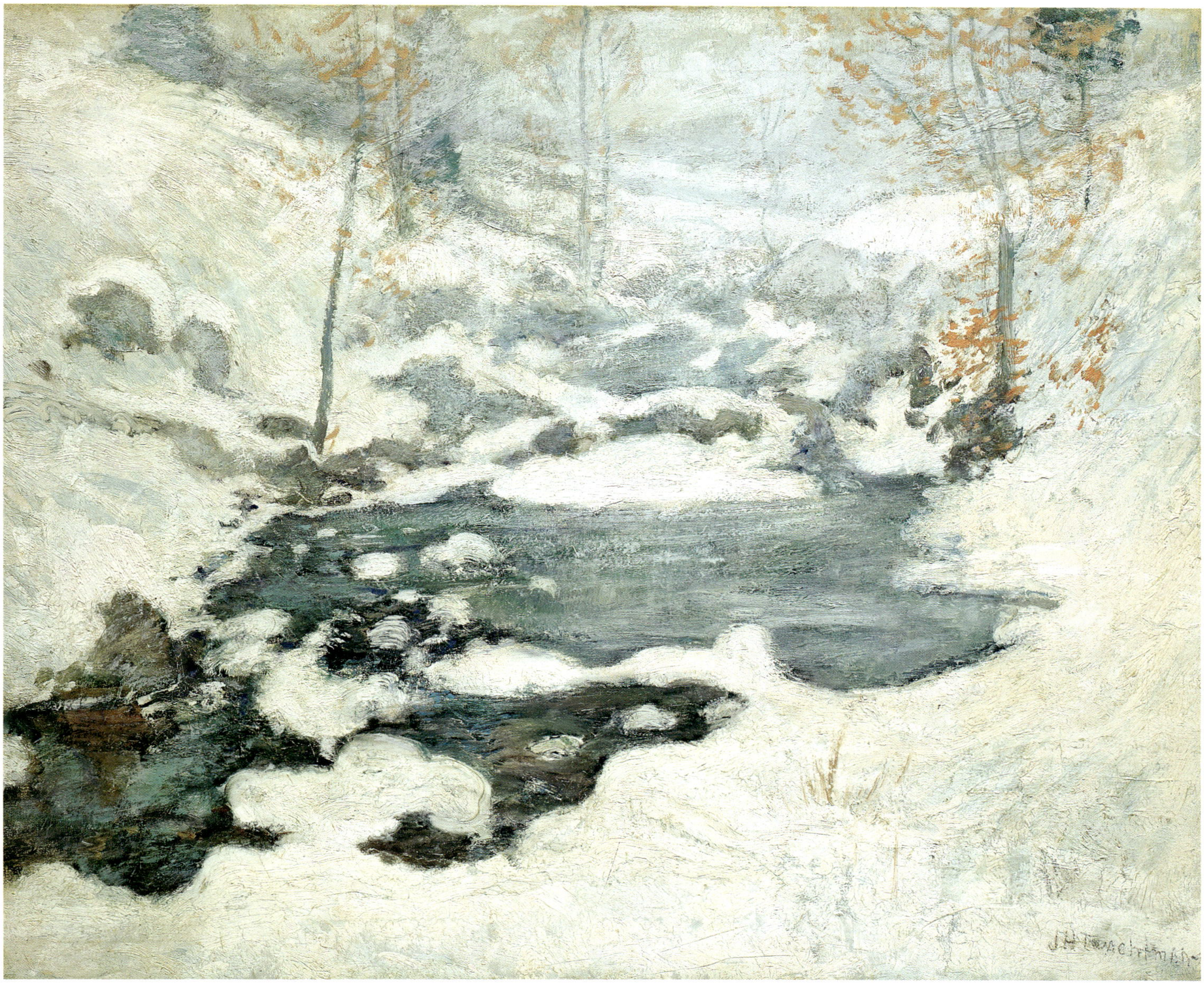

CAT. NO. 133

ments certainly correspond with the theme of the painting: "Mr. Twachtman's contribution . . . is of a nearly square format well-suited to the scene of a frozen brook in winter. Impressionism has brought forth these soft lavenders and blues, and this loving adulation of the icy winter air."[5]

The White Bridge, which Twachtman painted after *Icebound*, represents spring and depicts the bridge spanning Horseneck Brook. The artist built this bridge around 1895 and represented it at least five times over the course of the following seven years.[6] Unlike the relatively opaque, evenly handled snow in *Icebound*, the scene in *The White Bridge* is sketchily rendered in feathery strokes of green and rich brown pigment with expanses of unprimed canvas showing through. The vitality and renewal of spring are suggested by the energetic, short brushstrokes and by the transparent layers of freshly budding vegetation that seems to grow before one's eyes. The painting also demonstrates the artist's growing skill as an Impressionist and his commitment to working *en plein air* in extreme weather.

Twachtman's delight in depicting the same scenes again and again in different seasons, coupled with his loose handling and emphasis on effects of light, have prompted many to compare his work to that of Claude Monet. The comparison is apt considering that both men chose, in their later years, to explore the infinite and constantly changing beauty of a particular area that they continuously manicured—but Monet's work in series

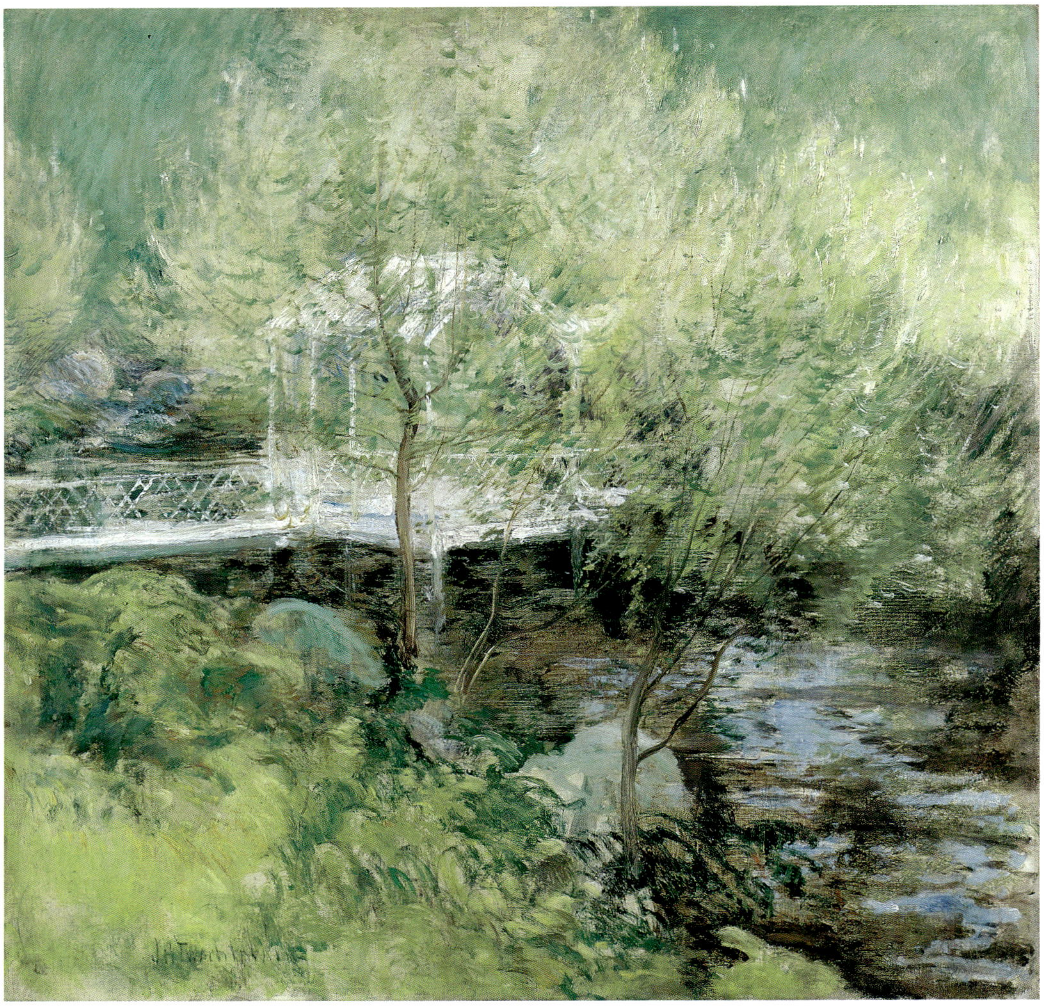

CAT. NO. 134

was more structured than Twachtman's. The French artist carefully choreographed his day, often working on more than one canvas, depending on the hour and the angle of the sun.[7] Twachtman seems to have worked more haphazardly, producing far fewer works than his prodigious French contemporary. However, Twachtman's work in Connecticut is significant in that it taps into the nascent "modernist" trend of examining a single subject from many points of view over time, creating a subtle range of effects within a limited framework.

NOTES

1. For more about Twachtman in Connecticut, see Deborah Chotner, Lisa N. Peters, and Kathleen A. Pyne, *John Twachtman: Connecticut Landscapes*, exh. cat. (Washington, D.C., National Gallery of Art, 1989).

2. See Kathleen A. Pyne, "John Twachtman and the Therapeutic Landscape," in Chotner, Peters, and Pyne (note 1), pp. 49–69.

3. See Deborah Chotner, "Twachtman and the American Winter Landscape," in Chotner, Peters, and Pyne (note 1), pp. 71–85.

4. Letter from John Twachtman to J. Alden Weir, Dec. 16, 1891; quoted in Dorothy Weir Young, *The Life and Letters of J. Alden Weir* (New Haven, Conn., 1960), p. 190.

5. *Chicago Herald Tribune*, May 3, 1889, p. 6. The Art Institute of Chicago, *Half a Century of American Art*, exh. cat. (1939), p. 48, states that a work entitled *Snow-Bound* was exhibited at the Art Institute in the second annual American Exhibition of 1889, under the title *Ice-Bound*.

6. Other images of the white bridge include *The White Bridge* (after 1895; Minneapolis Institute of Arts) and *The White Bridge* (c. 1900; Memorial Art Gallery of the University of Rochester, N.Y.). Lisa N. Peters speculated that the Art Institute's version is the one entitled "The New Bridge" shown in 1898 at the exhibitions of the Ten American Painters in New York and Boston; see Lisa N. Peters, "Twachtman's Greenwich Paintings: Context and Chronology," in Chotner, Peters, and Pyne (note 1), p. 40.

7. For Monet's series paintings, see Paul Hayes Tucker, *Monet in the Nineties: The Series Paintings*, exh. cat. (Boston, Museum of Fine Arts, 1989).

135. CHILDE HASSAM (1859–1935)

The Little Pond, Appledore, c. 1890

Oil on canvas; 40.6 x 55.8 cm (16 x 22 in.)

Signed, lower right: *Childe Hassam 1890*

Through prior acquisition of the Friends of American Art and the Walter H. Schulze Memorial collections, 1986.421

136. *New England Headlands*, 1899

Oil on canvas; 68.9 x 68.9 cm (27⅛ x 27⅛ in.)

Signed, lower left: *Childe Hassam 1899*

Walter H. Schulze Memorial Collection, 1930.349

Childe Hassam's vast body of work includes numerous views of late nineteenth-century seaside resorts, as in these paintings of Appledore Island (one of the Isles of Shoals located off the New Hampshire coast) and Gloucester, Massachusetts.[1] His sun-drenched scenes of these locales offer an optimistic view of the North American tourist landscape that celebrates the benefits of fresh sea air for physical, mental, and perhaps even aesthetic well-being. In formal terms, Hassam's depictions of Appledore and Gloucester also demonstrate his evolving Impressionist concerns as well as his ability to alter his style to suit the character of his chosen site.

Presided over by celebrated poet and gardener Celia Thaxter, Appledore Island attracted numerous artists and writers to its rocky shores during the nineteenth century.[2] Hassam may have first visited Appledore as early as 1884; he spent the summer of 1886 on the island, before making his second journey to Europe, during which he worked in Paris for three years. *The Little Pond, Appledore* dates from the artist's first summer on Appledore after his return from Paris and reflects his evolving interest in the bright palette, broken brushwork, and dramatic light effects that characterize Impressionist painting. The em-

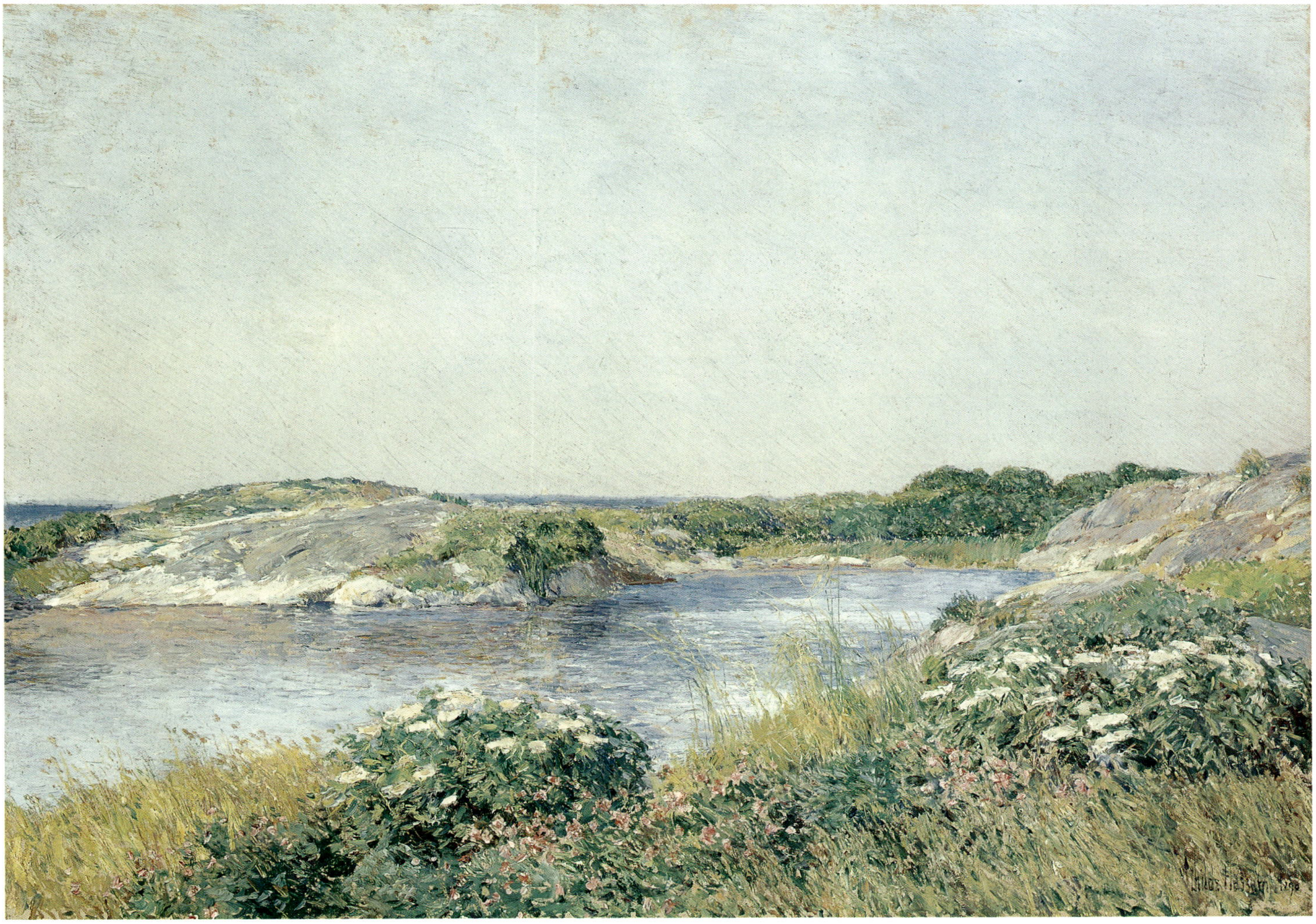

CAT. NO. 135

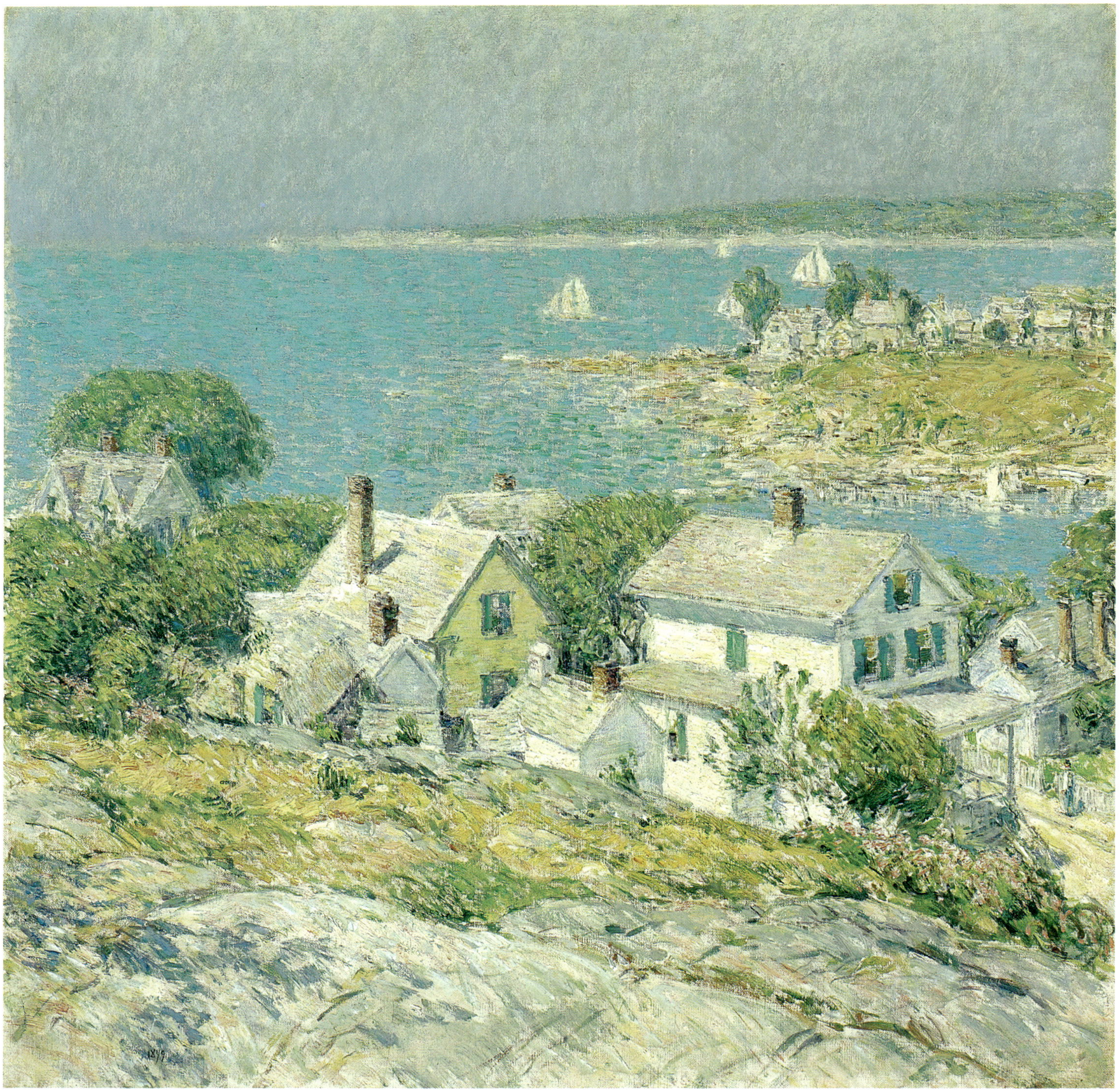

CAT. NO. 136

phasis on vegetation (white yarrow, water grasses, and perhaps scarlet pimpernel) and depiction of an identifiable site are characteristic of his Appledore paintings.

Bursting with color and freely composed, *The Little Pond, Appledore* and other early images of the island were inspired by Thaxter's extensive horticultural development of its distinctive landscape as well as her cultivation of its intellectual climate. The pond is probably the small reservoir behind Thaxter's cottage where artist William Morris Hunt drowned in 1879.[3] While Hassam typically emphasized the vivid reds and blues of the poppies and hollyhocks that Thaxter grew in her pleasantly crowded garden, here the artist worked with a delicate, pastel palette to create a more modulated, less vivacious mood in keeping with the associations with the site he must have had.

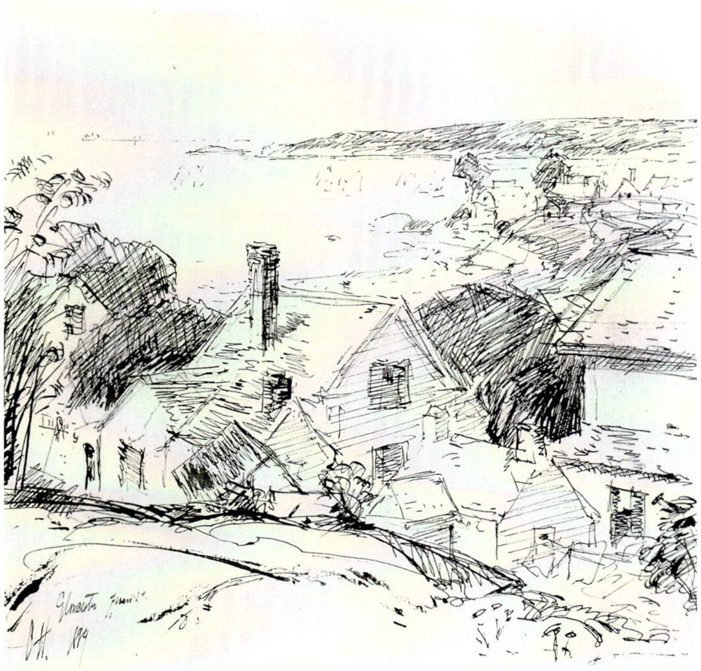

FIG. 72. Childe Hassam (1859–1935). *Gloucester, Outer Harbor*, 1899. Ink on paper; 21 x 21 cm (8¼ x 8¼ in.). Carnegie Museum of Art, Pittsburgh, Andrew Carnegie Fund (07.14.12).

As in other works by Hassam, the pond is enclosed and veiled by vegetation with a sliver of open sea visible in the distance. The effect he achieved here is that of an island within an island, a protected haven.

Like Appledore, Gloucester was one of Hassam's favorite summer haunts; he shared this predilection with artists such as John Twachtman (see cat. nos. 133–34) and Frank Duveneck.[4] Painted almost a decade after *The Little Pond, Appledore*, *New England Headlands* presents a more populated landscape, perhaps reflecting the hustle and bustle of Gloucester's fishing industry, although not directly portraying it.[5] The later work is also more daringly painted, with its broken, spasmodic brushwork and use of bare canvas as a compositional device. Bright, saturated blues and crisp whites underscore the maritime nature of the work, while the square canvas helps structure the space, as in Twachtman's work.

According to a note written by Hassam in 1920 found attached to the frame of *New England Headlands*, "This picture was painted in Gloucester Massachusetts in July 1899—This part of the town (really East Gloucester) then had many examples of the small New England frame houses painted white with green blinds which are seen in the foreground—The little promontory on the right is Rocky Neck and at the point of land in the distance is Normans Woe celebrated in the poem by Longfellow."[6] Hassam, like many artists who painted in East Gloucester during the summer months, chose to emphasize the picturesque aspects of the town—quaint buildings and sailing vessels—rather than the plants for drying and packing fish that figured prominently in the landscape.[7] Hassam painted this site more than once, and at least one related sketch survives (fig. 72). It reveals that, in the final paintings, the artist subtly shifted the point of view to increase the sense of depth, although he did not change the configuration of the houses and distant landscape.[8]

Hassam's Appledore scene looks inward, and his Gloucester view outward, which is appropriate to the character of each site: the first is an island and the second a bustling fishing center. Although the numerous houses and sailboats in the Gloucester scene suggest the presence of humanity, both are unpeopled landscapes that focus on the attractions of place rather than the activities of tourists and natives and that emphasize the timeless and picturesque variety of locales along the eastern seaboard of the United States. Hassam's Impressionist technique imbues these scenes with a modern sensibility that unites the traditional with the innovative.

NOTES

1. David Park Curry suggested that depictions of the Isles of Shoals comprise ten percent of Hassam's oeuvre; see Curry, *Childe Hassam: An Island Garden Revisited*, exh. cat. (Denver Art Museum, 1990), p. 13.

2. For more about Celia Thaxter and Hassam's personal and artistic relationship with her, see Curry (note 1), pp. 17–57.

3. Hunt was fifty-five years old at his death. A photograph of the reservoir that corresponds to the view in the painting is reproduced in *A Stern and Lovely Scene: A Visual History of the Isles of Shoals*, exh. cat. (Durham, N.H., University Art Galleries, University of New Hampshire, 1978), p. 110.

4. For more information about artistic activity in Gloucester at the turn of the century, see *Twachtman in Gloucester: His Last Years, 1900–1902*, exh. cat. (New York, Ira Spanierman Gallery, 1987); and H. Barbara Weinberg, Doreen Bolger, and David Park Curry, *American Impressionism and Realism: The Painting of Modern Life, 1885–1915*, exh. cat. (New York, Metropolitan Museum of Art, 1994), pp. 122–33.

5. Hassam's images of the Isles of Shoals from around 1900 also use panoramic effects and, like *New England Headlands*, depict views toward the sea.

6. Note dated June 1, 1920, East Hampton, N.Y., Files of the Department of American Arts, The Art Institute of Chicago. The poem Hassam referred to is Henry Wadsworth Longfellow's "The Wreck of the Hesperus" (1841).

7. Weinberg, Bolger, and Curry (note 4), p. 125.

8. Other Gloucester scenes by Hassam include *Gloucester Harbor* (1899; Norton Museum of Art, West Palm Beach, Fla.) and *Gloucester* (c. 1902; Vose Galleries of Boston, Inc., as of 1984).

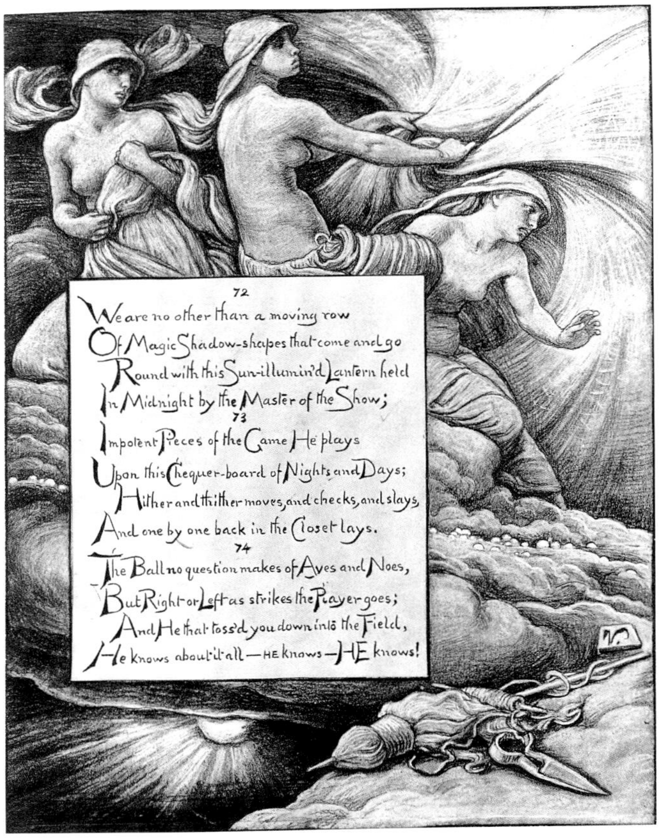

FIG. 73. Illustration by Elihu Vedder published in Edward FitzGerald's translation of the *Rubáiyát of Omar Khayyám* (Boston, 1884).

A smaller oil version of this work is in the Art Museum of Princeton University, and figure studies are in the Corcoran Gallery of Art, Washington, D.C. The Ryerson and Burnham Libraries of The Art Institute of Chicago contain a copy of Vedder's illustrated version of the *Rubáiyát of Omar Khayyám.*

NOTES

1. The others include *The Pleiades* (1884/85; Metropolitan Museum of Art, New York); *The Soul Between Doubt and Faith* (c. 1887; Herbert F. Johnson Museum of Art, Ithaca, N.Y.); *The Cup of Love* (1887; private collection); *The Cup of Death* (1885/c. 1911; National Museum of American Art, Washington, D.C.); *Love Ever Present* (1887; private collection); *The Last Man* (c. 1886/87; location unknown); and *Sphinx of the Seashore* (1879/80; private collection).

2. Elihu Vedder, *The Digressions of V.: Written for His Own Fun and That of His Friends* (Boston, 1910), p. 404.

3. Letter from Elihu Vedder to Joe Millet, June 28, 1883, Houghton and Mifflin Archives, Houghton Library, Harvard University, Cambridge, Mass.

4. Ibid.

5. *Rubáiyát of Omar Khayyám, the Astronomer-Poet of Persia* (Boston, 1884).

6. William Howe Downes, "Elihu Vedder's Pictures," *Atlantic Monthly* 59 (June 1887), pp. 842–46.

7. One specific reference to the poem that does not appear in the illustration is the checkerboard pattern found on the band of the spindle.

8. Quoted in Jane Dillenberger, "Between Faith and Doubt: Subjects for Meditation," in *Perceptions and Evocations: The Art of Elihu Vedder*, exh. cat. (Washington, D.C., National Collection of the Fine Arts, Smithsonian Institution, 1979), p. 132.

9. For information on spiritualism in the United States, see Peter Washington, *Madame Blavatsky's Baboon: A History of the Mystics, Mediums, and Misfits Who Brought Spiritualism to America* (New York, 1996). Judging from reviews and sales, Elihu Vedder's work was better received in Boston than in New York, where he also consistently exhibited. More than any East Coast city, Boston was a center for alternative spiritual practices. This painting was originally owned by Henry Melville Whitney of Brookline, Mass.

138. FREDERICK WILLIAM MacMONNIES (1863–1937)

Nathan Hale, modeled in plaster 1890, cast in bronze after 1890

Bronze; h. 72.4 cm (28½ in.)

Foundry (stamped, left rear): E. Gruet Jeune, Paris

Inscribed on right side of base: *F. MacMonnies 1890*

Gift of Robert Allerton, 1923.1840

139. *Bacchante and Infant Faun*, modeled 1894, cast after 1894

Bronze; h. 86.3 cm (34 in.)

Foundry (stamped): Jaboeuf & Rouard, Paris

Inscribed on base: *F. MacMonnies, 1894*

Restricted gift of Brooks and Hope B. McCormick Foundation, 1984.571

Frederick MacMonnies was the youngest of the triumvirate of sculptors who dominated turn-of-the-century American monument making. His elder colleagues, Augustus Saint-Gaudens (see cat. nos. 130–32) and Daniel Chester French (see cat. nos. 113 and 174–75), paved the way for MacMonnies' success by creating a market for both large- and small-scale bronze statuary, and all three artists benefited from Parisian training and high-profile public commissions. Like French's bronzes of Abraham Lincoln and Saint-Gaudens's *Amor Caritas*, MacMonnies' *Nathan Hale* and *Bacchante and Infant Faun* are reductions of larger works that demonstrate the artistic and entrepreneurial prowess as well as the popularity of their creator.[1]

MacMonnies received his first instruction in Saint-Gau-

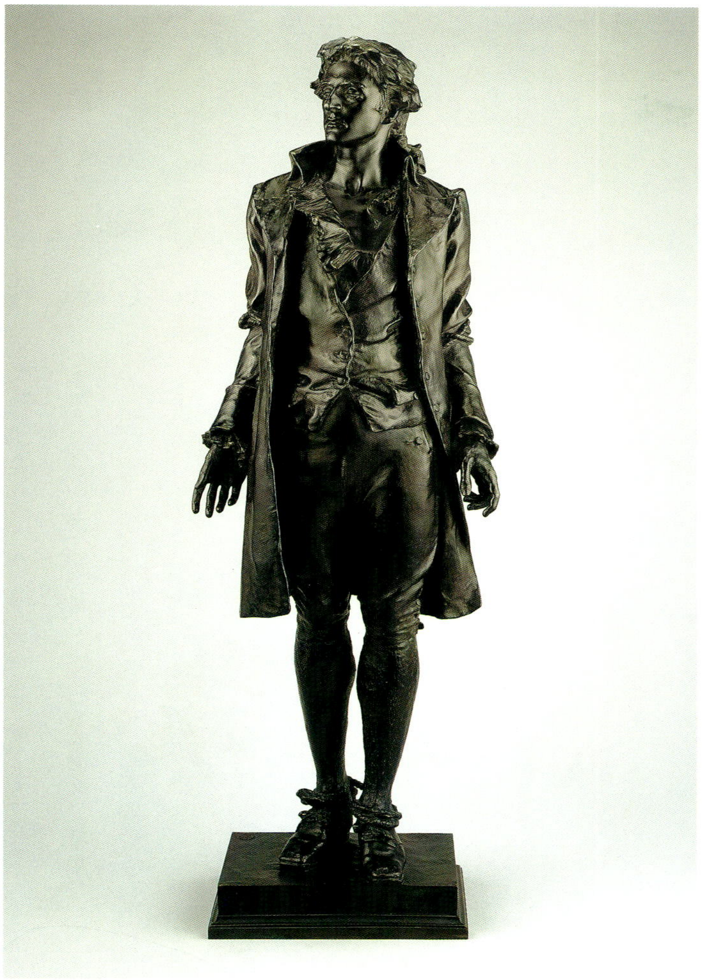

CAT. NO. 138

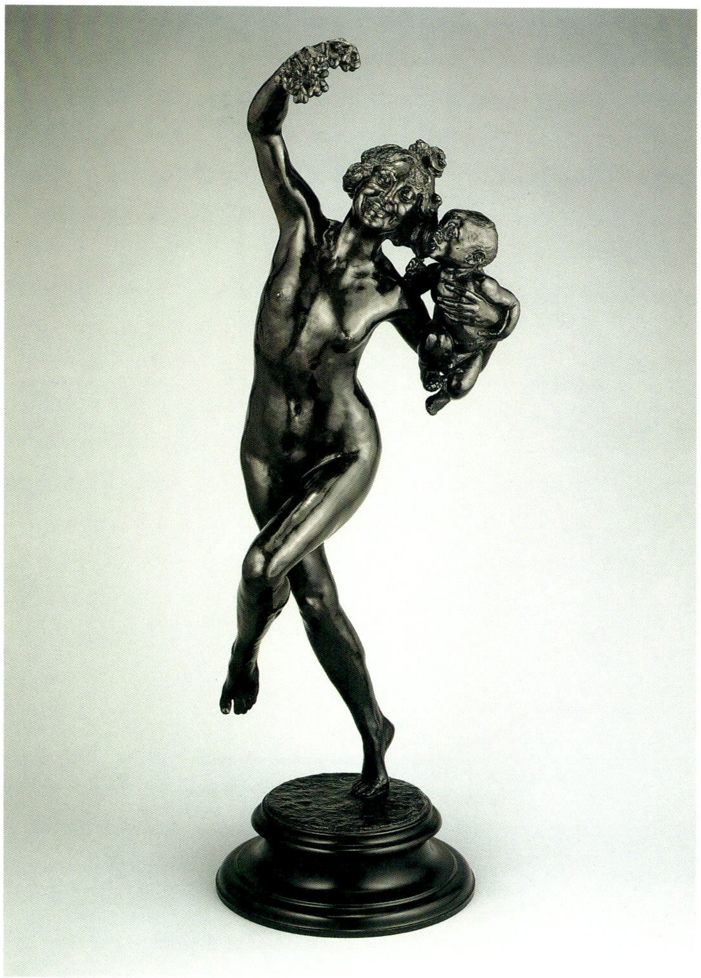

CAT. NO. 139

dens's studio when he was a teenager and followed up this early training with a stint at the École des Beaux-Arts in Paris, where he joined Jean-Alexandre-Joseph Falguière's atelier in May 1886.[2] MacMonnies resided in Paris for more than thirty years, but regularly received American commissions for public statuary; among the earliest of these was *Nathan Hale*, which he designed in 1890 for the Sons of the Revolution of the State of New York and which still stands on its original site in City Hall Park in New York City. An early version of the piece was exhibited at the 1891 Paris Salon to wide acclaim, followed by the official dedication of the monument in 1893. Numerous reductions such as the Art Institute's were cast by the E. Gruet Jeune Foundry in Paris.[3]

MacMonnies' statue depicts the Revolutionary War martyr hung by the British as a spy in the moments before his death.[4] Although his arms and feet are tied, Hale stands proudly upright, as if intoning his famous words "I only regret that I have but one life to lose for my country." Royal Cortissoz commented in an early biographical article about the sculptor: "Hale is a patriot held in love and reverence by his countrymen. In his own land any image of him would waken urbane greetings. If the statue by Mr. MacMonnies has roused enthusiasm, however, it has been for his own sake as much as for that of his subject."[5] The remarkably expressive and lively surfaces of the sculpture bespeak the sculptor's French training, but the statue was at first criticized by some Americans for these romantic, picturesque qualities. MacMonnies' unique vision set a fresh tone for monumental statuary. Hale is depicted as a sensual, sensitive hero, in period costume; this characterization differs greatly from those found in many other public monuments, which sought to instill national pride and awe in the viewer by presenting stoic, classicized heroes.

Subsequent to the *Nathan Hale* commission, MacMonnies increased his renown by contributing a huge sculpture, *Barge of State*, to the World's Columbian Exposition in Chicago in 1893. After that, he sculpted *Bacchante and Infant Faun*, which was reproduced in three sizes and two media during MacMonnies' lifetime. The sculptor presented one of his life-size bronze versions of the *Bacchante* to architect Charles Follen McKim in 1894, who in turn offered it as a gift to the Boston Public Library the following year.[6] The sculpture was installed in the library's garden court, but, unlike his previous public statues, it was eventually rejected by the institution because of public protests staged by the Women's Christian Temperance Union, which did not approve of the statue's depiction of drunkeness and frank female nudity.[7]

The bacchantes—mythological female followers of Bacchus, the god of wine, and symbols of libidinous abandonment—were considered unsuitably frivolous and amoral adornments for a public building. After the Boston debacle, McKim offered the statue to the Metropolitan Museum of Art in New York, where it resides today. Despite the public scandal, bronze reductions of *Bacchante and Infant Faun* were quite popular and cast in two sizes (approximately sixteen and thirty-four inches in height) by at least four different foundries in Paris and the United States. The Art Institute's piece is part of a group cast by the Jaboeuf and Rouard foundry in Paris; other versions of this group are in the Cleveland Museum of Art, the Philadelphia Museum of Art, and the New-York Historical Society.[8]

Poised gracefully on one foot, the bacchante dances gleefully, dangling grapes (symbolic of wine) to entice the infant she clutches in her left arm. An abundance of curves and supple surfaces informs the figure, which has been modeled naturalistically. Unlike most classically inspired sculpture, MacMonnies' *Bacchante* has visible muscles and bones. The model for the statue was Eugénie Pasque, a young French woman who also modeled for one of the figures on *Barge of State*. Like *Nathan Hale*, this statue challenges expectations for public statuary by imbuing bronze with sensuality and passion. In their reduced forms, neither work loses its power, allowing viewers to share the drama and liveliness of the subjects.

NOTES

1. The Art Institute has three other works by MacMonnies in its collection: *Diana* (bronze; modeled 1889, cast after 1900); *Pan of Rohaillon* (bronze; modeled 1890, cast after 1894); and *Self-Portrait* (oil on canvas; 1897/1915).

2. For more biographical information about MacMonnies, see Robert Judson Clark, "Frederick MacMonnies: An American Sculptor in Paris and New York," *Record of the Art Museum, Princeton University* 43, 2 (1984), pp. 7–25; and E. Adina Gordon, *Frederick William MacMonnies (1863–1937), Mary Fairchild MacMonnies (1858–1946): Deux Artistes américains à Giverny*, exh. cat. (Vernon, France, Musée Municipal Alphonse-Georges Poulain, 1988).

3. Bronze reductions of the Nathan Hale statue can be found in the Metropolitan Museum of Art (New York) and the Mead Art Museum (Amherst, Mass.), among other public and private collections.

4. The monument stands near the spot where Hale was hanged.

5. Royal Cortissoz, "An American Sculptor: Frederick MacMonnies," *Studio* 6, 30 (Oct. 1895), p. 21.

6. Another early life-sized bronze was exhibited at the 1894 Paris Salon and purchased by the French government. A complete list of life-sized versions of this sculpture can be found in Kathryn Greenthal, Paula M. Kozol, and Jan Seidler Ramirez, *American Figurative Sculpture in the Museum of Fine Arts, Boston* (Boston, 1986), p. 296.

7. For more about the Boston scandal, see Jonathan Leo Fairbanks, "MacMonnies' Bacchante: Its Trial, Condemnation and Restoration," *Sculpture Review* 42, 4 (Mar. 1993), pp. 29–31; and Walter Muir Whitehill, "The Vicissitudes of Bacchante in Boston," *New England Quarterly* 27, 4 (Dec. 1954), pp. 435–54.

8. Hildegard Cummings, "Chasing a Bronze Bacchante," *Bulletin of the William Benton Museum of Art* 12 (1984–85), p. 19.

140. CECILIA BEAUX (1855–1942)

Dorothea and Francesca, 1898

Oil on canvas; 203.5 x 116.8 cm (80⅛ x 46 in.)

Signed, lower left: *Cecilia Beaux*

A. A. Munger Collection, 1921.109

In 1899 William Merritt Chase publicly praised Cecilia Beaux as "not only the greatest living woman painter, but the best that has ever lived."[1] Painted in 1898, *Dorothea and Francesca* attests to Beaux's prominence in the art of fashionable portraiture, a field dominated by John Singer Sargent, and her burgeoning interest in complex double-portrait compositions that display psychological depth and painterly bravura. The portrait depicts the two older of Richard Watson Gilder's three daughters, Dorothea and Francesca.[2]

Richard Watson Gilder, a poet and editor of the *Century Magazine*, was an eminent member of New York society. He and his wife Helena hosted many important events in their Fifteenth Street home, referred to as The Studio, including the inaugural meetings of the Society of American Artists, in 1877, and the Authors' Club, in 1882. Cecilia Beaux met the Gilders in Paris in 1896 and became close to them after moving from her native Philadelphia to New York City.[3] Beaux often painted members of the Gilder family, especially the sisters. In addition to the Art Institute's work are, for example, *Dorothea in the Woods* (1897; Whitney Museum of American Art, New

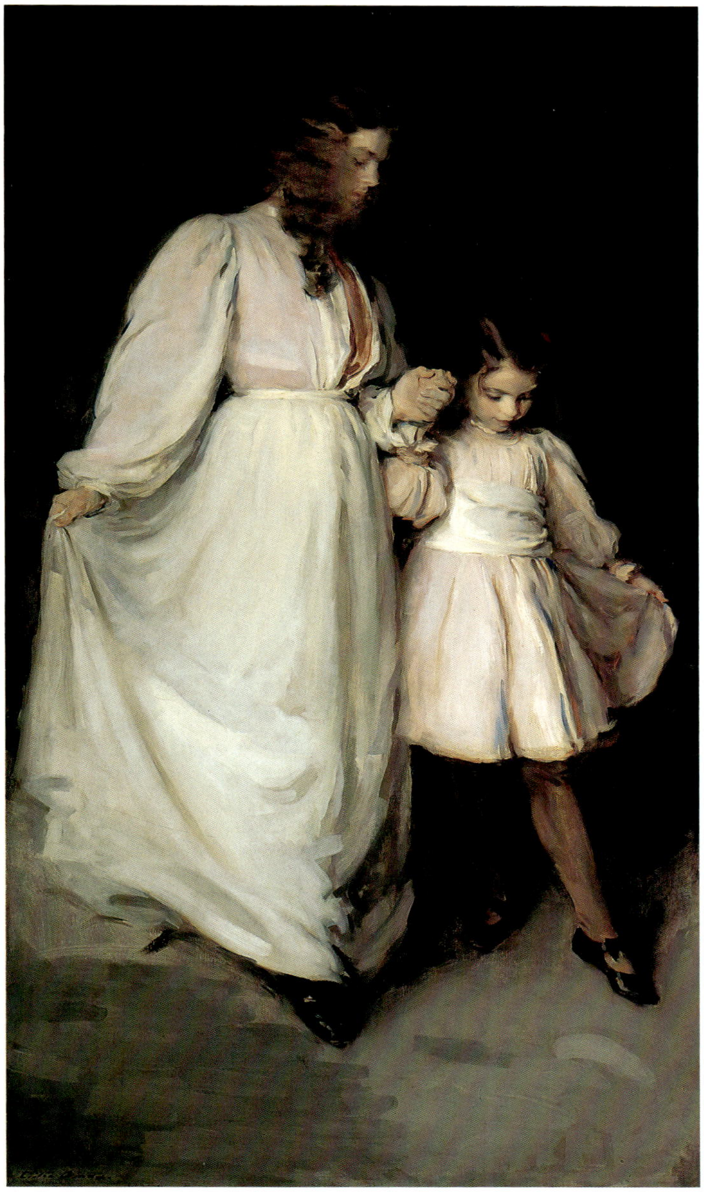

CAT. NO. 140

York) and *After the Meeting* (1914; Toledo Museum of Art, Ohio).[4]

In her autobiography, Beaux described painting *Dorothea and Francesca* in a converted tobacco barn at the Gilders's farm, Four Brooks, in Tyringham, Massachusetts:

> The big and little sisters, Dorothea and Francesca, used to execute a dance of the simplest and all too circumscribed design, invented by themselves, and adorned by their unconscious beauty alone. This was the subject. I built a platform with my own hands, as the girls could not move easily on the bare earth. When it rained hard, in September, the orchard let its surplus water run down the hill and under the barn-sill, so that, as my corner was rather low, I put on rubber boots and splashed in and out of my puddle, four inches deep. October was difficult, for it grew bitterly cold. But valiant posing went on, though the scenic effect of the group was changed by wraps. Summer, indeed, was over, when on a dark autumnal night, in the freezing barn, the picture was packed by the light of one or two candles and a lantern.[5]

Francesca Gilder Palmer recalled "very vividly 'sitting' or rather standing, for [*Dorothea and Francesca*] in Cecilia Beaux's studio. . . . It was a rather fatiguing pose and I longed to be out in the fields, riding the farm horses . . . and otherwise pursuing the wonderful farm activities of the summer months."[6] Rosamond Gilder, the youngest sister, remembers that her two sisters sometimes did not pose together, revealing the artifice of Beaux's portrait: "My sister . . . Francesca . . . remembers very well standing in that pose holding a wooden structure the right height for her right hand while Beaux painted her figure. Of course they often stood together but when only one was available—dragged from the joys of riding or haying on the farm—the rack or stand was used."[7]

Beaux's staged scene of elegance is an exercise in refinement of both style and subject matter. Dorothea Gilder, sixteen years old in 1898, is shown patiently teaching her younger sister to dance. The two are compositionally connected by their gesture, gaze, and clasped hands. The younger girl's tentative pose and intent downward gaze toward her outstretched foot echo her sister's steady and graceful posture. Each mirrors the other; Francesca gives us a glimpse into Dorothea's girlhood while Dorothea foreshadows Francesca's adolescence. Beaux avoids sentimentality, however, by omitting contextual details and employing lively brushwork to focus on the mood conveyed by this elegant dance.

The painting was first exhibited in December 1898 at the National Academy of Design and earned the praise of critic Charles Caffin, who wrote: "the movement in the two figures is most charmingly expressed, and there is a refined vivacity running through the whole picture, which is painted with great freedom and breadth."[8] This early praise is indicative of the acclaim the painting would generate through its lengthy exhibition history. Other commentators emphasized the gender connection between Beaux and her subjects. One noted, "only an artist who was in perfect sympathy with the ambitions of girlhood could have painted 'The Dancing Lesson'. . . . These sisters . . . show the perfection of grace and naturalness."[9]

The assertion that only a woman could have painted a "feminine" subject with such sensitivity to the proper deportment and behavior of upper-class young women reveals the lingering prejudice critics harbored toward women artists in the late nineteenth century.[10] In many ways, however, Cecilia Beaux worked against the grain of gender expectations during her career. She never married, for she believed marriage might compromise her work; she aggressively pursued professional acclaim with an ambitious exhibition schedule; and she was the first female instructor appointed to the faculty at the Pennsylvania Academy of the Fine Arts, in 1895. Moreover, when she enrolled at the Académie Julian in Paris, she focused on the study of the human figure, which was then largely viewed as a male domain.

Cecilia Beaux considered *Dorothea and Francesca* one of her finest compositions and chose to exhibit it frequently.[11] The painting won the Mr. and Mrs. Frank G. Logan Medal at the Art Institute's "Thirty-Fourth Annual Exhibition of American Paintings and Sculpture" in 1921 and was immediately purchased by the Friends of American Art for the museum's permanent collection.

NOTES

1. Quoted in Judith Stein, "Profile of Cecilia Beaux," *Feminist Art Journal* 4, 4 (winter 1975–76), p. 25.

2. Dorothea Gilder lived from 1882 to 1920, and Francesca Gilder from 1888 to 1984. Rosamond Gilder was the youngest of the daughters.

3. For more information on Beaux's relationship to the Gilders, see Tara Leigh Tappert, *Cecilia Beaux and the Art of Portraiture*, exh. cat. (Washington, D.C., National Portrait Gallery, 1995), p. 54.

4. For a more complete list of Beaux's paintings and drawings of the Gilder family, see Pennsylvania Academy of the Fine Arts, *The Paintings and Drawings of Cecilia Beaux* (Philadelphia, 1955), pp. 59–64.

5. Cecilia Beaux, *Background with Figures* (Boston, 1930), p. 218.

6. Letter from Francesca Gilder Palmer to Linn Hardenburgh, Mar. 14, 1977, Files of the Department of American Arts, The Art Institute of Chicago.

7. Letter from Rosamond Gilder to Milo Naeve, Aug. 28, 1981, Files of the Department of American Arts, The Art Institute of Chicago.

8. Charles Caffin, "New York Portrait Exhibition," *Artist* 24 (Jan. 1899), p. vii.

9. Lorinda Munson Bryant, *American Pictures and Their Painters* (New York, 1917), pp. 203–04.

10. For a fascinating study of Beaux criticism in the light of gender issues, see Sarah Burns, "The 'Earnest, Untiring Worker' and the Magician of the Brush: Gender Politics in the Criticism of Cecilia Beaux," *Oxford Art Journal* 15, 1 (1992), pp. 36–53.

11. During Beaux's lifetime, *Dorothea and Francesca* was exhibited no fewer than fifteen times—for example, at the International Society of Sculptors, Painters and Gravers in London (1899), the Pan-American Exposition in Buffalo (1901), and the Panama–Pacific Exposition in San Francisco (1915).

141. JOHN SINGER SARGENT (1856–1925)

Mrs. George Swinton (Elizabeth Ebsworth), 1897

Oil on canvas; 62.2 x 43.8 cm (24½ x 17¼ in.)
Signed, lower left: *John S. Sargent*
Wirt D. Walker Collection, 1922.4450

Mrs. George Swinton epitomizes the painterly virtuosity that established John Singer Sargent as the favored portraitist of fashionable Europeans and Americans in the late nineteenth century. The novelist Henry James, a close friend of the artist and a fellow expatriate living in London, wrote of Sargent's prowess: "His work has been almost exclusively in portraiture, and it has been his fortune to paint more women than men; . . . and if it has mainly been his fortune . . . to commemorate the fair faces of women, there is no ground for surprise at this sort of success on the part of one who had given so signal a proof of possessing the secret of the particular aspect that the contemporary lady (of any period) likes to wear in the eyes of posterity."[1] Produced when Sargent was at the peak of his popularity, this work exemplifies Sargent's typical working methods—his skillful use of props, poses, and painterly effects to suggest the class and gender roles of his sitters.

At the time this portrait was executed, Sargent had been living in London for ten years. His Parisian career had been abruptly halted by the scandal surrounding his portrait of Madame Gautreau, also known as *Madame X* (1884; Metropolitan Museum of Art, New York), whom he portrayed with an indiscreet sensuality that disturbed contemporary audiences. Retreating to London, the artist established his studio at 33 Tite Street in Chelsea, where he received a variety of clients who paid an average of one thousand guineas, or five thousand dollars, for a full-length portrait.[2]

Mrs. George Swinton was commissioned by the subject's mother, Mrs. Henry Edward Ebsworth, on the occasion of her daughter's engagement to Captain George Swinton in 1895.[3] Owing to Sargent's busy schedule and his insistence upon having numerous sittings in order to capture accurately his subject's likeness, the portrait was not begun until April 1896. By the time the work was completed, a year later, the subject was far from a bride-to-be; she had been married for two years and had given birth to one child. Elizabeth "Elsie" Swinton commented on the long gestation period of her portrait: "It took a

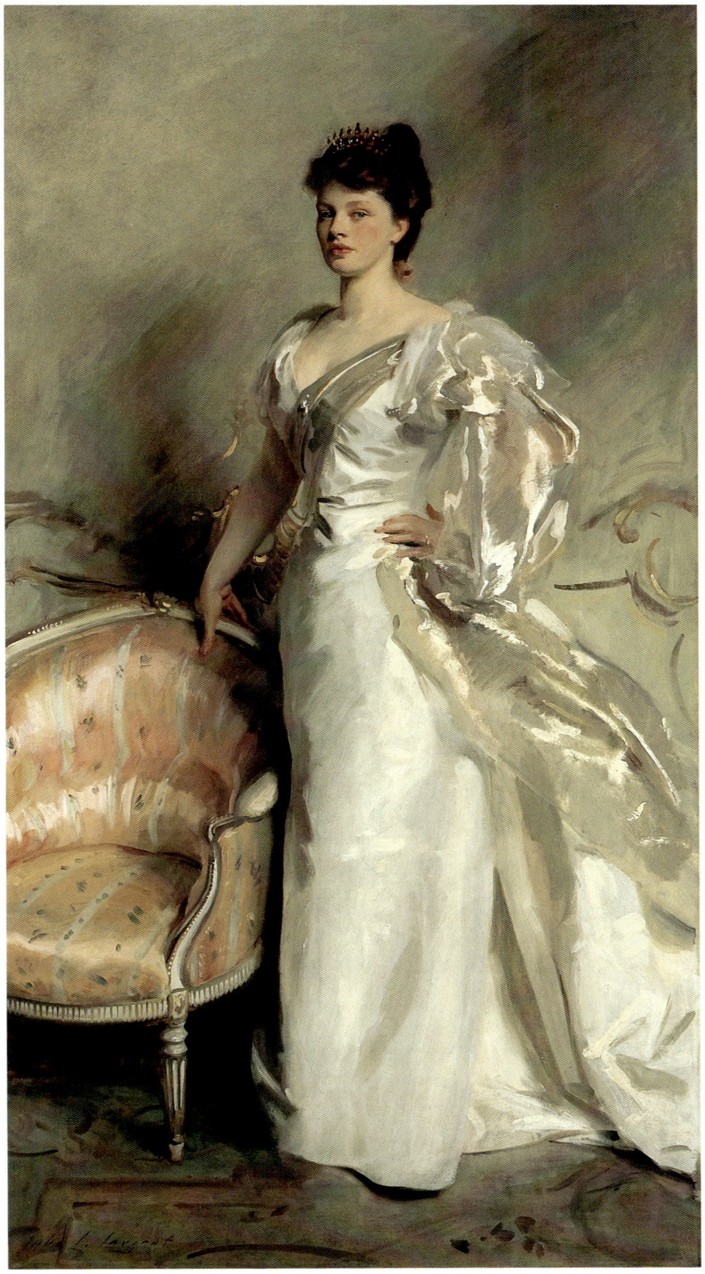

CAT. NO. 141

great many sittings as we wasted a lot of time playing the piano and singing instead of getting on with the picture."[4] Sargent always kept a piano in his studio and often played for his sitters. Musical themes proliferate in Sargent's oeuvre, ranging from portraits of singers (Elizabeth Swinton herself was a well-known singer) to Impressionistic renderings of the Parisian Pasdeloup Orchestra (see cat. no. 97).[5]

Swinton began performing professionally as a singer in 1906 and enjoyed a successful career until World War I.[6] Her repertoire consisted primarily of French, German, Italian, and Russian songs and she performed mainly in London at Bechstein Hall, Aeolian Hall, Queen's Hall, and private houses. Sir Osbert Sitwell described her talents: "The incomparable warmth of her voice cast a strange spell. . . . Her beauty, as she sang, [was] a beauty of an unusual and moving kind."[7] Yet it would have been deemed inappropriate for a woman of her upper-class social background to be too closely associated with a working profession, no matter how leisurely it was undertaken. Consequently, Sargent depicted her according to her physical attractions and wealth rather than her musical acumen.

Although Sargent did not explicitly depict Elsie Swinton singing, her pose suggests both the poise of a performer and the countenance of a fashionable and worldly woman.[8] Sargent chose an appropriate dress from her wardrobe and props from the collection in his studio to complement the composition. Mrs. Swinton's stance is one Sargent often used to suggest assertiveness. With one arm resting firmly on the back of a Rococo-style chair, the other akimbo, the subject turns to address the viewer with a cool gaze. In *Mr. and Mrs. I. N. Phelps Stokes* (1897; Metropolitan Museum of Art, New York), Mrs. Stokes adopts a similarly authoritative pose, in this case signifying the American subject's emancipation and free spirit.

In writing about *Mrs. George Swinton*, critics have commented most frequently on the extravagant color and brushwork displayed in her dress. "It is a pyrotechnical display of great sweeping brush-strokes," wrote one commentator, who added, "[t]here are blues, greens, pinks, lavenders—every tint of the pearl in its most glowing display of color, so often concealed, but in this case rapturously revealed."[9] This type of painterly performance was central to Sargent's success, as was his ability to present an image of his sitter that adhered to social standards dictated by class and gender expectations.

NOTES

1. Henry James, "John S. Sargent," in John L. Sweeney, ed., *The Painter's Eye: Notes and Essays on the Pictorial Arts by Henry James* (Cambridge, Mass., 1956), p. 218.

2. Trevor Fairbrother, *John Singer Sargent* (New York, 1994), p. 76. Fairbrother estimates that this was the equivalent of U.S. $86,000 in 1993 dollars.

3. See James Lomax and Richard Ormond, *John Singer Sargent and the Edwardian Age*, exh. cat. (London and Leeds, Leeds Art Gallery, 1979), pp. 59–60, for thorough documentation of the commissioning of this portrait.

4. Quoted in letter from Thomas Gerrity, M. Knoedler and Company, to Robert B. Harshe, June 17, 1924, The Art Institute of Chicago.

5. For more information on Sargent's portrayal of musical personalities and subjects, see Wilfrid Mellers, "Sargent in the Salons of Music," in *The Portrait of a Lady: Sargent and Lady Agnew*, exh. cat. (Edinburgh, National Gallery of Scotland, 1997), pp. 57–67.

6. Letter from David Greer, Department of Music, University of Durham, England, to Anndora Morginson, Oct. 10, 1993, Files of the Department of American Arts, The Art Institute of Chicago. All information pertaining to Swinton's singing career is taken from this source.

7. Sir Osbert Sitwell, *Left Hand, Right Hand!* (Boston, 1944), p. 257.

8. See Suzanne Raitt, "The Singers of Sargent: Mabel Batten, Elsie Swinton, Ethel Smyth," *Women: A Cultural Review* 3, 1 (spring 1992), pp. 23–29, for more information on this theme in Sargent's work. Raitt mistakenly asserts, however, that the portrait was commissioned for Mr. George Swinton.

9. Rose V. S. Berry, "John Singer Sargent: Some of His American Work," *Art and Archaeology* 18, 3 (Sept. 1924), p. 89.

142. DANIEL CHESTER FRENCH (1850–1931)

Truth, 1900

Plaster; h. 148.6 cm (58½ in.)

Restricted gift of Brooks McCormick, and Ethel T. Scarborough Fund, 1984.531

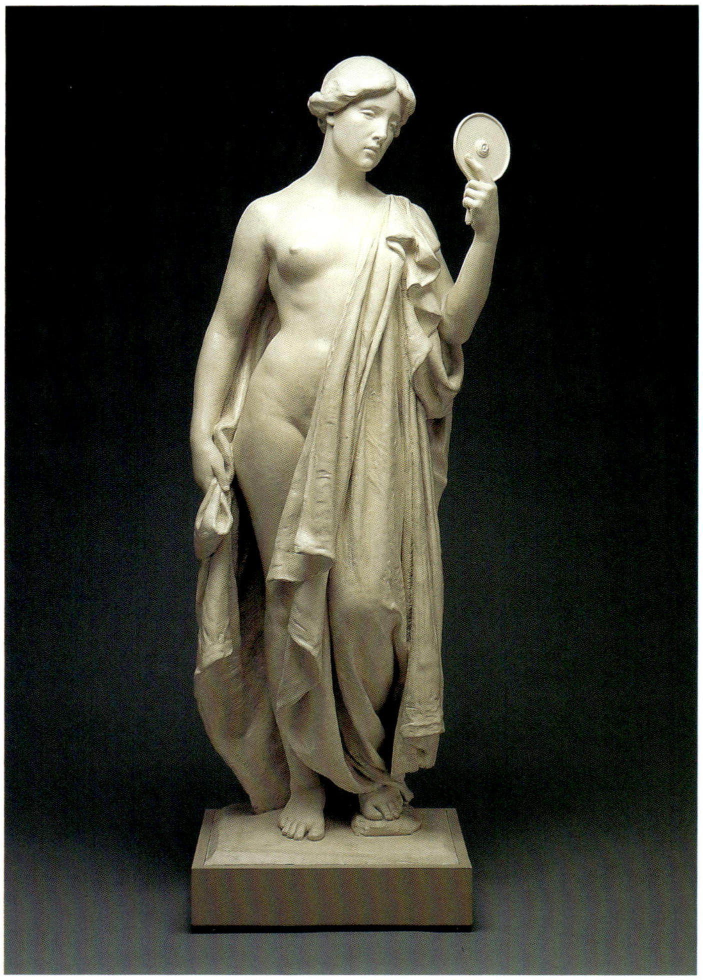

CAT. NO. 142

In 1898 the state of Minnesota commissioned Daniel Chester French to create six allegorical figures to adorn the facade of the Minnesota State Capitol in St. Paul: *Truth*, *Bounty*, *Wisdom*, *Prudence*, *Courage*, and *Integrity*. Architect Cass Gilbert, who devised the iconographic scheme for the capitol, described his design: "It is an inspiration toward patriotism and good citizenship, it encourages just pride in the state, and is an education to on-coming generations to see these things, imponderable elements of life and character, set before the people for their enjoyment and betterment."[1] Representative of moral and civic virtues, these statues served both a decorative and a didactic purpose. The Art Institute's statue *Truth* is French's model for the larger version on the facade of the Minnesota State Capitol.

The proliferation of classically inspired art and architecture at the turn of the twentieth century is often referred to as the American Renaissance—a term that signifies a style as well as a philosophy.[2] For the 1893 World's Columbian Exposition, a "White City" of grandiose Beaux-Arts showcase buildings was constructed in the swamplands on the South Side of Chicago that tipped the balance of American architecture in favor of classical and Renaissance design ideals. After the Columbian Exposition ended, artists and architects adhered to the idea that classically designed works of public art and architecture could serve as exemplars of national and state character. Beaux-Arts-style buildings dominated America's urban centers during this period, and painters, sculptors, and architects collaborated on projects such as the Boston Public Library (1894), the Library of Congress (1896), and the Minnesota State Capitol (1905).

Daniel Chester French was well versed in the art of civic sculpture, having been chosen to create monuments for the World's Columbian Exposition. Adhering to the tone set by Burnham and Root's Beaux-Arts exhibition halls, French designed three allegorical pieces for the fair: the sixty-foot-high *Republic*, which towered over the Court of Honor, *The Triumph of Columbus*, and *Agriculture* (with Edward Potter). Like many statues and mural paintings destined for public buildings, French's work for both the Fair and the Minnesota commission used female figures as allegories to represent abstract concepts. Traditionally, representations of the Virtues have been female. French drew from these sources and from representations in the nineteenth century of women as inherently good and adaptable to faceless allegory.[3] Of the six allegorical statues French designed for the Minnesota State Capitol, four depict women: *Truth*, *Bounty*, *Wisdom*, and *Prudence*.

Truth is defined by the figure's nudity and the mirror she holds in her left hand—symbolic elements that derive from classical and Renaissance sources.[4] Her mirror represents an unembellished reflection of her unadorned state, "the naked truth." She is paired with *Integrity*—a half-draped male figure—and the two form a symbolic union of moral virtue. While working on his model for *Truth*, the sculptor wrote to Cass Gilbert, "[i]f 'Truth' is too naked for public opinions, do not hesitate to say so!" referring to the stereotypically conservative midwesterner.[5] French pursued this theme further in the bronze doors he produced for the Boston Public Library. On the doors, which were dedicated in 1904, a partially clothed *Truth* is represented in bas-relief holding a mirror in one hand and a globe in the other. For this figure, however, French chose a different aesthetic form; the strict neoclassicism of the Minnesota State Capitol statue was exchanged for a flowing, serpentine Art-Nouveau design.

Between 1898 and 1900, French worked on the half-size plaster models in his New York studio, sending progress reports to Gilbert at intervals. The sculptor shipped the finished models to St. Paul on April 11, 1900. Two days later he wrote to Gilbert: "I had them all stained and waxed, so that they will make the best possible appearance if you exhibit them."[6] This accounts for the matte pinkish-brown hue of the surface of the Art Institute's *Truth*, and is evidence of French's wish that his plaster model be seen not only as an architectural ornament but as a finished statue with its own aesthetic merit. There are, however, formal characteristics that make it clear that the statue was an unfinished model for a more monumental, finished marble version. The statue lacks detail, particularly in the hair and crudely modeled extremities. Additionally, the classical proportions of the figure are ampler than usual to compensate for the final, monumental sculpture's height and distance from the viewer. The head is disproportionately small; it does not carry the important symbolic meaning associated with the partially nude body. The back of the figure is unfinished and slightly concave.[7] Nonetheless, *Truth* expresses French's mastery of the ideals of the American Renaissance.

NOTES

1. Cass Gilbert, "The Greatest Element of Monumental Architecture," *American Architect* 136 (Aug. 5, 1929), p. 144.

2. For an overview of the period, including its decorative and fine arts, see Richard Guy Wilson, Diane H. Pilgrim, and Richard R. Murray, *The American Renaissance, 1876–1917*, exh. cat. (New York, Brooklyn Museum, 1979).

3. For an excellent discussion of the use of female figures in late nineteenth-century allegorical images, see Bailey Van Hook, "From the Lyrical to the Epic: Images of Women in American Murals at the Turn of the Century," *Winterthur Portfolio* 26, 1 (spring 1991), pp. 63–80.

4. Marina Warner, *Monuments and Maidens: The Allegory of the Female Form* (New York, 1985), pp. 314–21.

5. Letter from Daniel Chester French to Cass Gilbert, Apr. 5, 1899, Cass Gilbert Papers, Minnesota Historical Society, St. Paul.

6. Letter from Daniel Chester French to Cass Gilbert, Apr. 13, 1900, Cass Gilbert Papers, Minnesota Historical Society, St. Paul.

7. That the Art Institute's statue is a model for a more permanent work is further suggested by the fragility of the plaster medium: the left index finger and the mirror had broken off at some point and were replaced in the early 1980s.

143. LORADO TAFT (1860–1936)

The Solitude of the Soul, modeled in plaster 1901, sculpted in marble 1914

Marble; h. 231.1 cm; base 129.5 x 105.4 cm (91 in.; 51 x 41½ in.)
Signed: *Lorado Taft Sc 1914*
Friends of American Art Collection, 1914.739

One of Chicago's most celebrated sculptors, Lorado Taft was a talented artist, educator, and sculpture historian.[1] Initially published in 1903, his book *The History of American Sculpture* continues to be a valuable resource for artists, art historians, and general readers. Taft did not begin his training as a sculptor until after he graduated with a master's degree in fine arts, in 1880, from what is now the University of Illinois at Urbana-Champaign. He subsequently traveled to Paris and enrolled at the École des Beaux-Arts, where he studied for three years. He returned to America in 1884 and completed his education independently in Chicago.

At the École des Beaux-Arts, Taft received a conservative, classical training grounded in the study of the human figure with an emphasis on depicting mythological, historical, and literary characters.[2] Although early in his career Taft used his training to build a reputation as a successful sculptor of portrait busts and soldier monuments, he is best remembered today for large allegorical works such as *The Solitude of the Soul.* In fact, the shift in Taft's output began around 1900 when he started working on the idea for this work, which he described

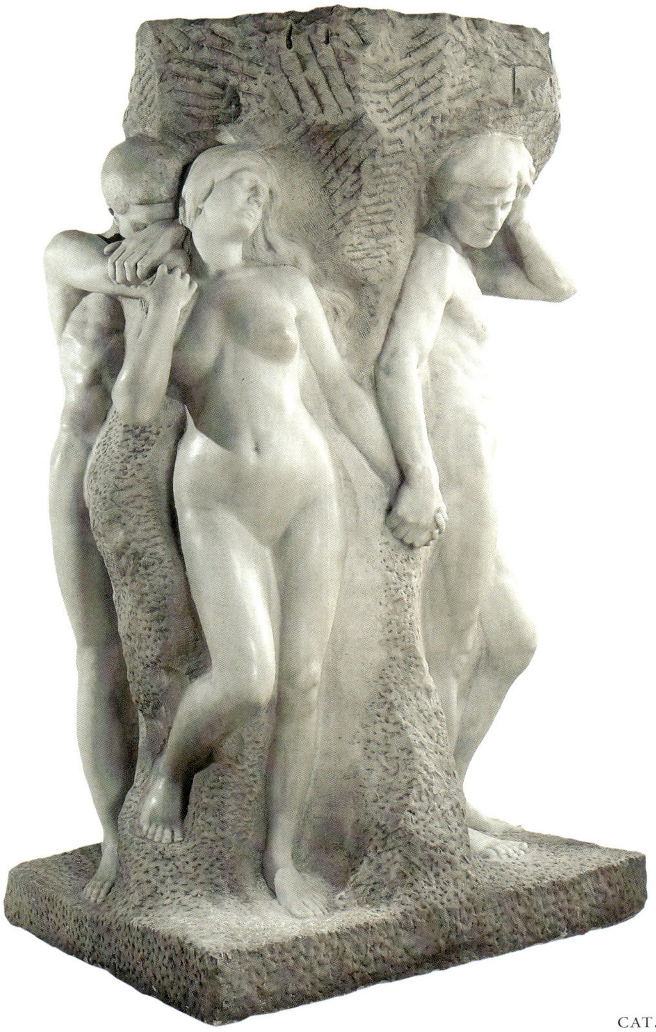

CAT. NO. 143

at the time as "a group of four figures, blind, groping, and clinging to each other."[3] The success of the finished composition was exceptional; the plaster version won a silver medal at the 1901 Buffalo Pan-American Exposition and a gold medal at the 1904 Louisiana Purchase Exposition in St. Louis. This recognition marked a transition in Taft's career and increased the number of commissions he received for public statuary in the Chicago vicinity; these works have become the mainstay of the sculptor's reputation and can still be seen dotting the city's landscape.[4]

In 1902 Taft wrote a letter to his friend Hamilton Gibson in which he explained the symbolism of *The Solitude of the Soul*: "[T]he thought is the eternally present fact that however closely we may be thrown together by circumstances, family ties, etc., we are *unknown* to each other. We grope, we cling to each other, but our eyes are 'hollow.' The young girl gazes in wonder, attempting to solve the impossible riddle of life; presently she will give it up and close her eyes like the others. Don't think me a pessimist! Quite the contrary; life seems to me very beautiful. This group is merely one comment on it—a gray-day picture."[5]

To illustrate his elusive and poetic idea, Taft created a sculpture in the round featuring four nude figures, two female and two male, who emerge in varying degrees from the rough-hewn stone. They are united by touch rather than vision: one woman's eyes are closed, one of the men buries his head in his hands, and the other gazes down. Two figures are shown frontally and two are shown from the side, providing multiple views of the human body that mimic a person moving in a circle. This composition abstracts the forms without detracting from their realism and instead relies upon the contrasting textures and varied surfaces of the stone to suggest the sense of personal alienation that Taft hoped his sculpture would communicate to audiences.

By questioning human beings' ability to know one another intimately, Taft broached a thoroughly modern subject linked to widespread apprehension about urbanization, technological innovation, and immigration. It was believed that, left unchecked, these modern circumstances alienated people from one another rather than promoted community. The Friends of American Art recognized the significance of both Taft and his sculpture to the history of the medium and commissioned the artist to translate his fragile plaster version into durable marble in 1913; the original plaster is now in the collection of the Dayton Art Institute in Ohio.[6]

NOTES

1. For more on Taft's biography and oeuvre, see "Lorado Taft: A Retrospective Exhibition," *Krannert Art Museum Bulletin* 8, 2 (1983); and Lewis W. Williams II, "Lorado Taft: American Sculptor and Missionary" (Ph.D. diss., University of Chicago, 1958).

2. On sculpture training at the École des Beaux-Arts, see Anne M. Wagner, "Learning to Sculpt in the Nineteenth Century: An Introduction," in Peter Fusco and H. W. Janson, eds., *The Romantics to Rodin: French Nineteenth-Century Sculpture from North American Collections*, exh. cat. (Los Angeles, Los Angeles County Museum of Art, 1980), pp. 9–20.

3. Letter from Lorado Taft to Mr. J. Hartmann, Mar. 18, 1901, Frances Ootheal Teall Memorial Collection, Eau Claire Public Library, Eau Claire, Wis.

4. Some of Taft's notable public sculptures in the Chicago area include *Fountain of the Great Lakes* (1913; The Art Institute of Chicago) and *Blackhawk* (1911; Oregon, Ill.).

5. Letter from Lorado Taft to Hamilton Gibson, Aug. 15, 1902, Files of the Department of Twentieth-Century Painting and Sculpture, The Art Institute of Chicago. Later in life, Taft recollected that the concept for the sculpture came from Susan B. Anthony: "The group was made . . . from a thought that came to me . . . suggested no doubt by a conversation with Miss Anthony. . . . The idea of human beings, thrown together by circumstance, yet practically unknown to each other, their eyes closed, they seek sympathy and comprehension wherever it may be found." For this and other reminiscences by Taft, see "Sermons in Sculpture," *Illinois Journal of Commerce* 18 (Apr. 1936); quoted in Williams (note 1), pp. 82–83.

6. For an account of the commission, see "Friends of American Art," *Bulletin of the Art Institute of Chicago* 8, 2 (Oct. 1914), p. 22.

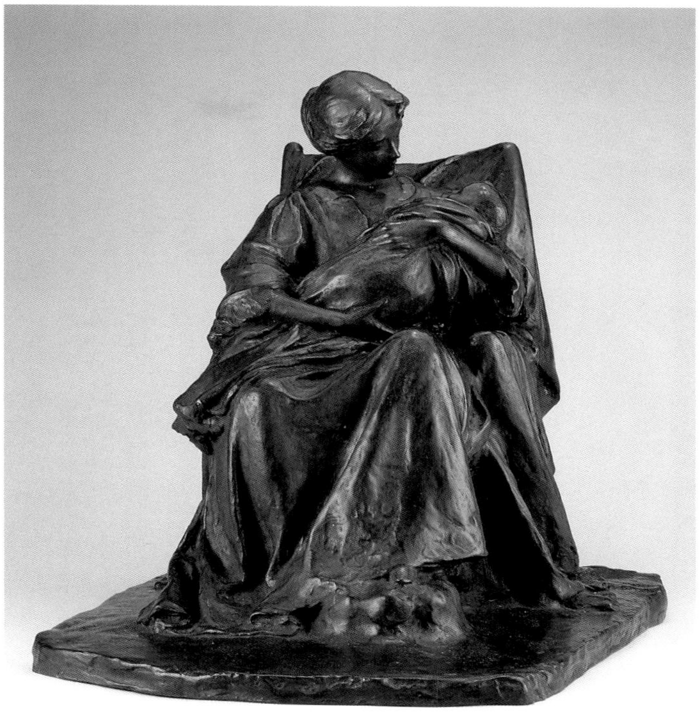

CAT. NO. 144

144. BESSIE POTTER VONNOH (1872–1955)

The Young Mother, modeled 1896, cast in bronze 1903

Bronze; 35.6 x 38.1 cm (14 x 15 in.)

Foundry: Roman Bronze Works, New York, N.Y.

Inscribed on base: *Bessie O. Potter / No. XX copyright 1903*

William C. Seipp Fund, 1915.193

145. *Girl Dancing*, 1897

Bronze; h. 36.2 cm (14¼ in.)

Foundry: Roman Bronze Works, New York, N.Y.

Inscribed on base: *Bessie Potter / copyright / No. XXVIII*

William C. Seipp Fund, 1915.194

Bessie Potter was born in St. Louis, but moved to Chicago with her widowed mother in 1876. During a childhood of lonely invalidism, the young future sculptor taught herself to model in clay. In 1886, when she was just fourteen years old, Potter met Lorado Taft, a sculptor and teacher at The Art Institute of Chicago. Taft, who had just returned from five years of study at the École des Beaux-Arts in Paris, allowed Potter to use his studio. Three years later she became his pupil at the Art Institute, where she continued to study until 1892. In 1894 Potter opened her own studio in Chicago, called the "Little Room," which became a meeting place for artists, writers, and musicians such as Eugene Field, Hamlin Garland, Edwin MacDowell, and, of course, Taft.[1] In 1899 she married painter Robert Vonnoh and moved to New York.

Although Potter's first professional commission was to sculpt an eight-foot allegorical figure of Art for the Illinois State Building at the 1893 World's Columbian Exposition in Chicago, she is best known for her small statuettes of female subjects.[2] She chose to represent the contemporary life of women in the form of "statuettes twelve inches in height, and in busts six inches," and years later she described her youthful philosophy as a radical one that sought after "beauty in the every-day world, to catch the joy and swing of modern American life."[3] Sometimes sculpted in tinted terracotta, her popular small statuettes became known as "Potterines." She concentrated on themes of young mothers and children, and dancing women in contemporary dress. Women friends served as her models in her Chicago studio. Around the turn of the twentieth century, Potter exhibited these small groups at numerous venues, including the National Sculpture Society in 1898, and the Paris Exposition Universelle in 1900.[4]

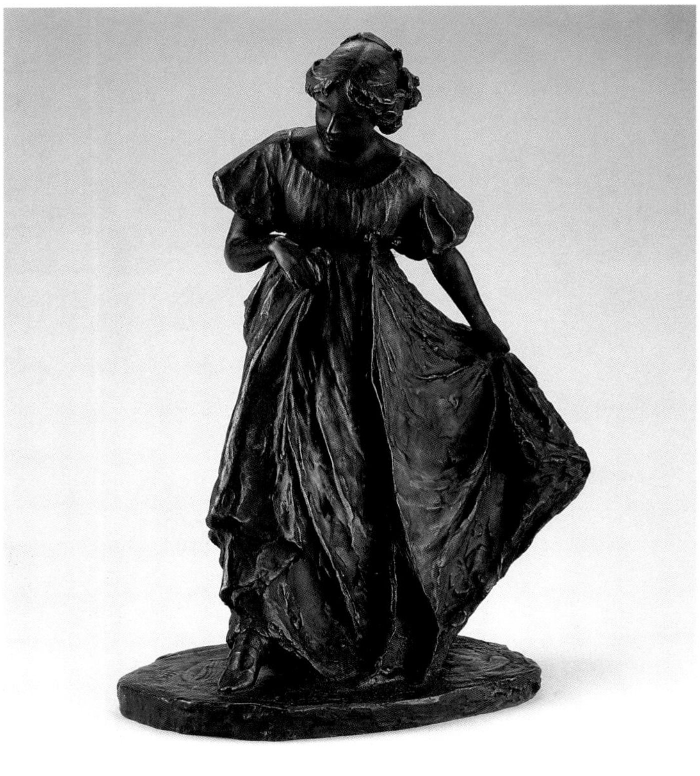

CAT. NO. 145

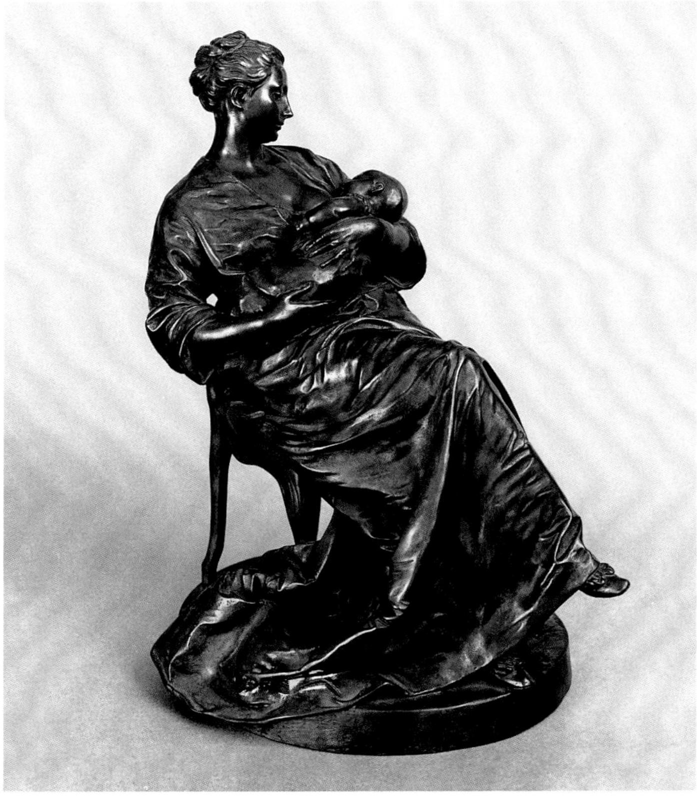

FIG. 74. Aime-Jules Dalou (French, 1838–1902). *Maternal Joy*, 1871–72. Bronze; h. 58.4 cm (23 in.). Baltimore Museum of Art, Gift of Lawrason Riggs (BMA 1945.51).

First modeled in 1896, *The Young Mother* is the earliest of Potter's mother-and-child groups and won a bronze medal at the 1900 Paris Exposition Universelle. It was completed a year after Potter's three-month trip to Paris, on which she was accompanied by Taft, his sister Zulime, and Potter's mother. In Paris, the young sculptress visited the studio of Auguste Rodin and absorbed the lessons of French naturalism. No doubt she also saw the bronzes of Aime-Jules Dalou (1838–1902). Her interpretation of motherhood in *The Young Mother* parallels Dalou's *Maternal Joy* (fig. 74) in its simplicity and directness of modeling. Dalou's original terracotta was executed in bronze in a reduced version in 1880 and was later copied in porcelain by the Sevres factory.

Potter delighted in the grace and rhythm of her small statuettes that depicted dancing women. *Girl Dancing* (1897) portrays what Lorado Taft felt was lacking in most contemporary American sculpture—"pleasure."[5] When the statuette was first completed, the art critic Lucy Monroe echoed Taft's assessment: "The personification of the modern skirt dance, . . . the simplicity and beauty of the action are exceptional—the curve of the back, the fall of the lifted skirt, the long line of the ribbons accenting the bend of the draperies, and the flexibility of the lithe, joyous young body."[6] Potter's impressionistic modeling technique is particularly evident in the rendering of the elegantly clothed young woman's upward gesture, which highlights the tactile folds of her empire-style dress.

By the early years of the twentieth century, however, Bessie Potter Vonnoh's statuettes of women became increasingly classical in pose and costume. Indeed, one critic emphasized the affinities between Potter's statuettes and ancient Greek Tanagra figures.[7] Like other sculptors influenced by the Renaissance Revival, such as Daniel Chester French (see cat. nos. 130–32) and Augustus Saint-Gaudens (see cat. nos. 113 and 174–75), Vonnoh not only clothed her figures in Grecian draperies, but gradually made her compositions more static and symbolic. But her change in style did not affect the popularity of her early subjects, which continued to be exhibited across the country. The Art Institute acquired both *The Young Mother* and *Girl Dancing*, along with four other small bronzes by Vonnoh, from a 1915 exhibition held at the museum.[8] In the 1920s and 1930s, Vonnoh moved to larger-scale sculpture and executed some fountain groups, and after the death of her husband in 1933, she gave up her career as a sculptor.

NOTES

1. Janis Conner and Joel Rosencranz, *Rediscoveries in American Sculpture: Studio Works, 1893–1939* (Austin, Tex., 1989), p. 168 n. 9.

2. The figure of Art was commissioned while Potter served as one of Taft's assistants to work on his sculptural groups for the Horticultural Building. She also submitted two plaster portraits for display in the Fine Arts Building. For more information on Potter's work at the Columbian Exposition, see Conner and Rosencranz (note 1), pp. 161–62.

3. Bessie Potter Vonnoh, "Tears and Laughter Caught in Bronze," *Delineator* 107 (Oct. 1925), p. 9.

4. Wayne Craven, *Sculpture in America* (New York, 1968), p. 502.

5. Lorado Taft, "The Exhibition of the National Sculpture Society," *Brush and Pencil* 2, 3 (June 1898), p. 127.

6. Lucy Monroe, "Bessie Potter," *Brush and Pencil* 2, 1 (Apr. 1898), pp. 33–34.

7. Alice Severance, "Talks by Successful Women: 10. Miss Bessie Potter, Sculptress," *Godey's Magazine* 133 (Oct. 1896), pp. 359–60.

8. The other bronzes by Vonnoh in the Art Institute's collection are *In Grecian Draperies*, *Motherhood*, *On the Sandman's Trail*, and *Daphne*.

146. ARTHUR WESLEY DOW (1857–1922)

Boats at Rest, c. 1895

Oil on canvas; 66 x 91.4 cm (26 x 36 in.)
Signed, lower left: *Arthur W. Dow*
Through prior acquisition of the Charles H. and Mary F. S. Worcester Collection, 1990.394

Arthur Wesley Dow was influential in the American art world as a painter, printmaker, curator, and educator. Born in Ipswich, Massachusetts, Dow studied at the Académie Julian in Paris between 1884 and 1889. During these years he spent time in Pont-Aven, France, experimenting with plein-air landscape techniques.[1] Pont-Aven, a small coastal town in Brittany, attracted European and American landscape painters, including Paul Gauguin, from around 1860 until the turn of the century. An early biographer of Dow observed that the artist examined Pont-Aven "with eyes trained to see the utmost possibility of any landscape."[2] When Dow returned to his hometown of Ipswich in 1889, he adapted this concentrated interest to the local landscape, producing painted works such as *Boats at Rest* that combine regionalist subjects with Asian-inspired compositions and vividly juxtaposed colors.

In Ipswich, a fishing town on the northern coast of Massachusetts, Dow discovered scenes of salt marshes, mud flats, haystacks, and brightly colored boats that provided him with ample raw material on which to base his paintings and woodcuts. Dow was particularly moved by the ever-changing colors of the fishing boats, and described this phenomenon vividly: "A yellow boat with a dark green stripe is likely to appear next season as a bright emerald green with a blue stripe, or a pure white, or lavender and gray."[3] The fishing boats in *Boats at Rest* delineate this phenomenon with their hulls of blue, green, and orange.

Boats at Rest marks a pronounced departure from the style Dow perpetuated in Pont-Aven, which emphasized suffused light and tonalist effects rather than the startling color and skewed composition of the Art Institute's painting. Dow's discovery in 1891 of Japanese prints, particularly those of Hokusai, may account for this stylistic change. Upon his return to the United States, Dow began to study non-Western arts and became a self-taught expert in Japanese prints. He pursued this field so avidly that in 1893 he was hired as Assistant Curator of Japanese Art at the Museum of Fine Arts, Boston, under Ernest Fenollosa.

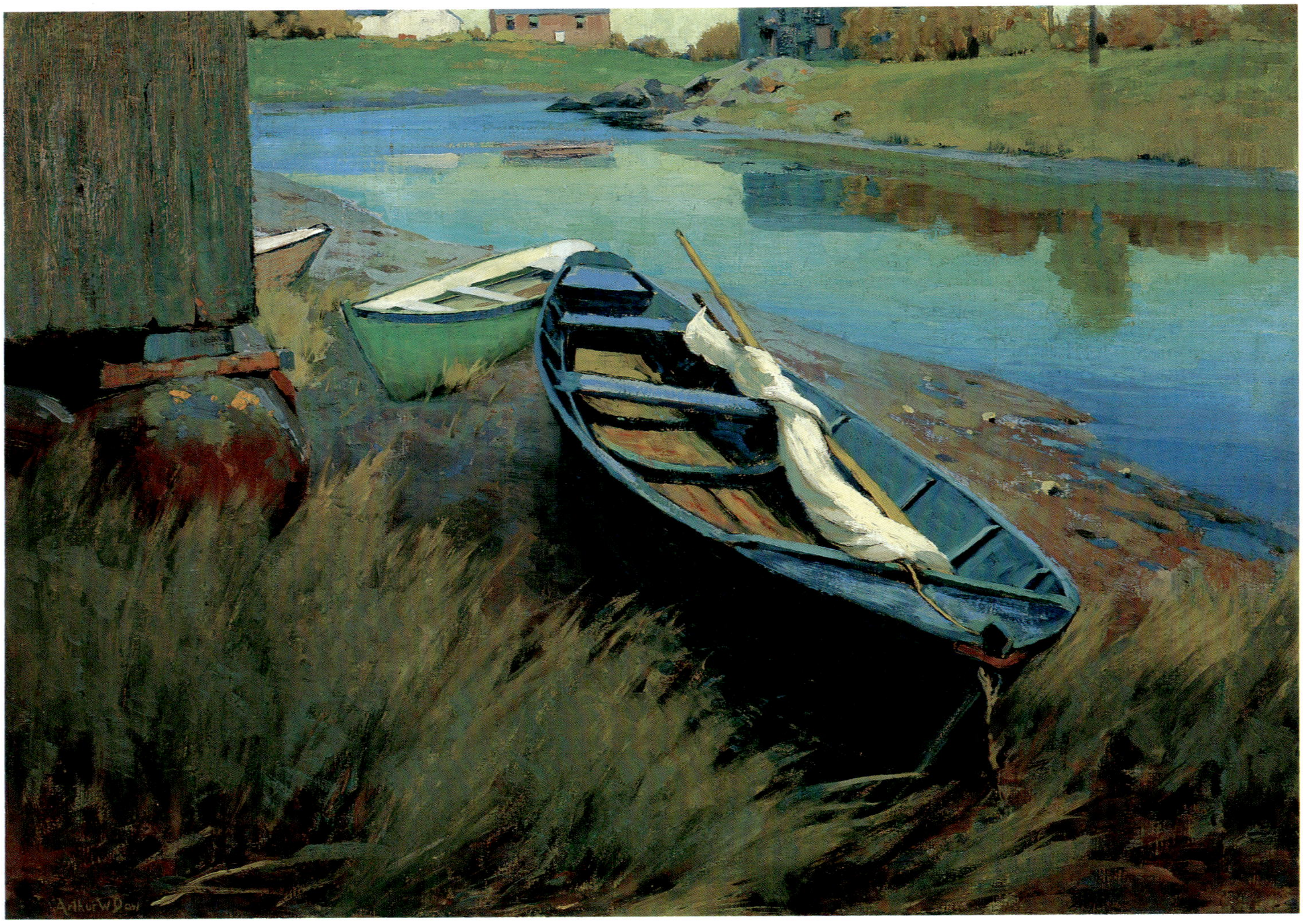

CAT. NO. 146

Dow's study of Japanese prints affected his artistic output during the 1890s, when it seems that he was more interested in printmaking than in painting. The paintings he did produce, however, such as *Boats at Rest*, do correspond to his prints both compositionally and coloristically.[4] Dow adopted Japanese techniques for his woodcuts, and applied the Asian aesthetic principles of line, color, and *notan* (harmony) to his prints and paintings. The forceful cropping of *Boats at Rest* and the strong diagonals of the boats and river correspond to compositional devices used by Japanese printmakers. The high-keyed palette of jarring color, however, is more akin to the work of French Post-Impressionist painters like Paul Gauguin, whose time in Pont-Aven coincided with Dow's, although there is no firm evidence of a link between the two artists.[5]

During the 1890s Dow also became interested in photography; *Boats at Rest* is perhaps indebted to the artist's practice of transposing photographic compositions to canvas. The artist began actively taking photographs in the early 1890s, mostly of Ipswich scenes. Dow's photograph of Essex Shipyard, taken sometime in the 1890s, bears a strong resemblance to *Boats at Rest*: both show small fishing boats angling away from one another, long marsh grasses blowing gently in the breeze, and ramshackle shanties.[6] The photograph, like the painting, is sharply cropped in the foreground and on the sides. Dow's combination of sharp focus on the buildings and boats, and the reflective river with softly blurred grasses also lends a photographic quality to the painting. Although it is unclear whether Dow used this photograph as an aid for the composition of *Boats at Rest*, it is likely that photography, as well as Japanese prints, played a role in its inception.[7]

As a teacher at the Pratt Institute in Brooklyn, the Art Students League in New York, and Teachers' College at Columbia University (where Georgia O'Keeffe was one of his students), Dow encouraged his students to combine eastern and western artistic modes in their work. In 1899 Dow published *Composition*, which became a standard teaching text for art instructors at all levels. Dow also worked as an instructor at the Ipswich Summer School between 1891 and 1907; he and his wife, Minnie Pearson, taught both fine arts and craft classes, emphasizing the importance of both. Dow was one of the most versatile and progressive American artists of his time, and *Boats at Rest* demonstrates his wide range of interests as well as his commitment to his native landscape.

NOTES

1. For more information about Dow's years in Pont-Aven and the Pont-Aven art colony in general, see David Sellin, *Americans in Brittany and Normandy, 1860–1910*, exh. cat. (Phoenix, Ariz., Phoenix Art Museum, 1982).

2. Arthur Warren Johnson, *Arthur Wesley Dow: Historian-Artist-Teacher* (Ipswich, Mass., 1934), p. 43.

3. Quoted in Frederick C. Moffatt, *Arthur Wesley Dow, 1857–1922*, exh. cat. (Washington, D.C., National Collection of the Fine Arts, 1977), pp. 15–16.

4. *Boats at Rest* corresponds to prints such as *The Dory* (c. 1895; Ipswich Historical Society, Mass.). See Moffatt (note 3), pp. 51–80; and Nancy E. Green, *Arthur Wesley Dow and His Influence*, exh. cat. (Ithaca, N.Y., Herbert F. Johnson Museum of Art, Cornell University, 1990), for more about Dow's prints.

5. See Sellin (note 1), pp. 52–53, for a description of Gauguin's first stay in Pont-Aven, in 1886.

6. This photograph is reproduced in Green (note 4), p. 9.

7. An untitled and undated photograph in the collection of the Ipswich Historical Society also corresponds to Dow's composition; this photograph is reproduced in the Arthur Wesley Dow Papers, roll 1027, Archives of American Art, Smithsonian Institution, Washington, D.C.

147. GEORGE INNESS (1825–1894)

The Home of the Heron, 1893

Oil on canvas; 76.2 x 115.2 cm (30 x 45 in.)

Signed, lower right: *G. Inness 1893*

Edward B. Butler Collection, 1911.31

During the final years of his life, George Inness and his family spent their summers in Tarpon Springs on the Gulf Coast of

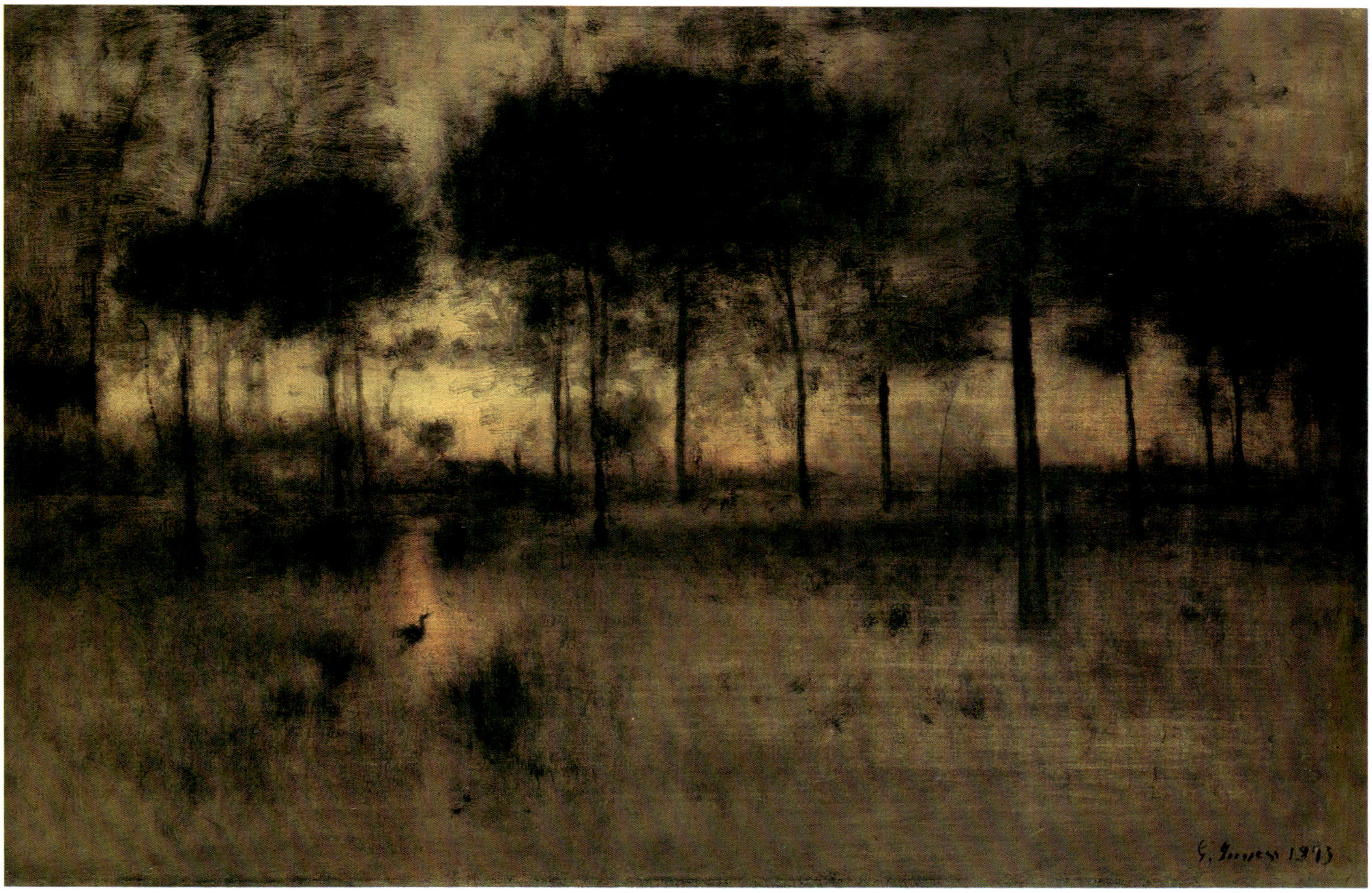

CAT. NO. 147

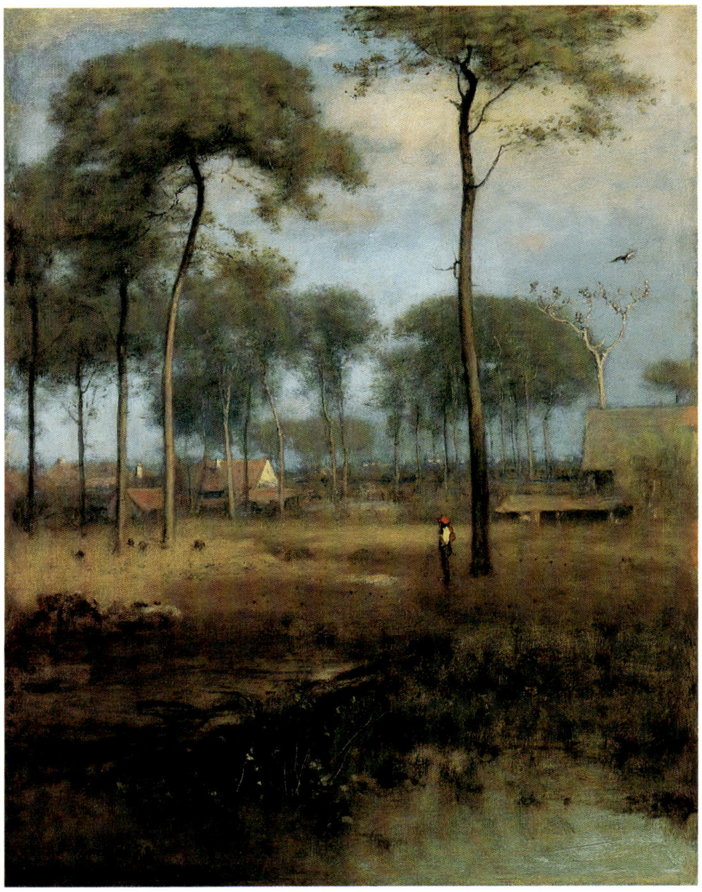

FIG. 75. George Inness (1825–1894). *Early Morning, Tarpon Springs*, 1892. Oil on canvas; 107.2 x 82.1 cm (42¼ x 32⅜ in.). The Art Institute of Chicago, Edward B. Butler Collection (1911.32).

Florida. Although his health was failing, Inness continued to paint in Florida and produced some of his most subtle, evocative work there.[1] *The Home of the Heron* was inspired by the marshy landscape and seemingly endless sunsets of the South, and its spare composition captures the artist's modern sensibilities. Inness's spiritual beliefs, the guiding force of his work, are also evident in this canvas.

If *Catskill Mountains* (cat. no. 75) represents the early stages of Inness's integration of Swedenborgian theological themes into his art through the spare use of symbolic color, *The Home of the Heron* exhibits his spirituality and artistic style.[2] Inness's use of atmospheric devices such as haze and mist to blur boundaries between earth and sky, treetops and clouds, unites the various landscape elements.[3] Although he did not use any explicit Swedenborgian symbols in this painting, the seamless blending of the composition does suggest one of the religion's basic tenets: the unity and harmony of the universe reflect with God's presence. By adopting modes of abstraction to convey spiritual associations, Inness successfully conveyed the otherworldliness of the Florida marsh at sunset.[4]

The Home of the Heron appears to be influenced by Asian sources as well, although Inness, unlike many of his contemporaries, did not collect Japanese prints or ink paintings. Inness balked when critics grouped him with the Impressionists, the group of artists most closely associated with the influence of Asian art, but he may have absorbed Eastern sources through his religious experiences. Swedenborg borrowed from eastern religions, particularly Buddhism and Daoism, when conceiving his theological philosophy and assimilated into his doctrine their ideas about the relationships between man, nature, and deity. The artist's use of thin, black washes of paint that resemble ink and spacious, spare compositions punctuated by a deeply sensitive feeling toward nature certainly correspond to Asian brush painting. They may also correlate with Swedenborg's theological teachings.

Inness's musical sensibilities are also apparent in this work. As Nicolai Cikovsky has suggested: "[I]n paintings like [*The Home of the Heron*], proportion and measure, size and interval, seem carefully determined and exactly plotted. . . . Although we know that Inness was interested in mathematics and numerology, this was mathematics internalized as an instinctive, almost musical sense of rhythmic relationship, cadenced order, and melodic line."[5] Early modernist painters such as Wassily Kandinsky and Georgia O'Keefe would incorporate such musical correspondences and inspiration into their work as well; Inness is not so much their progenitor as their distant and fondly remembered cousin.

Early Morning, Tarpon Springs (fig. 75), another late Florida painting, exhibits similar religious and musical qualities. This painting, however, is oriented vertically rather than horizontally, and the landscape clearly is one touched by humans. Inness accommodated and accentuated the tall, gangly trees in his composition and allowed them to dwarf the houses built in their shadows. The lone figure dwindles in comparison to nature, yet, like the trees that surround him, he is not overcome by his marshy surroundings. The overarching tone of the painting is serene and contemplative; the landscape strange and sublime, but not threatening.

Florida was a place Inness visited during the last years of his life, and the experience of aging may have inspired the wistful poetry of his works done there. Sunset and sunrise seem to have preoccupied the artist during these years, and these subjects suit the suffused tone of the paintings. By painting exotic landscapes during his final years, Inness may have been preparing himself for death and its mystery; indeed, aptly, *The Home of the Heron* was retitled *The Sun's Last Reflection* in an 1895 memorial exhibition of Inness's late work.[6] A less romantic, more pragmatic interpretation is that because the artist was under contract to produce paintings up to the time of his death, he was forced to keep hard at work. Whatever the case, Inness's body of late work exemplifies both his need to apprehend the spiritual through painting and his continued desire to succeed professionally.

NOTES

1. For more on Inness in Florida, see *Artists of the Florida Tropics*, exh. cat. (Gainesville, University of Florida Gallery, 1965); and *George Inness in Florida, 1890–1894, and the South, 1884–1894*, exh. cat. (Jacksonville, Fla., Cummer Gallery of Art, 1980).

2. For more about Swedenborg's ideas, see the entry on Inness's *Our Old Mill* and *Catskill Mountains* (cat. nos. 74–75).

3. Marilyn S. Kushner, "George Inness," in *George Inness: The Spiritual Landscape*, exh. cat. (New York, Borghi and Company, 1991), p. 9.

4. For an exploration of the Swedenborgian influence on Inness, see *George Inness: Presence of the Unseen*, exh. cat. (Montclair, N.J., Montclair Art Museum, 1994).

5. Nicolai Cikovsky, Jr., and Michael Quick, *George Inness*, exh. cat. (Los Angeles, Los Angeles County Museum of Art, 1985), p. 194.

6. *Catalogue of Paintings by the Late George Inness*, exh. cat. (New York, Fifth Avenue Art Galleries, 1895), cat. no. 69.

148. FREDERIC REMINGTON (1861–1909)

The Advance Guard, or the Military Sacrifice, 1890

Oil on canvas; 87.3 x 123.1 cm (34⅜ x 48½ in.)

Signed, lower left: *Frederic Remington / 1890*

George F. Harding Collection, 1982.802

149. *Coming Through the Rye (Over the Range)*, modeled 1902, cast in bronze 1902/06

Bronze; 72.4 x 71.1 x 47 cm (28½ x 28 x 18½ in.)

George F. Harding Collection, 1982.810

Raised in northern New York state, Frederic Remington's formal artistic training was scant: he spent a year and a half at the Yale School of Art and a few months at the Art Students League in New York City.[1] But even with limited training, he managed to become a myth-maker and entrepreneur whose images of the American West during the late nineteenth century made him rich and famous. Remington's art perpetuated popular, romanticized notions of Native Americans, cavalry soldiers, and cowboys who lived and did battle on the varied terrain of the "old" West.[2] *The Advance Guard* and *Coming Through the Rye* are characteristic works that not only represent the artist's skills as a storyteller and self-promoter, but also reveal important connections between his art and his journalistic enterprises.

Painted in 1890, *The Advance Guard* appeared as an illustration in *Harper's Weekly* three years later and was accompanied by an article authored by Remington. The text describes the scene of the painting and argues for the strategic necessity of using an advance guard when battling Native Americans.[3] Describing the painting's central figure, the artist wrote: "He hears a report, feels a shock, reels in his saddle, while his stricken horse plunges under him, and then the dull brain reels and faints."[4] Remington positioned himself not only as a first-hand observer, but as an expert on the history of the use of the advance guard. His authoritative voice helped establish the image's perceived authenticity and, in turn, made Remington an artist well known to a variety of turn-of-the-century audiences. It also heroicized the actions of the cavalry and maligned those of Native Americans fighting to maintain control over their land.

Although Native Americans are not visible in this painting, the violence associated with their presence is clear in both the image and Remington's accompanying text. He imagined how the Sioux were able to ambush the cavalry with their knowledge of this otherworldly terrain, which, he wrote, was "like the bottom of the sea in contour, taking strange forms, but dry and verdureless. . . . A Sioux can lay along a clay butte and 'pump a Winchester' into an advancing trooper, and can only be dislodged or 'developed' by the advance of a heavy body of troops."[5] The treacherous landscape in *The Advance Guard* suggests a deviousness on the part of the Native Americans, who hide within it, and throws the heroism of the cavalry, who face their enemy in the open, into sharp relief. The title of the work also emphasizes the protagonist as a martyr who has sacrificed his life in the service of westward expansion.

Remington's text and image were published in 1893, the year that marked the opening of the World's Columbian Exposition in Chicago, where Frederick Jackson Turner presented a lecture entitled "The Significance of the Frontier in American History." This leading American historian charted how the

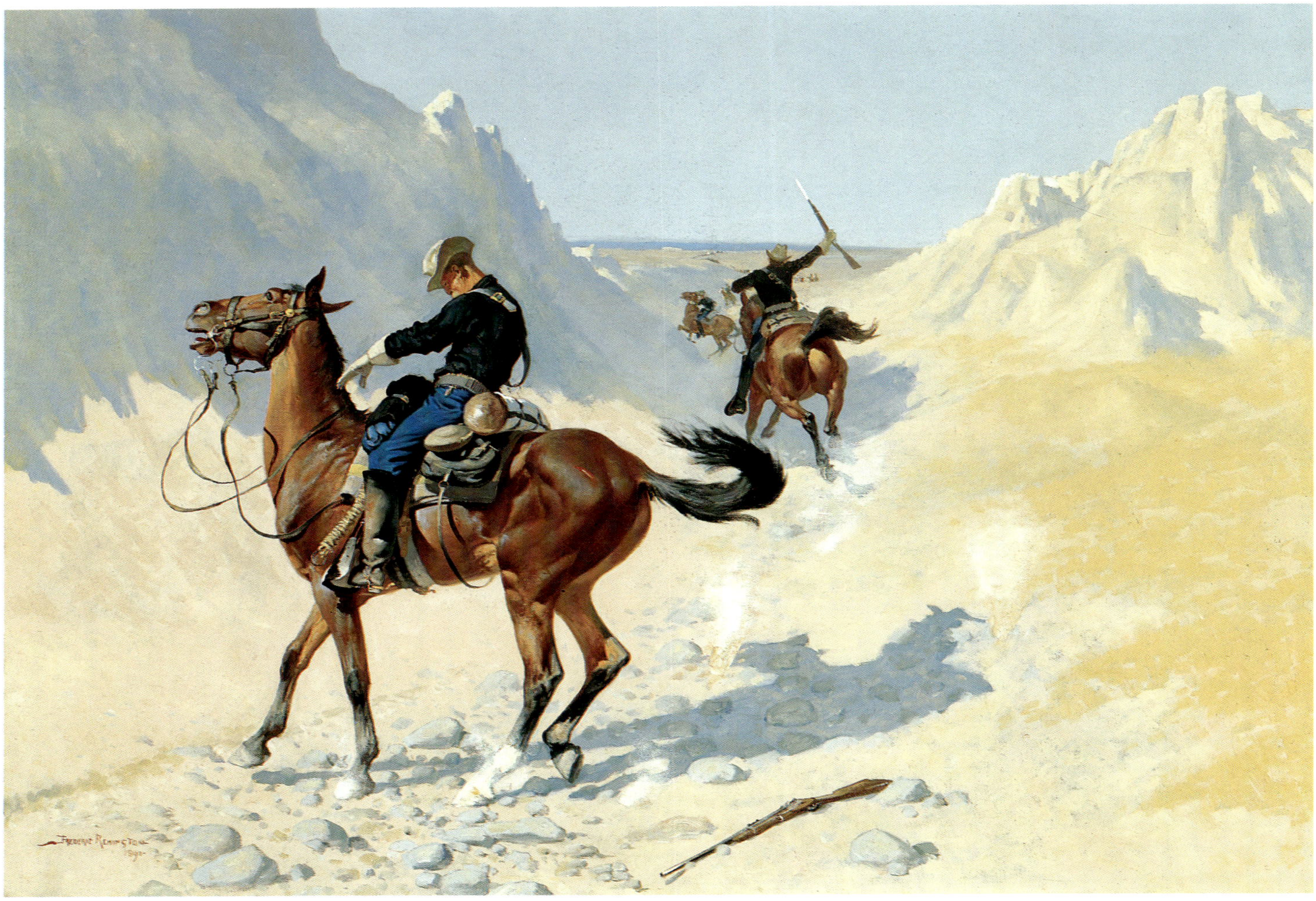

CAT. NO. 148

expansion westward across the frontier affected the national character. Turner ended his paper: "And now, four centuries from the discovery of America, at the end of a hundred years of life under the Constitution, the frontier has gone, and with its going has closed the first period of American history."[6] Remington, too, visited the Columbian Exposition and reported on it for *Harper's Weekly*, although he concentrated mostly on its carnivalesque attractions.[7] *The Advance Guard* served as a rebuttal to the presumption that the frontier had closed not only by keeping it alive through the representation of a martyred cavalryman, but also by recreating a historical period whose mythology resonated deeply with contemporary audiences.

Coming Through the Rye does for cowboys what *The Advance Guard* does for the cavalry—it provides them with a permanent place in the American imagination as synonymous with the West. Remington turned to bronze as a medium in 1895 in order to increase his earning potential and experiment with a new material. As a result of their serial production and widespread dissemination, Remington's bronzes are probably better known today than are his paintings.[8] *Coming Through the Rye* was copyrighted in 1902, and this unnumbered version was probably cast between 1902 and 1906. Remington wrote to Ricardo Bertelli of the Roman Bronze Works in 1902: "I have reconstructed the right hand man & made it much better with a foot on the ground. So—now I have six horses feet on the ground and 10 in the air."[9] The Art Institute's version of *Coming Through the Rye* conforms to Remington's description.[10]

Both *The Advance Guard* and *Coming Through the Rye* entered the Art Institute's collection from the George F. Harding Collection. Harding, a Chicago resident, was a collector of Remington paintings and sculpture as well as of arms and armor. The Art Institute's Remington collection also includes grisaille paintings done as illustrations for the artist's published stories, including the novel *The Way of an Indian*, which appeared in *Cosmopolitan* magazine between November 1905 and

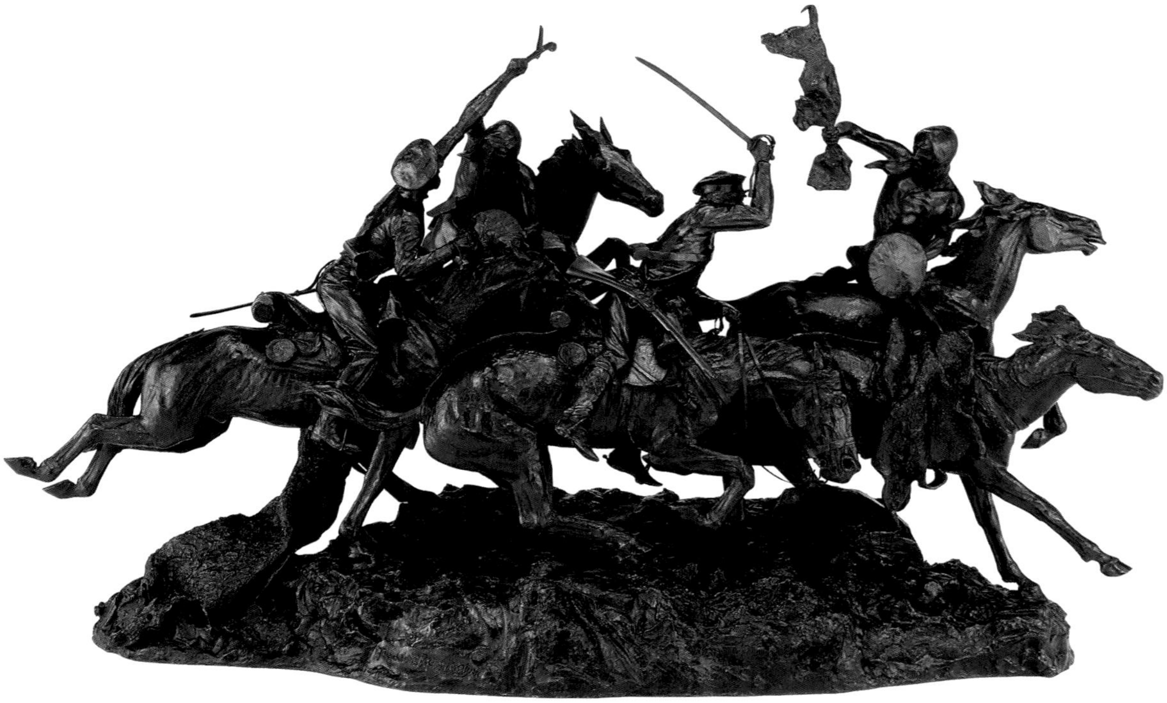

CAT. NO. 149

March 1906. Remington's art provides important evidence of how the "frontier era" was mythologized for the contemporary audience.

NOTES

1. For more biographical information on Frederic Remington, see Peggy and Harold Samuels, *Frederic Remington: A Biography* (Garden City, N.Y., 1982).

2. See Alexander Nemerov, *Frederic Remington and Turn-of-the-Century America* (New Haven, Conn., and London, 1995), for a provocative discussion of Remington's relationship to late nineteenth-century American ideas about social evolution, westward expansion, and masculinity.

3. Frederic Remington, "The Advance-Guard, or the Military Sacrifice," *Harper's Weekly* (Sept. 16, 1893), pp. 886, 888–89; reprinted in Peggy Samuels and Harold Samuels, eds., *The Collected Writings of Frederic Remington* (Garden City, N.Y., 1979), pp. 109–10.

4. Remington (note 3), p. 886; Samuels and Samuels (note 3), p. 109.

5. Ibid.

6. Frederick Jackson Turner, "The Significance of the Frontier in American History," in Graham Clarke, ed., *The American Landscape: Literary Sources and Documents* (Mountfield, Eng., 1993), vol. 1, p. 560.

7. Frederic Remington, "A Gallop Through the Midway," *Harper's Weekly* (Oct. 7, 1893), p. 963; reprinted in Samuels and Samuels (note 3), pp. 111–13.

8. For more information about Remington's bronzes, see Michael Edward Shapiro, *Cast and Recast: The Sculpture of Frederic Remington*, exh. cat. (Washington, D.C., National Museum of American Art, 1981).

9. Letter from Frederic Remington to Ricardo Bertelli, 1902, McCracken Collection of Remington Letters, St. Lawrence University, Canton, N.Y.; quoted in Michael Edward Shapiro, *Bronze Casting and American Sculpture, 1850–1900* (Newark, Del., 1985), p. 141.

10. By 1906 the artist had again altered the sculptural arrangement so that only five hooves touched the base. The four rollicking cowboys in the composition also appear in an 1888 ink drawing of the same title (private collection) and the painting *Cowboys Coming to Town for Christmas* (1889; private collection). For illustrations of these works, see Patricia Janis Broder, *Bronzes of the American West* (New York, 1974), p. 144; and James K. Ballinger, *Frederic Remington* (New York, 1989), p. 106.

150. DAVID WOLCOTT KENDALL (1851–1910)

Armchair, 1895/97

Green-stained oak with caned inserts;
86 x 75 x 56 cm (33⅞ x 29½ x 22 in.)
Gift of the Antiquarian Society through Morris and Jane Weeden, 1995.101

The Arts and Crafts movement's spirit of reform was seen not just in Chicago, but throughout the Midwest. In Grand Rapids, Michigan, the major furniture-producing center of the nation, David Wolcott Kendall designed unadorned furniture that could be easily manufactured by machine.[1] His stained oak

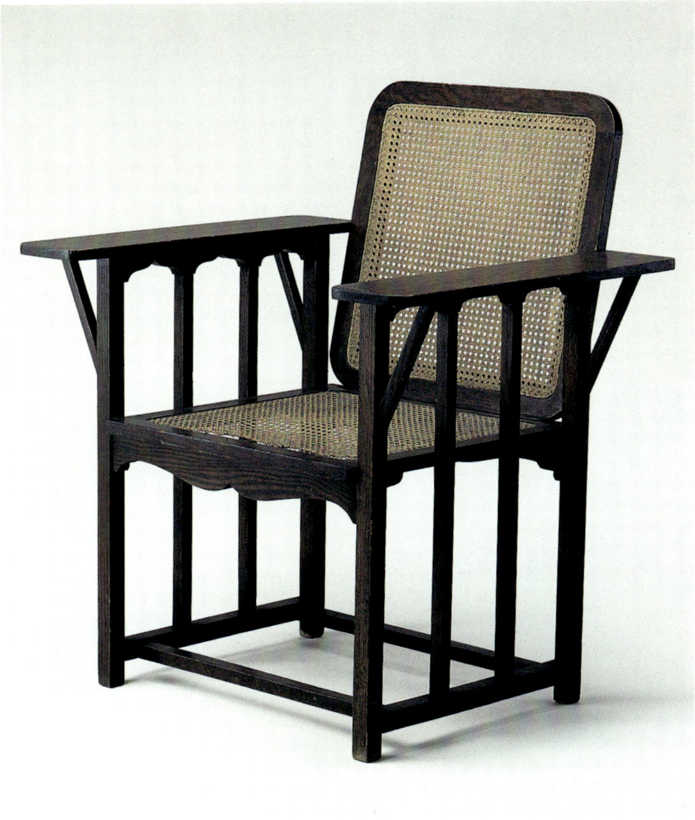

CAT. NO. 150

armchair, first designed for the Phoenix Furniture Company around 1895, was an early departure from the heavily carved walnut, rosewood, and mahogany furniture then prevalent. The caned seat adds lightness to the already spare, geometric simplicity of the design. Were it not for the gothic-arched detailing, which points to its nineteenth-century origins, this modern-looking chair could well have been made during the 1920s.

When introduced to the market in the mid-1890s, this chair was named for President McKinley, who was presented with a prototype for his offices at the White House.[2] The McKinley chair was one of Kendall's most successful endeavors, gaining him praise from the furniture-manufacturing community for its forward-looking design. Books and magazines from the early twentieth century reveal that the chair was still used in a variety of settings for decades after it was first produced.[3] Kendall's chair perhaps influenced Frank Lloyd Wright's geometric, caned birch chairs for the Sherman Booth House (1912; Glencoe, Illinois), which are now in the collection of the Chicago Historical Society.

In the nineteenth century, oak was thought of as a common material, lacking the dark rich color and smooth grain characteristic of the more expensive woods. But because of the increasing scarcity of walnut and the prohibitive expense of mahogany, Kendall turned to oak, which could be had in abundance from the forests of Indiana. At first, Kendall developed a number of brightly colored finishes, like yellow, copper, and malachite green, which hid the oak used in his furniture. Later, Kendall set out to develop a series of stains that would darken the color of the wood and highlight the open grain. Because of his immense success, other manufacturers designed oak furniture and copied finishes developed by Kendall.[4] His most imitated stain, known as the "Belgian finish," was used on this chair. Its green color was used in textiles, ceramics, metalwork, and other furniture of the period.[5]

NOTES

1. Kendall was the principal designer and manager of the Phoenix Furniture Company from 1879 until his death in 1910. During his early career as a draftsman for the Bromley, Hunn, and Smith Furniture Company, he studied drawing, painting, mechanical drawing, architecture, sculpture, and modeling. Before going to Grand Rapids, Kendall worked for William Wooton, maker of the patented Wooton desk. He worked in Chicago from 1873 to 1879 and was perhaps in the employ of the Fairbanks Furniture Company. Kendall joined the Phoenix firm in 1879 and was soon made a designer. He founded his own furniture company in Detroit in 1886, but returned to Phoenix in 1889 as chief designer. For further information on Kendall and the Phoenix Furniture Company, see the entry by Catherine Zusy in Wendy Kaplan, ed., *"The Art That Is Life": The Arts and Crafts Movement in America, 1875–1920*, exh. cat. (Boston, Museum of Fine Arts, 1987), pp. 150–51; Frank E. Ransom, *The City Built on Wood: A History of the Furniture Industry in Grand Rapids, Michigan, 1850–1950* (Ann Arbor, Mich., 1955); and Jane Perkins Claney and Robert Edwards, "Progressive Design in Grand Rapids," *Tiller* 2, 1 (Sept.–Oct. 1983), pp. 35–37.

2. Claney and Edwards (note 1), p. 48.

3. It appeared in a Frank Lloyd Wright house in Wilmette, Illinois, and in the Trellis Room at the Colony Club in New York, decorated by Elsie de Wolfe. See Robert L. Ames, "A West Suburban House," *American Homes and Gardens* (Mar. 1912), p. 88; Elsie de Wolfe, *The House in Good Taste* (New York, 1913), p. 270; and "Before and After," *House Beautiful* 17, 5 (Apr. 1905), p. 32.

4. The stenciled number underneath the seat rail of the Art Institute's chair corresponds to numbered furniture designs now in the library at the Kendall School of Design in Grand Rapids; the number authenticates this chair as one manufactured by the Phoenix firm. The chair design was one of only three to be patented by Phoenix. The patent was filed on July 24, 1897 (pat. no. 27,597); see Claney and Edwards (note 1), n. 37. Joseph McHugh and Company of New York, Paine Furniture of Boston, and J. S. Ford, Johnson and Company of Chicago all copied the chair design for their trade catalogues. See Kaplan (note 1), p. 150, cat. no. 35; and Don Marek, *Arts and Crafts Furniture Design: The Grand Rapids Contribution, 1895–1915*, exh. cat. (Grand Rapids, Mich., Grand Rapids Art Museum, 1987), pp. 29–30.

5. Claney and Edwards (note 1), pp. 43–45. For more on the Belgian finish, and others Kendall developed, see "Modern Finishes," *Michigan Artisan* (1904), p. 4.

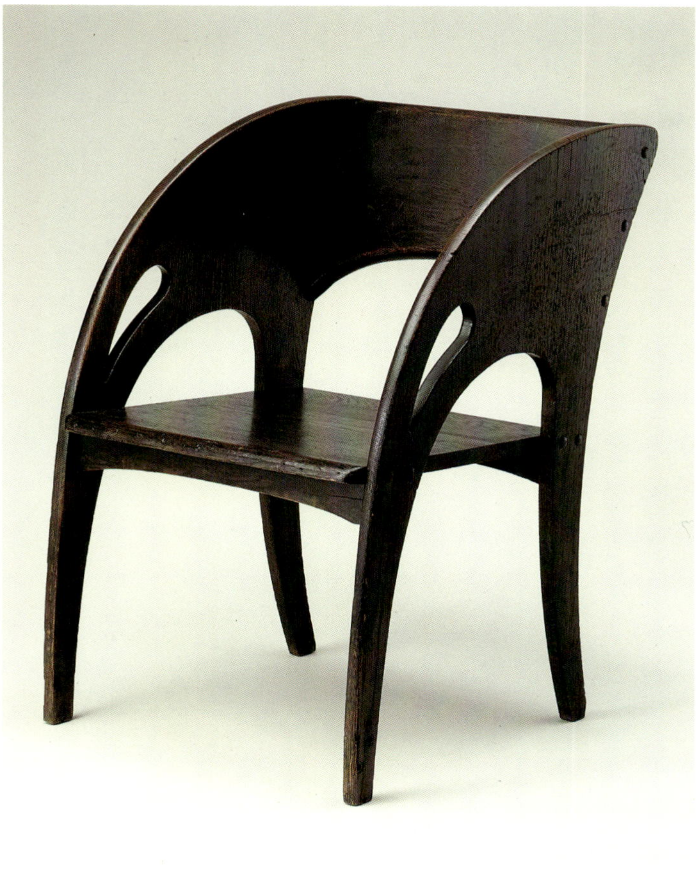

CAT. NO. 151

151. J. S. FORD, JOHNSON AND COMPANY

Armchair, 1904/05

Brown-stained oak; 81 x 52 x 50 cm (31⅞ x 20½ x 19⅝ in.)
Restricted gift of Gilda and Henry Buchbinder, 1995.100

Headquartered in Chicago, with divisions in Indiana and Massachusetts, J. S. Ford, Johnson and Company was one of the largest chair manufacturers in the country. It was one of several Chicago-based furniture-manufacturing businesses that expanded its scope of operations at the end of the nineteenth century to include all steps of production, from cutting trees to placing chairs on the showroom floor.[1] During the mid-1880s, the company showcased more than three thousand varieties of chairs, and used interchangeable parts.[2] Ford, Johnson used such parts to maintain its vast selection of designs.[3] From the start, the company was mostly involved in producing lines of office furniture, but by the turn of the century several new styles, such as this chair, were introduced for residential use.

This design, numbered 3051, was introduced in the 1904–05 trade catalogue as part of a suite of furniture that also included a settee and a rocking chair. A customer could purchase an individual chair or the entire suite.[4] Several different versions could be had: a plain style, like the Art Institute's chair; one with a strapped-down cushion; and one with an upholstered seat and back. Though the chairs were mass-produced, the exposed wooden rivets reveal an affinity with hand craftsmanship, and form a connection to California coppersmith Dirk Van Erp's designs.[5] The bold, crisp lines of the chair were also inspired by the work of two other European designers who produced similar chairs, the Englishman Robert Oerley in 1899 and the German-born Joseph Urban in 1902.[6] The creation of such a fresh, artistic design by a firm that mass-produced over three thousand different chair designs, mostly institutional ones, illustrates the skill of the firm's designers and the development of a simplified, organic, modern style in Chicago and the Midwest.[7]

NOTES

1. Sharon Darling, *Chicago Furniture: Art, Craft, and Industry, 1833–1983* (New York, 1984), p. 114.

2. A. T. Andreas, *History of Chicago* (Chicago, 1886), vol. 3, p. 735; and Darling (note 1), p. 115.

3. In 1904, the year the Art Institute's chair was introduced, the firm reportedly sold over 21,000 square feet of chairs. To aid in the production and distribution of their products, the firm acquired several other businesses, including Philander Derby and Company of New York and Boston and the Hitchcock Chair Company of Indiana, both of which produced Ford, Johnson designs, and the Stoll and Barnes Company of Chicago, which specialized in the sale and distribution of chairs. See David A. Hanks with Jennifer Toher, "Tradition and Reform," in Hanks et al., *High Styles: Twentieth Century American Design* (New York, 1985), p. 37; and Andreas (note 2), p. 735. A similar chair in the collection of the Wolfsonian Foundation, Miami, bears the paper label of Philander Derby and Company of New York.

4. J. S. Ford, Johnson and Company, *1904–1905 Special Catalogue: Fiber Rush, Imported Malacca and Mission Furniture* (Chicago, 1904). This volume is in the collection of the Winterthur Museum Library, Winterthur, Del.; a photocopy is in the Files of the Department of American Arts, The Art Institute of Chicago.

5. Hanks et al. (note 3), p. 37.

6. Letter from Dr. Barry Harwood, Associate Curator of Decorative Arts at the Brooklyn Museum of Art, to Seth A. Thayer, Department of American Arts, The Art Institute of Chicago, May 1, 1995.

7. Other Ford, Johnson chairs of this design are in the Baltimore Museum of Art; Brooklyn Museum of Art; Metropolitan Museum of Art, New York; Victoria and Albert Museum, London; and Wolfsonian Foundation collection in Miami.

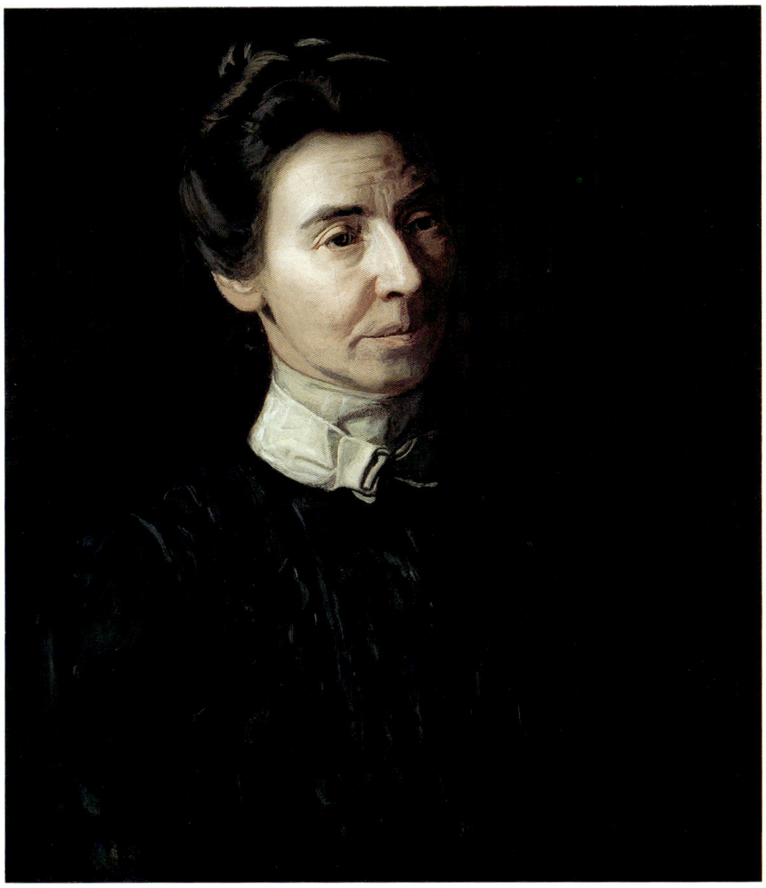

CAT. NO. 152

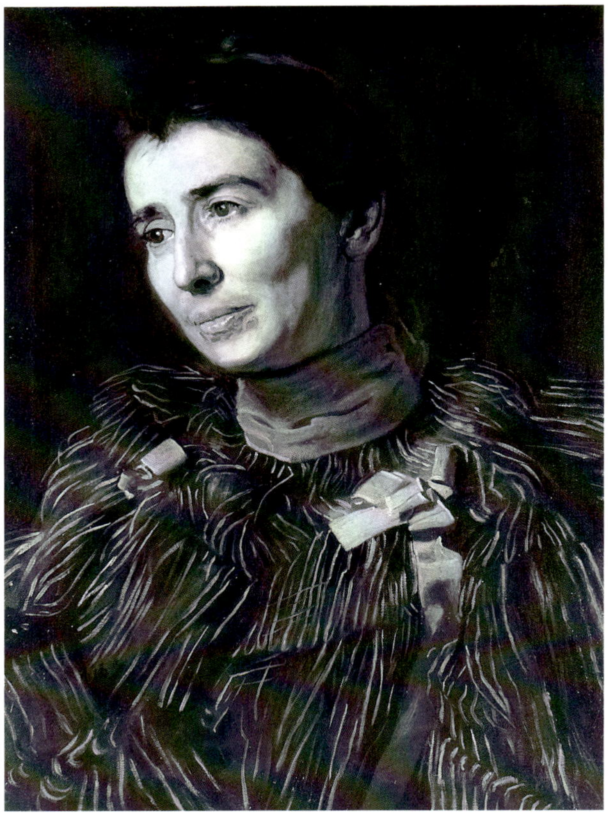

FIG. 76. Thomas Eakins (1844–1916). *Addie (Mary Adeline Williams)*, 1900. Oil on canvas; 61.3 x 46 cm (24⅛ x 18⅛ in.). Philadelphia Museum of Art, Gift of Mrs. Thomas Eakins and Miss Mary Adeline Williams (29.184.10).

152. THOMAS EAKINS (1844–1916)

Mary Adeline Williams, 1899

Oil on canvas; 61 x 50.8 cm (24 x 20$\frac{1}{16}$ in.)
Friends of American Art Collection, 1939.548

Thomas Eakins produced more than two hundred portraits, of which only twenty-five were commissioned.[1] At the turn of the century, when he painted *Mary Adeline Williams*, Eakins was entering the final phase of his embattled and controversial artistic career. In 1886 he had been dismissed from the teaching staff of the Pennsylvania Academy of the Fine Arts for removing a loincloth from a nude male model during a drawing class for female students. In 1895 the Drexel Institute of Art, Science, and Industry fired him for his continuing insistence that women be allowed to study nude models.[2] In the face of these difficulties, Eakins created some of his most intensely felt and personal portraits.

Little biographical information about Mary Adeline Williams survives. She was a childhood friend of Margaret, one of Thomas Eakins's sisters. She grew up in Fairton, New Jersey, and worked as a seamstress for Wanamaker's department store in Philadelphia, as well as a corset maker. Eakins mentioned her as early as 1867 in a letter to his sister Fanny, written while he was studying in Paris: "How did you like little Addie Williams? She is a pretty little girl & I guess just as good as she is pretty, or she belies her blood. We owe a great deal to her father & mother for their unvarying and disinterested kindness to us whenever we have been there and to little Addie too. Try to make her welcome whenever she comes to town."[3] After living with her brother in Chicago for six years, Williams returned to Philadelphia around 1897, and wrote to Eakins to renew their friendship.[4]

On Sunday, February 26, 1899, the artist's wife, Susan Macdowell Eakins, wrote in her diary, "Tom starts portrait of Addie."[5] Susan Eakins faithfully recorded each of Williams's portrait sittings and offered an intimate glimpse of her relationship with the Eakinses.[6] For example, on Saturday, April

29, she noted, "Addie poses for 7th time. . . . Tom takes Addie out riding on bicycle."[7] The contrast between Williams's appearance in the portrait—straightlaced, severe, and spinsterish—and descriptions of her in the diary—riding bicycles, going to art exhibitions, and lunching out—is striking and demonstrates that no single portrait could represent the complexity of these individuals and their relationship. Almost a year after Eakins undertook the Art Institute's portrait, Williams moved into the Eakins's large residence at 1729 Mount Vernon Street. She took the room left vacant by the death of Thomas's father, Benjamin Eakins, at the end of December 1899.[8] She inherited one quarter of Thomas Eakins's estate upon his death in 1916.

Eakins executed a second portrait of Williams (fig. 76) in 1900, during the first year of her residence in the Eakins home. In this painting, the subject is turned toward a light source that erases her wrinkles and softens her features. Her hair is slightly disheveled; she wears a billowing striped frock festooned with bows that is a remarkable departure from the severe, schoolmarmish garment she wears in the 1899 portrait.

There has been much speculation concerning the discrepancies between these two portraits. Some conjectured that Eakins and Williams had an affair, which led him to soften his second rendering.[9] Others proposed that, once she moved in with the Eakinses, she had less to worry about financially and could relax.[10] David Lubin, however, suggested that these ideas "rely on traditional assumptions about female fulfillment, as though nothing short of the love of a man or the ambience of a family could account for such an apparent transformation."[11] He proposed that, between the two portraits, Eakins simply may have become familiar with another side of her personality and evoked it. As in many portraits of his male friends, Eakins responded to Williams as a thoughtful, complex human being.

Mary Adeline Williams was acquired by the Art Institute from the sale of Susan Macdowell Eakins's estate in 1939. Two exhibitions were mounted in conjunction with the sale—one at the Babcock Gallery and the other at Kleeman Gallery, both in New York. Critics noted at the time that the Babcock show (in which the Chicago portrait figured) contained primarily works of personal significance to Susan and Thomas Eakins.[12]

NOTES

1. Elizabeth Johns, *Thomas Eakins: The Heroism of Modern Life* (Princeton, N.J., 1983), p. xix.

2. For more complete descriptions of these incidents, see Lloyd Goodrich, *Thomas Eakins*, 2 vols. (Cambridge, Mass., and London, 1982); William Innes Homer, *Thomas Eakins: His Life and Art* (New York, 1992); and Johns (note 1). For more about the Drexel Institute incident, see cat. no. 153.

3. Thomas Eakins Papers, roll 640, Archives of American Art, Washington, D.C.

4. Charles Bregler's Thomas Eakins Collection, Pennsylvania Academy of the Fine Arts, Philadelphia, microfiche I 7/E/4–5; letter dated Feb. 12, 1897.

5. Bregler Collection (note 4), microfiche II 4/G/12–II 5/E/11.

6. According to Susan Eakins's diary, Mary Adeline Williams sat for her portrait on Feb. 26; Mar. 26; Apr. 9, 16, 23, 29, 30; and May 14, 1899.

7. Bregler Collection (note 4), microfiche II 4/G/12–II 5/E/11.

8. The Eakins family had invited Williams to reside with them previously, but she declined because Thomas Eakins, then unmarried, was still living at home.

9. See Homer (note 2), p. 174, and Goodrich (note 2), vol. 2, pp. 224–25, for more on this assertion.

10. Goodrich (note 2), vol. 2, p. 174.

11. John Wilmerding, ed., *Thomas Eakins (1844–1916) and the Heart of American Life*, exh. cat. (London, National Portrait Gallery, 1993), p. 161.

12. One writer commented that "most of the items are pictures which the widow would not sell during her life time, feeling that they were intimate keys to her husband's famous works." "Last of Eakins," *Art Digest* 14 (Oct. 1, 1939), p. 14.

153. THOMAS EAKINS (1844–1916)

Riter Fitzgerald, 1895

Oil on canvas; 193.7 x 163.2 cm (76¼ x 64¼ in.)
Signed, lower left, on base of bookcase: *EAKINS 95*
Friends of American Art Collection, and the Goodman Fund, 1950.1511

This portrait is one of a large number of works by Thomas Eakins that depict scientists, doctors, writers, and artists in thoughtful poses, surrounded by objects alluding to their intellectual life.[1] Riter Fitzgerald was the art, music, and literary critic for the *Philadelphia Evening Item*—a prominent newspaper founded by his father, Thomas Fitzgerald—who championed Eakins's work and publicly defended his controversial teaching methods.

Eakins executed *Riter Fitzgerald* soon after his dismissal from the Drexel Institute of Art, Science, and Industry in 1895 for displaying a nude male model in front of female students (see entry on cat. no. 152). Defending Eakins in the *Evening Item* after he was fired, Fitzgerald recorded the only public statement the artist made about the controversy: "Professor Eakins tells me positively that there was never any arrangement

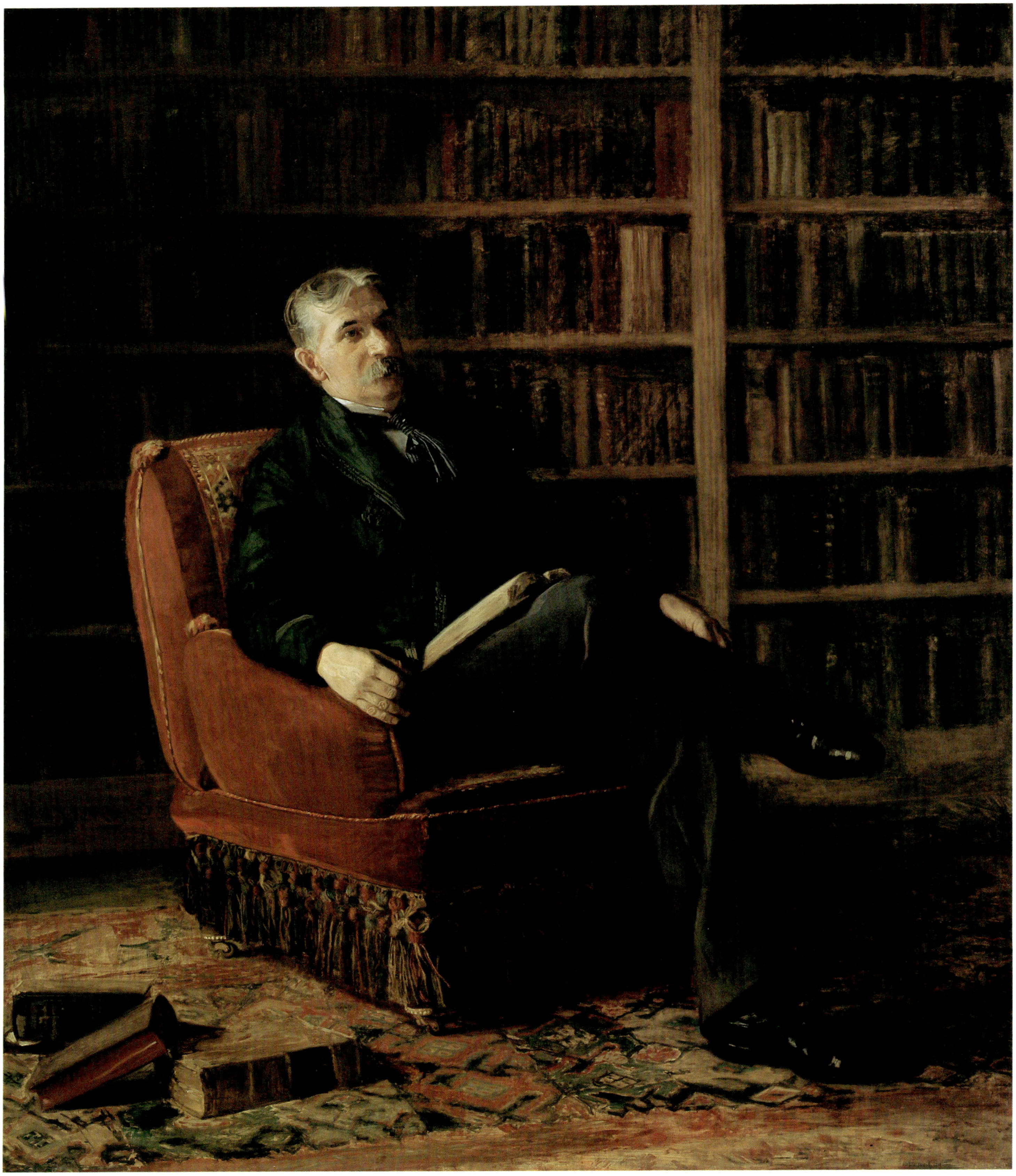

CAT. NO. 153

with him forbidding the introduction of a nude model. 'I would not have consented to deliver the lectures had such a proposition been made,' he said. 'I never discovered that the Nude could be studied in any except the way I have adopted. All the muscles must be pointed out. To do this all drapery must be removed.'" The writer agreed with Eakins and posed a question in the article indicative of his liberal views about art: "If the Trustees . . . are going to 'play propriety' with Art, what kind of artists do they expect to turn out?"[2]

Eakins's portrait of Fitzgerald captures the spirit of the journalist's open-minded opinions and commitment to intellectual life. He is portrayed as a genteel figure enjoying a leisurely and contemplative lifestyle. An open book in his lap, he thoughtfully gazes into the distance, apparently lost in the realm of ideas. The rich palette of deep red, tinged with blue and green, heightens the warmth and comfort of the scene. The casually strewn books at Fitzgerald's side; the worn, tasseled velvet chair; and the smoking jacket the sitter wears over formal attire all contribute to the perceived spontaneity of the scene.

Riter Fitzgerald was one of four works submitted by Eakins to the 1895 annual exhibition of the Pennsylvania Academy of the Fine Arts. Fitzgerald, who reviewed the exhibition for the *Sunday Item*, recognized that the apparently casual setting of the portrait was in fact artfully composed. "The chair is placed diagonally across the painting, giving the artist an excellent opportunity not only to paint it effectively, but to pose his subject in a most natural and unaffected manner." He commented further on Eakins's use of props, noting in a somewhat biased manner that, "where these are skillfully combined with a perfect likeness, a great picture is the result."[3] A preparatory oil sketch for the painting (fig. 77) also attests to Eakins's painstaking efforts to achieve a balanced composition.[4]

In this review and others, Fitzgerald positioned himself as a spokesman for Eakins's work. When the painter mounted the only one-man show of his career at the Earles' Galleries in Philadelphia in May 1896,[5] the critic drew attention to the artist's method of depicting his sitters in their own homes. About this practice, he quoted Eakins verbatim: "The home surroundings have the effect of giving a natural look to the picture which I think will add to its value."[6] This was the only notice of any length devoted to the Earles' Galleries exhibition. Fitzgerald continued to be Eakins's mouthpiece and defender. This portrait is a testament not only to the crucial role Fitzgerald played in the latter part of the artist's career, but to his integrity, intelligence, and commitment to the defense of art that presents its subjects with "imperfections, blemishes, and all."[7]

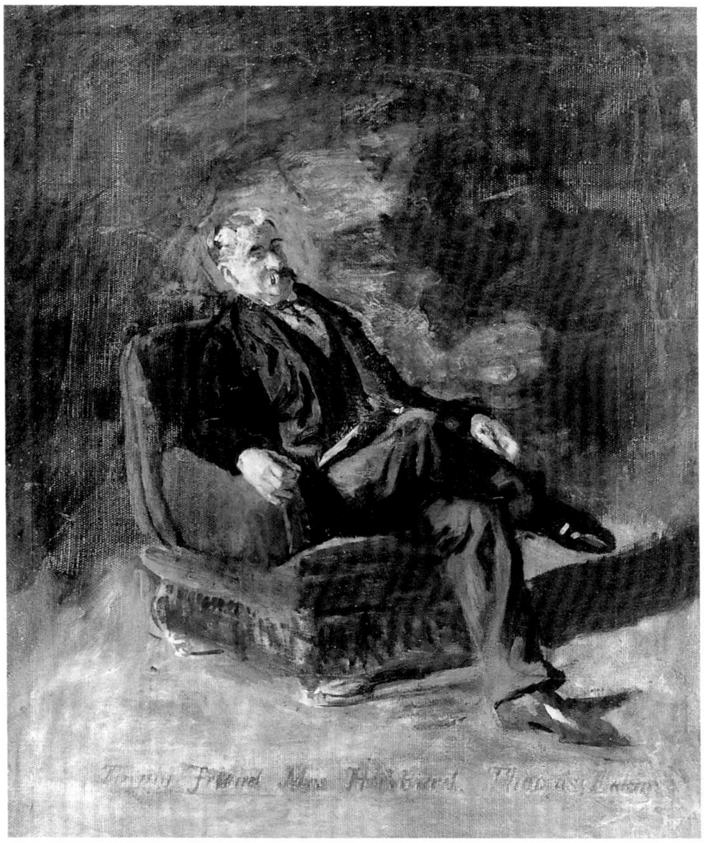

FIG. 77. Thomas Eakins (1844–1916). *Sketch for the portrait of Riter Fitzgerald*, c. 1895. Oil on canvas; 55.9 x 45.7 cm (22 x 18 in.). Photograph courtesy of the Huntington Library, Art Collections and Botanical Gardens, San Marino, Calif.

NOTES

1. See, for example, *Professor William D. Marks* (1886; Washington University Gallery of Art, St. Louis) and *Dr. Horatio C. Wood* (c. 1890; Detroit Institute of Arts). Both portraits depict men seated at a desk in their study or library surrounded by books. For more about Eakins's paintings of prominent figures, see Elizabeth Johns, *Thomas Eakins: The Heroism of Modern Life* (Princeton, N.J., 1983).

2. Riter Fitzgerald, "Nude Models," *Philadelphia Evening Item,* Mar. 14, 1895, p. 1.

3. Riter Fitzgerald, "A Great Exhibition," *Philadelphia Sunday Item,* Dec. 22, 1895, p. 8.

4. This version is inscribed, *To my Friend Mrs. Hubbard Thomas Eakins.* Another smaller (13 x 10½ in.) sketch of *Riter Fitzgerald* is in a private collection. Eakins also painted a portrait of Mrs. Hubbard, Fitzgerald's sister. It was destroyed by Mrs. Hubbard's daughter. Both are documented in Lloyd Goodrich, *Thomas Eakins: His Life and Work* (New York, 1933), p. 186.

5. See Evan H. Turner, "Thomas Eakins: The Earles' Galleries Exhibition of 1896," *Arts Magazine* 53 (May 1979), pp. 100–107, for a complete assessment of this exhibition.

6. Riter Fitzgerald, "Thomas Eakins," *Philadelphia Evening Item,* May 12, 1896, p. 1.

7. Fitzgerald (note 2), p. 1.

154. JAMES McNEILL WHISTLER (1834–1903)

Arrangement in Flesh Color and Brown: Portrait of Arthur Jerome Eddy, 1894

Oil on canvas; 209.9 x 92.4 cm (82⅝ x 36⅜ in.)
Signed, middle right: butterfly monogram
Arthur Jerome Eddy Memorial Collection, 1931.501

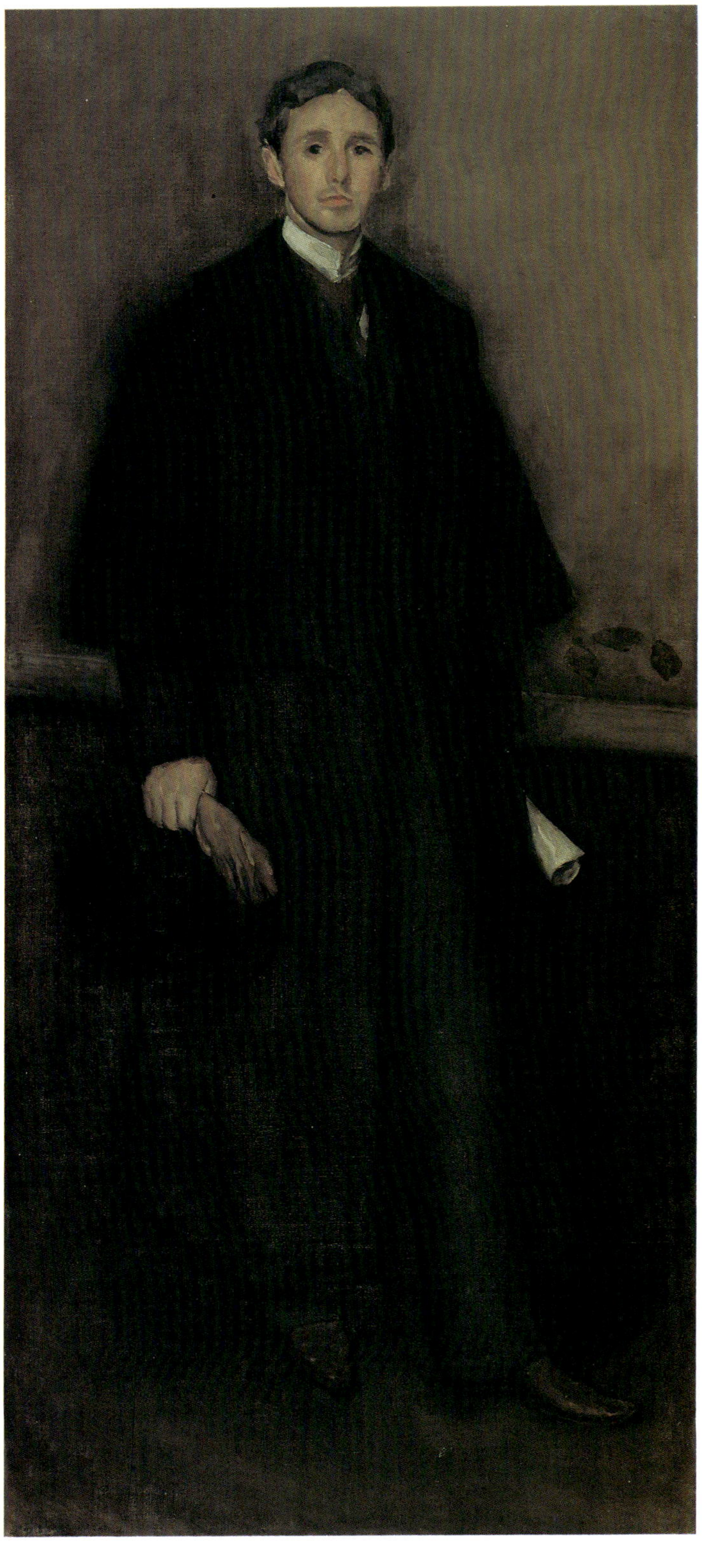

CAT. NO. 154

Full-length portraits such as this one depicting Chicago lawyer and art collector Arthur Jerome Eddy comprise a significant portion of James McNeill Whistler's artistic output. Like his tonally spare, musically titled landscapes (see cat. no. 101), Whistler's portraits interpret their subjects as much through color and form as through likeness. These portraits are often called "arrangements," linking them to musical composition and to the conscious shaping of space.[1] Eddy, a friend and admirer of Whistler as well as an astute and sensitive art critic, wrote: "Whistler's art was purely sensuous, as the finest music is sensuous. He had no interest whatsoever in the many problems of life and death, in the story of any person or the traditions of any place."[2]

Eddy commissioned this portrait in 1893, and it was initially painted in the artist's Paris studio over the course of six weeks. During his sitting, Eddy made notes on Whistler's method that he turned into a book-length recollection upon the death of the artist in 1903.[3] An early collector and champion of European modernism of the early twentieth century, Eddy went on to write the first American book on Cubism and abstract art in 1914; he also lectured on modern art at the Art Institute, and at least twice his subject was Whistler.[4] The relationship between the two men seems to have been a fond and aesthetically compatible one. Although Whistler labored over Eddy's portrait long after his subject returned to the United States, Eddy did not lose patience with the painter. He wrote to Whistler on November 20, 1894: "I can not tell you how glad I am to hear the picture is finished to your satisfaction. That is news I did not expect. All the trouble of the posing was recompensed in the delightful hours spent with you."[5] After receiving and hanging the portrait, he wrote: "The portrait is here on the wall at my right. . . . I am more than pleased with it. . . . Mrs. Eddy admires it greatly as a picture but thinks it does not do me justice as a portrait—my friends hold various and conflicting views as to the likeness . . . but nothing said disturbs my conviction that it is fine—both as picture and portrait."[6]

Whistler depicted Eddy as he did many of his sitters: in a muted palette against a gray background, projecting an elegant, subdued air. Eddy commented on the magic of Whistler's technique: "And so the portrait would really grow,

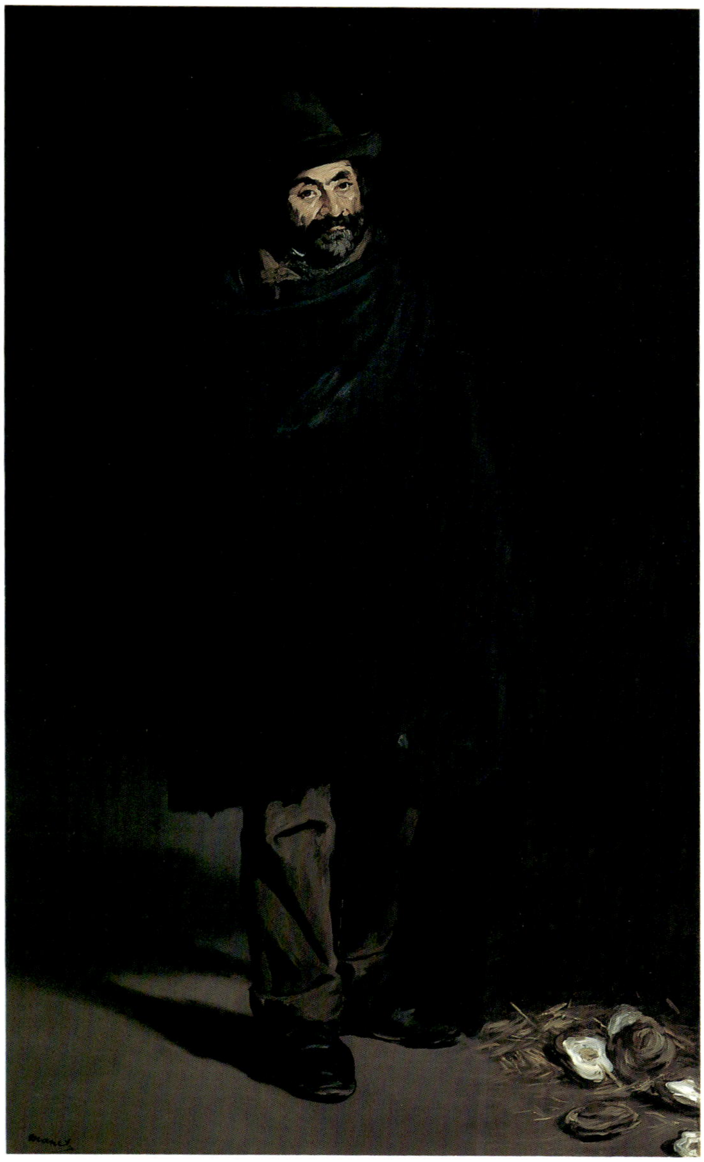

FIG. 78. Édouard Manet (French, 1832–1883). *Philosopher (with Hat),* 1865/67. Oil on canvas; 187.3 x 108 cm (73¾ x 42½ in.). The Art Institute of Chicago, Arthur Jerome Eddy Memorial Collection (1931.504).

really develop as an entirety, very much as a negative under the action of the chemicals comes out gradually—lights, shadows, and all from the first indications to their full values. It was as if the portrait were hidden within the canvas and the master by passing his wands day after day over the surface evoked the image."[7] Whistler's portrait style, like the styles of many of his contemporaries, was indebted to that of the Spanish master Diego Velázquez, who painted assertive portraits using bravura brushwork, usually placing his subjects against a flat gray or brown backdrop rather than setting them in an elaborate landscape or interior. Édouard Manet also used a similar technique to great effect in his single-figure compositions, one of which, *The Philosopher* (fig. 78), Eddy owned. This work is a fanciful, ironic rendering of an indigent man wearing the cape and carrying the walking stick of an urban sophisticate.

Whistler also pursued the connection between himself and Velázquez in an earlier painting now in the Art Institute: *The Artist in His Studio* (fig. 79).[8] He originally intended a monumental, ten-foot-high version of this painting that would consciously refer to the Spanish master's *Las Meninas* (1656; Museo del Prado, Madrid), the Spanish artist's controversial exploration of artistic identity, but never realized his ambition.[9] What remains is a rather languid accounting of Whistler's obsessions: his self-image, his collection of Asian art, and his lover Joanna Hiffernan, seated on the chaise wearing a white dress similar to the one she wears in *Symphony in White, No. 1* (1862; National Gallery of Art, Washington, D.C.).

Whistler appears less confident in this painting than in many other self-portraits, and seems to define himself less by

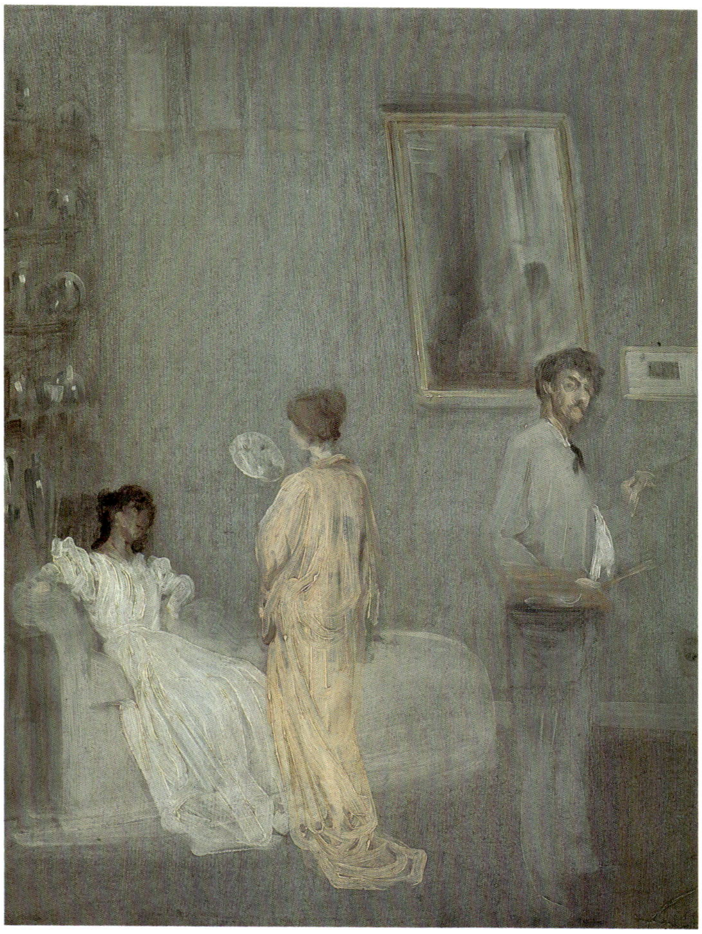

FIG. 79. James McNeill Whistler (1834–1903). *The Artist in His Studio,* 1865/66. Oil on paper, mounted on panel; 62.9 x 46.4 cm (24¾ x 18¼ in.). The Art Institute of Chicago, Friends of American Art Collection (1912.141).

his likeness than by the objects of beauty with which he has surrounded himself. He holds a brush and palette in his hands, but we cannot see what he is painting; perhaps it is the viewer he has taken as his subject, as he peers straight out of the canvas as if at his sitter. Compared to those in the Eddy portrait, the colors in Whistler's self-portrait are lighter and applied in clearly identifiable gestures that lend a certain spontaneity and sketchiness to this scene. Yet both canvases transcend mere likeness, and convey an aura of enigma and subtle indulgence in their sensuous presentation.

NOTES

1. The title of this work comes from an inscription in Whistler's hand on the canvas verso: *Arrangement in / Flesh Colour & Brown, / Portrait of Arthur J. Eddy. / of Chicago.* [butterfly monogram] *Painted in my Studio in / Paris. October. 1894. / J. McNeill Whistler.*

2. Arthur Jerome Eddy, *Recollections and Impressions of James A. McNeill Whistler* (Philadelphia and London, 1903), p. 179.

3. Ibid.

4. Letters from director William M. R. French to Arthur Jerome Eddy, Aug. 6 and 16, 1907, Archives, The Art Institute of Chicago. For more on Eddy as a collector, lecturer, and writer, see Paul Kruty, "Arthur Jerome Eddy and His Collection: Prelude and Postscript to the Armory Show," *Arts Magazine* 61, 6 (Feb. 1987), pp. 40–47.

5. Letter from Arthur Jerome Eddy to James McNeill Whistler, Nov. 20, 1894, Glasgow University Library, Glasgow, Scotland.

6. Letter from Arthur Jerome Eddy to James McNeill Whistler, Dec. 5, 1894, Glasgow University Library, Glasgow, Scotland.

7. Quoted in Robin Spencer, *Whistler* (London, 1990), p. 132.

8. A second version of this work, painted on cardboard and titled *The Artist's Studio* (c. 1865), is in the Hugh Lane Municipal Gallery of Modern Art, Dublin.

9. For more information on this connection, see Eric Denker, *In Pursuit of the Butterfly: Portraits of James McNeill Whistler*, exh. cat. (Washington, D.C., National Portrait Gallery, 1995), pp. 55–58.

155. FRANK LLOYD WRIGHT (1867–1959)

Library Table, 1896

Manufactured by John W. Ayers, Chicago

Oak and pine; 77.9 x 121.3 cm (30⅝ x 47¾ in.)

Gift of Roger White in memory of Charles E. Roberts, 1966.389

Like those of his Prairie School colleagues, Frank Lloyd Wright's principles of architecture and design developed from

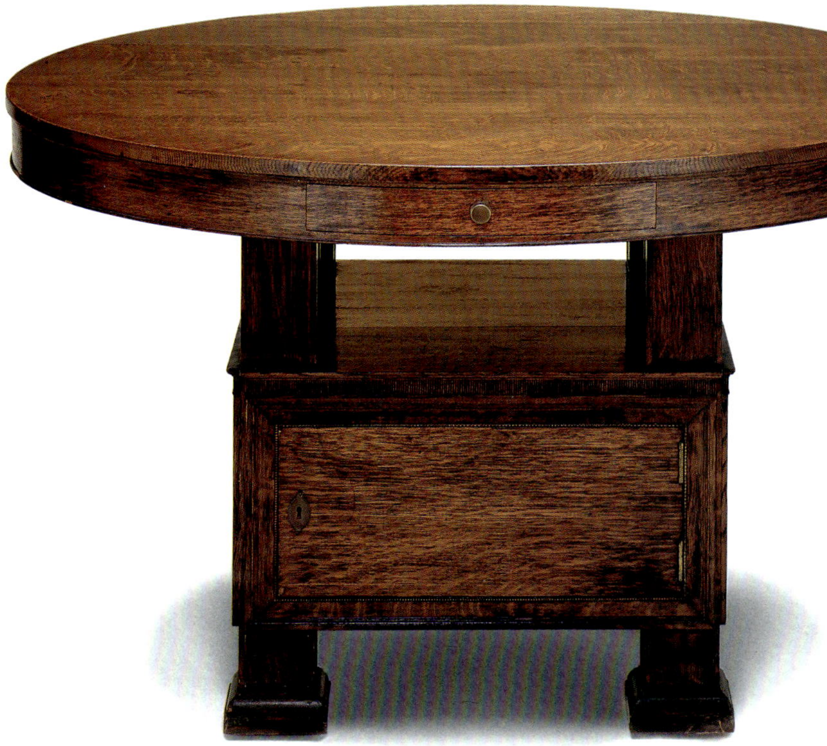

CAT. NO. 155

the English Arts and Crafts movement. The Prairie architects shared the Arts and Crafts philosophy of simplicity of design, visually understandable construction, and plain, high-quality materials. Wright's approach differed from the artisanal one of his English colleagues, however, in that he championed the use of machinery in making well-designed objects.

Wright became a charter member of the Chicago Arts and Crafts Society in 1897, and like other Arts and Crafts practitioners, he lamented the decline of craftsmanship and good design. Many English and American proponents of the Arts and Crafts philosophy advocated a return to medieval design principles and handcrafted work as the only solution. By 1901, however, Wright believed that machinery could be used to simplify and improve design. His radical departure from traditional Arts and Crafts philosophy was summarized in his now famous address entitled "The Art and Craft of the Machine."[1]

Wright believed that the machine could be used to simplify design, and strip it of unnecessary ornament. He also maintained that the machine could be used to preserve the nature of materials and that beauty was drawn from design itself. Wright's library table designed for the remodeling of the Charles E. Roberts House is similar to many English Arts and Crafts designs,[2] although it is far more geometric and balanced in its massed horizontal and vertical lines. Lack of ornamentation emphasizes the beauty of the fumed oak surface. While machinery was extensively used to make this table, the hand of the craftsman is also apparent in the beading.

At this early date, Wright was designing his furniture to match the building environment. The Roberts library table is of the same wood and contains the same detailing as the paneled room for which it was intended.[3]

NOTES

1. Wright gave his address "The Art and Craft of the Machine" on March 1, 1901, to the Chicago Arts and Crafts Society. It was reviewed in the *Chicago Tribune* on March 4, 1901, and reprinted in the exhibition catalogue of the Chicago Architectural Club in 1901. The date of the lecture was erroneously published in H. Allen Brooks, *The Prairie School: Frank Lloyd Wright and His Midwest Contemporaries* (Toronto, 1972), as March 6.

2. See especially Philip Webb's library table illustrated in David A. Hanks, *The Decorative Designs of Frank Lloyd Wright* (New York, 1979), p. 34.

3. Most of his furniture designs prior to 1907 were manufactured by cabinetmaker John W. Ayers of Chicago. See David A. Hanks, "Introduction: The Art and Craft of the Machine," in *Frank Lloyd Wright: Art in Design* (New York, 1983), pp. 10–11.

156. FRANK LLOYD WRIGHT WITH GEORGE MANN NIEDECKEN (1878–1945)

Desk, 1908

Oak; 144.9 x 102 x 60.6 cm (57 x 40⅛ x 23⅞ in.)
Restricted gift of the Graham Foundation for Advanced Studies in the Fine Arts, 1972.304

Wright considered his design of the Avery Coonley House (fig. 80) to be one of his most successful. It reflected the partnership between a liberal client and a great designer, which was cemented by trust. The Coonleys were a sophisticated couple: they were progressive thinkers, publicists and practitioners of Christian Science, and they were drawn to Wright because they admired his rational planning and "the countenance of principle."[1] The Coonley House was one of the architect's most completely conceived interiors; he designed everything in the house including the carpets, table service, and linens.[2]

The Art Institute's desk was intended for the rear guest room of the Coonley House and echoes the facade's geometric forms and broad cantilever. Small square doors with decorative banding suggest the casement windows, and applied horizontal moldings across the base supports echo those on the exterior of the building.

A watercolor rendering of the desk by interior architect George Mann Niedecken (fig. 81) shows the collaboration between Wright and the president of the interior design firm of Niedecken-Walbridge Company, Milwaukee.[3] The two probably met through the Arts and Crafts Society, and Niedecken worked in Wright's studio in 1904.[4] Scholars disagree about the amount of autonomy Niedecken had in designing furniture for Wright's houses. While Niedecken made finished renderings such as this one, he probably worked from Wright's sketches. He may also have finished details of the Coonley House interior after Wright left for Germany in 1909. Indeed, the moldings that form the desk's feet are typical of Neidecken's designs rather than Wright's simpler conceptions. Niedecken was a capable designer in his own right, designing murals, special fixtures, and furniture.[5] His sympathy for the Prairie School's integration of the building with its furnishings and natural environment made him an ideal choice for collaborations with architects such as Wright, George Grant Elmslie, and George W. Maher.

Niedecken's asymmetrical wash drawing with floating

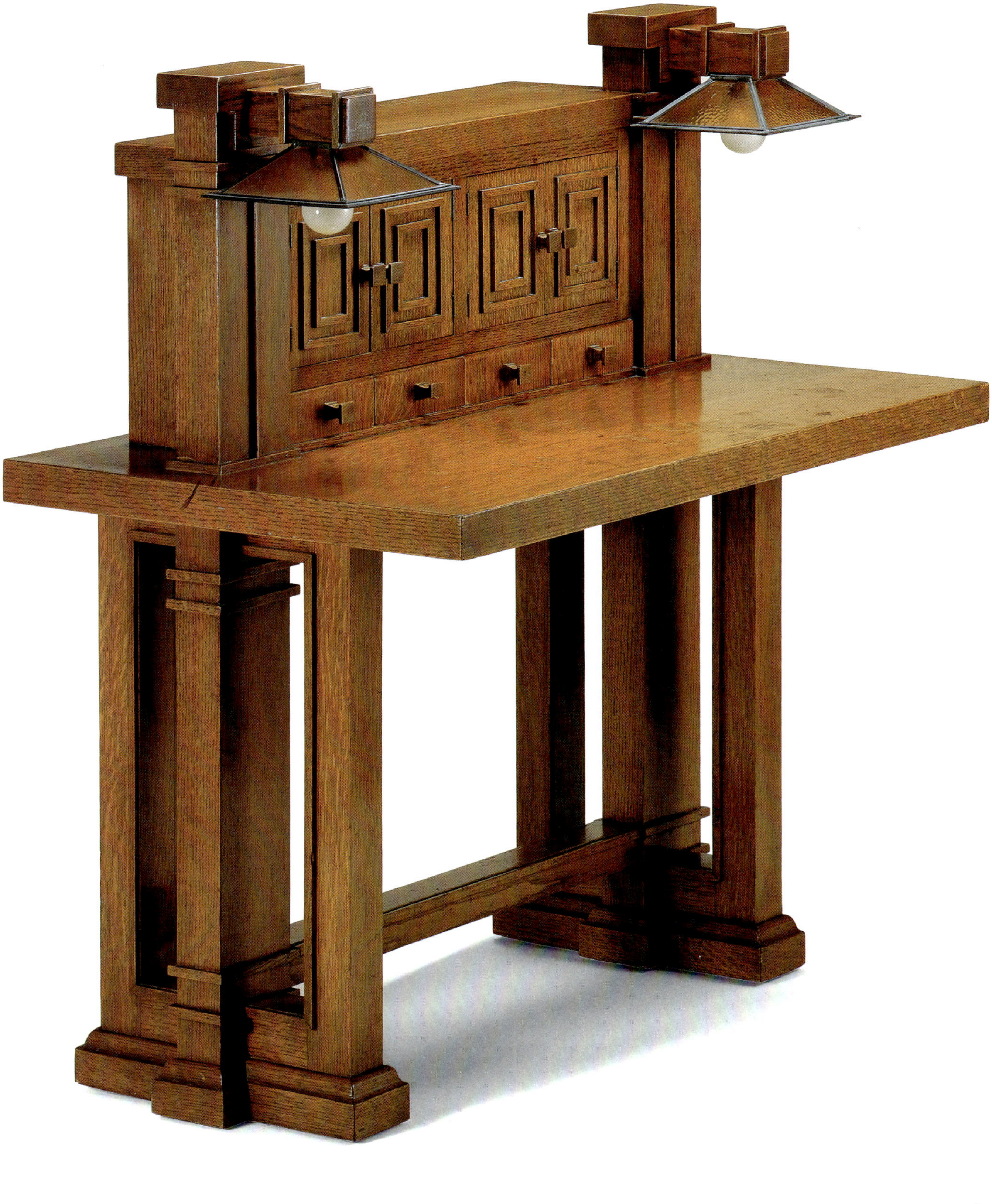

CAT. NO. 156

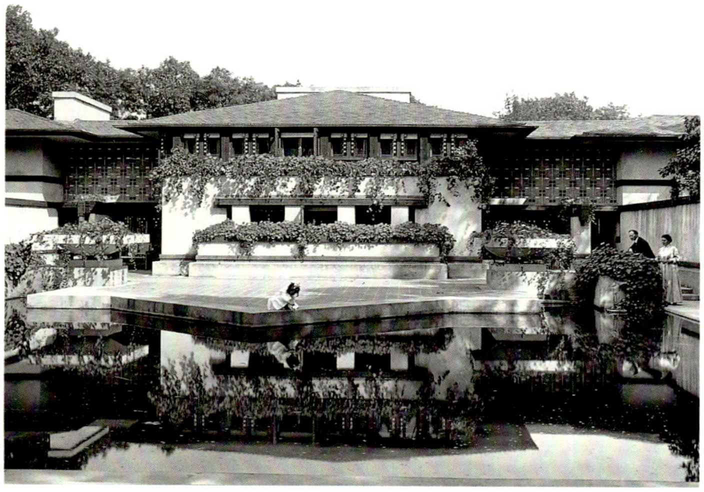

FIG. 80. Frank Lloyd Wright. Avery Coonley House, Riverside, Ill., 1908. Photograph by Henry Fuermann.

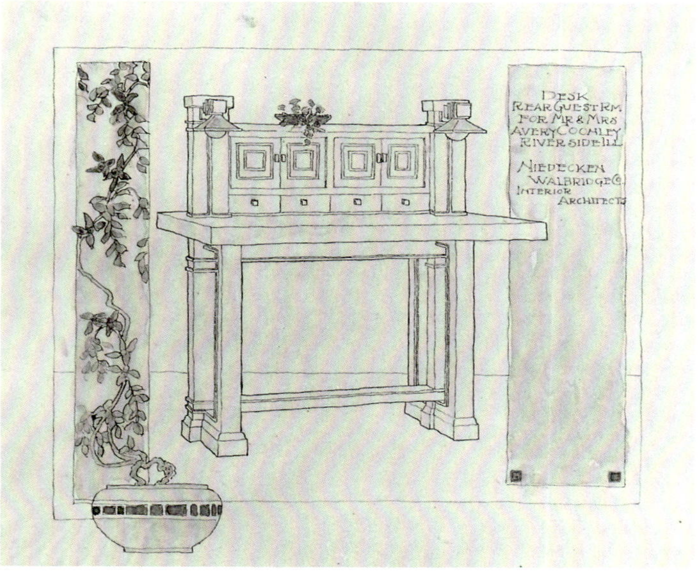

FIG. 81. George Mann Niedecken (1878–1945) for Frank Lloyd Wright (1867–1959). *Rendering of a Desk for the Avery Coonley House*, c. 1907. Ink and watercolor on paper; 27.9 x 39.4 cm (11 x 15½ in.). The Art Institute of Chicago, Gift of Mr. and Mrs. James Howlett (1990.41).

panels in overlapping planes, a meandering vine, and flattened decorative elements recalls Japanese woodblock prints. The repeated squares of the doors, handles, and pottery also echo the influence of the Vienna Seccessionist designs of Josef Hoffmann and Koloman Moser.

NOTES

1. Leonard K. Eaton, *Two Chicago Architects and Their Clients: Frank Lloyd Wright and Howard Van Doren Shaw* (Cambridge, Mass., 1969), pp. 82–84.

2. John Lloyd Wright, *My Father Who Is on Earth* (New York, 1946), pp. 41–42.

3. John Ayers's workshop, where furniture designed by Wright was made, burned in 1907; after that date, Wright used Niedecken-Walbridge for furniture manufacture.

4. Nancy Morris Smith, ed., "Letters, 1903–06, by Charles E. White, Jr., from the Studio of Frank Lloyd Wright," *Journal of Architectural Education* 25, 4 (fall 1971), pp. 104–12.

5. See Cheryl Robertson, *The Domestic Scene, 1897–1927: George M. Niedecken, Interior Architect*, exh. cat. (Milwaukee Art Museum, 1981), pp. 69–94. Niedecken was not a cabinetmaker, but he made drawings for furniture factories. Many of his renderings were manufactured by the F. H. Bresler Company.

157. GEORGE GRANT ELMSLIE (1871–1952)

Side Chair, 1910

Oak, laminated wood, leather, jute webbing, and horsehair (original upholstery);
127.3 x 48.9 x 41.2 cm (50⅛ x 19¼ x 16¼ in.)
Mrs. William P. Boggess II Fund, 1973.342

George Grant Elmslie was born in Scotland and emigrated to Chicago with his family in 1884. In 1887 he studied architecture in the office of Joseph Lyman Silsbee, where the staff included George Maher and Frank Lloyd Wright. In 1888 Wright joined the office of Louis Sullivan, and persuaded Elmslie to join him. Wright left the firm in 1893, and Elmslie became Sullivan's chief draftsman for the next fifteen years. As Sullivan's trusted colleague, Elmslie translated Sullivan's ideas into finished designs. Elmslie designed the ironwork entrance and the modular five-ply sawn-wood screens for the Schlesinger and Mayer (now Carson Pirie Scott and Company) department store in Chicago (1900–1903).[1]

Elmslie hired the Oak Park native William Gray Purcell in 1903. Purcell left the firm after five months, but the friendship between the two men continued. As early as 1907 Purcell and Elmslie corresponded about Purcell's residential designs, and in 1909 Elmslie left Sullivan's office to join Purcell and his Cornell classmate George Feick, Jr., in Minneapolis. The partnership of Purcell, Feick and Elmslie lasted until Feick's departure in

1913, after which the firm was known simply as Purcell and Elmslie.[2]

Purcell, devoted to the theory of organic architecture, rendered his ideas in notes and drawings that delineated overall structure. Feick attended to specifications and engineering problems. Elmslie translated these ideas into detailed graphic designs, and usually provided the drawings for furniture, terracotta, leaded glass panels, stencils, and other decorative arts.

While still in the employ of Sullivan, Elmslie designed a series of armchairs for residential use. Variations of tall-backed side chairs with cut-out splats were used at the Harold C. Bradley House (1909; Madison, Wisconsin; now Sigma Phi Alpha Society House of Wisconsin); the E. L. Powers House (fig. 82); the Mrs. T. B. Keith House (1910; Eau Claire, Wisconsin); the Amy Hamilton Hunter House (1916; Minneapolis); and as a wedding gift for his wife, Bonnie Hunter Elmslie.[3] Throughout the Powers House, the details of the space were tied together by the triangular, geometric motif seen in the chair backs and continued in the wall stenciling, terracotta detail in the front entrance, and sawn-wood design of the front door.

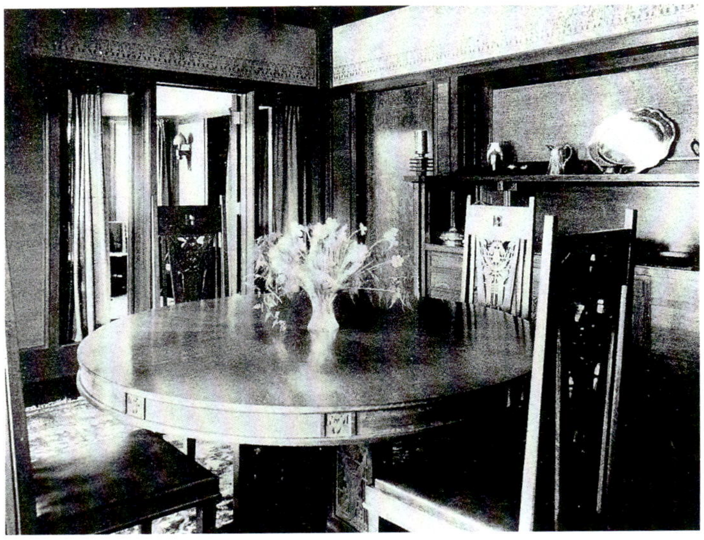

FIG. 82. Purcell, Feick and Elmslie. Dining room in E. L. Powers House, Minneapolis, 1916. Photograph from *Western Architect* 19, 1 (Jan. 1913), p. 19.

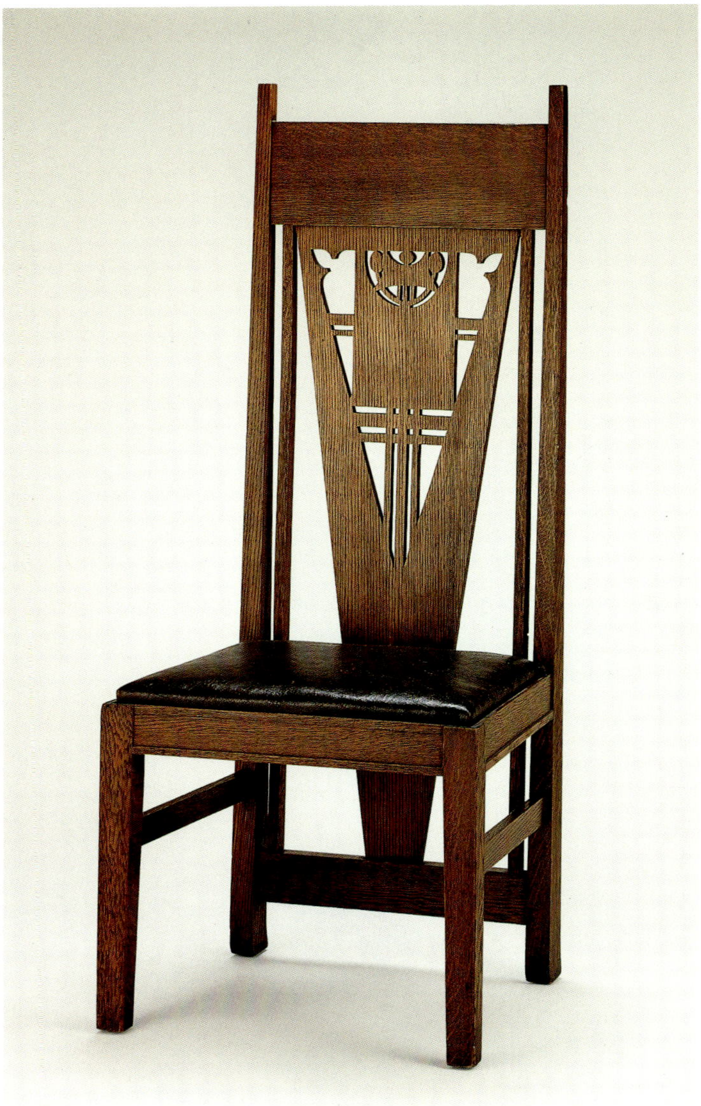

CAT. NO. 157

An oral provenance linked the Art Institute's chair to the Charles Purcell House in River Forest, Illinois (1909), but there is no documentary evidence that Elmslie designed furnishings for the house of his future partner's father.[4] However, an Elmslie drawing for the Mrs. T. B. Keith House dated June 1910 (fig. 83), which is now in the collection of the Northwest Architectural Archives at the University of Minnesota Libraries in St. Paul, matches exactly the pattern of the Art Institute's side chair.

The rectilinearity used in Elmslie's designs was also favored by other Prairie School architects such as Wright and European designers such as Charles Rennie Mackintosh.[5] Elmslie's chair designs show a strongly graphic sensibility.

NOTES

1. William Gray Purcell described watching Elmslie design these screens. See William Gray Purcell Papers, Correspondence (C: 124), Northwest Architectural Archives, University of Minnesota Libraries, St. Paul. Quoted in Mark Hammons, "Purcell and Elmslie, Architects," in Michael Conforti, ed., *Minnesota 1900: Art and Life on the Upper Mississippi, 1890–1915* (Newark, Del., 1994), pp. 220–21 n. 19.

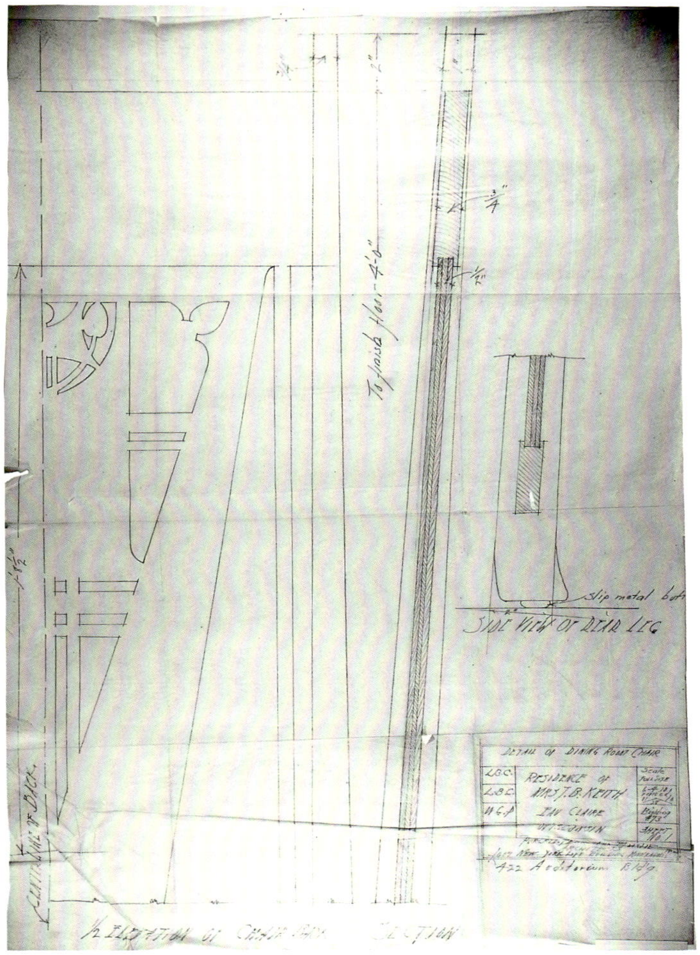

FIG. 83. George Grant Elmslie (1871–1952) of Purcell, Feick and Elmslie. *Full-Size Detail of Dining Chair for the Mrs. T. B. Keith House, Eau Claire, Wisconsin,* 1910. Photograph courtesy of the Northwest Architectural Archives, William Gray Purcell Papers, University of Minnesota Libraries, St. Paul.

2. David Gebhard, "William Gray Purcell and George Grant Elmslie and the Early Progressive Movement in American Architecture from 1900 to 1920" (Ph.D. diss., University of Minnesota, 1957).

3. Elmslie's furniture was fabricated by the Jean B. Hasswer Company, Chicago; John S. Bradstreet and Company, Minneapolis; and George M. Niedecken, Milwaukee. This chair bears no manufacturer's label, but is marked on the rear rail with the number 3.

4. Hammons (note 1), p. 256.

5. Edward S. Cooke, Jr., in Wendy Kaplan, ed., *"The Art That Is Life": The Arts and Crafts Movement in America, 1875–1920,* exh. cat. (Boston, Museum of Fine Arts, 1987), p. 204.

158. ROBERT RIDDLE JARVIE (1865–1941)

Candlesticks, 1905/15

Silver; 35.7 x 8.1 cm (14 x 3 3/16 in.)

Engraved in script on base of one candlestick: *Jarvie / I*

Bessie Bennett and Mrs. Herbert Stern funds, 1973.377–378

159. *Pitcher,* 1911

Silver; 26 x 20.3 cm (10 1/4 x 8 in.); diam. of base 16 cm (6 5/16 in.)

Engraved on underside: *PRESENTED TO / CHARLOTTE AILEEN HENRY / ON HER WEDDING DAY / OCTOBER THE TENTH / NINETEEN HUNDRED AND ELEVEN / BY / ALBERT AND MARY GRAY / ROBERT AND LILLIAN JARVIE / SAMUEL AND WINIFRED GRACIE / JAMES WILBUR GRAY and Made by the Shop of Robert Jarvie Chicago / STERLING*

Gift of Raymond W. Sheets, 1973.357

160. *Punch Bowl, Ladle, and Tray,* 1911

Silver; punch bowl: 25.7 x 39.3 cm (10 1/8 x 15 1/2 in.); ladle: 45.7 cm (18 in.); tray: diam. 52.7 cm (20 3/4 in.)

Embossed on rim: *PRESENTED TO JOHN J. HATTSTAEDT BY THE FACULTY OF THE AMERICAN CONSERVATORY OF MUSIC ON THE TWENTY-FIFTH ANNIVERSARY OF ITS FOUNDATION . . . 1886–1911*

Gift of Mr. and Mrs. John R. Hattstaedt in memory of his father, John J. Hattstaedt, 1974.293a–c

Robert Riddle Jarvie was a self-taught metalsmith who showed his work at the Chicago Arts and Crafts Society in the early years of the century. He exhibited candlesticks and lanterns in the Chicago Arts and Crafts Society's 1900 exhibition and soon came to public notice. At the same time he advertised in the Chicago publication *House Beautiful* as "the Candlestick Maker."[1] Jarvie fashioned the majority of his candlesticks in copper or cast bronze, and patinated their surfaces with brush polishing and acids to produce a green finish. The Art Institute owns a pair of Jarvie's thick, tubular, hammered copper candlesticks as well as this attenuated pair of silver candlesticks (cat. no. 158), which suggest a continuity and harmony between candlestick and candle.[2] The elongated sticks also take their inspiration from natural flower forms, reflecting the influence of the English Arts and Crafts movement. Jarvie's candlestick designs were elegant in geometry and proportion and were widely, if less successfully, imitated.

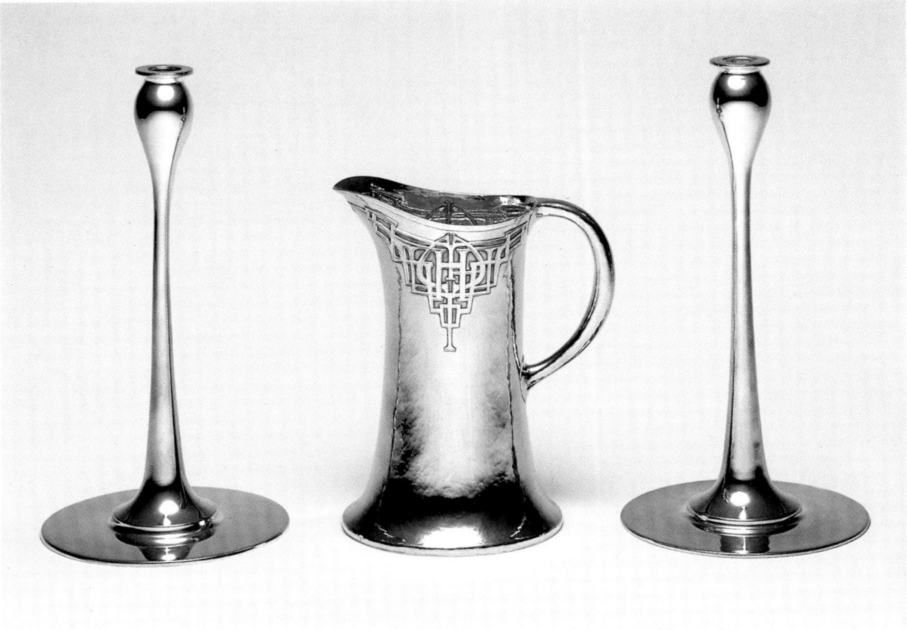

CAT. NOS. 158, 159

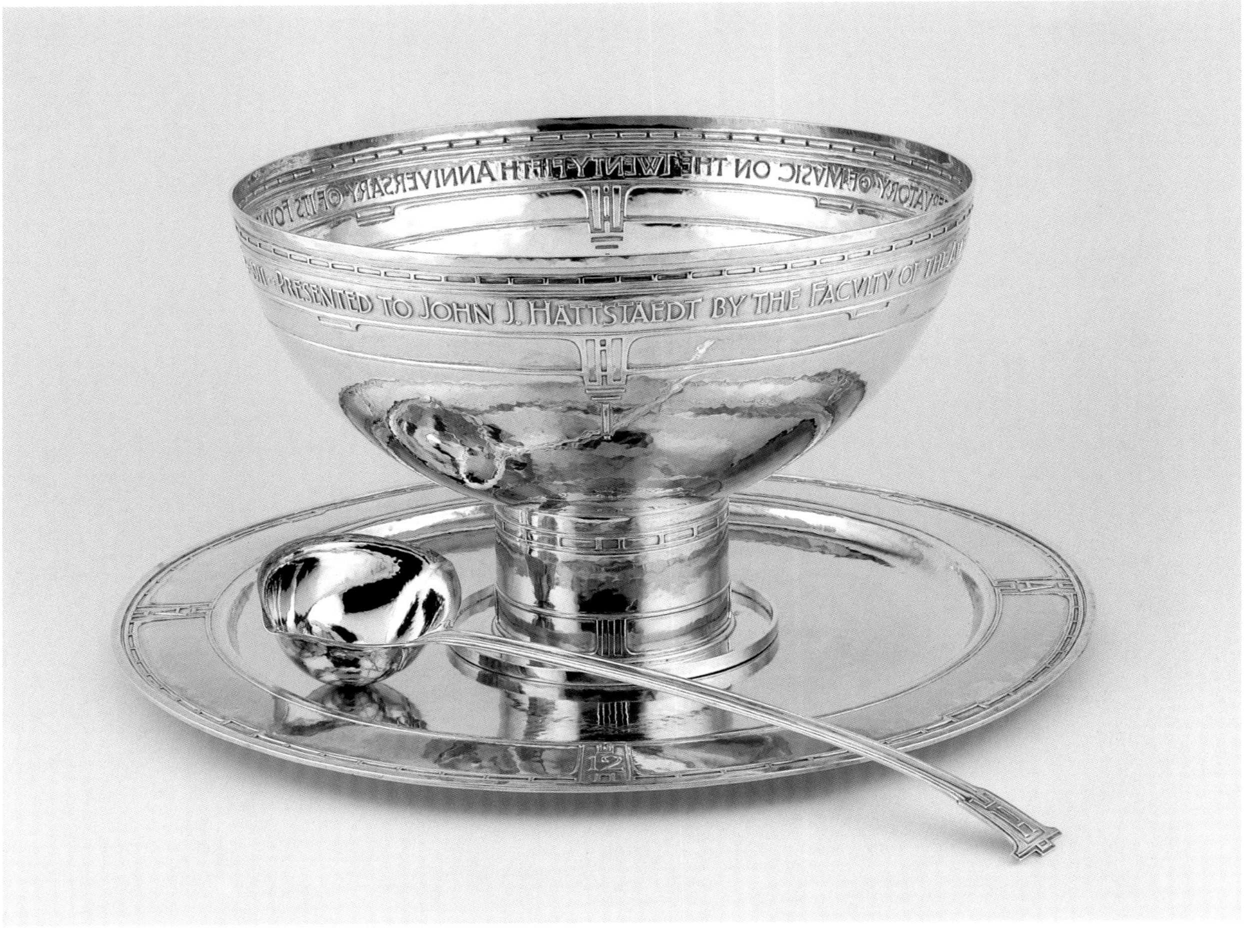

CAT. NO. 160

By 1905 he had opened the Jarvie Shop in the Fine Arts Building in Chicago, and in 1912 he moved his workshop to the Old English Cottage Building at the Chicago Stockyards.[3] There he fashioned trophies commissioned by Stockyards President Arthur G. Leonard to be given as awards at stockyard events. His presentation silver is some of his most innovative work. In the boldness of its footed form and broad expanses of unadorned surface, the Art Institute's Jarvie silver punch bowl (cat. no. 160) is indebted to English Arts and Crafts designers such as C. R. Ashbee. Its rectilinear, abstract decoration, however, reflects Jarvie's knowledge of the spare, linear fretwork designs of fellow Scotsman Charles Rennie Mackintosh. Jarvie's work after 1911, especially in trophies and presentation pieces is more closely tied to the geometric and abstract than to the naturalistic.

Jarvie's silver water pitcher (cat. no. 159), a wedding gift, incorporates the bride's initials, C.A.H., in an inverted heart within an embossed, Celtic-inspired design. The interlaced motif upon a stippled ground is perfectly balanced; the curve of the heart echoes the sweeping handle. Applied, interlaced strapwork designs were favored by Chicago metalsmiths.

Jarvie's ornamental style is draftsmanlike, possibly reflecting the influence of his friend and colleague George Grant Elmslie. Indeed, Jarvie's design on this pitcher is similar in feeling to some of the simplified arabesques and interlaced, abstracted designs Elmslie produced for the Babson House the following year (see cat. nos. 164–65).[4]

Jarvie went out of business sometime between 1917 and 1920. He was employed at C. D. Peacock, a Chicago jewelry store, until his retirement in the 1930s to the Scottish Old People's Home, where he died in 1941.

NOTES

1. See *House Beautiful* 9, 1 (Dec. 1900), pp. 2–8; and *House Beautiful* 10, 5 (Oct. 1901), p. 322.

2. W. Scott Braznell, in Wendy Kaplan, ed., *"The Art That Is Life": The Arts and Crafts Movement in America, 1875–1920*, exh. cat. (Boston, Museum of Fine Arts, 1987), p. 278.

3. Sharon Darling, *Chicago Metalsmiths: An Illustrated History* (Chicago, 1977), p. 61.

4. George Grant Elmslie's wife, Bonnie, worked in Jarvie's shop, and Elmslie executed some designs for Jarvie commissions. Those commissions, such as the trophy and commemorative book for the retiring University of Michigan president (1909), are far more organic, naturalistic, and curvilinear. See Edward J. Vaughn, "Sullivan and Elmslie at Michigan," *Prairie School Review* 6, 2 (1969), pp. 22–23.

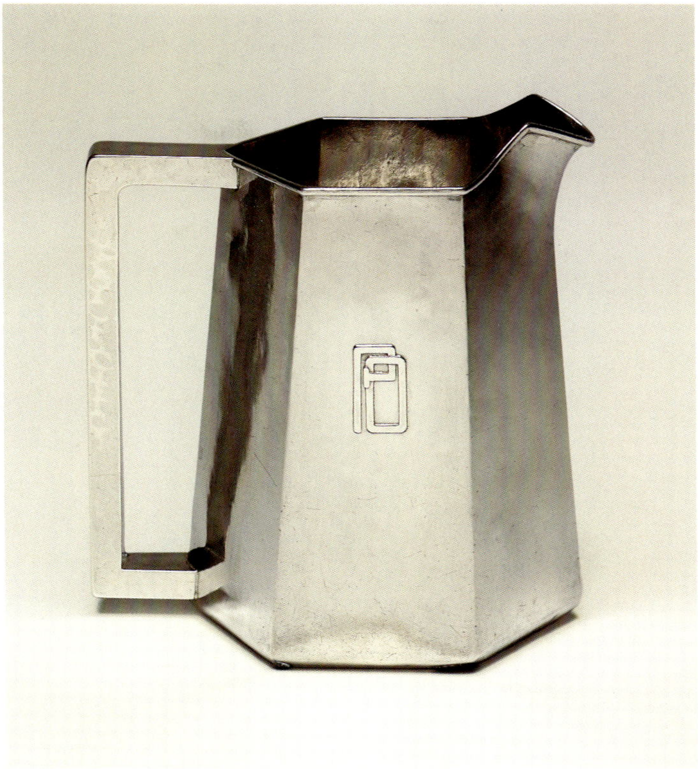

CAT. NO. 161

161. KALO SHOP

Water Pitcher, 1910

Silver; 18.4 x 16.5 cm (7¼ x 6½ in.)

Inscribed on base: *STERLING / HANDBEATEN / AT / KALO SHOPS / PARK RIDGE / ILLS. / 6863*

Gift of Mrs. Eugene A. Davidson, 1973.345

Founded by Clara P. Barck in 1900, the original Kalo Shop was one of the earliest silversmithing enterprises in Chicago. Barck graduated from the School of the Art Institute and chose the name Kalo, a Greek word meaning beauty, for the name of her shop. After her marriage in 1905, she became Clara Barck Welles and moved her craft community to rural Park Ridge, Illinois, still maintaining a retail shop downtown. At the height of the shop's operation, twenty-five artisans were employed—both men and women, for Welles was an advocate of women's involvement in the Arts and Crafts movement. Welles served as designer, teacher, and smith; and the shop's production included pitchers, bowls, trays, desk accessories, and jewelry in copper, brass, and silver.

The overall simplicity and hammered texture of early Kalo silver bespeaks its Arts and Crafts philosophical and aesthetic origins, yet the bold, geometric modern shape of this pitcher shows the influence of Prairie School aesthetics. Like the Prairie School architects who designed machine-made furniture, the Kalo Shop favored the look of hand-raised silver but often fashioned objects from machine-rolled sheets of metal. This seamed pitcher was fashioned in this way.

Early Kalo designs show the influence of the Englishman C. R. Ashbee's Guild of Handicraft. Products from Ashbee's guild were exhibited at the Art Institute in 1898, and two years later he lectured at the Art Institute.[1] Ashbee favored paneled designs such as this pitcher, and this motif is often found in Chicago art silver.[2] Like Robert Riddle Jarvie's work, the ornament is well integrated and balanced with the body of the object. The intertwined initials which subtly echo the overall silhouette of the piece were a favorite Prairie School decorative device.

NOTES

1. See *First Exhibition of the Chicago Arts and Crafts Society*, exh. cat. (The Art Institute of Chicago, 1898), p. 133; and Alan Crawford, *C. R. Ashbee: Architect, Designer, and Romantic Socialist* (New Haven, Conn., and London, 1985), pp. 96–98.

2. W. Scott Braznell, in Wendy Kaplan, ed., *"The Art That Is Life": The Arts and Crafts Movement in America, 1875–1920*, exh. cat. (Boston, Museum of Fine Arts, 1987), p. 280.

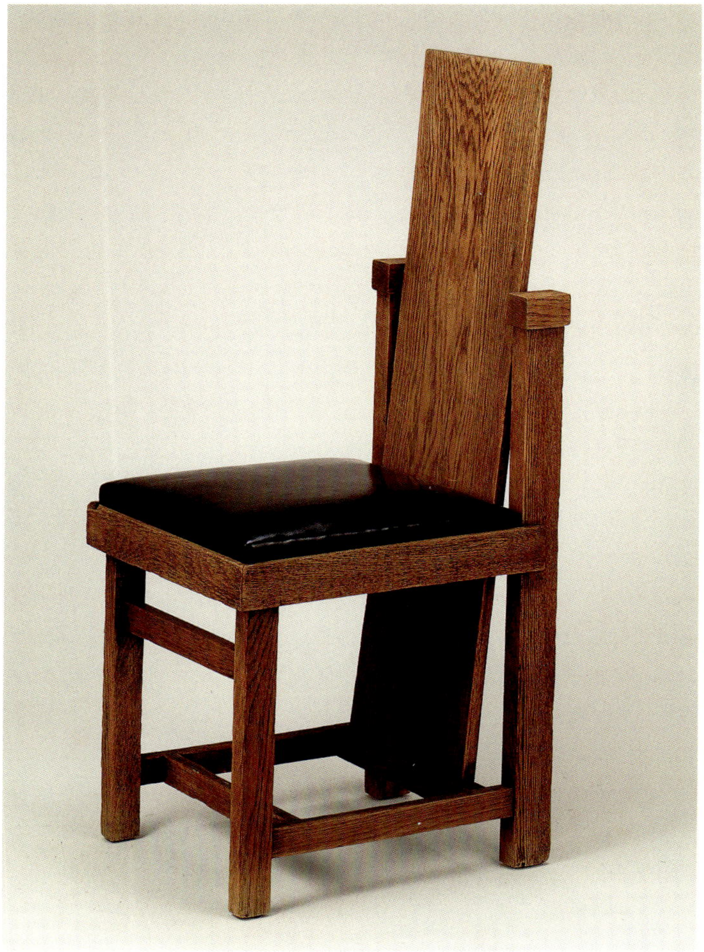

CAT. NO. 162

162. FRANK LLOYD WRIGHT (1867–1959)

Side Chair, 1904

Oak; 95.4 x 35.6 x 49.5 cm (37½ x 14 x 19½ in.)
Bessie Bennett Fund, 1977.523

The Larkin Administration Building (1902–06; Buffalo, New York; demolished 1950) and its furnishings were utilitarian. For the building itself, Wright designed a large central courtyard lit by a skylight. In this area, employees shared long desks with legless metal chairs attached, which were, in effect, self-contained work stations. Wood furniture, however, was also found throughout the building. The Art Institute's oak side chair was probably used in the employee dining area of the company[1] and is an early expression of Wright's designs that maximized the use of machinery. Simple oak boards were joined in such a manner that their intersecting planes became the design itself.

Wright's inspiration may have been examples by Christopher Dresser published in *Principles of Decorative Design* in 1873. In his illustrations for chairs, Dresser showed a slanting backboard joined to a seat frame and commented that "it cannot be doubted that a well-constructed work, however plain or simple it may be, gives satisfaction to those who behold it—while a work of the most elaborate character fails to satisfy if badly constructed."[2]

Wright's chair design for the Larkin Building developed the geometric balance and spatial effects that Charles Rennie Mackintosh also explored in the high-backed oak chairs designed for the Glasgow School of Art the same year. Years later, Wright's early conception of planar, rectilinear seating reached its apogee in Gerrit Rietveld's 1918 classic *Red-Blue Chair*. Wright used the Larkin Building chair, with minor variations, and usually with taller back posts, for other buildings. Other related chairs were designed for Wright's Oak Park, Illinois, studio (1904),[3] Unitarian Church (1904; Oak Park), and Hillside Home School (1903; Spring Green, Wisconsin).

NOTES

1. See Coy L. Ludwig, *The Arts and Crafts Movement in New York State, 1890s–1920s* (Hamilton, N.Y., 1983), p. 106.

2. Christopher Dresser, *Principles of Decorative Design*, 4th ed. (London and New York, [c. 1880]), p. 57.

3. See Leslie Greene Bowman, *American Arts and Crafts: Virtue in Design*, exh. cat. (Los Angeles, Los Angeles County Museum of Art, 1990), pp. 92–93.

163. FRANK LLOYD WRIGHT

Armchair, 1908

Oak; 86.9 x 58.5 x 57.1 cm (34¼ x 23 x 22½ in.)
Gift of Mrs. and Mrs. F. M. Fahrenwald, 1970.435

Square in plan, the Ray W. Evans House (1908) was built in the Beverly neighborhood on Chicago's South Side, and was another of Wright's integrated Prairie compositions. Wright, who hated radiators, designed radiator covers composed of vertical slats that allowed efficient heat circulation. In keeping with such utilitarian objects, Wright designed chairs and tables that extended the vertical-slat theme. Wright had created massive, square solid-oak armchairs for the B. Harley Bradley House (1900; Kankakee, Illinois), one of which is in the collection of the David and Alfred Smart Museum of Art at the University of Chicago. The Evans armchair is a more sophisticated interpretation of the form; Wright used positive and negative space to lighten the oak mass, and L-shaped feet to strengthen and broaden the chair's design. These feet, compared to the ball feet of a vertical-slat armchair designed by Purcell, Feick and Elmslie, for the Merchants Bank in Winona, Minnesota (now in the collection of the Art Institute), give the chair a monumental presence. Where Purcell, Feick and Elmslie's chair seems tight and self-contained, Wright's armchair seems to expand into the space around it.

The Art Institute also owns a library table from the Evans House that repeats the square, solid-oak mass penetrated and lightened by vertical elements.

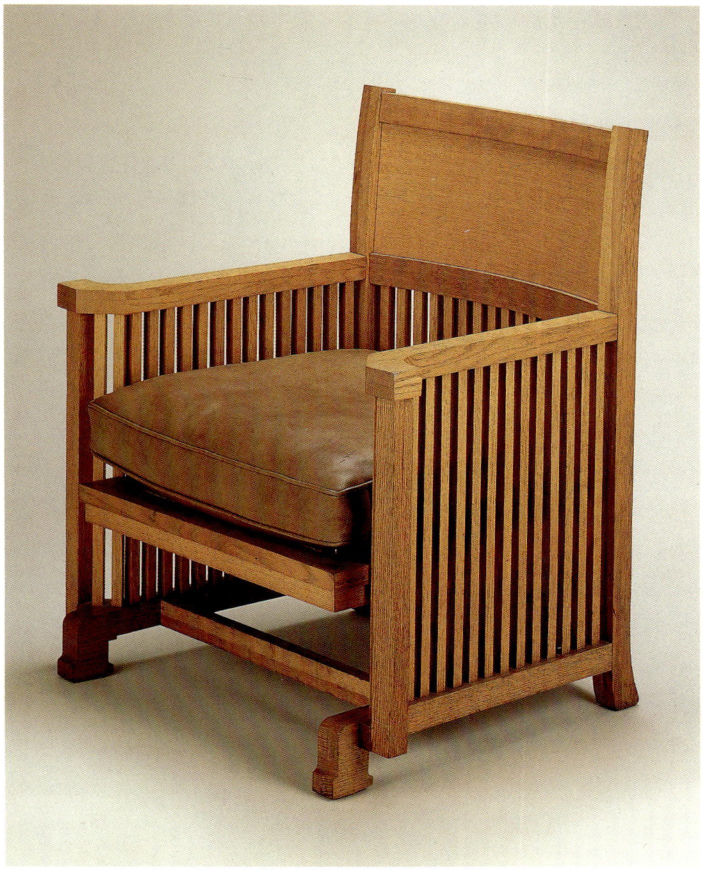

CAT. NO. 163

164. GEORGE GRANT ELMSLIE (1871–1952)

Tall Clock, 1912

Manufactured by the firm of Niedecken-Walbridge, Milwaukee
Mahogany with brass inlay; 213.3 x 66 x 40 cm (84 x 26 x 15¾ in.)
Restricted gift of Mrs. Theodore D. Tieken, 1971.322

165. *Andirons*, 1912

Brass, bronze, and cast iron;
26.5 x 20 x 72.4 cm each (10 7/16 x 7⅞ x 28½ in.)
Gift of Mrs. George A. Harvey, 1971.788a–b

George Grant Elmslie had been responsible for the built-in and freestanding furnishings of the Henry Babson House in Riverside, Illinois (1907), while still employed as Louis Sullivan's chief designer. In 1912 Babson asked Purcell and Elmslie to design eight pieces of furniture for this same structure.[1] One of these was a tall clock for a corner in the entrance hallway (cat. no. 164). Illustrated in the *Western Architect* in July 1915 (see fig. 84), the clock contained a cast-bronze face modeled by Chicago's Kristian Schneider, and the original hands were made by Chicago Arts and Crafts metalsmith Robert Riddle Jarvie.[2]

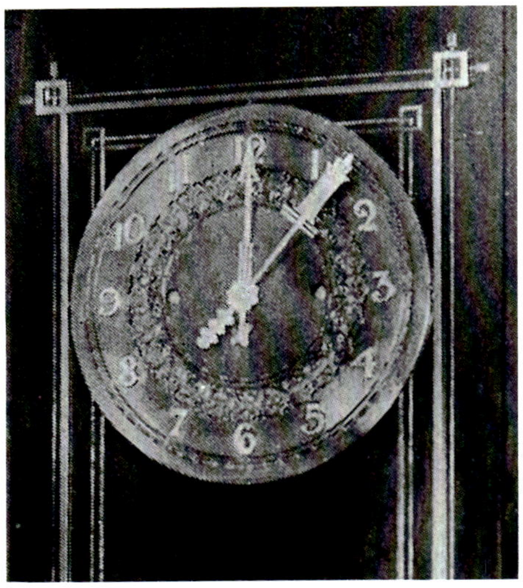

FIG. 84. George Grant Elmslie (1871–1952). Face of *Tall Clock* (cat. no. 164); cast bronze face modeled by Kristian Schneider; original hands made by Robert Riddle Jarvie. Photograph from *Western Architect* 22, 1 (July 1915), p. 9.

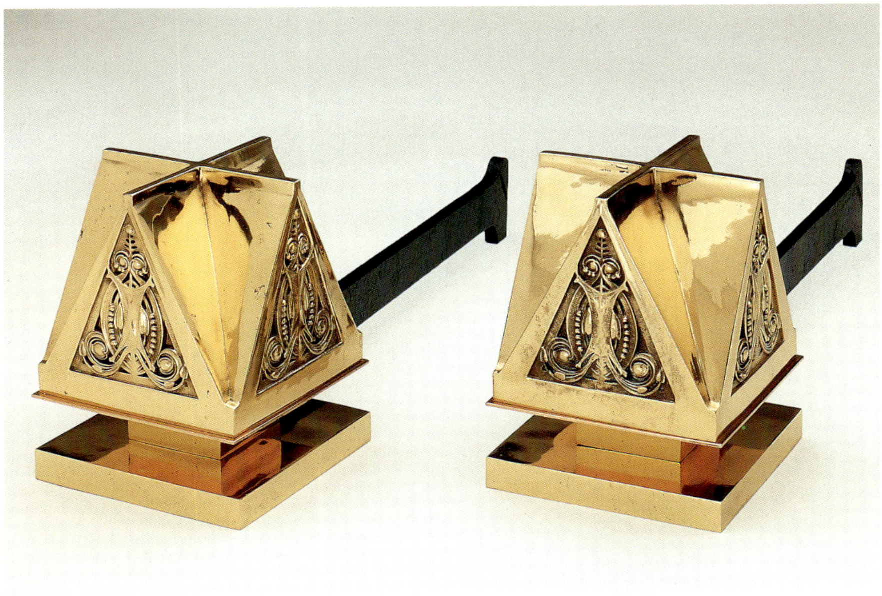

CAT. NO. 165

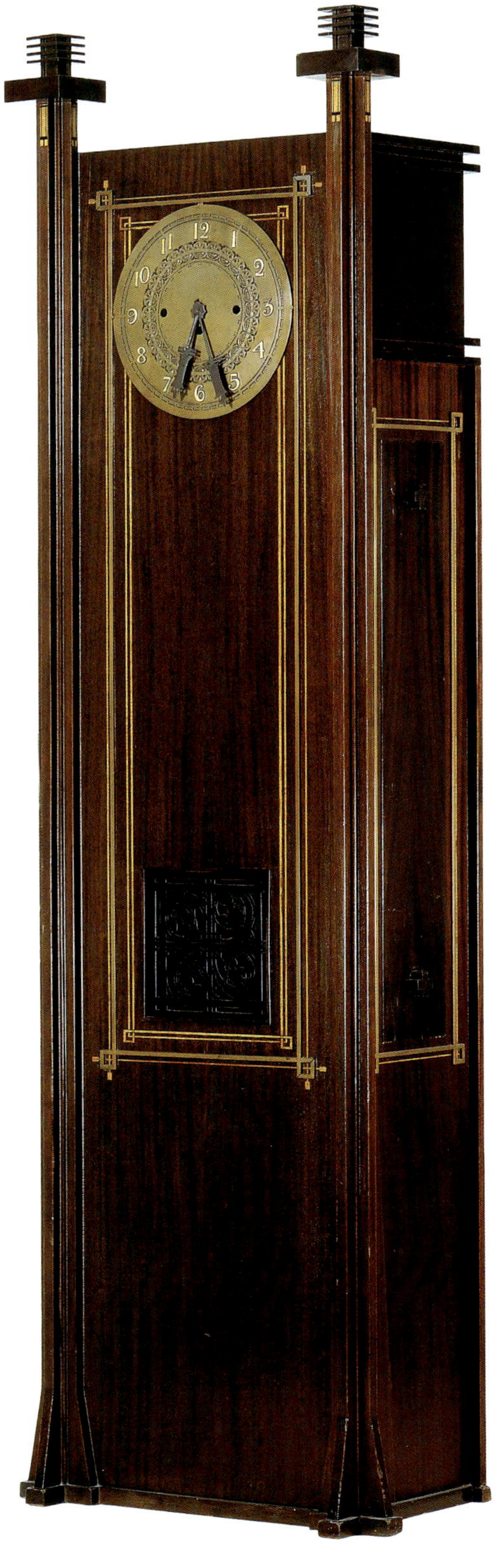

CAT. NO. 164

Made of mahogany, the case front is pierced by the familiar sawn-wood decorative technique favored by Elmslie. The piercing allows a view of the pendulum. The clock reflects the predilection of Purcell and Elmslie for decorative harmony—they often used a basic geometric form, usually rectilinear, tempered by a flowing organic motif drawn from nature. The rectilinear severity, perhaps inspired by Japanese temples, is softened by the four-part, sawn-wood design that repeats curling, natural tendrils arranged in subtle rotation.

Among the decorative motifs used at the Babson House, the four-part division emerges again in the fireplace andirons (cat. no. 165) designed for the hearth adjacent to what was the sleep-

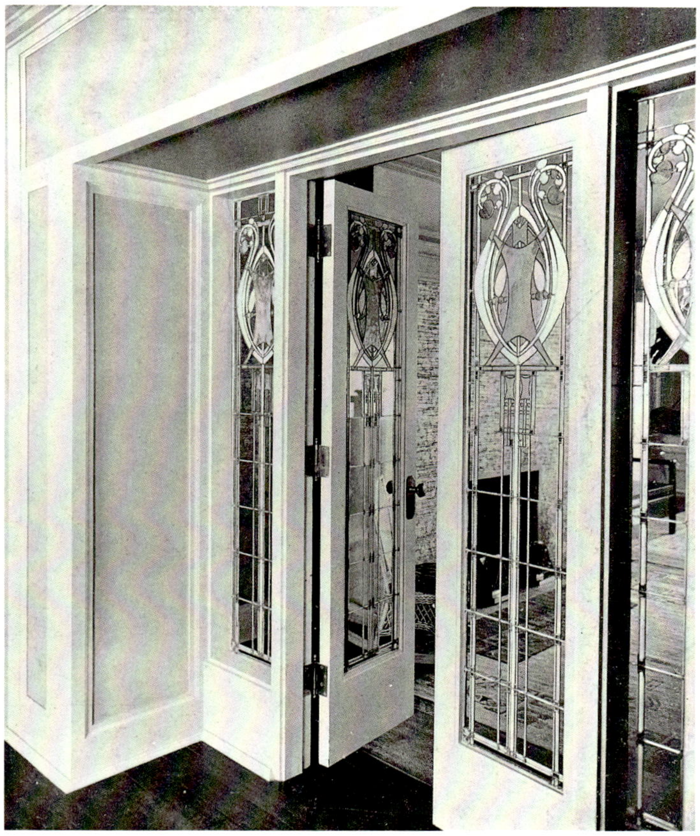

FIG. 85. Purcell, Feick and Elmslie. Sitting room doors for Henry B. Babson House, Riverside, Ill., 1912. Photograph from *Western Architect* 22, 1 (July 1915), pl. 5.

ing porch. The original sleeping porch was closed in during the 1912–14 renovations. The glass doors of the porch illustrated in the July 1915 issue of the *Western Architect* show the unified decorative plan. The motif on the andirons matches that of the doors. The andirons themselves are barely visible through the doors (see fig. 85). A third work from the Babson House in the Art Institute's collection is a carpet designed by Elmslie (fig. 86).

Henry Babson tried unsuccessfully to sell his house to the town of Riverside around 1960. Before the house was demolished, interior fittings, windows, and furnishings were salvaged.

NOTES

1. Sharon S. Darling, *Chicago Furniture: Art, Craft, and Industry, 1833–1983* (New York, 1984), p. 256.

2. The clock is described in William Gray Purcell, *Parabiography for 1912*, commission 142b, located in the Architectural Records, Purcell and Elmslie Archives, William Gray Purcell Papers, Northwest Architectural Archives, University of Minnesota Libraries, St. Paul. A blueprint drawing of the clock with the architects' embossed seal was in the George M. Niedecken Collection of the Prairie Archives, Milwaukee Art Center, and is now in a private collection.

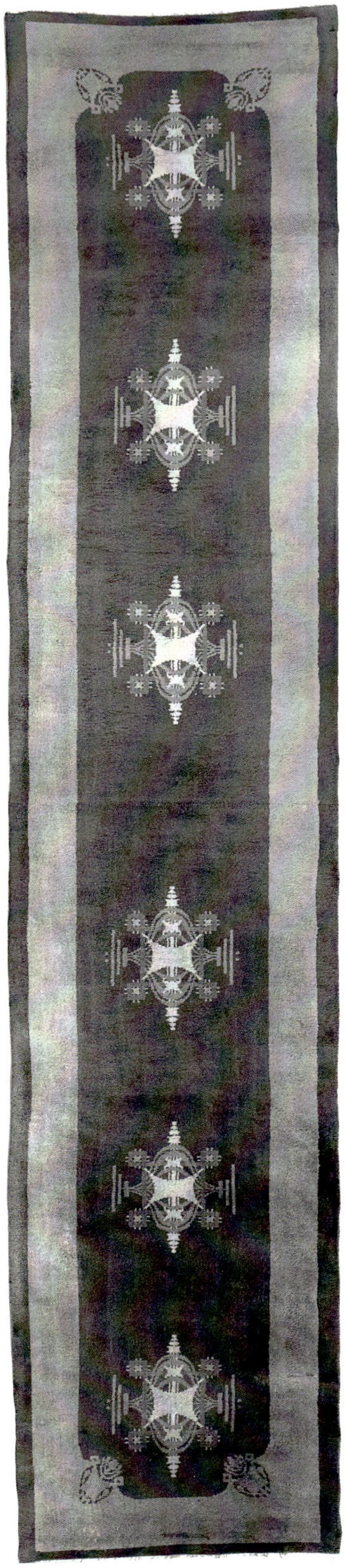

FIG. 86. George Grant Elmslie (1871–1952). *Carpet for Henry B. Babson House, Riverside, Illinois*, 1908/12. Linen, cotton, and wool, plain weave with "Ghiordes knots" cut pile; 560.1 x 115.7 cm (18 ft. 4½ in. x 3 ft. 9½ in.). The Art Institute of Chicago, Restricted gift of Mrs. Theodore D. Tieken (1972.1144).

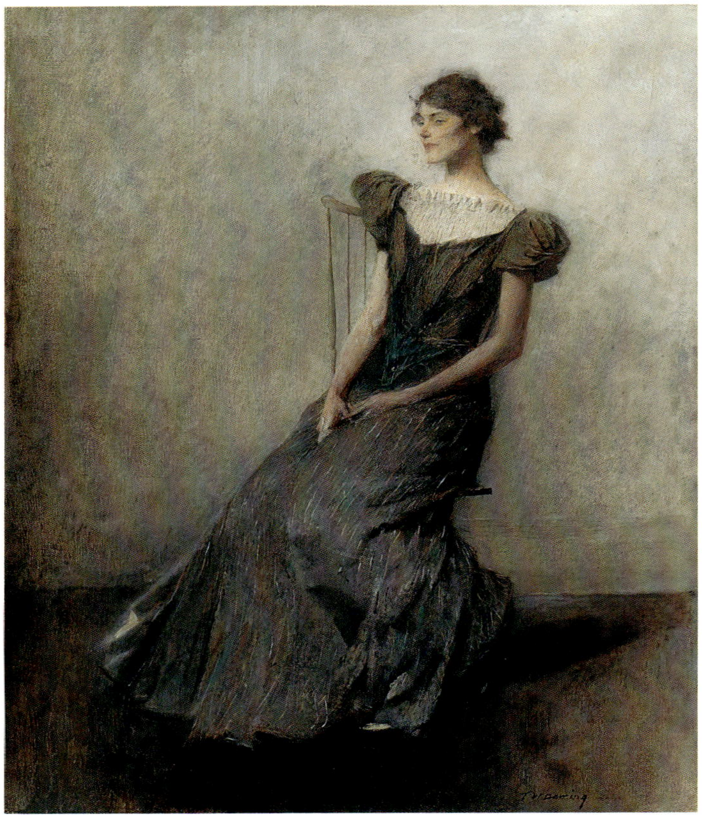

CAT. NO. 166

166. THOMAS WILMER DEWING (1851–1938)

Lady in Green and Gray, 1911

Oil on canvas; 61.3 x 50.8 cm (24⅛ x 20 in.)
Signed, lower right: *T W Dewing*
Friends of American Art Collection, 1911.5

Thomas Wilmer Dewing's enigmatic paintings of women in interiors have been assigned diverse meanings by critics and art historians. Some see them simply as symbols of beauty; some as symptoms of a patriarchal society that valued women for their status as fashionable consumers; and others as emblems of fin-de-siècle evolutionary theories that emphasized refinement.[1] *Lady in Green and Gray* speaks to all of these interpretations, if only indistinctly. The painting depicts an impossibly long-limbed woman seated sideways in a spindly chair placed in a bare room. What viewers make of her reveals their personal assumptions about women's status, feminine beauty, and art as a conduit for these ideas.

In many ways Dewing's career epitomized that of an artist who achieved renown during the latter part of the nineteenth century. Trained in Paris, he had a New York studio and a house in the country (Cornish, New Hampshire); an advantageous marriage to an intellectual, affluent artist (Maria Oakey); and famous friends who were also patrons (Charles Lang Freer, John Gellatly, and Stanford White).[2] His paintings often reflect these circumstances, creating a distinctly personal atmosphere that is difficult to decipher. Much of the artist's work confounded critics, who found it vague and affected, yet it profoundly appealed to the aesthetic sensibilities of men such as Freer who were rapt with admiration for Asian art and the tonalist, poetic canvases of James McNeill Whistler.

Dewing began painting women in interiors, the bulk of his oeuvre, in 1886 when he produced *Lady with a Lute* (National Gallery of Art, Washington, D.C.). He usually worked from models, a technique he doubtless developed as an art student in Paris. Dewing, however, distinguished his works from portraits by stating, "I merely use [the model] as a suggestion."[3] Although the women in these paintings are "suggestions" and are not identified in the predominantly descriptive titles, many of them can be identified as professional models, the artist's friends and lovers, and actresses.[4] For example, art historian Susan Hobbs has discovered that the woman depicted in *Lady in Green and Gray* is Gertrude MacNeill, an actress who frequently posed for Dewing between 1911 and 1917.[5]

The Art Institute's painting appears to be the first for which MacNeill posed and is the most austere of Dewing's many works that feature her countenance. A study of tone and form, the painting creates a mood rather than a narrative, just as it depicts a female presence rather than a particular woman. MacNeill wears an olive-green dress with pencil-thin gray stripes and a white ruffled bodice. The dress is flecked with deep red and the gray background has a matching rosy cast that unifies the composition and demonstrates Dewing's sophisticated sense of color. The artist strengthens his composition further by visually rhyming MacNeill's form with that of the chair in which she sits, situating the model at an angle that makes the affinity clearly visible. This likeness suggests that the chair and the model are both decorative art objects that function as compositional devices.

It has been suggested recently, however, by Barbara Dayer Gallati that the tone of Dewing's work is ironic and, in fact, disruptive of the standards of beauty espoused in his era.[6] She notes that Dewing's paintings register a shift from subject to paint surface as a site of beauty. Like *Lady in Green and Gray*, many of the artist's most powerful canvases rely on paint layering and stippling that creates a soft, rich, and subtle surface. This tendency, combined with Dewing's insistence upon returning to the same subject again and again and thwarting narrative impulses, provides a modernist context for viewing the artist's work. Reformulating a ubiquitous artistic subject—the woman—Dewing asserted his place in the early twentieth-century art world.

NOTES

1. For examples of these different perspectives, see Sarah Lea Burns, "The Poetic Mode in American Painting: George Fuller and Thomas Dewing" (Ph.D. diss., University of Illinois at Urbana-Champaign, 1979); Martha Banta, *Imaging American Women: Ideas and Ideals in Cultural History* (New York, 1987), pp. 345–47; and Kathleen Pyne, "Evolutionary Typology and the American Woman in the Work of Thomas Dewing," *American Art* 7, 4 (fall 1993), pp. 12–29.

2. For a complete biographical account of Dewing's life, see Susan A. Hobbs, "Beauty into Art: The Life of Thomas Wilmer Dewing," in Hobbs, ed., *The Art of Thomas Wilmer Dewing: Beauty Reconfigured*, exh. cat. (New York, Brooklyn Museum, 1996), pp. 1–49.

3. Quoted in Barbara Dayer Gallati, "Beauty Unmasked: Ironic Meaning in Dewing's Art," in Hobbs (note 2), p. 62.

4. Dewing's models who have been identified include Julia "Dudie" Baird, Mollie E. Chatfield, and Ingi Olsen.

5. Hobbs (note 2), p. 181. Gertrude MacNeill also posed for *Lady with a Mask* (1911; Corcoran Gallery of Art, Washington, D.C.), *Lady with a Fan* (1911; Peabody Institute of the Johns Hopkins University, Baltimore, Md.), and *Portrait of a Lady Holding a Rose* (1912; Daniel J. Terra Collection).

6. Gallati (note 3), pp. 51–82.

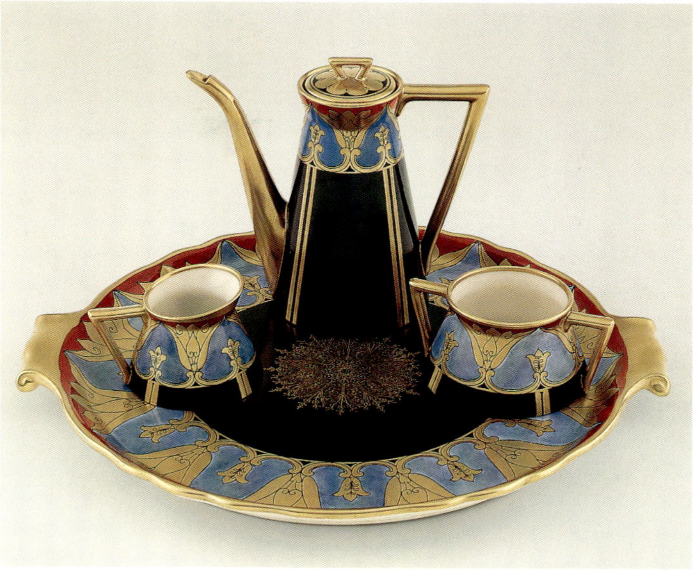

CAT. NO. 167

167. LENOX, INCORPORATED (FOUNDED 1889)

Coffee or Chocolate Set, 1906/10

Trenton, New Jersey

Belleek porcelain; coffeepot: h. 16.8 cm (6⅝ in.)

Gift of Gilda and Henry Buchbinder, 1995.103.1–4

Walter Scott Lenox began his career in ceramics as the manager of Ott and Brewer, a Trenton, New Jersey, manufacturer of ironstone china. Under Lenox's guidance, Ott and Brewer became the first firm in America to develop an equivalent to Irish belleek ware, an ivory-colored porcelain that is more durable than bone china.[1] Created from a mixture of white clay, silicate, flint, feldspar, and potash—the last three ingredients of which contributed to its characteristically smooth ivory color—belleek ware could be made thinner than other porcelains and thus was an excellent material for artistic forms.[2] After developing an artistic division at Ott and Brewer, Lenox moved to the Willets Manufacturing Company, which primarily produced utilitarian hotel and restaurant china. Lenox organized an artistic division there as well, and began producing high-style wares to compete with Ott and Brewer.[3]

In 1889 Lenox founded the Ceramic Art Company solely to manufacture decorative porcelains for the home, the first firm in Trenton to do so. Lenox used the belleek formula he had helped develop at Ott and Brewer, and along with catalogues showcasing the Ceramic Art Company's artistic designs, Lenox also published quarterly catalogues of whiteware—undecorated forms that were sold to artists. Much of the firm's business, in fact, involved selling such white forms to amateur and professional artists who would execute their own designs and sell the forms independently.[4]

In 1905 Frank G. Holmes replaced the nearly blind Walter Scott Lenox as the principal designer and manager of the firm. The Ceramic Art Company was reorganized and renamed Lenox, Incorporated. A new division of the firm began production of fine tablewares while another kept up the production of artistic wares. In 1910 the firm produced several specialized catalogues outlining the variety of forms available to the public, among which was one that highlighted "Tea, Coffee, Mocha, and Chocolate Sets."[5] That same year, the company introduced a line of tablewares made from belleek clay. The popularity of the belleek wares was quickly apparent: by 1919 it accounted for three-quarters of Lenox's products. Experts agreed that for the first time an American firm manufactured ceramics that were equal in quality to those produced in Great Britain.[6]

Lenox's own ambition was to employ china painters who could create images on porcelain bodies. His encouragement of experimentation among his painters explains why many of the early designs of Lenox, Incorporated, are unique pieces, unrecorded in the pattern files of the firm's archives. The pieces from the Art Institute's coffee set appear undecorated in the 1909 Lenox price guide. Each was sold separately under its individual form number, as marked on the bottom of three of the four pieces in the set.[7] Customized services could then be combined and decorated accordingly by one of the artists at Lenox.[8]

While the cool color scheme and lotus-blossom motif of this coffee set are indebted to the emphasis of the Arts and Crafts movement on abstract natural themes, the severe shapes and geometric decoration show the influence of the Vienna Secession, particularly the work of Josef Hoffmann.[9] The late nineteenth and early twentieth centuries were a time of innovation by American firms. By the turn of the century, American porcelain products—specifically Lenox items such as this coffee set—had begun to reflect a new sophistication of design.

NOTES

1. For more information on Ott and Brewer, see James Mitchell, "Ott and Brewer: Etruria in America," *Winterthur Portfolio* 7 (1972), pp. 217–28.

2. Ellen Paul Denker, *Lenox China: Celebrating a Century of Quality, 1889–1989*, exh. cat. (Trenton, New Jersey State Museum, 1989), p. 37.

3. Alice Cooney Frelinghuysen, *American Porcelain, 1770–1920*, exh. cat. (New York, Metropolitan Museum of Art, 1989), p. 48.

4. Denker (note 2), p. 35.

5. Ibid.

6. Hanna Tachau, "American-Made Pottery Exemplified in Lenox China," *International Studio* 67 (May 1919), p. xciii.

7. The tray is form 955, the creamer is form 544, and the sugar bowl is form 543. Although the teapot is not marked, it appears as form 542½ in the 1909 price guide. The pattern number 477 appears on the bottom of three of the pieces. Lenox archivist Marge Exton graciously provided this information.

8. The tray for this breakfast set is pictured with a matching fluted vase and compote, with a design scheme different from that of the Art Institute's breakfast set. See Tachau (note 6), p. xciv.

9. For examples of Hoffmann's work, see Kirk Varnedoe, *Vienna 1900: Art, Architecture, and Design*, exh. cat. (New York, Museum of Modern Art, 1986).

168. CHARLES ROHLFS (1853–1936)

Hall Chair, c. 1900

Buffalo, New York

Oak with original black stain;
144.8 x 48.3 x 38.7 cm (57 x 19 x 15¼ in.)

Stamped twice, once in red and once in black, on front apron within a bow saw: *R*

Gift of the Antiquarian Society through Mrs. Eric Oldberg and Mr. and Mrs. Morris S. Weeden, 1998.2

Charles Rohlfs, the son of a New York cabinetmaker, left school at the age of twelve when his father died. He supported his family through a series of odd jobs before taking a position at a local foundry. Rohlfs also attended night classes at the Cooper Union, New York's tuition-free college, where he excelled in drafting, chemistry, and ornamental design. His experiences at the Cooper Union led Rohlfs into a career as a designer of cast-iron stoves and furnaces; he spent his spare time pursuing an acting career.[1] Following his marriage in 1884 to novelist Anna Katharine Green, Rohlfs abandoned his dream of a career on the stage. The couple moved to Buffalo, where Rohlfs took a job managing a foundry, and, as a hobby, he made furniture for their home. Soon, friends who admired his work were commissioning pieces as well, and in 1897 Rohlfs's cabinetmaking enterprise outgrew the attic where he had worked with minimal space and equipment, and he opened his own shop.[2] His business grew rapidly; in January 1900, an article in *House Beautiful* featured Rohlfs's furniture on display at Marshall Field and Company in Chicago and thrust him into the spotlight.[3]

Rohlfs exhibited his furniture at the 1901 Pan-American Exposition in Buffalo and garnered an invitation to participate in the International Exposition of Modern Decorative Art in Turin, Italy, the following year. He was the only American furniture craftsman invited to show his work. Critics from Germany and Austria were particularly attentive and complimentary. "So far as furniture is concerned, Buffalo can claim to hold the most original man in America. . . . Without planning to create a new style he has created one," wrote the *Norddeutscher Allgemeine Zeitung* of Berlin, while another reviewer announced: "Among the art workers of America . . . Charles Rohlfs ranks first."[4]

While scholars have cited sources for Rohlfs's work as far reaching as Louis Sullivan's Guaranty Building in Buffalo, designs by Arthur Mackmurdo and Edward Colonna, and even

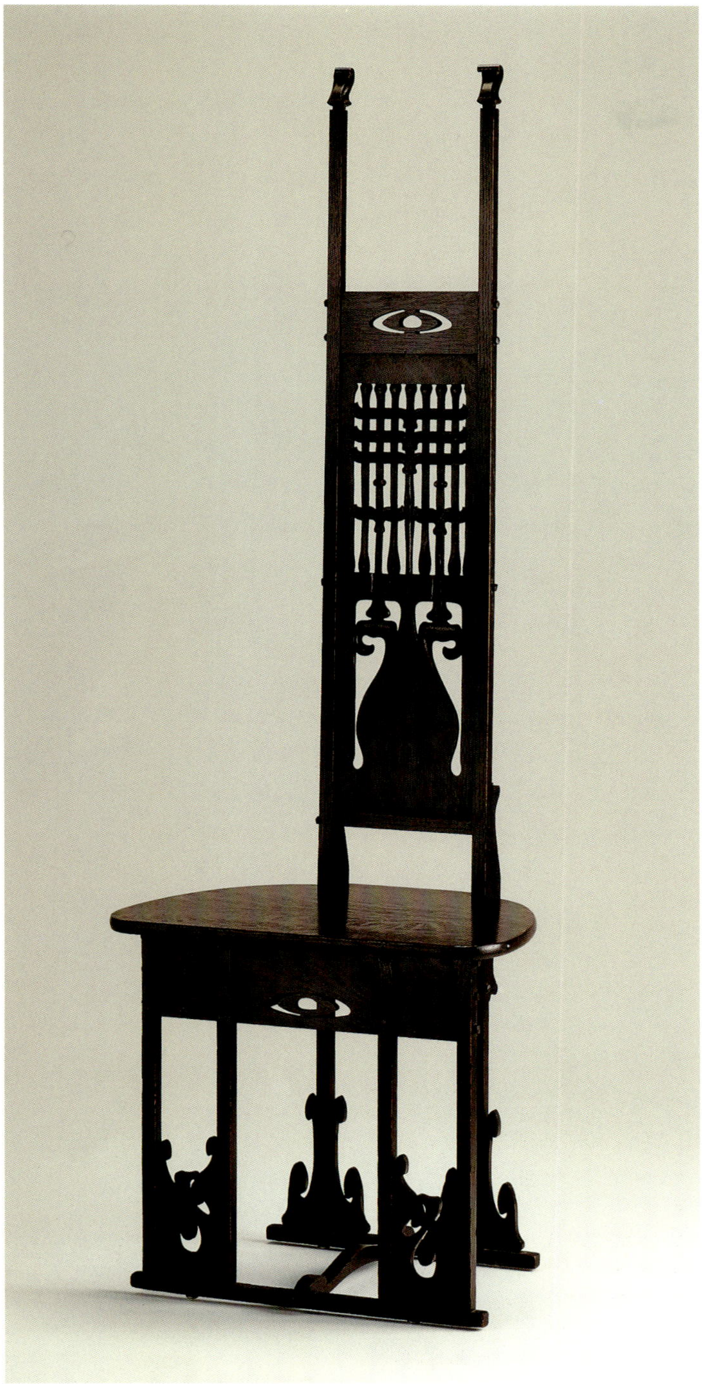

CAT. NO. 168

the curls in Rohlfs's own pipe smoke, Rohlfs himself—in a 1900 interview—boldly denied that he had any influences: "My designs are my own. I evolve them. They are like those of no other period nor people. . . . I do not read Ruskin nor anybody nor anything that might influence my ideas. I never get them from books."[5] Looking at the body of Rohlfs's work, however, one can see a reinterpreted mixture of styles and influences organized in a unique statement. Nature plays the most important role in inspiring his craftsmanship. Organic forms of flowers and grasses repeatedly appear, as can be seen in the budding flowers on the back splat of this hall chair and in the growing grasses around its base. The chair's dramatically high back certainly brings to mind the designs of Charles Rennie Mackintosh. Indeed, though the two men developed their high-backed styles at approximately the same time, photographs of Mackintosh's tea room interiors of 1896–98 with high-backed chairs in situ were published in numerous magazines where Rohlfs could have seen them.

Rohlfs produced work only upon commission, for he disliked the mass-produced quality of American furniture in the Mission style. He designed each piece according to the needs of the individual client and only reproduced a design upon request, altering it slightly in each instance. While he used machines to cut the boards for his pieces, the finish work and carving were executed by hand. He employed between eight and twelve craftsmen in his shop, and, believing in the dignity of labor, he referred to them as "fellow-laborers" and not as employees. He considered work to be a process from which to gain satisfaction rather than simply a means to an end.[6]

The chair retains its original black stain over oak and bears two of Rohlfs's distinctive stamps. It is one of only five known examples of his hall chairs.

NOTES

1. Tod M. Volpe and Beth Cathers, *Treasures of the American Arts and Crafts Movement, 1890–1920* (New York, 1988), p. 40.

2. His first outside commission was from Louis B. Hart, a future New York State Supreme Court justice, who was a young law clerk at the time. See Michael L. James, *Drama in Design: The Life and Craft of Charles Rohlfs*, exh. cat. (Buffalo, N.Y., Burchfield Art Center, 1994), p. 33.

3. Marshall Field bought a large desk from the exhibition, and later furnished several rooms in his home with pieces from the Rohlfs workshop. See Volpe and Cathers (note 1), p. 42; and James (note 2), p. 69.

4. These and other notices are quoted in James (note 2), p. 66.

5. Volpe and Cathers (note 1), p. 44; Leslie Greene Bowman, *American Arts and Crafts: Virtue in Design* (Los Angeles, Los Angeles County Museum of Art, 1990), p. 58; Robert Judson Clark, ed., *The Arts and Crafts Movement in America, 1876–1916* (Princeton, N.J., 1972), p. 28. The interview is quoted in James (note 2), p. 48.

6. Michael L. James, "Charles Rohlfs and 'The Dignity of Labor,'" in Bert Denker, ed., *The Substance of Style: Perspectives on the American Arts and Crafts Movement* (Winterthur, Del., 1996), pp. 229–41.

169. WILLIAM GLACKENS (1870–1938)

At Mouquin's, 1905

Oil on canvas; 121.9 x 99.1 cm (48 x 39 in.)
Signed, lower left: *W. Glackens*
Friends of American Art Collection, 1925.295

William Glackens was one of The Eight, a group of artists who challenged the traditional selection and display practices of the National Academy of Design. In response to frequent rejections of their work under this system, they promoted and exhibited their art independently.[1] Their name derived from the title of a 1908 exhibition of their work at the Macbeth Gallery in New York City (see cat. no. 172). When *At Mouquin's* was shown at The Art Institute of Chicago in 1908 as part of a traveling exhibition of works by The Eight, one Chicago art critic sardonically asked, "Can a Scotch highball or a Manhattan cocktail figure in a beautiful painting?" The same critic noticed that Glackens and his colleagues were extending the boundaries of art, not so much by their means of expression (figurative and "realistic"), but by their choice of subject matter: portraits of the urban populace and scenes of life in New York City.[2] Like John Sloan in *Renganeschi's Saturday Night* (cat. no. 173), Glackens knew the subject of the canvas intimately: Mouquin's was a French restaurant located at Twenty-eighth Street and Sixth Avenue, close to the artist's Thirtieth Street studio. The scene of Glackens's painting and its emphasis on drinking, however, reveal that Mouquin's catered to a clientele very different from the one that frequented the Italian eatery Sloan depicted. Glackens's painting is further distinguished by its resemblance to nineteenth-century French art, particularly to Édouard Manet's paintings of modern life.[3]

Glackens visited Paris in the company of fellow painter Robert Henri (see cat. nos. 177–78) in 1895 and 1896. Prior to this trip, Glackens was primarily a landscape painter. While in Paris, he reportedly studied the work of Manet and his contemporaries in the Gustave Caillebotte collection on view at the Musée du Luxembourg.[4] Although his palette is dark, the scenes he produced of Parisian street life, and those of people enjoying leisure time in urban and suburban locales, attest to this influence. After his sojourn in Europe, Glackens settled in New York City; while establishing himself as a painter, he resumed working as a newspaper and magazine illustrator, a career he had begun in Philadelphia. By 1905, the year *At Mouquin's* won an Honorable Mention at the Carnegie Institute's Tenth Annual Exhibition of American Art, Glackens had established himself as both an illustrator and a painter.

In his correspondence with family and friends, Glackens often referred to Mouquin's and the male protagonist of his painting, James B. Moore. A lawyer by training, Moore owned the Café Francis on West Thirty-fifth Street and advertised his restaurant as "New York's Most Popular Resort of New Bohemia," in order to attract the artists and writers he sought as his friends. The fashionable woman intimately sharing the banquette with Moore has not been identified; perhaps she is one of the young women with whom Moore kept frequent company and referred to as his "daughters."[5] Two other figures reflected in the mirror have been identified: Glackens's wife Edith, whose head is positioned between Moore and his companion, and on the far right side, the art critic and early champion of Glackens's work, Charles Fitzgerald. Judging from the angle of their reflections, Edith Glackens and Fitzgerald appear to be engaged in a conversation from which Moore has momentarily turned away. Humorously, he brandishes a glass of liquor in order to draw the attention of his somewhat bored-looking companion, who has yet to touch her cocktail.

Like the barmaid in Édouard Manet's *Bar at the Folies-Bergère* (1881–82; Courtauld Institute of Art, London), the lavishly bedecked woman in *At Mouquin's* is inscrutable; what attracts her gaze remains the mystery that sustains the tension of the composition.[6] She is also its most visually arresting element: her vivid blue dress and silvery gray cloak are painted with a confident bravura and creamy texture that caused some writers to dub Glackens the "American Manet."[7] The artist's inclusion of a tabletop still life of flowers, glasses, and liquor bottles is reminiscent of the French realist's work as well, particularly his Folies-Bergère scene, which includes a similarly virtuoso still-life arrangement.

In New York and Chicago, critics perceived this picture as "sensational" and "vulgar," focusing on its candid depiction of drinking ("the man does not look like a Prohibitionist") and on the sexually charged side of social intercourse between men and women.[8] Whereas this type of scene was commonplace in French painting by the turn of the century, North American audiences and artists were only on the brink of accepting sophisticated scenes of modern life that broached themes of sexuality and license as subjects for art. *At Mouquin's* remains one of Glackens's most renowned and accomplished paintings, both for its style and for its subject matter. Looking closely at his own milieu, the artist devised a scene that combines por-

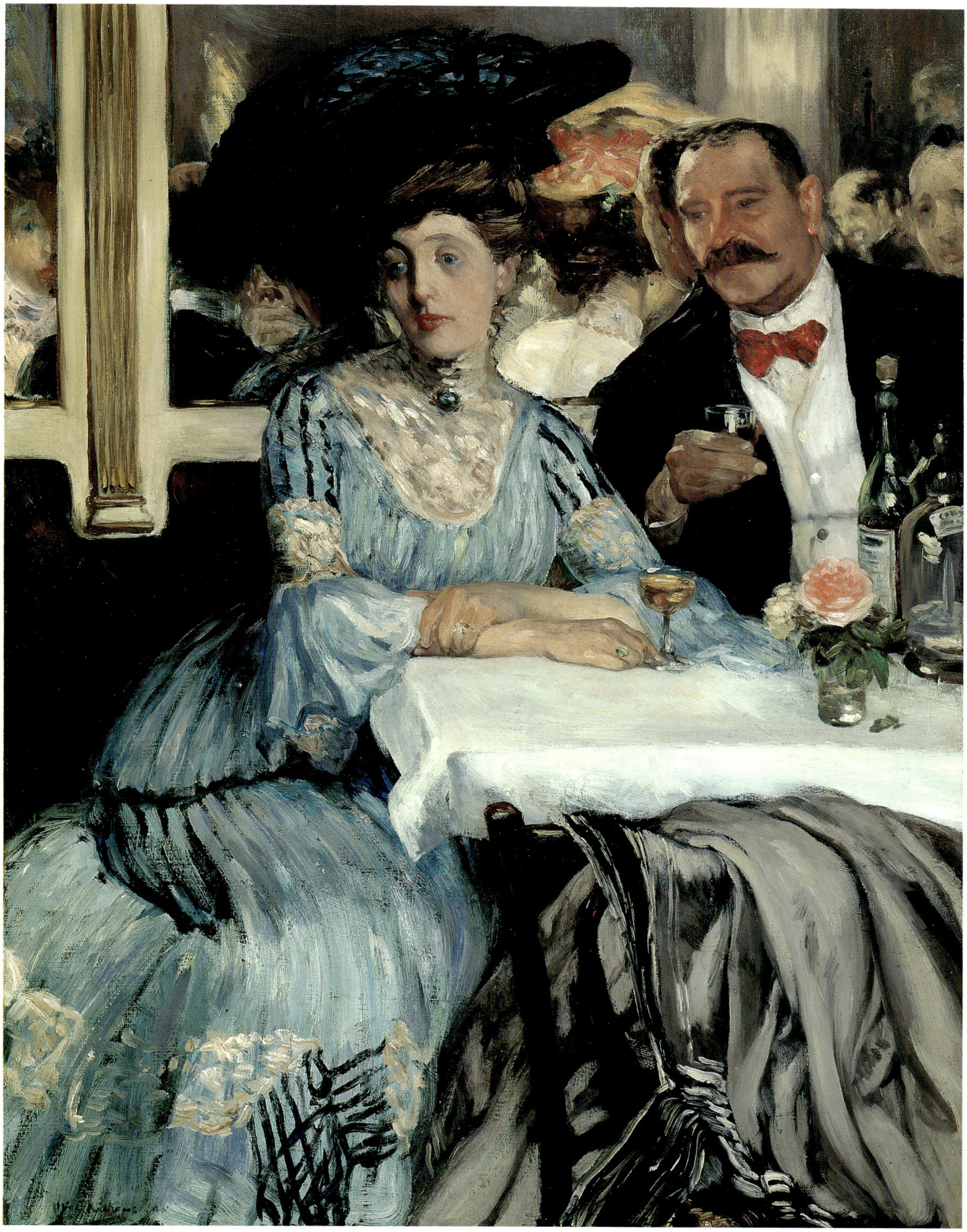

CAT. NO. 169

traiture with genre painting, eschews clear narrative conventions, and ushers in a mode of painting appropriate to the pleasures and perils of the age.

NOTES

1. For more about the political impact of The Eight as a confederation of artists, see Rebecca Zurier, "The Making of Six New York Artists," in Rebecca Zurier, Robert W. Snyder, and Virginia Mecklenburg, *Metropolitan Lives: The Ashcan Artists and Their New York*, exh. cat. (Washington, D.C., National Museum of American Art, 1995), pp. 68–69.

2. *Chicago Post*, Sept. 29, 1908.

3. For more about Mouquin's, see H. Barbara Weinberg, Doreen Bolger, and David Park Curry, *American Impressionism and Realism: The Painting of Modern Life, 1885–1915*, exh. cat. (New York, Metropolitan Museum of Art, 1994), pp. 223–24.

4. For a complete overview of Glackens's career, see William Gerdts, *William Glackens*, exh. cat. (Fort Lauderdale, Fla., Museum of Art, 1996).

5. "[James Moore] had numerous young ladies about, whom he referred to as his 'daughters,' and it was one of these who posed with him in 1905 for W.G.'s painting 'Chez Mouquin.'" See Ira Glackens, *William Glackens and The Eight: The Artists Who Freed American Art* (New York, 1957), p. 54.

6. It is not known whether Glackens ever saw *Bar at the Folies-Bergère*, but similarities between Manet's painting and *At Mouquin's* suggest that he was familiar with the work. Glackens had at least two opportunities to see Manet's great painting, in New York and in Paris. The canvas was shown in March 1895 at the Durand-Ruel Gallery in New York (*Manet, 1832–1883*, exh. cat. [Paris, Galeries Nationales du Grand Palais, 1983], p. 478). In March 1896, the estate of Emmanuel Chabrier, the painting's first owner, was sold at the Hôtel Drouot, Paris, where it was certainly placed on public view. On the Chabrier sale, see Anne Distel, *Impressionism: The First Collectors* (New York, 1990), p. 220.

7. Gerdts (note 4), p. 15.

8. *Chicago Post* (note 2).

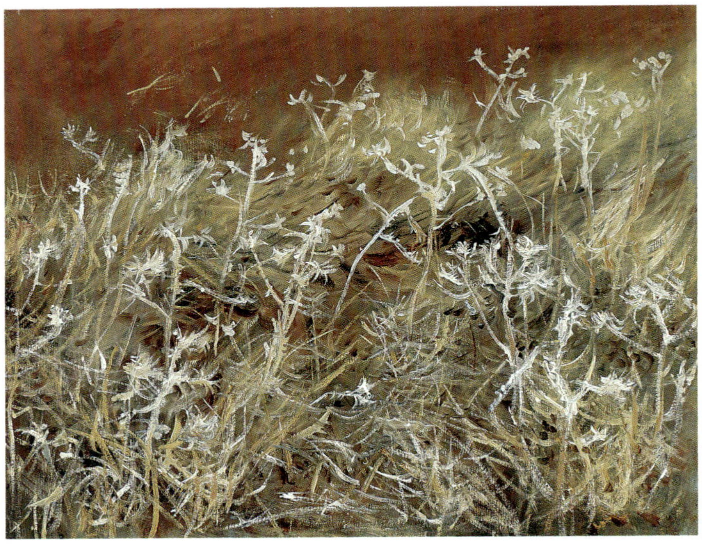

CAT. NO. 170

170. JOHN SINGER SARGENT (1856–1925)

Thistles, 1885/89

Oil on canvas; 55.9 x 71.8 cm (22 x 28¼ in.)

Gift of Brooks McCormick, 1996.446

171. *The Fountain, Villa Torlonia, Frascati, Italy*, 1907

Oil on canvas; 71.4 x 56.5 cm (28⅛ x 22¼ in.)

Signed, lower left: *John S. Sargent*

Friends of American Art Collection, 1914.57

Thistles is an exceptional example of John Singer Sargent's work *en plein air* and was probably painted between 1885 and 1889 during one of the artist's regular outdoor sketching excursions in the Worcestershire region of England. Sargent's trips to Worcestershire began after he took up residence in London following the scandalous exhibition of *Madame X* (1884; Metropolitan Museum of Art, New York) in Paris in 1884 (see entry on Sargent's *Mrs. George Swinton* [cat. no. 141]). Another expatriate American, Edwin Austin Abbey, introduced Sargent to Worcestershire in September 1885 when they traveled together to Broadway, a Cotswolds town where artists such as Francis David Millet and Edwin Howland Blashfield had formed an artists' colony.[1]

The pastel-hued stalks of *Thistles* criss-cross in a delicate grid that captures an abstract aspect of the natural world. At

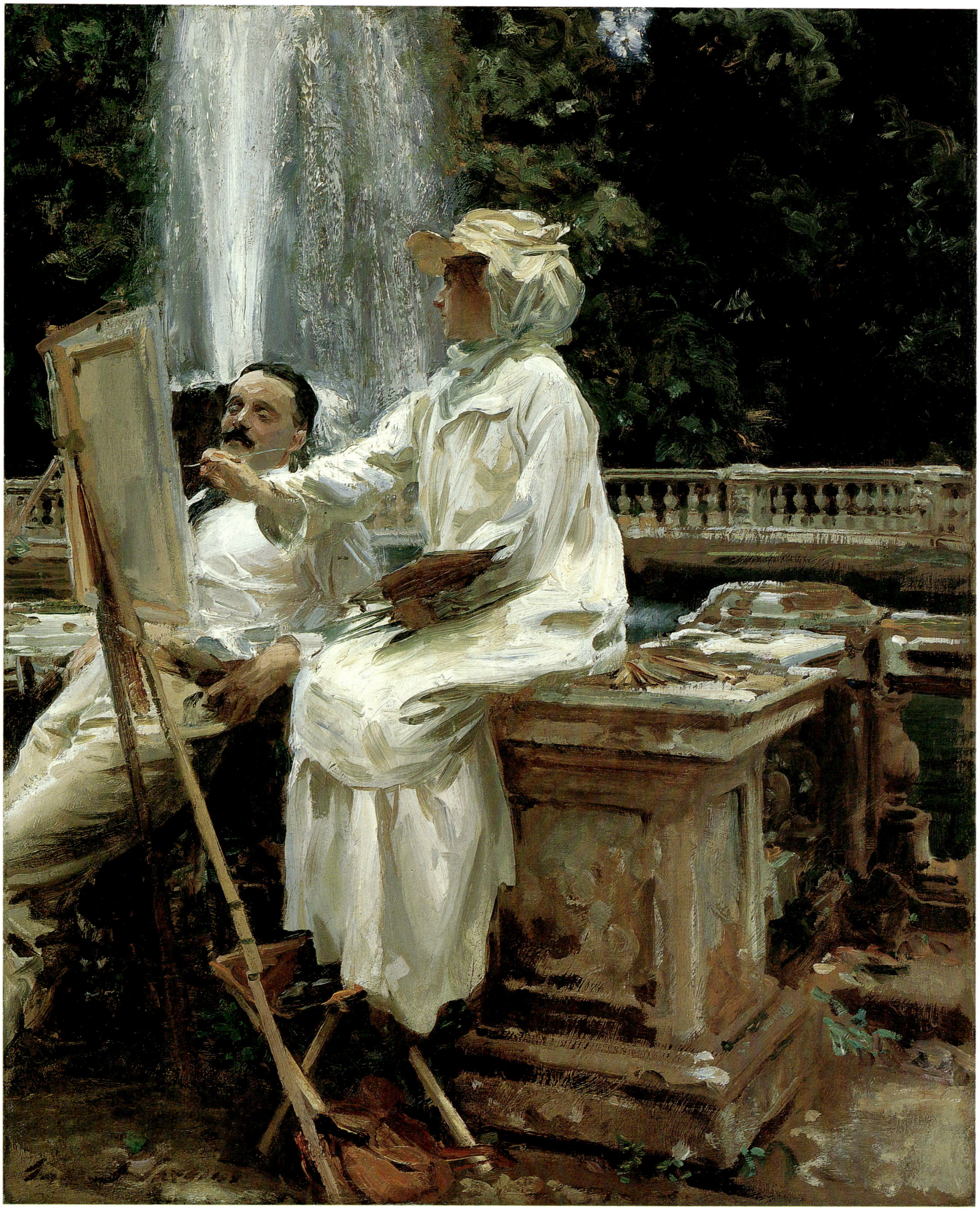

CAT. NO. 171

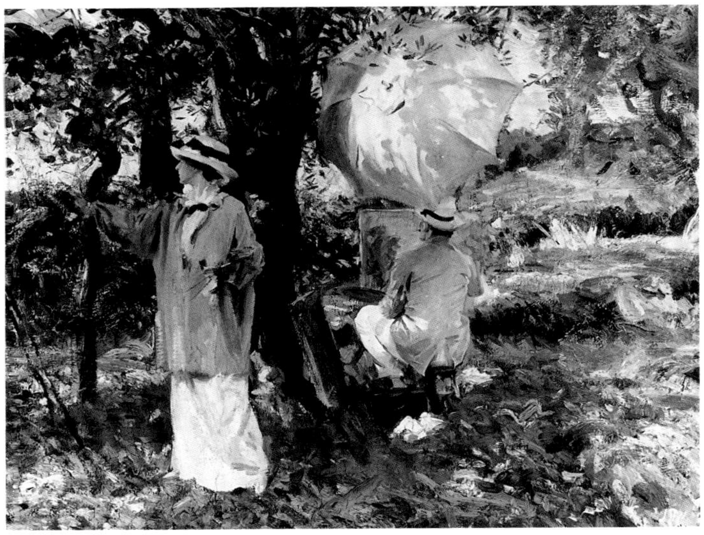

FIG. 87. John Singer Sargent (1856–1925). *The Sketchers*, 1914. Oil on canvas; 55.9 x 71.1 cm (22 x 28 in.). Virginia Museum of Fine Arts, Richmond, Arthur and Margaret Glasgow Fund (58.11). © 1998 Virginia Museum of Fine Arts.

first, this composition appears uncharacteristic of the works Sargent produced during his summers and autumns in the English countryside, many of which depict boating parties, women with parasols, and friends at work on their own plein-air paintings. Indeed, a well-known and typical Sargent painting from this period, *Paul Helleu Sketching with His Wife* (1889; Brooklyn Museum of Art), shows a couple languidly seated among the reeds by a stream.[2] Close examination, however, reveals similarities between the palette, staccato brushstrokes, and emphasis on grasses and greenery in the two works.

Though painted two decades later, Sargent's *The Fountain, Villa Torlonia, Frascati, Italy* shares an important kinship with *Thistles*; both paintings celebrate plein-air painting excursions. *The Fountain*, however, is a more aesthetically complex work that integrates figures into a richly rendered landscape. Completed in Italy during an autumn holiday, the canvas documents a painting excursion Sargent and his close friends Jane and Wilfrid von Glehn took to the famous Villa Torlonia in Frascati, located about fifteen miles southeast of Rome. The party traveled there in October 1907, and all three painted scenes of the villa's elaborately landscaped grounds.[3]

After 1906 Sargent decreased his production of portraits and concentrated largely on works such as *The Fountain* that combine informal, intimate portraiture with light-saturated, impressionistic landscapes. However much he intended this work to convey spontaneity, Jane von Glehn's description of posing for it suggests a very different atmosphere: "Sargent is doing a most amusing and killingly funny picture in oils of me perched on a balustrade painting. It is the very 'spit' of me. He has stuck Wilfrid in looking at my sketch with rather a contemptuous expression. . . . Poor Wilfrid can't pose for more than a few minutes at a time as the position is torture after a while."[4] The painting was composed over several days that were frequently interrupted by rain, and thus it was a composite creation. Evidently Sargent's impulses as a portrait painter continued to guide his approach to painting, which included multiple sittings, contrived poses, and appropriate props.[5] *The Fountain* is distinguishable from Sargent's earlier indoor portraits, such as *Mrs. George Swinton (Elizabeth Ebsworth)* (cat. no. 141), however, by the Impressionist effects—such as that of the play of bright sunlight on a variety of surfaces—that suggest the artist's prowess with rich, rapid, painterly execution. The von Glehns and the plume of water behind them comprise a study of whites set off by the deep green of the dense trees and the variegated browns and grays of the architectural details. A later, more matter-of-fact canvas shows both Jane and Wilfrid painting out-of-doors (fig. 87), absorbed in their work. *The Sketchers*, however, is a spontaneously produced landscape study and does not represent the same complex narrative as does the Art Institute's painting.

Sargent's attraction to Italy as a subject dates back to his earliest years as a painter and continued into his final years (see cat. no. 98). The works he created at the Villa Torlonia, a highly regarded example of landscape and villa architecture, link Sargent and his subjects to a long tradition of American artists who traveled to Italy to bask in the glow of its history. Although Jane von Glehn had hoped that Wilfred would purchase *The Fountain*, Sargent instead sent it off for exhibition, first at the New English Art Club, in 1907, and then to The Art Institute of Chicago, in January 1914, where it was purchased by the Friends of American Art for the permanent collection.[6]

NOTES

1. For more information on Sargent and the art colony in Worcestershire, see Marc Simpson, "Reconstructing the Golden Age: American Artists in Broadway, Worcestershire, 1885 to 1889" (Ph.D. diss., Yale University, 1993).

2. French artist Paul Helleu and his wife, Alice, visited Sargent in Fladbury, near Broadway, in 1889, where Helleu painted landscapes not unlike Sargent's. For more information on their interaction, see Donelson F. Hoopes, "John S. Sargent: The Worcestershire Interlude, 1885–89," *Brooklyn Museum Annual* 7 (1965–66), pp. 74–89.

3. Sargent painted at least six views of the Villa Torlonia during this trip. For more information on the cultural significance of the Frascati region at the time, see Erica E. Hirshler, "John Singer Sargent, *The Fountain, Villa*

Torlonia, Frascati, Italy," in Theodore E. Stebbins, Jr., ed., *The Lure of Italy: American Artists and the Italian Experience, 1760–1914*, exh. cat. (Boston, Museum of Fine Arts, 1992), pp. 255–56. According to Hirshler, Frascati, famous for its wine, was a hillside resort popular with foreign tourists, who traveled there for its healthy environment and stunning views of the Campagna.

4. Letter from Jane von Glehn to Lydia Emmet, Oct. 6, 1907, quoted in Patricia Hills, "'Painted Diaries': Sargent's Late Subject Pictures," in Patricia Hills, *John Singer Sargent*, exh. cat. (New York, Whitney Museum of American Art, 1986), p. 191. A von Glehn family member later related: "[Wilfrid] had just walked over to see how his wife was getting on when Sargent said 'stay there, Wilfrid, you look just like an Italian loafer'"; see letter from Dr. Norman A. de Bruyne to Linda J. Cohn, Nov. 15, 1982, Files of the Department of Twentieth-Century Painting and Sculpture, The Art Institute of Chicago.

5. Jane von Glehn reported to her sisters that Sargent brought costumes along on these trips and painted his friends and family posing in them; see Hills (note 4), p. 186.

6. "Gifts of the Friends," *Bulletin of the Art Institute of Chicago* 7, 4 (Apr. 1914), p. 64.

172. EVERETT SHINN (1876–1953)

The Hippodrome, London, 1902

Oil on canvas; 66.9 x 89.3 cm (26 5/16 x 35 3/16 in.)
Signed, lower right: *E Shinn*
Friends of American Art Collection, 1928.197

The Hippodrome, London is one of eight paintings, all depicting theatrical subjects, that Everett Shinn showed at the landmark exhibition of the group of American painters known as The Eight at the Macbeth Gallery in New York City in 1908.[1] A souvenir of his only trip to Europe, this work is presumably the first oil painting Shinn devoted to what would become his signature subject: popular forms of entertainment, including the circus, vaudeville, and the theater. The artist's idiosyncratic use of perspective and choice of subject matter correspond to

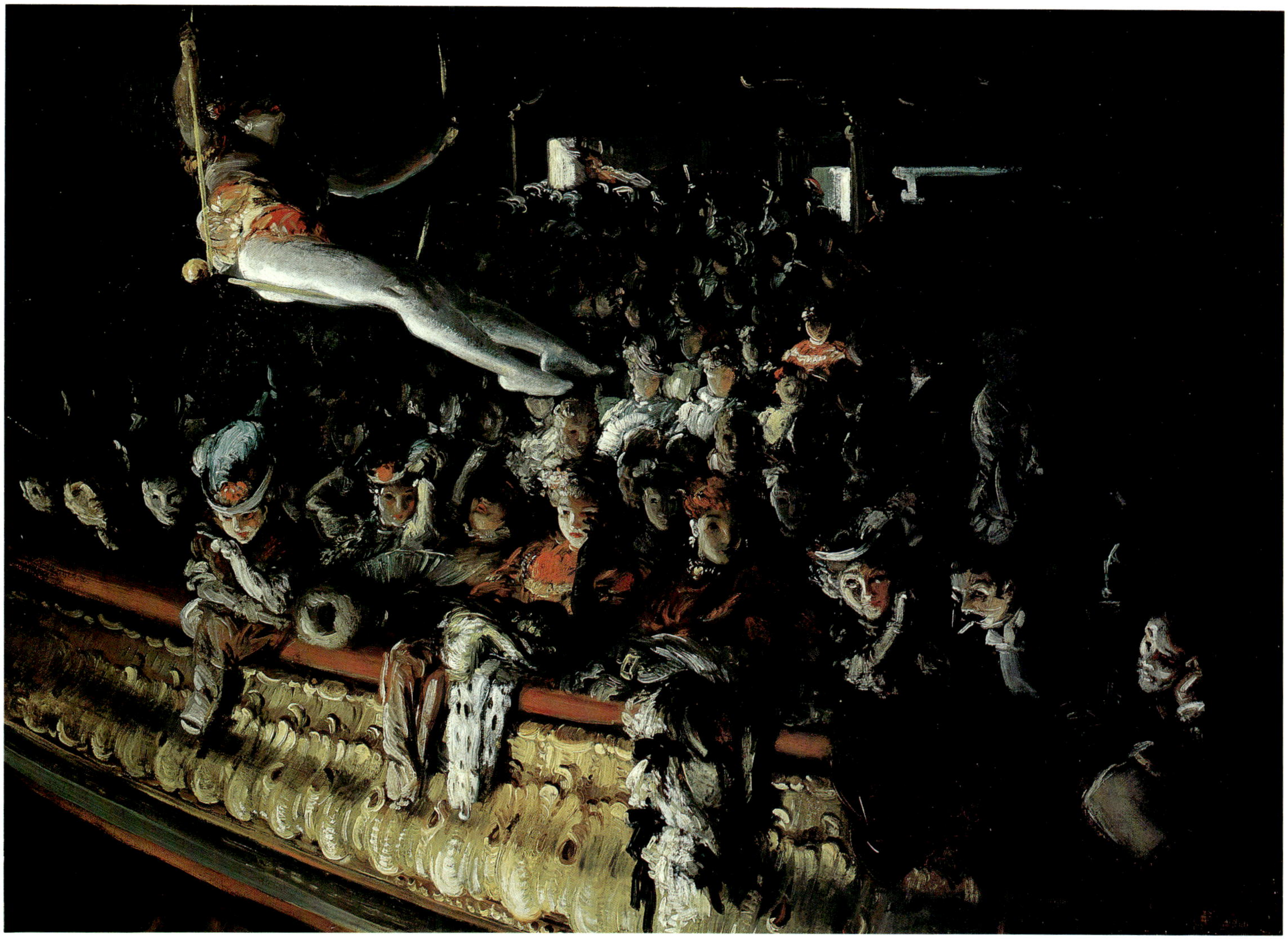

CAT. NO. 172

French Impressionist and Post-Impressionist work by artists such as Edgar Degas and Henri Toulouse-Lautrec. Shinn's commitment to this type of scene, however, is also linked to his interest in theater and early career as an illustrator for popular periodicals.

Shinn, like fellow Ashcan artists and members of The Eight such as George Luks, William Glackens (see cat. no. 169), and John Sloan (see cat. no. 173), began his career as a newspaper illustrator in Philadelphia.[2] He moved to New York in 1897 and soon found work with *New York World* and, later, *Ainslee's Magazine*. During these first years in New York, Shinn began working in pastel, pursuing primarily street and theatrical scenes. By the time he painted *The Hippodrome, London* in 1902, Shinn had developed a style and a reputation for masterful pastels that he hoped to translate into oil painting.

Little is known about Shinn's stay in Europe, and the only evidence of his visit to London is the Art Institute's painting.[3] The Hippodrome opened in January 1900 as a circus and was transformed into a music hall a decade later. Presumably, Shinn attended a performance there during the first year of its existence, and although he was probably in London during the summer, he includes a fur muff and ermine stole resting casually on the ledge of the balcony.[4] These fashionable garments belong to the women in the first row of the balcony, who exhibit a variety of responses to the performance taking place above and below them. Their disparate gazes indicate the coincident diversity of the performance: one woman looks up at the trapeze artist swinging overhead, one leans over to look down at the scene below, and others look off to the sides at other portions of the spectacle.

The women and men seated in the front row are the most defined members of the audience. Their faces are finely delineated and contrast sharply with the masklike faces of the people in the crowd behind. Shinn uses the white accents of the spotlight and a limited palette of red, blue, and gold to unify the audience, and relates the women in the front row to the trapeze artist through the use of red and white. This formal connection could simply be the extension of a compositional motif, but it may also suggest that the women are prostitutes, who, like the trapeze artist, are paid to entertain. They are, after all, without male escorts, over-dressed, and sitting in the cheaper balcony seats.[5]

The spectators' response, or lack thereof, to the trapeze artist who flies perilously close to their heads suggests the audience's close acquaintance with public spectacle, a representative feature of modern life in large cities such as London, Paris, and New York.[6] Many critics writing about Shinn's work, however, chose to linger over the artist's indebtedness to French artists, writing, for example, that "between the personality . . . he is endeavoring to express and the sympathetic but unprejudiced eye there stand the brilliant figures of Degas and Forain."[7] They never commented on the relationship between audience and performer, arguably the most interesting facet of Shinn's work.

By 1910 Shinn was producing fewer canvases and began to work directly with the theater through stagecraft. He designed his own studio playhouse in the back of his residence, where he created theatrical effects and put on private plays with a troupe that included his wife, Florence Shinn, and friend William Glackens. As the motion picture industry developed, Shinn began a second career as a set designer and art director in Hollywood, where he worked from 1917 to 1923. Throughout his life, his work reflected an abiding interest in theatricality, spectacle, and the relationship between performers and audiences.

NOTES

1. Shinn also showed *Gaieté Montparnasse, Rehearsal of the Ballet, White Ballet, Leader of the Orchestra, The Gingerbread Man, Trapeze Artist,* and *Girl in Blue* at Macbeth's. When the show traveled to the Art Institute and other venues that same year, he showed a different series of paintings that did not include *The Hippodrome, London.* At the Art Institute he showed *The Song, The Dance Step, In the Orchestra Pit, Man with Umbrella, Ballet Girl Tying Slipper, Ballet Girl Resting,* and *The Last Song.* For more information on the exhibition history of Shinn's theatrical subjects, see Linda Ferber, "*Stagestruck*: The Theater Subjects of Everett Shinn," *Studies in the History of Art* 37 (1990), pp. 51–67.

2. See Edith DeShazo, *Everett Shinn, 1876–1953: A Figure in His Time* (New York, 1974), for the most complete biographical information on Shinn.

3. Ferber (note 1), p. 54. Shinn probably spent the summer of 1900 in Europe; Paris and London are the only documented locations.

4. Ferber has noted: "although Shinn was abroad during the summer months, he often depicted Paris in the snow, a device he had found very successful in his New York subjects and which he apparently did not hesitate to apply to his French views"; see Ferber (note 1), p. 66 n. 26.

5. For more information on images of prostitutes, see Hollis Clayson, *Painted Love: Prostitution in French Art of the Impressionist Era* (New Haven, Conn., and London 1991).

6. For more information on popular entertainment at the turn of the century, see Robert W. Snyder and Rebecca Zurier, "Picturing the City," in Zurier, Snyder, and Virginia M. Mecklenburg, *Metropolitan Lives: The Ashcan Artists and Their New York*, exh. cat. (Washington, D.C., National Museum of American Art, 1995), pp. 156–71.

7. "New Pictures by American Artists and Some Old Prints," *New York Tribune*, Feb. 5, 1908; quoted in Ferber (note 1), p. 64.

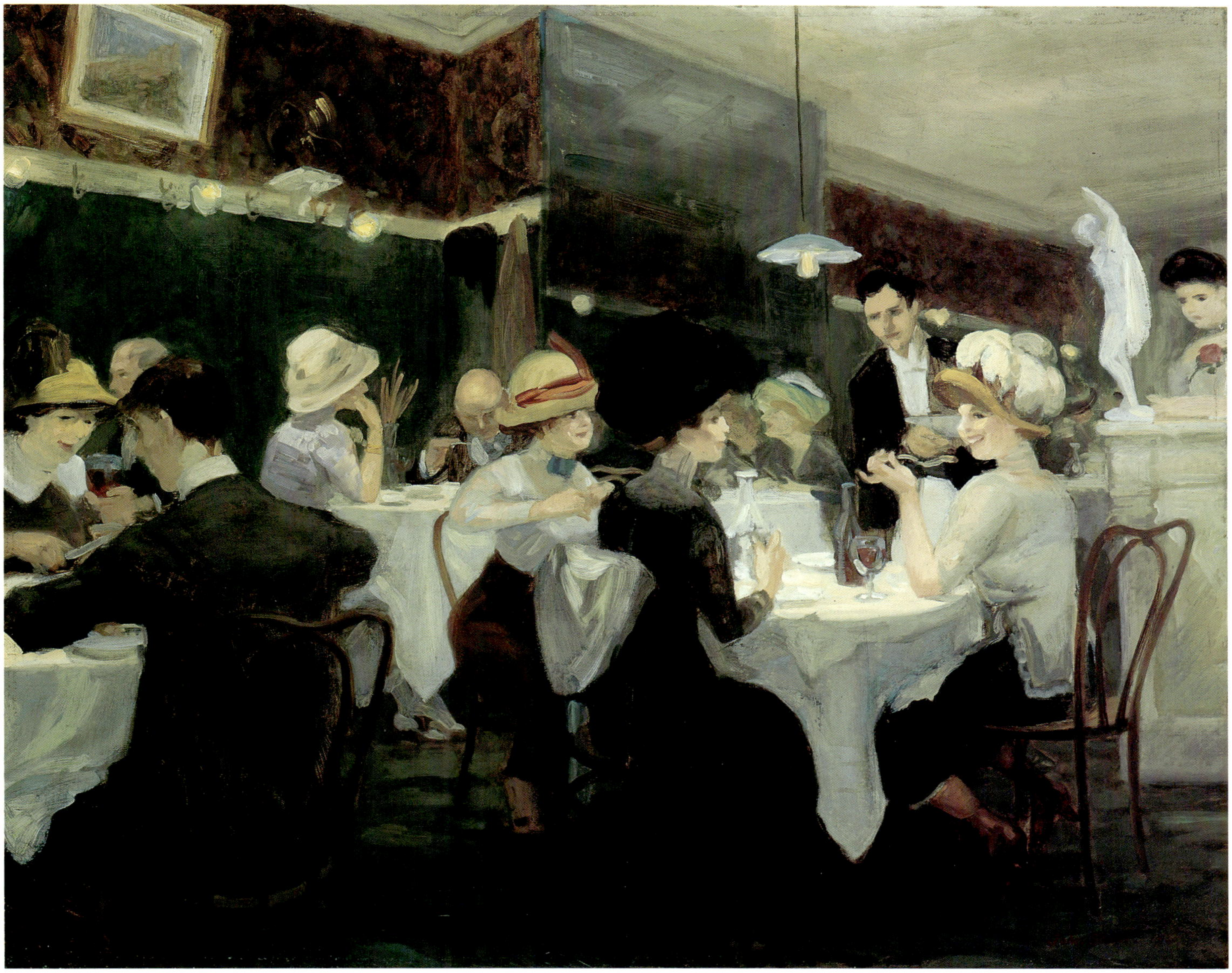

CAT. NO. 173

173. JOHN SLOAN (1871–1951)

Renganeschi's Saturday Night, 1912

Oil on canvas; 66.7 x 81.3 cm (26 ¼ x 32 in.)
Signed, lower right: *John Sloan 1912*
Gift of Mary Otis Jenkins, 1926.1580

Renganeschi's Saturday Night depicts the popular Italian restaurant on West Tenth Street in New York City in full swing—the tables are full, people are eating and drinking with gusto. The artist John Sloan frequented Renganeschi's; he perhaps even tried to pay a bar tab with this painting.[1] He recalled in 1939 that "Renganeschi's was and still is, I believe, located on West Tenth Street, a stone's throw from Jefferson Market jail. The quality of light and sense of the place, as well as the life of the dining room—quite satisfactory."[2] His lively rendering of the restaurant and its customers exhibits his familiarity with the scene, as well as his enthusiasm for representing the daily lives of New Yorkers, especially working women.

A native of Philadelphia, Sloan studied at the Pennsylvania Academy of the Fine Arts. He was the last of the loosely connected group of artists known as the Ashcan School—which included Bellows (see cat. no. 186), Glackens (see cat. no. 169), Henri (see cat. nos. 177–78), Luks, and Shinn (see cat. no. 172)—to settle in New York, which he finally did in 1904. Like many of the Ashcan artists, Sloan was preoccupied with the depiction of modern city life and had a dual career as a painter and periodical illustrator. In 1908 the Ashcan artists—minus George Bellows, the youngest of the group—sponsored an independent exhibition of their work, along with that of Arthur B. Davies, Ernest Lawson, and Maurice Prendergast, dubbing themselves The Eight. The most politically active of the group, Sloan became in 1912 the art director for the Socialist magazine *The Masses*, a post he held until 1916, when he resigned from both the paper and the party. Sloan tried to distance his political activity from his art, claiming, "while I am a Socialist, I never allowed social propaganda to get into my paintings." Works such as *Renganeschi's Saturday Night*, however, bear a distinct formal and thematic resemblance to a number of the illustrations he produced for *The Masses* around the same time.[3]

With the steady influx of immigrants into New York City in the early twentieth century, ethnic restaurants became a staple of that city's life.[4] In *Renganeschi's Saturday Night*, Sloan alluded to the Old World, immigrant identity of the restaurant by depicting a watercolor of an Italian landscape that Signor Renganeschi kept on the wall to remind himself of home.[5] The emphasis in the painting, however, is not on the decor of the restaurant. Instead Sloan focused on the establishment's clientele, and in particular on the three women who sit together at

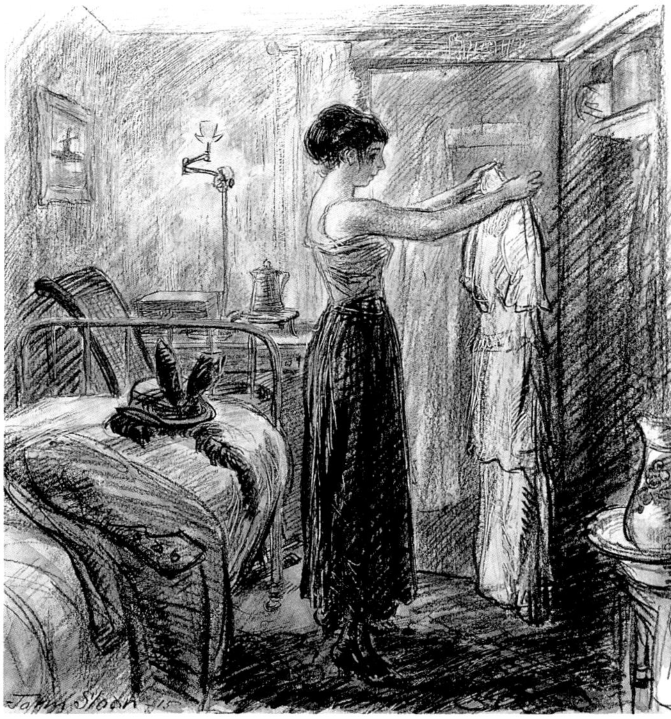

FIG. 88. John Sloan (1871–1951). *Bachelor Girl*, 1915. Black crayon and watercolor on paper; 35.5 x 35.5 cm (14 x 14 in.). The Art Institute of Chicago, Olivia Shaler Swan Memorial Fund (1941.826).

the table in the foreground, apart from the surrounding tables occupied by couples.

These women represent a newly visible component of the urban work force—single women typically employed in the garment district or as secretaries and referred to as "bachelor girls." They were regular subjects for Sloan, who emphasized their independence and confidence in the face of the financial constraints of their inadequate wages. A 1915 drawing by Sloan for *The Masses*, titled *Bachelor Girl* (fig. 88), features a young woman preparing to leave her small, meagerly furnished apartment for a night of entertainment, perhaps prefacing a scene like *Renganeschi's Saturday Night*.[6] In the painting, the women's relaxed but "unladylike" postures and gestures—feet splayed under the table and wrapped around chair rungs—indicate their social class without being judgmental. Sloan celebrated their newfound freedom to socialize in public (with money they earned themselves) and to enjoy each other's company without appearing to seek male companionship. Rather than displaying their bodies to the viewer, Sloan represented them seated, facing one another, and absorbed in conversation. *Renganeschi's Saturday Night* is unusual for Sloan, however, because in it he does not voyeuristically observe his female protagonists or include male figures who show interest in them.[7]

Sloan's informal style and loose brushwork enliven this scene of casual leisure with a sense of immediacy. The skilled composition and lighting of the setting—in which a single ceiling lamp illuminates the women's table—highlight the scene of independent womanhood that is the focus of this work. The Art Institute's painting, and the many others like it in the artist's oeuvre, provide us with a view of changing social customs, as well as painting practice, during the first decades of the twentieth century.

NOTES

1. A member of the Renganeschi family wrote: "The original painting was painted for my grandfather by John Sloan in 1912. Sloan tried to give it to grandpa in lieu of payment of a bar tab at Renganeschi's. The painting was not accepted." See letter from Maude Renganeschi to Lieschen Potuznik, June 3, 1992, Files of the Department of Twentieth-Century Painting and Sculpture, The Art Institute of Chicago.

2. John Sloan, *Gist of Art* (New York, 1939), p. 237.

3. Quoted in Robert W. Snyder, "City in Transition," in Rebecca Zurier, Robert W. Snyder, and Virginia M. Mecklenburg, *Metropolitan Lives: The Ashcan Artists and Their New York*, exh. cat. (Washington, D.C., National Museum of American Art, 1995), p. 45; on the same page is an illustration of *The Return from Toil*, a cover Sloan designed for *The Masses* in July 1913 which shows a group of working women out for a night on the town, much like those depicted in *Renganeschi's Saturday Night*.

4. On dining out in New York during the nineteenth and early twentieth centuries, see H. Barbara Weinberg, Doreen Bolger, and David Park Curry, *American Impressionism and Realism: The Painting of Modern Life, 1885–1915*, exh. cat. (New York, Metropolitan Museum of Art, 1994), pp. 221–33.

5. Sloan (note 2), p. 237.

6. Robert W. Snyder and Rebecca Zurier, "Picturing the City," in Zurier, Snyder, and Mecklenburg (note 3), p. 173.

7. Sloan's more typical strategy can be seen in *Sunday Afternoon in Union Square* (1912; Bowdoin College Museum of Art, Brunswick, Me.), in which two women stroll in the park engaged in conversation while two men admire them from behind. The women, however, seem oblivious to this attention and remain focused on one another.

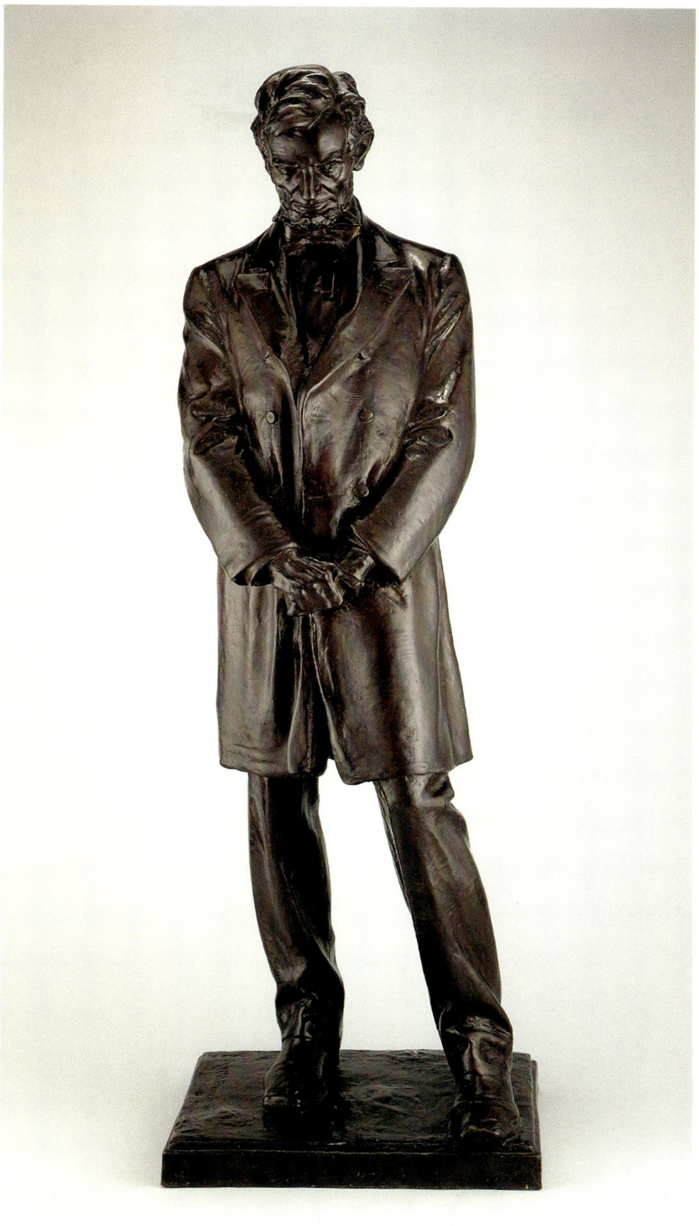

CAT. NO. 174

174. DANIEL CHESTER FRENCH (1850–1931)

Abraham Lincoln, modeled in plaster 1912, cast in bronze after 1912

Bronze; h. 95.2 cm (37½ in.)
Foundry: Roman Bronze Works, New York, N.Y.
Inscribed, top of base at left: *Daniel C. French Sc. / 1912*
Gift of Mrs. Philip D. Sang in memory of Philip D. Sang, 1984.1130

175. *Abraham Lincoln*, modeled in plaster 1916, cast in bronze after 1916

Bronze; h. 83.8 cm (33 in.)
Inscribed, top of base at back right: *Daniel C French / March 1916*
Bequest of the Arthur Rubloff Trust, 1991.324

Monumental statues of Abraham Lincoln are common in the United States, marking places as diverse as Newark, New Jersey, and Wabash, Indiana, with the dignified, thoughtful presence of America's sixteenth president.[1] Artists such as Augustus Saint-Gaudens and Paul Manship have immortalized Lincoln with powerful likenesses. The best-known statues, however, were made by Daniel Chester French when, late in his career, he collaborated with the architect Henry Bacon to fashion two important national monuments: one in Lincoln, Nebraska, and the other, more renowned memorial, in Washington, D.C. The Art Institute's two bronzes replicate the monuments on a small scale and were produced to capitalize on both the popularity of Lincoln memorabilia and the reputation of their sculptor.

Throughout the course of French's career he excelled in the production of public statuary, creating works for the World's Columbian Exposition in Chicago, the Boston Public Library, the Customs House in New York City, the Minnesota State Capitol (see cat. no. 142), and numerous other municipal monuments.[2] French received the Nebraska commission for the standing *Abraham Lincoln* in 1909, six years after the state legislature passed a bill initiating the formation of the Abraham Lincoln Centennial Memorial Association. The sculptor responded enthusiastically to the commission, but expressed some doubts about his ability to represent Lincoln: "I pray that

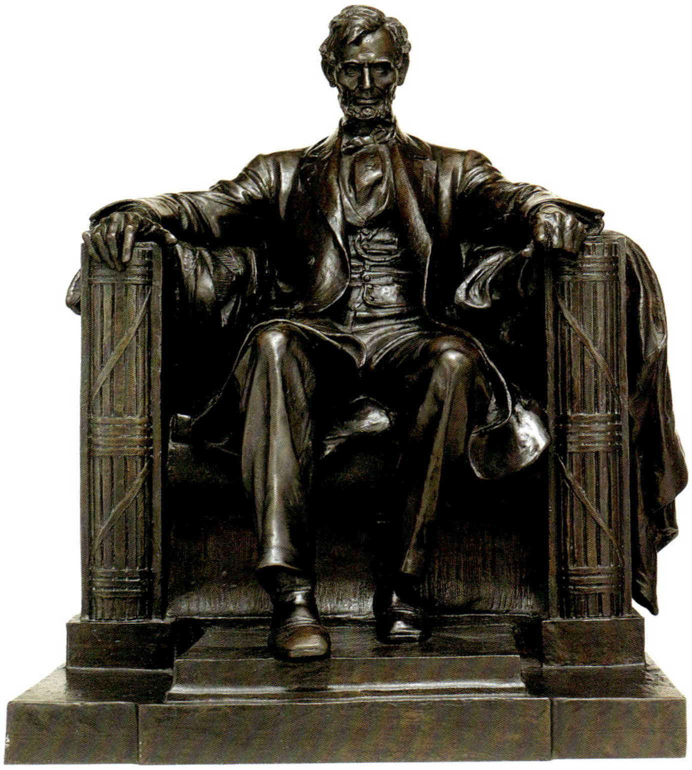

CAT. NO. 175

I may rise to the occasion. . . . The confidence that [the members of the committee] have in this manner, manifested, in my ability, will be another incentive to me to make this statue worthy of the subject."[3]

French and Bacon submitted their plans for the monument to the Lincoln committee in January 1911 and signed a contract the following month. Their plans specified a bronze statue of the president standing in front of a large slab of granite on which the text of the Emancipation Proclamation was to be carved. The confluence of word and image in the monument presents an image of Lincoln as a powerfully moving orator remembered not only for his deeds, but also for his words.[4] French pursued his subject's likeness by studying photographs by Mathew Brady and a life mask of the president by Leonard Volk, cast in April 1860.[5] He completed his Lincoln after much revision early in 1912, and unveiled it in Nebraska that autumn.

French petitioned the committee to allow him to produce bronze copies of his working model in lieu of the final installment of his contract payment; at least twelve bronzes, smaller and less complex than the monument, were cast.[6] Michael Richman has designated these bronzes "unquestionably the best of all the bronze multiples that French produced during his career," as they capture, in French's words, "Lincoln bearing the burdens and perplexities and problems of the Great War."[7] With his head bowed, hands clasped, and one knee bent, French's Lincoln personifies contemplation.

Several years later, French created a very different image of the president for the Lincoln Memorial in Washington, D.C., that conveys the intense moral fortitude of "honest Abe" rather than his sensitive, solitary thoughtfulness. The sculptor wrote, "[W]hat I wanted to convey was the mental and physical strength of the great President and his confidence in his ability. . . . If any of this 'gets over,' I think it is probably as much due to the whole pose of the figure and particularly to the action of the hands as to the expression of the face."[8] French received the commission in December 1914 and again collaborated with Bacon, who had signed his contract with the Lincoln Memorial Commission a year earlier. The carving of French's model in marble began in November 1918 and was finally completed a year later; the memorial was dedicated in 1922.

As many as nine bronze replicas of the Lincoln Memorial statue were cast during French's lifetime, and others were produced posthumously with authorization from the sculptor's daughter, Margaret Cresson French.[9] The appeal of these pieces lies not only in their association with the majesty of the Lincoln Memorial, but in their suggestion of Lincoln's understated strength. Lincoln sits in a thronelike chair with a flag draped over its back, his fiercely clenched hands belying the guarded expression on his face and revealing the agony of the issues he faced while in office. It is not an image of martyrdom like Frederick MacMonnies' *Nathan Hale* (see cat. no. 138), but one of moral force designed to instill a sense of awe and national pride in the viewer.

NOTES

1. For documentation of public statues of Lincoln, see F. Lauriston Bullard, *Lincoln in Marble and Bronze* (New Brunswick, N.J., 1952); Donald Charles Durman, *He Belongs to the Ages: The Statues of Abraham Lincoln* (Ann Arbor, Mich., 1951); and George Tice, *Lincoln* (New Brunswick, N.J., 1984).

2. For more about French's body of work, see Michael Richman, *Daniel Chester French: An American Sculptor*, exh. cat. (New York, Metropolitan Museum of Art, 1976).

3. Letter from Daniel Chester French to Frank M. Hall, June 28, 1909, Nebraska State Historical Society, Lincoln; quoted in Richman (note 2), p. 121.

4. The carved text does not appear in the Art Institute's small-scale replica.

5. The Art Institute's collection includes bronze casts by Leonard Volk of Lincoln's hands and death mask.

6. Richman (note 2), p. 126.

7. Ibid., pp. 126–27.

8. Letter from Daniel Chester French to Charles Moore, May 13, 1922, box 5, Charles Moore Papers, Library of Congress, Washington, D.C.; quoted in Richman (note 2), p. 184.

9. Richman (note 2), p. 186 n. 48. It is unclear to which category the Art Institute's bronze falls.

176. HENRY OSSAWA TANNER (1859–1937)

Two Disciples at the Tomb, c. 1905

Oil on canvas; 129.5 x 106.4 cm (51 x 41⅞ in.)
Signed, lower left: *H. O. Tanner*
Robert A. Waller Fund, 1906.300

Henry Ossawa Tanner was one of the most renowned religious painters at the turn of the twentieth century. His achievements were recognized both in America, where he first took up painting, and in France, where he lived most of his adult life. *Two Disciples at the Tomb* is one of Tanner's most celebrated paintings and shows his interest in Christian themes so important to African-Americans at the time. The work illustrates a passage from the Gospel of St. John in which the disciples Peter and John learned that Jesus' body was no longer in its tomb and visited the site to see for themselves what had happened: "Peter therefore went forth, and that other disciple, and came to the sepulchre. So they ran both together: and the other disciple did outrun Peter, and came first to the sepulchre. And he stooping down, and looking in, saw the linen clothes lying; yet went he not in."[1]

Like many of Tanner's paintings, the Art Institute's canvas focuses on individual responses to the miraculous events relating to the resurrection. Upon reaching Christ's empty tomb on Easter morning, Peter (the older, bearded man on the left) looks downward with a somber gaze, holding his entwined hands pensively across his chest. In contrast, John's angular face and chest are bathed in a golden light that signifies the presence of Christ's spirit and resurrection. The entrance to the tomb and the background landscape are muted and dark, emphasizing the stunning, powerful realism of the figures.

The recurrence of themes of resurrection in Tanner's work corresponds with his sense of African-American identity.[2] As the son of a prominent minister of the African Methodist Episcopal Church, Tanner was familiar with the importance of Christian symbolism to African-Americans. Specifically during the late nineteenth century, the theme of resurrection was an important symbol of the new life brought by the Emancipation Proclamation of 1863. W. E. B. DuBois noted in 1903, "For fifty years Negro religion . . . transformed itself with the dream of abolition. . . . Thus, when Emancipation finally came, it seemed to freedmen a literal Coming of the Lord."[3] Under these circumstances, the discovery of Christ's resurrection in Tanner's painting becomes a modern allegory of the salvation of African-Americans from slavery. In a brief autobiography from 1913, Tanner himself described how he invested his paintings with meaning, making them more than mere illustrations of the Bible: "I choose religious subjects not primarily because I believe they will interest people, nor because I consider them most salable. I am very glad if they do interest the people, and certainly am glad to sell them. Yet, I have chosen the character of my art because it conveys my message and tells what I want to tell to my own generation and leave to the future."[4]

The symbolism of Tanner's work reveals that he was committed to the personal expression of his heritage. But he was also concerned that the art world would not accept him as an artist without regard to stereotyped notions about his race. Although well educated and possessing social status within his community, Tanner still encountered prejudice and discrimination while studying at the Pennsylvania Academy of the Fine Arts in the 1880s. Seeking an environment with less racial discrimination, he completed his training in Paris at the Académie Julian in 1891, where his friend Hermann Dudley Murphy made a portrait of him during his student years (fig. 89). He returned to the United States in 1893 to recoup after a bout with typhoid fever and that same year presented a paper entitled "The American Negro in Art" at the Congress on Africa, an auxiliary congress at the World's Columbian Exposition in Chicago. Tanner returned to Paris in 1894 and subsequently made his home there because he found it more comfortable to live and work in its more tolerant atmosphere.

From his home in France, Tanner achieved his greatest successes, receiving honorable mention in the Paris Salon of 1896 and additional recognition in the Salons from 1897 to 1901. Many of Tanner's religious paintings from this period, including *Two Disciples at the Tomb*, were purchased by major art institutions in the United States and abroad soon after they were completed, earning the artist international recognition for these subjects.[5] *Two Disciples at the Tomb* was painted in Tanner's Parisian studio and first exhibited in 1906 at that city's

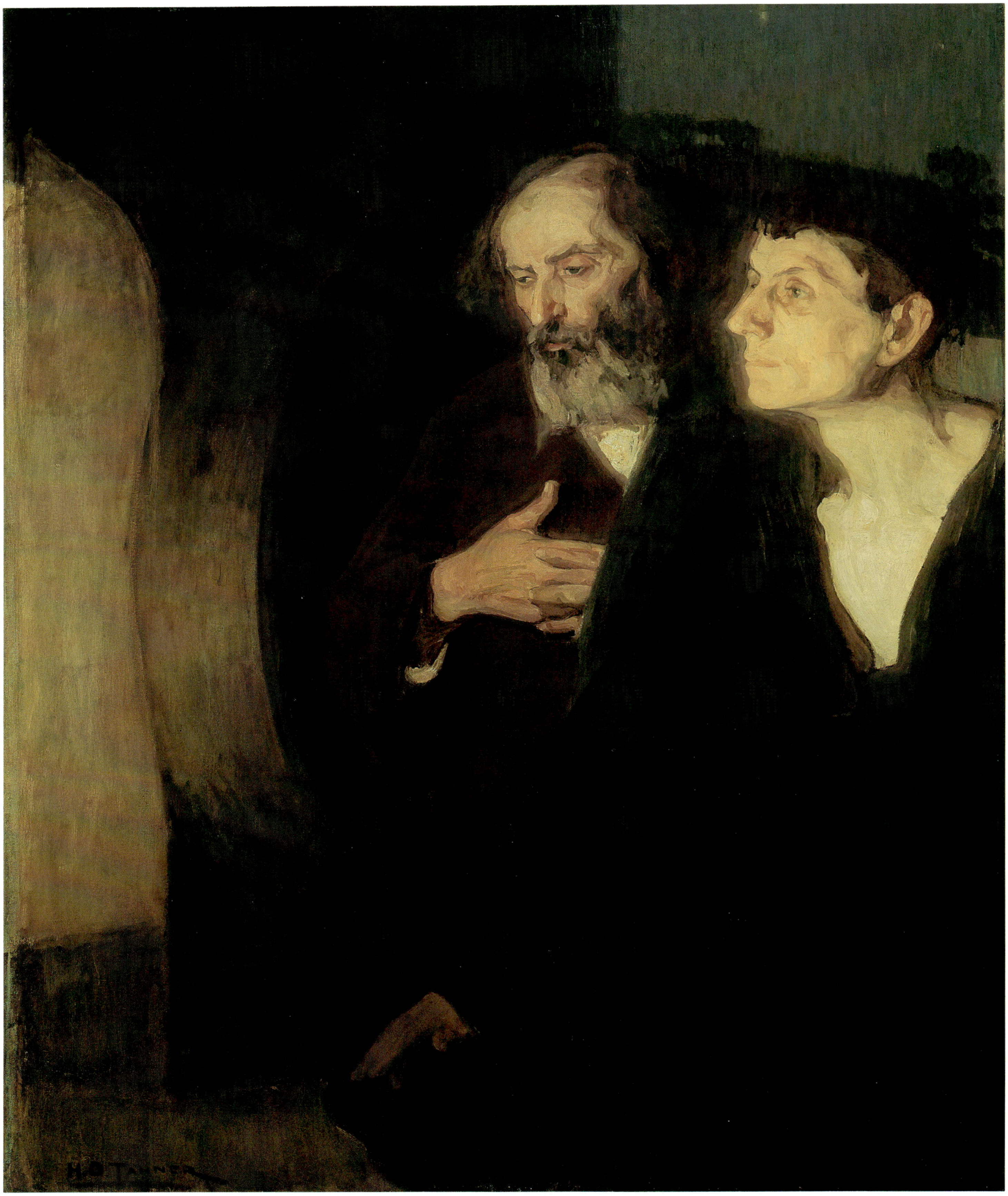

CAT. NO. 176

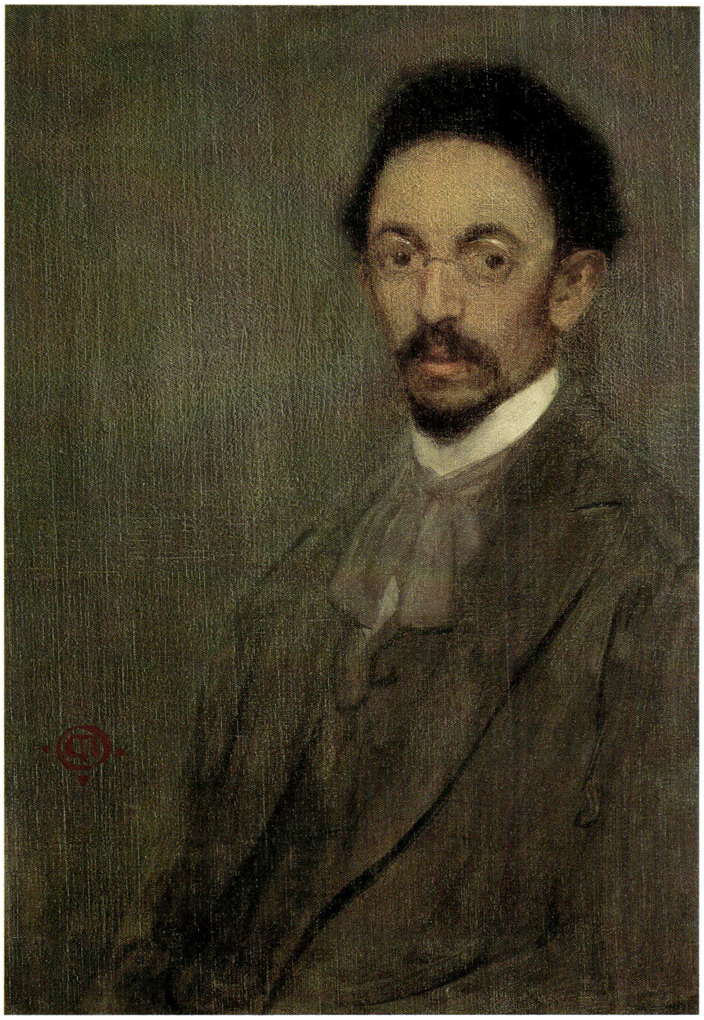

FIG. 89. Hermann Dudley Murphy (1867–1945). *Henry Ossawa Tanner*, 1891/96. Oil on canvas; 73 x 50.2 cm (28¾ x 19¾ in.). The Art Institute of Chicago, Friends of American Art Collection (1924.37).

American Art Students' Club. Later that year it was exhibited at the Art Institute's Annual Exhibition of American Art, where it won the Harris Prize for "the most impressive and distinguished work of art of the season," and was purchased by the museum.[6] One critic noted it as a "quite remarkable achievement of strength, dignity, and impressiveness," and another that "after careful consideration of all this gathering of excellence [at the Chicago exhibition], the jury of award was unanimous in selecting Mr. Tanner's picture as the best."[7] Despite the discrimination he felt living in America, Tanner could at least be satisfied with the positive reception of his art in his home country.

NOTES

1. John (20:2–6), cited in Dewey F. Mosby, Darrel Sewell, and Rae Alexander-Minter, *Henry Ossawa Tanner*, exh. cat. (Philadelphia Museum of Art, 1991), p. 192.

2. For more information on Tanner, his African-American identity, and the role of race in his art, see Dewey F. Mosby, *Across Continents and Cultures: The Art and Life of Henry Ossawa Tanner*, exh. cat. (Kansas City, Mo., Nelson-Atkins Museum of Art, 1995).

3. Quoted in Mosby (note 2), p. 40.

4. From Henry O. Tanner, "An Artist's Autobiography," *Advance* (Mar. 20, 1913), pp. 2012–14; quoted in Mosby (note 2), p. 44.

5. Among these works are *The Resurrection of Lazarus* (1896; Musée d'Orsay, Paris); *Nicodemus Visiting Jesus* (1899; Pennsylvania Academy of the Fine Arts, Philadelphia); and *Disciples at Emmaus* (1906; Musée d'Orsay, Paris).

6. Kathleen James and Sylvia Yount, "Chronology," in Mosby, Sewell, and Alexander-Minter (note 1), p. 45.

7. Florence L. Bentley, "Henry O. Tanner," *Voice of the Negro* 3, 11 (Nov. 1906), p. 480; cited in Mosby, Sewell, and Alexander-Minter (note 1), p. 192.

177. ROBERT HENRI (1865–1929)

Himself, 1913

Oil on canvas; 81.9 x 66.4 cm (32¼ x 26⅛ in.)
Signed, lower left: *Robert Henri*
Walter H. Schulze Memorial Collection, 1924.911

178. *Herself*, 1913

Oil on canvas; 81.3 x 66 cm (32 x 26 in.)
Signed, lower middle: *Robert Henri*
Walter H. Schulze Memorial Collection, 1924.912

Robert Henri is usually recognized as the rebellious leader of The Eight, but unlike his younger colleagues William Glackens (cat. no. 169), Everett Shinn (cat. no. 172), and John Sloan (cat. no. 173), the artist did not specialize in painting urban scenes. Instead Henri excelled at portraiture and sought to express his attitudes toward modern life by depicting a wide spectrum of humankind. He painted his portraits, which were mostly uncommissioned, during his travels in Europe and the United States. He produced *Himself* and *Herself* in 1913 on Ireland's Achill Island, where the artist and his wife had spent the summer; the canvases depict fisherman Johnnie Cummings and his wife.[1] Using Irish terms of endearment for husband and wife as titles, these portraits reflect Henri's empathic attitude toward his subjects. "[M]y love of mankind is individual,"

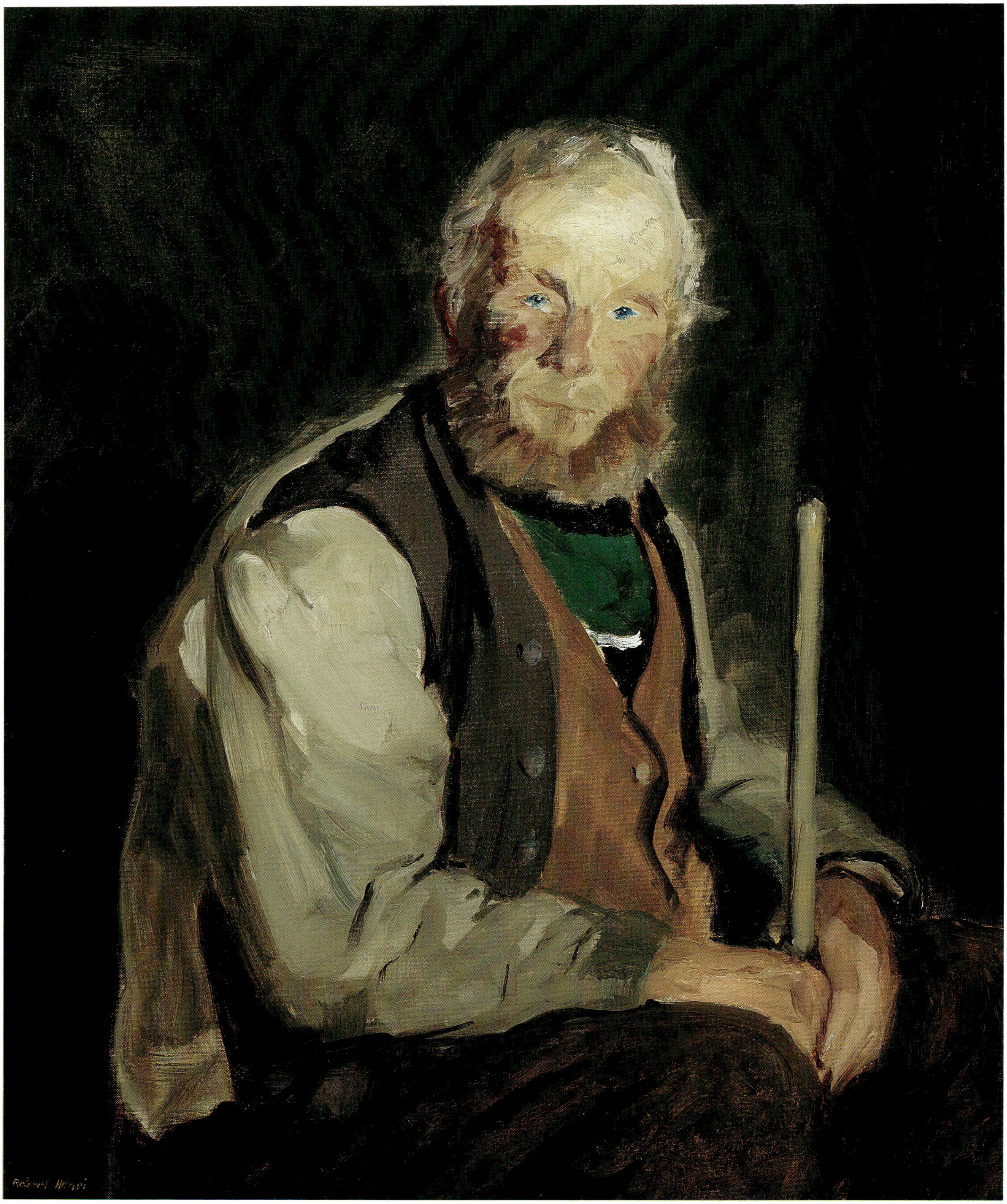

CAT. NO. 177

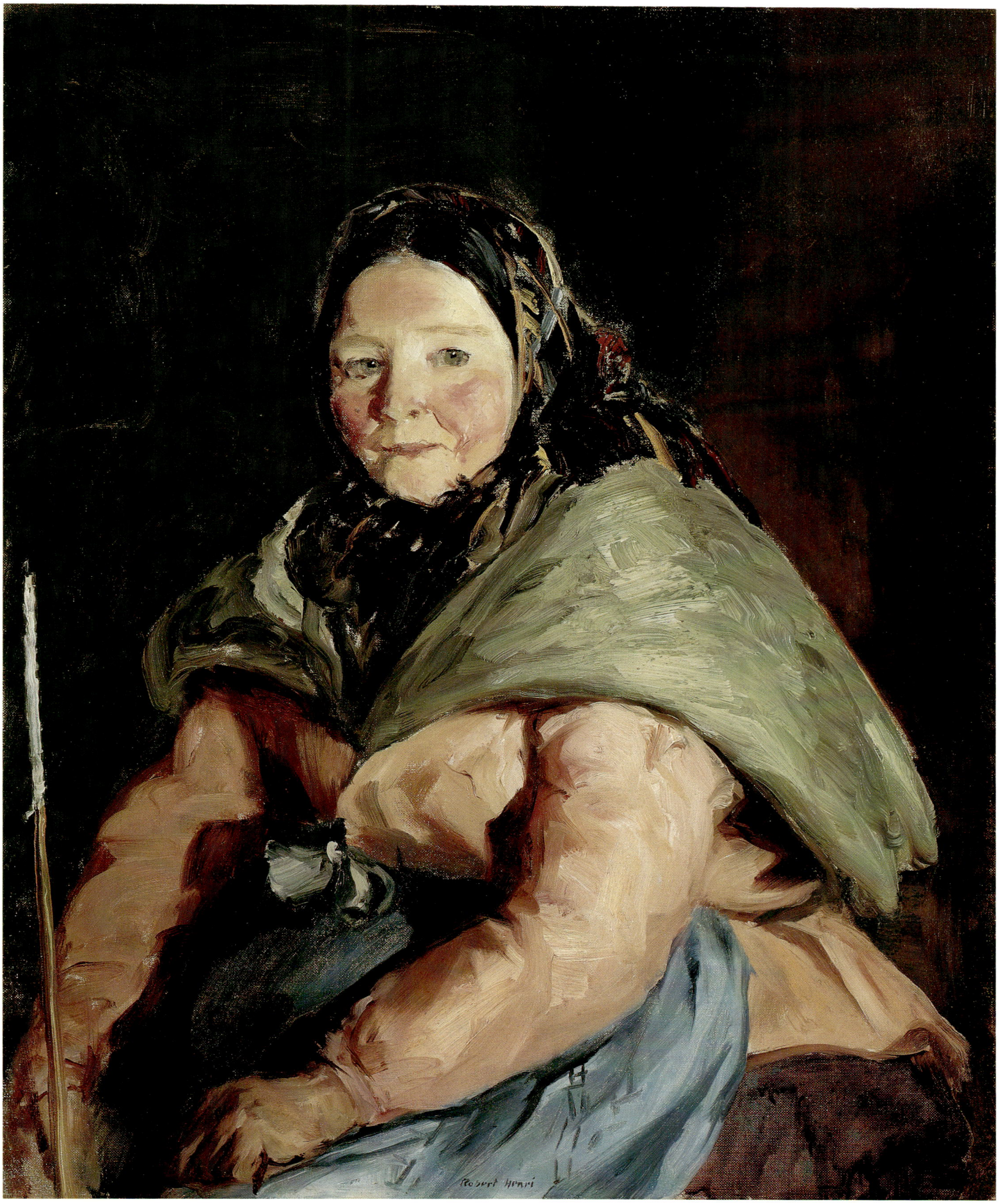

CAT. NO. 178

he wrote. "It intensifies before the Irish peasant whose love, poetry, simplicity, and humor have enriched my existence, just as completely as though each of these people were of my own country and my own hearthstone."[2]

Henri's artistic influences were many and diverse; he was inspired by the art of Frans Hals, Édouard Manet, Diego Velázquez, and the American artists Thomas Anshutz, Thomas Eakins, and Thomas Hovenden. Although Henri received the bulk of his artistic education in Paris at the Académie Julian, he had previously trained at the Pennsylvania Academy of the Fine Arts in Philadelphia; his lifelong commitment to teaching stemmed from his earliest academic experiences.[3] The artist also sowed the seeds of artistic dissent in Philadelphia, turning his studio into a meeting place for young artists such as Glackens, Shinn, and Sloan, who questioned the conservative expectations of established art institutions such as the Pennsylvania Academy and New York's National Academy of Design. Henri continued to foster this spirit of independence after moving to New York City in 1900, through his aggressive attempts to find venues for exhibiting new art. Not only did he organize the 1908 Macbeth Gallery exhibition of The Eight, but he also participated in both the legendary 1913 International Exhibition of Modern Art, or Armory Show, and the 1916 Forum Exhibition at the Anderson Galleries—all in New York City.

Henri and his wife departed for Achill Island soon after the furor over the Armory Show subsided; they settled in a fishing community called Dooagh. Although the people he painted during this trip were rustically picturesque, Henri's paint handling, palette, and naturalistic tendencies strip the portraits of sentimentality. *Himself* and *Herself* are accomplished studies of texture and color that capture in a straightforward manner the artist's sympathy for his subjects. These works are a marked departure from Henri's early full-length portraits (see fig. 90), on which he established his reputation and which have often been compared to James McNeill Whistler's elegant, more muted full-length depictions (see cat. no. 154).[4]

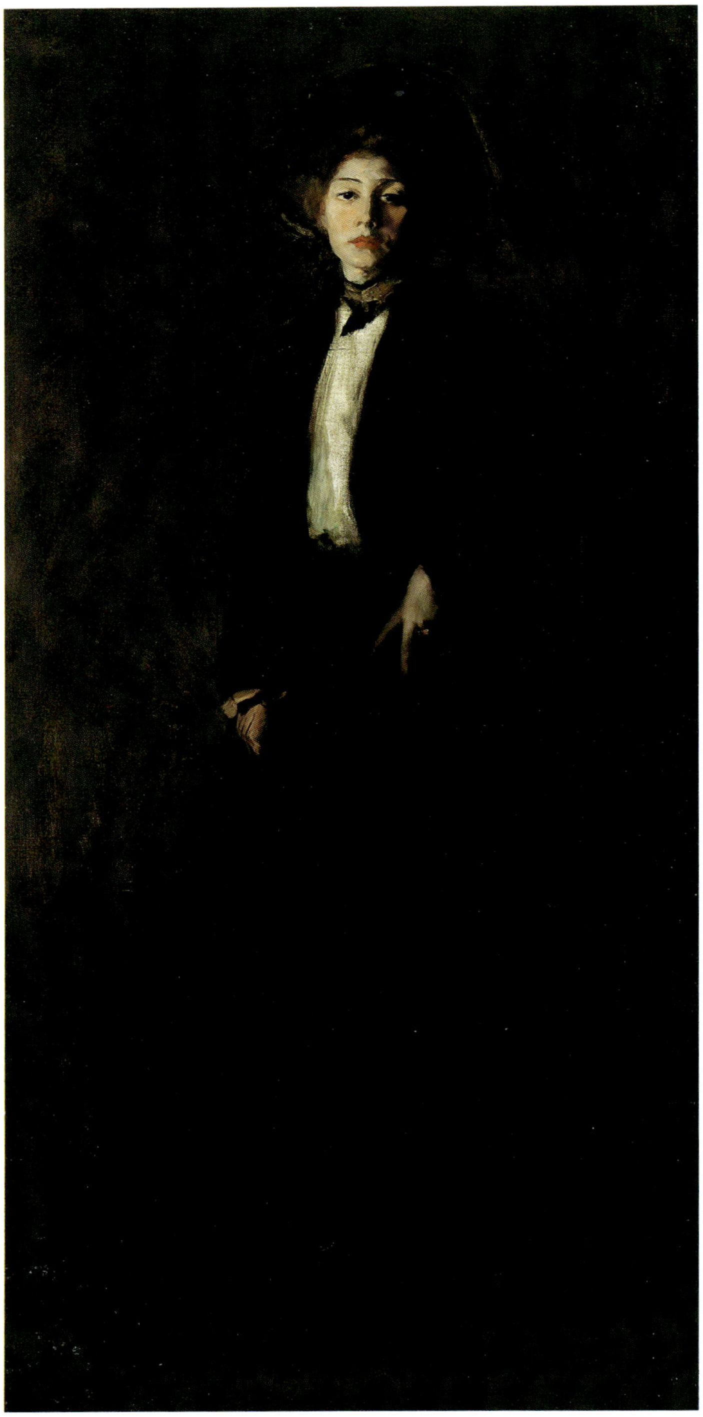

FIG. 90. Robert Henri (1865–1929). *Young Woman in Black*, 1902. Oil on canvas; 195.6 x 97.8 cm (77 x 38½ in.). The Art Institute of Chicago, Friends of American Art Collection (1910.317).

Four of Henri's Irish paintings were exhibited at the Annual Exhibition of the Pennsylvania Academy of the Fine Arts in 1916, among them *Herself*, which received a gold medal. In this painting, Henri combines a masterful command of color with a complex rendering of expression to produce an engaging yet complex image.[5] Mrs. Cummings wears a rosy pink shirt, slate blue apron, and dove gray shawl; the colors of her clothing are repeated in her kerchief. Henri applied the paint thickly and with facility, augmenting the immediacy of the likeness. The subject's expression, however, is elusive and defies description. While Mrs. Cummings appears shy and skeptical, she allows a tight smile to play across her lips.

Johnnie Cummings—the subject of *Himself*—on the other hand, is more soberly dressed, in shades of brown; his countenance is enlivened by his shining blue eyes, bright green shirt, and forthright, friendly expression. Again Henri used thick, lush paint to model his sitter's face, adding depth to the portrait. The bodies of both subjects are seen in three-quarter view, with their heads turned toward the viewer. This pose suggests something of the tension involved in depicting models who are unaccustomed to sitting quietly and still less to posing for a portrait.

Henri continued in the tradition begun by Eakins (cat. nos. 107–08 and 152–53), who painted portraits to gain psychological and physical insight into humankind. Henri, however, enlarged his project by depicting diverse types of peoples. He explained these interests in humanitarian terms, which paralleled contemporary reformist ideals: "I am looking at each individual with the eager hope of finding . . . kindness, something of the order that will rescue the race and the nation."[6] Painted during a period of great change in the arts and just before the onslaught of World War I, *Himself* and *Herself* express Henri's optimism about the power of modern art to effect change and to promote tolerance.

NOTES

1. At the same time, Henri painted at least two other portraits of Johnnie Cummings and his wife: *Old Johnnie* (Baltimore Museum of Art) and *Old Johnnie's Wife* (Detroit Institute of Arts).

2. Robert Henri, "My People," *Craftsman* 27, 5 (Feb. 1915), p. 459.

3. Henri's long career as a teacher included periods at the New York School of Art (formerly the Chase School of Art) and the Art Students League. He also operated his own establishment, the Henri School of Art, between 1909 and 1912. On Henri's teaching methods, see Robert Henri, *The Art Spirit* (Philadelphia, 1923).

4. On *Young Woman in Black*, see Valerie Ann Leeds, *My People: The Portraits of Robert Henri*, exh. cat. (Orlando, Fla., Orlando Museum of Art, 1994), pp. 17–18.

5. Henri was concerned with color theory throughout his career; he may have relied on the ideas of Hardesty Gillmore Maratta in the conception of these paintings. Maratta developed the idea of manufacturing and packaging paint in the colors of the spectrum to allow artists a system for mixing a range of colors. On Henri and color theory, see Michael Quick, "Robert Henri: Theory and Practice," in Leeds (note 4), pp. 47–62.

6. Henri (note 2), p. 467.

179. ARTS AND CRAFTS SHOP OF SHREVE, CRUMP AND LOW COMPANY

Two-Handled Dish, 1902/14

Boston

Sterling silver and stones; 5.7 x 29.2 x 10.8 cm (2¼ x 11½ x 4¼ in.)

Marked: *SHREVE, CRUMP, / & LOW CO. / STERLING* (eagle); inscribed: *RLA*

Mr. and Mrs. Robert Kubicek Fund, 1982.206

180. MARY CATHERINE KNIGHT (1876–c. 1928)

Sauce Set, 1902/08

Made at the Handicraft Shop, Boston

Silver and champlevé enamel; bowl: h. 5 cm (2 in.), diam. 10.5 cm (4⅛ in.); plate: h. 1.2 cm (½ in.), diam. 14 cm (5½ in.); ladle: 11.4 cm (4½ in.)

Marked: *sterling* (struck shield enclosing *K* and knight on horseback)

Americana Fund, 1982.205a–c

181. ELIZABETH E. COPELAND (1866–1957)

Covered Box, c. 1920

Boston

Silver, painted enamels, cloisonné, and applied cabochon stones 7 x 14 x 10.2 cm (2¾ x 5½ x 4 in.)

Marked: *EC* (on bottom in applied wire)

Laura S. Matthews Fund, 1982.1291

The English influence of the Arts and Crafts movement was initially most apparent in Boston and Chicago, in part because of British designer Charles Robert Ashbee's tours of the United States. In 1896 he made the first of four lecture tours. Beginning in 1894, his articles on silversmithing and enameling and on the Guild of Handicraft appeared in the *Art Journal* and in *Studio* magazine.[1] His silver and jewelry produced at the Guild of Handicraft were displayed at The Art Institute of Chicago in 1898 in the first exhibition of the Chicago Arts and Crafts Society at the museum. His experiments with the crafts commune the Guild of Handicraft in the rural English setting of Chipping

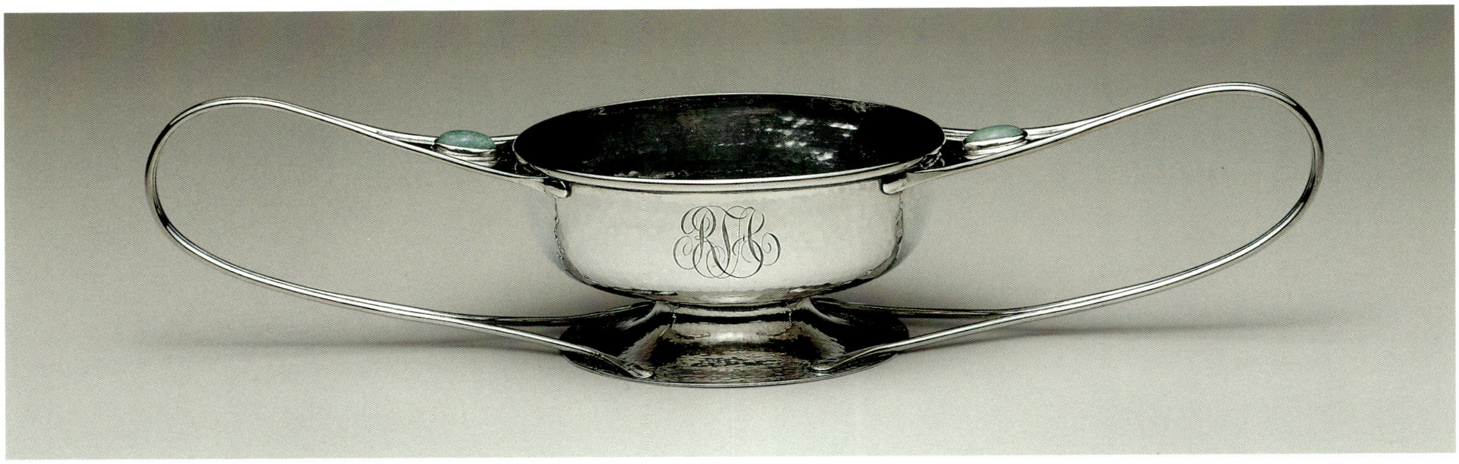

CAT. NO. 179

Camden no doubt inspired similar societies such as the Kalo community in Park Ridge, Illinois, and the Handicraft Shop in Wellesley Hills, Massachusetts.

The two-handled footed bowl (cat. no. 179) produced by Shreve, Crump and Low Company between 1902 and 1914 demonstrates that English Arts and Crafts designs were readily available in the United States. Ashbee's footed dishes, first made around 1888, were inspired by the ancient Greek kylix, a type of drinking bowl. They had been imported into the United States and were also seen in printed materials.[2]

Boston has a long history of silversmithing that began in the seventeenth century. The craftsmanship of John Hull and Robert Sanderson set a standard, followed by eighteenth-century silversmiths such as Edward Winslow and Jacob Hurd, for elegant simplicity and complex yet restrained design. At the end of the nineteenth century, the ideals of the Arts and Crafts movement joined with Boston tradition to produce another style of sophisticated silversmithing. The Boston Society of Arts and Crafts and its subsidiary, the Handicraft Shop, were influential organizations that promoted Arts and Crafts ideals and offered outlets for work produced by women.

Mary Catherine Knight was a designer of Gorham silver, and had been a pupil of Mary Ware Dennett at the Drexel Institute in Philadelphia. After Dennett helped to found the Handicraft Shop in 1901, Knight became a managing supervisor for the shop. Like the Kalo Shop in Chicago, the Handicraft Shop was a cooperative venture, and the male silversmiths were born mostly outside the United States. Unlike

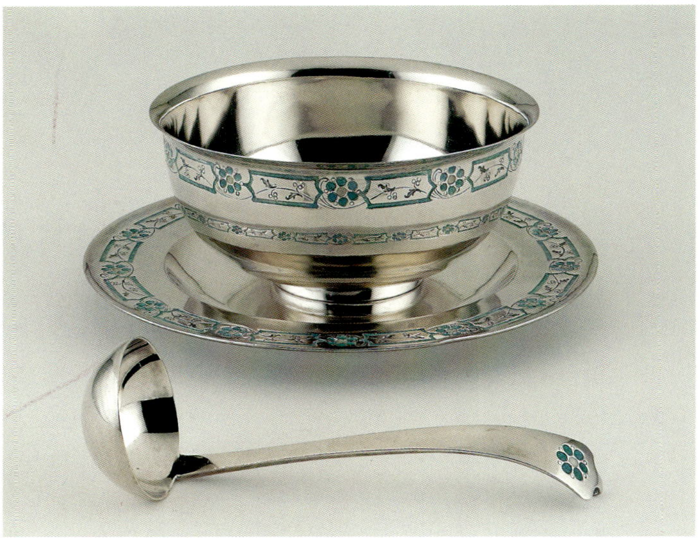

CAT. NO. 180

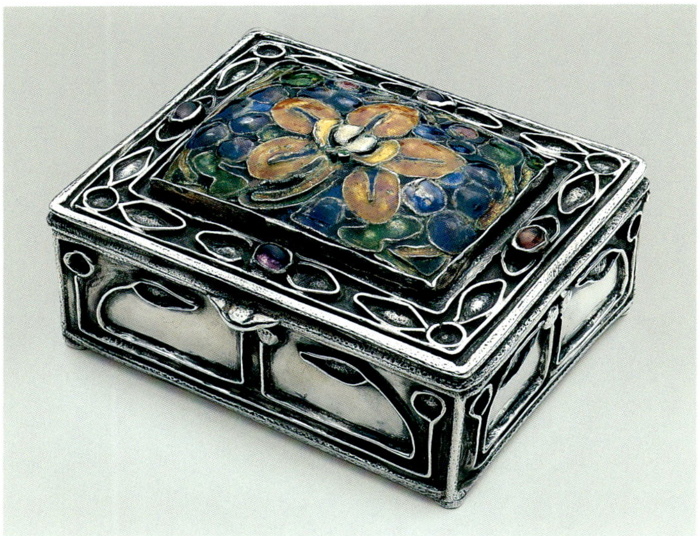

CAT. NO. 181

silversmiths such as Robert Jarvie (cat. nos. 158–60) and Clara Barck Welles (cat. no. 161), who usually created innovative, streamlined designs, the Boston Handicraft silversmiths often reinterpreted traditional forms. The strapwork and floral-band design used on this sauce set (cat. no. 180) are similar to those used on seventeenth-century Boston beakers.[3]

Knight exhibited regularly at the Boston Society of Arts and Crafts. Although her date of death is not known, she last exhibited there in 1927.[4] She also exhibited with her Handicraft Shop colleague George C. Gebelein at the first Arts and Crafts exhibition held at the Art Institute in 1902 and won a medal at St. Louis in 1904.[5]

Born in Boston, Elizabeth Copeland worked in enamel, silver, and other metals. A pupil of the noted illustrator and designer Amy Sacker, she also studied at the Cowles Art School and learned metalworking from fellow student Laurin H. Martin. Copeland's work was admired by a founding member of the Boston Society of Arts and Crafts, Sarah Choate Sears. Sears arranged for Copeland to study in London with Alexander Fisher, one of the finest enamelists of the time. Copeland returned to work for the Handicraft Shop, and then established her own shop in 1904. She exhibited in major Arts and Crafts exhibitions around the country, including those in Chicago and Detroit, and won a bronze medal at the Panama–Pacific Exposition in 1915. She retired in 1937.[6]

Copeland's enameled coffer (cat. no. 181) reflects the medievalist impulses of the Arts and Crafts movement. It recalls the enameled reliquaries covered with precious gems and exhibiting extraordinarily skilled craftsmanship associated with medieval art. In addition to applying semi-precious stones such as the purple cabochons on the outer edge of the lid, she attached thin wires to form raised divisions and accentuate contrasting light and dark areas. The brilliantly enameled colors of the lid form an orange five-petaled flower surrounded by blue grapes and green leaves.[7]

NOTES

1. C. R. Ashbee, *Modern English Silverwork: An Essay*, ed. Alan Crawford and Shirley Bury (London, 1974), p. xxiii.

2. See Leslie Greene Bowman, *American Arts and Crafts: Virtue in Design* (Los Angeles, 1990), pp. 19–21; and Charles L. Venable, *Silver in America, 1840–1940: A Century of Splendor* (Dallas, 1995), p. 351.

3. W. Scott Braznell, in Wendy Kaplan, ed., *"The Art That Is Life": The Arts and Crafts Movement in America, 1875–1920*, exh. cat. (Museum of Fine Arts, Boston, 1987), pp. 272–73.

4. Karen Evans Ulehla, ed., *The Society of Arts and Crafts, Boston Exhibition Record, 1897–1927* (Boston, 1981), p. 128.

5. See The Art Institute of Chicago, *Catalogue of the First Annual Exhibition of Original Designs for Decorations and Examples of Art Crafts Having Distinct Artistic Merit*, exh. cat. (1902), p. 40.

6. Braznell (note 3), p. 268; and *Who's Who in American Art*, vol. 3 (Washington, D.C., 1940), p. 145.

7. The Art Institute also owns an inkwell made by Elizabeth Copeland.

182. SHREVE AND COMPANY (FOUNDED 1852)

Pitcher, c. 1910

San Francisco

Sterling silver; h. 39.4 cm (15½ in.)

Marks, struck incuse: *SHREVE AND CO. / SAN FRANCISCO / STERLING / 6¼ PINTS*

Gift of the Antiquarian Society, 1988.216

183. *Vase*, 1910/20

San Francisco

Sterling silver and ceramic; 21.8 x 11.8 cm (8⅝ x 4⅝ in.)

Marks, struck incuse: *SHREVE AND CO. / SAN FRANCISCO / STERLING*

Gift of the Antiquarian Society through Mrs. Robert Hixon Glore, 1984.246

Founded in 1852, Shreve and Company had become a large, mechanized silver manufacturer by the end of the century. Like many other Arts and Crafts silversmiths, Shreve produced "handcrafted" Arts and Crafts designs that were actually spun on a lathe, with hammer marks added later.[1] The medieval inspiration of the Arts and Crafts movement is obvious in the strap handle of this pitcher (cat. no. 182) as well as in the applied strapwork patterns and rivets. These adornments were most often used on Arts and Crafts furniture, but were also used on silver, copper, and even ceramic vessels.[2] The Art Institute also owns a Shreve tea and coffee service with a tray in the popular "XIVth Century" pattern. Produced after 1911, this Gothic-inspired design has a lightly hammered strapwork motif, which contrasts with its broad, smooth, expansive, and unembellished silver surfaces.

Shreve produced silver-mounted ceramic objects as well. These earthenware and silver combinations reflect the marriage of the Arts and Crafts movement with the Asian influences of the West Coast. The glazed stoneware body of this vase (cat. no. 183) is unmarked. It has been thought that

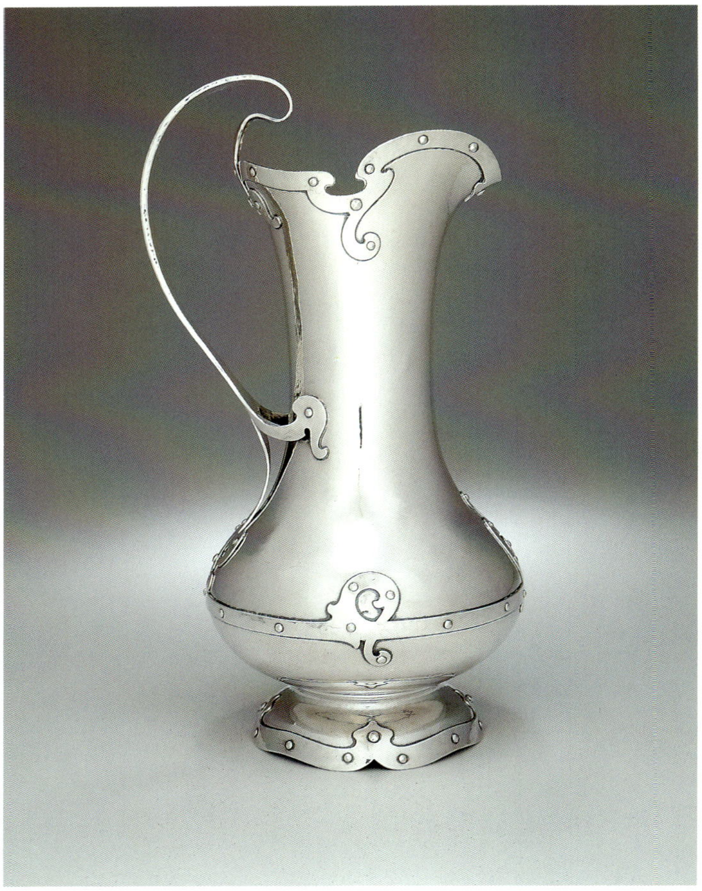

CAT. NO. 182

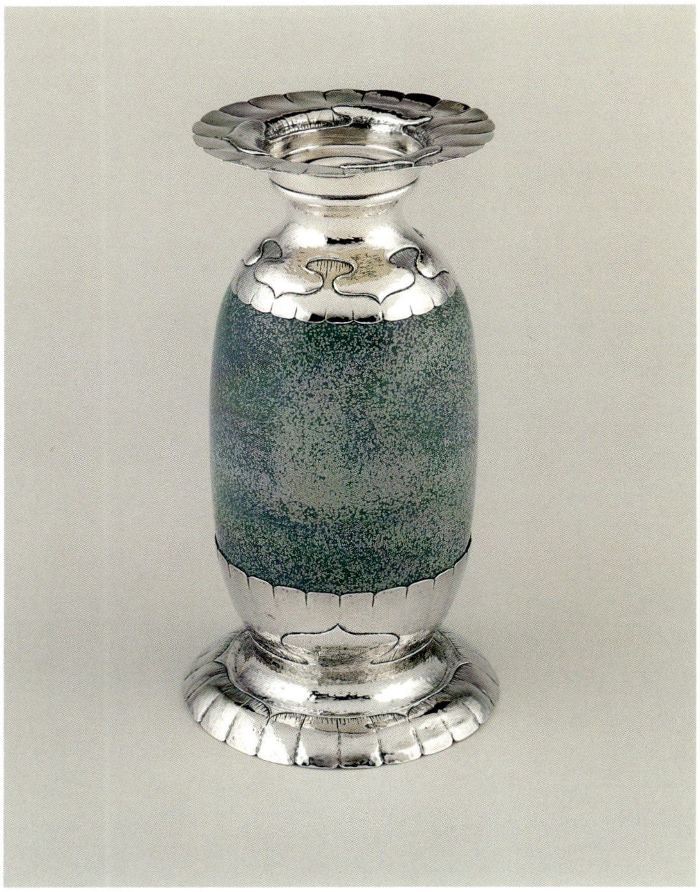

CAT. NO. 183

such ceramic bodies were imported from Japan. It is also possible that Shreve's well-traveled clients brought back objets d'art from China and Japan that Shreve then mounted.[3]

The silver mounts surrounding this vase, with their abstracted, curvilinear leaf forms around the neck and foot rim, reveal the lingering influence of Art Nouveau aesthetics in the 1910s. These flowing, organic shapes are punctuated by a regular pattern of vertical lines and slightly rounded edges, making the vase a quiet, balanced, contemplative object.

NOTES

1. Leslie Greene Bowman, *American Arts and Crafts: Virtue in Design*, exh. cat. (Los Angeles County Museum of Art, 1990), p. 116.

2. Gorham silver also used silver mounts over art pottery.

3. During the early twentieth century, Shreve and Company produced silver compotes that held Japanese Satsuma earthenware bowls. See Kenneth R. Trapp, *The Arts and Crafts Movement in California: Living the Good Life*, exh. cat. (Oakland, Calif., Oakland Museum 1993), p. 144; and Edgar W. Morse, ed., *Silver in the Golden State: Images and Essays Celebrating the History and Art of Silver in California*, exh. cat. (Oakland, Calif., Oakland Museum 1986), p. 20.

184. PAUL MANSHIP (1885–1966)

Indian and Pronghorn Antelope, 1914

Bronze; *Indian*: h. 33.3 cm (13 in.); *Antelope*: h. 31.4 cm (12¼ in.)
Foundry: Roman Bronze Works, New York, N.Y.
Inscribed on *Indian*: *Paul Manship c 1914*
Friends of American Art Collection, 1914.823 a-b

185. *Dancer and Gazelles*, 1916

Bronze; h. 78.7 cm (31 in.); base 84.5 x 25.4 cm (33¼ x 10 in.)
Inscribed: *Paul Manship c 1916*
Friends of American Art Collection, 1916.444

Born in St. Paul, Minnesota, Paul Manship had decided to become a sculptor by the time he was fifteen. With the encouragement of his family, he studied at the St. Paul Institute and in 1905 moved to New York City to attend classes at the Art Students League. There he studied briefly with the sculptor Hermon Atkins MacNeil before becoming an assistant to

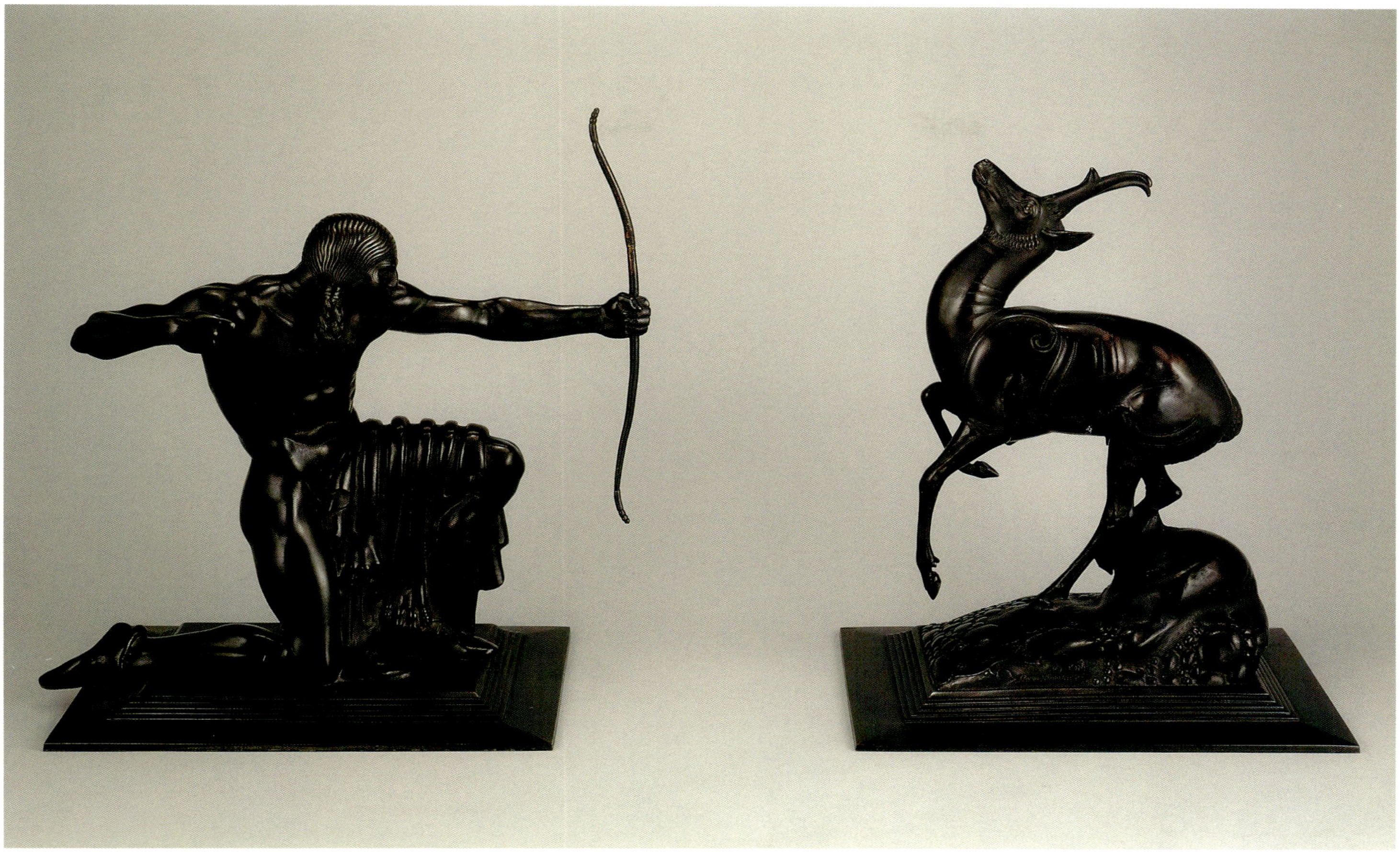

CAT. NO. 184

Solon Borglum, a renowned designer of equestrian statues. In 1908, after completing a life modeling course with Charles Grafly, Manship worked in the studio of the classically trained Viennese sculptor Isidore Konti, and in 1909 he won the prestigious Prix de Rome.

As a fellow at the American Academy in Rome, Manship traveled in Greece and Italy and found that he was especially drawn to archaic Greek statues and ancient Egyptian, Assyrian, and Minoan motifs. Rejecting the then-fashionable Beaux-Arts naturalism, the young sculptor found inspiration in the silhouettes, smooth planes, and stylized renderings of these ancient works, and combined them with modernist art forms to create a unique sculptural style. By the time he made his professional debut at the annual exhibition of the Architectural League of New York in 1913, his interest in archaism corresponded to the European modernists' interest in primitivism.[1] As one critic was to observe a few years later, in 1916: "Manship, while on his travels, learned a great lesson,—the essential unity of all primitive art, whether Greek, Assyrian, Gothic, Egyptian, or East Indian."[2] Manship was known both for his arresting linear compositions, celebrated for their modernistic appeal, and for his technical mastery. He deftly fused smooth, curved surfaces with exquisitely carved details in his sculptures, finishing them with rich, glowing patination.

Manship first exhibited *Indian and Pronghorn Antelope* along with thirteen other sculptures in 1914 at the Pennsylvania Academy of the Fine Arts. In these pendant pieces, Manship excelled at capturing the force and power of the hunt in small scale, expertly making use of positive and negative space through the physical separation of the two sculptures. The arrow that appears to have flown through the central space connects the two works, which together form a circular composition.[3] Manship copyrighted the design for *Indian and Pronghorn Antelope*, originally created for his mantelpiece, in 1914, and consigned the work to the Gorham Foundry in Rhode Island; the sculptures became extraordinarily popular as decorative ornaments for both house and garden.[4] Later that year, Manship transferred the consignment to the Roman Bronze Works in New York City, where all subsequent casts were produced. When an expanded version of the Academy

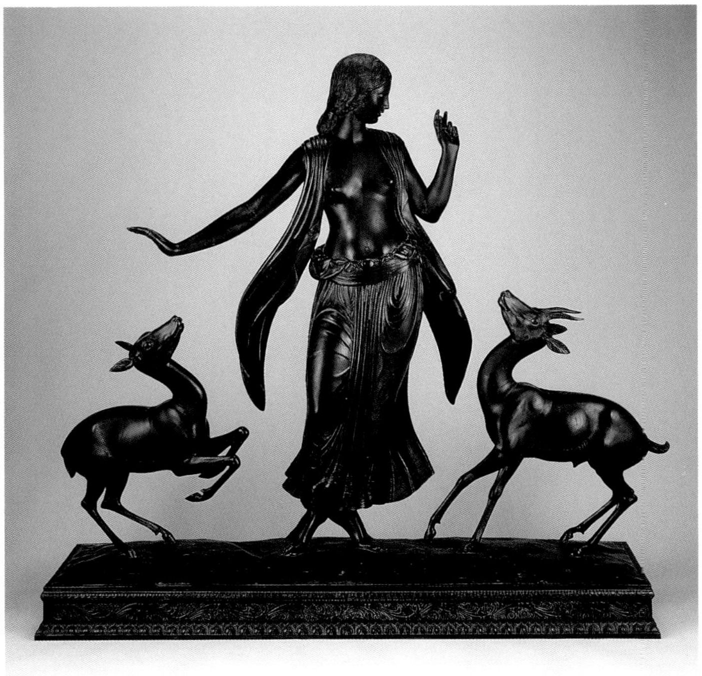

CAT. NO. 185

show traveled to The Art Institute of Chicago in August 1915, the Friends of American Art ordered a version of *Indian and Pronghorn Antelope* for the museum's collection.[5]

In 1916 Manship had his first one-man show in New York City, at the Berlin Photographic Company. Included among his designs was the model for *Dancer and Gazelles* (1916), whose composition reflects the artist's interests in East Indian subjects and modern dance.[6] When A. E. Gallatin, the noted art critic and collector, first saw the sculpture, he commented that, with its rhythmic play of positive and negative space, it "possess[es] a smoothness and vitality one very rarely finds outside of Indian art."[7] The combination of sources used to create a seemingly simple composition, however, proved unique. Even more successful than the earlier group, *Dancer and Gazelles* was a widely popular sculpture and in 1918 won Manship his second Barnett Prize from the National Academy of Design in New York.[8]

NOTES

1. For a discussion of Manship's archaic sources and their relationship to modernism, see Susan Rather, *Archaism, Modernism, and the Art of Paul Manship* (Austin, Tex., 1993).

2. Martin Birnbaum, "Paul Manship," *Introductions: Painters, Sculptors, and Graphic Artists* (New York, 1919), p. 53.

3. Harry Rand, *Paul Manship*, exh. cat. (Washington, D.C., National Museum of American Art, Smithsonian Institution, 1989), p. 36.

4. Rather (note 1), p. 92.

5. *Indian and Pronghorn Antelope* was illustrated on the front cover of the exhibition's small catalogue; see *Catalogue of an Exhibition of Sculpture by Paul Manship*, exh. cat. (The Art Institute of Chicago, 1915).

6. Paula M. Kozol, "Paul Manship (1885–1966)," in Kathryn Greenthal, Paula M. Kozol, and Jan Seidler Ramirez, *American Figurative Sculpture in the Museum of Fine Arts, Boston* (Boston, 1986), p. 400.

7. Quoted in Rather (note 1), p. 119.

8. Janis Conner and Joel Rosenkranz, *Rediscoveries in American Sculpture: Studio Works, 1893–1939* (Austin, Tex., 1989), p. 135.

186. GEORGE BELLOWS (1882–1925)

Love of Winter, 1914

Oil on canvas; 82.6 x 102.9 cm (32½ x 40½ in.)
Signed, lower right: *Geo Bellows*
Friends of American Art Collection, 1914.1018

The spirit of bold experimentation that pervades George Bellows's work was evident to both critics and viewers of his 1914 exhibition at The Art Institute of Chicago. An art critic for the *Bloomington (Illinois) Bulletin* reported overhearing a visitor comment: "Isn't this strong, vital stuff?" Another critic wrote that "no one can enter the room where [Bellows's paintings] are exhibited without feeling the grip of their strange quality or admiring the cleverness of the artist's handling."[1] *Love of Winter* was among the works in this exhibition, which also included numerous Maine seascapes by Bellows. The Friends of American Art acquired this painting for the museum directly from the exhibition, attesting to their progressive taste and commitment to promoting modern American art.[2]

Although he did not participate in the 1908 group exhibition at the Macbeth Gallery, Bellows is usually considered alongside the artists of the Ashcan School because of his interest in social realism and modernist painting methods. He studied with Robert Henri (see cat. nos. 177–78), the iconoclastic leader of the group, at the Chase School of Art (founded by William Merritt Chase) after withdrawing from Ohio State University in 1904.[3] This brief period at the Chase School appears to be his only instance of formal training. However, like Henri, Bellows remained engaged with art theory throughout his career and often relied upon innovations in color theory and composition to invigorate his work.[4]

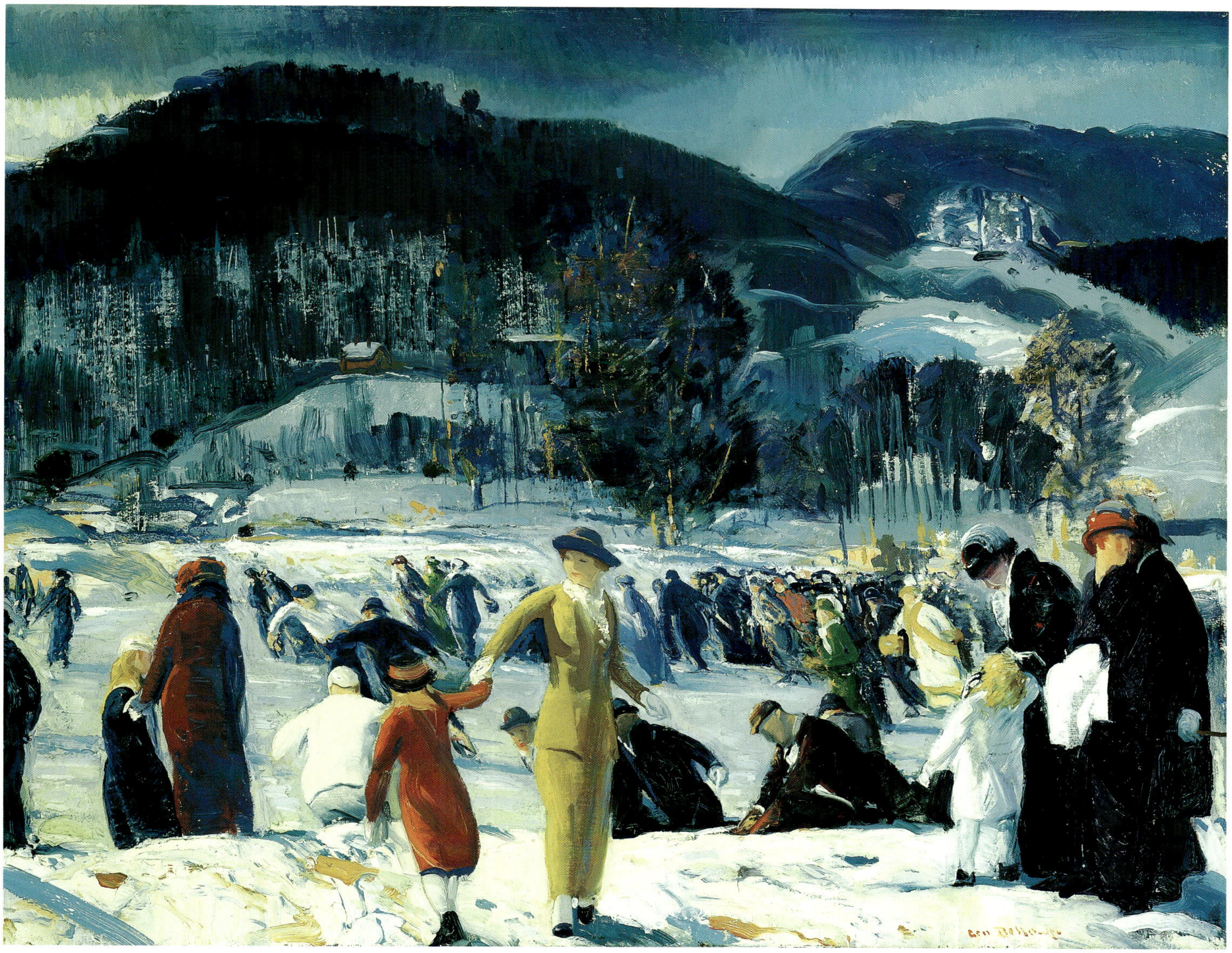

CAT. NO. 186

Love of Winter shows Bellows pushing at the boundaries of his style while reaffirming his interest in certain types of subject matter and methods of paint application. Between approximately 1911 and 1915, he immersed himself in the color theories espoused by the paint manufacturer Hardesty Gillmore Maratta, who marketed a set of pigments designed to assure harmoniously balanced color compositions by allowing artists to choose palettes based on musical notation.[5] Bellows composed *Love of Winter* following the enormously productive summer he spent on Monhegan Island in 1913. In these months, using the Maratta system, he painted seascapes perfectly suited to the closely related blues and greens advocated by the theorist. The Art Institute's painting departs from the balanced, nuanced shades of the seascapes and introduces brighter, jarring color combinations that nonetheless derive from Maratta's ideas: red-purple, red-orange, yellow, and blue. The artist supplemented his color scheme with pale, icy blues, greens, and lavenders that intensify the winter scene and offset the saturated hues in the foreground.

The thickly applied paint, winter scenery, and urban setting of *Love of Winter* are common in Bellows's work. Lavish and varied, the brushwork defines the solidity of the snow and the speed of the skaters, while creating a surface that firmly roots the artist in modernist art practice. Art historian Michael Quick commented that, "as Bellows, like some other Henri students, began to use the palette knife more and more, he found in snow the opportunity to create numerous textures in unusually high impastos."[6] In January 1914, the artist wrote to

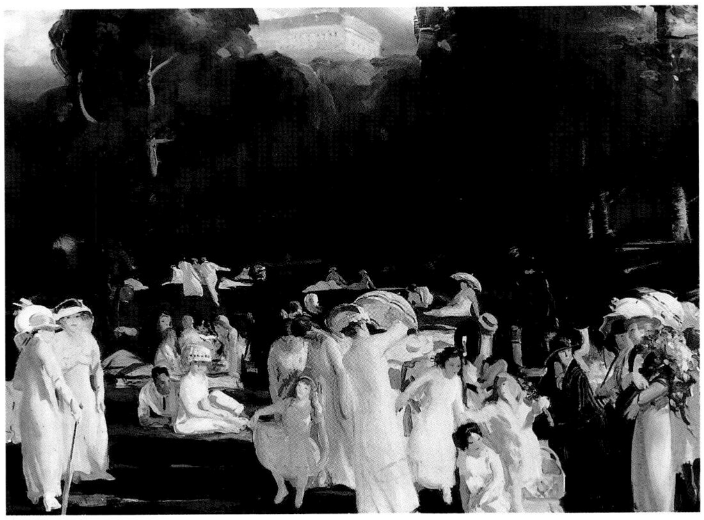

FIG. 91. George Bellows (1882–1925). *A Day in June*, 1913. Oil on canvas; 106.7 x 121.9 cm (42 x 48 in.). Detroit Institute of Arts, Detroit Museum of Art Purchase, Lizzie Merrill Palmer Fund.

a friend just before painting this work: "There has been none of my favorite snow. I must always paint the snow at least once a year."[7] Then, on February 13, a major blizzard hit New York City, allowing Bellows to paint *Love of Winter*.[8]

The Art Institute's painting corresponds in many ways to the artist's 1913 work *A Day in June* (fig. 91); both are outdoor scenes of public leisure activities featuring multiple groupings of women and children. Although many have assumed that the location of both works is Central Park, the size of the hills in the background of *Love of Winter* suggests a different site or that Bellows contrived a composite view. The themes of these two works and their vigorous style link them to many other Ashcan School paintings such as John Sloan's *Renganeschi's Saturday Night* (cat. no. 173) in which leisure is explained in a reportorial, but emphatically experimental, fashion.

NOTES

1. *Bloomington (Illinois) Bulletin*, Dec. 15, 1914, in Chronological Scrapbooks, Ryerson Library, The Art Institute of Chicago, roll 5; and *Chicago Herald*, Dec. 17, 1914, in Chronological Scrapbooks, roll 5.

2. In this respect, a critic for the *Chicago Herald* commented that "the Friends of American Art are hovering about the exhibit bent on purchase" (*Chicago Herald*, Dec. 17, 1914, in Chronological Scrapbooks [note 1]).

3. For Bellows's biography, see Charles H. Morgan, *George Bellows: Painter of America* (New York, 1965).

4. Michael Quick explained in depth this long-ignored facet of Bellows's work in "Technique and Theory: The Evolution of George Bellows's Painting Style," in Quick et al., *The Paintings of George Bellows*, exh. cat. (Fort Worth, Tex., Amon Carter Museum, 1992), pp. 9–95.

5. Ibid., pp. 33–42.

6. Ibid., p. 27. Other winter scenes by Bellows, totaling twenty-six paintings, are catalogued in David Setford and Nancy Barrow, "George Bellows's Winter Paintings: A Chronological Checklist," in Setford, *George Bellows: Love of Winter*, exh. cat. (West Palm Beach, Fla., Norton Museum of Art, 1997), pp. 111–15.

7. Letter from George Bellows to Joseph Taylor, Jan. 15, 1914; quoted in Quick et al. (note 4), p. 47.

8. Setford (note 6), p. 104.

GLOSSARY OF DECORATIVE ARTS TERMS

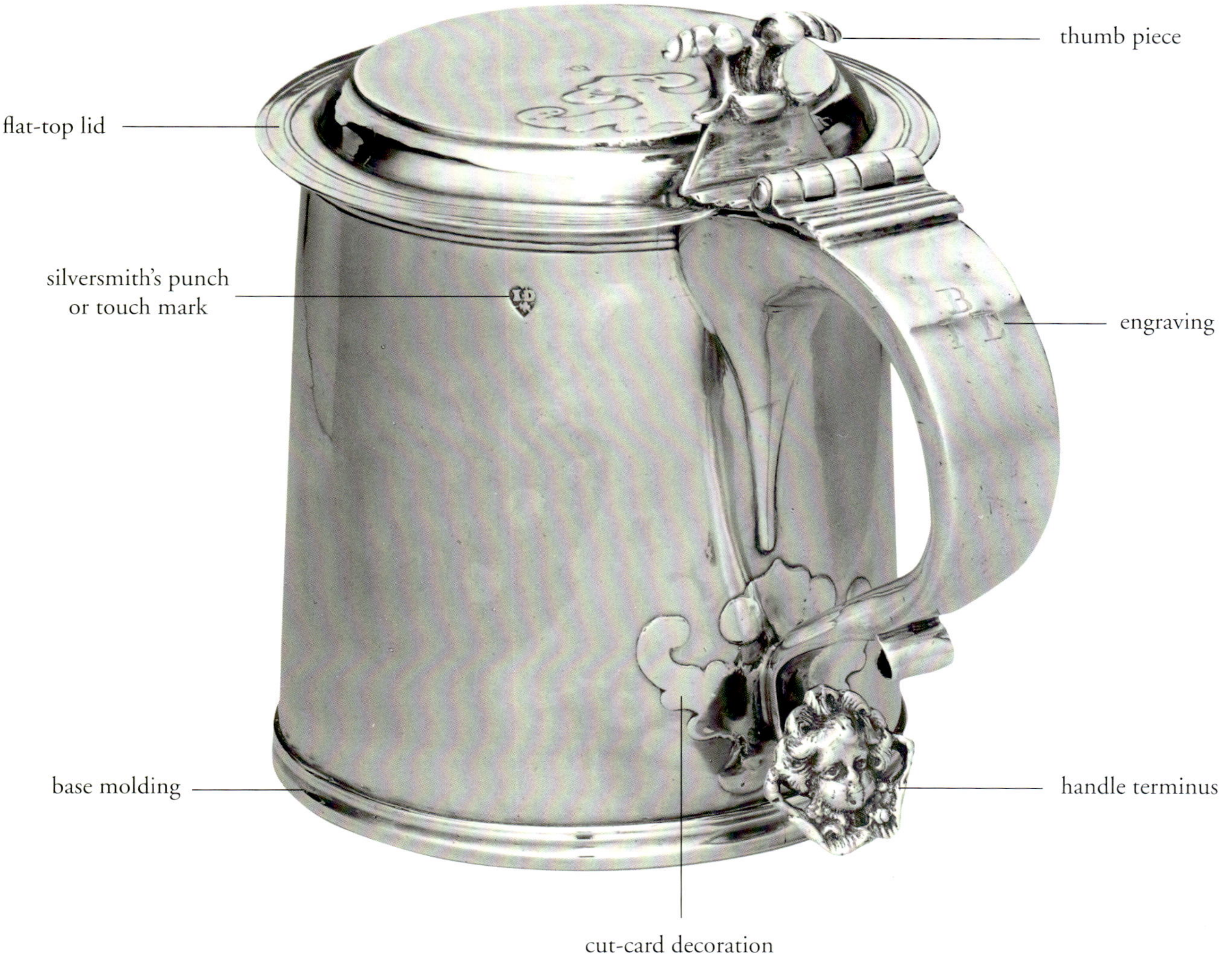

CAT. NO. 6

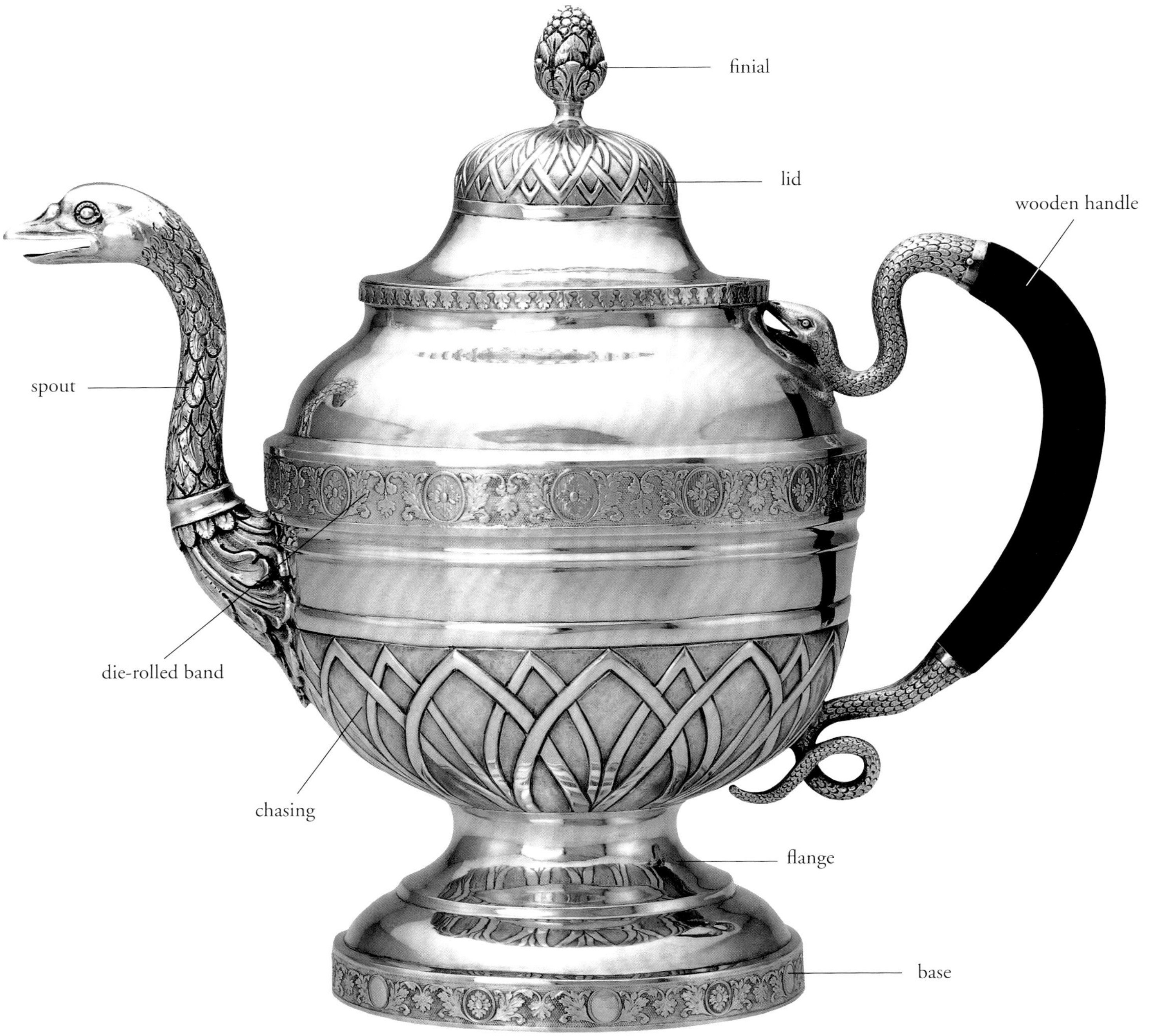
finial
lid
wooden handle
spout
die-rolled band
chasing
flange
base

CAT. NO. 55

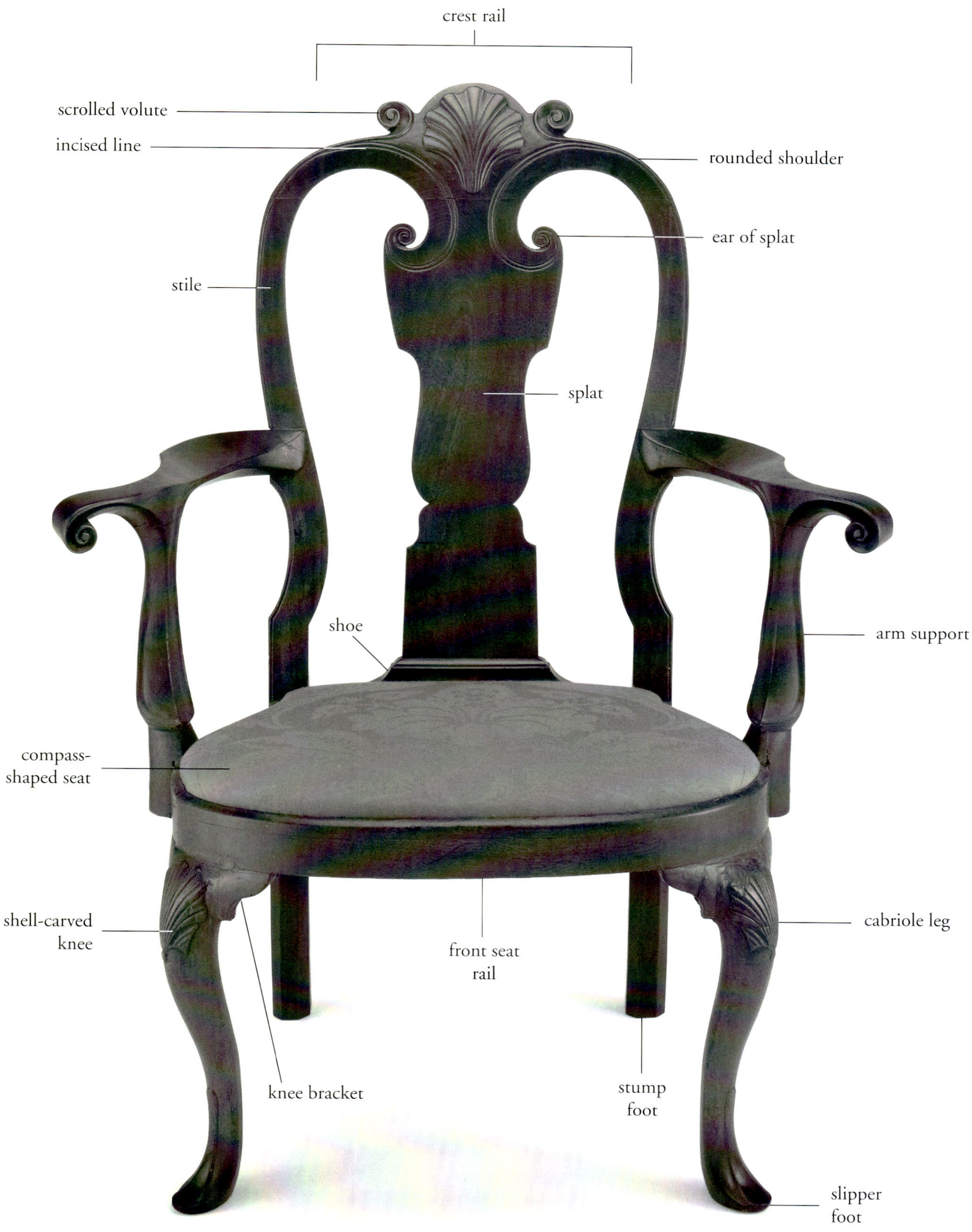
crest rail
scrolled volute
incised line
rounded shoulder
ear of splat
stile
splat
shoe
arm support
compass-
shaped seat
shell-carved
knee
front seat
rail
cabriole leg
knee bracket
stump
foot
slipper
foot

CAT. NO. 13

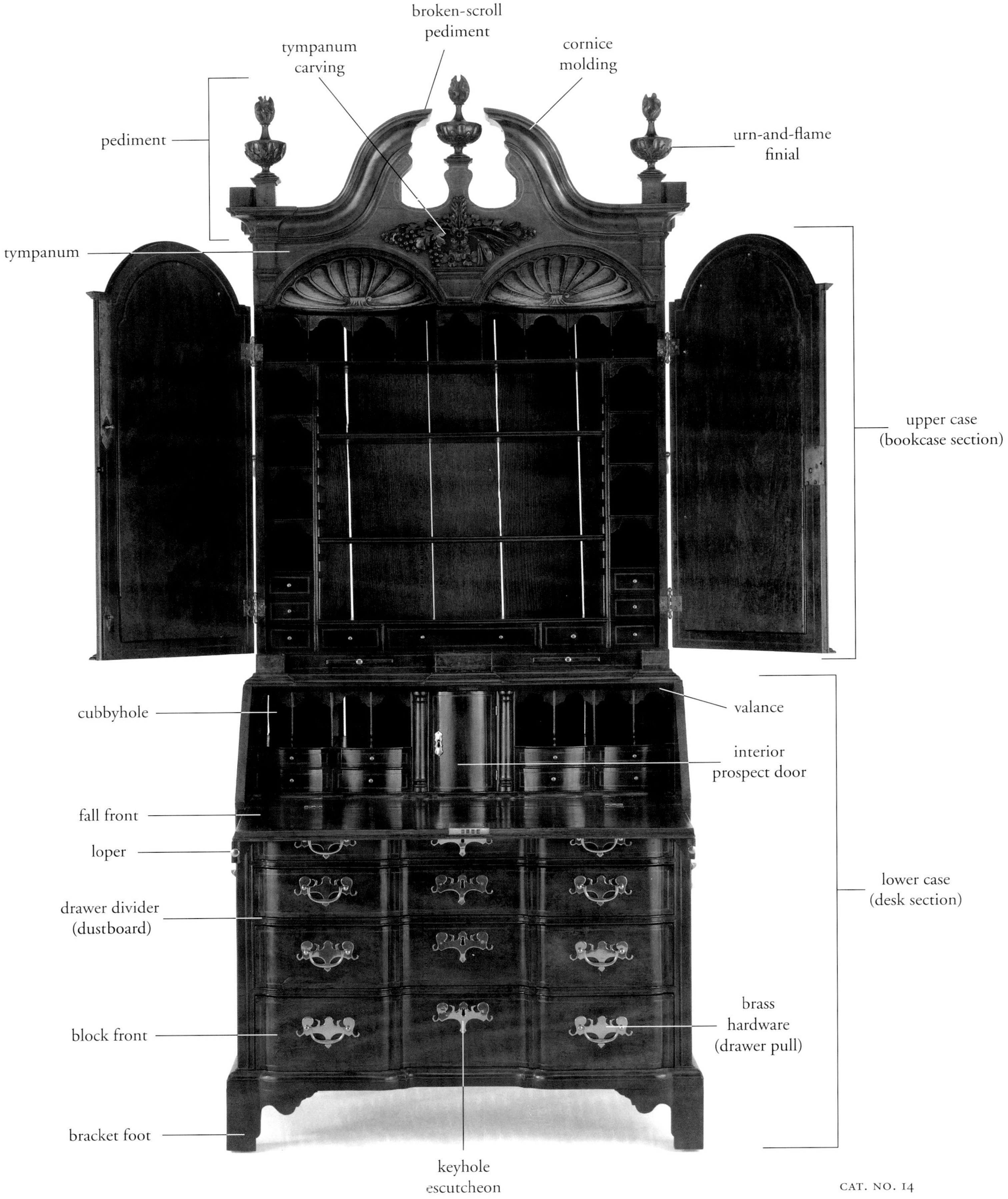
broken-scroll pediment
tympanum carving
cornice molding
pediment
urn-and-flame finial
tympanum
upper case (bookcase section)
cubbyhole
valance
interior prospect door
fall front
loper
lower case (desk section)
drawer divider (dustboard)
block front
brass hardware (drawer pull)
bracket foot
keyhole escutcheon

CAT. NO. 14

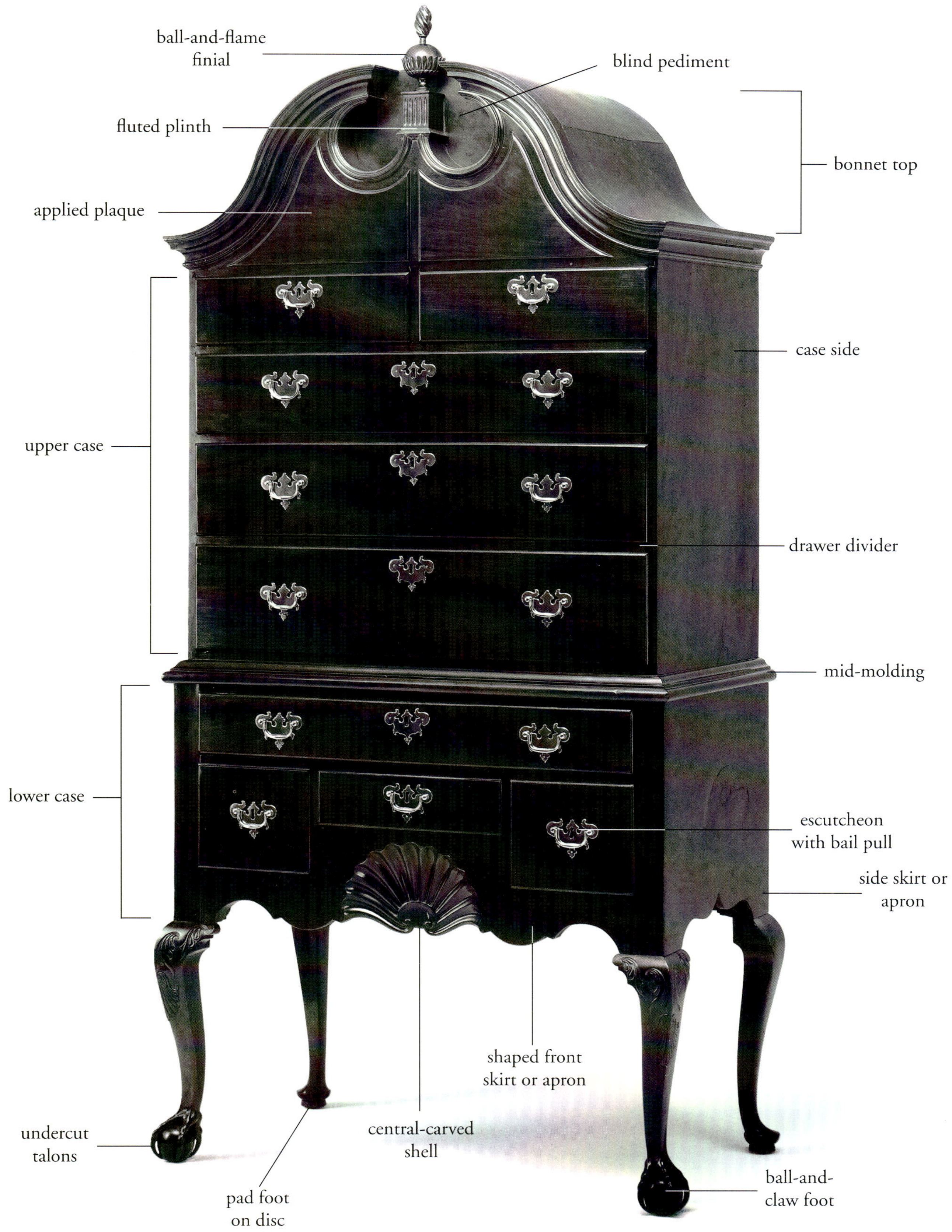
ball-and-flame finial
blind pediment
fluted plinth
bonnet top
applied plaque
case side
upper case
drawer divider
mid-molding
lower case
escutcheon with bail pull
side skirt or apron
shaped front skirt or apron
undercut talons
central-carved shell
pad foot on disc
ball-and-claw foot

CAT. NO. 22

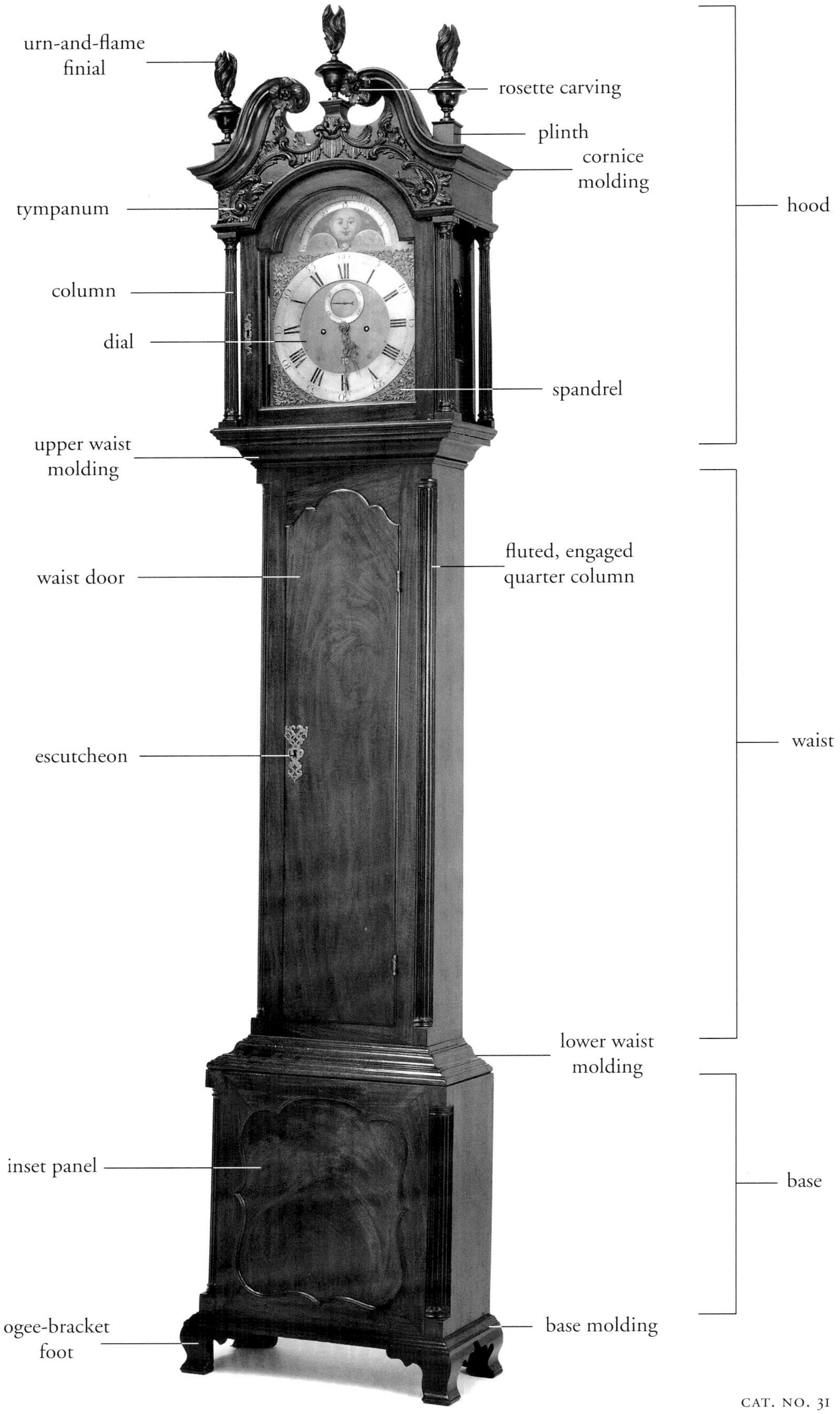
urn-and-flame
finial
rosette carving
plinth
cornice
molding
tympanum
hood
column
dial
spandrel
upper waist
molding
waist door
fluted, engaged
quarter column
escutcheon
waist
lower waist
molding
inset panel
base
ogee-bracket
foot
base molding

CAT. NO. 31

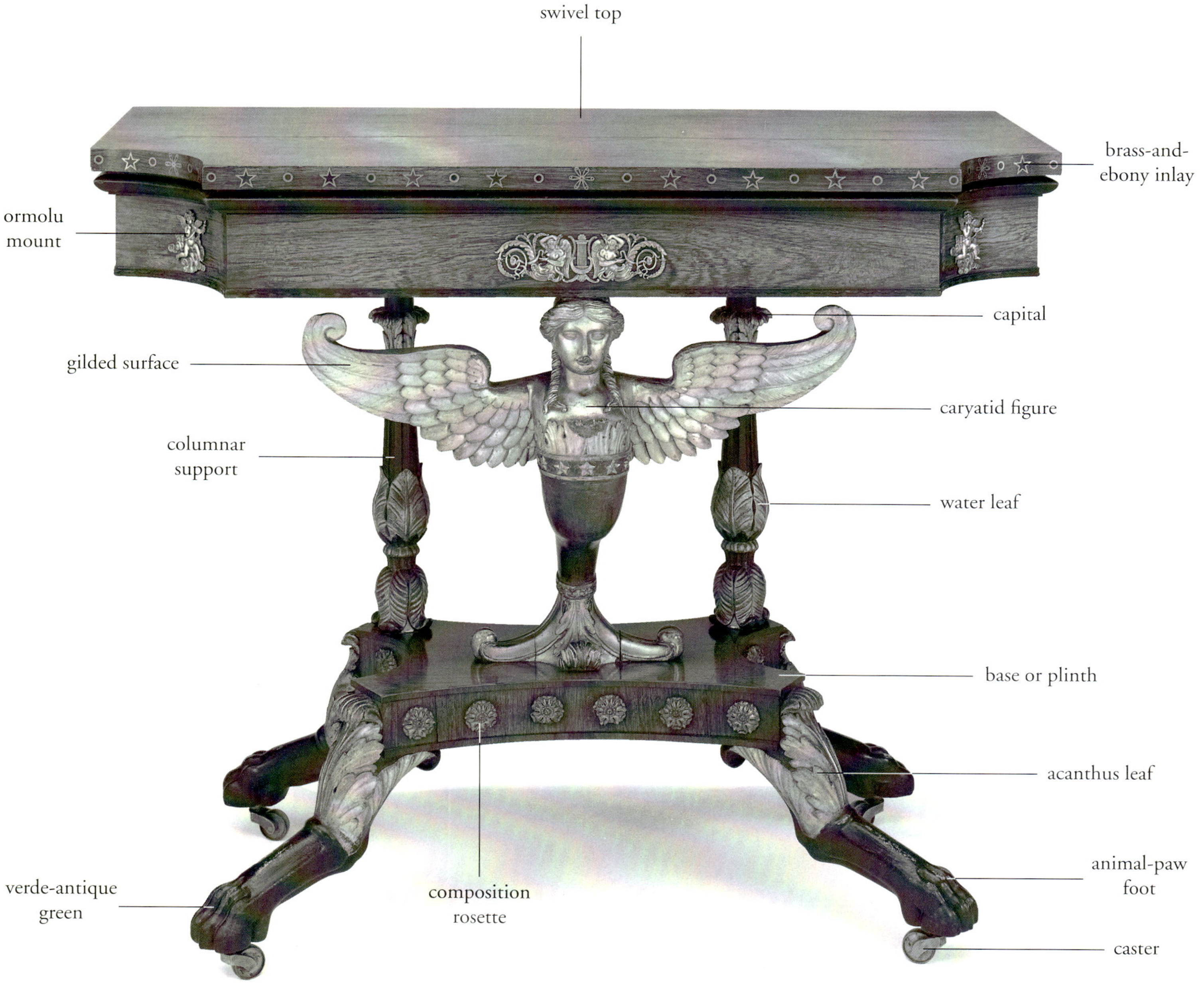
swivel top
brass-and-ebony inlay
ormolu mount
capital
gilded surface
caryatid figure
columnar support
water leaf
base or plinth
acanthus leaf
animal-paw foot
verde-antique green
composition rosette
caster

CAT. NO. 52

INDEX

Page numbers in **bold** refer to illustrations.

Abbey, Edwin Austin, 322
Académie Julian, Paris, 270, 282, 289, 331, 336
Ackermann, Rudolph, 159–60
Repository of Arts, Literature, Fashions, Manufacturers, &c., 159–60, **160**, 181
Adam, Robert, 113, 120
The Works in Architecture of Robert and James Adam, 113
Addams, Jane, 26
Aestheticism, Anglo-Japanese, 241, 247
Aesthetic Movement, 236
"Alabama Claims" lawsuit, 220–21
Alexander, Cosmo, 74, 138
Alexander Grant (cat. no. 18), 71, **73**, 74–75
Allen, Harold, 40
Allerton, Robert, 17, 34
Allston, Washington, 155
American Art Association, New York, 34
American Art Bronze Foundry, Chicago, 18
American Art-Union, 168–69, 171–72
American Institute of Architects, 33
American Renaissance, 284–85
Andirons (Elmslie) (cat. no. 165), 37, 313–15, **314**
antiquarianism, 29
Antiquarian Society of The Art Institute of Chicago, 14, 34–35, 37–38, 40
Archambo, Peter
Wine Fountain, **100**
Archibald, George. *See* Emmons, Thomas, and George Archibald
Armchair (1670/1700, New York area) (cat. no. 5), **53**, 53–54
Armchair (1730/40, Philadelphia) (cat. no. 13), **64**, 64–65
Armchair (c. 1815, New York) (cat. no. 53), 131, **132**, 133–34
Armchair (1840/60, New York) (cat. no. 81), **180**, 180–81
Armchair (Ford, Johnson and Company) (cat. no. 151), 297, **297**
Armchair (Hunzinger) (cat. no. 102), **219**, 219–20
Armchair (Kendall) (cat. no. 150), 295–96, **296**
Armchair (Pottier and Stymus; Guerin) (cat. no. 111), **235**, 235–37
Armchair (Wright) (cat. no. 163), 37, 313, **313**
Armory Show (1913), 28–29, 31, 336
art, Asian, influence of on American artists, 292, 339–40. *See also* art, Japanese; *japonisme*
art education, 14, 176, 336
in Munich, 18, 208–09, 250, 270
in Paris, 215, 268, 270, 316. *See also* Académie Julian, Paris; École des Beaux-Arts, Paris
art, English, influence of on American artists, 74, 109, 140, 143. *See also* furniture, English and Irish
art, French, influence of on American collectors, 14–16, 21, 146. *See also* furniture, French
Art Institute of Chicago, **12**, **16**, **17**, **18**, **35**, **36**, **39**
acquisition of contemporary art, 27–28, 342. *See also* Friends of American Art
acquisition of decorative arts, 30–35
administration of, 30
building, 17
Daniel F. and Ada L. Rice Building, **12**, 38, **39**, 40
Department of American Arts, 37–38
Department of Industrial Arts, 33
Department of Textiles, 31
exhibitions
annual exhibitions of American painting and sculpture, 16, 27, 29, 36, 282, 333
Arthur Jerome Eddy Memorial Exhibition (1922), 29
Arts and Crafts exhibitions, 26, 30, 337
Century of Progress Exhibition (1933), 36, **36**
of decorative arts, 34
"From Colony to Nation: Exhibition of American Painting, Silver, and Architecture from 1650 to the War of 1812" (1949), 36–37
"Half a Century of American Art" (1939), 36
Harper memorial exhibition (1910), 27
"Hudson River School and the Early American Landscape Tradition" (1945), 36
"James McNeill Whistler" (1968), 37
loan exhibition of American furniture (1926), 34
"Sargent, Whistler, and Mary Cassatt" (1954), 37
Field-McCormick Galleries of American Arts, **12**, **39**, 40
J. Peter McCormick Sculpture Court, **12**, 40
Stickney memorial gallery, 16, **16**
See also Antiquarian Society of The Art Institute of Chicago
Artistic Houses, 20, **20**
art, Japanese, influence of on American artists, 25, 212, 217, 231–32, 247–49, 263, 270, 289–90, 307. *See also* japonisme
Art Journal, 25
Art-Nouveau style, 25–26, 249, 285, 340
Arts and Crafts movement, American, 26, 30, 295–96, 311–12, 318, 339–40. *See also* Boston Society of Art and Crafts; Chicago Arts and Crafts Society; Prairie School design
Arts and Crafts movement, English, 13, 25–26, 305, 309–10, 337
Ashbee, C. R., 25, 311–12, 337. *See also* Guild of Handicraft
Ashcan School, 327–28, 342
Atlan Ceramic Club, 30
Authors' Club, 280

Bacher, Otto, 19
Bacon, Henry, 329–30
Baker, Isaac F., 157. *See also* Cornelius and Company
Girandoles (cat. no. 69), **157**, 157–59
Baltimore, 123
baptism, 76
Baptismal Basin (Edwards) (cat. no. 20), 75–76, **76**
Barber, Edwin Atlee, 31
Barbizon School, 21, 228
Barck, Clara, 26, 37, 311. *See also* Kalo Shop, Chicago
Barney, Natalie Clifford, 31
Baroque style, 57, 60, 62, 65
Barrett, Thomas, 123
Bartholomew, Edward Sheffield, 172–74
Hagar and Ishmael (cat. no. 77), 40, 172–74, **173**
Shepherd Boy, 173, **174**
Bartolini, Lorenzo, 177
Bartram, John, 64
Barye, Antoine-Louis, 18
Bastien-Lepage, Jules, 268
Bayou Bend Collection, Houston, 63–64
Beaux-Arts style, 17, 38, 284
Beaux, Cecilia, 280–82
Dorothea and Francesca (cat. no. 140), 280–82, **281**
Beckwith, J. Carroll, 19
Beest, Albert Van, 203
Behrends, Mr. and Mrs. B. A., 34
belleek ware. *See* porcelain, belleek
Bellows, George, 27, 36, 342–44
A Day in June, 344, **344**
Love of Winter (cat. no. 186), 28, 342–44, **343**
My Mother, 29
Belter, John Henry, 182–83
"Belter style," 183
Bennett, Bessie, 30, 33
Benson, Frank Weston
Rainy Day, **28**
Bermuda, 71
Betts, Louis
Martin A. Ryerson, **22**
Bierstadt, Albert, 190, 192
Mountain Brook, 190, **192**
Mountain Brook (cat. no. 87), 40, 190, **191**, 192–93
Binon, J. B.
Portrait Bust of Major-General Henry Dearborn, **139**, 139–40
Blackburn, Joseph, 71, 74
Abigail Chesebrough (Mrs. Alexander Grant) (cat. no. 17), 71, **72**, 74–75
Mrs. David Chesebrough, 74, **74**
Blackie and Son
The Cabinetmaker's Assistant, 182, **183**
Black, William, and Erastus O. Tomkins
Tea Caddy, 113, **113**
Blair, Helen Bowen. *See* Helen Bowen Blair Fund
Blum, Robert Frederick
Venetian Lacemakers, 214
Blythe, David Gilmour
Old Virginia Home, **194**, 195
Boardman, Langley, 118
(attr. to) *Serpentine-Front Chest of Drawers* (cat. no. 44), 117–19, **118**
(attr. to) *Serpentine-Front Chest of Drawers* (cat. no. 45), **35**, 117–19, **118**
bombé furniture. *See* furniture, Boston bombé
Borglum, Solon, 341
Boston, 60, 82, 86, 93–94, 337–38
Boston and Sandwich Glass Company, 199–200
(possibly) *Clear Strawberry Diamond Bowl with Cross* (cat. no. 67), **154**, 154–55
Double-Plated Lamp (cat. no. 91), 40, **199**, 199–200
Boston Public Library, 18, 284–85
Boston Society of Arts and Crafts, 338–39

bowls, **154**, 154–55, 197, **198**, 199, 309, **310**, 311
Box (1650/1700, Massachusetts), 34, **34**
boxes, 34, **34**, 337–39, **338**
Bradford, William, 202–04
The Arctic Regions, 203
The Coast of Labrador (cat. no. 93), 202–04, **203**
The Schooner Jane of Bath, Maine, **204**
Bradley, Will, 26
Brasher, Ephraim
Urn with Cover (cat. no. 33), 35, **99**, 99–100
Breton, Jules, 15, 228
Brooks and Hope McCormick Foundation, 40
Browne, Charles Francis, 27
Brown, Henry Kirke, 171–72, 193
Choosing of the Arrow, 172
The Filatrice (The Spinner) (cat. no. 76), 40, **171**, 171–72
Bryant, William Cullen, 36, 149
Bullwer-Lytton, Edward
The Last Days of Pompeii, 177
Burch, Cornelius van der, 49
Caudle Cup (cat. no. 1), 35, **49**, 49–50
Bureau Table (attr. to Townsend) (cat. no. 23), 80–82, **81**, **82**, 104
Burne-Jones, Edward, 276
Burnham and Root, 14
Burnham, Daniel
"Chicago Plan," 25
Burt, Benjamin
Communion Dish (cat. no. 19), **75**, 75–76
Butler, Edward, 27

Cabinet (Herter Brothers) (cat. no. 119), 38, 245, **247**, 247–48
Candlesticks (Jarvie) (cat. no. 158), 309, **310**, 311
Cann, John, and David Dunn
(designed by) *Pitcher* (cat. no. 80), **179**, 179–80
card playing, 90
Card Table (1755/90, New York) (cat. no. 28), **90**, 90–91
Card Table (Lannuier) (cat. no. 52), 40, 128–31, **129**, **130**
card tables. *See* tables
Carolus-Duran, Émile Auguste, 214, 253
case furniture, 65, 68
Cassatt, Mary, 21–25, 36, 206, 208, 263, 265
After the Bullfight (cat. no. 95), 206, **207**, 208
The Child's Bath (cat. no. 128), 25, 263, **264**, 265
The Lamp, 24, **24**
Modern Woman, 23
Offering the Panal to the Bullfighter, 206, **208**
On a Balcony (cat. no. 127), **262**, 263
series of prints "à la Japonaise," 263
Young Mother, 21
Caudle Cup (Burch) (cat. no. 1), 35, **49**, 49–50
Centerpiece (Dominick and Haff) (cat. no. 113), **237**, 237–38
Center Table (top by Cremer) (cat. no. 89), 195–97, **196**
Central Church, Chicago, 31. *See also* Gunsaulus, Frank W.
Centennial Exhibition, Philadelphia (1876), **194**, 195, 240–41
Japanese pavilion, 248
Ceramic Art Company, Trenton, New Jersey, 317. *See also* Lenox, Incorporated
Chadbourne, Emily Crane, 31–32, 40
Chair from Baldishol Church (c. 12th century, Norway), 53, **54**
chairs
arm-, **53**, 53–54, **64**, 64–65, 131, **132**, 133–34, **180**, 180–81, **219**, 219–20, **235**, 235–37, 295–97, **296**, **297**, 312–13, **313**
hall, 318–19, **319**
side, **62**, **63**, 62–64, 84, **85**, 91–95, **92**, **93**, 102–04, **103**, 110–11, **111**
Windsor, 32, 105
Chap-Book (Chicago), 26
Chapin, Aaron, 102
Chapin, Eliphalet, 102
Chapin school
Pair of Side Chairs (cat. no. 35), 102–04, **103**
Chase, William Merritt, 15–16, 250–51, 342
Alice, 18, **18**
A City Park (cat. no. 121), **250**, 250–52
Prospect Park, 251, **251**
Chaudron, Jean-Simon, and Anthony Rasch, 134–36
Tea and Coffee Service (cat. no. 55), **134**, **135**, 134–36,
Chest (1700/1710, Hatfield or Deerfield, Mass.) (cat. no. 4), 51–53, **52**
Chest of Drawers (attr. to Cogswell) (cat. no. 24), 37, 82–84, **83**
Chest of Drawers (1878/84, New York) (cat. no. 116), 38, 241–43, **242**
chests of drawers, 52, 68–69, **68**, **69**, 78–80, **79**, **80**, 82–83, **83**, 117–19, **118**, 241–43, **242**
Chicago
as design center, 25, 296–97, 337–38
as frontier, 38
immigrant population of, 14
modernist art in, 27
See also Art Institute of Chicago
Chicago Academy of Fine Arts, 14
Chicago Arts and Crafts Society, 26, 305, 309, 337
Chicago Society of Decorative Art, 13–14. See also Antiquarian Society of The Art Institute of Chicago
Chippendale, Thomas
Gentleman and Cabinet-Maker's Director, 84, 93, **94**, **96**, 96–97, 180
Church, Frederic Edwin, 188–89, 203
View of Cotopaxi (cat. no. 86), 188–90, **189**
Civic Opera, Chicago, 31
Clark, Alson Skinner
Coffee House, **26**, 27
Clark, Thomas Curtis
"Chicago," 41
Clarkson, Ralph, 26–27
classical antiquity, 114
Clear Strawberry Diamond Bowl with Cross (Boston and Sandwich Glass Company or New England Glass Company) (cat. no. 67), **154**, 154–55
Cliff Dwellers Club, Chicago, 26–27
Clifton, Henry, 84
clocks, **95**, **96**, 95–97, **231**, **232**, 231–33, 313–15, **314**
coffee drinking, 101
Coffee or Chocolate Set (Lenox, Incorporated) (cat. no. 167), **317**, 317–18
Coffeepot (Richardson) (cat. no. 34), **101**, 101–02, 114
Coffin, William, 210
Cogswell, John, 82–83
(attr. to) *Chest of Drawers* (cat. no. 24), 37, 82–84, **83**
Coleman, Samuel, 20
Cole, Thomas, 20, 149, 151
Distant View of Niagara Falls (cat. no. 64), 149–51, **150**, 188
New England Scenery, **116**, 117
Niagara, Two Miles Off, 150, **151**
Colonial Dames, 34
colonial period, 49, 54, 101
Colonial Williamsburg, Virginia, 30, 63
Communion Dish (Burt) (cat. no. 19), **75**, 75–76
Compote (1830/50, Massachusetts) (cat. no. 90), 197, **198**, 199
Coney, John
Tankard, 35
Congregational churches, 75–76
Cook, Clarence, 245
Cooper and Holt
Sideboard, **244**, 245
Cooper, James Fenimore, 36
Last of the Mohicans, 157–58
Cooper Union, New York, 318
Copeland, Elizabeth E., 339
Covered Box (cat. no. 181), 337–39, **338**
Copley, John Singleton, 86
Daniel Hubbard (cat. no. 26), 37, 86, **87**, 89
Mrs. Daniel Hubbard (Mary Greene) (cat. no. 27), 37, 86, **88**, 89
Mrs. John Amory (Katherine Greene), 86, **89**
Cornelius and Company, 157–158. *See also* Baker, Isaac F.
Girandoles (cat. no. 69), **157**, 157–59
Courbet, Gustave, 215–16
Covered Box (Copeland) (cat. no. 181), 337–39, **338**
Covered Sugar Bowl (New England Glass Company) (cat. no. 66), **154**, 154–55
coverlets, 31, **31**
Cowell and Hubbard Company, Cleveland, Ohio
(retailers) *Centerpiece* (cat. no. 113), **237**, 237–38
Cox, John, and Co.
(retailers) *Pitcher* (cat. no. 80), **179**, 179–80
Crane, Richard T., 31
Crane, Walter, 25
Cremer, Joseph, 195–96
(top by) *Table* (cat. no. 89), 40, 195–97, **196**
croquet, 223–25
cups
caudle, **49**, 49–50
two-handled, **48**, 49–50, 76
curators, changing role of, 30
Curran, Charles Courney, 16
Curry, John Steuart, 36
Cutbush, Edward, 147
Cylinder Desk (1800/10, Baltimore) (cat. no. 48), **123**, 123–24
Cylinder Desk and Bookcase (1800/10, northeastern Mass., poss. Boston) (cat. no. 47), 120, **121**, 122

Dalou, Aime-Jules, 288
Maternal Joy, 288, **288**
Dannat, William Turner, 15
David, Jacques Louis
Portrait of Madame Récamier, 31
Davies, Arthur B., 24, 27, 31, 36
Deakin's Art Rooms, Chicago, 25
Dearborn, Henry, 138–40, **139**
Deering, Charles, 18–19, **19**
Deering, James, 19
Degas, Edgar, 21, 212, 263, 326
Denon, Dominque Vivant, 160
Voyage dans la Basse et la Haute Egypte, 160, **160**
Desk (1770/90, Norwich, Conn.) (cat. no. 36), **104**, 104–05
Desk (Wright and Niedecken) (cat. no. 156), 305, **306**, 307
Desk-and-Bookcase (1700/35, Boston) (cat. no. 10), 60–61, **61**
Desk-and-Bookcase (1740/50, Boston) (cat. no. 14), 65–67, **66**, **67**
Desk-and-Bookcase (Salem, Mass.), **34**, 35
desks, **34**, **35**, 60–61, **61**, 65–67, **66**, **67**,

104, 104–05, 120–24, **121**, **123**, 305, **306**, 307
Dewing, Thomas Wilmer, 316–17
Lady in Green and Gray (cat. no. 166), 28, **316**, 316–17
Dixon, Wesley, 40
Doll and Richards, Boston, 269
Dominick and Haff, 237–38
Centerpiece (cat. no. 113), **237**, 237–38
Dominick, Henry Blanchard, 237
Donoghue, John, 17
Young Sophocles Leading the Chorus of Victory after the Battle of Salamis, 17, **17**
Double-Plated Lamp (Boston and Sandwich Glass Company) (cat. no. 91), 40, **199**, 199–200
Dow, Arthur Wesley, 289–91
Boats at Rest (cat. no. 146), 289–90, **290**
Downing, Andrew Jackson, 179, 181
The Architecture of Country Houses, **181**, 181–82
Drach, Rudolph
Dish, **31**
Dresser, Christopher, 248, 312
Principles of Decorative Design, 312
Dressing Table (1750/70, Salem, Mass.) (cat. no. 16), **70**, 70–71
dressing tables, 70, **70**
Drexel Institute of Art, Science, and Industry, Philadelphia, 298–99, 338
Drinking Glass (1700/20, English), 57, **58**
DuBois, W. E. B., 331
Duchamp, Marcel
Nude Descending a Staircase, No. 2, 29
Dummer, Jeremiah, 55, 57
Caudle Cup, 35, 49
Tankard (cat. no. 6), 54–56, **55**
Dunn, David. *See* Cann, John, and David Dunn
Durand, Asher B., 190
Durand-Ruel, Paul, 16, 22
Dutch Reformed Church, 50
Dutch West India Company, 50
Dyer, Uriah, and Silas Hoadley, 231–32
Tall-Case Clock (cat. no. 109), **231**, **232**, 231–33

Eagle's Nest art colony, Oregon, Ill. *See* Taft, Lorado
Earl, Ralph, 109
Mrs. Noah Smith and Her Children, **109**, 109–10
Noah Smith (cat. no. 39), **108**, 109–10
Eakins, Thomas, 29, 36, 229–30, 298–99, 301
Addie (Mary Adeline Williams), **298**, 299
Knitting (cat. no. 108), 29, 229–31, **230**
"The Laws of Sculptured Relief," 229
Mary Adeline Williams (cat. no. 152), 37, 298–99, **298**
Riter Fitzgerald (cat. no. 153), 299, **230**, 231
Spinning (cat. no. 107), 29, 229–31, **230**
The Zither Player, 37
Eastlake, Charles L.
Hints on Household Taste, 244
École des Beaux-Arts, Paris, 253, 268, 279, 285
École Impériale et Spéciale de Dessin, Paris, 215
Eddy, Arthur Jerome, 29, 302
education, 120. *See also* art education
Edwards, Samuel
Baptismal Basin (cat. no. 20), 75–76, **76**
Edwin A. Seipp (Mr. and Mrs.) Fund, 35
eglomisé panel, 120
Egyptian Revival, 235–38
Eight (The), 320, 325–26, 333, 336
Elliott, John, 84
Elmslie, George Grant, 25, 305, 307–08, 311, 313–15. *See also* Sullivan and Elmslie
Andirons (cat. no. 165), 37, 313–15, **314**
Carpet for Henry B. Babson House, Riverside, Illinois, 315, **315**
Full-Size Detail of Dining Chair for the Mrs. T. B. Keith House, Eau Claire, Wisconsin, 308, **309**
Side Chair (cat. no. 157), 37, 307–09, **308**
Tall Clock (cat. no. 164), 37, 313–15, **314**
Emancipation Proclamation, 193–95, 330
Emerson, Ralph Waldo, 205
"Nature," 205
Emmons, Thomas, and George Archibald, 144
Pier Table (cat. no. 60), 40, 143–44, **144**
Empire style, 129, 136, 143
Enlightenment, 120
Erp, Dirk Van, 297
Erving, Henry Wood, 51
Étagère (1850/70, New York) (cat. no. 82), **182**, 182–83
etching revival, American, 19
expatriate artists, American, 15, 19, 27, 172, 215, 265. *See also* Paris; Rome
Exposition Universelle, Paris
of 1878, 249
of 1889, 15–17
of 1900, 269, 288
evangelical movement, 161
Faber, John
Mary Finch, Viscountess Andover, 86, **89**
Falguière, Jean-Alexandre-Joseph, 279
Fan-Back Windsor Chair (1760/70, Philadelphia) (cat. no. 38), 105–06, **106**
"Federal" style. *See* neoclassical style
Field, Erastus Salisbury
Woman with Green Book, 120, **122**
Field, Marshall, 40
Field, Mrs. Henry (née Lathrop), 18
Field Museum of Natural History, Chicago, 31
Firescreen (1850/60, New York) (cat. no. 83), 182–83, **183**
Fisher, Alexander, 339
Fitzgerald, Charles, 320
FitzGerald, Edward. *See* "Rubáiyat of Omar Khayyám"
Flagon (attr. to Will) (cat. no. 21), 77, 77–78
folk art, 32, **33**
Ford, Henry, 30
Ford, Johnson and Company, 297
Armchair (cat. no. 151), 297, **297**
Forum Exhibition, Anderson Galleries, New York (1916), 336
Foujita, Tsugouharu
Portrait of E. C. Chadbourne, 31, **32**
Fowler, Samuel, 81
frames, molded white pine, 86
Francis, John F., 184–85
Wine, Cheese, and Fruit (cat. no. 84), 40, **184**, 184–85
Frank G. Logan Prize, 29, 282
Franklin, Benjamin, 122
French and Indian War, 95
French, Daniel Chester, 14, 21, 26, 284–85, 329–30
Abraham Lincoln (cat. no. 174), **329**, 329–31
Abraham Lincoln (cat. no. 175), **329**, 329–31
Truth (cat. no. 142), **284**, 284–85
French, William M. R., **14**, 14–16
Friends of American Art, 27–28
furniture, 32
Boston bombé, 82
English and Irish, 65–66, 133, 244
French, 82, 129, 187, 195–96, 245
Newport, 68, 70, 78–81, 82, 104
Rhode Island, 63, 79, 104

Gaines, John, III
(attr. to) *Side Chair* (cat. no. 11), 62, **62**
Galland, Pierre-Victor, 245
Gallatin, A. E., 342
Garland, Hamlin, 26–27
Garvan, Francis P., 33–34
Gauguin, Paul, 31
Gautier, Théophile
Un voyage en Espagne, 206
Gebelein, George C., 339
gendered roles
mens', 185, 224–25
womens', 185, 224–27, 260, 316, 328
Gérôme, Jean-Léon, 206, 253, 259
Gibson, John, 176
Gignoux, Régis François, 168
Gilbert, Cass, 284–85
Gilder, Richard Watson, 280–81
Gillinder and Sons
Covered Compote in the Pioneer Pattern, **40**
Gilmor, Robert, 149–50
Girandoles (Cornelius and Company; Isaac F. Baker) (cat. no. 69), **157**, 157–59
Giverny, 252–53
Glackens, William, 36, 320, 336
At Moquin's (cat. no. 169), 28, 320, **321**, 322
glass
blown, 30, 32
molded, 30
plated, 200
pressed, 31, 40, 154–55, 197
silvered. *See* mirrors
Venetian, 213
Glessner, Mrs. J. J., 13
Gleyre, Charles, 215
Goddard, John, 63, 79–80
(attr. to) *High Chest* (cat. no. 22), 37, 78–80, **79**, **80**
Goddard–Townsend school, 63, 79–80
Godwin, E. W., 247
Gonse, Louis
L'Art japonaise, 25
Gordon, Patrick, 105
Gossett, Isaac, 122
Gothic Revival, 180–81, 244, 339
Grainger Fund, 40
Great Depression, 30
Great Fire of 1871, 13
Greek Revival style, 143
Greenfield Village, Dearborn, Mich., 30
Greenough, Horatio, 155, 157
Abdiel (cat. no. 68), 17, 155, **156**, 157
Washington, 158
Guerin, Pierre E.
Armchair (cat. no. 112), **235**, 235–37
Sofa (cat. no. 112), 236, **236**
Guild of Handicraft, 25–26, 312, 337
Gunsaulus, Frank W., 31

Hadley chests, 51
Haff, Leroy B., 237. *See also* Dominick and Haff
Hall Chair (Rohlfs) (cat. no. 168), 318–19, **319**
Hallowell, Sara Tyson, 21–22, **21**, 268
Hals, Frans, 336
Hamill, Ernest, 18

Hamilton House, South Berwick, Maine, 32, **33**. *See also* Vaughan, Elizabeth Tyson
Handicraft Shop, Boston, 338–39. *See also* Boston Society of Arts and Crafts
Hanks, David, 37
Harding, George F., 38
Harnett, William M., 256, 258
For Sunday's Dinner (cat. no. 124), 256, **257**, 258–59
Just Dessert (cat. no. 125), 256, **258**, 258–59
(after) *The Old Violin*, 256, **259**
Harper, William A., 27
Normandy Pines, **27**
Harroun and Bierstadt
Gems of American Scenery, **192**
Harshe, Robert, 30
Hassam, Childe, 273
At the Florist, 266, **266**
Gloucester, Outer Harbor, 275, **275**
The Little Pond, Appledore (cat. no. 135), **273**, 273–75
New England Headlands (cat. no. 136), **274**, 275
Haussmann, Georges Eugène, 25, 251
Hawthorne, Nathaniel, 29, 176
Heade, Martin Johnson, 254
Magnolias on Light Blue Velvet Cloth (cat. no. 123), 254, **255**, 256
Study of a Single Magnolia Bud, 254, **255**
Study of Three Blossoms of Magnolia, 254
Helen Bowen Blair Fund, 37
Henri, Robert, 27, 333, 336–37, 342
Herself (cat. no. 178), 28, 333, **334**, 336–37
Himself (cat. no. 177), 28, 333, **335**, 336–37
Young Woman in Black, 28, 336, **336**
Henry, Edward Lamson, 29
Attack on the Chew House, 29, **30**
Hepplewhite, George, 118
The Cabinet-Maker and Upholsterer's Guide, 110, **111**, 113, **123**, 123–24
Herculaneum, 114, 177
Herst, Gertrude and Perry, 38
Herter Brothers, 235, 243–45, 247
Cabinet (cat. no. 119), 38, 245, **247**, 247–48
Sideboard (cat. no. 117), **243**, 243–45
Side Chair (cat. no. 118), 245, **246**, 247–49
Herter, Christian, 243–45, 247
Herter, Gustave, 235, 243
Heun, Arthur, 30–31
High-Back Windsor Chair (1760/68, Philadelphia) (cat. no. 37), **105**, 105–06
High Chest (attr. to Goddard) (cat. no. 22), 37, 78–80, **79**, **80**
High Chest of Drawers (1745/65, Mass., poss. Salem), **68**, 68–69
High Chest of Drawers (1760/65, Salem, Mass.), 68, **69**
high chests. *See* chests of drawers
Hinton, John Howard
The History and Topography of the United States, 150
Hitchcock, George, 265–67
Annunciation Lilies, 15
Flower Girl in Holland (cat. no. 129), 265–67, **266**
Hoadley, Silas, 231. *See also* Dyer, Uriah, and Silas Hoadley
Hodge, Emma B., 31, 34, 40
Hoffmann, Josef, 307, 318
Hogarth, William
Analysis of Beauty, 71
Hokusai, Katsushika, 249
Chinese Bell Flowers and a Dragonfly, **249**
Iris and Grasshopper, 249, **249**
Holmes, Frank G., 317. *See also* Lenox, Incorporated
Homer, Winslow, 36, 223–25, 233–34
After the Tornado, Texas, 24, **24**
Coast of Maine, 29, **29**
Croquet Scene (cat. no. 104), 37, 223–25, **224**
A Game of Croquet, 224, **225**
The Herring Net (cat. no. 110), 24–25, **233**, 233–34
Mount Washington (cat. no. 105), 225–27, **226**
Study for The Herring Net, 234, **234**
Hope, Thomas
Household Furniture and Interior Decoration, 147
Hopper, Edward, 36
Hoschedé, Ernest, 263
Hosmer, Harriet, 174, 176
Zenobia, Queen of Palmyra (cat. no. 78), 40, 174, **175**, 176–77
Hotchkiss, Thomas, 238
House Beautiful, 25
Hubbard, Daniel, 86
Hudson River School, 117, 149–50
Hull House, Chicago, 26
Hull, John, 55, 338
Humboldt, Alexander von, 188–89
Cosmos, 188–89
Humphries, Richard, 114
Huntington, Ebenezer, 104
Hunzinger, George Jakob, 219–20
Armchair (cat. no. 102), **219**, 219–20
Hurd, Jacob, 338
Sauce Boat, 35
Hutchinson, Charles L., 15, **15**, 23, 27
Hutchinson, Mr. and Mrs. William Y. *See* William Y. Hutchinson (Mr. and Mrs.) Fund
Huth, Hans, **37**
immigration, 30, 328. *See also* Chicago, immigrant population of
Impressionism, American, 23, 253, 273, 324
Impressionism, French, 251, 253, 263, 326
collectors of, in America, 21–25, 217
exhibitions of, in America, 22
exhibitions of, in France, 212
Inness, George, 20, 27–28, 168–71, 291–93
Catskill Mountains (cat. no. 75), 168–71, **169**
Crossing the Ford, 169, **170**
Early Morning, Tarpon Springs, 292, **292**
The Home of the Heron (cat. no. 147), 28, **291**, 291–93
The Mill Pond, **28**
The Old Mill (cat. no. 74), 28, 168–69, **169**
Peace and Plenty, 169–70
installations, 15–16
International Exhibition of Modern Art (1913). *See* Armory Show (1913)
International Exhibition of Modern Decorative Art, Turin (1902), 318
internationalism, 25
International Studio, 25
Inter-State Industrial Expositions
Chicago (1885), 21
Chicago (1890), 15, 22
Irving, Washington, 36
Isham, Ralph, 13
Ives, Halsey, 22

Jackson, Andrew, 147, **148**
James, Henry, 15, 282
japonisme, 25, 263
Jarves, James Jackson, 194
Jarvie, Robert, 26–27, 309, 311, 313
Candlesticks (cat. no. 158), 309, **310**, 311
Pitcher (cat. no. 159), 309, **310**, 311
Punch Bowl (cat. no. 160), 37, 309, **310**, 311
Jarvie Shop, Chicago, 311
Jefferson, Thomas, 138–39
Jennys, William
Dr. William Stoddard Williams, **37**
Jeurgens and Anderson, 30
Johnson, Eastman, 228
Husking Bee, Island of Nantucket (cat. no. 106), **227**, 227–29
Husking (Study for Corn Husking), 228, **228**
Johnson, Mrs. Justus, 31
Jouffroy, François, 268

Kalo Shop, Chicago, 26, 37, 311–12
Water Pitcher (cat. no. 161), **311**, 311–12
Kandinsky, Wassily, 292
Kast (1650/1700, New York area) (cat. no. 3), **50**, 50–51
Kelmscott Press, 25
Kemeys, Edward, 17–18, 26
Lions, 18, **18**
Kendall, David Wolcott, 295–96
Armchair (cat. no. 150), 295–96, **296**
Kensett, John Frederick, 202–05
Near Newport (cat. no. 94), 204–06, **205**
Kent, Rockwell, 36
Khayyám, Omar. *See* "Rubáiyát of Omar Khayyám"
Kierstede, Cornelius, 55
Tankard (cat. no. 7), 54–56, **55**
Two-Handled Covered Cup (cat. no. 2), 35, **48**, 49–50
kindermaal, 49
Kneller, Godfrey, 58
Knight, Mary Catherine, 338–39
Sauce Set (cat. no. 180), 337–39, **338**
Kuniyoshi, Yasuo, 36

LaMotte, Ellen, 31–32
lamps, **199**, 199–200
landscape architecture, 251
landscape painting, 128, 168, 188, 205, 238–39
Lannuier, Charles-Honoré, 128–29
Card Table (cat. no. 52), 40, 128–31, **129**, **130**
Lathrop, Bryan, 18
Leigh, W. Colston, 200
Lenox, Incorporated
Coffee or Chocolate Set (cat. no. 167), **317**, 317–18
Lenox, Walter Scott, 317
Leprince, Ringuet
Sideboard, 187, **187**
Library Company of Philadelphia, 64, 96, 122
Library of Congress, Washington, D.C., 284
Library Table (Wright) (cat. no. 155), 304–05, **304**
Lincoln, Abraham, 329–30. *See also* Emancipation Proclamation
"Little Room," 288. *See also* Potter, Bessie
Livingston, Robert, 91
London, 216
Longfellow, Henry Wadsworth, 29
Looking Glass (1790/1810, New York) (cat. no. 46), **119**, 119–20
looking glasses. *See* mirrors
Loudon, John Claudius
The Encyclopaedia of Cottage, Farm and Villa Architecture and Furniture, 181
Louvre. *See* Musée du Louvre, Paris
Luks, George, 27, 326

Macbeth Gallery exhibition, New York (1908), 336. *See also* Eight (The)
Mackintosh, Charles Rennie, 308, 311–12, 319
MacMonnies, Frederick William, 278–80
Bacchante and Infant Faun (cat. no. 139), 278, **279**, 280
Nathan Hale (cat. no. 138), 29, 278–79, **279**, 330
MacMonnies, Mary Fairchild, 23
Portrait of Mlle. S. H. (Sara Tyson Hallowell), **21**
Primitive Woman, 23
MacNeil, Herman Atkins, 26, 340
Maher, George Washington, 25, 305
Manet, Édouard, 206, 303, 320, 336
Bar at the Folies-Bergère, 320
Departure from Boulogne Harbor, 217, **217**
Olympia, 31
The Philosopher, 303, **303**
Manship, Paul, 340–42
Dancer and Gazelles (cat. no. 185), 340–42, **342**
Indian and Pronghorn Antelope (cat. no. 184), 340–42, **341**
maquetry, 195–97
Maratta, Hardesty Gillmore, 343
Marcotte, Leon, 242
Cabinet, 242, **242**
Marot, Daniel
Nouveaux Livre d'ornements, pour L'utillitée des Sculptures, et Orfèvres, 100, **100**
Martin, Eloise, 38
Marx, Samuel, 33
Masses (The), 328
Matisse, Henri, 31
McCormick, Brooks, 40
McCormick, Mrs. Cyrus J., 13
McCormick, Roger, 40
McEwen, Walter, 19
McIntire, Samuel, 110
(carving attr. to) *Pair of Side Chairs* (cat. no. 40), 110–11, **111**
McKim, Charles Follen, 280
Meissen porcelain. *See* porcelain, Meissen
Melchers, Gari, 19, 265
Charles L. Hutchinson, **15**
Merritt, Susan
Anti-Slavery Picnic at Weymouth Landing, **33**
Mésangère, Pierre de la, 144
Collection des meubles et objets de goût, 129–30, **131**
Metropolitan Museum of Art, New York, 34–35, 193
mezzotint, 86
Miller, Dr. and Mrs. C. Phillip, 35
Milles, Carl, 33
Millet, Jean François, 26
Millet, Louis Julian, 16, 26, 30
Milton, John
Paradise Lost, 155, 157
miniatures, 126, 137
Minnesota State Capitol, 284–85
mirrors, 70, 119–20, 157
Moeller, Henry, 16
Monet, Claude, 271–72, 253
Monroe, Harriet, 29
Moore, Edward C., 249. *See also* Tiffany and Company
Morris, William, 13. *See also* Kelmscott Press
Morris, William, and Company, 25
Moser, Koloman, 307
Mount, William Sidney, 152–53
Bar-room Scene (cat. no. 65), pp. 152–53, **153**
Mowbray, Henry Siddons, 16
Mozier, Joseph, 201–02
Pocahontas (cat. no. 92), 40, **201**, 201–02
Müller, Karl L. H., 241
Poet's Pitcher (cat. no. 115), **240**, 240–41
Murphy, Hermann Dudley, 331
Henry Ossawa Tanner, 331, **333**
Musée du Louvre, Paris, 16
Museum of Fine Arts, Boston, 35
Muybridge, Eadweard, 229

Naeve, Milo, 37–38
Napoleonic Campaigns, 129, 238
National Academy of Design, New York, 16, 152, 190, 193, 205, 224, 253, 320, 336
National Sculpture Society, 193
Neal, David
Interior of St. Mark's, Venice, 20, **20**
needlework, 182
neoclassical style, 93–94, 98, 113–14, 118, 131, 147, 172, 174–75
at World's Columbian Exposition, 17–18, 284
"neo-grec" style, 220, 222
neo-Renaissance style. *See* American Renaissance; Renaissance Revival
New Amsterdam (now Manhattan), 53
New England County Seat, 116, **116**
New England Glass Company
(possibly) *Clear Strawberry Diamond Bowl with Cross* (cat. no. 67), **154**, 154–55
Covered Sugar Bowl (cat. no. 66), 154–55, **154**
New Netherland colony, 50
Newport, Rhode Island, 63, 71, 78. *See also* furniture, Newport
New York, 131
Niagara Falls, 149, 150, 327–38
Nickerson, Mrs. S. M., 13
Nickerson, Samuel Mayo, 20
Niedecken, George Mann, 26, 305, 307
Desk (cat. no. 156), 305, **306**, 307
Rendering of a Desk for the Avery Coonley House, 305, **306**
Noble, Louis
After Icebergs with a Painter, 203
Norris, Frank
The Pit, 13

Oerley, Robert, 297
O'Keeffe, Georgia, 36, 292
Onckelbag, Gerrit, 49
Orchestra Hall, Chicago, 27
orientalism, 18, 248
Ott and Brewer, Trenton, New Jersey, 317

Paestum, 114
Pair of Side Chairs (Chapin school) (cat. no. 35), 102–04, **103**
Pair of Side Chairs (carving attr. to McIntire) (cat. no. 40), 110–11, **111**
Palmer, Bertha Honoré (Mrs. Potter), 13, 15, 21–24, **21**, **22**, 217
Palmer, Erastus Dow
Indian Girl, or the Dawn of Christianity, 201
Palmer, George Smith, 104
Palmer, Potter, 21, **22**
Palmer, Potter, Jr., 15
Pan-American Exposition, Buffalo (1901), 26–27
Paris, 14–16, 210, 251, 320, 331. *See also* art education, in Paris
parlors, 182, 200
Parris, Alexander, 144
Pasdeloup, Jules Ètienne, 212
Passe, Crispin de, the Younger
Officina Arcularia, 51, **51**
pattern books, 51, 84, 93, 96–97, 100, 110, 113, 129, 133, 180
Patti, Tom
Red Lumina with Concentric Disc, 40
Peale, Charles Willson, 124, 137–38
"An Essay to Promote Domestic Happiness," 124
John Nicholson, 126, **126**
Mrs. John Nicholson (Hannah Duncan) and John Nicholson, Jr. (cat. no. 49), 124, **125**, 126, 128
Peale, James
Mary (Polly) Lawton Bringhurst (cat. no. 50), 124, **126**, 128
Peale, Raffaelle, 128, 137–38
Still Life—Strawberries, Nuts, &c. (cat. no. 56), 40, **137**, 137–38
Peale, Rembrandt, 128, 137
Samuel Fisher Bradford (cat. no. 51), 40, 124, **127**, 128
Pelham, Peter, 86
Pennell, Joseph, 19
Penniman, John Ritto, 115–17
Meetinghouse Hill, Roxbury, Massachusetts (cat. no. 43), **115**, 115–17
Pennsylvania Academy of the Fine Arts, Philadelphia, 206, 230, 282, 298, 331, 336
Percier, Charles, and Pierre F. L. Fontaine
Recueil de décorations intérieures, 129, **130**, 136, **136**
pewter, 77
Pezzicar, Francesco
The Freed Slave, 195
Philadelphia, 64–65, 84, 95–96, 101, 105, 157
Phillips, Ammi, 161
Cornelius Allerton (cat. no. 71), 161, **162**, 164
Mrs. Reuben Allerton (Lois Atherton) (cat. no. 72), 161, **163**, 164
Phoenix Furniture Company, 295
photography, 229, 290, 330
stereoscopic, 192
Phyfe, Duncan, 131, 133
Pianoforte (Stewart) (cat. no. 62), 143–44, 146–47, **146**, **147**
Pier Table, 32, **32**
Pier Table (Emmons and Archibald) (cat. no. 60), 40, 143–44, **144**
"Pilgrim" pieces, 34
Pistataqua River Valley, 62, 117–18
Pitcher (designed by Cann and Dunn) (cat. no. 80), **179**, 179–80
Pitcher (Jarvie) (cat. no. 159), 309, **310**, 311
Pitcher (Shreve and Company) (cat. no. 182), 339–40, **340**
Pitcher (Tiffany and Company) (cat. no. 120), 248–50, **249**
pitchers, **179**, 179–80, **240**, 240–41, 248–50, **249**, 309, **310**, **311**, 311–12, 339–40, **340**
plate. *See* silver
Platt, Charles Adams, 19
Poet's Pitcher (Union Porcelain Works; Müller) (cat. no. 115), 240–41, **240**
Pompeii, 114, 177
Pond, Irving, 27
Pont-Aven, France, 289
porcelain, 240–41
belleek ware, 317–18
Chinese export, 32, 138
Meissen, 197, **198**, 199
portraiture, 74, 86, 109, 120, 126, 127–28, 143, 149, 161, 280, 282, 298–99, 301–02, 333, 336–37
Post-Impressionism, French, 326
Potter, Bessie, 26, 287–89
Girl Dancing (cat. no. 154), **288**, 288–89
The Young Mother (cat. no. 144), **287**, 288–89
"Potterines," 288
pottery, Turkish, 52
Pottier and Stymus, 235–36

(attr. to) *Armchair* (cat. no. 112), 235–37, **235**
Pottier, Auguste, 235
Powers, Hiram, 167–68, 201
America, **167**, 168
America (cat. no. 73), **166**, 167–68
Greek Slave, 193
Mrs. Potter Palmer, 21, **22**
Potter Palmer, 21, **22**
Prairie School design, 25–26, 37, 304–08, 312
Pre-Raphaelites, American, 190
Pre-Raphaelites, English, 276
Price, William, 61
Pugin, Augustus Charles, 181
Pugin, Augustus Welby Northmore, 181
Punch Bowl (Jarvie) (cat. no. 160), 37, 309, **310**, 311
punch pots. *See* urns
Purcell, Feick and Elmslie, 307–08
furniture for Henry Babson House, Riverside, Ill., 313–15, **315**
E. L. Powers House, 308, **308**
Purcell, William Gray, 307–08

Quakers, 63, 65, 79–80
quilts, 31

realism, 161, 193, 215, 230, 266
Reinhardt, Henry, 27
religion. *See* Congregational churches; evangelical movement
Remington, Frederic, 293–94
The Advance Guard, or the Military Sacrifice (cat. no. 148), 293–95, **294**
The Broncho Buster, 38
Coming Through the Rye (Over the Range) (cat. no. 149), 293–95, **295**
grisaille series *for Cosmopolitan Magazine*, 38
The Rattlesnake, 38, **38**
The Way of an Indian, 294–95
Renaissance Revival, 17, 185, 197, 236, 289
Restoration style, 143. *See also* Greek Revival style
Richardson, Francis, 101, 114
Richardson, Joseph, 101, 114
Coffeepot (cat. no. 34), **101**, 101–02, 114
Richardson, Joseph, Jr., and Nathaniel Richardson, 114
Salver (cat. no. 42), **114**, 114–15
Richards, William Trost, 20
Rickman, Thomas
An Attempt to Discriminate the Styles of English Architecture . . . , 181
Rietveld, Gerrit
Red-Blue Chair, 312
Roberts, Howard, 268
Robinson, Theodore, 252–53
On the Cliff, 253, **253**
The Valley of Arconville (cat. no. 122), **252**, 252–54
Rockefeller, John D., 30
Rococo Revival, 179, 263
Rococo style, 93–94, 96–98, 100–01, 106, 183, 197
Rodin, Auguste, 288
Rogers, Meyric, 33–37
Rogers, Randolph, 177
Nydia, the Blind Flower Girl of Pompeii (cat. no. 79), 17, 177, **178**, 179
Rohlfs, Charles, 318–19
Hall Chair (cat. no. 168), 318–19, **319**
Romanesque Revival, 14
Rome, 172, 174–75, 177, 201, 341
Rookwood Pottery, 33
Rousseau, Jean Jacques, 124
Roux, Alexander, 185, 187
Sideboard (cat. no. 85), 38, 40, 185, **186**, 187–88
Sideboard, 187, **187**
Royall, Isaac, 76
Rubáiyát of Omar Khayyám (trans. by Edward FitzGerald), 276
Rush, William, 147, 149
Portrait of Andrew Jackson (cat. no. 63), 40, 147, **148**, 149
Ruskin, John, 218, 245
Ryder, Albert Pinkham, 36
Ryerson, Martin A., **22**, 23–25, 34
Ryerson, Mrs. Martin, 13, 34

Saint-Gaudens, Augustus, 19, 267–69, 278–79
Amor Caritas (cat. no. 132), 260, 267, **268**, 269–70
Jules Bastien-Lepage (cat. no. 130), 267–70, **268**
Violet Sargent (cat. no. 131), 19, 40, 267, **267**, 269–70
St. Louis Universal Exposition (1904), 27
Salver (Richardson and Richardson) (cat. no. 42), **114**, 114–15
Salver (Winslow) (cat. no. 8), 35, 56–58, **57**
salvers, 56–58, **57**, **114**, 114–15
Sanderson, Robert, 338
Sargent, John Singer, 18–19, 35, 210, 212, 214, 282–83, 322, 324
Flower, **212**, 213
The Fountain, Villa Torlonia, Frascati, Italy (cat. no. 171), 28, 322, **323**, 324–25
Madame X, 282, 322
Mrs. George Swinton (cat. no. 141), 282–84, **283**
murals for Boston Public Library, 18
Rehearsal of the Pasdeloup Orchestra at the Cirque d'Hiver (cat. no. 97), 210, **211**, 212–13
Rehearsal of the Pasdeloup Orchestra at the Cirque d'Hiver, **212**, 212–13
The Sketchers, 324, **324**
Study from Life, 18, **19**
Thistles (cat. no. 170), 322, **322**, 324–25
Venetian Glass Workers (cat. no. 98), 24, 213–15, **214**
Venetian Water Carriers, 214, **215**
Sauce Set (Knight) (cat. no. 180), 337–39, **338**
Scammon, Mrs. J. Young, 13
scenic touring, 226. *See also* tourism
Schneider, Kristian, 313–14
Schultze, Paul, 28
Sears, Sarah Choate, 339
Secrétaire à Abattant (Boston, 1820/25) (cat. no. 61), 143–45, **145**
Seipp, Mr. and Mrs. Edwin. *See* Edwin Seipp (Mr. and Mrs.) Fund
Serpentine-Front Chest of Drawers (attr. to Boardman) (cat. no. 44), 117–19, **118**
Serpentine-Front Chest of Drawers (attr. to Boardman) (cat. no. 45), **35**, 117–19, **118**
Settee (1815/20, New York) (cat. no. 54), 131, **133**, 133–34
Sheeler, Charles, 36
Shepley, Rutan and Coolidge, 17
Sheraton, Thomas
Cabinet-Maker and Upholsterer's Drawing-Book, 113, 120, **122**
Shinn, Everett, 325–26, 336
The Hippodrome, London (cat. no. 172), **325**, 325–36
Shinnecock Hills Summer School, 251. *See also* Chase, William Merritt
Shirlaw, Walter, 208–10
Bell Foundry, Germany, **209**, 210
Toning the Bell (cat. no. 96), 18, 208–10, **209**
Shreve and Company, San Francisco, California, 339–40
Pitcher (cat. no. 182), 339–40, **340**
Vase (cat. no. 183), 339–40, **340**
Shreve, Crump and Low Company, 338
Two-Handled Dish (cat. no. 179), 337–39, **338**
Sideboard (1825/35, Philadelphia or Baltimore) (cat. no. 70), **159**, 159–61
Sideboard (Herter Brothers) (cat. no. 117), **243**, 243–45
Sideboard (Roux) (cat. no. 85), 38, 40, 185, **186**, 187–88
Side Chair (1730/60, Newport, Rhode Island), **63**, 63–64
Side Chair (1750/55, Philadelphia) (cat. no. 25), 84, **85**
Side Chair (1742/70, New York area) (cat. no. 29), 91–93, **92**
Side Chair (1770/85, Boston) (cat. no. 30), 37, **93**, 93–95
Side Chair (Elmslie) (cat. no. 157), 37, 307–09, **308**
Side Chair (attr. to Gaines) (cat. no. 11), 62, **62**
Side Chair (Herter Brothers) (cat. no. 118), 245, **246**, 247–49
Side Chair (Wright) (cat. no. 162), **312**, 312–13
side chairs. *See* chairs
Silsbee, Joseph Lyman, 307
silver, 34–35, 55, 75, 98, 112–14, 136, 237–38, 248–49, 338–39
slavery, 193–95
Sloan, John, 27, 327–28, 336
Bachelor Girl, 328, **328**
Renganeschi's Saturday Night (cat. no. 173), **327**, 327–29
Smibert, John, 58, 74
Richard Bill (cat. no. 9), 58, **59**, 60
Smith, Thomas C., 240. *See also* Union Porcelain Works
Society for the Preservation of New England Antiquities, 32
Society of American Artists, 16, 280
Sofa (Guerin) (cat. no. 112), 236, **236**
Soligny, Eugene J., 223
The Geneva Tribunal (cat. no. 103), 38, 40, 220–23, **221**, **222**. *See also* Tiffany and Company, New York
spiritualism, 276
Starr, Ellen Gates, 26
Steinfeld, Fern and Manfred, 38
Stein, Gertrude, 31
Stewart, James, 146–47
Pianoforte (cat. no. 62), 143–44, 146–47, **146**, **147**
still-life painting, 137, 184–85, 254, 256, 258
Stone and Kimball (publishers), 26
Stone, Herbert S., 27
Stuart, Gilbert, 74, 138–40
Major-General Henry Dearborn (cat. no. 57), 138–40, **139**
Stymus, William, 235–36. *See also* Pottier and Stymus
Sugar Dish with Cover and Cream Pot (Woodcock) (cat. no. 32), 97–99, **98**
Sullivan and Elmslie. *See also* Elmslie, George Grant; Sullivan, Louis
Babson House, Riverside, Ill., *37*
Sullivan, Louis, 25, 307
Sully, Thomas, 140, 143
Dr. Joseph Klapp (cat. no. 58), 140, **141**, 143
Mrs. Klapp (Anna Milnor) (cat. no. 59), 140, **142**, 143
Swedenborg, Emanuel, 27, 170
Swedenborgianism, 27, 170–71, 292
Sweet, Frederick A., 36–37, **37**
Symbolism, French, 276

table rugs, 200
tables, **32**, 80–82, **81**, **82**, 143–44, **144**, 195–97, **196**, **304**, 304–05
card, 82, **90**, 90–91, 128–31, **129**, **130**

Taft, Lorado, 17, 26–27, 195, 285–87
Eagle's Nest art colony, Oregon, Ill., 26–27
Solitude of the Soul (cat. no. 143), 26–27, 285–87, **286**
Talbert, Bruce, 244
Gothic Forms Applied to Furniture, 244, **244**
Tall-Case Clock (Dyer and Hoadley) (cat. no. 109), **231**, **232**, 231–33
Tall-Case Clock (Wood) (cat. no. 31), 37, **95**, **96**, 95–97
Tall Clock (Elmslie) (cat. no. 164), 37, 313–15, **314**
Tanagra figures, 289
Tankard (Dummer) (cat. no. 6), 54–56, **55**
Tankard (Kierstede) (cat. no. 7), 54–56, **55**
tankards, 54–56, **55**
Tanner, Henry Ossawa, 27, 36, 331, 333
"The American Negro in Art," 331
Two Disciples at the Tomb (cat. no. 176), 27, 331, **332**, 333
Tea and Coffee Service (Chaudron and Rasch) (cat. no. 55), **134**, **135**, 134–36
Tea Caddy (Black and Tomkins), 113, **113**
temperance, 153, 185
Thaxter, Celia, 273
Thayer, Abbott Handerson, 259–60
Winged Figure (cat. no. 126), 259–60, **260**
Thorvaldsen, Bertel, 155
Tieken, Mrs. Theodore, 37
Tiffany and Company, New York, 220–21, 223, 248–49, 269
Candelabra No. 3180, **223**
The Geneva Tribunal (cat. no. 103), 38, 40, 220–23, **221**, **222**
Hammering, Mounting, and Engraving Design for Pitcher No. 5051, 249, **249**
Pitcher (cat. no. 120), 248–50, **249**
Tiffany, Charles L., 249
Tomkins, Erastus O. *See* Black, William, and Erastus O. Tomkins
Toulouse-Lautrec, Henri, 326
tourism
in America, 149–50, 192, 225–27
to Egypt and the Holy Land, 237
Townsend, Job, 63, 80, 225–27. *See also* Goddard–Townsend school
Townsend, John, 80
(attr. to) *Bureau Table* (cat. no. 23), 70, 80–82, **81**, **82**, 104
Townshend Acts, 101
Transcendentalism, 205
trompe l'oeil, 256
Turner, Frederick Jackson, 38, 293–94
"The Significance of the Frontier in American History," 293–94
Twachtman, John, 16, 36, 270–72
Icebound (cat. no. 133), 28, 270–72, **271**
The White Bridge (cat. no. 134), 24, 270–72, **272**
Two-Handled Covered Cup (Kierstede) (cat. no. 2), 35, **48**, 49–50
Two-Handled Dish (Shreve, Crump and Low) (cat. no. 179), 337–39, **338**
Tyson, Russell, 32

Union Centrale des Arts Décoratifs, 25
Union Porcelain Works, 240–41
Poet's Pitcher (cat. no. 115), **240**, 240–41
University of Chicago, 26–27
Urban, Joseph, 297
urn form, 114
urns, **99**, 99–100
Urn with Cover (Brasher) (cat. no. 33), 35, **99**, 99–100
utopian tradition, in Midwest, 26

Vance, Mrs. Herbert, 40
Vase (Shreve and Company) (cat. no. 183), 339–40, **340**
Vaughan, Elizabeth Tyson, 32, 40
Vedder, Elihu, 15, 20, 238–39, 276
The Cumean Sibyl, 239, **239**
Fates Gathering in the Stars (cat. no. 137), 15, 276, **277**, 278
illustration published in the *Rubáiyát of Omar Khayyám*, 276, **278**
Storm in Umbria (cat. no. 114), 20, 238–39, **239**
Velázquez, Diego, 206, 214, 303, 336
Las Meninas, 303
Vienna Secession, 307, 318
Vonnoh, Bessie Potter. *See* Potter, Bessie
Vonnoh, Robert, 288
Voorhis, Daniel Van, 112–13
Tea Set (cat. no. 41), **112**, 112–13
Voysey, C. F. A., 25

Ward, John Quincy Adams, 172, 193–95
The Freedman (cat. no. 88), 40, **193**, **194**, 193–95
Warner, Olin Levi, 268
War of 1812, 138–39
War of Spanish Succession, 60
Water Pitcher (Kalo Shop) (cat. no. 161), **311**, 311–12
weather vanes, 32
Weber, Max, 36
Wedgwood, Josiah, 122
Welles, Clara Barck. *See* Barck, Clara
West, Benjamin, 128, 138
Wheeler, Candace, 13
Whistler, James McNeill, 19, 29, 36, 247, 302–04, 336
Arrangement in Flesh Color and Brown: Portrait of Arthur Jerome Eddy (cat. no. 154), 29, **302**, 302–04
The Artist in His Studio, **303**, 303–04
Gray and Silver: Old Battersea Reach (cat. no. 99), 29, 215–19, **216**
Nocturne: Blue and Gold—Southampton Water (cat. no. 101), 215–19, **218**
Nocturne in Black and Gold: The Falling Rocket, 218
Study for Arrangement in Gray and Black, No. 2: Thomas Carlyle, 32
Symphony in White, No. 1, 303
Trouville (Gray and Green, the Silver Sea) (cat. no. 100), 29, 215–19, **217**
White Mountains, 190, 192, 225–27
White, Stanford, 269
Willets Manufacturing Company, 317
William and Mary style. *See* Baroque style
William Y. Hutchinson (Mr. and Mrs.) Fund, 38
Willing, J. H., 18
Willis, John, 76
Will, John, 77–78
Flagon, 77, **77**
Will, William, 77–78
(attr. to) *Flagon* (cat. no. 21), 77, **77–78**
Teapot: with mark of maker; wood handle, 78, **78**
Wilson, Alexander, 128
wine drinking, 57
wine fountains. *See* urns
Winslow, Edward, 57, 338
Salver (cat. no. 8), 35, 56–58, **57**
Wister, John, 84
Woodcock, Bancroft, 97–98
Sugar Dish with Cover and Cream Pot (cat. no. 32), 97–99, **98**
Wood, Grant, 36
Wood, James N., 38
Wood, John, Jr.
Tall-Case Clock (cat. no. 31), 37, **95**, **96**, 95–97
World's Columbian Exposition, Chicago, 15–19, 21–23, 38, 268, 284, 288
Congress on Africa, 331
Department of Fine Arts, 22
Woman's Building, 22–23
Wright, Frank Lloyd, 25, 296, 304–05, 307
Armchair (cat. no. 163), 37, 313, **313**
"The Art and Craft of the Machine," 305
Avery Coonley House, 305, **307**
Desk (cat. no. 156), 305, **306**, 307
Larkin Administration Building, Buffalo, New York, 312
Library Table (cat. no. 155), **304**, 304–05
Ray W. Evans House, Chicago, 313
Side Chair (cat. no. 162), **312**, 312–13

Yale University, 34–35

Zorn, Anders, 19
Mrs. Potter Palmer, **21**
Reading: Mr. and Mrs. Charles Deering, **19**

*The text for this book was digitally set in Adobe Garamond and Monotype Perpetua.
The text stock is Aberdeen, manufactured by Donside Paper; the endleaf is Gainsborough
pewter, by Fox River. This book has been printed in an edition of 4,000 copies.*